SPAIN

THE BLUE GUIDES

ENGLAND
LONDON
SCOTLAND
WALES AND THE MARCHES
IRELAND
NORTHERN ITALY
ROME AND ENVIRONS
VENICE
SICILY
GREECE
CRETE
PARIS AND ENVIRONS
LOIRE VALLEY, NORMANDY, BRITTANY
BELGIUM AND LUXEMBOURG
MALTA
SPAIN: The Mainland
MOSCOW AND LENINGRAD

BLUE GUIDE

SPAIN

The Mainland

IAN ROBERTSON

With Maps, Plans, and Atlas

ERNEST BENN LIMITED
LONDON AND TONBRIDGE
RAND McNALLY & COMPANY
CHICAGO, NEW YORK, SAN FRANCISCO

Southern Spain and Portugal FIRST EDITION 1929
Southern Spain SECOND EDITION 1964

Northern Spain FIRST EDITION 1930
Northern Spain SECOND EDITION 1958

Spain, the Mainland THIRD EDITION (first in
this form) 1975
Spain, the Mainland FOURTH EDITION 1980

Published by Ernest Benn Limited
25 New Street Square, London EC4A 3JA
& Sovereign Way, Tonbridge, Kent TN9 1RW

Rand McNally & Company
Chicago, New York, San Francisco

© Ernest Benn Limited 1980

Set by Cold Composition Ltd.,
Tonbridge, Kent

Printed in Great Britain by
Fletcher and Son Ltd,
Norwich

ISBN *Library*   0 510-01629-4   0 528-84614-0 (USA)
ISBN *Paperback*   0 510-01630-8   0 528-84610-8 (USA)

PREFACE

This fourth edition of the BLUE GUIDE TO SPAIN: THE MAINLAND follows the successful pattern set by the third edition of five years ago, which, virtually re-written, had established itself as the accepted general guide to the country. Since then many changes have taken place, not least the passing of the Franco Era, forty years of 'Unenlightened Despotism', political repression, and intellectual stagnation, and a new 'democratized' generation seeking integration with modern Europe is rapidly growing up. The ubiquitous Yoke and Arrows symbol of the Falange has been torn down for kindling; and since then some inevitable changes in street names—particularly those of heros and martyrs of the 'Movimiento'—have taken place, which have probably gone unnoticed in this edition. Now more seasonable than ever is Richard Ford's injunction that 'the traveller in Spain cannot be too often counselled to lay aside his preconceived prejudices and foregone conclusions, the heaviest of all luggage'.

Although there is now much more widely spread material prosperity, the cost of living has also risen dramatically, and what was once the comparatively low cost of a holiday in Spain is no longer a consideration. In general, roads continue to be improved, but others have been allowed to deteriorate. The system of motorways or *autopistas* continues to expand, and while these may often facilitate the rapid communications between certain centres, they will not necessarily allow the visitor to see more of the country in the time at his disposal unless used with caution, and some suggestions in this respect have been made. Often it is only by very deliberately breaking away from the track beaten by the majority of tourists that one may get a deeper feeling for the country, for this is not a guide to the sophisticated delights of crowded beaches. Like others in the *Blue Guide* series, it is intended for those who wish to take a closer look at the country, its architecture and monuments, the very diversity of which should satisfy the demands of the most enthusiastic traveller, for, as Joseph Baretti observed some 200 years ago: 'Innumerable are the objects of curiosity up and down this large kingdom that deserve to be seen, examined and described'.

The romantic concept of building castles in Spain has taken on with a vengeance a new and unequivocal meaning, for in the last two decades the Spanish obsession with 'urbanización' has altered out of all recognition a large number of once attractive townscapes, and has likewise disfigured extensive stretches of the over-exploited coast. Too many fine and characteristic vistas have been irremediably blighted by unsightly and perfunctorily controlled speculative development. Too often the harmony of an urban scene has been destroyed by the Philistine erection of a brash new block of a bank, offices, or flats, which is then left stranded for an interminable time in a sea of plastic, rubble, and refuse. This lack of civic pride is also noticeable in the non-disposal of garbage in many places, often obvious at the entry and exits of towns and villages; but this trait, together with the pollution of the sea in the vicinity of many resorts, is just one more problem of civilization to be solved.

In the absence of any form of a political 'Arts Council', a Ministry of Culture has been meanwhile established to accommodate more functionaries, and although there appears to be considerable doubt in many minds as to what in fact constitutes culture, certain departments function remarkably well considering the more pressing demands on the public purse. The so-called *Patrimonio Nacional* (see p.89) has yet to be incorporated, as it should, in the *Patrimonio Artistico, Archivos y Museos*.

There is still little general understanding of the principle of democracy, in spite of widespread 'liberalization', and a not untypical remark is that made in the hearing of the Editor, when it was suggested: 'What we need is *Democracy,* like under Tito in Yugoslavia, where people are told exactly what they should do'! But government in Spain has always been a butt. Ford maliciously retold the story of Fernando III, who being a saint, escaped Purgatory when he died, 'and Santiago presented him to the Virgin, who forthwith desired him to ask any favour for beloved Spain. The monarch petitioned for oil, wine, and corn—conceded; for sunny skies, brave men, and pretty women— allowed; for cigars, relics, and bulls—by all means; for a *good government*—"Nay, nay", said the Virgin, "that never can be granted; for were it bestowed, not an angel would remain a day longer in heaven".'

Spain is now making up for the fact that she was never on the well worn track of the 'Grand Tourist' of the 18th century. Indeed, it was not until some decades after the Peninsular War that Spain, with a reputation somewhat tarnished by civil war and banditry, attracted the 19th-century tourist, who was warned by Richard Ford in his indispensable *Hand-Book for Travellers in Spain* of 1845, that a (riding) expedition in Spain for civilians was almost equivalent to serving a campaign. It may be of interest to know that this book (reprinted in 1966), the most accurate and comprehensive guide to *any* foreign country that had yet been written, and one of the famous *red* guides published by John Murray, was the direct forerunner of the first *Blue* Guide to Spain, edited by *Findlay Muirhead*, the second 2-volume edition of which was revised and enlarged by *John H. Harvey* and edited by *L. Russell Muirhead* (1896–1976).

Wherever necessary the text has been revised, the amount of alteration varying from very minor correction to the addition of considerable new matter, while in order not to increase the bulk of the volume, certain sections have been judiciously pruned. Most of the revisions have been made from personal observation on the spot during recent extensive tours in the service of this edition, but not every locality can be visited by the Editor for every edition of such a comprehensive guide to so large a country. The readers' continuing assistance is therefore solicited; and any constructive suggestions for its correction or improvement will be gratefully welcomed, and acknowledged by the Editor, who alone is responsible for all inexactitudes, shortcomings, inconsistencies, and solecisms. No one is better aware of the difficulty of avoiding errors both of omission and commission. To quote Henry Swinburne, writing in the 1770s after his tour of Spain, one may 'be detected in many mistakes, because a foreigner must often be exposed to receive partial accounts of things from the natives, who have an interest in hiding the nakedness of their country, and exaggerating its advantages'.

The introductory essays, and the section of Practical Information have been updated; and the maps and plans corrected, the cartography having been again undertaken by *John Flower*. The Atlas Section, although not intended to take the place of large-scale motoring maps, shows the general lie of the land, and should facilitate the planning of tours. Not all routes described are necessarily intended to be travelled in a day, but they indicate a general direction which may be followed; and some overlap from one region to another—from Estremadura into Andalucía, for example. Towns are described for sightseeing on foot, while the description of mountain regions is limited to an indication of available excursions and winter-sporting facilities: serious climbers and skiers will have their more specialized sources of information. Some of the events foreseen as imminent in 1975 have still not come to pass. Only *two* rooms of the *Municipal Museum* in Madrid have been opened (after a period of two decades) while the considerable reorganization of the *Prado Museum* is at present undergoing makes it more sensible to leave the previous description as an indication of what *may* be on view rather than to incorporate merely a provisional distribution. A number of new museums—such as that devoted to *Contemporary Art* in Madrid, and to *Miró* in Barcelona—have been opened, and are described. The section describing the Gothic painting in the *Museo de Arte de Cataluña* in Barcelona has been retained, although—for no good reason—it is at present closed. Many other collections are being rearranged, but while endeavouring to keep abreast of all the most recent changes, inevitably the very latest information is not always forthcoming.

There have been signs of a salutory reaction to the building of large hotels fettered to the exigencies of tour operators, although there are still too many with pretentions to the category of 'Luxury', providing unnecessary amenities which most travellers will never use but are nevertheless obliged to pay for. The existence of reasonable accommodation is indicated after each town, but individual hotels, with the exception of the State run *Paradores*, are not specified. Tourist Offices in Spain and abroad can provide up-to-date lists of various types of accommodation available, and there are annual commercial publications also listing a wide selection.

As with the previous edition, this concentrates exclusively on the mainland, as it is considered that most travellers to the Balearics and the Canaries would prefer separate and slighter guides to those islands rather than a bulky volume largely devoted to the Peninsula.

Since the publication of the last edition there has been a reorganization of certain government departments, and the *Secretaria de Estado de Turismo (S.E.T.)* is no longer under the aegis of the disbanded Ministerio de Información y Turismo, this department being now controlled by the *Ministerio de Comercio*, as travellers entering many countries are now considered by their respective governments as being merely 'invisible exports'! Government itself is being decentralized, and many regions are promised a degree of autonomy.

The continuing practice of 'starring' the highlights always comes in for some criticism, but although the system is subjective and inconsistent, such asterisks do help the hurried traveller to pick out those things which the general consensus of opinion (modified occasionally by the Editor's personal prejudice, admittedly) considers he should not miss. In certain cases a museum has been starred, rather than individual objects among those described, when the standard of its contents is remarkably high.

Selection is the touchstone by which guide-books are judged, and it is hoped that this edition will provide a comprehensive and balanced account of most aspects of the country without intentionally neglecting any that might appeal to the intelligent resident or visitor, and without being so exhaustive as to leave him no opportunity of discovering additional pleasures for himself; and yet, in the words of Ford: '... how often does the wearied traveller rejoice when no more is to be "done"; and how does he thank the faithful pioneer, who, by having himself toiled to see some "local lion", has saved others the tiresome task, by his assurance that it is not worth the time or trouble'.

A number of brief quotations from the works of earlier English travellers have been included in the text, when apt, amusing, or interesting, particularly when trenchantly underlining some of the many unchanging aspects of the country.

Gratitude must be expressed to *Evilio Verdera y Tuells,* ex-Director General del Patrimonio Artistico, Archivos y Museos of the Ministerio de Cultura for easing this path; to *Francisco Giron Tena,* Subdirector General de Promoción del Turismo, *Esperanza Aguirre y Gil de Biedma,* and *Juan Sánchez Lorenzo* of the Secretaría de Estado de Turismo for invaluable practical help; to *Rodolfo Nuñez de las Cuevas,* Director General del Instituto Geográfico Nacional, *Ildefonso Nadal Romero,* and *Francisco Vázquez Maure,* for their assistance. Facilities have also been kindly granted to the Editor by the Directors or Curators of a number of museums, etc., among them—in Madrid—by *Alfonso E. Pérez Sánchez* (Museo del Prado); *Luis Vázquez de Parga* (Real Academia de la Historia); *Martín Almagro* (Museo Arqueológico Nacional); and *Joaquín de la Puente* (Museo Espanol de Arte Contemporaneo); in Seville—*Fernando Fernández Gómez* (Museo Arqueológico); *Joana María Palou Sampol* (Museo de Bellas Artes); and *Antonio Limón Delgado* (Museo de Artes y Costumbres Populares); in Barcelona—*Carmen Farré de Ruiz Combalia,* and *María Teresa Palau Ribes* (Museo de Arte de Cataluña); *Trinidad Sánchez Pacheco* (Ceramic Museum); and in Granada—*Antonio Fernández Puertas* (Museo Nac. de Arte Hispano-Musulman).

While it may be invidious to single out the few ecclesiastical authorities who have offered any help, thanks are due to Don *Constancio* at Salamanca; Don *Rafael* at Osera; and *Cyrilio Martínez,* and *Jesús Garcia* at Monforte de Lemos: nor will Sr. *Peña* at the Ayuntamiento of Osuna, and the guardians of the castle at Loarre, S. Pedro de Arlanza, and Quintanilla de las Viñas, be forgotten; while among Managers of S.E.T. offices or delegations, those in Toledo, Granada, Cuenca, Santander, and Oviedo, and in particular *Mari-Carmen Sánchez* in Salamanca, and *Montserrat Ballart* at Barcelona, have offered every assistance.

The Editor is again indebted to many friends in both Spain and England for new information and advice, other than those mentioned by name in the previous edition who have continued their interest: among them *Bernard Bevan,* author of the article on Spanish Architecture in earlier editions of this guide; *Tobias Rodgers; Luis Marín; Alejandro Masso* (on Spanish organs); *Manuel Eléxpuru* (on Spanish wines); *Richard de Willermin; Eileen Ascroft; Dereck Kelso; Richard Hitchcock; Brinsley Ford; Robert Wade-Gery; Elisabeth de Stroumillo;*

Henry Bailey-King; and in particular to *Paloma Bazán.*

In the preparation of this edition, the Editor must reiterate his special obligation to *Paul Langridge,* General Editor of the Blue Guides since 1975, for his patient criticism and continued encouragement; to *Olga* and *Paco Mayans,* for much help and kindness both in Madrid and Trujillo; and to *Marion* and *Arthur Boyars,* whose hospitable Mews (well shelved and roofed) is a second home to him on his peregrinations; while this guide could not have been completed without my wife, *Marie-Thérèse,* constantly at the wheel, who has shared the many tribulations of intensive travel as well as its pleasures.

CONTENTS

PRACTICAL INFORMATION

I THE BASQUE PROVINCES AND NAVARRE

II ARAGÓN AND CATALONIA

III MADRID, OLD CASTILE, AND LEÓN

IV THE ASTURIAS AND GALICIA

V NEW CASTILE AND ESTREMADURA

VI NEW CASTILE, VALENCIA, AND MURCIA

VII ANDALUCÍA

MAPS AND PLANS

TOWN PLANS

GROUND PLANS

HISTORICAL INTRODUCTION

Traces of Prehistoric man in the Iberian Peninsula are many and varied, and the caves in which they have left their mark are widely distributed. Important Neolithic sites exist in the province of Almería, specifically at *Los Millares* (dated by radio-carbon tests to 2340+85 B.C.) and at *El Algar*. In the neighbourhood of Antequera are several Megalithic monuments, such as the remarkable *Cueva de Menga,* while of the Magdalenian period the murals at *Altamira* (near Santander) are outstanding.

Among the emerging culture-groups were the LIGURIANS, related to those of N. Italy, who are thought to have settled in the centre; the IBERIANS, who may have come from N. Africa, and settled in the southern half of the country before spreading to the centre, and the CELTS, who penetrated Spain viâ France in the 6C B.C., and settled in the North and West; but the term Celto-Iberian, which was given to the inhabitants of the centre, does not indicate any fusion of the races. From the earliest times these peoples lived in tribes and did not unite to form a nation, a lack of union that was to be a marked characteristic throughout their history. Some tribes left their trace in the names of districts, such as the ASTURES in the Asturias. Of the BASQUES, who have to a large extent preserved their language, it is not possible to state the origin, although some have been tempted to connect them with the Iberians on account of certain affinities between the Basque language and that of the native tribes in N. Africa, and the similarity between the unusual blood-groups of the Berbers and Basques.

The first people known to have had commercial relations with Spain were the PHOENICIANS, who founded the port of *Cádiz* c. 1100 B.C., hence establishing further settlements at *Abdera* (Adra), *Malaca* (Málaga), *Onuba* (Huelva), and *Tarsis* (Tharsis), etc. Also attracted by the mineral wealth of the country were the CARTHAGINIANS, who also settled in the Guadalquivir valley at *Corduba* (Córdoba) and *Hispalis* (Seville), and at *Carteia* (near Algeciras). Meanwhile, from 630-570 B.C. the GREEKS had settled along the E. coast, specifically at *Emporion* (Ampurias) and *Dianium* (Denia).

Expelled from Sicily by the Romans, the Carthaginians adapted Spain as a base of action against their rivals, *Hamilcar Barca* eventually subjugating much of the country south of the Ebro, while *Hasdrubal* founded *Nova Carthago* (Cartagena). In 221 B.C. Hasdrubal was succeeded by *Hannibal,* who precipitated the Second Punic War by attacking Rome through her ally *Saguntum,* an action which was to bring about the ruin of the Carthaginian Empire. Rome, now the predominant power, endeavoured to colonize the peninsula, but it took them almost 200 years to pacify the intractable tribes of the centre and North, who continued to resist imperialist expansion and exploitation with inflexible stubbornness. *Viriathus* defied Rome for six years until assassinated c. 140 B.C., while the obstinate defence of *Numancia* (near Soria), eventually reduced by *Scipio Aemilianus* in 133 B.C., was to become legendary.

Nevertheless, Roman Spain prospered both commercially and politically. Under Augustus, the two earlier provinces of HISPANIA CITERIOR and HISPANIA ULTERIOR were rearranged to form *Tarraconensis* (the N., N.W., and central area), *Lusitania* (roughly modern Portugal), and *Baetica* (S. Spain). Spain produced four Emperors *(Trajan, Hadrian, Theodosius I,* and *Honorius,* while *Marcus Aurelius* was of Spanish parentage); the two *Senecas, Lucan,* and *Columella* were also born in Spain of Roman parents, but both *Martial* and *Quintilian* were probably of Hispanic stock.

Between A.D. 264 and 276 the Hispanic provinces were barbarically devastated by the FRANKS and the SUEVI, and in 409 these raids were followed by significant invasions by the Suevi, ALANS, and VANDALS, who after pillaging the country, turned to fighting among themselves. The Visigoths, operating from Toulouse, undertook to restore order on behalf of Rome, but when they were themselves defeated by the Franks in Gaul, they sought refuge South of the Pyrenees, and eventually set up their own capital at *Toledo.* There were at this time between 80,000 and 100,000 Goths occupying the central plateau, who under *Leovigild* (568-86) unsuccessfully attempted to assimilate the 3 or 4 million Hispani who lived along the Mediterranean coast and in Baetica, for basically they remained an exclusive military aristocracy and would not mix with the natives. Their own tenuous unity was destroyed by civil war breaking out between religious factions, which continued in a desultory manner until 585 when Leovigild's son *Hermenigild,* the leader of the Catholic Party, was executed. However, Leovigild's successor, *Recared,* renounced Arianism, and at the Third Council of Toledo in 589, Catholicism became the officially enforced religion of the Visigothic kingdom. Nevertheless, in spite of apparent religious unity, the country was still a prey to political disturbances for which the elective system of the monarchy was partially responsible.

The Caliphate and Moorish Rule. In 711, taking advantage of this state of affairs, and at the invitation of either the political opponents of *Roderic* (who had been elected king the previous year), or by *Count Julian* (whose daughter had been seduced by Roderic), an expeditionary force of some 7000 Berbers under *Tariq,* a lieutenant of *Musa,* governor of Mauretania, landed near Gibraltar and was shortly reinforced. The Visigothic army was defeated at the battle of the *Guadalete,* and the 'Moors', reinforced by Arabs of two rival tribes, rapidly extended their conquest over almost the entire country, leaving only scattered remnants of the Christian army in the inaccessible mountains of the Asturias. They subsequently invaded Gaul, but in 732 were decisively repulsed at *Poitiers* by *Charles Martel.* The Moors were generally welcomed, and the majority of the Christian inhabitants submitted to their tolerant masters. Those choosing to retain their faith were known as *Mozárabes,* but were subjected to a capitation tax, to avoid which many became Moslems, forming a class known as *Muladies.*

In 756, *Abderrahman,* sole survivor of the OMAYYAD dynasty at Damascus, took possession of Córdoba and obtained recognition of his independent emirate from the Caliph of Baghdad. His reign (until 788) was filled with a succession of wars with rebellious Berber states and minor chiefs, and it was not until the caliphate of *Abderrahman III* (912-61), a man of great political and military energy, that some semblance of unity was established in Moslem Spain. During this reign, and that of *Hakam II* (961-76), Córdoba became perhaps the most civilized city in Europe: encouragement was given to literature and science; schools of philosophy and medicine were founded, and libraries formed. Military glory was gained by *Almansor,* the prime minister of *Hisham II* (976-1013), who arrogated to himself all the power, and he indulged in numerous summer campaigns *(aceifas)* in which he ravaged Barcelona, León, and Compostela, and again forced back the Christians to the Pyrenees and into the mountain ranges of the North-West. It is supposed that Almansor was eventually defeated at *Calatañazor* (near Soria), but there is little evidence that such a battle ever took place. He died in 1002, to the relief of the northern kingdoms, but the militarism fostered by him was continued by his successors. Anarchy, however, soon set in. Provinces declared themselves independent and split up into petty *'taifas',* but these, themselves distracted by perpetual civil wars, never consolidated their power, and were often obliged to pay tribute to Castile and León. Eventually the Moors turned to N. Africa for aid, and towards the end of the 11C a contingent of ALMORÁVIDES, Berber tribes united by religious fanaticism, entered Spain, to be followed in 1147 by another dynasty, the ALMOHADES.

The Reconquest. Following the symbolic victory of *Covadonga* in 718 (in which a small probing force of Moors were repulsed), the Christians, led by *Pelayo,* rallied, and set up the kingdom of the Asturias with their capital first at Cangas de Onís, and later at Oviedo. *Alfonso I, the Catholic* (739-57) crossed the Cantabrian mountains and descended on León, but the Christian capital was not established there until 914. *Alfonso II, the Chaste* (791-842) continued with the slow acquisition of territory, and at his death the kingdom of León consisted of the Asturias, Santander, Galicia, N. Portugal, and part of the modern province of Burgos. The reputed discovery of the body of Santiago in Galicia started a great cult which later grew to be an important contributory factor in the reconquest, Santiago 'Matamoros' (the Moorslayer) becoming a redoubtable Christian champion. Meanwhile *Ramiro I* (842-50) beat back attacks made on the Spanish coast by the Normans, and castles (which later gave the name to Castile) were constructed as bastions against fresh Moorish incursions. Courts were appointed by León to govern this new territory, and by the middle of the 10C *Count Fernán González,* one of many who had gradually tended to assert their independence, obtained a measure of autonomy for Castile. His son married *Sancha,* sister of *Bermudo III* of León, and received the title of King as dowry. Sancha, soon widowed, then married a son of Sancho the Great of Navarre, who as *Fernando I* reigned as king of Castile from 1037 to 1065. He also seized his father-in-law's kingdom of León, and extended his own to the south, making the Moorish kings of Toledo and Zaragoza his vassals.

Another focus of resistance against the Moors was in the Pyrenees. The Basques, beating off both Moors and Franks, had set up the kingdom of Navarre in the 9C, which under *Sancho the Great* (1000-35), whose territories stretched as far as Catalonia, was for a time the most powerful of the northern kingdoms. The boundaries of Catalonia itself, set up as a border county by Charlemagne, were extended by *Ramón Berenguer I* (1035-76), while *Ramón Berenguer III* (1096-1131), opening relations with Italy, laid the foundations of Catalan naval power in the Mediterranean. *Ramón Berenguer IV* (1131-62) married *Petronila,* heiress of Aragón, and their son, who took the name of *Alfonso II* (1162-96), united the sovereignty of Aragón with Catalonia.

Meanwhile Fernando I of Castile who, like his father, had divided his territory among his children, had died, precipitating a fratricidal war finally won by *Alfonso VI* (1072-1109), during whose reign Toledo fell to the Christians (1085). Nine years later Valencia was captured, temporarily, by the followers of the *Cid Campeador* (*Rodrigo Díaz de Vivar*, c. 1043-99). Shortly afterwards the dependency of Portugal, given by Alfonso to his daughter *Teresa* on her marriage to *Count Henry of Burgundy,* became a separate kingdom. Castile continued to be ravaged by civil war, both during the reigns of queen *Urraca* (1109-26) and of her son *Alfonso VII* (1126-57), order being eventually restored by *Alfonso VIII* (1158-1214). Alfonso then marched against the Almohades and was defeated at *Alarcos* in 1195. In 1212, Alfonso having united with the kings of León, Aragón, and Navarre, in a general crusade, was able at the battle of *Las Navas de Tolosa* (between the pass of Despeñaperros and Bailén), to cripple Moorish power in the peninsula for good. Castile was finally united with León in the person of *Fernando III* (1217-52), son of Alfonso IX of León and Berenguela, daughter of Alfonso VIII of Castile. The reign of Fernando III, who was later canonized, was decisive in the long-drawn-out reconquest. In 1236 Córdoba fell; in 1241, Murcia; and in 1248, Seville. Universities were founded, and the building of the cathedrals of Burgos and Toledo was begun.

Concurrently, the kings of Aragón had been active. In 1118 *Alfonso I, el Batallador* (1104-34) entered Zaragoza, and later captured Tarazona, Calatayúd, and Daroca, while Tortosa and Lérida, among many other towns, fell to *Ramón Berenguer IV. Alfonso II* gained possession of Albarracín, and founded Teruel, and was succeeded by *Pedro II* (1196-1213), who, involved in the Albigensian Wars, was killed at the battle of Muret. The long reign of *Jaime I, el Conquistador* (1213-76), was one of the most brilliant in the history of Aragón. The Balearics fell to him in 1229; he regained control of Valencia in 1238; and by 1266 Alicante was in his hands. His son *Pedro* or *Pere III* (1276-85) inherited Aragón, Catalonia, and Valencia; another son, *Jaime,* was left the Balearics, Roussillon, and the Cerdagne. In 1282, after the massacre of the French known as the 'Sicilian Vespers', Pedro became king of Sicily at their invitation, a consequence of which was a French invasion of Aragón. This was unsuccessful, and their fleet was defeated by the Aragonese at Las Hormigas. On the death of his brother, Jaime inherited Sicily, while Pedro's son *Alfonso III* (1285-91) inherited his Spanish possessions. During the following reign, of *Jaime II* (1291-1327), a Catalan expedition took place to Constantinople and Asia Minor, which although successful against the Turks, aroused the jealousy of the Greeks, and Paleologos had its leaders assassinated. Later, however, the Catalans gained control of Athens, and formed a Grand Duchy of Athens, which was to survive until the end of the 14C. *Pedro IV, the Ceremonious* (1336-87) was able, after the battle of Épila, to discipline the recalcitrant Aragonese nobles who had forced concessions from Alfonso III, and did much to strengthen royal authority. Majorca and Roussillon were united with Aragón. *Juan I* (1387-95) was succeeded by *Martin* (1395-1410), who left no male heirs, and the Infant of Castile known as *Fernando de Antequera* was elected king (1410-16). His son *Alfonso V, the Magnanimous* (1416-58), invited by Joanna II of Naples to help her to defend her kingdom against Louis of Anjou, was adopted by her as heir to Naples. Although defeated by the French at the naval battle of Ponza, Alfonso was able to regain Naples, and his illegitimate son Fernando was recognized as king. On the death of Alfonso V, the Crown of Aragón passed to his brother *Juan II* (1458-79), who was involved in a quarrel with his own son, the *Príncipe de Viana*. The latter died in mysterious circumstances, at which the Catalans rose up in revolt, while Louis XI of France took possession of Roussillon. Juan died in 1479, leaving as his heir *Fernando V*, who had already, in 1469, married Isabel of Castile.

The history of **Castile** from the death of Fernando III to the accession of the Catholic Kings is one long record of Civil War. The reign of Fernando's son, *Alfonso X, el Sabio* ('the Learned, but *not* Wise'; 1252-84) was more memorable for the lustre of his literary court than for political success, although he captured Cartagena, Cádiz, and Sanlúcar. *Sancho IV, el Valiente* (1284-95) was followed by *Fernando IV* (1295-1312) and *Alfonso XI* (1313-50), but the minorities of the last two were again periods of political turmoil. In 1350 *Pedro I, the Cruel*, succeeded to the throne, who after quelling an insurrection stirred up in Castile by his bastard brother *Enrique de Trastámara*, declared war on Pedro IV of Aragón. The latter, in conjunction with Enrique, called in the White Companies from France led by *Du Guesclin*, while Pedro the Cruel obtained assistance from the English under the *Black Prince*. Pedro defeated Enrique at *Nájera* (or *Navarrete)* in 1367, but lost the battle of *Montiel* (1369), and was murdered in De Guesclin's tent.

Enrique de Trastámara, as *Enrique II* (1369-79), was forced to grant various concessions to the nobles in order to maintain his position, but was strong enough to refuse the demands of *John of Gaunt*, who claimed the throne through his wife, a daughter of Pedro the Cruel. *Juan I* (1379-90) legitimized his line by marrying his son *(Enrique III*, 1390-1406) to John of Gaunt's daughter. He also attempted to unite Portugal to Castile, but was beaten by the Portuguese at *Aljubarrota* in 1385. In 1391 there was a general pogrom of Jews in Spain. *Juan II* (1406-54) preferred to leave the government of Castile in the hands of *Alvaro de Luna*, Grand Master of the Order of Santiago, who aimed at making the monarchy supreme. The refractory nobles were at first defeated at *Olmedo* (1445), but a later intrigue, supported by the queen, was successful, and the favourite was seized and executed (1453). *Enrique IV* (1454-74) was likewise faced with rebellion by the nobles, who proclaimed his brother Alfonso king, but a compromise was reached on Alfonso's death, when Enrique, ignoring his daughter *Juana ('La Beltraneja')*, whose legitimacy was disputed, named his sister *Isabel* heir to the throne. She, however, refused to accept the crown during the lifetime of her brother, who, offended by her marriage with her cousin Fernando, heir of Aragón, annulled the pact and left the succession uncertain.

The Catholic Kings. The joint rule of *Isabel I of Castile* (d. 1504), 'la Católica', and *Fernando V of Aragón* (d. 1516), 'el Católico', partially unified the country: both kingdoms were considered of equal importance. Civil war, however, was immediately provoked by the partisans of 'La Beltraneja', whose claim was supported by the king of Portugal, but after the indecisive battle of *Toro* (1476) the Portuguese withdrew, leaving Fernando and Isabel firmly established. Numerous reforms were introduced, especially with regard to justice and legislation, and the revival of the Santa Hermandad constituted an effective police force which also formed the nucleus of a standing army. Although Councils were formed for the government of the kingdom, which met for consultation, the final decision rested with the sovereigns, and in accordance with the same centralizing policy, the grand-mastership of the great military orders were vested in the crown. Royal revenues were reorganized, and encouragement was given to the MESTA, a wealthy and powerful guild of sheep-owners. The sheep themselves had been cross-bred with Moroccan sheep of the Banū Marīn, and were known for their 'merino wool' as early as 1307. A political and commercial treaty between England and Spain was signed at Medina del Campo in 1489. The extreme bigotry of the rulers, and their ardour for the purity of the Catholic faith, was attested by the establishment of the Inquisition (in Castile in 1480; in Aragón in 1487), which was to become another powerful and predatory arm of the crown.

Once order had been established, the Catholic Kings turned their attention to the conquest of the Nasrid kingdom of Granada, the only remaining possession of the Moors in Spain. The subsequent war of attrition lasted ten years, until, finally isolated, *Boabdil (el Rey Chico)* capitulated, and on 2 January 1492, the Catholic Kings entered Granada in triumph. At first, toleration was shown to the vanquished Moors, but sterner measures were later advocated. In Castile, the MUDÉJARES (Moors under Christian rule) were in 1502 confronted with the alternative of accepting Christian baptism or expulsion. A similar edict had been issued against the Jews in 1492, when between 150,000 and 400,000 were forced to abandon their country or suffered persecution. The Moors who conformed were known as MORISCOS: converted Jews were known as CONVERSOS, or New Christians; those expelled from Spain (and from Portugal in 1497) were known as SEFARDIES.

In the same year as the conquest of Granada, the Genoese navigator *Columbus* discovered America, thus opening a vast new field for Spanish enterprise. In Europe, the foreign policy of the Catholic Kings was to form strong alliances by skilfully arranged marriages. *Isabel,* their eldest daughter, became queen of Portugal; *Juana,* the second, married Philip of Burgundy, son of the Habsburg emperor Maximilian; while *Catherine of Aragón* the youngest, was the first wife of Henry VIII of England. In 1494 Charles VIII of France invaded Italy and took Naples. Later, the Spanish agreed to join the French in dismembering the country, but quarrelled with them over the division of territory.

The Spaniards, under the leadership of *Gonzalo de Córdoba (el Gran Capitán)* were everywhere victorious, and Naples remained under Spanish control. At the death of Isabel in 1504, her daughter Juana, heiress to the throne of Castile, (and known as *Juana la Loca,* 'the Mad'; 1479-1555), being considered mentally unfit to rule and her son, Charles, an infant of only four years old, Fernando of Aragón became regent. Although briefly superseded by Philip of Burgundy, Fernando remained regent until his death in 1516. In 1512 Fernando took possession of southern Navarre, the territory to the north of the Pyrenees passing to the House of Albret. As Charles was not twenty years old, and in Flanders, when his grandfather died, *Card. Cisneros* was appointed regent of Spain, while *Adrian of Utrecht* (later Pope Adrian VI) represented the young prince, who had shrewdly insisted on being proclaimed king during the lifetime of his mother.

The House of Habsburg. On his accession, *Charles I* (1516-56), perhaps better known as the *Emperor Charles V,* inherited Flanders, the Low Countries, Artois, the Franche-Comté, all the possessions of the crown of Aragón, and Castile, together with the empire in America. Once comparatively isolated from the rest of Europe, and almost exclusively occupied with her own territorial problems, Spain now became the centre of European politics, and after the election of Charles as Emperor in 1520 she was linked for thirty-six years with the interests of the German Empire. Charles, born at Ghent, was a complete stranger to his Spanish subjects, and when he arrived in Spain in 1517 with a train of Flemish favourites, trouble soon ensued. The reign was disturbed first by the revolt of the COMUNEROS (1519-20), in which the 'cities' were supported by disaffected nobles. The insurgents, under *Acuna, Bp. of Zamora* and *Juan de Padilla* (1484-1521) came near to success against Adrian of Utrecht, but were subsequently defeated at *Villalar* (1521). Charles was then able to turn his attention against his rival, Francis I of France. Hostilities between them opened in Italy, where the campaign ended to the advantage of Charles, Francis being taken prisoner at *Pavia* (1525), but war with France continued intermittently until 1547. Meanwhile, perturbed by the growing influence of the Ottoman Turks, and by the activity of the Barbary pirates in the Mediterranean, Charles endeavoured to sever all contact between the Moors of N. Africa with those still in the Peninsula, and in 1535 led a successful expedition to Tunis against Barbarossa; but an attempt to reduce Algiers six years later ended in disaster. Charles abdicated at Brussels in 1556, and passed the last two years of his life in the monastery of Yuste, near Plasencia, where he died.

Concurrently, the opening up of the New World progressed with astonishing rapidity. The history of the sanguinary exploits of *Hernán Cortés* (1485-1547) in Mexico, and of *Francisco Pizarro* (1476-1541) in Peru during the years 1531-32, added extraordinary lustre to the reign. Chile was conquered by *Pedro de Valdivia* and *García de Mendoza;* Buenos Aires was founded in 1534. In 1519 the Portuguese navigator *Magellan* had set sail from San Lucar with a fleet of five ships, and after doubling Cape Horn, had reached the Philippines, where he was murdered by the natives; but one ship returned, commanded by *Sebastián Elcano,* the first to sail round the world.

Philip II (1556-98), although free from the burdens of the German Empire, inherited many political problems, including continued rivalry with France, and growing discontent in the Low Countries. Philip, born at Valladolid, was essentially a Spaniard. At first allied with England through his marriage with Mary Tudor (d. 1558), and possessing Milan and Naples, and with all the wealth of the Indies, he was in a most advantageous position when hostilities broke out in Italy. The seat of war was later transferred to the frontier of Flanders, where the Spaniards won notable victories at *St. Quentin* (1557) and at *Gravelines.* Peace was signed at Cateau-Cambrésis (1559), and Philip married Elizabeth of Valois. The two main objects of his policy, to which he devoted all his resources and energy, were to maintain his inheritance intact and to stamp out heresy. In 1559, leaving Flanders under the regency of Margaret of Parma, Philip returned to Spain, which he never left again. In 1571 the Spaniards under *Don Juan of Austria,* Philip's illegitimate half-brother, and the Genoese *Admiral Doria,* won a decisive victory over the Turkish fleet at *Lepanto*. In 1580, on the death of the aged Card. Henry, king of Portugal, Philip claimed the Portuguese crown through his mother, the eldest daughter of King Manuel. Meanwhile, the situation in the Low Countries grew more serious. At first Philip paid little attention to the demands of his Flemish subjects, but when the population reacted to his indifference by desecrating churches, he despatched the *3rd Duke of Alba* to crush the rebellion; but on the introduction of a special tax, members of both religions united to resist, supported by the Protestants of England, France, and Germany. The Northern Provinces declared themselves an independent Republic at The Hague in 1581, even if only recognized as such in 1609. The religious question, the assistance given to the insurgents, the unchecked piracy of English sea captains, together with Philip's plots in favour of Mary, Queen of Scots, led inevitably to war. Philip decided to invade England. At great expense, the *Armada* was ready to sail in 1588, but incompetently led by *Medina Sidonia,* and encountering adverse weather, if fell an easy prey to the superior seamanship of the English, and the expedition ended in disaster. During Philip's reign the Moriscos also revolted. In spite of the milder measures proposed by *Mondéjar,* Philip persisted in his intransigence, and in 1568 the Moriscos, after seeking the support of the king of Fez, prepared to resist in the Alpujarras and the mountains of Granada. Don *Juan* of Austria, after a difficult campaign, was able to suppress the rising in 1570. The survivors were dispersed throughout Spain.

Philip III succeeded his father in 1598, but preferred to leave the management of the State entirely in the hands of the *Duke of Lerma* (1553-1625), the first of a succession of unscrupulous royal favourites who were to exercise their baneful influence on Spain. In 1609 Philip decreed the expulsion of some 275,000 Moriscos (of some 500,000) of the estimated total population of c. 9,000,000, while the Thirty Years War in Germany, during which Spain supported the house of Austria, was an additional drain on the diminishing resources of the country with no compensating benefits.

Philip IV (1621-65) handed over the direction of affairs to the ambitious *Conde-Duque de Olivares* (1587-1645), who struggled to maintain the authority of the dynasty, but in spite of the victories of *Spinola* in the Low Countries, Spain was rapidly losing ground. In 1630 her hold over Italy was seriously undermined, and the victory of the French at *Rocroi* in 1643 destroyed the prestige of the Spanish infantry or *tercios.* In 1640 Olivares was faced with a serious rebellion in Catalonia, while in the same year Portugal, after sixty years of forced union, also revolted, and its subsequent separation from Spain hastened his downfall. The Catalans returned to their proper allegiance in 1643, but it was not until 1659 that the province was completely pacified. By the Treaty of the Pyrenees, signed in that year on the marriage of the Infanta María Teresa with Louis XIV, the French king renounced all claims to the Spanish throne for his descendants, but the obligations undertaken by Spain were never completely carried out, and the treaty became a dead letter.

Philip left one legitimate son, the sickly *Carlos II* (1665-1700), who succeeded at the age of four. The eleven years of his minority were disturbed by feuding between the Regent Mariana of Austria and the king's half-brother Don Juan, while Carlos's marriage to Marie-Louise of Orleans caused equally bitter rivalry between the French and Austrian factions at court. On her death (1689), he married Maria of Neuburg, and it seemed likely that the Austrian cause would triumph, but through the ability of d'Harcourt, the French Ambassador, Carlos, who was childless, was persuaded to bequeath his throne to Philip, Duke of Anjou, grandson of Louis XIV and María Teresa.

The House of Bourbon. With the accession of the Bourbons in 1700 there began a century during which Spain was to be dragged into nearly all the political conflicts of Europe. *Philip V* (1700-46) entered Madrid in 1701 without opposition, but the **War of the Spanish Succession** broke out immediately. The *Archduke Charles of Austria* invaded Spain, assisted by British troops, commanded by *Peterborough, Galway,* and *Stanhope,* and naval forces commanded by *Rooke, Byng, Leake,* and *Shovel.* Gibraltar fell into British hands in 1704. The war was carried on with varying fortunes until the death of the emperor in 1711. At the Peace of Utrecht (1713) Philip was recognized by the Powers as King of Spain. French methods and institutions were introduced, and a number of reforms were carried out. The *Duc de Saint-Simon* visited the court at Madrid in 1721-22, of which he left an amusing account. *Fernando VI* (1746-59) was succeeded by *Carlos III* (1759-88), and the country enjoyed a period of comparative prosperity, while considerable improvements in the administration were made by a succession of able ministers, including *Aranda, Campomanes,* and later, *Floridablanca* and *Jovellanos.* In April 1767 the Jesuits were expelled from Spain, their schools abolished, and their revenues seized.

By a Family Compact (1762) with the Bourbons of France, Spain had entered into a closer alliance with her neighbour, and was drawn again into intermittent war with England. At the Peace of Versailles (1783) Spain recovered Minorca and Florida. Among travellers from England during the latter half of the century the following may be mentioned: *Edward Clarke* (1760-61); *Joseph Baretti* (1760, and again in 1768-69); *Richard Twiss* (1773); *Henry Swinburne* (1775-76); and *Joseph Townsend* (1786-87). Soon after *Carlos IV* (1788-1808) succeeded to the throne, Spain came into conflict with the revolutionary powers in France. Carlos and his minister *Godoy*—the favourite of *María Luisa,* his lascivious queen—were unable to save Louis XVI from the scaffold. Godoy, entitled 'Prince of the Peace' after his negotiations at the Peace of Basle (1795), was no match for Napoleon, and by degrees Spain was involved in Napoleonic schemes to the extent of active co-operation, which led, in 1805, to her fleet being shattered by *Nelson* at *Trafalgar.* Popular indignation led eventually to the overthrow of Godoy at Aranjuez (1808), which was followed by the abdication of Carlos IV. The royal family was decoyed to France, while Murat was sent to Madrid, where, on 2 May 1808 (*'el Dos de Mayo'*) he suppressed a popular rising with the utmost brutality. Napoleon's next step was to place his brother Joseph on the Spanish throne.

Meanwhile revolutionary *juntas* had been set up in the provinces, numerous pockets of resistance defied the French, and so commenced the sanguinary **Peninsular War,** known in Spain as the *War of Independence.* After their initial success at *Bailén,* the Spaniards carried on the war largely by guerrilla methods. As their invitation, a small British army under *Sir John Moore* entered Spain, but were forced back to *La Coruña* by *Soult* (1809). They were replaced shortly by another expeditionary force commanded by *Wellesley,* known after the battle of *Talavera* (1809) as *Wellington.* In Spain, other famous battles of the war were those of *Fuentes de Oñoro* and *Albuera* (1811), *Salamanca* (1812), *Vitoria* and *Sorauren* (1813). The sieges of *Zaragoza* (1808 and 1809) and *Gerona* (1809) are memorable for the extrordinary tenacity of the Spanish defenders. Later sieges of significance were those of *Badajoz* and *Ciudad Rodrigo* (both 1812) and *San Sebastián* (1813).

Meanwhile, the Spanish American colonies began to assert their independence, and one by one detached themselves from Spain. In 1812 the Cortes at Cádiz had enacted a constitution for a limited monarchial government, but in 1814, on his restoration, this was repudiated by *Fernando VII,* who was more preoccupied in stifling all Liberal aspirations, and to this end his obnoxious administration enforced a rigid censorship, re-established the effete Inquisition, and readmitted the Jesuits. A revolt broke out in 1820 under *Gen. Riego,* and there followed a Liberal government until 1823, when Fernando was restored to power by the armed intervention of the French led by the *Duc d'Angoulême.* However, Fernando's policy of persecuting the Liberals was unchanged, and the country continued to suffer under his repressive absolutism until 1833. On Fernando's death, his brother *Don Carlos,* basing his claim to the throne on the Salic Law, contested the rights of his niece *Isabel II* (1833-68), then a child under the regency of her mother *Cristina.*

In the **First Carlist War,** the civil war which followed, Don Carlos was supported by the Church party, the reactionaries, and the Basques, whereas Cristina could rely on the Liberals and the army, but for some time the issue seemed doubtful. A British Auxiliary Legion, commanded by *de Lacy Evans,* also fought for Cristina in the Basque Provinces. The Carlists possessed some good guerrilla leaders, among whom were the ferocious *Cabrera,* and *Zumalacárregui,* but eventually the Cristino generals *Espartero* and *Narváez* were able to bring the war to a successful conclusion after the Treaty of Vergara (1839). Cristina resigned the regency in 1840, and for three years the country was under the dictatorship of Espartero. Literacy was merely 10% in 1841, which rose to 25% in 1860, and progressively to 47% by 1901. The population of Spain in 1857, according to the first official census, was 15,500,000. Among English visitors to Spain during the post Peninsular War period were *Samuel Cook,* later *Widdrington* (1829-32, and again in 1843), *Richard Ford* (1830-33; author of the famous 'Hand-Book for Travellers in Spain', first edition published in 1845), and *George Borrow* (1836-40; author of 'The Bible in Spain').

In 1843 *Isabel II* was declared of age, but the remainder of her reign was a period of political confusion and constitutional crises. The conservative policy of Narváez was followed by the liberal régime of *O'Donnell.* The government, being at the mercy of any *pronunciamiento,* was unstable, and popular dissatisfaction increased. In 1868, when *Prim* and other liberal generals raised a rebellion in the South, the queen was forced to abdicate. After a brief interregnum, *Amadeus of Savoy* was invited to the throne, but abdicated three years later, in 1878. For a short period Spain tried the experiment of a Republic (1874-75), but anarchy in the South made it impossible for the successive presidents, *Pi y Margall, Salmerón,* and *Castelar,* to carry their progressive theories into practice.

Meanwhile, the **Second Carlist War** had broken out in the North, but by a *pronunciamiento* at Sagunto, *Martínez Campos* restored the Bourbon dynasty in the person of *Alfonso XII* (1874-85), the eldest son of Isabel. In 1876 a new constitution was formed, establishing a limited monarchy with the power vested in two chambers. Alfonso died in 1885, leaving the country under the regency of *María Cristina*. During this period of comparative calm, Spain was ruled by the alternating governments of the conservatives under *Cánovas del Castillo,* and the radicals under *Sagasta.* In 1898, as a result of the war with the United States of America, Cuba, the Philippines, and Porto Rico were lost to Spain. *Alfonso XIII* was declared of age in 1902, and the alternating party system continued, with the conservative ministries of *Silvela, Maura,* and *Dato,* and the radical ministries of *Canalejas* and *Count Romanones.* During the Great War of 1914-18, Spain remained neutral. In 1921 an insurrection broke out under *Abd-el-Krim* in the Riff, a Spanish protectorate, which was not brought under control until 1926. Meanwhile, in 1923, *Gen. Primo de Rivera* had established a military dictatorship, abolished the Cortes, and governed with a council of ministers. Although there was an increase in material prosperity, the imposition of a strict censorship of the press caused deep dissatisfaction, especially among the intellectuals, and opposition to the regime increased.

Although various attempts to supplant the dictators failed, the devious and hostile attitude of the king made his fall inevitable, and he was compelled to resign in 1930, and died soon after. But support for the crown also disintegrated rapidly, and new political factions began to take shape: the Liberal Republican Right was founded by *Alcalá Zamora,* while the Socialists were grouped under *Largo Caballero.* The result of the municipal elections of April 1931 were indeed largely anti-monarchist, and upon the proclamation of a republican régime in Barcelona, Seville, and other centres, Alfonso acceded to Alcalá Zamora's demand that he should abdicate.

The Civil War. A *Constituent Assembly* was elected and empowered with the function of drawing up a new constitution, which was completed and ratified in Dec. 1931, when Alcalá Zamora was duly elected president of the Republic. Meanwhile, Catalonia had declared herself independent of the Madrid government and proclaimed herself a republic, while strong movements in favour of home rule sprang up in the Basque Provinces and in Galicia. The rigorous reforms introduced by the Constituent Assembly provoked discontent, and resulted in the formation of various conflicting parties, notably Acción Popular and Acción Católica, which greatly contributed to the undermining of the strength of the regime. Recent research has also confirmed that political activists of the Spanish Church were also very largely responsible for fomenting the later rebellion against the government. Radical reforms, long overdue, affecting the structure of the army introduced by the Minister for War, *Manuel Azaña,* aroused resentment among the officers. In spite of sweeping agrarian reforms, and a new Law of Labour Contracts brought in by Largo Caballero, such measures did little to appease the various factions.

A general state of unrest accompanied by widespread strikes set in throughout the country. An insurrection in Seville sponsored by *Gen. Sanjurjo* was quickly suppressed. A far more serious rebellion of miners and workers flared up two years later in the Asturias (October 1934), and after much loss of life, and damage, the movement was brutally stamped out by *Gen. López Ochoa* and *Col. Yagüe*, directed from Madrid by *Gen. Francisco Franco* (1892-1975). After the elections of February 1936, Azaña again became Prime Minister: Alcalá Zamora was compelled to resign and was succeeded as president by Azaña with *Casares Quiroga* as Prime Minister. But disorders became increasingly frequent, and numerous strikes virtually paralysed the normal activities of the population. The imprisonment of *José Antonio Primo de Rivera*, son of the late dictator, and leader of a militant right-wing organization, the *Falange*, and the assassination of the monarchist leader *Calvo Sotelo*, increased the tension between the rival parties.

On 17 July 1936, the garrison in Morocco rebelled under the leadership of *Gen. Franco*, and this was followed by military risings against the government throughout the country—notably under *Gen. Queipo de Llano* in Seville and by *Gen. Mola* in Pamplona. Franco captured Algeciras with airborne troops, and within a short time, after subjugating Badajoz and Mérida with his legionaries and 'moros', he was able to join forces with Mola, but the intended attack on Madrid was delayed in order to relieve the beleaguered alcázar at Toledo. Although at first the European Powers had agreed to adopt an attitude of non-intervention, arms and equipment poured into Spain from all sides, and soon the Civil War ceased to be a strictly national affair. The right-wing Nationalists received considerable military aid from Nazi Germany and Fascist Italy, both in men (c. 17,000 and 75,000 respectively) and material, while the Republican government obtained equipment from Communist Russia and manpower in the form of 'International Brigades' (some 35,000, including c. 2,000-3,000 Russians). After the initial successes of the Nationalists, the territories held by the two sides were roughly equal in geographical extent.

Gen. Franco installed himself by a 'coup d'état' as Head of State, confirmed 'by decree' at Burgos on 1 Oct., while on 20 Nov. José Antonio was shot at Alicante. Although the government retained Madrid (which was to be defended to the last), Valencia, Barcelona, Murcia, Almeria, Alicante, Santander, and Bilbao, the government itself withdrew to Valencia. Largo Caballero was ousted to make way for *Negrin*, while by now Azaña was virtually a prisoner in the hands of Communist extremists. Vigorous attempts made by Franco to storm the capital and cut the Madrid-Valencia road failed. After the capture of Málaga in February 1937, the Italian brigades launched a lightning attack on Guadalajara, only to be routed, but in the North, shortly after the bombing of Guernica by the German Condor Legion on 26 April, Bilbao and Santander fell. At the end of the year Republican government troops entered Teruel, which was recaptured by Franco in February 1938. In the July of that year Republican forces attacked with success along the river Ebro and were able to maintain important strategic positions until November, but fell back before Franco's counter-thrust into Catalonia; Barcelona capitulating the following January. Shortly after these events the situation in Madrid became desperate. *Col. Casado*, commander of the central forces, was in favour of opening negotiations with Franco, but *Gen. Miaja*, insisted that opposition should continue, although by the end of March 1939 organized armed resistance had ceased.

Vindictive reprisals followed, Franco himself showing as heinous a lack of magnanimity as had his revengeful Nationalists at the fall of any town or village, when barbaric proscriptions were frequent, but—to quote Gerald Brenan—'In class wars, it is the side that wins, who kills most'; and, in addition, some two million persons were to pass through concentration camps or prisons during the next three years alone. Indeed, there is no denying that Franco was ultimately responsible for confirming more death sentences than any other statesman in the history of Spain.

Not directly involved in the Second World War, Spain was able to lick her sores and attend to her own disrupted internal affairs undisturbed, but corruption was rife, and there was much suffering. Franco withstood German pressure (interview with Hitler at Hendaye, 23 Oct. 1941), and apart from the anti-Communist gesture of sending the 'Blue Division' to fight against Russia, Spain was able to remain in a state of non-belligerency; indeed she was too weak to do otherwise.

The new regime maintained order by authoritarian methods, which in the course of decades were progressively relaxed, although there was little political freedom as understood by Western democracies. Only one party, known as the 'Movimiento', was permitted, and various forms of censorship rigidly enforced. By a Law of Succession, Franco continued as head of state *(caudillo),* governing with a Council of the Realm. The Cortes, consisting of a single chamber composed ostensibly of representatives of the main national institutions, including the Catholic Church, the Universities, professional syndicates, labour unions, etc., was reintroduced in 1942. In 1956, independence was granted to Spanish Morocco, which in 1957 itself appropriated Spanish Sahara. In 1969 *Juan Carlos*, grandson of Alfonso XIII (who had died in Rome in 1941) was nominated heir to the vacant throne, an expedient considered anachronistic by some, but which met with the approbation of others as being preferable to the alternatives. In Dec. 1973 *Adm. Carrero Blanco*, the reactionary President of the Government, was assassinated. In Nov. 1975, after a valedictory exhibition of inflexibility in convicting impatient 'extremists' without any proper trial (at Burgos; 1970), and again in Aug. 1975, which exposed him to the execration of the World, Gen. Franco died. Juan Carlos I was invested with the trappings of sovereignty—after an interregnum of almost 45 years—being accepted by the populace in general, knowing the monarchy to be limited, while the fabricated myth of the late dictator being the saviour of his country very rapidly evaporated, his fly-blown portraits being replaced overnight by those of the new Head of State, who has since maintained his popularity.

In Dec. 1976 a referendum overwhelmingly confirmed the wish of the much abused Spanish people for political reform. Press censorship was lifted in April 1977, and in the June of that year the first general election for over 40 years returned a government professing to be 'of the Centre'. Nevertheless, demands for political amnesty were only partly granted, and eventually a measure of autonomy was conceded to Cataluña and the Basque Provinces. The latter had been humiliated by repressive measures rigorously enforced by the military and police—still far too often in evidence—some of the more aggressive of whom have been assassinated in retaliation by members of ETA and other more fanatic organizations such as GRAPO, etc. The ultra Right, known as the

Fuerza Nueva, has reacted in an obnoxious and provocative fashion rather than coming to terms with reality.

Meanwhile, progressive forces continue to seek fuller integration with the rest of Europe, behind which Spain has lagged so long, but the intellectual and political desert left behind by Franco has only been partly irrigated; certainly the Universities have much lost ground to make up. The influence of the Church is progressively weakening, although divorce is still difficult to obtain. Freemasonry is now (just) tolerated, while the para-ecclesiatical 'Opus Dei' continues its devious course. Each province still boasts a 'Military' Governor as well as a Civil Governor, but any tarnished prestige the Armed Forces may have enjoyed under the dictatorship, has plummeted.

Whether the government of *Adolfo Suarez,* returned to power in the election of March 1979 under the new 'Democratic' constitution (yet still governing 'by decree')—with a strong Socialist opposition, as confirmed by the municipal elections of that April—will be able to harness the powers of and steer the disparate and separate Spains through the anfractuosities of the modern world, remains to be seen. It has never been an easy task. As Edward Clarke astutely observed in 1763: in Spain they travelled in a 'clumsy coach, drawn by six mules, with *ropes* instead of traces', and 'as the last two only are reined, or rather roped, they run on with the coach with their heads pointing four or five different ways. This is but a trifling circumstance, yet even the merest trifles may sometimes serve to shew the turn and genius of a people'.

ARCHITECTURAL INTRODUCTION

Compared with Spain, few countries have preserved so much evidence of their medieval greatness. Her artistic patrimony has survived comparatively unscathed, and an immense number of fine churches, castles, and palaces still remain, although many buildings have suffered from neglect, which has probably caused more loss than the ravages of war. For although her history has been stormy, and the Napoleonic invasion robbed her of many of her more portable treasures, she has been spared upheavals comparable to the Protestant Reformation or the French Revolution, as well as both World Wars. Even the Civil War did surprisingly little damage to ancient buildings, although there were some serious losses, such as at Sigena. It has been estimated that only 150 churches were entirely destroyed and about 1,850 others seriously damaged. Whether many of these had sufficient architectural merit for their destruction to be considered a cultural loss rather than a loss to the cult, is a matter of speculation.

Spain, partly for climatic reasons, is almost a continent in herself. While the storks of the chilly north cling obstinately to the chimneys of the Escorial, and an icy wind beats against the soaring pinnacles of the cathedral at León, the narrow winding streets of Toledo, the troglodyte villages near Guadix, and the sun-scorched flat-roofed mud-built houses of the south are purely African. In Spain, being then the meeting-point of both Christian and Moslem civilizations, one will find, built at the same time, such masterpieces as the Pórtico de la Gloria at Compostela, a superb example of late Romanesque, and the Giralda at Seville, one of the finest minarets in existence; while among the many other Moorish relics, the Mezquita at Córdoba, and the Alhambra at Granada, are world famous. Moorish Spain possessed a higher civilization than Christian Spain: Córdoba, the capital, was one of the largest cities in the world, and the centre of a tradition, both cultural and material, compared with which the level of the Christians in the north was almost barbarous. Nevertheless, the story of Christian architecture in Spain is equally fascinating. In the first place, in the 9-10C, in almost the only corner left to them in the Peninsula, the rulers of the kingdom of the Asturias produced in and around Oviedo, a number of remarkable little churches and other buildings the like of which is to be found in no other country, and which are far superior to contemporary Saxon work in Britain or to anything of that date in France. In the period immediately following, Spain should no longer be thought of as merely two countries divided by race and religion, for Christian Spain was subdivided into several states with constantly changing frontiers open to various influences from abroad. Thus, while a slowly decreasing portion of southern Spain remained Moslem for over 700 years, and open only to African or Near-Eastern influences, for some four centuries Castile and the north in general became architecturally a French province, while Catalonia looked to Italy for inspiration and itself became a centre of a traditional style spreading into Languedoc.

The position has been well summed up in the phrase: 'The art of Spain is alluvial'—implying, not only that waves of foreign influence broke upon her shore, left their impress and receded, but also that the Spaniards failed to take advantage of the new learning. It is certainly true that French monasteries dictated the usual sequence of Romanesque and Gothic, while later, Renaissance architecture and the principal elements of Baroque were imported directly from Italy. It is also true that in no other Western country were so many foreign artists employed. In the 12th and 13Cs their names usually proclaim them as French. By the 14C, Frenchmen, Burgundians, Flemings, Germans, Italians, and even a few Englishmen—skilled architects, sculptors, ironworkers, glass-workers, or silversmiths—jostled one another in the race to supply this 'new' country with expert technique. In the Renaissance and Baroque ages, Italians, and later Frenchmen, formed the bulk of these foreign technicians, while many Spaniards went to Italy for instruction.

The Spaniards, with the peculiar and immensely vital creative spirit of their own, inevitably found a way to adapt and modify the various styles imported, which soon became characteristically Spanish. No one, standing in the cathedrals of Burgos or Toledo, whose interiors are predominantly French, could suppose he was anywhere but in Spain. Spanish Renaissance and Baroque also have a flavour very different from the Renaissance and Baroque of Italy.

The Spanish were intensely conservative in architecture. This is due, perhaps, not so much to a question of temperament, as to the subdivision of the Peninsula into disunited provinces, separated from each other by arid wildernesses and mountain ranges, both thinly populated, and to the subsequent extreme difficulties of contact and transport in so vast a country. Whatever the precise explanation, fashion in architecture changed very slowly and once implanted, underwent little spontaneous or conscious development. This is most noticeable with Romanesque, which survived for more than three centuries, and long after the introduction of Gothic. Here one cannot resist the conclusion that most Spaniards, not without reason, felt that Gothic, developing towards walls of glass, was wholly unsuited to a country of blinding sunlight. But when Gothic was supplanted by Renaissance, they were equally loath to change—for example, the Gothic cathedrals at Salamanca and Segovia were not begun until well into the 16C, the latter only being finished in 1592, seven years after the completion of the Escorial, a monument of the High Renaissance. This was further complicated by the existence of two hybrid styles peculiar to Spain: firstly, the *Mozarabic*, brought by Christian refugees fleeing from persecution in Córdoba, whose beautiful mosque-like churches, founded on the great *mezquita* in their former home, form one of the most curious chapters in Western art. Their horseshoe and lobed arches were even reproduced in France before the style was cut off in its prime by Cluniac Romanesque. The second hybrid, *Mudéjar,* is a whole family of styles, regional and chronological, brought to Christian Spain as the reconquest developed, by captured moslems and their descendants who stayed on in their native towns after surrendering, or who, as artisans and workmen particularly skilled as bricklayers, plasterers, and carpenters, migrated, in some cases, to the north. Their style of work, although originating mainly in pure Moorish building, is usually blended, according to period and region, with Romanesque, Gothic, or Renaissance. The precise degree of blend differs in almost every building and has a charm entirely its own. It appealed so much to the Christians that several of even the greatest 15th and 16C architects and decorators—foreigners as well as Spaniards—succumbed to its spell and included typically Moorish elements in their designs. It is thus because of Mudéjar that one finds obvious Moorish workmanship and taste in the north of Spain, e.g. in the vaulting, plasterwork, and ceilings at Las Huelgas at Burgos. Mudéjar likewise explains the curiously Arabic appearance of Toledo, although in Christian hands since 1085. And to this day, in almost the whole of Aragón, Moorish taste, as translated for us by the Mudéjars, is still the dominant feature of the landscape; indeed the national taste is perhaps more deeply permeated with this tradition than is often willingly admitted.

Spanish buildings undoubtedly possess a unique 'atmosphere'. One can attempt to summarize the essential characteristics as follows: first, a predilection for solidity of construction: hence, the heaviness and austerity of Spanish Romanesque together with its long duration; hence, too, the massiveness of the Herreran, much of the Baroque, the Neo-Classic, and domestic architecture throughout.

Secondly, a curious partiality for square blocks: buildings as lofty and as wide only as they are long, or precisely twice the length of their height and width. Or again, a preference for squareness in decoration; for instance, rectangular frames for anything, such as octagons, equilateral triangles, stars, and round-headed arches, that can be fitted into a square. Such proportions lead to a sense of calm and repose, an absence of fussiness in even the most ornate and ostentatious interiors. This squareness, noticeable in the Alhambra, in many Renaissance works, and in all forms of decoration, is the very antithesis of French Gothic with its emphasis on the vertical. It accounts for what might be called Horizontal Spanish Gothic, for the solid squareness of Spanish towers, for twin windows arranged in pairs *(ajimez)* and for the characteristic square drip-stone *(alfiz)* over doorways.

Thirdly comes an inclination to divide a space into compartments. Long, uninterrupted vistas do not appeal to Spaniards. Whether in the Alhambra, in churches, or in lengthy rooms, such vistas are broken up by series of columns, by screens, or curtains, and alcoves become a predilection. Hence, too, perhaps, the custom of alternating the barest plain surfaces with squares or bands of rich surface decoration, as in Moslem work, and in low relief, as in Isabelline and Plateresque.

Finally, a curious tendency towards hanging decoration. It originates, possibly, from Moslem stalactite ceilings and fringed arches; it appears in veritable tapestries of stone, stucco, or marble hanging from ceilings, vaults, and domes. Again, ornament seems to hang with no visible support from carved altarpieces, from façades and portals. Examples include the 16C façades of *S. Gregorio,* Valladolid, the *University* at Salamanca, and the Baroque *Hospicio de S Fernando,* Madrid.

To generalize, perhaps the most striking feature is contrast: austerity with exuberance; massive stone buildings decorated with lace-like plasterwork; the simple grandeur of plain surfaces contrasted with sumptuous and extravagant decoration. It is true also that one finds a certain theatrical exaggeration and ostentation: exaggerated formality in the Herreran and Neo-Classic; exaggerated ornament in Late Gothic and Plateresque; and pure sensationalism in the Churrigueresque. There is no denying that for rich, and even sumptuous effects Spanish architecture has no parallel; and it also has unrivalled dignity.

ROMAN AND PRE-ROMANESQUE

The history of architecture in Spain begins in Roman days, although the Cossetanians, an Iberian tribe, are remembered for their cyclopean walls of unhewn stone at *Tarragona,* and the Greeks have left vestiges of colonies of the 6C B.C. at *Ampurias* and elsewhere on the Levant coast. In comparison with earlier civilizations the Romans are well represented, although remains are scarce considering the importance and duration of their dominion. The best preserved are those for which succeeding ages found a use. Temples and theatres fell into ruin, but engineering works were constantly repaired and long served their original purpose. The aqueduct at *Segovia* is, with the possible exception of the Pont du Gard, the finest Roman aqueduct surviving. Others are seen at *Tarragona* and at *Mérida,* and smaller ones at *Almuñécar,* and between Seville and Alcalá de Guadaira. *Mérida* is a complete Roman city, with a theatre, and amphitheatre, a triumphal arch, the bridge of Augustus, half a mile long—the longest in the Roman Empire—a circus, a stadium, an artificial reservoir, and temples dedicated to Diana and Mars. Amphitheatres or theatres are also to be seen at *Itálica, Tarragona, Clunia* (Coruña del Conde), and *Ronda.* That at Itálica was, after the Colosseum, the largest in the Empire, but the best preserved is at *Sagunto.* City Walls remain at *Tarragona, Astorga,* and *Lugo;* there are remains of a bridge at *Martorell,* and other works at *Barcelona, Valencia,* and *Vic,* while the bridge spanning the Tagus at *Alcántara* is one of the most remarkable examples of civil engineering and the loftiest Roman bridge in existence. There remain also a few triumphal arches such as that at *Medinaceli,* and the *Arco de Bará* near Tarragona, while mausoleums exist at *Tarragona, Fabara* (near Caspe), and *Sádaba.* Inevitably these buildings were pillaged by later builders, and Roman columns and capitals became normal features in almost all pre-Romanesque churches.

The Visigoths, with their close relations with the Near East, brought to Spain a medley of influences. Traffic in small objects, particularly consular ivories, had some effect upon Visigothic decoration, but local constructional ideas were in part based upon monuments in Persia, Syria, and the north coast of Africa, at this time Christian (Arian), and in part upon Roman works they found in Spain. They were also conversant with contemporary works in Italy. There are remains of 5C baptisteries at *Gabia la Grande* (Granada) and at *Centelles* (Tarragona), but the best example is that now called *S. Miguel* at *Tarrasa,* which recalls both Roman work and early Christian buildings at Ravenna.

Some examples of Visigothic sculpture may be found at the 'Conventual' and Museum at *Mérida,* housing lintels, pilasters, and bands of ornament of typical decadent Roman type, some of them markedly Eastern Roman rather than Western. Here one finds the earliest *ajimez* to twin horseshoe window in Spain with the lights divided by a colonnette, as well as the 'Maltese' cross, helices, stars, and the 'cable border', all of which are regarded as the most characteristic features of Visigothic ornamentation. One should note that it was not the Moslems who introduced the horseshoe arch into Spain, although they adopted it, modified it, giving it a point, and used it almost to the exclusion of all other forms. It is to be found (always round-headed) as a decoration on nearly sixty Spanish Roman stelae of the 2nd to 5C, and the Visigoths, owing to their contact with the Near East, where it was known as early as 300 B.C., used it constructionally and also in plan. But there is a subtle difference between the Visigothic and Moorish horseshoe, which is highly technical and has been explained in several conflicting ways, but is fairly obvious to the eye, for the Moorish horseshoe appears to be carried down further, and therefore to be more 'pinched' at the base than the Visigothic. One of the finest Visigothic churches is that of *S. Juan* at *Baños de Cerrato* (Palencia), although it contains little in decoration that foreshadows Moslem taste beyond tiny horseshoe windows and a splendid nave arcade of slightly horseshoe arches. They spring from bastard Corinthian capitals and Roman columns taken from the neighbouring baths, and it appears that the whole interior of the church was originally veneered with marble. Of other Visigothic churches one need only mention three: the crypt of *Palencia Cathedral,* possibly built in 673; *Sta Comba de Bande,* remotely situated in the province of Orense; and *S. Pedro de la Nave,* near Zamora.

Asturian. In the 8C nearly all Spain was in Moslem hands, but in Galicia and in the Asturias, shielded from the invaders by the Cantabrian mountains, the Christians reorganized their forces and set up a kingdom with Oviedo as their capital. Here, in an area only some 40 miles by 30, they erected a group of pre-Romanesque buildings of the highest interest. In style, they continue the Visigothic tradition, with debased classical ornament, but carved in a manner perhaps even more rustic than that used by the Visigoths themselves. The earliest of these are the Cámera Santa, now incorporated into the *Cathedral* at *Oviedo,* and *S. Julián de los Prados,* or *Santullano;* both built by an architect named Tioda for Alfonso the Chaste (791-842), while from the reign of Ramiro I (842-50) there remain *S. Miguel de Lillo,* and *Sta Maria de Naranco,* just outside Oviedo. Among later Asturian buildings should be mentioned *Sta Cristina de Lena* (905-12), *S. Salvador de Valdedios,* and *S. Salvador de Priesca.* One may well inquire how so vital and robust a style should have come to an untimely and sudden end. The answer is that with the moving of the capital from Oviedo to León, and the increasing importance of regions easily accessible from France, the importation of French Romanesque soon stifled it. But first there came an artistic invasion from the south.

Mozarabic. For over a hundred years after the Moorish invasion, the Christians of S. Spain were permitted to keep their religion, to elect bishops, and to build churches. Many spoke arabic, they dressed like Moors, and they assimilated Moorish culture. Unfortunately, there now survives, it seems, only two churches thus built under Moslem domination: *Sta Maria de Melque,* near S. Martín de Montalbán (S.W. of Toledo), and *Bobastro,* N. of *Alora* (Málaga). All other examples of Mozarabic architecture are the work of refugees who fled from Córdoba in the 9-10C to Aragón, Galicia, the Asturias, and León, and they naturally brought with them the style of architecture of their former home. This exodus of 'arabized' Christians had the effect of enriching the north of Spain, where the finest examples of their art are to be found, and not, as one would expect, in the south. They vary greatly in type, but nearly all include features borrowed direct from the Mezquita at Córdoba, and the typically Moorish horseshoe arch is almost universal both in construction and decoration. It is used in the nave arcades, which are often supported on monolithic columns with 'broken palm-leaf' capitals, and the chancel arches (also horseshoe) are usually copied from *mihrab* fronts; while the sanctuaries, horseshoe in plan and roofed with 'melon' domes, are copies from the mihrab itself. Other domes have parallel ribs as in the *maqsurah* at Córdoba, and windows and doorways are framed with the typical Moorish rectangular label known as an *alfiz*. Wooden roofs are often supported on curious corbels or eaves brackets decorated with stars and helices. One of the most accessible of these churches is *S. Miguel de Escalada*, S.E. of León, consecrated in 913. Other striking examples are *S. Cebrián de Mazote* (Valladolid), and *Sta Maria de Bamba; Santiago de Peñalba*, and *Sto Tomás de las Ollas*, near Ponferrada; *S. Miguel de Celanova*, S. of Orense, and *Sta Maria de Lebeña*, near Potes. In Catalonia, there remain the less striking examples of *S. Quirce de Pedret, Sta Maria de Marquet*, and *S. Miguel de Olérdola*, all of them 10C. More interesting are those in Castile, namely *S. Millán de la Cogolla, S. Baudel*, near Berlanga del Duero, and *N.S. de las Viñas* at *Quintanilla*, near Salas de los Infantes. Small decorative features of Mozarabic art, such as lobed arches and miniature horseshoe arches occasionally persisted in Spanish Romanesque, and are found in Southern France in buildings, for instance at Le Puy, and in Limoges enamels, while Mozarabic manuscripts were to influence French manuscript painting almost until the Gothic period. It is noticeable how many modern Spanish words concerning buildings are of arab derivation, apart from the builder *albañil* and architect *alarife* themselves. Houses were often made of sun-dried bricks, *adobe*, adorned with blue tiles, *azulejos*, with terraces, *azoteas*, alcoves, *alcobas*, portico, *zaguán*, and provided with culverts, *alcantarillas*, and *algibes*, water conduits, etc.

Moorish Architecture

Islamic or Moslem art covered a larger area of the world than medieval Christianity, and had as many subdivisions, including such well-defined regional variations as the Syrian, the Egyptian, the Persian, the Ottoman, the Indian, and the Moroccan. But to only two of these belong the so-called Moorish buildings in Spain. The first style, as shown at Córdoba, originates primarily from buildings in Syria, Egypt, and on the north coast of Africa. The second style, as shown in the Alhambra, is that of the Maghreb, which included Tunisia and Algeria as well as Morocco and Southern Spain. The Alhambra is in fact the principal monument of the Maghreb.

Art of the Caliphate. Once the invaders of the early 8C, Berbers and Arabs, settled down in the land of their adoption, Córdoba became the capital of the Western Moslem world. It soon rivalled Baghdad and Constantinople in the splendour of its monuments, and was in fact, after the latter, the largest town in Europe, with a population estimated at between 500,000 and a million. Its bronze-founders, gold- and silver-smiths, and ivory carvers produced some exquisite work which is still preserved in the treasuries of Spanish cathedrals and the principal museums of Europe and America. There was a direct trade in textiles and pottery with Baghdad (such textiles being also imported from Andalucía by the Christian monarchs of the north), while Near-Eastern pottery exercises an influence upon Spanish peasant pottery to this day.

The importance of Córdoba stems from the fact that in A.D. 756 Abderrahman made a deliberate attempt to fix the religious centre of Islam in the West, after breaking away from the Baghdad Caliphate. Architecturally, the *Mezquita* or Mosque of Córdoba incorporated a number of audacious constructional features, based chiefly on Damascus and Kairawan (in Tunisia), among which may be mentioned first the double rows of arches supporting the wooden roof; all of them of ultra-semicircular horseshoe form, and of white stone alternating with red brick. Secondly should be noted the 10C innovations in the *maqsurah* or vestibule of three bays in front of the *mihrab;* these include intersecting arches, lobed and multifoil arches, true composite piers and lofty domical vaults with massive coupled ribs intersecting to form star patterns in the centre. All these features eventually found their way into Christian Spain, where in both Romanesque and Gothic one can continue to trace their 'descendants' for centuries. Similar vaulting, but on a diminutive scale, can be seen in the miniature mosque in Toledo which was converted on the recapture of the city into the church of *Santo Cristo de la Luz.*

It is unfortunate that the only great civil monument of this period, the summer palace of the Caliphs at *Medina Azahara,* just W. of Córdoba, was destroyed in the 11C, but recent discoveries and reconstructions show that its decoration was quite as rich as anything in the mosque. Among other surviving monuments may be mentioned the sovereign's private mosque in the *Aljafería* at *Zaragoza.* On the decline of the Caliphate and the rise of the warring *tâifa* kingdoms, much rebuilding of city walls took place. These usually consisted of a double enceinte, and the towers, square or polygonal, were built either of stone, brick, or cement encrusted with pebbles, and the crenellations are of a distinctive Moorish type. To this epoch we owe much of the surviving fortifications of Córdoba, Seville, Almería, Jaén, Ronda, Málaga, and the castle of Alcalá de Guadiara.

Art of the Maghreb. With the coming of the Almohades (1147-1235), the capital was transferred temporarily to Seville, and we fortunately retain from this period the *Giralda,* which with its trellis-like diaper of pink brickwork (reminiscent of Marrakesh and Rabat in Morocco) is by far the finest minaret not only in Spain, but in the whole Maghreb. According to tradition, Fernando III, during the siege of Seville of 1248, threatened the Moorish population with annihilation if one brick of the Giralda were loosened. On the fall of Seville, Moslem Spain became concentrated in the kingdom of Granada. Pleasure and repose rather than vitality became the keynote of their style, and their monuments show them to have been ornamentalists rather than architects. Even the late 12C *Patio del Yeso* surviving from the original Seville *Alcázar,* already exhibits the arabesque and stucco decoration typical of the Alhambra. Henceforward the Andalusian interiors are as sumptuous as their exteriors, for fear of the Evil Eye, are bare. The walls of the *Alhambra* (1232-1408) embroidered in plaster, hung with gesso tapestries below delicate stalactical pendatives and surrounded by dados or richly coloured *azulejos,* contribute to produce an insinuating sensation of splendour and voluptuousness rarely experienced in occidental buildings.

ROMANESQUE ARCHITECTURE

Catalonia. By the end of the 9C Catalonia had developed close contact with Languedoc, Provence, and N. Italy, and it is here that the earliest Romanesque churches in the Peninsula are to be found. There remain at least seventy-five, but most are small, aisleless, built of undressed masonry and roofed with timber, and they have little sculpture. Where aisles occur, single columns or plain rectangular piers support equally plain round-headed arches. The exteriors of these churches are distinguished by Lombard blind arcading and pilasters, and by tall square belfries, also typically Italian. Fine examples survive at *S. Miguel de Cuxá* (1040), *Breda,* and *S. Miguel de Fluviá.* There are also examples of unorthodox planning, such as trefoil-shaped apses, while stone barrel vaults were already known before 950 and certain vaulting improvements seem to have been made before their adoption in either France or Italy. The five-aisled basilica of *Ripoll,* with its worn but richly sculptured W. Doorway, is the largest example of the style. Others are *S. Vicente de Cardona* and *S. Llorens del Munt,* with their typically Lombard polygonal cupolas. In neighbouring Aragón, the castle and chapel of *Loarre,* and the monastic church of *Leyre,* are also important. Indeed sculpture plays an integral part in later Catalan Romanesque. There are many fine 12C cloisters, for example at the *Cathedral* and *S. Pedro de Galligáns* at *Gerona, S. Cugat de Vallés, Estany, Ripoll,* and *S. Benito de Bages,* in which one finds capitals splendidly carved with interlacing floral ornament or with figures and scenes, the workmanship very like that at Arles.

Castile. In contrast to Catalonia, Romanesque influence in Castile was a comparatively sudden penetration. During the reign of Sancho the Great of Navarre (1000-35), the Benedictine monks of Cluny entered the country, immediately set about the reorganization of the Spanish Church, and fostered a series of Crusades. Before 1100 fourteen such expeditions set out from France, and another fifteen before 1150. They also established on an international scale the pilgrimage to Santiago de Compostela, which before had only been a local concern. With royal support, the Benedictines constructed roads from Bordeaux and Toulouse, viâ Roncevaux and the Somport respectively, to Nájera, Santo Domingo de la Calzada, Burgos, and León, and dotted this road with monasteries, churches and hospices, so that pilgrims could make the 500-mile journey along the *Camino Francés,* as it was known, significantly—in Spanish the *Camino de Santiago,* or the 'Milky Way'— in thirteen full-day stages from the frontier. Both at the beginning and at the end of the road they built at precisely the same time, two great churches almost identical in their chevets and general proportions, St Sernin of Toulouse and *Santiago de Compostela.* The latter, although masked outside with Baroque trappings, remains comparatively unaltered inside and is the earliest and most uniform Cluniac work in Spain, begun in 1075 and materially completed in 1128. Other early churches on the Pilgrimage Road are the *Cathedral* at *Jaca, S. Martín* at *Frómista,* and *S. Isidoro* at *León.* By the beginning of the 12C N. Spain had become the most flourishing province of the Cluniac Order outside France. Fernando I himself became a lay brother, and gave to the Order three important monasteries, *Carrión de los Condes, Sahagún,* and

Frómista. His son, Alfonso VI, self-styled 'Sovereign of the Two Religions' and father-in-law of Raymond of Burgundy, appointed his confessor, a Frenchman named Bernard de Sédirac, first abbot of Sahagún (to which eventually 130 Spanish monasteries became subject) and later as first archbishop of Toledo and Primate of Spain. In his turn Sédirac appointed thirteen French bishops in the country.

One would expect the Cluniac monks to have planted innumerable derivatives of their mother church at Cluny, or at least to have introduced Burgundian Romanesque; and it is true that they have left a few examples in Spain such as *S. Vicente* at *Ávila*. But curiously enough they introduceed much more often the variants of Romanesque found in W. and S.W. France. For instance at *Sto Domingo* at *Soria* and at *Sangüesa*, one finds the arcaded west fronts of Poitou; at *Salamanca* the stone-shingled spire from Poitiers itself; and at *Silos*, at *León*, and on the Pta de las Platerías at *Compostela* a type of sculpture typically Toulousain. But one also finds a great number of churches in which the origins are inextricably confused and difficult to identify. At a somewhat later stage too one finds local Spanish schools of Romanesque, eclectic in origin but sufficiently individual to be classed as new variants, which is not surprising considering that over 700 Romanesque churches are said to survive in Spain. Outstanding among these variants are the Galician, often with remarkable rose windows not unlike the Sicilian; the Segovian, with large W. and lateral porches; the Zamoran, with curiously massive sculpture; and finally the several regions where brick was the only building material—Sahagún, Arévalo, Cuéllar, etc.—in which Mudéjar features make their first appearance. Here, too, one should note the 12C cloister at *Silos,* in which, although the bas-reliefs are Toulousain, the capitals, unsurpassed for their wealth of invention and their perfect execution, are so finely chiselled as to be attributed even to Moorish slaves.

In due course each important cathedral set a local fashion and had its derivatives. For instance, in Galicia, the model of Compostella served for those of *Lugo, Orense,* and *Túy,* the latter partly fortified as was Compostela at one time. The only essential difference was the introduction of pointed instead of round barrel-vaulting, but the transverse ribs remained as massive as before. As remarked earlier, the Spaniards were strangely conservative. Although the pointed arch was occasionally introduced in connection with vaulting almost as early as in France—e.g. at *La Oliva,* begun in 1164, and *Veruela*—its constructional advantages do not seem to have been appreciated. There was no obvious evolution from Romanesque to Gothic. While it is understandable that the Spaniards did not want to build churches of glass as in France, it would seem that they preferred a ponderous solidity of construction to forms that 'fly'. The result is that Spain has a number of magnificent but massive churches which, although Transitional and employing the pointed arch, are still Romanesque in spirit, among them the *Old* Cathedral at *Salamanca,* and those at *Zamora, Toro,* and *Ciudad Rodrigo*. The first three also have remarkable central lantern towers, derivatives of which are also found in the chapter house at *Plasencia* and in the Cathedral at *Évora* in Portugal. In the late 12th and early 13C there rose in N.E. Spain another series of massive Transitional cathedrals: *Tarragona, Lérida, Sigüenza, Santa Domingo de la Calzada,* and *Tudela*. All have Gothic vaulting and pointed arches, but are still Romanesque in their solidity, their small windows, and their fortress-like aspect. There is no doubt that in these the influence of the Cistercians was of great importance. Just as former sovereigns had summoned the Cluniac Benedictines to Spain, so Alfonso VII imported the Cistercians. The first monks from Clairvaux arrived in 1131 at *Moreruela,* and there began a Cistercian 'invasion' almost as thorough as that of the Cluniacs. Few countries can claim so fine a collection of Cistercian abbeys. Altogether, more than sixty were founded, and more than half are still standing in whole or in part, among them *Fitero, La Oliva, Veruela, Piedra, Rueda, Gradéfes,* and *Las Huelgas; Osera, Melón, Meira,* and *Oya* in Galicia; and in Catalonia the two great monasteries at *Poblet* and *Santes Creus,* which have preserved their conventual dependencies almost complete. Most of the simplicity, sobriety, and vigour of later Spanish Romanesque is due to the Cistercians, who also introduced quadripartite, sexpartite, and octopartite vaulting. But the Spaniards made no attempt to act on the new building principles involved. Walls remained massive and windows small, and flying buttresses were not constructed.

Early Gothic Architecture

French Gothic in Castile. By the 13C the influence of the Benedictine and Cistercian monks had waned, although there are a few minor masterpieces of early Gothic for which the Cistercians were directly responsible, such as the refectory at *Sta Maria de la Huerta.* The secular bishops, many of whom travelled abroad, now took the place of the monastic orders as patrons of art. Another generation of French architects entered the country, and the foundations were laid of three immense cathedrals: *Burgos, Toledo,* and *León.* They belong to the great cosmopolitan Gothic style which had been founded in the Domaine Royale of France and which spread throughout Western Europe. The Spanish examples may not be as lofty as those of France, nor as long as those of England, but they are magnificent expressions of French Gothic and none the less inspiring for being set as exotic flowers on the barren plains of Castile. Apart from *Cuenca* cathedral, which has many northern features, the first Gothic cathedral in Spain was *Burgos* (1221). Six years later *Toledo* Cathedral, the metropolitan church, was begun, while that at *León,* completed c. 1303, was the first in Spain to have a glazed triforium throughout, and in which the clerestory windows fill the whole space between the vaulting shafts, fulfilling the French ambition to construct a church with walls entirely of glass. Curiously enough the beauties of León created no architectural tradition in Castile and there are no important derivatives. Burgos, on the other hand, had many—such churches as *Támara, Aguilar de Campóo, Sta Maria del Campo, Sasamón,* and the Cathedral of *El Burgo de Osma,* and *Palencia* Cathedral, another fine example of later French Gothic, completed, however, in Flamboyant. Finally *Sta Maria* at *Castro-Urdiales* and *Pamplona* Cathedral are both rich in fine French sculpture of a type repeated at *Vitoria.*

Catalan Gothic. In the late 13C Barcelona was the capital of a great Mediterranean Empire. An expansion in trade and population led to an increase in building activity and to the patronage of art on a generous scale. Here there was no direct importation of northern French architects as in Castile. Catalan architects, rational and sophisticated, soon evolved a purely regional, scientifically-planned variation of Gothic.

As in many other parts of Europe where the 'hall church' was beginning to appear, the great Catalan churches were built for public, not monastic worship, and the prime objective in construction was to make the high altar visible to the entire congregation. The Catalans found two ways of doing this; first to build very wide aisleless churches with no columns to block the view, and secondly, churches with immensely wide central naves divided by tall slender columns from very narrow collaterals. For both types a wide vault was necessary and, to support this, massive oblong buttresses were provided, between which were placed side-chapels, their outside walls flush with the ends of the buttresses. These buttresses do not show from the outside except above the aisle roof and hence become 'internal', Artistically it was not a happy solution and the long unbroken wall surfaces of Catalan churches cannot vie with the picturesquely broken outline of northern churches, but they are remarkably capable works of engineering. The earliest example of the aisleless type, Sta Catalina in Barcelona, begun in 1223, no longer exists, but there remain many others, including *Sta María del Pino*, and *SS. Justo y Pastor* in *Barcelona* itself, and the plan was copied throughout southern France where the outstanding example is at Albi.

The foremost Catalan architect was **Jaime Fabre,** a Mallorquin, who seems to have been the genius responsible for the *Cathedral* at *Barcelona,* and *Sta María del Mar,* in turn used as models for other churches such as *La Seo* at *Manresa,* and *Tortosa* Cathedral. In every one, the triforia and clerestories are sacrificed in order to give added height to the main arcade, and the columns, often octagonal, rise unbroken to nearly twice the height of those in any northern church of this period. The supreme example of Catalan constructional engineering is *Gerona* Cathedral. Here, to a three-aisled chevet with a corona of radiating chapels, **Guillem Bofill** or *Boffy* added a gigantic single nave with a clear span of 22 m, the widest vault of any Gothic church.

In Catalonia civil architecture was also noteworthy, beginning with the *Tinell Hall* of the Royal Palace in *Barcelona* and the *Hall of the Hundred,* which have wooden roofs supported on wide semicircular arches. Then comes a series of *Lonjas* or Exchanges, such as those at *Barcelona,* the earliest, and at *Valencia, Palma,* and later, at *Zaragoza.*

Mudéjar Architecture

We must retrace out steps to deal with the *Mudéjar* style. Although between the 12th and 14C the Christians had recovered almost the whole country, Moors and Jews continued to live on their native soil. More than a hundred towns possessed ghettos or *aljamas* in which these subject Mudéjars (and Jews) were segregated, and although not allowed to build or possess mosques, many clung to their religion, and were not converted until the 16C. Yet the Christians showed toleration towards Moorish art, using it even for their tombs. The lace-like canopies of those at *Cuéllar* and *S. Juan de la Penitencia* at *Toledo,* or the chapel of the Annunciation in *Sigüenza* Cathedral, are outstanding examples of Mudéjar blended with Florentine Renaissance, and proof of the sentiment 'they lack our faith but we their works', as expressed by Card.

Cisneros, and remember also Charles V's rebuke on seeing the new cathedral erecting in the Mezquita at Córdoba. While the great cathedrals and abbeys were built largely in the French styles, the Mudéjars were employed mainly on the smaller churches, to which their art was more suited. Of this class are the *Casa de Mesa*, the *Taller del Moro*, and the two *synagogues* at *Toledo*. The earlier of these, *Sta María la Blanca*, with its octagonal pillars and round-headed horseshoe arches, is derived from the Caliphate style, but the rich plasterwork of the second, *El Tránsito*, recalls later Andalusian buildings. Toledo alone preserves no less than nine Mudéjar churches, their apses and towers with trefoil, horseshoe, and intersecting arches, as well as the *Pta del Sol*.

A second medium of influence was the court. Christian kings had seized Moslem palaces at Toledo, Huesca, Zaragoza, Lérida, and Valencia, and found them more comfortable than Romanesque or Gothic dwellings, and Pedro the Cruel actually rebuilt and restored an earlier palace at Seville in imitation of the Alhambra. This predilection for Moorish art is also seen in the north, in the convent-palaces of *Astudillo*, and *Tordesillas*; and all through the 14C it was the custom for nobles, even in the far north, to decorate the interiors of their castles with Mudéjar brick and plasterwork. In the south, Mudéjar decoration in stucco persisted until it gradually merged with that of the Renaissance as in the so-called *House of Pilate* (Seville), built in the reign of Charles V. The garden pavilion, also of this date, at the Alcázar, still preserves perfectly the proportions of a Moorish building, and throughout southern Spain Mudéjar work remained remarkably pure in style. At *Sahagún*, one of the first northern towns to employ Mudéjars, two Romanesque churches, *S. Tirso* and *S. Lorenzo*, are decorated with simple recessed panels of bricks. Almost contemporary are *S. Lorenzo* at *Toro*, *La Lugareja* at *Arévalo*, and *S. Salvador* at *Cuéllar*, all with towers that slope slightly inwards like many minarets. Other strange examples are the 13C cloisters of *S. Juan de Duero* at *Soria*, with their interlacing and horseshoe arches, and the cupola of *S. Miguel* at *Almazán*, with coupled ribs derived from the *maqsurah* at Córdoba.

Of Mudéjar mingled with Gothic there are numerous examples in Castile; one of the most interesting is the brick cloister at *Guadalupe*. Even more curious than Castilian Mudéjar, is that of Aragón. Here the belfries, often detached, like minarets, from the buildings they serve, form a striking feature of the landscape. The earliest (13C) are square, and at *Teruel* some of their wall surfaces patterned in brick and decorated with coloured tiles, stand astride the streets, forming town gates as well as belfries. The 14th and 15C towers are usually octagonal, and survive at *Tarazona*, *Daroca*, *Alarcón*, *Ateca*, *Utebo*, *Tardienta*, and *Calatayúd*. At *Tobed*, *Torralba de Ribota*, and *Morata de Jiloca*, there are windows of two or three lights with flamboyant tracery in the heads but stone jalousies below, and the walls are lined with patterned gesso.

Of the Spanish minor arts due to the Mudejáres none was so important as ceiling construction. Although of many varied types, flat, peaked, polygonal, deeply coffered and in the form of domes, usually called *'media naranja'*, the designs upon them are made from tiny pieces of wood to form interlacing geometrical patterns. Extremely rich in effect, for they are also painted and gilded, and sometimes rise from stalactite cornices, they are found all over Spain.

MILITARY AND LATER GOTHIC ARCHITECTURE

Castles. That 'châteaux en Espagne' should be synonymous with chimeras appears to be due to the unfulfilled expectations of foreign knights whom the Spaniards urged to help them in local crusades against the Moors. The phrase is found in French literature as early as the 13C and in English in the 14C. Spain is particularly rich in castles; however, comparatively few of those still standing were built by the Christians to prevent the return of the Moors, and of purely Moorish citadels not many survive. First and foremost should be mentioned the *Alhambra*, then *Alcalá de Guadaira, Málaga* with its castle of *Gibralfaro, Carmona* with its horseshoe gateway, *Tarifa, Almería,* and *Almodóvar del Rio.* All these are in the south, while in the north *Gormaz* (S.W. of Soria) is outstanding. It is believed that there were some 400 Moorish castles in Spain, and what little remains is sufficient to suggest that in the art of fortification the Moors were more advanced than the Christians, and that certain features that were first adopted in Palestine by the crusaders (e.g. pentagonal towers) were repeated in Spanish castles earlier than elsewhere in Western Europe. Particularly striking is the Moorish appearance of many Christian castles near Toledo, for instance *Almonacid,* and the use made, as at *Escalona* and *Montalbán* in the same region, of colossal wedge-shaped towers projecting from the inner walls right over the outer walls, lofty pointed arches allowing communication through the 'lices'.

Romanesque military architecture is represented by the unrivalled monument of *Ávila,* which still looks like the city of an illuminated manuscript, girt with battlemented walls in perfect preservation, dating from the last decade of the 11C. At *Astorga, León,* and *Lugo,* are other Romanesque city walls, in part on Roman foundations. The fortified monastery of *Loarre* is also of the 11th and 12C, while the fine stretch of curtain wall at *Berlanga de Duero* appears to date from the 13C. At *Madrigal de las Altas Torres* the walls formed a perfect circle c. 700 m. in diameter. *Seville* and *Niebla* have also preserved stretches of wall and several gateways, but of later walled towns should be mentioned *Albarracín* and *Morella,* and *Daroca,* where the gates are Mudéjar. *Toledo* retains gateways and two fortified bridges over the Tagus, while other examples of town gates are those of *Valencia, Burgos,* and *Vivero.*

Most of the great castles now to be seen in Spain—and they form a very impressive array—date from the 15C, and were erected either by kings or by powerful nobles jealous of royal and other interference. Of the royal castles, the most imposing is the vast castle-palace, somewhat of the type of the Papal Palace at Avignon, erected by Charles the Noble of Navarre at *Olite* (now a Parador). Of the many castles erected later in the 15C, two of the most famous are the Fonseca strongholds of *La Mota* at *Medina del Campo,* and *Coca,* both of brick. Nearly all the internal decoration of these castles is Mudéjar, with patterns in stucco, also repeated in the neighbouring castle of *Segovia.* Nearby, at *Turegano,* built by the Knights Templar, is another exceptional castle, enclosing a three-aisled church. Two other outstanding castles are those of *Manzanares el Real* and *Belmonte,* but many lesser known fortresses were equally formidable: *Valencia de Don Juan, Ampudia, Montealegre, Barco de Ávila, Davalillo, Fuensaldaña, Torrelobatón,*

Villafuerte, Peñafiel, Barciense, Illescas, and *Grajal de Campos.* Most of these have imposing square or oblong keeps known as *Torres de Homenaje,* with bartizan turrets and heavy machicolations.

National Gothic and Isabelline. One final and magnificent burst of Gothic, this time of Flemish-Burgundian origin, was reserved for the 15-16C. Contemporary with Flamboyant in France, and with Perpendicular in England, it became a National Gothic despite its northern sources, and the difference, characteristically Spanish, is immediately evident in the stress given to horizontal rather than vertical lines. Seville cathedral, begun in 1402, was the first to show Flemish influences. By the middle of the century, Flemish, Dutch, and German architects flocked to Spain as Frenchmen had done before them. Outstanding among them were Jan van der Eycken of Brussels, whose name became hispanicized as *Anequín de Egas,* and Hans of Cologne, who became known as **Juan de Colonia.** Anequín had worked on the town hall of Louvain and is chiefly remembered for the lofty spire that he added to *Toledo* Cathedral, assisted by Juan Guas (or Wass) who became one of the most original Isabelline architects. Anequín was also the father of a still greater architect, *Enrique de Egas.* Hans of Cologne was brought to *Burgos* by the converso bishop, Alonso de Cartagena, on his return from the Council at Basle. He is chiefly known for the spires of Burgos cathedral (which recall those of Freiburg in Germany); he was also the founder of a dynasty of architects, and with the help of his son, *Simón,* and another foreigner named *Gil de Siloée,* introduced the star-patterned vaults for which Burgos is famous. Their successor here was a Burgundian from Langres, named *Felipe Biguerny* or *Vigarni.*

With the marriage in 1468 of Fernando and Isabel, the final conquest of the Moors at Granada in 1492, and the discovery of America, there followed an era of intense building activity. The hall-church cathedrals of *Astorga* and *Plasencia* date from this period, and work on the cathedrals of *Salamanca* and *Segovia* commenced, the chief architects for both being **Juan Gil de Hontañón** and his son *Rodrigo,* and displaying full stellar vaulting derived from Germany, they were the final expression of Gothic in Spain, unless we include the cathedral planted in the Mezquita at *Córdoba,* and the imposing 16C hall-churches of *S. Millán de la Cogolla, Berlanga de Duero,* and *Barbastro* Cathedral, in which the details are frankly Renaissance. Isabelline ornament, as derived from Flanders and Burgundy, consists of highly naturalistic sculpture in rather low relief, accompanied by lace-like ornament, often beneath ogee or other curiously shaped arches and elaborately fringed canopies. Perhaps the best example in Spain is the portal (attri. to *Enrique de Egas)* of the *Capilla Real, Granada.* Another, attributed to both *Gil de Siloée* and *Simón de Colonia,* is the façade of the church at *Aranda de Duero.*

Before the recapture of Granada, the Catholic Kings had intended Toledo to be their burial-place, and **Juan Guas,** pupil of Anequín, had already begun the Chapel Royal there, known as *S. Juan de los Reyes.* It is in the work of Guas that one finds the most fantastic and Spanish variation of this over-rich Isabelline ornament. Whatever his origin—he described himself as born in France—this architect added to the typically Flemish-Burgundian repertory of florid Gothic an extreme emphasis on heraldry and at the same time a strange medley of Mudéjar designs. Thus in S. Juan de los Reyes there are not only vast heraldic achievements but also stalactite cornices, and his Gothic tracery has a distinctly Moorish look. Moreover, his work shows so great an antipathy to plain surfaces that walls are covered with a sort of tapestry in plaster or stone. He is known to have designed also the castle of *Manzanares el Real* and the *Infantado palace* at *Guadalajara.* In much the same style too are the retablo-like façades of *S. Gregorio* and *S. Pablo* at *Valladolid,* a palace at *Úbeda,* and the *Medinaceli palace* at *Cogolludo.* The style, which recalls the Manueline of Portugal, is bizarre and opulent rather than beautiful. Perhaps all that can be said for it is that it set the stage for the next development, the introduction of Renaissance ornament in rather the same manner; the style known as 'Plateresque'.

RENAISSANCE ARCHITECTURE

Plateresque. Early in the 16C it became fashionable for Spanish nobles and ecclesiastics to commission their tombs in Italy, particularly at Genoa. Both tombs and sculptors were imported, and soon the delicately sculptured amorini, garlands, fruit, flowers, medallions, grotesques, and candelabra with which the effigies were surrounded, were copied by Spanish silversmiths and architects.

With silver and gold pouring in from the New World, silverwork or *platería* for shrines, custodias, and church ornaments in general, became exceedingly important; but it is untrue to say that early Renaissance architectural ornament was derived from silverwork. Both came from the same source, namely Lombard sculpture; the architects called their work *'obra del Romano'* and the term Plateresque, not applied to architecture until later, was perhaps derisive. The important point is that both silversmiths and architects used the new carefully chiselled ornament in much the same way: as an appliqué decoration. The structure of neither silver tabernacles nor of stone buildings was affected. The sole difference was that the new Lombard repertoire took the place of the florid Gothic crockets and finials beloved by Isabelline architects, and was indiscriminately applied, but often with immense charm.

Although several 'schools' were formed, the principal architects of the period travelled all over the country, and were at work on several buildings at the same time. The two greatest Plateresque architects from Toledo were **Enrique de Egas,** son of Anequín, and **Alonso de Covarrubias,** who married Enrique's niece and succeeded him as master of the works at Toledo Cathedral. Both Egas and Covarrubias were members of an architectural commission for Salamanca Cathedral, and Egas was probably responsible for the plan (in Gothic) of *Granada* Cathedral, where he was succeeded by *Diego de Siloée.*

The first patrons of Plateresque were the Catholic Kings and the prelates Mendoza, Cisneros, and Fonseca. For the former Enrique erected the royal hospitals of *Santiago de Compostela* and *Granada,* where he was also in charge of the *Capilla Real.* He began the *Hospital de Santa Cruz* at *Toledo,* completed by *Covarrubias,* who made an almost exact replica of it in the *Archbishop's Palace* at *Alcalá de Henares.*

Most of the work of Egas is a subtle blend of Gothic construction with Italian ornament. *Alonso de Covarrubias,* on the other hand, was an architect in whom the evolution of style can be easily traced. Among his Plateresque works may be mentioned the *Cap. de los Reyes Nuevos* in *Toledo* cathedral, and the *Sacristy* in *Sigüenza* cathedral. His style is closely related to that of **Lorenzo Vázquez**, an architect about whom little is known but who seems to have been responsible for much Plateresque work at *Sigüenza, Guadalajara, Cogolludo,* and *Mondéjar,* and to whom the palace at *Peñaranda de Duero* is sometimes attributed.

Salamanca is a museum of 16C architecture, and the superb façade of the *University* is a masterpiece of Plateresque. No architect has yet been credited with the design, nor with that of other outstanding Plateresque works in this town, the *Escuelas Menores,* the two *Fonseca palaces,* and the *Monterrey palace.* Other fine Plateresque works are the façade of the *University* at *Alcalá de Henares,* by *Rodrigo Gil de Hontañón,* and the façade of *S. Marcos* at *León.* In Andalucía, we should note particularly the *Ayuntamiento* at *Seville,* begun by *Diego de Riaño,* the *'House of Pilate',* and the collegiate church at *Osuna.*

At *Burgos,* the chief architect of the period was **Francisco de Colonia** (son of Simón and grandson of Hans of Cologne) to whom are due the sacristy doorway of the *Constable's Chapel,* and the *Puerta de la Pellejería* in Pseudo-Florentine style but with ungainly bell-shaped capitals and arches decorated with acanthus—peculiarities found also at the above-mentioned palaces at Cogolludo and Peñaranda de Duero. The *Hospital del Rey* at Burgos, the belfry at *Sta María del Campo,* and the palace at *Saldañuelo* also come within this group. Burgos is important also as the birthplace of **Diego de Siloée** (c. 1495-1563), son of the sculptor and perhaps pupil of Simón de Colonia. His first known work is the Plateresque *'Golden Staircase'* in the Cathedral. In 1524 he accompanied Bartolomé Ordóñez, the sculptor, to Naples, and his work thereafter is very different. First he was occupied with *S. Jerónimo* at *Granada,* which he took over from a certain *Jacobo Florentino L'Indaco,* who is said to have been a pupil of Michelangelo. Siloée also succeeded Enrique de Egas as master of the works at *Granada* Cathedral, and he designed a number of important works, including the *Great Sacristy* at *Seville* Cathedral, *El Salvador* at *Úbeda* (which was actually built by **Andrés de Vandaelvira,** chief architect of *Jaén* Cathedral), and the courtyard of the *Irish College* at *Salamanca* (executed by *Pedro de Ibarra*). He also had a hand in the design of the cathedrals at *Málaga* and *Guadix.* None of these later works can be classed as Plateresque, and in fact, in Granada Cathedral, the Classical repertoire is used constructionally. While the ground plan with nave, double aisles, and ambulatory is still Gothic, despite a central dome, the details are all classical. The cathedrals of Málaga, Guadix, Jaén, and Cádiz all show the influence of this 'Granadine' Renaissance, the half-way step to full comprehension of the Italian principles.

The High Renaissance and Herrera. The first building in Spain of true Classic inspiration is the huge square palace which Charles V erected in the Alhambra. The architect chosen was **Pedro Machuca,** a Spaniard who, trained in Rome, had absorbed many of the best principles of the Italian Cinquecento. The next work is the *Tavera Hospital* at *Toledo* (1541-99) by *Covarrubias.* The same architect designed the courtyard of the *Alcázar* at *Toledo.* There are, of course, many lesser examples of Classical inspiration by the middle of the century such as the Palladian windows of the *Ayuntamiento* at *Baeza,* and the Corinthian

Ayuntamiento of *Jerez de la Frontera,* but all these are of little account compared with the *Escorial.* The first architect was *Juan Bautista de Toledo,* who had worked with Michelangelo on St Peter's in Rome, and was summoned from Naples in 1559 to make the plans. In 1563 the corner stone was laid, but he died four years later and was succeeded by his assistant **Juan de Herrera** (1530-97).

Although the Escorial was his life work, Herrera also designed the courtyard of the *Lonja* at *Seville* (executed by *Juan Mijares),* the *Puente de Segovia* at *Madrid,* and the unfinished cathedral at *Valladolid.* For a long time Herrera, who enjoyed an awesome reputation for his great work on the Escorial, was royal inspector of monuments, and everywhere there appeared churches, palaces, and public buildings in the dominating *'estilo desornamentado',* often reproducing the Escorial's corner towers capped with sharply-pointed slate-roofed spires. Examples on the grand scale are the *Ducal Palace* at *Lerma,* built by *Francisco de Mora,* the sombre ruined palace at *Renedo de Valdeteja,* N.E. of León, and the *Ayuntamiento* at *Toledo,* by *Jorge Theotocopulos.* But in general it was the frigidity of the style that was reproduced, and not its grandeur.

BAROQUE

A reaction to the austerity of this style came spontaneously, and found its expression in the Baroque. The Baroque of Spain was perhaps the most sensational and most imaginative of all European variations and was surpassed in these respects only by that of her own colonies, in particular Mexico.

In many places it was Italian Baroque that held sway, for instance in the pantheon of the Escorial, entrusted by Philip III to *Giovanni Battista Crescenzi,* and his style was followed in the grand church planned for the Jesuits at *Loyola,* their founder's birthplace. In *Madrid,* the plan of the Gesù at Rome was copied for *S. Isidro el Real.* In eastern Spain, again under Jesuit influence, Neapolitan Baroque is often recognizable, for instance in nearly all the churches of Valencia, but these influences are very mixed. The lavish stucco decoration in *Los SS. Juanes* at *Valencia* was due to a Milanese, *Jacopo Barthesi,* the W. Front of the Cathedral to a German pupil of Bernini named *Conrad Rudolf,* the tower of *La Seo* at *Zaragoza* to another Italian, *Contini,* and the Borrominesque façade of *Murcia* Cathedral to *Jaime Bort,* perhaps also a foreigner.

But these Italianate works are outside the main stream of Spanish tradition. During most of the 17C comparative simplicity reigned, for instance in several Madrid churches of this epoch, and in the work of *Juan Gómez de Mora,* who designed the *Pl. Mayor* at *Madrid,* and the *Jesuit College* at *Salamanca.* The same simplicity, indeed heaviness, is found in *Alonso Cano's* work, above all in the W. Front of *Granada* Cathedral. A minor masterpiece of interior decoration is the sacristy of *Guadalupe,* with its perfect co-ordination of ornament.

Far more interesting is the Baroque of the 18C, especially the variations of what is loosely termed *Churrigueresque.* Its originality is unquestionable; it is emotional, an architecture of fantasy, sometimes inspired, sometimes merely intoxicated. But it was a most successful protest against the rules of Vitruvius and the ascetic Herreran, and in its use of striking ornament in bold relief, often crowded on to one small portion of a building—usually the portal—it showed true appreciation of light and shade.

José Churriguera (1665-1723) after whom the style is named, and who was later said to have defiled stone with his pernicious and ill-directed genius, was a comparatively mild innovator, and his own work, for instance the planned village of *Nuevo Baztán,* was restrained. However, himself the son of a sculptor of retablos, he had four brothers, all of them architects or sculptors, and at least three of his sons followed the same profession. Their works have not yet been disentangled and moreover they often collaborated with another dynasty of architects, the **Quiñones,** and it is to this group as a whole that we owe the style, Churrigueresque. They specialized in huge gilt polychromed retablos, peopled with ecstatic saints, but also produced a number of other dramatic and distinguished works as well, particularly at *Salamanca,* where *Joaquín Churriguera* and *Andrés García Quiñones* completed the Cathedral dome, while *Alberto Churriguera* carved the choir stalls. To Quiñones and the younger Churrigueras we owe the *Pl. Mayor* at *Salamanca,* one of the finest squares in Europe, and to Alberto Churriguera the partial completion of *Valladolid* Cathedral.

In *Madrid* an architect perhaps equally original, **Pedro Ribera** (1683-1742) constructed the *Puente de Toledo* and the portal of the *Hospicio Provincial,* while at Valencia a painter named *Hipólito Rovira* erected for the Marqués de Dos Aguas a palace with a remarkable portal carved by *Ignacio Vergara.* At *Santiago,* **Fernando Casas y Nóvoa** dressed the W. Front of the Cathedral in Baroque trappings, and here too was evolved a sort of 'Plattenstil' with abstract ornament—the *Conv. de Sta Clara* by *Simón Rodríguez* is the best example—a kind of protocubist fantasy. One of the most extraordinary compositions of the age is the *Transparente* by *Narciso Tomé* in *Toledo* Cathedral.

Meanwhile, in *Seville,* another dynasty, the *Figueroas,* were responsible for many attractive but unorthodox buildings, including the *Archbishop's Palace,* and the *Pal. de S. Telmo* with its imposing portal. But the most revolutionary Andalusian was **Francisco Hurtado Izquierdo** (1669-1728), who died at *Priego,* where numerous Baroque works by his pupils survive. Among his rich interiors is the Sancta Sanctorum at *El Paular* where he introduced a motive inspired by the interlacing arches of the Mezquita at Córdoba, and the Sacristy of the *Cartuja* at *Granada,* a fantastic domed hall surrounded by fretted pilasters surging with delirious ornament.

The styles at court in this period were very different. To the Bourbon Philip V (grandson of Louis XIV) and his Italian queen Isabella of Parma, Spanish fashions in dress and architecture must have seemed outmoded, and in their new palaces they immediately attempted to rival the spendours of Versailles, and called in foreigners to do the work. The old Habsburg palace of *Aranjuez* was taken in hand in 1715, and later Carlos III added further wings. Next came the mountain palace of *La Granja,* begun in 1721 by a German, *Theodor Ardemans,* where the garden front was rebuilt in 1735 for Philip V by the Italians *Juvara* (a pupil of Bernini) and *Giovanni Battista Sacchetti,* while the gardens in the style of Le Nôtre were planned by *Etienne Boutelou,* with ornamental statuary by several other Frenchmen. Juvara and Sacchetti were responsible also for the *Royal Palace* at *Madrid,* rebuilt between

1738 and 1764, while its interior was decorated by other foreigners, mainly Italians, the greatest of whom was *Giambattista Tiepolo* (1696-1770)—fresh from Würzburg. But the style remained a fashion of the Court only, and in architecture Spain never appreciated the taste of the Bourbons.

THE NEO-CLASSIC

Despite the fact that Spain remained curiously aloof from the French styles in architecture and interior decoration that swept over most of Western and Central Europe, the Bourbons were in a sense responsible for the Classic Revival in Spain. By founding academies of art modelled on the Academy in Paris—namely a national school for architects (1744) and the Royal Academy of San Fernando (1752)—they set new standards in art and exercised virtual control. A royal decree prohibited the erection of any public building the plans for which had not been approved by the Royal Academy, where the professors of architecture were *José Hermosilla*, the translator of Vitruvius, and *Ventura Rodríguez*, an architect steeped in Classicism. As a result, buildings as severe and massive as those by Herrera rose on every side. By Rodríguez himself may be mentioned the church of the *Augustinian Convent* at *Valladolid*, the façades of *Lugo* and *Pamplona Cathedrals*, and significant alterations to the Basilica of *El Pilar* at *Zaragoza*. In *Madrid* some of the best work of the period was by *Francesco Sabatini*, who built the *Ministerio de Hacienda*, and by *Juan de Villanueva*, who built the *Prado Museum*, and the *Observatory*, while the *Casita del Principe* at the *Escorial*, another at the *Pardo*, and the *Casa del Labrador* at *Aranjuez* were decorated in the Pompeian style for Carlos IV.

The Peninsular War saw the destruction or dilapidation of a number of ancient buildings, while in the mid-1830s when church property was expropriated, many monasteries—including Santes Creus and Poblet—fell into ruin, but to balance this there was little loss by excessive and unscholarly restoration. The late 19C and early 20C saw a tremendous building activity and a revival of many styles—including for instance Moorish and Mudéjar for Bullrings and Railway stations—but few individual buildings display any great originality, except perhaps for certain works by *Antonio Gaudí* (1852-1926).

It has been remarked of the last edition of this guide that reference to Spanish architecture after 1800 had been virtually dismissed, to which the Editor can but reply that had there been any examples of great significance, they would have been described. No doubt there are a number of erections of interest to architects specifically, and indeed certain buildings conform to the best quality of stylistically eclectic but aesthetically uninteresting modern architecture, but such can be seen in any country, and hardly merit inclusion here, with the exception of a very few structures, which are pointed out in passing. Both before and after the Civil War a grandiose neo-Herreran style was imposed on many of the newly erected ministerial and University buildings, while conventional 'modern' blocks of flats, offices, barracks, and hotels continue to proliferate unchecked.

Meanwhile, while there is still time, strenuous efforts are being made in the face of the stronger forces of Philistine materialism to preserve Spain's architectural heritage, and legislation has gone some way in an attempt to protect individual buildings—often tastefully converted into museums, or State-owned Paradores—apart from 'monumental districts' of towns, picturesque villages, archaeological sights, and panoramic views. Much remarkable work of restoration of damaged or derelict buildings of historic or architectural interest has been carried out in recent years. Also, one should add, too many churches have also been virtually rebuilt, which hardly deserved such attention. Advertisement hoardings, T.V. aerials, a profusion of cables and wires, etc. still scar most townscapes. Whether those few imbued with the spirit of conservation are able to redress to any extent the depredations and encroachments of a more prosaic era, is debatable, but a special note of admiration should be recorded for the important work of preservation being done and every encouragement should be given to those entrusted with the task, even if, in their enthusiasm they may, in over-restoring, destroy the patina of ages.

GLOSSARY OF ARCHITECTURAL AND ALLIED TERMS

AJARACAS. Brickwork in trellis pattern.
AJIMEZ. Two-light Moorish window divided by a slender column.
ALCÁZABA. Moorish citadel.
ALCÁZAR. Moorish fortified palace.
ALFIZ. Rectangular moulding, often round a horseshoe arch.
ALHÓNDIGA. Corn Exchange.
ALICATADO. Mosaic of glazed tiles.
ARTESONADO. Wooden coffered ceiling.
ATALAYA. Watch-tower.
AUDIENCIA. Law Court.
AVITOLADO. Imitation of brick courses, noticable in Seville.
AYUNTAMIENTO. Town Hall.
AZULEJO. Glazed tile.
BÓDEGA. Cellar
BOVEDA, Vault.
CAMARÍN. Shrine of an image.
CAPILLA MAYOR. Chancel containing the High Altar.
CASA CONSISTORIAL. Municipal Building.
CHURRIGUERESQUE. Name given to extreme Baroque architecture (after José Churriguera, 1650-1723).
CIMBORIO. Cupola, Lantern.
CLAUSTRO. Cloister.
CONVERSO. A Jew converted to Catholicism. The term Marrano has a derogatory connotation.
CORO. Choir, usually in the centre of the nave, but sometimes over the W. entrance (Coro alto).
CRUCERO. Crossing of a church, transept.
CUARTEL. Barracks.
CUBO. Semicircular tower.
CUSTODIA. Monstrance, in which the Host is kept, or carried in procession.

ERMITA. Hermitage, or chapel.

ESMALTE. Enamel.

FACHADA. Façade.

FACISTOL. Lectern.

HERRERAN. A Post-Plateresque and pre-Baroque style of architecture, named after *Juan de Herrera* (1530-97).

IGLESIA. Church.

LONJA. Exchange building.

MAMPOSTERÍA. Rubble masonry.

MARFIL. Ivory.

MARMOL. Marble.

MEDIA NARANJA. Half-orange (of cupola).

MÉNSULA. Corbel, console.

MIRADOR. Balcony, belvedere.

MOZÁRABE. Christian subject to the Moors; a term extended to their architecture. The term *Muwallad* or *Muladi* denotes a Christian converted to Islam.

MUDÉJAR. Moslem subject to the Christians; a term extended to their architecture. The term *Morisco* describes a Moor nominally baptized as a Christian.

PALACIO. Royal mansion; in the Asturias, any mansion.

PASEO. Promenade or Parade.

PATIO. Courtyard, quadrangle.

PAZO. Country manor, in Galicia.

PLATERESQUE. Name given to an exuberant and ornate form of Renaissance architecture in Spain influenced by that of Lombardy.

PLAZA. Place, or Square.

REJA. Iron grille, usually guarding a chapel.

RESPALDOS. Exterior side-walls of the Coro.

RETABLO. Large altar-piece, sculptured, carved, or painted, or all three.

SAGRARIO. Sacristy; also sanctuary, or monstrance.

SILLERÍA. Choir stalls; ashlar masonry.

SOLAR or CASA SOLARIEGA, Old town mansion.

TAPIA. Earthen wall, or of sun-baked brick.

TRASALTAR. Wall behind altar facing ambulatory.

TRASCORO. Exterior end-wall of the Coro.

TRASSAGRARIO. Back of the high altar; ambulatory behind the Cap. Mayor.

VERJA. Railing round a tomb.

YACENTE. Recumbent effigy.

ZÓCALO, Base, plinth, or dado.

INTRODUCTION TO SPANISH PAINTING

'Spain, if visited by some of our artists, would, I am persuaded, open new, astonishing, and unexamined treasures to their view...'. Such was the reaction of Edward Clarke, who entered the country in 1760; an impression confirmed by the small but growing number of English travellers, collectors, and amateurs who traversed Spain in succeeding decades. But the depredations of the French during the Peninsular War—both in actual destruction and blatant appropriation—the sequestration of ecclesiastical property in the mid-1830s, when some but by no means all works of art found their way into museums; the blight of unskilled restoration; the iconoclastic proclivities of extremists and the church-burnings of the early 1930s; the recent Civil War; sheer neglect and decay over the decades: all have since taken their toll.

Certainly the Spain depicted in the lithographs of John Frederick Lewis, David Roberts, and George Vivian—to name but three English artists of the 'Romantic' period—and in the topographical drawings of Richard Ford himself, is no longer. But following in the footsteps of J. A. Ceán Bermúdez (whose admirable *Diccionario histórico de los más ilustres profesores de las bellas artes en España,* published in 1800, was a godsend to the French in search of canvases). Ford described her unplundered treasures to English readers in his great *Hand-Book for Travellers in Spain* of 1845. Three years later appeared both Sir Edmund Head's *Hand-Book of the History of the Spanish and French Schools of Painting,* and William Stirling's *Annals of the Artists of Spain.* Spanish Painting was no longer the great unknown. In spite of the gradual dissipation of her works of art, a very high proportion remained in Spain, and did not cease to astonish by its spendour and variety.

Now a new spirit of conservation has set in; old collections are being reformed, and new museums opened; and there is today a more general appreciation in Spain herself of the quality of her artistic heritage, which, due to the strenuous efforts of scholars, is being properly described and catalogued, and questionable attributions corrected.

Many pages could be devoted to the Arts of Spain—to her sculpture; to leather-work, textiles, and tapestries; furniture, both ecclesiastical and domestic; glass and ceramics; jewellery, ivories, and jet; the art of the metalworker, armourer, and silversmith; miniatures and illuminated manuscripts, etc.—but to describe each facet would make this introductory study unwieldy; and many are the subject of specialized monographs.

Apart from such cave-paintings as those at *Altamira,* perhaps the earliest known surviving examples of mural decoration that the traveller will come across, from the pre-Romanesque period, is that in *S. Julián de los Prados* or *Santullano* (Oviedo) of c. 830, in which the traditional Byzantine splendour of effect secured by the use of mosaic was reproduced by elaborate fresco decoration, unfortunately much decayed. Northern Spain was indeed in the vanguard of European Romanesque painting, however much her contribution to its development may be disputed, and a relatively high percentage of this 12C painting to survive is unrivalled outside Spain, one masterpiece of which is the apse of *S. Clemente de Tahull* (now in the *Museo de Arte de Cataluña,* Barcelona), which is dated by an inscription 1123, where the basic colours of the Mozarabic art of illumination, red and yellow, are emphasized by strong black outlines. The Mozarabic church of *S. Baudel* at Berlanga, S.W. of Soria, was completely decorated with Biblical scenes; those surviving are now displayed in the *Prado Museum,* Madrid; but the largest and most important example is the decoration of the *Panteón de los Reyes* in *S. Isidoro* (León), probably executed in the reign of Fernando II, who is portrayed in the painting.

Altar frontals conformed to international standards, and were often built of wooden panels on which were moulded stucco or gesso in low relief to imitate as closely as paint and gold and silver leaf could simulate, certain frontals executed for the few wealthy sees by Limoges enamellers in solid gold, enamel, and precious stones. These painted substitutes, which almost alone survive, are usually designed to show Christ in Majesty or the Virgin Enthroned, within a mandorla, occupying the centre, while rows of saints or apostles, or scenes from religious legends are arranged in static groups on either side. These frontals gradually gave way to *retablos,* which grew in size as the crucifix was placed higher above the altar upon a painted panel, which became a diptych, then a triptych, and by the end of the 14C the Spanish retablo proper had evolved, rambling and asymmetrical, to occupy the entire eastern end of the church.

Spanish medieval art has only in recent decades become the object of serious study. We know little about the early executants, and until the middle of the 15C, half the extant works remain anonymous despite the labours of scholars, who have rescued scores of paintings and painters from oblivion. In signing his wall-paintings in the Old Cathedral in Salamanca in 1262, *Antón Sánchez* of Segovia was one of the first to prove the existence of an individual artist proud of his personal achievement and capacity as a painter. These Castilian murals are in a marked Franco-Gothic style, found also in the majority of paintings executed about 1300 both in Aragón and Catalonia.

The artistic impulse of Catholic Spain moved slowly south in the wake of the intermittent reconquest of Moorish Spain, and schools of painting developed from the Catalan in Valencia, and later in Seville, with the shifting of commercial activity. Eventually they waned, for when the court was centred on Madrid, the capital became the focus of interest and seat of patronage. If Salamanca, Ávila, Toledo, and Granada are omitted from such a brief summary, it is because the relative importance of the various centres can be judged only by the works that have survived.

CATALAN SCHOOLS. By the 14C Barcelona had already developed a rich, independent merchant class which vied with the king and Church in fostering local talent, with the result that Catalan artists enjoyed almost a monopoly of work in the realm of greater Aragón until the 15C. The recognized head of the Catalan School was **Ferrer Bassa** (active 1324-48), whose frescoes have survived in the *Convent of Pedralbes* in Barcelona. He was a versatile artist, having ten years earlier been engaged by Alfonso IV as a miniaturist. His manner and style are a blend of the art of Giotto, Simone Martini and Lorenzetti, and it is presumed that he was trained at Florence and Siena. But their Giottesque element is not handed on to his successors, *Arnau de la Penna* (1355-85), *Jaume* and *Pere Serra* (active 1363-99), and their pupil *Luis Borrassá* (active

1388-1424), who may all be studied in Barcelona and Vic. Their works show more the influence of the French, Avignon, and Sienese Schools, and retain a somewhat naïve provincial character, but are marked by a rich display of contemporary costume and a taste for genre. It was in this century that towering retablos, with their gilded pilasters and pinnacles encasing innumerable panels of bright tempera and gold, came into their own. The artist who transformed the international Gothic style practised by Borrassá and his successor *Ramón de Mur* into a genuine Catalan Gothic, which was to survive until the end of the 15C, was *Bernat Martorell* (active 1427-52), combining the naturalistic elements of Gentile da Fabriano in Italy with those of the Franco-Flemish movement centred in the Limburg brothers at the court of Jean, Duc de Berri.

Three years after Jan van Eyck's visit to Spain in 1428, Alfonso V sent **Luis Dalmau** (active 1428-60), one of his court painters, to Flanders, where in Ghent in all probability he saw Van Eyck's great 'Adoration of the Lamb', then newly unveiled. Years after his return, Dalmau, in his one certain work executed for the city councillors of Barcelona in 1443-45, defied tradition by substituting a typically Flemish landscape for the customary gold background, and it is largely through Dalmau that the realism of the Flemish School was introduced to **Jaime Huguet** (c. 1414-92), who dominated the Catalan School from the 1460s. Even the workshop of *Rafael Vergós* and his brother *Pablo,* artist of the 'Retablo of Granollers' (of 1495), is now proved to have merely reflected the models of Huguet, their master. Even contemporary painting in ARAG-ÓN was merely a provincial ramification of his style, which, inherited from Martorell, also incorporated many Flemish elements. But Huguet was unable to rid himself of the Catalan predilection for covering backgrounds with gilded motifs in stucco relief, and his work incorporates and summarizes most of the qualities, styles, defects, and idiosyncrasies of the mature Catalan School, colourful, realistic, and robust.

Meanwhile, in adjacent VALENCIA, where Alfonso V had established his court, there developed a flourishing school of painting, more Italianate, in the person of *Lorenzo Zaragoza* (1365–1402) and *Pedro Nicolau* (fl. 1390–1410). Perhaps inspired by the Florentine *Gherardo Starnina,* whose frescoes once decorated the walls of Valencia Cathedral, their brilliantly coloured altar-pieces introduced the international Gothic style into the region, while *Andrés Marzal de Sax* (active 1394–1410), who probably came from Germany and who collaborated with Nicolau, brought with him a tendency towards exaggerated realism, which corresponded to an inherent trait in the Spanish character, and was soon assimilated by their artists. Recent research has clarified the main lines of development of the Valencian School, although to attempt any minute identification of painters is not always possible, the difficulty being to connect the contracts which have been unearthed with the altarpieces they prescribe, now so often dismembered. One of the principal figures was *Jacomart (Jaime Baço;* active 1409/17-61), who was court painter to Alfonso V for ten years in Naples, where he introduced the Hispano-Flemish style. One of his surviving works is in the Diocesan Museum at Segorbe, but the 'Catí Altarpiece' has now been proved to be by *Joan Reixach* (1431-84/92). In these we find superficial Italian Renaissance borrowings as in the architectural niches, and the Flemish love of counterfeiting jewellery and textiles, together with the Northern landscape backgrounds.

Bartolomé Bermejo (active 1474–95), a Cordoban painter who lived successively in Daroca, Zaragoza, and Valencia, before settling in Barcelona in 1486, greatly encouraged the transformation of the Gothic to the Renaissance style in Aragón and Valencia, and it was once customary to link his name with another Cordoban, *Master Alfonso,* whose fame rested on the 'Martyrdom of S. Cucufat' (in the Museo de Arte de Cataluña), which has now been proved to be the work of a German painter, *Ayne Bru.* Bermejo was one of the first exponents of oil-painting in Catalonia, although he exploited this strange medium more as an adjunct to than instead of tempera, which he controlled with such finesse that it is sometimes difficult to decide which medium he has used, or, when both are present, where tempera ends and oil begins.

With the partial unification of Spain under the Catholic Kings, a great programme of public building was initiated together with attendant commissions to artists both foreign and indigenous. In CASTILE, the two foreign influences—Flemish and of Florence—were also at work. *Starnina,* already referred to in Valencia, was painting for Juan I at Salamanca in 1380, and was followed there by his compatriot *Nicolás Florentino* (active in Spain 1433–70), whose altar-piece of 1455 in the *Old* Cathedral, is outstanding. In León, the partially reassembled retablo mayor of 1434, clearly inspired by Italian trecento models, was painted by a French artist, *Nicolás Francés* (1425–68). One of the first works of definitely Flemish character to be produced in Castile was executed in 1455 by *Jorge Inglés,* an artist of uncertain nationality, despite his name; while in Zamora and elsewhere **Fernando Gallego** (active 1466–1507) was imitating with deceptive facility the technical skills of Roger van de Weyden, Campin, and Dirk Bouts. His altarpieces are quite Flemish in character, with the addition of a certain angularity of form and heightened sense of drama. Throughout the century there was a steady importation of devotional paintings of these masters, of Gerard David, and Isenbrandt, and their influence was dominating, except perhaps in Valencia, geographically nearer to Italy and Naples. In 1472 the Cathedral chapter invited two Umbrian artists to settle in Valencia, where the influences of the Renaissance affected the styles of local painters, among them *Rodrigo de Osona* (father and son; active 1464–1513).

The Castilian **Pedro Berruguete** (active 1477–1504) set the fashion for Spanish artists to visit Italy, not always with happy results. In 1477 Berruguete was working in Urbino under Justus of Ghent and Melozzo da Forli, and influenced by Signorelli: he later became court painter to Fernando and Isabel, settling at Toledo (1483–95) before moving to Ávila, where he worked on the high-altar in the cathedral. His son *Alonso Berruguete* (1486–1561), who had also trained in Italy under Michelangelo, became court painter to Charles V.

The altar-piece of Valencia Cathedral (1507), by *Fernando de los Llanos* and *Fernando Yáñez,* is another example of the overwhelming effect of a great tradition, in this instance that of Leonardo da Vinci and the Florentines who they studied in Italy, which lacks any indigenous Spanish character. They were succeeded by another hybrid, *Juan Vicente Macip* (c. 1475–1550) and his son *Juan de Joanes* (1523–79), whose altar-pieces abound in Valencia.

SEVILLE. A great number of Sevillian paintings still hang in the city's churches, convents, hospitals and in the Cathedral, and a representative collection can be seen in the *Museo de Bellas Artes*. Among the first to achieve popular success was *Alejo Fernández* (active 1498–1543), who introduced the Renaissance style into his own serene and balanced compositions with their elegant idealized types. Apart from being a miniaturist, he also superintended the decoration of Seville for the entry of the Emperor Charles V in 1526. His contemporaries *Pedro de Campana* (*Kempeneer* of Brussels, 1503–80), *Fernando Sturm* (active 1537–57), and *Frans Frutet*, also trained in Italy, were for a few years also at work in Seville, where, after twenty-eight years' travel in Italy, they were joined by *Luis de Vargas* (c. 1502–68), a native of Seville, whose altar-piece known as 'La Gamba' in the Cathedral (1551–53), shows how thoroughly he had absorbed the art of the Roman Mannerists. *Luis de Morales* ('*el Divino*'; active 1546–86) from Badajoz, also subjugated his own natural capacity for religious expression to the fashionable mannerisms of the moment.

Another artist whose style sprang from Italian Mannerism, was **El Greco** (*Domenico Theotocopoulos, 1540–1614*), a Greek from Candia. He received his 'Western' training directly from Titian in Venice, and later travelled to Spain, possibly in the hope of securing lucrative employment at the Escorial, and in 1575 settled for life in Toledo, where two years later he started on one of his first commissions, 'The Disrobing of Christ', Towards 1580 he entered into competition with some of the established favourites—*Carvajal, Sánchez Coello, et al.*—but his unorthodox drawing and design, and vivid, indeed, too frequently *livid* colouring, was more than Philip II could stomach, and it was banished to the chapter room. His only other commission for the Escorial, 'The Dream of Philip II', with its ochreous reds and greys, is low in tone by comparison. Every eccentricity of his style is foreshadowed in another of his early masterpieces, 'The Burial of the Count of Orgaz', painted for Santo Tomé at Toledo in 1586/8, where it still hangs. It is remarkable for the row of *hidalgos* across the lower half of the composition, which reveals El Greco as a portrait painter of rare mastery and insight. It was one of the few paintings which impressed George Borrow— admittedly no connoisseur—who considered it a work by a 'most extraordinary genius'. The Prado contains another series of individual portraits in which El Greco has rendered with singular charm the grace, pride, and aloof temper of these Castilian gentlemen. His repetition of favourite designs at different periods, and consequent reversion to earlier types and elongated proportions make his work difficult to arrange chronologically. It was not until comparatively recently that there has been any general appreciation of his qualities. Richard Ford considered him very unequal: 'what he did *well*, was excellent, while what he did *ill*, was worse than anybody else. He was often more lengthy and extravagant than Fuseli, and as leaden as cholera morbus'. El Greco handed on little to his pupil *Luis Tristán* (c. 1585–1624) or to his son *Jorge Manuel*, who was mainly an architect and sculptor.

One of the most powerful factors in the evolution of the Spanish School of the so-called 'Golden Age' of painting (lasting roughly from 1550 to 1650) was the formation of the Royal Collections under Charles I (the Emperor Charles V), Philip II, and Philip IV—the latter acquiring a number of masterpieces sold from the collection of Charles I of

England. The cosmopolitan emperor patronized Titian to the exclusion of all other 'face-painters', and began that magnificent collection of the great Venetian's portraits and scriptural and mythological works, which Philip II continued in the Titian nudes, which now form one of the glories of the Prado Museum. Philip II, having failed to entice Veronese from Venice to decorate the Escorial, and not appreciating El Greco, still would not trust to native talent. This neglect may have retarded progress in Castile, but, much as his unpatriotic and expensive importations of such showy representatives of Italian Mannerism as Zuccaro, Cambiaso, and Tibaldi has been deplored, it seems true to say that this importation was only of slight significance. Even the failure of *Juan Fernández Navarrete, 'el Mudo'* (1526–79) to justify to the king his title of the 'Spanish Titian' cannot be wholly attributed to the noxious influence of these Italians among whom he worked. Nevertheless, he did help to translate Italian Mannerism into the Spanish idiom, and he and his ESCORIAL SCHOOL were the first of the *'tenebrist'* painters, so famous in the 17C, especially in Seville.

But the true founder of the SEVILLIAN SCHOOL was *Francisco Pacheco* (1564–1654), an Andalusian who in 1611 met El Greco in Madrid, and in the following year returned to Seville, where until 1617 he was the master of young Velázquez, to whom the shrewd Pacheco married his daughter, as he relates whith engaging complacency in his *'Arte de la Pintura',* a curious blend of useful biography and rules for religious painters. In 1623–25 Pacheco was in Madrid, accompanying Velázquez, and his house became an informal meeting-place for writers and painters, who here copied engravings, and studied the painting of still life, and painted directly from nature, a reaction against Mannerism. Even *Herrera the Elder* (c. 1576–1656) was basically under this influence, which can also be observed in his contemporary *Juan de las Roelas* (1558/60–1625), who, from being an apostle of the Venetian, Bolognese and Roman Mannerists, became the exponent of a broader technique and a Baroque style, and his insistence on naturalistic details in his subsiduary figures led to the genre pictures of the 17C Seville School.

It is convenient to consider here the impact on this school of the Catalan **Francisco Ribalta** (1551–1628), and the Valencian, *Ribera.* Ribalta, born at Solsona, spent his youth in Barcelona, and later, from 1582, painted in Madrid, until he settled in Valencia in 1599. There is no evidence that he studied in Italy, or ever went there, nor that he studied under the Carracci, nor that he was the channel of Caravaggesque 'tenebrism'. His use of chiaroscuro, realistic details, and 'tenebrism' is merely a development of the Escorial School of Navarrete and the Italian Mannerists. Only after 1615 do his works in Valencia show the true impact of the Caravaggesque style, by which time the works of the Caravaggesque School were in Spain. His latest works show the influence of Ribera, who cannot ever have been his pupil.

José Ribera, *'el Españoleto'* (1591–1652), who was born at Játiva, went to Italy at an early age, and after a prolonged study of Titian, Corregio in Parma, and the Carracci in Rome, settled for life in Naples in 1616. He arrived at exactly the right moment to cull from Caravaggio those qualities of sensational lighting and unshrinking realism which were best calculated to display his dramatic gifts and to gratify the taste of the Neapolitans (and Spanish residents) for savage and sinister martyrdoms. His influence and great fame reached Spain with his works sent over by Spanish viceroys, and had a share in the formation of Murillo and his fellow painters in Seville. Unlike most Spaniards, Ribera was a daring and able designer and an accomplished figure draughtsman, and his method of placing the great bodies of his saints and their tormentors right across the foreground gives great force and verisimilitude to his grim representations. His 'Martyrdom of St. Bartholomew' (1630)—the year he was visited by Velázquez—which is in the Prado, admirably illustrates this, while at Salamanca, in the *Augustinas,* one can see Ribera's celebrated 'Conception' of 1635, whose tall Virgin and golden glow appear later in the works of Alonso Cano and Murillo respectively.

In Seville itself—and excepting *Velázquez* (see below), whose work done in his native city has long since gone elsewhere—the most important figure, and perhaps the finest representative of Spanish religious painters, was **Francisco Zurbarán** (1598–1664). He travelled extensively in Spain, moving from cloister to cloister, illustrating saintly legends for the monks whose aspirations he shared. The dissolution of the monasteries scattered most of these works, but at least three series are still fairly complete and accessible, one devoted mainly to the Life of St Jerome, which has remained at Guadalupe since 1639; another depicting Carthusian legends, now removed from the Cartuja at Jérez to the Cádiz Museum, and (attrib. to his school) a number of female saints to be seen at the Museo de Bellas Artes at Seville. His early acquaintance with polychrome sculpture in the studio of *Pedro Díaz de Villanueva* in Seville, where he was apprenticed in 1614–16, strongly affected his practice, as may be seen in the Crucifixions in the Museum and in the S. Pedro Nolasco series divided between Seville Cathedral and the Prado, in which figures and draperies resemble painted wood sculpture rather than human beings and woven stuffs. Later he was a pupil of Juan de las Roelas but he was also greatly influenced by the 'tenebrists', by Ribera, and even by the young Velázquez. The application of Ribalta's chiaroscuro to his early training in naturalism produced Zurbarán's characteristic style of composition and side lighting. He borrowed, more than any other Spanish painter, new ideas from early 17C Antwerp engravings by Theodor Galle, Schelte, and Bolswert, a pupil of Rubens. Many of his compositions derive from 16C German prints by Dürer, Beham, and Salomon, as in the series of 'The Labours of Hercules' (in the Prado), painted in Madrid in 1634. Among his more attractive and original creations are the two large canvases in the Seville Museum depicting Carthusian brothers respectively kneeling beneath the wings of the Virgin's cloak and visited in their refectory by St Hugo; in particular the Refectory with its cool fresh colours, still life paintings of loaves and blue and white pottery. Many of his single figures, ostensibly of saints in meditation, are actually searching and candid portraits of his monkish friends: his solitary monks at prayer are more obviously creatures of his imagination.

A striving after realism had been a particular characteristic of the Seville School and the secret of its independent existence. **Bartolomé Esteban Murillo** (1617–82) arrived as an anticlimax, and just when the possibilities seemed greatest, reinstated academic standards, and, indirectly, Italian idealism, and introduced the mawkish and 'picturesque' note which, in contrast to the masculine force of Zurbarán, contributed so much and for so long to his popularity—the urchins, beggars, and flower-girls of both his genre and religious compositions—and gave him an unrivalled place in public affections. He was long held in great esteem, and was highly regarded by Reynolds. He was also perhaps the first of the Spanish Baroque painters to achieve a convincing effect of figures floating up to heaven. A bitter theological controversy having provoked demonstrations in favour of the doctrine of the Immaculate Conception, Murillo, with easy conviction, took up the profitable role of 'Pintor de Concepciónes' to 'La Tierra de María Santísima', as the Sevillians called their province. But his success was his undoing. Possessing little imaginative power or creative invention, his run of commissions involved him in endless repetition of well-worn themes. In his later years his compositions are blurred by his *estilo vaporoso'*, in which an enveloping yellow haze seems to suffuse every part, perhaps the most impressive examples of which are those paintings executed for the church of the *Caridad* at Seville in 1670–74.

Murillo's contemporary, *Juan de Valdés Leal* (1622–90), copiously represented in Seville, grafted the 'estilo vaporoso' upon a technical method derived from the Venetians, of which the most prominent and unpleasant feature—common to a number of Andalusians—is the tricky use of a hot red ground, which has since forced its way to the surface. But inequalities of handling and design, and a love of violent movement mar his works, and the Sevillian School virtually ended with *Esteban Márquez,* a heavy-handed academic imitator of Murillo's late work, and *Clemente Torres,* who reverted to the standards and tastes of the 16C.

Alonso Cano (1601–67), who also an architect, studied sculpture with *Montañes,* and painting under Pacheco, and with his assistants, composed the short-lived SCHOOL OF GRANADA. His first signed known work in Seville is dated 1624, but in 1638 he was summoned to Madrid by the Conde-Duque de Olivares, and here he continued to train himself on the Titians, Rubenses, Van Dycks, and Riberas in the royal collections and churches of Castile. He later moved to Granada, his birthplace, where his seven vast canvases illustrating the Life of the Virgin (in the Cathedral) are among the most important and imposing examples of his work as an artist. He was also perhaps the most celebrated of Spanish draughtsmen, but his drawings are scattered throughout the world.

Many huge dull votive paintings in Seville are enlivened by admirable portraits of their donors, but portraiture as a distinct branch did not exist in the early 16C outside the capital, where it was introduced on the accession of Philip II, who brought *Antonio Moro (Anton van Dashort Mor;* active 1544–76), a Dutchman from Utrecht and pupil of Scorel, to be his court painter. Mor is hard to find in England, despite the fact that he painted Mary Tudor in 1554, but he is superbly represented in the Prado, where he deserves careful study both for his own sake and because he established a tradition lasting until Velázquez, and even affecting the latter's youthful works. His pupil *Sánchez Coello* of Valencia (c. 1531–88), who had been with him in Flanders, succeeded him as painter-in-ordinary to Philip. The division between Mor and Coello is sometimes difficult to mark, so deeply imbued with his master's spirit was Coello and so well trained in the transparent Flemish technique and the Flemish tradition of drawing. After Mor's departure, however, and under the influence of the king's Venetian portraits, he considerably broadened his handling and strengthened his colour; moreover, in his authentic works he has a very individual and engaging sense of aristocratic distain and insolent humour which is quite different from Mor's burgher gravity. *Juan Pantoja de la Cruz* (1553–1608) studied under Coello, and stepped into his shoes during the next reign; and Pantoja's successor was his imitator *Bartolomé González* (1564–1627), who was to serve Philip IV.

Although there are a number of fine works in England, the first visit to the Velázquez rooms at the Prado is an exciting experience, for nowhere else is there such an array of his masterpieces, from the naturalism and sombre tones of 'The Adoration', of 1619, painted in Seville, to his 'Las Hilanderas', painted nearly forty years later. In his early years **Diego Velázquez de Silva** (1599–1660) was much influenced by Caravaggio and Rubens, who he met in Madrid the year before he set out for Venice.

During his first visit to Italy (August 1629 to early 1631) he found much that was suggestive in Titian, Tintoretto, Guido Reni, and Massimo Stanzioni. In Italy he painted 'The Forge of Vulcan' and 'Joseph's Coat', and later, on returning to Madrid, he started work on 'Las Lanzas' (or 'The Surrender of Breda'), completed in 1640. It is interesting to note that the composition of the two last derive from two woodcuts by Bernard Salomon in a book printed in Lyons in 1553. From 1649–51 Velázquez was in Rome, and on his return his work shows a steadily growing emphasis on colour, and, as exemplified in 'Las Meninas', his range and power, his subtlety and resource in his last phase can hardly be overestimated. And last of all, about 1660, is the enchanting even if unfinished portrait of the little Infanta, in her coral pink and flashing silver gown. Almost all his full-dress portraits of the royal family were copied, sometimes more than once, for presentation to foreign courts. These replicas, which are not always easily to be distinguished from the originals, were chiefly the work of his studio assistant and son-in-law *J. B. del Mazo* (?1612–67)—who was also a notable copyist of Titian, Tintoretto, and Veronese—and *Juan Carreño* (1614–85). For a painter trained under the eye of Velázquez, Mazo in his original work is strangely uncertain in draughtsmanship, dull in colour, and weak in design, but his most serious defect is the faulty proportions of his figures, which are quite inadequately supported by their tapering legs and absurdly small feet. He had a pleasant feeling for landscape, deriving his interest and his sombre style not from his master but from the contemporary romantic school of Salvator Rosa. Carreño shows much more enjoyment of people, and more understanding of Velázquez, whom he took as his model when he turned to professional portraiture after long practice of religious painting in the manner of Van Dyck.

Strictly speaking, Velázquez did not belong to the SCHOOL OF MADRID, which had an independent origin and existence and pursued different ends. It was a numerous and prolific school, devoted mainly to historical, allegorical, and religious painting, and was grounded upon the Prado Titians, Rubenses, and Van Dycks which were then in various royal houses—hence its conflicting aims and lack of local character. But one of the painters most affected by Velázquez was *Juan Bautista Maino* (1578–1649), who could never have been the pupil of El Greco as some claim, although he worked at Toledo and became a member of the Dominican monastery there in 1612. Other individual members of the school were *Antonio de Pereda* (1608–78), and *Jusepe Leonardo* (?1605–

-56): and, primarily religious painters, *José Antolínez* (1635–75), and *Mateo Cerezo* (1626–66), who were able draughtsmen and admirable colourists in the tradition of Van Dyck. Last in the line is *Claudio Coello* (1642–93), who is reputed to have spent seven years on his elaborate masterpiece, 'Carlos II worshipping the *Sagrada Forma*', now in the Sacristy of the Escorial.

Philip V, a Bourbon, who built the 'Spanish Versailles' at La Granja, brought *Michel-Ange Houasse* from Paris, and later came *Jean Ranc,* and *Michel Van Loo;* while from Italy *Luca Giordano* (1632–1705) had already reached Madrid by 1692. These artists and their fellows were so pampered, and their performances so exalted, that the listless native craftsmen simply aped them as paragons. In 1761 the Bohemian *Antón Rafael Mengs* (1728–79), settled in Madrid, and for the next two decades was the arbiter of taste. His portraits, which have perhaps been underestimated, where to influence Goya. Among the more important Spanish painters of the epoch may be mentioned the Catalan *Antonio Viladomat* (1678–1755), *Luis Meléndez* (1716–80), whose still lifes or *'bodegones'* are remarkable, *Luis Paret y Alcázar* (1746-99), an elegant painter of landscapes and court subjects. *José del Castillo* (1737–93), *Mariano Maella* (1739–1819), *Antonio Carnicero* (1748–1814), and *Augustin Esteve* (1753-1820?). Meanwhile, in the 1740s, a Royal Academy of Arts had been established in the capital, and later others were set up in some of the main cities of Spain, which did much to improve the general standard of work in the arts and crafts, while the growing merchant class began to commission and collect paintings, and artists were no longer so dependent on royal patronage and the dictates of the Church.

Between 1776 and 1790 **Francisco de Goya** (1746–1828), encouraged by Mengs, was designing cartoons for the royal tapestry factory, illustrating popular outdoor scenes, which were remarkable for their variety, originality, and colour. Some were influenced by the French School of the period, and perhaps by prints of Hogarth's works; others by *G. B. Tiepolo* (1696–1770), who had come to Madrid in 1762 to decorate the new royal palace. Goya had also, in collaboration with his brother-in-law *Francisco Bayeu* (1734–95), worked on ceiling frescoes in Zaragoza between 1772 and 1783. He then started painting portraits, of which one of the earliest, and characteristic of his personal 'grey' style, is that of the Osuna family of 1787, to be followed by one of Bayeu (in the year of his death), and of the actress 'La Tirana' (1799). In 1799 Goya was made first painter to Carlos IV, but the devastating veracity of his portraits of the king, María Luisa, and the court, were very far from flattering. They are, however, suffused by a new richness of colour, while the composition and pose of some other examples, such as of General Urrutia of 1798 and Doña Tomasa Palafox (1804), recall such English 18C masters as Reynolds and Gainsborough. His later portraits are more sombre in style, but are no less impressive.

The entry of the French into Madrid, and the atrocities Goya witnessed at first hand in May 1808 and later, were to be the basis of some of his most dramatic paintings, and also inspired a grim series of etchings, 'The Disasters of War'. An earlier series—satires on the licentious nobility and the ignorant and unprincipled priesthood—known as 'The Caprichos', were followed by a bull-fighting series, 'The Tauromachia', and by the so-called 'Proverbs'. Goya also decorated his house, the '*Quinta del Sordo*'—for he had been almost stone deaf since the age of 47—with a remarkable series of saturnine murals, known as the 'Black Paintings', which have been transferred to the Prado. Whether they were the fruit of his own despair and isolation is hypothetical. In 1824, Goya retired to Bordeaux where he died, but his remains were not brought back to Madrid until 1919, where they rest in *S. Antonio de la Florida,* frescoed by himself in 1798, and which is now his mausoleum. The range, vitality, and impact of his work is indeed immense. Gautier remarked that in Goya's tomb was buried ancient Spanish art—'all the world, which has now for ever disappeared, of torreros, majos, manolas, monks, smugglers, robbers, alguazils, and sorceresses; in a word, all the colour of the Peninsula. He came just in time to collect and perpetuate these various classes. He thought that he was merely producing so many capricious sketches, when he was in truth drawing the portrait and writing the history of the Spain of former days . . . '.

Among 19C painters, many of them portrait, or genre. painters (*Costumbristas*), were *Vicente López* (1772–1850) *José* and *Federico de Madrazo* (1781–1859, and 1815–94 respectively: from 1838–57 the former was a director of the Prado Museum, which had opened in 1819); *Antonio Esquivel* (1806–57); *José Elbo* (1804–44); *Leonardo Alenza* (1807–45); *Genaro Pérez Villaamil* (1807–54), and *Francisco Parcerisa* (1803–75), both best known for their topographical works; *Joaquín Espalter* (1809–80); *Eugenio Lucas* (1824–70); *José Casado del Alisel* (1832-86); *Eduardo Rosales* (1836-74); *Mariano Fortuny* and *José, Joaquín,* and *Valeriano Domínguez Becquer* (1809–41, 1817–79, and 1834–70 respectively). A later generation included the impressionists *Aureliano de Beruete* (1845–1912), and *Darío de Regoyos* (1857–1916); the Valencian *Joaquín Sorolla* (1862–1923), who achieved popularity with his sunny beach scenes; *Ramón Casas* (1866–1932); the Basque *Ignacio Zuloaga* (1870–1945), who exploited two distinct branches, fashionable portraiture, and peasant genre in combination with turbid landscapes; *Isidro Nonell* (1873-1911); the mural painter *José María Sert* (1874–1945); *Daniel Vázquez Díaz* (1882–1969); *Julio Romero de Torres* (1885–1930), known for his lush 'Cordobana' versions of 'Nell Gwyn'; *José Gutiérrez Solana* (1886-1945); and the Cubist *Juan Gris* (1887-1927).

The most internationally famous, prolific, versatile (and some would say overrated) 20C Spanish artist was **Pablo Ruíz Picasso** (1881–1973), long exiled from his native country; among others, perhaps the most notable are the Surrealists *Joan Miró* (1893-   ), and *Salvador Dalí* (1904-   ).

While it may be invidious to name other living contemporaries, among the more accomplished are the following; how many will survive the fluctuations of fashion remains to be seen: *Rafael Canogar, Luis Feito, Juan Genovés, José Guinovart, Ginés Liebana, Antonio López García, César Manrique, Lucio Muñoz, Pablo Palazuelo, Benjamin Palencia, Manuel Rivera, Antonio Saura, Eusebio Sempere, Ramiro Tapia, Antonio Tàpies, Gustavo Torner, and Fernando Zobel.*

Among sculptors, are *Miguel Ortiz Berrocal, Eduardo Chillida, Julio López Hernández, Jorge de Oteiza,* and *Pablo Serrano.*

BIBLIOGRAPHY

Grouped below are a number of books in English about Spain which may be found useful or of interest to the average traveller, and any will themselves contain bibliographies for further or more specialized reading. Some will be out of print, but may be obtained through a Public Library. The *Spanish Institute Library*, 102 Eaton Square, the *Hispanic Council Library*, 2 Belgrave Square, London S.W.1, and the *Library of the Hispanic Society of America*, 613 West 155th St, New York, should not be overlooked.

TOPOGRAPHICAL AND GENERAL. Among older works of particular value, although the Spain they depict has greatly changed, are: *Joseph Baretti*, A Journey from London to Genoa (1770, reprinted 1970); *Richard Ford*, Gatherings from Spain (1846, reprinted 1970), Hand-Book for Travellers in Spain (1845), the latter, of outstanding importance. was reprinted in its entirety in 1966; *George Borrow*, The Bible in Spain (1843), and The Zincali, or Gypsies of Spain (1841), are frequently reprinted. A Guide to Spain by *H. O'Shea* (1865) and English editions of *Baedeker's* Spain and Portugal (last edition 1913) are still of interest, while the once-restricted British Naval Intelligence Geographical Handbooks (1941: 1944) contain much curious information.

Havelock Ellis, the Soul of Spain (1908), *Rafael Shaw*, Spain from Within (1910), and *Mario Praz*, Unromantic Spain (1929) contain interesting interpretations of aspects of the country.

Among other earlier descriptions of Spain, the following are the most notable: Private Correspondence of *Sir Benjamin Keene* (1933); *Henry Swinburne*, Travels through Spain (1779); *Joseph Townsend*, A Journey through Spain (1792); *Alexander Jardine*, Letters from Barbary (1788); *F. A. Fischer*, Travels in Spain (1802); *J. Bourgoing*, The Modern State of Spain (1808); *Lady E. Holland*, The Spanish Journal of (1910); *J. Blanco White*, Letters from Spain (1822); *A. Sliddell-Mackenzie* (the '*Young American*'), A Year in Spain (1831), and Spain Revisited (1836); *Anon [Henry Southern]* Madrid in 1835 (1836); *S. E. Cook*, later *Widdrington*, Sketches in Spain (1834), and Spain and the Spaniards (1844); *C. Rochfort Scott*, Excursions in the Mountains of Ronda and Granada (1838); *G. Dennis*, A Summer in Andalucia (1839); and *T. M. Hughes*, Revelations of Spain (1845); the majority of these are the subject of a forthcoming study by *Ian Robertson* of English Travellers in Spain, 1760–1855, the Spanish translation of which, entitled 'Los Curiosos Impertinentes', was published in Madrid in 1977.

More recent works include: *Gerald Brenan*, The Face of Spain, and South from Granada; *V. S. Pritchett*, the Spanish Temper; *Sacheverell Sitwell*, Spain; *H. V. Morton*, A Stranger in Spain; *Robin Fedden*, The Enchanted Mountains (Pyrenees); *H. Myhill*, the Spanish Pyrenees; *Hilaire Belloc*, The Pyrenees (1909); *Laurie Lee*, A Rose for Winter; *Walter Starkie*, Spanish Raggle Taggle, The Road to Santiago, and Don Gypsy; *Rose Macaulay*, Fabled Shore; *J. Langdon-Davies*, Gatherings from Catalonia; *Fernand Braudel*, the Mediterranean; *R. Way*, Geography of Spain; *J. M. Houston*, The Western Mediterranean World; *P.E. Russell* (Ed.), Spain, a Companion to Spanish Studies (6th rev'd edition); *A. Boyd*, Madrid and Central Spain (Companion Guide Series), *James A. Michener*, Iberia (somewhat turgid, and to be read with caution).

GENERAL HISTORY. *H. N. Savory*, Spain and Portugal, the Prehistory of the Iberian Peninsula; *C. H. V. Sutherland*, The Romans in Spain, 217 B.C.-A.D. 117; *H. V. Livermore*, The Origins of Spain and Portugal; *E. A. Thompson*, The Goths in Spain; *R. Menéndez Pidal*, The Cid and his Spain; *Américo Castro*, The Structure of Spanish History (Rev'd edition entitled The Spaniards); *G. Jackson*, The Making of Medieval Spain; *W. Montgomery Watt*, History of Islamic Spain; *D. W. Lomax*, The Reconquest of Spain; *Peter Linehan*, The Spanish Church and the Papacy in the Thirteenth Century; *J. F. O'Callaghan*, History of Medieval Spain; *J. N. Hillgarth*, The Spanish Kingdoms 1250–1516; *Angus Mackay*, Spain in the Middle Ages; *P. E. Russell*, The English Intervention in Spain and Portugal in the time of Edward III and Richard II; *J. Vicens Vives*, Economic History of Spain, and Approaches to the History of Spain; *J. H. Elliott*, Imperial Spain, 1469–1716, and The Revolt of the Catalans, 1598–1640; *H. Kamen*, The Spanish Inquisition, and The War of the Succession in Spain (1700–15), the political and economic background; *G. Mattingly*, The Defeat of the Spanish Armada; *J. H. Parry*, The Spanish Seaborne Empire; *J. Lynch*, Spain under the Habsburgs. 1516–1700; *A. Domínguez Ortiz*, The Golden Age of Spain, 1516–1659; *R. Herr*, The 18th Century Revolution in Spain; *G. Marañon*, Antonio Perez; *A. A. Neuman*, The Jews in Spain; *Y. Baer*, History of the Jews in Christian Spain; *E. Allison Peers*, Handbook to the Life and Times of St. Teresa and St. John of the Cross; *G. W. C. Oman*, History of the Peninsular War (7 vols), and Wellington's Army; *J. Weller*, Wellington in the Peninsula; *E. Longford*, Wellington, the Years of the Sword; *A. Bryant*, The Great Duke; *E. Holt*, The Carlist Wars in Spain; *R. Carr*, Spain, 1808–1939; *H. J. Chaytor*, History of Aragon and Catalonia; *A. D. Francis*, the First Peninsular War, 1702–1713; *J. Read*, the Moors in Spain and Portugal; *W. N. Hargreaves-Mawdsley*, Eighteenth Century Spain; *C. E. Kany*, Life and Manners in Madrid, 1750–1800; *Claudio Sánchez-Albornoz*, Spain, a historical enigma (Madrid, 1976); *S. Harcourt-Smith*, Alberoni, or the Spanish Conspiracy; *Michael Glover*, The Peninsular War, 1807–14.

Among earlier works of interest are: *W. H. Prescott*, History of Ferdinand and Isabella (1842), and History of Philip II (1878); *Butler Clarke*, Modern Spain (1906); *A. Parnell*, The Wars of the Succession in Spain (1888), and *R. Dozy*, Spanish Islam, Trans. by F. G. Stokes (1913)

MODERN HISTORY. *B. Bolloten*, The Grand Camouflage; *F. Borkenau*, The Spanish Cockpit; *Gerald Brenan*, The Spanish Labyrinth; *G. Hills*, Spain (Nations of the Modern World); *G. Jackson*, The Spanish Republic and the Civil War; *Salvador de Madariaga*, Spain; *George Orwell*, Homage to Catalonia; *S. G. Payne*, The Falange, The Spanish Revolution, Politics and the Military in Modern Spain; *Hugh Thomas*, The Spanish Civil War (1977 edition); *R. A. H. Robinson*, The Origins of Franco's Spain; *D. T. Cattell*, Communism and the Spanish Civil War; *P. Broué* and *E. Témime*, The Revolution and the Civil War in Spain; *Arturo Barea*, The Forging of a Rebel (autobiography); *Paul Preston*, Spain in Crisis, and The Coming of the Spanish Civil War; *Ronald Fraser*, Blood of Spain; the Experience of Civil War; *Raymond Carr* and *J. P. Fusi*, Spain: Dictatorship to Democracy.

ART AND ARCHITECTURE, ETC., but not including works on specific artists or merely picture books. *Bernard Bevan,* History of Spanish Architecture, the standard work in English, an extended edition of which is in preparation; *W. M. Whitehill,* Spanish Romanesque Architecture of the 11th Century; *J. H. Harvey,* The Cathedrals of Spain; *A. N. Prentice,* Spanish Renaissance; Architecture and Ornament, 1500–1560 (Rev'd edition, 1970); *Pedro de Palol* and *M. Hirmer,* Early Medieval Art in Spain; *C. Oman,* The Golden Age of Spanish Silver, 1400–1665; *A. W. Frothingham,* Spanish Glass; *J. Lees Milne,* Baroque in Spain and Portugal; *G. Kubler* and *M. S ria,* Art and Architecture in Spain and Portugal and their Spanish Dominions, 1500–1800; *Sacheverell Sitwell,* Southern Baroque Art, and Spanish Baroque Art; *Royall Tyler,* Spain, a Study of her Life and Arts (1909); *C. R. Post,* A History of Spanish Painting (14 vols); *J. W. Waterer,* Spanish Leather.

Among outstanding earlier works is; *G. E. Street,* Some Account of Gothic Architecture in Spain (1855; rev'd edition 1914, since reprinted); also of interest, and available in Spain are *A. Gámir* (Ed.), Richard Ford; Granada, an account with unpublished original Drawings; and *Brinsley Ford,* Richard Ford en Sevilla (Spanish text and 48 plates); also Richard Ford in Spain (a catalogue of a loan exhibition at *Wildenstein's* in 1974). Also of interest for the large number of plates they contain are *Muirhead Bone,* Old Spain (folio ed.; 1936), an outstanding work; and *Fernando Chueca,* Historia de la Arquitectura Española; likewise in Spanish the six volumes of *Carlos Flores,* Arquitectura popular española, and *Luis Feduchi,* Itinerarios de Arquitectura Popular Española, all profusely illustrated.

LITERATURE. *W. J. Entwistle,* The Spanish Language; *Gerald Brenan,* The Literature of the Spanish People; *E. Allison Peers,* The Romantic Movement in Spain; *N. D. Shergold,* History of the Spanish stage (to 1700); *R. O. Jones* (Ed.), A Literary History of Spain (in 8 vols).; *George Ticknor,* History of Spanish Literature (1849 and later editions). *F. W. Chandler,* Romances of Roguery (1899; reprinted 1961); *D. L. Shaw,* The Generation of 1898 in Spain; *José Alberich,* Bibliografía Anglo-Hispánica, 1801–50; *Philip Ward* (Ed.), The Oxford Companion to Spanish Literature.

No one will forget Don Quixote (of modern translations, those of Samuel Putnam or Walter Starkie are preferred); *Le Sage's* Gil Blas; and *Washington Irving's* Chronicle of the Conquest of Granada, and The Alhambra, however romanticized.

NATURAL HISTORY. *Guy Mounfort,* A Portrait of a Wilderness (Coto Doñana); *R. Peterson, G. Mountfort* and *P. A. D. Hollom,* A Field Guide to the Birds of Britain and Europe; *O. Polunin and B. E. Smythies,* Flowers of South-West Europe; *O. Polunin* and *A. Huxley,* Flowers of the Mediterranean; *Abel Chapman* and *W. J. Buck,* Unexplored Spain (1910), and Wild Spain (1893; recently reprinted in Spain), are still of interest.

MISCELLANEOUS. *M. Defourneaux,* Daily Life in Spain in the Golden Age; *J. Pitt-Rivers,* The People of the Sierra; *Violet Alford,* Pyrenean Festivals; *Rodney Gallop,* Book of the Basques; *A. Livermore,* Short History of Spanish Music; *J. Read,* the Wines of Spain and Portugal; *J. Jeffs,* Sherry; *Croft-Cooke,* Sherry.

For Maps, see p.72.

PRACTICAL INFORMATION

APPROACHES TO SPAIN AND TRANSPORT IN SPAIN

Spain may be reached directly from Great Britain by a variety of ways, but it is recommended that the traveller intending to tour in the Peninsula should take his own car, as it is the only practical way of seeing large areas of the country. Except during a bad Winter, or in the main Summer season, when roads are crowded, the overland routes across France can be very pleasant, and not necessarily as expensive as has been made out. Advantage may also be taken of the Car Ferry Service direct from England to Spain, or the Car-Sleeper Expresses. Air services offer by far the quickest, but least interesting, means of transit; there are also a number of rapid rail services from London or Paris to the Spanish frontier (also through trains to Madrid and Barcelona), and beyond to the more important centres.

Travel Agents. General information may be obtained gratis from the Spanish National Tourist Office at 57-58 St James's St, London S.W.1, while in most of the larger towns of Spain one will find, usually well indicated by sign-posts, offices of the *Secretaría de Estado de Turismo* S.E.T.) or municipal tourist offices. Both can provide information regarding accommodation, admission to museums, entertainment, etc. The manager (*administrador*) of any *Parador Nac.* (see p.76) should also be able to advise travellers concerning matters of local interest.

The Spanish Nat. Tourist Office in *New York* is at 665 Fifth Av., with branches at 180 N. Michigan Av., *Chicago;* 3160 Lyon St, *San Francisco;* and also at *St Augustin* (Florida). The Canadian office is at 660 Bloor St W., *Toronto.*

Any accredited member of the *Association of British Travel Agents* will sell travel tickets and book accommodation.

Among general travel agents are *Thomas Cook & Son,* 45 Berkeley St, W.1., with many branches in Central London; *American Express,* 6 Haymarket, S.W.1., 89 Mount St, W.1., and 82 Brompton Rd, S.W.3; and Powell Duffryn, 170 Piccadilly, W.1., 12 Tower Place, E.C.4, and other branches.

Numerous and frequent **Passenger** and **Car Ferry Services** between England and the Continent are operated by British and French Railways (S.N.C.F.), also known as *Sealink;* Townsend Thoresen, Southern Ferries, Normandy Ferries, and Brittany Ferries, etc.; for the latest information with regard to services available, enquiries should be made to the *Car Ferry Centre,* 53 Grosvenor Gardens, London S.W.1. The only direct ferry between England and Spain at present in operation (1979) is that between Plymouth and Santander (Brittany Ferries; Millbay Dock, Plymouth). Those wishing to make use of the **Hovercraft** services should be warned that these may be erratic in adverse weather conditions.

Motorists will save much trouble by joining the *Automobile Association* (Fanum House, Basingstoke, Hants RG21 2EA), the *Royal Automobile Club* (83 Pall Mall, London S.W.1), the *Royal Scottish Automobile Club* (17 Rutland Sq., Edinburgh), or the *American Automobile Association.* These organizations will provide any necessary documents, as well as information about rules of the road abroad, restrictions regarding Caravans and trailers, advice on routes, and arrangements regarding delivery of spare parts, insurance, etc. Motorists who are not the owners of their vehicle should possess the owner's permit for its use abroad. *The Real Automóvil Club de España* has its head office at 10 C. Gen. Sanjurjo, Madrid.

The *latest* edition of the *Michelin* Map of France (No. 989) or the Carte Routière of France published by the *Institut Géographique National* are recommended for those disembarking at the Channel Ports, while the *Blue Guide to the Loire Valley, Normandy, and Brittany* will not come amiss. For further information regarding maps, and on touring in Spain, see pp.67-73

While it may be convenient to travel to Spain **by Rail,** and to use the *Spanish Railways* (RENFE—*Red Nacional de Ferrocarriles Españoles*) for long through journeys, they are not recommended as a means of touring, except by enthusiasts.

The *British Railway Travel Centre,* Rex House, Lower Regent St, London S.W.1, provides travel tickets, sleeping berth tickets, seat reservations, etc., on Continental (as well as British) transport services. Make certain that the 'global' price has been offered, including *all* supplements, etc., and check on the validity of return tickets.

In Spain there are a number of *Express* trains, and the articulated *Talgo,* running between the major cities, which if speed is a consideration, are always preferable to those designated *Rápido,* etc. In general the Spanish rail services, at least between the main towns, have been much improved and modernized in recent years.

The *'Puerta del Sol'* travels overnight between Paris and Madrid, and the *'Barcelona Talgo',* between Paris and Barcelona, changing bogies at the frontier, thus avoiding a change of carriage, the gauge of Spanish railways being broader than the French.

Regular **Air Services** between England and Spain are maintained by *Iberia,* working in conjunction with *British Airways.* Full information regarding flights may be obtained from British Airways, Dorland House, Lower Regent St, London S.W.1, and from Iberia, 169 Regent St, W.1. Flights are also provided by Charter companies, while internal or domestic services are maintained by *Iberia* or *Aviaco.*

There are also regular flights from most European capitals and larger cities to Madrid, and in certain cases with intermediate landings at, or direct flights to, Barcelona, Málaga, Alicante, etc. There are also regular direct services from New York, and Montreal, to Spain, and from many other non-European countries.

From airports there are bus services to the town termini, and in many cases motor coach connections with other towns or resorts in the area. Taxis will also meet planes, and many car-hire firms have offices at airports.

There are now numerous regular **Bus Services** (*Coches de Linea; autobuses*) in Spain, between the main towns, apart from additional Tourist Services during the season, and fares are moderate. On the important routes vehicles are comfortable, and convey a reasonable amount of luggage, but bone-shakers are still found on some rural roads.

Careful inquiry should be made in advance from local Tourist Offices as to the times and place of departure, but it is always as well to have this confirmed and booked in advance at the Bus Station (*Estación de autobuses*) as seating is limited. Tickets, which are usually for a numbered seat, can sometimes be booked for the return trip (*ida y vuelta*—there and back).

Taxis, pronounced '*Tassi*', no longer inexpensive, display the sign 'LIBRE' when disengaged. In Madrid, where they are numerous, they are recognizable by a red horizontal line on black coachwork, while Minicabs (*Microtaxis*), less frequently seen, have a yellow line on blue coachwork. These distinguishing marks vary from town to town. A tip of 10 per cent is more than sufficient. Surcharges apply for drives outside town, to stations, airports, and for luggage placed in the boot.

Beware of *'Gran Turismo'* taxis, without distinguishing lines, which lurk in areas frequented by tourists, and charge exorbitantly.

Horse Cabs may still be found in the main tourist areas of some Andalucían cities, and elsewhere. A very definite bargain should be made beforehand as to the *duration* of the drive and *total* cost.

GEOGRAPHY OF SPAIN AND PLAN OF TOUR

For the discriminating tourist it is often a problem to plan a suitable itinerary which will take in a representative selection of historic towns and monuments, at the same time passing through regions of scenic beauty or grandeur. This is partly because of the sheer size of the country, which is only very slightly smaller than France. Likewise it should be remembered that Spain, after Switzerland, is the highest and most *mountainous* country in Europe (the average height is just under 2000 ft above sea-level), a point that is not usually appreciated, and the time required to cover a particular route can easily be underestimated.

Briefly, the main physical feature of Spain is a vast elevated plateau or *meseta*—two-fifths of the country—divided by a central chain of mountains (the sierras of Guadarrama, Gredos, and Gata) running west from the Iberian Mountains. It has been estimated (in the 1960s) that 33.7 per cent of the soil produced virtually nothing. The northern section comprises a large area of Old Castile and León; the southern part includes most of New Castile and Estremadura. The Northern Meseta, also known as the Duero basin, is cut off from the Atlantic coast to the north by the Picos de Europa and the Cantabrian Mountains, a westward extension of the main Pyrenean chain, while to the N.W. the Montes de León combine to make remote Galicia difficult of access. Between France and Spain rears up the formidable barrier of the Pyrenees, c. 400 km. long and well over 5000 ft for most of its length, and with a maximum height of 11,169 ft (*Pic d'Aneto*). On the Spanish side, foothills of the range extend some distance into Aragón and Catalonia before reaching the wide depression of the Ebro valley. To the W. and S. of the Ebro, a further range, the Iberian Mountains, runs S.E. from Burgos to the coast near Valencia, providing a watershed between the Duero and Ebro, and including in its complex the Sierra de Demanda, Sierra de Moncayo, the Montes Universales, and the Sierra de Gúdar. South of Madrid, the rivers Tagus and Guadiana run west through the southern meseta, separated from each other by the lower Montes de Toledo and Sierra de Guadalupe. To the S., beyond the broad and broken Sierra Morena, extends the wide low-lying valley of the Guadalquivir. Still farther S., rising abruptly from the Mediterranean coast, and running roughly parallel to it for over 550 km., are the complex ranges composing the Betic Cordillera, the main chain of which, the Sierra Nevada, rises S.E. of Granada to 11,420 ft (*Mulhacén*), the highest summit in Spain. All these mountain ranges provide a variety of scenery amply compensating for the occasional monotony of the undulating plateau.

The Pyrenees may be crossed at a number of points, and are passed with ease at either end. From its western extremity, travellers must climb through the broken and mountainous Basque Provinces before entering Old Castile N.E. of Burgos, while from Barcelona the Ebro valley is ascended as far as Zaragoza before the road climbs through the Iberian Mountains to approach Madrid. Almost all these ranges are traversed by reasonably surfaced and improved roads, and although during winter months some passes or *puertos* are intermittently blocked by falls of snow, there is now little difficulty in getting about the country. In the past the problems of communication contributed to the localism of towns and separation of provinces, indifferent to common preoccupations. Climatic conditions further emphasize the physical divisions. The Basque Provinces, the Asturias, and Galicia—humid, green and often thickly wooded—are in striking contrast to the calcined plains and keen air of adjacent Castile and León. Modern methods of irrigation, reafforestation, etc. have combined to obscure these differences, but they still remain. Whatever the season, travellers are advised to consider carefully the routes they wish to follow. As far as roads are concerned, there has been a very considerable improvement as to their general quality during recent years, although in many areas—in Galicia particularly—there is still work to be done. Too often an important major road has been allowed to deteriorate, while a rarely used minor road has been entirely resurfaced.

The net of Motorways (*autopistas*; see also below) has been considerably extended during the last few years, as part of the general Continental system of Europe, which have done much already to facilitate communications. They are numbered with the prefix A (e.g. A 2), and their position is best studied on the *latest Michelin* map of Spain (No. 990) or on that published by *Firestone* (No. EU-2).

Six main highways radiate from Madrid, forming part of the National network, and are given Roman numbers (e.g. N IV). Other main roads (*carreteras*) are given Arabic numerals (e.g. N 234), while the more important local roads are classed C. (comarcales), and are numbered likewise (e.g. C 456). The general condition of by-roads (usually marked as *Camino Rural* or *Camino Forestal*) can usually be relied on, but the surface of some minor cross-country roads still leaves much to be desired. Many are in a perfectly satisfactory state, even if narrow and winding, but occasionally they deteriorate unaccountably into rough stony tracks and continue so for many kilometres.

In the bitter experience of the Editor, it cannot be emphasized too often that the apparently direct road between two points *is by no means* always the easiest or fastest, particularly off the beaten track. Some roads (indicated as reasonably good on maps) wind and climb through hilly country for hours, while others will lead for considerable distances across the level *meseta* in half the time.

As few maps indicate the *contour* of the area to be traversed, or how mountainous and broken up it may be, ascertain if possible the quality of the road to be followed from someone likely to have travelled on it in the recent past: the police or a garage are the most reliable judges, but *few will admit that they don't know* when asked such a question or even when asked directions. Some maps (such as those published by the Ministerio de Obras Públicas) are inexcusably misleading, indicating a

Key to Basque Provinces.
1 Vizcaya
2 Guipúzcoa
3 Aláva

FRANCE

NGADAS
PROVINCES

2

NAVARRE

ANDORRA

roño

Huesca

Lérida

Girona

CATALUÑA

Barcelona

ia

Zaragoza

ARAGÓN

Tarragona

dalajara

Teruel

Castellón

Cuenca

VALENCIA

Valencia

Albacete

Alicante

Murcia

MURCIA

Almería

winding road as being straight, and a tortuous mountain road as having merely a few 'wriggles'.

In some villages the surface is non-existent, a situation aggravated by rain washing away the dust and rubble that has accumulated in its potholes. Many roads are hilly and even mountainous, and brakes (*frenos*) should be checked. Although there are many new garages and petrol stations on the main roads, elsewhere they are still few and far between, and it is advisable to top up where one can. It is often convenient to ask for so many pesetas-worth of petrol (*gasolina*) rather than by the litre. The 96 octane '*Super*' is always preferable. A request to fill up the tank is 'Rellenar, por favor'.

When traversing mountainous districts in winter, and even as late as May, care should be taken to ensure that the passes are open. Signs are displayed at the beginning of the ascent of many indicating whether they are closed (*cerrado*) or open (*abierto*) in which case chains (*cadenas*), which are *obligatory*, may be required. The weather on any high mountain road can suddenly deteriorate, and the driver may find himself in a blizzard within minutes. The police are often in a position to advise the motorist of road or snow conditions, while a telephone advisory service is available in Madrid and in the provincial capitals.

When travelling in summer, motorists should if possible avoid driving due west during the late afternoon. Towards evening the glare of the setting sun can be most unpleasant and even dangerous. And while most tourists will plan to reach their destination in daylight, particularly if travelling off the beaten track, when driving at dusk or after dark, a sharp look-out should be kept for unlit carts, bicycles, and donkeys, etc. Lorry-drivers are usually co-operative in allowing themselves to be overtaken. Passing motorists invariably stop to assist a car in trouble, but should the breakdown (*avería*) be serious, it is advisable to contact the nearest *Auxilio en Carretera*, or garage.

The Highway Code conforms to the general Continental system. The use of seat-belts is compulsory outside towns. A high proportion of the drivers of private cars in Spain will not have had them for long; many have comparatively little experience, and they are not always as considerate on the road as they might be. It should be noted that the responsibility for accidents to pedestrians is thrown almost entirely on the motorist. One's insurance should include a 'Bail Bond'.

When planning a tour, the intending traveller should not assume that many provincial capitals, even if writ large on maps—especially Spanish maps (such as those given out by the S.E.T.)—are necessarily of any great interest or importance if one is seeking a city replete with old-world charm. Many, whatever their past history, are now little more than administrative centres of regions, and as such are very likely to have been spoiled by recent development. Although it may be invidious to particularize, the following—even if described briefly in the text, which should be scanned first for what *may* be seen—can be by-passed without the traveller feeling that he is missing very much: *Albacete, Badajoz, Castellón, Ciudad Real, Guadalajara, Huelva,* and *Teruel. Santander* (were it not for its position), and *Lérida* (were it not for its restored cathedral) would be likewise included in this list.

The main **Motorways** (*autopistas*) in Spain at present (1979) completed—or nearly so—are as detailed below:

The **A 1,** crossing the French border from Bayonne at Behobia to Burgos. A section shortening the present route—which turns S. at Bilbao (**A 68**)—bearing S.W. near Eibar to rejoin the completed section near Miranda de Ebro, is still being constructed.

From this latter junction, the **A 68** (from Bilbao) leads S.E. to Zaragoza, while an extension from Bilbao to Santander is planned.

The **A 15**, at present commencing at Irurzun, and which will eventually lead N. to San Sebastián, by-passes Pamplona and joins the **A. 68** W. of Tudela.

The **A 17**, now crossing the French border from Perpignan at La Jonquera, leads S. past Girona to Barcelona, which is also by-passed. From Barcelona the **A 2** leads S.W. past Villafranca del Penedés and W. past Lérida, to Zaragoza. Near Vendrell the **A 7** turns S. and skirts the Levante coast to Valencia (to be by-passed), shortly continuing S. to Alicante. An extension hence to Murcia and Cartagena is planned.

In the Asturias there are at present only short stretches joining the centres of Oviedo, Gijón, and Avilés; its extension S. from Oviedo to León, is planned.

In Galicia, the stretch between La Coruña and Santiago (**A 9**) is virtually completed, and that between Pontevedra and Vigo. Further stretches are planned from La Coruña to El Ferrol, from Santiago to Pontevedra, and from Vigo to Túy.

From Madrid, the **A 2** approaches Alcalá de Henares, while the **A 3** (leading S.E.) has hardly extended beyond the city limits. The **A 6** leads 105 km. N.W. towards Arévalo.

In Andalucía, the **A 4** has been completed between Seville and Cádiz, and the **A 49** leads W. from Seville towards Huelva.

A paragraph describing the route taken by each stretch of motorway following approx. the same line as the main route, has been incorporated at the head of each such route.

Obviously it is impossible to take a motorway and at the same time hope to visit many of the adjacent towns and villages, which it deliberately by-passes, however many exits and entrances there may be, and they should therefore be avoided if the traveller wishes to explore any number of sites and monuments near the usual road and route described. Nevertheless, in certain areas they are recommended, in spite of the cost of the toll (*peaje*), not only when the saving of time is a consideration. In many cases they can in themselves provide an interesting, attractive, and less tiring route (between San Sebastián and Bilbao, for instance) or because they avoid a comparatively dull coast and by-pass a number of ugly towns (as between Tarragona and Sagunto), and in the latter case both Tortosa and Peñiscola can be approached with ease.

Other sections, which may be followed by tourists wishing to avoid some of the worst excesses of coastal development, are those behind Benidorm and Alicante. Others recommended are those between Seville and Jérez; La Junquera (from Perpignan) to Gerona, and from Gerona to Barcelona; the stretches between Barcelona and Lérida (from which Santes Creus and Poblet may be visited), and from Lérida to Zaragoza; likewise the Bilbao-Burgos motorway, and that between La Coruña and Santiago.

But any detailed study of the use of motorways will be reserved for the next edition of this Guide, by which time many more will be in operation, and the routes at present followed may well require adjustment, taking into consideration the improvement, or otherwise, of other roads.

On entering towns, and parking. Most large towns in Spain, and many of the smaller ones, are unpleasantly congested, particularly in the centre, where most of the monuments of interest to the traveller, and hotels, are likely to be. This area will be marked '*Centro Ciudad*' at the approach to the town, but such directional signs may well peter out later. Having once found a vacant site for parking it is as well to remain there as long as it is conveniently near where one wishes to make one's base, for with the proliferation of one-way streets, an excess of traffic-lights, and cars, it is no longer a pleasure to drive in towns. Some car-parks are attended (*vigilado*), at least during the day. Underground parking (*subterráneo*) is available in some of the larger cities. It is not advisable to leave visible any articles of value in a parked car. In Blue Zones (*zona azul*) a parking disk, obtainable at some garages, should be set at the hour one parked. Ill-parked foreign cars are towed away by the *Grua* as ruthlessly as native ones and may take hours to recover. In addition, there will be a fine to pay.

Most **Frontier Posts** are open between 7.00 and 22.00 or 24.00 in Summer, and between 7.00 or 9.00 and 21.00 or 24.00 in Winter, with the exception of the following, which are open day and night throughout the year: Hendaye-Irún, Behobie-Behobia motorway, Bourg-Madame-Puigcerdá, and Le Perthus-La Junquera (also the motorway). In addition Cerbère-Port-Bou, Fos-Les, Urdos de Béarn-Canfranc, and Behobie-Behobia are open day and night in the Summer. All such times are liable to alteration. During the last few years cars have also been stopped at police check-points inside the frontier, particularly in the Basque provinces.

Hikers and mountaineers in the Pyrenees should carry their passports, and should note that although there is no specific regulation prohibiting the crossing of the range in remote zones, the Editor has been informed by the authorities that it is 'not recommended'!

MAPS

Both the quality and availability of maps of Spain has improved in recent years, but with few exceptions, there are not many good up-to-date town plans, the rapid growth of some towns making any new edition almost obsolete on publication. But there should be no excuse—now that the *Instituto Geográfia Nacional* (I.G.N.; C. Gen. Ibañez de Ibero 3, Madrid-3) has inaugurated its *Centro de Información y Documentación*—for the traveller to find 'by chance' (as did Widdrington in 1843) a good plan of Granada in Málaga, although no bookshop in Granada had heard of it!

Perhaps the most reliable planning maps for general purposes are those on a single sheet, of which it is essential to obtain the *latest* edition, showing new *autopistas* and other improvements, among them are those published by *Firestone* (No. EU-2), by *Michelin* (No. 990), and by the *I.G.N.* (Peninsula Ibérica), all at 1:1,000,000, the latter giving a better indication of physical features than most, but not including road distances. Others available are the 'Mapa General de Carreteras' published by the Spanish *Min. de Obras Publicas* (1:800,000); by *Freytag and Berndt* (1:1,000,000); by *Bartholomew* (1:1,125,000); by *Kümmerly & Frey* (No. 1144 at 1:1,000,000); by *Reise- und Verkehrsverlag* (No. 85 at 1:800,000); by the *Touring Club Italiano* (Nos. 9-13 in their Europa Series at 1:500,000); and by the *British Min. of Defence* (Series 1301—GSGS at 1:1,000,000), etc.

Spain is also covered by a series of 9 sectional motoring maps published by *Firestone* (1:500,000), which may be supplemented by their 11 Mapas Turisticos covering the main holiday areas (mostly coastal) at 1:200,000. The latter now have town plans, etc. on their reverse side. *Michelin* maps of N.E. Spain and the Pyrenees (Nos. 42 and 43 at

1:400,000) and Nos. 85 and 86, covering the frontier areas at 1:200,000, may also be found useful.

The I.G.N. have recently completed the publication of a series of *Provincial Maps* (Mapa oficial de España: Conjuntos Provinciales) at 1:200,000, showing contour, but for some inexplicable reason this is not shown beyond each provincial boundary! They also issue two series of maps at 1:500,000 covering the whole peninsula in 11 and 13 sheets respectively.

Spain is also covered in a series of c. 1,050 sheets of the Mapa Nacional Topográfico of varying quality (depending on the date of their last revision) at 1:50,000, and work has commenced on the production of maps at 1:25,000. Some large scale maps for mountaineers are published by *Alpina*, while those of the Pyrenees issued by the French *Institut Géographique National* will also be found useful: but see paragraph on p.72, with regard to frontier posts.

Spanish military maps of varying quality are published by the *Servicio Geográfico del Ejército*, details of which may be obtained through the Spanish I.G.N., some of which may at present be available only as black and white photoprints.

The Atlas section of this guide may be supplemented by the Obras Públicas *Mapa Oficial de Carreteras* (1:400,000), which also includes a number of town plans, but it is by no means as reliable as it should be, and no contour is indicated. *Firestone* likewise produce a small Atlas (P-43) at 1:1,000,000 with town plans indicating the main thoroughfares. *Almax* also publish detailed plans of some cities.

The annual *Red Michelin Guide* for Spain and Portugal can also be of assistance, containing useful town plans for the motorist, indicating the latest points of entry and exit, one-way streets, parking sites, and the position of the main hotels and restaurants, etc.

Almost all these maps and guides, apart from those of a more specialist nature, will be available or may be ordered through *Stanford*, 12-14 Long Acre, London W.C.2; *Geographia*, 63 Fleet St, E.C.4; the *A.A.*, Fanum House, Leicester Square, W.C.2; *Sifton Praed*, 54 Beauchamp Place, Brompton Rd, S.W.3, and any good bookshop.

FORMALITIES AND CURRENCY

Passports are necessary for all British and American travellers entering Spain, and must bear the photograph of the holder. British passports (£10) valid for ten years, are issued at the Passport Office, Clive House, Petty France, London S.W.1, or may be obtained for an additional fee through any tourist agency. No visa is required for British or American travellers to Spain.

Visitors wishing to remain in Spain for more than three months should apply for a police permit (*Permanencia*) before the three months have elapsed.

Consuls, etc. At present (1979) there are *British Consuls* or *Vice-Consuls* in mainland Spain at: C. Fernando el Santo 16, Madrid (the Embassy); Diagonal 477, Barcelona; Alameda Urquijo 2, Bilbao; Av. Fr. Franco 11, Algeciras; C. Canalejas 1, Alicante; C. Duque de Parcent 8, Málaga; Pl. de Compostela 23, Vigo; C. Santian 4, Tarragona; and Pl. Nueva 8, Seville.

British Chambers of Commerce: C. Marqués de Valdeiglesias 3, Madrid; Paseo de Gracia 11, Barcelona; Alameda de Mazarredo 5, Bilbao; and C. Alfonso el Magnánimo 15, Valencia.

U.S. Consulates will be found at C. Serrano 75, Madrid (the Embassy); C. Layetana 33-34, Barcelona; Paseo de las Delicias 7, Seville; and Av. del Ejército 11-3, Deusto, Bilbao. *U.S. Chamber of Commerce,* C. Padre Damián 23, Madrid.

Customs House. Except for travellers by air, who have to pass the customs at the airport of arrival, or those travelling on international expresses, where their luggage is examined in the train, luggage (*equipaje*) is scrutinized at the frontier or port of disembarkation. Provided that dutiable articles are declared, bona-fide travellers will usually find the Spanish customs authorities (*aduaneros*) courteous and reasonable: no longer can they be condemned, as they were by Ford, as gentlemen 'who pretend to examine baggage, in order to obtain money without the disgrace of begging, or the danger of robbing ...'. It is as well to check in advance with the Spanish Consulate as to the latest regulations with regard to the importation of firearms, whether sporting or otherwise.

Currency Regulations. In October 1979 the British Government announced the suspension of exchange controls. There are now no restrictions on the amount of sterling the traveller may take out of Great Britain.

Money. The monetary unit is the *peseta* (pta), divided into 100 *céntimos*. Bank notes for 100, 500, 1000, and 5000 ptas are issued by the Banco de España, together with silver coins of 100 ptas (not often seen), nickel coins of 5 (still frequently referred to as a '*duro*'), 25, and 50 ptas, and a bronze coin of 1 pta. Also an alloy jeton of 50 céntimos. The 2½ ptas coin and those of 10 céntimos are rarely in circulation.

Banks. Branches of Spanish banks and foreign banks in Spain are to be found near the centre of most towns, and are open from 8.30 to 14.00. only. A sign is usually displayed outside indicating that change (*cambio*) is given, and there is now little difficulty in changing Travellers' Cheques, although sometimes there is an unconscionable delay, particularly in the larger banks. Paradores and the larger hotels will also accept them, but give a lower rate of exchange. Exchange Bureaux are also to be found at airports and points of entry into Spain, often providing a 24-hour service. It is advisable to obtain a small supply of Spanish change for incidental expenses before leaving home.

At present most Spanish banks provide minimal facilities compared with most of their Continental counterparts, when it comes to accepting bank cards, etc., a situation which is slowly improving. Motorists are advised to carry sufficient money to cover at least minor expenses on the road, apart from petrol, as garages only accept cash.

Security. Travellers are warned that there appears to be a recrudescence of the blight of the '*ratero*', or small-time thief in many of the larger cities of Spain—Seville, Granada, Málaga, Barcelona, Valencia, Madrid, etc. No objects of any value should be left visible in the interior of cars parked overnight near hotels, for example, apart from any other time. Ladies using handbags with shoulder straps should beware of bag-snatchers operating on motorcycles. In general, it is advisable to deposit any valuables with the manager of one's hotel, against receipt, rather than tempting providence. Normally, however, with a reasonable amount of circumspection (and without over-preoccupation) the tourist will find his property respected. The police should be applied to immediately in case of any such trouble.

POSTAL AND OTHER SERVICES

Postal Information. The main Post Office in Madrid operates a limited 24-hour service; others are usually open from 8.00 to 12.00 and from 17.00 to 19.30. Post Offices (*Correos*) and Telegraph Offices are not invariably in the same building. Correspondence marked '*lista de correos*' or '*poste restante*' (to be called for) may be addressed to any post office and is handed to the addressee on proof of identity (passport preferable). The surname of the addressee, especially the capital letter, should be clearly written, and no 'Esq.' added. Letters (*cartas*) of importance should be registered (*certificado*). A postcard is a *tarjeta postal*. Postage-stamps (*sellos*) may also be obtained from tobacconists, see p.90. Pillar or post-boxes are now painted bright yellow.

Telephones. The Spanish telephone service is maintained by the *Compañia Telefónica Nacional,* or *Telefónica,* which is still, anachronistically, a private monopoly, not a nationalized service, a situation which it is hoped will be rectified shortly. It is thus still distinct from the postal or telegraph services, although they will accept telegrams dictated over the telephone for dispatch. All towns have an office from which local, trunk, and international calls (*conferencias*) may be made, but many of these offices have recently been moved from a convenient central site to an obscure suburb, and its whereabouts unknown by most citizens, and much time can be wasted trying to locate it. There are, however, more telephone cabins to be seen in the streets from which calls can be made, apart from call-box instruments in bars and restaurants, etc. constructed to take special tokens (*fichas*), which have to be bought at the counter near which it is installed. Spain is now, except in some rural areas, in automatic or S.T.D. communication with the rest of Europe, etc.

It should be noted that in Telephone Directories and other alphabetical lists that names beginning with Ch are printed in a separate section after the Cs. It is also advisable to make sure one knows the full name of the person required; i.e. Federico *García* Lorca, as this will be indexed under the second name, which is the first part of the surname.

When answering the telephone the expression *Diga* or *Digame,* literally 'Speak to me', should be used, while *Oiga* (listen) meaning 'hallo!' or 'are you there?' is the usual interrogation.

HOTELS AND RESTAURANTS

Hotels. The standard of comfort, efficiency, and cleanliness of Spanish hotels is now comparatively high. All have been officially graded by the S.E.T., who issue an annual *Guia de Hoteles*, which may be perused at all Tourist Offices.

Hotel accommodation falls into eight categories; Hotels, from 1-star to 5-star, and Hostels and Pensions from 1-star to 3-star. In addition there exists an extensive and growing network of tourist establishments—mostly 3- or 4-star—managed by the S.E.T., and known as: *Paradores Nacionales*, which often occupy historic buildings, or premises specially constructed in positions of outstanding scenic beauty or cultural interest; *Albergues de Carretera*, wayside inns strategically placed on main roads; *Refugios*, upland inns and centres for mountaineering, shooting, and fishing, and *Hosterías*, which are restaurants *only*, with no sleeping accommodation on the premises. Very similar in style to the Paradores are the luxury hotels at Seville (Alfonso XIII), Santiago (Los Reyes Católicos), León (San Marcos), and El Paular (Santa María), etc. The *latest* map showing Paradores should be requested from a S.E.T. office, who can advise on any recently opened.

The Paradores are more adapted for longer stays than the Albergues, which cater principally for the passing tourist, and which provide some form of meal service at any reasonable hour, although not invariably so. In both, the bedrooms (with private bathrooms) and public rooms are comfortable, and usually tastefully furnished. Their safe 'international' menu also introduces a number of regional dishes to the cautious traveller, for not all are like Joseph Baretti, who remarked: 'Let it be dinner-time, and I care not a fig for the difference between macaroni and roast-beef, herring and frogs, the olla and the sourcrout; a very cosmopolite in the article of filling one's belly'. Nevertheless, the menu can pall if Paradores are resorted to habitually, and the quality of food rarely merits the prices now charged.

Unfortunately, owing to the misdirected pretensions of a late minister, some of the more recent Paradores (among them Segovia and Salamanca) have been large modern buildings some distance from town centres, of very little intrinsic interest, and in striking contrast to the discreet and intimate, which was part of the charm of some earlier establishments. The advice of their managers should be sought, should there be no local office of the S.E.T. open.

The recession of the tourist boom has had the effect of improving the quality of many hotels—the fittest have usually survived. Others have come to realize that the 'Sacred Cow' of 'Turismo' could not be milked indefinitely without offering compensating benefits, although regrettably a number of shoddy establishments still remain. And some of the internal walls of many of the newer buildings are embarrassingly thin, lacking any sound insulation.

In the main cities and coastal resorts there are large luxury hotels providing cosmopolitan comfort at corresponding charges, while the ordinary first-class hotels in the medium-sized towns are usually excellent. Hotels are still few and far between in many inland areas, but satisfactory accommodation can almost always be found at short notice. In areas frequented by tourists—particularly 'Package Tourists'—hotels are likely to be crowded during the season.

In an increasing number of comparatively modest hotels one will now find bathrooms (*cuarto de baño*) and running water in the bedrooms, and the lower category establishments with one or two stars only (which were in certain cases known previously as *Fondas, Posadas,* or *Ventas*) should not be scorned by the unexacting traveller. Although simple, they are invariably scrupulously clean, however inelegant the décor, and uninviting their exterior appearance, and they often serve good meals in the traditional local style. There may be a lack of comfort in the public rooms (where only too often the ubiquitous television is the centre of attraction), a disadvantage against which may be placed the opportunity of seeing a characteristic side of Spanish life.

Should no accommodation be found in the only local hotel or boarding-house (*Casa de Huéspedes*—C.H.), a bed in a nearby private house may obligingly be found, and if food is required, an omelette (*tortilla*) or eggs and bacon (*huevos con jamón*) can almost always be produced at short notice.

Every bedroom (*habitación*) must display a notice giving details of the maximum price applicable to the room, and this is *inclusive* of all service charges and taxes. Rarely are the prices lower than the maximum, although in theory this is allowed. Extra gratuities are *not* normally expected, although porters, etc. in some of the larger hotels, may hang about hopefully, but (to quote Baretti again) 'where every trifle may be turned into money, money will be expected for every trifle'. Such notice of prices must also be displayed at the Reception desk. No charges higher than the maximum may be made for reasons such as festivals, special local events, etc., except in certain very specific cases (such as at Seville during Semana Santa and the Feria).

Any client staying more than 48 hours in a hotel has the right to receive the full board rates from the time of his arrival. All hotels are allowed to charge the minimum price for a Continental Breakfast, whether or not the client has it. More substantial breakfasts can be provided if requested. It is hoped that a decision will soon be made to supply *natural* orange-juice automatically without making it 'an extra'.

It will be noticed that in Spain hotels *still* demand the traveller's passport on arrival, at which moment it might be convenient to request garage space, at least when staying in towns, for parking facilities near hotels are rarely adequate.

Clients are not obliged to accept full board except in the case of Pensions. 1-star hotels and 1- or 2-star Hostels or Pensions are entitled to charge an additional 20 per cent over the maximum price for the room if the client fails to have at least one of the two main meals on the premises. A demi-pension system sometimes operates, details of which may be discussed with the management.

If no single room (*sencilla*) is available, a double room may be offered, for which the price is less 20 per cent of the maximum. Some (even well-known) hotels dishonestly choose to assume that single tourists prefer the latter, and this point should be checked. Comparatively few Spanish hotels have actual double-beds. When accommodation is limited, it may be convenient to ask for an extra bed to be fitted into a single room; the additional charge for this may not be higher than 60 per cent of the maximum price for the room, or 35 per cent in the case of a third bed in a double room. The management must inform guests as to any reduced prices available in the case of children, servants, etc.

Despite the official categorization, the quality of hotels can still vary widely. At the more popular resorts and tourist-conscious towns it will often be found that a hotel of lower category is superior in comfort and service than one flaunting four or five stars, which can be pretentious in manner but indifferent in performance. The independent traveller will realize that here, as elsewhere, many hotels are geared to package tours and coach groups, the result being a standard stabilized at a mediocre or take-it-or-leave-it level, and it has been suggested that it would be helpful if such hotels were so indicated in the *Guía de Hoteles,* that they might be avoided by the individual traveller.

An **Official Complaints Book** (*Libro de Reclamaciones*) is a requirement of every establishment offering accommodation, and in the case of serious irregularity or indifferent service *should be requested without compunction.* Complaints may also be made to the Provincial Delegations of the Ministry or direct to the *Dirección General de Empresas y Actividades Turísticos, Sección de Inspección y Reclamaciones,* C. Alcalá 44, Madrid.

In this edition of the *Blue Guide,* the inclusion of the words *Hotel/s* and/or *Parador* after certain towns, indicates the existence of reasonable accommodation throughout the year in the town or in the vicinity. On the coast particularly, there are numerous other establishments which only operate during the season. Hotels are *not* indicated in certain coastal routes when the majority of places described contain numerous hotels, and these routes are so indicated at their commencement.

Omission of a hotel does not imply any adverse judgement; the inclusion equally implies no guarantee of statisfaction. Up-to-date lists of local hotels are obtainable from any Tourist Office, who can also advise which have private swimming-pools, etc.

Although professional *limpiabotas* may still be found at many cafés and bars, visitors wishing to have their shoes cleaned at the hotel should instruct the maid, and not leave them outside the bedroom door. Similarly laundry and ironing should be given to the maid, and is normally returned within 48 hours; a small supplement is charged for urgent work. Hotels can usually recommend a good hairdresser (*peluquería*).

Youth Hostels. Information regarding Spanish Youth Hostels may be obtained from the *Red Española de Albergues Juveniles,* Inst. Nac. de la Juventud, Min. de Cultura, Generalísimo 39, Madrid.

Camping. Sites are numerous from the Costa Brava to Alicante and between Almería and Tarifa; less so in the Pyrenees and along the Biscay coast, and they are still scarce in other parts of the country. Details may be obtained from the *Agrupación Nacional de Campings de España* (A.N.C.E.), C. Francisco de Rojas 5, Madrid 10.

Restaurants. Spaniards have always eaten to live rather than lived to eat, and it is idle to pretend that the general standard of Spanish cooking will please the gourmet; indeed there are only a handful of eating places in the whole country of any gastronomic merit. Nevertheless there are many good restaurants, often providing interesting and palatable regional dishes, well-prepared, and at reasonable cost, and often the traveller will have better value for money in the less pretentious establishments. Unfortunately there is a tendency for restaurants of all categories, particularly in areas frequented by tourists, to serve stereotyped meals of a mediocre quality for the price charged. As in hotels, an Official Complaints Book is at the disposal of dissatisfied customers. Likewise, all restaurants in Spain have been officially graded into four classes plus De Luxe establishments, but often the categorization refers to the number and variety of dishes available and the maximum price to be charged for the Touristic Menu, rather than to the quality of food and service provided. It should be noted that the bill (*la cuenta*) includes service, but it is still customary to leave a small gratuity to the *Camarero* or *Camarera* for *good* service.

The restaurants of all Paradores and many hotels are open to non-residents. Breakfast (*desayuno*), from 8.00 to 11.00, may be served in one's room if requested. Lunch is usually served between 13.30 and 15.30; and dinner between 20.30 and 23.00, both à la carte and at a fixed price, or on a '*Menu Turistico*', and the bill of fare is displayed at the entrance.

Portions are often generous, particularly with the Hors d'oeuvre (*entremeses*), and one *ración* is often enough for two. Spanish cookery is apt to contain rather more olive oil (*aceite de oliva*) than the visitor is used to, and should be treated with respect; however the local wine is often a good counteragent. Although tap water (occasionally over-chlorinated) is usually safe, some tourists are induced to drink mineral water, which may be ordered '*con gas*' or '*sin*' (without) gas. Light Spanish beer (*cerveza*) may be ordered by the small bottle (*botellín*), large size (*doble*), or draft (*caña*). Cider (*sidra*) should be tasted along the N. coast of Spain, regarded as the original home of cider-making, whence the process was derived by the Normans, who brought it to England.

There is no lack of smaller and more convivial establishments—*bars, tascas, tabernas, cervecerias*, etc.—open throughout the day, many of which display an excellent selection of dishes from which one may chose one's *tapas*, eating them at the bar or adjacent table. The charge for food and drink at a table, or out in the open, is often slightly more expensive. The word *aperitivos* or *tapas* always applies to appetizers, not just drinks, and covers an occasionally bewildering range of hot or cold dishes from smoked ham, cheese, salted almonds, olives (*aceitunas*), sardines, *chorizo*—a dried spiced pork sausage, mushrooms, tunny, peppers, etc., to more exotic and invariably extremely tasty prepared dishes such as *salpicón de mariscoes,* with eggs, onion, peppers, olive oil, and shellfish, etc.

Refreshments are also available at most cafés. All are popular points of rest, particularly during the heat of the midday sun and the evening *paseo*, and remain open until well after midnight. They are usually found in or near the main square, and many entertaining hours may be spent sitting in the open, but in the shade, observing the passing throng. It is also likely to be less noisy, and the T.V. and inevitable background music may be avoided. Here one may have a snack (*merienda*) or sandwich (*bocadillo*), meet one's friends, and rest one's weary feet. Coffee—at a price—may be ordered black (*solo*), with a dash of milk (*cortado*), or white (*con leche*); a large cup is a *doble*.

Horchaterias, properly speaking only places selling 'horchata', a drink made from a ground nut known as *chufa,* are not now so common.

Food and Wine. While the *Paella Valenciana* is not always found at its best in Valencia, the traveller should have no hesitation in savouring most regional dishes, preferably in establishments patronized by the locals, and he will rarely be disappointed. When touring, much time and money may be saved by having picnics en route, sampling the local bread, cheese, sausage, and wine, etc. It is as well, however, to wash first all fruit and vegetables. 'Spanish Tummy', with which some visitors are occasionally afflicted, is usually caused by over-eating and a higher consumption of wine than normal, and the heat, or an over-indulgence in cold drinks during excessive heat. Alka-Seltzer will usually clear it up, while the advice of a chemist (*farmacéutico*) is generally knowledgeable. It is also as well to note that the increasing pollution of some nurseries of shellfish has produced unpleasant repercussions.

Wine (*vino*) is the national drink, and wines of quality may be found in almost every bar, *tasca, taberna,* and restaurant in the country. Almost every region produces wine, much of it now controlled by a 'Consejo Regulador de la Denominación de Origen', similar to the French 'Appellation Controlée'.

The majority of the wines (white, *blanco*; red, *tinto;* and rosé, *clarete* or *rosado*) are regional, and will be found only in the area of their production. Probably the only wine which is sold throughout Spain (with the exception of *Sherry;* see p.560), is the *Rioja,* more expensive than the regional wines, and normally only available in bottles or half-bottles, not usually being sold by the glass as are the local *vinos 'del país'* or *'de la casa'.*

In the Rioja, situated in the Ebro valley between Pancorbo (to the N.W.) and Alfaro (to the S.E.), with Logroño as its centre, wines of great quality are produced, similar to a Bordeaux or Burgundy, but with a higher alcoholic content, which is one of the characteristics of most Spanish wines compared with those of most other European countries. There are some dozens of companies producing a variety of Riojas (mostly red) at a variety of prices. In the Rioja itself one may drink the young wines *'de cosechero'* of good quality and inexpensive. A local connoisseur can advise, but in general the ratio of quality to price is reasonably balanced.

As far as other Spanish wines are concerned, among the better known are the following: in Galicia and León, the dry white *Albariño,* the white *Condado,* and also the *Ribeiros* (a heavy red; and white), *Cacabelos* (red and rosé), and the red *Bierzo* or *Valdeorras.* The Asturias however, produce no wine, only cider (*sidra*).

Further S., in the Duero valley, are the red wines of *Toro,* the white *Rueda,* and those of *Cigales* (rosé) and *Las Navas* (white). Further up the Duero, E. of Valladolid, one finds the famous (and dear) *Vega Sicilia* (red), and the adjacent rosés of *Ribera de Duero,* which are less expensive, are found between Peñafiel and Aranda de Duero.

Returning to the N., in the Basque Provinces one will find *Chacolí* (both red and white), somewhat acid and an acquired flavour; while adjacent Navarre and Aragón, abutting the Rioja, are both important wine-growing areas, producing strong red and rosé wines such as *Campanas, Murchante, Cariñena, Jalón,* and *Barbastro.*

Continuing E., we reach Cataluña, and the Mediterranean coast, where a great variety of wines will be met with, the best known of which are those of *Ampordá* (red and rosé), *Alella* (dry or sweet whites), the white *Penedés,* and those of *Tarragona,* such as the *Priorat* (with a high alcoholic content). One of the specialities of Cataluña are the Champagne-like sparkling wines, produced brut, sec, and demi-sec, and some of them are not bad. Once again, the choice should be made based on price if there is no other source of information.

Further down the coast we reach the old provinces of Valencia and Murcia, producing a variety of wines such as *Manchuela* (red and white); those of *Utiel* and *Requena* (reds), *Monóvar* (likewise red), and *Jumilla* (strong reds).

Towards *Málaga* are the famous sweet dessert wines; while in inland Andalucía, near Córdoba, the white *Moriles* and *Montilla,* similar to those lesser known white wines of *Condado,* near Huelva.

And lastly, there is the extensive central region, dominated by the wines of La Mancha, especially the cheap *Valdepeñas* (reds and whites), the largest producers of wine in Spain, the consumption of which in the bars of Madrid being very considerable. Also in this area are interesting wines for their price such as *Mentrida* (reds) in Toledo, and also the red and rosé *Cebreros*; and nearer Madrid, those of *Navalcarnero* (red). In Extremadura to the W., one will find the light red *Aloque* and *Montánchez, Almendralejo* and *Salvatierra* (reds).

In general, it is suggested that the traveller drinks the wines 'de la casa' or 'del país', and on occasions in restaurants, a good bottle of Rioja or other '*reserva*' of any of these regions.

There is a wide range of good Spanish brandies available, and other spirits (*aguardientes*), which vary from province to province, from the *Orujos* of Galicia and Santander to the *Anis de Chinchón, Cazalla,* or *Ojén, dulce* (sweet) or *séco* (dry), the latter a very powerful liquor. Spanish-produced 'whisky' is best avoided.

Sangria is a summer cup composed basically of red wine, lemon juice, sugar, brandy, soda-water, cinnamon, and ice (*hielo*)—a cool, refreshing, but somewhat heady drink.

Bota and Porrón. The former is a large pear-shaped leather pouch for carrying wine. At the neck is a turned wooden cup in which a small hole is stopped by a spigot. By raising the neck of the *bota* to the level of the mouth—but without touching the lips—and then gradually raising the bag, a thin stream of wine will flow out. Similarly with the *porrón,* found mainly in Catalonia, which is a cone-shaped glass bottle with a long narrow spout; but both require a little practice, otherwise wine will flow down one's neck rather than into one's mouth.

The MENU which follows contains a number of the more common dishes to be met with:

Entremeses, Hors d'oeuvre

Spaniards often sustain themselves with *tapas* (see above) at a bar before returning home or going on to a restaurant, where they may continue to pick at similar dishes, or sliced sausages (*embutidos*). These include:

Chorizo, a hard dry spiced pork sausage
Longaniza, a longer and darker variety
Salchicha, fresh pork sausage
Salchichón, large hard dry sausage with paprika
Jamón (pronounced Hamón) *Serrano,* lean ham, which with *lomo,* sirloin of pork, are both cured in salt
Butifarra, Catalan pork sausage
Morcilla, fresh black pudding
Sobresada, soft lard and pimento
Fiambres, cold meats

Sopas, Soups

Gazpacho, a most refreshing cold soup, originally from Andalucia, composed of tomato, cucumber, olive oil, vinegar, garlic, pimento, bread, water, and ice.
White gazpacho has a base of ground almonds
Caldos, broths or consommés
Sopa de ajo, a substantial soup of garlic, bread and paprika (*pimentón*)
Caldo gallego, containing white beans, potatoes, cabbage, dried bacon fat, and pig's trotters

Huevos, Eggs

These may be ordered *pasado por agua,* lightly boiled
cocido, hard-boiled
frito, fried
escalfado, poached
revuelto, scrambled
à la Flamenca, fried with peas and *chorizo* etc.
Tortilla, omelette, of which there are any number of varieties

Pescados y Mariscos, Fish and Shellfish

Anguila, eel; *Angulas,* elvers
Boquerónes, fresh anchovies, often provided as a *tapa*
Sardinas, sardines, delicious grilled
Pulpos, octopus
Sepia, cuttlefish
Calamares (called *Chipirones* in the Basque Provinces) *en su tinta,* squid in its own ink, or *á la Romana,* fried in egg and flour.
   A wide variety of fresh fish, both on the coast, and brought inland by overnight lorries, are to be seen, including:
Besugo, sea bream
Chanquetes, whitebait
Lenguado, sole
Lubina, bass
Merluza, hake
Mero, brill
Rodaballo, turbot
Salmonetes, red mullet
Pez espada, sword-fish
Bonito, tunny; also *atún,* see below
Trucha, trout
Arenque, herring
Rape, monk-fish
Atún à la plancha, grilled tunny-fish, or *Marmitako,* stewed with tomatoes, potatoes, green peppers, and bread
Bacalao, dried—or occasionally fresh—cod, *al pil-pil,* slowly simmered, or *à la Vizcaina,* with garlic and red peppers
Of shellfish, also known as *moluscos* or *crustáceos,* there are a great variety, often known by other names in different regions. These include
Quisquillas, shrimps
Gambas or *Camerones,* prawns
Cigalas, Dublin Bay Prawns
Langostinos, larger prawns
Langosta or *Bogavante,* lobster
Cangrejos del rio, crayfish
Cangrejo or *Nécora,* sea-crab
Centolla or *Changurro,* spider-crab
Almejas, clams
Mejillones, mussels
Ostras, oysters
Percebes, goose-barnacles
Vieiras, scallops
   The term *en escabeche* means pickled, soused, or marinaded.

Carne, Meat

In Castile, particularly, you will find good *Cordero*, lamb; *chuletas* are chops, *Ternera*, veal, *Cerdo*, pork, and *Cochinillo*, sucking-pig, usually served *asado*, roasted. Meats are also prepared *á la chilindrón*, stewed with tomatoes and paprika; *al horno*, baked or roasted; *á la parrilla* or *á la plancha*, grilled, etc.

There is a variety of stews, *cazuelas, calderetas, cocidos, guisadas, pucheros*, etc., and also the *olla podrida*, hot-pot, while the *Fabada Asturiana*, butter beans stewed with *chorizo, morcillas*, and *lacón* (partially salt-cured pig's trotters) should not be overlooked.

Callos, tripe, *à ta Madrileña*, is always very appetising.
Riñones, kidneys

Aves y Caza, Poultry and Game

Pollo, chicken, also *gallina*
Pavo, turkey
Pato, duck
Perdice, partridge
Cordonice, quail
Conejo, rabbit
Liebre, hare
Jabali, wild boar

Verduras, Vegetables

Ensaladas, salads: *lechuga*, lettuce
Pisto, fresh vegetables slightly and slowly fried in oil
Menestra, similarly stewed, but with the addition of ham, etc.
Pulses are the basic ingredients of a number of *potajes*, stews, and include *Judias blancas*, haricot beans; *judias verdes* are French beans
Grelos, turnip tops (in Galicia)
Ajo, garlic
Col, cabbage
Rábano, radish
Acelgas, Swiss beet, chard
Remolacha, beetroot
Cebolla, onion
Puerros, leeks
Setas, mushrooms
Habas, broad beans, often served with chopped ham
Alubias, dried beans; *alubias blancas*, butter beans
Garbanzos, chickpeas
Lentejas, lentils
Alcachofas, artichokes
Espinacas, spinach
Berejenas, aubergines
Pepino, cucumber
Zanahorias, carrots

Quesos, Cheeses

While they cannot compare in quality or variety with those of France, are nevertheless, full-flavoured and worth investigating. They range from the soft white *queso de Burgos*, and *Villalón*, and the breast-shaped Galician *Tetilla*, to the smoked *Idiazabal*, hard *Roncal*, and ubiquitous *Manchego*, which is found *fresco*, fresh, *curado*, smoked, and *en aceite*, somewhat oily. *Cabrales* is a strong Asturian cheese.

Postres, Sweets, etc.

Flan, cream caramel
Arroz con leche, rice pudding
Nata, Whipped *cream*
Natillas, custard

Carne de membrillo, a rich sweet quince cheese
Yemas, a rich sweet candied yoke of egg
Churros, a confection, usually eaten in the morning, of dough mixture piped into
   boiling olive oil, and often served with hot chocolate together with a glass of
   cold water.
Turrón de Jijona, a nougat-like confection of ground almonds and honey; *Turrón
   de Alicante* is much harder, and with whole almonds
   There is also any number of sweet confections, such as *polverónes, mantecadas,*
   etc., which may be bought at *Pastelerias* and *Confiterias.*
Mermelada is merely jam. Those preferring marmalade for breakfast should ask
   for *mermelada de naranja;* even 'Old English' marmalade *mermelada de
   naranja amarga* (bitter) is now being manufactured in Spain.
Miel, honey
Mantequilla, butter

Frutas, Fruit

Fresas, strawberries; also *Fresón*
Frambuesas, raspberries
Higos, figs
Peras, pears
Uvas, grapes
Manzanas, apples
Cerezas, cherries
Ciruelas, plums or prunes; *Claudias,* greengages
Melocotón, peach; *en almibar,* in syrup
Sandia, water-melon
Albaricoques, apricots
Pomelo (or *Toronja*), grapefruit
Piña, pineapple
Plátanos, bananas
Nueces, nuts
Naranjas, oranges; *jugo de naranja,* orange-juice, which *should* always be served
   natural, or fresh, not tinned.

GENERAL INFORMATION

Season. Climatically the best seasons for visiting Spain in general are
the spring and autumn, although the Atlantic coast enjoys a
comparatively temperate summer, and the Mediterranean coast a mild
winter. The elevated central meseta is subject to a continental climate,
parched and dusty in summer, and mainly dry but often bitterly cold in
winter, although fine crisp days are frequent. Then, even when the sun is
shining, visitors to Madrid, for example, should be on their guard
against the biting wind descending from the nearby snow clad sierras.
Indeed, for winter travelling, an overcoat is essential, while even in
summer, some warm clothing should always be carried as a precaution
against sudden drops in temperature. Between June and September,
when light clothes are equally essential, many towns of obvious historic
or artistic interest such as Toledo, are crowded, and the heat can be
stifling, indeed, it is often better to avoid staying in the larger centres,
which may be visited from smaller towns, where it is still possible to
observe a more characteristic and provincial way of life. Almost all
forms of dress are now seen in all but the remotest regions. There is no
longer any officious 'supervision' on the beaches, where the briefest
costumes are common, but sun lovers are *warned* against over-exposure
which can be both unpleasant and dangerous, but perhaps less so than
bathing in the cloacal Mediterranean, which can result in some nasty
skin complaints, etc.

Manners and Customs. Attention should be paid by the traveller to the more formal manners of Spaniards. It is customary to open conversations in shops, etc., with the courtesy of *buenos días* (good day), *buenas tardes* (good afternoon), and the phrases *dígame usted* (please tell me), and *deme usted* (please give me), *tiene usted* (have you got), and *muchas gracias* (many thanks) should be used. It will also be noticed that the greeting *Adiós,* literally 'Goodbye', is used on occasions when we would say 'Hallo'. In shops and offices a certain amount of self-assertion is taken for granted, since queues are not the general rule, and it is incumbent on the inquirer or customer to get himself a hearing. The handshake at meeting and parting is also usual, but such standing on ceremony is becoming progressively relaxed in many circles.

A stranger is rarely allowed to play host to a native and may find, if he tries, that the bill has been settled over his head by his Spanish 'guest'.

Sightseeing. Whether visiting monuments or museums, or when driving from one town to another, an early start is strongly advised. Not only will the traveller be able to see far more during the morning before such buildings close for their midday siesta, and before the heat of the sun becomes overpowering, but accommodation for the night may be found in good time.

Indeed, many tourists may be at a loss in some towns during the early afternoon. But by this time, particularly in the South in Summer, the heat may force one to remain indoors. Even in the 18C, according to Thomas James, the Spanish had a saying 'that none but a dog and an Englishman will be seen out in those four hours: which is literally true, for I have been barked at, from one end of the village. . . to the other'!

What is also time-wasting is the present anarchy in opening times of museums, cathedrals, and other monuments. An attempt to list such times of admission as far as they apply to Madrid has been made (see p.243), while in Barcelona almost all museums are closed on Mondays.

One wll find doors closed when one would expect them to be open, and vice versa, and while the local office of the S.E.T. should be applied to, they also may be shut. It is hoped that some simple rule will be laid down before too long, which may also be applied to municipal and ecclesiastical museums, and those in private hands.

A pocket-compass may be found helpful at times, also a pocket-torch when exploring the darker recesses of some churches and cathedrals, which are rarely lit by more than weak light-bulbs or guttering candles. A small pair of field glasses will also be found of value.

Begging, which is still occasionally met with, and the importunate demands of gypsies, who can be a nuisance, and touts, together with uninvited offers of guidance (see below), should be refused with firmness but without rudeness.

Language. While a knowledge of Spanish is not essential in the main tourist resorts, the attempt to speak it in itself will enlist the native courtesy of the Spaniard to the assistance of the visitor in difficulties.

No longer is the Englishman placed in the predicament of the two who, in the 1840s, while travelling post to Madrid, were said to 'make themselves understood by signs, placing themselves on all fours when they wished to indicate their want of locomotive quadrupeds, and putting their fingers in their mouths when they desired it to be known than they wanted to eat. They were followed, of course, everywhere, by crowds', wrote T. M. Hughes, 'but beyond being stared at suffered no particular inconvenience'. CASTILIAN (*Castellano*) is spoken and understood throughout the country, but the visitor will often hear accents or dialects which can be confusing, such as the Galician or Andalucían.

VOWELS in Castilian are pronounced (a=ah, i=ee, etc.); in the syllables *gue, gui, que, qui,* the *u* is silent, unless marked by a diaeresis. CONSONANTS are pronounced more or less as in English, with the following exceptions: *c* before e or i like th in think; *ch* as in chapter; *d final* is scarcely sounded; *g* before e or i as a guttural h (e.g. Gerona=Herona); *h* is mute; *j* is roughly aspirated (Jaén=high-en); *ll* like the French l-mouillé (as in cotillon); *ñ* like the French gn (señora=senyora); *r* is trilled; *s* is sharp, *z* like th in think.

It has been estimated that over 4,000 words in Castilian derive from the Arabic, including most commencing with Al-, including *alcohol* (for make-up), *alcalde* (mayor), etc.: see also p.34.

ACCENTS. Words of more than one syllable ending in a vowel, in ia or io, regarded as diphthongs, or in n or s are accented on the penultimate syllable, those ending in other consonants on the last syllable. Exceptions to these rules are indicated by an acute accent.

The complex BASQUE language, known as *Vascuence* to the Spaniards, but as *Euskera* to the Basques, and still heard in the northern Basque provinces, is an idiom of no known derivation, but it is believed to be a relic of the Iberian tongue spoken throughout the Peninsula before the Roman conquest.

The CATALAN language, a form of Provençal, spoken in various forms along the Mediterranean seaboard from Prpignan to beyond Valencia, is subject to rules of pronunciation different from the Castilian: *c, g,* and *j* are pronounced as in French; *ch*=k; *ny,* even at the end of a word, is pronounced as the Spanish ñ; *x*=sh; in *ll* the l-sound almost disappears, leaving a strong consonantal y-sound; *ig* at the end of a syllable=tch. E.g.: *xampany*=champagne; *puig*=putch; *Ripoll*=ripó-ye; *Bell-lloch*=bey-yók; *Vich*=Vick, now written Vic.

It may be useful to know that the signs *Dones* and *Homes,* in Cataluña, indicate 'Women', and 'Men' respectively.

With the lifting of censorship and the granting of limited autonomy there has been a marked increase in the number of titles published in Catalan and Basque, apart from those in the Galician dialect, or *Galego*.

Guides. Henry Swinburne, in the 1770s—and, with few exceptions, little has since changed—complained that 'one of the greatest vexations a curious person experiences in travelling in Spain, is the scarcity of tolerable *ciceroni;* those you meet are generally cobblers, who throw a brown cloak over their ragged apparel, and conduct you to a church or two, where they cannot give you the least satisfactory information concerning its antiquities or curiosities'. Baedeker, equally cynical, remarked, when describing the Alcázar at Seville some 65 years ago: 'The traveller should reject the services of the official guides, who are always in too much of a hurry'—indeed, only too often one would do better being escorted by the famous Cornelio (the well-informed but *blind* guide of the Escorial in the second quarter of the last century) who would describe one picture and point to the next!

However, travellers requiring the presence of an English-speaking official guide (who will have passed some form of examination) should apply to the local S.E.T. office, but should be forewarned that all articles bought at 'recommended' shops are likely to have their prices inflated to cover the guide's commission. Do not be 'taken in' by unofficial guides—plausible and insinuating individuals—who haunt some areas frequented by tourists, who may attempt to guide one round the sites or museum, and then charge an exorbitant amount. It is as well to request to see their credentials first.

Churches. Those of importance, including the larger cathedrals, are generally open all day except for c. 2-3 hours in the early afternoon, although some (as at Oviedo) may remain shut in the afternoon in Winter. The less-visited churches are now usually kept locked. Although the priest or sacristan may be found, the loss of time incurred in locating him is a serious factor to be taken into account when planning ecclesiological tours, and not infrequently all attempts to gain entry will be disappointed.

It will be noticed that the altars of many churches have been moved from their traditional place to a more central position nearer the crossing, in accordance with recent liturgical reform.

Twiss, visiting Seville in 1773, complained that the friars, who he had hoped might direct him to some paintings in the churches, 'were either asleep, or so lazy that they would not give themselves the trouble of shewing them. . . '. On a recent visit to the museum at Segorbe, the present Editor, having later (impatiently) to listen to the sacristan's burden of pious fictions and travesties of truth, was first informed that he might take photographs, *but not notes!*

But do not be too easily dissuaded, for such difficulties have always risen up before the traveller in Spain, should it be any consolation. Richard Ford, in one of his many brilliant passages, referring to his own experiences—experiences often shared by the Editor—reiterated that whatever apparently impregnable barriers, unexpected obstacles, and impediments official keepers might make, the search should not be given up. '"No", may be assumed to be their natural answer; nor even if you have a special order or permission, is admission by any means certain. The keeper, who here as elsewhere, considers the objects committed to his care as his own private property and source of perquisite, must be conciliated: often when you have toiled through the heat and dust to some distant church, museum, library, or what not, after much ringing and waiting, you will be drily informed that it is shut, can't be seen, that it is the wrong day, that you must call again tomorrow; and if it is the right day, then you will be told that the hour is wrong, that you are come too early, too late; very likely the keeper's wife will inform you that he is out, gone to mass, or market, or at his dinner, or at his *siesta,* or if he is at home and awake, he will swear that his wife has mislaid the key, "which she is always doing". If all these and other excuses won't do, and you persevere, you will be assured that there is nothing worth seeing, or you will be asked why you want to see it? As a general rule, no one should be deterred from visiting anything, because a Spaniard of the upper classes gives his opinion that the object is beneath notice. . .'. Elsewhere he attests to the absence of any *disinterested* appreciation of the beautiful by the incurious pococurante Spaniards, who lacked the organs of veneration and admiration 'for anything beyond matters connected with the first person and the present tense'.

The ecclesiastical authorities have stooped to follow the mercenary practice of collecting together paintings and any other movable objects in their cathedrals and churches and placing them in a so-called 'museum' for which an admission charge is made. This pernicious system, which is particularly noticeable on routes frequented by tourists, may apply likewise to locked chapels, choirs, cloisters, towers, and treasuries, etc., indeed to *anything* that can be used to extort money from the interested visitor; and the quality of the 'treasures' displayed rarely merits even the moderate charge imposed. In some churches and convents a charge is made at the end of an accompanied visit!

The most blatant examples of such rapacity is the sealing off of such outstanding buildings as the Capilla Real at Granada, and the *old* Cathedral at Salamanca. There seems to be considerable doubt as to whether these are now places of worship or museums: if the latter, they should, with their contents, pass into the more secure and competent hands of the secular authorities: indeed, there is a strong move to place the conservation of the fabric also of all cathedrals, convents, and churches in more qualified hands than those of the clergy. The quantity of religious 'art' carefully stored up, *but of no aesthetic quality whatsoever,* has to be seen—as much of it has been by the present Editor—to be believed. And even when the items are of *some* interest and value, little has been done in the past to protect them, with the inevitable consequence that they have become a tempting prize (as at Murcia, and Burgos) or objects of vandalism (as at Oviedo), while at Zamora the beautiful tapestries are hung in conditions which should make a bishop blush.

In extenuation, there are now perhaps fewer canvases rotting on damp walls than there were. In waves of anticlericalism—in Barcelona in 1909 and in many areas just prior to the Civil War—certain 'works of art', much of it of a very meretricious nature, were destroyed, but before that the cupidity of their custodians was such that even Baedeker complained that 'Every year art-treasures find their way out of the country without the fact being generally known. Thus objects mentioned in our Handbook may sometimes have disappeared'. Indeed, the acquisitive tendencies of delinquent dilettanti would not demur at gutting buildings, Romanesque churches of their murals, and absconding with paintings by the score.

Few visitors would baulk at contributing to the upkeep of the fabric of such monuments as the Mezquita at Córdoba, among many others, but only too often one has the unfortunate impression that as little as possible is spent on the ecclesiastical buildings concerned, which are invariable unkempt, and often—even at Toledo—the retablo mayor is hidden under a shroud of dust, while grass-grown precincts are as unsightly as the inappropriate display of political symbols and slogans still to be seen on many façades.

The main **Church Festivals,** marked both by striking and solemn ceremonial and theatrical exuberance, are those of Holy Week (*Semana Santa*) and Corpus Christi, when the frequent religious processions with their *pasos*, or floats, often bearing astonishingly lifelike Baroque carvings of the principal actors in the Passion, etc., are a curious relic of an age in which the visual impact of the paraphernalia of religion was essential to the propagation of the Faith. See also p. 539. Animated crowds still flock to witness the objects of their devotion, and the spectacle can be impressive, although there are many who will agree with Alexander Jardine, who when writing of such festivities some two centuries ago, remarked: 'Any details of their religious or superstitious ceremonies, I should think rather unworthy of your attention'. Accommodation, particularly at Seville, and at Granada, is likely to be difficult to find at short notice at any price, and it is well to bear in mind when planning a tour, and check in advance, the dates of local festivals and *fiestas* (see below) in order to avoid such places. The cult of 'Folklore', not only in Andalucía, has been likewise overplayed in recent years, but almost anything is preferable to the proliferation of 'majorettes' which invaded a local fiesta at Oropesa attended by chance by the Editor.

Museums. Much has been done in recent years to increase the number of museums in Spain, and to modernize and reform the older establishments, and work is still in progress. In these, exhibits are well displayed and labelled, and the entry charge correspondingly increased. In smaller towns, particularly those off the beaten track, the official opening hours are not always adhered to, and when the custodian lives on the premises foreigners may be admitted outside the prescribed hours, if any.

There are a small number of comparatively important monuments which were once royal property, such as the Pal. Real and the Conv. de las Descalzas Reales (Madrid), and parts of the Escorial, which have been expropriated by and are now conserved and patrolled by a doctrinaire organization known as the *Patrimonio Nacional*. These buildings may only be visited in dragooned 'groups', taken on a conducted tour by a guide (often English-speaking) with a 'basic' knowledge of the exhibits, who expects, but should not receive, a gratuity. Time must be allowed for such a group to accumulate, after which, invariably, it is herded round the building at a breakneck speed. While it is appreciated that the supervision of crowds presents a problem of organization, the present stultifying expedient is quite deplorable, and all attempts by a guide to hurry one past the exhibits should be strongly resisted. Regrettably, this organization (which has deservedly been the butt of criticism for its predatory policies in the recent past) seems to assume that all visitors, without distinction, are perfectly satisfied by the most cursory glance at the objects displayed, and the uniformed functionaries concerned are not authorized to grant any facilities to those wishing to study undisturbed.

Until there is a radical change in policy, one may apply in person, or write well in advance, to the *Inspección General de Museos*, Palacio de Oriente, Madrid 13, specifically requesting permission to visit the museums, etc. of the Patrimonio Nacional '*con detenimiento*'—without restraint and at leisure—at the same time giving a valid reason for wishing to do so, but sadly the reply is rarely but negative!

It should also be mentioned that although visitors are allowed—if given time—to peruse their own guide-books, cameras must be handed in at the entrance, it being presumed that the Patrimonio Nacional's own highly-coloured post-cards and other publications, which are noticeably well displayed, will provide propitiatory mementos of the works of art one may very likely have missed seeing.

It is hoped that in the near future these properties and their contents will pass into the hands of the Ministry of Culture, where they belong.

Public Holidays. Official holidays are now 1 Jan.; 6 Jan. (*Dia de los Reyes,* Twelfth Night or Epiphany—Christmas presents to children); 19 March: Good Friday (*Viernes Santo*); East Sunday (*Dia de Pascua*); 1 May; Corpus Christi; 25 July (Santiago); 15 Aug.; 12 Oct.; 1 Nov.; 8

Dec., and 25 Dec. (Christmas Day or *Navidad*). Whenever these happen to fall near a weekend, a 'long weekend' is taken, known as a 'puente' or bridge!

Working Hours. Government and business offices, and shops, are normally open on weekdays from 9.00 to 13.00, and from 16.00 to 19.30, but from May to Oct. from 16.30 to 20.00. In Summer, many offices work a 'jornada intensiva', i.e. they open earlier and close at 15.00. Some of the larger shops are now open during the lunch hour, when 'mad dogs and Englishmen' may avoid the midday sun and wasting time waiting for the 'siesta' to end. There is a tendency towards following the European pattern (except perhaps in the Summer), but habits in this respect are hard to change.

Newspapers. Foreign newspapers and magazines are only found, at an inflated price, at kiosks in the main tourist areas of the larger towns, but stocks are usually small. The main Spanish newspapers are now *El País, Vanguardia* (in Cataluña), *Informaciones, A.B.C.,* and *Diario 16;* while among the more informative magazines are *Triunfo, Cambio 16,* and *Cuadernos para un dialogo.* Until very recently the censorship and prevarications of certain sections of the Spanish Press exposed it to the taunt of Richard Ford, who, writing of the *Gaçeta* (the official paper, founded in 1661; government owned since 1762), remarked that its pages—the French *Moniteur* only excepted—'were the greatest satire ever deliberately published by any people on itself'. The other media of communication—Radio and T.V.— rarely propagate other than the views of the Establishment.

Tobacco. The manufacture and sale of Tobacco is a state monopoly, and many excellent brands of cigarettes (*cigarrillos,* or *pitillos*) and cigars (*puros*) are available in the *tabacaleras* or *estancos,* which display the Spanish colours—red, yellow, red—above their entrances. Foreign tobaccos, cigarettes, etc., are also available at these estancos, apart from most hotels, restaurants, bars, etc. Matches are *cerillas*.

Note that tobacconists also sell postage-stamps (*sellos*), and some have a post-box (*buzón*) inside the shop, although these are now usually in the street, and are painted yellow.

Entertainment. *Theatre* performances, details of which may be found in the daily papers, often begin at a late hour and last until after midnight, and times should be checked carefully. *Tablao Flamenco,* exhibitions of authentic gypsy dancing, occasionally exceptionally good, commence even later, and end in the early hours. *Cinemas* are found in most towns, and some, in the main cities, specialise in showing foreign films (*salas especiales*), which are usually dubbed. It was the custom (which is dying out) to give a *small* tip to the usher who shows you to a seat.

Tipping. However anachronistic may be this system of rewarding waiters, taxi-drivers, cloak-room attendants, et al, it still persists. However, many restaurants and hotels have replaced it by adding a percentage to the bill, leaving little room for discussion, even when the service has been indifferent, or merely perfunctory. Any serious irregularity should be reported, without compunction, to the manager and/or the director of the local S.E.T. office.

Sports. Information on sports in general may be obtained from the *Sección de Deportes del Secretaría de Estado de Turismo,* Alcalá 44,

Madrid, who also produce various booklets on different sports, or from any S.E.T. office in the main towns; likewise from *Spanish Nat. Tourist Offices* (see p.64).

Winter Sports. The four main areas are the Cantabrian Cordillera and the Picos de Europa, the Central and Eastern Pyrenees, the Central Guadarrama and Eastern Gredos ranges, and the Sierra Nevada. Details of slopes and Ski Schools may be obtained from the *Federeción Española de Esqui*, C. Modesto Lafuente 4, Madrid, or from the *Fed. Deportes de Invierno*, C. Claudio Coello 32. Information regarding mountaineering may be obtained from the *Fed. Española de Montañismo*, C. Alberto Aguilera 3, Madrid. Amateurs should seek local advice before setting out on any high expedition, and when on foot in mountainous areas it is advisable to leave word of your intended route at the expected place of arrival or return.

Hunting, Shooting, and Fishing; and Ecology in general. For regulations and full information, apply to the *Instituto Nacional para la Conservación de la Naturaleza* (ICONA), Gran Via de S. Francisco 35, Madrid, or to an office of the S.E.T. Other useful addresses are those of the *Fed. Española de Caza*, C. Ortega y Gasset 5, and the *Fed. Española de Pesca*, C. Navas de Tolosa 3, both in Madrid.

Golfing. The address of the Spanish Golfing Federation is C. Capitán Haya 9, Madrid. A number of good Golf Courses are to be found in Spain, the majority of them situated on the Costa del Sol.

Bull-fights (*Corridas de Toros*) are still the favourite 'sport' of the populace— apart from football—and all attempts in the past to abolish it have failed. Lady Holland wrote that such was the rage for the sport, that women sold 'their shifts, and finally *persons*, to procure sufficient to obtain a seat'. Jardine stigmatized those who took part in the undefying spectacle as 'hired gladiators, who are generally butchers by profession'.

Every town of any consequence—and many of no consequence—has its bull-ring (*Plaza de Toros*), in which *corridas* take place throughout the season, opening with the Easter corrida in Seville and lasting until mid-October. *Novilladas*— fights between young bulls and less experienced *toreros*—should not be confused with the corrida proper. An *encierro*, in which the bulls are driven through the streets from an enclosure in the suburbs to the *corral* of the plaza de toros, is again different, the most vaunted occuring at Pamplona during the fiesta of S. Fermin (5-16 July). The side streets are barricaded off, and those that take part in the encierro run before the bulls, watched from crowded balconies along the route. Serious accidents are not infrequent, and only the foolhardy tourist should participate.

The bull-ring is an open amphitheatre on the Roman plan, with the arena separated from the rising tiers of seats by a stout stockade, with narrow openings through which the toreros may escape when hard pressed. Occasionally a bull will leap over this barrier into the narrow passage behind! The *barreras, contrabarreras* or *delanteras* are the most expensive seats nearest the arena, and are favoured by the *aficionados*, the experts and fans, who arrive armed with *bota* and cigar; but the *tendidos* or *gradas* behind these afford an even better general view and are cheaper. In hot weather it may be preferable to get seats in the *sombra*, the shady side of the ring. Tickets should be obtained in advance from agents in the town.

On the ethics of bull-fighting each must decide for himself. It is part of the 'sub-culture' of Spain, and may be condemned just as fox-hunting may be condemned, with the difference that while the odds are heavily against the bull, which is invariably killed, the danger to human life is considerable. The great blot was formerly the treatment of the horses, usually worn-out crocks exposed unprotected to be gored by the infuriated bull. Now they are provided with padded plastrons or *petos*, but harrowing scenes still occur, and one must be prepared for the sight of trailing entrails. It is difficult to judge to what extent Gautier was exaggerating when he wrote that he saw 24 bulls and 96 horses killed in three days! Much of the interest of the corrida lies in the elegance with which the different manoeuvres or *pases* are executed by the toreros, and the varying methods employed in dominating bulls of different temper.

The leading *torero* (*not* toreador), the *matador*, or *espada*, who eventually dispatches the bull, often a popular and extravagantly-paid idol, is assisted by his *cuadrilla*, consisting of *banderilleros*, who plant darts into the bull's shoulders, and *picadores*, or mounted lancers. Other toreros, occupied in wearying the bull with their *Capas* or cloaks, or distracting his attention at critical moments, are known as *monos*, or *Chulos*.

The corrida opens with the processional entry of the toreros to the strains of a *paso-doble*, led by the mounted *alguazils* in costumes of the time of Philip II, and followed by the gaily-caparisoned mule-team whose later function is to drag out the slaughtered bulls from the arena. The president, who occupies a central box facing the *toril* or enclosure, tosses the key to the alguazils, the toril is opened, and the bull, decorated with the colours (*devisa*) of the *ganadería* or ranch on which he was bred, charges into the ring. Fighting bulls are now usually between 3 and 5 years old, younger and lighter than the huge beasts used previously. Usually six bulls are killed at each corrida, the fate of each being settled in c. 20 minutes; the evenings spectacle lasting 2½-3 hours.

As a preliminary the toreros tease and tire the bull by playing him with their magenta, yellow-backed, capas, the bull (which is colour blind) invariably attacking the moving cloak and not the man. The first act is the *Suerte de Picar* or *de Varas*, in which picadores, their legs protected by greaves, and mounted on blindfolded hacks, enter the arena armed with short steel-pointed lances (*puyas* or *varas*). The bull is incited to charge the horses protected right side, and irritated by the stab of the lance, lunges furiously at the horses belly, occasionally lifting both mount and rider and sending them sprawling in the sand. However his attention is immediately distracted by the chulos, and the second picador enters. The intention is to damage and weaken the bull's neck muscles, while the loss of blood will further exhaust him. This is followed by the *Suerte de Baderillas*, for which the beast is manoeuvred into the centre of the ring to encounter the *banderilleros*, which he charges, while they skip aside after plunging two barbed darts ornamented with streamers into the shoulders of the bull. Three pairs should be thus planted.

Eventually we reach the *Suerte de Matar*, in which the matador, after exhibiting his full repertoire in playing the bull with his cape, exchanges this for a scarlet cloth or *muleta*, attached to a short rod, and prepares to dispatch the bull with his *estoque* or short sword. Inviting but evading attack, his aim is to kill at a blow by thrusting this sword between the bull's shoulders or withers, to the heart, which is only possible when the beast's feet are close together and its head held low. The feat, if successful, is the matador's triumph, but several thrusts are often necessary before the bull succumbs, or it may have to be killed by plunging a special sword, the *verdugillo*, into the nape of the neck. This action is known as the *descabello*. Usually the coup de grâce is given to the prostate bull by a dagger or *puntilla* by the attendant *puntillero*. The carcase is dragged out, the sand is raked smooth, and the next bull enters.

Not the least interesting feature of the corrida is the reactionof the aficionados, swift to greet a sluggish bull or clumsy torero with whistles, catcalls, and ironical clapping in a slow triple time (*palmas de tango*); while a brilliant display of dexterity will receive an immense ovation, shouts of '*olé*', waving of white handkerchiefs, and a flurry of hats, *botas*, etc., thrown into the arena. A good kill is rewarded by the president with one or two ears and the tail of the bull, which are cut off and presented to the torero as trophies.

In recent years interest in an older form of corrida has gained ground, the main variation being that the combat is waged on horseback, calling for brilliant horsemanship on the part of the 7rejoneador. Needless to say, the quality of the mount in no way compares with the poor hacks of the picadores.

There is a remarkable and extensive vocabulary of the bull-ring, naming with precision all the *pases*, as well as the age, colour, horns, and temper, etc. of the bull. There is also a considerable literature on the subject, historical, descriptive, and technical. And every season there is much argument among the aficionados and in the press regarding malpractices (such as shaving the bull's horns, causing it to aim short, etc.). Perhaps the best handbook in English is 'To the Bullfight Again' by *John Marks*; *Ernest Hemingway's* 'Death in the Afternoon', although containing curious detail, is dated.

Population. The population figures in this Guide are given in round figures according to the census of December 1975, and should be sufficient to give an idea of the size and likely amenities of a town. It should be noted that these are for municipalities, and often include a number of nearby villages, while in highly populated conurbations they will *not* take into account adjacent municipalities.

The movement of population from the smaller towns (less than 50,000 inhab.) and villages to the larger urban areas, continues. During the last 15 years the population of all *provincial capitals* has continued to increase. Tarragona, Gerona, and Vitoria have more than doubled in size, while Alicante, Bilbao, Burgos, Castellón, Guadalajara, León,

Lérida, Logroño, Madrid, Pamplona, and Valladolid have grown dramatically. But in spite of this the total population of both the provinces of Burgos and León has declined during the last five years, as have those of Albacete, Cáceres, Ciudad Reál, Córdoba, Jaén, Lugo, Orense, Salamanca, and Toledo. Among other towns that have seen considerable growth during the past five years—other than those on the outer rim of Madrid and Barcelona—are Elche (124,000 to 148,000), Gijón (184,000 to 236,000), and Vigo (199,000 to 233,000). The *provinces* of Ávila, Badajoz, Cuenca, Guadalajara, Huesca, Lugo, Orense, Palencia, Segovia, Soria, Teruel, and Zamora have a lower population than they did in 1920, during which time Spain's total population has increased by over 50 per cent. That of the mainland is now almost 34,000,000; the Balearics and Canaries, etc. contain slightly over 2,000,000, making a combined total of 36,000,000.

Those interested in past statistics may note that the population of Spain in 1715 was approx. 6,000,000, which by 1768 had risen to 9,307,000 (of which 176,000 were monks, nuns, friars, and secular clergy) and by 1791 had reached the figure of 10,143,000. Among these were 27,500 foreign *heads of families*, including 13,332 French, 1,577 Germans, and 140 English. By 1800-01 the total population is given as 12,000,000.

Police. Althoagh Spain no longer admits to being a police state, the police are still very much in evidence, and visitors may well be confused with regard to the different types. In most towns traffic is controlled by blue or brown-uniformed *Municipal* police, much addicted to whistling and hand-waving (some of whose duties have been taken over by women), who may be mounted on motor-cycles, as are the *Cuerpo de Vigilantes de Carreteras*, patrolling the main highways. In the countryside, where they now serve little purpose, their place is taken by the ubiquitous olive-green-uniformed *Guardia Civil*, always patrolling in pairs (and known familiarly as '*La Pareja*', the couple), wearing incongruous but distinctive patent leather tricorn hats. Formed in 1844, members of this strong but singularly ineffective arm of the law, raised originally to combat rural banditry, and who have since regularly intimidated the peasantry, are seldom officious, but are not invariably civil; nevertheless within their limited capacity they try to be helpful when their advice or assistance is required, and as *Auxilio en Carretera*, also patrol roads in Landrovers.

In addition, but normally only seen in urban areas, particularly when students, Basques, crowds, demonstrations, or 'manifestations' may in their opinion require 'supervision', are the autocratic police *armada*, recently designated '*Policia Nacional*', and in the process of changing from a grey uniform (when they were familiarly known as '*Grises*') to a brown (and already called '*chocolate con porras*'—the latter being a truncheon-shaped fritter!). They also guard embassies, ministries, ministers, nervous capitalists, stations, banks, and post-offices, etc. Some of them have met with a violent death in recent anti-authoritarian disturbances.

There are also plain-clothes police, and it is worth mentioning that passports or other proofs of identity are occasionally demanded by them. This inquisitorial and undemocratic examination of papers has been a feature of Spanish life under most political regimes, and however intolerable, is best accepted while it lasts as a mere formality. Although ostensibly not a para-military force, *all* Spanish police are obtrusively armed. Recently seen in Madrid are *green-helmeted* police, on the lookout for vehicles further polluting the already contaminated streets.

Serenos, a dying race of private night-watchmen (not police), were first established in Valencia in 1777, and in Madrid twenty years later.

EXPLANATIONS

TYPE. The main routes are described in large type. Smaller type is used for branch-routes and excursions, for historical and preliminary paragraphs, and (generally speaking) for descriptions of greater detail or minor importance.

ASTERISKS indicate points of special interest or excellence.

Total and intermediate DISTANCES are measured in kilometres, and total route distances are also given in miles. Road distances along the routes themselves record the approx. distance between the towns and villages, etc. described, but it should be noted that with the realignment of many roads it is almost certain that these distances will vary slightly from those measured by motorists on their milometers. Measurements of buildings are given in metres (m); ALTITUDES of passes and mountains are still expressed in feet, a compromise which may well suit the instinctive preferences of most English readers.

PLACE-NAMES. The names of a number of towns and villages in Cataluña have recently reverted to their Catalan spelling, many of which have been incorporated into the text of this edition, but travellers should have little difficulty in recognizing the names of others indicated on the new sign-posts.

ANGLICIZATION. For the sake of consistency, most place-names and the names of kings have been given their Spanish form, except in a few cases, as with Seville rather than *Sevilla*, and Philip rather than *Felipe*, where the English equivalent is much more familiar. It is hoped the compromise will be acceptable.

ABBREVIATIONS. In addition to generally accepted and self-explanatory abbreviations, the following occur in the guide:

> Av. = *Avenida,* Avenue
> C = Century
> C. = *Calle*, street or road
> Cap. = *Capilla*, chapel
> Conv. = *Convento*, convent
> Ctra. = *Carretera,* highroad
> Est. = *Estación*, station
> Gta = *Glorieta,* roundabout
> l. = left
> N.S. = *Nuestra Señora*, Our Lady
> Pal. = *Palacio*, palace
> Pl. = *Plaza*, Square or place *or* Plan. The
>   Pl. Mayor is always the main square
>   of any town or village.
> Pta. = *Puerta*, door, gate
> Pte. = *Puente*, bridge
> Pto. = *Puerto*, mountain pass, not
>   abbreviated when referring to ports
>   and harbours.
> r. = right
> Rte. = Route
> S. *or* Sta = *San, Sant* in Cataluña; *Santa,*
>   Saint
> SS. = Saints
> S.E.T. = *Secretaria de Estado de Turismo*

For Glossary of architectural and allied terms, see p.48.

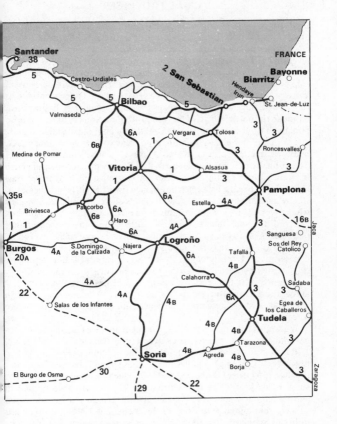

I BASQUE PROVINCES AND NAVARRE

   The **Basque Provinces** (*Las Provincias Vascongadas*) of *Guipúzcoa,
Álava*, and *Vizcaya*, together with northern Navarre, provide an
unexpected view of Spain to most travellers entering the country at the
western extremity of the Pyrenees. The countryside is exceedingly hilly
and thickly wooded when not mountainous, and communications are
not easy, although the main roads are good, and the state of repair of
minor roads is improving continually. Solid wide-gabled farms or
caserios, their doors and shutters often painted dark green or maroon,
are seen dotted over the steep green slopes of the broken ranges that fom
here a natural barrier between France and the Castilian plateau, and
overlook the highly-populated industrial valleys to which they offer a
strong contrast. Many of the older stone-built houses still display carved
escutcheons, a proud reminder of the Basques assumption of nobility,
which was secured for them by the mere fact of being born in these
provinces. Even in the smallest villages, and often abutting the
churchyard—some of which preserve their characteristic discoidal

95

tombstones—one will see an open court with one high wall, the ubiquitous *frontón*. Here is played their national ball-game of *pelota*, resembling fives, utilizing in one of its forms, a large basket-work glove or *chistera*. The Basque national costume is now represented only by their beret or *boina*, and rope-soled shoes or *alpargatas*. Their lanluage (*Euskera*; see p.86) is still frequently heard in Guipúzcoa, eastern Vizcaya, and northern Navarre, but less so in Álava. Guipúzcoa, with its capital at San Sebastián, is perhaps the most completely Basque area, although the northern half of Navarre, with Pamplona as its capital, also remains Basque in customs. Álava, relatively poor in natural resources, and with a less abundant rainfall, produces excellent wine along the N. bank of the Ebro, the Rioja Alavesa, while Vizcaya possesses exceptionally rich mineral deposits. The Basque provinces are also rich in agricultural produce, in fruit, and timber, while from time immemorial Basque fishermen have sailed from her ports into the Bay of Biscay and far beyond to the Cod-fisheries of Newfoundland, and their whaling industry was famous. The industrious, enterprising, materialistic, and intensely individual Basques, the autochthonous inhabitants of this rugged corner of Spain, a race of unknown origin, have always been energetic in preserving their independence, and until comparatively recently enjoyed certain privileges of self-government, safeguarded by ancient '*fueros*', or codes of law, which they jealously maintained over the centuries against the centralizing policy of their autocratic Castilian overlords. As recently as 1975, and since, certain over-policed areas resembled provinces under occupation by foreign forces.

Without taking into account the many who have emigrated, or who have sought political asylum elsewhere, the Basques now number c. 1,500,000, of whom 250,000 live in the adjoining *French* Basque provinces. The total population of the *Spanish* Basque provinces (including Navarre) is about 2,560,000, which has more than doubled since 1920. 170,000 of Álava's total of 238,000 are concentrated in Vitoria alone, while over 750,000 live in Bilbao and its industrial suburbs, but a high proportion of this increase is due to the organized influx of Spaniards from poorer provinces, an expedient considered by some Basques as a deliberate attempt to dilute their blood!

The Basques, or *Vascones*, who long resisted Roman incursions, long gained themselves notoriety for plundering travellers in the western Pyrenees, and it was they who brought about the disaster at Roncesvalles. The influx of pilgrims to the shrine of Santiago de Compostela also brought them much booty. From the 11C onward the three northern provinces were restless vassals of Castile, but it was not until the 19C that they played a prominent part in Spanish history. In the Carlist Wars of 1833-39 and 1872-76 the Basques supported the rebels and showed some of their skill in guerrilla warfare in defence of a hopeless cause; as a punishment many of their fueros, including the cherished right of exemption from military service, were revoked. Until then, in Jardine's words (1777), these provinces were 'the only remaining asylums in the peninsula for liberty'. During the last Civil War the majority of the autonomous Basques were cut off from the rest of the Republican zone, as reactionary Navarre adhered to the Nationalists, and suffered severely in the campaign mounted by Gen. Mola. Indeed, the Navarrese militia or *requetés* earned themselves an unenviable reputation for ferocity during the war. The destruction of Guernica by

German bombers was an outrage which excited the sympathy of the non-fascist world.

Basque nationalists claim that over 21,000 Basques died in the post-war repression. In recent years a small militant extremist group known as ETA (*Euzkadi Ta Azkatasuna*, or Freedom for the Basques) has agitated too violently for home rule, which invited repressive counter-measures instituted by Franco causing world-wide recrimination. More recent measures against ETA, which still has considerable local support (and other independent groups taking advantage of the disturbed state of the provinces), have spectacularly failed, underlining the incapacity of the Madrid government, who still think that a show of force can cow rather than exacerbate nationalist feelings, but regional autonomy is likely to be granted after the referendum of Oct. 1979.

Meanwhile, some Navarrese, more traditionally minded than the more hard-headed Basques of Guipúzcoa and Vizcaya, still champion the outmoded cult of Carlism.

Navarre has had a somewhat different history from the other Basque provinces. The kingdom established here in the 9C. despite Frankish and Moorish attacks, reached its zenith under *Sancho the Great* (1000-35), after which its political importance declined. For a time a dependency of Aragón, it eventually separated and was ruled by its own kings until Sancho VII died in 1234 without heirs. The Navarrese elected Thibaut V, Count of Champagne, and this dynasty ruled until 1285, when it became a dependency of the French crown. In 1328 it passed to the House of Evreux. In 1434 Leonor of Navarre married Gaston de Foix, and later the throne passed to the House of Albret. In 1512 Fernando the Catholic annexed the whole of Navarre south of the Pyrenees. It was anciently divided in six '*merindades*', with capitals at Pamplona, Sangüesa, Tudela, Estella, Olite, and St-Jean-Pied-de-Port, the last representing French Navarre, which was eventually united to France at the accession of Henry IV.

1 FROM (BAYONNE) IRÚN TO BURGOS

Total distance, 251 km (156 miles). N 1. 22 km. **San Sebastián**— 27 km. **Tolosa**— 44 km. *Alsasua*—45 km. **Vitoria**— 25 km. *Pancorbo*— (25 km. *Briviesca*)—63 km. **Burgos.**

Motorway. The French A63 *autoroute*, which will circumvent *Bayonne*, drives S.W. from that city, by-passing both *Biarritz* and *St-Jean-de-Luz*, to cross the Bidassoa a short distance E. of the *Behobie* border-crossing (see below), and is recommended, particularly during the Summer, when the two coastal roads are congested, as a faster and less tedious approach to *San Sebastián*. Thence (Customs) the *autopista* (A1) drives W. through magnificent scenery, traversing a number of tunnels, and crossing the deep wooded gorges of the region in a series of viaducts, with occasional views of the sea, towards *Eibar*, and *Bilbao*. The stretch of the A1 bearing S.W. just prior to Eibar to rejoin the completed road near *Miranda de Ebro*, has yet to be constructed, but those wishing to continue on motorways may turn S. at Bilbao onto the A68. This also converges on Miranda before turning S.W. through *Pancorbo* and *Burgos*. The latter stretch is recommended in Winter as preferable to the main road climbing to the Pto. de la Brújula.

From Bayonne the N 10 drives S.W. to *St-Jean-de-Luz* before climbing a spur of the Western Pyrenees, with a good view (l.) of *La Rhune*, before descending to *Behobie* (Customs).—An alternative road skirts the rocky coast S.W. of St-Jean to *Hendaye*, there crossing the *International Bridge* (Customs) immediately N. of *Irún* (see below). Hence a fine view may be had (r.) of Fuenterrabia at the mouth of the Bidassoa and below Mte Jaizquíbel (see Rte 2) and (l.) of the triple peak of the Peñas de Aya.

From *Behobia* we bear r. for (2 km.) *Irún*, which may also be by-passed, while the direct road for Pamplona (C 133) turns off to the l. (see Rte 3). We pass (r.) the unprepossessing *Iles des Faisans*, or *Ile de la Conférence*, on neutral ground in the river bed.

Here negotiations between Louis XIV of France and Philip IV of Spain put an end to hostilities between their nations in the Thirty Years' War (1659). Velázquez contracted a fever here, when fitting up the saloon of conference, from which he later died. Earlier international meetings had taken place between Louis XI and Enrique IV of Castile in 1468; and in 1615 between Isabel, daughter of Henry IV of France, destined to be the wife of Philip IV, and the latter's sister Ana (of Austria) who was on her way to Paris to marry Louis XIII.

Irún (50,900 inhab.; *Hotel*) badly damaged in 1936, has been largely rebuilt. The Paseo de Colón leads to the Pl. del Mercado at the entrance of the old town, with a 16C *Ayuntamiento* in the Pl. de S. Juan, beyond which stands *N.S. de Juncal* (1506-8), typical of the Renaissance architecture of Guipuzcoa, with an overladen altarpiece (1647). *Fuenterrabía,* see p. 107, lies some 3 km. N.W.

Leaving Irún, the N I runs S.W., parallel to Mte. Jaizquíbel (r.) before entering industrial *Rentería* (46,400 inhab.) with a 16C fortified church containing a Jasper retablo designed by *Ventura Rodríguez* (1784). The town merges with the land-locked port of *Pasajes*, see p.106-7.—After a short climb, we descend gently towards (20 km.) **San Sebastián** (see Rte 2), passing *Mte. Ulia* on the r.

After crossing the Urumea and skirting the curving bay of *La Concha*, the road bears S., shortly meeting the interchange for the autopista for Bilbao.—At 7 km. the N 634 for Bilbao diverges r. (see Rte 5).— Following the beautiful wooded valley of the Oria, but polluted by paper-mills, the N I by-passes (8 km.) *Andoain*, with a Renaissance church, and the birthplace of Manuel de Larramendi (1690–1766), the Basque grammarian.

20 km. **Tolosa** (18,500 inhab.). In *Sta María* are good carvings and paintings, and a 19C organ by Stolz, while *S. Francisco* contains a retablo by *A. Bengoechea*; the *Armería* is 12C.

The direct road to Pamplona (N 240) bears l. on leaving the town (see Rte 3); while diverging r. 1 km. beyond Tolosa, an attractive mountain road (C 6324) runs through *Régil* (*Hotel*; Views from the *Balcón de Guipúzcoa*) to (25 km.) *Azpeiia* and the Sanctuary of Loyola, see p.122.

14 km. *Legorreta*, with an arcaded mansion and 16–17C retablo in its church.—By-passing (4 km. r.) *Villafranca de Ordizia, Beasain*, and *Villazábal* (with a Trans. church), the road commences to climb, shortly traversing a short tunnel.

FROM VILLAFRANCA TO ESTELLA (69 km.). 1 km. beyond this tunnel a picturesque but hilly road (C 130) leads S.E. across country, following the Argaunza valley past (6 km.) *Ataun*, entering Navarre by the Pto. de Lizarrusti, to (21 km.) *Echarri-Aranaz*. Hence we follow the N 111, climbing S.E. to the Alto de Lizarraga (pierced by a tunnel) commanding splendid views.—24 km. *Abarzuza.*—7 km. *Estella*, see p.114.

FROM VILLAFRANCE TO VITORIA VIÂ VERGARA (69 km.). This route follows the old coach road, which is reached by turning r. at 4 km. for *Ormáiztegui*, birthplace of the Carlist guerrilla leader Tomaso Zumalacárregui (1788–1835) whose house and furniture are kept as they were in his day.—After 10 km. we enter *Zumárraga* (12,400 inhab.: *Hotel*) on the l. bank of the Urola, with an attractive Pl. Mayor and 16C church and birthplace of Adm. López de Legazpi (c.1510–72) conqueror of the Philippines.—On the opposite side of the river lies *Villarreal de Urrechua*, with a late 16C hall-church, overlooked by Mte Irimeo, and the castle of *Ipenarrieta* (1605).—To the r. the C 6317 descends the wooded gorge of the Urola to (14 km.) *Azcoitia* (see p.122), while the main road turns l. and then r. to climb the Pto. de Descarga.—From the latter junction the l. fork leads 15 km. S.W. to *Oñate* (see below) viâ *Legazpia*, whose church of *La Asunción* has a fine porch and contains an ancient iron cross, and then climbs the Alto de Udana, from which we may see *Mte. Aloña*, or *Gorgomendi* (4259 ft).—At 8 km., near *Anzuola*, in the hamlet of *Uzárraga*, is an ancient Templar Church.

3 km. **Vergara** (16,200 inhab.). Here was founded, in 1756 by the Conde de Peñaflorida (1729–85), the '*Real Sociedad Bascongada de los Amigos del País*', first of a number of Economic Societies which flourished throughout Spain in the late 18C, which did much to foster interest in education, agriculture, commerce and industry. Vergara was also the scene of the Convention which brought an end to the First Carlist War (1839).

The town contains a number of old houses, including the *Casa de Jáuregui*, and a 17C *Ayuntamiento*. *S. Pedro* contains a Christ by *J. M. Montañés* (1657), while Gothic *Sta Marina*, beyond the lower bridge across the Deva, has a painting of the Christ of Burgos by *Mateo Cerezo*. In the *Seminario* (1776) is a statue of S. Ignacio by *Greg. Fernández*; outside the town is the *Pal. de Olazaeta* (1549–53).

At 5 km. a road leads 7 km. S.E. up the Aránzazu valley to **Oñate** (10,900 inhab.) famous for its former *University*, founded by Bp. Zuázola of Ávila in 1539. Fine buildings remain, decorated with sculptures by *Pierre Picart* and with a statue of the founder, whose Renaissance tomb of Parian marble is in 15C *S. Miguel*. This contains also, in the University Chapel on the N. side, a retablo (1536) by *Gaspar de Tordesillas*, and tombs of the Counts of Oñate, a Plateresque cloister, and a tower by *Manuel de Carrera* (1779–83). In the Franciscan *Conv. de Bidaurreta* (1509) is another retablo; the convents of the *Sacro Corazón*, and of *Sta Ana*, the latter with the pulpit of S. Francisco Borja and a retablo bearing a statue of Sta Ana by *Greg. Fernández*, are also of interest. In the *Ayuntamiento*, with a good front to the Pl. Mayor, is a solid gold ciborium, formerly in the University Chapel. Oñate, which was the birthplace of Lope de Aguirre (c.1511–61), the conquistador, retains a number of mansions and tower-houses, especially along the Aránzazu road. The road goes on to (9 km.) the modern *Conv. de Aránzazu*, whence *Mte. Aitzgorri* (4954 ft) may be ascended. Among the works of art in the basilica is a St Anthony, by *Greg. Fernández*.

4 km. beyond the turning for Oñate we enter *Mondragón*, (25,200 inhab.) with an *Ayuntamiento* of 1746, and noted for an iron-mine that has been worked from remote antiquity, while in *S. Juan*, S. Vicente Ferrer preached in 1408. It was the birthplace of the Basque historian Estéban de Garibay (1539–99).—We pass the spas of *Arechavaleta* and *Escoriaza* and climb through woods roughly parallel to the route of the new motorway to the Pto. de Arlaban.—At *Ullibarri-Arrazua* is a Trans. church with a finely carved portal.—*Landa* preserves early Gothic *S. Bartolomé* and the ruined Romanesque chapel of *S. Miguel*.—At *Mendizábal*, to the S.E., is *S. Pedro* with Romanesque grotesques, and further on, early Gothic *S. Pedro de Nanclares de Gamboa*.—Skirting the N. bank of the Zadorra reservoir, we descend gently to *Durana*, with an early Gothic church, and scene of a defeat of the Comuneros in 1521.—At *Arzubiaga*, 2 km. E., is a church with a Trans. carved doorway.—On the N. outskirts of Vitoria, we pass *Betoño*, with a Trans. church, and another to the N.W. at *Gamarra Mayor*, containing the tomb of Fr. de Gamarra, chaplain of Philip III and Bp. of Ávila.—At *Giamarra Menor* is the late Romanesque chapel of *S. Juan*.—35 km.. *Vitoria*, see p.100.

Beyond the Villafranca tunnel, the N I continues to climb steeply to reach the *Pto. de Echegarate* (2100 ft).

At 3 km. the old road across the Alto de Sta Barbara diverges r. to (8 km.) *Cegama*, in the church of which is the tomb of Zumalacárregui (see *Ormaiztegui*, above).

22 km. *Alsásua* (7,300 inhab.; *Hotel*) overlooked from the S.E. by the barren *Sierra de Urbasa* (4000 ft)—The chapel of *S. Pedro* to the N.E. is the legendary place of election in 717 of Navarre's first king, García Jiménez. Crossing the Araquil, the main road turns abruptly W.

FROM ALÁSUA TO PAMPLONA (49 km.). The N 240 diverges l. through (9 km.) *Echarri-Aranaz*, and (2 km.) *Arbizu*, with a good church and large tower-house, to (5 km. l.) *Huarte-Araquil*, between the Sierra de Aralar (N.) and the Sierra de Andia, with the Romanesque church of *S. Marcial*.—A bridle path leads (4 km. N.) passing the Romanesque church of *Zamarce*, and further on (l.) a dolmen, to the Romanesque chapel of *S. Miguel*, cons. 1098, with a retablo (c. 1200) in Limoges enamel. (View from the summit of the range above the chapel.)—10 km. *Villanueva-Araquil*, in a district full of prehistoric remains.—3 km. E. is *Echarren* with old houses, and nearby, the Romanesque church of *Chisperri*, now the Ayuntamiento of the Araquil valley.—1 km. *Irurzún* where we bear r. for (20 km.) *Pamplona*, see p.109.

At 13 km. a road leads r. off the N I to (3 km.) *Zalduendo*, containing a mansion with a remarkable classic frontal and carved arms.—We shortly pass (r.) the dolmen of *Eguilaz*, and the early Gothic church of *Mezquia*.—6 km. r. **Salvatierra**, a picturesque village (3400 inhab.) once surrounded by walls. Arcaded streets lead to the Pl. Mayor, the *Pal. Municipal* of 1606, and the *Casa de los Eulates*. Late 15C *Sta María* contains a 14C St Anne and a retablo mayor of c.1600 by *Lope de Larrea; S. Juan*, has a Renaissance porch and tower.

Gaceo, 3 km. W., has a Trans. church, and 2 km. beyond, at *Ezquerecocha*, the early Gothic church has exuberant carvings and a stone reredos.—15 km. S.E. lies *Contrasta*, once a frontier town, with a fortified church; in the Romanesque chapel of *N.S. de Elizmendi* is a carved Gothic triptych.

The N I shortly approaches the S. rim of the Zadorra reservoir.— 2 km. r. stands the *Castillo de Guevara*, modelled in the 15C on that of Sant'Angelo at Rome, but burnt in 1889.

At 14 km. a road (l.) passing *Argomániz* (*Parador Nac.*) leads to (6 km.) *Alegria*, Roman *Tullonius. S. Blas* has an 18C tower by *Olaguibel*, while the chapel of *N.S. de Ayala* is an unspoilt Trans. work of the 13C with pointed barrel vault, an arcaded S. portico, and a 15C statue of the Patroness.—2 km. S. of Alegria lies *Gauna*, where the palace of the Counts of Salvatierra (now the *Ayuntamiento*) has an ancient church.

11 km. **VITORIA** (169,800 inhab.; 36,000 in 1920; 69,000 in 1960; *Hotels*), the capital of Álava, is divided into an upper quarter (1730 ft) of narrow lanes and old mansions, with a rapidly growing industrial town surrounding it. The old nucleus, '*El Campo Suso*', stands on a height (Basque, *beturia*) that gives the town its name.

History. The early town of *Gazteiz*, perhaps of Visigothic origin, lay on the hill. After the victory of Las Navas (1212) it was enlarged and surrounded with a new wall, remaining independent until the union of Álava with Castile in 1332. From 1366 to 1413 it passed into the hands of Navarre. Near Vitoria a battle was fought in 1367 between Pedro the Cruel, supported by English troops, and Enrique de Trastamara; for the *Battle of Vitoria*, see below. During the First Carlist War many men of the British Legion perished here of cold and fever. Pero López de Ayala (1332–1407), chronicler, and chancellor of Castile, Fray Fr. de Vitoria (c.1483–1546), defender of the Indians of America, Gen. Alava (1771–1843), aide-de-camp to Wellington; and Ramiro de Maeztu (1874–1936), the philosopher and essayist, were born here.

The C. de Dato, the main street of the new town runs S. from the central arcaded PL. DE ESPAÑA, built 1781–91 by Justo Antonio de Olaguíbel, on the N. side of which is the *Ayuntamiento*. From the adjoining *Pl. Vieja* steps ascend to 14C *S. Miguel*, with a Baroque retablo (1632) by *Greg. Fernández*. In front of the principal door stands the 14C statue of the *Virgen Blanca*. In the nearby *Pl. de Machete* is the *Pal. de Villasuso*, with a Renaissance doorway. To the E. is *S. Vicente* (15C, with a tower of 1865), containing a tomb of 1349 and a

Churrigueresque retablo. In the Sacristy and the *Cap. de los Pasos* are a Crucifixion and Mater Dolorosa by *Valdivielso* (1760–1822).

Following the ancient C. de la Cuchillería we pass (r.) the *Casa del Cordón* (No. 24, restored) containing a museum, and the *Pal. de Bendaña* (Nos. 58–60), both of c.1500, before reaching the 14C Gothic **Sta María,** a cathedral since 1862. The vaulted W. Portico shelters a magnificent * *Doorway* of c.1400 in the Franco-Navarrese style.

Within are 15C effigies, a Descent from the Cross attr. to *Caravaggio*, and two kneeling alabaster figures (16C). The retablo mayor is by *Olaguíbel*, with an Assumption in high relief by *Valdivielso*. In the central chapel of the ambulatory is the silver Virgin of the Rosary, brought from Flanders in 1510, and in a chapel next to the sacristy the early-Gothic seated Virgin and Child known as N.S. de la Esclavitud. The sacristy contains a Descent from the Cross attr. to *Van Dyck* but more probably by *Gaspar de Crayer* (1582–1669), and a Conception by *Juan de Carreño*, from the destroyed Conv. de S. Francisco. The Treasury contains a silver processional cross attr. to *Benvenuto Cellini*. In the *Cap. de Santiago* are works by *Valdivielso*.

To the N.W. of the Cathedral is the *Casa del Portalón*, C. de la Correría 151, an old timbered house with overhanging stories, with a small museum devoted to the Battle of Vitoria. At No. 116, opposite, are collections of Armour and Archaeology from the Provincial Museum, see below.

The concentric streets of the old town, on the E. side of which stood the *Judería*, contain many ancient houses and palaces, among which may be mentioned those in the C. de la Correría and the Herrería, in the Cuchillería and the Zapatería. In the C. del Fray Zacarías Martínez are the Plateresque *Pal. de Escoriaza-Esquivel*, and the *Episcopal Pal.*, with Renaissance windows. Near the N. end of the C. de la Pintorería is the façade of the *Conv. de la Santa Cruz*. The *Hospicio* has a Renaissance door and its chapel contains a figure of the founder, Martín de Salvatierra (1589), attr. to *Greg. Fernández*.

Returning from the cathedral along the W. side of the old town, we pass *S. Pedro* (14C) with a fine portal. The *Altar de los Reyes* is a curious Plateresque retablo with carvings in high relief, and, among tombs of the 16C are two bronze effigies of members of the family of Álava, cast in Milan in 1526 and 1540. In the sacristy is a Flemish Pietà.

We descend to the Pl. de la Provincia, and the *Diputación*, containing a Crucifixion by *Ribera* and other paintings. On the S. side of the PL. DE LA VIRGEN BLANCA, W. of the Pl. de España, is the *Conv. de S. Antonio*, begun in 1604. The statues on the front are attr. to *Greg. Fernández*; in a side chapel is the Romanesque Virgen de los Remedios from the Conv. de S. Francisco. Just beyond stands the undistinguished 'new' *Cathedral* (begun 1906), and the gardens of *La Florida*. To the N. is the *Conv. de las Brígidas* with a rebuilt neoclassic front (1784) by *Olaguíbel*, while to the S. is the Paseo de Fray Francisco, where the *Casa de Alava* houses the *Provincial Museum* and Library.

The museum contains a collection of triptychs, polychrome statues of the Virgin (14th and 15C), a 14C figure of Christ from Zurbano and a number of Renaissance paintings, notably a Conception by *Alonso Cano*, paintings by *Ribera*, and works attr. to *Murillo* and *Morales*; here also are some important early statuary; a marble Goddess (2C A.D.) from Iruña, and other Roman carvings, altars and mosaics; Romanesque sculptures, including a Column from Zurbano, some 5 km. N.E. of Vitoria, bearing grotesque figures (? c. 1200).

There are a number of interesting churches in the vicinity of Vitoria, see al
p.127-8, but which may be difficult to find in the still growing conurbation.
Lopidana, c. 3 km. W. is an early-Gothic church with a carved Renaissar
retablo—3 km. S.W. on the Trevino road, at *Lasarte* (*Hotel*). *Sta Maria* has
Romanesque sanctuary with richly carved windows.—3 km.. S.E. of Vitoria li
Otazu, with a good Trans. church, while at *Monasterioguren* (S.W. of Otazu),
Pedro has a remarkable open portico and pointed barrel vaults.

3 km. S.W. of Vitoria, to the l. of the N I in the hamlet of *Armentia*, birthplace
St Prudentius (6C), *S. Andrés* (c. 1181), unfortunately rebuilt in 1776, retai
remarkable reliefs in the porch, carved capitals in the choir, and statues of t
Evangelists at the crossing.— 4 km. S.W. to the r. of the N I, lies *Zuazo de Álav*
with a pure Romanesque church, while another turning (r.) 4 km. beyond, lea
past *Iruña*, the ancient *Suisacio*, preserving Roman remains, but the objec
discovered during excavations have been removed to the Provincial Museum.
Further W. lies *Badaya*, with ruins of a 15C Hieronymite monastery. There a
dolmens in the neighbourhood.—After 4 km., at *Mendoza*, rise the *Towerhous*
of the Duke of Infantado (restored) and of the Count of Orgaz, while to the N.V
are the Romanesque chapel of *Urrialdo* and the twin villages of *Hueto de Aba*
and *Hueto de Arriba*, the former with an early Gothic church; the latter has
Romanesque apsidal church with a carved font (13C).

For routes from Vitoria to *Estella* and *Legroño*, see pp.127-8.

Beyond Vitoria the road passes (r.) the battlefields of 136
(*Inglesmendi*, where English troops fought for Pedro the Cruel), and o
1813, leaving on the r. the ancient bridges of *Trespuentes* and *Villoda*
over the Zadorra.

The *Battle of Vitoria* (21 June 1813) in which Wellington defeate
Jourdan and secured the mastery of the Basque Provinces, took plac
W. of the town, on either side of the road to Nanclares.

After a day's heavy fighting, during which the French lost over 8,000, compare
to the Allies 5,000, the French army, with Joseph Bonaparte and his cou
retreated E., leaving behind 143 guns and a prodigious amount of plunder whic
delayed the pursuit. The pictures from the royal Spanish collection found in Kir
Joseph's carriage are now in Apsley House, London.

At 10 km. a road leads 2 km. r. to *Nanclares de Oca*, with th
Romanesque church of *La Asunción*.—We descend the Zadorra valley
with the castle of *Arganzón* on the r. to (6 km. r.) *Puebla de Arganzón*
whose church has a 16C retablo. We pass *Manzanos*, across the rive
from *Estabillo*, with its Isabelline church, and *Armiñón*, with a
picturesque bridge, and enter the upper valley of the Ebro.—At 8 km
the N 232 to *Logroño* diverges l. (see Rte 6A), while the N I bears S.W
shortly entering Old Castile, at 9 km. by-passing **Miranda de Ebro**
before crossing the river. A ruined castle commands the town (35,60
inhab.; *Hotel*), an important railway junction, which also contains *St*
María, late Gothic, and *S. Nicolás*, on the l. bank, with a door of 1316
and Romanesque apse.

At 8 km. l., is the Cistercian *Conv. of Bujedo*, with a Romanesque
apse (1172) and 17C buildings. We shortly meet the N 625 from Bilbac
viâ Orduña converging from the r., see Rte 6B.—The N I, together with
the A1, now enters the narrowest part of the impressive **Pass of
Pancorbo**, cutting through the Montes Obarenes. The Madrid railway
line also threads its way through the gorge by a succession of tunnels and
viaducts, while the road itself tunnels through an immense splintered
cliff before passing the village of *Pancorbo* (2090 ft; 700 inhab.; *Hotels*).
Above the pass are a ruined Moorish castle and remains of the fort of *Sta*
Engracia (1794).—The N 232 branches l. for *Logroño*, see Rte 6B.

PANCORBO TO MEDINA DE POMAR (67 km.). After 8 km. the N 232 forks r. pas
Santa María Ribarredonda, with a hall-church of 1583, and *Cubo de Bureba*, wit

a star-vaulted hall-church rebuilt in 1734, to skirt the S. flank of the sierra.—At 20 km. l. *Cornudilla*, is an early seated wooden Virgin.

An interesting alternative road, in good weather, is that climbing r. 6 km. beyond *Cubo*, leading through a defile before reaching *Frias*.

9 km. **Oña**, with a Benedictine abbey of *S. Salvador*, founded in 1011, and now a house of Jesuits. The remarkable church, with Romanesque remains, has a 13C nave containing restored 13–14C murals, Gothic choir-stalls, Isabelline cloisters, and royal tombs. A single-arched Roman Bridge, called *La Horadada*, spans the Ebro to the N.—At 4 km. a road leads r. viâ (8 km.) *Trespaderne*, to **Frías** (14 km. E.), picturesquely situated with its rock-set castle, and with a rare *Bridge* retaining its central gate-tower.—19 km. N. of Trespaderne is the late Romanesque chapel of *S. Pantaleón de Losa*, with carvings dated 1207, while 18 km. N.W. lies **Medina de Pomar** (4,200 inhab.), where the 15C *Castle*, with its two towers (the view of which is spoilt by new buildings) contains ruins of a palace with Mudéjar stucco-work, while in the *Conv. de Sta Clara* are Renaissance tombs of the Dukes of Frias. *Sta Cruz* is an unusually fine hall-church (?14C).—*Espinosa de los Monteros* (see p.126) lies 21 km. N. of Medina.

The landscape changes character as the road crosses the monotonous plain of *La Bureba*, part of the plateau of Old Castile, and many will agree with William George Clark, who (traversing the gorge in 1849) remarked that 'it is only on emerging from the Defile of Pancorbo that the traveller feels himself to be indeed in Spain'.

12 km. *Berzosa*, with a Romanesque church.—10 km. **Briviesca** (4600 inhab.; *Hotel*), now by-passed, where in 1388 Juan I established the honour of Prince of the Asturias as the title of the king's eldest son.

A number of old mansions flank its streets, and a picturesque *Ayuntamiento* stands in the arcaded Pl. Mayor. The N. side is occupied by *S. Martín*, with star-vaulting, a carved early Renaissance pulpit and a N. chapel containing a good tomb (1513) and retablo. To the E. lies the *Hosp. de Sta Clara* with a *Church* (1525–65), begun by *Juan Gil de Hontañón* and finished by *Pedro de Rasines*, consisting of a single nave and polygonal sanctuary covered by a wide stellar vault. It contains a Retablo by *Diego Guillén* and *Pedro López de Gámiz. Guillén* also carved a retablo (1524) for the S. chapel of *Sta María la Mayor*, further S., which has a Gothic Virgin and Child in a niche of the neo-classic W. front.—Some 8 km. W. lies the pilgrimage chapel of *Sta Casilda*.

Shortly after passing (r.) *Prádanos de Bureba*, whose church contains a curious terracotta Virgin, and Romanesque *N.S. del Valle*, the N I climbs to (20 km.) the *Pto. de la Brújula* (3219 ft; *Hotel*). As the outer industrial areas of Burgos are approached, we may see on a ridge to the l. the towerless *Cartuja de Miraflores*; and ahead, the twin spires of the *Cathedral.*—Entering the suburbs we pass (l.), at *Gamonal*, *N.S. de la Antigua*, begun c.1296 in a markedly English style, with a square buttressed tower and ridge-ribbed vaults. 43 km. **Burgos**, see Rte. 20A.

2 SAN SEBASTIÁN AND ENVIRONS

SAN SEBASTIÁN (166,250 inhab.; 63,000 in 1920; 111,000 in 1950; numerous *Hotels*), the agreeable capital of the province of Guipúzcoa, and long the most fashionable summer resort in Spain, is in danger of losing its old-world charm as its natural beauties are exploited. The *Parte Vieja*, or old town, commanded by *Mte. Urgull* with its castle, stands on a rocky peninsula and was once a strong fortress, but its landward defences on the isthmus were demolished in 1865–66. To the

W. is the impressive semi-circular bay of *La Concha*, protected from the open sea by the *Isla de Sta Clara*, while on the E. side flows the Urumea It enjoys a mild climate, but sudden showers or a *'siri-miri'*(Scotch mist are not infrequent, and in winter it is depressingly damp.

History. The early history of San Sebastián is obscure. Its old Basque nam would seem to have been *Izurum*, and it was later known as *Donostia*. After th union of Guipúzcoa with Spain, San Sebastián became a bulwark against Frenc incursions. Among its many sieges the most disastrous was that of 1813, when Gér Rey with 3,000 veterans held out for six weeks against Gen. Graham with a Anglo-Portuguese force of 10,000. After several fruitless assaults, involving grea loss, the English succeeded in fording the Urumea under cover of a heav bombardment from the r. bank and Mte. Ulia, and entered the breache meanwhile a fire, initially started by the French to keep the besiegers at bay, cause much damage to the town, which Rey evacuated. Driven into the castle, h surrendered some days later with all the honours of war. The English were late reproached for deliberately setting light to the town out of commercial jealousy. I 1835–37 it was successfully defended against the Carlists with the aid of the Britis Auxiliary Legion under the command of de Lacy Evans. Its defences were largel demolished c.1865. The town only became 'fashionable' after 1886, when th Spanish Royal family commenced spending their summers there. It has not lost it cachet, but in recent years has been somewhat slighted and over-policed.
Natives of San Sebastián are Antonio de Oquendo (1577–1640), the admira Catalina de Erauso (1585–c.1650) known as *'La Monja Alférez'*('the nun-ensign' who, after escaping from a convent, had a romantic and successful military caree in Spanish America without her sex being discovered; and Pio Baroja (1872–1956 the novelist.

From the W. end of the ALAMEDA DE CALVO SOTELO, which lies across the isthmus S. of the Parte Vieja, the *Puerto* is reached by a short stree N. of the *Ayuntamiento*, the former Casino, passing the Club Nautico From the mole a good view is obtained of the small but animated fishing harbour, and the bay.—Skirting the N. side of the port and passing a terrace of fishermen's cottages sheltering under the bulk of *Mte. Urgull*, we reach the *Aquarium* and *Museo Naval Oceanográfico*, devoted to the history of the Basque fishing industry. By car, this may only be approached by the Paseo José Antonio, a pleasant drive round the seaward side of the hill, commencing at the E. side of the peninsula.

From the Puerto an archway leads into the **Parte Vieja**, the thronged narrow streets of which are best explored on foot. Many of the most characteristic bars and restaurants are found here.—On reaching the C. Mayor, to the l. is seen the elaborate sculptured façade of *Sta María*, a spacious hall-church reconstructed in 1743–64, and restored.

The architects were *Pedro Ignacio de Lizardi* and *Miguel de Salazar*. Th paintings of the retablo mayor are by *Roberto Michel*, the statues of Sta Barbar and S. Pío by *Diego Villanueva*, and the retablos of S. Pedro and S. Antonio b *Felipe Arizmendi*. The statue of Sta Catalina and group of the Holy Family are b *Juan de Mena*. It contains a huge Cavaillé-Coll organ.

Mte. Urgull (425 ft) is best climbed (c.½ hr) by a footpath to the r. of Sta María, although a steeper path ascends from behind the puerto. After c.20 min. we pass on the l. the *English Cemetery*, with tombs of officers of the British Legion. Above rises a monument to British soldiers who fell in the Peninsular War. The *Castillo de la Mota*, on the summit, containing an apology for a military museum, is a good example of the 16C transition from the castle to the bastioned fortification of the Renaissance. The *Views are extensive, but the hill itself is disfigured by a monumental statue of Christ.

From Sta María the C 31 de Agosto leads E. to Gothic *S. Vicente* (1507) with a retablo mayor of 1584 by *Ambrosio de Bengoechea* and

PASEO NUEVO

Mte. Urgull

Castillo de la Mota

Sta. S. Telmo
Maria Museo

S. Vicente

Aquarium

Arch

PARTE VIEJA

Mercado

Pte. del
Kursaal

AV. DEL
GENERALISIMO

Puerto

ALAMEDA DE
CALVO SOTELO

Barrio de
Gross

Ayuntamiento

Parque
Alderdi-Eder

Pte. de
Sta. Catalina

Diputacion

SFT

AV. DE ESPAÑA

Playa de la Concha

PASEO DE LA CONCHA

ZUBIETA

Catedral

PO

Estacion

Pte. de
Maria Cristina

C. VICTORIA ERNA

Estacion

PLAZA DE
CENTENARIO

FRANCE

RIO URUMEA

REPUBLICA ARGENTINA

PASEO DE LOS FUEROS

AV. DE FRANCIA

AV. DE SANCHO EL SABIO

San Sebastián

| 0 yards | 400 |
| 0 metres | 400 |

Environs

0   1 km

Mte. Igueldo

SANTA
CLARA

Mte.
Urgull

Mte.
Ulia

Bay of Biscay

Bahia de l.
Concha

San
Sebastián

Pasajes
S. Pedro

Rio Urumea

BILBAO PAMPLONA & MADRID

Juan de Iriate. To the N. stands the former *Conv. de S. Telmo* (1531–51), founded by Alonso de Idiáquez, Secretary of State to Charles V, and built to the plans of *Fray Martín de Santiago* in Isabelline style; the Renaissance cloister is by *Juan Santesteban*. The buildings house the *Municipal Museum*.

From the cloister, which contains early discoidal tombstones, the Picture Galleries are reached, with a good collection of the Spanish School on the FIRST FLOOR, while above are modern paintings, furniture, etc. The exhibits include a S. Dominic by *El Greco*, Fernando VII by *Vicente Lòpez*; and *Goya's* portrait of Gen. Alexander O'Reilly (see p. 565). A room displays works by *Zuloaga*.

In the upper galleries of the cloister are archaeological and historical collections, with rooms devoted to the Carlist Wars, etc. A separate section contains the collections of Basque Ethnography, comprising furniture and tools, reconstructions of a traditional room and kitchen, etc. The former *church*, with recumbent effigies at the door of the founder and his wife, has been decorated by *José-María Sert* with a series of paintings representing the life of the Basque people.

Walking S. from the W. end of S. Vicente and turning r., we enter the *Pl. del 18 de Julio*, with the old *Ayuntamiento* (1829–32).

S. of the Alameda the wider streets of the new town between the *Parque Alderdi-Eder* overlooking the Concha to the W., and the Urumea to the E., are lined with fashionable shops and cafés, particularly in the *Av. de España*, reached by any street running S.

The C. Hernani, to the W., approaches the church of *El Buen Pastor* (begun 1888), now the Cathedral, while the C. El Cano leads to the *Pl. de Guipúzcoa*, an arcaded square with the *Diputación* (housing a good Library) on its W. side. Further E., the C. Oquendo and the tree-lined Av. de la Republica Argentina, skirting the l. bank of the Urumea, lead S. to the Paseo de los Fueros and to new and growing suburbs hemmed in by low green hills.

On the E. bank of the river Urumea lies the Barrio de Gros, which may be approached from the Alameda by the *Pte. de Kursaal* and from the Av. de España by the *Pte. de Sta Catalina*, while to the S. the *Pte. de María Cristina* crosses to the railway station. The summit of **Mte. Ulia** (820ft), to the N., affording panoramic views, may be ascended by a road off the Av. del Gen. Mola, climbing past the villas on its lower slopes.

From the W. end of the Av. de España we approach the *Paseo de la Concha*, an esplanade overlooking the *playa*, resplendent with its *toldos*, or sun-shades, in summer. The C. Zubieta skirts the beach and tunnels beneath the garden of the *Pal. de Miramar* (1889–93; designed by the English architect Selden Wornum), once the royal residence, standing on a rocky cliff separating *La Concha* from the *Playa del Antiguo* or *de Ondarreta*.— Passing the tunnel, the main road bears S.W., resuming its course as the N I, for *Vitoria* (see Rte 1), off which, some 7 km. S., forks the coast road for *Bilbao*, see Rte 5.

The Av. de Satrustegui diverges r. to the foot of **Mte Igueldo** (650ft), and climbs steeply to the summit (panoramic *Views), now surmounted by a hotel. The ascent may also be made by funicular. Beyond lies the village of *Igueldo*, with a 12C church; after 7 km. the road peters out at the foot of *Mendizorrotz* (extensive views from its summit).

FROM SAN SEBASTIÁN TO PASAJES AND FUENTERRABÍA (23 km.) We follow the N I, direction Irún.—At 3 km. we may turn l. into *Pasajes San Pedro*, now a crowded suburb (22,300 inhab.) N. of the port, but affording a good view of *Pasajes San Juan* on the opposite bank of the narrow entrance of the land-locked bay, the safest harbour between

Bordeaux and Bilbao. There is a regular ferry across the estuary.—After 4km. turn l. for *Lezo*, with old houses and the *Basilica de Santo Cristo*, rebuilt in the 17C.—After 2km. we reach **Pasajes San Juan**, huddled between the slopes of Jaizquíbel and the shore, and threaded by a single narrow street. A visit on foot is almost obligatory. The alley continues past (r.) the 16C church, with a good retablo, to a ruined fort of 1621 and the mouth of the bay.

At No. 59 Victor Hugo lived in 1843. From the 10th to the 16C Pasajes was a centre of the Biscay whaling industry, together with St Jean de Luz and San Sebastián. From here Lafayette embarked for America in 1776, while during the closing stages of the Peninsular War it was Wellington's main port of supply.

The road for Fuenterrabía climbs steeply just short of the village entrance and runs along the humpback of **Mte. Jaizquíbel** (1916ft.; *Hotel*; orientation table) with a panoramic *View from the summit; in the foreground the Valley of the Bidassoa, beyond which, in France, rises *La Rhune*; to the r. is the *Peña de Aya* among the Montes de Bidassoa, foothills of the Pyrenees. Passing the chapel of *N.S. de Guadalupe* we descend towards (16km.) **Fuenterrabía**, a characteristic old town (11,000 inhab.; *Parador Nac.* and *Hotel*), at the mouth of the Bidassoa, somewhat spoilt by modern accretions, including a series of tower-blocks buttressing the sea-flank of Jaizquíbel.

This frontier fortress was once powerful enough to withstand a siege by the French under the Prince of Condé in 1638, but was taken by Francis I in 1521 and in 1719 by the Duke of Berwick. Crossing the Bidassoa from Fuenterrabía by an unsuspected ford, Wellington was able to surprise and turn the strongly defended French right flank (7 Oct. 1813).

From the *Pta. de Sta. María* in the 15C walls, the picturesque *C. Mayor* climbs past (l.) the *Ayuntamiento* and several ancient mansions to *N.S. de la Asunción*, 11C but altered at the Renaissance. At the upper end of the C. Mayor is the *Pal. de Carlos V*, founded in the 10C, but dating mainly from the 14th to 16C, and restored to accommodate the *Parador Nac.* From the lower town of *La Marina* the road goes on to the lighthouse on Cabo Higuer, passing the remains of the *Castillo de S. Telmo* or *de los Piratas*, bearing a large royal escutcheon.

Turning S., the road shortly enters *Irún* (see p.98) after passing the small airport. An attractive alternative to returning to San Sebastián by the N I may be made by branching l. 2km. S. of Irún for (5km.) **Oyarzún** (7,600 inhab.), with a 17C church, the ancient *Oeasso*, capital of the Basques during the Roman occupation of Spain, standing on the old post road to Madrid.

Hence a road runs due S. (14km.) to the *Collado de Bianditz,* with panoramic views, while the summit of the *Peñas de Aya* or *Las Tres Coronas* (2677ft) may be reached from the Lesaca road climbing S.E. from Oyarzún, which, after passing through a tunnel, winds through the mountains for 24km. before descending to *Lesaca* (see below).

9km. S.W. of Oyarzún lies *Astigarraga*, and 3km. beyond, **Hernani** (28,100 inhab.) containing old mansions in the C. Mayor, with striking balconies and escutcheons. In the church is the tomb of Juan de Urbieta (d. 1553), who captured Francis I at Pavia; among the retablos, several are Churrigueresque. The British Legion was defeated here by the Carlists in 1837 and the town suffered severely during the Carlist War of 1874.—From both Astigarraga and Hernani roads lead back to *San Sebastián*, c. 10km. to the N.

FROM SAN SEBASTIÁN TO ELIZONDO (69 km.), AND (24 km. beyond) DANCHARINEA. We take the N I to Irún, there turning r. for (20 km.) *Behobia*. Following the C 133 along the r. bank of the Bidassoa, which here forms the frontier, we pass below the heights of *S. Marcial*, the site of a battle during the Peninsular War, in which a Spanish force led by Gen. Freire, unsupported by British troops, repulsed Soult's attempted relief of San Sebastián (31 Aug. 1813).—Perched high on the French bank is the village of *Biriatou*, long the haunt of smugglers.—When the road crosses the river at *Enderlaza*, we enter Navarre, where points precipitous banks are in Spanish territory.

13 km. **Vera de Bidassoa** (3200 inhab.), lies in a green valley below the S. flank of *La Rhune*, taken by Wellington's forces ascending the Bayonet ridge among others, in Oct. 1813. The church, the old bridge of *S. Miguel*, the *Ayuntamiento* (1776), and ruined *castle of Alzate* are of interest, while 'Itzea', the home of Pio Baroja (1872–1956) and Julio Caro Baroja, is one of many attractive houses in the town.—At 4 km. a road leads r. (2 km.) to **Lesaca** (3000 inhab.) Wellington's headquarters during the crossing of the Pyrenees, containing a number of tower-houses, while in the church are medieval carvings covered with gold plating in the 16C.—At 2 km. a road leads to *Echalar* (Customs; *Hotel*), and climbs up through the thickly wooded valley towards the border, beyond which is the French village of *Sare*.—We pass the *Ventas de Yanci*, scene of fierce skirmishing during Soult's retreat from Sorauren, and (13 km.) picturesque *Sumbilla*, noted for its trout fishing, with an ancient Bridge, before by-passing (3 km. r.) **Sanesteban** (Basque *Doneztebe*).—The curious village of *Donamaria* (4 km. S.), with a fine tower-house and round-towered church, and *Zurbieta* (7 km. W.) remain almost entirely Basque in this wild and mountainous corner of Navarre.—Both road and river turn abruptly E. and we soon enter (5 km.)*Oyeregui*, with old houses and bridge.—At *Oronoz-Mugaire*, the main road to Pamplona (N 121) diverges S., see Rte 3.—Passing (6 km.) *Irurita*, with senorial mansions, at 3 km. we reach the resort of *Elizondo* (650ft; *Hotel*); the main town of the rich *Val de Baztán*, once an independent republic like Andorra, with the 16C *Pal. de los Gobernadores*. Continuing up the valley, we shortly pass *Elvetea*, with a curious church, and solidly-built mansions.

At 4 km. a road (r.) leads viâ the picturesque village of *Ariscun*, to *Errazu* (Customs) before climbing to the Pto. de Izpeguy (2205 ft). Beyond, in France, lies (20 km.) *St-Etienne-de-Baigorry* and (11 km. further E.), *St-Jean-Pied-de-Port*. Near Ariscun an ostracized community lived in previous centuries, known as Cagots, which are believed to have descended either from an isolated settlement of Goths or, more probably, from ancient leper colonies.

At 2 km. a turning (r.) leads 2 km. to *Maya*, with a ruined castle.—The main road ascends to the *Pto. de Otsondo* or *Col de Maya* (1975 ft), fiercely but unsuccessfully defended by part of Wellington's forces at the commencement of Soult's advance to the relief of besieged Pamplona. Good views over France, and of *Urdax* in the valley below, with a 15C church and the birthplace of Piarres de Axular (1556–c.1640), author of Basque devotional works, are obtained as the road descends steeply to the frontier at (15 km.) *Dancharinea* (Customs).—Just short of the border a road leads l. 6 km. to picturesque *Zugarramurdi*, once renowned for its witches.

3   FROM SAN SEBASTIÁN TO PAMPLONA AND ZARAGOZA

Total distance, 268 km. (166 miles) N I 27 km. **Tolosa**—turn l. onto N 240; 64 km. **Pamplona**—N 121; 38 km. *Olite*—59 km. **Tudela**—N 232; 80 km. **Zaragoza.**

Motorway. An *autopista* is planned to connect the N I not far S. of *San Sebastián* with a completed section commencing at *Irurzun*, N.W. of *Pamplona*. From Pamplona it drives S. between *Tafalla* and *Olite* (exit; and for *La Oliva*) to join the A 68 just W. of *Tudela*, some 90 km. N.W. of *Zaragoza*.

An alternative but longer route runs from San Sebastián to *Pamplona* viâ *Irún* and (55 km.) *Sanesteban* (see above), 5 km. beyond which we turn S. onto the N 121 and climb steeply through fine mountain scenery to the *Pto. de Velate* (2779 ft) before descending to (27 km.) *Olague*.—Hence a road leads l. across country to 19 km. *Zubiri* on the Roncesvalles-Pamplona road—12 km. *Sorauren*. To the l. rise the ridges on which the sanguinary battles of 28–30 July, 1813, were fought, when Soult's thrust across the Pyrenees in an attempt to break the Allied blockade of Pamplona was successfully repulsed by Wellington.—5 km. *Villava*, with ruins of a Romanesque monastery, and Renaissance houses. Crossing the Arga we enter *Pamplona*, see below.

Another attractive route, but by a minor mountain road, ascends the valley of the Urumea to (10 km.) *Hernani*. Hence, turning S.E., we climb into Navarre.—At 14 km., perched above us, lies *Arano*, commanding extensive views. Leaving Mte. Urdaburu on the l. we follow the valley S. through (8 km.) *Goizueta*, with ancient timbered houses, (20 km.) *Leiza*, the starting point for an excursion to (12 km.) *Ezcurra*, in the wild valley of the Basaburúa Menor, and (13 km.) *Lecumberri*, where we meet the N 240, see below. Leiza may also be approached from Tolosa (19 km. N.W.) by taking a minor road viâ *Élduayen* and *Berástegui*, entering Navarre at the Pto. de Urto.

See also the sub-route from *Sangüesa* to *Tauste*, p.190.

We follow the N I (Rte 1) as far as (27 km.) *Tolosa*, there turning l. onto the N 240—20 km. *Betelú*, with a 15C church and ancient houses.— After climbing to the Pto. de Azpiroz (1929 ft) we enter (10 km.) *Lecumberri* (1800 ft), with a Gothic church and picturesque streets.— 2 km. E. is *Echarri*, with old houses.—We pass between the craggy peaks known as Las Dos Hermanas to reach (14 km.) *Irurzún*, with an old church. On the peak of La Trinidad (N.E.) is a chapel containing a 14C stone carving of the Trinity, while at *Larumbe* (6 km. S.E., l. of the Pamplona road) is an important 13C church.—5 km. *Sarasate*, with a beautiful Cross, and (2 km.) *Erice*, with an old church and palace, are traversed before we enter (6 km.) *Berrioplano* (*Hotel*) with Romanesque and Gothic churches.

7 km. **PAMPLONA** (1475 ft; 163,200 inhab.; 33,000 in 1920; 93,000 in 1960; *Hotels*), known to the Basques as *Iruña*, and capital of the ancient kingdom of Navarre, stands on rising ground in the midst of the Concha de Pamplona, a broad valley among the Pyrenean foothills. Part of its ancient fortifications have been levelled to make room for the extension of the fast growing city, to the S. of which lies the *Opus Dei University* (founded 1952).

Fiestas. The boisterous fiesta of *S. Fermín* (5–16 July) is the most exploited (see p.91); also 'El Chiquito' (25–30 Sept.).

History. Pamplona, a city of the Vascones rebuilt in 68 B.C., by the sons of Pompey and named *Pompeiopolis*, was taken by Euric the Goth in 466 and by the Frankish king Childebert in 542. It was held by the Moors (who corrupted its name to *Bambilonah*) from c. 738 to 748, when it was captured by Count Garcia Iñigo. Charlemagne, who had been called into Spain apparently to settle a dispute between two Moorish factions, sacked the city in 778 by way of payment for his services, in revenge for which the Navarrese massacred his rearguard at Roncesvalles, In the middle of the 9C Pamplona became capital of the county of Navarre, which was raised to the dignity of a kingdom by Sancho I in 905.

During succeeding centuries the city prospered, especially under Sancho III (1000–35) and Carlos III (1387–1425), although the cathedral was sacked by French troops in 1276. In 1512, during the reign of Catalina, wife of Juan de Labrit (Jean d'Albret), Spanish Navarre was overrun by Castile, and Pamplona became the seat of a viceroy. In 1521 Jean d'Albret, aided by the French, attempted to regain his former capital, and at this siege the young captain, Iñigo López de Recalde, afterwards S. Ignacio de Loyola, received the wound which had so momentous an effect upon the history of the church (see p.122).

Philip II, by erecting the citadel in 1571, made Pamplona the strongest fortress in N. Spain, and relieved the town from further assaults, until in 1808 Gén. d'Armagnac's division treacherously seized the citadel. In 1813 the fortress fell to Wellington after a four months' blockade in spite of Soult's attempt to relieve it. The battle of Sorauren was fought 9 km. N., just E. of the Bayonne road, see p.108. Pamplona was never captured by the Carlists, and in the fortress ditch Santos Ladrón de Guevera was shot in 1839 for proclaiming Don Carlos king at Estella. Among natives of Pamplona are St Firminus (S. Fermín; martyred at Amiens c. 300), and Pablo de Sarasate (1844–1908), the violinist.

Crossing the Arga, the N 240 enters the town by the Av. de Guipúzcoa, passing (r.) the *Taconera gardens*: beyond rises the *Citadel*, a pentagonal fortress built for Philip II by *Jorge Palearzo* in imitation of that of Antwerp. The N 111 from Logroño also enters at this point. On the l. the Paseo de Sarasate leads to the arcaded PL. DEL CASTILLO, the main square, passing *S. Nicolás*, with 12–13C details, and at the E. end, the *Diputación* (1847), the Throne Room of which contains portraits of Kings of Navarre.

In a later wing to the r., behind a garden, is the *Archivo de Navarra*, containing the ancient book of the Fueros, a fragment of the chain of Las Navas (below), and other objects relating to the history of Navarre, including an illuminated MS. of the English Coronation ritual sent to Carlos III of Navarre in the late 14C by Richard II, whose portrait appears as an initial. Further on, the rebuilt *Basilica de S. Ignacio* covers the spot where the saint was wounded (see history).

From the N.E. corner of Pl. del Castillo the C. de la Chapitela leads N., at the far end of which we turn r. to approach the Gothic ***Cathedral**, with details strongly reminiscent of the French 14C style.

The first cathedral on this site, begun in 1023 and finished in 1102, fell into decay c.1390, and the present church was begun in 1397 and finished c.1525. The classical façade, designed by *Ventura Rodriguez*, was completed in 1783, and replaced the only remaining part of the original Romanesque church. Baretti, who passed this way in 1768, remarked that the arches over the two lateral gates of the cathedral exhibited 'many small naked figures of men and women placed in such postures, as it is not fit to tell'!

The *Coro* has been removed from the nave, and the stalls (1597) by *Miguel Ancheta*, placed in the *Cap. Mayor*. The nave contains the *Tomb of Carlos III (d. 1425) and his queen, Leonor (of Castile, d. 1416), by *Jean de Lomme* of Tournai, a fine example of the Burgundian type, with a procession of 'mourners' on the pedestal. Several painted and sculptured retablos are in the side chapels, notably in those of the ambulatory.

The *Cap. Mayor* is enclosed by a *Grille* by *Guillermo Ervenat* (1517). On the high altar is the Virgen de los Reyes, an ancient image before which the kings of Navarre kept vigil before their coronation. The curious plan of the apse, with one advancing and two re-entrant angles, should be noticed.

The large and lofty **Cloisters**, on the S., was begun in the early 14C by Bp. Arnaud de Barbazán. Over the *Pta. del Amparo*, by which we enter, is a relief of the Death of Mary (1356). On the N. side is the tomb of Don Leonel (d. 1443), son of Charles the Bad and his wife Epifania de Luna, and just beyond is an Adoration by the sculptor *Jacques Pérut* (14C). On the S. side is the *Pta. de la Preciosa*. The *Sala de la Preciosa* was once the meeting-place of the Cortes of Navarre. Built out into the S.W. corner of the cloister is the *Cap. de la Santa Cruz*, whose iron grille was forged from tent-chains captured at Las Navas de Tolosa in 1212, and on the W. side is the tomb of the guerrilla general Espoz y Mina (1781–1836).

The *Refectory of the Canons*, now the *Diocesan Museum*, contains a lector's pulpit and an attractive doorway. Adjacent is th *Kitchen*, with a large central chimney.

Leaving the cathedral by the N. Door, we soon reach the ramparts (fine views of the Arga valley), which we may follow to the l. as far as the *Pta. de Francia* (or Zumalacarregui) of 1553, the last survivor of the 16C town gates.

By turning half-l, at the N. end of the C. de la Chapitela (see above) we reach the Baroque *Ayuntamiento* (1741). Behind is 16C *Sto. Domingo*, with a good retablo mayor, and brick cloister. Beside this is the *Col. de S. Juan* (1734) housing the *Museo Histórico*, with mementoes of the Carlist Wars.

A short distance N.W. of the Ayuntamiento is the **Museo de Navarra**, with good archaeological and ethnological collections, carved capitals from the Romanesque cathedral, paintings (14–18C) including *Goya's* portrait of the Marqués de San Adrián, armour, etc.

From the Ayuntamiento a street leads S.W. to *S. Saturnino*, (13–14C), on the spot where St Saturninus or Sernin is said to have baptized 40,000 pagan citizens of Pamplona. The N. door, with a Last Judgement in relief, is its most remarkable feature.

The C. Mayor leads from S. Saturnino to the *Paseo de Taconera*, passing the 18C doorway of the Carmelite church. In *S. Lorenzo* is a statue of S. Fermín. The C. de Eslava (l.), leads to the Pl. S. Francisco, in which is the *Cámara de Comptos* (c. 1364), the royal treasury.

S.E. of the Pl. del Castillo stands the *Plaza de Toros*, S. of which the new town, laid out on a regular plan, is bisected by the Av. de Carlos III (leading from the Pl. del Castillo to the Pl. Conde de Rodezno) and the Av. del Gen. Franco, the main road to Bayonne (N 121). These intersect at the Pl. del Gen. Mola, the latter extending W. to the Pl. del Príncipe de Viana, from which roads to San Sebastián, Logroño, Jaca, and Zaragoza may be reached.

FROM PAMPLONA TO (47 km.) RONCESVALLES AND (28 km. beyond) ST-JEAN-PIED-DE-PORT. This mountain road (C 135) ascends the Arga valley viâ (6 km.) *Huarte*, with a church containing a marble Virgin, Parisian work of the early 14C, given to the town in 1349, (11 km.) *Urdániz*, with a 13C church, and (3 km.) *Zubiri*, with a Roman Bridge. We cross a ridge and descend to *Erro*. The road goes on through *Viscarret* and *Espinal*, formerly halting-places for pilgrims to Compostela.—At 22 km., just before *Burguete*, with old houses, a side road runs 7 km. S.E. to *Garralda*, noted for its trout, and *Arive*, in the Irati valley, while from Burguete the C 127 runs S. 26 km. to *Aóiz*, passing (16 km.) *Arce*, with a Romanesque church.

5 km. **Roncesvalles** (*Roncevaux*), a hamlet surrounding a restored Augustinian abbey founded by Sancho the Strong of Navarre (c. 1230). The zinc-roofed church contains Sancho's tomb and that of his wife, Clemencia, valuable reliquaries, and a 13C Virgin. The cloisters were rebuilt after a fire in 1400. In the treasury are a Flemish triptych, a pair of 16C slippers, a gold-embroidered Cope given by St Elizabeth, Queen of Portugal, and a Holy Family by *Morales*.—Opposite the abbey is the *Cap. del Espíritu Santo* of the 12C, altered in the 15th. Here are also the parish church of *Santiago* and an ancient church known as *Itzandegula*, now a hay-barn.

It was in the Pass of Roncesvalles in 778 that the rearguard of Charlemagne's retreating army, led by Roland, was cut off and overwhelmed with rocks hurled by the Basques from the crags above. Louis the Debonair, in 810, preserved his army from a like fate by forcing the wives and children of the peasantry to accompany him through the defile. The Black Prince led his troops this way in Feb. 1367 to the battle of Nájera or Navarrette; and in 1813 Soult attempted to relieve Pamplona after forcing his way through the pass.

At the summit of the *Pass of Roncesvalles* or *Pto. de Ibañeta* (3648 ft) are remains of the early chapel of *S. Salvador*, and thence we descend the defile of the Nive to (17 km.) *Valcarlos*, beyond which is the Spanish custom house. Crossing the Nive by the Pte. de Arneguy we enter France and shortly reach *St-Jean-Pied-de-Port*.

Leaving Pamplona by the N 121, at 5 km. we take the r. fork—the l. leads to Jaca and Huesca, see Rte 16B—and beyond *Noain* we pass an 18C *Aqueduct* by Ventura Rodríguez, which crosses the Rio Elorz on the site of a Roman bridge.—At 7 km. we bypass (l.) *Tiebas*, with a Trans. church and ruins of a 13C castle.—In the hills to the E. is the 12C Romanesque chapel of *Sto. Cristo de Catalain*.—At 10 km. the road bypasses the twin villages of *Garinoain* and *Barasoain*, both containing ancient houses.

10 km. **Tafalla** (9700 inhab.; *Hotel*), an ancient capital known as 'La Flor de Navarra', dominated by the fortress of *Sta Lucía*; little remains of the 15C palace of the kings of Navarre, but there are several mansions,

and in *Sta María*, a Renaissance retablo carved by *Miguel de Ancheta*; while in the *Conv. de la Concepción* is a retablo from La Oliva by *Rolam de Moys*.

A road leads N.W. to (11 km.) **Artajona** (1800 inhab.), an impressive medieval town with a remarkable circuit of walls and tall square towers known as *El Cerco*; mid-13C fortified *S. Saturnino*, with a sculptured front and a 15C retablo; *S. Pedro*, with a Trans. porch; and the 17C chapel of *N.S. de Jerusalén*, containing a Byzantine Virgin of enamelled copper brought back from the Crusades by a companion of Godfrey of Bouillon, are of interest.

To the E. of Tafalla, the C 132 runs to (10 km.) *San Martín de Unx*, with old walls, in whose Gothic church there survives an earlier Crypt.—9 km. beyond is the hilltop village of **Ujué** with the late 14C fortified church of *Sta María* preserving earlier apses (c. 1089 and c. 1150) and containing a 12C Virgin and Child of silver plates on wood, and the heart of Carlos II of Navarre (d. 1387), who had been responsible for the great nave of a single wide span. The tower commands an extensive view.

6 km. **Olite** (2900 inhab.) with the principal *Castle* (c. 1400–19) of the kings of Navarre, an imposing rambling ruin, with many tall square towers (restored) and housing a *Parador Nac.* In addition to huge vaulted halls, it once possessed a roof garden, a lions' den, and an aviary. *S. Pedro* is a 12C church with a Romanesque portal and cloister and Gothic spire; *Sta María la Real* preserves a richly sculptured portal and remains of a cloister (14C), a splendid 15C retablo, and an organ of c. 1780, its case conforming to the shape of the vault.

At 16 km., the C 124 leads E. along the bank of the Aragón to (9 km.) *Santacara*, commanded by a Roman tower, and (8 km.) *Carcastillo* close to the famous Cistercian *Abbey of **La Oliva**. Founded in 1134 and built in 1164–98, the church with its pointed arches is regarded as the earliest example of Gothic style in Spain. There is a 13C Chapter house and 15C cloister. The monastery has been restored and re-occupied by the Cistercian Order. Note the sculpted band above the main door, and the capitals in its austere interior.

We soon cross the Aragón and pass *Caparrosa*, with an 11C castle, while the hill-top church of *Santa Fé* has a ruined Gothic nave and a 16C Mudéjar tower.—The road now traverses the deserted region of the Bárdenas Reales, reaching crossroads at 20 km. The new main road continues ahead, and after crossing the Ebro meets, at 9 km., the Logroño-Zaragoza road (N 232), where we turn l. for (19 km.) *Tudela*, see below.

By bearing l. at these crossroads we may follow the old road viâ *Valtierra*, with ruins of a castle, ancient houses, and cave dwellings, to (6 km.) *Arguedas*, where the church of *S. Miguel* is a converted mosque. The district is rich in prehistoric sites, and by-roads lead N.E. to the chapel of *N.S. del Yugo* and the ruined castle of Doña Blanca de Navarra.—To the E. just beyond Arguedas, are the remains of a Roman town. At (6 km.) *Murillo de las Limas* is Romanesque *N.S. de la Huerta*.

14 km. **TUDELA** (23,400 inhab.; *Hotel*), stands at the head of a curious 13C *Bridge* over the Ebro with 17 irregular arches, and formerly fortified.

The second city of Navarre, Tudela's origins go back to a remote past; taken by the Moors in 716, it was reconquered by Alfonso I of Aragón in 1114 and passed to Navarre in the reign of his successor. It was the last place in Spanish Navarre to yield to Fernando the Catholic in 1512. Among its natives were the poet Judah Ha-Levi (c. 1075-after 1140); the Jewish traveller Benjamin of Tudela (1127–73); Sancho VII (the Strong) of Navarre, and Miguel Servet (Michael Servetus; 1511-53), forerunner of Harvey in the discovery of the circulation of the blood.

The *Colegiata*, built in 1194–1234, is an attractive early Gothic church, with a W. Door of 1260 whose 116 sculptured groups depict the Last Judgement. Internally well proportioned, the church has important contents; a *retablo mayor* (1489–94) painted by *Pedro Díaz* of Oviedo; 16C *choir stalls* by *Étienne d'Obray*; a Baroque altarpiece in the chapel of Sta Ana; and a 13C Statue of the Virgin, by the S.E. pier of the crossing. The S. chapel of the transept, *Cap. de la Esperanza*, closed by a 15C reja, houses the Tomb of the Chancellor Fr. de Villaespesa (d. 1422) and his wife, by *Jean de Lomme* of Tournai, and two painted retablos (15C) of 28 and 21 panels. On the S. side of the church is a Romanesque *Cloister* with admirably carved capitals, containing the tomb of Don Fernando, son of Sancho 'el Fuerte' (the Strong), and remains of a 9C mosque.

Nearby is the *Ayuntamiento*, with notable archives, and the 18C painted travelling coach of the Marqués de S. Adrián. Close to the Colegiata, at No. 13 C. de Sáinz, is the Renaissance *Casa del Almirante*; among other mansions are Nos. 3, 9 and 29. At the N. end of the street is *S. Nicolás*, where Sancho the Strong lay from 1234 until his reburial at Roncesvalles. Largely rebuilt c. 1733, the church retains a 12C carved tympanum and interesting retablos. At the head of the bridge is *La Magdalena* (13–16C) with a sculptured door (c. 1200), a Romanesque tower, and a 16C retablo.

To the S.E. of the Colegiata are the picturesque C. del Portal and, at No. 10 in the C. de Magallón, the *Pal. of the Marqués de S. Adrián*, with a Renaissance patio and superb staircase. Other buildings of interest are the Plateresque *Bishop's Palace* next to the Colegiata, the *Hospital* (1549), and *S. Jorge*, with Baroque retablos. Among many mansions now shops or tenements, No. 14 C. Villanueva may be noted.

For the road from Tudela to *Soria*, see p. 118.

For a detour to *Tarazona* and *Veruela*, p. 119.

Beyond Tudela the Moncayo massif is seen on the r. Following the N 232 we pass (4 km. l.) *Fontellas*, with the 16C church of *S. Carlos Borromeo*, and at *El Bocal del Rey* (l.) is the intake of the Imperial Canal from the Ebro, begun in 1528, with a palace of Carlos V.—18 km., l. *Cortes*, with a castle-palace of the Dukes of Granada.

At 6 km., a road (l.) leads 6 km. to *Gallur*, with a conspicuous church tower, and (8 km.) *Tauste*, see p. 191.

Entering Aragón, we pass (18 km.) *Pedrola*, where in the palace of the Duke of Villahermosa, Don Quixote and Sancho Panza were entertained; while at nearby *Alcalá de Ebro* occurred the adventure of the enchanted barque.—8 km. l. *Alagón*, with an octagonal brick tower to its parish church, and *S. Antonio de Padua*, with a variegated brick dome.—10 km. l. *Utebo*; *Sta María* is a Mudéjar work begun in 1514 by *Antonio de Sariñena*, with a brick tower and glazed tiles finished in 1544 by *Alonzo de Loznes*. We shortly reach the outskirts of **Zaragoza**, see Rte. 17.

4   FROM PAMPLONA TO SORIA

A   Viâ Logroño

Total distance, 198 km. (123 miles). N, 111; 44 km. **Estella**—48 km. **Logroño**—106 km. **Soria.**

The road from Logroño to Soria viâ the Pto de Piqueras is often snowbound for some months during the Winter, and it is as well to check before setting out.

As far as Logroño this forms part of the principal medieval pilgrimage road to *Santiago de Compostela*, which entered Spain by St-Jean-Pied-de-Port and Roncesvalles, see p.111. At Estella it was joined by another important route from the Somport Pass, which ran W. from Jaca through Sangüesa and Tafalla, see pp.190; 194. From Logroño it bore W. to Burgos see p.116.

An ALTERNATIVE ROAD FROM PAMPLONA TO ESTELLA (47 km.), reached by turning l. off the San Sebastián road (N 240) soon after crossing the Arga, runs N. of and parallel to the main route.—6 km. *Arazuri*, with a castle, and Trans. church containing an enamelled Romanesque Crucifix.—2 km. *Ororbia*, with a Gothic church retaining fine retablos and a 16C Cross. We pass *Ibero*, where Roman mosaics have been found, and (4 km.) *Echauri*, with several tower-houses, before the road climbs to the Pto. de Echauri, with retrospective views of Pamplona and the Pyrenees beyond.—On the r., at *Salinas de Oro*, stands the castle of the Dukes of Granada. At 28 km., after passing (l.) the Embalse de Alloz, we reach *Abárzuza*, 2 km. N.W. of which lies the Cistercian Abbey of *Iranzu*, mainly 12–13C. Parts of the ruined buildings (over-restored), including the church, chapterhouse, cloister and kitchen, have been re-occupied.—7 km., *Estella*, see below.

We leave Pamplona by the N 111. At (5 km.) *Cizur Mayor* are ruins of a 12C castle and a church containing a fine retablo and verja, 4 km. W. of which, at *Gazolaz*, is a curious Romanesque church of c. 1100.—5 km. *Astrain* with the Sanctuary of *N.S. del Perdón*. The road crosses the Sierra del Perdón and the country becomes mountainous before we descend into the Arga valley.—At 10 km. a turning (l.) leads 2 km. to *Obanos*, with old mansions, while 2 km. further at *Muruzábal*, stands a Renaissance palace and the 12C octagonal Templar church of *Sta María* at *Eunate*, surrounded by a cloister arcade.

3 km. *Puente la Reina* (2000 inhab.; *Hotel*), with an old main street, retains some 13C walls, and the churches of *Santiago* (12, 15, and 18Cs), with a good porch, Romanesque *S. Pedro*, the ruins of *La Trinidad*, and the Templar church of *Del Crucifijo* (c. 1150, rebuilt 15C), and a medieval *Bridge* over the Arga.

A road runs S.E. viâ *Artajona* to (24 km.) *Tafalla*, passing (7 km. r.) *Mendigorria*, with an old bridge and imposing church with a good tower.

4 km. *Mañeru*, with ancient senorial houses and neo-classic *S. Pedro*, with a fine tower. In the district are several Romanesque chapels.—2 km. *Cirauqui*, with *Sta Catalina* and *S. Román*, the latter having a richly carved doorway. To the l. are remains of a Roman road and bridge.—8 km. *Villatuerta*, with Romanesque *S. Miguel*.

7 km. **ESTELLA** (1385 ft; 11,300 inhab.), the ancient *Gabala*, residence of the kings of Navarre throughout the Middle Ages, and Carlist H.Q. during the civil wars of 1833–39 and 1872–76. It contains several fine churches, particularly *S. Pedro de la Rua*, S.W. beyond the bridge over the Ega, with a 12C front in the style of Poitou, a half-ruined Romanesque cloister, and a 12C bronze crozier with Limoges enamels in the treasury. Also outstanding among the Romanesque churches is *S.

Miguel; the doorway has a carved tympanum and original doors with 12C wrought ironwork; the retablo is by *Martín Periz* (1406). *S. Juan Bautista*, in the Pl. de los Fueros, has a Romanesque N. Porch and contains the 13C Virgen de las Antorchas, a large retablo mayor and other Baroque retablos.

Sta María Jus del Castillo retains its Romanesque apse, while the Gothic doorway (1328) of derelict *Sto Sepulcro* survives below the ruined *Conv. de Sto Domingo* (13C) on the r. bank of the Ega. Also worth visiting are the *Capuchin Convent*, the 12C chapel of *N.S. de Rocamadour*, and on a height above the town, *N.S. del Puy*, containing a 13C Virgin and a painted coffer. Later religious houses include 17C *S. Benito* and *Sta Clara*, and the 18C *Monjas Recoletas*. The *Audiencia, formerly the palace of the Dukes of Granada de Ega, is one of the most remarkable 12C buildings to survive in Europe. The *Ayuntamiento* (1571) and the Renaissance *Pal. of the Counts of S. Cristóbal*, are noteworthy among the mansions which range from the 14th to the 18C. The old *Judería* contains some picturesque alleys.

THE SALVATIERRA ROAD RUNS N.W. from Estella, to the r. of which at (16 km.) *Zudaire*, are the ruins of the castle of *Gollano* (1473), while 6 km. W. of Zudaire is the picturesque village of *Eulate*, with a ruined palace, close to several stalactite caves.

To the S., the C 123 runs to (36 km.) *Lodosa* on the Ebro, with a large church and ancient houses, from which, at 9 km., a side road (r.) leads to *Dicastillo*, whose church preserves a figure of the Virgin, a retablo, and woodwork from the monastery of Irache.—From (4 km.) *Allo*, with old mansions, another road (l.) leads down the valley of the Ega to (10 km.) *Lerín*, where the church of 1572 has a good brick tower, interesting choir-stalls, and tombs of the Dukes of Alba.

We pass, 3 km. W. of Estella, the monastery of **N.S. de Irache**, a foundation of c. 1200 which sheltered a University until 1833. The church is of Transitional Gothic with Romanesque apses and has a remarkable *media-naranja* Cupola, like that at Zamora, over the crossing, interesting tombs, and a Plateresque cloister.—At 3 km. a road leads to *Igúzquiza* (2 km. N.W.) with a *Pal. of the Marqués de Vessolla*, while after 4 km. *Villamayor* is seen on the r. with the ruins of the castle of *Monjardín* on an eminence.

10 km. **Los Arcos** (1500 inhab.; *Hotel*), with a picturesque plaza surrounded by brick houses, entered through a 17C gateway. In the imposing church of *La Asunción*, which has a 15C cloister, are a Baroque retablo, a 14C Virgin of French style, a very beautiful organ, possibly by Juan Otorel, and interesting paintings and woodwork.—To the r. a road runs to (9 km.) *Sorlada* and the sanctuary of *S. Gregorio Ostiense*, a 17C basilica with a Baroque portal, and retablos by *Lucas de Salazar*.—Our road now traverses a group of towns known as LAS CINCO VILLAS DE SANSOL, of which the first is (6 km. l.) *El Busto*, in whose church is a notable Romanesque crucifix. To the r. is *Torres de Sansol*, or *del Río*, with the octagonal Templars' church of *El Sepulcro*, Romanesque, with a Mudéjar dome (late 12C).

A road leads to (29 km. N.W.) *Santa Cruz de Campezo* (p.128) viâ (10 km.) *Azuelo*, with a church of the first half of the 12C.

12 km. **Viana**, (3200 inhab.), formerly of some importance as the capital of a principality formed in 1423 by Carlos III of Navarre as the appanage of the heirs to the throne, retains many old mansions, ruins of its walls, and the *Torre de S. Pedro*. In *Sta María*, restored in the 16C,

was buried Cæsar Borja, slain in a petty skirmish in 1507; his tomb has been violated. The magnificent Renaissance Portal was begun in 1549 by *Juan de Goyaz* and completed by *Juan Ochoa de Arranótegui* in 1567. The town gave his title to the Prince of Viana (1421–61), son of Juan II of Aragón (Juan I of Navarre).—8 km, *Oyón* (*Hotel*), 3 km. r., has an Isabelline church with a good portal and an 18C tower.

2 km. **LOGROÑO** (1275 ft; 96,500 inhab.; 28,000 in 1920; *Hotels*), the Roman *Julia Briga*, stands on the river Ebro near the junction of Old Castile, the Basque province of Álava, and Navarre, and has recently attracted some light industry, which has not improved its appearance.

It is the centre of the wine-growing district of *La Rioja*, taking its name from the Rio Oja, which flows into the Tirón just above Haro. It also produces cereals and olive oil. Logroño was the birthplace of the painter Juan Fernández Navarrete (1526–79; nicknamed 'El Mudo', the Dumb), and Martín Zurbano (1788–1845), the guerrilla leader. Gen. Espartero (1792–1879) also resided here after his marriage to a local heiress.

Crossing the Ebro by the Pte. de Hierro (the iron bridge of 1884) we enter Logroño by the C. de Sagasta to reach the hub of the town, the Paseo del Espolón. To the E., downstream, is the stone bridge of 1770, and between the bridges on the S. bank an arch of the old bridge, built in 1138 by S. Juan de Ortega. To the W. of the iron bridge is *Santiago el Real*, with a wide and lofty single nave of the early 16C, containing a good Gothic sculpture of the Virgin, while near the stone bridge stands *Sta María del Palacio*, founded in the 11C, rebuilt at the end of the 12th, and in the 16th enlarged. The 13C spired tower is known as the *Aguja del Palacio*; it contains the image of N.S. de la Antigua, and a Renaissance retablo by *Arnao de Bruselas*. The restored Gothic cloister has 17C frescoes by *José Vexes*.—Further S. is *S. Bartolomé* (early 13C) with a W. Doorway (14C) of Franco-Navarrese style, a 17C brick tower, and noteworthy tombs.

To the S.W., in the C. del Gen. Mola, stands **Sta María la Redonda**, a hall-church (15–16C) with star vaults springing from tall shafts without capitals, and side-chapels between the buttresses in the Catalan fashion.

Later additions have been made at both ends: the *Gran Cap.* or *Redonda* (1742–60), to the W., has a Churrigueresque portal between twin towers by *Martín de Beratúa* (1769) while at the E. end is the tomb of Espartero. In the *Cap. de la Cruz*, r. of the S. door, is the Renaissance monument of Diego Ponce de León; there are some fine wrought-iron verjas, a figure of the Magdalen of the school of Juan de la Mena, and, in the Chapter House, a retablo by *Pantoja de la Cruz*.

Among the old mansions is the handsome Baroque palace once inhabited by Espartero, in the C. S. Agustin, which will house a Museum.

FROM LOGROÑO TO BURGOS (115 km.). We drive S.W. on the N 120, and at 11 km. by-pass *Navarrete*, a village of ancient houses. In the 16C church are a retable in Churrigueresque style, a Flemish triptych and goldsmiths' work. Of *Sto Sepulcro* there remains a good Trans. doorway.—15 km. **Nájera** (5600 inhab.; *Hotel*), has a ruined castle, and the church of *Sta María la Real*, once a burial-place of the royal house of Navarre, where Fernando III was crowned in 1217. The church (cons. 1056) was rebuilt in 1422–53; the *coro* (1495) is delicately carved and there are good retablos. The most important tomb is that of Blanca, queen of Sancho III (1157–58); the cloister dates from 1517–28. To the N.E. of Nájera took place the battle of 1367 in which the Black Prince helped Pedro the Cruel to regain his throne by defeating Enrique de Trastamara and his ally Du Guesclin.

FROM NÁJERA TO SALAS DE LOS INFANTES (94 km.). The C 113, a mountain road, climbs S.W. between the Sierra de la Demanda (r., 6995 ft) and the Sierra de Urbión, following for the main part the valley of the Najerilla.

At 5 km. a road (r.) leads 12 km. S.W. to **San Millán de la Cogolla**, with a Benedictine abbey founded in 537, rebuilt on its present site in 1554, and known for its magnificence as the 'Escorial de la Rioja'. The retablo of the hall-church (1504–40), by *Juan Rizi*, depicts the life and miracles of S. Millán (d. c. 564), and the chest in which his ashes were preserved is shown.—Near by, at a higher level, the more interesting Mozarabic church of ***S. Millán de Suso** (923–29), partly dug out of the mountainside, contains the tombs of the Infantes de Lara. Gonzalo de Berceo (?1190–?1264), the earliest known Castilian poet, was a native of Nájera and a priest at S. Millán.—Hence a road leads 19 km. N.W. to *Santo Domingo de la Calzada* (see below), passing at 5 km. near the Cistercian nunnery of *Sta María de Cañas*, founded in 1171, begun in 1236, but only a presbytery and transepts were built, with a vaulted chapter house containing the fine tomb of the Abbess Urraca López de Haro (c. 1260).

Continuing S. on the C 113 we pass (15 km.) *Anguiano*, with a good church, while at 9 km. a by-road diverges r. 5 km. to the Benedictine monastery of *Valvanera*, reconstructed since 1883, with an over-restored 11C carved Virgin.— At 12 km. a road leads l. to the pretty villages of *Viniegra de Abajo* and (12 km.) *de Arriba*.— 18 km. *Canales de la Sierra*, with a Romanesque church.—We cross the Pto. el Collado and at 35 km. enter *Salas de los Infantes* on the Burgos-Soria road (N 234) see Rte 22. For *Santo Domingo de Silos* (22 km. S.W.), see p.232.

20 km. **Santo Domingo de la Calzada** (5600 inhab.; *Parador Nac.*), is dominated by its ***Cathedral**, begun in 1168 by Alfonso VIII and finished in 1235, with a detached Baroque *Belfry* (1762–67) by *Martín Beratúa* beside the ancient chapel of *N.S. de la Plaza*, S. of the Cathedral. The remarkable *W. Doorway* has seven orders of mouldings carried round the arch without capitals.

Entering by the S. Door, we see the shrine (1513–17) of the saint (a local hermit) beneath the enormous vault of the transept, enlarged when the presbytery was reconstructed in 1529 by *Juan Rasines* to the designs of *Felipe Vigarní*. The 13C vaults of the nave have ridge-ribs, suggesting English influences. The retablo mayor of carved walnut (1537–41) was the last work of *Damián Forment*, while the stallwork of the coro was made (from 1531) by *Andrés de Nájera* after patterns by Guillén de Holanda. There is a Plateresque screen of 1517 to the chapel of *La Magdalena*, and several other chapels contain retablos of interest. Further chapels surround the *Cloister* (c. 1380) and by the door of the *Chapter House* is a monument recording the heart-burial of Enrique de Trastamara, who died here in 1379. Within are two triptychs of the late 15C, one Flemish, the other German. The great curiosity of the Cathedral is the chamber opening from the W. wall of the S. transept, and closed by a grille, in which are kept a live cock and hen killed and replaced each May 12th, in remembrance of a miracle in which a youth's innocence was proved by a roasted cock crowing on the table.

Beside the Cathedral is the *Hosp. del Santo*, a hostelry built for the reception of pilgrims to Compostela. At the W. end of the town lies the *Conv. de S. Francisco*, built in the 16C by Juan de Herrera; the church contains a stone retablo and the alabaster tomb (1587) of the founder, Padre Bernardo de Fresneda, confessor of Philip II. In the *Conv. de Bernardas* is a tomb of the Manso de Zúñiga family. Remains of the town walls and towers built in 1367 by Pedro el Cruel can be seen here, and also ancient houses.

14 km. S. lies *Escaray* (*Hotel*), a summer resort at the foot of the Cerro de S. Lorenzo (5990 ft), with several retablos in its 15C Gothic church.—19 km. N. of Santo Domingo lies *Haro*, see p. 129.—*Bañares*, 5 km. N.E. of Santo Domingo, contains Romanesque *Santa Cruz*, and *Sta María*, with a Gothic nave.

At 6 km. we pass *Grañón*, with remains of walls and the castle of *Mira-Villa*, and at 6 km. and 10 km. respectively the churches of *Castildelgado* and *Belorado* contain Gothic retablos. *Belorado* retains an arcaded plaza and remains of walls and gates.—11 km. *Villafranca Montes de Oca* has a good parish church and two chapels.—At 15 km. a road leads r. 4 km. to *S. Juan de Ortega*, whose church (c. 1138, restored in the 15C) encloses the saint's flamboyant shrine, surrounded by a nasty grill replacing the Plateresque verja. The marble of the district was once highly prized.—2 km. *Zalduendo*, 5 km. N. of which lies *Atapuerca*, where in 1057 García of Navarre was killed in battle by his brother Fernando I of Castile. 19 km. **Burgos**, see Rte 20 A.

Leaving Logroño, the N 111 ascends the valley of the Iregua.—At 5 km. a road leads l. to (12 km.) *Clavijo*, site of the victory of Ramiro I over the Moors in 844, and famous for a legendary apparition of St. James, 'Santiago Matamoros', and preserving ruins of its castle.—At 10 km. a road leads r. to (6 km.) *Entrena*, with a good 16C church. We pass an ancient bridge at *Viguera* to reach (14 km., r.) *Torrecilla de Cameros*, whose parish church contains a fine triptych and embroidered pallium. It was the birthplace of Práxedes Sagasta (1827–1903), founder of the Spanish Liberal party. In the neighbourhood are the chapel of *N.S. de Tómalos* and the stone-age *Cueva Lóbrega*.—At 13 km. a road leads 3 km. r. to picturesque *Ortigosa de Cameros*, while at 5 km. a side-road diverging W., leads 3 km. to *Villoslada de Cameros* in the Sierra de Freguela.

8 km. S.E. is the remote mountain chapel of *N.S. de Lomos de Orios.*—A circuitous road leads W. from Villoslada to (10 km.) *Montenegro de Cameros*, the starting point for climbs to the *Pico de Urbión* (7310 ft) and the adjacent *Laguna de Urbión*.

We climb in zigzags to (20 km.) the **Pto. de Piqueras** (5610 ft), in the austere Sierra Cebollera, often snowbound in winter months.—At 21 km. a road leads W. to the attractive village of *Sotillo del Rincón*, nestling beneath the S. slope of the Sierra Cebollera, passing *Tera*, with the *Pal. of the Marqués de Vadillo.*—11 km. *Garray*, with the Romanesque *Cap. de los Santos Mártires* (dated 1231); and in the parish church a 14C Florentine retablo.

Hence a side-road climbs to the excavated site of wind-swept **Numancia**, the Iberian city which resisted Scipio Aemilianus and his Roman legions for nearly a year (134–133 B.C.). Excavations have laid bare the regular plan of the city, but most of the antiquities discovered date from the Roman town which rose on the ruins of the Iberian, beneath which are traces of a still older prehistoric settlement.

7 km. **Soria**, see Rte 29.

B   Viâ Tafalla and Ágreda

Total distance, 189 km. (118 miles). N 121, 93 km. **Tudela**—21 km. **Tarazona**—N 122, 20 km. **Ágreda**—55 km. **Soria**. An alternative and more direct route (179 km.)—but missing Tudela and Tarazona—may be followed by forking r. at 76 km. on to the C 101, which regains the N 122 just N.E. of Ágreda, see p. 120; and for the route **Tafalla**—*Arnedo*—**Soria**.

We follow the same road as that of Rte 3 as far as (93 km.) *Tudela* (see p. 112), where we bear S.W., still on the N 121, and after 9 km. pass (r.)

Cascante, ancient *Cascantum*. A curious covered way leads to *N.S. del Romero* (17C), while Plateresque *La Asunción* contains a retablo of 1596 carved by *Pedro González de San Pedro* of the school of Miguel Ancheta.—3 km. *Tulebras*, with the oldest convent of Cistercian nuns in Spain, founded in 1215.—3 km. beyond is *Monteagudo*, with a brick church tower, and a centre of Roman ruins and prehistoric sites.

6 km. **TARAZONA**, an ancient episcopal city (11,400 inhab.; *Hotel*), famous among the Romans as *Turiaso*, where a handful of Romans defeated a Celtiberian army. Reconquered from the Moors in 1118 by Alfonso I of Aragón, it remained a frontier town of importance and a royal residence until the 15C; here Card. Cisneros was consecrated Abp. of Toledo in 1495.

The **Cathedral* built in 1152–1235, enlarged and reconstructed between 1361 and 1500, is surmounted by a curious *lantern* (1543–45) of patterned brick by *Juan Botero*; the *Cloisters* (1504–29) are likewise a remarkable example of brickwork, as is the Mudéjar S.W. Tower, begun c. 1500 by *Ali el Darocano* and finished in 1588.

Internally, the brick nave with its star-vaulting is a fine specimen of Aragonese style, and the details are well designed. The Cap. Mayor (1560) contains a retablo of 1603. The side chapels have some notable tombs of the 16C; that of *Santiago* has a painted retablo (1497), and that of *La Purificación* (adjacent) one by *Martín Bernat* (1493) and a reja (1505) by *Guillén de Turena*. The 1st chapel of the N. Ambulatory contains a painted retablo of 1462 and two Gothic alabaster tombs. The *Library* is rich in illuminated MSS.

On the hill S. of the cathedral is the *Conv. de Sta Ana* with a Renaissance N. door. To the N.W. is the *Pal. of the Counts of Algira*, and further on the old *Pl. de Toros*, now converted into dwellings but retaining its three arcaded and balconied stages above the arena. By this stands the 16C brick chapel of *N.S. del Río*, with strange cupolas. *S. Francisco* (13C), has a single nave and brick steeple, late Gothic stellar vaulting, Renaissance side chapels, and a good retablo mayor.

Most of the old city is on the opposite bank of the Queiles, dominated by the Mudéjar tower of *La Magdalena*, which has a Romanesque E. end. Above is *S. Atilano*, whose street front is a remarkable work of the Renaissance. The adjoining *Bishop's Palace* (14–15C) was formerly the Alcázar of the Kings of Aragón. Not far off is late Gothic *La Concepción*, and on the top of the hill that of *S. Miguel* (early 16C), with another brick belfry and Plateresque retablos. *La Merced*, nearby, is of the 17C. Half way up the hill is the 16C **Ayuntamiento*, with decoration in high relief and a frieze of figures running the whole length of the building, representing the taking of Granada.

10 km. S.E. of Tarazona—the landscape dominated by the massive *Sierra del Moncayo* (see below)—a road leads r. off the the N 122 for 6 km. to the fortified **Abbey of Veruela*, one of the oldest Cistercian houses in Spain (1171–1224), with an early Gothic church and chapter house, and 14C cloisters. There is a remarkable Baroque door to the sacristy. The abbey, now a Jesuit College, contains a small museum.—The road goes on to *Añón*, with a notable castle, whence the Moncayo may be climbed.—Another ruined castle (15C) stands at *Trasmoz*, N.W. of Veruela.

The N 122 continues S.E. to (13 km.) *Borja*, with the ruined castle of the Borja family, which after migrating to Játiva in the 14C, acclimatised itself in Italy as the Borgias. An old palace is under restoration here.—6 km. beyond lies *Magallón*, with two Mudéjar churches, *St. Domingo* and *S. Francisco*.—The N 232 is reached 8 km. beyond, some 45 km. W. of Zaragoza.

Our route climbs S.W. from Tarazona to (20 km., l.) **Ágreda**, (3600 inhab.), Iberian *Ilurci* and Roman *Graecubis*, an old frontier town, dominated by the *Castillo de la Muela*. It retains fragments of Moorish walls, with a horseshoe-arched gateway (mid-10C), a bridge of a single arch, picturesque remains of the *Judería*, and the Barrio de los Castejones with a medieval watch-tower and ruined palaces. The 12C *Pal. de los Castejones* in the C. Tudor is crowned with brick towers, and near the Pta. de Añaviejo is another fortified tower.

N.S. de la Peña (1193) has twin naves and painted retablos, one Aragonese of the 14C; another of five panels of the mid-15C; and later remains of a fine example of the Valencian school. *S. Miguel* (15C) retains its Romanesque tower; the cap. mayor, with its Plateresque retablo, is of 1519; that of Sta Ana dates from the late 14C. *S. Juan* (15C) has a Baroque high altar and Gothic and Plateresque retablos. *N.S. de Magaña* has three naves with fine Gothic ribbed vaults, a 15C retablo, and a Romanesque font. *N.S. de los Milagros* (16C) preserves a polychromed 'black' Virgin of the 14C, and 15C Aragonese retablos.

In the *Conv. de la Concepción*, S. of the town, is the tomb of Sor María (1602–65), mystic and valued adviser of Philip IV, who visited her in 1643 and corresponded with her on state affairs for twenty-two years, although it is now assumed that she was merely acting as the mouthpiece of her Franciscan confessor!

Ágreda is a centre for the ascent of **Sierra del Moncayo** (7600 ft), with fine views of the Pyrenees. The journey on horseback by the direct mule-track takes some 5 hrs. to the sanctuary of *N.S. del Moncayo* (open mid-June–mid-Sept.), where there is a hostelry. From the sanctuary to the summit is a climb of c. 1½ hr.—An alternative route is by car to *Cueva de Ágreda*, 6 km. from the summit, which can be scaled in about 3 hrs.

At 4 km. a road leads 2 km. l. to *Muro de Ágreda*, with Roman walls and a Romanesque church.—At 5 km. another leads r. 16 km. to the village of *Magaña*, with a 13C castle, and panoramic views.—The N 122 continues to ascend the bleak and stony 'Parameras' to the Pto. del Madero before entering the basin of the Duero. We commence the gradual descent to (46 km.) *Soria*, see Rte 29.

From Pamplona to Soria viâ Citruénigo (184 km.). This alternative route bears r. at 74 km. S. of Pamplona, and after bridging the Ebro crosses the N 232 just S.E. of *Alfaro*.—At 15 km. we pass (2 km. r.) **Corella**, (6200 inhab.). *S. Miguel* dates from the 13C, and *N.S. del Rosario* from 1579; and the town contains many old mansions, notably the *Casa de las Cadenas*. In the *Benedictine nuns' church* (1671) is an Assumption by *Juan Ant. de Escalante*, and in that of the *Carmelite Fathers*, a series of patrician tombs.—5 km. *Citruénigo*, with the 16C church of *S. Juan Bautista*.

Hence we may visit, 6 km. up the Alhama valley, **Fitero**, with a church formerly the Cistercian abbey of *Sta. María la Real* (1152–1287). It contains important tombs, a square Chapter house of nine bays, and cloister (early 16C). In the Treasury is an ivory coffer of the 10C and a 13C enamelled reliquary.—The hot springs of *Los Baños de Fitero*, and cold springs of *Grávalos* lie to the W.—Regaining the C 101 we join the N 122 31 km. S. of *Citruénigo* and 4 km. N.E. of *Ágreda* (see above).

From Pamplona to Soria viâ Arnedo (183 km.). The road follows that of Rte 3 as far as (35 km.) *Tafalla* (see p.111), 3 km. beyond which we fork r. onto the C 115.—At 22 km. a road leads E. 4 km. to *Marcilla*, with a fine but over-restored castle, and remains of a monastery, c. 7 km. S. of which lies *Villafranca*, with Renaissance mansions.—12 km. The Moorish castle of *Milagro* lies 6 km. E.—We shortly cross the Ebro, and at 5 km. meet the N 232. Turning W. we continue on the C115 past (2 km.) *Aldeanueva de Ebro*, with a 16C retablo by *Pierre de Troas* (Troyes) and *Arnao de Bruselas* in the parish church.

20 km. **Arnedo**, an old town (10,900 inhab.; *Hotels*) with ruins of a castle, an aqueduct, and the church of *S. Tomás* (c. 1500).—*Quel*, 4 km. E., was the birthplace of the playwright Manuel Breton de los Herreras (1796–1873). 11 km. beyond is *Arnedillo*, with hot springs, lying at the foot of Mte. de la Encienta. In Jan. 1932 six demonstrating strikers were mown down here by the terrified

Guardia Civil in retaliation for the murder of five guards at Castilblanco in
Estremadura a week earlier. We follow the road up the valley of the Cicados.
32 km. *Yanguas*, with medieval walls, a Romanesque tower of 1146, Moorish
castle, and ancient houses, *S. Miguel* contains an elaborately carved altar-piece. At
(18 km. l.) *Oncala* are preserved ten Flemish tapestries (17C) from cartoons by
Rubens.—At 10 km. a road leads r. 10 km. to the picturesque village of *Narros*, and
6 km. beyond, *Suellacabras*, with a late Iron Age site, and the Visigothic cemetery
of *Los Castillares*.—At 16 km. we meet the N 111 from Logroño at *Garray*, passing
Numancia (see p.118), before descending to (7 km.) *Soria*, see Rte 29.

5 FROM SAN SEBASTIÁN TO BILBAO AND SANTANDER

Total distance, 226 km. (140 miles). N 1 for 7 km.—N 634, 19 km. *Zarauz*—10 km.
Zumaya—15 km. *Deva*—20 km. *Eibar*—18 km. *Durango*—30 km. **Bilbao**—33 km.
Castro Urdiales—26 km. *Laredo*—30 km. *Solares*—17 km. **Santander**.
Motorway. See description at the head of Rte 1. *Bilbao* may now be reached
from San Sebastián in approx. one hour, a very considerable saving of time, if that
is the consideration, but one will miss most of the places described below—except
for occasional plunging views—which are more easily approached from the 'old' N
364. There are sufficient exits, nevertheless, that at *Deva* being taken by those
wishing to follow the coast road thence. A continuation of the motorway, from
Bilbao to *Santander*, is projected.

Leaving San Sebastián by the Av. del Gen. Zumalacárregui, at 7 km.
we fork r. off the N 1 onto the N 634, and follow the wooded valley of the
Oria through the picturesque village of (3 km.) *Usurbil*, with the old
Casa de Soroa and *Pal. de Samaniego*.—10 km. *Orio*, a fishing village
with a curious 16C church; 8 km. S. at *Aya*, is another of the same
period.—Crossing the Altos de Orio we descend to (5 km.) **Zarauz**, a
fashionable resort (14,000 inhab.; *Hotels*), at the foot of Mte. Sta
Bárbara, with old houses in the C. Mayor, notably the *Torre Luzea*,
early 15C, with a half-ruined tower. In 18C *Sta María la Real* is a
Baroque retablo. Overlooking the W. end of the beach is the *Pal. del
Marqués de Narros* (15C) where Isabel II in 1868 received the news of
her deposition.—Hence a road climbs S.W. direct to (13 km.) *Cestona*,
see below.—The road now clings to the rocky coast and at 5 km. enters
Guetaría, another fishing village renowned for its cider, and connected
by a breakwater to the *Isla S. Antón*, known as the *Ratón* (mouse), with
attractive views of the coast. Here was born Juan Sebastián de Elcano
(d. 1526), whose ship, the first to circumnavigate the globe (1519–22),
was the sole survivor of Magellan's fleet of five. *S. Salvador* was largely
rebuilt c. 1429; the inner porch is of 1603–5, by *Domingo de
Cardaveraiz,* and in the interior are retablos carved in 1625 by *Domingo
de Goroa*. The tower, begun in 1526 to designs by *Pedro de Alzaga*, was
still unfinished in 1673.

At 5 km. we cross the Urola, at the mouth of which stands **Zumaya**, of
Roman foundation, a summer resort, (7200 inhab.), where Gothic *S.
Pedro* contains a wooden statue of the Virgin, a retablo by *Anchieta*,
and a triptych and paintings of the 15–16Cs; also worth visiting are the
basilica of *S. Telmo* and the chapel of *N.S. de Arritokieta*. Among the
fine mansions may be mentioned those of *Ubillos*, with a good patio,
Olozábal, and *Uriarte*.

Zumaya was the home of Ignacio Zuloaga (1870–1945). The *Villa Zuloaga* (E. of
the river) includes, besides the painter's house, the 12C chapel of *Santiago Echea*,
with a small cloister, a shrine visited by Compostelan pilgrims, and a museum
containing a selection of *Zuloaga*'s own works; five paintings by *El Greco*;

portraits by *Goya* of the Marquesa de Baena, of Gen. Palafox, and of the artist's brother; and two santas attrib. to *Zurbarán*.

FROM ZUMAYA TO ELGÓIBAR VIÂ AZPEITIA (34 km.). Soon after leaving the town the C 6317 bears S. past the spa of *Cestona*, with the imposing Gothic *Pal. de Alércia* or *Lili*, to (16 km.) **Azpeitia** (12,200 inhab.). In its 16C hall-church of *S. Sebastián* are the font at which S. Ignacio de Loyola was baptized (the silver cover of which was carried off by the French in 1794), and the tomb of Bp. Zurbano (d. 1510). Opposite is the 15C *Casa de Anchieta* with brick façades in the Moorish style. Other old houses are the *Casa de Emparán* and the *Casa de Bazozábal* beside the Urola, while the churches include 16C *N.S. de la Soledad*, and the *Conv. de la Concepción* with a Baroque retablo by *Azpiazu*. The composer Juan Anchieta (d. 1523) was born here.

Bearing W. we shortly pass the *Sanctuario de Loyola*, birthplace of Iñigo López Recalde (1491–1556), canonized as S. Ignacio in 1622, founder of the Jesuit Order, a society (in the words of Baretti), whose members were 'indefatigable accumulators of riches they do not want'. The so-called *Santa Casa*, a fragment of the tower-house (1387–1405) of the Loyola family, is entirely enclosed in the huge convent.

Over the entrance is an effigy of a bear; on the 1st floor is shown the room in which the saint was born; on the 2nd floor is the room (now the Chapel) where he recovered from the wounds received at Pamplona and where, due to the inactivity thus enforced, he began those studies which led to his great missionary project and the foundation of the order. The bold carvings and reliefs illustrating his life and the altar and decorations, are noteworthy. On the 1st floor is shown the chasuble of S. Francisco Borja, embroidered in 1551 by his sister, and on the 2nd floor are personal relics of S. Ignacio, and an 18C ceiling of gilded wood.—The large and overdecorated *Church* was designed by *Carlo Fontana* for Mariana of Austria, wife of Philip IV, and built in 1686–1738. It contains a good Cavaillé-Coll organ, as does the church at *Azcoitia* (see below).

5 km. **Azcoitia** (10,900 inhab.), where *Sta María la Real* has a retablo in its S. transept with eight paintings done at Seville in 1568. The *Pal. de Balda* includes an ancient tower-house; there are a number of other old mansions, and a fine *Ayuntamiento*.

By turning r. onto the C 6324 the main Bilbao road may be regained at (13 km.) *Elgóibar* (see below) after passing (r.) the village of *Madariaga*, and crossing the Alto de Azcarate.

At 9 km. we pass *Iciar*, a mountain village whose 14C church shelters a Plateresque retablo, attr. to *Araoz*, and a figure of the Virgin (?8C), venerated as the Patroness of Basque seafarers.—6 km. **Deva** (5000 inhab.; *Hotel*), attractively situated and built on a regular plan. *Sta María* has a fine 13C Portal, interesting retablos and tombs, and a graceful 15C cloister, but most of the church dates from the rebuilding completed in 1629 by *Juan Ortiz de Olaeta* to the plans of *Juan de Aróstegui*.

FROM DEVA TO BILBAO BY THE COAST ROAD (88 km.). Although offering many impressive vistas of land and seascapes, it should be emphasized that the winding road is narrow and hilly, and the going will be slow. Crossing the Rio Deva, we turn onto the C 6212 and shortly enter **Motrico** (5100 inhab.) named from the rocky spur (Basque *tricu*, hedgehog) that commands it, and surrounded by wooded hills. It was the birthplace of Adm. Churruca (1761–1805) who fell at Trafalgar. It is famous for its fruit, and for the cider and red *chacolí* wine of the district.—8 km. **Ondárroa** a fishing port (12,000 inhab.) with picturesque houses and a 14C church raised upon arcades.

From Ondárroa the C 6213 leads S.W. to Durango (29 km.), passing through (6 km.) *Berriatúa*, with the medieval tower-house of *Arancibia*, and close to the curious polygonal sanctuary of *S. Miguel de Arrichinaga*, before reaching (13 km.) *Marquina*, with a 16C hall-church containing a retablo that belonged to Charles V.—9 km. N.W. lies *Murélaga-Aulestia*, with a good crenellated tower-house.—At 3 km. the road forks, the r. fork leading to Guernica and Bilbao, viâ (2 km.) *Bolívar*, whose church contains a 14C wooden crucifix. The ancestors of the Liberator of South America took their name from this village.—*Cenarruza*, S.W. of Bolívar, has a noble collegiate church (c. 1380) and a cloister (mid-16C) by *Miguel de Zengoitia* and *Juan de Beznón*—The famous *Viewpoint known as the

Balcón de Vizcaya is c. 10 km. W. of Bolivar.—From Marquina, the Durango road zigzags across the hills to the E. of *Mte. Oiz* (3366 ft).

Hugging the rocky coast we reach (12 km.) **Lequeitio** (7100 inhab.; *Hotel*), another fishing village, with *Sta María* rebuilt in 1488–1508, and old houses, including the picturesque *Casa de Adán*. A fine single-arched *Bridge* spans the river.

A detour of 30 km. may be made by forking r. 3 km. W. of Lequeitio, following the hilly coast road through the fishing villages of *Ea* and *Elánchove*, with its old church of *S. Nicolás*; then the E. bank of the Ría de Guernica to regain the direct road from Lequeitio at *Arteaga*, with a 15C castle (partly restored by the Empress Eugénie).

At 19 km. we pass *Cortézubi*, near which is the *Cueva de Basondo* containing rock-paintings.—3 km. **Guernica** (17,500 inhab.) standing in the beautiful valley of the Mundaca, was the seat of the Basque Parliament until the repudiation of the *fueros* in 1876. Their meeting-place was beneath a venerable oak (the *'Guernikako Arbola'*, which gives name to the Basque national anthem, by José María de Iparraguirre), a fragment of which has been preserved alongside a younger tree sprung from one of its acorns. The town has been rebuilt since its deliberate devastation by German bombs on 26 April 1937, and is now of little interest. In the hall-church of *Sta María* (c. 1470–1518) is a chapel, enclosed by a grille, containing a fine statue of the Virgin.—The C 6313 now descends the l. bank of the Ría to (14 km.) **Bermeo** (17,800 inhab.), in which the *Torre de Ercilla*, survives, while in the church of *Sta Eufemia* the kings of Castile used to swear to uphold the 'fueros' of the Basques.—The coast road continues past the *Cabo de Machichaco*, to *Baquio*, with the castellated mansion of *Elizalde*, and *Plencia* (p. 125), but the C 6313 climbs inland to the Alto de Sollube and (18 km.) *Munguia*, with the tower of the *Pal. de Abajo* (1360) and Gothic *S. Pedro*.—14 km. **Bilbao**, see below.

From Deva, the N 634 turns inland along the valley to (13 km.) *Elgóibar*, preserving in its cemetery the 15C porch of a demolished church, 4 km. beyond which a road leads 13 km. S.E. to *Vergara*, see p. 99.—7 km. **Eibar**, an industrial town of 37,900 inhab. (*Hotel*), largely rebuilt since 1937, which has long been famous for damascened iron, as had the village of *Placencia*, to the S.E. The 17C church contains a retablo by *Araoz* and 15C bronze lecterns. It was the birthplace of the early Basque novelist, Juan Antonio Moguel y Urquiza (1745–1804).— We shortly enter Vizcaya, passing (10 km.) *Zaldivar*, with an old church.

2 km. *Olacueta*, where a road leads 6 km. S.E. to **Elorrio** (7900 inhab.; *Parador Nac.* projected), with numerous Renaissance mansions, and a hall-church (16C) containing the early tombs of the Arguineta (6–11C).—3 km. to the W. lies *Apatamonasterio*, with an old church, and further along the road to Durango, **Abadiano**, with the tower-house of *Muncharaz*, the Abbey of *S. Torcas*, and the *Pal. de Trana-Jaúregui*.

8 km. **Durango** (25,700 inhab.), birthplace of Fray Juan de Zumárraga (c. 1475–1548), the first bishop of Mexico. *S. Pedro de Tavira* is among the oldest churches in the Basque provinces, with a Plateresque retablo and two curious tombs. On its S. side is the arcaded *Market Hall*. The high altar in *Sta Ana* is by *Ventura Rodríguez* (1774) while Baroque *Sta María de Ulibarri* contains a richly ornamented coro (late 16C). A remarkable stone cross (c. 1442) stands in the suburb of *Crutziaga*.

FROM DURANGO TO VITORIA (40 km.). A picturesque road (C 6211) leads S. to *Izurza* and its medieval tower-house of *Echaburu*, at 10 km. climbing the mountains separating Vizcaya from Álava at the Pto. de Urquiola (views).—We pass (7 km.) *Ochandiano*, with the old church of *Sta Marina*, to meet the N 240 from Bilbao to Vitoria at (7 km.) *Villareal de Álava*, see p. 127.

The church of (10 km.) *Amorebieta*, with a Baroque steeple, rises picturesquely above the river Ibaizábal, while at 6 km., in industrial

Galdácano (24,100 inhab.), stands 13C *Sta María*, with a fine doorway and additions of c. 1500.—Approaching (14 km.) *Bilbao*, we may follow the road skirting the Nervión, or take the r. fork uphill—by-passing the old town—which then descends steeply from the N., crossing the river by Pte. Gen. Mola. Another approach road takes a wider circle and enters central Bilbao at the N. end of the Alameda de Recalde.

BILBAO (431,300 inhab.; 115,000 in 1920; *Hotels*), known to the Basques as *Ibaizábal* ('broad river'), is a thriving industrial town, its population having doubled during the last 25 years, while its port handles more traffic than any other in Spain. Much of its prosperity derives from the rich veins of hematite in which the surrounding countryside abounds, and from its position astride the navigable Nervión. It can hardly be credited that in the late 18C Bilbao was considered by William Bowles (see p.267), who had lived there for some years, to be 'one of the neatest towns in Europe'!

Having suffered greatly from bombardment and fire during the Carlist wars, old Bilbao offers little to interest the antiquary, but its natural situation is imposing. At one time the town lay entirely on the r. bank of the Nervión, but since 1874 the new quarter has eclipsed it in size and importance. The climate in summer is temperate, but the prevalent *siri-miri* or Scotch mist makes it depressingly damp in winter; and the atmosphere is somewhat polluted. The old English words *bilbo* (cutlass) and bilboes (iron fetters) testify to the fame of Bilbao as an ironworking town, and one which always has had strong commercial ties with England, but it was not until c. 1870 that the deposits of iron-ore at *Somorrostro*, to the N.W., were actively exploited. The first dry dock was constructed in 1896, when a revival of shipbuilding was initiated.

Airport at *Sondica*, c. 6 km. N.

History. Bilbao was founded in 1300 by Diego López de Haro and enjoyed an uneventful history until the 19C. Sacked by the French in 1808, it was besieged three times in the civil wars later in the century, which gave the town its name of '*Ciudad de los Sitios*'. In June 1835, Don Carlos, the pretender, anxious to score a striking success, despatched the famous 'guerrillero' Zumalacárregui against Bilbao. Seizing the heights of Begoña, the general prepared to assault the town, when he was mortally wounded. A second assault in October was repulsed with the help of the British Legion. In 1873, during the second Carlist war, the inhabitants were also able to beat off the besiegers. In the Civil War Bilbao held out for a year, until June 1937, against the Nationalists. It was the birthplace of the composer J. C. de Arriaga (1806–26), Miguel Unamuno (1864–1936), author and philosopher, and José Antonio de Aguirre (1904-60), the Basque President from 1936.

The centre of old Bilbao is the *Arenal*, a pleasant promenade on the r. bank of the Nervión, which is here crossed by the Pte. de la Victoria. To the E. stands the large but uninteresting 18C church of *S. Nicolás de Bari* containing statues by *Juan de Mena*, and in the Pl. de Arriaga on the S. side of the bridge approach, is the unwieldy *Teatro de Arriaga*. Further downstream, beyond the *Ayuntamiento* on the road to Las Arenas, is the tree-planted *Campo Volatin*.

From the *Arenal* we may enter the old town—preferably on foot—by taking the C. de los Fueros to the arcaded *Pl. de los Mártires*. From the opposite corner a short street leads to the C. de la Cruz and the *Museo Historico*, with an archaeological collection containing an extraordinary cross from Durango, and a Romanesque tympanum from Santurce. Also in the C. de la Cruz is *SS. Juanes*, with a good retablo mayor, while a short distance S.W. stands *Santiago*, mainly c. 1379–90, with a fragment of a later cloister on the N.E. side, and modern W. Front and tower; the S. Porch is dated 1571. The Tendería leads to the riverside market-place and 15C *S. Antón*, designed by *Guillot de Beaugrant*, a Fleming, but spoilt by restoration. The C. de Achuri leads E. to the Dominican church of *La Anunciación* (15C, altered in the 17C).

On a height to the E. stands Gothic *N.S. de Begoña* (c. 1511, with a modern tower and cloister) containing immense paintings by *Luca Giordano*, and the Pilgrimage to Begoña by *Echena*.

The Pte. de la Victoria crosses the Nervión into modern Bilbao, meeting the *Gran Vía* at the *Pl. de España*, to the N. of which is *S. Vicente*, a 16C hall-church in the traditional style. In the Gran Vía we pass (l.) the *Diputación*, containing archives of the province and a historical museum, to approach the Pl. Frederico Moyúa or López de Haro, the oval hub of the town. Hence the C. Elcano leads N.W. towards the *Parque de Doña Casilda de Iturriza*, and the **Museo de Bellas Artes.**

On the ground floor are displayed Primitives and Old Masters, including works by *Q. Metsys, C. Engelbrechtsen*, and *Mabuse*, while the later Italian and Flemish Schools are also well represented. The collection includes a number of paintings by *El Greco, Ribalta, Roelas, Ribera, Fr. Herrera the elder, Orrente, Zurbarán, Cano, Fr. Rizi*, and *Valdés Leal*. Among the portraits are *Velázquez*, Philip IV; *Carreño*, Doña Teresa Francisca Mudarra; *Claudio Coello*, Carlos II; Maria-Anna de Neubourg; *Goya*, María-Luisa de Parma; and the poet Moratín, and engravings. Sculptures include a seated Virgin by *Juan de Mena*, and there are some good pieces of ancient furniture. Other rooms contain 19C Spanish paintings, while on the First Floor is the *Museo de Arte Moderno*, with works by *Sorolla, Solana, Zuloaga*, etc.

The street continues N.W. towards the *Pte. del Generalísimo*, spanning the Nervión, on the far bank of which are the *Universidad Commercial* and the adjacent Jesuit *Universidad de Deusto*. A new University has been built some 15 km. N. of the town.

At the far end of the Gran Vía stands the *Casa de Misericordia* in the buildings of the old *Conv. de S. Mames*, from which the broad Av. de José Antonio leads S.W. to meet the N 634 leaving the town to the W., while just S. of this junction the entrance to the autopista.

FROM BILBAO TO PLENCIA (25 km.). Crossing the Pte. del Generalísimo, we shortly bear r. to *Asúa*, to the E. of which lies the airport of *Sondica*.—7 km. E. of this junction lies *Zamudio*, with a 16C hall-church and the tower-house of *Malpica*.—Turning l., we pass *Erandio*, with a 15C church and the tower-house of *Martiatu*. We reach the sea after passing through the residential districts of *Las Arenas* (at the E. end of the Pte. Vizcaya, see below), *Neguri*, and *Algorta*, just N. of which, at *Guecho* is another medieval tower-house, also called *Martiatu*.— *Plencia*, a fishing port founded by López de Haro, is now a small resort, as is *Gorliz*, 2 km. beyond. At Plencia, Sta María Magdalena is of some interest.—A nuclear-power station is under construction at *Lemonitz*, 7 km. to the E., which has provoked considerable opposition, not only in the immediate area.—7 km. inland stands the 13C castle of *Butrón*, almost entirely modernized.

FROM BILBAO TO SANTURCE. The W. bank of the Nervión may be followed by driving W. along the N 634, and after crossing the Rio Cadagua, forking r. onto the C 639. This threads its way through the industrial and port districts of *Baracaldo*, *Sestao* (with a battlemented tower-house) and the blast furnaces of *Los Altos Hornos*, *Portugalete*, and *Santurce*, with a combined population of c. 275,000. Overlooking *Portugalete* stands Gothic *Sta María*, with a carved oak retablo, while to the r. is the *Pte. Vizcaya*, a lofty transporter bridge (1893).

We leave Bilbao by the N 634, climbing W. past *Abanto*, with the ancient church of *S. Pedro*, and (19 km.) *Somorrostro*, centre of an extensive mining area.—A turning (r.) leads to *San Julián de Musqués*, with a ruined chapel, 15C castle, and 16C palace.

The N 634 bears N.W., winding above the indented rocky coast before descending to (14 km.) **Castro Urdiales**, (12,600 inhab.; *Parador Nac.* projected), an attractive fishing port of Roman foundation (*Flaviobriga*) built partly on a peninsula at whose extremity stands *Sta María* (13–14C), with unfinished towers, an apse with large buttresses, and monumental brasses. Near by is a ruined house of the Knights Templar. The Black Prince was nominal lord of the town in 1366–70. Antonio Hurtado de Mendoza (1586–1644), the poet and dramatist, was born here. Prehistoric paintings have been discovered in a cave near *Sámano*, 2 km. S.

We continue to skirt the coast, turning abruptly S. before crossing the Aguera, beyond which the road ascends through well-wooded country before climbing down steeply to (26 km.) *Laredo*, see below.

From Bilbao to Laredo by the inland route (78 km.). Leaving Bilbao by the N 634, we shortly fork l. onto the C 6318, which winds up the valley of the Cadagua into the Cantabrian highlands.—20 km. *Güeñes*, with a 17C palace and Gothic church, where we bear r. onto the C 6210, passing *Zalla*, with a tower-house, and (6 km. r.) *Avellaneda*, where the *Casa de Juntas*, a medieval tower-house of a type commonly met with in the district, contains the regional museum of Las Encartaciones, a rugged country of hills and glens.—14 km. *Carranza*, with the tower-house and bishop's *Pal. of Aedo*, and cave-paintings at *Venta la Perra*. We cross the Asón, at 9 km. entering *Gibaja*.—4 km. S.W. at *Ramales de la Victoria*, scene of Espartero's victory in 1843, is a ruined 16C palace.—Joining the C 629, we descend the valley to (3 km.) *Rasines*, birthplace of the architect Juan Gil de Hontañón (f. 1500—26), and (7 km.) the fishing village of *Limpias*.—5 km. beyond we meet the coast road at *Colindres*, 4 km. S.W. of *Laredo*, see below.

From Bilbao to Espinosa de los Monteros (60 km.). At *Güeñes* (see above) we continue to follow the C 6318 to (9 km.) **Valmaseda**, a pleasantly situated town (7900 inhab.) with three old bridges and two medieval churches.—15 km. *Villasana de Mena*, where in the church of the Franciscan nunnery is the tomb of a canon of Seville showing the Giralda as it was before the 16C alterations.—A road bears S. for 16 km. to *Vigo-Siones*, with the richly carved 12–13C church of *Sta María*, passing Romanesque *S. Lorenzo* (c. 1185–1200) at *Vallejo de Mena*.—At 7 km. we reach the C 629 from Burgos to Santoña viâ Villarcayo.—9 km. S.W. lies **Espinosa de los Monteros**, the scene of the defeat of Blake by Victor in 1808, and headquarters of the Monteros de Espinosa, the personal bodyguard of the Kings of Castile, established by Count Sancho García in honour of a huntsman of Espinosa who saved his life. It is an attractive old town (2700 inhab.), retaining a number of old houses, many with glazed balconies, while the Plateresque hall-church has an unusual sanctuary.

Laredo (11,300 inhab. out of season; *Hotels*), once described as a decayed seaport, with a fine beach—a wide spit of sand jutting towards Santoña on the opposite side of the bay—has recently been developed into a summer resort of huge proportions. The ancient town, to the N.E., retains some old houses and the remains of two monasteries. Charles V landed here in 1556 on his way from Flanders to Yuste, and presented two bronze eagle lecterns to the Church (a 13C building with double aisles). The *Ayuntamiento* is 16C.—4 km. *Colindres*, with ancient houses.

At 5 km. we may bear r. for (5 km.) *Santoña*, (10,300 inhab.;*Hotel*) another resort, with a 13C church, lying beneath an imposing rock, the only Spanish fortress from which the French were not driven during the Peninsular War. It was the birthplace of the mariner and cartographer Juan de la Cosa (d. 1509).—12 km. N.W. lies *Noja*, while 8 km. further W. at *Bareyo*, are two Romanesque churches, and in the *Conv. de S. Sebastián de Anó*, the tomb of Barbara Blomberg (d. 1597), mother of Don Juan of Austria.—*Ajo*, 2 km. N. of Barejo, preserves 14–16C houses.—Hence we may skirt the coast or drive S.W. to rejoin the main road at Solares.

19 km. *Hoznayo,* and *Villaverde de Pontones,* 4 km. to the N., have 7C palaces, while (4 km.) *Solares,* on the Rio Miera, is well known for ts mineral waters.—*La Cavada,* 5 km. S., preserves an 18C cannon oundry, 4 km. W. of which at *Liérganes,* are some 17C mansions.

Travellers wishing to by-pass Santander and follow the N 634 along the Asturian coast, will bear S.W., see below. For the road from Santander to *Torrelavega* and beyond to *Oviedo, La Coruña,* and *Santiago,* see Rte 39.

At Solares we bear r., and crossing the Ría de Solla, fork r. past *Astillero,* a shipbuilding centre in the days of wooden vessels, to follow the line of the bay, passing (r.) the airport of *Parayas,* and (10 km.) *Muriedas,* with an *Ethnological Museum* installed in the *Casa Velarde,* before entering the outskirts of (7 km.) **Santander,** see Rte 38.

FROM SOLARES TO TORRELAVEGA (32 km.). We pass *Sobremazas,* with the interesting *Casa de los Cuetos,* and *Penagos,* near which is the Baroque *Pal. de Elsedo* (1710) with a remarkable chapel.— 12 km. *Sarón,* S. of which lies Romanesque *Sta Maria de Cayón,* 17 km. beyond which is *Villacarriedo,* with the magnificient Baroque *Pal. de Soñanes,* built in 1718–22 by the Italian *Cosimo Fontanelli* round the ancient solar of the Diaz de Arce family, while at nearby *Selaya* is the *Pal. de Donadio,* and other interesting old houses.—The N 634 continues W. through attractive country, passing (7 km.) *Castañeda,* with a Romanesque church with Gothic and 18C additions.— We drive through (3 km.) *Vargas,* on the intersection of the Santander/Burgos road (N 623) and wind down to (10 km.) **Torrelavega** (51,000 inhab.; *Hotels*) an industrial centre, with an arcaded Pl. Mayor; near the old church is the *tower-house* of the family of Garcilaso de la Vega.—*Santillana del Mar* lies 7 km. N.W., see p.386.

6   FROM BILBAO TO ZARAGOZA

A   VIÂ VITORIA AND LOGROÑO

Total distance, 320 km. (199 miles). N 634 for 11 km.—N 240. 54 km. **Vitoria**—N I, at 25 km. turn l. on to N 232—18 km. *Haro*— 42 km: **Logroño**—49 km. *Calahorra*— 41 km. *Tudela*—80 km. **Zaragoza.**

Motorway. The A 68 (its remaining sections almost completed) climbs S. from Bilbao towards *Miranda de Ebro* (off which a good road leads to *Vitoria*). At Miranda it connects with the A 1 for *Burgos.* Turning S.E. through the Rioja, it then by-passes *Haro, Logroño, Calahorra,* and *Tudela,* running roughly parallel to the N 232 to *Zaragoza.*

At 11 km. S.E. of Bilbao we fork r. off the San Sebastián road (N 634) onto the N 240 ascending the wooded valley of the Arrati past (13 km. r.) *Elejabeitia,* with a curious church, and *Villaro,* whose church of *La Piedad* and *Pal. of the Marqués del Riscal* are of interest.—4 km. *Ceánuri,* with an old church, is passed as we climb steeply to the Alto de Barazur (2275 ft), with views (r.) of the Pico de Gorbea, and descend to (24 km.) *Villareal de Álava,* on the Embalse Sta Engracia, thence running roughly parallel to the old road from *Vergara* (p.99) to (13 km.) **Vitoria** (see p.100) which may be by-passed to the W.

3 km. S. of *Villareal* is *Urbina,* close to *Gojain* with a simple church of great age, while at *Urrunaga,* to the W., is a Trans. Church with a richly carved doorway; also *Nafarrate,* with an early church.—At *Miñano Mayor,* S. of Urbina, is the fine Romanesque and early Gothic church of *S. Vicente.*

FROM VITORIA TO LOGROÑO, VIÂ LAGUARDIA (60 km.). Leaving Vitoria by the C. de Rioja, the road passes, at 3 km., *Gardélegui,* with a church of great antiquity, whence a track leads to the *Campo de los Palacios* with remains of a Romanesque chapel, and to the prehistoric sites of *Olárizu,* or *Crucemendi.* The MONTES DE VITORIA are crossed at the Pt. de Vitoria.—In the hills to the E. of (9 km.) S.

Vicentejo is the Romanesque chapel of *S. Vicente de los Olleros*.—At 4 km (Ventas de Armentia) is a cross-road leading E. to Logroño viâ *Bernedo*, see below The valley of the Ayuda is traversed and the road again climbs through picturesque country to (10 km.) walled *Peñacerrada*, in whose church of *La Asunción* are notable tombs and retablos. Climbing in zigzags the road crosses the Sierra de Cantabria to the *Pto. de Herrera* (3640 ft), with a magnificent *View over the upper Ebro valley. Descending steeply into the RIOJA ALAVESA, we meet the road from Briñas (N 232) near *Leza*, p.128.—18 km. *Laguardia*; 16 km.**Logroño**, p.116.

FROM VITORIA TO LOGROÑO VIÂ BERNEDO (63 km.). At Ventas de Armentia (see above) we turn l. and follow the valley of the Ayuda to *Albaina*.—Hence a road runs N.E. to *Marquínez*, where the chapel of *S. Juan* (1226) is dated example of the transition from Romanesque to Gothic.—Beyond Albaina the road crosses the Montes de Izquiz, a region of caves and ancient chapels to (39 km.) **Bernedo** with the ruins of a castle, and a parish church with a fine Gothic doorway of 8 recessed orders.—N.E. is the chapel of *S. Bartolomé de Angostina* with a 13C seated Virgin and Child.—Crossing the Sierra de Cantabria the road runs S. to (24 km. **Logroño**.

FROM VITORIA TO LOGROÑO VIÂ LOS ARCOS (90 km.). 3 km. E. of Vitoria we fork r. off the N I onto the C 132, with the hills of the Condado de Treviño (3855 ft) or the r.—7 km. r. *Aberásturi*, with a Romanesque church (12C) retaining a good doorway. Adjacent is *Argandoña*, with a Trans. church, to the N. of which stands the restored Romanesque church of *Estíbaliz*, with a 13C door and font and remains of the statue of the Virgin as Patroness of Álava, which until 1332 was taken to *Arriaga*, just N. of Vitoria, for the sittings of the provincial diet.—1 km *Anúa*, with the pilgrimage chapel of *Sta Lucia*, containing an unusual early Gothic polygonal apse and a door with carved capitals.—2 km. *Eguileta* has a good Romanesque church containing a Flemish triptych, N.E. of which lies *Erunchun* where the church has an early Gothic porch and two Romanesque chapels. Beyond, among wooded hills, lies *Gáceta*, whose Trans. church preserves ancient vestments and an early coffer covered with a tapestry of country scenes.—After crossing the Pto. de Azaceta, the road descends to (12 km.) *Maestu*, with the Trans. chapel of *N.S. del Campo*, an early Gothic doorway in the ruined chapel of *S. Martín*, and antiquities kept in the sacristy of the parish church.—At *Leorza* and *Cicujano*, not far N., are Romanesque churches, and at *Igoroin* an early church of simple Cistercian Gothic.—At (15 km.) *Santa Cruz de Campezo* the church contains a collection of 16C embroideries; the parish church of *S. Vicente de Arana* (9 km. N.) has 15C Gothic retablos. At 9 km. we turn r. at *Acedo* for (13 km.) *Los Arcos* (see Rte 4A), 28 km. N.E. of **Logroño**.

At Vitoria we join the N I, which we follow S.W.— described on p.102—until, 25 km., we diverge l. onto the N 232, soon passing *Zambrana*, with an old church and ruins of two castles, and (12 km. l.) *Salinillas de Buradón*, with ruined walls and ancient castle—2 km. *Briñas*, has a medieval bridge, and a church with carvings by *Matiás el Francés*, Vigarni's assistant.

FROM BRIÑAS TO LOGROÑO VIÂ LAGUARDIA (43 km.) Turning l. at Briñas, we may take an alternative road to Logroño throught the fertile district of the RIOJA ALAVESA, on the N. bank of the Ebro, through **Labastida** (1100 inhab.) containing many old houses, the Romanesque fortress-chapel of *El Cristo* (with Renaissance additions), and a church with 17C porch and 18C tower.—Nearby are the ruined 12C chapel of *S. Martín de los Monjes*, with curious rock-cut graves, the castle of *Toloño*, and remains of the Franciscan friary of *S. Andrés de Maya* with a 13C cloister and ruins of the conventual aqueduct.—8 km. *S. Vicente de la Sonsierra* has a hill-top castle, a pilgrim's hospice, and in the well-vaulted church of 1520–50, a retablo by *Damián Forment*. Nearby, Romanesque *Sta María de la Piscina* was founded in 1136 by Don Ramiro of Navarre, son-in-law of the Cid.—5 km. *Abalos*. The *Pal. del Marqués de Legarda* houses important works of art; in the 15C church is stallwork from the destroyed monastery of La Estrella at *S. Asensio* and a carved Renaissance lectern.—Martín Fernández de Navarrete (1765–1844), the biographer of Cervantes, was born here.—A side road leads 2 km. S. to *Leza* with a 15C gateway and late Gothic *S. Martín*.—Following the direct road, we pass (11 km. r.) *Páganos*, with a curious church, before reaching (3 km.) **Laguardia**, a hill-top village (1500 inhab.; *Hotel*), of ancient houses surrounded by walls and towers and surmounted by ruins of a castle. Gothic **Sta María de los Reyes** has a

ine 15C *Porch* with polychrome sculpture, a Life of the Virgin and Apostles attr.
to *Greg. Fernández,* and a *Retablo* of 1632 by *Juan de Arismendi, Juan de Iralzu*
and *Juan Vascardo,* known as the 'retablo de los tres Juanes'. *S. Juan,* or *El Pilar,*
has vestiges of Romanesque work but was transformed in Churrigueresque style in
1731–41.—At *Elvillar* (6 km. N.E.) is the largest dolmen of the Pyrenean region,
while at nearby *Berrena* are Roman remains.—We descend into the Ebro valley
and after passing the Roman site of *Asa* and ruins of the Roman bridge of
Mantible, enter (16 km.) **Logroño.**

4 km. **Haro,** an agricultural and vinious town (8600 inhab.) at the
junction of the Tirón with the Ebro, gave a title to Luis Méndez de Haro
(1598–1661), the minister of Philip IV. It was the birthplace of the art
critic and educator Manuel Bartolomé Cossio (1858–1935). The *Cerro
de Lorenzo* (5990 ft) is conspicuous to the S. and to the N.E. is the *Peña
Cerraca* (4145 ft). In the Pl. de la Paz is the *Ayuntamiento* of 1769, while
notable among many ancient houses, is the 16C *Casa de Paternina. Sto
Tomás* is a large hall-church with a large Plateresque Porch (1516) by
Felipe de Vigarní; work on the structure was still in progress under
Pedro Rasines in 1564. Behind the high altar is a tabernacle with
sculptures of 1757. The 18C basilica of *N. S. de la Vega* contains an
ancient image of the Virgin, retablos and paintings. Also of interest is
Gothic *S. Nicolás.*

7 km. **Briones** is also noted for its wine. The town (1100 inhab.), well-
sited on its hill, and surrounded by old walls, retains a ruined castle and
stone mansions, notably the *Pal. de Marqués de S. Nicolás;* the hall-
church, completed in 1546 to the designs of *Juan Martínez,* has
interesting chapels and an 18C Baroque tower by *Martín Berratíua.*—
4 km. r. *S. Asensio,* has a retablo (1569) by *Pedro Arbulo Marguvete* in
its church.—The castle and chapel of *Davalillo* are finely situated on a
bend of the Ebro, while at *Torremontalvo* we pass the remains of
another castle.—From (11 km. r.) *Cenicero* a road crosses the Ebro to
Laguardia (see above), 11 km. N.E. viâ *Elciego,* birthplace of the
chronicler Manuel Navarrete Ladrón de Guevara, Bp. of Mondoñedo.
The chapel of *S. Vicente,* by the Ebro, contains a 15C wooden Christ,
and the parish church has enormous Churrigueresque retablos.—8 km.
Fuenmayor, with a 16C hall-church.—12 km. **Logroño,** see p.116.

Beyond Logroño lies (13 km. l.) *Agoncillo,* with the ruins of Roman
Egon and a castle with four square towers. On the r. is a broken precipice
of reddish rocks which continues as far as *Alcanadre,* with an early 16C
parish church which may be reached by turning l. at 11 km. On the l.
beyond Alcanadre is seen a considerable fragment of the Roman
aqueduct which supplied Calahorra with water.

25 km. **Calahorra** (16,400 inhab.; *Parador Nac.*) is an ancient town at
the confluence of the Cidacos with the Ebro, well-sited, but largely
ruinous, and any relics of Roman walls have been demolished in the
interest of modern development, mostly towards the N.W.

The Celtiberian stronghold of *Calagurris Nassica,* unsuccessfully besieged by
Pompey in 75 B.C., was taken by Afranius four years later after a famine so
dreadful that it became proverbial. Quintilian (c. 35–100 A.D.) was a native of the
town, as was the Christian poet, Aurelius Prudentius (fl. 350–75), and Juan
Antonio Llorente (1756–1823), the historian of the Inquisition. The see, founded
in 1045, has been united with Logroño since 1890. Here Enrique de Trastamara
was proclaimed King of Castile by Bertrand Du Guesclin in 1366.

The **Cathedral,** by the bridge, was restored in 1485, after a serious
flood, by *Maestro Juan;* the *Cap. Mayor* was built in 1621 by *Juan Pérez
de Solarte;* the main portal and façade and the *Epifania chapel* were

altered under Philip V. The N. Door is a mixture of Gothic and Renaissance styles, while the curious W. Front with its oblong tower dates from 1680–1704. The *Nave* is a fine example of pure late-Gothic, with stellar vaults springing direct from octagonal piers. The *Cap. de la Visitación* and *Cap. de S. Pedro* have early Renaissance altarpieces, and the latter a 15C Reja; in the *Cap de los Mártires,* off the ambulatory at the E. end, entered between two 18C confessionals, is a Churrigueresque retablo with the martyrdom in high relief. The *Sacristy* contains a beautiful Custodia of the mid-15C, known as 'El Ciprés', and a copy of *Titian's* Sta Margarita de Cortona. Note the carved octofoil font.

The other churches are of little interest. *S. Andrés,* late Gothic, has a brick tower and curious W. Door; *Santiago* is a domed building of classic design. In the *Carmelite Convent,* nearer the cathedral, is a Flagellation by *Greg. Fernández.*

At 22 km. we by-pass **Alfaro,** (8400 inhab.; *Hotel*), where the brick-built Colegiata of *S. Miguel* (16C) contains finely carved choir-stalls, a Plateresque reja, and a good statue of N.S. de los Dolores. In the town are many ancient houses of Aragonese type, notably the *Casa de los Frías* and the *Pal. Abatial,* built in the late 18C to plans by *Ventura Rodríguez.*—19 km. *Tudela* (p.112), after which we follow the route described on p.113 to reach (80 km.) **Zaragoza,** see Rte 17.

B Viâ Orduña and Pancorbo

Total distance, 332 km. (206 miles). N 634 for 6 km.—N 625. 36 km. *Orduña*—at 52 km. turn on to N 232—26 km. *Haro*—42 km. **Logroño**—49 km. *Calahorra*—41 km. *Tudela*—80 km. **Zaragoza. Motorway.** see head of Rte 6A.

Leaving Bilbao by the San Sebastián road (N 634), we turn r. at 6 km. onto the N 625 to by-pass *Arrigorriaga,* with an 11C church erected in memory of a battle between the Basques and Ordoño, Infante of Castile (848). We keep to the W. bank of the Nervión, which now flows through a narrowing valley, passing (9 km. l.) *Miravalle,* with the church of *S. Pedro.*—20 km. **Amurrio,** an industrial town (6900 inhab.), retains a Romanesque church and ancient houses including the *Pal. de Guinea* with a Gothic front.—At *Murga* on the N.W. outskirts are the restored remains of a palace of 1270.—*Maroño,* some 6 km. to the W., has a good late Romanesque church.

From Amurrio to Arceniega (15 km.). At Amurrio the road up the Nervión valley is crossed by the C 6210.—In the direction of Valmaseda (N.W.) this passes through (5 km.) *Respaldiza,* with a medieval mansion, and tombs of the Counts of Ayala in its church.—A road leads 3 km. S.W. to *Quejana* where the 14C fortified church contains besides other tombs of the Ayalas, the noble Tomb of the Chancellor Pero Lopez de Ayala and his wife in the Cap. de N.S. del Cabello (1399), and in an enamelled triptych a golden reliquary.—The C 6210 continues to (10 km.) *Arceniega,* with a Plateresque palace and the sanctuary of *N.S. de la Encina* containing a 13C apse-painting and a 16C Gothic retablo as well as the effigy of Cristóbal de la Cámara y Murga, Bp. of Salamanca.—At nearby *Sojoguti* is a grand castle keep.

From Amurrio to Vitoria (40 km.) The second half of this route is now followed by an improved road. C 6210 climbs S.E. past (4 km.) *Lezama,* with a Romanesque church and the Renaissance *Pal. of Larraco,* through picturesque country to (18 km.) *Murguia,* in the Zuya valley, just beyond which a road leads E. past *Manurga,* with the *Berástegui palace,* to *Murúa,* whence the caves of *Mairu Elegoretta* in the Sierra de Gorbea, with prehistoric sites, may be visited.—At 5 km. we pass *Olano,* with the Romanesque church, while at 9 km. a road (r.) leads to *Forondo,* with a palace, beyond which, at *Legarda,* is a Romanesque church with a good tower.—4 km. **Vitoria.**

Beyond Amurrio we enter the fertile Concha de Orduña, a broad
basin dotted with prosperous farms. 7 km. **Orduña** (935 ft), an ancient
own (4700 inhab.) with a picturesque *Plaza,* from which ten streets
diverge. An older Orduña, once the only city in the Basque provinces,
tood nearer the mountain *La Peña de Orduña* (6400 ft). Buildings of
interest include the old *Aduana, Sta Maria la Antigua, S. Juan Bautista,*
and the *Colegiata of the Jesuits* with a 16C front.

Not far S. is the *Gorge of Tertrago* and the cascade of the Nervión, and the most
southerly part of the famous Orduña gradient, where at one point the railway
track, making a sweeping curve round the valley, can be seen high up on the l., only
550 m. away from its starting point.

FROM ORDUÑA TO HARO VIÂ SUBIJANA (68 km.) A side road leading E. to
Murguía, passes (8 km. r.) *Unzá*; (l.) *Oyardo* and *Gujuli*; and (7 km. r.) *Belunza,* all
with Romanesque churches, the latter with richly carved windows and a fine early
Gothic doorway of five orders.—The road turns S., passing *Izarra* to reach
Andagoya, with a Romanesque church containing a 13C seated Virgin, and
Catadiano, with a Trans. church.—9 km. *Zuazo de Cuartango* has an early Gothic
church with a good doorway. We traverse the defile of the Techas, through which
Wellington manoeuvred a body of his forces at a critical moment before the battle
of Vitoria, and descend the lovely valley of the Bayas to (11 km.) the picturesque
twin villages of *Morillas* and *Subijana,* linked by an ancient bridge, the latter with
the *Pal. de Anda.* Continuing S. at 10 km. we meet the N I 3 km. N. of its junction
with the N 232 for *Haro,* 18 km. beyond.

Leaving Orduña, the N 625 climbs steeply S. by a series of zigzags to
the *Pto. de Orduña* (2935 ft), with fine retrospective *Views.—9 km.
Berberana, from which the ascent of the Peña de Orduña may be
made.—At 11 km. a side-road leads W. to *Villanañe* with its fortified
palace and the chapel of *N.S. de Angosto,* and to the remote villages of
the Gobea valley, among which *Valdepuesta* is noted for its 14C
*Colegiata.—3 km. *Espejo,* a picturesque village, whence a road leads E.
to the Romanesque chapel of *Tuesta* with a good doorway, and the
curious salt-pans of (6 km.) *Salinas de Añana,* whose church possesses a
remarkable early triptych.

At 6 km. a more direct road (C 122) bears l. past *Fontecha,* with the *Pal. of the
Counts of Orgaz,* the prehistoric site of *Molinilla* and *Cambriana,* with Roman
ruins, at 12 km. entering *Miranda* (see p.102). Here we may take either a road N. of
the Ebro to meet the N 232 8 km. beyond, or continue on the C 122 along the S.
bank to (18 km.) *Haro.*

The main road (N 625) crosses the Ebro, and shortly passes *Sta Gadea
del Cid,* with a restored plaza, dominated by the ruins of a castle and
preserving a Romanesque church and remains of town walls.—At
23 km. the Madrid road (N I) is reached just N. of the defile of Pancorbo
(see p.102).—At 4 km., having traversed the pass, we diverge l. onto the
N 232.—At 12 km. a road leads E. to Haro, passing (12 km. N.)
Sajazarra, with a wooden seated Virgin and a picturesque castle with a
turreted curtain wall and keep, and *Anguciana,* with a Gothic tower-
house of the family of Blanco de Salcedo.—3 km. r. *Cuzcurrita de Río
Tirón* with a castle, the Gothic chapel of *La Sorejana,* and baroque *S.
Miguel* (1753-1800).—At (5 km.) *Casalarreina* are the Plateresque
Conv. de Dominicanas (1508) with a remarkable portico, a Renaissance
Pal. of the Constables of Castile, and other mansions.—13 km. to the S.
lies *Santo Domingo de la Calzada* (see p.117), while at *Zarratón,* 4 km.
S.E., is the monastery of *Herrera,* retaining a Romanesque cloister, and
a parish church with a fine coro.—6 km. N.E. lies Haro (see p.129),
beyond which we follow Rte. 6A.

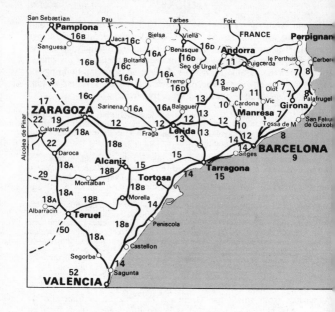

II ARAGÓN AND CATALONIA

Catalonia, in Spanish *Cataluña,* in Catalan *Catalunya,* divided into the four provinces of Gerona, Barcelona, Tarragona, and Lérida, is an ancient principality differing widely in character, climate, and language from the rest of the country. Separated from central Spain by the barren plains of eastern Aragón and by the mountains south of Ebro, the Catalans have always looked upon the Mediterranean as their natural outlet. The soil of Catalonia is almost everywhere fertile, producing excellent wine, oil, fruit, and even where, as in the upland province of Lérida, the climate is less favourable, the hardworking peasantry surmount the difficulty and 'make bread out of stones'. The enterprising and mercantile Catalans generally pay strict attention to business, and their capacity to take advantage of modern industrial methods can be seen in the flourishing factories around Barcelona, and many other towns.

Meanwhile, the aspect of the **Costa Brava,** the once attractive rocky coastline of the province of Gerona, has changed radically during the last three decades (since wonderfully described, as it *was,* in the first fifty pages of Rose Macaulay's *Fabled Shore* in 1949), and rarely for the better; and even some of the once attractive inland villages, such as Besalú, are in danger of losing their charm. There has also been a growth of winter sporting on the southern slopes of the Pyrenees. The population of Catalonia, which has more than doubled in the last half century, is now over 5½ million, 3,000,000 of which (including a large number of non-Catalans), are concentrated in Barcelona, its industrial uburbs, and the main towns of the province. Once escaping from these, ne enters some of the most beautiful countryside in Spain, of wooded ills, and rich agricultural regions dotted with stone-built farms or *nasias,* and also endowed with a pleasant climate during most of the ear.

Barcelona was recaptured from the Moors in 801, and the province vas first governed by feudatories of the Frankish king, but the counts chieved effective independence in 874, and in 987 were recognized as overeign princes after the brief recapture of Barcelona by Almanzor. he principality remained hereditary in the line of Wilfred *'el Velloso'* the Hairy; 857–902), whose descendants in 1137 acquired the throne of Aragón by marriage. Thenceforward the fate of the province was linked, ven if tenuously, to that of Spain, but the Catalans clung obstinately to he partial independence embodied in their ancient *'usatges'* or code of ights. Both in 1640–43 and during the War of the Spanish Succession, Catalonia took the opportunity of rebelling against Castile, indicative of desire for separation which has persisted. Even in the late 18C they vould talk of making a journey *into* Spain, as they would of into France. he futile wars of the 19C, hampering their commercial activities, again rove them to fury against the central government, and Carlism, epublicanism, and anarchism were in turn espoused by an energetic eople deprived of a peaceful safety-valve. In 1931, a Catalan Republic vas proclaimed under the presidency of Francesc Macià (1859–1933), nd Catalan autonomy was guaranteed by the new Spanish onstitution, together with the official use of the Catalan language (see .86), a form of Provençal, and possessing an extensive literature of its wn: outlined in Arthur Terry's *History of Catalan Literature.*

During the Civil War of 1936–39, Catalonia supported the Republicans, and afterwards lost its autonomy. For some years the ffects of the disastrous struggle were felt more seriously here than in ome other parts of the country, part of a deliberate policy of Nationalist evenge, but the recent prosperity of Spain has directed the natural nergy of Catalonia back into its normal channel.

Since the death of the late dictator a certain measure of autonomy has gain been introduced, the *Generalitat* being re-established in Sept. 1977 ınder its president-in-exile Josep Tarradellas. The Catalan language ıow appears to be used to an increasing extent, and most place-names ıave reverted to their earlier spelling.

To the west lies **Aragón,** comprising the modern provinces of Huesca, Zaragoza, and Teruel, which extends over the Middle Ebro basin from he Pyrenees to the North to the Sierras de Javalambre and of the Maestrazgo to the South and South-East. To the West, the Sierras de Cebollera, Moncayo, and the Montes Universales, separate Aragón rom the Castiles. Thus surrounded on all sides by mountains, the plain s subject to a continental climate, with torrid summers and icy winters. The N.W. wind (*cierzo*), and that from the S.E. (*bochorno*), cold and hot espectively, are robbed of all moisture by the mountains they traverse, ınd rainfall is consequently very scanty. On either bank of the Ebro xtend semi-desert, sparsely inhabited, pasture lands, although hydro-lectric schemes harnessing the Pyrenean rivers, and conserving their vaters, have increased the prosperity of certain districts. The barren Aragonese Pyrenees themselves, have been comparatively little xplored, and offer some impressive scenery, while their flora and fauna vill interest the naturalist.

The Aragonese national dance, the brisk and jerky *Jota,* may still b seen at fiestas, but their costume of knee-breeches supported by a sash white stockings, and red handkerchief covered by a broad-brimmed hat is now only very occasionally noticed in remoter districts.

The Christian Goths, at first driven into the Pyrenean fastnesses of the Sobrarbe, there rallied, and eventually repulsed the Berbers who had occupied their territory. Like the Basques, the Aragonese had their *fueros,* which strictly limited the powers of the king they elected; in addition, they also appointed a Justiciar, to whose supreme authority any dispute involving their infringement was referred. The parchmen on which these fueros were inscribed was cut to shreds by Pedro IV in 1348, which won for him the name *'el del Puñal'*(him of the dagger), bu the Aragonese, being naturally pertinacious, persisted in their rights even after the union with Castile, until 1591, when Philip II, enraged by the justiciar Juan de Lanuza, who had protected his scheming secretar Antonio Pérez, marched into Zaragoza, expelled the judge, and revoked their fueros.

Indeed, they have long had a reputation for obstinacy—so *testarudo* that they were said (in the words of Ford) 'to drive nails into walls with their heads, into which when anything is driven nothing can get it out'

In 1137 Aragón was united with Catalonia, and their stubborn martial vigour, coupled with the trading capabilities of the Catalans, soon made their name respected throughout the Mediterranean. For their resistance to the French during the Peninsular War, see p.199.

The total population of Aragón (1,164,000) has changed little during the last half century, although there has been a considerable drift from the provinces of Huesca and Teruel, while Zaragoza has increased from 499,000 to 794,000. The city of Zaragoza itself, now with 528,000, ha increased by 224,000 in the last 15 years!

7   FROM (PERPIGNAN) LA JONQUERA TO GIRONA AND BARCELONA

Total distance, 156 km. (97 miles). N II. 25 km. *Figueres*—37 km. **Girona**—N I and then C 251 for 94 km. **Barcelona.**

Motorway. The A 17, continuing the French B 9 from *Perpignan* across th frontier (Customs) near *La Jonquera,* is the recommended route to be followed far as *Girona,* travellers wishing to do so making their exit at *Figueres* for the Bad de Roses and the N. part of the Costa Brava (see Rte. 8), or inland towards *Besal* Note the curious pyramidal construction (1976; by *Ricardo Bofill*) marking th border. S. of Girona there are a number of exits leading towards the coast resorts, but unless one wishes to explore the few sites described off the C 251 (som of which can be approached from the motorway), it is as well to remain on th motorway as far as *Barcelona*. Those wishing to by-pass Barcelona, are able to d so by veering off some 20 km. N. of the city.

Crossing the frontier from *Le Perthus,* our route follows the N II from *La Jonquera* (2200 inhab.; *Hotels*; Customs), whose church has a Romanesque door, to (25 km.) **Figueres** (28,100 inhab.; *Hotels*) founded in 1267. To the N.W. it is dominated by the *Castillo de S. Fernando,* a fort laid out in the style of Vauban by Fernando VI, but seriously damaged in 1936 (now barracks). Townsend, who in 1786 spent his first night in Figueres on 'three boards laid upon trestles to support a mattress', considered it a wasteful occupation building fortifications to

ep people *out* of a country, and that the time and energy would have
en better employed in 'mending roads, to invite strangers into Spain',
 idea which has now taken root. In 1701 Philip V was married to
aria Luisa of Savoy in 14C *S. Pedro*, restored, with a Romanesque
wer, octagonal lantern, 16C doorway, and modern windows. A few
eps N. of the tree-shaded Rambla in the town centre, with the *Museo
l Empordà*, is a meretriciously embellished *Museo-Teatro*, now
commodating a collection of the works of the surrealist artist and
hibitionist Salvador Dalí, born in Figueres in 1904. Adjacent, to the
 ., is a 15C palace.

The C 252 leads to *Vilabertrán* (2 km. N.E.) with an old palace and a collegiate
urch (cons. 1101), with a fine bell-tower and 14C processional cross.—Further
 is (3 km.) *Perelada*, birthplace of Ramón Muntaner (1265-1336), the Catalan
ronicler, with a 14C castle, the Romanesque cloisters of the former Dominican
ary, and, in the Gothic *N.S. del Carmen* (founded 1206), carved capitals from S.
 re de Roda (p.139). The castle contains an important library and works of art
revious authorization to visit necessary).—Some 15 km. N.E. of Perelada,
ached by a rough track, lie the remains of the monastery of *S. Quirze de Culera,*
1ose church was consecrated in 935 and again in 1123.
12 km. E. of Figueras lies *Roses*, see Rte.8.—The C 260 leads S.W. from
igueres to (25 km.) *Besalú* (p.137) off which at 10 km., a roads leads r. 4 km. to
.edó, with the basilican church of *Sta Maria* (1081-89).—From 4 km. S. of
igueres the C 252 leads 19 km. S.E. viâ Viladematt to *Ampurias (Empúries)*, see
 140.

At 26 km. we pass *Medinyà,* with a 14C church and early castle, and
 km. l.), the castle of *Montagut,* before descending into the valley of the
 er, which we cross after 6 km. Skirting the park of *La Dehesa,* and
 .rning l. under the railway bridge, we enter the provincial capital and
 owing industrial centre of **GIRONA** (75,100 inhab.; 18,000 in 1920;
 2,000 in 1960; *Hotels*) previously known as *Gerona*.

History. *Gerunda,* a city of the Ausetani, was a Moorish possession from the late
 C to 1015, and later gave a title to the eldest sons of the kings of Aragón. Its
 1story is a tale of sieges for the most part successfully withstood. The most famous
 ' these was the French assault of 1809 when a force of 35,000 commanded by
erdier, Gouvion St-Cyr, and Augereau was kept off for seven months by the
 1habitants aided by a small garrison and a few English volunteers. The women
 1rolled themselves into a company dedicated to Sta Barbara, patroness of
 rtillery. When the commander, Mariano Álvarez de Castro (1770–1810), broke
 own under the strain of privation and anxiety, the town surrendered, its food and
 mmunition exhausted. It was here that, in 1802, Lady Holland experienced for
 1e first time the 'extreme derision and scorn with which a woman is treated who
 oes not conform to the Spanish mode of dressing'! It was the birthplace of the
 oubadour Cerverí de Girona (fl. 1250–80).

It is preferable to visit the narrow winding streets of the old town on
 oot. This area lies to the E. of the river Oñar (which joins the Ter just N.
 ' the town), which may be crossed by the *Pte. de Piedra* or the new
 ambla de José Antonio. From either point, or from footbridges
 irther N., a good view may be had of the picturesque but decrepit old
 ouses overhanging the river. Crossing to the E. bank we reach the Pl. de
 ispaña with the *Ayuntamiento,* in part of 1642, and the *Casa Carles,*
 ontaining the *Museo Diocesano,* a good local collection.

Of particular interest are wall-paintings from Pedriñá (12C) and S. Juan de
 iellcaire (13C), and a 12C painted beam from Cruilles, the Retablo of Púbol
 (437) by *Bernat Martorell,* a 14C tomb relief from Crespia, and the important
 Retablo of Cruilles, by *Lluís Borrassà* (1416), among others of the 15C. Other
 ooms are of more local interest, but include two pen-drawings by *Goya,* a fine
 1S. copy of the Homilies of Bede, with miniatures (early 12C), and a magnificent
 luminated martyrology (14C).

Hence the C. de los Ciudadanos leads N. towards the Cathedral passing No. 19 (l.) the *Casa de la Fontana de Oro* (13C), restored t house a museum, and (r.) the *Casa de Solterra,* to reach the small Pl. de Oli. Here stands the *Casa de Foizá,* and on the l. of the street of step ascending to the r., the 17C *Casa de los Agullanas* or *Pal. de Vizcondado.* At the top of the steps is *S. Martín* (1606–10), with a goo front, and beside it the door (1599) of the *Seminario.* Climbing anothe steep lane and steps we reach the *Conv. de Sto Domingo* (1253–1349 restoration in progress. To the N. stands the former *University* (1561 70) and behind it remains of a cyclopean *Wall* rebuilt in the 3C A.L From here narrow lanes lead to the Pl. Lladoners, the S. Door of th Cathedral, and the *Pal. Episcopal* with Renaissance windows. Fror beneath the palace a lane leads uphill to the ruins of the 14C *Torre a Gironella* (view).

The direct route from the Pl. del Oli keeps to a lower level, passin the C. de la Força, with the Renaissance *Casa de Sambola,* to the base of the monumental staircase (1607–90) ascending to the *W. Front* of th Cathedral. On the r. is the 14C building of the *Pia Almonina* (restored and to the W. is the *Audiencia* (1599).

The Gothic **Cathedral,* one of the finest buildings in Catalonia, date in its present form from 1312–1598, with 17–18C alterations.

The first church, founded by Charlemagne in 786 and desecrated by the Moor was rebuilt in 1016–38, but the only important survival is the *N. Tower,* called th *Torre de Carlomagno,* of 1038–1117. It was with stones from a steeple of this ol cathedral that the clergy of Girona celebrated Easter 1278 by bombarding th adjacent *Judería!* The present cathedral was begun when the apse chapels wer constructed (1312–47) by *Maitre Henri* and *Jacques Favran.* The plan for the ne nave, begun c. 1350–86, and whose huge vault was designed in 1416 by *Guillerm Bofill,* was considered unsafe by the chapter and was adopted only on the advice of a jury of twelve architects. The tower was built in 1580–81 and the W. FRONT, t the designs of *Pedro Costa,* in 1730–33. The S. Door, recently restored, was begu in 1394 by *Guillén Morey*; of the original terracotta statues of the Apostles b *Antonio Claperós* (1548) only two survive.

The *INTERIOR is an apsidal hall surrounded by chapels and covere by Bofill's vault, the widest Gothic vault known (22 m), 3.3 m wide than the similar vault at Albi in Languedoc, while the internal buttresse supporting it are 6 m. thick. Some windows retain glass of 1380 by Llu Borrassá, and there is much of the 15C.—The *Sillería* in the Cor though altered in the 16C, preserves some original 14C stalls and Bishop's Throne, carved in 1351 by Maestro *Aloy.*—Cap. Mayor. Th High Altar, with a retablo of 1320–25 covered with silver plate an enamel, is surmounted by a remarkable wooden Baldacchino, likewis plated with silver, supported on shafts ornamented with enamelle escutcheons. The work was carried out by Maestro *Bartomeu,* bu altered (1357) by *Pedro Bernes* of Valencia, who also made the whole c the bottom range of the retablo. To the l. is the Tomb of Bp. Berengue Anglesola (d. 1408), by *Pedro Oller,* with a fine series of weepers.– Among other tombs are those of Bernard de Pau (c. 1457) in the 1st N Chapel, probably by Lorenzo Mercadente de Bretaña, and of Coun Ramón Berenguer II (d. 1082), nicknamed Cap d'Estopa ('Tow-Head' over the door of the sacristy, and that of his wife Ermesendis (d. 1057 on the S. Wall nearly opposite, these two of the 14C.

The *Sacristy* and *Chapter Rooms* contain crosses and reliquaries of the 15–16C an illuminated Apocalypse dated 974; an alabaster Statuette of 'Charlemagne' or Pedro IV of Aragón, c. 1350, by *Jaime Cascalls* of Berga, a pupil of Maestro Aloy; a 13C Bible annotated by Charles V of France. *The Creation', a magificent piece of early 12C embroidery, etc.—The irregular Romanesque *CLOISTER of c. 1180–1210, has elaborately carved capitals.

Turning r. on descending the Cathedral steps, we pass between two arge semi-circular towers called the *Portal de Sobreportas*, and on the l. stands the collegiate church of **S. Feliú**. The presbytery dates from 1313–18, the nave from 1318–26. The steeple, truncated by lightning in 1581, vas begun by *Pedro Zacoma* in 1368–69, and completed by *Pedro Ramón* in 1383–92. Embedded in the chancel wall are eight sarcophagi, wo of them Roman (Rape of Proserpine; Lion Hunt), the rest of them 4-5C. A sarcophagus above the altar contains the body of St. Felix of Girona (d. 303); the retablo illustrates his life.—In the domed *Cap. de S. Narciso* (1782–92) on the N. side are a tomb of 1328 by Maestro *Juan*, while in the *Cap. de Sta Afra* is an alabaster recumbent Christ (mid-14C), perhaps by *Jaime Cascalls*.

By turning r. after passing the Portal de Sobreportas, we reach neo-classic *S. Lucas* (1724–29), and beyond it the '*Arab Baths*', recorded in 1194 but in their present form dating from the 13C.

Hence we may follow the *Paseo Arqueológico*, which climbs through gardens, allowing good views of the fortress of *Montjuich* (1653), which commanded the town until destroyed in 1809, and the exterior of the Cathedral. At the far end we reach the *Walls*, which may be followed some distance along the perimeter of the old town.—On the hill above lie more ruined forts blown up by the French in 1809.

To the N., beyond a bridge over a small stream, is Romanesque **S. Pedro de Galligans,** finished c. 1131, with an octagonal tower; the apse forms a bastion of the town-wall. The *cloister* (c. 1154–90) is occupied by the *Museo Provincial*, containing prehistoric finds, Greek and Roman sarcophagi, etc., from Ampurias, and medieval sculpture including the polychrome alabaster Virgen de Besalú (14C). On the N. of S. Pedro is the restored Romanesque chapel of *S. Nicolás* (late 12C).

A path leads up the valley of the Galligans to the monastery of *S. Daniel,* whose late 11C church stands above a crypt containing the saint's shrine with an effigy of 1345. There is a 15C door and a *cloister* of c. 1200 with a late Gothic upper gallery.

The only objects of interest in the new town which has grown up W. of the Oñar are the *Hosp. de Sta Catalina* (1666) and opposite, the *Hospicio* of 1776–85, by *Ventura Rodriguez*, which stands S.W. of the Rambla de José Antonio.

FROM GERONA TO OLOT (55 km.). 4 km. N. of Gerona the C 150 forks l. off the N II to (14 km.) **Banyoles,**(11,100 inhab.; *Hotel*), with the restored church of *Sta María dels Turers*. In the conventual church of *S. Esteban* is a 15C retablo; the *cloisters* contain 12–16C tombs of the abbots; among the old houses is the *Pía Almoina*, begun in 1307, and containing an archaeological museum.

We follow the road skirting the W. bank of the lake of Banyoles, passing at *Porqueres*, Romanesque *Sta María* (cons. 1182) before climbing to (7 km.) *Serinyà*, with a 12C church and a series of caves containing remarkáble paintings, notably in the *Cueva dels Encantats*.

A direct but secondary road to Olot diverges W. of the lake and follows a picturesque route past the Renaissance church of (6 km.) *Mieres*, and (10 km.) *Sta Pau*, an ancient village with an early castle and 15C church.—The 9C *Santuario dels Archs* is c. 2 km. distant, while from the chapel of *S. Aniol de Finestras* splendid views are obtained.—We pass through a region of strange volcanic formations, cut by ravines known as '*grederas*' to (10 km.) *Olot*, see below.

8 km. **Besalú** (2000 inhab.) still retains a number of reminders of its past, including an (over-restored) fortified *Bridge* (12th and 14C), some porticoed streets and squares, and old houses, while among its churches are restored *S. Vicente* (1018–13C), ruins of Romanesque *Sta María* (? 1055), while the 11C

Hospital, and late 12C *Monastery of S. Pedro* are of interest, as is the recently discovered and restored vaulted *Jewish Baths* or *Mikwah* (11–12C), in the lower town. Among early 13C troubadours was Ramon Vidal de Besalú.—Near (14 km.) *Castellfollit de la Roca,* perched on some curious basalt cliffs, is a *Roman Bridge* of two storeys.—3 km. N. lies *S. Cristi de Palera* (cons. 1085).

8 km. **Olot** (23,200 inhab.; *Hotel*) the birthplace of the composer Antonio Soler (1729–83), is now an unattractive industrial town encircled by mountains, once a volcanic area. In *S. Esteban* (18C) are a retablo by *Juan Panyó,* and in the sacristy Christ carrying the Cross by *El Greco,* and a 15C processional cross. The *Hospicio* contains a small archaeological museum, while in the *Torre Castany* is a museum of Catalan art.—At *S. Joan les Fonts,* 5 km. N., is a Romanesque church and a curious basaltic formation.

From Olot the C 150 climbs W. to the Collado de Coubet. with a fine view of the Pyrenees, and again from the Pto. de Santigosa, as we descend to *Sant Joan de les Abadeses* (see p.166).—The C 153 leads N. W. through the ancient villages of the Vall de Vianya to (16 km.) *Sant Salvador de Bianya,* with a church of 1170. *Camprodón* (p.166) lies 14 km. beyond, on the far side of the Pto. de Capsacosta.

Driving S. from Olot (C 152) we may return to Girona, passing, after 18 km., on a spur of the Sierra de Finestres, the castle of *Hostoles,* and (11 km.) *Amer,* with a Romanesque church. Crossing the Ter, leaving the Embalse d'El Pasteral on out r., we meet the N 141 at (9 km.) *Anglès,* a picturesque walled village, where we turn l. and follow the river to (17 km.) *Girona.*

From Girona to Sant Feliú de Guixols (35 km.) The direct road (C 250) drives S.E. through (13 km.) *Caça de la Selva,* containing a 15C church with a Renaissance front, before entering (7 km.) *Llagostera,* with remains of a 14C castle, 16C church, and old houses.—Here the road diverges l. (C 253) for (15 km.) *Sant Feliú* and r. for (4 km.) *Tossa,* see p. 141.

From Girona to Palafrugell (40 km.) The C 255 driving N.E. from Girona. circles the wooded slopes of the Sierra de les Gavarres. We shortly bear S.E. to (28 km.) *La Bisbal (Hotel)* with a 14C castle of the bishops of Girona, passing (3 km. W.) *Cruilles,* with the monastic church of *S. Miguel* (mid-12C) with a 10C cloister. At *Vulpellac* (1 km. E.) is an interesting church and 14C castle, 5 km. N.E. of which lies *Peratallada,* a walled village; further N. at *Ullastret,* is an important Iberian settlement, with cyclopean *Fortifications; a small archaeological museum has been installed in a 14C hermitage.—The mozarabic church of *S. Julian de Buada* lies to the E.—12 km. *Palafrugell,* see p.140.

Quitting Girona, the N II drives S. past the airport, and (16 km. l.) a turning for *Caldes de Malavella* (2900 inhab.; *Hotels),* the 'Vichy Catalan', with medicinal springs, ruins of Roman thermae, and medieval castle. Leaving the Sierra de les Gavarres behind us to the l. we approach (r.) the Sierra de Montseny.—At 3 km. the road forks: l. to the coast N. of *Calella* (see p.141), off which, at 4 km., a road leads direct to (17 km.) *Llóret de Mar,* and at 6 km. another leads, 2 km. r., to *Maçanet de la Selva,* with old houses and a ruined 12C castle.—The r. fork (C 251) follows the valley of the Tordera to the S.W., running parallel to the coast, between the Montseny massif, and the Sierra de Montnegre.

At 3 km. the C253 leads W. 9 km. to *Santa Coloma de Farners,* with a picturesque ruined castle (12-14C) and the chapel of *N.S. de Farners.*—A minor road leads further W. to (12 km.) *Sant Hilari Sacalm,* a small spa. From the chapel of *S. Miguel* (3950 ft) there is a splendid view.—*Arbúcies,* 11 km. S. of *Sant Hilari,* is a starting point for the ascent of *Montseny* (5585 ft).—Beyond *Sant Hilari,* a road climbs down to (36 km.) *Vic,* see p.164.

9 km. l. *Hostalric,* a picturesque but dilapidated walled village above the Tordera valley surrounded by plantations of cork-oaks.—At 7 km. a road leads r. 4 km. to *Breda,* noted for pottery. The Gothic parish church retains a fine tower of 1068, and nearby are the ruins of the Benedictine *Conv. de S. Salvador.* To the N.W. stands the ruined castle of *Montsoliu.*—6 km. *Sant Celoni,* where the church (cons. 1106) has a

emarkable Baroque front of painted plaster.—A tortuous road climbs
N.W. to (22km.) *Sta Fé del Montseny* set among mountain lakes,
passing the church tower of *Fogars de Montclús*.—At 2km. another
mountain road ascends to the village of *Montseny* (13km. N.W.; *Hotel*)
and winding through the centre of the range, descends its W. slope to
(27km.) *Tona,* see p. 164.—7km. **Llinars,** dominated by a severe castle
of 1551–58, 7km. N.W. of which is the church of *S. Pedro de Vilamayor,*
with a tower of c. 1500. We now emerge into the fertile valley of the
Congost.—11km. **Granollers,** an industrial town (36,500 inhab.; *Hotel*)
with a 14C church and ruined walls of 1366–77.—The ruined castle of *La
Roca* stands 4km. S.E.; 8km. S., at *Montmeló,* are remains of a
Carolingian church.—At 3km. we join the N 152 from Puigcerda, see
Rte. 11.—27km. **Barcelona,** see Rte. 9.

8   THE COSTA BRAVA: PORTBOU TO BLANES

This 'route' is printed more as a convenience to describe the area rather than one
which should be methodically followed. Except for the most northerly part of this
indented coast, the rest is perhaps more easily approached by turnings off the A 17
motorway, as described at the head of Rte. 7. As almost all the coastal resorts are
plentifully supplied with *hotels* of every category, even if some are closed out of
season, their presence will not be indicated in this route.

Cerbère, the French customs post, lies 47km. S.E. of Perpignan, the
main focus of traffic. Passing the Pto. d'els Balitres, we shortly reach the
Spanish customs station at *Portbou,* once a fishing port, beyond which
we have panoramic views of the coast towards Cap de Creus.

After 14km. of narrow winding road, we reach *Llançà,* with a
Baroque church.

Hence the improved C 252 leads S.W. near *Perelada* (p.135) to (21km.)
Figueres, off which (at 9km.), after passing the ruined castle of *Carmansó,* we may
turn l. and l. again at *Vilajuiga,* to climb a secondary road to (9km.) **S. Pere de
Roda,* on a ridge of the Sierra de Rosas. The ruined abbey (12C) and nearby castle
of *S. Salvador* (which may also be approached by a bridle path from Llançá)
command extensive views.—From *Vilajuïga* the main road leads 11km. S.E. to
Roses, see below.

Beyond (7km.) *El Port de la Selva,* overlooked to the S.W. by the 10C
tower of *Selva de Mar,* the road climbs steeply S.E. through a region of
slatey terraced hills to (8km.) to high-lying crossroad, from which we
make a twisting descent to attractively-sited (5km.) **Cadaqués** (1500
inhab. out of season), with a 17C church containing a richly gilt organ-
case, and the *Museo Perrot-Moore,* devoted to the graphic arts.—
Rough lanes lead to adjacent *Port-Lligat,* home of Salvador Dalí (see
Figueres).

A track climbs N.E. to *Cap de Creus* (the ancient *Aphrodision*) and another
leads round the S. side of the peninsula to Roses.

Regaining the main road, affording many splendid views, we climb
down to (12km.) **Roses** (7100 inhab.), occupying the site of the Greek
colony of *Rhoda.* Visigothic remains have been found at *Puig de las
Murallas.* The ruined citadel (1543), once a fortified monastery (cons.
1022), after undergoing numerous sieges, was blown up by Suchet in
1814.—The road now crosses the Empordà plain, skirting the sandy bay
of Roses, to (9km.) **Castelló d'Empúries** (2100 inhab.) with a Bridge
over the Muga built in 1354 by *Berenguer Brunet.* The church (13–14C)

has a square battlemented tower and a fine early 15C Doorway by Antonio Antigoni. The alabaster Retablo of 1483–85 is by *Vicente Borrás*. The Cavaillé-Coll organ was restored in 1976. Adjacent is the 13C *Lonja*, restored. Also in the town is the *Conv. de Sta Clara*, and disused *Sto Domingo* with a Renaissance and Baroque cloister.—The C 260 leads W. to *Figueres*, but we bear S.—At (8km.) *Sant Pere Pescador*, a road leads W. 9km. to **Sant Miguel de Fluvià**, with a beautiful church (cons. 1066) of a Benedictine abbey, with an 11C belfry and a front begun in the 15C and finished in 1533.—At (7km.) *Viladamat* we veer E. towards L'Escala, but after 3km. may make a detour by turning l. for the picturesque village of *Sant Martí*.—Hence, descending abruptly to the shore we reach the important and extensive *Ruins* of **Ampurias**, or *Empúries*, the Greek and Roman port of *Emporion*, where Gnaeus Scipio landed during the Iberian expedition in the Second Punic War (218 B.C.).

Excavations have laid bare part of the harbour, fragments of the Roman wall and earlier Cyclopean wall, and the outline of many of the streets. There is a museum, but the most striking discoveries have been removed to Barcelona and Gerona. Many mosaic pavements remain in situ, and the site, on a gentle slope overlooking the bay, is impressive.

1km. S. lies the resort of *L'Escala* (3500 inhab.) with a good 18C church.—We now circle the flank of *Montgri*, surmounted by a fine castle begun in 1294, passing (7km., r.) the ruined late-13C castle of *Belcaire*.—At 3km. we turn l. for (3km.) **Torroella de Montgri** (5300 inhab.), with remains of walls and gates, a 14C church and Ayuntamiento, and medieval and Renaissance palaces.—5km. S.E. lies the resort of *Estartit*, with a view of the offshore ILLES MEDES.—Leaving Torroella, we cross the Ter and pass (9km. r.) *Pals*, an old village with ruined walls and towers, partly restored, beyond which the road climbs E. to (7km.) **Begur** (2200 inhab.), surrounded by five atalayas commanding the coast.

From Begur roads descend: N. to *Sa Riera;* E. to (7km.) *Aiguafreda;* while to the S. shortly after leaving the town, another climbs down to *Fornells* and (6km.) *Aigua Blava (Parador Nac.).*

Regaining the main road, we continue S. to (6km.) **Palafrugell** (13,800 inhab.), birthplace of Josep Plá (1897–), the historian and journalist, whose library has been donated to the town, with remains of Moorish walls, and Baroque *S. Martín*, with a 17C retablo.—A picturesque road leads down through pine woods to the sheltered village of *Tamariú*, while another descends S.E. to *Llafranch*, and the playa of *Calella de Palafrugell*, 2km. S. of which at *Cap Roig*, are attractive botanical gardens.

From Palafrugell to *Girona* see p. 138.

From Palafrugell the C 255 drives S., shortly passing at *Montras*, a church of 1599 with a fortified belfry known as the *Torre Simona*, to (9km.) **Palamós**, founded in 1277, a growing resort (11,350 inhab.) with a 14C church altered and enlarged in the 16th and 18Cs, and a small Museum. The coast between Palamós and Sant Feliú de Guixols has been irreparably spoilt; little attempt has been made to control the ruthless exploitation by the tourist industry of its natural beauty.— 7km. *Platja d'Aro;* 3km., *S'Agaró*, with remains of a 14C cloister incorporated into the modern church.

3 km. **Sant Feliú de Guixols,** an old port (14,200 inhab.), whose staple industry was exporting the products of the surrounding cork-oak forest, is now a tourist centre retaining a pleasant paseo, a 14C church, near which are the 11C *Porta Ferrada* and the Baroque *Arco de S. Benito,* remains of a vanished monastery. The museum contains prehistoric remains and a collection of paintings and sculpture.—The chapel of *Sant Elm* on the summit of Mte. Castellar to the S.W., was built as a landmark in 1452.

A scenically attractive road (C 253) turns inland to avoid the cornich between Sant Feliú and Lloret de Mar, off which (at 6 km.) a road leads N. 7 km. to *Romanyá de la Selva,* near which is the important megalithic monument known as the *'Cueva d'en Dayna'.*—The C 253 may be regained just short of (8 km.) *Llagostera,* beyond which we bear S.W. to meet the N II near (14 km. r.) *Vidreres.* The autopista for Barcelona may also be conveniently reached from this point. Alternatively we may continue S. to approach the coast again S.W. of *Blanes,* see below.

From *San Feliú* the coast road climbs steeply to the *Ermita de la Grau,* with panoramic views, before winding down to (22 km.) **Tossa** (2600 inhab. out of season) preserving some medieval walls which protected it against the Barbary pirates, remains of a castle, a Baroque church of 1755, and museum. Beyond *Tossa* the road continues its serpentine course, but further back from the sea, from which by-roads descend to a series of small beaches and coves.

12 km. *Lloret de Mar.* (8200 inhab.), with the church of *S. Quirico* (1079), beyond which the road straightens out and by-passes **Blanes** (18,500 inhab.), with a 14C church occupying an old palace.—We cross the Tordera and after passing the ruined castle of *Palafólls,* meet the N II just N. of (13 km.) *Malgrat.*

A string of resorts of little interest follow almost without interruption: *Pineda; Calella; Sant Pol de Mar,* with a chapel known as *La Ermita;* slightly inland lies picturesque *Sant Cebrià de Vallalta; Canet de Mar* retains the medieval castle of *Sta Florentina* and 15C atalayas.—15 km. *Arenys de Mar.* In the church is a retablo by *Pablo Costa* (1706–14).—On a hill stands *Arénys de Munt,* whose church of *S. Martín* is of 1531–44.—By the road to *S. Celoni* stands the dolmen of *Vallgorguina.*—Passing (r.) the *Baños de Titus* and the *Torre dels Encantats,* on its hill, we reach *Caldetes,* with a 13C church and houses of the 14–16C.—To the r. is the ruined castle of *Nofre Arnau.*—At *Llavaneres,* 2 km. inland, is *S. Andrés,* with a 17C Italian retablo, and ruins of a castle.

12 km. **Mataró,** the ancient *Iluro,* of which the Roman villa of *Torre Llauder* has been excavated, is now a manufacturing and shipbuilding centre (92,100 inhab.), above which lay the walled medieval town. The railway hence to Barcelona was the first to be laid in Spain in 1848.—4 km. inland are the springs of *Argentona,* with an early 16C church and the ruined castle of *S. Vicente de Burriach* (15C).—From Mataró the A 19 autopista leads directly to Barcelona, running parallel to the coast and by-passing (r.) *Villassar,* with a Gothic church, old castle and several atalayas, and (l.) *Montgat,* famous for the defence of its castle against the French in 1808.—4 km. inland from Montgat lies *Tiana,* near which is the former *Cartuja de Montealegre* (founded 1344), which commands a wide sea-view.

19 km. **Badalona** (203,700 inhab.) an industrial suburb of Barcelona, is the ancient *Baetula*, a town of even greater antiquity than its flourishing neighbour. Excavations have brought to light part of the Roman town plan, and finds dating from the 2C B.C. to the 4C A.D. On the *Puntigalá*, a cliff W. of the town, is carved an inscription to Apollo; nearby is the ruined abbey (15C) of *S. Jerónimo de la Murta*, while a short distance W. lies *Santa Coloma de Gramenet*, where stands the *Torre Pallaresa* (c. 1530), a late-Gothic country house.—10 km. **Barcelona.**

9   BARCELONA AND ENVIRONS

BARCELONA, capital of the ancient principality of Catalonia and modern province of Barcelona, and with a population of 1,751,100 excluding populous adjacent municipalities, is the most prosperous city in Spain, and one of the most interesting and exuberant, and many would agree with Rose Macaulay, when she wrote, three decades ago, of Barcelona: 'More, perhaps, than any city in the world (Marseilles and Naples are near rivals) it gives an impression of tempestuous, surging, irrepressible life and *brio*'.

Barcelona enjoys as fine a situation as any town on the Mediterranean. The plain on which it stands is bounded on the N.E. by the river Besós, on the S.W. by the Llobregat, and is overlooked from the landward side by an amphitheatre of hills, culminating in the summit of *Tibidabo*, while immediately S.W. of the harbour rises *Montjuich*. The winter temperature is mild, while the sultry summer heat is tempered by sea breezes.

P.O. Pl. de Cataluña
Tourist Offices S.E.T., Gran Via 658; *Centro Excursionista de Cataluña*, C. Paradis 10; *Municipal Offices* at Av. Pto. del Angel 8; Pl. S. Jaime, Est. de Francia; and Estación Marítima.
British Institute, C. Amigó 83.
Railway Stations: *Est. de Francia*, for Port Bou and France, to Zaragoza viâ Caspe, and to Tarragona and Valencia; *Est. de la Pl. de Cataluña* (underground), for most trains to Puigcerdà, and Montserrat, stopping also at Arco de Triunfo, near the *Est. del Norte*, the new bus station. Also the *Est. Paseo de Gracia*, for Valencia.
Airport at Prat de Llobregat, c. 12 km. S.; *Air Terminus* (by train) at *Sants* station, just W. of the Pl. de España; *Iberia*, Rambla de Cataluña, 18. There is now a regular air-bus service operating between Barcelona and Madrid.
Regular steamer services and car ferries to the Balearic Islands.
Motor Launches. Frequent '*Golondrinas*' from the Puerta de la Paz to Barceloneta, and '*Gaviotas*' to the Rompeolas.
Hotels. Barcelona is plentifully supplied with hotels of every category, but travellers are advised to assure, if possible, that their hotel is reasonably near the 'Barrio Gotico' for many of the newer establishments are some distance away, and much time can be wasted in travelling to the centre.
Note. *All* the museums of Barcelona are *closed on Mondays,* with the exception of the *Museo Picasso,* which is open on Monday afternoons.
Employment of Time. For the hurried visitor, the principal objectives will be the *Barrio Gotico, Sta. Maria del Mar* (p.151) and the nearby *C. Montcada* and its museums; the *Ramblas* and the adjacent *Reales Atarazanas* (p.149), and *Montjuich* with its fortress and museums (p.154).

History. The Carthaginian city of *Barcino,* founded by Hamilcar Barca c. 230 B.C., occupied Mont Taber, the low hill on which the cathedral now stands. There appears to have been a previous city, Iberian or perhaps Phocæan, on this site, but of its history little is known. After the expulsion of the Carthaginians from Spain by the Romans (206–201 B.C.) Barcino became capital of Layetania, and a district of Hispania Tarraconensis, and under Augustus was distinguished by the title *Colonia Julia Augusta Pia Faventia*. It was destroyed by the Franks in A.D. 263, but retaken by the Romans and fortified with a great wall. The Visigothic leader Ataulf made it his capital in 415 A.D., and it is probably to this that Catalonia owes its name (*Gothalania*); but in 713 the city surrendered to the Moors on honourable terms. Early in the 9C Louis the Debonair, son of Charlemagne, drove the Moors out of Catalonia and appointed a dependent count to rule the Spanish marches.

In 874 Wilfred '*el Velloso*' ('the hairy'), Count of Barcelona, was given independence by Charles the Bald, in return for services rendered, and his descendants prospered for many years. In 985 Almanzor burnt the town, but was driven out in the same year by Borrell II. Ramón Berenguer I (1018–25) compiled the '*Usatges*', Catalan equivalent of the '*fueros*', or privileges of Aragón and the Basque provinces. Ramón Berenguer IV, by his marriage with Petronila, daughter of Ramiro '*el Monje*' of Aragón, united that kingdom to his domains (1137) and assumed the title of King of Aragón. The Consejo del Ciento (Council of the 100), founded by Jaime I, promulgated in 1259 the *Consulat del Mar,* the earliest code of European maritime laws, which served as model for other Mediterranean states.

The marriage of Fernando and Isabel (1474) brought Barcelona beneath the Castilian yoke, and marked the end of its independence. At Barcelona the Catholic kings received Columbus on his return from the discovery of America (June 1493). In 1640 an attempt by Philip IV to ignore the 'usatges' drove the Catalans to seek the assistance of France (the War '*dels Segadors*'), but in 1705 Barcelona espoused the cause of the Archduke Charles against Philip V, the nominee of Louis XIV. The city was taken and sacked by Marshal Berwick (1714) and its ancient privileges abolished. Barcelona was occupied by the French from 1808 to 1813.

Throughout the 19C it was a focus of unrest, declaring itself as a matter of course opposed to any constituted authority. In 1827 and 1868 it supported the Carlists, and in 1835 it was a centre of anti-monastic agitation, while in the early years of the present century it was a hotbed of anarchist plotting, and anticlericalism and outbreaks of violence occurred in 1908–9, and again in the immediate post-war period in reaction to the repressive governorship of Martínez Anido. By 1920 its population (c. 115,000 in 1800) had risen to 706,000. In 1923 Gen. Primo de Rivera published at Barcelona his Pronunciamiento declaring the establishment of a military dictatorship. But Catalonia remained a centre of disaffection, and on 14 April 1931 the Catalan Republic was proclaimed. In 1936 Gen. Goded arrived from Majorca to raise the garrison for the Nationalists, but the attempt failed after violent street fighting, and it was not until Jan. 1939 that Nationalist forces entered Barcelona. Many of its churches were gutted by fire during this Republican period.

The Generalitat was re-established in Sept. 1977, and with a greater measure of autonomy the city, as well as the province, materially flourishes.

Among its natives are the writers Juan Boscan (1487/92–1542); Antonio Capmany (1742–1813); Jacinto Verdaguer (1843–1902); Joan Maragall (1860–1911); Josep Carner (1884–1970); and Carles Riba (1897–1959). Among painters, Antonio Viladomat (1678–1755); Francisco Javier Parcerisa (1803–75); and Joan Miró (1893-). Also Francisco Pi y Margall (1824-1901), President of the first Spanish Republic; and Francisco Ferrer (1849–1909), the radical reformer.

The nucleus of the town is the ancient *Barrio Gotico,* around which the medieval city grew, which was in turn surrounded by defensive walls (demolished 1868), the approx. line of which lay along the '*Paralelo*' to the S.W.—commanded by a fortress of Montjuich—the Ronda de S. Antonio, the C. de Pelayo, and the Ronda de S. Pedro; while to the N.E. it was later defended by the Ciudadela. The only wide street was the Rambla, until the Via Layetana was driven through the town as part of the grandiose Plan Cerda of 1854, when the New Town or *Ensanche* (extension) was laid out in a grid beyond the Old, connecting it with outlying communities.

The '*Diagonal*' intersects this grid, N. of which lies an extensive and fashionable residential and shopping district climbing the lower slopes of Tibidabo and Vallvidrera, an area not sufficiently appreciated by the visitor, who will naturally concentrate on the Barrio Gotico, and may

well assume that there is little of interest beyond the intervening lattice of
streets now primarily a commercial area.

A   The Barrio Gotico

The narrow congested alleys of the old town are best visited on foot.
Underground car-parks are available outside.

Specifically, the *Barrio Gotico* is the area once enclosed by the 4C town walls,
considerable sections of which may still be seen. There is an ambitious and well
conceived project under way to uncover and restore an almost complete circuit of
walls as derelict houses abutting the demolished, but this may well take some
decades to come to fruition.

From the Av. de la Catedral we have a good view of the W. Front of
the *Cathedral* and the huge square bastions of the walls to the r., and the
Pta. Nueva, with cylindrical towers on Roman foundations facing the
Pl. Nueva. The ***Cathedral** (Pl. 10), a magnificent example of Catalan
Gothic, is known to the Catalans as *La Seu.*

The octagonal towers above the transepts date from 1385–89, the clock-tower
being slightly older. The W. Front, for which a design (still preserved) had been
made in 1408 by the French master *Carli,* was only completed in 1890–92, but the
openwork spires harmonize well with the older work. The original church, possibly
built on the site of a pagan temple, was desecrated by Almansor in the 10C. Of the
rebuilding of 1046–58 by Ramón Berenguer II nothing remains but the *Pta. de S.
Severo* in the S. Transept and the entrance to the Cap. de Sta Lucía outside the
S.W. corner of the cloister. The N. entrance to the Cathedral, the *Pta. de S. Ivo*
(above which are reliefs depicting the combat of the Knight of Vilardell with a
dragon), is flanked by inscriptions relating to the building of the present church,
which was begun in 1298 and finished as far as the W. end of the coro in 1329, with
Jaime Fabre of Majorca as master of the works from 1317 to 1339. The W. end and
cloister were built between 1365 and 1448 under *Bernard Roca, Bartolomeu Gual*
and *Andrés Escuder.*

INTERIOR. From the central door of the W. Front its fine proportions
—now well-lit—can be appreciated. Behind two massive 15C columns
supporting the cimborio (1418–22 by *Gual*) is the TRASCORO, decorated
with marble reliefs of the Life of Sta Eulalia, by *Bartolomé Ordoñez*
(1517–20) and *Pedro Vilar* (1563–64). On either side, above the row of
chapels, is a deep triforium surmounted by a rather inadequate
clerestory, many of whose windows contain good 15C stained glass.—In
the CORO (after 1390) the high *Stalls,* each surmounted by a delicately-
worked canopy, are by the German artists *Michael Lochner* and
Friedrich (1483–90), the lower by *Matías Bonafé* (1457).

The coats of arms on the upper tier are those of the Knights of the Golden Fleece
who assembled at the first and last Chapter of the Order held here by Charles V in
1519, and include royal arms of Sweden and Poland, the devices of the Prince of
Orange, and the Duke of Alba, etc.—On the l. is *Lochner's* Pulpit, reached by a
stair by *Pere Ca-Anglada,* who designed also the Bishop's Throne (r.).

Most of the numerous SIDE CHAPELS contain retablos of the 16–18C;
mostly in poor condition, separated from the aisles by well-wrought
grilles.—The 1st S. Chapel (after 1405, by *Arnau Bargués*), has a fine
Grille and the tomb of St. Olegarius (d. 1136), Abp. of Tarragona. The
effigy of 1406 is by *Ca-Anglada,* but the tomb dates from 1678–79. Here
is the crucifix carried by Don Juan of Austria on the prow of his flagship
at Lepanto.—The 2nd chapel (l. wall) contains the tomb of Sancha
Jiménez de Cabrera (1446, by *Pere Oller*).—In the 5th S. Chapel is the
early 14C sarcophagus of S. Raimundo de Peñafort (d. 1275), general of
the Dominican order and confessor of Jaime el Conquistador. On the r.

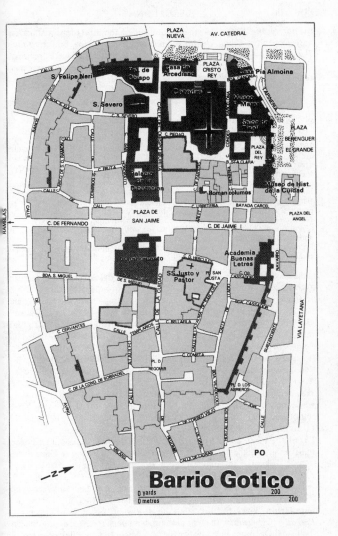

Barrio Gotico

0 yards 200
0 metres 200

above the sacristy door, are the wooden sarcophagi of Ramón Berenguer I (d. 1025) and his wife Almodis.—The 3rd, in the AMBULATORY, has a 15C Retablo by *Bernat Martorell*. In the 4th chap. is a 16C carved retablo. The last chapel in the ambulatory contains the sumptuous tomb of Bp. Ramón de Escales (d. 1398), finished in 1409 by *Antoni Canet*.—Beneath the *organ* (1539) in the N. Transept are two huge Moors' heads; the transepts and crossing were completed in 1329.—To the N. of the W. Door is the *Baptistery,* with a white marble font of 1433 by *Onofre Juliá,* a Florentine, and glass of 1495, designed by *Bartolomé Bermejo.*—From the foot of the altar-steps a staircase descends to the *Cripta de Sta Eulalia,* an apsidal chapel built by *Jaime Fabre* in 1318–39 to contain the relics of the patroness of Barcelona, translated thence from Sta María del Mar. The marble tomb has bas-reliefs by *Giovanni Pisano.*

The SACRISTY, entered by a Gothic door on the r. of the ambulatory, contains the *Treasury,* including a reliquary of gold and silver (15C), the silver-gilt Throne of Don Martín el Humano (1396–1410), an enamelled processional cross by *Francesc Villardell* and, among illuminated MSS., the 15C Missal of Sta Eulalia.

By the adjoining Romanesque *Pta. de S. Severo,* we enter the **Cloister**, begun in 1382 by *Bernard Roca* and finished by *Andrés Escuder* in 1448, with irregular arches and curious capitals. On the r. is the *Pabellón de S. Jorge,* a graceful arcaded pavilion (note the vault-boss of St. George carved by *Joan Claperós*) sheltering a fountain, adjoining which is the *Fuente de las Ocas,* a pool with an enclosure for the 'Capitoline' geese kept as a reminder of the Roman greatness of Barcelona. On the W. side of the cloister is the *Chapter House* of c. 1400, by *Arnau Bargués* containing paintings, notably a Pietá (1490) by *Bermejo* and in the N.W. corner is an entrance to the *Cap. del Santísimo Sacramento.* In the *Secretaria del Capitulo* is the tomb of the 15C archdeacon Lluís Desplá, while the N.W. walk contains those of canon Francisco Desplá (d. 1457)) and of Mossèn Borra, knight, ambassador and court jester, who died at Naples in 1477.—It is worth while to leave the cloister by the S.W. door to see the Romanesque *Door* of the *Cap. de Sta Lucía* (1257).

Facing the W. side of the cloister is the **Casa del Arcediano** or former archdeacons' house of c. 1495–1510, now occupied by the *Archivo Histórico de la Ciudad.* It preserves a charming courtyard with some decorated windows and a Renaissance doorway.—To the l. the *Pal. del Obispo* incorporates some Romanesque portions of the original bishop's palace begun in 1255. In the Pl. Garriga stands *S. Servero,* by *Jaime Arnaudies,* completed in 1708, with Baroque decorations, while a turning (r.) between the two last leads to *S. Felipe Neri* (1721–22) with neo-classical altars (1776–78). Adjacent is the *Museo del Calzado,* devoted to footwear. Following the C. del Obispo Irurita we pass the *Pta. de Sta. Eulalia,* a fine Gothic doorway to the Cathedral Cloister, while the *Pta. de la Piedad,* at the angle of the apse and the cloister, has a sculptured Pietá (15C) in the tympanum. We continue past the 14C *Casas de los Canónigos* (restored) and turn down the narrow C. de Paradis. At No. 10, the *Centro Excursionista de Cataluña,* in a house built on the highest point of the old city, where stood a Corinthian temple dedicated to Augustus, four *Roman columns* are displayed in situ, and may be seen from the vestibule.

Following this alley, we enter (on the site of an ancient cemetery) the **Pl. de S. Jaime** (Pl. 10), the heart of the barrio. To the r. stands the **Diputación,** which together with the *Audiencia,* occupies what was the *Pal. de la Generalitat,* the seat of the ancient parliament of Catalonia. In the C. del Obispo is the entrance to the **Audiencia,** a building of 1416–18 by *Marc Safont* with a plain façade (finished in 1540) surmounted by a Medallion of St. George and the Dragon carved in 1418 by *Pere Johan.*

The building (restored) of the *Diputación* was begun in the 15C, but the main front on the Pl. de S. Jaime was not built until 1597–1600 by *Pedro Blay.*—From the courtyard a flight of steps with an elaborate balustrade ascends to the delicately arcaded gallery of the first floor. Hence we may enter the *Patio de los Naranjos,* an upper courtyard overlooked by finely carved windows and curious gargoyles.—On the r. is the *Cap. de S. Jorge,* also by *Safont,* an interesting work of 1432–34, containing 16C Flemish tapestries and the mid-15C embroidered altar-frontal of St. George (S. Jordi in Catalan) together with a copy in silver. Opening off the gallery of the main patio is the classical *Salón de S. Jorge;* while on the l. of the Patio de los Naranjos are the richly decorated *Salón de Sesiones,* or council chamber, and other rooms of the former courts of justice. The Archives comprise a remarkable series of legal records dating from 1372.

On the opposite side of the plaza stands the **Ayuntamiento** (1847) preserving on the N.E. side the *façade* of the old Gothic town hall of 1399–1402, by *Arnau Bargués,* which bears sculptures by *Jordi de Déu.* The statues on the front, by *José Bover,* represent Jaime el Conquistador and Conceller Juan Fivaller, upholder of the Catalan fueros. Among the numerous finely furnished and decorated rooms on the first floor is the *Salón de Ciento,* where councillors are elected, a Gothic chamber 27 m. long (1369–73) entered by a Renaissance doorway with twisted columns (1550). The *Salón de las Crónicas* is decorated with paintings by *José María Sert* of the Catalan expedition to the East under Roger de Flor. The *Chapel* of 1409–10 was the original home of the retablo 'dels Concellers' painted by *Luis Dalmau* in 1445 (comp. p.156).

To the S. of the Ayuntamiento, in the shadow of its simple but incongruous modern extension, stands the 15C *Pal. de Centellas,* with a good patio.—Behind the new council offices, the C. de Ataulfo leads to the *Cap. de los Templarios* (1245) close to the *Cap. del Palau* (1542; retablo of 1580), the only vestige of the former Pal. Real Menor.—The C. Templarios and C. de la Ciudad lead us to *SS. Justo y Pastor,* a building of 1345–60 (restored) claiming to occupy the oldest ecclesiastical site in Barcelona, with fine vault bosses, and in the *Cap. de S. Felix* a retablo (c. 1530) by *Pedro Nuñes.*—Opposite, a passage leads to the *Pal. de Academia de las Buenas Letras,* with an attractive patio. Following the C. de Lladó, turning l. and l. again, we may see part of the exterior Town Wall which has recently been exposed.

Passing the S.W. side of the Pl. del Angel we reach the Pl. DE BERENGUER EL GRANDE from which a good view may be obtained of the ancient **Walls** buttressing the chapel of *Sta Águeda* and the old palace. These may be reached by retracing our steps to the Pl. del Angel and turning r. and r. again. We pass at the S.E. corner of the Pl. del Rey, the 16C *Casa Pedellás,* brought from the C. de Mercaders and re-erected, in which has been installed the *Museo de Historia de la Ciudad.* Steps descend to subterranean galleries displaying extensive remains in situ of a Visigothic and Roman town. Excavations are continuing, particularly on the 4C Christian Basilica and 11C Cathedral. The first and second floors are devoted to the history of Barcelona, its craft guilds, and minor arts; collections of plans and drawings illustrating the development of the city from the 16C to the 19C, and including the original sketch by *Luis Dalmau* (1443) for the Virgen dels Concellers (see above).—From the first floor we may enter the **Chapel Royal of Sta Águeda,** built in 1302–19 by *Bertrán Riquer,* with an octagonal belfry, and containing a retablo of the Epiphany (1464–66) by *Jaume Huguet.*

Adjacent to the museum is the picturesque Pl. DEL REY, on the site of the old palace of the counts. Across the N. corner of the plaza stairs ascend under a lofty arch to enter the *Pal. Real Mayor* and the great hall, known as the *Salón de Tinell,* where Fernando and Isabel received Columbus on his first return from America. The hall (1359–70), by *Guillén Carbonell,* with a span of 17 m., was converted into the conventual church of Sta Clara in 1716, but was purchased by the muncipality in 1940 and restored. In the earlier part of the palace are remains of wallpaintings of c. 1300.—The hall is surmounted by an unusual tower (1557) consisting of five superimposed galleries, known as the **Mirador del Rey Martín.**

Leaving the Pl. del Rey, we turn r. towards the apse of the Cathedral, and follow the C. de los Condes. Immediately on our r. stands the **Pal. de Lloctinent,** erected in 1549–57 by *Antonio Carbonell* for the viceroy of Catalonia. Off the dignified courtyard ascends a staircase with a superb coffered ceiling. The building houses the *Archives of the Crown of Aragón* (founded in 1549), comprising over 4 million documents, dating back to A.D. 844.

Opposite the *Pta. de S. Ivo* (N. entrance of the cathedral) is the ***Museo Marés,** installed in former conventual buildings, containing the important collections formed by the sculptor *Federico Marés* (1896-) and donated by him to the city.

The ground floor contains over four hundred medieval sculptures in polychromed wood, well displayed and described. From Room 1 we descend to the *crypt,* where among stone sculpture of the 10–16C, a fine Romanesque portal from the destroyed church of *Anzano* (Huesca) has been incorporated into the building. Some Roman remains are also displayed in situ.—The FIRST FLOOR contains over one thousand examples of Spanish sculpture from the Early Middle Ages to the end of the 19C, remarkable both for its range and for the quality of the exhibits. The SECOND and THIRD FLOORS constitute a museum of bygones, illustrating everyday life, including collections of Locksmith's work; Female costume; Fans, parasols, purses, combs, scissors, and jewellery; Male costume; watches, sticks, braces, etc.; games, dolls, and playing-cards; the *Sala del Fumador,* with a unique collection of pipes, snuff-boxes, match-boxes (15,000 specimens), cigarette papers, etc.; and minor religious art; reliquaries, ex-votos, Holy-water stoups, etc.—The collection of Arms and Armour is housed in the *Military Museum* on Montjuich.

We now return to the Pl. de Cristo Rey, by the W. Front of the Cathedral, where stands the 15C *Casa de la Pia Almoina,* containing the Cathedral Archives, and incorporating on its far side part of the City Wall.—Just N. of the Pl. Nueva is the modern building of the *College of Architects,* with a frieze designed by *Picasso* (1960), to the l. of which, in the C. del Archs, stands the *Casa Bassols* (16C) housing the Cercle Artístic. Hence the Av. Pta. del Angel leads directly to the Pl. de Cataluña.

B   THE RAMBLAS

These are best visited on foot from the PL. DE CATALUÑA, the liveliest square in Barcelona, and a hub of the city, lying between the old town and the new. From its S. corner, we enter the tree-lined **Ramblas** (Pl. 6; 10), the principal thoroughfare of the old town and favourite promenade, which extend to the Pl. Pta. de la Paz, overlooking the harbour.

The Ramblas (from the Arabic *raml,* sand) occupy the site of the Riera de la Malla, a seasonal torrent whose channel was used in the dry season as a roadway. Nevertheless, by 1366 a covered sewer existed along its length.

The *Rambla de Canaletas* is succeeded by the *Rambla de los Estudios,* also known as '*dels Aucells*' (oiseaux) from the bird-market held here. On the r. is *N.S. de Belén,* formerly a Jesuit church in the Baroque style (1681–1732), by *Jozep Juli.*

Opposite the arcaded *Pal. de Moya* (l., 1774–90) we may turn down the C. de Carmen towards the former **Hosp. de la Sta Cruz.** We first turn into a courtyard with the *Academia de Medicina* of 1762–64, containing a collection of ancient surgical instruments and, in the chapel, a Baroque altarpiece from the Cartuja de Scala Dei.—Opposite stands the *Casa de Convalecencia* (1629–38), the exterior of which, to the W., is decorated with statues (1662–77) by *Lluís Bonifas.*—Inside the Hospital we may see some remarkable azulejos by *Llorens Pasoles* (1672–84) and *Ramón Porcioles* (1665). From the Gothic cloister we may enter the *Biblioteca Central*, housed in the great wards of the Hospital, built in 1401–15 around a central courtyard.—The *church*, altered in the 18C, contains a group representing Charity by *Pere Costa.* The main front of the building is best seen from the C. del Hospital, S. of the courtyard.

The C. del Carmen leads S.W. to the C. S. Antonio Abad, passing the Romanesque *Cap. de S. Lázaro*, the remains of a Leper hospital founded c. 1150. Retracing our steps, we turn r. along the *Rambla de S. José* or 'de las Flores', the flower-market, passing No. 99, the **Pal. de la Virreina** (1772–78) by *José Mas* and *José Ribas*, accommodating miscellaneous collections (including a *Postal Museum*) and occasional exhibitions. The Rambla de S. José ends at the *Liceo*, the opera-house, rebuilt after a fire in 1861.

By turning r. into the C. S. Pablo, we reach, after some minutes' walk through a poor and populous district, **S. Pablo del Campo,** (Pl. 9), the oldest church in Barcelona, founded before 977 by Guibert Guitard for Benedictine monks, restored in 1117–27, and again since the Civil War. The façade (13C) is notable for the capitals of the entrance, probably brought from an earlier building, and for the symbolic carvings of the tympanum. The plain interior is in the shape of a Greek cross with a central octagon tower and three apses. The diminutive 13C *cloister* has arches of three and five lobes supported on twin columns. The 14C Abbot's House is now the Rectory.

Just beyond lies the '*Paralelo*', once considered the 'Montmartre' of Barcelona, but now a somewhat depressed and seedy area.

The *Rambla Capuchino* ends at the Pl. del Teatro, while to the r. at Nos. 3 and 5 C. Conde del Asalto, is the *Museo del Teatro*, housed in the *Pal. Güell* (1885–89) by *Gaudí*, devoted to the history of the stage, but particularly to the Liceo.

The *Rambla de Sta Mónica* ends at the PL. PTA DE LA PAZ, in the centre of which rises the ugly *Columbus Monument*, a column 52 m. high, erected in 1882-90 from the designs of *Cayetano Buigas.* To the r. are the ***Reales Atarazanas** (Pl. 13), the remarkable medieval covered shipyards (well-restored), housing the ***Museo Maritimo.**

The collections include numerous ships' models; photographs and drawings illustrating the history and sociology of the maritime settlements of Catalonia; maps, navigating instruments and ships' figureheads, among them the 'Blanca Aurora', a portrait of the owner's daughter. A full-size replica of the Galera '*La Real*', which fought at Lepanto (1571) was built here in 1971 to celebrate the quatercentenary of the battle.

On the far side (S.) of the *Atarazanas*, in the *Paralelo*, part of the old *Town Wall*, may be seen. Crossing the plaza, we reach the harbour. To the r. lies the *Estación Maritima.* Before us floats a replica of the 'Santa María', surprisingly diminutive, in which Columbus set sail in 1492 on his first voyage of discovery.

Hence we may follow the palm-lined but otherwise undistinguished PASEO DE COLÓN, on the site of the Muralla del Mar or old sea-wall. Cervantes is said to have once occupied a house on a site now covered by the *Gobierno Militar.* Behind the *Capitana General*, at a central point in the paseo, lies *La Merced*, of 1765–75 by *José Mas*, preserving a façade of 1516 from demolished S. Miguel. At 26 C. Ancha, is the *Casa Larrard* or *Pal. del Duque de Sesa* (1772–78) by *José Ribas,* and in the neighbourhood are many ancient mansions.—Just N. of *La Merced* we may turn into the C. de Aviño and along the *C. Escudellers* back to the Ramblas. This route takes us through the disreputable '*barrio Chino*', a colourful and cosmopolitan port area of narrow alleys and innumerable bars, crowded night and day, by those seeking and offering diversion.

Turning r. on regaining the Ramblas, we may enter (r.) the arcaded *Pl. Real,* with a palm-shaded garden. From its N. end we follow (r.) the C. de Fernando past Gothic *S. Jaime* (1393), built on the site of an ancient synagogue, and then turn l. into the C. Baños Nuevos. After crossing the C. Boqueria (closed to wheeled traffic), we turn l. into the Pl. S. José Oriol.

Opposite is the N. façade of *Sta. María del Pino (c. 1320–1400; restored since damaged in 1936–39) with a Romanesque door, standing on the site of an older building, named after a pine-tree that grew in the Pl. del Pino. The W. Portal and rose window are well designed, and there is a handsome octagonal tower. In the *Sacristy* is an Adoration by *Antonio Viladomat* (1678–1755), who is buried in the 3rd S. Chapel. The chapter house, by *Bartomeu Mas,* was finished in 1468.

By following the C. Petritxol, opposite the W. entrance, and crossing the C. Puertaferrisa, we enter (viâ the C. del Bot) the PL. VILLA DE MADRID, where excavations of a Roman road and tombs are displayed in situ. A short alley leads N. into the C. Sta Ana. The church of *Sta Ana,* founded in 1146 but altered in later years, has a portal of c. 1300. The interior, burnt out in 1936, but restored, contains the tomb of Miguel de Bohera, commander of the Spanish troops at the battle of Ravenna (1512). Adjoining is a two-storied *cloister* (15C), passing which we return viâ the C. Rivadeneyra to the *Pl. de Cataluña.*

C   N.E. QUARTER (ON FOOT).

From the Av. Catedral we may follow the C. Tapineria E., passing the Pl. Berenguer el Grande (see Pl. p. 145) to reach the Pl. def Angel. Here we cross the Viâ Layetana (see Pl. p. 291) and enter the C. de Carders, some short distance along which we see (r.) the façade of the 12C *Cap. de Marcús* (restored) with attractive blind arcading on the exterior. Here we turn r. across the C. de la Princesa, into the **C. Montcada** (Pl. 11), containing several interesting medieval mansions. No. 15, the *Pal. Aguilar,* together with the adjacent building, now houses the *Museo Picasso.

This important but still unrepresentative collection of the works of *Pablo Ruíz Picasso* (1881–1973), donated by the artist to Barcelona in 1970, is of particular interest in that it enables one to follow the successive stages of his development during his earliest years in Málaga (1889–90), La Coruña (1891–95), and Barcelona (1895–1904). The works are displayed (but as yet not well labelled) in a series of over 30 rooms, at present arranged as follows:

R3 *Early drawings and notebooks, including a Portrait of his father José Ruiz Blasco, a Self-portrait, and Landscapes (1896–97). **RR4-5** Nude studies. **R6** Copy of Velazquez's portrait of Philip IV. **R7** Portrait of Tía Pepa. **RR8-10** Religious themes, sketches for 'Science and Charity', and the final work (1897); note the storage jars in situ in **R11**.—Stairs ascend from R13 to the FIRST FLOOR, and (r.) **R14** 'La Chata', and Lola, the artist's sister, and figure studies in the manner of Toulouse-Lautrec (more in R17). **R15**   Menu for El Quatre Gats restaurant (Barcelona, 1900). **R16** Preliminary studies for 'El clam de las Verges', and carnival themes. **R17** The kiss, and Margot. **R18** 'Desemparats'(Mother and child, 1903), The madman (1904). **R19** (a richly decorated salon) displaying a Portrait of Señora Canals (1905). **R20** Studies for 'La Vida'. **R21** 'La Salchichona', Harlequin, and El paseo de Colón (all 1917). **R22** A series on the theme of Las Meninas of Velázquez (58 works in all, 1957), studies for which are in **R23**. **RR24-25** Studies of doves at windows. **R28** *Ceramics* (1948–57). **R29** Portraits of Jaime Sabartés (1881–1968; donor of many works to the museum). —SECOND FLOOR, and **R30** Portrait of Dora Markovitch. **R33** Head of a young girl. **R34** Youth, Head of a goat, Toad, and Hen. **R31** Illustrations for the Metamorphoses of Ovid (Skira, 1931). **R32** Portraits of Françoise Gilot, Fauns and centaurs, etc.

Opposite, in the 14C *Pal. de Lljó* (No. 12), is the *Museo de Indumentaria* (Costume), or **Coleccion Rocamora* after its founder Manuel Rocamora. This remarkable collection of over 4,000 items is of fundamental importance to the study of Spanish costume. Additional sections are devoted to dolls, shoes, fans, socks and stockings, purses and wallets, handkerchiefs, etc.

Continuing down the C. de Montcada, we pass three more 15C houses (Nos. 14, 23 and 25), while No. 20, *Casa Dalmases* (17C) contains a Baroque courtyard and staircase, and soon reach **Sta María de Mar*, the finest church in Barcelona after the cathedral.

Begun in 1329 and completed in 1383, it shows the wide nave typical of Catalan Gothic, and was apparently designed by *Jaime Fabre*, the second architect of the cathedral. The E. Door dates from 1542; the N. Tower was finished in 1495, the S. Tower not until 1902. The fine W. Portal is flanked by statues of SS. Peter and Paul.—The aisles are as high as the nave and are very narrow. The chapels are lighted by good stained-glass windows, notably that of the Last Judgement (1494), by Senier *Desmames* of Avignon, and the Coronation of the Virgin in the W. rose, Fired in 1936, the church lost its Baroque fittings, and shows its original simple lines, but some chapels have been disfigured since by the addition of tasteless modern statues. On each side of the chapel beneath the organ (N. side) is a curious little tomb.

Leaving by the S. Front we turn l. to the *Pl. de Palacio*. On our r. stands the **Lonja** or *Exchange*, built to the design of *Juan Soler Faneca* in 1774–94 on the site of the Lonja del Mar, where the **Exchange* hall, a Gothic room of 1380-92, by *Pedro Arvey*, has been preserved, and may be entered from the courtyard opening off the C. Consulado. — On the S.E. side of the plaza stands the *Escuela Náutico*, behind which the Paeeo Nacional leads to the port quarter of *Barceloneta*, a regularly planned suburb laid out by the Marqués de las Minas in 1753–55, beyond which lies the Paseo Maritimo and an insalubrious beach. Its church of *S. Miguel del Puerto*, of the same date, is by *Pedro Mártir Cermeño*.

Viâ the Paseo Nacional we may also reach—but preferably by car—the recently extended quay or breakwaters known as the *Rompeolas,* protecting the harbour from the E., from which we get a fine view of Barcelona and its amphitheatre of hills. From the *Torre de S. Sebastián* a cable-car crosses the harbour to Montjuich.

On the far side of the Pl. de Palacio is the so-called *Aduana*, formerly the Custom House, but now occupied by the Gobierno Civil. It was built originally for Godoy, who never occupied it. The Av. de la Marqués le Argentera leads N.E. past the *Estación de Francia* towards the PARQUE DE LA CIUDADELA, laid out after 1869 on the site of the citadel built for Philip V in 1715. The park still contains a small group of buildings which

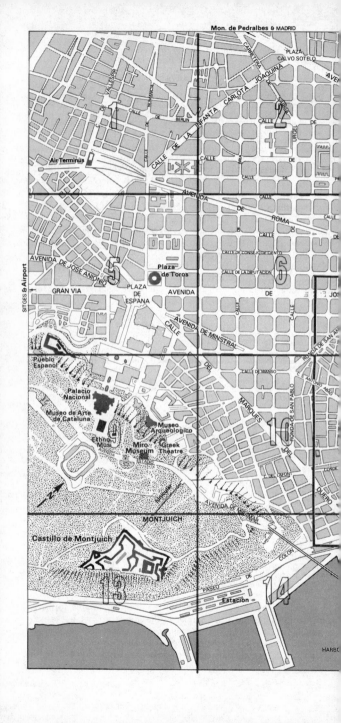

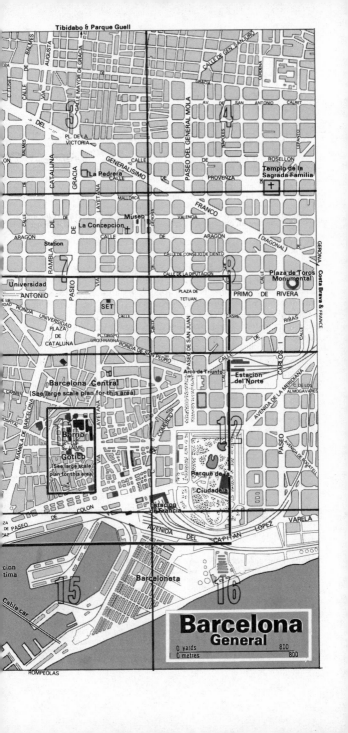

Barcelona
General

| 0 yards | 800 |
| 0 metres | 800 |

were left standing, including a chapel and the old Pal. Real of the Bourbons. Two wings were added to the latter in 1915, which now houses the misleadingly named **Museo de Arte Moderno** (Pl. 16), devoted mainly to the school of Catalan art of the final decades of the 19C and the Madrid School of the early years of the 20C. Only two small rooms contain recent work.

The Museo accommodates canvases by such individual artists as *Nogués*, *Pidelaserra*, *Sunyer*, *Canals*, *Fortuny*—including his huge Battle of Tetuan—and another room of drawings and watercolours; and *Sert*, with sketches and models of his work in Vic Cathedral (see p.164). A number of paintings by *Alsina*, *Casas*, *Mir*, *Nonell*, and *Rusiñol*, among others, are exhibited, but *Dalí*, *Miró and Tàpies* are only represented by one work each. The collection contains few individually important works: noteworthy are *Sorolla*, Portrait of Elena and María; and *Zuloaga*, My Cousins; and among the sculpture, a bronze by *Rodin*, 'L'Age d'Airain'.—The first floor, where some furniture of the period is displayed, also houses the *Gabinete Numismático de Cataluña*.

Behind the Museo is a small *Zoo* (with an albino gorilla) and *Aquarium*, and the park also contains an ornamental *Cascade*, an early work by *Gaudí*. Further W. is the *Museo Martorell*, a geological collection, to the N. of which is the *Museo de Historia Natural*.—A short distance to the W. of the park, is *S. Agustín el Viejo*, with a 17C portal and one aisle of a 14C cloister.

N.W. of the park, on the r. of the Salón de Victor Pradera, stands the *Pal. de Justicia* (1903), containing fine 16C tapestries, and beyond, a brick *Arco de Triunfo* erected for the Exhibition of 1888. Before reaching this, we may turn l. down the C. Baja de S. Pedro, off which, in a small plaza, stands *S. Pere de les Puelles* (mid-10C), which has suffered many partial destructions and alterations since it was built on the site of an older foundation of Louis le Debonnaire's. The main rebuilding took place in 1147, but the E. end is of 1498.

Hence we follow the C. Alta de S. Pedro, passing (r.) the *Pal. de la Música*, a concert hall built by *Luis Domènech y Muntaner* in the fantastic and uncompromising 'modern' style of its time (1908), to regain the Viâ Layetana. Here, on our r., is a pargetted house built in 1759–63 by *Juan Garrido* for the Gremio de Velers, a guild of silk-weavers, whence we may return to the Cathedral, or viâ the C. Condal opposite, to the Pl. de Cataluña.

D   MONTJUÏCH

The **Montjuïch** (700 ft; Pl. 9, 13), which rises steeply above the harbour, derives its name either from a shrine of Jupiter (*Mons Jovis*) or from a colony of Jews (*Mons Judaicus*). Its Catalan spelling is Montjuïc.

In 1929 the park on the N. slope of the hill was occupied by an International Exhibition, planned on a grandiose scale. Among the many buildings erected was the *Pal. Nacional* (see below); and the *Spanish Village* (see p.157) has likewise remained a permanent attraction, while the stadium, with a seating capacity of 60,000, is still the scene of many sporting events. Between the Pal. Nacional and the Pl. de España lie exhibition halls in which the city's numerous Trade Fairs are held.

Approaches: The buildings on Montjuïch (well-signposted) may be reached with ease by car from the *Pl. de España*, or from the *Pl. Pta. de la Paz* viâ the Paseo de Colón, from which a road climbs to the Miramar, the W. terminus of the cable-car crossing the harbour. Hence the Carretera de Montjuïch leads to the Citadel on the summit. This may also be approached by Funicular from the S. end of the C. Conde del Asalto.

The **Citadel** was erected in 1640, when Barcelona sided with the French against Philip IV. It was brilliantly surprised and captured by Lord Peterborough in 1705 during the War of Succession. In 1808, French troops under Gén. Dufresne, who had entered in the guise of allies, suddenly evicted the Spanish garrison and made themselves masters of Barcelona. The Montjuïch was held in 1842 by Espartero, who bombarded the city thence during the insurrection of that year. During the Civil War it was used as a prison. In 1960 it was handed over to the city by the military authorities, since when a *Military Museum has been installed in its cavernous casements, entered from the Pl. de Armas.

Of particular interest are the numerous plans and models of the castles of Cataluña displayed in R 4, while in R 6 is shown the arms collection of Federico Marés (see p. 148). RR 7-9 are devoted to the early military history of Cataluña, and RR 10-13 to the history of the fortress during the War of the Spanish Succession, and the Peninsular and Carlist Wars (in Cataluña).—Steps from the Pl. de Armas ascend to the roof, from which panoramic Views of the city and port may be obtained.

Descending from the citadel, we turn l. along the Av. de Miramar, to reach the **Fundación Joan Miró**, by Josep Lluís Sert.

The effective open-plan edifice (1975), also incorporating the *Centre d'Etudis d'Art Contemporani*, with exhibition halls, book and print shop, library and documentation centre, and auditorium, Archives (containing over 5000 drawings), etc. ranged round a series of internal and external patios, contains a representative collection of the art and sculpture of Joan Miró (1893-). Note also Chillida's sculpture, 'Meeting-place', and *Calder's* Fountain of Mercury (1937).

Beyond is the *Pal. Nacional* (Pl. 9), a mausoleum of a building, but housing the *Museo de Arte de Cataluña,* one of the most important collections of medieval painting in the world, and also a comprehensive collection of Spanish **Ceramics** (see p.157).

The rooms to the r. of the entrance hall constitute the *Galerías Románicas*, a series of reconstructions of church interiors, incorporating mural decorations, from remote villages in the Catalan Pyrenees. Most of these were covered by later fittings and some were actually being removed from the country when their transport to Barcelona was undertaken in 1919.

The Romanesque section has been re-arranged and its contents are particularly well displayed. Among the more outstanding exhibits are: **R 1** Visigothic and pre-Romanesque capitals and stone-carvings. **R 2** Apse from the chapel of the castle of *Marmellar* (mid-12C). **R 3** Mural of the Stoning of Stephen from *S. Juan de Bohí* (11C). **R 4** Apse from *S. Pedro, Seo de Urgel*; paintings from *S. Juan de Bohí*; polychrome wooden Christ in Majesty. **R 5** 12C Frontals from *Durró* (Lérida). **R 6** Apse from *Ginestarre de Cardós*; 12C Christ on the Cross. **R 7** Photographs of early churches and of the process of transferring the paintings. **R 10** Apse paintings from *Argolell*; wall-paintings from *S. Quiricio de Pedret*; apse, with the parable of the Wise and Foolish Virgins (12C); paintings from the chapel of the castle of *Orcau*. **RR 11-12** 12C wood-carvings, including the 'Batllo' Majesty, with a tunic decorated with Islamic motifs. **R 13** A series of 12-13C wooden seated Virgins, including one from *Gerp* (Gerona); altar frontal 'de los Obispos' (12C) from *S. Sadurní de Tavernoles, Anserall* (Lérida). **R 14** Pantocrator, from the apse of *S. Clemente de Tahull* (note foreshortening); pine sedilia from *S. Clemente.* **R 15** Apse from *Sta Maria de Tahull*; frontal from *Sta María.* **R 16** Aisle paintings from *Sta*

Maria de Tahull; four figures from a Descent from the Cross from *Sta Maria* (12C); wooden crucifixion dated 1147 from the diocese of Urgel; wooden Virgin from a Calvary, *Durró* (12C); wooden St John and a Virgin from *Erill la Vall.* **R 17** Capitals from *Tavernoles* (12C). **R 18** Apse from *Esterri de Cardós* (12C), and a frontal from the same church. **R 19** Eight wooden Virgins. **R 20** Wooden crucifixion of S. Pedro (13C); the **Ceramic Museum** is reached by a staircase ascending from hence. **R 21** Apse from *Sta Eulalia de Estaon* (Lérida); altar frontal from *Mossoll* (12C), altar frontal from the *Valle de Arán* (early 12C); 12C altar from the chapel of *La Vila d'Encamp* (Andorra); frontal from *Aviá* (13C); reconstruction of a baldacchino with 12-13C fragments from *Tosas* (Lérida). Between **RR 21** and **R 22** are fragments of the cloister of *S. Pere de les Puelles* (Barcelona, 12C). **R 22** Apse from *S. Miquel d'Engolastres* (Andorra), cons. 1163; three polychrome figures from *Vilanova de l'Aguda* (Lérida); polychrome female saint from *S. Martí Sarroca* (13C); four panels from a group of the Virgin and Magi, with heads in relief (13C). **R 23** Keystone from *Ripoll.* **R 25** A collection of capitals. **R 26** Painting from the Sala Capitular of the Monastery of *Sigena* (see p.185), and five tombs from *Sta María de Matallana* (Valladolid). **R 27** Chivalric scenes (c. 1200). **R 28** Murals from *S. Pedro de Arlanza* (Burgos). **R 29** Navarro-Aragonese frontals (12-13C). **R 30** Apse from *Toses* (Girona). **R 31** Apse from *Andorra la Vella* (13C) and a fine collection of bronze and copper crucifixes, censers, croziers, chests, etc., many enamelled. **R 32** Retablo of S. Miguel by the *Master of Soriguerola.* **R 33** 13C murals of the assault on Palma de Mallorca by Jaime I, and the battle of Porto-Pi, both from the Pal. Aguilar in the C. Montcada (Barcelona); artesonado panels from Aragón (c. 1400); wooden reliquary chest with stucco reliefs (13C shrine of S. Candido) from *S. Cugat del Vallés.* **R 34** Baldacchino from *S. Sadurni de Tavernoles.*

R 35 Panels from *Mahamud* (Burgos, 13-14C); frontals from *Sta María de les Monges.* **R 36** *Arnau Bassa* (?), Annunciation and Magi from the Collegiata, Cardona. **R 37** works by the *Serra* family; predella from Tortosa Cathedral (late 14C) by *Pere Serra*; retablo from Sigena (late 14C); retablo of S. Esteban from Gualter (Lérida); retablo of Sta Catalina, Castellbó (14C), by the *Master of Castellbó;* Epifany, by *Jaume Cabrera* (1399–1427), from Alzina de Ribelles (Lérida). **R 38** *Joan Matas,* S. Sebastián; Resurrection, by the *Serra brothers* and *Guerau Gener,* but finished by *Lluis Borrassá,* SS. Estaban y Juan, school of Borrassa. **R 39** *Bernat Martorell,* retablo of S. Vicente from Menarguens, and retablo of S. Juan Bautista and S. Juan Evangelista, 1440, Vinaixa (Tarragona); early 15C triptych of S. Esteban (Castilian school); retablo of Sta Bárbara (Valencian, early 15C), and another by the *Master de los Martir de Torres.* R 40 the *Dalmau room;* the great retablo of the Virgen dels Concellers, undergoing restoration, is replaced temporarily by an oil painting; portraits of kings by a Valencian painter (early 15C). **R 41** retablo of Sta Ursula, by *Joan Reixach,* from Cubells (Lérida); early 15C retablo of S. Martín (Catalan-Valencian school); retablo of the Epifany, by *Joan Reixach*; and fragments of works by the *Master of Xàtiva* (Valencian school). **R 42** *Fern. Gallego,* Adoration. **R 43** *Pere García de Benabarre,* Salome (from S. Juan Bautista, Lérida); 14C sculpture of the Annunciation (Catalan school).

Outstanding paintings in the following rooms, (the numbering of which does not follow their layout), are: **R 56** Anon. portrait of the

Conde Luis de Nassau; Annunciation and Visitation (Flemish school, both c. 1500); retablo of the Martyrdom of S. Jorge from S. Cugat, by *Ayne Bru*; triptych of the Baptism of Christ by the *Master of Frankfurt* (c. 1500); *Hans van Wechlen*, Calvary. **R 61** *Zurbarán*, S. Francis of Assisi; *Ribalta*(?), Ramon Llull, and S. Jerónimo; *El Greco*, SS. Peter and Paul, and Christ carrying the Cross; *Ribera*, Martyrdom of St Bartholomew; *Velázquez*, St Paul. **R 62** *Andrea Vaccaro*, Tobias and the Fish; *Tintoretto*, Marqués de Santa Cruz. **RR 63-64** are devoted to the work of *Ant. Viladomat* (1678–1755).

With the recent addition of the Fontana Donation, the museum has acquired a Nativity by *Guerau Gener* and *Lluís Borrassà*; *Jaume Ferrer II*, Calvary, St Jerome, St Martin, and St Sebastian; *Pere García de Benebarre*, Virgin and Child with S. Vincente Ferrer and donors, Birth of the Virgin, and a Nativity, among other works.

The magnificent collections of the ***Ceramic Museum**, now in the process of being entirely reformed under the auspices of an enlightened curator, and well displayed and labelled, provide a comprehensive view of Spanish decorative pottery and ceramics from the 13C to the present. The collection of 16-18C lusterware is outstanding.

R1, the first of the three rooms completed, is devoted to Arabic and early Catalan examples, 23 pieces having been found in Palma de Mallorca in 1937. **R2** concentrates on ceramics decorated in green, blue, and purple from Paterna, Manises, Teruel, and Barcelona, and also contains a remarkable collection of tiles, etc. **R3** displays lustreware from Manises, and also from Barcelona, Reus, and Muel, and a further collection of decorative tiles, many with coats of arms, etc., zocalos or dados, and plaques. The opening of further rooms is awaited with impatient interest.

———————

A short distance to the W. of the Pal. Nacional lies the *Pueblo Español* (1929).

This 'Spanish Village' contains full-size replicas or façades of famous and characteristic buildings (and plazas) from provincial towns and villages. Regrettably, this well-contrived and picturesque architectural anthology has developed into a shop-window and bazaar for souvenirs and handicraft, only a small proportion of which are manufactured on the premises.

Not far E. of the Pal. Nacional, but on a lower level, is the **Museo Arqueológico**, with notable prehistoric and Greco-Roman collections.

Left of the vestibule are RR I-III displaying Palaeolithic material. R IV, Neolithic, with exhibits from the Cueva de la Fou de Bor at Bellver (Lérida), Cueva Fonda at Salomó (Tarragona), etc. R V is devoted to the Megalithic culture; RR VI-VIII to the Bronze Age culture of El Argar, and R IX to the Hallstatt period. RR X-XIV contain Hellenic and Carthaginian objects from the Balearic Isles, including notable jewellery.

In Room XV is a scale model of part of the excavations at Ampurias, objects from which are in RR XVI-XVII, containing Greek vases, glassware, fragments of painted stucco and a noble Statue of Asclepios (4C B.C.). Other important sculptures are a bronze panther's head (6C B.C.), the *Venus of Ampurias*, and a head of Artemis of the school of Scopas. Among exhibits of technical interest are the unique fittings of a Roman Military Catapult.

A series of rooms contain minor objects from the classical perdiods; RR XVIII-XIX, Greek and Etruscan vases; R XX, Iberian culture; R XXI, Roman bronzes and a Mosaic of Bellerophon; RR XXII and XXIII, Roman glassware and pottery. Returning through these rooms, we enter R XXIV, with exhibits of Roman religious life and then R XXV, whose walls are covered with Mosaics of racing chariots found at Barcelona and Gerona. The dome displays a reproduction of the mosaic covering the early Christian mausoleum of Centcelles (Tarragona).R XXVII contains a reconstruction of a kitchen, while R XXVIII is arranged as an atrium. In R XXIX is the *Venus of Badolona*. R XXXIII displays furniture from Early Christian and Visigothic tombs. Additional exhibits will be displayed in the N. wing, at present being reformed.

Nearby, to the S., lies the *Greek Theatre,* built for the 1929 Exhibition, and the *Ethnological Museum*, containing collections from Africa, Spanish America, the Philippines, and Japan. Its Spanish section is accommodated in the *Pueblo Espanol* (see above).

E THE NEW TOWN

Some 230 m. W. of the Pl. de Cataluña, facing the Gran Via and surrounded on three sides by a botanic garden, stands the unpretentious *University* (1863–73), which now houses only certain Faculties, for a UNIVERSITY CITY has been built some distance W. along the Diagonal near the Pal. de Pedralbes (see below). Just S. of the Pl. de la Universidad, in the C. de Tallers, stands *S. Severo y S. Carlos Borromeo* of 1710, with Baroque altars. Two blocks N.E. of the University, the wide tree-lined PASEO DE GRACIA leads N.W. to meet the Diagonal at the *Pl. de la Victoria* (Obelisk), beyond which the C. Mayor de Gracia climbs to the Pl. de Lesseps and the 16C church *de los Josepets*. Hence the Av. Republica Argentina ascends towards Tibidabo.

At the lower end of the *Paseo de Gracia* (No. 43, 1.) stands the *Casa Batlló* (1905-7) by *Gaudi*. Adjacent is the *Casa Amatller* by *Puig y Cadafalch*, and three buildings to the S., the *Casa Lleó Morera* by *Domènech y Muntaner,* monuments of the 'Modernist' period of Catalan architecture. Turning r. into the C. de Aragón, we pass in the third block, the church of *La Concepción* (built in 1293–1448), with an oblong cloister of c. 1400, brought to its present site when the monastery of Junqueras in the old town was demolished. Returning to the Paseo de Gracia, and turning r., we come to the *Casa Milá* (1905–10), popularly known as *'La Pedrera'* (the Quarry), by *Gaudi*.

By turning N.E. again along the C. Provenza and crossing the Diagonal, we approach a plaza above which rears the unfinished **Templo de la Sagrada Familia** (Pl. p.152/4), one of the most extraordinary of Catalan buildings. Its most obvious features are four curious spires (over 100m. high), the stalactite-like canopies over the triple porches of each façade, and the luxuriant carving over the whole surface. Threading our way through a builder's yard, we may visit a small exhibition in the crypt of plans and models for the building, which was begun in 1882 by *Villar*, and continued by *Antonio Gaudi* (1852–1926).

Between 1936 and 1954 it was practically abandoned, but work has since been resumed, causing further controversy, the argument being that any attempt to follow Gaudi's original designs would be contrary to his conception of the finished work, for he would invariably make changes during building operations, rarely conforming to the prototype. Whether there is sufficient support for this misguided scheme remains to be seen; uncompleted, it could have remained both a monument to its architect and an assertive symbol for a vital city.

The devotee of Gaudi will find other examples of his work, apart from the *Pal. Güell* (p.149) and those in the *Paseo de Gracia* (see above) listed below: *Casa Calvet* (1898–1904) at 48 C. Caspe, near the intersection of the Gran Via and C. del

Bruch; N. of the Diagonal at 24-26 C. Carolinas; to the W. of the C. Mayor de Gracia, is the *Casa Vicens* (1878–80). Further N. lies the *Parque Güell*—best approached from the Pl. de Lesseps (see above) containing the Hall of a Hundred Columns, terraces and fountains, and a Gaudí museum; *Casa Figueras* (1900–02) n the C. Bellesguard (see below); the *Col. de Sta. Teresa de Jesús* (1899), 41 C. de Ganduxer (off the Paseo de la Bonanova); and the gates, walls and pavilions of the *Finca Güell* (1887) off the Av. de la Victoria (N. of the Pal. de Pedralbes).

Some little way N. of the Sagrada Familia lies the *Hosp. de S. Pablo* (1905) designed by *Domènech y Muntaner*, with the rebuilt front of the Baroque *Cap. de Sta María* (1735) brought from the old city.
S.E. of the Sagrada Familia, and just W. of the junction of the Gran Via with the Diagonal, is the *Plaza de Toros Monumental*, with seats for 22,000, which has succeeded the *Arenas* as the principal bull-ring of Barcelona. Further E., in the suburb of *Clot*, stands *S. Martín de Provensals* of the later 15C, retaining a doorway of 1432.

From the Pl. de Victoria we may turn W. along the Diagonal, at No. 373 in which the *Museo de Música*, with a good collection of ancient and modern instruments, has recently been installed. To our l. in the Rambla de Cataluña, is the late 14C church of *Montesión*, brought here from the Pl. de Sta Ana and re-erected. On our r., the *Via Augusta* leads uphill to *Sarría* after crossing the C. de Balmes. The latter continues to climb through the district of S. GERVASIO built round the hill of Putxet, to meet the Paseo de S. Gervasio.

N. of this junction lies *Bellesguard*, the remains of an ancient summer-palace of the kings of Aragón. Hence we may also approach the lower end of the Funicular ascending to the summit of Tibidabo itself. The range has been pierced by three tunnels to improve communications with outlying towns to the N.W.—By turning r. at the Paseo de S. Gervasio we soon meet (1.) the Carretera de S. Cugat which winds up the crest of **Tibidabo** (1745 ft), the highest of the hills encircling Barcelona, and which commands a magnificent *View. In the forefront are the Catalan mountains of Montserrat, Montseny, and S. Llorens del Munt; to the N. are the Pyrenean summits of Canigou, Puigmal, and Pic de Costabona, while in clear weather the peaks of Mallorca are visible out to sea.—From Tibidabo the road continues S.W. to the lower hill of *Vallvidrera*, before descending to Sarría. Vallvidrera may also be reached by Funicular, the lower station being approached from Sarría.

At the main crossroad of *Sarría* stands *S. Vicente* on the site of an earlier church founded in 980 and rebuilt in 1379.—Hence the Paseo Reina Elisenda leads W. to the ***Monasterio de Pedralbes**, one of the most interesting and attractive buildings in Barcelona. The interior may only be visited between 12.00–14.00 on Sundays, but the church is open to the city public daily. The monastery of *Sta María de Pedralbes* was founded in 1326 by Elisenda de Moncada (d. 1364), queen of Jaime II. The fine Catalan Gothic church contains good choir-stalls and beautiful stained glass by Mestre *Gil*, while in the choir lies one half of the foundress's richly carved tomb. On the far side of the wall, in a small chapel off the cloister, the other half may be seen, less elaborate, and of stone. Off the impressive three-storied *cloister*, with clustered columns supporting ogival arches—26 on each side—is a vaulted *Chapterhouse* of c. 1412–19, with a finely carved keystone and good glass of 1419, containing an interesting small museum. In the *Cap. de S. Miguel* are important murals by *Ferrer Bassa* (1345–46).—Near the entrance, within the monastery wall, the façade of a demolished monastery from Breda (near Hostalrich) has been reconstructed.
The Av. de la Victoria, opposite, leads downhill towards the Diagonal, passing (r.) the gates of the *Finca Güell* by *Gaudí*. Turning r.

at the Diagonal we shortly reach the entrance of the *Gardens* of the *Pal de Pedralbes,* designed by *Novo Miguel* (1924-25), presented by the city to Alfonso XIII, and later a residence for visiting dignitaries; it was Negrín's H.Q. during the latter part of the Civil War.

Many of the faculty buildings of the new *University City* are situated on either side if this section of the Diagonal, while to the E., on both sides of the avenue as it descends gently towards the *Pl. de Calvo Sotelo,* rise blocks of luxury flats and offices. Beyond this plaza, a rendezvous for the *señoritos* of Barcelona society, we pass (1.) *C. Tuset,* one of the more fashionable shopping streets in an elegant area, before returning to the Pl. de Victoria.

EXCURSIONS FROM BARCELONA

Within 40 km. (25 miles) of Barcelona there are a number of towns and monuments of interest, which may be visited with ease. Taking the road to Tibidabo (see p.159) we turn r. before reaching the summit and descend through pine woods to (18 km.) *Sant Cugat de Valls* (29,200 inhab.) on the site of the Roman *Castrum Octavianum.* The Benedictine Abbey of **S. Cugat,** one of the oldest in Spain (said to have been founded by Charlemagne or Louis the Debonair), and in some need of restoration, has an attractive Romanesque *cloister* (c. 1190) by *Arnal Gatell.* The *Church,* with a notable W. Rose Window, contain the engraved monument of Abbot Estruch, and some 14–15C paintings, while in the chapterhouse is a small museum containing *Pere Serra's* Retablo de Todos los Santos (1375).

Viâ (4 km.) *Rubí,* we reach (11 km.) industrial Terrassa (161,000 inhab.), close to ancient *Egara.* Its most interesting building is *S. Miguel,* in the suburb of S. Pedro (N.W.), made up of two Romanesque churches and a baptistery conjoined. The marble columns of the square baptistery are Roman and support Roman and Romanesque capitals. The church was built before 450 but reconstructed in the 9C. The crypt has 12C wall-paintings. In *S. Pedro,* with a curious 3-lobed apse of the 9C and a 12C vaulted nave, are important inscriptions. *Sta Maria,* also with a 9C apse and a nave consecrated in 1112, contains a painted stone retablo of the 10C and late 12C wall-paintings of St. Thomas Becket. In the museum are the Retablos of S. Pedro (1411) by *Lluís Borrassa,* and of SS. Abdon and Sennen (1459–60), a masterpiece of *Jaume Huguet.* The old buildings of Terrassa include the *Torre del Palau* of the castle and the late Gothic *Casa Consistorial.* In the crypt of the modern church of *Santo Espíritu* is an alabaster tomb of 1544 by *Martín Díaz de Liatzasolo.* The *Museo Soler y Palet* contains medieval paintings and sculpture, and Catalan ceramics, while in the *Museo Biosca* is a fine collection of early textiles.

Nearby stands the *Cartuja de Vallparadis* (restored), also known as the *Castle of the Caballeros de Egara,* begun in 1110 but rebuilt after 1344, with a Gothic gallery of 1415–32.—From a point 6 km. N. of Terrassa, on a mountain riddled with caverns, the ruins can be reached of the Benedictine monastery of *S. Llorenç del Munt,* cons. 1064, and partly restored in the 14C.—At 22 km. N.E. of Terrassa lies *Caldas de Montbui,* (9700 inhab.; *Hotels*), with hot springs: a barrel-vaulted Roman bath survives. The parish church has a Baroque front of 1701 by *M. Fiter* and houses a noble 12C Christ known as La Santa Majestad. A new road now connects Terrassa with (17 km.) *Monistrol* (see below).

We may return to Barcelona viâ **Sabadell** (182,900 inhab.), 15 km. S. of Caldas and 10 km. E. of Terrassa, containing a good *Museum* of archaeology, ceramics, and Catalan paintings, and a collection of fans, parasols, and textiles. The *Museo Sellarés y Pla* also contains 15-19C textiles.—Just S. of Sabadell we pass *Sta Maria de Barbará,* with a Lombardic parish church (late 11C) with wall-paintings of c. 1200.

10   FROM BARCELONA TO MONTSERRAT, MANRESA AND SOLSONA

Total distance, 133 km. (82 miles), including the ascent to Montserrat. 27 km. *Martorell*—shortly turning r. onto the C 1410 for *Monistrol*—(*Montserrat* lies 7 m. S.W.)—18 km. *Manresa*—33 km. *Cardona*—18 km. *Solsona.*

BY RAILWAY. From the Pl. de España (Barcelona) a direct line leads to *Monistrol*. Adjoining the station is the lower terminus of the rack-railway which will convey one to the monastery in a few minutes.

We follow the autopista S.W. as far as (27 km.) *Martorell* (see p. 167), obtaining intermittent views of the Montserrat massif ahead, there diverging onto the N II. At 14 km., after passing the Romanesque church of *Sta María del Puig*, we turn r. and cross the flank of the mountain, descending into the Llobregat valley. At (9 km.) *Monistrol* we fork l. and commence a steep zig-zag climb of c. 7 km. up to the *Monastery of Montserrat* (2378 ft), obtaining spectacular views of the mountain from numerous points on the ascent.

Notable for its strange physical appearance, the *Montserrat* is one of the famous mountains of the world. The range itself (4072 ft), an isolated ridge running from S.E. to N.W., raises its reddish-grey mass of sandstone and conglomerate 3600 ft above the Llobregat, which flows below its S.E. and E. slopes. The serrated summit of the ridge (whence it derives its name *Mons Serratus*), thrusts up at irregular intervals a series of barren pinnacles, formed by erosion and separated by fissures of varying depth. Further down, below a bewildering chaos of buttresses, gorges, and hanging boulders, the mountain has been worn into terraces owing to the differing hardness of its rock-strata.

History. The origin of the *Monastery*, according to legend, dates from 880, when an image of the Virgin, which had been brought to Barcelona in A.D. 50 by St. Peter and hidden in a recess of the mountain at the time of the Moorish invasion (717), was rediscovered by shepherds. Gondemar, Bp. of Vic, attempted to remove the image to Manresa, but on reaching the ledge where the monastery now stands, it refused to proceed further. The chapel erected here was reinforced by a nunnery, replaced in 976 by a Benedictine convent.

Centuries of prosperity ensued, especially under the auspices of the Spanish popes Benedict XIII (Luna) and Alexander VI (Borgia), the former of whom 1410) raised the abbot to the dignity of a mitre, with independence of episcopal authority. From 1499 it was the seat of a printing-press, one of the earliest in Spain. In 1522 S. Ignacio Loyola kept vigil before laying his sword upon the altar and dedicating himself to the Virgin as her knight. Philip II bestowed many favours on Montserrat and completely rebuilt the church. During the Peninsular War the abbey was sacked by the French under Suchet, after having been fortified by the Somatenes', the Catalan guerrilleros. In 1835 the monastery was suppressed and the image removed to Esparraguera, but in 1874 it was reinstated. The Montserrat legend also inspired Wagner's 'Parsifal'.

The principal pilgrimages take place on 27 April and 8 Sept.

Visitors expecting some serene sanctuary in the mountain fastness of the Montserrat massif will be disillusioned: the commercialization of the cult is at once apparent in the shops and restaurants near the basilica.

On either side of the entrance are the *Aposentos*, lodging for 2000 pilgrims, (also *Hotel*), beyond which we enter a courtyard; on the l. are fragmentary remains of the old monastery, consisting of one wall of a *Cloister* (after 1476), a 17C belfry (unfinished), and a Romanesque doorway. Straight ahead is the cloister built under Fernando VII that precedes the façade (1900) of the present *Basilica*, a commonplace Renaissance building (1560–92). Above the high altar is seen the dark complexioned 12C wooden Virgin and Child—blackened by the smoke of candles smouldering over the centuries—seated on a silver throne (1947) in the centre of the *Camarín*, or sanctuary.

This sumptuous oval chamber in the apse (1880), is reached through the *Sacristy*, which contains the treasury, made up mostly of modern gifts. Several museums are housed in the buildings, as well as a library of over 200,000 volumes. Behind the church is the *Escolanía*, or music-school.

Those wishing to regain the Madrid road further W. in the direction of Igualada may turn l. some short distance off the road by which the Monastery was approached.

Numerous signposted footpaths lead from the monastery into the massif itself, affording ggood views of the fantastic rock formations of the mountain and of the plains of Aragón and Catalonia, and from Los Degotalls and S. Jerónimo or S. Geroni, a magnificent *View of the Pyrenean chain from Canigou as far W. as the Maladetta. The majority of the hermitages—mostly ruined—which are scattered over the mountain are not particularly interesting.

The following excursions are recommended for the less energetic: (a), the hermitage of *S. Juan*, by the funicular, from which the view S. is very fine; (b), *Los Degotalls*, reached by a path ascending from the road at the E. end of the Monastery. Hence we may either descend to the Igualada road and return to the Monastery, or go on to *Sta Cecilia*, with a small 11C church of an ancient monastery which may also be approached direct from the Igualada road; (c), from this road, near Sta Cecilia, we may take the 'teleferic' to the *Ermita de S. Jerónimo*, from which an easy path climbs to the *Turo de S. Jerónimo*, the highest peak, commanding a similar view to that from the Degotalls, but including also a curious panorama of the range itself and a glimpse over the dizzy N.E. precipice. On clear days one may see Mallorca.

Returning to Monistrol, we cross the Llobregat by a Gothic *Bridge*, and turn onto the C1411 for (18 km.) **Manresa** (66,000 inhab.; *Hotel*) the ancient *Munorisa*, now an industrial town above the l. bank of the Cardoner. Immediately below the ruins of 18C *S. Ignacio* is the cave in which the saint is said to have written his 'Spiritual Exercises' (1522), cloisters house the *Municipal Museum*. Crowning a rocky bluff is **Sta Maria de la Seo**, most of which dates from the reconstruction begun in 1328 by Berenguer de Montagut, but not completed until the mid-16C. The Tower dates from 1572-90; the ugly W. Front from the 19C. The INTERIOR, though the main vault is excelled in width by that of Gerona, shows the greatest breadth across nave and aisles of any church with aisles and clerestory; it contains remarkable stained glass. In the S. Nave Aisle is the Retablo of the Holy Ghost, by *Pere Serra* (1394). On the N. side is a cloister, and baptistery (under restoration), part of the original building of 1020.

In the town are *Sto Domingo* (1318–1438) and 16C *N.S. del Carmen*.

Near *Sant Fruitós de Bages* (5 km. N.E. on the N141), N.E. of which is a medieval bridge, is the ruined monastery of *S. Benito* with a lanterned church of c. 1225 and early Gothic chapter house entered from a Romanesque cloister with carved capitals signed 'Bernardus'—At *Rocafort*, 14 km. E. of Manresa, is the remarkable Romanesque church of *Sta Maria de Marquet*, with a vault on horseshoe arches (late 10C).

FROM MANRESA TO GUARDIOLA DE BERGA (69 km.) We take the N 141 in the
rection of Vic, 52 km. N.E. (see below).—At 4 km. we turn l. on to the C 1411,
assing (4 km. l.) *Santpedor*, whose church has a fine 12C tympanum and a
ottingham alabaster of St. Michael.—15 km. *Balsareny* has a hilltop castle
4C).—At 14 km. we may diverge 6 km. l. for *Casserras*, with the church and
oister of *S. Pedro* (c. 1006).

18 km. **Berga**, a mining town (12,300 inhab.), has a ruined castle and the Gothic
onv. *de S. Francisco* (1333   ).—In a 17C chapel 5 km. N.W. is the 13C image of
, *S. de Queralt*.—5 km. N.E. is the Mozarabic church of *S. Quirze de Pedret* (late
th and 12C).—We now approach the Sierra de Cadi (8324 ft).—18 km.
uardiola de Berguedà, 2 km. N.W. of which, at *Bagá*, are a ruined castle and
omanesque church, while 10 km. E. at *La Pobla de Lillet*, is a 12C Majesty.—
ome 10 km. S.E. across country, best approached from the Berga-Ripoll road, is
Jaume de Frontanyá, Romanesque, with a lantern and lobed apse of c. 1070.—
rom *La Pobla de Lillet* a picturesque, but difficult road crosses the Sierra de
1ontgrony to (24 km.) *Ripoll* (p.165) passing (15 km.) *Gombrèn*, with medieval
ouses near the ruined castle and Romanesque church of *Montgrony*, and (4 km.)
, *Llorent*, with an early square church tower.

The road (N141) leading N.E. from Manresa to (52 km.) *Vic* is recommended for
s *Views*, both as it gently climbs towards the Puerto de La Pullosa, and also for
1e extensive vistas on the descent into the Ter valley, and may be followed as an
lternative to that described in the first part of Rte 11. After 26 km. we reach *Moià*,
ith a Baroque church, 8 km. N. of which, at *L'Estany*, is a Trans. church (c. 1124–
3) with a 14C polychrome alabaster Virgin and a Romanesque cloister.

From Manresa the road winds up the valley, passing potash mines at
uria, to (33 km.) **Cardona** (6700 inhab.; *Parador Nac.*), commanded by
s *Castle* (1475ft; now incorporating the Parador; Views), the *Chapel
f which (1020–40) contains tombs of the Dukes of Cardona, the first
onstables of Aragón.

The town, with a parish church cons. in 1397, is perhaps more famous for its
alina, nearer the river, an extraordinary surface deposit of salt, indeed famous in
1e days of Strabo, and which may be visited on application to the director of the
orkings. Objects carved in rock-salt are liable to melt if transferred to damper
limates.

The road continues to climb, with extensive views N. towards the
yrenees, at 12 km. passing near the 16C sanctuary of *El Milagro*, with a
aroque retablo (1768) by *Carlos Morató*, before descending to (6 km.)
olsona (6000 inhab.; *Hotel*), the Roman *Setelix*, made a bishopric by
'hilip II in 1593, and now a Summer resort. Francisco Ribalta (1563–
628) was a native. The ruined *Castle* is of the 12C–13C, and the town
self retains remains of ramparts.

Near the bridge over the Rio Negro (replacing one of 12 arches
estroyed during the Civil War) stands the dark single-naved *Cathedral*
f 1161–63, rebuilt in the 14–15C. It contains 15C stall-work (against the
pse wall), and in the overladen S. transept, a 12C Virgin.

It is said that the *Museo Diocesano* (usually closed) in the adjacent *Abp's Palace*
17C; by *Francisco Pons*) houses the frescoes (11–12C) from S. Quirce de Pedret;
he 13C decorations of a wall-tomb from S. Pablo de Casserras, by the *Master of
lusanés*, and 12C panels from the altar of Sagars, of the Ripoll School. Gothic
ainting is represented by the 13C retablo of S. Jaime de Frontanyá, and the Last
upper of *Jaime Ferrer I*. The sculpture includes fragments from the cathedral and
apitals from S. Pedro de Madrona, by *Mirus*; a 14C tomb of an abbot of
Serrateix; and the Tomb of Hugo de Copons (d. 1354), from Llor.

Olius, 4 km. E., has a church cons. in 1079, and a 13C watermill.

32km. N. of Solsona in the former Benedictine church of *Sant Lorenc de
Morunys*, are retablos by *Pere Serra* (1380–85) and *Jaime Cirera* (c. 1425–50) and
1 the chapel of La Piedad is one by *Franc. Solives*, a follower of Huguet, of 1480.

From Solsona, a road descends into the Segre valley to meet the
C 1313 at (25 km.) *Bassella*, see Rte 13. The C 149 leads N.E. from

Solsona to *Berga* (see below) whence we may follow the Llobregat vall
to *Manresa*, or alternatively take the C 154, an attractive road offerir
good views, to *Vic* (p.164), from either town returning to Barcelona

Another lonely road leads S. from Solsona, later descending past *Montfal
Murallat* (see p. 168) to (53 km.) *Cervera*.

11   FROM BARCELONA TO PUIGCERDÀ (AND ANDORRA)

Total distance, 172 km. (107 miles). N 152. 69 km. **Vic**—38 km. *Ripoll*—65 k
Puigcerdà.

From the Pl. de las Glorias we turn N. onto the N 152, and pass (9 km
at *Reixach,* a ruined castle, once the stronghold of the Moncada famil
At 17 km. the road by-passes *Granollers* (see p.139), but on the old roac
4 km. N. of the town, lies *Llerona*, with a 12C church, and nearb
Romanesque *S. Feliú de Canovellas*. The roads converge near (13 km
La Garriga, where *S. Esteban* has a retablo of the school of Huguet (
1490) and the chapel of *Sta María del Cami* (12C).—*Bigues*, 5 km. W
contains some Gothic houses, some 8 km. N.W. of which is the 15
sanctuary of *S. Miguel del Fay* over-looking the finest waterfall i
Catalonia.—We now thread the narrow wooded valley of th
Congost.—17. km., l. *Centelles*, an old town with an unfinished 18
castle of the Duke of Solferino, beyond which we obtain a distant vie
of the Pyrenees.—4 km. *Tona* (*Hotels*), with a ruined castle and 11
church.—At *Seva*, 5 km. E., is another 11C church; 4 km. beyond is th
Romanesque church of *El Brull*.

9 km. **VIC** (1575 ft), lying in an amphitheatre of hills, an episcopa
town of 27,600 inhab. (*Parador Nac.* 13 km. N.E., attractively sitec
overlooking the Pantano de Sau), was the ancient capital of th
Ausetani.

At the S.E. corner of the PL. MAYOR is a 16C *Palace* and th
Ayuntamiento of 1495–1509, with a later tower (1679). The C. de Rier
descends towards the **Cathedral**, rebuilt by *José Morató* in 1780–1803
and interesting as a complete neoclassical design.

Of the old building (cons. 1038) there remain the crypt, the tower called '
Cloquer' (1180), and cloister, although the latter was taken down and re-erected
1806. The N. Chapels also survive from the work of 1633–80 by *Jaime Vendrell;*
the 6th is the silver sarcophagus by *Juan de Matons* (1728) of Bp. Bernardo Calv
(d. 1243). The gilt screen of the chapel dates from 1685. In the ambulatory is a
alabaster Retablo of 1420–27 by *Pedro Oller*, and opposite, the same sculptor
tomb of Canon Desputjol (d. 1434).

The Cathedral also contains wall-paintings by *José María Sert*, who had twi
before decorated the church with murals, in 1900–15 and 1926–30, but these earli
series were burned in 1936 when the cathedral was sacked. The present series we
not quite completed at the painter's death (1945), and the lunettes above th
cornice were painted from Sert's sketches by his pupil *Miguel Massot*.

The Cloister is of two storeys, the lower 12C, the upper, notable for its larg
windows with elaborate tracery, built between 1318 and 1400. Awkwardly plac
in the centre is a monument (1865) to the philosopher Jaime Balmes (1810–48). O
the N.E. corner is the *chapter house*, by *Bartolomé Ladernosa*, finished in 1360 an
further S. the domed chapel of *Sta. María de la Redonda* with a Baroque retabl
and statue of the Virgin (1632).

The *Museo Episcopal, N. of the cathedral, contains an impressive collection of early Catalan paintings on wood, including works by *Ferrer Bassa* (1324–48), *Pere Serra, Jaime Ferrer I* and *II*, the *Maestro de Rubió* (c. 1350), the *Maestro de Fonollosa* (c. 1420), *Ramón de Mur* (1402–35), including his masterpiece, the Retablo of Guimerá, *Bernat Martorell, Jaume Huguet*, and *Juan Gasco*. The collection of sculpture includes, besides early Calvaries, among them one from Erill-la-Val, a carved retablo from S. Joan de les Abadesses by *Bernat Saulet* (1341). Other rooms contain a good collection of embroidered vestments, and other fabrics, *guadamecils*, ceramics and glass, metalwork, coins, drawings, crucifixes, coffers (some ivory), and furniture, mostly ecclesiastical.

The cella of a 3C *Roman Temple*, discovered during the demolition of the Moncada palace, has been restored to house a lapidary collection.

The town contains a number of old houses and several churches of some interest; *S. Justo* (late 15 and 17C); *S. Teresa*, finished in 1646, with a Baroque retablo of 1698–1704; *N.S. de la Piedad*, by *José Morató*, who also designed in 1753 the church of the *Hosp. de Santa Cruz*, a 16C building.

At *Sant Julià de Vilatorta* (5 km. E.) are ruins of a castle and a house of the Templars (cons. 1050), while further S. is *Villaleóns* with a late 11C church.—From S. Julià a picturesque but difficult road runs on to (31 km.) *S. Hilari Sacalm*, see p. 138.—At *Tavèrnoles*, 7 km. N.E. of Vic, off the N141, is *S. Esteve*, a well-preserved Lombardic church of 1078, while at *Sta Eugenia de Berga* (6 km. S.E.) is another 11C church (cons. 1183).—The C 154 leads to *Berga* (p.163; 59 m. N.W.), viâ (30 km.) *Prats de Lluçanès*, 5 km. N. of which is 11C Lombardic *Sta Maria de Llucanes*, with a 12C cloister. A mountain road (C 153) leads N.E. from Vic to (60 km.) *Olot* (p.138), passing at 28 km. the villages of *Rupit*, and nearby *San Juan de Fabregas*, both with Romanesque churches.

Leaving Vic, the N 152 passes the ruined castle of *Gurp*, and ascends the Ter valley. Near (25 km. r.) *Sant Quirze*, stands the castle of *Montesquiú*, and beyond are the ruins of the castle of *Besora* (2953 ft).

13 km. **Ripoll** (2230 ft; 11,700 inhab.) an ugly town situated in the angle between the Ter and the Fresser, is famous for its Benedictine *Monastery*, founded in 888 by Count Wilfred 'el Velloso', and consecrated in 935 and 977. After being ravaged by a fire in 1835, it was almost completely rebuilt. The heavily restored *church* (1020–32), with its square tower, is preceded by a narthex, now hidden behind a glazed conservatory', within which is the *W. Doorway* of 1160–68, a remarkable example of rich Romanesque carving with grotesque monsters and bands of sculpture illustrating the Scriptures.

The INTERIOR is plain with double aisles and massive square piers dating from the foundation; the short apsidal chancel and the apses on the E. side of the transepts are slightly later.—The tombs include those of Counts Borrell II (d. 992) and Ramón Berenguer III (d. 1113).—The *Cloister* is of two storeys, the lower gallery Romanesque (c. 1172–1206) with storeyed capitals, the upper (c. 1382–1408) with foliated capitals and carved abaci.

Above 14C. *S. Pedro*, a cavernous edifice with nave and aisles of nearly equal height, is an extensive but miscellaneous ethnological museum, with an interesting collection of firearms manufactured in Ripoll in the 16-18C. The church itself is under restoration.

At the picturesque village of *Vallfogona* (12 km. E. of Ripoll) are remains of a castle and a church of 1756 preserving its 12C front, beyond which the C 150 leads over the Collado de Coubet (fine views) to (19 km.) *Olot*, p.138.

FROM RIPOLL TO CAMPRODÓN (24 km.). 10 km. N.E. lies **S. Joan de l Abadesses** (2580 ft; 4200 inhab.), with a restored medieval *Bridge* over the Te dating from 1130. The remarkable collegiate church of *S. Joan* was founded in 887 by Count Wilfred, whose daughter was the first of the abbesses, and consecrated in 1150. In the N. Chapel is the strange wooden *Calvary* (1250 known as 'las Brujas' (witches). Note also the capitals, and the 14C alabaster retablo in the S. Transept. A small museum of Religious art has been established adjacent. The delicately columned cloister was begun in the 14C and finished 1445.—The ruined church of *S. Pol* has a Romanesque W. Door and trefoil aps

The C 151 continues to ascend the Ter valley to (14 km.) *Camprodón* (2950 2300 inhab.) a summer resort with an old church, and birthplace of the compos Isaac Albéniz (1861–1909). The 16C bridge has a square defensive tower, while the church of the restored monastery of *S. Pedro* was consecrated in 904 and again 1169.—At *Baget* (12 km. E.) is 11C *S. Cristobal* with an early tower and 11 Crucifixion known as La Magestad.—*Llanás*, 2 km. N.W. of Camprodón, has church consecrated in 1168.—From Camprodón we may cross the frontier v *Molló*, whose Romanesque church has a remarkable tower, and the Col d'Arre (4290 ft), to *Prats-de-Mollo* in France.

From Ripoll the road ascends alongside the Freser amid fine mountain scenery.—4 km. *Campdevánol*, with a ruined Romanesque church. We pass an old Gothic Bridge before reaching (10 km.) *Ribes de Freser* (2980 ft).—8 km. N. of Ribes, at *Queralbs,* is a 10C church beyond which at 6513 ft, reached by rack-railway, is the sanctuary of *N.S.de Núria* (partly 11C), whence we may climb E. to the Ull de Te refuge (7625 ft). W. of Ribes de Freser and beyond the Collada de Tose (5906 ft), which may be closed by snow in Dec.-March, lies *La Molin (Hotels)* and *Masella,* both being developed as winter sports centres.

51 km. **Puigcerdà** (3900 ft; 6000 inhab.; *Hotels*), was founded in 117 by Alfonso II as capital of the Cerdaña, or Cerdagne, a district divided between France and Spain by the Treaty of the Pyrenees (1659). The town stands on a hill in the centre of a mountain-girt plain. The 15C *Ayuntamiento*, damaged in the civil war, has been restored; of *S. Maria* only the fine tower and a 14C carved doorway survive. *Sto Domingo* (13C), restored, preserved its 15C Front of grey marble.

Puigcerdà is connected by an international bridge (frontier—Spanish customs) with *Bourg-Madame*, in France.

A 'neutral road' connects Puigcerdá with (3 km. N.E.) **Llivia** (800 inhab.; *Hote* the ancient *Julia Livia*, and capital of the Cerdagne until 1177. Thanks to a quibb in the Treaty of the Pyrenees by which the villages but not the towns of the Uppe Cerdagne were ceded to France, Llivia, once the haunt of smugglers, occupies Spanish enclave within France. The balconied streets are entirely Spanish in styl and the church is fortified. Its *pharmacy* is one of the oldest in Europe (c. 142￼

FROM PUIGERDÁ TO SEU D'URGELL (48 km.) The C 313 descends the Segre valley with the Sierra de Cacli on the l. through (5 km.) *Bolvir* with a Romanesqu church, and (12 km.) *Bellver,* also preserving an old church and a ruined castle.— At 8 km. a road climbs N. to the small spar of *Lles,* beyond which is the Romanesque church of *Aransa.*—At 19 km. we leave on our r. the road to *Estimariú,* with the half-ruined basilica of *S. Vicente,* and beyond, with an ear belfry, *Bescaràn.*—4 km. Seu d'Urgell, see Rte 13.

From PUIGCERDÀ TO SEU D'URGELL VIÀ ANDORRA (86 km.) After passin through FRANCE for 36 km. on the N 20 we climb in steep zig-zags to the *Pto. Envalira,* on the high E. frontier of Andorra.

ANDORRA, officially the *Neutral Valleys of Andorra*, the last survivor of the independent states of the Pyrenean valleys, occupies an area of 450 km² in the upper basin of the Valira and a population of 26,500, having almost quadrupled i the last 15 years. The completion in 1931 of a motor-road from France, the establishment of hydro-electric power stations in the main valleys, and the openin of a wireless station, have robbed the state of most of its attractive isolatior Smuggling was once the principal source of revenue, but it now subsists largely o a particularly obnoxious form of Tourism. However, the upper valley sti preserves some wild romantic scenery, a backcloth to the unattractive boom-town

elow, the streets of which are lined with hotels, garages and shops supplying
verything from souvenirs to untaxed luxury goods.

History: A longstanding dispute between the counts of Foix and the bishops of
rgel as to which had the prior right to the suzerainty of the Andorran valleys was
rranged in 1278 by arbitration or 'paréage' to the effect that the inhabitants
ould be independent under a joint suzerainty. This arrangement still holds good,
e crown and later the government of France being the heirs of the counts of Foix.
he French President and the Bp. of Urgel each appoint a 'Viguier' or Vicar,
ainly for judicial functions, while the administration is in the hands of a Council
f Twenty-four (elected every four years) who appoint a Syndic-General from
mong their number.

From the **Pto. de Énvalira** (7905 ft) the highest road-pass in the Pyrenees, we
limb down to *Soldeu* (5985 ft) the highest village in Andorra. 6 km. beyond lies *S.
an de Casellas*, a primitive Romanesque chapel with a Catalan retablo. We soon
ach *Canillo* (5125 ft), with a good church tower, beyond which a path ascends to
e sanctuary of *Meritxell*, a 16C chapel containing a 12C Virgin.—6 km. *Encamp*
715 ft) with a Romanesque belfry and the curious quarter of La Mosquera.—At
km. we enter *Les Escaldas* (3625 ft) above which rises the isolated Romanesque
apel of *S. Miguel d'Engolasters;* its frescoes are now in the Museo de Arte de
ataluña, Barcelona.

From Les Escaldas a road ascends the Valira del Norte to (17 km.) *El Serrat*
050 ft), passing between the peaks of *Coma Pedrosa* (9665 ft) to the W. of *La
assana* by the Arinsal Valley, still the haunt of the ibex, and E., the *Pic de
asamanya* (9090 ft), an easy climb from *Ordino* (4270 ft) via the Col d'Ordino,
hich leads to Canillo.

2 km. **Andorra la Vella** (3475 ft) is the capital of the state. In the central square is
Romanesque church with altars gilded in the Catalan style. To the S. stands the
asa de la Vall (16C). the scat of the administrative council, where, on the first
oor, is the Council Chamber, with the archives enclosed in a chest with six locks,
ne for each parish.

Just S. of the town stands the chapel of *Sta Coloma*, with a round tower, 12C
all paintings, and horseshoe chancel arch.—There is another round-towered
hurch at *Ars*, S.W. of *Sant Julià*, reached by a rough road diverging r. on the
panish side of the frontier.—4km. *Sant Julià de Loria* (3125 ft) has a
omanesque church tower, beyond which we pass, at *Anserall*, the ruined church
f *S. Sadurni de Tabérnoles* (c. 1040), with a curious apse and a Lombard tower.—
t 4 km. we cross into Spain (customs post) and at 9 km. enter *La Seu d'Urgell,* see
te 13.

12   FROM BARCELONA TO LERIDA
AND ZARAGOZA

otal distance, 294 km. (182 miles). N II. 100 km. *Cervera*—54 km. **Lérida**—140
m. **Zaragoza**.

Motorway. The A2 autopista from Barcelona to *Lérida* and *Zaragoza* has now
een completed. The first half, diverging to a point some distance S. of the N II,
rovides a faster route, off which the monasteries of *Santes Creus* and *Poblet* may
e visited with ease. From Lérida, the motorway is recommended as allowing one
o traverse the monotonous Monegros more rapidly.

Leaving Barcelona by the Diagonal, we join the autopista just W. of
e city and descend into the Llobregat valley.—At *Molins de Rei* the
oad until 1972 turned abruptly across the river by a bridge of 1764,
hich, badly damaged by floods, was dismantled recently and replaced
y the viaduct which spans the valley nearer Martorell. On the W. bank
f the river (between Molins de Rei and Martorell), at *Papiol,* is a castle
nd Romanesque church, and at *Pallejá*, a 16C castle.

27 km. **Martorell** (14,700 inhab.) with a view (r.) of the *Pont del
iable*, an ancient bridge across the Llobregat restored in 1768 by
arlos III, but almost destroyed during the Civil War. Here is a

Triumphal Arch erected (according to a modern inscription) b
Hannibal in honour of Hamilcar Barca, A.U.C.535 (218 B.C.).

The *Museo Santacana* contains architectural material, while the *Muse
Municipal*, installed in the 18C *Conv. de Capuchinos*, displays sculptures a
azulejos.—The parish church of *Gélida*, 8 km S.W., is built into the ruins of an o
castle, said to be Roman.

9 km. we by-pass *Esparraguera*, 5 km. beyond which the road t
Monistrol and Montserrat forks r., see Rte 10. At 28 km. we by-pas
Igualada (30,000 inhab.; *Hotel*), with a venerated figure of Christ in th
church of *Sta María*, and a *Museum* largely devoted to the leathe
industry, tanning, etc.

From Igualada the C 241 leads S.W. to (25 km.) *Sta Coloma de Queralt* with
good medieval parish church as well as that of *Sta María de Belloc* (13C) wi
tombs of Sta Coloma (c. 1370) and of Pedro VI, lord of Queralt, and Alamanda
Rocaberti, made c. 1350–70 by *Pedro Aguilar* of Lérida and the local master *Ped.
Ciroll.*

At 8 km. a by-road (r.) approaches the fortified church of *Rubi*
Jorba, with a late 14C retablo, and the C 1412 leads N. 18 km. to *Cala⸗*
with ancient ramparts and a ruined Moorish castle.

28 km. **Cervera** (6200 inhab.; *Hotel*), retains the huge decayin
buildings, by *Luis Curiel*, of the *University* created by Philip V in 171
on the suppression of those of Lérida and Barcelona, and removed t
Barcelona in 1841. Here in 1760, Joseph Baretti, on entering its porta
without first begging permission from the obstreperous students, was
hissed at, and subjected to a shower of stones! It now contains a sma
museum of ethnology. The *Dominican Church* has a good cloister; th
Ayuntamiento, by *Francisco Puig* (1677–88), contains a collection o
paintings; while *Sta María*,(c. 1200–1487) has an octagonal tower (1431
by *Pedro de Vallebrera*, a 13C statue known as the Virgen del Coll,
processional cross of 1435 by *Bernat Llopart* of Barcelona, a fin
altarpiece in the *Cap. de S. Martín* (1378–80) and a tomb of 1382, bot
by *Jordi de Deu*. Other buildings are the 11C *Pta. de S. Martín*, th
round church of *S. Pere le Gros*; *S. Antonio*, with a Baroque doorwa
and the remains of Gothic *Sta María Magdalena*.

6 km. N.E., on a hill near the village of *Olujes* stands **Montfalcó Murallat,**
houses enclosed by a huge wall with only one gateway, and nearby, the ruine
Moorish castle of *Santa Fé.*—Beyond (9 km.) at *Portell*, is the *Conv. de S. Ramó
Nonato*, with a Baroque altarpiece by *Pedro Costa* (1741).—11 km. N.E.
Cervera is *Llor*, with a Romanesque church and later castle, while at 14 km. N. li
Guissona, with a 14-17C church and a late-Gothic mansion (1505–15) called '*Ob.
de Fluvia*'.—To the N.W. at *Montcortés* is a Renaissance castle, and *Concabel*
with a Romanesque church and old houses.—*Pallargues*, 15 km. N.W. of Cerver
and *Florejacs*, beyond, have medieval castles, and *Pelligals*, a Romanesqu
church.

At (10 km.) **Tàrrega** (10,600 inhab.) we reach the monotonous Llan
d'Urgell, watered by the Cervera. The parish church has 17C Gothi
star-vaulting.—*Verdú*, 5 km. S., has a 14C castle and a church with
Romanesque portal, and rose window.—At 3 km. we pass *Vilagrassa*
with a good Romanesque church doorway, and nearby *Anglesola*, wit
12-14C statues in its church.—8 km. **Bellpuig** (3,600 inhab.), by-passed
in the parish church of which is preserved the elaborately sculptes
Tomb of Ramón de Cardona, Viceroy of Sicily (d. 1522), by *Giovann.
di Nola* (1526–31), with its armed effigy.—1 km. S., in what was a 13C
Franciscan Convent (refounded by Ramón in 1507), is a degraded three
storeyed *Cloister*, late Gothic below, Renaissance (1614) above, with

newel staircase.—*Vilanova de Bellpuig*, 5 km. S.W., has an Aragonese retablo in its church.

The road now traverses a rich area of orchards before the hill-top cathedral of Lérida comes into view.

33 km. **LÉRIDA** (in Catalan, *Lléida*; 100,900 inhab.; 38,000 in 1920; 52,000 in 1960; *Hotels*) is a busy but, except for its *Old* Cathedral, not very interesting town consisting of an insalubrious old centre traversed by two long streets running parallel to the Rio Segre, intersected by steep lanes descending from the fortress-hill 300 ft above, surrounded by modern suburbs. The Old Cathedral may be approached with ease by car.

History. The ancient *Ilerda*, one of the keys of Catalonia, has from time immemorial been the theatre of sieges and war. It was held for Pompey by Afranius and Petreius until they were outgeneralled by Caesar, and soon after it became a municipium and the seat of a university; its inconvenience was such, however, that the recusant youth of Rome used to be threatened with rustication thither. The vicissitudes of the Moorish occupation ended with the victory of Ramón Berenguer V in 1149. The university was re-established in 1300; S. Vicente Ferrer, and Calixtus III (Alfonso Borja) were among its pupils.

In 1640 Lérida declared for Louis XIII and it was taken by Philip IV in person, after an unsuccessful siege by Gen. Leganés. The Grand Condé was unable to recapture it in 1644. Berwick and Orleans sacked the town in the War of Succession (1707). Philip V, the claimant whom they supported, was routed at *Almenar* (22 km. N.) by Stanhope in 1710, and barely escaped with his life; in revenge he transferred the university to Cervera. In the Peninsular War the citadel was induced to surrender by Suchet (1810), who drove the defenceless citizens on to the glacis, where they were exposed to the fire of both sides until the governor capitulated. It was the birthplace of the composer Enrique Granados (1868–1916), and Salvador Seguí (1885–1923), the syndicalist leader.

Opposite the N. end of the principal bridge (on Roman foundations) spanning the Segre stands an old gateway, leading to the arcaded Pl. de la Pahería. To the E. is the Pl. de España; to the W., turning towards the C. Mayor (closed to traffic), is the *Ayuntamiento*, with a 13C front, and containing a small archaeological collection, a retablo by *Jaime Ferrer VI* (1439), and a 14C Codex of the Constitutions of Catalonia illuminated by *Ramon Destorrents*. On the N. side of the C. Mayor further W. is the *Cathedral Nueva*, a plain Corinthian building to the designs of *Pedro Mártir Cermeño* (1760–81), gutted in 1936 but restored, and preserving some 15-16C Tapestries. Opposite is the *Hosp. de Sta Maria* (1454–1512), now housing a museum of local interest. *La Sangre*, some distance beyond, has a Plateresque portal. To the N. of the Catedral Nueva is *S. Lorenzo* (1270–1300, with a 15C tower) said to occupy the site of a Roman temple converted into a mosque, and containing 14-15C retablos. At its W. end is a Baroque extension.

The Seminario, adjacent, houses the *Museo Diocesano* (at present closed). Outstanding works include painted frontals (13C) from Tresserra and Berbegal, and the abbess's throne (c. 1330) from Sigena. Painting of the 14C is represented by a panel of the Virgin and Child and a Franciscan retablo from Castelló de Farfanyá; while later retablos are largely the work of the Ferrer family, notably the panel by *Jaime Ferrer 11* of a medieval knight out hunting. The sculptures include a 13C frontal from Buira, a series of reliefs from Corbins (late 14C), and fragments from the Old Cathedral, also a wooden model of the New.

The C. Tallada climbs E. (to the N. of which is 13C *S. Martín*; to the S. the *Instituto*, in a 15C convent with an 18C patio to reach gardens laid out to the W. of the **Castle**, known as *La Zuda*, mid-13C and enlarged by Simón de Navers in 1336-41. We enter through the *Puerta del León* in the outer wall erected in 1826 to reach fortifications built by the French during the War of the Spanish Succession.

Contained in the fortifications, and used as barracks between 1707 and 1948, since when it has been gradually restored, is the *Seo Antiguo* or *Catedral Viejo, dominated by its tall tower. Appalling damage was done in its 240 years of military occupation. Partitions separated the crossing from the nave, which was once used for machine-gun instruction; the aisles were converted into dormitories, being divided horizontally just below the level of the capitals by a floor, below which were the stables, while the kitchen and canteen were contained in the cloister!

Begun in 1203 by *Pedro Decumbo* for Pedro II, it was consecrated in 1278 and remains a fine example of the transitional style from Romanesque to Gothic, but the cloister was still under construction in 1350, and the octagonal *Tower* was not finished until 1416 by *Carlos Galter* of Rouen. The roofs are of stone, and for this reason the building was once used as a magazine. The S. Doorway, called *Porte dels Fillols* like that of St. Sernin at Toulouse, is the finest of three portals; its outer porch (1386) was built by the Flemings *Bartolomé de Bruselas* and *Esteban de Gostant*. The curious *Capitals within repay examination as do the details of the carving in the cloister. One the S. side of the presbytery is the tomb of Archdeacon Berenguer de Barutell (d. 1432), while on the walls opposite are battered line drawings (c. 1300) of New Testament scenes (under restoration). It has five apses, but with only three bays in the nave, while over the crossing is an octagonal lantern rising on conical squinches. Both the transepts and W. Front have rose-windows. The Cloister, to the W., with its 12 traceried windows, is entered from the W. by the *Puerta de los Apóstoles,* while to the S. five traceried bays provide a mirador overlooking the plain.

---

22 km. S. of Lérida is *Cogul*, with prehistoric cave-paintings in the Covacho de Cogull beside the Rio Sed. Off the N 230, also leading S., is (28 km.) *Torrebeses* where the Romanesque church has a 14C stone retablo. At *Granadela*. 14 km. further S.E., is a picturesque Baroque church-tower.

16 km. due N. of Lérida, at *Albesa*, the church contains a 14C stone retable, while mosaics may be seen in the nearby Roman villa of Romeral.

From just E. of Lérida, the C 1313 leads N.E. to *Seu d'Urgell, Andorra,* and *Puigcerdà,* see Rte 13. The N 230 and C 147 (viâ Balaguer) lead N. into the Pyrenees and to *Viella,* see Rte 16D. For the N 240 driving N.W. to *Huesca,* Rte 16A.

Quitting Lérida, the N 11 bears S.W. past (11 km.) *Alcarràs* with remains of ramparts, and, crossing the Sierra de la Mezquita, soon enters Aragón. A rapid descent brings us to (16 km.) **Fraga** (10,600 inhab.) on the Rio Cinca, famed for its figs and for the obstinacy of its inhabitants. 12C *S. Pedro* has a late-Gothic vault and a tall tower and spire. Beneath one of the altars is a remarkable 14C carving of the Three Living and the Three Dead, re-used as a frontal.—There is an important Roman site at *Pilaret de Sta Quiteria,* 4 km. N.W. The C 1310 also leads N.W. along the valleys of the Cinca and Alcandre to (58 km.) *Sariñena,* see p. 185.

Mequinenza, 20 km. S., with a castle dominating the confluence of the Segre and Ebro, was of importance during the War of the Spanish Succession, and was sacked by the French in 1811.

We now cross the sterile salitrose district of Los MONEGROS, passing (24 km.) *Candasnos,* with a church containing an imposing early-16C altarpiece, and by-pass (22 km.) *Bujaraloz.*

Hence the C 230 turns S. to (33km.) *Caspe* (p. 209); 29km. beyond which lies *Alcañiz*.—The C 230 runs N. towards (41 km.) *Sariñena*, passing through (16 km.) *Castejón de Monegros*, with a ruined castle and a 14C church enlarged in 1591, and (14 km.) *Pallaruelo*, where the parish church (1258) has remains of an altar-piece of 1485.

48 km. *Alfajarín* (*Hotel*) dominated by a ruined castle and chapel, has a Mudéjar church with a good brick front and an octagonal tower of 1486 by *Andalla de Brea* and *Mahoma Muferriz*.—19 km. **Zaragoza**, see Rte 17.

13   FROM LA SEU D'URGELL TO LÉRIDA AND TARRAGONA

Total distance, 224km. (139 miles). C1313. 50km. *Bassella*—32km. *Artesa*—(24km. *Balaguer*)—27km. **Lérida** N 240. 45km. *Vimbodi* (for Poblet)—27km. *Valls*—19km. **Tarragona**.

Motorway. It may be convenient to make use of the motorway *between* the exits for *Montblanc* and *Poblet*, and that for *Santes Creus*, thus avoiding the Coll de Lilla between Montblanc and *Valls*.

For the road from *Puigcerdà* to *Seu d'Urgell*, see Rte 11. The Spanish customs post for *Andorra* (p.166) is 2km. N. of Seu d'Urgell.

La Seu d'Urgell (9400 inhab.; *Parador Nac.*) an ancient town called after its episcopal see founded in 820, is now surrounded by modern buildings. The ***Cathedral** (1131-c. 1182) dedicated to St Odo, is by *Raimundus* the Lombard, and had a fine *Cloister*—one side of which has been destroyed—W. and S. Doors, and Apse. Ponce, a mid-13C bishop, had the reputation of being the father of ten children and a 'deflorator virginam', and was even more flagrant in satisfying his desires than was usual in that age. The *Museo* contains a MS of the Apocalypse of Beatus de Liébana (11C). From the cloister we may enter *S. Miguel* (1010–35). The 14C church of the former Dominican convent, and the old *Casa Municipal* are also of interest.

From the W. side of the town the C 1313 turns S. past *Castellciutat*, dominated by three forts, and soon enters the narrow gorge of Garganta de Organyà, with cliffs nearly 2000 ft high.—23 km. r. *Organyà*, with a good Trans. church; at *Figols*, on the opposite bank of the Segre, is an interesting Romanesque church. We follow the W. bank of the Embalse d'Oliana, passing (5 km. r.) *Coll de Nargó*, with *S. Clemente* of c. 1000, from which a rough mountain road leads W. over the Collado de Boixols to (58 km.) *Tremp*, see p.197—S. of the reservoir we cross to the E. bank of the Segre and pass (15 km.) *Oliana*, with a church door supported by two monolithic Doric columns.—7 km. *Bassella*, where we meet the road from Solsona.—16 km., r. *Gualter*, with the noble church of *Sta María*, completed c. 1205—2 km. *Ponts* (*Hotel*), with a ruined church of c. 1100.—14 km. **Artesa de Segre** (3400 inhab.) with a 13C church.—*Vilanova de Meià*, 15 km. N.W., has a fine Gothic church-portal.

FROM ARTESA TO MONTBLANC (69 km.). From Artesa the C 240 leads directly S. viâ (15 km.) **Agramunt**, where *Sta María* of c. 1163–1250, has a magnificent portal dated 1283 although in the Limousin Romanesque style, and (16 km.) *Tàrrega*, see p.168.—At 14 km. a road leads E. past the ruined castle and monastery of *Ciutadilla* to (5 km.) the castle and Gothic church of *Guimerà*, while another forks W. to (6. km.) *Sant Martí de Maldá*, whose Baroque church has a belfry of 1774 by

José Prat.—4 km. beyond, at *Maldà*, is a ruined 14C castle, 7 km. S.E. of which lies
Vallbona de les Monjes, with a nunnery founded c. 1173 having a noble W. Tower
and an octagon (c. 1340–48), the tomb of Doña Violante, queen of Jaime el
Conquistador, and a fine *cloister* of c. 1220–1445.—We may regain the main road
11 km. S.E.—24 km. *Montblanc* (p. 173), 10 km. E. of *Poblet*, see below.

10 km. *Cubells*, with a Romanesque church door and 13-14C
sculpture. At 14 km. *Balaguer* lies 2 km. to the W., see p. 196. The
Tarragona road may be joined without entering (27 km.) *Lérida*,
p.169.—Approx. 1 km. after meeting the N II, where we turn r., we fork
l. onto the N 240, after 26 km. passing *Les Borges Blanques* (5000 inhab.)
and (14 km.) *Vinaixa*, where the early-14C church has remains of
sculptures by *Guill. Saguer* (1340).—3 km. W. at *Albi*, is a palace of c.
1600.—8 km. *Vimbodi*, the chief centre of rioting against Poblet in 1835,
with a church containing retablos from the monastery, where we turn r.
for (5 km.) *Poblet*; at *Milmanda*, 2 km. S., is a castle which was the
summer residence of the abbots.

The once wealthy and powerful *Monastery of Poblet,* or *Sta Maria
de Poblet*, was founded by Ramón Berenguer IV in 1149 and populated
by Cistercian monks from Fontfroide near Narbonne.

It takes its name not from the legendary hermit, Poblet, but from a poplar-grove
(populetum). It was favoured by kings of Aragón who chose it as their burial-place
But the brotherhood of Poblet became in time a preserve for the sons of the
aristocracy and a den of dissipation, while its abbots ruled their lands with
inflexible severity.

Swinburne tells an undefying story that these immense lordships served 'as so
many nurseries and seraglios for them, where the wives and daughters of their
vassals are humbly devoted to their pleasures', continuing: 'some years ago, a set of
wild young officers, who owed the fathers a grudge, carried thither a bevy of
common strumpets drest out like ladies, and contrived matters so, that while the
men of the party went up into the hills to see prospects, the females were left to be
comforted by the Bernadines. The hot-livered monks employed the time of absence
to the best advantage, but smarted so severely for the favours they obtained from
the good-humoured nymphs, that for many months afterwards the chief
dignitaries of the house were dispersed about the neighbouring towns, under the
care of the barber-surgeons'.

Not surprizingly, in 1835 the 'constitutionalist' Catalans suspected the abbey to
be a nest of Carlism and a mob from neighbouring villages invaded it, burning the
library and archives and smashing the monuments.

Now admirably restored, the monastery and 18C buildings are again occupied
by Cistercians. Philip, Duke of Wharton (1698–1731), Jacobite and ex-president
of the 'Hell-Fire Club' died there in extreme poverty; as Duke of Northumberland
he had visited Madrid in 1726 to urge a Spanish descent on England in favour of
the Stuarts.

Entering the outer gate we see (r.) before the inner *Pta. Dorada*, the
Cap. de S. Jorge (1442). Within the gate (1480–99)) on the l. is the
Romanesque *Cap. de Sta Catalina*, dating from the time of Ramón
Berenguer IV. In front is the elaborate W. FRONT of the church (1716),
with statues of St. Benedict and St. Bernard, and the Virgin above,
flanked on the l. by the castellated *Pta. Real* (1309). On either side rise
tall watch-towers; to the r. are the ruins of the 18C abbots' palace.

We enter the monastery proper (conducted tour): to the r., above the
huge wine-vaults, is the *Pal. del Rey Martín*, begun by Martín I (1395–
1410) as a retreat for his old age, and continued by Philip IV in 1632. We
next enter the beautiful *Cloister* (late Romanesque and Gothic), off
which open the *Refectory* and *Kitchen*, and the *Chapter House*, a finely
proportioned Gothic square. On the N. side of the cloister is the
Glorieta, a hexagonal fountain pavilion very similar to that at Santes

Creus, comp. p.173. The *Upper Cloister*, seen from the Dormitory, is still derelict.

From the S. side of the cloister we enter the **Iglesia Mayor* (begun after 1166), cathedral-like in its dimensions, containing royal tombs of the House of Aragón, which stand on either side of the crossing, on depressed arches erected by Pedro IV in 1367. The tomb-chambers beneath were inserted in 1661, by the Duke of Cardena y Segorbe.

On the N. side are the tombs of Jaime I (d. 1276), Pedro IV (d. 1387) and his two queens, Fernando I (d. 1416), and Martín I; on the S. those of Alfonso II (d. 1196), Juan I (d. 1395) and Juan II (d. 1479) with their wives. After 1835, parts of the broken tombs were removed to Tarragona, but all that survived has now been returned. The bodies of the kings and queens were reburied here in 1952, and the tombs restored, embellished with effigies by *Federico Marés.*

The high altar was made (1527–29) for Charles V by *Damián Forment.* The *Sacristía Nueva*, on the S. side of the church, dates from c. 1705–34. Other buildings of interest are the *Library* and *Archives*, beyond the N.E. corner of the cloister, and the enormous **Dormitory*, a vaulted hall 87 m. long, reached by steps directly from the choir of the church. Behind the apse are ruined cloisters and the *Chapel of S. Esteban* (Romanesque), not on view.

The main road may be regained just E. of *Espluga de Francolí*, while at *Fuente de Hierro*, on the outskirts, are a Gothic church with a doorway of 1297, and the medieval *Hosp. of S. Juan.*

5 km. **Montblanc** (5000 inhab.; *Hotel*), is a decaying town with remains of gates and **Ramparts* of 1366–72. The church of *Sta María* begun in 1352 by the English mason, *Raynard 'Fonoyll',* has a plateresque portal (1668); while *S. Miguel* (Romanesque) is restored. Among other ancient buildings is the *Casa Aguiló*, with a Romanesque front and Gothic windows, the *Hosp. de Sta Magdalena*, with a 16C cloister, and N. of the town, a medieval *Bridge* over the Francolí.

The C 240 continues due S. through (15 km.) *Alcover*, with a Romanesque church known as La Mezquita, and by-passes (5 km. r.) *La Selva*, famous for its wines, with a 16C church designed by Canon Blay.—9 km. *Reus*, see p.184.—At 6 km. we meet the N 340 (the Tarragona-Valencia road) before reaching the coast at (3 km.) *Salou.*

The N 240 now climbs to the *Coll de Lilla* (views) and descends steeply to (17 km.) **Valls** (16,700 inhab.), birthplace of the novelist Narcís Oller (1845–1930) and the composer Roberto Gerhard (1896–1970), preserving a wide-naved church of the Gerona type (1570), a ruined castle, ancient ramparts, and one or two picturesque streets.—From Valls a road leads N. to *Plà de Cabra*, with a cruciform Romanesque church with a carved doorway; 14 km. beyond, on the Igualada road, is the ruined castle of *Querol.*

The excursion to *Santes Crues* may be easily made from **Valls** by driving E. on the C 246. After 10 km. we turn N. to reach (7 km.) the Cistercian Abbey, still surrounded by its ancient walls. Founded in 1150, **Santes Creus* was moved to this site in 1158 by Ramón Berenguer IV. It was badly damaged in the anticlerical rising of 1835, and is undergoing restoration. In the courtyard is the *Cap. de Sta Lucía* (1741). The reconsecrated **Church* of 1174–1221, with a fine rose window and massive square piers, contains in its transepts the tombs of the kings of Aragón, Pedro III (el Grande; d. 1285) by *Master Bartomeu* and *Guillem d'Orenga* (1285–1302); and Jaime II (d. 1327), with his wife Blanche of Anjou, the work of *Jaume Lorana de Montmeló* and *Bertrán*

Riquer, with effigies by *Francesc Muntflorit* (1310–15). At the feet of Pedro III is the tomb of Roger of Lauria (d. 1304), the admiral who destroyed Charles of Anjou's fleet in 1284 and that of Frederick of Sicily in 1299. In the *coro* are the tombs of Ramón and the Guillermo de Moncada who fell at the taking of Mallorca (1229). The central lantern is of c. 1314, while the tower was added in 1575.

The charming *Cloister* likewise contains remarkable tombs; on its s. side is a six-sided fountain-pavilion (comp. Poblet). It was begun in 1313. The S. walk was designed (1331–41) by an Englishman, *Raynard 'Fonoyll'*. The *Chapter House*, *Dormitorio*, and other conventual buildings are of interest, together with remains of the *Palace* of Pedro III and Jaime II, and the Romanesque *Old Cloister* of 1163. The *Pal. of the Abbots* (c. 1570–90) is now the Ayuntamiento.

From Santas Creus, the road S. leads directly to (32 km.) *Tarragona*.

From Valls, we follow the N 240 due S. along the E. bank of the Francoli, at 19 km. entering *Tarragona*, see Rte 15.

14   FROM BARCELONA TO TARRAGONA, TORTOSA, AND VALENCIA

Total distance, 345 km. (214 miles). N 430. 48 km. *Vilafranca del Penedès*—21 km. ·*Vendrell*—30 km. **Tarragona**—(at 72 km. **Tortosa** lies 13 km. to the r.)—90 km. *Benicarlo*—26 km. **Castellón**— 35 km. *Sagunto*—23km. **Valencia.**

Motorway. The A7, avoiding the Pto. de Ordal, may be taken as far as *Vendrell*, after which the N 340 should be followed to pass the *Arco de Bará* and *Torre de los Escipiones*, before entering *Tarragona*. Thence one may revert to the motorway and remain on it as far as *Sagunto*. Exits may be made to *Tortosa* and *Peñiscola*, but in fact it offers a much pleasanter drive than the main road, and by-passes *Castellón*.

FROM BARCELONA TO VENDRELL viâ SITGES (68 km.). This alternative route along the coast is followed by driving S.W. from Pl. de España on the C 246. We cross the Llobregat and (10 km. l.) pass the airport of *Prat*. Skirting the coast and traversing pine woods, at 14 km. we meet the C 245.—This latter road is approached from the W. end of the Diagonal, and by-passes *Hospitalet* (282,100 inhab.; part of greater Barcelona) with a 12C church and ancient chapel of *Sta Eulalia*; it then crosses the suburb of *Cornellá*, with remains of a 10C church and a medieval castle, before continuing S.W. past the ruined castle of *Arampruña*, to *Castelldefels* (20,100 inhab.; *Hotels*) with a Romanesque church and the Torre del Homenaje of its former castle.—The C 246 climbs to the corniche of the Costas de Garraf.

17 km. **Sitges** (11,100 inhab.; *Hotels*). N. of the parish church is the *Museo del Cau Ferrat*, containing a collection of local ironwork, and paintings, including a Magdalen by *El Greco*. The adjacent *Museo Maricel* is also of interest, while in the *Casa Llopis* is a *Mueso Romántico*, with Empire and Restoration furniture and fittings. The chapel of the modern *Hosp. de S. Juan Bautista* contains a retablo by *Jaime Forner* (1544).—8 km. **Vilanova i la Geltrú** (41,400 inhab.), with the *Museo Balaguer*, a good collection of antiquities and art, including an Annunciation by *El Greco* in the restored castle of *La Geltrú* (12-15C). The church of the old quarter has a Renaissance retablo mayor.—4 km. *Calafell*, dominated by a 12C castle.—4 km. *Vendrell*, see below.

We follow the autopista as far as the bridge at Molins de Reí, crossing which we climb S.W. on the N 340 to the Pto. de Ordal.—At 17 km. a road leads W. 7 km. to *Corbera de Llobregat*, where 11C *S. Pons* has a 14C polychrome Virgin and child.—At 23 km. a road leads E. c. 10 km. to *Olesa de Bonevalls*, with remains of a fortified pilgrim-hospice of 1262.

8 km. **Vilafranca del Penedès**, (20,200 inhab.; *Hotel*) the centre of a fertile wine-growing district, preserves a few old mansions, including that of the barons of Rocafort and the Palace of the kings of Aragón, containing a *Museo del Vino*, which should not be missed by the connoisseur. The town was taken from the Moors in 1000 and made a 'free town' in order to attract settlers. *Sta María* (before 1285) has been much altered; the old *Conv. de S. Francisco* (now a hospital) contains a Retablo by *Luis Borrassá*. The chapel of *S. Juan de los Hospitalarios* was begun in 1307. Its most famous native was the medievalist Manuel Milà i Fontanals (1818-84).

At *Sant Marti Sarroca*, some 10 km. N.W. is an attractive Romanesque church (12C), with a Retablo by *Jaime Cabrera*.—At **Olérdola**, 4 km. S. of Vilafranca, are ruins of a castle, possibly the stronghold of *Carthago Vetus*, the first Punic settlement in Catalonia, but the existing walls are those built by Cato in 197 B.C. The church of *S. Miguel* has a chapel cons. 925, nave and transepts of 991, and vaults and lantern finished in 1108.

5 km. *Sta Margarita dels Monjes* has a Romanesque church.—8 km. *L'Arboç; S. Julián,* with an interesting façade, contains a carved retablo.—8 km. *Vendrell* (10,600 inhab.), birthplace of the 'cellist Pablo Casals (1876-1973), and where he is now interred.

Hence the C 246 leads W. to (30 km.) *Valls*, off which, at 21 km. *Santes Creus* (p.173) lies 7 km. N. *Poblet* (p.172) lies 22 km. N.W. of Valls.

At 8 km. the road passes round the **Arco de Bará**, a Roman arch with a span of 5 m. and four fluted pilasters on either face, built astride the old Via Maxima by L. Licinius Sergius Sura, a friend of Pliny the Younger (2C A.D.). Damaged in the Civil War, it has since been restored.—12 km. *Altafulla*, with three ruined castles, one on the cliff-edge, beyond which lies *Tamarit*, with a well-restored castle (12-13C) with a small museum, a late Romanesque church, and the *Torre de Mora* (1562), while on the r. we pass the *Cantera del Médol*, a Roman stone-quarry.—At 4 km. stands the so-called *Torre de los Escipiones*.

This square monument nearly 9 m. high bears on one face two mutilated male figures in high relief and traces of an inscription, but as it dates from the latter half of the 2C. A.D., it is not likely that it commemorates the brothers Scipio who were killed at *Anitorgis* (Alcañiz) in 212 B.C.

The hill and old walls of **Tarragona** may be seen from some distance as we approach the city, entered at 7 km., see Rte 15.

Passing through the centre of the town, we cross the Francoli and continue S.W. through an industrial area with cracking plants, and traverse the undulating Campo de Tarragona.—A road shortly bears l. to the Cabo de Salou, and the extensively developed coast. **Salou** (12,300 inhab.; *Hotels*) ancient *Salauris*, was the seaport whence Jaime el Conquistador set sail for the conquest of Mallorca in 1229. The nearby chapel of *La Pineda* has 14C remains.—17 km. *Cambrils*, Roman *Oleaster*, has a church-tower fortified for coast-defence. The orchard-covered plain, dominated by the Sierra de Llaveria, narrows, while perched on the summit of the *Mola* (2625 ft), the castle of *Escornalbou* (p.184) may be discerned. The landscape changes and we cross a desolate health, passing (15 km. l.) *Hospitalet de Infante*, taking its name from a hospice founded in 1314 for pilgrims who had crossed the mountains from Zaragoza. On the r. rises the Sierra de Balaguer (2992 ft.). S. of Cala Justell we pass (l.) a nuclear power-station.—At 18 km., we by-pass the resort of *L'Ametllá de Mar*. To the r. is the castle of *Perelló*, and ahead the Montsiá.—At (13 km.) *Ampolla* the road crosses the neck of the extensive Ebro delta, which may be seen to the l., dotted with lagoons and intersected by canals, largely given over to market-gardening and the cultivation of rice.— 5 km. a road leads E. to *La Cava*, on the N. bank of the Ebro, and beyond to Cap de Tortosa.

At 4 km. the C 235 bears r. for (13 km.) Tortosa, from which we may regain the main road at *Vinaroz*, see below.

TORTOSA (47,200 inhab.; *Parador Nac.*; *Hotel*), a dull old town, retaining some walls and commanded by its castle, lies on both banks of the Ebro, here 220m. wide, allowing small sea-going vessels to ascend to its quays.

History. The Roman colony, *Dertosa Julia Augusta*, was sufficiently important to possess a mint. Except for a few years after Louis the Debonair's successful assault in 811, it was held by the Moors until 1148, when Ramón Berenguer V took the town with the aid of the Genoese and the Knights Templar. A counter assault in the following year might have been successful had not the women manned the battlements while the men sallied out and drove off the besiegers. In 1708 it was taken by the French under Orleans and in the Peninsular War it surrendered to Suchet in 1811. In the Civil War the Ebro formed the front between Nationalists and Republicans for almost a year (1938–39) and Tortosa suffered serious damage. The Carlist general Cabrera (1810–77) was born here; likewise Felipe Pedrell (1841-1922), the composer and musicologist. Adrian Dedel (d. 1523), the Dutch tutor of Charles V and inquisitor-general of Aragón, was Bp. of Tortosa from 1516 until his election in 1522 to the papacy as Adrian VI.

Commanding the W. end of the town is the *Citadel*, in the extensive ruins of which the *Parador* has been accommodated, from which panoramic **Views* of the rich plain to the S., ringed by mountains, may be gained. The ancient *Judería* of Tortosa lay to the W. below the castle hill.

The **Cathedral** was founded in 1158 by Bp. Gaufredo on the site of a mosque built by Abderrahman III in 914, and the present building begun in 1347 by *Benito Dalguayre*. The massive unfinished façade, added in 1705–57, is out of harmony with the Gothic interior whose double **Ambulatory*, with pierced stone screens, is one of the most beautiful in Spain. The reliefs on the pulpits and the iron choir-screen deserve notice. The *Cap. de Santa Cinta* (1672–1719) is embellished with precious marble, and in that of *Sta Candia* are preserved tomb-inscriptions of the first four bishops (1165–1245). The *Sacristy* contains a Moorish ivory casket, but it is rarely on view, and the sacristan ossified. The 13-14C *Cloister* is entered through a portal at its W. side, while opposite the main entrance is the 14C *Bishop's Pal.* (restored), retaining an attractive patio.

A few old houses may be seen in the C. de la Rosa and C. Moncada, in which stands Baroque *La Purísima*. The old *Ayuntamiento* has a front of 1768. To the r. is the *Col. de Sto Domingo*, housing the *Museo Municipal*. Close by is the *Conv. de S. Luis*, founded in 1544 by Charles V, with a Renaissance front by *Juan Anglés* and a three-storeyed patio enriched with 38 busts of the kings and queens of Aragón. The 14C open *Lonja* has been rebuilt in a park S. of the railway bridge.

Some 12 km. N. lies *Cherta*, the scene of combats in the Carlist wars, preserving an ancient '*azud*', or wheel to raise water from the river to the irrigation channels.—A nature reserve is maintained at *Paúls* to the N.W., while in the hills to the N.E. are the baths of *Cardó*, accommodated in a 17C monastery.

FROM TORTOSA TO VINAROZ (43 km.) We may regain our route by crossing the Ebro and turning S. along the inland road traversing the huerta of Tortosa, backed by the imposing mountain chain culminating in *Mte. Caro* (4750 ft), and with the ridge of *Montsiá* on our l.—30 km. *Ulldecona* has a Gothic church with an octagonal tower, and a retablo by *Sariñena*.—24 km. to the W. lie the ruins of the Cistercian *Abbey of Benifazá* (1264–76), with a nave of 1430–1518 by *Barceló de Vallibona*, a 13C chapter house, and cloister of 1347–79.—At 13 km. we meet the N 340 at *Vinaroz*, see below.

The N 340 crosses the Ebro—which here enters the Mediterranean after a course of 466 miles—just E. of (6 km.) *Amposta* (13,500 inhab.) by-passed by the main road.—At 10 km. lies *San Carlos de la Rapita* (9,700 inhab.) situated on the Puerto de los Alfaques and sheltered by the S. lobe of the delta, on which salt is still produced. Here Carlos III had planned a great Mediterranean port of which fragments remain, including a mansion with Salomonic columns, but the project was abandoned after his death (1788).—22 km. **Vinaros**, a fishing port (16,800 inhab.; *Hotels*) on an open bay, noted for its sturgeons and lampreys. The Duc de Vendôme, who won the battle of Villaviciosa for Philip V in 1710, died here in 1712 from a surfeit of the local fish.— Hence the N 232 climbs inland to (64 km.) *Morella*, see p.209.—7 km. **Benicarló** (15,700 inhab.; *Parador Nac.*), once fortified, with an 18C octagonal church-tower and a dome covered with blue azulejos.—A road leads 7 km. W. to *Cálig*, and (7 km.) *Cervera del Maestre*, both with medieval churches; near the latter stands the ruined *Castillo de Montesa*.

We may make a short detour along the shore to (7 km.) **Peñiscola** (2800 inhab.; *Hotels*) jutting out into the Mediterranean. This fortified seagirt promontory was until recently only accessible from the mainland by a narrow sand-spit, but the exigencies of tourism have converted it into a 'picturesque' resort and it has since become spoilt by over-exploitation, many views have been obliterated by the erection of tower-blocks, etc.

History. Conquered at an early date by the Phoenicians, Peñiscola was named *Tyriche* from its resemblance to Tyre, and was later known to the Greeks as *Chersonesos*. Here young Hannibal swore eternal hatred to the Romans. Taken in 1234 from the Moors, Jaime el Conquistador gave it to the Templars. Here the schismatic pope Benedict XIII (Pedro de Luna, 'Papa Luna') resided from his deposition by the Council of Constance in 1417 until his death in 1423. It played no prominent part in history until 1811, when it withstood for 11 days a siege by the French under Suchet.

The (over-restored) *Castle* was built by the Templars and altered by Benedict XIII, but still contains imposing Gothic rooms.

From the entrance we pass (l.) stables, with a guardhouse to the r. Vaulted stairs ascend to a central platform. Above the stables is a vast hall, and adjacent is the chapel. Steps descend to the *Sala de Conclave*. A further series of rooms may be visited, and the parapets command extensive sea views.—The parish church dates from 1739.

We may regain the main road 5 km. S. of Benicarló, passing a ruined castle.

21 km. *Alcalá de Chisvert*, whose 18C church has an octagonal belfry and a retablo with paintings (17C) by *J. J. Espinosa*.—26 km. *Oropesa del Mar* (1600 inhab.; *Hotels*), on a height crowned by the ruins of its castle.—Skirting the development of *Benicasim* (3300 inhab.; *Hotels*) strewn along the shore, we enter the fertile plain of Castellón, with its orange, olive and carob trees.—To the r., among limestone hills, rises

the *Desierto de las Palmas*. A track climbs to the 18C monastery (2392 ft) set among pines, from which the main road may be regained by bearing S. past the chapel of *La Magdalena* and ruins of the Moorish castle of *Castalia*.

24 km. **CASTELLÓN DE LA PLANA,** (108,650 inhab; 34,000 in 1920; 75,000 in 1960; *Hotels*), although a provincial capital, a centre for the export of oranges and wine, and the manufacture of azulejo tiles, is of very little interest, and is better by-passed. The old town, to the N., was captured from the Moors by Jaime I in 1233 and refounded by him on its present site.

In the central *Pl. de España* are the high octagonal belfry (1591–1604) and the church of *Sta María* (1409–1549) designed by *Miguel García* destroyed in 1936 and since rebuilt. There are a S. Roch by *Ribalta* and a 15C, Nativity in the *Ayuntamiento* (1689–1716), while the C. Mayor, behind the church, leads to the Gobierno Civil, occupying the *Conv. de Sta Clara* and the remains of the church of *La Sangre*. Nearby, the *Museo* (in the Diputación) contains paintings by *Ribera, Ribalta* and *Bermejo*, among others, and ceramics from Alcora. To the E. is the *Conv. de las Capuchinas*, whose high altar has paintings by *Zurbarán*. Also in the C. Mayor is *S. Agustín* (1650), gutted in 1936.

Immediately N.E. of the town is the *Santuario de Lidón* (1731), while near *El Grao*, the port of Castellón, is the chapel of *S. Roque de Canet* (1650).—Some 30 miles out to sea lie the *Columbretes*, a group of volcanic islands with a lighthouse.

From Castellón we may follow the C 232 due W. to (21 km.) **Alcora**, (7850 inhab.), famous for its ceramics, with a *Ribalta* and medieval sculptures in the chapel of *La Sangre*, and (13 km.) **Lucena del Cid**. a hill-town with the ruined castle of the Duque de Híjar, from which the Peña Golosa (5948 ft) may be climbed. In the parish church is a triptych by the '*Master of the Miracle of Cologne*', and in the neighbourhood are the cressquely situated chapels of *S. Antonio* and *S. Vicente* and ruins of an Iberian tower of the 3C. B.C. at *Los Foyos*.—A winding road leads W. to *Mora de Rubielos* and *Teruel*, see p.207.

At 7 km. we by-pass **Villarreal** (36,600 inhab.), with orange-groves irrigated by the Mijares, here crossed by an 18C stone bridge. The town was founded by Jaime I on a grid plan in 1272, and its principal church (1752-59) with an octagonal brick tower, contains paintings by *Pablo de San Leocadia*.

Some 10 km. S.W. lies *Bechí*, birthplace of Antonio Ponz (1725–92), author of 'Viaje de España' (18 vols; 1784–94), the first important topographical 'guide' to large areas of Spain.— 6 km. S.E. lies **Burriana** (23,900 inhab.) preserving some walls and a 16C church, while its adjacent harbour is mainly occupied with the export of oranges.

14 km. W. of Villarreal lies **Onda** (16,300 inhab.) with factories of azulejos. There is a ruined castle, and paintings adorn the parish church (18C) and the *Iglesia de la Sangre*, which retains a Romanesque doorway. In the chapel of *El Savador*, to the N., is a polychrome wooden Christ by *Juan de Joanes*.

11 km. *Nules* (10,200 inhab.) has a 16C church, in the sacristy of which is a retablo of 1418. The road is dominated by the Sierra de Espadán as we near the ruined castle of *Almenara*, once the key to Valencia, where Jaime I defeated the Moors in 1238. On nearby *Mte. del Cid* are a Roman camp and and remains of a Temple of Venus. We approach Sagunto, the citadel of which rises up before us on a ridge to the W. of the main road, off which at 16 km. a road leads l. 4 km. to *Canet de Berenguer*, with a palace (17–18C), and church containing a good retablo and paintings by *Vergara* and *Espinosa*.

17 km. **Sagunto** (52,000 inhab.) proverbial for its stubborn heroism, and whose red pottery and sailcloth were famous in Roman times.

History. Although almost certainly of Iberian foundation, it is possible that *Saguntum* took its name from a colony of Greeks from the island of Zacynthus who are said to have allied themselves with Rome in the 3C B.C., and excavations, which have laid bare masonry of the type common at the Greek settlement of Emporion, tend to confirm this. In 219 B.C. Hannibal attacked Saguntum and after a siege of eight months, during which the Saguntines vainly appealed to Rome for assistance, entered the citadel, but not without having to contest every foot of ground. It was recaptured by the Romans five years later, but never regained its importance, and with the fall of the empire Saguntum fell into decay and became known simply as '*Muri veteres*' or 'old walls'.

The Moors, who built an alcázar on the castle hill, called it *Murbiter*, and the name *Murviedro* was in use until 1868, when the old name was revived. The citadel made a stubborn resistance under Andriani in 1812, but was isolated by Blake's defeat by Suchet in the plain of Valencia. It was the scene of Martínez Campos's pronunciamento in 1874, which restored the Bourbon dynasty. The composer Joaquín Rodrigo (1902) was born at Sagunto.

From the main road we turn r. up the C. José Antonio passing *S. Salvador*, a rebuilt Gothic church with a Romanesque door. We follow the C. Mayor past the Moorish *Pta. Ferrisa* and (l.) *S. Miguel* with a doorway and azulejos of 1746, to reach the Pl. Mayor, its arcades in part supported by Roman columns taken from the ruins.—To the N., beyond gardens, are insignificant remains of a *Roman Circus*.—The S.W. corner of the Pl. Mayor is occupied by *Sta María*, built in 1334 on the site of a mosque, and renovated within in the 18C. The N. Doorway preserves Gothic sculptures. To the S.E., in the C. de Tras Sagrario, are remains of a so-called *Temple of Diana*.

From the Plaza we ascend the C. del Castillo, in which stands the solar of the dukes of Gaeta, passing near the chapel of the *Virgen de los Dolores* to reach the **Roman Theatre**, and a small museum. The theatre, long used as a rope-walk, was damaged by Suchet's soldiers in 1808, and although undergoing restoration, remains one of the best preserved monuments of the kind in existence.

It dates from the late 2C A.D. The 33 rows of seats in the auditorium, divided into three tiers, may still be traced, together with the rock-cut passage from which they were entered; but the topmost gallery was destroyed in 1812, and of the buildings of the stage and orchestra little remains but the foundations.

A road ascends from the theatre to the drawbridge by which we enter the **Castillo** or *Acropolis*, a series of fortified works occupying the ridge which dominates Sagunto.

Since 1921 excavations have been proceeding intermittently and portions of Roman and pre-Roman masonry are now to be seen. Practically all the walls above ground-level are of Moorish construction or later. We emerge on the Pl. de Armas; to the l. are further excavations, including a circular medieval mill resting on Roman foundations, beneath which a large section of Iberian wall has been uncovered. Further on is the Pl. de Almenara, the E. crest of the citadel, which commands a fine view, likewise from the W. crest, or Pl. de S. Fernando, which has been partially excavated.—To the N. of the town, near *Los Valles*, an Iberian sanctuary of Bacchic type has been discovered.

5 km. S. of Sagunto we fork l., and skirting the Mediterranean, enter **Valencia** at 23 km., see Rte 52.

15 TARRAGONA AND ENVIRONS

TARRAGONA (100,800 inhab.; 28,000 in 1920; 42,000 in 1960; *Hotels*) stands on a limestone rock 260 ft above the sea, N. of the river Francoli. The old town, surrounded by cyclopean walls and partially dismantled more modern fortifications, commands a fine view of the coast from Barcelona to the Ebro delta. The modern town to the S. and around the harbour, is of little interest, except as the export centre for Tarragona wine.

History. The Carthaginian fortress of *Tarchon*, built on the site of the Iberian stronghold of *Cosse*, whose cyclopean walls (3C B.C.) still survive in part, became under the Romans one of the most important cities in Spain. First occupied by Publius and Gnaeus Scipio, *Tarraco* was made the capital of Hispania Citeror, or Tarraconensis (with the titles of *Colonia Julia Victrix Triumphans*), by Augustus, who wintered here in 26 B.C., after his Cantabrian campaign. The fertile plain and sun-baked shores ('aprica littora') are praised by Martial, and the wines of 'vitifera Laletania', rivals of the Falernian, are described by Pliny. Though it suffered at first from the Gothic invaders, the city regained its prosperity later, and it was the scene of the death of St. Hermengild, beheaded by his Arian father, King Leovigild, for adhering to the Roman faith. The city was razed by the Moors in 714 and remained practically deserted until the end of the 11C. The archbishopric, founded early in the Christian era but transferred by the Goths to Vic, was restored in 1089, and in 1118 the city was granted to the Norman adventurer Robert Burdet.
· Tarragona joined the revolt of 'Els Segadors' in 1640; it was reduced in 1643, but its commercial importance passed to Barcelona and Valencia. It was captured and burnt by the British in 1705, and by 1775, when visited by Swinburne, it had 'contracted to a very trifling city', covering only 'a small portion of the Roman enclosure'. In 1811 it was one of the few cities in Spain that resisted the invading French army, and when at length taken by Suchet it was ruthlessly sacked. The retreat of Sir John Murray before Soult's approach to Tarragona in 1813 was described by Napier as 'an operation perhaps the most disgraceful that ever befell the British arms'. The monks of Grande Chartreuse migrated here in 1903, where they established a liqueur factory.

The Barcelona road climbs to the S.E. perimeter of the old town and runs parallel to the *Ramble del Generalisimo,* a tree-lined promenade separating it from the new.—From the end overlooking the sea ('El Balcon'), we may follow the Paseo Calvo Sotelo along the line of the cliff.

Below on the r. in the Parque del Milagro is the *Roman Amphitheatre* (2-3C A.D.), long used as a quarry, while built within the ruins are fragments of the 12C church of *Sta Maria del Milagro.*—Following the Rambla de S. Carlos for a few paces, we turn r. along the Bajada de Pilatos to the remains of the Roman *praetorium*, known as the *Pal. de Augusto* or *Torreón de Pilatos*, names referring to Augustus's visit and to the fable that Pontius Pilate was praetor of Hispania Tarraconensis. Hadrian stayed here in A.D. 121.—Immediately N. of the praetorium stands the new **Museo Arqueológico**; housing an important collection of Roman and medieval antiquities; the mosaics are particularly fine.

From the Pl. del Rey to the N., with the late 16C church of *La Sangre*, we pass by the *Pta. de la Portella*, one of the original gateways in the Cyclopean wall, to approach the *Pta. de S. Antonio*, adorned with 18C trophies, through which we pass out to the Av. de la Victoria. Turning l. and skirting the wall, disfigured here by the superimposition of old houses, we reach the N. entrance of the ***Paseo Arqueológico.**

This attractive walk leads S.W. between the ancient walls and later fortifications built during the Wars of the Spanish Succession under the direction of English engineers. Planted with trees and adorned with antique fragments (including a bronze statue of Augustus presented by Italy in 1936), the Paseo provides a close exterior view of the walls.

Entering the Paseo and passing the *Minerva tower*, we see one of the finest sections of the *Wall before reaching the *Cabiscol tower*, beyond which is a Cyclopean gateway. Another is passed near the base of the square *Torre del Arzobispo*, standing at the central point in the paseo. The Cyclopean walls and their Roman superstructure continue to the W. end of the Rambla de S. Carlos.

Leaving the Paseo, we pass through the *Pta. del Rosario* into the Pl. Pallol, with a Roman gateway, possibly once the entrance to the Forum. The *Museo de la Ciudad* here is undergoing reformation. Ascending (l.) the Bajada del Rosario, we approach the *Archbishop's Palace* (1814–27) incorporating a considerable section and tower of the Roman walls. Beyond is the *Seminario*, in the W. courtyard of which stands the chapel of *S. Pablo*, fabled to be built on the spot where St Paul preached to the citizens of Tarraco in A.D. 60. It appears to have been rebuilt in part by

1243, but the W. Front, with its square door, round window, and elaborately corbelled cornice, is probably older. Nearby are the 13C church of *La Enseñanza*, the *Cap. de S. Magín* (1776), with a 16C wall-painting, and late 16C *S. Lorenzo*, with an altar-piece of 1499. We now turn S. along the C. Vilamitjana, noting at the corner of the C. Sta Tecla the remains of a Romanesque church built into a house. The *Casa de los Concilios* dates from 1584. Turning r. we reach the unfinished W. Front of the Cathedral, the exterior of which is cluttered by outbuildings.

The **Cathedral*, of considerable architectural interest, shows the transition from the late Romanesque style of the closing years of the 11C to the early Gothic of the 13th.

Begun in 1171 on the site of a mosque, which may have occupied the emplacement of a Roman temple of Jupiter, the first parts of the cathedral, built with an eye to a possible return of the Moors, were well adapted for defence, and the apse has the simplicity of a bastion. Work continued throughout the 13C under the direction of Frater *Bernardus* (d. 1256), and the building was consecrated in 1331.

The W. FRONT rises in two stages, the uppermost containing a huge rose-window between buttresses intended to be crowned by pinnacles. In the niches of the Gothic Portal (1278–89) are statues of prophets and apostles, while the tympanum is filled with elaborate tracery. The doorway itself, with monolithic jambs and lintel, is divided by a figure of the Virgin, below and above which are curious bas-reliefs. The statues of the portal are by *Bartolomé* or *Barthélemy 'le Normand'*; those on the flanking buttresses are later additions by *Jaime Castayls* of Zaragoza (1375). The doors themselves are of 1510. On either side of the central door are smaller Romanesque doors, that on the S. surmounted by a relief of the Passion, that on the N. by an early Christian sarcophagus. Over each is a wheel window. The Tower (1292), square below and octagonal above, and the eight-sided cimborio, are best seen from the E. end of the church.

The INTERIOR (103m. long, 45m. across the transepts, 32m. across the nave) is dark and severe, with piers massive to the point of clumsiness but redeemed by the delicacy of their bases and capitals. The nave is almost twice as high as the aisles. Some of the fine *Stained glass* in the windows of the clerestory and transepts is the work of *Juan Guas*. In the *Coro* the walnut *Sillería* is a late Gothic work by *Francisco Gomas* and his son (1478), while the *Organ* was designed by *Jaume Amigó* of Tortosa (1561–63), carved by *Jerónimo Sancho* and *Pedro Ostris*, and painted by *Pere Serafí* (16C). It is under restoration.

To the N. of the *Coro* are the chapels of *El Santo Sepulcro*, with a polychrome group and a marble Christ by *Fr. Gomar* on a Roman sarcophagus, and of *Sta Lucía*, with medieval wall-paintings and a late-14C statue of St Hippolytus.—The 1st chapel on the N. side contains a good retablo, and in the 2nd is the Italian Renaissance tomb of Abp. Pedro de Cardona (d. 1530), and an altarpiece ascribed to *Lluís Borrassá*.—The 3rd chapel, by *Juan Coastas*, is Baroque; the retablo is by *Domingo Rovira*. In the wall between the 4th and 5th is the tomb of Abp. Juan Terés (d. 1603), beneath a Corinthian pavilion by *Pedro Blay*.

S. side. The S.W. Chapel, or *Baptistery* (1341), contains as a font a medieval marble basin. Beyond the chapel of *S. Miguel* (1360; retablo of 1432 by *Ramón de Mur*) is the elaborate Baroque chapel of *Sta Tecla* (1760-65), by *José Prats*. Passing two late 16C chapels, we enter the *Transepts*, lighted by the low octagonal cimborio. On the E. side of each transept is a small Romanesque apse. On the r. between the S. Transept and the Cap. Mayor, is the Romanesque *Pta. de Sta Tecla*. In the *Cap. de Sto Tomás de Aquín*, off the S. Transept, is the Cristo de la Salud (1508), with polychrome statues.

In the *Cap. Mayor* (1171–1226), which has an early reja (1438), is a magnificent Retablo by *Pedro Juan de Vallfogona* and *Guillermo de la Mota* (1426–34). Behind the altar is the Romanesque apse.

On the N. side of the Cap. Mayor, near a Byzantine doorway, is the *Cap. de los Sastres* (Tailors) of c. 1360–80, with a relief of the Virgin.— Adjoining is the entrance to the cloister. This round-arched double *Doorway, the finest in the cathedral, has, on the cloister side, some expressive sculptures.

The **Cloister**, of c. 1195–1215, based on that of Fontfroide near Narbonne, is disfigured by unattractive grilles placed within each arch. Each side is composed of six bays with three round arches to a bay and two circular openings above, some of which retain their tracery. Most of the capitals are foliated, but some are adorned with quaint reliefs, including the well-known '*procesión de las ratas*' (at the end of the 2nd bay going E.) where a cat's funeral conducted by rats is rudely interrupted by the awakening of the 'deceased'. The old *Chapter House*, in the S.E. corner, contains figures of saints (c. 1330). On the E. side are the chapels of *La Piedad* (1520) and of *Sta Magdalena*, with curious reliefs of her life (16C). In the W. wall are embedded fragments of Roman sculpture and a small Moorish arch with a Cufic inscription bearing the date 349 (A.D. 960). At the S.W. corner is the *Cap. del Santísimo Sacramento*, built by Abp. Ant. Agustín (d. 1586), with a doorway brought in part from the Roman forum. The founder's tomb within is by *Pedro Blay* (1590); the 16C statues and bronzes on the altar are noteworthy. In the N. walk are the chapels of *N.S. de las Nieves*, with a reja of 1414, of *Sta Tecla* (1535), and of *N.S. del Claustro*, with an image of the early 14C and tombs.

The MUSEO DIOCESANO comprises a collection of 14-15C retablos, sculptures and plate, and archbishops' portraits (in the old Chapter House); among others, the 15C Tapestry, called La Buena Vida (in the 18C Chapter House); prehistoric and Roman finds etc. The Cathedral archives were burnt by Suchet.—A gate just outside the S. Transept doorway leads to Romanesque *Sta Tecla la Vieja*, on the site of the 12C cathedral, retaining some contemporary details.

In the Llano de la Catedral, No. 6 is the *Museo Molas*, with Roman antiquities and medieval ceramics and coins; and the *Camarería* is a 14C mansion. Built into the front of No. 6 in the nearby lane of the Escribanías are Roman fragments and a Hebrew inscription. The *Judería* lay between the cathedral and the E. wall of the town. Descending the Cathedral steps, we pass (1.) the picturesque arcaded *C. Mercería*, leading to the Pl. del Foro. The C. Mayor slopes steeply to the Pl. José Antonio. To the r., in the C. Cabelleros, a *Museo Romántico* is being formed. The *Ayuntamiento* of 1862 stands at the W. end of this plaza, formerly known as the Pl. del Fuente, from the 'cyclopean'(more likely medieval) well situated there. On this site formerly stood the *Roman Circus*, and some of its arches may still be seen built into the houses of the Pl. de los Cedazos a few steps N.E., the Pescadería, and neighbouring alleys.

Leaving the S. side of the Pl. José Antonio, and crossing the Rambla de S. Carlos, we regain the Rambla del Generalísimo. Diggings are in progress in the C. de Cervantes, three streets to the S., which have uncovered extensive remains of the *Roman Forum*, while at the W. end of the Av. de Ramón y Cajal, in the grounds of the Tobacco factory, a *Romano-Christian Cemetery* (3–6C A.D.) has been excavated. The chief finds are in the adjacent *Museo Paleo-Cristiano*, but there are also remains of a basilica and two interesting crypts.

Hence the Paseo de la Independencia leads S. to the harbour, begun in 1491 for Fernando the Catholic and since greatly extended. Some of the mooring posts on the *Dique de Levante* are Roman columns from the Forum.

4 km. N., to the r. of the Valls road, stands the **Acueducto de las Ferreras**, locally known as the Pont del Diable, a portion of the Roman aqueduct that brought water to Tarraco from the river Gayá. It was destroyed by the Goths and, though partly restored by Abp. de Santián y Valdivieso in the 18C, the water-channel has disappeared. Two tiers of arches (25 above, 11 below), however, remain, tanned a deep ochre by the sun. The length is 217 m, the height 24 m.

Immediately after crossing the Francoli, a by-road leads N.W. to (7 km.) *Constantí*, near which are the remains of the 4-5C baptistry of *Centcelles*, with a small museum of Roman finds.

FROM TARRAGONA TO ALCAÑIZ (149 km.). After crossing the Francoli, to the W. of the town, we turn r. onto the N 420, and at 5 km. pass a turning (l.) to *La Canonja*, with the 16C mansion of *La Boella*, before reaching (7 km.) **Reus** (71,500 inhab.; *Hotels*), a wool-weaving town and the principal market for the rich wines of the Priorato. Most of the commerce of Reus dates from 1750 when an English settlement was established here. The inhabitants distinguished themselves in 1835 by coldblooded murders in the anti-monastic rising, and since then the town has often been a centre of industrial disturbances. Among its natives eere Gen. Prim (1814–70) and the painter Fortuny (1838–74).

The *Casa de la Ciudad* and several old mansions, including the 17C *Casa de Bofarull*, are of interest, while *S. Pedro* with an altar by *Perris Ostris*, an Austrian, commands a good view from its tower (1520–62) by *Benito Otger* of Lyon. The *Museo 'Prim Rull'* is at present undergoing restoration.—A little S. of the town is the sanctuary of the *Virgen de la Misericordia* (c. 1593–1603).

24 km. S.W., approached viâ *Riudoms* and *Montbrió*, stands the restored castle of *Escornalbou* on a commanding height, incorporating remains of an Augustinian house founded in 1162, notably the Trans. church (1165–1240) and a Romanesque cloister, from which a splendid view is obtained.

At 7 km. a picturesque road (C. 242) leads r. into the Sierra de Montsant. After 1 km., N. of the Embalse and to the E., lies the village of *Ciurana*, with a Romanesque church and ruins of a 13C castle.—At 6 km. a by-road leads r. for 9 km. to *Prades*, with old churches and houses, and from the chapel of *N.S. de la Abellera* on a precipice, a fine view.—20 km. N.E. of Prades lies *Poblet*, see p.172.

19 km. *Falset* with a prison which was formerly the palace of the dukes of Medinaceli, is noted for its lead-mines, and is the centre of the wine-growing district of the Priorato, which takes its name from the priory of *Scala Dei*, a charterhouse (1163) whose ruins lie c. 25 km. N., near *Vilella Alta*.—At 18 km. we cross the Ebro at *Móra la Nova*, and at 10 km. a road (r.) leads 12 km. to *Ascó*, with a ruined castle, and (8 km. beyond) *Flix*, (5000 inhab.) on a bend of the Ebro, with a Moorish castle.—10 km. S.W. of Mora stands the castle of *Miravete*.

11 km. **Gandesa**, (2800 inhab.), centre of the Battle of the Ebro in 1938, retains a church with a late 12C porch in the Limousin style,—At 7 km. the C 221 leads r. 49 km. to *Caspe* (p.209) viâ *Maella*, 10 km. N.E. of which lies *Fabara*, with the finest example of a Roman funerary monument in Spain.—19 km. **Calaceite**, with a Baroque church, picturesque *Ayuntamiento* and Pl. Mayor; the remains of the Iberian town of *San Antonio*, and other Iberian sites are nearby, while there are more near *Mazaleon*, on a road off to the r. at 7 km.—At *Cretas*, 12 km. S of Calaceite, the church has a Renaissance font.— 9 km. beyond lies **Valderrobres**, (2000 inhab.), an ancient town with a 12C church, the impressive ruined Castle of the Kings of Aragón (1390–1410), and a 17C *Ayuntamiento*.—There is fine scenery among the mountains further S., as at *Beceite* and the *Pantano de la Peña*, 7 km. S., and 9 km. S.W., respectively. The main road may be regained by following a road N.W. viâ the attractive village of *Fresneda*, containing some arcaded streets and ancient houses— At 16 km. we meet the N 232 from Zaragoza and Alcañiz to Morella and Vinaros, see Rte 18B.—15 km. *Alcañiz* (p.208) and from thence to *Monreal del Campo*, p.206.

16   THE CENTRAL PYRENEES

Note. Hikers and mountaineers should refer to the paragraph on p.72 with regard to frontier posts, etc.

A   FROM LÉRIDA TO HUESCA

Total distance 118 km. (73 miles). N 240. 67 km. *Barbastro*—51 km. **Huesca.**

FOR THE ALTERNATIVE AND MORE SOUTHERLY ROUTE VIÂ SARIÑENA (134 km.), we follow the N II W. to (27 km.) *Fraga* (p.170), 2 km. beyond which we turn r. onto the C 1310, passing (12 km.) *Velilla de Cinca* with an early 13C chapel, and 12 km., *Chalamera*, with the Trans.*Ermita de la Virgen.* Some 8 km. to the N.W. lies *Alcolea de Cinca*, birthplace of the novelist Ramón Sender (1902–).—18 km. *Villanueva de Sigena*, just beyond which (l.) is the **Conv. of Sigena** (partly restored), founded in 1188 by Alfonso II of Aragón and Sancha of Castile.

Within a picturesque group of buildings of varying dates stands the church (1188), which has a fine Romanesque doorway. Opening off the S. Transept is a Mudéjar chapel dating from 1354, and off the N. Transept is the chapel of *S. Pedro*, containing the tombs of Pedro II and knights who fell at Muret (1213). In other parts of the church are the sepulchres of prioresses of the convent. Great destruction was wrought here during the civil war and only fragments of the important paintings (c. 1321–47) survived to be taken to the Museo de Arte de Cataluña, Barcelona.

2 km. *Sena*, with a 16C *Ayuntamiento*; 14 km. *Sariñena* (4100 inhab.) S.W. of which rises the abandoned *Cartuja de las Fuentes*, with a huge church and conventual buildings dating from 1732.—At *Lanaja*, 17 km. W. on the C 129, the Gothic church has remains of a fine 15C altarpiece.

The C 1310 turns N. from Sariñena past (12 km.) *Alberuela de Tubo*, 4 km. l., with a ruined castle and chapel enshrining a 12C Virgin.—13 km. *Sesa*, with a late Romanesque church, 13 km. S. of which lies *Grañén*, with a ruined castle and a 16C church containing a retablo mayor by *Cristóbal de Cardenosa* and *Pedro de Aponte* (1511-12).—6 km. *Novales*, with a 12C church; (6 km.). *Albero Alto*, whose Gothic church contains a Plateresque retablo. Soon after passing (16 km.) *Monflorite*, with a ruined church of 1176, a by-road leads l. to *Las Casas*, near which is the late-Romanesque chapel of *Pompién*, whose wall-paintings (c. 1315) transferred to canvas, are in private hands close by. At 6 km. we enter *Huesca*, see p.188.

At *Binéfar*, 39 km. N.W. of Lérida o the N 2440, a road leads 12 km. E. to **Tamarite de Litera**, where the *Colegiata*, a ruinous basilica in the Poitevin style, has a 14C lantern and additions of 1619, while ruined *S. Miguel* preserves Romanesque doorways.—*Albelda*, 5 km. E. on the Balaguer road, has a church of the early 16C with exquisite star-vaulting and 15C retablos.—10 km. **Monzón**, an industrial town (14,200 inhab; *Hotel*) at the confluence of the Sosa and Cinca, overlooked by a dismantled castle of the Templars, with *S. Juan* (15C), a Colegiata rebuilt c. 1500, and 13C *S. Francisco*. Monzón was the birthplace of Joaquín Costa (1846–1911) the political writer.—14 km. N. at *Fonz* are a ruined castle of the 12C, a 14C hospital, a late 15C church with good woodwork, and old houses.

A by-road direct to Huesca, by-passing Barbastro, leads due W. from Monzón through (7 km. r.) *Selgua*, with a late-Romanesque wall-tomb in the chapel of *S. Salvador.*—12 km. *Berbegal*, with a Romanesque colegiata containing the 14C statue of Sta María la Blanca.—The early 13C church of *Peralta de Alcofea*, 7 km. S.W., has a fine carved portal.—5 km. *La Perdiguera* has a Gothic church with a tower finished by *Benito de Toloseta* in 1553.—7 km. *Pertusa* has another collegiate church (1575) designed by *Juan de Herrera* and covering a circular 12C crypt.—5 km. *Antillón* has a Romanesque church. At 13 km. we join the N 240 16 km. short of Huesca.

18 km. **Barbastro**, an ancient city (12,900 inhab.; *Hotel*) destroyed by Pompey but rebuilt and renamed *Brutina* by Decius Brutus. In 1064 it was taken from the Moors and sacked by Guillaume de Montreuil, 'le bon Normand', an ally of the Catalans and Aragonese in the 'crusade' urged by Alexander II. The **Cathedral**, built in 1500–33 by *Balt. de Barazábal* to the designs of *Juan de Segura*, has a separate six-sided tower and notable vaulting sustained by six pillars. It contains retablos by Damián Forment and his pupils (c. 1560–1604), and stalls (now placed round the apse) by *Jorge Commón* and *Juan Jubero* (1582–94). There are also some Baroque additions.—The new *Ayuntamiento* cloaks the late 15C building by *Farag de Gali*, the Moor. Lupercio de Argensola (1559–1613), poet and statesman, and his brother Bartolomé (1562–1631), poet and historian, and Gen. Antonio Ricardos (1727–94), were born here.

23 km. N.W. lies **Alquézar**, a Moorish-looking village (300 inhab.), once the Roman *Castrum Vigetum,* with a picturesque *Pl. Mayor,* a fine 12C *Castle,* and a *Colegiata* (1525–32) by *Juan Segura,* containing a 17–18C organ, and paintings by *Alonso Cano,* 15C retablos and a 13C wooden crucifixion, and flanked by remains of a Romanesque cloister.

From Barbastro to Bielsa (102km.). From Barbastro the C 138 leads N. along the r. bank of the Cinca to (18 km.) *El Grado,* with a 15C Colegiata, standing at the S. end of the Embalse de El Grado, where we leave the road to Benabarre and Benasque on the r., see p. 195. 11 km. *Naval,* with its ruined castle and 16C parish church.—At 22 km. a road leads l. 6 km. to *Castejón de Sobrarbe,* where the 15C church contains remarkable processional crosses.—We now skirt the Embalse de Mediano, passing (l.) a track to *S. Martín de Buil,* with an interesting 11C church.

13 km. **Ainsa** (1920 ft; 1100 inhab.), the walled capital of the old mountain kingdom of Sobrarbe, stands on a height above the modern village, and the confluence of the Cinca and the Ara, and preserves a picturesque porticoed *Pl. Mayor* surrounded by dark grey schist houses, slate-roofed (restored), a tiny *Colegiata* (12C and later additions), and to the W., the remains of the royal palace.—The monastery of *S. Victorián,* a 9C foundation, with an 18C church, lies some 10 km. across country to the N.E.—The C 140 leads 30 km. E to meet the C 139 from Barbastro to Benasque, see p.187. For the road from Ainsa to Boltaña, Ordesa, and Biescas, see p.186.—We pass (9 km.) *Escalona* before traversing the Desfiladero de las Devotas and reaching (22 km.) *Salinas,* from which excursions may be made over the *Col de Tella* (4430 ft) to (4 hrs) *Escuaín* in the Valle de Tella, above which is the impressive *Garganta de Escuaín.*—The most repaying ascent is that of the *Cotiella* (9548 ft; 7 hrs. S.E.; guide essential) descending to *Plan de Gistain,* see below, 4½ hrs.

7 km. **Bielsa** (3555 ft; 550 inhab.) the chief village of the valley, but damaged during the Civil War, with a 16C *Ayuntamiento.* The *Parador Nac. Mte. Perdido* lies c. 10 km. to the W.

A road now climbs due N. from Bielsa to the new Tunnel pierced below the Pto. de Bielsa, to meet the French N 129 S.W. of *Arreau* on the mountain road (N 618) between *Bagnères-de-Bigorre* and *Bagnères-de-Luchon,* providing and alternative route through the Pyrenees W. of the Viella tunnel.

Passes. The *Port de Pinède* (7992 ft) leads from the head of the Cinca valley to the *Cirque d'Estaubé* and (9½ hrs) *Gèdre,* in France. *Aragnouet,* in the Neste valley, is reached in 8 hrs. either viâ the *Port de Bielsa* (7887 ft), due N. at the source of the Cinca de Barrosa, or viâ the *Circo de Barrosa* and the *Paso de Barrosa* (N.W.; 8340 ft); the *Port de Moudang* (N.E.; 8160 ft) leads to (8 hrs) *Fabian;* and the easy *Port d'Ourdissétou* (W.; 7875 ft) to (5¼ hrs) the *Hospice de Rioumajou* and *St.-Lary,* 12 km. S. of *Arreau,* see above.

From *Salinas* (see above) a bridle-path on the r. ascends the Cinqueta valley to (2½ hrs) *Plan de Gistain* connected with France (*Hospice de Rioumajou,* 5¾ hrs) by the *Pto. del Plan* (8060 ft; mule-track), and with *Benasque* (see below; 4½ hrs) by the *Col de Gistain* (8280 ft).

FROM BARBASTRO TO BENASQUE (9 km.). We follow the C 138 to *El Grado* and turn E., passing (27 km. l.) *La Puebla de Castro*, Roman *Labitolosa*, whose Romanesque church contains a retablo of 1303, and enter the Esera valley.

An alternative route is that turning E. 9 km. from Barbastro, which threads a series of tunnels past impressive gorges, skirting the W. bank of the Barasona reservoir, and passing a medieval bridge before entering (after a further 20 km.) *Graus*.

At 7 km. the C 1311 leads 19 km. E. to *Benavarri*, see p.195.— 1 km. **Graus** (3700 inhab.), with an arcaded plaza, old houses and Romanesque *S. Miguel*, containing a crucifix of *S. Vicente Ferrer*.—To the S.W. is the strikingly situated 16C hermitage of *N.S. de la Peña*.—The early 13C church of *Capella*, 6 km. N.E., has a retablo mayor (1527) by the Portuguese *Pedro Núñez*, 6 km. beyond which we meet the road from Benavarri to *Roda d'Isavena*, see p.195

The main road continues to ascnd the valley of the Esera, crossed by a number of medieval bridges, passing the attractively-sited village of *Perarrúa*, with its ruined castle before reaching, at 26 km., the turning for *Ainsa*. This road (C 140), now the main route from Barbastro to the Bielsa tunnel, climbs W. to the *Pto de Foradada* (views) before descending past a number of largely uninhabited hamlets, to (30 km.) *Ainsa*, see above.

At 21 km. the C 144 climbs E. to *Pont de Suert*, see p.195.—At 28 km. we pass *Villanova*, with a curious 16C retablo in its church, and at 10 km. enter **Benasque** (3750 ft, 700 inhab.) with a 13C church, some picturesque old houses, and a gloomy castle surrounded by ravines on three sides.—*Cerler*, to the N.E. of Benasque, is being developed as a winter-sports centre.

ASCENTS. *Benasque* is the starting-point for some of the finest climbs in Spain. To the N.E. rises the massif of the *Montes Malditos*, or *Monts Maudits*, the 'accursed mountains' so called from their utterly barren appearance. Chief of these is the **Pica d'Aneto** (11,168ft) or *Pic de Nethou*, the highest summit of the Pyrenees, usually climbed in 2 days.—The route ascends from the *Hosp. de Benasque* (see below), whence we cross the Plan des Etangs S.E. to (2 hrs) the *Refuge de Rencluse* (6972ft), where the night may be passed. The actual ascent crosses the Maladeta glacier to (2½ hrs) the *Brèche du Portillon* (9540 ft), whence we traverse the main Aneto glacier to (4½ hrs) the *Pte. de Mahomet*, the narrow granite arête by which the summit is attained.—The *Pico del Medio* or *Pic du Milieu* (11,004 ft) and the *Pico de la Maladeta* (10,967 ft), the other two main summits of the group, each take 4½ hrs from the refuge.

The **Pic des Posets** (11,047 ft), or *Punta de Lardana*, the second highest summit of the Pyrenees, is a fatiguing climb of 8½ hrs (guide necessary) from Benasque. The route ascends the Valle d'Astos, which leads N.W. from the main valley at the Pte. de Cubere. The final ascent is usually made from (3 hrs) the *Turmes Hut* (5512 ft). The view is even more extensive than that from the Aneto. The descent may be made in 5¾ hrs viâ the S.E. slopes and *Eristé*, 3 km. below Benasque.—Further S. is the *Pico de Eristé* (10,027 ft; 7¾ hrs).—A slightly easier ascent is that of the *Pico Gallinero* (8918 ft; 4¾ hrs), affording a good view of the Maladeta, which may be combined with the excursion to *Senet* (see below) viâ the *Col de Bassibé*.

PASSES. *Senet* on the Noguera Ribagorzana, is reached in 10½ hrs either viâ the *Pto. de Bassibé* (6628 ft) and *Pto. de las Salinas*, or viâ the *Pte. de Cubere* (see below) and the *Pto. de Malibierne* (8682 ft) on the S. flank of the Maladeta. The descent from the latter pass leads past the numerous lakes of Llauset.—The *Pico de Malibierne* (10,063 ft; fine view) is climbed from the col in 1½ hrs. The VALLÉE DU LYS, above *Luchon*, may be reached in 8¾ hrs viâ the *Turmes Hut* (see above) and the *Port d'Oô* (9555 ft).

The track to the Pto. de Benasque ascends the l. bank of the Esera. At (1 hr) the *Pte. de Cubere* (4006 ft), cultivation ends and the Maladeta comes into view. A bold bridge carries the track up the Valle d'Astos across the stream. Waterfalls and rapids succeed each other as we ascend past the mouth of the Valle de Malibierne (r.) and through a gorge to the *Pte. del Campamiento*.—On the r. is the narrow Querigueña gorge, an unfrequented approach to the Montes Malditos, which ascends to the large *Lago de Querigueña* (8718 ft). On the l. the Valle de Literola leads up to the *Pico Perdighero* (10,565 ft).

2 hrs *Baños de Benasque* (5585 ft) a small sulphur spa perched on a precipice on the r., passing on the l. the impressive Aguas Pasa waterfall, we reach (2¾ hrs) the *Hosp. de Benasque*.— 5 hrs; the **Pto. de Benasque** or *Port de Venasque* (8032 ft), the frontier pass, is a narrow, wind-swept cleft, commanding a fine view of the Maladeta across the Plan des Etangs. A road is now under construction between

Benasque and Luchon. The *Pic de Sauvegarde* (8977 ft; 1 hr. W.) commands an even wider view than the pass.

A path on the r. below the pass leads into the VALLE DE ARÁN (p. 196) by the *Pto. de la Picada* (7907 ft; 5 hrs to *Las Bordas*) viâ the *Güelh de Juéu*, the most copious of the 'sources' of the Garonne, and the hermitage of *Artiga-Telin*. Colour tests have proved that the Güelh was merely a resurgence and that the true source of the river was the Trou del Toro, a deep hollow at the foot of the glacier on the S.E. side of the Pic d'Aneto (1½ hrs from the Rencluse hut).

The descent into France leaves on the l. four little lakes and crosses (6½ hrs) the *Culet*, a rock cleft traversed by waterfalls (dangerous avalanches in spring). 7 hrs *Hospice de France* (4550 ft) and thence to (14 km.) *Luchon*.

Soon after leaving Barbastro by the N 240, we pass (r.) the *Santuario del Pueyo*, a 14C centre of pilgrimage.— At 20 km. a road leads 11 km. N. to *Bierge*, and further E., *Adahuesca*, both with Romanesque churches, the former with 13C wall-paintings.—At 6 km. a road leads 6 km. N. to the Cistercian monastery of *Casbas*, badly damaged in 1936.

At 8 km. another road leads 3 km. r. to *Liesa*, where the parish church has an early-14C painted frontal, and *Sta María del Monte* (Romanesque and 15C) with 13C wall-paintings. More important are the wall-paintings (c. 1305) at *Ibieca*, 4 km. beyond, in *S. Miguel de Foces* (1259), which contains an 11C font and 12C Virgin. 10 km. further N.E. viâ *Aguas*, lies *Panzano*, where the Romanesque church has a tall tower.

4 km. *Siétamo*, preserving the 14C *Pal. de Aranda*, and birthplace of the Conde de Aranda (1719–98), minister of Carlos III and 'the hammer of the Jesuits'.

At 5 km. a road leads r. to *Loporzano*, where late-Gothic *S. Salvador* contains a Plateresque retablo from Mte. Aragón and a Crucifixion of the school of Rubens.—6 km. to the E. lies *Arbaniés*, with early 14C paintings in its church, while 6 km. N. of Loporzano lies *Barluenga*, with a 16C church and a cemetery chapel with an artesonado ceiling and 13C wall-paintings.—6 km. to the N.E. is *Sta Eulalia la Mayor*, with a Romanesque chapel and a ruined 12C monastery.

We pass (r.) the ruined monastery of *Monte Aragón*, burial place of Alfonso el Batallador (d. 1134), largely rebuilt by *Sofí* in the late 18C, before entering **HUESCA** (8 km.) (1530 ft; 36,500 inhab.; 14,000 in 1920; 23,000 in 1960; *Hotels*) which stands on a hill in the centre of its 'hoya' or huerta irrigated by the Isuela, and commanded to the N. by the barren ridges of the southern Pyrenees.

History. *Osca*, capital of the Vescitani, was chosen by Quintus Sertorius as headquarters against the partisans of Sulla, and here he established a university in 75 B.C. Overrun by the Moors in 789, the city was recaptured by Pedro I in 1096, after Sancho Ramírez had been slain beneath its walls in 1094, and it ranked as the capital of Aragón until the recapture of Zaragoza. The four kings' heads on the city arms are those of the Berber sheikhs killed at the siege. As a Nationalist out-post, Huesca suffered severely in 1936–38.

We enter from the E. by the C. del Coso Bajo, which with its continuation, the Coso Alto, follows the line of the old wall which circled the S. and W. of the town. On the Coso Bajo, to the E., are the brick churches of *Sto Domingo* (1687–96) and *S. Lorenzo* (1607–24), the latter with a 17C retablo mayor by *Seb. de Ruesta* of Barbastro. Nearby stands *S. Pedro el Viejo*, the oldest church in Huesca, begun c. 1134 by *Mateo de Agüero* and finished in the 13C. It has a slender six-sided tower and its nave and aisles each end in an apse. The grotesque capitals of the Romanesque *cloister* (many restored) are interesting. In one chapel on the S. side is the tomb of Ramiro II (d.1137); in another a

14C painted Crucifixion.—To the W., at Coso Alto 18, is *S. Vicente el Real* (18C), with a brick Baroque front, and at No. 63 is the 16C *Casa de Climent*.

The roads for Pamplona (N 240) and Jaca (C 136) lead N. from the Coso Bajo.

To the E., uphill, lies the **Cathedral**, well-restored and cleaned, a late-Gothic building begun in 1497 by *Juan Olózaga*, and completed in 1515. It incorporates much of an earlier church (begun in 1278) to which belonged the fine W. Portal (c. 1300–13). Above is Olózoga's florid frontal surmounting a curious Mudéjar gallery of brick. The octagonal tower commands a wonderful view.

The INTERIOR, with aisles much lower than the nave, contains a *High Altar*, whose *Retablo* (1520–34) is the masterpiece of *Damián Forment*. Beneath the 1st S. chapel, under a cupola of 1646, is the armoured effigy of the founder Vicencio Lastanosa (1665); and in the *Cap. Mayor* is a tomb erected by *Forment* (1522) to a pupil. In the sacristy is a custodia (1596–1601) by *José Velázquez*, and in the archives are silver panels from a retablo of 1367.

An attractive doorway leads from the N. Aisle into the *Cloister*, which preserves two Gothic walks (1411–59) and curious wall-tombs. Battered fragments of the original Romanesque cloister are visible in the yard below. In the *Parroquia*, entered through the Bishop's Palace, is the *Retablo de Monte Aragón* (1506–12), attr. to *Gil de Morlanes the elder*. The palace has 15C timber roofs; and the *Museo Diocesano* contains primitives collected from churches in the region.

In the Pl. de la Catedral are the *Ayuntamiento* (1577–78) and the *Col. de Santiago*, with a front of 1610–12 by Mendizábal, containing some panels from the retablo of Sigena. The C. Quinto Sertorio leads N. to the Pl. de la Universidad, on the l. of which is the *Instituto*, in the building formerly occupied by the *Pal. de los Reyes* and the University (refounded by Pedro IV in 1354) now housing the *Museo Provincial*.

Beneath the Instituto is the *Sala de la Campana*, a vaulted 12C chamber named from a stratagem of Ramiro II who, in 1136, summoned his insurgent nobles to consult on the casting of a bell (*campana*) which should be heard throughout Aragón. As each entered the palace Ramiro caused his head to be struck off and his body flung into the vault. Adjacent is a late-12C chapel called the *Sala de Doña Petronilla*.

Opposite the Instituto is a doorway with a curious 16C wooden tympanum, formerly painted.—On the ramparts to the N.W., near the bridge over the Isuela, is the Gothic convent-church of *S. Miguel* (c. 1200–1350).

From the S.E. corner of the city a rough road leads to the Romanesque *Ermita de Salas*, the most interesting of the seven hermitages of Huesca, largely rebuilt in 1772 by *José Sofi*, but retaining a good doorway and a huge circular window.—The *Ermita de S. Jorge*, W. of the town, built on the site of the battle of Alcoraz against the Moors, and reconstructed in 1554, commands a good view. A road leads N. 10 km. to *Apiés*, with a late Romanesque church; 13 km. beyond lies the Pantano de Belsué.

B   FROM PAMPLONA TO HUESCA

Total distance, 164 km. (102 miles). 41 km. (*Sangüesa* lies 5 km. S.)—6 km. *Yesa*. (*Leyre* lies 4 km. N.)—89 km. *Ayerbe*. (*Loarre* lies 7 km. N.E.)—28 km. **Huesca**.

We follow the Zaragoza road (N 121) for 6 km. before forking l. on to the N 240.—At 10 km. a road (l.) leads 6 km. to *Artaiz*, with a

Romanesque church with remarkable carvings, and a number of tower-houses, and 4 km. beyond, *Urroz*, with an interesting church.—8 km. E. of Urroz lies *Aoiz*, where *S. Miguel* contains a retablo by *Ancheta* and a fine font.

Thence the Irati may be followed past the Embalse de Usoz and the forest of Irati extending N. across the frontier into France.—3 km. N. of Aoiz we may fork r. for the picturesque village of (14 km.) *Oroz-Betelu*, 8 km. beyond which we meet the road from Burguete, see p. 111.—2 km. *Arive*, beyond which is (6 km.) *Orbaiceta* and (9 km.) the Embalse de Irabia.

From Arive a road leads E. to (20 km.) *Ochagavia*, with a parish church containing a late-16C retablo carved by *Miguel de Espinal* and gilded by *Mateo de Zabalza*. Nearby are the castle of *Ezperun* and the 13C Romanesque basilica of *N.S. de Musquilda*.—The road crosses the watershed of the Alto de Lazar (fine views) before descending to *Isaba* in the Roncal valley, see p. 191.—9 km. E. of Ochagavia a road (customs post) crosses the *Port de Larrau* (4520 ft) to *Larrau* in France.

3 km. *Monreal*, with the *Monastery of S. Cristóbal*, and (4 km.) *Idocin*, birthplace of the guerrilla general, Espoz y Mina (1784–1836).—12 km. a road leads N.E. 4 km. to *Lumbier* (1700 inhab.), ancient *Illumberri*, starting-point for the ascent of Mt. Arrangoiti.

From Lumbier a road ascends the picturesque Valle de Salazar to (20 km.) *Navascués*, with a fine Gothic doorway in the parish church and a well-preserved Romanesque chapel.—28 km. *Ochagavia*, see above.—From Navascués a road leads 15 km. E. to *Burgui*, see p. 191.

The r.-hand turning at the above junction leads 6 km. to **Aibar**, an old town (1000 inhab.) of arcaded street and Gothic doorways, with slight ruins of a castle of the Prince of Viana and dominated by its church.—8 km. further S. at *Cáseda*, is a retablo by *Juanes de Anchieta* in the church of *Sta María*, while S.E. of Cáseda is the 13C chapel of *S. Zoilo* (off the road to *Carcastillo*, see p. 112).—From Aibar we may directly approach Sangüesa, 7 km. due E.

At 6 km. a r.-hand turning leads 5 km. S. to *Sangüesa* (see below), passing (r.) the ruined castle and walls of *Rocafort*, Roman *Sancossa*.

Sangüesa (4500 inhab.) is an ancient town on the l. bank of the Aragón. by the bridge stands *Sta María la Real* (mainly 13C), with an impressive sculptured *Doorway* (signed by Leodagarius in c. 1170), a notable custodia, and a slender octagonal tower and spire. Among other churches are Romanesque *Santiago*, with a battlemented tower, and *S. Salvador*, 14C Gothic with a Romanesque door. *S. Francisco* and *El Carmen* retain Gothic cloisters. In the town centre the *Ayuntamiento* occupies part of the former castle of the princes of Viana. To the S. is the *Pal. de Vallesantoro*, an imposing Baroque mansion. Among other buildings of interest are the 15C palaces of the Counts of Guaqui and of the Dukes of Granada, and the *Casa de Paris*.

7 km. N.E. lies *Javier*, formerly *Xavier*, with a medieval castle, birthplace of S. Francisco Xavier (1506–52); in the parish church are the font in which he was baptized, a good statue of the Virgin, and discoidal tombstones.

From Sangüesa to Zaragoza viâ the 'Cinco Villas' (147 km.). We bear S.E. shortly passing the chapel of *S. Adrián*, formerly belonging to the Templars, and climb to (11 km.). *Sos del Rey Católico* (1150 inhab.; *Parador Nac.*), an ancient walled town (under restoration), preserving the *Pal. Sada*, birthplace of Fernando the Catholic (1452–1516), but altered in the 16–17C. Among many other mansions in the narrow streets is the Gothic *Pal. de Camporreal*. From *S. Estebán* (11–13C), with a crypt, and doorway carved c. 1190, we can ascend to the *Castillo de la Peña Feliciano*, with a tall clock-tower. Sos is one of the Cinco Villas, five villages—*Sádaba, Ejea de los Caballeros, Uncastillo*, and *Tauste* being the others—which Philip V raised to the rank of towns for their services in the War of Succession.—From Sos we climb 5 km. to (24 km.) **Uncastillo** (1200 inhab.), medieval in appearance, where Romanesque *Sta María* has a Gothic tower with bartizan turrets and pinnacled spire, a Plateresque cloister, and on its W. Front an early carved tympanum of the Magi identified as the source of the famous whalebone relief in the Victoria and Albert Museum, London; note also the apse and the well-carved S. Porch. *S. Miguel* and *S. Lorenzo* are destroyed; *S. Andrés* is being restored; while *S. Juan* retains 13C wall-paintings.—Hence we bear S.W. past (13km.) *Layana*, near the remains of the Roman aqueduct of *Los Bañales*, before entering (2km.) **Sádaba** (2100 inhab.), with an imposing *Castle* and very slight remains of a synagogue. The 2C tomb of the Atilia family, known as the *Altar de los Moros*, can be found by turning r. off the direct Sos road immediately after crossing a canal, and following the lower track.—From Sádaba we turn S.E. again to (21km.) brick-built **Ejea de los Caballeros** (15,200 inhab.; *Hotel*), once walled, with the fortified Romanesque church of *S. Salvador*, cons. 1222.—Driving S., at 23km. we reach **Tauste** (7250 inhab.), where the Mudéjar church has a good tower (1243) and 16C carved and painted retablos.—Hence we approach the main road for Zaragoza at *Alagón*, see p.113.

From the Sangüesa turning,, our route leads E. to (6km.) *Yesa*, at the foot of the great reservoir of the Aragón, 4km. N. of which stands the Cistercian monastery of ***S. Salvador de Leyre**, with a very ancient church, the burial place of the kings of Navarre. The crypt belongs to the work consecrated in 1057 while the apsidal sanctuary and its aisles are of 1098; to these was added in the late 13C a single nave (comp. Gerona Cathedral), with later ribbed vaults. The monastic buildings (17-18C) were restored in 1950, and are now reoccupied by a hospitable Benedictine community (guest house).

At 18km. the C 137 leads N. through the gorge of the Esca to reach the *Valle de Roncal*, until recently the most remote and beautiful of the Navarrese valleys, where old Basque costumes are occasionally seen.—16km. *Burgui*, with the chapel of the *Virgen de la Peña* and the ivy-clad ruins of the 9C monastery of *Burdaspal*.—At 9km. a road leads 19km. E. to *Ansó* (see below).—2km. **Roncal** (400 inhab.), ancient houses and a picturesque church; its cheese should be tasted.—From (8km.) *Isaba*, whose fortified church contains a retablo of 1540 by *Simón Pérez de Cisneros*, a road leads N. to the *Venta de Arraco*, whence tracks lead across the French frontier to Ste-Engrâce by the *Gorge of Kakouetta*, and by the Collado de la Peña de S. Martin to *Bedous*. The inhabitants of this French valley have delivered at the frontier, every June 13th since 1365, a tribute to Roncal of three cows and a sum in gold coins.

At 16km. a road leads N. 24km. to *Ansó* (600 inhab.), famous for its traditional costumes, with a late Gothic church containing a good retablo.—.At 8km. another road ascends the parallel valley to (26km.) **Hecho**, a prosperous village (1200 inhab.), developing as a winter-sports centre, and 2km. beyond, *Siresa*, with the 9C monastery of *S. Pedro*; the church, begun in 1082, contains 15-16C retablos.

From the last-mentioned junction the N 240 bears S., climbing to the Pto. de Sta Bárbara, while the C 134 forks l. towards (19km.) *Jaca* (see below), skirting the S. side of the Valley of the Aragón, off which, at 10km. a road climbs 4km. to **Sta Cruz de la Serós**. The curious Romanesque **Church* has a tall square tower (c. 1095), while the tiny neighbouring parish church of *S. Caprasio* is of 848. Hence a passable track leads steeply up to *S. Juan de la Peña*, see p.192, some 6km. S.

At 25km. the N 240 passes the Embalse de la Peña, where the N 330 leads N.E. to Jaca, see Rte 16C. W descend parallel to the river Gállego, which flows in a deep gorge, at 8km. passing *Murillo de Gállego*, with a 12C church.—**Agüero**, 4km. N.W., has a 13C parish church with a 15C custodia and 18C organ (restored 1970), and **Santiago*, an unfinished church of c. 1200 (reached by a track to the r. just prior to the village), well-sited, and with finely carved archivolts and capitals (key at parish church, but the interior is of less interest).

To the l. a road leads to *Riglos*, with the 12C *Ermita de Sta María de Concilio*, retaining Romanesque wall-paintings, nestling beneath the detached masses of ruddy perpendicular cliffs known as *Los Mallos* (the ninepins) *de Riglos.*—11 km. **Ayerbe** (1600 inhab.), with its *Ayuntamiento* in a 15C mansion, and the *Torre de S. Pedro* (12C).

7 km. N.E. is the village of **Loarre**, with a spired Romanesque church Above, on an outcrop of rock commanding a wide *View, and well worth visiting, is the well-restored 11–13C *Royal Castle*, with its curtain wall, and enclosing an impressive Romanesque *Church with carved capitals. Enquire first at the village for the guide and key.

At (10 km.) *Plasencia del Monte* we pass a conspicuous ruined castle. The nearby ruined villages of *Anzano* and *Castejón de Becha* have late Romanesque chapels with fine carvings.—At *Bolea*, 6 km. N., the vast hall-church (1535–56) by *Bart. de Barazábal* contains a carved retablo painted by *Pedro de Aponte* (1507–11), another retablo of S. Sebastián, and reja.—The church of *Aniés*, 6 km. beyond, has a 15C altarpiece.—18 km. **Huesca**, see p.188.

C   FROM ZARAGOZA TO JACA

Total distance, 143 km. (89 m.). N 123. 72 km. **Huesca**—N 136. 71 km. **Jaca**.

We leave Zaragoza by the N 123, passing (l.) the Military Academy buildings, and drive N. parallel to the W. bank of the Gállego across the dreary Llanos de Violada viâ (27 km) *Zuera*, where the road bears N.E. to (26 km. l.) *Almudévar*, whose 18C church contains 16C retablos by *Gabriel Jolí* and two painted altarpieces of 1498, while neighbouring *N.S. de Violada* has a retablo of 1500. In the *Ayuntamiento* is a late-13C diptych.—A road leads 8 km. E. to *Tardienta*, where the parish church has an octagonal belfry and panels from a retablo of c. 1440.—19 km. **Huesca**, see p.188.

N. of Huesca we follow the C 136, passing (5 km.) *Yéqueda*, (3 km.) *Igriés*, and (6 km.) *Nueno*, with Romanesque churches, the last with a 16C brick tower. After climbing the Pto. de Monrepós, the road commences a serpentine descent to meet the Gállego, 9 km. S. of (44 km.) *Sabiñánigo* (8750 inhab.; *Hotel*), where we turn W. onto the C 134 for (18 km.) *Jaca*, see below. Petroleum deposits have been found in the area (1979), which will be exploited.

FROM HUESCA TO JACA VIÂ AYERBE (89 km.). This alternative route follows the N 420 through *Ayerbe* (see p.192) to a point 47 km. N.W. of Huesca, where we turn r. on to the N 330, which climbs laboriously up to (22 km.) *Bernués*, where a l.-hand turning continues the ascent (11 km.; 3658 ft.) to the *New Monastery* of *S. Juan de la Peña* (1693–1714), destroyed by Suchet's troops, with a Baroque front by *Pedro de Onofre*. Not far off is a Mirador, commanding a magnificent *View of the Pyrenees. A short distance beyond, huddled beneath a huge overhanging cliff (and near the city of Pano destroyed in the 8C by the Moors) is the 'Old' monastery of *S. **Juan de la Peña**. Founded before 858 and, although many times wasted by fire, and plundered by Suchet in 1809, it still preserves its fine Romanesque *Church*, encircled by a fortified wall.

It was at S. Juan that the Santo Cáliz, now in Valencia cathedral, was preserved during the Dark Ages, giving rise to the romances of the Holy Grail. Here in 1071 the Roman rite was first introduced into Spain by the legate of Alexander II. Carlos III in 1770 constructed in the interior a Pantheon for the heroes of Aragón and decorated it with tombs and reliefs.

From the entrance steps descend (r.) to a Crypt, above which is a courtyard which we cross to reach the *Church*, its three apses under the impending rock, on the far side of which is the partially restored Romanesque *Cloister* (note capitals), to the l. of which is the *Cap. de S. Victoriano* of 1426–33.

Hence we may descend to *Sta Cruz de la Serós* (see p. 191), and thence to *Jaca*, 9 km. E.

Beyond *Bernués*, the road climbs over the shoulder of pine-clad *Monte Oroel* (5775 ft). On its W. slope is the chapel of *La Virgen de la Cueva*, at the entrance of a cave in which 300 lords of Sobrarbe in 724 swore to drive the Moors out of Spain, and which is regarded as the cradle of the Kingdom of Aragón. The summit commands a good view of the Pyrenees, and S.W. towards the Moncayo. The road descends towards *Jaca*.

30 km. **JACA** (2687 ft; 10,300 inhab.; *Hotels*) an ancient frontier fortress, famous as the first headquarters of the Christians in the re-conquest of Aragón from the Moors. Like Huesca, it bears the heads of four sheikhs on its coat-of-arms.

History. Jaca was taken by M. Porcius Cato in 194 B.C. and surrounded by a wall, fragments of which still remain. About 716 it was overrun by the Moors, but the Aragonese, who had taken refuge in the Pyrenean fastnesses, retook it c. 760, under García Iñigo, legendary King of Sobrarbe, and Count Aznar. A Moorish counter-attack in 795 was beaten off, with the assistance of the women of Jaca, at the battlefield of Las Tiendas, along the Pamplona road, where the victory is still commemorated by the local girls in a sham fight on the 1st Fri. in May. The fueros of Jaca, dating from the 8C and confirmed in 1063 by Sancho Ramírez IV of Navarre, are among the oldest in Spain.

The town stands above the l. bank of the Aragón on a hill surrounded by turreted ramparts. The E. side has been laid out as a promenade with fine mountain views. From the N. it is commanded by the *Citadel* constructed after 1592.

A few steps to the E., opposite the citadel, stands the massive ***Cathedral,** founded in 814, dating mainly from 1054–63, but it has been considerably altered; the chapels and aisle-vaults are by *Juan de Segura* (c. 1530), the nave-vault by *Juan de Bescós* (1596). Many of the capitals and corbels are well carved. The silver shrine of the patroness, St Orosia (1731) lies below the altar, below the octagonal cupola of the crossing and in front of the deep central apse, on either side if which are chapels closed by 12C wrought iron screens. The *Cap. S. Miguel*, on the S. side, has a Plateresque portal by *Giovanni Moreto*, who also carved the *Sacristy* doorway (1521–23). The 17-18C organs have been restored.

The *Diocesan Museum* contains the recently discovered Romanesque mural from *S. Juan Evangelista de Ruesta*, among others.

The *Casa Consistorial* in the C. Mayor, by *Dom. Lasarte* and other Biscayan masters (1528–45), contain the 'Libro de la Cadena', the chained 13C book of the local fueros.

At the E. end of this street is the *Benedictine Convent*, in which is preserved the sarcophagus of Sancha (d. 1096), daughter of Ramiro I. The 15C *Torre del Reloj* (restored) stands just S. of the Casa Consistorial; *Sto Domingo*, further S., with 11C remains, has been virtually rebuilt; *El Carmen* retains a late 17C façade and tower.—1 km. to the W., the Aragón is crossed by the medieval *Pte. de S. Miguel*, on the old pilgrims' road.

From Jaca to the Somport (32 km.): Beyond Jaca the N 330 ascends the Valley of the Aragón.—At 7 km. a track (r.) leads to *Acin*, near which is the remote chapel of *N.S. de Iguacel*, of importance as a dated building by a named designer, *Galindo Garcias*, begun soon after 1063 and completed in 1072, with good carving and 12C wrought ironwork.

As we approach *Canfranc*, we obtain a fine view N.E. of the conspicuous *Peña Collarda* (9457 ft). 16 km. *Canfranc* (3410 ft; 700 inhab.) with the Spanish Customs house, has a well-preserved castle built by Philip III. Here is the S. entrance of the *Somport Tunnel* (almost 8 km long) opened for rail traffic in 1928. The road, which may be impassable between Nov. and May, ascends the upland valley of Aragón passing near the summit the ruins of a hospice built in 1108 by Gaston VI of Bearn to shelter pilgrims bound for Compostela. We pass the winter sports development of *Candanchu* (*Hotels*) before reaching (9 km.) **Somport** (5380 ft), the Roman *Summus Portus*, and the pass by which the greater part of Abderrahman al Gâfaqî's Moors crossed into France in 732. We descend to (14 km.) *Urdos* (2493 ft), the first French village, with the custom-house—41 km. *Olorón-Ste-Marie*.

From Jaca to Biescas, the Pto. de Portalét, and Panticosa. We drive E. on the C 134 for 14 km., and turn N., by-passing *Sabiñánigo*, to meet the C 136, and ascend the Gállego valley, or Val de Teña.—At 11 km. a track (r.) leads shortly to *Oliván*, and the well-preserved 11C church of *S. Pedro de Lárrede*.—5 km. **Biescas** (2853 ft; 1400 inhab.) a Summer resort, with a parish church built by the Knights Templar.—We shortly pass (r.) the fort and hermitage of *Sta Elena* on a precipitous rock, and the *Pico de Tendeñera* (9350 ft).

For *Panticosa* and beyond, see below.

The C 136 continues N. past (16 km.) *Escarilla*, with a fortified church and fine bridge, and through a gorge to (8 km.) **Sallent** (4288 ft; 1000 inhab.; *Hotels*), a Spanish Customs post, with a church of 1525-37 by *Juan de Segura*. The road ascends past *Formigal*, and the pyramidal *Peña Foradada* (r. 7687 ft) and soon reaches (8 km.) the **Pto. de Portalét** (5468 ft)— closed Nov.-June— between the *Pic d'Anéou* (7149 ft) on the l., and the *Pic d'Estremère* (6924 ft), where the frontier is marked by a dry stone wall. The view ahead of the *Pic de Midi d'Ossau* behind the *Pic de Peyreget* is splendid; behind on the r. is the gloomy ridge dividing the Gállego valley from the Aragón, and to the l. the dark wall of the Enfer massif with the Tendeñera behind. We descend the Vallée d'Ossau, which gradually grows less barren.—15 km. *Gabas* (3379 ft) is the first French village.—8 km. *Eaux-Chaudes* (2215 ft; French custom-house.)

At Escarilla we may diverge r. past *Panticosa* (3950 ft) to ascend the side valley of the Caldares. We thread the gorge of El Escalar (retrospective view) to reach the *Balneario de Panticosa* (5370 ft), one of the highest inhabited spots in the Pyrenees and a centre for winter-sports, and for the exploration of the surrounding mountains (guide preferable).

An easy ascent is that of the *Pico de Baldairan* (8845 ft; S.E.). To the N.W. is the *Pico de las Aruelas* (10,043 ft) and to the N.E. the *Pico de Brazato* (8983 ft; View), which may be combined with the excursion to Gavarniè, see below.

Passes. The *Col de Marcadau* (8386 ft) leads to *Cauterets* in c. 9 hrs. The route ascends the church at Panticosa, and follows the course of the Torrente de Bachimaña, with numerous lakes and waterfalls. After 4 hrs we cross the frontier between the *Péterneille* (9085 ft. l.) and the *Grande-Fache* (9868 ft). The view towards Spain is magnificent, and includes the Pico de Tendeñera and Pico de las Aruelas. About 1¼ hrs beyond the pass we reach the *Refuge Wallon* (6122 ft); 7½ hrs *Pont d'Espagne*, and thence to *Cauterets*.

A fine route leads S.E. to Bujaruelo (7½ hrs) viâ (3 hrs) the *Col de Brazato* (8385 ft; E.) between the *Pico de Brazato* (l., see above) and the *Pico de Bacias* (8918 ft). To the N.E. the impressive S. face of the **Vignemale** (10,821 ft) is seen in all its grandeur. We descend to (4 ½ hrs) *Plalaube*, an upland pasture basin, whence a track on the r. descends to (7½ hrs) *Bujaruelo* and the *Pte. de los Navarros*, see below.

From Biescas to the Parque Nac. de Ordesa, and to Ainsa. We turn E. onto the C 140 and ascend the *Pto. de Cotefablo* (5358 ft; tunnel) from which the *Puig de Buey* (S., 6555 ft) may be climbed. At 23 km. we meet the C 138. For the road S. to *Broto, Boltaña* and *Ainsa*, see below.

Turning N. we pass through **Torla** (3380 ft), an old village with smoke-blackened houses of the 13-16C.

Beyond the *Pte. de los Navarros*, where our road bears r., a by-road continues N. past the chapel of *Sta Elena*, in a wooded gorge, to *Bujaruelo* (4350 ft) at the E. foot of the Tendeñera, where the road ends. A zigzag uphill climb to the N.E. brings us in 2½ hrs to the *Port de Gavarnie* (7390 ft), the frontier pass, with the *Gabiétou* (9950 ft) on the r. and a lower ridge on the l. The descent to (4 hs) *Gavarnie* is straight-forward and commands a fine view of the *Cirque de Gavarnie* on the r.

From the *Pte. de Navarros* we follow the road E. along the N. side of the Valle de Arazas, into the **Parque Nac. de Ordesa**, from which we may ascend the main valley to the Cueva de Arazas, passing on the l. the red walls of the cirque of *Cotatuero*.—Climbers may go on from the Cueva to Gavarnie (9 hrs) viâ the *Gaulis huts* (7050 ft) and the so-called *Brèche de Roland* (9200 ft), a cleft 100 m. deep and 40-60 m. wide, hewn by the Paladin Roland with one blow of his sword Durandal. To the N. of the hut rises **Monte Perdido** (Mont Perdu; 10,998 ft), with the *Cylindre de Marboré* (10,915 ft) to the l. These two dangerous ascents are better attempted from the French side.—From the Gaulis huts (guide advisable) we may go due W. over the *Pto. de Fanlo* (7136 ft) to the *Fon Blanca hut* at the head of the Val de Niscle and thence by the *Pto. de Niscle* (8104 ft) into the valley of the Cinca (or de Pineta) and the *Parador Nac.*, see p.186.

Turning S. off the C 140 at 23 km., after 2 km. we enter *Broto* (2935 ft; 600 inhab.) with a doorway of 1578 to its parish church, while the chapel of *S. Blas* dates from the 12C, and 2 km. beyond, at *Sarvisé*, is a 12C church-tower.

Hence an interesting track ascends (l.) the Jalle valley to (4 hrs) *Fanlo* (3765 ft), with a curious retablo of St. Michael, and then descends the bridlepath down the Rio Aso, to the S.E. In 3 hrs from Fanlo we reach the magnificent gorge of the *Bellos*, or *Val de Niscle*. The track goes on S. to (4 hrs) *Vio* and thence S.E. to (7 hrs from Fanlo) *Escalona*, through unfrequented pasture-lands.

Beyond (27 km. r.) *Fiscal* (2560 ft) we traverse the curious gorge of *Jánovas* to (25 km.) **Boltaña** (2340 ft; 950 inhab.) preserving a *Colegiata* of 1544 and slight ruins of a castle, and overlooked to the S. by the *Sierra de Guara* (c. 6500 ft).—At 9 km. we reach *Ainsa* on the road from Barbastro to *Bielsa* and *Pte. Perdido*, see p.186.

D FROM LÉRIDA TO VIELLA

Total distance, 162 km. (100 miles). N 230. 65 km. *Benavarrí*—57 km. *Pont de Suert*—40 km. *Viella*, or 219 km. (136 miles). C 1313: 29 km. *Balaguer*—C 147. 66 km. *Tremp*—16 km. *Pobla de Segur*—29 km. *Sort*—79 km. *Viella*.

There are two routes, which are connected by a road (C 144) between *Pobla de Segur* and *Pont de Suert*. The newer road (N 230) to the W., drives directly N. from Lérida and approaches the Pyrenees by the valley of the Noguera Ribagorzana viâ *Benabarre* and *Pont de Suert* and passes through the tunnel beneath the Pto. de Viella.

The alternative and longer route, by the C 147 (see p.196), runs roughly parallel. viâ *Balaguer* and *Tremp* as far as *Pobla de Segur*, and then follows the Noguera Pallaresa through *Sort* and *Esterri d'Aneu* before crossing the Pto. de la Bonaigua and descending into the Valle d'Arán.

VIÂ BENAVARRÍ (162 km.). Leaving Lérida by the N 230 (N.W. of the town), at 25 km. we meet the cross-road (C 148) from Tàrrega and Balaguer to *Binéfar* (see p. 185), by which, if approaching from Barcelona, Lérida may be by-passed. We turn N.W., circling round the Embalse de Canelles, to (40 km.) **Benavarri** (2300 ft; 1200 inhab.) with a castle and old houses.—Hence the C 1311 turns N.W. to *Graus*, see p.187.

A by-road leads N. along the Isábena valley passing (19 km. r.) near the fine mid-16C church of *Lascuaire*, to (11 km.) **Roda d'Isàvena**, with a small *Cathedral* of 1063–67 with a 12C cloister, and containing a carved folding chair (9C) and a rare organ dating possibly from c. 1500, although modernized c. 1600, and still playable, among other treasures. The *Pal. Episcopal* is a late 15C mansion.—At the head of the valley lies *Calvera*, with the 11C monastic church of *Obarra*. The road has been continued to meet the C 144 near its junction with the N 230.

Our road bears N.E. on leaving Benavarrí to (9 km.) *Tolva*, with a church consecrated in 1130, before entering the valley of the Noguera Ribagorzana, which we ascend, skirting the W. bank of the Embalse de Escales and threading our way through a series of tunnels to (48 km.) **Pont de Suert**, (2600 inhab.), close to which are the ruins of the monastery of *Labaix.*—Just S. of the Embalse, near *Sopierna*, is the monastery of *Alahón*, founded in 835, in whose church (cons. 1123) is an ancient wooden Virgin; the sacristy has 14C wall-paintings.—At Pont de Suert the C 144 from Pobla de Segur, after crossing the Sierra de Pinyana, joins our route, see p.197.

At 3 km. a road ascends N.E. up the valley of the Noguera de Tor to the spa of (19 km.) **Caldas de Bohí** (4300 ft.) We pass (l.) at 16 km. the Romanesque churches of *Erill-la-Val*, with a slender tower, and (r.) *Bohí*, with a six-storey tower, containing reproductions of the original murals which are preserved in the Museo de Arte de Cataluña, Barcelona. Similarly replaced, are those in the remarkable little Lombardic basilicas (both cons. 1123) in **Tahull**, high up the valley side to the E. *S. Clemente* is at one end of the village, while at the other stands *Sta María*, with a curious octagonal dome and leaning tower. The churches at *Barruera* and *Durro*, lower down the valley, are also of interest.

At 4 km. the C 144 climbs W. over the mountains towards *Benasque* (p.187), while our road continues to ascend the valley past the *Hosp. de Viella* of 1509 (5335 ft.), base for the ascent of the *Pico di Mulleres* (9860 ft; guide essential), the E. spur of the Maladeta, which commands a magnificent view of the highest peaks. Here we enter the Tunnel which pierces the Mtes. Malditos beneath the Pto. de Viella, emerging 5 km. beyond, before descending to *Viella*, passing (r.) the *Parador Nac.*

33 km. **Viella** (3150 ft; 2250 inhab.; *Parador Nac.* and *Hotels*) delightfully placed at the confluence of the Rio Negro and the Garonne, contains a massive church with an octagonal tower and an ornate interior, and many old houses.—The church of *Gausach*, N.W., contains a Roman stele.

The *Valle de Arán*, or upper valley of the Garonne, is a Spanish outpost on the N. slope of the Pyrenees, and until the completion of the road in 1924, was connected with the rest of Spain only by bridle-paths. Practically independent until the 18C it was annexed to France by Napoleon in 1808, but finally recognized as Spanish in 1815.

FROM VIELLA TO ST BÉAT (37 km.) After crossing a bridge over the Garonne we pass (l.) the Gothic chapel of *Mitg-Arán* (i.e. mid-Arán), the remnant of a once powerful monastery, and on the other side of the road a huge monolith (? an ancient altar). *Vilach* (r.) has a 13C church, and *Aubert* a Romanesque one with wall-paintings.—Beyond (11 km. l.) the mouth of the Valle de Barrados we pass *Las Bordas* and the track leading up the Garona de Juéu to *Aritiga.*

Further on, at 4 km., just short of Bosost, a road diverges l. to (18 km.) *Bagnères de Luchon* (Spanish Customs post), climbing steeply in zig-zags to the *Pto. de Portillon* (4292 ft) on the frontier. The descent of the French valley of the Burbe, passing the Cascade Sidonie, is equally steep.

1 km. *Bosost* (2500 ft), overlooked by a ruined castle, has a fine 12C church with a spire and a carved doorway.—4 km. *Lés* (2085 ft;, *Hotel*), with the Spanish custom house, is the starting-point for the *Col d'Aouéran* (7090 ft) which leads to (8 hrs E.) *Sentein*. We cross the frontier by a rebuilt bridge at (5 km.) *Pont-du-Roy.*—3 km. *Melles-Seriail*, with the French custom-house.—8 km. *St Béat* where the road turns W. to (5 km.) *Cierp*, to join the N 125 16 km. N. of *Luchon.*

VIÂ TREMP (219 km.). This alternative route turns N. from the N 1 just E. of Lérida onto the C 1313 following the E. bank of the Segre. At 27 km., **Balaguer** (12,200 inhab.; *Hotels*) which lies 2 km. to the W., has an attractive arcaded Pl. Mayor and several churches: *Sta Maria* (late Gothic; 1351–c.1550), *S. Salvador* (good retablo), *N.S. de Almater*, with a 16C figure of Christ, and the *Conv. de Sto Domingo*, with a cloister of c.1323–50 by *Jaime Fabre.*—8 km. W. is a ruined castle, and 14C church with a fine retablo at *Castelló de Farfanya.*

Our road bears N.W., but the eventual completion of the C 147 N. from Balaguer beyond Camarasa into the valley of the Noguera Pallaresa, will avoid this detour.—19 km. *Les Avellanes*, near the beautiful Premonstratensian monastery of *Sta Maria de Bellpuig* (1166), with a Romanesque cloister and 14C church. We now cross the Port d'Àger and descending, turn abruptly E. through (10 km.) *Ager*, with a ruined *Colegiata* and other churches. With the *Sierra del Montsec* (5495 ft) on our l., and the Embalse de Camarasa on our r., we enter the defile of the Noguera Pallaresa, emerging from which we skirt the W. bank of the Embalse dels Terradets in the fertile Conca de Tremp.

At 30 km. a road leads 8 km. W. to the Augustinian sanctuary of *Mur* or *Moró*, in a fortified precinct including a 12C Romanesque cloister with arches now blocked, which once contained important apse-paintings in its church (regrettably removed to Boston); 11C ruins of the castle survive.

Just S. of Tremp are crossroads: the C 1311, a narrow mountain road, leads W. to meet the N 230 some 24 km. E. of *Benabarre*, while the r.-hand turning leads to *Artesa de Segre* (p.171) viâ (18 km.) *Isona*, with a richly sculpted 12C church portal, N.E. of which a track leads to the Romanesque basilica of *Abella de la Conca*, with a retablo by *Pere Serra* (c. 1375). Also near Isona are *Llordá* with an early castle and church of 1040, and *Covet*, to the S.E., with a carved doorway of c. 1100.

7 km. **Tremp**, the principal town (5800 inhab; *Hotel*) of the valley, with remains of old walls and a church of 1638–42 with fine Gothic vaulting, stands at the foot of the Embalse de S. Antonio or de Tremp. Our route passes the picturesque village of *Talarn*, preserving a good 18C organ (restored), to reach (16 km.) **La Pobla de Segur** (3200 inhab.).

Here the C 144—a mountain road—diverges l. to meet the N 230 at Pont de Suert, thereby approaching the Viella tunnel and avoiding the Pto. de Bonaigua— A turning off to the r. 10 km. N. of Pobla de Segur leads up the valley of the Flamicell to (19 km.) *Cabdellá*, with a Romanesque church containing remains of 13-14C murals.—13 km. *Viu de Llevata*, with a 12C monastic church.—10 km. *Pont de Suert*, see p.195.

The C 147 continues to ascend the Noguera Pallaresa, passing through the impressive **Pas de Collegats** to (16 km.) *Gerri*, with a Romanesque church (cons. 1149) and the sanctuary of *N.S. de Arboli*.

13 km. **Sort** (2375 ft; 1500 inhab.; *Hotel*), with a ruined castle and remains of fortifications, is the capital of the mountain district of *Pallarés*.—*Llesui*, 15 km. N.W., has been developed as a winter-sports centre.—There are small Romanesque churches at *Vilamur* to the S.E. of Sort, and at *Surp*, N.W. of (4 km.) *Rialb* (500 inhab.; *Hotel*) which we pass before entering (11 km.) *Llavorsi* (2675 ft; 350 inhab.).

From Llavorsí a poor road, later a track, ascends the valley of the Noguera de Cardós (N.E.) to *Ribera de Cardós*, with its Romanesque church; *Esterri de Cardós*, with another; and (20 km.) *Tabescán* (5000 ft), a curious village connected by passes with *Ustou* (8¼ hrs) and *Aulus* (8½ hrs) in France. Several obscure smugglers' paths lead from the E. tributary valleys of the Val de Cardós into Andorra.

We bear N.W. and pass (9 km.) *Escaló*, near the 11C monastery of *S. Pedro de Burgal*.—At 3 km. a turning leads 7 km. W. to *Espot* (*Hotel*), now being developed as a winter-sports area. It is also a good centre for excursions into the *Parque Nac. de Aigües Tortes* and the deserted craggy peaks of the *Sierra del Encantados* or *dels Encantats*, so well described in Robin Fedden's 'The Enchanted Mountains'.

From (6 km.) *Esterri d'Àneu* (3185 ft) the road begins a steep and winding ascent of a side valley, leaving the upper valley of the Noguera Pallaresa to the r.

This may be followed to the Pto. de Salau, first climbing to (12 km.) *Alós*, passing *Isabarre*, where the Romanesque church has wall-paintings, and *Isil*, with a fine church earlier than 1095.—Beyond Alós a bridle-path leads along the E. bank of the Noguera. After c. 1 hr we turn uphill to the r. to the *Pto. de Salau* (6733 ft), the frontier pass between the *Pic de Portabère* (N.) and the *Pic de Péguille*, commanding a fine view S. of the Piedrafita massif. We may descend to *Salau* (2760 ft), in France, 32 km. S. of *St Girons*.

2 km. *València de Àneu* has a church with wall-paintings and a broach spire, and there is another steeple at *Son del Pino*, 3 km. S.—2 km. r., *Sorpe*.—We climb steeply to (19 km.) the **Port de la Bonaigua** (6800 ft), there crossing the main watershed of the Pyrenees. To the N. is the *Pico de la Lanza* (8724 ft), to the S. the almost unexplored ranges of *Saboredo* and *Colomés* (9613 ft). We descend steeply into the valley of the Garona (Garonne), past *Tredòs*, where, regrettably, the wall-paintings from the 12C church have been removed to New York.

15 km. **Salardú** (4160 ft), picturesquely situated on a promontory between the Garonne and the Iñola, surrounded by remains of ramparts, retains its castle. Its 13C church contains the important 12C Cristo de Salardú. Among the ancient houses the *Casa de Berentete* (1580) is notable; even better is the 14C fortified *Casa de Bastete* at *Unyá* (N.E.; 4330 ft), where there is also a 12C church. To the N. is the winter-sports development of *Baqueira-Beret*.

Salardú is a good base for excursions in the Piedrafita massif to the E. (*Roca Blanca*, 8775 ft) and in the lake-studded Sierra de Montarto to the S.W. (*Bizberri*, 9245 ft).—A fine and easy round leads viâ (1¾ hrs) the *Pto. de Beret* (6102 ft), on the far side of which is the Source of the Noguera Pallaresa. We follow the stream down and reach (c. 4 hrs) *N.S. de Mongarri* (5420 ft). *Sentein*, due N. in the French valley of the Lez, is reached in 8 hrs by either the *Port de la Hourquette* (8350 ft) or the *Port d'Urets* (8365 ft); *Castillon* is 8 hrs from Mongarri viâ the *Port d'Orla* (7753 ft).

Below Salardú the valley widens.—2 km. *Arties* (*Parador Nac.*), has sulphur springs and an old church.—At the head of the valley to the S. is the *Lago de Ríos* (3½ hrs), the largest of the Pyrenean tarns.—We pass *Escunyau* and *Betren*, both with interesting churches, before entering 6 km. *Viella*, see p.196.

17   ZARAGOZA

ZARAGOZA, anglicized as *Saragossa* (528,700 inhab.; c. 40,000 in 1800; 140,000 in 1920; 304,000 in 1960; *Hotels*), capital of the ancient kingdom of Aragón, and of the modern province, has a reputation for the stubborn valour of its people. It possesses two cathedrals—the ancient church of La Seo and the more modern shrine of the Virgin del Pilar, whose towers and multicoloured domes rise above the S. bank of the Ebro. Zaragoza has grown rapidly in recent years, and is now surrounded by industrial and residential suburbs. Beyond its richly cultivated huerta, irrigated by the Ebro and the Canal Imperial, rise the desert hills of Aragón, overlooked on the W. by the Moncayo and on the N. by the Pyrenean foothills.

Fiestas. The main festival is that of the Virgen del Pilar (12 Oct.).

History. The celtiberian city of *Salduba* won the favour of Augustus (25 B.C.) and was called *Cæsaraugusta* (later corrupted to *Sarakusta* by the Moors). It was always a 'colonia immunis', or free city, and became a seat of assizes, and a mint.

From 466 the city was in the hands of the Goths, and legends tell of a stubborn resistance to the besieging Frankish armies of Childebert and Clothair. In the 8C it fell to Berber allies of the Moors, who, in 777, quarrelling with the Caliph of Córdoba, requested aid from Charlemagne at Paderborn. But in the following year they refused to admit Charlemagne's troops within their gates, and his retreating army was attacked by the Basques at Roncesvalles. Zaragoza throughout the 10th and 11Cs was a centre of the Beni-Kasim, a Moorish culture hostile to Córdoba, and as often as not in alliance with Castile against Aragón. The Beni-Hud family of kings were philosophers and scholars.

In 1115 or 1118 Alfonso el Batallador recaptured Zaragoza after a five years' siege. The union with Barcelona in 1137 and the conquests of Jaime el Conquistador made Zaragoza capital of a great maritime power. Fernando the Catholic on his marriage with Isabel of Castile was able to maintain the equality of his kingdom and to insist on the observance of the ancient 'fueros' of Aragón. In 1590, however, when Antonio Pérez took refuge in Zaragoza from the anger of Philip II, the king forced the Justiciar, Juan de Lanuza (*el Justiciazgo*), to flee, and revoked the fueros, insisting at the same time on the introduction of the Inquisition.

On May 25th, 1808, at the commencement of the Peninsular War, Gén, Lefebvre, who had been sent to attack the town, met with an unexpectedly stubborn resistance; the citizens, organized by the peasant leader Jorge Ibort, had placed themselves under the command of José Palafox, a young Aragonese nobleman, and resolutely withstood the assault, which began in earnest on June 15th. On June 30th the French would have forced an entrance at the Portillo, but for the bravery of Agustina de Aragón, Byron's 'Maid of Saragossa', who when her lover fell by the side of his gun, seized the match from his hand and worked the gun herself. On Aug. 13th the French defeat at Bailén temporarily relieved the town and Lefebvre was forced to retire. In December the place was again invested, this time by an army of 30,000, commanded by Lannes, Mortier, Moncey and Junot. Fire and pestilence broke out, but the French continued to press forward, storming each house separately while the women and children hurled tiles upon them from the roofs, and it was not until 20 Feb. 1809, that the city surrendered, a mass of smoking ruins. When Ford passed through, in 1831, he condemned it as a 'dull, old-fashioned, brick-built town'. During the Civil War it adhered to the Nationalists and was little damaged.

Among natives of Zaragoza were Avempace (d. 1138), the Almoravid philosopher; Jerónimo de Zurita (1512–80), the historian; Ignacio Luzán (1702–54), poet and critic; Francisco Bayeu (1734–95), the painter, and Miguel Asín y Palacios (1871–1944), the arabic scholar.

The **Pl. de España**, a focus of life in Zaragoza, lies halfway along the C. del Coso, which follows the line of the old city wall. Hence we follow the C. de Don Jaime I towards the river. On the l. is Baroque *S. Gil*, with a Mudéjar tower (c. 1350) and a rich high-altar retablo by *Ancheta* (1570–85). In the C. S. Jorge (r.) stands Mudéjar *SS. Juan y Pedro*, with a square brick tower and 16C retablos, and the *Conv. de la Enseñanza*, built on the site of the Lanuza palace, destroyed by order of Philip II. In this area stood the ancient *Judería*.

At No. 7 in the C. de Clavel is an old palace, while on the l. is *Santa Cruz* (1678–80), by *Agustín Sanz*. Near its end the C. de Don Jaime I intersects the Pl. DEL PILAR connecting the cathedrals. On the r. are the *Seminario Conciliar* (1834), the *Pal. Arzobispal* (1787), and the *Seo* itself. It is worth while to walk round the narrow alleys surrounding the Seo, to see the *Muro Mudéjar* and the old mansion in the C. Domer with its deep cornice, and patio.

The ***Cathedral of La Seo**, the oldest and most interesting church in Zaragoza, was erected as a mosque on the site of an older church during the Berber occupation. In 1119 it was reconstructed by Bp. Pedro de Librano and during succeeding centuries it has been greatly altered, especially outside. In 1318 it was appointed the metropolitan church of a new archbishopric detached by Pope John XXII from that of Tarragona. Its archives and library have been the object of spoilation.

The EXTERIOR, varied in style and period, is notable for its *Muro Mudéjar*, at the N.E. angle, where the wall is covered with a mosaic of brick and azulejo tiles. Above the adjoining apse, which shows traces of Romanesque work, rises the *Cimborio*, erected in 1412 by Pedro de Luna (Benedict XIII) and rebuilt by *Juan Botero* in 1498–1520. The main N.W. façade was built by *Julián de Yarza* in 1683, and the tall tower beside it (1682–90) by *J. B. Contini*. The usual entrance is by the 16C S.W. door in the C. de Pabostría, which admits to the *Pavordería*, a vestibule with a Gothic vault.

INTERIOR. The building is nearly square, with double aisles and a row of external chapels on all four sides. The slender pillars, whose capitals are sculptured with figures of children, support a lofty pointed vault with foliated keystones. The present form of the cathedral is due mainly to the extensive rebuilding of 1546–59 by *Charles de Mendivi*. The marble floor is picked out with a design reproducing the vault-plan.— Facing the S.W. entrance is the front of the *Trascoro*, a rich example of the Plateresque style (1538–57) by *Arnau de Bruselas* and *Tudelilla*, decorated by *Juan Sanz* and sculptured in plaster by *Juan de Bruselas* (1560).—In the centre is an 18C baldacchino with twisted columns (*Cap. del Santo Cristo*), by *Juan Zábalo*, marking the spot where the Cristo de la Seo is said to have spoken to Canon Funes.

The *Coro*, fenced by a 16C grille, contains stalls of the 15C by *Juan Navarro* and *Fr.* and *Ant. Gomar* and a lectern of 1413, the gift of Benedict XIII.—In the *Cap. Mayor* the magnificent alabaster * *Retablo* was begun by *Pere Johan* in 1431 and continued by Maestro *Hans de Suabia* in 1467–77; the lantern above it is by *Gil Morlanes* (1488). The interior cupola of the cimborio was completed by *Enrique de Egas* in 1520.—On the l. of the altar are the tombs of Abp. Juan de Aragón (brother of Fernando the Catholic; d. 1475), and of Pedro López de Luna, first abp. of Zaragoza (14C).—The black slab in the wall near by marks the burial place of the heart of Don Baltasar Carlos (the Infante so often painted by Velázquez), who died of small-pox at Zaragoza in 1646. The organ (1413) was rebuilt in the 18C.

CHAPELS. On the r. of the high altar is the Renaissance chapel of *SS. Pedro y Pablo*, beyond which is the semicircular doorway of the *Sacristy*, whose effect is marred by the Baroque framework.

The **Sacristy** contains a small museum, with reliquaries, a Plateresque custodia probably designed by *Damián Forment* (1537–41) and vestments, including an English chasuble embroidered with Adam and Eve, from Old St. Paul's London. In the *Chapter House* are paintings by *Ribera*, *Zurbarán* and *Goya*, while the *Museum* has 15–18C tapestries, Gothic paintings, and designs by the *Bayeus* and others for the decoration of El Pilar.

The next chapel is that of *S. Pedro Arbués*, an inquisitor murdered near the S. pulpit in 1485 (canonized 1867). The 16C chapel of *S. Gabriel*, with a Plateresque portal and screen, was founded by the rich merchant Gabriel Zaporta for his burial-place. The first chapel beyond the Pta. de la Pabostría, *S. Bernardo*, contains the Tombs of Abp. Fernando de Aragón, grandson of Fernando the Catholic, and of his mother Ana de Gurrea. The tombs are by *Bernardo Pérez* and *Juan de Liceire* (1553–75), of the school of Morlanes, and the centre retablo is by *Pedro Moreto*.—The chapels on the N.W. side, especially the last one, *Santiago*, contain a profusion of Churrigueresque ornamentation. In the chapel of *N.S. la Blanca*, on the l. of the high altar, are preserved some gravestones of early bishops, transferred hither when the cathedral was repaved. The chapel of *S. Miguel*, with a bronze grille by *Guillén Tujarón* (16C) contains the Tomb of Abp. Lope de Luna (d. 1382), a Gothic work by *Pere Moragues* of Barcelona.

Leaving La Seo by the N.W. door we see, on the opposite side of the plaza, the **Lonja**, a plain rectangular hall (1541–51) by *Gil Morlanes the Younger* and *Juan de Sariñena*, Gothic in plan and Plateresque in adornment, with a fine cornice. Within, the 24 Ionic columns and

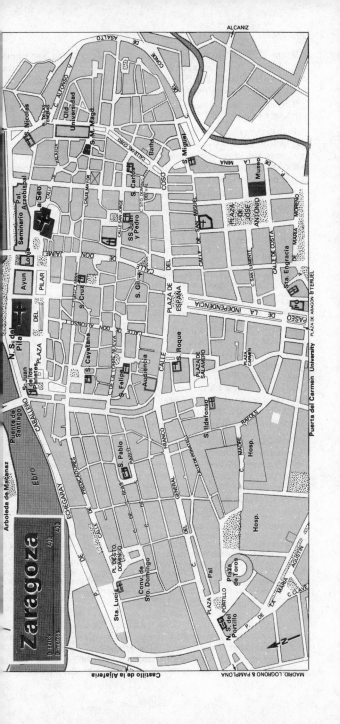

pilasters are encircled by a band of curious ornamentation, and round the walls, level with the capitals, runs a frieze-inscription recording the erection of the building.—Beyond are the *Ayuntamiento* and *Gobierno Civil*, facing the huge *Pl. del Pilar*.

To the N. is the *Pte. de Piedra* with seven pointed arches, rebuilt in 1401–37 and often since strengthened and restored.

Flanking its plaza, the unwieldy bulk of the **Basilica of N.S. del Pilar**, the seat of the archbishop and chapter for six months of every year, enshrines the cherished cult-image of Zaragoza, which is also the patroness of the Guardia Civil. Its restoration is projected, which may feel is an unmerited extravagance.

History. Legend relates that St. James the Great (Santiago), while preaching in Spain (A.D. 40), saw here a vision of the Virgin who descended from Heaven on a marble pillar, supported by angelic hosts, and commanded him to build on this site a temple in her honour. The chapel then erected was replaced by a church in the 13C; the present building was begun after a fire in 1434, but of that church only the high altar and the coro remain. *Fr. Herrera el Mozo* began his rebuilding in 1681 and a further remodelling was undertaken in 1754–66 by *Ventura Rodríquez* and *José Ramírez*.

EXTERIOR. Attention is diverted from the uninspired lines of the main mass to the picturesque group of ten cupolas roofed with brightly-coloured tiles, which surround the central dome. At the ends rise four slender towers surmounted by cupolas, provided for in Herrera's plan, although the spire of the W. Tower and almost the whole of the E. Tower were not completed until 1903. A Romanesque tympanum from the earlier chapel is built into the S. Front.

INTERIOR. In plan it is a rectangle divided into three aisles of seven bays each, every alternate bay being surmounted by a cupola. The enormous square piers, faced with Corinthian pilasters, give a monotonous effect of a solidity too ponderous for the height of the vaults.—At the W. end is the *Coro*, a Renaissance work (1554–64) by *Juan de Moreto*, a Florentine who sculptured the three rows of stalls after designs by *Etienne d'Obray* who produced also the organ-case (1529). The Reja is the masterpiece of *Juan Celma* (1574–79). The *High Altar* is by *Damián Forment* (1509-15).

The **Santa Capilla**, near the E. end of the church, is an oval temple surrounded by columns of broccatello marble. Protected by a silver reja are three altars. On the r.-hand altar, on a marble pillar, stands the image of the Virgin, a black wooden figure (comp. Montserrat, p.162) in a gold-embroidered cloak.—The outer dome is frescoed by *González Velázquez* (1793); one of the spandrels is by *Goya* (the Virtues), the rest by *Fr. Bayeu* (1781–82).

At the back of the chapel, to the l. of an 18C alabaster relief by *Carlos Salas*, is an opening through which the credulous kiss the pillar. The 16C Christ on the altar facing the relief is ascribed to *Damián Forment*. In the vault beneath the chapel is buried the engineer Ramón Pignatelli (1734–93).

The encircling chapels contain monuments of the 18-19C. Facing the N. side of the Santa Cap. is the *Sacristía de la Virgen*, containing the offerings of wealthy pilgrims. Among the contents of the treasury is a late 15C Reliquary-bust of Sta Ana. Of the tapestries, the most notable is a Flemish work of the late 15C representing the Coronation of the Virgin.

From the S. side of the Pl. de la Catedrales the C. de Don Alfonso I leads back to the Coso. In the C. Espoz y Mina (l.) the *Casa de Pardo* (No. 31) has a Renaissance patio (restored), and No. 36 preserves 15-16C patios. From the C. Alfonso I we take the C. de la Torre Nueva (r.), named after a famous leaning clock-tower, 90 m. high, dating from 1504, demolished in 1894. In the Pl. S. Felipe, in a college attached to *S. Felipe* (by *Miguel Jiménez*, 1686–91), is the *Pal. del Conde de Morata* (known as '*de los Condes de Argillo*') which preserves a fine wooden cornice and interesting patio (1659–63). The adjoining church contains an Ecce Homo of 1525 and a rich custodia. In the surrounding streets are several curious 'solares' (e.g., in the C. de Candalija, the 15C *Casa Fortea* and the *Pal. del Conde de Guara*). To the N. is Baroque *S. Cayetano* (by *Villanova*; 1681–1704), with the tomb of Juan de Lanuza, beyond which, towards the river, stand remains of the *Real Pal. de la Azuda*, the residence of Alfonso el Batallador in the 12C, now incorporating the church and college of *S. Juan de los Panetes* with a Churrigueresportal (1720) by *Fr. Gaspar Lafiguera* and a 13C brick tower.—To the N. is the new *Pte. de Santiago* crossed the Ebro and the *Arboleda de Macanaz*, a riverside park.

S.W. of *S. Juan* we may follow the C. de S. Pablo to **S. Pablo**, the most interesting church in Zaragoza after La Seo. Founded after 1266 and enlarged in the 16C, it has the appearance of a Gothic church of the latter date. The W. Door has been modernized, but the N. Door is a good example of late Gothic, sheltered by a Renaissance cornice of wood. The 13C *Mudéjar Tower* is among the most remarkable of the many towers of Zaragoza.

The dark interior is notable for the wooden *Retablo Mayor* by *Damián Forment* (1511–29), at the back of which the *chapel of N.S. del Pilar*, with a reja by *Jaime Tejedor* (1527), contains another retablo in the style of Forment. The stalls were begun in 1569 by *Jerónimo de Cósida*; the organ is of 1572; while the sacristy contains a rich treasury, and tapestries after Raphael.

The C. de S. Blas, with a Plateresque mansion at No. 32, leads W. to the *Conv. de Sto Domingo* (partly 15C), and 16C *Sta Lucia*. Between the C. de Predicadores and the Ebro is the *Pal. del Duque de Villahermosa*, once the prison of the Inquisition.

At the W. end of the old city in the Pl. del Portillo. *N.S. del Portillo* (1722–31) is by *Fr. Pontón* and *Marcos de Tarazona*. Beyond the Portillo stands the castle of *La Aljafería, once the palace of the Berber sheikhs, and the residence of the Kings of Aragón, named after its builder, *Abu Ja'afar Ahmed* (1039–81). After a period as the seat of the Inquisition it was partly destroyed by Suchet (1809) and was used as barracks, then as a hospital, a prison, and later in military occupation. It has recently been restored.

Little remains of Moorish days except the *Mezquita*, or mosque (11C), entered by a horseshoe arch, and the *Torreta del Trovador*, said to have been the prison of Manrico (in Verdi's 'Il Trovatore'), and, more certainly, the study of the inquisitor Pedro Arbués. Noteworthy also are the *Grand Staircase* (1492), with Moresque ornaments and the badges of Fernando and Isabel; the *Sala de Sta Isabel*, birthplace of Elizabeth of Portugal (1271–1336), daughter of Pedro III; and the *Salón del Trono*, both these rooms, especially the latter, having artesonado ceilings with pendant ornaments.

We may return to the centre by the C. Gen. Franco, to the S. of which is the *Pl. de Toros* and the *Hospicio Provincial* (1669).—The church of the *Escuelas Pías*, to the N.W. as we regain the C. del Coso, has a 17C brick front. Within are ceilings painted by *Coello*, who decorated also the *Col. de Escolapias* (1663–66), further S. near *S. Ildefonso*, begun in 1661 by *Dom. Zapata*.

The *C. del Coso*, which girdles the old town on the S., contains many old mansions. At its W. end stands the **Audiencia** (1537) formerly the mansion of the Condes de Luna, a distinguished family to which Benedict XIII and the wicked count in 'Il Trovatore' belonged. The house was sometimes known as the '*Casa de los Gigantes*' from the colossal figures guarding the entrance (1551–54). The chapel contains a 17C wooden Christ and there are several artesonado ceilings.—On the r.

as we walk towards the Pl. de España are the palaces of the *Condes de Fuentes* (No. 54), whose patio is now occupied by a bank, and of the *Condes de Sástago* (No. 56) now a Casino; at No. 29 is the beautiful courtyard of the former mansion of the *Condes de Azara*.—In the Pl. de S. Roque is 18C *S. Roque*, with two brick towers.

Keeping on along the Coso beyond the Pl. de España, we may diverge r. to visit *S. Miguel* (14C), with an ornamented Mudéjar tower (c. 1260) and a Renaissance altar-piece (1519) by *Damián Forment* and *Jolí*. A chapel contains paintings by *José Luzán*.—On the other side of the Coso, in the C. Sto Dominguito del Val, is the 17C doorway of the *Pal. de Sora*, and in the Pl. de S. Carlos, adjoining, is the 16C *Casa de los Morlanes*, the home of the sculptor Gil de Morlanes and others of the family. The church of the *Seminario de S. Carlos* (1570) has decorations of 1723 and good paintings, including a S. Francisco Borja by *Ribera*.— The so-called *Baños Árabes* of c. 1300, at No. 146 in the Coso, are really the baths of the *Judería*, while not far off, in the C. del Cíngulo, is the *Casa del Rabino*. Further along the Coso are some of the buildings of the *University*.

Its foundation dated from 1474, and the present buildings were begun in 1587 They were largely destroyed by the French in 1809, together with the nearby church of S. Augustín, and little of the original work remains. Other faculties are housed in the Paseo de Pamplona, while the new *Ciudad Universitaria* is further S.W. at the end of the Gran Via. The university possesses a collection of Rheims Tapestries (15-17C).

To the l. of the University stands 14C *Sta María Magdalena*, with a lofty Mudéjar *Tower*. The retablo of the Santo Cristo chapel is ascribed to *Forment*, while that of the high altar is by *Juan de Yarza* (1727-30) with carvings by *Ramírez*.—The *Conv. del Sepulcro*, further N., is on the site of the old Castillo de Don Teobaldo and preserves a section of the Roman walls.—A Churrigueresque chapel in *S. Nicolás*, adjoining, has good azulejos and paintings on copper. The C. del Sepulcro leads through a characteristic quarter back to La Seo. In the parallel C. de Palafox is the house of the hero of 1809, with the classical *Aduana Vieja* opposite. To the S. of La Seo are the *Pal. de Azara* and the *Casa de la Maestranza* (c. 1537-47), with splendid artesonado ceilings.

The S. QUARTERS are more modern. The shady PASEO DE LA INDEPENDENCIA, lined with arcades, leads from the Pl. de España to the Pl. de Aragón, to the W. of which is the *Pta. del Carmen*, a gateway of 1782, by *Agustín Sanz*, bearing scars of the sieges of 1808-9. The *Conv. de Jerusalén*, at No. 19 in the Paseo, has an interesting front.

On the opposite side of the Paseo is **Sta Engracia**, built after 1493 and restored in 1891–98. The Plateresque **Portal* with kneeling figures of Fernando and Isabel, the founders, is by the *Gil Morlanes*, father and son (1515–19), and in the crypt is a 14C sarcophagus which passes for the tomb of Sta Engracia.

Further E. is the Pl. de José Antonio and the **Provincial Museum**.

On the ground floor is the MUSEO ARQUEOLÓGICO, containing Roman sculpture; mosaics, arabesques and florid Gothic fragments from the Aljafería; fragments from Sta Engracia, including a St Stephen ascribed to *Gil Morlanes* (early 16C), late 14C tombs of the Duque de Hijar and his wife, and a series of 15C wooden corbels, and choir-stalls, from Veruela.

The SALA DE LOS PRIMITIVOS contains panel-paintings, including eight by *Jaime Serra* (14C) from the retablo of Santo Sepulchre; two predella paintings from the retablo of Sigena (1425); the Retablo of Santa Cruz de Blesa (15C) by *Miguel Jiménez* and *Martín Bernat*; and Virgin and Child with an angel, by *Jaime Huguet*.

On the first floor is the *Museo de Pinturas*, a rather indifferent collection but including works by *Rolán de Moio, Pedro Pertus, J. Vicente Cósida, Ysenbrandt, Ant. Martinez, Ribera, El Greco, Lucas van Leyden, Claudio Coello, Luca Giordano, Mengs,* and *Bayeu.* Also displayed are a self-portrait, and portraits of Fernando VII, and the Duque de San Carlos, by *Goya*, and of Calomarde by *V. López*, and among 19th and 20C works, paintings by *Sorolla* and *Zuloaga*.

The suburb of *Torrero* was the scene of Stanhope's victory of 1710, which gave the Archduke Charles the mastery of Zaragoza, and on the Cabezo Cortado, a hill above the canal to the E., was posted one of the French batteries during the siege of 1808. In the other direction below the Cabezo de Buenavista to the N.W., is the Parque de Buena Vista, with an 18C fountain; while further on, beyond the canal bridge over the Huerva, is the *Casa Blanca*, with the canal locks and a fountain built by *Pignatelli*. Here in 1809 Marshal Lannes signed the terms for the surrender of Zaragoza.

An *Ethnographical Museum* has been installed in the *Casa Pirenaica* of the Parque de Primo de Rivera, reproducing the interior of a house from Ansó (p.191), with furniture, etc., and models in folk costume.

The *Cartuja de Aula Dei*, 12km. N. of Zaragoza, on the E. bank of the Rio Gállego, was built in 1564–67, and after damage in 1808–9, restored by Carthusians, but the eleven frescoes (1771–72) by *Goya* in the church have been repainted.—*Villamayor*, 9km. N.E., has a Mudéjar church-tower.

18   FROM ZARAGOZA TO VALENCIA

A Viâ Teruel

Total distance 326 km. (202 miles). N 330. 80 km. *Daroca*—(at 84 km., *Albarracín* lies 26 km. S.W.) —17 km. **Teruel**—91 km. *Segorbe*—31 km. *Sagunto*—23 km. **Valencia**.

We drive S.W. on the N 330 parallel to the W. bank of the Huerva to (24 km.) *Muel* with a Roman fountain, now at the *Ermita de N.S. de la Fuente*, with saints painted by *Goya* (1771).—11 km. *Longares*, where the hall-church (c. 1580) retains a 14C tower and an untouched 16C organ of quality.—8 km. **Cariñena** (2030 ft; 3000 inhab.), noted for its wines, considered 'most excellent' by Baretti, who passed that way in 1760. The church tower is a relic of a fortress of the Knights of St. John, while the *Cap. de Santiago* is a former mosque. Note the 18C organ.—7 km. N. lies the Baroque sanctuary of the *Virgen de las Lagunas*, while 25 km. to the E. on the C 221 lies *Fuendetodos*, a poor village where the painter Francisco Goya (1746–1828) was born; his birthplace has been preserved.—The road now climbs past (6 km.) *Paniza*, with a 15C church and Mudéjar belfry, to cross the Pto. de Paniza (3209 ft).—18 km. *Mainar*, with a fine 16C church-tower.—c. 31 km. E., approached by a circuitous route, lies *Herrera de Navarros* with a 14-15C Mudéjar church.—At 10 km. the road from Calatayúd joins our route from the N.W., see Rte 22, p.234.

3 km. **Daroca** (2700 inhab.; *Hotel*), a town of great antiquity in the most fertile part of the valley, between the *Sierra de Sta Cruz* (4670 ft) on the W., and the *Sierra Palarda* (4895 ft) on the S.E. It is surrounded by a *Wall* (13-16C) with 114 towers, while the neighbouring hills are crowned with ruined castles. From its position in the narrow valley it is subject to floods, and a tunnel (*La Mina*, 700 m. long) to carry off the superfluous water, was dug in 1560 by *Pierre Bedel*, the N. entrance of

which is a short distance S.E. of the *Pta. Alta*. Hence the C. Mayor, flanked by old houses, leads W. past the *Casa de la Cadena* (15C) and *Casa de Trinitarios* (13C). Uphill to the r. is the Pl. Mayor and the *Colegiata de Sta María,* begun in the 13C, altered for Juan II (1458-79), and rebuilt by *Juan de Marrón* (c. 1587). It has a Mudéjar tower of 1441 and a doorway with 13C reliefs, and also houses a good *Museum of ecclesiastical art*, including a Custodia of 1388 and a number of 15C retablos, among them those of S. Pedro, S. Martín, and Sto Tomás.— The ancient *Ayuntamiento*, close by, is now the gaol. Interesting churches are *S. Andrés* (Gothic), *S. Juan* and *S. Miguel* (both Romanesque, with good medieval paintings), and *Sto. Domingo de Silos* with a Mudéjar tower and a superb Retablo, by *Bart. Bermejo*. At the far end of the C. Mayor is the *Pta. Baja*, roofed with glazed tiles and flanked by 14C turrets.

Hence we may regain the main road, which slowly ascends the Valley of the Jiloca to (30 km.) *Calamocha*, with a Moorish bridge and tower, facing the hill of El Poyo (3960 ft) and (9 km.) *Caminoreal*, where the N 211 from Alcañiz and Montalban joins our route, see Rte 18B.—7 km. **Monreal del Campo**, (2600 inhab.) founded in 1120 by Alfonso I to keep in check the Moors of Daroca who were not subdued until 1122. Here the C 211 bears W. towards *Molina de Aragón*, see p.233. To the E. rises the *Sierra Palomera* (5016 ft) and on the W. the foothills of the Sierra de Albarracín.

At 38 km. a road leads W. 3 km. to *Cella*, with a church containing a fine plateresque retablo, where we bear S.W., and at 26 km., after following the l. bank of the Turia, enter picturesque and well-sited *Albarracín* (1245 ft; 2800 inhab.; *Hotel*). Now much shrunken, this walled Moorish city was the capital of an independent state from 1165 to 1333, when it was annexed to Aragón. From the *Pl. Mayor* (restored) we may ascend narrow rambling streets of timbered houses with overhanging storeys to the small *Cathedral*, rebuilt c. 1531 and internally classicized in the late 18C. It contains a set of six Brussels tapestries by *François Geubels* (16C), a fine rock-crystal Fish, and notable retablos, one by *Joli*.—There are important rock-paintings in the prehistoric shelters of Callejón del Plou and El Navazo, a short distance S.E.

For the route from Albarracín to *Cuenca*, see p.439, reversed.

Returning on our tracks for 18 km., we fork r. to regain the N 330 9 km. S. of where we diverged.

17 km. **TERUEL** (3000 ft; 23,300 inhab.; 12,000 in 1920; *Parador Nac.* 2 km. N.; *Hotel*), largely brick-built, with remnants (restored) of castellated walls and Mudéjar towers just visible among the blocks of the modern town, rises above the banks of the Turia in a well-wooded vega, surrounded by fissured hills and vertiginous cliffs of barren red clay. Its climate in winter is particularly severe.

History. Teruel, Iberian *Turba*, was destroyed by the Romans as a reprisal for Hannibal's sack of Saguntum. It became a centre of Moorish power and large numbers of Moors continued to live there after the reconquest of the city in 1171. Jews also formed an important part of the population until 1486, when, after a massacre, the remnant was expelled. In the Civil War Teruel was held as a salient by the Nationalists until 14 Dec. 1937, when it was taken and sacked by the Republicans, to be recaptured a fortnight later. At one time during the battle the temperature fell to 18°C. below zero!

From the Zaragoza road from which a by-pass veers r. to avoid the town, we fork l., passing (l.) Gothic *S. Francisco* (1392-1401) and ascend to the Paseo del Generalísimo. Continuing S. along the line of the old fortifications, we reach the *Viaducto de Calvo Sotelo*, off the far end of which forks the Valencia road. We may follow the ronda further to the E. to see (l.) the remarkable polygonal tower known as the *Castillo de Ambeles*. Entering the town N. of the Viaduct, we pass through the modern Pl. Gen. Varela and follow the C. Ramón y Cajal to the arcaded Pl. Carlos Castel. Hence the C. Muñoz Nogués leads to the dark **Cathedral**, built in 1248–78, altered in 1596–1614, with Churrigueresque additions of c. 1658–85. The central lantern is by *Martin de Montalbán* (1538). The *retablo mayor* (1535-38) is by *Gabriel Jolí*; the coro has good stalls and a bronze reja. The nave is roofed by a remarkable painted *artesonado* of c. 1260–1314. The Treasury and Sacristy may also be visited.

Passing beneath the Mudéjar tower of the cathedral we reach the Pl. del Venerable, named after the patriot friar Francés de Aranda (1346–1438). The *Bishop's Palace* here has an interesting Renaissance entrance and patio. From the Pl. Fray Anselmo Polanco, behind the cathedral, with the porticoed *Casa de la Comunidad* and other old houses, the street on the l. leads to *S. Miguel* (17C) beyond which (r.) is the remarkable *Aqueduct* (Los Arcos de Teruel), built by the French engineer *Pierre Bedel* in 1537–58. The ruinous church of *La Merced*, in the suburb below has a good brick tower. From S. Miguel we may follow the C. del 22 de Febrero and C.S. Martín to the Mudéjar *Tower of *S. Martin* (restored by Bedel in 1589–91 and again recently), beyond which is the *Pta. de la Andaquilla*. Adjacent is a small provincial *Museum*. We may return to the centre by the C. Yagüe de Salas, passing the *Seminary*, *Sta Teresa* (18C), and (r.) the Mudéjar tower of *S. Salvador*. The church contains the Cristo de las Tres Manos.

From the E. side of central Pl. Carlos Castel the stepped C. de Hartzenbusch leads to *S. Pedro*, a restored Gothic church with a Mudéjar tower. Refitted in Churrigueresque style in 1741, S. Pedro retains an altarpiece by *G. Jolí* (16C) and a 14C cloister.

In an adjacent chapel are the remains of the 13C 'Lovers of Teruel' (Isabel de Segura and Juan Diego Martínez de Marcilla), who died of grief at being separated, and were buried on one tomb. The popular legend has inspired many dramas, perhaps the best known being by Tirso de Molina (1635) and by Hartzenbusch (1837).

Further S. is *S. Andrés*, with a rebuilt tower and the tomb of Sánchez Muñoz the antipope Clement VIII elected at Avignon in 1423.

For the road to *Cuenca*, see p.439, in reverse.

Quitting Teruel, our route ascends to (16 km.) the Pto. de Escandón (3996 ft) and (7 km.) *La Puebla de Valverde*, a chilly upland town with Moorish walls.

Hence the C 232 winds 128 km. S.E. to the coast at *Castellón* through the attractive old village of (18 km.) *Mora de Rubielos* (1500 inhab.) and (13 km.) *Rubielos de Mora* (800 inhab.). At Mora the 15C *Colegiata* was burnt during the Civil War, while the *Castillo de Fuentes* (c. 1490) is under restoration. Rubielos has ancient houses and a 15C retablo in the church.—25 km. N. of Rubielos lies *Linares de Mora*, a picturesque hill-village.—The road goes on to (19 km.) *Cortes de Arenoso*, notable for the late-15C Valencian triptych in its church, and is prolonged viâ (44 km.) *Lucena de Cid*, see p. 178.

14 km. *Sarrión*, among pine-woods, to the r. of which rises the *Pico de Javalambre* (6627 ft). The Baroque church contains a 15C retablo, a Virgin by *Pedro Nicolau* (1408), and a 15C enamelled cross and custodia.—At 4 km. a road leads S. 2 km. to *Albentosa*, with another retablo by *Nicolau*.—We now descend through the rugged Sierra de

Espiña, the new road avoiding the steep Cuesta de Radudo, to (34 km.) *Viver*, with an old tower and containing numerous Roman inscriptions, and 4 km. beyond, **Jérica** (2000 inhab.), with ruined walls and castle, a small museum, and three old churches; *S. Roque* (1395), with a retablo by *Lorenzo Zaragoza*, the parish church with an elaborate portal and a Mudéjar tower, and *El Socorro*, with 16C paintings and tombs (1600–09) of the Coverio family.

12 km. **Segorbe**, an ancient cathedral city (7300 inhab.) of Roman origin (*Segobriga Edetanorum*) stands in a side valley above the Palancia, with relics of 14C walls and commanded by two castles. The ugly *Cathedral* (1483-1534, but entirely 'modernized' in 1791-95) has been largely restored in recent years, as has its 15C cloister.

Works by *Vicente Masip*, *Juan de Juanes*, his son, and of *Jacomart*, may be seen in the *Museo Diocesano*, otherwise a very miscellaneous collection of ecclesiastical art collected from churches in the area devastated during the Civil War, but containing a good Limoges enamel triptych; other works are displayed in the octagonal vaulted chapter-house.—Some 5 km. to the W. lie the ruins of the *Cartuja de Valdecristo*, founded in 1385.

Beyond Segorbe we leave the hills and enter the fertile huerta of Sagunto, at 31 km. passing the fortified acropolis of *Sagunto* (p. 178), where we join the N 340 and turn r. for (23 km.) **Valencia**, see Rte 52.

B Viâ Alcañiz and Morella

Total distance, 345 km. (214 miles). N 232, 59 km. *Azaila*—42 km. *Alcañiz*—74 km. *Morella*—35 km. turn r. onto C 238—70 km. *Castellón*—65 km. **Valencia**.

Driving S.E. from Zaragoza on the N 232 along the S. bank of the Ebro, we pass (9 km. l.) *La Cartuja*, a curious village formed out of the ruins of a charterhouse begun in 1651 and reconstructed in 1781.—6 km. beyond, near *El Burgo de Ebro*, is a group of buildings known as *Zaragoza la Vieja*.

At 5 km. a road turns S. to (29 km.) *Belchite*, the scene of serious fighting in 1936-38, where a new town has been built adjacent to the extensive ruins of the old, deliberately left standing as a macabre monument to the horror of Civil War.

At 23 km. a by-road crosses the Ebro and turns r. to (9 km.) *Velilla de Ebro*, with the ruins of the Roman colony of *Julia Lepida*.—16 km. *Azaila*, with Iberian and Roman ruins and a Celtic cemetery.

The C 221 leads E. 18 km. to *Escatron*, to the N. of which lies the important *Abbey of *Rueda del Ebro* founded in 1182 by Alfonso II, abandoned in 1835, with a church of 1225–38 and an early 14C cloister, and recently restored.—We may regain our route by following a by-road S.W. viâ *Samper de Calanda*, picturesquely situated, with a 17C church.

At (14 km.) *Hijar*, the church, burnt out in 1936 but restored, contains interesting retablos.—6 km. S.W. at *Albalate del Arzobispo* are ruins of a fine castle (c. 1300–10) incorporating a Mudéjar chapel.—The road bears S.E. and approaches (28 km.) **Alcañiz** (11,100 inhab.; *Parador Nac*), the ancient *Anitorgis*, where Hasdrubal defeated the Scipios in 212 B.C. It remains a pleasant and picturesque town, commanded by its castle, with a pointed barrel-vaulted chapel (12C) and later porch; the main building of 1728 has been converted to house the *Parador*.

The Renaissance façade of the *Ayuntamiento,* the arcaded 14C *Lonja* adjoining (restored) and grandiose *Sta María,* with a monumental Baroque Portal, flank the Pl. Mayor. *N.S. del Carmen,* with a Baroque retablo and concha, and the *Bridge,* are also of interest. The journalist Francisco Mariano Nifo (or Nipho; 1719–1803) was born here.

For the road from Alcañiz to *Tarragona,* see the route on p.184, in reverse.

29 km. N.E. of Alcañiz on the C 231, lies **Caspe** (8300 inhab.) at the junction of the Guadalope with the Ebro, an ancient town on the Roman road from Tarragona to Zaragoza. Here in 1412 the 'Compromise of Caspe' settled the problem of the Aragonese succession by placing on the throne a junior branch of the Castilian house of Trastamara. The church, a Romanesque and Gothic building of the 13–14C, was damaged in 1936–38. The Civil Guards here used the wives and children of local trade union members as a human barricade when endeavouring to resist Republican columns in 1936.

FROM ALCAÑIZ TO MONREAL DEL CAMPO (145 km.). 3 km. W. of Alcañiz we turn l. from the N 232 on to the N 420. 17 km. *Calanda,* in the centre of an olive-growing district with a 17C church and the birthplace, in 1900, of Luis Buñuel, the film-maker.—At (15 km.) *Alcorisa,* the church of *Sta María,* with a good doorway and tall tower, the *Pal. de Lalinde,* and the Pl. de los Arcos, are of interest, beyond which the road crosses the steppe-like desert or Tierra Baja of Teruel, and the Pto. Traviesas to (47 km.) **Montalbán** (2100 inhab.), with a fine Pl. Mayor and a church in Mudéjar-Gothic style (c. 1210–14C) enriched with polychrome bricks.—At 3 km. the N 420 bears S. 41 km. to *Teruel* (p.206), off which, at 22 km., after passing the Pto. de S. Just, a road leads E. 18 km. to *Aliaga* (the *Laxia* of Ptolemy), with a medieval castle surrounded by a towered curtain-wall.—At 10 km. the C 222 leads 32 km. N. to *Muniesa,* with a Mudéjar church-tower.—We cross the Pto. Minguez and at 46 km. meet the main Zaragoza-Teruel road at *Caminoreal.* Here we turn l. and after 7 km. reach *Monreal del Campo,* see p.206.

At 15 km. we fork r.—To the N. is the Cueva del Charco de Agua Amarga, with remarkable rock-paintings.—After 1 km. a road leads 22 km. S.E. to *Valderrobres* (see p.184)—26 km. *Monroyo,* where a road leads 9 km. E. to *Peñarroya de Tastavins,* with a good Mudéjar church (14C) and another of 1556.—7 km. S. of Peñarroyo is the Gothic *Castillo de Herbes,* a noble fortified mansion, near which is a standing cross (1390–1420) by *Antonio Arbó* and *Pedro Crespo.*—We climb to the Pto. Torre Miro and cross the Sierra de S. Marcos as we approach the commanding height on which Morella stands.

33 km. **Morella,** (3300 inhab.; *Hotel*), an old frontier fortress with steep arcaded streets, 14C wall and towers, and a castle held by the obstinate Carlist leader Cabrera from 1838 until its capture by Espartero in 1840. Morella is identified with the Roman *Castra Aelia,* the winter quarters of Sertorius. Beside the Alcañiz road runs the *Gothic aqueduct* (c. 1273–1318). The *Town Walls* are in perfect preservation and include 14 towers and 4 gates, among the latter the *Pta. de S. Miguel* of 1360, by *Domingo Zoroball.* From the *Castle,* which dominates the town, there is an extensive *Panorama over the surrounding hills.

The outstanding church of *Sta María la Mayor (1265–1330) has fine carved doorways of c. 1355–80 and a raised coro of 1406–26 by *Pedro de Segarra* who also (1414–25) built the belfry; the vault beneath the coro was added in 1430–40 and the winding staircase, decorated by *Antonio Sancho,* in 1470; the trascoro is by the Italian *José Beli.* In the *Cap. Mayor* is a retablo of 1657–77 and Churrigueresque decoration (1677–85) by *Vicente Dolz,* who was also responsible for the stalls of 1672. Some windows contain excellent Stained Glass of 1384–86 by the Valencians *Juan Gascó* and *Pedro Ponc.* The 18C organ, with a beautiful tone, has been recently restored. There is a museum in the

Sacristy, including a Visitation by *Joan Reixach*, vestments of 1410, and a S. Roque by *Ribalta*. *S. Juan* is of 1450–70, and the former *Franciscan Convent* preserves a cloister of c. 1280–90 and a church (cons. 1390) with neoclassical additions (1800); *S. Miguel*, by *José Palau*, was built in 1712–29. Among the civil buildings the most interesting are the *Ayuntamiento* (1361–1414) and the *Almudin* of c. 1260.

Morella is a good centre for excursions in the wild and picturesque hill-country of the MAESTRAZGO. To the N. is a series of grottoes, notably the Cueva del Roble containing prehistoric paintings; while at *Chiva de Morella* (11 km. N.W.) is a painting of c. 1400 in the Ayuntamiento.

14 km. W. of Morella lies *Forcall*, an ancient town of arcaded streets with a 13C church and Baroque belfry (1760) by *José Ayora*.—3 km. further W. is *Todolella* with an old castle.—N. of Forcall stands the castle of *Ortells*, and 13 km. beyond *Zorita del Maestrazgo*, whose rock-cut chapel of *N.S. de la Balma* has a Churrigueresque portal and a fine verja (1490–1510).

FROM MORELLA TO TERUEL (145 km.). This mountain road runs S.W. to (14 km.) *Cinctorres*, with a church of 1758 by *José Ayora* of Morella, containing three panels of 1441 by *Bernardo Serra* and a processional cross.—16 km. S. lies *Castellfort* with a Baroque church (1725–34) and the 13–14C chapel of *S. Pedro* and 12 km. beyond, the hill-top village of *Ares del Maestre*, near important prehistoric caves.—19 km. *La Iglesuela del Cid*, with an attractively arcaded Ayuntamiento.—10 km. S. E. is *Villafranca del Cid*, an old walled village whose Ayuntamiento (13-14C) contains a fine custodia and a panel painting (1455) by *Valentín Mantoliu*. In the sacristy of the parish church (1567–72) by *Pedro Maseres Navarro* and *Ramón Pertasa*, are a 15C processional cross and reliquary. *Puebla de Ballestar*, nearby, has a retablo of 1429 by *Bernardo Serra* in its 13C church.—26 km. S. of *La Iglesuela*, on the far side of the range, lies *Mosqueruela*, with ancient walls and houses. The road leads on to *Rubielos de Mora*. see p.207.

Following our road W. of La Iglesuela we climb to (13 km.) **Cantavieja** (900 inhab.) with a picturesque arcaded plaza, and retaining much of its walls. The huge parochial church dates from 1664–1746.—A road passes through the arch of an octagonal church tower towards *Mirambel*, 15 km. N., also walled, 8 km. beyond which lies *Olocau del Rey*, with 16C public buildings and a Gothic church containing medieval vestments.—Beyond Cantavieja we cross the Puertos de Cuarto Pelado, de Villarroya and de Sollavientos, N. spurs of the Penarroya massif (6625 ft), often snowbound in winter, to (48 km.) *Allepuz* and (51 km. **Teruel**, see p. 206.

Leaving Morella, the N 232 bears E.—good retrospective views— from which at 11 km. a road leads 16 km. N.E. to *Vallibona*, whose church has a retablo of c. 1360 and a fine 14-15C painted artesonado roof—The road zigzags steeply down from the Pto. de Querol past (r.) the 18C *Santuario de Vallivana*.

At 13 km. a road leads S. 8 km. to *Catí*, an ancient village damaged during the Civil War. The 13C parish church contains an altarpiece of 1460 by *Joan Reixach*, and a processional cross of 1471–75. The Italianate *Ayuntamiento* is of 1427, the *Casa Abadia* of 1373–78, the *Casa del Delme* is early 15C, and the *Casa de Miralles* (c. 1452–55) is by *Pedro Crespo of* Santander.

At 11 km. we turn r. onto the C 238 and after 5 km. enter **San Mateo** (2100 inhab.)—From this crossroad, the N 232 continues due E. for 29 km. to *Vinaroz*, see p.177. The *Iglesia Arciprestal* of San Mateo has a nave and apse of 1350–60, an octagonal tower and a fine doorway (both 13C); in the 1st chapel (l.) are remains of a retablo of c. 1400, while the Plateresque retablo mayor is by *Pedro Dorpa*, a pupil of Damián Forment; the sacristy contains a processional cross of 1397. In the town are a Gothic *Ayuntamiento*, the *Casa de Borrull*, and the Plateresque *Pal. de Villores*.

At 20 km. a road leads 14 km. W. to *Albocácer*, with the 13C church of *S. Juan* and the *Parroquia Alta*, also remains of a Templar castle, and on the outskirts, the chapels of *S. Pedro* and *S. Pablo*, with wall-paintings. There are prehistoric rock-paintings at *Valltorta* off the road N. to *Tirig*, while 16 km. W. lies the walled village of *Benasal*.

At 4 km. we pass the Cuevas de Vinromá, prehistoric shelters containing rock-paintings, while at (19 km.) *Cabanes* is a Roman arch. After traversing a picturesque defile we reach (19 km.) *Borriol*, with a Roman milestone in the chapel of *S. Vicente*, beyond which we meet the main road (N 340) at (8 km.) *Castellón de la Plana*, see p.178. Here we turn r. and follow the route described on pp.178-9 to (65 km.) **Valencia**, see Rte Rte 52.

19   FROM ZARAGOZA TO MADRID

Total distance, 327 km. (203 miles). N II. 86 km. **Calatayúd**—57 km. *Sta María de la Huerta*—29 km. *Meinaceli*—17 km. *Alcolea del Pinar*.—79 km. *Guadalajara*—59 km. **Madrid**.

We follow the N II S.W.—At 34 km. from Zaragoza a road leads r. 9 km. to *Épila*, with the *Pal. de los Jímenez de Urrea*, where Pedro IV defeated the Aragonese nobles in 1348.—6 km. N. lies *Rueda de Jalón*, with the Moorish castle of *Rota* on a rock honey-combed with cave-dwellings.—12 km. *Calatorao*, 3 km. to the W., built on Roman foundations, has a castle where Urraca, queen of Alfonso the Batallador, is said to have died.—5 km. *La Almunia de Doña Godina* (*Hotel*), to the N. of which is the *Santuario de la Virgen de Canañas*, with an artesonado ceiling and 12C frescoes; beyond lies *Ricla*, with a Mudéjar belfry on a 16-18C church.—At 8 km. a crossroad leads S.E. to (16 km.) *Tobed*, with a church begun in 1359 with Mudéjar decorations incorporating the Islamic confession in Arabic; while 16 km. to the N.W., at *Mesones*, is a palace of the antipope Benedict XIII (Pedro de Luna, c. 1330–1423).—At 8 km. a road (r.) leads to (9 km.) *Saviñan*, where in the *Pal. de Argillo* is preserved de Luna's skull, while 14 km. beyond, at *Illueca*, is the immense 14C palace in which he was born.—15 km. To the r. stood the Iberian city of *Bilbilis*, a Roman municipium and birthplace of the poet Martial (43–104 A.D.) who returned here to die after 35 years in Rome. Bilbilis was also the scene of a victory of Metellus Pius over Quintus Sertorius (73 B.C.). Its insignificant ruins lie partly under a chapel on the Cerro de Bámbola.

4 km. **CALATAYÚD** (1750 ft; 17,200 inhab.; *Hotel*), at a crossroad of the Burgos-Soria-Daroca route, see p.234, imposing in outline and dull in colour, merges into the surrounding crumbling clay hills, some of which, in the quarter called *La Morería*, contain caves still populated. This name and that of the city itself (*Kalat Ayub*, 'the castle of Job') betrays the Moorish origin of the place, which was founded in the 8C by Ayub, nephew of Musa.

The town contains two collegiate churches: *Sto Sepulcro*, to the N.E., once the Spanish headquarters of the Knights of St. John, was founded in 1141 and rebuilt in 1613; *Sta María la Mayor*, in the centre, has a fine portal of 1525–28 and a lofty tower, octagonal in its upper tiers. The ancient *Judería* lay in the area behind the church. Many of the other churches have Mudéjar towers, including *S. Andrés* (late 15C), *S. Pedro Mártir,* with azulejos in the coro, and *S. Martín,* with a charming patio. The *Conv. of Sto Domingo,* E. of the town, has a fine three-storeyed patio, with part of the exterior enriched with Mudéjar patterns.

At *Belmonte de Calatayúd,* 11 km. E., was born Baltazar Gracian (1601–58) author of 'El Criticón', etc.

FROM CALATAYÚD TO MOLINA DE ARAGÓN (75 km.) 28 km. S.E., off the C202 and not far beyond *Nuevalos,* picturesquely situated at the S. end of the Embals de la Tranquera, is the famous *Monastery of Piedra* (2579 ft). Founded in 1194 b Cistercians from Poblet, it was moved to its present site on the opposite bank o the Rio Piedra in 1218. It was damaged in the anticlercial rising of 1835, but ha been restored and converted into a *Hotel.*

The *Church* was refaced in the 17C, but the 13C *Cloister* and the *Grand Staircase,* with a remarkable vault of the 14–15C., were not altered; the othe monastic buildings are also interesting. Not the least of the charms of Piedra is it delightful situation in a wooded valley, with grottoes, pools, and cascades. Fines of all is the lowest fall, the Cola del Caballo (53 m. high), which may be viewed from a subterranean passage.

From Nuevalos we may regain the N 11, by skirting the W. bank of the Embalse at *Elhama de Aragón.*—The C 202 continues S. past (18 km., r.) the old village o *Milmarcos.*—At 18 km. the C 211 leads 15 km. N.E. to *Embid,* with a well preserved castle.—2 km. *Rueda de la Sierra,* where the 12C church has a lat Gothic chapel and a retablo of c. 1500.—9 km. *Molina de Aragón,* see p.223.

Our route follows the Jalón past (8 km.) *Terrer,* with a Mudéjar church, and (7 km.) *Ateca,* with two imposing towers, one (13C) above a converted mosque, the other belonging to the *Ayuntamiento,* formerly a castle.—14 km. The spa of **Alhama de Aragón** (1500 inhab.; *Hotels*), Roman *Aquae Bilbilitanae;* the towering *Alcázar* recalls the rediscovery of the springs by the Moors.—6 km., r. *Cetina,* has a castle with a Mudéjar chapel containing an early 15C retablo.—8 km. *Ariza,* also with a castle, S.W. of which is the site of an Iberian town.—At 7 km. the C 116 leads to *Almazán,* 45 km. N.W., see p. 337.

After passing the *Albergue Nac.,* we reach (7 km.) **Sta María de la Huerta** (700 inhab.), preserving the impressive remains of a great Bernardine *Monastery,* with a huge sexpartite vaulted *Gothic Refectory* (1215–23). The well-proportioned *Church* (1179 et seq.) with a restored rose-window, contains the grave of Abp. Rodrigo Jiménez, who fought at Las Navas de Tolosa and a two-keyboard organ (18C). There is an interesting octagonal chapel of 1747–50 off the S. Transept, while from the N. Transept, containing the tomb of the Cid's grandson, we pass into the 13C *Cloister* and thence by a monumental staircase of 1600–91 to the Renaissance *Upper Cloister* (1531–47) and the cloister of the hostelry (1582–1637).

After (10 km.) *Arcos de Jalón* with a medieval castle, the road traverses the gorge of the Jalón past (19 km. r.) *Medinaceli* (p.337) on a commanding height to the W. Crossing the Pto. de Esteras, we shortly approach the road junction of (17 km.) *Alcolea de Pinar.* For the road hence to *Sigüenza,* p.338.

From Alcolea we bear S.W.

At 34 km. a r.-hand turning leads S., after 13 km. passing 3 km. N.E. of *Valderrebollo,* with a small Romanesque church and remains of the monastery of *Ovila,* much of which, regrettably, has been removed to the U.S.A.—9 km. further S.E. lies *Cifuentes* ('hundred fountains'), with 1800 inhab., a large ruined castle (1324), Renaissance convents, and *El Salvador,* with a notable door of c. 1261–68 and rose-window.—10 km. S.E., on the Tagus, stands *Trillo,* with a sulphur spa nearby.

At 19 km. a road leads 9 km. S.E. to **Brihuega** impressively sited on a hill above the Tajuña, an old fortified town (3700 inhab.)—the *Pta. de Cozagón* remains—with four Romanesque churches, including *Sta María de la Peña*, and *S. Felipe* (restored), and commanded by a prominent building designed as a cloth-factory by Carlos III. The so-called *Cuevas Arabes* are worth visiting. Here and at *Villaviciosa de Tajuña*, 5 km. N.E., took place the battles of Dec. 1710, in which the Duc. de Vendôme's victory over the Austrian troops established Philip V firmly on the Spanish throne.

5 km. *Trijueque*, with remains of 13C fortifications and a 16C church.—5 km. *Torija*, with a Renaissance church containing interesting tombs, a 16C Pillory, and remains of a once-famous 13C castle, blown up in 1811.

17 km. *Guadalajara*, for which, and the road hence to (59 km.) **Madrid**, see p.288, and pp.286-8 in reverse.

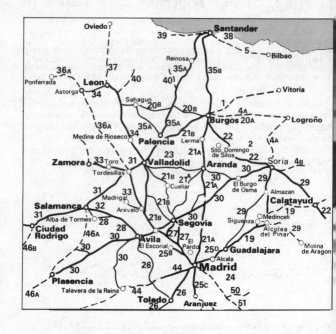

III   MADRID, OLD CASTILE, AND LEÓN

The characteristic landscape of **Old Castile** (*Castilla la Vieja*) is a limitless undulating plateau or *meseta*, scattered with earth-coloured villages, the skyline being only occasionally broken by a thin line of poplars, flat-topped hills, or distant mountain ranges. The soil is generally fertile, indeed, the area is one of the granaries of Spain, but the rainfall is scanty, although less so than in New Castile, and the main source of water is found in the Duero and its tributaries fed by the snows of the Cantabrian mountains to the north, the sierras of La Demanda, and Cebollera to the N.E., and of Guadarrama and Gredos on the S. The outlaying district of the Rioja, in the upper Ebro valley, with its rich vineyards and orchards, borders the less austere landscape of Navarre and the Basque country. Similar to Castile is the rolling *meseta* of León, bleak and wind-swept, and equally subject to violent variations in temperature. In the N.W. of the province is the remote mountain district of the Bierzo, resembling Galicia in its characteristics, while its western frontier touches Portugal, from which for many miles it is separated by the Duero and its tributory the Agueda. To the S. the Sierra de Gata and Peña de Francia wall off Estremadura and the Tagus basin.

Although Madrid, Toledo and certain other towns of New Castile (see p.429) are described in this section, historically and sentimentally, Old Castile is the heart of Spain. Its early counts and later kings were among the first to make an organized resistance to the Moorish power, and it owes its name to the many castles (*castillos*) erected as successive bulwarks against Islam. First Burgos, and then Valladolid, was the

capital of the expanding Christian kingdom, until later conquests
enabled the kings to advance their headquarters further south.

Concurrently, emerging from the Asturian mountains after the first
Moorish advance, in the 9C Alfonso the Catholic of León overran the
country to the west as far south as the river Tormes, but the capital was
not established in León until c. 910. In the meantime internal strife arose
between León and the Christian kingdoms of Castile and Navarre, the
former nominally subject to León, fostered by the unwise habit of the
Leonese kings of dividing their territory among their sons. The Moors,
taking advantage of this, pressed northwards again in the 10C and
ravaged the whole kingdom, and were not driven out until the following
century.

The ancient kingdom of **León** includes the modern provinces of León,
Zamora, and Salamanca; those of Palencia and Valladolid are usually
referred to as being part of Old Castile, which is comprised of the
provinces of Burgos, Logroño, Soria, Segovia, and Avila. Santander is
also included politically in Old Castile, but it resembles more its
neighbouring province of Oviedo (or the Asturias) both in topography
and in its people, and is described in Section IV.

The three most southerly provinces of Castile—Soria, Segovia, and
Ávila—all with a high proportion of rural population, have each
experienced a severe decrease in numbers during the last 15 years, from a
total of 607,000 to 449,000. In the province of Burgos the rural
population has dropped from 328,000 to 218,000 in the last 25 years,
while in the same period Burgos itself has more than doubled. Valladolid
has likewise grown significantly, from 119,000 to 286,000 (76,000 in
1920), but the rest of the province has decreased from 299,000 to
164,000. Both Palencia and Zamora have also suffered depopulation
during recent decades, but there has been less change in León and
Salamanca, except for the growth of their capitals during the last two
decades from 59,000 to 113,000 (22,000 in 1920); and from 74,000 to
131,000 (32,000 in 1920) respectively.

20   FROM BURGOS TO LEÓN

A   BURGOS AND ITS ENVIRONS.

BURGOS (2800 ft; 132,900 inhab.; c. 9000 in 1800; 32,000 in 1920;
81,000 in 1960; *Hotels*), the ancient capital of the kingdom of Castile and
León, is famous for its cathedral and for its historical associations as the
residence of Fernando III, el Santo, Alfonso the Wise (el Sabio), and the
Cid. Its climate, however, is more notorious for its extremes than that of
Madrid.

History. Burgos claims as its founder Diego Porcelos, who c. 884, at the
command of Alfonso III, built a castle on the bank of the Arlanzón as a check to
the Moors. The city remained subject to the kings of León until 926, when the
citizens elected two judges to govern them. Among these magistrates and
celebrated in historical ballads were Laín Calvo, who repelled the attacks of León
and the Asturias, and Nuño Rasura, his son-in-law. The first independent
sovereign was Fernán González (c. 950), who bore the title of count of Castile. His
great-grandson, Fernando I, assumed the title of king of Castile, and by his
marriage with Sancha, heiress of León, united the two crowns. In 1087 Alfonso VI
removed the court from Burgos to Toledo, recaptured from the Moors two years
before, and disputes as to precedence between these two cities ended only when,

after the fall of Granada in 1492, the royal residence was transferred to Valladolid, and later to Madrid. Burgos was unsuccessfully besieged by Wellington in 1812, but in the following year the castle was blown up by the French prior to their retreat to Vitoria. In 1937 it was the temporary capital of Nationalist Spain. The 'Burgos Trials' of dissident Basques (Dec. 1970) brought notoriety to the town. It is a curious coincidence that Lady Holland, when visiting Burgos in 1804, remarked that prayers were then being said in the cathedral for the success of the royal arms against the Biscayans during some trivial commotion, which Godoy was supposed to exaggerate, 'that he may have the honor of quelling them and receive from the deputies of Biscay a good round sum to prevent the soldiery from committing excesses'.

In most famous native is Rodrigo or Ruy Díaz de Bivar (1026–99), called *El Cid* (i.e. the Arabic title Sidi) *Campeador* (surpassing in valour), whose true character, apparently that of an unscrupulous mercenary leader, is veiled in the romantic language of the '*Poema del Cid*', the epic of Spanish heroism. Pedro I of Castile (1333–69), known alternatively as 'the Cruel' and 'the Lawgiver', was likewise born at Burgos, as was the architect Diego Siloée (c. 1495–1563), the blind musician Francisco Salinas (1513–90) and Francisco de Enzinas (hellenized to 'Dryander'; 1520–52) the humanist and disciple of Luther.

Immediately to the N. of the *Pte. de S. Pablo* lies the *Pl. del Gen. Primo de Rivera*, where the roads from Vitoria and Santander converge, while just S. of the river Arlanzón the road bears r. for Valladolid, off which, at the Pl. de Vega, the Madrid road (N I) turns l. Leading W. from the Pl. del Gen. Primo de Rivera is the *Paseo de Espolón*, a popular promenade, which takes us to the *Pte. de Sta María*.

Facing the N. end of the bridge is the **Arco de Sta María**, an imposing castellated gateway, originally part of the 11C fortifications, the masonry of which may be seen at the rear of the gate. The decorative river front, with its two flanking towers and four turrets, was erected in 1534–36 in honour of Charles V. The statues represent him in company with the five Burgalese heroes: Porcelos, Rasura, Calvo, Fernán González, and the Cid.

Beyond the gate stands the *Cathedral (Sta María).

History. The archiepiscopal see of Oca (36 km. N.E.) was transferred to Burgos in 1075 by Alfonso VI, but the cathedral was not founded until 1221, when Fernando III, in honour of his marriage with Beatrice of Swabia, laid the first stone, and by 1230 some part of the new church was sufficiently advanced to be used for services. To judge from the unusual Angevin vault of the only remaining original chapel (E. of the N. Transept), the first architect may have been the Anglo-Angevin *Ricardo* who was working at Las Huelgas before 1203, and still living near Burgos in 1226. By c. 1235 the master was *Enrique*, also architect of León Cathedral and probably a Frenchman; at his death in 1277 the original church must have been substantially complete, having been consecrated in 1260. The top stages and spires of the W. Towers were added by *Juan de Colonia* in 1442–58, and the Cap. del Condestable in 1482–94 by *Simón de Colonia*, his son, while the central lantern was not completed until 1568 from the designs (1540) of *Francisco de Colonia*, son of Simón.

EXTERIOR. The W. FRONT, although its lower storey was unhappily deprived of most of its decoration by an 18C restorer, preserves two reliefs by *Juan de Poves* (1653). The rose-window is flanked by the two openwork spires, 90 m high. The transeptal façades are unaltered; on the N. the C. Fernán González, reached by the steps opposite the W. Façade, skirts the cathedral at a high level, passing the *Pta. Alta de la Coronería* (kept closed to prevent the use of the cathedral as a thoroughfare) with statues of the Apostles, completed in 1257, surmounted by an open arcade and affording a closer view of the stone lacework of the *Spires*, and central *Lantern*, 55 m. high, a mixture of Gothic and Renaissance motives, completed by *Juan de Vallejo* (1568). Further on we descend by a flight of steps to the level of the cathedral floor, to visit on the E. side of the N. Transept, the Plateresque *Pta. de la Pellejería*, a profusely ornamented work of 1516, by *Francisco de Colonia*.

We complete the circuit, after skirting the Condestable chapel and the cloisters, with a view of the *Pta. del Sarmental* (before 1250), another finely decorated composition of the 13C, probably the work of *Enrique*, the second master.

The INTERIOR is 106 m. long with the Condestable chapel, and 58 m. wide across the transept, but the effect of length is impaired by the central *coro* which extends halfway down the nave. The main arcade of the NAVE is in the pure 13C style, but the unusual triforium, with five or six lights in each bay surmounted by a semicircular arch, was later rebuilt or cloaked with Flamboyant work. The ridge-ribs running along the length of the high vaults betray English influence on their design. The immense piers of the crossing, rebuilt to support the great lantern, have Renaissance panels at their bases, and the apse piers were decorated with scrollwork to match them. In the pavement below the cimborio a slab marks the tomb of the Cid and his wife Jímena.

The Cid was originally buried at *S. Pedro de Cardeña* (p.223), but during the Peninsular War the tomb was rifled by Prince Salm-Dyck, and some of the bones were carried off to Sigmaringen. They were rediscovered and returned to Burgos at the instance of Alfonso XII, and were finally interred here in 1921.

The *Pta. Alta de la Coronería*, high above the N. Transept floor, is approached by the *Escalera Dorada* (1519–23), a magnificent double staircase by *Diego de Siloée*, with an iron balustrade by the French 'rejero' *Hilaire*. The rose-window in the S. Transept contains fine late-Gothic glass. The *Retablo* of the HIGH ALTAR was designed by *Rodrigo* and *Martín de la Haya, Domingo de Berriz,* and *Juan de Ancheta* (1562–80).

Surrounding the Virgin (1461) is a series of statues and reliefs, and smaller subjects on the predella below. On the N. side are three 14C tombs of infantes, including Don Sancho, brother of Enrique II, who was a prisoner in England in 1347.—At the back of the presbytery are reliefs of the Passion: the three in the centre by the Burgundian *Philippe de Vigarni* (1498–1513), the others by *Pedro Alonso de los Rios* (1679).

The central CORO (apply to the Sacristan), enclosed by a grille of 1602 and decorated on the outside with paintings by *Juan Rizi* (1654–59), contains 103 walnut *Stalls* carved by *Vigarni* (1499–1512); the seats are ornamented with box inlay. In the centre is the tomb (1260) of Abp. Maurice (d. 1238), an Englishman, with a wooden effigy covered with gilt and embossed copper, retaining part of its original Limoges enamelling.

The CHAPELS that encircle the church in picturesque irregularity are varied in period and style. Beginning in the N.W. corner, beneath the 16C clock with its mechanical jaquemart, known familiarly as 'Papamoscas' (i.e. fly-catcher), is the *Cap. de Sta Tecla*, a profusely decorated work by *Fr. de Bastigueta* (1731–34) with all the characteristic over-elaboration of the followers of Churriguera. The font dates from the 13C.—The *Cap. de Sta Ana*, built by *Simón de Colonia* in 1477–82, contains a fine *Retablo* of painted wood by *Gil de Siloée* and *Diego de la Cruz*, but unsatisfactorily restored. Here is the tomb of Bp. Luis de Acuña (d. 1495), carved in alabaster in 1519 by *Diego de Siloée*, and that of the archdeacon Fernando Díez (d. 1492) by *Simón de Colonia*.— Beyond the N. Transept is the *Cap. de S. Nicolás*, with its Angevin octopartite vault; the Isabelline tomb of Pedro Fernández de Villegas (d. 1536), translator of Dante, and the chapel of *La Natividad*, with its elliptical dome (1571). Next come two beautiful 13C chapels (*La Anunciación* and *S. Gregorio*), the latter containing the tomb of Bp. Gonzalo de Hinojosa (1307–20), with finely carved mourners and reliefs.

At the E. end, entered from the Trassagrario, is the opulent *Cap. de Condestable*, grandest of them all, built by *Simón de Colonia* in 1482–9 for Pedro Hernández de Velasco, hereditary Constable of Castile. We enter through a magnificent *Reja* by *Cristóbal Andino* (1523). The eight sides of the chapel and the elaborate vault repay detailed study. The retablo of the main altar is by *Vigarni* and *Diego de Siloée* (1523–32); on the l. is the Plateresque altar of S. Jerome by *Diego de Siloée*, and a triptych (school of Gerard David); opposite are an Ecce Homo with a Dutch inscription, and inlaid stalls. In the centre is the tomb of the founder (d. 1492) and his wife, Mencia de Mendoza (d. 1500), of Atapuerca marble with figures of Carrara marble, carved by a Genoese master (c. 1560). The huge marble slab adjoining was intended as a base for the tomb. The Sacristy of the chapel, finished in 1512, contains a Magdalen by *Giampetrino*, and an oval alabaster relief of the Virgin.

Note also the small 17C organ, unusual in having no trumpets. A small portative organ (16C), of ivory and ebony, is preserved in the Cap. de S. Nicolas.

The *Cap. de Santiago* (by Juan de Vallejo; 1524–34). S.E. of the apse has ribbed vaults which are outstanding examples of the period. Beyond the *Sacristia Mayor*, with richly carved oak panelling and presses, is the *Cap. de S. Enrique*. Off *Cap. de S. Juan de Sahagún*, the first in the S. nave aisle, opens the domed *Relicario*, housing the Virgen de Oca, etc. The large *Cap. de la Presentación*, founded by Canon Lerma in 1519, contains his Tomb (1524), by *Vigarni*. The altarpiece is a Virgin by *Seb. del Piombo*; the Rejas are by *Andino*. The *Cap. del Santísimo Cristo* is dedicated to an ancient leather-covered image with articulated limbs, the Cristo de Burgos, at least as old as the 13C.—On the way to the cloister we visit, in the S.W. corner of the transept, the *Cap. de Sta Isabel* or *de la Visitación* (1442), perhaps by *Juan de Colonia*, containing the tomb (1446–47) of Bp. Alonso de Cartagena (d. 1456; of Jewish origin and son of Bp. Pablo de Santa María).

The CLOISTERS (c. 1300–24), containing the MUSEO DIOCESANO, are reached by a sculptured doorway in the S. Transept. The small head on the l. at the spring of the outer arch is said to be a portrait of S. Francis of Assisi. The fine door of 1495 is by *Simón de Colonia*, while beneath the four-light arcade (c. 1300) are statues and tombs. On the l. of the entrance are statues of Alfonso X and Violante of Aragón, his wife, opposite which is the chapel of *S. Jerome*, with a Renaissance retablo. Further on are some 15C Flemish Tapestries.—Off the E. Walk open three chapels. The *Cap. de Sta Catalina*, or *Old Sacristy* (1316–54), with a remarkable ribbed vault like those of English polygonal chapter houses, resting on finely carved corbels, is entered between two 13C statues, with a Descent from the Cross above the door. It is decorated with 18C woodwork and contains a museum of vestments, plate, incunabula, and MSS, including parchments of 972 and 978 with Visigothic lettering, and the marriage settlement of the Cid.—The *Cap. del Corpus Christi*, with the supposed tomb of Juan Cuchiller (14C), page to Enrique III, and the 13C sepulchre of the Count and Countess of Castañeda, contains also supported high on the wall, the *Cofre del Cid*, an iron bound chest which the Cid filled with sand and pledged to the Jews as full of gold as surety for a loan of 600 marks, afterwards honestly redeeming the pledge.—*The Chapter House* adjoining, has a flat wooden ceiling of Moorish character, a Crucifixion attr. to *Mateo Cerezo*, a Flemish 15C triptych, and paintings of the late 15C Spanish School. At the end of this gallery is a Romanesque tomb (Sepulcro de Mudarra dated 1105) from S. Pedro de Arlanza. In the S. Walk are tombs including that of Canon Diego Santander, by *Diego de Siloée* (1523).—Beneath the cloister is a gallery (seen from the C. de la Paloma), of simple ribbed vaults of the end of the 13C.

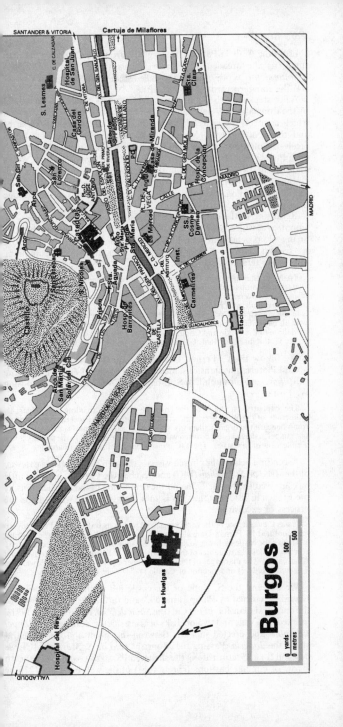

From the C. de la Paloma, leading N.E. from the Cathedral, we may enter (r.) the arcaded *Pl. Mayor*. Beneath the S. arcade, in the *Ayuntamiento*, is preserved the so-called Chair of the Judges of Castile, and the standard yard (*vara*) of Castile.

A few steps E. of the Pl. Mayor is the **Casa del Cordón**, begun in 1482 by the Constable de Velasco. Its name refers to the cordon of St Francis, which connects the arms of Velasco on the façade with the royal arms and those of his wife, Mencia de Mendoza. Fernando and Isabel received Columbus here in 1496, and here Philip I died in 1506. The C. de la Puebla leads E. to the front of the former *Hosp. de S. Juan*, with a doorway of 1479, and opposite the church of *S. Lesmes*, with a late-Gothic S. Doorway, and fine retablo in the S. aisle, carved c. 1510 by an unknown Fleming. Near by in the C. de Calzadas is a Plateresque mansion.

Returning to the old town, we follow the C. de S. Juan to the C. S. Lorenzo, in which is the spacious Baroque church of *S. Lorenzo* built on an ingenious octagonal plan. Further N., to the E. of the *Arco de S. Gil*, we ascend steps to **S. Gil** (1399, with later alterations) containing interesting retablos and tombs.

To N. of the high altar the *Cap. de la Buena Mañana* contains Gothic and Plateresque tombs and a finely carved 15C retablo; another retablo is in the *Cap de los Santos Reyes*. The *Cap. de la Natividad* in the N. aisle, added in 1586, has an interesting vault, and retablo and a Flemish Deposition. The wrought-iron pulpi is in the late-Gothic Style. In the vestibule of the sacristy are two effigies of slate with alabaster faces and hands, in a style peculiar to Burgos. An early Renaissance medallion of the Virgin and Child, probably by *Diego de Siloée*, forms an addition to the Gothic tomb of Juan García de Burgos and his wife (1479).

We follow the C. Fernán González towards the cathedral, passing several Plateresque mansions, including the so-called *Pal. del Conde de Castilfalé*, and turn uphill to **S. Esteban** (1280–1350), with an imposing W. Front.

The baptistry on the l. of the entrance has good arcading and reliefs; the balustrade of the W. gallery is effective late-Gothic work; and the pulpit and the tomb beneath the organ gallery are good specimens of Renaissance carving. The last chapel in the S. aisle is covered with beautiful arabesques. In the sacristy is kep a collection of tapestries. The 14C cloister has been sadly mutilated.

Ascending behind the church we pass through the horseshoe gateway of the *Arco de S. Esteban* (14C) and reached the **Castillo**, of which little has survived the fire of 1736 and the demolition of the fortifications by the French in 1813, but the view is good. Subterranean works are in the process of excavation.

It was the residence of the early kings, and within its walls García IV of Navarre was confined by Fernán González, and Alfonso VI of León by the Cid. Alfonso VIII gave the castle in dower to his queen, Eleanor of England. Here Fernando III received S. Casilda, daughter of the Moorish king of Toledo, who was converted to Christianity. The marriages of the Cid and Jimena (1074) and that of Edward I of England (aged 15) and Leonor of Castile (1254) were celebrated here.

We descend the S. slope of the castle hill to the *Arco de Fernán González,* erected by Philip II in 1592, and turning r., reach the site of the ancestral mansion of the Cid (the *Solar del Cid,* demolished in 1771), marked by a stele and two obelisks bearing shields, designed by *Manuel Campillo* and erected in 1791. Between this point and the cathedral stood the *Judería*. Passing the Moorish *Arco de S. Martín* (14C), we descend (l.) and return along the sheltered PASEO DE LOS CUBOS, beneath a row of circular bastions (*cubos*=tubs) of the wall begun in 1276 by

lfonso X. Passing (r.) the *Hosp. de Barrantes* (founded 1627, gateway
f 1661), we re-enter the walled town.

S.W. of this point lies the *Paseo de la Isla,* in which stands the re-erected
Romanesque doorway from the church of Cerezo de Riotirón (on the eastern
oundary of the province), and an Arcade of six Plateresque arches given by the
onde de Castilfalé.

Passing on our l. the old *Prison,* with an early Renaissance front
earing the arms of Charles V, we follow the C. de Sta Águeda to 15C
ta Águeda or *Sta Gádea,* in whose predecessor Alfonso VI was forced
y the Cid to swear that he had no part in the slaying of his brother
Sancho before Zamora. An iron copy of the silver lock by which he
wore is fixed over the door. The church possesses a 15C chalice, several
6C monuments, and carvings and paintings of some interest.

S. Nicolás, just N.W. of the cathedral, (and best seen in the
fternoon), begun in 1408, is remarkable for the magnificent **Retablo
f the high altar* (1505) by *Francisco de Colonia.* Incorporated in the
ase are the canopied tombs of (l.) Alfonso Polanco (d. 1490) and his
vife, and (r.) of Gonzálo Polanco (d. 1505) and his wife Leonor de
Miranda (d. 1503). The retablo in the N. aisle is in the Hispano-Flemish
tyle, and there are several tombs.—Just beyond and opposite the front
f the cathedral is the *Pal. de Castrofuerte,* with an early Renaissance
ortal and patio.

Crossing to the S. bank of the Arlanzón by the *Pte. de Sta María* and
urning l., we reach in the C. de la Calera, first passing the *Casa de
Angulo,* with turreted entrance and decorated windows, the restored
Casa de Miranda (1545). This picturesque specimen of a nobleman's
esidence, with an attractive patio and imposing staircase, now houses
he *Provincial Museum* and Library.

Most of the rooms on the ground floor are devoted to local archaeology,
sculpture and mosaics from *Clunia,* Visigothic sarcophagi, a carved altar-support
rom *Quintanilla de la Viñas,* and an inscribed stone recording the refounding of
Lara (era 900: A.D. 862), etc., while in R V, E. of the patio, are Gothic and
Renaissance tombs, among the finest of which are those of Juan de Padilla (d.
1492) by *Gil de Silóee,* of Antonio Sarmiento (d. 1533) and his wife María de
Mendoza, dated 1548, and attr. to the Dutchman *Rodrigo de la Hava;* also those of
María Manuel, mother of Bp. Luis de Acuña, Gómez Manrique and his wife
Sancha de Rojas (early 15C), Pedro Girón (1504), Jerónimo de Aranda (d. 1531),
nd 14C polychrome wooden effigies.—In the gallery of the patio are numerous
carvings, capitals, and sculptures from old monasteries and palaces of province.
UPPER FLOOR. R VII is devoted to Moorish and Mudéjar art, including a carved
Ivory Case for a ball-game (Córdoba, 10C), an Ivory Casket carved with fabulous
beasts in Persian style by Mohamed ben Zeyan at Cuenca in 1026, bearing added
Limoges enamel plaques (12C), and a copper **Reliquary-casket* from Silos (13C).
R VIII contains a Frontal with enamelled bronze figures of Saints (late 12C) from
Silos, Spanish work influenced by Limoges, while adjacent rooms display an
enamelled processional cross (14C), the 14C Treasure of Briviesca, including a fine
silver dish, etc. R XI contains a Virgin and Child of the School of Memling, and
Berruguete's Mass of St Gregory; R XII, eight panels of the Passion from Oña
(15C); R XVI, a carved and gilt walnut retablo from La Merced (17C). Other
rooms contain works by *Jan Mostaert, Bayeu, Luca Giordano, Juan Ricci* among
others; a portrait by the latter shows a view of Burgos and its vanished castle in the
background. Among the 17C paintings is one of Philip IV and his family in the
gardens of Buen Retiro. There is also a watercolour view of Burgos in 1802 by
Pedro Telmo Hernández. Other rooms display a selection of 16–17C furniture,
while on the 3rd floor are more archaeological remains, including in R XXXIII
recent finds from the cave of *Ojo de Guareña;* and a collection of ceramics.

Continuing S.E. we reach the Conv. church of *Sta Clara*, with a finel
proportioned vaulted interior and a carved boss of the Coronation of the Virgin ir
the N. chapel.—Further S., beyond the railway, to the r. off the Madrid road, ar
the remains of the *Conv. de las Agustinas* (now in military occupation) with a late
Gothic cloister of great purity of design, while to the W. is 15C *Sta Dorotea*, witl
tombs of Alfonso (d. 1501) and Juan de Ortega (d. 1515), and *S. Pedro y S. Felip*
(14C), with good goldsmiths' work in the sacristy.—Turning W. from Sta Clara
the C. del Gen. Mola passes the *Hosp. de la Concepción* finished in 1561, with a
fine N. door by *Juan de Nates*. Nearby is *SS. Cosme y Damián*, with a Plateresqu
doorway, Baroque retablo, and tomb of Cristóbal Andino, maker of the reja of the
Cap. del Condestable in the Cathedral. In the sacristy is an ivory crucifix (15C).—
Opposite is a Plateresque mansion.—The C. de la Concepción leads to the
Instituto founded in 1570 as the *Col. de S. Nicolás*. The severe entrance front, the
chapel, and the patio, form a good example of a Renaissance college.—To the W
is the late Baroque church of the *Carmelites*.—Turning E. to the Pte. de Sta Maria
we pass *La Merced*, with an attractive 15C doorway.

EXCURSIONS FROM BURGOS

To the CARTUJA DE MIRAFLORES (c. 3 km. E.). Turn l. at the S. end o
the Pte. de S. Pablo. The C. Conde Vallellano, passing the *Convent o,
the Carmelitas Descalzas*, leads to the shady Paseo de la Quita, at the E
end of which we turn r. and crossing the railway, ascend to the *Cartuja
de Miraflores*, a Charterhouse built in 1441–51 by Juan II on the site of a
palace begun by his father Enrique III but burnt down in 1452. The
CHURCH, overlooking a garden-patio, was designed in 1454 by *Juan de
Colonia* and continued by his son *Simón*. It was completed by Isabel the
Catholic in 1488 as a memorial to her parents. The elaborate parapet
and pinnacles were added in 1539 by *Diego de Mendieta*. The late-
Gothic doorway (1486), admits to an interior divided in the Carthusian
manner into three sections from W. to E.: for the public, the lay-
brethren, and the monks. In front of the high altar is the *Monument of
Juan II and Isabel of Portugal*, his queen, one of the most elaborate
examples of sculpture in Europe. Designed by *Gil de Siloée* in 1486, it
was carried out between 1489 and 1493, when it was surrounded with its
wrought iron screen by *Fray Francisco de Salamanca*.

The recumbent figures of the king and queen (who died in 1454 and 149
respectively) in their robes of state, lie on the star-shaped tomb, whose plan is tha
of two intersecting squares. The face of the king is regarded as a genuine, althougl
posthumous, portrait. At the corners 16 lions support the royal arms, and the
spaces between are filled with New Testament subjects.

In a recessed arch on the l., entwined with vine leaves, is the *Tomb of
the Infante Don Alfonso* (1453–68), their son, whose death opened the
succession to Isabel. Originally buried at Arévalo, his body was moved
in 1492 to this tomb made at the same time as that of his father. The
kneeling statue much resembles that of Juan de Padilla (p. 221). The
spectacled figure low down on the l. of the prince's tomb is the alleged
portrait of the sculptor, whose masterpiece this is. The same artist, with
the help of *Diego de la Cruz*, executed also the elaborate Retablo of the
high altar (1496–99), with kneeling statues of the king and queen at the
foot. On either side are the monks' stalls, carved by *Martín Sánchez*
(1486–88); the officiating priest's stall on the r. is especially delicate.—
The stalls of the lay-brethren's choir are by *Simón de Bueras* (1558); the
figure holding a child in a chalice (the third on the r.) is St Hugh of
Lincoln. The chapel contains an Annunciation by *Berruguete*, a triptych
attr. to *Juan de Flandes*, and a Magdalen by *Ribera*. The stained glass
was brought from Flanders in 1484, except that of the apse, which is
Spanish work of 1657.

The chapel of *St Bruno*, near an Annunciation by *Mateo Cerezo,* contains a ooden figure of the saint, by *Manuel Pereira* (d. 1667). The image of the Virgin, in ne otherwise unattractive *Chapel of Miraflores,* is worth notice.

The convent of **S. Pedro de Cardeña,** 10 km. beyond Miraflores, traditionally ounded in 537 by Queen Sancha, but more probably in 917, is celebrated as the urial place of the Cid and Jimena. The Cid's favourite charger Babieca was buried utside the gates (1099). The hero's empty monument (comp. p.217) stands in a de chapel, modernized in 1736. Of the 11C buildings, the tower and cloisters -main; the church of 1447 has been restored, and was handed back in 1950 to the istercian order. Some of the conventual buildings were destroyed by fire in 1967.

THE MONASTERIO DE LAS HUELGAS and the *Hosp. del Rey* lie S. W. of ne town, and are approached by following the Valladolid road (N 620), ff which we fork l. after passsing (r.) the Pte. de Castilla.

The ***Monasterio de Las Huelgas,** a Cistercian nunnery, was founded y Alfonso VIII (1187) on the site of a country residence (*huelga*=repose) f the Castilian kings, at the request of his wife Eleanor, daughter of lenry II of England.

The convent, to which only ladies of the highest rank were admitted as nuns, as granted extraordinary privileges. The abbess was a princess-palatine, second nly to the queen, and, as *'señora de horca y cuchillo'* (gallows and knife), ossessed powers of life and death over 51 manors. Many Castilian kings were nighted in the church, beginning in 1219 with Fernando III; here Edward I kept igil and was knighted by Alfonso the Wise (1254); and here the Black Prince was dged in 1367 after the battle of Nájera.

The church was built c. 1180–1230 in a plain English-looking Gothic tyle by a certain master, *Ricardo,* either English or Angevin. Visitors nter by a cloister-porch on the N. side, adjoining the tower, with little astles crowning its buttresses to represent the city arms, and with an ttractive double wheel-window. In the porch are four tombs (c. 1210– 0), one on the r. being particularly fine.—Within, the transept and anctuary are accessible throughout the day; on either side of the high ltar are kneeling figures of Alfonso VIII and his queen Eleanor of ingland, and above are 16C Gobelins tapestries. The octopartite omical vaults of the crossing and chapels, of Angevin type, deserve pecial notice.

The gilt iron pulpit, pivoted so as to direct the preacher's voice either towards the uns' choir or towards the public part of the church, dates from the 16C.

We enter the N. Aisle (*Nave de Sta Catalina*) from the transept, etween the tombs (r.) of Enrique I (d. 1217) and (l.) of Fernando de la 'erda (d. 1275), eldest son of Alfonso X, el Sabio, surmounted by a culptured Crucifixion (15C). The remaining tombs in this aisle are nostly of infantes; the sixth on the l. is that of Leonor (d. 1244), aughter of Alfonso VIII and queen of Jaime I of Aragón. In the *Nuns' 'hoir* (the structural nave), at the E. end of the Renaissance stalls, is the louble tomb of the founders, Alfonso VIII and Eleanor (both d. 1214), etween those of (N.) their eldest daughter Berenguela (d. 1246), wife of Alfonso IX, and (S.) Margaret of Savoy. Further E. are the carved arcophagi of (N.) Berenguela, daughter of Fernando III, and abbess of Las Huelgas (1241-1279), and (S.) Blanca (d. 1325), daughter of Alfonso III of Portugal. The S. Aisle contains tombs of royal ladies, ncluding (E. end, opposite the cloister door) Constanza 'la santa' (d. 243), daughter of Alfonso VIII.

From the S. Aisle we enter the CLAUSTRO MAYOR (with wooden doors y Mudéjar craftsmen), built in the mid-13C in Gothic style, but with ecently exposed remains of richly polychromed Mudéjar stucco work

in the vaults, dated to 1275. The *Sacristy* is entered by doors of eve
greater magnificence, perhaps brought from Seville; the early-Gothi
Chapter House, of nine bays, is vaulted from four shafted columns c
markedly English appearance. Here are kept the *'pendón'* of Las Navas
in fact the tent-flap of the Moorish king, and flags from ships under th
command of Don Juan of Austria at Lepanto, and several paintings

In the *Zaguán* is arranged the *Museo de Ricas Telas,* a unique collection
early textiles, jewellery, and arms discovered in royal tombs; of great richness a
variety, they display many types of Christian, Moorish, and Oriental stuffs a
brocades, and the court costume of Castile from the 12th to the 14C. The mc
remarkable exhibits are those (Cases 8–11) from the tomb of Fernando de la Cer
(d. 1275), the only burial of the series left undisturbed by Napoleon's troops; the
include his sword, spurs, belt (bearing English heraldry), and ring. Also shown
the historic Cross of Las Navas, with its case of embossed leather.

We pass on to the *Romanesque Cloister* or *Claustrillas* (c. 1180–87) c
round arches on coupled shafts with stiff foliated capitals, at whose N.E
corner stands the Moorish *Cap. de la Asunción* (c. 1200), and enter th
garden, from which there is a view of the E. end of the church. In a corne
of the garden is the *Cap. de Santiago,* Andalusian in style and entere
through a pointed horse-shoe arch of brick. Within is the 13C
articulated *Statue of Santiago,* seated on a throne and holding a swor
in the counterbalanced right hand, said to have been made to enabl
Fernando III to avoid receiving the accolade of knighthood from a
inferior (1219).

The **Hospital del Rey,** N.W. beyond Las Huelgas, approached through the gro
of El Parral, was founded by Alfonso VIII for poor pilgrims. An elaborate
decorated Platersque archway of 1526 admits to the Renaissance court rich
ornamented with shields and medallions. To the r. is the pilgrims' hospice (Casa
los Romeros); on the l., the church, entered by a restored 13C porch.

B   FROM BURGOS TO LEÓN

Total distance, 201 km. (125 miles). N 120. 83 km. *Carrión de los Condes*—44 k
Sahagún—74 km. **León.**

This is a continuation of the Pilgrimage route described on pp. 116–8
Following the Valladolid road (N 620), at 6 km. we bear r. onto the N
120.—At 8 km. a road turns N. to (12 km.) *Miñón,* on the Rio Urbe
with a 12C church.—At 7 km. a turning (r.) leads 8 km. to *Pedrosa de
Páramo,* with a battlemented pele-tower, and *Villadiego,* 11 km
beyond, with a Romanesque church, fortified tower and porticoe
houses, was the birthplace of the historian Enrique Flórez (1702–73)
14 km. S.W. of which at *Grijalba,* is a good late-13C church.—11 km
Olmillos de Sasamón, with a ruined castle (15C) and a 16C hall-churc
containing a good Renaissance retable.—2 km. N. lies **Sasamón** (220
inhab.), Roman *Segisamo,* seat of a bishop in the 11C, and retaining th
noble church of *Sta María la Real* (13–15C) with a portal imitated fron
the S. Transept of Burgos Cathedral, and a dilapidated late-Gothi
cloister.

At this point an alternative route, following more exactly the old road
Santiago, diverges l. past *Villasilos,* with a hall-church of c. 1550, W. of whic
across the Odra, lies *Villaveta,* whose church has fine stellar vaulting.—11 kr
Castrogeriz, the seat of the Council of Castile in the 16C and birthplace of th
composer Antonio de Cabezón (c. 1500–66), preserves a ruined castle, a Tran
Colegiata in the sacristy of which the remains of a 16C Flemish portative orga

ave been transformed into a cupboard; there is also the early 16C hall-church of
. Juan with a 12C tower (note fish-scale tiles) and cloisters, and *Sto Domingo*
vith 16C tapestries.—Not far off are the early 14C ruins of the monastery of *S.
Antón.*—On leaving Castrogeriz the road turns N.W. for 3 km, and then S.W. to
23 km.) **Frómista** (1250 inhab.), on the N 611 (see Rte 35A), with the restored
Romanesque church of *S. Martín* (1035–66), with its octagonal lantern and twin
urrets, *S. Pedro*, with 14–16C paintings, and *Sta María del Castillo*, mainly
'lateresque, with a 16C Hispano-Flemish altarpiece of 29 panels.—We now turn
N.W. to *Villalcázar de Sirga* (see below) and rejoin the main route at (20 km.)
Carrión de los Condes.

6 km. *Villasandino* has two star-vaulted hall-churches, one (*La
Asunción*) with an earlier presbytery (c. 1400). The rare unpainted 16C
organ was possibly used by Cabezon in his youth. It was enlarged by
Pedro Merino de la Rosa in 1739.—7 km. *Padilla de Abajo* has an
interesting church of 1573, while at (6 km.) *Melgar de Fernamental* is a
ate-Gothic church of cathedral proportions, enlarged in the 16C, and
containing an organ of 1884 by Juan Otorel, preserving part of the 17C
instrument, and restored in 1977; its 'chamade' is outstanding.

We cross the Pisuerga and at 8 km. turn l. on meeting the N 611, and
pass (r.) *Osorno* (*Hotel*) with a conspicuous church-tower and two
chapels with artesonados, but its organ (17–18C) has been recently
unsatisfactorily restored. We turn r., shortly passing *Villadiezma*, with a
signed tomb of 1400.

24 km. **Carrión de los Condes** (2800 inhab.), the seat of the cowardly
infantes de Carrión (Diego and Fernando González, born c. 1075, and
sons of a Conde de Gonzalo Ansúrez) who married the daughters of the
Cid and afterwards maltreated them, with dire consequences to
themselves; see also p. 341. Here was born the poet Marqués de
Santillana (1398-1458), while Shem Tov Ardutiel (Santob; c.1290-
.1369), compiler of 'Proverbios morales', was rabbi here. Romanesque
Sta María del Camino has a notable façade and tombs; 12C *Santiago*
has a remarkable carved frieze; while *N.S. de Belén* is Gothic. Of the
Benedictine *Conv. de S. Zoilo* there remain cloisters begun in 1537 by
Juan de Badajoz and completed in 1604 with an upper storey by *Pedro
Torres*. In the curious classical hall-church of *S. Andrés* are choir-seats
rom the nearby ruined abbey of *Benevivere* founded in 1165.

At **Villalcázar de Sirga**, or *Villasirga*, 7 km, S.E., is *Sta María la Blanca*, built
early in the 13C by the Templars, with a square E. end and ridge-ribs suggesting
contacts with England. The porch is richly carved, and in the S. Transept are the
impressive royal *Tombs of Don Felipe (d. 1274), who was first married to
Christina of Norway (see Covarrubias), and of his second wife Leonor Ruiz de
Castro.

At *Nogal de las Huertas*, 6 km, N.W. of Carrión, are the scant remains of the
Benedictine *Conv. de S. Salvador;* a nave and doorway of 1163–96; and the parish
church has a wooden Crucifix of the 11C.—Also N.W. of Carrión on the C615,
beyond (16 km.) *Renedo de la Vega*, near the Múdejar ruins of *Sta María de la
Vega*, lies (9 km.) *Saldaña*, a picturesque village with a *Bridge* of 23 arches over the
Carrión. The remains of the 11C *Castle*, and the 16–18C church of *S. Miguel*, are
of interest, while the nearby sanctuary of *N.S. del Valle* contains an 8C Byzantine
Virgin. The church of *Bahillo*, 14 km. N. of Carrión, has a 15C doorway.

Continuing W. on the N 120; we pass (5 km.) *Calzada de los Molinos*
and (12 km.) *Cervatos de la Cueza*, both with churches with fine
artesonados. The road now bears N.W. to (27 km.) **Sahagún** (i.e. S.
Facundo). This decayed town (2600 inhab.) was the starting point of the
retreat of Sir John Moore to La Coruña (Nov. 23rd, 1809). Pablo de
Olavide escaped to France from prison here in 1780. It possesses the ruin

of what was once one of the greatest Benedictine abbeys of Spain, th
retiring-place of the kings of León, and fragments remain of Mozarabi
S. *Juan*, founded by Alfonso III in 907, rebuilt in 1121–1213, on th
designs of Guilllaume, a Norman master, and burned in 1810 and 183!
The *Cap. de S. Mancio* retains the tomb of Alfonso VI (d. 1109) and o
his Moorish wife, Zaida, and in the treasury is a custodia by *Enrique d'
Arfe*.—The early 12C Mudéjar brick tower of *S. Tirso*, restored, and th
13C churches of *S. Lorenzo* and *La Trinidad* are interesting; th
Franciscan Convent preserves horseshoe arches, and the *Santuario de l'
Peregrina* (1257) has a good doorway.—5km. S. is the Benedictin
abbey of *S. Pedro de las Dueñas* (begun c. 1110).

We cross the Cea and, at 34km., meet the N 601, the main Madrid
León road. Here we turn r. for (21 km.) the walled village of *Mansilla d'
las Mulas*, with a porticoed plaza.—To the W., after crossing the Esla, i
the Benedictine abbey of *Sta. María de Sandoval*, with early ribbe
vaults (c. 1200–06) in the church, which was lengthened in 1462.

At 2km. a road (r.) leads 12km. to *S. **Miguel de Escalada**,
remarkable church built in 913 by refugee Mozarabic monks fror
Córdoba, who have used the horseshoe arch throughout, even in th
plan of the apses. A feature is the arcaded exterior gallery; the aisle
nave is of c. 930, the tower of the 11C.—*Gradefes*, further up the Esla
has a Romanesque church (begun 1177) of a Cistercian nunnery.

17km. **León**. see Rte 37.

21   FROM BURGOS TO MADRID

A   Viâ Aranda

Total distance, 237 km. (147 miles). N I. 37 km. *Lerma*—44 km. *Aranda*—39 km
(*Sepulveda* lies 12 km. W.)—43 km. *Buitrago*—74 km. **Madrid**.

We climb S. on the N I., from which at 8km. the N 234 forks l. for
Soria, see Rte 22. For *Covarrubias* and *Sto Domingo de Silos*, the
detour to which may be conveniently included in this route, see pp. 231-3
Beyond this turning, the road traverses the rolling plateau of Old Castile
to (29km.) **Lerma** (2400 inhab.; *Hotel*), an old town on the Arlanza.

Passing through the town gate, we may ascend through the old town
dominated by the huge *Palace* of the Dukes of Lerma, with its four
corner towers, built by *Francisco de Mora* (1605–17) for the Card.
Duke of Lerma (c. 1550–1625). It was sacked by the French in the
Peninsular War, but it had been visited by Lady Holland in Sept. 1804
It is now little less than tenements. It is connected by a covered walk tc
the *Colegiata de S. Pedro*, a hall-church of 1570–1616, containing ar
impressive bronze *Monument* (1603), completed by *Lesmes Fernández
de Moral* in the style of Pompeo Leoni to Abp. Cristóbal de Rojas y
Sandóval of Seville, uncle of Philip III's favourite. Here took place ir
Jan. 1722, in the presence of the Duc de Saint-Simon, the marriage
between the twelve-year-old Louise Elisabeth d'Orléans and the young
Prince of the Asturias (1707-24), who as Luis I, reigned for eight months
before his death.

There is a simple Romanesque church at *Ruyeles del Agua*, 4 km. W

Descending into the Duero valley we by-pass (33 km. l.) *Gumiel de Iizan,* where what was a fine organ has been almost destroyed by restorers of the building, and its pipes stolen; it is now a ruin.—We nortly enter (11 km.) **Aranda de Duero** (24,400 inhab.; *Hotels.*). The *S. ront of *Sta María* (under restoration) is a magnificent work by *Simón e Colonia,* bearing the insignia of Fernando and Isabel; the interior, of nusual splendour, contains a pulpit attrib. to *Juan de Juni,* and a arved font (14C). *S. Juan,* at the W. end of the town, has a S. Doorway f eight recessed orders (c. 1400) and a good W. Tower.

For the road to *El Burgo de Osma,* 58 km. E., see p. 341, in reverse.

FROM ARANDA TO VALLADOLID (94 km.). We drive W. on the N 122, cutting cross a bend of the Duero, on the bank of which to the N. lies *Roa,* with a large 'lateresque *Colegiata,* with star-vaults and the remains of a Gothic porch. It was ere that Card. Cisneros died in 1517, and where the guerrilla general Juan Martín Díaz (El Empecinado; 1775–1825) met his death.—39 km. **Peñafiel** (4900 inhab.; *Iotel*), dominated by its remarkable *Castle on a high ridge flanked by ramparts begun 1307), and with an imposing 15C keep. *S. Miguel* is ascribed to *J. de Ierrera; Sta María* has a 16C retablo, while the *Conv. de S. Pablo* (1324) is Mudéjar and Gothic Plateresque in style. The curious *Pl. del Cosa,* S. of the town, rrounded with shuttered wooden loggias, should not be overlooked.—22 km. Quintanilla de Onésima,* with a star-vaulted 16C hall-church, 17 km. N. of which is ne derelict 15C castle of *Villafuerte.*—6 km. E. of Quintanilla,on the N. bank at Valbuena,* is the imposing Cistercian abbey of **Santa María** (under restoration) ounded in 1190, with a splendid 13C and Renaissance cloister, and an impressive efectory with a pointed barrel vault.—Near *Sardón de Duero* lies the abbey of Retuerta (Premonstratensian; c. 1200), with a fine chapterhouse.—At 19 km. we ross the river at *Tudela de Duero,* with a hall-church of 1555, and 14 km. beyond nter **Valladolid,** see Rte 23.

The C. 111 leads 18 km. N.E. from Aranda to **Peñaranda de Duero** (1000 inhab.) ominated by a medieval square keep, with a 15C carved stone pillary opposite its . Gate. By the restored Pl. Mayor stands the impressive Renaissance *Pal. de los Condes de Miranda* (also restored) with Plateresque additions of c. 1530 by *Fr. de Colonia* or *Lorenzo Vázquez;* it is now a school, but adm. to the 17C Pharmacy hould be requested. The *Colegiata* is of 1732.—15 km. beyond lies the extensive rchaeological site of *Coruña del Conde,* preserving the name of Roman *Clunia,* vith a rock-cut theatre at *Peñalba del Castro,* 3 km. N.E. and a Castle.

FROM ARANDA TO SEGOVIA VIÂ TUREGANO (106 km.). Just S. of Aranda the C 003 bears S.W.—At 29 km. a by-road leads W. to (11 km.) *Sacramenia,* with— .3 km. E. of the village—the impressive remains of a Cistercian *Abbey* of c. 1200. ts cloister (13–15C) was acquired by William Randolph Hearst in 1925, and was ater rebuilt at Miami Beach.

Fuentidueña, 10 km. S., is dominated by a ruined castle and Romanesque hurch (restored), and retains a ruinous medieval gate. The church of *S. Martín* as been removed to New York—We continue S. through pinewoods viâ (20 km.) Cantalejo,* whence the Romanesque priory of *S. Frutos* (c. 1100; enlarged a entury later) lying some 18 km. N.W., may be approached over rough roads.— 15 km.) **Turégano** (1200 inhab.) with a Romanesque church and an interesting 5C *Castle* founded by Fernán González in the 10C, retaining the 13C church of *S. Miguel,* which fills most of its keep.—At *Aguilafuente,* 12 km. N.W., is a brick Romanesque church (restored), and castle, 2 km. S. of which, on the site of a Roman villa, an extensive Visigothic necropolis has been discovered.—16 km. Cantimpalos (r.) is renowned for its *chorizos.* On meeting the N 601 at 9 km., we urn l. for (9 km.) **Segovia,** see Rte 27.

FROM ARANDA TO SEGOVIA VIÂ SEPULVEDA (108 km.). 39 km. S. of Aranda we urn off the N 1 for (12 km.) **Sepúlveda,** the ancient *Septempublica,* still a omparatively unspoilt town (1800 inhab.) surmounting a craggy hill in a loop of he Rio Duratón. Its *fueros* dates from 1076. The Arco de la Villa, a survivor of the riginal seven town gates, was needlessly demolished only recently to allow a freer low of its slight traffic. At the W. end of the Pl. Mayor stands the old Ayuntamiento (restored), which will house a small museum. From the E. end of he plaza steps lead up to Romanesque *S. Bartolomé.* To the N. is *S. Justo,* with a Mudéjar artesonado ceiling, a Baroque retablo, and 12C carvings in the crypt; to the S. is ruined *Santiago*, with a brick apse and, over the later S. door, a statue of 1200. *El Salvador*, above the W. end of the town, dating from 1093, has a gallerie portico (perhaps the earliest of its type) and a detached belfry. To the N.W. is *N. de la Peña*, a sanctuary church with a Romanesque tympanum and a tower begu in 1144.

Shortly after leaving the town by the Segovia road we climb again in stee zigzags before turning sharp l. off the main road, with panoramic views of tʰ sierra ahead. We pass (11 km. l.) the castle of *Castilnovo*, of Moorish foundatio but largely rebuilt in the 15C.—At 11 km. a road leads E. 2 km. to **Pedraza de Sierra** *(Hosteria Nac.),* a picturesque walled village perched on an isolated h offering an extensive view of the Guadarrama range, and entered by a fortifie gateway, but its charm is in danger of over-exploitation. It preserves the *Castle* the Condestable de Velasco, in which the sons of Francis I were held hostage aft Pavia (with Ronsard's father as their majordomo), and later used as a studio ᵇ Zuloaga; two Romanesque churches (one in ruins), and a *Pl. Mayor* of gre character.—Regaining our road, we soon pass (l.) *N.S. de las Vegas* (Romanesqu before meeting (10 km.) the N 110 (see Rte 30, p. 342), off which, after passing ne (l.) the ruined priory of *Sta Maria de la Sierra* (c. 1200), at 6 km. (r.) lies *Sotosalba* with a fine Romanesque church. The road soon descends to (19 km.) **Segovia**, s Rte. 27.

From Aranda we continue on the NI S. towards the Sierra dᵉ Guadarrama, obtaining panoramic views as we approach the grea barrier range. At 53 km. the N 110 from Soria (see Rte 30, p.341) join our road, and 5 km. beyond bears r. for *Segovia*. We now commence tʰ improved climb to the **Pto. de Somosierra** (4757 ft; *Hotel*), scene of tʰ charge of Polish lancers (29 Nov. 1808) who scattered the Spaniard holding the pass, allowing Napoleon's troops to enter Madrid five day later. The road descends in sweeping curves into the Lozoya valley tᵉ (26 km.) **Buitrago**, an ancient walled and reservoir-moated village with 14C castle altered in the 15C by the Marqués de Santillana, and showin Mudéjar features, as does the 15C church and brick-built *Hospital.*—A 7 km. the C 604 leads r. up the valley to (26 km.) *Rascafria* and tʰ *Monastery of El Paular*, see p. 322.—At 2 km. we by-pass *Lozoyuela*

Hence the C 102 leads S.E. through (3 km.) *Sieteiglesias*, with the castle ᵈ *Mirabel*, and *El Berrueco*, with a stone pillory dated A.D. 1000 in its plaza.—⁄ (15 km.) **Torrelaguna**, the Roman *Barnacis*, with Moorish walls, Card. Cisnerᵉ (1436–1517) was born. The church has a good retablo, while among the mediev buildings are a Gothic *Ayuntamiento* and the Cardinal's *Granary (Pósito)* of 149 In a stalactite cave at *Patones*, to the N.E., are Aurignacian carvings; while ᵃ *Uceda*, 9 km. E., is the lovely but ruinous church of the *Virgen de la Varga* (c. 122ˢ 40).—10 km. *Talamanca* has early walls, a Roman bridge, and a medieval churc while there is a late Gothic church (1625) at (5 km.) *Valdetorres*, and interestiʳ examples at (7 km.) *Fuente el Saz* and (5 km.) *Algete*, 8 km. E. of the N I.

Just W. of (8 km.) *Cabrera (Hotel)*, is the ruined *Conv. de S. Antonic* and a rock-crystal grotto. The N I by-passes (18 km.) *El Molar*, with 13C church, before the autopista commences some 32 km. N. of Madric leaving on the r. *San Sebastián de los Reyes* (27,500 inhab.), with church of 1506 with a good timber ceiling, while at adjacent *Alcobenda* (50,250 inhab.)—now little more than a scruffy suburb of Madrid—is 16C church and Romanesque *Ermita*.

Madrid soon presents itself, in the words of Michael Quin, wh entered it from this direction 150 years ago, 'standing almost, lik Palmyra, in the midst of a desert . . . no shady groves, no avenues, n country seats, bespoke the approach of a great capital'.

Shortly, the N I veers off to the r. towards the N. suburb oᶠ *Fuencarral*, with a large church of 1654, but it is recommended to folloʷ the l.-hand road at this junction, from which we may turn off to meet tʰ Av. del Generalísimo N. of the Pl. de Castilla. The road continues S xtended by the Av. de la Paz (see Pl. on p. 254-5), which now virtually y-passes the centre, and a sharp lookout is necessary when attempting o follow directional signs. For **Madrid,** see Rte 24, and plan on p. 292-3.

B   Viâ Valladolid

otal distance, 311 km. (193 miles). N 620. (76 km. **Palencia** lies 10 km. W.).— 4 km. **Valladolid**—N 430. 110 km. *Villacastín*—81 km. **Madrid.**

Quitting Burgos by the N 620, we descend the valley of the Arlanzón, assing (19 km.) *Estépar,* with a fortified 13C church, 9 km. N.W. of hich, at *Iglesias,* is a small but finely proportioned hall-church.

At 12 km. a turning leads 11 km. S. to *Sta María del Campo,* a picturesque village 800 inhab.) retaining one of its battlemented gates. The church (15C) is dominated y a good Plateresque tower designed by *Diego de Siloée* and *Felipe Vigarni* (early 6C) and contains fine tombs and stallwork, and a parochial cross and plate in the acristy.—At *Villahoz,* 8 km. further S.E., the Isabelline parish church has a square anctuary, star vaulting and good W. and S. doors.

At 5 km. a road leads 2 km. S.E. to the unspoilt village of *Palenzuela,* ith the Plateresque hall-church of *S. Juan* with interesting retablos, a 5C *Hospital,* ruins of *Sta Eulalia* (13C), and the monastery of *S. rancisco.* There is a large late Gothic church at *Tabanera de Cerrato,* km. S.—6 km. *Villodrigo;* a pyramid marks the site of the monastery here King Wamba died (680), whence his remains were taken to oledo.—At 10 km. a crossroad leads l. through *Quintana del Puente,* ith an ancient bridge, to (4 km.) *Herrera de Valdecañas,* with a late-3C church.—Turning r. at this intersection, we reach (8 km.) *Valbuena e Pisuerga,* whose 18C church has a Churrigueresque high altar and a 5C panel-painting. Close by is *S. Cebrián de Buena Madre,* with a othic church, and a mansion with an imposing front and towers.—At *ordovilla la Real,* 5 km. W. of the main road, are a Plateresque church, bridge of 1778, and remains of the abbey of *S. Salvador del Moral.*— fter passing (r.) the confluence of the Arlanza and the Pisuerga, we each (13 km.) *Torquemada.* The Inquisitor-general Tomás de orquemada (1420–98) who was perhaps born here, restored *Sta ulalia;* also of interest are the 11C cemetery chapel and the old *Bridge* f 25 arches.

6 km. S.E. lies *Hornillos de Cerrato,* with a ruined castle and church containing a 2C Christ, on the road to (13 km.) *Baltanás,* with a church containing important reasures and the *Hosp. de Sto Tomás,* with a Baroque front.—12 km. beyond, on he C 619, at *Cevico Navero,* the Romanesque capitals and Trans. front of the hurch are noteworthy.—6 km. W. of Torquemada lies *Villamediana,* with 13C alls and good ironwork on the door of its Romanesque church, while 6 km. eyond, at *Valdeolmillos,* another Romanesque church treasures a processional ross.

10 km. *Magaz* has a ruined castle, and 4 km. E., *Reinoso de Cerrato* as remains of a castle and a Renaissance church containing a Gothic arving of the Virgin and St Anne, while *Villaviudos,* 4 km. beyond, has a Gothic church with a Churrigueresque altarpiece.—1 km. past Magaz he N 610 turns r. for **Palencia,** 10 km. W., see p. 364.

At 8 km. the road by-passes (l.) *Venta de Baños,* a railway junction *Hotel),* with, 1 km. E., the little Basilica of **S. Juan Bautista* (restored) t *Baños de Cerrato* (7100 inhab.), built by the Visigothic king Recceswinth in 661, largely of materials from the Roman temple of the ot springs which gave the place its name.

On the road to *Tariego*, (2 km. S.E.), is a medieval *Bridge* over the Pisuerga. The road continues to (9 km.) *Cevico*, beyond which lies *Vertavillo*, with a church consecrated in 1192, and *Castrillo de Onielo*, the Celtiberian *Arcilasis*, with Gothic church and old walls. From Cevico a road leads S.E. to (6 km.) *Alba d Cerrato*, with an enormous castle and a 15C church.

The N 620 passes (l.) the partly Romanesque church (with a rebuilt nave) of the *Conv. de S. Isidro*, known locally as *La Trapa*, founded in 911; the hill on the r. contains cave-dwellings. After crossing the Carrión we by-pass (7 km.) **Dueñas**, scene of the first meeting between Isabel of Castile and Fernando de Aragón only a few days before their marriage in 1469. In 13C *Sta María* are Isabelline wall-tombs, carved stalls, a 16C Gothic retablo and a processional cross.—At (16 km.) *Aguilarejo*, the priory (1213–54) of *Sta María de Palazuelos* contains Gothic tombs.— Nearby lies *Cabezón*, a village built into the flank of the barren Montaña de Altamira, with a ruined castle, and a bridge, near which Bessières defeated the Spaniards under Cuesta in 1808.—At *Cigales* (3 km. W. *Hotel*, on the main road), is a Renaissance hall-church by *Juan de Herrera*.—14 km. **Valladolid**, see Rte 23, p. 234

FROM VALLADOLID TO SEGOVIA viâ CUÉLLAR (111 km.). Leaving by the N 601 we pass (23 km.) *Arrabal del Portillo*, whose 16C church contains a retablo of 161: *Portillo*, close by, is dominated by the keep of its castle (14–15C).— 27 km *Cuéllar*, a shrunken town (8900 inhab.) with ancient walls and a fine castle (la 15C), under restoration, with a courtyard of 1558. Romanesque *S. Esteban* has brick apse with decorative arcading and contains Mudéjar tombs; *S. Martín* likewise Mudéjar Romanesque; *S. Andrés* contains a wooden calvary, while the door of the *Hosp. de María Magdalena* is also of interest. Cuéllar was the birthplace of Diego Velázquez de Cuéllar (1461/6–1524), the conquistador. W bear S. through pine-woods, with a wide view of the Guadarrama mountains as w approach them.—33 km. *Carbonero el Mayor*, where *S. Juan Bautista* contains retablo by disciples of Ambrosius Benson.—4 km. r. *Tabanera*, with a church containing a wooden calvary from El Paular(?).—At 24 km. we enter *Segovia*, se Rte 27, with a panoramic view of the town from the N.E. as we descend into the valley of the Eresma.

Leaving Valladolid by the N 403 we pass (5 km.) a modern Dominican convent and cross the rivers Duero, Cega, and Eresma at 4, 11, and 10 km. respectively.—At 13 km. (r.) lies **Olmedo** (3100 inhab.; *Hotel*) an old walled town of former importance: 'He who would be master of Castile must have Olmedo and Arévalo on his side'.

It also gave its name to Lope de Vega's famous tragedy. 'El Caballero d Olmedo' (1641), among others. It was in the venta here that Gautier was s astonished to see a handsome girl suckling a puppy: she was a *Pasiega* (from the valley of the Rio Pas, S. of Santander) going to Madrid, as did many women from this region, to take up a situation as a wet-nurse, and was afraid that her supply c milk might otherwise run dry!

13C Mudéjar *S. Andrés* has a restored retablo, the first important work by *Alonso Berruguete* (1514). Protruding from the town walls, is *S. Miguel*, also 13C, built over a crypt; it contains some attractive painted ceilings. *Sta María* preserves a Romanesque doorway, a retablo of 1550, and a curious reliquary retablo of 49 compartments. To the N.W. lies the *Conv. de la Mejorada*, with a somewhat derelict late-15C Mudéjar chapel.—At *Iscar*, 16 km. N.E. on the road to Cuéllar, are a castle-keep and a Mudéjar brick church.

FROM OLMEDO TO SEGOVIA (63 km.) We follow a road S.E. to (15 km) **Coca** (2100 inhab.) ancient *Cauca*, an Iberian town sacked by the Romans in 180 after characteristically obstinate siege. The *Arco de la Villa* is the main relic of it medieval walls. The imposing ***Castle** (restored) of mampostería and pink brick with typical clustered bartizan turrets, and defended by a deep dry moat, was built the early 15C and belonged to the powerful Fonseca family, dukes of Alba. It now contains a Forestry Commission School. In *Sta María,* remarkable for its 14-ded sanctuary, are four 16C tombs of the Fonsecas, by *Bart. Ordóñez,* the finest eing that of Bp. Juan Rodríguez de Fonseca.—Continuing S.E. we reach (17 km.) a María la Reál de Nieva. In the Gothic *Cloister of Sta María le Real,* founded by atherine of Lancaster in 1393. Enrique IV convened the Cortes of 1473 in which e rescinded the popular privileges granted during the previous ten years.—We ow follow the C 605, off which (at 4 km.) a road bears r. 4 km. to *Paradinas,* with a te-Gothic hall-church.—At 19 km. the road forks. Both roads lead to (8 km.) egovia: that to the l. passes the *Sanctuary of Fuencisla,* beyond which we may ither turn r. at the first bridge and circle S. of the town, obtaining a fine view of the row of the Alcazar, or crossing the second bridge, follow the wooded Ronda de ta Lucía towards the Aqueduct. Bearing r. at the junction, we soon meet the N 110 om Ávila, and turning E. enter **Segovia,** see Rte 27.

8 km. *Almenara de Adaja* lies to the r. where a Roman villa with rich iosaics has been excavated.—At 12 km. a road leads 13 km. S.W. to *révalo,* see p. 353.—13 km. *Martín Muñoz de las Posadas* has a palace uilt in 1566–72 by *J. B. de Toledo* for the Inquisitor Diego de Espinosa, hose tomb is in the church.

At 7 km. the N 403 bears r. for *Ávila,* 41 km. S., through a region of ilex groves, nd at (29 km.), *Mingorria,* a district strewn with granite boulders. We enjoy a fine iew of the walls of *Ávila* as we approach the town, see p. 329.

At (3 km.) *Adanero,* we join the N VI (Madrid to La Coruña), or the utopista under construction.—5 km. *Sanchidrián* has a church by *Juan e Herrera* and a late 18C fountain.—At 19 km. we by-pass **Villacastín** (700 inhab.; *Albergue Nac.*) with old granite houses, an *Ayuntamiento* f 1687, *S. Esteban,* an imposing hall-church begun in 1529 with a fine etablo mayor, interesting tombs, a 16C organ, and a pulpit of 1596; the *urisima chapel* has a good reja and a carved retablo of 1608.

Beyond Villacastín the road is described in reverse in Rte 28. The utopista may be joined at 21 km., which by-passes *San Rafael* and iortly enters the Guadarrama tunnel. Approaching **Madrid** from the .W. we enter the capital (see Rte 24) at the Pta. de Hierro and pass irough the University City.

22   FROM BURGOS TO SORIA, AND DAROCA FOR TERUEL

otal distance, 274 km. (170 miles). N 1 9 km. N 234(60 km. *Sto Domingo de Silos* es 19 km. W.)—84 km. **Soria**—91 km. **Calatayúd**—39 km. **Daroca.** Teruel lies 9 km. beyond.

We follow the N1 S., and at 9 km. fork l. onto the N 234, passing *arracin,* close to the Italiante *Pal. of Saldañuela* (1520–30) which icorporates a medieval tower, and *Olmos Albos,* with a castle, and a hurch containing embossed leather-work.

After c. 11 km. some 2 km. beyond *Hontoria de la Cantera,* there is an nmarked track to the l. as the road again descends, which leads 3 km. E. o approach the ruined monastery of *S. Quirce,* preserving two sets of iteresting carved panels, and well-carved Romanesque capitals in its iterior.

Some 7 km. beyond this turning is *Cuevas de San Clemente,* where by earing r. we gain the direct road to (12 km.) *Covarrubias,* see below, but is preferable to remain on the main road for another 7 km. in order to isit the important Visigothic chapel of *N.S. de las Viñas,* some 4 km.

E., just beyond the village of *Quintanilla de las Viñas* (first collecting th
guide and key in the village). Only a square apse and transepts remain o
what was once a three-naved building blending Asturian and Mozarabi
styles, and which may date from as early as the 7C, even if certain carve
stones are dated from the early 10C. Of particular interest are th
horizontal bands of carving on the exterior, the horseshoe arch of th
sanctuary, its imposts resting on Roman columns and carved wit
angels supporting the moon (l.) and sun. Other Visigothic reliefs are als
preserved here.—Further E. on a height, are the remains of a Celtiberia
settlement, and to the S.E. the ruins of a castle of Fernán González, an
near *Campolara,* the remains of an Ibero-Roman city. Anothe
Celtiberian fortress has been discovered in the Sierra de las Mamblas, t
the W. of the main road, to which we return, and turn l.

7 km. *Hortigüela.* Hence the more interesting road to *Covarrubia*
leads W. along the beautiful valley of the Arlanza, shortly passing th
extensive and impressive ruins of the monastery of *S. Pedro d
Arlanza,* the original resting place of Fernán González, begun in 108
but largely rebuilt in the 15C. The fortified tower is well-preserved, an
may be ascended. Note the shields high up at each corner. There is
project to remove carvings and parts of the building to a higher site, wit
the construction of a reservoir further E., the waters of which may cove
the ruins.—Continuing up the valley we reach **Covarrubias,** 13 km. fro
the main road. This attractive if somewhat over-restored village (80
inhab.; *Hotel*), retains a gatehouse of 1575, an unusual *Tower* (10C
showing considerable batter, in which Doña Urraca was imprisoned b
Fernán González, and remains of walls. The *Colegiata* (14–15C
containing a large number of well-carved tombs, among them those c
Fernán González (to the l. of the high altar), moved here from S. Pedr
de Arlanza in 1841 (see above), and of his wife, opposite; also of intere
is the tomb of Christina of Norway (d. 1262). who had been married f
four years to Philip, son of Fernando III. The beautiful 17C orga
containing some wooden pipes, has been recently restored. The Cloiste
is 16C. Also to be seen in the museum is a painted and carved triptyc
attrib. to *Gil de Siloée* and what is thought to be an old Flemish copy of
lost Virgin and Child by *Van Eyck,* apart from MSS and vestment
etc.—To the N. of the village stands *Sto Tomás* (15C), und
restoration.

Lerma (see p. 226) lies 22 km. to the W.

From Covarrubias we turn S. across the Arlanza and climb pa
(14 km.) *Santibáñez,* near which are the 10 or 11C chapels of *Sta Cecil*
and *S. Pedro de Tejada,* 4 km. beyond which we reach the village an
*Monastery of Sto Domingo de Silos (reoccupied since 1881), famou
for its beautiful two-storeyed Romanesque cloister and for its school c
Gregorian chant.

Founded by Fernán González in 919 and originally dedicated to S
Sebastian, the convent, sacked by Almanzor, was rebuilt in 1042 b
Domingo, a monk from Cogolla, who became its parton saint (not to b
confused with Sto Domingo de Guzman; see below).

Tickets are obtained at the main entrance (car park), from which w
walk round to the entrance of the 18C church by *Ventura Rodrígue*
replacing a Mozarabic church, and of little interest. Hence we descen
through a Romanesque doorway, a relic of the latter, and are escorte

do not be hurried) round the lower gallery of the *Cloister (c. 1150) with ts single secular cypress. The columns and capitals, of varying and laborate design (some worn) deserve close inspection, as do the corner ilasters decorated with reliefs recalling those at Moissac, near Toulouse. Note also the 14C painted Mudéjar ceilings (in part restored). The upper storey was added in the late 12C. We are shown a vault at a lower level containing a *Museum,* with a painted Guzmán tomb, a Mozarabic silver chalice, ivory perfume cases, and a 12C copper retablo, tc.; also a rather nasty replica of the enamel frontal in the Burgos Museum. The old *Pharmacy* is of some interest.

Travellers wishing to regain the N I may drive S.W. through an impressive gorge iâ (19km.) *Caleruega,* birthplace of Sto Domingo de Guzman (1170–1221), ounder of the Dominican Order, to (24km.) *Aranda,* see p. 227, or alternatively, ›n the C 111 from a point 13km. S. of *Silos,* viâ *Coruña del Conde* and *Peñeranda de Duero,* see p. 227. We may regain the N 234 19km. E., and 5km. S. of *Salas de os Infantes,* see below.

Driving E. also through an imposing gorge, we regain the N 234 after 9km., some 5km. S. of *Salas de los Infantes,* itself 13km. S.E. of Hortigüela (see p. 232). A l.-hand turning between the two leads 11km. N.E. to *Vizcainos,* which with adjacent *Jaramillo de la Fuente,* preserve 2C churches of some interest.

Salas was famous for the legend of the seven Infantes de Lara, killed by the Moors in 970; the tomb of their father, Gonzalo Bustos, is in the hall-church of *Sta Maria* (1549). For the road hence to *Nájera,* see p. 117 in reverse.

After 13km. (or 8km. from the Silos road) a r.-hand turning leads S.W. through pine-woods to (13km.) *Huerta del Rey,* and beyond to Coruña del Conde and Peñeranda del Duero: see p. 227.—22km. *San Leonardo de Yague,* with a 16C castle.—Hence an attractive road, with wide views, leads S. to (19km.) *Ucero* (p.341) and *El Burgo de Osma* (p.340) 16km. beyond.

The N 234 bears E., through pine-woods leaving the Sierra de Urbión to the N. After passing the Pto. Mojón Pardo we descend to (28km.) Abejar with a good 18C organ in its church, the key of which is retained n Madrid! 10km. N. lies *Molinos de Duero,* with ancient houses. Vinuesa, 4km. further N. and also on the Pantano de la Cuerda del Pozo, contains a 16C council house and other mansions. Molinos may lso be approached by a direct road running E. from Salas, which at Duruelo de la Sierra, passes only a few kms. S. of the source of the Duero.—To the S. rises the Peñon de Acenilla, and the abrupt Pico Frentes. At 18km. a turning leads N. 9km. to *Hinajosa de la Sierra,* with he *Hurtado de Mendoza Palace.*—At 5km., a road leads r. 2km. to *La Mongia,* with a Romanesque church, part of a ruined monastery.— 5km. *Soria,* see Rte 29, p. 334.

An alternative road from Soria to Teruel (for Valencia) is that viâ Medinaceli and Molina de Aragón, described on p. 337 as far as (76km.) *Medinaceli,* where we cross the N II, bearing S.E. to (26km.) *Maranchón,* and (8km.) *Mazarete,* with a monolith known as 'El Huso' (the spindle), 23km. S.W. of which, at *Riba de Saelices,* is a Romanesque church-door, near which the *Cueva de los Casares* contains prehistoric engravings.—29km. **Molina de Aragón,** an ancient town (3950 inhab.), incorporated with Castile in 1293 by the marriage of its lady Doña Blanca, with Sancho IV. It preserves it 12–13C *Castle,* with tall square towers and an extensive curtain wall, a medieval bridge, and notable churches: *S. Martín* is of the 12C, as are the ruins of *Sta Maria del Conde; Sta Clara* is Trans.; *S. Francisco* dates from 1284; while in *S. Gil* is the tomb of Doña Blanca.—In a wild gorge c. 12km. W. is the sanctuary of *N.S. de la Hoz* (1130).

11km. *Castellar* has a Churrigueresque church and an interesting Romanesqu
chapel (La Carrasca).—At 11km. a road leads directly S.E. for 68km. t
Albarracín (p. 206), viâ (28km.) *Alustante*, where the fine church dates from 140C
and (8km. r.) *Orihuela de Tremedal*, nestling among the pinewoods of the Sierr
de Albarracín (6090 ft).—9km. to the S.E. lies *Bronchales*, a small spa. To th
S.W. rise the peaks of the MONTES UNIVERSALES (5540 ft), so called from being th
source of rivers which water almost every part of Spain, including the Tagus, th
Turia, and tributaries of the Ebro.— The N 211 goes on over the Sierra Mener
and descends to (26km.) *Monreal del Campo*, see p. 206. Here we meet the N 33
and turn r. for (56km.) **Teruel**, see Rte 18A.

Driving E. From Soria we shortly bear r. (still on the N 234) and
traverse a poor wind-swept region overshadowed by the mass of the
Moncayo to the N.E. (7600 ft, see p. 120), passing (75km.) *Cervera de la
Cañada*, where Gothic Mudéjar *Sta Tecla* was built by Maestre
Mahoma Ramé (1424–26), and (5km. l.) *Torralba de Ribota*, with *S.
Félix,* in the same style, begun in 1367.—11km. **Calatayúd,** see p.211

Beyond, the N 234 ascends the verdant valley of the Jiloca, thickly
planted with orchards, to (8km.) **Maluenda,** with the important
Mudéjar church of *SS. Justa y Rufina* (c. 1413), and *Sta María*, with a
Mudéjar tower and rebuilt nave.—At 5km., r. *Morata de Jiloca,*
Mudéjar *S. Martín* (14C) has unusual vaults, while at 5km., *Fuentes de
Jiloca,* is a good hall-church of 1580.—21km. *Daroca*, see Rte 18A, and
for the road continuing S.E. to (99km.) Teruel and Valencia.

23   VALLADOLID

VALLADOLID, whose name has been derived from the Arabic
Belad-Walid (land of the governor), lies on a plain (2100 ft) at the
confluence of the Esgueva with the Pisuerga. The city (286,000 inhab.; c
21,000 in 1800; 76,000 in 1920; 151,000 in 1960; *Hotels*) of growing
industrial importance, is also the centre of the Castilian corn trade. The
town is distinctly modern in appearance, but contains some fine old
buildings, and a wealth of 16C sculpture.

The layout of Valladolid may confuse the visitor at first, containing as
it does a number of buildings of secondary interest spread out over a
large area, and still gives the impression of being 'a large rambling city. .
run up in a hurry', to quote Swinburne, who passed through in June
1776. Likewise, great care must be taken on making one's exit from the
city, the sign-posting of which is exceptionally bad.

History. A favourite seat of the Castilian kings from the 12C, it was not unt
after the conquest of Granada that Valladolid temporarily supplanted Burgos a
the official capital, and here Columbus died in 1506. But in 1560, Philip I
although born here, finally established the court at Madrid. A brief renewal c
importance under Philip III (1601–21) ended with the accession of Philip IV an
the confirmation of Madrid as 'the only court'. It suffered severely at the hands c
the French in the Peninsular War, when many of the finest buildings were strippe
of their treasures.
Among its natives (or Valisoletanos) were Panfilo de Narváez (1478–1529
explorer of Florida and the lower Mississippi; Hernando de Acuña (1520–80), th
soldier-poet; Valentín Llanos Gutiérrez (1795–1885; author of novels written i
England, where he was exiled, and married Fanny Keats); José Zorrilla (1817–93
the poet and playwright; and the exiled poet Jorge Guillén (1893).

From the N 620, by-passing it to the W., we may cross the Pte. Mayor
to the W. of which is the early 17C church of *La Victoria* by *Fr. de*

Praves. The road then skirts the E. bank of the Pisuerga before bearing S.E. towards the Campo Grande, at the N. end of which the Pl. de Zorilla is a focal point for traffic. Hence we may regain the N 620 (for Salamanca), see Rte 31. p. 343, or join the N 403 for *Madrid*, see pp. 230-1. For the road to *Segovia* viâ *Cuéllar*, see p. 230.

From the Paseo de Isabel la Católica we may turn l. along the C. de S. Quirce, passing the *Pal. de los Condes de Benavente* (1518), once a royal residence, and close by, on the N. of the Pl. de la Trinidad, the massive church of *S. Nicolás*, begun in 1624 by *Marcos de Garay* and containing a sacristy with early 18C Churrigueresque fittings. A little to the S. stands the *Conv. de Sta Catalina*, where Juan de Juni is buried; mainly of the 16C, the interior has a Christ by *G. Fernández*, another by *Juni*, and fine Renaissance doors and ceilings. Nearby stands the *Monasterio de S. Agustín*, founded 1407, and transformed in 1619-25 by *Diego de Praves*. On the E. side of the Plaza is the *Monasterio de S. Quirce*, begun by *Fr. de Praves* in 1620, and with late-17C retablos.—Further N. lies the *Conv. de Sta Teresa*, founded by the saint herself in 1569; the retablo mayor by *Crist. Veláquez*, has sculptures by *Greg. Fernández*.—The C. de Exposito leads S. to the **Casa de Fabio Nelli** named after its owner, the Maecenas of Valladolid (d. c. 1612); its two-storeyed portal and Corinthian court are imposing; the patio and staircase were begun by *Fr. de la Maza* in 1582, the front by *Pedro Mazuelos* in 1594. The chapel of the *Puríşma Concepción*, has a good late-16C retablo. The building now houses the *Archaeological Museum.*

Among the items displayed are: Oriental textiles from the tomb of Alfonso, son of Sancho IV; Panels from the retablo of S. Benito el Real (c. 1420); Ceramics from the Bronze Age; Renaissance azulejos from the Palace, by *Hernando de Loaysa*; and Wall-paintings from *S. Pablo*, Peñafiel (early 14C).

Opposite is the *Pal. Valverde* (1503, altered 1763) and the old *Casa Fernández de Muras*. Nearby *S. Miguel* was designed by *Diego de Praves*, and contains a retablo (1595) by *Adrián Álvarez*, with sculptures by *Fr. del Rincón* and *Greg. Fernández*, and tombs of the Counts of Fuensaldaña.—We follow the C. Fabio Nelli to the Pl. de Sta Brigada, where the *Conv. de la Brigadas* (1637–95) includes remains of the *Pal. de Butrón* (c. 1570).

Nearby is *S. Pablo, partly rebuilt by *Juan de Torquemada* (1463) and continued in 1601–17 by the Card.-Duke of Lerma, whose arms are seen on the upper part of the *Façade,* above the Gothic portal of 1486-92. In the convent attached, the inquisitor Tomás de Torquemada (nephew of Juan) took the Dominican habit. The interior, restored since it was ruined by the French in 1809, contains tombs by *Berruguete* and *Leoni,* and two handsome transeptal doorways, transitional between Gothic and Plateresque.

Facing S. Pablo is the *Pal. Real,* built by the Marqués de Camarara in the mid-16C, with a patio by *Juan de Aquiles* and *Alejandro Mayner.* The palace was bought in 1600 by Lerma, who sold it to Philip III. It was Napoleon's residence in 1809, and is now the *Capitanía General.* The galleries of the dignified patio are adorned with busts of Roman emperors (? by Berruguete) and the arms of the provinces of Spain.

Beyond S. Pablo is the *Col. de S. Gregorio, founded in 1480 by Fray Alonso de Burgos but completed only in 1496. On the splendid façade, rich in heraldic ornament, is an elaborate portal flanked by *maceros,* or mace-bearing wild hairy men, which runs up into an armorial tree. In the first court is a window with stucco decoration in the Moorish style; in the second is a rich Plateresque gallery surmounted by a frieze bearing the arrows and ox-yoke of the Catholic kings.

The buildings now house the *Museo Nac. de Escultura Religiosa, an important collection of cloyingly realistic Castilian sculpture from the 13th to the 18C, originally formed between 1828–35. Adm. during the morning only.

On the r. of the entrance hall (with local paintings of the 16–17C) are RR I-II containing what remains of the colossal Retablo carved by *Alonso Berruguete* in 1527–32 for S. Benito el Real.—R IV *Greg. Fernández* (1566–1636); *Pieda* (1617), polychromed by *Fr.* and *Marcelo Martínez*; the Magdalen; Baptism; Sta Teresa (1627), etc.; also the sculptor's portrait by *Diego Valentín Díaz.*—R V *Greg. Fernández*, a recumbent Christ; attrib. to *Mena.* St Francis.—We ascend the stair to R VI. attr. to *Jorge Inglés*, Retablo of St Jerome; *Nuño Gonçalves*, Apostles: and other primitives.—R VIII *Adrián Álvarez* and *Pedro de Torres*, Remains of a retablo for S. Benito (1596–1601); St Mark; recumbent figure of Justice.—R IX *Pedro de la Cuadra*, Sculptures from a retablo (1597) of the Conv. de la Merced Calzada. R X *Alonso de Villabrille*, Head of St Peter (1707); bust of Bl. Mariana de Jesús; etc.—RR XI-XIV, minor 16–18C works; the first room has a good 18C artesonado ceiling.—R XV *Greg. Fernández*, St Peter enthroned, from Abrojo.— R. XVI *Pompeo Leoni*, Fragments of a retablo from S. Diego (1665).—R XVI Paso de los Durmientes by *Alonso de Rozas* (1679) and Angels by *José de Rozas* (1696).—R XVIII Flemish retablo (late 15C) from the Conv. de S. Francisco; small altarpiece, Adoration (1446).—R XIX *Gasp. de Tordesillas*, another fragmentary retablo from S. Benito.—R XX *Andrés de Nájera*, Stalls from S. Benito, with details by *Diego de Siloée* and *Guillén de Holanda.*—R XXI *Juan de Juni* (fl. 1550 -80), Entombment; Reliquary bust of St Anne; St Anthony of Padua; St John the Baptist.—The Pasos carried in Holy Week, some by *Greg. Fernández* (1614) are not now on show.—In the garden are some rebuilt arches from the Romanesque cloister of S. Agustín.

To the l. of the entrance is the **Chapel** (1487–88), by *Juan Guas*, with fine lierne vaults and carved bosses, containing a Renaissance Retablo (coarsely retouched) carved by *Berruguete* in 1525–26 for the monastery of La Mejorada (Olmedo), the master's first recorded work. In the presbytery are kneeling statues of gilt bronze by *Juan de Arfe* after *Pompeo Leoni* (1602–8).

Here are also: a Crucifixion by *Antonio Moro;* the Tomb of Bp. Diego de Avellaneda by *Felipe Vigarni;* and (in the antechapel) Death, once attr. to *Gaspar Becerra*, but probably not Spanish; an Annunciation (1596), painted by *Greg. Martínez* for Fabio Nelli's chapel in S. Agustín; and colossal statues of Sta Mónica and Sta Clara de Montefalco (17C). In the raised choir are Baroque Stalls from S. Francisco, finished in 1735 by *Pedro Sierra*.

Further along the C. de S. Gregorio stands the *Casa del Sol*, with a fine doorway of 1540, once the residence of the Conde de Gondomar, ambassador to the court of James I of England, and now a convent, with the church of *S. Benito el Viejo* (1583–99).

We may follow a street S.E. to the *Audiencia*, on the site of the Palace of the Viveros, where Fernando and Isabel were married in Oct. 1469. The present building is mainly of 1562 but contains a late-15C patio, and a Christ by *Bartolomé de Cárdenas* (1624). Also exhibited are some illuminated grants of arms from the Archivo de la Real Chancillería.
To the E., lies the old *Prison*, an early-17C building in the style of Herrera, and beyond is *S. Pedro*, by *Rodrigo Gil de Hontañón*, with a retablo mayor of 1788. Opposite the *Audiencia*, the *Conv. de Descalzas Franciscas* (c. 1600–15), begun at the expense of Margaret of Austria, has retablos by *Juan de Muniátegui.* Also in the N.E. quarter are the *Conv. de Sta. Clara*, with buildings of 1489–95 (church transformed within in 1747); and 17C *El Carmen.*

Opposite S. Gregorio is the *Casa del Marqués de Villena*, now the *Gobierno Civil*, a mid-16C mansion with an Ionic patio; while across the C. Fray Luís de Granada is the *Casa de Zorrilla*, now the *Ateneo*, with mementoes of the poet. At the S.E. corner of the plaza is a house of

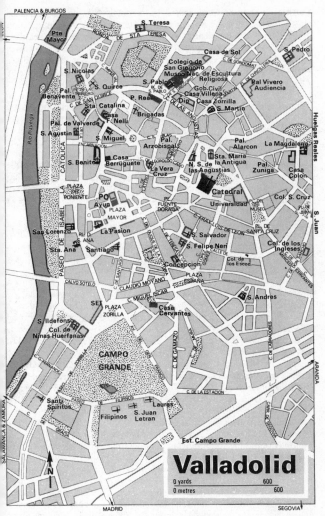

PALENCIA & BURGOS

MADRID   SEGOVIA

Valladolid

0 yards   600

0 metres   600

c. 1500 (now the *Diputación*), where Philip II was born in 1527.—We
follow the C. de las Angustias, noting on the l. in a side street, the early-
13C tower of *S. Martín.* The church was rebuilt by *F. de Praves* before
1621 and contains a retablo by *Pedro Gutiérrez* (1672); a group by *Greg.
Fernández;* and (in the sacristy) a Piedad by *Juan de Juni.* At the corner
of the C. S. Martín is the house where the irascible painter Alonso Cano
is said to have killed his wife. The neighbouring *Hosp. de Esgueva*
preserves a polychrome Mudéjar ceiling and a 14C Annunciation.

Further on, opposite the *Teatro Calderón*, is **N.S. de las Angustias** (1597–1604) by *Juan de Nates*, a pupil of Herrera, with an Annunciation of 1602–05 over the high altar by *Cristóbal Velázquez* and the theatrical 'Virgen de los Cuchillos' by *Juan de Juni*, so called from the seven knives (symbolizing the Seven Sorrows) which pierce her breast. Other sculptures are by *Greg. Fernández*, while the statues on the front are by *Fr. del Rincón* (1605).

To the W. lies the handsome *Pal. Arzobispal*, formerly the *Casa de Villasantes* (mid-16C), in the C. del Rosario, with a chapel containing a Retablo of c. 1500. The street takes its name from the former *Hosp. del Rosario*, of which the patio, begun in 1604 by *Juan de Nates*, survives in the *Casa Sacerdotal*. In the C. de Leopoldo Cano (r.), at the angle of the Rúa Oscura, is *La Vera Cruz*, begun by *Diego de Praves* in 1595 and showing Baroque motives; it was altered by *Juan Tejedor* in 1667–81. Within are sculptures by *Greg. Fernández* (the Dolorosa of the retablo mayor, and a Descent from the Cross, 1623), and *Alonso Manzano* (Christ at the Column, in a Baroque retablo of 1693). The C. de la Platería leads to the Pl. Mayor.

Not far E. of N.S. de las Angustias stands early-14C Gothic **Sta Maria la Antigua**, with three parallel apses and a campanile (early 13C), Lombard in form, but with northern mouldings. The retablo of the high altar is an exaggerated work by *Juan de Juni* (1556). To the N. is a Romanesque Cloister (restored).

From behind the church, the C. Don Juan Membrillo, containing a number of old mansions, leads E., and bearing l. we soon reach *La Magdalena*, designed by *Rodrigo Gil de Hontañón* (1566), with a huge coat of arms on its façade, and with a retablo mayor (1571–75) by *Esteban Jordán*; the *Cap. de los Corrales* (1538–47) by *Juan de la Cabañuela* has a Renaissance reja, and a retablo by *Fr. Giralte* (c. 1547). Beyond is the Prado de la Magdalena, with the *Hosp. Provincial*, the chapel of which contains a Resurrection by *Pantoja de la Cruz* (1609). Behind are the *Seminario Conciliar* and the *Conv. de Jesús y María*, both with interesting retablos. To the E. are remains of the Mudéjar *Pal. de Doña María de Molina*, next to the *Conv. de las Huelgas*, with a church of 1579–1600 (by *Mateo de Elorriaga* and *Juan de Nates*) containing the late-14C tomb of María de Molina and a retablo of 1613–16 by *Greg. Fernández*. The C. de Colón, with the restored *Casa de Colón* (Columbus) containing an apology for a museum, leads S.W. to the restored **Col. de Santa Cruz,** begun in 1487 in Gothic style by *Pedro Polido* and finished in 1491 by *Lor. Vázquez de Segovia* in the Plateresque style—the earliest Renaissance work in Spain. The windows of 1768 are insertions by *Ventura Rodríguez*. A group of the founder, Card. Pedro González de Mendoza, surmounts the entrance, beneath which (r.) is the chapel containing the Cristo de la Luz, by *Greg. Fernández,* and a Mater Dolorosa, by *Pedro de Mena*. The first floor is occupied by the *University Library*, with 18C shelving, and contains an illuminated MS. of Beatus (970).

To the S.E. beyond the Pl. de S. Juan, stands *S. Juan*, with Baroque retablos and late-17C paintings, while in the nearby C. de Don Sancho is the **Col. de los Ingleses,** or *de S. Albano*, a red brick building by Sir Francis Englefield who retired to Spain in 1559, and (at the instance of the Jesuit Robert Parsons) endowed with many privileges by Philip II in 1590 as a seminary for English priests who were to reconvert their country. The cloisters, by *Ant. López*, were building in 1614, but most of the rest was executed by *Pedro Bibanco* in 1671–80, to the designs of the Jesuit *Manuel de Calatayúd* and *Pedro Matos*.

From the Pl. de Santa Cruz we turn N., passing on our l. the *University* (17C) with a façade by *Narciso* and *Diego Tomé* (1715) embellished by statues of the sciences. Founded in the mid-14C, the University attained its greatest influence in the 16–18Cs.

To the N.W. rises the **Cathedral** begun by *Juan de Herrera* in 1580, but left unfinished at the death of Philip II (1598). Of the four projected towers the only one completed fell in 1841, but was rebuilt in 1880–85; and the rest of the exterior was unsuccessfully remodelled by *Alberto Churriguera* (1729). A model of Herrera's original design may be seen among the cathedral archives.

In the plain interior are some inlaid stalls, designed by *Herrera* for the Conv. de S. Pablo, and the tomb (end of N. aisle) of Count Pedro Ansúrez (d. 1119). The 3rd S. chapel contains 17C statues of the Veneros, the 4th has a reja of 1765; at the end of the aisle is a Transfiguration by *Luca Giordano*. The *Retablo Mayor* is by *Juan de Juni* (1551). In the sacristy is a silver **Custodia*, the masterpiece of *Juan de Arfe* (1590).—The gardens contain remains of *Sta Maria la Mayor* (12–14C).

From the Cathedral we may make our way S.W. viâ the *Pl. de Fuente Dorada* to the PL. MAYOR, rebuilt after a great fire in 1561, where spectacles, executions, and bull-fights used to take place.

In this square Berenguela abdicated in favour of her son, Fernando III, in 1217; here, Charles V formally pardoned the Comuneros in 1521; and here in 1559 Philip II held the first of many memorable *autos de fé*. Just N., to the r. of the *Ayuntamiento*, is the site of the Ochavo (octagon) where in 1452 Álavaro de Luna, the minister of Juan II, was beheaded, after 30 years of virtual dictatorship. Behind is the church of *Jesús* (1664–70). The *Caballo de Troya* inn (remodelled), where George Borrow put up, stands in the C. de Correos. The *Conv. de S. Benito*, beyond the N.E. corner of the plaza, founded in 1389, has a cloister of c. 1600 by *Juan Ribero Rada*, while the church by *Juan de Arandia* (1499–1504) has a porch by *Rodrigo Gil de Hontañón* (1569–72) and reja by *Juan Tomás Celma* (1571). Opposite is the 16C *Casa Alonso Berruguete*, and in the C. de la Encarnación, just to the N., is the *Conv. de Sta Isabel*, where the mid-16C church has Gothic vaulting, and contains a retablo mayor by *Fr. Velázquez* (1613–14) with a relief by *Greg. Fernández*, and another retablo of St Francis by *Juan de Juni*.

From the Pl. de Fuente Dorada, the C. de Teresa Gil leads S. past *S. Felipe Neri* (1658–75), with a retablo mayor of 1689 and Churrigueresque chapels containing *pasos*.—The *Conv. de la Concepción* (1521), opposite, has a fine retablo mayor and a pierced gesso screen to its raised choir. The street passes the 15C *Casa de las Aldabas*, birthplace in 1425 of Enrique IV of Castile, who later gave the house the right of sanctuary (whence its name, *aldabas*, door-knockers).—Further on is the *Conv. de Porta Coeli* (1598–1614), with paintings by *Horacio Borgiani* and statues of the Calderón family.

Behind S. Felipe Neri is *El Salvador*, completed in 1576 by *Juan Sanz*, with a brick tower (1618) by *Bart. de la Calzada*, and, in the late-15C chapel of S. Juan Bautista, a carved Flemish Altarpiece with wings painted by a pupil of Quentin Massys, presented in 1501.

The C. del Salvador leads to the *Col. de los Escoceses*, founded at Madrid by Col. William Semple in 1627 and transferred here in 1771, but of the original buildings only the Baroque façade survived a fire in 1929. Beyond it is the *Santuario Nac. de la Gran Promesa*, built early in the 17C as the church of the Col. de S. Ambrosio. It contains the Cristo de Burgos (1570), by *Est. Jordán*, a retablo of 1627, altarpieces by *Berruguete*, etc. To the N., at C. de Fray Luis de León 21, is the *Casa Escudero Herrera*, with a front of c. 1530. S. of the Santuario, in the C. de la Manteria, is *S. Andrés*, with a retablo mayor of 1741–42 by *Pedro Correas*.

At the S. end of the C. de Teresa Gil is the Pl. de España, off which the C. Miguel Iscar leads W., passing the *Conv. de Capuchinos*, with a retablo of 1610 in its simple church. On the l., beyond a garden, is the *Casa de Cervantes*, occupied by the author of 'Don Quixote' in 1605, and containing a small museum. In the garden is a 16C fountain, and at the side a rebuilt fragment of the Hospicio de la Resurrección, frequently mentioned by Cervantes.—We shortly reach the Pl. de Zorilla at the N. apex of the CAMPO GRANDE, the large and attractive gardens occupying the site where in 1809 Napoleon reviewed his Peninsular army of 35,000 men.

Within the garden are remains of the 12C cloister of the Templars of Ceinos de Campos, while on the S. side are the *Conv. de las Lauras*, with a chapel of 1606; the *Conv. de S. Juan Letrán*, a Baroque work of 1675–1739, by *Lozano;* and the *Col. de Agustinos* (1759), by *Ventura Rodríguez*, with a museum of the Philippine mission.
S.W. of the Pl. de Zorilla stands the *Cavalry Academy*, and beyond, the *Col. de Niñas Huérfanas* (1621–29), by *Sancho de la Riva* and *Fr. de la Peña*, containing paintings by *Diego Valentín Díaz;* nearby is *S. Ildefonso* (1618), by *Fr. de Praves*, and the *Conv. de Sancti Spiritus* (1520), with a reja of 1582 by *Álvaro de la Peña* and retablo mayor by *Est. Jordán*. Juan de Juni (d. 1586), the sculptor, and, later, his fellow artist, Greg. Fernández (1566–1636), lived and died at C. Greg. Fernández 39, which leads from the W. side of the Campo Grande.

From the Pl. de Zorilla the C. de Santiago leads back to the Pl. Mayor, passing the *Col. de Dominicas Francesas*, with a patio of 1506–47 and church of 1730, and *Santiago* (1490–1505) by *Juan de Arandia*, with a good tower and a small retablo by *Berruguete*.

To the W. of the Pl. Mayor is *La Pasión*, a Baroque church of 1666–71, restored to house a *Museum of Sacred Art* containing works by *Vicente Carducho* and *Greg. Martínez* among others, and beyond, in the Pl. de Sta Ana, is the *Conv. de Sta Ana*, a neoclassical rebuilding of 1780 by *Fr. Sabatini*, with a church containing three religious paintings by *Goya*. Nearby is *S. Lorenzo* (1485–1512; altered 1602–21), containing a Byzantine Virgin, and a Holy Family (1620) and a Virgin by *Greg. Fernández*.—From the Pl. del Poniente, to the N., the shady Paseo de Isabel la Catolica is soon reached.

24   MADRID

MADRID (3,228,000 inhab. including outer suburbs; 729,000 in 1920; 1,096,000 in 1940; 2,177,000 in 1960), the highest capital in Europe (average altitude 2000 ft), is situated at almost exactly the centre of the Iberian Peninsula, on a bare and exposed upland plateau—still largely a 'hideous, grassless, treeless, colourless, calcined desert'—with no visible limit except the Sierra de Guadarrama to the N. It is an animated and flourishing town with all the characteristics of a cosmopolitan capital, but apart from its political significance, its main attractions for the traveller are the unrivalled collections of the Prado Museum, among many others.

Recent changes have increasingly tended to obliterate Madrid's national characteristics and peculiarities. Richard Ford (when describing Madrid) had reproached the unheeding Spaniards for doing their best 'to *denationalize* themselves, and to destroy with suicidal hand their greatest merit, which is in being *Spanish*; for Spain's best attractions are those which are characteristic of *herself;* here all that is imitated is poor and second-rate, and displeases the foreigner, who . . .

hopes to find again in Spain . . . all that has been lost and forgotten elsewhere'. It is certainly no longer the 'blanche ville aux sérénades' of Musset; the residential quarters which have grown up in every direction, are impersonal, unlike the narrow winding streets of Old Madrid that are still to be found near the Pta. del Sol and in the S.W. quarter. On the W. and S. the low hills occupied by the town are skirted by the dirty and insignificant *Manzanares* (now canalized), 'a rivulet with the reputation of a river' as Cervantes calls it, spanned however, by several handsome bridges, but whose narrow banks are no longer white with the town's washing as they were when first seen by Robert Southey in Jan. 1796.

The climate, although hot and oppressive in summer and cold but dry in winter, is not so trying as is sometimes represented. Spring, although it has many delightful days, can be rainy, but autumn is usually fine. It is proverbial that the subtle air of Madrid 'which will not extinguish a candle, will put out a man's life', and even on sunny days visitors should be on their guard against abrupt falls in temperature at sunset or in passing from the sunny to the shady sides of streets.

Dense but not aggressive traffic flows mercurially along widened and once dignified tree-lined avenues. Underground car-parks, one-way streets, and fly-overs proliferate, as do new banks, hotels, blocks of flats and offices, and suburban estates. An elaborate series of ring roads under construction promises to ease the communication problem, of which the Av. de la Paz is now virtually completed.

Recent years have seen an extraordinary growth of the town. Its *chabolas,* depressing shanty slums, have to a large extent been demolished, only to be replaced by tower blocks, and factories and industrial installations are now found in most outlying areas except to the W., where the 'green belt' of the *Casa del Campo* offers some slight protection from the encroaching metropolis.

Nevertheless, considering what architectural riches other Spanish towns have to offer, there are many who would agree with Ford that 'those who the soonest shake the dust off their feet, and remain the shortest time in Madrid, will probably remember it with most satisfaction'.

Airport at *Barajas,* 13 km. E., with regular bus services from the underground Terminus at the Pl. de Colon (Pl. p. 293/8).

Railway Stations. The main station is now *Chamartin,* at the N. end of the town, also communicating with *Atocha,* at the S. end of the Paseo del Prado. The *Est. del Norte* (or *del Principo Pío*) now concentrates on local services, apart from being the terminus for lines to the N.W.

Buses. Urban routes are subject to alteration, and are not often of use to the tourist, while long-distance coaches start from a number of different points, although new termini have been constructed: latest details may be obtained from Tourist Offices.

A handy plan of the *Underground* or **Metropolitano** is available at most stations.

P.O.; the main office is at the Pl. de la Cibeles (24 hour service, but not in all departments). **Telephones;** the head office is at Av. José Antonio 28.

S.E.T. Tourist Offices: C. Alcalá 44; C. Princesa 1; and at the airport. *Municipal office,* Pl. Mayor 2. *RENFE,* Alcalá 44. *Iberia,* Av. José Antonio 57, and Pl. de Canovas 4.

Embassies. *British,* C. Fernando el Santo 16; *United States,* C. Serrano 75. For Consulates and Chambers of Commerce, see p. 73-4.

British Institute, C. Almagro 5; *British American Hospital,* Paseo de Juan XXIII (just E. of the Ciudad Universitaria).

History. The earliest mention of *Majrit* or *Magerit* occurs under Ramiro II (930–50), and it was merely an outpost of Toledo when it was captured by Alfonso VI of León in 1083. In the gradually growing town the Cortes met for the first time in 1309 under Fernando IV and again in 1335 under Alfonso XI. Enrique IV replaced the Moorish alcázar by a new palere c. 1466. Enrique III (1390–1407) is said to have been crowned at Madrid. Charles V benefited from its keen air, and here after the battle of Pavia (Feb. 1525), his defeated rival Francis I of France was confined until the Treaty of Madrid in 1526. Philip II (1558–98) decided to establish the seat of government in this central spot; in 1561 he declared Madrid the *'única corte'*, when its limits were extended, and in 1625 it was surrounded by a mud or 'tapia' wall, which reconstructed in 1782, was only demolished late in the 19C. It also has maintained its rank as capital, in spite of abortive attempts by Philip III to prefer Valladolid (1601–07) and Carlos III to prefer Seville.

In 1605 the first part of 'Don Quixote' was published at Madrid; and in the 17C. under Philip III (d. 1621) and especially under Philip IV (d. 1665), the capital enjoyed its golden period when Cervantes (d. 1616), Lope de Vega (d. 1635), Velázquez (d. 1660), and Calderón (d. 1681) lived and worked there. Hither El Greco came c. 1575 hoping for employment on the Escorial; and here Rubens and Velázquez met in 1628. In 1623 the visit of Prince Charles Stuart (afterwards Charles I of Britain), suitor for the hand of the Infanta María, sister of Philip IV, was celebrated with bull-fights and festivals, although political reasons prevented the match. The reign of Carlos III, in which the building of the Prado Museum was begun, saw many other embellishments and improvements in the capital. Here in 1766 took place riots against the Marqués de Esquilache, the king's Italian minister, who attempted to control the length of cloaks and brims of hats. According to the census of 1787, its population was then 156,000. In 1808 the insurrection of the *Dos de Mayo* took place, and Joseph Bonaparte, known as 'Tio Pepe', or 'Rey Plazuelas', from the clearances he made in the congested town occupied the palace until ousted in 1812 by Wellington.

Often the scene of pronunciamientos, during the 19C, Madrid proclaimed the Republic in 1931, but after the outbreak of the Civil War the seat of the government was transferred to Valencia. Meanwhile Madrid underwent a protracted siege (Oct. 1936–March 1939), in the course of which the new University City, in the front line, was destroyed.

Although it was again the administrative capital under the dictatorship, and the scene of the assassination of Adm. Carrero Blanco in 1973, and of the lingering death of Gen. Franco in 1975, little of any historical moment has occurred since until in April 1979 a Socialist Mayor again took office, and May Day 'manifestations' were again tolerated, replacing the military processions and political demonstrations of loyalty to the Fascist cause previously imposed on the populace.

Famous natives include the writers Alonso de Ercilla y Zúñiga (1533–94) author of the epic poem 'La Araucana'; Lope de Vega (1562–1635), Tirso de Molina (Fray Gabriel Tellez; 1572–1648); Francisco Gómez de Quevedo y Villegas (1580–1645); Alonso Jerónimo Salas Barbadillo (1581–1635); Fray Juan Eusebio Nieremberg (1595–1658); Calderón de la Barca (1600–81); Pérez de Montalbán (1602–38); Francisco Santos (1623–98; author of 'Dia y Noche de Madrid' 1663); Ramón de la Cruz (1731–94); Nicolás (1737–80) and his son Leandro Fernández de Moratin (1760–1828); Manuel José Quintana (1772–1857); Agustín Duran (1789–1862; literary critic and editor of the 'Romancero general'); Ramón de Mesonero Romanos (1803–82; 'costumbrista' and topographer, who wrote a guide to Madrid in 1831); Juan Eugenio Hartzenbusch (1806–80); Mariano José de Larra (1809–37); Jacinto Benavente (1866–1954); José Ortega y Gasset (1883–1955); Gregorio Marañón (1887–1960; endocrinologist and author); and Pedro Salinas (1892–1951); while Benito Pérez Galdos (1843–1920) lived most of his life in the capital.

Among painters were Claudio Coello (1621–93); and José Gutiérrez Solana (1886–1945). Among composers, Domenico Scarlatti died in Madrid in 1757, having written much of his music in Spain, and Luigi Boccherini died here in 1805. The English ambassadors Richard Fanshawe (1608–66) and Benjamin Keene (1697–1757) both died in office in Madrid. Washington Irving was appointed to the American Legation in Madrid in 1826 and remained in Spain until 1829.

Employment of Time. Visitors making a short stay in Madrid will probably commence with their first visit to the *Museo del Prado* (Pl. 12). A day may easily be spent exploring an area of the old town to the W. of the *Pta. del Sol,* concentrating on that part within and surrounding Pl. 10, including the *Pl. Mayor,* also seeing at least the exterior of the *Royal Palace* (Pl. 9). A further day may be occupied visiting the *Archaeological Museum* (Pl. 8) the *Museo Lázaro Galdiano* (N. of Pl. 4), or the *Artes Decorativas* (Pl. 12), or others, depending on one's interest, bearing in mind that (until a more enlightened policy is in operation) a number are only open during the mornings: see below. The main shopping streets, apart from the *Gran Via* (N. of the Pta. del Sol) are those perpendicular and parallel to the *C. Serrano* (Pl. 4, 8), areas perhaps best visited in the late afternoon.

Hours of admission to the main Museums, etc. In the following table the more important collections are indicated in bolder type. The hours of admission are very liable to change, opening and closing later during Summer afternoons. Some may be closed in August.

	MAP. REF.	OPEN	DESCRIBED ON PAGE
Acad. de Bellas Artes C. Alcalá 13; but see p. 250	293:11	10.00; 14.00	245
Museo de America Av. Reyes Católicos near entrance to Ciudad Universitaria	254	10.00-14.00	265
Arqueológico C. Serrano 13	293:8	9.30-13.30	250
Army Museum (del Ejército) C. Mendes Nuñez	293:12	10.00-14.00 (closed Mon.)	248
Art Contemporáneo C. Juan Herrera 2, near entrance to Ciudad Universitaria	254	10.00-18.00 (closed Mon.); 10.00-14.00 only on Sun.	265
Artes Decorativas C. Montalbán 12	293:12	10.00-17.00 (closed Mon.);10.00-14.00 only on Sat. and Sun.	246
Casón de Buen Retiro C. Felipe IV 13, just E. of the Museo del Prado	293:12	10.00-14.00; 17.00-20.00	247
Cerralbo C. Ventura Rodíguez 17, N.W. of the Pl. de España	292.5	9.00-14.00 (closed Tues.)	264
Descalzas Reales, Conv de las N. of the C. del Arenal	292:10	10.30-12.45; 16.00- 17.15 (mornings only on Fri., Sat., Sun., and holidays)	259
Encarnación Conv. de la N.E. of the Pl. de Oriente	292:6	10.00-13.00, 16.00- 18.00 (closed Sun.)	259
Lazaro Galdiano C. Serrano 122	255	9.30-14.15	252
Municipal C. Fuencarral 78	293:7	10.30-13.30 (closed Mon. and holidays)	267

Naval Museum C. Montalbán 2	293:12	10.30–13.30 (closed Mon.)	246
Palacio Real, Armoury and Library,etc; Pl. de Oriente	292:9	10.00–12.45; 15.30– 17.15 (16.00–18.25 in summer, 10.00–13.30 only on Sun., and holidays	259
Prado, Museo del Paseo del Prado	293:12	10.00–17.00; 10.00–14.00 on Sun.	268
Romántico C. S. Mateo 13	293:7	10.00–18.00 (closed Mon. 10.00–14.00 only on holidays	267
S. Antonio de la Florida Paseo de la Florida, N.W. of the Est. del Norte	254		263–4
Valencia de Don Juan, Inst. de C. Fortuny 43	255	10.00–14.00 on Wed. and Fri. at other times by appointment	268

More specialist collections include, among others, the *Ethnological and Anthropological Museum*, C. Alfonso XII, 68; the *Academia de la Historia*, C. León 21; the *Bullfighting Museum*, at Las Ventas Bullring; the *Theatre Museum*, Teatro Real (introduction required); the *Museo Sorolla*, C. Gen. Martinez Campos 37; the *Carriage Museum*, near the Est. del Norte; the *Fábrica de Tapices*, C. Fuenterraba 2; and *Numismatic Museum*, at the Mint. C. Dr. Esquerdo 36.

The *Museo del Pueblo* has not yet been reopened.

Madrid is described in six sections: **A** (S.E.), p. 245; **B** (N.E.), p. 249; **C** (S.W.), p. 256; **D** (Western), p. 258; **E** (N.W.), p. 264; and **F** (Northern), p. 267, while section **G** is devoted to the *Prado Museum*, see p. 268.

It may be useful to note that Madrid's streets were numbered in 1833, beginning at the end nearest the Pta. del Sol, with even numbers on the right, and the odd on the left.

The Topography of Madrid can be best understood by taking the **Pta. del Sol** (Pl. 10) as a focal point. This irregular space—not a gateway—from which ten streets radiate, is still a centre of life, and the historic heart of the town, on the S. side of which, in the entrance hall of the unimposing *Police Headquarters* (Seguridad; 1786), is a stone slab indicating Kilometric Zero, from which all distances in Spain are calculated. This building, designed by *Jacques Marquet* as the Gen. Post Office, was later famous as the Ministerio de la Gobernación. It is surmounted by a clock donated by its maker, Losada, a Spaniard resident in London, and placed there in 1866. At the E. side of the Pta. del Sol stood the chapel of the Buen Suceso, whose façade bore the figure of the Sun which gave the square its name, while opposite was the emplacement of the famous fountain known as 'La Mariblanca'. It was by the adjacent *Liberia San Martín* that the politician Canalejas (1854–1912) was assassinated.

The *Carrera de S. Jerónimo* leads E. hence past the *Pl. de Canalejas*, veering half-r. before widening as it continues downhill towards the *Pl. Cànovas del Castillo* (p. 246) and the *Prado*.

In the C. de Carretas, leading S. from the plaza, stood the well-known bar. *El Pombo*. To the W. of the Seguridad stood the convent of *S. Felipe el Real* and the *Gradas de S. Felipe*, once a famous rendezvous, below which were toy-stalls known as the *Covachuelas*. Opposite the Seguridad stood the *Inclusa* (foundling hospital) or *Niños Expósitos*.

A   S.E. MADRID

C. de Alcalá, Paseo del Prado, El Retiro.

On the l. of the **C. de Alcalá,** leading E. from the Pta. del Sol, is the *Hacienda* (Min. of Finance), built in 1769 as the *Aduana* (Customs House).

Adjoining it is the **Real Academia de Bellas Artes** founded in 1752 as the *Academia de Nobles Artes de S. Fernando,* and displaying a classical front of 1774 by *Diego de Villanueva.* While many of the finest canvases were transferred to the Prado in 1902, it normally contains a number of important works which deserve notice.

These include *Goya;* Burial of the Sardine; Scene in a madhouse; Bull-fight; Inquisition scene; Penitents; Portraits of Leandro Fernández de Moratín, the architect Juan de Villanueva, La Tirana (the actress Rosario Fernández), Godoy 'Prince of the Peace', Fernando VII, José Luis Muñarriz, secretary of the Academy, and a self-portrait of 1815. Among others of interest are: *V. López,* Fernando VII; *Mengs,* Duquesa de Llano in Aragonese costume; *Carreño,* Magdalene, Mariana of Austria; *Cano,* Crucifixion, Pietà; *Ribera,* St Jerome, Ecce Homo; *Zurbarán,* portraits of Monks of the Order of Mercy. There is also a collection of drawings.— It also houses the *Calcografía Nacional,* where old engravings from original plates are on sale.
The building is at present undergoing restoration; but see p. 250

Next door (No. 15), is the *Casino de Madrid,* a leading club with an appropriately ornate entrance hall.—Before reaching the junction of the Gran Via we pass the church of *Las Calatravas* (c. 1686) with a Baroque retablo by *Pablo González Velázquez.*—On the opposite side, near the corner of C. del Marqués de Cubas. Gen. Prim was assassinated in 1870.—On the l. stands rococo *S. José,* finished 1742. From this point there was a fine vista towards the *Pta. de Alcalá,* but the skyline is now dominated by a tower block at the N.E. corner of the Retiro park.—A few paces to the N., at the W. end of the Pl. del Rey, stands the almost entirely reconstructed *Casa de las Siete Chimeneas* on the site of the original 16C building attrib. to Juan de Herrera, and residence in 1623 of Prince Charles Stuart, Buckingham, Sir Kenelm Digby and Endymion Porter; of Sir Richard Fanshawe in 1664–66; and in the mid 18C of the Marqués de Esquilache. It now houses the Collection of the *Banco Urquijo.*

Among the paintings displayed on the upper floors are: *El Greco,* Annunciation; *Méndez,* Marqués de Leganes; and *Picasso,* Conde-Duque de Olivares. There is a small collection of Alcora ware, and furniture.

Returning to the C. de Alcalá, we pass (l.) the *Min. de Ejército* (War Office), which occupies the former *Pal. da Buenavista,* built in 1772 by *Pedro Arnal* and in 1805 given to Godoy. In 1841–43 it was the residence of Espartero, and in 1869-70 that of Prim.—The C. de Alcalá intersects the Prado at the spacious **Pl. de la Cibeles** (Pl. 8), so named from the *Fountain of Cybele* (1780) by *Fr. Gutiérrez* and *Robert Michel.* The Plaza is bounded on the S.W. by the *Banco de España* (built on the site of the Palace of the Dukes of Béjar), adjacent to which is a S.E.T. *Tourist Information Office.* To the S.E. of the *General Post Office* (1913), a pretentious 'wedding-cake' edifice facetiously known as the *'Palacio de Comunicaciónes',* or *'N.S. de Comunicaciónes',* or even *'Casa de tócame Roque'* (or Do as you Please).

The long C. de Alcalá—passing (l.) the famous *Café Lion*—gently climbs to the PL. DE LA INDEPENDENCIA, in the centre of which rises the **Pta. de Alcalá** (1778), a triumphal arch by *Fr. Sabatini* erected in honour of Carlos III, before continuing its eastward course N. of the Retiro Park, see p. 249.

At one time a bull-ring stood just N.E. of the Pta de Alcalá, but this was replaced in 1874 by another further E., superseded in 1928–29 by the present *Plaza de Toros,* also built in a Mudéjar style', accommodating 22,700 spectators, and with a *Bullfighting Museum,* which stands over 1 km. to the N.E.

From the Pl. de la Cibeles we may turn S. along the **Paseo del Prado,** a broad tree-shaded boulevard laid out by Carlos III's minister Aranda after 1767 and planted with rows of trees in the 1780s on the 'pratum' (meadow) of S. Jerónimo. long the most fashionable promenade of Madrid. The most frequented part, once the animated and crowded scene of fashion, flirtation, and elegant lounging described by so many travellers, was the Salón del Prado, between the Fountain of Cybele on the N. and the *Fountain of Neptune* on the S., passing half-way the *Fountain of Apollo* (by *Ventura Rodríguez;* 1777–80). On the E. side is the *Ministerio de Marina,* housing a **Naval Museum.**

Among numerous models of ships are a Flemish galleon of 1593 (16C); the three-decker 'San Antonio' of 1799; here also are the Chart of *Juan de la Cosa* (1500), the earliest known map to show America; the Code of Signals invented by the Marqués de la Victoria (1687–1772) and Table designed by him for the instruction of his officers, a predecessor of the War Game. Among the portraits is that of Gabriel de Aristizabal, by *Goya.* There is a collection of navigational instruments, and among books displayed are the rare 'Arte de Navegar' of *Pedro de Medina* (1545) and the 'Breve Compendio' of *Martin Cortés* (1551). The library contains 15,000 charts, plans and drawings, and a valuable collection of naval documents.

At No. 12, on the r. C. de Montalbán ascending towards the Retiro, is the reformed ***Museo de Artes Decorativas,** consisting of five floors ranged around a central patio. Here, tastefully displayed, one may see representative examples of Spanish furniture of every period, while certain rooms are devoted to tapestries, embroideries, lace, and leatherwork; glassware, china and pottery; silver, and ironwork, etc. Of particular interest is the artesonado ceiling in R 16 on the 2nd floor, and the Manises tiled Valencian kitchen (18C) on the top floor (R 46).

Continuing S. along the Paseo del Prado, we shortly reach the leafy PL. DE LA LEALTAD, in which rises the *Monumento del Dos de Mayo.*

Madrid was occupied by the French under Murat on March 23rd, 1808, and on May 2nd the populace, alarmed by the removal of the royal princes from the palace, rose in revolt. Murat, with his Mameluke troops, repressed the rising with ruthless severity, and after trial by court-martial, executed some indiscriminate hundreds of the citizens on the Prado. Luis Daóiz and Pedro Velarde whose medallion portraits appear on the obelisk, were two artillery officers who fell rather than surrender their guns. Jacinto Ruiz, a third officer, is commemorated by a statue in the Pl. del Rey. Although the revolt failed, it led indirectly to the intervention of the British and the eventual liberation of the Peninsula.

The **Pl. Cánovas del Castillo** (Pl. 11), overlooked on the E. by the *Ritz Hotel* (see below) may also be reached directly from the Pta. del Sol by the Carrera de S. Jerónimo, which passes (l.) the front of the *Pal. de las Cortes,* with a portico of Corinthian columns, home of the Spanish Parliament or Cortes Españolas. An extension has been built to the W.

Erected in 1843–50 by *Narciso P. Colomer,* it is flanked by two bronze lions cast from cannon captured in the Moroccan campaign of 1860, which replaced stone lions, one of which was decapitated by a cannon-ball in the revolution of 1854.

Théophile Gautier, who did not admire the building, doubted whether good laws could be enacted in such a structure; and as to the statue of Cervantes in the triangular garden opposite, he remarked that, while it was praiseworthy to erect a statue to the author of 'Don Quixote', they might have erected a better one while they were at it.

The Carrera de S. Jerónimo ascends hence to the N.W. to regain the *Pta del Sol,* passing (l.) the front of the *Pal. de Miraflores* (c. 1725) by *Pedro de Ribera,* now business premises, and beyond, the C. de Principe, in which George Borrow's Bible showroom and warehouse was once situated.

From the S.W. corner of this triangular square we may ascend the C. del Prado past (r.) the *Ateneo de Madrid.* Founded in 1837, this influential Club and cultural centre, housing a fine library and small concert hall, was for many years a hive of Liberal activity and among its members have been an impressive number of outstanding political and literary figures. The street continues to climb to the Pl. de Sta Ana, with the *Teatro Español,* and beyond to the Pl. de J. Benavente.

Just past the Ateneo, in the C. de León (l.) on the corner of C. de Cervantes, stood the house in which Cervantes died in 1616.—In this last-named street, at No. 15, Lope de Vega lived intermittently from 1610 until his death (1635); the building (1587) is restored and furnished as it might have been in his lifetime.

Cervantes was buried in the *Conv. de las Trinitarias* (1668–96) in the adjoining C. Lope de Vega, although the site of his grave is not known. The site of the press where the first part of *'Don Quixote'* was printed is marked by a plaque at C. de Atocha 121, which may be reached by the C. de León, at the intersection of which with the C. de las Huertas stands the **Real Academia de la Historia,** in a building by *Villanueva.*

Among the paintings to be seen here are *Goya's* portraits of Carlos IV and Maria Luisa, of Fr. Juan Fernández de Rojas, and of Josef de Bargas y Ponce; also *Angelica Kauffmann's* portrait of the philologist Lorenzo Hervás y Panduro; and an *anon.* portrait of Isabel la Católica (similar to that in the Royal Palace). Note also the bust of Jovellanos by *Monasterio.* In the adjacent room is an interesting reliquary-retablo from the Monasterio de Piedra (1390), depicting angels playing musical instruments. Note also the reverse side of the doors. Here also is the silver *Disc of Theodosius* (A.D. 393), discovered near Almendralejo in 1847. Other rooms contain such antiquities as a painted map of Mexico City (1753); two palaeo-Christian sarcophagi (from Hellin); an illumniated document of Garcia de Najera (1054) from Pamplona; and a caliph's linen head-scarf from San Esteban de Gormaz. The Library preserves some important MSS, including items from San Millán de Cogolla, and San Pedro de Cardeña. The collection of medals is also of interest.

At the N.W. corner of the Pl. Cánovas stands the *Pal. de Villahermosa* (1806), reconstructed internally. Opposite, S.W. of the plaza, is the *Palace Hotel,* built on the site of the old Medinaceli Pal., destroyed in the 1890s, behind which is a showroom for publications of the C.S.I.C, see. p. 253.

S.E. of the plaza—in the centre of which is the *Fountain of Neptune* (1780) by *Juan Pascual de Mena*—stands the world-famous **Museo del Prado** (Pl. 12), see p. 268.—Hence the C. de Felipe IV climbs E. between the museum and the *Ritz Hotel,* where on 20 Nov. 1936 the famous anarchist Buenaventura Durruti died, having been mortally wounded near the Model Prison the previous day; the hotel had been converted into a hospital.

At the far end of the C. de Felipe IV stands the **Casón de Felipe IV** (restored, and with a new front added), designed in 1637 by *Alonso*

Carbonell as a dependence of the Retiro Palace, and intended as a ballroom. The ceiling of the main saloon is decorated by *Luca Giordano* (1694–95). It now houses subsidiary 19C collections of the Museo del Prado, including portraits by *Vicente López, Tejeo, F. Madrazo, Esquivel* (a fine portrait of Mendizábal), goyaesque Inquisition scenes by *Eugenio Lucas,* works by *Alenza, Valeriano Domínguez Bécquer, Eduardo Rosales, Fortuny, Sorolla, Pinazo, Beruete* (views of Madrid), *Regoyos, Muñoz Degrain, Alisel,* and *Gisbert* (execution of Torrijos, ref. p. 503), etc.

To the N. of the adjacent small square, is the **Army Museum** (*Museo del Ejército*), founded in 1803 and containing an extensive collection relating to Spanish military history, which since 1841 has been installed in this decrepit building, part of the former palace of Buen Retiro. It is particularly rich in examples of artillery and small arms from the earliest period.

Among relics of numerous wars are a sword of the Cid, called 'La Tizona'; the sword of the Alcaide of Loja; weapons and tunic of Boabdil; the miniature ivory triptych of Charles V, and his tent and furniture used on the Tunis expedition (1535); half-armour of Gonzalo de Córdoba, 'el Gran Capitán', when page and esquire to Isabel the Catholic, and a later Milanese set; the *boina* (beret) of the Carlist general Zumalacárregui, and souvenirs of Gen. Espoz y Mina, and Gen. Narváez; the swords and pistols of Palafox and coach in which Prim was assassinated. Individual rooms are devoted to the expulsion of the Moors from the Kingdom of Granada; the insurrection of 1808 and the Peninsular War; the Guardia Civil; and the Civil War of 1936–39. Among other exhibits are portraits of heroes and generals; flags, colours, decorations and uniforms; models of fortifications and bridges; armour; and a collection of lead soldiers.

Returning to the Prado viâ the C. de Felipe IV, we pass (l.) the *Real Academia Española,* founded in 1713, and now with 36 members, whose function is the study of the Castilian language and literature, and the revision and publication of the 'Diccionario de la Lengua', their first 'Diccionario de autoridades' (6 vols) being published in 1726–39. Behind it, in the C. de Ruiz de Alarcón, rises the conspicuous brick and white stone church of *S. Jerónimo el Real,* a Gothic building of 1503–05 with two lofty spires, but much restored. To the S. are the remains of a cloister of 1612 by *Miguel Martínez.* The church overlooks the E. façade of the *Museo del Prado,* the N. entrance of which may be reached by steps descending through what was once the orchard of the Hieronymites.

By passing along the W. façade of the museum, facing the Prado, we reach the Pl. de Murillo and the main entrance, by *Villanueva,* of the overgrown **Botanical Gardens,** founded in 1775 by Carlos III, removed to its present site in 1781, but sadly depleted by a cyclone in 1886. It is open from May to Oct, but is closed in wet weather. Ford reports that it was once inhabited by a brood of boa-constrictors that had escaped from the menagerie in the Buen Retiro, which, until winter killed them off, bolted any unfortunate cat or dog that unwittingly strayed in to study botany! The Library preserves the botanical drawings of *Celestino Mutis.*

The Paseo del Prado skirts the Botanical Gardens, along the S. side of which are to be found second-hand bookstalls, and ends at the GLORIETA DEL EMPERADOR CARLOS V, now a maze of flyovers, just S. of which is the *Estación de Atocha* (previously known as *de Mediodía*). The first railway hence, from an earlier building, ran to Aranjuez (1846), and the line to Alicante was inaugurated in 1851.

A short distance N.W. is the *Conv. de Sta Isabel* (restored), founded by Philip III, the church of which contains a Virgin by *Ribera* among other paintings.—The PASEO DE LA INFANTA ISABEL leads S.E., passing the *Museo Etnológico* to the *Basilica of Atocha* begun in 1873 as a national pantheon on the site of the chapel of a Dominican convent founded in 1523 by Hurtado de Mendoza, confessor of Charles V. The spot had long been a place of pilgrimage, and is the home of the black statue of N.S. del Buen Suceso; the pantheon contains monuments of famous 19C Spaniards, including Argüeles, Calatrava, Canalejas, Cánovas del Castillo, Castaños, Dato, Mendizábel, Palafox, Prim, and Sagasta.

Nearby, in the C. Fuenterrabía, is the **Reál Fábrica de Tapices,** where the Royal Tapestry Factory has stood since 1889, which is still in active operation after 200 years, and may be visited.—The Paseo de la Infanta Isabel is prolonged to the E. to join the Av. del Mediterraneo, and the commencement of the N III for Valencia.

Parallel to and E. of the Paseo del Prado is the C. de Alfonso XII, running S. from the Pl. de la Independencia and forming the W. limit of the well-shaded **Retiro Park** (119 hectares).

The site, already a royal domain in the time of Philip II (who intended it as a country seat for Mary Tudor), was laid out in 1636–39 by Olivares as a *Buen Retiro* or 'pleasant retreat' for Philip IV. The palace, begun c. 1621 and under later monarchs the scene of many lavish festivals, was burned down in 1764, and is now represented only by the *Army Museum* and the *Casón* (see above). The porcelain factory established in the park by Carlos III in 1759 with workmen brought from Capodimonte, near Naples, has likewise gone. Its site was towards the S. where now stands the statue of the *Fallen Angel*. Buen Retiro ware, marked with a fleur-de-lis, is similar in style to the Capodimonte productions. Here, in 1792, took place Vicente Lunardi's famous ascent by balloon. The park was injured by military operations during the Peninsular War, but was restored by Fernando VII. After the Revolution of 1868 the W. side (which reached to the Post Office) was cut off for urban extension and in 1876 the rest became public property.

From the entrances (for pedestrians) in the Pl. de la Independencia and the N. half of the C. de Alfonso XII, walks lead to the *Estanque Grande,* an oblong artifical lake, near the W. corners of which are the fountains of the Galapagos (Tortoises) and the Alcachofa (Artichoke), while on its E. bank stands the conspicuous equestrian *Statue of Alfonso XII* by *Benlliure.* To the S. of the Estanque stands the *Pal. de Valázquez,* an exhibition hall (1900; restored), and nearby, the *Pal. de Cristal.* Near the N.E. entrance of the park, a road passes (l.) the ruined Romanesque *Cap. de S. Isidoro,* brought here from Ávila, while above the S.W. corner of the park stands the colonnaded *Observatory* (1785–90) built for Carlos III by *Juan de Villanueva,* but gutted by the French; its restoration is projected.

B   N.E. MADRID

Museo Arqueológico, Museo Lázaro Galdiano

N. from the Pl. de la Cibeles extends the PASEO DE CALVO SOTELO, previously *Paseo de Recoletos* (taking its name from a former Conv. of the Franciscan Recollects), passing over the site of the famous garden of the Regidor Juan Fernández and of the old English Cemetery.—We pass (r.) the former residence of the Marqués de Salamanca, (1811–83), the entrepreneur who was responsible for the development of the area to the N.E. of this building, known as the Barrio de Salamanca. The mansion now houses the Banco Hipotecaria. The Paseo is prolonged to the N. by the PASEO DE LA CASTELLANA, but the ever-increasing volume of traffic has virtually banished the animated scene presented here formerly, and much of it is now flanked by ugly and ostentatious bank buildings.

On the r. stands a ponderous edifice (Pl. 8) accommodating both the **Biblioteca Nacional** and the *Museo Arqueológico Nacional.* The former, its main entrance facing the Paseo, was founded by Philip V in

1712 by adding the books that he had brought from France to the old Royal Library. It contains c. 1 million printed books, c. 2000 incunabulae, and over 100,000 MSS, drawings and engravings, some of which are occasionally on display.

A selection of paintings from the *Academia de Bellas Artes de San Fernando* (see p. 245) is at present on view here.

The *Museo Arqueológico Nacional, occupying the E. side, and entered from the C. Serrano, is still in the process of reconstruction and re-arrangement, the completion of which is eagerly awaited. Well-lit and spacious rooms have been opened, and show a quality of design which the objects displayed deserve.

At present the BASEMENT is largely devoted to Prehistory, those rooms concerning Spain being well laid out and their contents well labelled. Showcase numbers are given in brackets. The rooms are not a present actually numbered.

From R1 we turn l. into R2 containing displays of fauna of the *Quaternary period,* including a skull and tusks of early elephants from Piñedo (Toledo) and bones from Torralba and Ambrona (Soria), and from the Cueva del Castillo, Puente Viesgo (Santander); also artefacts found at the Cerro de S. Isidro (Madrid) in 1862, the first palaeolithic site excavated in Spain, near the banks of the Manzanares.—R3 (1 and 4) artefacts and incised bones (depicting the heads of horses and deer) from the Cueva del Castillo, and other finds from caves near (5) the Cantabrian and (6) Mediterranean coasts.—R4 *Neolithic period.* (1) Combed ceramics and bone bracelets; (2) esparto basket-ware, etc. and finds from the Cueva de los Murciélogos (Granada); (3) a large ovoid vase from the Cueva de Higueron (Málaga), and (4) hanging pots from the same site; (5) vase from the Cueva del Tesoro (near Torremolinos); (6) ceramics, axe and arrow-heads, and silex knives; (8-9) artefacts from Los Millares (above the Rio Andarax, off the Almería-Guadix road) including (11) stylized incised slate idol-plaques, with eyes, bronze knife and axe-heads, and zoomorphic vase, an anthropomorphic female figure, and shell and turquoise bangles and necklaces; (13) *cylindrical idol of alabaster, showing eyes (from Estremadura); (14) incised idol-plaques and bronze axe-heads from Garrovillas and the Granja de Cespedes.—R5 (1) decorated ceramics; (3 and 6) *ceramics from El Algar (Almería); (4) bronze swords, daggers, axes, etc., including moulds; (9) shell, bone, and bronze necklaces; (10) reconstructed urn-burial; inscribed stele or idol from Corao (near Cangas de Onis, Asturias); (13) bronze sword and gold handle (? from Guadalajara).—R6 Stone idols; (1) axes and moulds; (2) *swords, daggers, lances, etc. from a shipwreck near Huelva (825–800 B.C.); (8) *Late Bronze Age gold torques and spiral bracelets, etc.; (9) gold vases from Axtroki in the Bolivar valley (Guipúzcoa); (10) ceramics and moulds, including (15) some from Azaila (between Zaragoza and Alcañiz); (16) bronze support for a ritual bowl incorporating a sculpted horse.—R7 (1) bronze pectoral disk and other objects from the necropolis of Aguilar de Anguita (Soria-Guadalajara); (4) bronze daggers and sickles; (5) bronze fibulas, including one of a mounted horseman, belt-buckles, bits, etc. (7) gold torques, diadems, etc. from Cangas de Onis and Ribadeo, etc., some decorated with filigree work.—R8, to the l. (1) inlaid enamelled objects from the necropolis of Osera (Ávila).—R9 (1) *silver treasure from Salvacañete (Cuenca), Chao de Lamas (Miranda do Corvo,

Portugal), and torques, pectorals, earrings, fibulas, rings, and cups, etc. from Palencia and Guadalajara, etc.; (2) artefacts from Numancia (Soria), including a ceramic horn.—**R10** Objects from the Balearic Islands, including three *bronze bulls heads from Costig (Mallorca), and artefacts of the Talayot culture; and in **R11**, from the Canary Islands.

RR 12-18 display material from elsewhere besides Spain, among them in **R12**, artefacts from the W. Sahara (Morocco).—**R13** Collections from Egypt and Nubia, including numerous bronze statuettes of divinities, faience *ushabtis,* scarabs, amulets, necklaces, alabaster vases, sarcophagi, funeral masks, mummies, etc. Note (28) the alabaster canopic vase unearthed at Churriana (Málaga), and (29) the black basalt hawk-like statue of Horus.—**R14** is devoted to the archaeology of the E. Mediterranean, and Persia: note the bust from Cyprus (6C B.C.).—**RR 15-16** contain collections of red and black-figure vases, amphora, craters and other ceramics of the Greek and Roman period.—**R17** (1) bronze greaves, helmets, and breast-plates, and (3) ceramic ex-votos, and (6) heads, mostly from Calvi (Italy).—**R18** contains a number of bronze objects, including Etruscan vases and jewellery, mirrors, and scarabs, etc.

Hence we ascend to the GROUND FLOOR, and turn into **R I**, with finds from the necropolis of Tútugi, and Tugia; Celtiberic jewellery; the Treasure of Jávea (4C B.C.); the Treasure of Abengibre, silver plates inscribed in Greco-Phoenician (?); artefacts from Azaila; the Phoenician 'Sphinx of Balazote'; candlesticks from Lebrija; and the Treasure of Aliseda (Cáceres).—**R II** Temple sculpture (frieze) from Osuna; the *Dama de Baza (4C B.C.; discovered in 1971), preserving much painted decoration; the Greco-Iberian *Dama de Elche (? 3C B.C.) transferred here from the Prado, and standing female figures and heads from the Cerro de los Santos (Albacete).—**R III** Early Imperial sculpture; unfinished statue of Tiberius from Paestum; head of Lucius Verus; a huge mosaic pavement from Hellín.—**R IV** Mosaic of the Labours of Hercules; fine bronze plaques, the 'Lex Malacitana', etc.; bronzes and marbles of the 2C A.D.; glass; jewellery; Trajanic inscriptions from Cartagena;—**R V** marble sundial, and 3C Roman ensign; and the Madrid Puteal.—**R VI,** late Roman mosaics and sarcofagi; **R VIII,** Christian sarcofagi.

Ascending to the FIRST FLOOR we turn r. into rooms displaying Visigothic and medieval material, notable among which is the *Treasure of Gurrazar* (Toledo) including the votive crown of Reccesvinth (649–72), five other crowns, and several pendant crosses. An ivory crucifix offered in 1063 to S. Isidoro at León by Fernando I and Queen Sancha; a cylindrical box of ivory and silver with cufic inscriptions of 964 (the 'bote de Zamora'); the earliest known Astrolabe, made in Toledo in 1066; a bronze lamp (1305) from the Alhambra; two large vases from Hornos (Jaén, mid-14C), and Jerez de la Frontera (13C); pottery from Medina Azahara; and a collection of Hispano-Moresque azulejos and lustre-ware.

Other rooms are still (1979) in the process of a thorough reorganization, but in due course will again be open to the public.

Beneath the garden by the entrance one may visit a replica of the *Altamira Caves* (see p. 386).

On the large square site to the N. of the museum stood the Moneda (or *Mint,* now transferred to the Av. Dr. Esquerdo, and containing a Numismatic Museum), which was demolished to make way for the extension eastwards of the PL. DE CÓLON (Pl. 8). Here is the underground *Terminus* for buses to the airport at Barajas, and a car park. An extraordinary and ugly *Memorial* to the discovery of the 'New World' now effectively blocks off the E. side of the square, with its equally hideous lighting installations; on the W. side stands the *Columbus Column* (1885).

Parallel to the E. of the Paseo de Calvo Sotelo is the **C. Serrano,** a fashionable shopping street running N. from the Pl. de la Independencia. The C. Serrano, together with the C. Velázquez and C. Gen. Mola, further E., are the main thoroughfares of the BARRIO DE SALAMANCA, forming, with its wide avenues—many regrettably no longer tree-lined—an attractive residential district.

This was laid out in a grid by the Marqués de Salamanca in 1865–68 beyond the crumbling boundary walls of Madrid, which were thrown down in 1867. The built up area was later greatly extended.

Towards the N. end of the C. Claudio Coello (by No. 104), running parallel to the C. Serrano, Adm. Carrero Blanco, President of the Spanish Government, was assassinated in Dec. 1973.

The abduction and assassination of José Calvo Sotelo (1893-1936), taken from his home at 89 C. Velázquez on 13 July 1936, to a large extent precipitated the commencement of the Spanish Civil War.

Towards the N. end of the C. Serrano, after crossing C. Juan Bravo, and passing the *U.S. Embassy* block (No. 75, l.) stands (No. 122, r.) the former home of José Lázaro Galdiano (d. 1948), who bequeathed to the state his collection of works of art—including a high proportion of outstanding quality—which, as the ***Museo Lázaro Galdiano,** was opened to the public in 1951. An Art Library is accommodated in an adjoining building. Antonio Rodriguez-Moñino (1910-70), the bibliographer, was long the librarian of the Foundation, see Pl. p. 255.

From the Vestibule we enter R II (ahead) containing a magnificent collection of Limoges enamels, medieval ivory carvings and metalwork, notably a Parisian ivory Virgin and Child (c. 1300); R III plate; a group of chalices (15–16C); cup of Matthias Corvinus (1462); R IV Celtic diadem from Ribadeo; 14C gold collar from Granada; group of morses from cloaks; 14C German Paten; gold ear-rings by *Benvenuto Cellini;* a collar with medallion of the great Duke of Alba, by *Caradosso;* cup of rock crystal surmounted by an enamelled gold figure of Neptune, by the *Sarachi* of Milan (c. 1600); Group of 14 Byzantine cloisonné enamels (10–11C); rock crystal jar and dish (late 16C); Baroque and later jewellery.—R. V Terracotta Head of St John (16C Italian); R VI Terracotta bust of Christ, by *Verocchio; Leonardo da Vinci,* John the Divine (c. 1480); Renaissance bronzes, plaques, etc., including a Dancing Faun by *Sant' Agata.*
At the entrance to R VII stands a 15C Flemish statue of Sta Clara; Moorish inlaid decoration in agate (Granada, c 1300).—R VII enamelled glass mosque lamp (13–14C); bronze Persian bowl, made in Venice (early 16C) by *Mahmud the Kurd.*
We pass a rotunda displaying antique and Renaissance bronzes, and take the lift to the THIRD FLOOR. R XXXI Renaissance and Baroque plaques, vestments and embroidery; RR XXXII and XXXIII Swords and firearms; R XXXIV Moroccan and granadine fabrics; coins and dies; azulejos, and powder-flasks.—R XXXV Fans and cutlery.—R XXXVI Portraits of Philip II, and Philip III as a child, by *Pantoja;* R XXXVII Medals and medallions, and portraits of Lope de Vega; *Mengs,* self-portrait; and portraits by *Esquivel* and *Bayeu.*
We descend to the SECOND FLOOR. R XVIII Spanish and 15C painting; Virgin of Mosén Sperandeu (1439), from Tarazona; *Garcia del Barco,* Triptych of Ávila.— R XIX *Master of Cabanyes,* Panel in early Renaissance style; *P. Berruguete,* self-portrait; *Bart. de Castro,* St Dominic, Annunciation, Nativity, Epiphany, from S. Pablo, Palencia; Virgin of Columbus (c. 1540), with the unfinished cathedral of Santo Domingo in the background.—R XX *Gerard David,* Virgin; School of Bruges, Virgin of the Beautiful Landscape; *Joos van Cleve,* Leonor de Austria,

sister of Charles V; *H. Bosch,* St John in Patmos, the Vision of Tondal; *Dürer,* Virgin in a garden; *A. Ysembrandt,* Virgin; Portraits by *B. van Orley* (?), and by *P. Pourbus; Q. Massys,* Triptych; *Mabuse,* Triptych; *Master of the Half-lengths,* Virgin.—R XXI *Ludolf de Jongh,* Portrait of a Lady; *Rembrandt,* Portrait of Saskia (1634); Landscapes by *Wouwerman* and *Hobbema.*—R XXII Landscapes by *A. Cuyp* and *Teniers;* French chairs upholstered with Beauvais tapestry. R XXIII *Velázquez,* Luis De Góngora (1622), Juana Pacheco; *Zurbarán,* S. Diego de Alcalá; *El Greco,* St Francis with Brother Leo, St John and the Holy Woman, St Francis, Mater Dolorosa.—R XXVI *Murillo,* Sta. Rosa de Lima; *Ribera,* St Peter; *Carreño,* Carlos II; *Murillo* (?) head of a friar.—R XXV *Gainsborough,* Portrait of a lady; *Francis Cotes,* Portrait of a lady; *Allan Ramsay,* Princess Augusta of Saxony; *Lawrence,* Master Ainslie; *Reynolds,* Lady Sondes; *Romney,* The Widow; *Constable,* Four landscapes; *Bonington,* Seascapes.—R XXVI Miniatures 16–18C; *Turner,* Water-colours.—R XXVII *Tiepolo,* Portrait of his wife, Cecilia Guardi; *Guardi,* The Grand Canal—R XXVIII Escritoire of Maria Leczynska, queen of Louis XV; *Tiepolo,* portraits.—R XXX *Mengs,* Carlos III; portraits of Jovellanos; *Goya,* Descent from the Cross (1771–72); Cartoon for a tapestry of summer; Conde de Miranda (1777), the artist's first dated portrait, portraits and sketches, also portraits by *Maella* and *Esteve,* and a collection of clocks and watches, including Charles V's ivory hunting watch in the form of a cross.

FIRST FLOOR. R VIII *Lucas Gassel,* landscape; *P. Pourbus,* Portrait.—R IX Spanish primitives.— R XI Five baptismal cups.—R XII *Reynolds,* Mrs Damer; Gen. Stringer Lawrence; Landscapes and a portrait attr. to Gainsborough (?); Byzantine ivories, including a carved coffer of c. 1000; ivory and silver covered tankard of Charles, V.—R XIII Portraits by *V. López; F. Madrazo,* Gertrudis Gómez de Avellaneda. *Benv. Cellini*(?), Enriched case in form of a book, ordered by Pope Paul III for Charles V; Nautilus with bronze mounts; enamelled gold cup given by Archduke Albert to Gen. Spinola after the surrender of Breda; ivory medallion of Ferdinand II.—R XV Collection of arms and armour, but including a number of reproductions.—R XVI *Carreño,* Fernando de Valenzuela; Agate cup of the Roman period with Renaissance mountings, and a marquetry *bargueño;* 15C German Gothic cup of rock crystal.— R XVII Portraits; *Carreño,* Ines de Zuñiga, Condesa de Monterrey, and Conde de Aguilar; Italian School (c. 1550), Duque del Infantado; *Sánchez Coello* (?), Lady, also attr. to *Ant. Mor; Pantoja de la Cruz,* Duchess of Savoy; *Ant. Mor,* John III of Portugal (1552); and the 'Cup of Julius Caesar' (Augsburg, mid-16C).

A short distance to the W., in the C. de Pinar, stands the famous *Residencia de Estudiantes,* founded 1910, once administered by the Institución Libre de Enseñanza, which at one time counted among its residents, Lorca, Buñuel, Dalí, and Alberti; and among its teachers, Ortega-y Gasset and Unamuno.
   The *Instituto de Valencia de Don Juan* and the *Sorolla Museum* (see p. 286) lying to the W. of the Paseo de Castellana may be conveniently visited from here. Below the flyover crossing the Castellana, is an outdoor exhibition of representative contemporary Spanish sculpture.
   At 117 C. Serrano are the buildings of the *Consejo Superior de Investigaciones Científicas* (C.S.I.C.), containing an important research library, and the National Historical Archives. To the W. on a slope overlooking the Paseo de la Castellana and the Pl. de S. Juan de la Cruz, stands the *Natural History Museum.*

The Paseo de la Castellana is here prolonged by the wide AV. DE GENERALÍSIMO flanked (l.) by an extensive range of ministerial offices built on the site of the old Hipódromo or racecourse. Commenced in the early 1930s, these *Nuevos Ministerios* were intended to accommodate *all* the ministries of the time, but with the growth of bureaucracy they now house a mere fraction of Madrid's functionaries.
   Further N., some distance beyond both a flyover and roundabout, is No. 29 (l.), the *Pal. de Congresos y Exposiciones,* containing a Concert Hall, and No. 39, now the *Min. of Culture.* On the r. we pass the *Bernabeu Stadium,* home ground of the Real Madrid Football Club. Further N. is a modern business and residential area of little character, a section of it known facetiously as the 'Costa Fleming', named after the C. de Doctor Fleming.
   The Av de Generalísimo continues N. to the *Pl. de Castilla,* from which the C. de Agustin de Foxa bears half-r. to approach the *Estación de Chamartin,* the new, but uninspired main railway terminus for Madrid. Some distance beyond the Pl. de Castilla we approach a maze of flyovers, overlooked to the l. by *La Paz Hospital,* from which the autopista and N1 drives N. for Burgos and Irún.

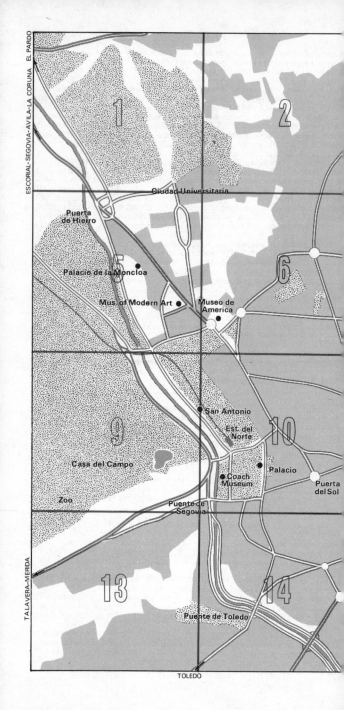

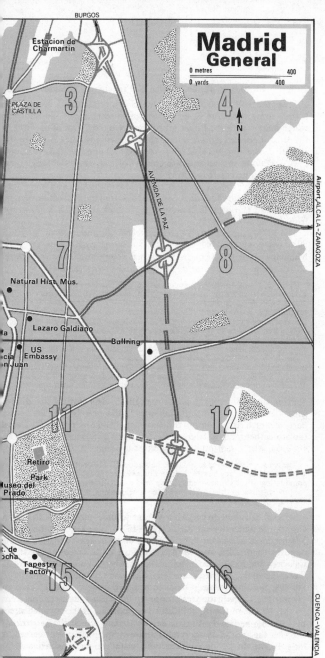

BURGOS

Estacion de
Charmartin

Madrid
General

| 0 metres | 400 |
| 0 yards | 400 |

PLAZA DE
CASTILLA

3

4

N

Airport-ALCALA-ZARAGOZA

AVENIDA DE LA PAZ

7

8

Natural Hist. Mus.

Lazaro Galdiano

Bullring

US
Embassy
n Juan

a

cia

11

12

Retiro

Park

Museo del
Prado

t. de
cha

Tapestry
Factory

15

16

CUENCA-VALENCIA

ARANJUEZ-CORDOBA-GRANADA

C   S.W. MADRID

Pl. Mayor, Pl. de la Villa, S. Francisco el Grande

From the S.W. corner of the Pta. del Sol, we enter the *C. Mayor,* and turn l. along the short C. de Esparteros to reach the Pl. de Sta Cruz which merges with the Pl. de la Provincia. On the S. side of the latter is the *Min. of Foreign Affairs,* accommodated behind a brick façade by the Italian, *J. B. Crescenzi* (1629–34), erected to house the *Audiencia,* and once containing the notorious *Carcel de Corte,* in which George Borrow was briefly incarcerated in May 1838.

We may enter the S.E. angle of the Pl. Mayor through a lofty archway to the r., although more direct approaches from the Pta. del Sol can be made viâ the C. Postas (still preserving the ancient *Posada del Peine)* or from the C. Mayor itself.

The **Pl. Mayor** (Pl. 10) is a spacious rectangle about 120 m. long and 90 m. wide, surrounded by arcades sheltering small shops (and the Municipal Tourist Office). In the centre is an equestrian *Statue of Philip III* (restored) by *Giovanni da Bologna* and *Pietro Tacca* (1615).

The plaza was formally inaugurated in 1620 under Philip III. From the balconied houses surrounding it (1617–19), built on a uniform plan by *Juan Gómez de Mora,* citizens assisted at the *autos-de-fé,* executions, bull-fights tournaments, festivals, and popular demonstrations of which the square was a frequent scene. One of the most brilliant festivals was the tournament held here in 1623 in honour of the Prince of Wales, afterwards Charles I. Another was that held to celebrate the Public Entry of Carlos III into his capital (1760), as described by Edward Clarke. Here, too, were played the religious *autos* of Lope de Vega.

To the N. is the *Casa Panadería;* recognizable by its ornamental façade, two towers and small spires, it succeeded in 1620 a municipal bake-house (*panaderia,* erected in 1590 and, with the exception of the porticus, was rebuilt after a fire in 1672. From this house the king used to survey the proceedings in the square below.

From the S. side of the plaza leads the *C. de Toledo,* flanked for a short distance by arcades. It continues S. through the '*barrios bajos*', parts of which retain some of the character of Old Madrid. On the l. rises the pro-cathedral of *S. Isidro el Real,* a large plain structure dating from 1662–64, with a Corinthian façade by the Jesuit *Fr. Bautista.*

The church is dedicated to S. Isidro Labrador (d. 1170), patron saint of Madrid, who passed his life as a humble labourer or servant. Though gutted in 1936, it still contains the silver shrine of the patron, and a crucifix by *Dom. Beltrán.*

Some distance to the E. at No. 10 C. de la Magdalena, is the *Pal. de Perales,* by *Ribera.*

Beyond S. Isidro, to the W., a market occupies most of the PL. DE LA CEBADA, in which Rafael Riego (1785–1823) was hanged by Fernando VII for his share in the Liberal rising of 1820. The short side streets opposite the market lead to the l. from the C. de Toledo to the Pl. de Cascorro and Ribera de Curtidores, an area better known as '*El Rastro*', the scene of an animated and characteristic rag-fair, particularly on Sunday mornings, when it tends to be overcrowded, although most of the 'antique' shops in the area are open at other times. By ascending steps on the W. side of the Pl. del Rastro, a good view of the crowded street may be obtained; and on a clear day, by looking due S., the *Cerro de los Ángeles,* the approx. geographical centre of Spain, may be discerned. A little E., in the C. de Embajadores, is the remarkable front of *S. Cayetano* (c. 1690) by *José Churriguera,* burnt out in 1936.

The C. de Toledo descends steeply to the *Pta. de Toledo,* begun in 1813 from the design of *Ant. Aguado* to commemorate the return of Fernando VII from captivity at Valençay, and opened in 1827. Thence it continues downhill to the Glorieta de as Pirámides and *Pte. de Toledo,* a massive stone bridge with baroque decorations 1718–35) by *Pedro de Ribera,* which crosses the canalized *Manzanares* in nine arches, only three of which have water beneath them. The old road shortly meets the Paseo de Sta María de la Cabeza, the S. W. extension of the Prado, and the main road to Toledo, (N 401), see p. 306 .

On the opposite bank lie a number of cemeteries, including that of *S. Isidro,* in which is buried Valdés Leal (d. 1691). The C. del Gen. Ricardos leads S.W. from the bridge to the *British Protestant Cemetery,* purchased in 1854. In this neighbourhood, to the r. of the bridge, take place the popular festivals (*Romerías*). he Burial of the Sardine on Ash Wednesday, etc., most notable among which is the Fiesta de S. Isidro which begins on May 15th. Remains of prehistoric settlements have been found in the vicinity.

Of interest in that it still retains much of the atmosphere of *old* Madrid, is the area between the C. Embajadores (forking l. off the C. de Toledo) and the C. de Atocha, further E. Here is the district of **Lavapiés,** and the ancient *Judería,* with the characteristic *La Corrala* or galleried tenements in the C. Mesón de Paredes, near which gardens have been laid out around the ruined church of the *Escolapios.*

From the S.W. corner of the Pl. Mayor we descend a flight of steps through the *Arco de Cuchilleros* to reach the C. Cava de S. Miguel. A fine view of the Arch and the towering exterior of the W. side of the plaza can be seen as we turn back N. towards the *C. Mayor,* in which, at No. 50, Lope de Vega was born (1562), and at No. 75 Calderón de la Barca lived and died (1600–81).—In the **Pl. de la Villa,** which opens to the l., stands the *Casa del Ayuntamiento* by *Gómez de Mora* (1640–70), with a açade of 1787 by *Villanueva* fronting the C. Mayor; the towers and doorways are by *Ardemáns.* Within are a handsome staircase, and a room containing an allegorical painting by *Goya,* among other works.— In the restored *Torre de los Lujánes,* opposite, with a late Gothic Portal, Francis I may have been confined for a year (1525) before he was removed to the Alcázar.—Just round the corner, in the C. del Codo, is a door with a horseshoe-arch; the *Conv. de las Carboneras,* behind the Torre de los Lujánes, has a good relief over the entrance to its church 1607).—To the S. of the plaza, stands the *Casa de Cisneros,* of 1537, but much restored.

The adjacent C. de Cordón leads to the small Pl. de Cordón; No 1 in the C. del Doctor Letamendi, issuing from this square, is the house of Juan Vargas, where S. Isidro is said to have lived as a servant.—The Arca de S. Isidro, a 14C coffer covered with leather, painted with the Saint's miracles, is preserved in the *Pal. Episcopal,* to the E.

The nearby *Cap. Pontificia de S. Miguel* is an interesting rococo work by the Italians *Giacomo Bonavia* and *Guarino Guarini* (1734–45). Crossing the C. de Sacramento we shortly reach the C. de Segovia.

This descends steeply to the W., passing under a viaduct and broadening out as it continues downhill to cross the river by the widened nine-arched *Pte. de Segovia,* built in 1584 by *Juan de Herrera* for Philip II. Beyond the bridge we approach the Av. de Portugal, and the N V for Talavera and Estremadura, see Rte 44. To the N. of the bridge stands the chapel of the *Virgen del Puerto,* finished in 1718 by *Ribera,* rebuilt since its destruction during the Civil War. Hence a good view of the W. açade of the Pal. Real from below the Campo del Moro may be obtained.

On the S. side of the C. de Segovia as approached from the C. del Doctor Letamendi stands *S. Pedro el Viejo* (14–15C) with a Mudéjar tower, and a retablo by *J. Churriguera.* Hence we climb the Costanilla de S. Pedro to the *Pta. de Moros.*—To the r. is *S. Andrés,* one of the oldest foundations in Madrid, although dating in its present form from

the 17C. The contents were destroyed in the Civil War. Adjoining on the
N. is the *Cap. del Obispo* (1520–35), one of the town's few Gothic
churches, which contains notable wood carvings and the Plateresque
tombs of Bp. Gutiérrez de Vargas of Plasencia and his parents, by
Francisco Giralte, who carved also the retablo mayor. The Pl. Marqués
de Comillas, to the N. of S. Andrés, is an attractive corner of the
Morería, the former Moorish quarter of Madrid.

From the S.W. corner of the Pta. de Moros the Carrera de S.
Francisco leads us to **S. Francisco el Grande,** recalling in its design the
Pantheon at Rome. The original convent church in which was buried
Doña Juana, queen of Enrique IV, made way for the present edifice
begun in 1761 by Friar *Fr. Cabezas,* and completed in 1785 by *Sabatini.*
The dome—32 m. in diameter, fractionally larger than St Paul's,
London—was designed by *Miguel Fernández.*

Intended in the mid-19C to be the national pantheon, for which it was soon
found to be unsuitable, the church was later restored and elaborately decorated
but without much taste (1889). The interior (admission fee) is a rotunda with
Cap. Mayor facing the entrance, and three domed chapels on each side. The cupola
and the chapel ceilings are frescoed by *Bayeu* and others.—In the first chapel on
the l. of the entrance, the carved doors of which should be noted, is displayed
Goya's somewhat academic St Bernardino of Siena Preaching (normally only lit
up by the guides when satisfied that their presence in conducting visitors
round the building, but light should be specifically requested).—The stalls at the E
end were brought from El Parral, Segovia, while the *Chapter House,* reached from
the third chapel on the l., contains finely carved stalls from El Paular in the Sierra
de Guadarrama. Miscellaneous paintings by *Pacheco* and other 18C artists line the
cloister. The building has recently been the object of restoration.

From S. Francisco we can return to the C. Mayor by the C. Bailén,
crossing the C. de Segovia by the Viaduct.—We may diverge for a
moment (l.) to the Pl. Gabriel Miró or Campillo de las Vistillas,
commanding what was once a famous view N.W. over the Manzanares
valley and of the Sierra de Guadarrama in the distance, but now not so
attractive. Steps, the Cuesta de los Ciegos (the blind) descend to the C.
de Segovia itself.—N.W. of the viaduct stands the still unfinished
Catedral de N. S. de la Almudena, an ambitious but commonplace
edifice designed by the *Marqués de Cubas* and begun in 1880, and which
would be better demolished rather than completed. Further N. is the
Pal. Real (see p. 259). On the r. is the *Gobierno Militar,* occupying the
former *Pal. de los Consejas* (Council of State), built under Philip III as a
mansion for the Duque de Uceda. Behind is the church of the *Bernardas*
Recoletas, built in 1671–1744, with a late-Gothic statue of the Virgen de
la Almudena. Opposite, the C. S. Nicolás leads to *S. Nicolás,* with a 12C
brick Mudéjar tower, the oldest building in Madrid.

D   WESTERN MADRID

Las Descalzas Reales, Palacio Real, S. Antonio de la Florida.

From the W. end of the Pta. del Sol the C. del Arenal leads past *S.*
Ginés, dating from 1465, but rebuilt in 1642–45, and since restored
containing *El Greco's* Expulsion of the Money-changers.

Borrow's Testaments were once used at the Sunday School in this church, one of
the best preserved in Madrid, with a richly decorated interior.

The vault beneath the chapel of the Cristo de la Esclavitud was formerly used by
penitents during Lent for spiritual exercises and mortification.

The C. de S. Martín, opposite, ascends to the Pl. de las Descalzas, and he *Conv. de las Descalzas Reales* (Pl. 10), steeped in the atmosphere of he mid-17C. Part of the convent now contains a museum of Religious rt.

We are conducted—do not be hurried—from the main cloister to an elaborately ecorated hall and ascend to an *Upper Cloister* surrounded by a series of chapels, he first containing a recumbent Christ by *Gaspar Becerra*. Among the more otable works displayed here are *Pedro de Mena,* painted figure of Our Lady of orrows; *Zurbarán,* St Francis; and *Brueghel the Elder,* Adoration of the Kings; vhile in the *Salón de los Reyes,* with a Mudéjar frieze, is an interesting collection of ortraits. Other rooms accommodate a series of 17C Brussels' tapestries from artoons by *Rubens,* and religious works of the Flemish school, and a chapel with rich display of reliquaries.—The main *Chapel* (1559–64; by *J. B. de Toledo*) is eached by a lower cloister, and contains the Tomb of the foundress, Juana of ustria, daughter of Charles V, by *Pompeo Leoni.* Tomás Luis de Victoria was hoir-master and organist here from 1586 to his death in 1611. By the late 18C natters had deteriorated: William Beckford complained, when he attended mass ere, of the 'wretched music' and 'vile stink'.

Opposite is the new building of the *Monte de Piedad* (1703), the nunicipal pawn-office, and *Caja de Ahorros* (Savings Bank, 1838), reserving a Baroque portal.

Returning to the C. de Arenal and turning r. we soon enter the PL. SABEL II. On the W. side is the *Teatro Réal,* by *Aguado* (1818–50), eopened as an opera house, on the site of the earlier Coliseo de los años de Peral, and accommodating the *Conservatory of Music,* and a *heatre Museum* (permission to visit should be sought in advance). ome rare Baroque viols left to the Conservatory in c. 1960 to form the asis of a 'Museo de Musica', were allowed to fall apart (the glue melting n the heat of summer) and were later jettisoned as bits not worth eeping!

Running N.W. from the plaza the short C. de Arrieta leads directly to he **Conv. de la Encarnación** (Pl. 6), by *Gómez de Mora,* with a tree-haded façade. The convent contains a few paintings of interest, while in he church the retablo mayor has an Annunciation by *Vic. Carducho;* he vaults are frescoed by *Bayeu;* and it contains a restored 18C organ.— .E. of the Encarnación lies the Pl. de Oriente, which may also be pproached from either side of the Teatro Réal, the W. entrance of hich faces the Palacio Real.

The **Pl. de Oriente** (Pl. 9), one of the largest open spaces in Madrid, as planned in 1811 under Joseph Bonaparte, but dates its present form om 1841, when the surface was levelled and trees planted.

The forty-four statues of Spanish kings and queens in the gardens were riginally intended, like those in the Retiro, for the top of the palace, for which, owever, they were too heavy. In the centre of the square is an equestrian *Statue f Philip IV,* modelled by *Montañés,* after a painting by Velázquez and cast at lorence by *Pietro Tacca* (with the help of calculations by Galileo). This fine atue, 'a solid Velázquez' as Richard Ford calls it, was presented to the king in 640 by the grand-duke of Tuscany, and until 1844 stood in the Retiro. The reliefs n the pedestal are modern.
S.E. of the plaza, on the E. side of the Pl. de Ramales, stands the church of *antiago* (1811) by *Juan Ant. Cuervo,* while in nearby C. de Santiago lived George orrow in 1837–38.

The **Palacio Real,** also known as the *Pal. de Oriente,* or *Pal. Nacional,* an imposing late Renaissance edifice in a commanding position on a eight that falls steeply to the W. and N. but so exposed to the chill vinter blasts from the Guadarrama range, it is said that sentinels were

constantly frozen to death! The main buildings form a square of
140 m., built about a central court, while two projecting wings on the ?
flank the *Pl. de Armas*. Above a rustic basement of granite rise th
many-windowed upper storeys, built of Colmenar stone and articulate
by pilasters and Corinthian columns, crowned by a balustrade original
intended to support statues (see above). The E. Façade is separated fro
the Pl. de Oriente by the C. de Bailén, and here is the *Pta. del Princip*
but the principal entrance is on the S. side, facing the Pl. de Arma
separated by a railing from the Pl. de la Armería. The W. wing
occupied by the *Armería Reál* (Royal Armoury), see p. 262.

In Ford's opinion this was 'one of the finest armouries in the world', and
greater interest than the palace itself, which while admittedly a truly royal o
'nothing is more tiresome than a palace, a house of velvet, tapestry, gold and bo
. . .' Ford repeats a story told of a young bodyguard at court who omitted to p
the usual salute to the Duque de Infantado, when excusing himself that he did r
know his rank, was told by his grace, more witty than most: 'my friend, the safe ru
is to suppose everybody in the palace who looks like a monkey to be a grandee
the first class'!

The exterior façades are closely related to Mansart's garden front to the cent
block at Versailles as well as to Vanvitelli's work at Caserta, while the windows a
entablature correspond exactly to Bernini's design for the Louvre. The courtyard
closer to the Farnese Palace in Rome and the Ducal Palace at Modena. T
present Palace, begun for Philip V in 1738 by *G. B. Sacchetti* of Turin a
substantially completed under Carlos III in 1764, replaced a previous pala
(founded by Enrique IV c. 1466, on the site, it is said, of a Moorish Alcázar) whi
burned down on Christmas Eve, 1734. A much more splendid scheme, designed
Felipe Juvara (d. 1735) was abandoned by Philip V on the score of expense, large
on the advice of his wife, Elizabeth Farnese. The main scheme of decoration w
begun in 1753 by *Corrado Giaquinto*, who in 1761 was followed by *Mengs* a.
G. B. Tiepolo. It was in this sumptuous palace that Napoleon remarked to I
brother Joseph. 'Vous serez mieux logé que moi aux Tuileries', adding, as he la
his hand upon one of the marble lions of the staircase, 'Je la tiens enfin, ce'
Espagne si désirée' In 1812, Wellington, on entering Madrid after his victory
Salamanca, took up temporary residence here.

The Royal Gardens below its lofty W. Façade, since June 1978 open to t
public, were originally laid out in 1566 on the former Campo del Moro, where t
Moors established a camp in 1109.

Visitors enter from the S. courtyard, and are conducted round th
apartments in groups (see p. 89). by guides curiously fascinated b
ceilings. We commence the tour from the foot of the Grand Staircas
Beyond lies the spacious central court, the main entrance to which is c
the E. Façade, which is surrounded by a porticus with statues of th
Roman Emperors of Spanish birth (Trajan, Hadrian, Theodosius, an
Honorius).—In a recess opposite the staircase is a statue of Carlos III a
a Roman emperor. The *Staircase,* with a painted ceiling by *Giaquin*
(1753–61), ascends to the guard-room or *Salón de Alabardero*
containing 16C Flemish tapestries and armour made for royal childre
(Philip III as prince, and others); the ceiling is by *Tiepolo*. The adjace
Salón de Columnas contains busts of Roman Emperors fro
Herculaneum, and 16C bronzes.

We enter the rooms in which Carlos III lived after taking possession i
1764; the *Saleta, Antecámara* and ***Salón de Gasparini,*** named after th
Neapolitan artist who decorated it. The last, with a fine marble floor an
a profusion of rococo stucco work in the 'Chinese' style, is one of th
most luxurious and beautiful in the palace. In the Antecámara are fo
portraits by *Goya* of Carlos IV and María Luisa, and a monument
clock of 1786.

From the adjacent gallery known as the *Tranvía* we pass to the *Salón*
e Carlos III, that king's bedroom, where he died. Its vault was painted
1828 by *Vic. López,* and there is a portrait of Carlos III by *Maella*
784). Next are the remarkable *Sala de Porcelana,* covered with
odelled plaques by Italian artists but made in the Buen Retiro factory,
1d the *Sala Amarilla,* or Yellow Room, with a ceiling painted by *Luis*
ópez (1829), and a fine suite of chairs. We continue through the *Gran*
omedor de Gala (State Dining Room) of 1879, preserving the painted
:ilings of the earlier Cuarto de la Reina by *Mengs, Fr Bayeu,* and
hers, to the *Music Room,* containing a tintinnabulous collection of
▸yal clocks of which both Carlos IV and Fernando VII were great
nateur collectors.

We enter the Galería surrounding the central court to reach a series of
▸oms at the N.W. corner of the palace now housing a collection of
intings.

R I (vestibule): *Van der Weyden,* Philip of Burgundy; *Bermejo,* Isabel la
atólica; R II attr. to *Caravaggio,* Salome with the head of John the Baptist; R III
.), works by *Goya,* including cartoons for tapestries, and two scenes of the
aking of gunpowder and shot in the Sierra de Tardieta during the Peninsular
'ar; also paintings by *V. López.*—R IV (l.), furnished as the bedroom of Carlos
/, with two landscapes by *Luis Paret* (San Sebastián and Pasajes); R V displays
elázquez, Caballero de la orden de S. Juan, and a study of a White Horse
estored); attr. to *Herrera ei Viejo,* Four doctors of the Church. The following
▸om (VI) contains an old copy of a Rembrandt portrait, portraits of Philip IV and
abella de Bourbon attr. to *Rubens,* and smaller works of the Flemish School.—
VII is dominated by *El Greco,* St Paul, among five works attr. to *Bassano.*
urning l. we pass through RVIII devoted to paintings by *M.-A. Houasse* (1680-
730) and containing two works by *Watteau.* The next salon displays *Ribera,*
ortrait of Don Juan José de Austria on horseback, portraits by *Bart. Gonzáles* of
hilip III and Margaret of Austria, and of historical interest, a view of the old Pal.
e Buen Retiro by *Del Mazo.*—Further rooms contains works of lesser interest,
ut lead to one displaying a fine collection of china, porcelain and glass.

Hence we approach the **Cap. Real,** built in 1749–57 by *Sacchetti* and
'*entura Rodríguez.* It is surmounted by a dome, has ceiling paintings by
'*iaquinto,* and an unfinished altarpiece by *Mengs.* The 18C organ is by
ie Majorcan *Jordi Borch.* Opposite the sacristy are two rooms
ontaining a reliquary given by Francis I to Charles V, another with
roups carved by *Berruguete,* the reliquary of the Lignum Crucis, and
ie shrine containing the bones of Fernando III (d. 1252; canonized
571).

From the chapel we enter the rooms of the E. Front, passing through
ie *Antesala, Antecámara, Cámara* and *Saleta de María Cristina,*
ontaining Spanish tapestries and 19C paintings and busts.—In the
'*omedor de Diario,* the dining room of the royal family from the time of
'arlos IV, took place on Easter Sunday the ceremony in which King and
ourt attended the blessing of a lamb and distribution of painted eggs.
he *Salón de Espejos* (mirrors) has a vault painted by *Bayeu* and
ontains Retiro porcelain.

The *Salón de Tapices,* with a ceiling painted by *Bayeu* in 1794, is
ntirely hung with tapestry, and leads to the *Salón de Armas,* in which is
ie Triptych of Isabel the Catholic, painted in 1496 by *Juan de Flandes*
nd others.—Passing through another *Tranvía,* with valuable
orcelains and miniatures, we enter a private suite of 17 rooms left as
iey were by Alfonso XIII when sent into exile in 1931. The contents of
is study characterize the man.

We return to the *Cámara* where the audiences were granted and when the ceremony of Recognition of the Princes of Asturias took place. The vault was painted by *Maella* in 1797.—*G. D. Tiepolo* painted the ceiling of the adjacent *Salón de Grandes,* whose walls are covered with blue silk in which are woven fleurs-de-lys and the cypher of Alfonso XII.

Between the Salón de Grandes and the Throne Room is the *Saleta,* to which persons of all classes who sought audience of the King had access.—The *Salón del Trono,* also known as the *Salon de Embajadores* or *De Reinos,* contains the gilt bronze lions cast in 1651 at Naples by *Finelli* for the old Alcázar and which, surviving the fire of 1734, now guard the steps of the throne.

It was here that Ford saw Fernando VII lying in state, 'his face hideous in life now purple like a ripe fig, dead and dressed in full uniform, with a cocked hat on his head, and a stick in his hand'. The Salón de Columnas (see above) was likewise temporarily converted into a 'capilla ardente' for Gen. Franco, in Nov. 1975.
The mirrors, from the glass factory at La Granja, in rococo frames, were designed by *Ventura Rodríguez* for the positions they occupy, but the intervening statues had been brought from Italy by Velázquez for Philip IV. The two large clocks in ebony and bronze cases are English, and there are some porphyry busts the 16C and two Roman busts. The ceiling painting (1764), by *G. B. Tiepolo* (then aged 78), represents the Majesty of Spain, and illustrates the different costumes its provinces. In the corners are stucco reliefs of the Seasons by *Robert Michel.* We return to and descend the Grand Staircase.

Of some interest is the **Royal Library,** at the N.W. angle of the Palace possessing more than 300,000 volumes and 4,000 manuscripts, as well as the Archives of the Royal House from 1479, and 265 incunables. One of the more remarkable items is the 15C *Book of Hours of Isabel the Catholic.* Among its earlier librarians was the arabist José Antonio Condé (1765–1820). Other collections include maps, prints, engravings and drawings, and medals, musical instruments (including some by Stradivarius), and scores, a selection of which are on display.

The Palace also contains a famous collection of *Tapestries,* beginning with several Flemish series of the late 15C, including those of the Passion, from designs by *Van der Weyden;* the Acts of the Apostles (*Raphael,* 1527); the Honours, and the Apocalypse (*Van Orley*); the Conquest of Tunis (*Van Aelst* and *Willem Pannemaker*), etc.

Near the entrance to the palace is the *Royal Pharmacy,* which may also be visited, containing curious retorts and other utensils, a distilling unit, a collection of Talavera ware, and china jars from the Buen Retiro factory.

The **Armería Real,** installed in the S. extremity of the W. wing of the palace, is a unique accumulation of arms and armour, the nucleus of which was the collection of Flemish and German armour brought to Spain by Charles V and housed in a separate building by Philip II.

Although the collection was plundered in 1808 and the old building was destroyed by fire in 1884, the most precious objects have survived, including the MS. catalogue of the collection of Charles V. Artistically, the most remarkable pieces are those of the early 16C, when the rivalry between the German and the Italian schools led to the production of decorative masterpieces, but from the point of view of general design, armour had reached its culmination somewhat earlier under Maximilian I and Philip the Fair, father of Charles V. Only at Vienna there a naturally formed body of arms and armour (as distinct from artificial collections) worthy of comparison; and it is in these two armouries alone that it is possible to study complete suites or 'garnitures' of armour, each consisting several suits for different purposes, and provided with spare parts. The collection at present accommodated on two floors, is neither well displayed nor adequately labelled, and a complete rearrangement is long overdue.

Among the more interesting exhibits are: in the main Salón, a room
0 m. long, suits of armour of Charles V by *Kolman Helmschmeid*
(471–1532) and his son *Desiderius* (1500–c. 1578) including (A 164)
rmour worn by the emperor at the battle of Mühlberg (1547) and
epicted by Titian in the equestrian portrait in the Prado. Among the
istoric pieces by famous armourers of the period are light armour worn
y Charles V at the taking of Tunis (1535), on the Algerian expedition of
541, and (A 188) that in Roman style (1546) by *Bart. Campi* of Pesaro,
resented to the emperor by Guid' Ubaldo II, Duke of Urbino; (A298)
lack and gold armour 'of Sebastian of Portugal' by *Anton*
'effenhauser of Augsburg; (A139) gold-decorated suit made by the
legroli brothers of Milan; (A291) armour made for Philip III by *Lucio*
'iccinino; (A16–17) tournament suits of Charles the Fair; (M10) steel
irban and breastplace of Barbarossa, the Barbary pirate, taken at
'unis in 1535; parade armour of Philip II; (A149) equestrian armour
iherited from Maximilian I, designed by *Hans Burgkmair* and made by
.. *Helmschmeid* with scenes in cut, engraved and inlaid steel. The arms
f Francis I taken at Pavia; swords of (G21) Fernando the Catholic;
329) Gonzalo de Córdoba, el Gran Capitan and (G35) Francisco
'izarro, are also remarkable.

Leading N. from the palace to the Pl. de España, the C. Bailén offers
anoramic views W. over the *Casa de Campo* beyond the Manzanares,
nd N.W. towards the Guadarrama mountains, now largely spoiled by
ae haphazard erection of suburban blocks. The C. Balién overlooks the
abatini Gardens, which may be reached by steps, on the site of the
oyal Stables.—To the r., in the Pl. de la Marina Española, stands the
ormer *Pal. de Godoy* (1776 by *Sabatini*).

Adjacent is the *Pal. del Consejo Nacional,* previously that of the
enate.

From the S.W. corner of the Pl. del España (see p.264), the Paseo de
Jnésimo Redondo descends steeply downhill beneath a flyover towards
ae *Pte. del Rey,* skirting the N. end of the royal gardens and passing (r.)
ae *Estación del Norte.* The entrance to the **Museo de Carruages**
Carriage or Coach Museum) lies to the l. just before crossing the bridge.

Among the miscellaneous exhibits, one of historical interest is that (built 1832)
n which Alfonso XIII and his English bride Victoria Eugenia (Ena) were returning
·om their wedding (31 May, 1906), when an assassination attempt was made on
nem as they were driving along the Calle Mayor, a bomb disguised as a bunch of
owers being hurled from No. 88 in that street, killing a number of guards and
pectators, but leaving the royal couple unharmed.

Beyond the river lies the well-wooded **Casa del Campo,** a royal park
.id out before 1623, and once surrounded by a wall, with an area of
,721 hectares; see Pl. p. 254.

One of the few open spaces remaining in the immediate vicinity of Madrid, its
osky heights afford panoramic views of the town, which was heavily bombarded
·om this quarter during the Civil War. A *Zoo* has been built here, close to an
.musement Park.—At the W. end of the *Pte. del Rey* the road diverges l. viâ the
.v. de Portugal to commence the N V (see Rte. 44), while to the r., the Paseo
Marqués de Monistrol shortly joins the N VI autopista heading N.W., see Rte 25B.

From the Estación del Norte the Paseo de la Florida leads N.W. to (r.)
. Antonio de la Florida, and is prolonged by the Av. de Valladolid, an
xtension of which, running parallel to the Manzanares, joins the N VI
t the Pta. de Hierro.

S. Antonio de la Florida (beyond Pl. 5), begun in 1792 by the Italian *Fr. Fontana,* is notable for the remarkable series of *Frescoes* painted on its ceiling by *Goya* (1798), which were received with enthusiastic admiration and won for the artist the post of first painter to the court. The church is now a monument to Goya, whose remains, brought from Bordeaux, were buried beneath the cupola in 1919.

Admirable in draughtsmanship, in colour, and in decorative effect, these frescoes are secular in spirit, and some have seen in them an expression of the artist's cynical attitude towards the Church. In his angels and other figures he is said to have mingled portraits of court ladies with those of less reputable models. The main subject (in the cupola), represents St Anthony raising a murdered man from the dead in order to name his murderer and so save an innocent accused.

In 1928 a new church, a copy of the old, was built for the service of the parish and stands a few paces N. Just to the N.E., beyond the railway line, is the *Hill of Principe Pio,* with a small cemetery where lie the victims of 3 May 1808, (see p. 246., and comp. Goya's painting in the Prado).

E   N.W. MADRID

From the Pta. del Sol the C. de Preciados (pedestrians only) and C. del Carmen, both busy shopping streets, leads N.W. to the Pl. de Callao, a central point in the **Gran Via** (officially *Av. de José Antonio*), an important commercial thoroughfare in which many of the large cinemas and cafés are situated. In the C. del Carmen stands the Herrera convent church of *N.S. del Carmen,* built in 1611–60 by *Miguel Soria* containing a polychrome group of the Dormition of the Virgin. The demolished convent was built in 1575 on the site of a brothel.—Cutting through a formerly congested but picturesque region, the Gran Via affords a direct route between the C. de Alcalá and N.W. Madrid viâ (l.) the **Pl. de España** (Pl. 5). This open space, formerly Pl. de S. Marcial, on the site of the old S. Gil Barracks, contains a *Monument to Cervantes* by *Coullaut Valera* (1927), preceded by the familiar figures (in bronze) of Don Quixote and Sancho Panza in search of chivalric adventure. At the *Torre de Madrid* (N. corner) is a S.E.T. Tourist Information Office.—A short distance N.E., in the Pl. del Conde Toreno, the church of the *Capuchinas* (c. 1650) contains paintings by *Ant. Pereda;* while in the C. de S. Leonardo is Baroque *S. Marcos* (1749-53), by *Ventura Rodrigue.*

The C. de Ferraz leads N.W. from the Pl. de España, passing (r.) the **Museo Cerralbo,** containing the private collection of the 17th Marque. de Cerralbo (d. 1922).

Among the paintings are *Zurbáran,* Conception; *Tintoretto,* Portrait of a Man (damaged); *Mengs,* 12th Duke of Alba; *Van Dyke,* Maria de Medici; genre scenes by *E. Lucas;* and, in the chapel, *El Greco, S.* Francis. The armoury contains some interesting pieces, and furniture and the minor arts are well represented.

To the W. stood the Montaña barracks, destroyed during the Civil War. Now laid out as gardens, this improbable site has been embellished with palm trees and the *Temple of Debod* (4C B.C.) recently given to Spain by Egypt.

Beyond (r.) runs the Paseo de Pintor Rosales, overlooking the attractive *Parque del Oeste,* commanding an extensive panorama

Hence a 'Teleferico' (cable cars) communicate with the Amusement Park in the *Casa del Campo* (see above).

Beyond the Pl. de España the Gran Via is prolonged by the C. de la Princesa, passing (r.) the rebuilt **Pal. de Liria** (Pl. 1), residence of the Alba family, and their protége; and housing their extensive private collections and archives. The original building was erected in 1770 on the site of the older palace of the Conde Duque de Olivares. It was damaged by Nationalist bombing in Nov. 1936, but most of its treasures were saved, some of which may be seen on prior application.

Among the most important contents are: the armour of the Conde Duque, and of the Great Duke of Alba, and portraits of the latter by *Titian, Sánchez Coello,* and others; also *Titian,* Portrait of the Duke of Mantua; *Fra Angelico,* Virgin of the Pomegranate; *El Greco,* Crucifixion; *Velázquez,* Infanta Margarita María; and works by *Palma Vecchio, Bronzino, Rubens, Rembrandt* (Landscape), *Ruysdael, Teniers* and *Reynolds,* among others. Also Brussels tapestries of his battles presented to the Great Duke by the city of Antwerp. The Library preserves a number of MSS of interest.

For the area to the N.E. see p.266.

At the far end of the street (l.) stands the Escorial-like *Air-Ministry,* on the site of the old Model Prison. Beyond is a memorial *Arco de la Victoria,* erected in the Fascist taste. It was near here that the great anarchist leader Durruti was mortally wounded in Nov. 1936.

Just N. of the Arch stands the **Museo de America** and the *Instituto de Cultura Hispanica.*

The former contains the Oñate Collection of Mexican and Peruvian terracotta vessels; the Larrea Collection of over 600 Inca ceramics and other specimens of Tihuanaco culture; Maya sculptures from Yucatán; a monument to the Mexican chief Tizoc; the Treasure of Las Quimbayas, gold objects found in Colombia, etc. Also displayed are two Maya MSS., the *Troana* and the *Cortesiano,* and paintings on mother-of-pearl by *Miguel González* (1698) depicitng the Conquest of Mexico. Among exhibits illustrating the colonial period are numerous wax figurines of local types, by *Andrés García* (c. 1800).

Some distance beyond the Arch is the entrance to the **Ciudad Universitaria;** see Pl. p. 254.

Founded in 1927, the new university was devastated in 1936–39, when it stood in the front line of the siege of Madrid, but it has since been largely rebuilt on a new plan, but hardly one of the buildings merit attention. Adjacent to the *School of Architecture* the Isabeline *Portal* of the old Hosp. de la Latina has been reconstructed. Among buildings destroyed and rebuilt in a dissimilar style is the *Pal. de Moncloa,* now the residence of the President of the Government ('Prime Minister').

From the Arch, the Av. de Pta. de Hierro (named after the 'Iron Gate' of 1753, at its far end) leads downhill to the N VI (the road for the Escorial, Segovia, Ávila, and the N.W.).

To the l. stands the undistinguished block of the **Museo Español de Arte Contemporáneo,** inaugurated in 1975, the internal distribution of which has also been much criticized. It is surrounded by gardens embellished with stone and (rusting) metal sculptures; see Pl. p. 254.

Exterior steps ascend to the ENTRANCE HALL, to the l. of which is the entrance to the museum. No section in the 'open-plan' is numbered, but by bearing round the building in an anticlockwise direction one will see all the paintings on display, which have been hung in approximately chronological order. Although it pretends to be a 'National' museum of contemporary art, much that is shown is hardly 'contemporary', and the collection is by no means representative of recent Spanish painting. The buildings also house an art library and archives.

We first pass (r.) *José María Lopez* (1883–1954). A chain of prisoners; *Ramón Casas* (1866–1932), 'El garrote vil'; *Ignacio Zuloaga* (1870–1945), 'Torerillos de pueblo', Cousin Cándida, Portrait of his father, Nude, The bleeding Christ, Landscape at Alhama, Mountains of Calatayúd; *Ricardo Baroja* (1871–1953), townscapes; *José Gutierrez Solana* (1886–1945), The fishermen's return, Chorus girls, The 'tertulia' and the Café de Pombo, The display cases, Funeral procession The bishop's visit; *Gustavo de Maeztu* (1887–1947), Pub love; *Valentín Zubiaurre* (1889–1963), The village authorities, Basque bersolaris; *Ramón Zubiaurre* (1882 1969), Santhi Andia, the fearless sailor; *Juan Echevarria* (1875–1931) Portraits c Pío Baroja, Valle Inclán, Azorin, Iturrino, Unamuno, and Self-portrait; *Fernand Alvarez de Sotomayor* (1875–1960), Portraits, etc.; *Julio González* (1876–1942 Two women; *María Blanchard* (1881–1932), The convalescent, Breton womer *Pablo Ruiz Picasso* (1881–1973), Woman in blue; *Salvador Dali* (1904–), Girl a the window, Girl's back; *Isidro Nonell* (1873–1911), Gipsy's head, '*La azotea*' c roof-terrace; *Daniel Vázquez Diaz* (1882–1969), Portraits of Unamuno, and c Dimitri Sapline the sculptor, A mother, Don Francisco and his double-bass, Th *cuadrilla,* Self-portrait, Blind musicians, Amazons (tapestry); *José Frau* (1898– Fairy-tale landscape; *Rosario de Velasco* (1910–) Adam and Eve; *Antonio Clav* (1913–), Still life; *Joan Miró* (1893–), Woman, bird, and star; *Juan Gonzale Bernal* (1908–1939), Man in chains; *Joaquin Sunyer* (1875–1956), Woma crocheting; *Francisco Gutiérrez Cossío* (1889–1970), Portrait of his mothe Tables; *Francisco Mateos* (1897–), Garden of the mad; *Rafael Zabaleta* (1907–60 Municipal garden at Quesada, Nocturne; *Benjamin Palencia* (1903–), Portrait c the poet Alberti, Portrait of Gutiérrez Solana; *Cirilo Martínez Novillo* (1921– Landscapes; *Francisco Arias Alvarez* (1912–) Roman theatre at Mérida; *Jua Guillermo Rodríguez Baez* (1916–68) Sheep wagon; *Godofredo Ortega Muño* (1905–), Chestnut trees; *Agustín Redondela* (1922–), Feria; *Menchu Gal* (1919– Portrait of the artist Zabaleta; *Ricardo Macarron* (1902–), Landscape, Portrait c a nun; *José Beulas* (1921–), Landscape near Huesca; *Antonio Tapies* (1923– Painting; *Manolo Millares* (1926–1972), Sacking!; *Modesto Cuixart* (1925– Montserrat, Fernandina, Omorká; *Manuel Viola* (1919–), Composition; *Manue Rivera* (1927–), Wire-mesh; *Rafael Canogar* (1935–), Painting No. 41; *Césa Manrique* (1921–), 'Lacran'; *Lucio Muñoz* (1929–), 'Sequeros', Black painting *Gustavo Torner* (1925–), Metallic composition; *Francisco Farreras* (1927–), Th junk, View of Cuenca; *Fernando Zobel* (1930–), Navacerrada; *Eusebio Semper* (1924–), Composition; *Manuel Mompo* (1927–), Composition; *Agustín Ubed* (1925–), Nobody blames the caliph; *Rafael Canogar* (1935–), Woman wit sombrero; *José Hernández* (1944–), Venetian opera; *Cristóbal Toral* (1940– Luggage, *Francisco Bores* (1898–1972), Portrait of Apraiz; *Pedro Bueno* (1910– Portrait of Mercedes Gal.

Among the sculptures are examples of the work of *Eduardo Chillida* (1924– *Pablo Serrano* (1910–), *Amadeo Gabino* (1922–), and *Martín Chirino* (1925–2

N. of the Pl. de España and E. of the Pal. de Liria stands the hug crumbling bulk of the *Conde-Duque barracks,* (which may be restore to house part of the Municipal Museum), with a portal of 1720 by *Pedr de Ribera* on its E. front, opposite which the C. del Cristo leads to th church of *Las Comendadores de Santiago* (1683–93) by *Manuel an José del Olmo,* and beyond, in the C. de S. Bernardo, the fine façade c the church of *Montserrat* (c. 1715–25).—To the N. lies the Glorieta d Ruiz Jiménez (or de S. Bernardo) which occupies the site of th *Quemadero,* where heretics were burned by the Inquisition; larg deposits of ashes and human bones were found nearby in 1868.

Turning downhill, we pass (r.) the undistinguished building of the ol University, formerly belonging to the Jesuits, and in 1842 used t accommodate the university which moved to Madrid from Alcalá d Henares in 1836. Most faculties have been transferred to the rebui *University City* (see above); others are being 'dispersed'.

The C. de S. Bernardo leads back to the Gran Via, but opposite th University the C. del Pez and its continuation, the C. de la Puebla, passe three interesting churches; *S. Plácido* (1641–61) with a recumbent Chris by *Greg. Fernández,* paintings by *C. Coello,* and frescoes by *Rico*

5. Antonio de los Alemanes, formerly *'de los Portugueses',* founded by Philip III in 1606 (and built in 1624–26 by *Pedro Sánchez and Fr. Seseña*), containing frescoes by *Carreño, Ricci,* and *Luca Giordano,* and a statue of St Anthony of Padua by *Pereira;* and, to the E., the *Mercedarias Descalzas* (1656). Hence we may regain the Gran Via by the *Telefónica* building (see below). Just S. of S. Antonio stands domed *S. Martín* (c. 1725–61).

Here was buried William Bowles (1705–80), the Irish author of an 'Introdución a a Historia Natural y a la Geografía Física de España' (1775), and for many years superintendent of the Spanish state mines.

F   NORTHERN MADRID

The busy C. de la Montera climbs N.E. from the Pta del Sol, passing (r.) in a street of the same name, the little basilical church of the *Caballero de Gracia* (1786–95), by *Villanueva,* built on the spot where in 1650 Cromwell's ambassador Antony Ascham had been assassinated by embittered royalists.—Opposite, to the W., is the tall *Telefónica* building, used by the Republicans as an observation post when defending Madrid during the Civil War.

After crossing the Gran Via at the Red de S. Luis, the road branches: the r. fork, C. de Hortaleza, leads N. to the Pl. de Alonso Martínez, while we follow the l. fork, the C. de Fuencarral. At No. 80 in the latter street, stands the former **Hospicio de S. Fernando,** with its elaborate stone *Doorway and red-brick front, housing the **Municipal Museum.** The building was erected in 1722–29 to the plans of *Pedro de Ribera,* while the statue of S. Fernando over the main entrance is by *Juan Ron.*

At present (1979) only a small part of its collections are on display, including a number of Views of Madrid and Maps of the capital between 1635 and 1835, among them those of Pedro Texeira (1656), Nic. Chalmandrier (1761), Ant. Espinosa de los Monteros (1769), and Tomás López (1785). Of more interest is the * *Model* or maquette of Madrid (5.20 m by 3.40 m) made by *León Gil de Palacio* in 1830, which gives a better idea of its topography at the time of Ford and Borrow than many written descriptions.

Opposite, the C. de la Palma runs W. to *SS. Justo y Pastor* or *Las Maravillas,* founded in the 17C, but largely rebuilt by *Miguel Fernández* (1770). To the N. lies the *Pl. del 2 de Mayo,* scene of the resistance of Daóiz and Velarde to the French occupation of Madrid (see p.246).

The C. de S. Mateo leads to the r. off the C. de Fuencarral just S. of the Municipal Museum. At No. 13 is the ***Museo Romántico,** established in 1924 by the Marqués de la Vega-Inclan in an old mansion.

This tastefully arranged collection contains many fine portraits of the period (c. 1800–60), notably: *Esquivel,* Nazario Carraquieri and Gen. Prim; *V. López,* Marqués de Remisa; *L. Alenza,* Augustín Argüelles; and works by *Cabral Bejarano, E.Lucas, J. Elbo, L. Ferrant,* and *J. Espalter,* among others. Also displayed are earlier paintings including *Goya,* St Gregory the Great; *Carnicero,* Godoy; and *Zurbarán,* S.Francisco Xavier. A room is devoted to souvenirs of Mariano José de Larra (1809–37) a young romantic who committed suicide; the library contains some autographs, and books and journals published during the Peninsular War.

Opposite the entrance we may cut through to the C. de Hortaleza, where, in *S. Anton* (to the r.) by *Pedro de Ribera,* is a painting by *Goya* of *The Communion of St. Joseph of Calasanz: apply at No. 53.—In the C. de Góngora, a little to the E., is the Baroque church of the *Mercedarias Descalzas,* better known as the *Góngoras,* founded by Philip IV and completed in 1689.—Continuing N. up the C. de

Hortaleza we may turn r. into the C. Fernando VI, which shortly leads to the Pl. de las Salesas and Baroque **Sta. Bárbara**, or *Las Salesas Reales*, with an elaborate façade (1750–58) by *F. Carlier* and *Fr. Moradillo* and containing the tomb of Fernando VI (1713–59) by *Sabatini.*

Baretti considered it the 'grandest' of Madrid's churches. Its altars were not, elsewhere, 'adorned with little nosegays of natural or artificial flowers, nor is hung with pretty cages of canary-birds, that keep chirping the whole day long, the great diversion of those who go to hear masses. . .'.

Adjacent is the *Pal. de Justicia,* occupying the site of a convent of Salesian nuns founded in 1750 by Bárbara de Braganza, consort of Fernando VI.—the C. Marqués de la Ensenada leads N. to the C. de Génova, crossing which and turning up the C. de Monte Esquinza, we reach at the junction of the C. de Fernando el Santo, the new cylindrical *British Embassy* (1966). Turning l. we approach the C. de Almagro, where at No. 5, opposite, is the *British Institute*—the first director of which, from 1940, was Walter Starkie (1894-1976)—and Library.—We continue N. for some distance along the C. Almagro, and after crossing the C. Eduardo Dato, take the first r., and r. again, to reach at C. Fortuny 43, the **Instituto Valencia de Don Juan** (Pl. p. 255).

This private museum was founded by Don Guillermo de Osma (d. 1922) and named by him in memory of his wife, the heiress of the Valencia de Don Juan family, and is notable for its Spanish Ceramics. The Textile Room has a rich collection ranging from Egyptian materials and Moslem stuffs of the 10C to 17C Spanish brocades. Notable in the Arabic collection is the 'bote de Cuéllar', a 14C inlaid box from Granada; while among the illuminations are the Statutes of the Order of the Golden Fleece, illustrated by *Simon Bening* in 1537. A 12C enamel book-cover from Silos, an Iberian silver Helmet, and an emerald dragon offered by Hernán Córtes to N.S. de Guadalupe, are other outstanding individual exhibits. In the rooms devoted to the **Ceramic Collection* are the great Azulejo made in Granada in the reign of Yusuf I (1408–17), known by the name of the painter Fortuny, a former owner; a fine series of Mansises, Paterna, Teruel, and Andalucian wares; heraldic glazed panels from Seville (13C); also jewellery and seals, and harness ornaments. Other rooms contain Buen Retiro and Alcora pottery and a Collection of Compostelan jet carvings; and paintings, including *El Greco,* Allegory; *Velázquez,* Portrait, wearing glasses, of Francisco de Quevedo.— A magnificent collection of Hispano-Moresque lustre ware is also to be seen. The coin collection is also important.

Opposite the N. end of the C. Fortuny is the **Museo Sorolla**, with personal belongings of the artist (1863–1923) and representative paintings donated to the State by his widow. They are perhaps best viewed on sunny days, when they can be seen to advantage.

G   THE PRADO

The ***Museo del Prado** (Pl. 12) in the Paseo del Prado, contains the national collection of paintings. It is open daily except on Jan. 1st, Good Friday, Oct. 1st, Nov. 1st and Dec. 25th. The usual entrance is at the N. end, and there is another in the middle of the long façade facing the Paseo del Prado. An early start is suggested, or alternatively during the early afternoon when many other museums are closed, but more than one visit is recommended, for, as Ford so rightly remarked, 'picture seeing is more fatiguing than people think, for one is standing all the while, and with the body the mind is also at exercise in judging, and is exhausted by admiration'.

The building (1785–1819) by *Juan de Villanueva,* originally intended as a natural history museum (though never so employed), has within the last few years been rearranged again, and a new series of admirably lighted rooms have been added; important changes and additional improvements are still being made, and work is in progress to further combat the hazards of contamination.

The collection owes its origin primarily to Charles V, whose enthusiasm for art was shared by Philip II. The royal collection formed by them was augmented by Philip IV, the patron of Velázquez, and Philip V imported many works of art from France. Further additions were made by Carlos III. Fernando VII assembled the paintings scattered among various royal palaces and installed them in the Prado Museum (1819). Some suffered in the following decades in a mania of unscholarly restoration. An important acquisition was the collection of primitives taken in 1836 from the suppressed monasteries in Madrid and the neighbourhood, and housed in the Conv. of La Trinidad until their removal to the Prado in 1872.

The following brief description of some of the more important paintings (which are not asterisked), will take the visitor over the whole gallery at present open to the public, but in an order that does not follow the numbering of the rooms (see plan, p. 271). A complete unillustrated catalogue, giving details of each painting in Spanish, is on sale at the bookstalls.

Note. The Prado Museum is at present (1979) undergoing a thorough modernization, including, the overdue installation of air-conditioning equipment, etc., and it was felt, rather than attempt to include any provisional distribution of the paintings, that it would be better to leave the description of its contents as printed in the last (1975) edition of this Guide, as an indication of what may be see. It is hoped that its reorganisation will have been completed by the time the next edition is called for, when the present description will be throughly revised.

It is possible that *Picasso's* 'Guernica' will be placed in the museum in the near future.

From the N. entrance on the **GROUND FLOOR** we traverse the Rotunda (**R 51**) displaying battle-pieces by *P. Snayers* (1592–1667), off which (l.) in **RR 51A** and **B** respectively, are 12C murals from the Ermitas de S. Baudel, Berlanga (Soria) and de la Cruz, Maderuelo (Segovia). **R 50** contains a number of fine retablos: 1321, from S. Benito el Real (Valladolid, c. 1420); 1332, from Arguis (Huesca, c. 1450); 1336, from Sigüenza Cathedral, by the *Maestro de Sigüenza*; 2545, by *N. Francés* (fl. 1434–68) from a chapel near La Bañeza (León); 2670–1, a Spanish Martyrdom of S. Vicente; and 2668–9, scenes from the life of Santiago (15C Aragonese or Catalan).

R 49, one of the principal galleries, is devoted to early paintings of the SPANISH SCHOOL and includes: 3017, *Pedro Machuca*, Descent from the Cross; 2171, *León Picardo*, Annunciation; 3110, *Juan de Borgoña*, Magdalen; 1339, *F. Yáñez*, S. Damian; *Juan Correa*, 689, Visitation; 672, Virgin and Child with St Ann; 690, Nativity; *Juan de Joanes*, 840 and 842, Martyrdom, and Entombment of St. Stephen; 846, Last Supper; 855, portrait of Luís de Castella de Villanova; *Juan Vicente Masip*, 843, Martyrdom of Sta Inés; 849–50, Calvary, and Descent from the Cross; 851,Visitation; and works by *Luis de Morales*, among others. **R 56B**, adjoining, contains work by *Pedro Berruguete*, and *Fernando Gallego*, including 3039, Martyrdom of Sta Catalina, by Gallego; and 1925, *Alejo Fernández*, Flagellation, while in **R 56C** are *Juan de Flandes*, 2935, Raising of Lazarus, and 2937, Ascension; and Passion scenes by *Rodrigo de Osona*. **R 55B**, 848, *Juan de Joanes*, Ecce Homo, leads to **R 55**, the first of many devoted to **Francisco de Goya y Lucientes** (1746–1828), which, together with **RR 56** and 57, contains his celebrated *Cartoons* for tapestries.

These were painted for the royal tapestry works of Sta Bárbara between 1776 and 1791. The designs were reproduced for the royal palaces of Madrid, the Escorial, and El Pardo. For many years the cartoons were stored in the cellars of the factory, but after repeated applications by successive curators of El Pardo, they were at length unearthed, restored, and exhibited.

The earliest series, painted for the rooms of the Prince of the Asturias at El Pardo, is perhaps the most attractive, and includes a number of holiday scenes in the neighbourhood of Madrid, e.g.: 768, Picnic on the banks of the Manzanares; 769, Dance at S. Antonio de la Florida. The later series were often touched up to suit the officials of the tapestry works, and are consequently often less perfect in design. Noteworthy are: 773, The Parasol; 778, Blind man with a guitar; 780, Earthenware seller; 784, Game of rounders; 799, Village wedding; 804, Blind man's buff; 790, Boy with a bird, and 798, Snowstorm. **R 57A:** 3047, bull-fighting scene; 2781-2, miniature oil paintings for cartoons nos. 796 and 804; 2785, the Colossus, or Panic; 739, the Duke of Osuna and family; 745, Crucifixion; 737, Carlos III. (comp. 2200 by Mengs in R 80); 750, La Pradera de S. Isidro; 2783, La Ermita de S. Isidro el dia de la Fiesta. **R 56A:** 754-67, *Mural Decorations* designed by Goya for his country house on the banks of the Manzanares, 'La Quinta del Sordo'. **R 55A:** 723, Self-portrait; 724 and 735, two contrasting portraits of Fernando VII; 725, Equestrain portrait of Palafox, defender of Zaragoza; 748-59, the 'Dos de Mayo', and the Fusillade of the 'Tres de Mayo'. In **R 53** are displayed the series known as the *Caprichos* and the *Disasters of War*, and a selection of his other prints, while further examples of Goya's work may be seen in **R 32** and **R 10** on the first floor, see p.273.

We pass through **RR 55, 54**, and **48**, turning l. into the W. entrance hall. Beyond, in **RR 75**, and **61B** to the l. are paintings by *Rubens* and his school (see also p.273) and **Sculpture** from the collection. Other examples are displayed in the rotunda (**R 74**), in the adjoining corridor (r. **R 70**), **R 72**, together with coins and medals, and l. in **R 71**: 47, Statuette of Athene (copy of the Athene Parthenos), Archaic Konros (6C B.C.), and bowl. **R 72**, 99, Bronze head (3C B.C.). **R 73** contains the **Treasure of the Dauphin**, comprising 16-17C goldsmiths' work and carved crystals brought to Spain by Philip V. Returning to and crossing R 74, we enter a parallel corridor (**R 68**) displaying 2045 and 2816, Snowscenes by *Brueghel the Younger*, the latter being a copy of a lost painting by the *Elder Brueghel*; Landscapes by *Momper*; 1446, 1854-55; by *Valckenborgh*; 1856, *Van Dalen*, and 1347-48, *Alsloot*, Festival of Ommeganck, in Brussels.

At the far end we turn l. into **R 67**, devoted to the art of *Jan Brueghel* ('de Velours', 1568-1628). **R 66**, genre paintings by *David Teniers II* (1610-90). **R 65** contains more examples of the Flemish School, while **R 64** displays a remarkable collection of portraits by **Antonio Moro** (Anthonis Mor Van Dashorst, c. 1519-76), including 2110, the Empress Maria of Austria, wife of Maximillian II (2111); 2114, the artist's wife; 2118, Philip II; 2109, Catalina of Austria; 2108, Mary Tudor, second wife of Philip II; and 2119, Woman with the Gold Chains. From **R 63**, containing 2567, *Reymerswaele*, Moneychanger and his Wife, **RR 63B** and **62B** should be taken in, accommodating further examples of the Flemish School: **R 63B** is devoted to *Snyders*, and 62B contains 1349, *Van der Meulen*, a General. Returning to and crossing **R 63** we enter **R 63A**, displaying 2217, *El Maestro de 1518*, Adoration of the Magi;

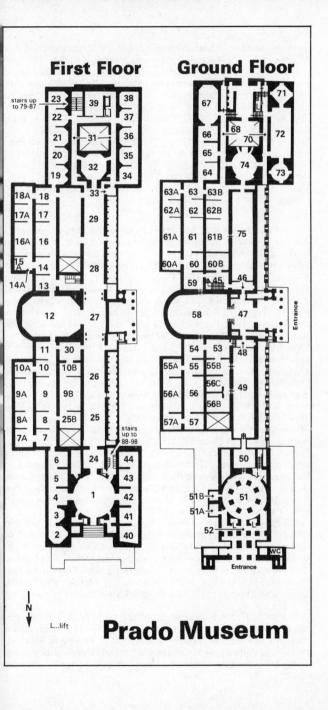

First Floor

stairs up to 79-87 →

23
22
21
20
19

39

31

32

33

38
37
36
35
34

18A | 18
17A | 17
16A | 16
15A | 14
14A | 13

29

28

12

27

11 | 30
10A | 10 | 10B
9A | 9 | 9B
8A | 8
7A | 7 | 25B

26

25

stairs up to 88-98 →

6
5
4
3
2

1

24

44
43
42
41
40

Ground Floor

67

66
65
64

68 | 70 | 71
72
73
74

63A | 63 | 63B
62A | 62 | 62B
61A | 61 | 61B
60A | 60 | 60B
59 | 45 | 46
58 | 47
75
Entrance

54 | 53
55A | 55 | 55B
56A | 56 | 56C
56B
57A | 57
48
49

50

51B →
51A →
52

51

WC

Entrance

N ↓

L...lift

Prado Museum

works by *Ambrosius Benson*, including 1933, The Virgin and Child with St Ann; and 2635; *Anon.,* the Birth and Infancy of Christ.

RR 62 and **61A** are devoted to the works of **José Ribera**, '*el Españoleto*' (1591–1652) including S. Francisco, and, S. Jerónimo: see also R 26. The former also contains 3009, *Zurbarán*, Fray Diego de Deza. In **RR 60A** and **60** are examples of *Ribalta, Orrente, Murillo* (see also RR 28 and 29), and 627, *Cano*, Virgin and Child. To the l., **R 61**: **Murillo**, including 973, the Conception; 975, the Virgin with a Rosary; and 989, St James the Great. **R 62**; Spanish School, including Landscapes by *Iriarte*. We return through **R 60** to **R 59**, containing works by *Carreño*, 645, Pedro Iwanowitz Potemkin, the Rusian Ambassador, and *Del Mazo*, 888, Empress Margarita of Austria; 1221, Don Baltazar Carlos; and 2571, La Cacería del Tabladillo, Aranjuez, concluding our tour of the Ground floor.

The **FIRST FLOOR** may be reached by a staircase in R 45, adjoining. Turning l., and then immediately r. at the top of the stairs, in the central section of the long gallery (**R 27**), we see part of the Prado's magnificent collection of **Diego Velázquez de Silva** (1599–1660): 1177, Margarita of Austria, wife of Philip III; 1178, Philip IV; 1213, Triton Fountain at Aranjuez, and in comparison, 1214, *Del Mazo,* Calle de la Reina, Aranjuez. We enter the principal Valázquez room (**R 12**) between these two paintings: 1181, Conde-Duque de Olivares; 1170, *Los Borrachos* (the Topers); 1171, Forge of Vulcan; 1192, Infanta María Teresa de Austria, daughter of Philip IV, aged ten; 1200, Jester of Philip IV, called 'Don Juan de Austria'; 1173, *Las Hilanderas*, a scene in the tapestry factory of Sta Isabel at Madrid: the painting was damaged by a fire in 1734; 889, View of Zaragoza, mainly by *Del Mazo*: the figures are probably by *Velázquez;* 1207, 1206, Menippus and Aesop, arbitrary titles for two strongly characterized types of low life in Madrid. 1208, Mars; 1189, Don Baltasar Carlos aged six; 1182, Philip IV; 1184, Philip IV in hunting costume; 1188, Don Carlos, second son of Philip III; 1191, Mariana de Austria, second wife of Philip IV; 1186, Don Fernando de Austria, brother of Philip IV; 1172, Surrender of Breda (1625), or *Las Lanzas*, in which we see Gen. Spinola, a Genoese in the service of Spain consoling the defeated Dutch leader, Justin of Nassau. The head of Velázquez himself is seen on the extreme r. 1180, Don Baltasar Carlos on Horseback; 1198, Pablo de Valladolid, jester of Philip IV; 1194, Montañés, the sculptor; 1193, Antonio Pimentel, Count of Benavente; 1178, Philip IV on horseback, at El Pardo.

RR 13 and **14** contain further examples of *Velázquez's* art, notably in R 13 2873, Ven. Mother Jerónima de la Fuente; 1167, Crucifixion; 1166, Adoration of the Magi (1619) an early work containing portraits of the painter's Sevillian contemporaries; 1196, Antonia Ipeñarrieta y Galdós, the child added after the death of Velázquez (?); 1224, Portrait of a man (probably self-portrait, c. 1623); *Del Mazo*, 888. Margarita de Austria, daughter of Philip IV; 1221, Don Baltasar Carlos, son of Philip IV, aged 16.

In **R 14**, 1201, 2, 4, 5, four dwarfs of Philip IV; El Primo, with an open book, Sebastián de Morra, simply stolid, 'El Nino de Vallecas', more than half an idiot, and 'El Bobo de Coria'; 1179, Isabella of Bourbon, first wife of Philip IV, on horseback; 1187, Infanta Doña María, sister of Philip IV, afterwards Queen of Hungary. **R 14A**, Philip IV, armed.

R 15, adjoining, is occupied solely by (1174) *Las Meninas*.

Painted in 1656, it represents the Infanta Margarita María attended by maids of honour (*meninas*) Agustina Sarmiento and Isabel de Velasco. In the foreground are the figures of the dwarf Mari Bárbola and Nicolasito Pertusato, and in the background at an open door stands José Nieto, the queen's chamberlain. On the l. is seen Velázquez himself engaged in painting the portraits of the King and Queen, whose figures are reflected in the mirror at the back. The red cross of Santiago worn by the painter is said to have been added by Philip IV himself—examine the reflection of the painting in the mirror which hangs in the opposite corner and enhances the effect of reality.

R 16A is devoted to a superb collection of portraits by **Anthony Van Dyck** (1599–1641), particularly 1486, Henry, Count of Berg; 1487, Musician; 1488, Unknown Man; 1489, the artist with Sir Endymion Porter; and 1484, Charles I of England, armed and on horseback. **R 17A** contains works by *Jordaens*, including 1549, his family in a garden, and 1493, *Van Dyck*, Policena Spinola, Marquésa de Leganés. In **RR 18A, 18**, and to the r. in **RR 17** and **16**, and (beyond R 18) in **RR 19, 20** and **21**, are accommodated further works of **Rubens**, notably, in **R 18A**; 1669, the Judgement of Paris; and 1670, the Three Graces, which dominate the room. **R 17**; 1865, Maria de Medici; 1686, Philip II on horseback; 1689, Anne of Austria and 1688, copy of Holbein's Sir Thomas More. **R 16**: 1643, the Supper at Emaus; and portraits of the Apostles; and 1692, a copy of Titian's Adam and Eve. **R 20** also contains 1954, *P. Van Somers* (1576–1621), James I of England.

Examples of the DUTCH SCHOOL are found in **RR 22**, including 1729, *Ruysdael*, Landscape, and 2974, *Koninck*, a philosopher; and **R 23**, *Wouwerman*; 2145, 2146 and 2151, among others; *Ostade*; 2121–2126 (2124-25 are copies); 2131, *Paul Potter*; 2978, *Van Goyen*; and 2103, *Metsu*. **R 23** also displays *Rembrandt*; 2132, Artemis, and 2808, Self-portrait; 1728, another *Ruysdael*; 2860, *Hobbema*; and more by *Wouwerman*.

From R 22 we turn r. along a corridor (**R 31**) containing *Esteve*; 2581, Joaquina Tellez-Girón, daughter of the Duke of Osuna; and 2876, Mariano S. Juan y Pinedo, aged 10; 2939, *Amiconi*, Marqués de la Ensenada; 2649, *Carnicero*, Doña Tomasa de Aliaga; and still-lifes by *Meléndez*.

We now enter **R 32**, the **Goya** Rotunda: 721, the painter Francisco Bayeu; 727, 728, Portraits of Carlos IV and María Luisa; 741, 742, *La Maja desnuda* and *La María Vestida*, certainly not the Duchess of Alba, who is said to have served as a model; 740, Tadea Arias de Enríques; 734, Maiquez, the actor; 720, María Luisa de Parma, wife of Carlos IV, on horseback; 2448, Marquesa de Villafranca (d. 1835); 729, Infanta María Josefa, daughter of Carlos III; 723, Portrait of the artist as a young man; 726, Carlos IV and his family, one of the most satirical portrait-groups ever painted; 2449, Duke of Alba; 719, Carlos IV on horseback; 731, Infante Carlos María Isidro, son of Carlos IV; 722, Josefa Bayeu de Goya (?); 736, Gen. Urrutia; and 2784, Gen. Ricardos.

After entering the parallel corridor containing 2329, *Ranc*, Portrait of Philip V. **R 35**; *Watteau*, 2353, Rustic Wedding, and 2354, View in the FRENCH SCHOOL, *Poussin* and *Claude Lorrain* (**R 36**), predominating. **R 34**; 2350, *Vernet*, View of Sorrento; 2269, *Houasse*, View of the Escorial; *Van Loo*, 2282, Infante Felipe, Duque de Parma, and 2283, the family of Philip V. **R 35**; *Watteau*, 2353, Rustic Wedding, and 2354, View in the Park of St. Cloud; *Rigaud*; 2337, Philip V; and 2343, Louis XIV; **R 36**,

2987, *Vouet*, Time vanquished by Youth and Beauty. **R 38**; 2291, *Mignard*, María Teresa, daughter of Philip IV; 1503, *Bourdon*, Christina of Sweden on horseback. From **R 37**, and passing 537, *Vouet*, Virgin and Child, we reach **R 39**, devoted to the *Tiepolos*. and also containing four fine inlaid tables.

Turning r. we ascend a staircase (**R 79**) to the SECOND FLOOR. **R 80** contains a number of fine historical portraits by **A. R. Mengs** (1728–79); 2200, Carlos III (comp. 737 by Goya in R 57A); 2201, Maria Amalia of Saxony; 2186, Maria Josefa of Lorraine, archduchess of Austria; 2188, Carlos IV, when prince; 2189 and 2568, María Luisa de Parma, princess of Asturias; 2190, Fernando IV, king of Naples; 2197, self-portrait; 2198 and 2199, Leopold of Lorraine, later Emperor, and his wife, María Luisa of Bourbon. In the corridor (**R 81**) to the r.; 2226, *Wertmüller*, Concepción Aguirre y Yoldi; 605-06, *F. Bayeu*, Madrilenian scenes; 2599, *R, Bayeu*, Cartoons, and 475, 2462-3 *Vanvitelli*, Venetian, and Neapolitan scenes. Turning l. and l. again into **R 82** we see 641, *Carnicero*, Ascent of the Montgolfier balloon over Madrid (1792); 2440, *Maella*, Carlota Joaquina, Queen of Portugal and daughter of Carlos IV; 2875, *Paret*, Masked ball; 2514, *Inza*, Tomás Iriarte. Passing through **R 83** (Spanish School) we enter **R 84** with works of the ENGLISH SCHOOL, a collection which is being gradually expanded, containing characteristic portraits by *Gainsborough*, *Oppie*, *Raeburn*, *Lawrence*, *Hoppner*, *Shee*, and *Romney*; and 2852-53, *David Roberts*, the Castle of Alcalá de Guadaira, and La Torre del Oro, Seville.—Returning to the entrance corridor (**R 81**) we pass 640, *Carnicero*, View of the Albufera lake (Valencia); and small paintings by *Canaletto*. **RR 86** and **87** (Spanish School) includes 1950, *Vidal*, Philip III; and 1126, *Rizi*, Auto de Fé in the Pl. Mayor, Madrid, 30 June, 1680, while to the r. **R 85** is primarily devoted to *Luca Giordano*.

Descending to the FIRST FLOOR, passing (l.) 2561, *J. F. Voet*, portrait of Luís de la Cerda,¨9th Duque de Medinaceli, we follow the corridor ahead which brings us back to the S. end of the principal gallery, the first section of which (**R 29**) accommodates further examples of *Cano* and *Coello*; and *Carreño*, 642 and 644, portraits of Carlos II and Mariana of Austria. Next (**R 28**) we see more paintings by **Bartolomé Esteban Murillo** (1618–82); 978, the Virgin appearing to St Bernard; 972, La Concepcion 'de El Escorial', and 2809, La Immaculada 'de Soult', so-called from its theft by Soult in 1813; 2834, Caballero de Golilla; 3008, Landscape. See also R 61, p. 272. Note also the fine Florentine inlaid table.

Passing the central section displaying the Velázquez described on p. 272, we turn r. into **RR 30** and **11**, devoted to **Fr. Zurbarán** (1598-1662); including a series of the Labours of Hercules, and 656, Defence of Cádiz against the English; 1236–7, Vision of St Peter of Nola, and Apparition of St Peter the Apostle to St Peter of Nola; 1239, Miracle of Sta Casilda; and 2803; Still-life. **R 10** contains works by *Goya* including 744, a picador; 2857, hunting scene; and 2862, María Luisa.

The next seven rooms, **RR 10A**, **9A**, **8A**, **7A**, **7**, **8** and **9**, accommodate fine examples of the ITALIAN SCHOOL, particularly *Bassano*, *Tintoretto* and *Veronese*, and above all, *Titian*, see also RR 2-6, p. 276. Among individual works; **R 8A**, 372 *Bordoni*, self-portrait; **R 7**: 288, *Giorgione*,

Virgin and Child between St Antony of Padua and St Roch; **R7**; 50, *Bellini*, Virgin and Child between two saints; 240, *Lotto*, Micer Marsilio and his wife, and 448, St Jerome. Among the **Titian's** are, in **R 7**: 434, Virgin and Child with St George and St Catherine; **R 8**, 427, Tcio; **R 9**, dominated by 409, Charles V with his dog, and 410, at the Battle of Mühlberg the latter shows the Emperor wearing a suit now in the Royal Armoury. Charles was so ill that he had to be lifted on to his horse, and his expression shows suffering controlled by an indomitable will; 407, self-portrait, when an old man; 408, Federico Gonzaga, Duke of Mantua; 415, Isabel of Portugal; 418, Bacchanal; 422, Venus and Adonis; 428, Salome with the head of John the Baptist; 429, Adam and Eve; and 432, '*La Gloria*', or the Apotheosis of Charles V.

We see the Emperor, his wife Isabel of Portugal, and their son and daughter-in-law, Philip II and Mary of Hungary. Below the royal group the painter has introduced his own portrait. This picture was brought from Yuste to the Escorial together with the body of Charles V.

Returning to **R 8**, we turn l., for **25A**, containing *Piombo*, 345, Christ bearing the Cross; 346, Christ in Limbo; 262, *Moroni*, a Soldier; before entering **R 9B**, devoted to **Doménico Theotocópulos** (1541–1614) a native of Candia (Crete), and better known as **El Greco**: notably 2445, S. Julián and a Knight of Santiago, and 2889, the Saviour, and in **R 10B**, adjoining, containing numerous fine portraits including 809, Gentleman with his hand on his chest; also 2644, Trinitarian Friar; and 822, Christ embracing the Cross.

From R 9B we re-enter the principal gallery at **R 26**, displaying **Ribera**: 1072, St Peter; 1100 and 1101, St Bartholomew, and his Martyrdom; and 1117, Jacob's Dream, among others. (See also R 61 and 62, desc. on p.272). The adjoining section (**R 25**) contains 2804, *Fr. Ribalta*, Christ embracing St Bernard; and 3044, *Juan Ribalta*, St John. **R 24**: *Sanchez Coello*, 1036, Philip II; 1136, Prince Don Carlos.

We now reach **R 1**, a rotunda accommodating some large works by *Carducho*, and a bronze of Charles V by *Leone Leoni* (1564), and turn l. for **RR 40-44**, with some outstanding early FLEMISH and GERMAN works. **R 42**: 1932, *Van Orley*, Virgin and Child with St John; l. for **R 43**; passing 2050-51 and 3085, *Bosch* (?), Triptych of the Temptation of St. Anthony; 1611; *Patinir*, Rest on the Flight into Egypt; 1614, St Jerome and the Lion; 1615, Temptation of St. Anthony; and 1616, Landscape, showing the Stygian Lake, Paradise, and Hell. **Hieronymus Bosch**, known in Spain as '*el Bosco*': 2048, Adoration of the Magi; 2049, Temptation of St Antony; 2052, the Hay Wain; 2056, Extraction of the Stone of Madness; 2695, a Crossbowman; 2822, Table of the Mortal Sins; 2823, the Garden of Delights, is shown in **R 44**, adjoining. Here we see 2182, *Van Cleve* or *Hans Holbein*, an Old Man; 1393, *Brueghel the Elder*, Triumph of Death; 2183 and 2184, two works by *Amberger*: 2177-8, *Dürer*, Adam and Eve, and 2179, Self-portrait (a replica of the Uffici portrait); 2180, Portrait of an unknown man; 2175-6, *Lucas Cranach the Elder*, the Hunt of Charles V and the Duke of Saxony at Moritzburg in 1544; 2219, *Hans Baldung Grien*, the Three Graces; 2220, Ages of Woman, and 2095, *Huys*, Hell. Passing back through R 42 to **R 41**: 2450 *Van der Weyden*, Pieta; 2825, Descent from the Cross; 1557, *Memling*, Triptych of the Nativity, Adoration and Presentation; 1543, Virgin and Child with angels; 1512 and 1537, *Gerard David*, two paintings of the Virgin and Child with St George and St Catherine; **R 8**, 427, Ticio; **R 9**,

Massys, Christ shown to the People, and 2702, an anon. Flemish Crucifixion. **R 40**: 1461, *Dirk Bouts*, Annunciation, Visitation, Nativity and Adoration; 1921, *Petrus Christus*, Virgin and Child.

Returning to the rotunda, we cross to a series of rooms devoted to the ITALIAN SCHOOL. **R 4** contains 15, *Fra Angelico*, the Annuciation; **R 5** (r.), 332, *Andrea del Sarto*, the artist's wife; *Correggio*, 111, 'Noli me tangere'; 112, Virgin and Child with St John; **R 6**, *Parmigianino*, 279-80, the Conde de San Segundo, and a Lady with three sons; 18A, *Barocci* Crucifixion. We turn back to **R 3**: *Botticelli*, 2838-40, three of four panels of the story of Nastagio degli Onesti ('Decameron' V. 8); 248, *Mantegna*, Death of the Virgin; and 3092, *Antonello de Messina*, Christ supported by an angel. **R 2** contains **Raphael**: 296, a miniature Holy Family with the Lamb; 297, the Virgin with the Fish; 301, Holy Family, known as '*La Perla*'; 299, portrait of a Cardinal; 298, Christ bearing the Cross, known as '*El Pasmo de Sicilia*' (painted for Sta Maria de Spásimo, Palermo).

From the N.W. corner of the Rotunda we may reach **RR 89-98** on the SECOND FLOOR, largely devoted to the later ITALIAN SCHOOLS. **R 89**: 34, *Bassano*, Last Supper; 2631, *Carracci*, Venus and Adonis. **R 90**: 147, *Gentileschi*, Finding of Moses. **R 91**: *Guido Reni*, 211, St Sebastian; 212, St James the Apostle; 219, St Peter; 220, St Paul; 3090, Hipomenes and Atalanta. **R 92** (passage); 2734-45, *Frans Franck*, Landscapes with Old Testament scenes; 2770, *Morales*, Ecce Homo; 2795-96, *Pillement*, Landscapes. **R 94**: *Carnicero*, 2786-87, Torero, and Maja; 2793-94, *Oudry*, Conde and Condesa de Castelblanco. **R 95**: 2754-56, *W. K. Heda*, still-lifs; 2820-21, *J. Ch. Vollardt*, Landscapes; 2788, *Jean de Boulogne*, negation of St Peter. **RR 96-8** also concentrate on the Italian School, **R 97** containing 324, *Salvador Rosa*, View of Salerno, and **R 98**: 63, *Cantarini*, Holy Family; 65, *Caravaggio*. David and Goliath; 2235, the Birdseller, by an anon. disciple of Carlo Saraceni; and 148, *Cecco de Caravaggio*, Woman with a Dove.

Returning to the Rotunda, we may make our exit.

A selection of the Prado's collection of 19C works is at present house in the nearby **Casón**, see p.247.

25   EXCURSIONS FROM MADRID

A   EL PARDO; B   THE ESCORIAL; C   ARANJUEZ;
D   ALCALÁ DE HENARES, AND GUADALAJARA.

The only short excursion of any interest in the immediate vicinity of Madrid is that to *El Pardo* (see below). but the capital is a good base for expeditions to the *Escorial* (see p.278), *Aranjuez* (p.284), *Alcalá de Henares* (p.286) and *Guadalajara*, p.288. For some travellers *Toledo* (Rte 26), *Segovia* (Rte 27), and *Ávila* (Rte 28), are more conveniently visited in day-trips from Madrid, while the Sierra de Guadarrama and Sierra de Gredos, N. and N.W. respectively, are also within easy range, although the roads are often crowded at weekends, particularly when returning on Sunday evenings.

A   EL PARDO

Follow the C. Princessa or Paseo de la Florida, the N. extensions of which converge near the *Pta. de Hierro* (Iron Gate) erected in 1753 at the entrance to the royal park. Here we bear r. through oak and ilex woods

affording cover for deer and other game, and pass a turning (r.) to the
Pal. de la Quinta, containing a collection of wall-papers, to reach
(14 km.) *El Pardo.* The village, founded by Carlos III, is divided by a
plaza from the **Palace,** a square edifice with a tower at each corner, and
surrounded by a moat. The principal entrance is on the S. side.

The present palace, which Clarke considered 'an indifferent seat for an English
country gentleman' is in fact a not inelegant building with pleasant patios and
colourful gardens. It was constructed on the site of a hunting lodge, built in 1405 by
Enrique III. This was replaced by a palace begun in 1547 by *Luis de Vega* for
Charles V and completed in 1558 by Philip II, who adorned it with many works of
art. This was almost entirely destroyed by fire in 1604, and the present building, by
Fr. de Mora, dates from the reign of Philip III. Enlarged by Carlos III—it once had
stabling for 800 horses and 1000 mules—it received its internal decoration under
Carlos IV and Fernando VII. The ceilings, with frescoes by various artists, and
stuccos by *Robert Michel,* are of some quality. Here in 1766 Carlos III found
refuge after the riots roused in Madrid by his unpopular Italian minister,
Esquilachi, and many winters he spent here hunting. It was the official residence of
the late dictator.

Its interior, which may be visited (guided groups only), is less elegant, although
certain formal reception rooms are attractively decorated (particularly one in the
'Chinese' taste) and tapestried (some *after Teniers*; others from *Goya's* cartoons).
The private apartments are furnished in a mean manner.

Just N. of the palace stands the restored ***Casita del Principe,** a
'cottage orné', built in 1786 for Carlos IV when Prince of Asturias as a
retreat from the severe etiquette of his father's court. From the entrance
rotunda we may visit a series of well-proportioned and elegantly
decorated and furnished rooms. The Yellow Room (l.) and (r.) a room
with frescoes by *Luca Giordano,* are particularly attractive, while a third
contains frescoes by *Gonzalez Pastor.* Some portraits by *Mengs,* and a
series of *Tiepolo* pastels are notable.

On a hill to the W. of the Manzanares (views) stands the convent church of *Sto
Cristo,* containing a painted Entombment in carved wood by *Greg. Fernández,*
and two paintings by *Ribera.*

On leaving the Pardo, the return to Madrid may be made by driving E.
through the park to meet (7 km.) the C 607, where we turn r., some 6 km.
N. of its junction with the N I. Here stands the chapel of *N.S. de
Valverde.*

The excursion may be extended by turning l. towards Colmenar
Viejo, 14 km. to the N. on a good new road.—After 4 km., a road leads r.
7 km. to the early castle of *Viñuelas,* which once belonged to the order of
St John.—**Colmenar Viejo** (15,500 inhab.) has a parish church (14C,
with Renaissance alterations), possessing a tall steeple, and a retablo by
Fr. Giralte (1579); here are also two old chapels and a Moorish fountain.
The road goes on, skirting the E. bank of the Embalse de Santillana to (l.
14 km.) **Manzanares el Real,** a good centre for the exploration of the
granitic hills of the Pedriza de Manzanares, with the *Castle of the
Mendozas, built in 1435–75 with additions including the Mirador of
1480 by *Juan Guas* for the Dukes of Infantado, and distinguished by
such Mudéjar features as honeycomb cornices, diamond-point in
plaster, and stone balls embedded.—The N VI may be reached at
Villalba, 17 km. to the W., and 40 km. N.W. of Madrid, or we may turn
N.E. to (15 km.) *Miraflores de la Sierra (Hotels),* with a retablo of 1557
in its church, whence we may bear S.E. and after 20 km. meet the N I
near *El Molar,* 42 km. N. of the capital.

B THE ESCORIAL

We drive N.W. on the N VI, leaving the Pta. de Hierro (see above) on our l., and shortly pass (r.) the *Hipódromo de la Zarzuela*, N. of which, in the park of El Pardo, lies the small palace, originally a hunting-box, of *La Zarzuela* (no adm.) built by Carlos IV and since reconstructed on the site of an earlier one, from which Spanish operettas, first performed here in the 17C, take their name of 'Zarzuelas'. It is now the residence of the Spanish royal family. At 13 km. we fork l. onto the C 505, and after c. 9 km., at Pte. de Retamar, the Escorial comes into sight under the jagged sierra. At (17 km.) *Galapagar*, the last intermediate halt of royal funerals, the present clergy-house was Philip II's residence during the building of the Escorial. One reason for the dearth of trees here is the fact that they were felled for the production of charcoal for the kitchens and braziers of Madrid in previous centuries, and no one even considered reafforestation. The road skirts *El Escorial de Abajo*, with the railway station, and climbs to (19 km.) the upper town (3280 ft) beside the monastery, with a combined population of 12,400 (*Hotels*). Regrettably the lower slopes of the range are now disfigured by new buildings, and the monastery no longer stands in almost splendid isolation.

The **Escorial*, the full title of which is *El Real Sitio de S. Lorenzo el Real del Escorial*, includes a monastery, a church, a royal palace, a royal mausoleum, and a famous library. Like the Royal Palace in Madrid, it is still conserved by the Patrimonio Nacional (see p.89). Since 1792 it has formed a 'ciudad' of itself. The huge and austere edifice, mainly Doric in style, is a rectangular parallelogram, 205 m. from N. to S. and 160 m. from E. to W., with towers at the corners, and loftier towers and the dome of the church rising in the centre. Statistics strive to convey an idea of its size; it contains 16 courtyards, 2673 windows of which 1100 are external, 1200 doors, 86 staircases, and 900 m. of painted frescoes.

Yet the edifice has little which is either royal, religious, or antique. The clean granite, blue slates, and leaden roof look almost new. The windows are too small, but had they been planned in proportion to the façades the rooms lighted by them would have been too lofty, and thus external appearance was sacrificed to internal accommodation. Nevertheless, the building has a certain grandeur of conception that had characterized the real arbiter of taste, Philip II, whose attitude is best summed up in his own instructions to Herrera; 'Above all do not forget what I have told you; simplicity in the construction, severity in the whole, nobility without arrogance, majesty without ostentation'. The reactions of travellers in the past have been mixed. Edward Clarke (1760-61) found it 'a large confused stupendous pile', while Gautier considered it 'the dullest and most wearisome edifice that a morose and suspicious tyrant could ever conceive for the mortification of his fellow-creatures'! Ford suggested that it might 'disappoint at first sight, for expectations have been too highly raised; but this is the penalty which the credulous hope of travellers must pay, who will go on expecting too much in spite of illusion-dispelling experience'.

Admission. Tickets are obtained at the N. and W. entrances; there is no charge to enter the church; but see p.89. The building is illuminated at weekends and at festivals.

History. The Escorial was built in 1563–84 by Philip II. His objects were to obey the wishes of his father Charles V by constructing a royal burial place and to fulfil a vow made at the battle of St Quentin, which was fought in 1557 on St Lawrence's day (Aug. 10th). The story that the ground-plan of the structure is intended to represent the gridiron on which St Lawrence was martyred is a later fancy, indifferently supported by the ground-plan itself. The first architect, *Juan Bautista de Toledo*, who had worked with Michelangelo on St Peter's in Rome, was summoned from Naples in 1559, and the first stone was laid on April 23rd, 1563, but Bautista died in 1567, and the work was completed by his pupil, *Juan de Herrera*, on Sept. 13th, 1584. The monastery was occupied by fifty Hieronymite monks, under whose direction was a Colegio or theological seminary. Here for fourteen years Philip II lived, half king, half monk, boasting that from the foot of a mountain he governed the world, old and new, with two inches of paper.

The palace, although enlarged and richly decorated by later monarchs, was intended by Philip as a simple appanage of the monastery, where he might spend his later days in religious peace. But for the decoration and enrichment of the rest vast sums were spent. Distinguished artists from Italy and elsewhere were invited to cover the walls with frescoes and paintings; rare books and MSS. made the library one of the most valuable in the world; while the church was enriched with paintings, statuary, countless vessels of gold and silver, and—the king being a relicomaniac—515 reliquaries enshrining (it is said) 7,421 relics. In 1671 the monastery and some of its valuable contents were damaged by fire; and in 1808 the building was plundered of its bullion by the French under La Houssaye, who left the relics in a pile on the floor. The exterior was also injured. Fernando VII did what he could to repair the damage, but after his death many of the best pictures were removed to Madrid. It ceased to be a royal residence c. 1861, and since 1885 the monastery has been occupied by Augustinian monks.

The principal entrance is in the centre of the main W. Façade, while on the l. is the entrance to the *Colegio*, on the r. that to the *Convent*. The main portal is surmounted by a colossal stone statue of St Lawrence, with head, hands, and feet of marble. Passing through the vestibule (within which, on the r., is the entrance to the *Library*), we enter the *Patio de los Reyes*, a spacious court taking its name from the six huge statues of Kings of Judah high up on the façade of the church immediately opposite us. These, like the statue of St Lawrence, are by *Monegro*.

A 'plate of gold' on a pinnacle above the church is said to have been placed there to show that the colossal expense of the Escorial had not exhausted the royal resources; but in 1949 the metal was found to be gilded bronze, engraved with prayers for protection against storms.

The *Church, or *Templo*, built in 1578–81, with two towers and a central dome surmounted by a lantern bearing a cross, 94 m. above the pavement, is entered through the dark *Coro Bajo*, or lower choir, whose flat vault (the '*boveda plana*'), a triumph of architectural skill, supports the upper choir. The interior of the church, square in plan, with four massive piers (8 m. square) supporting the central cupola (17 m. in diameter and 90 m. high), conveys by its fine proportions, its bold vaulting, and its granite simplicity, an impression of grandeur, even if badly lit.

Around the church are 42 subsidiary altars, with altar-pieces by *Navarrete*, *Zuccaro*, *Pellegrino Tibaldi*, *Luca Cambiaso*, *Michiel Coxcie*, and others. On the vaulting are eight large but mediocre frescoes by *Luca Giordano*. On the r. is the white marble *Christ, carved by *Benvenuto Cellini* in 1562, and given to Philip II by the Grand Duke of Tuscany in 1576, and carried here on men's shoulders from Barcelona.

The **Cap. Mayor**, adorned with precious marbles, is approached by a flight of steps. The *Retablo* of the high altar, 28 m. high, an elaborate design in marble and gilded bronze by *Giacomo Trezzo* of Milan, shows the four architectural orders and includes heroic statues and medallions by *Leone Leoni* and his son *Pompeo*, and paintings by *Pellegrino Tibaldi* and *Zuccaro*.—On each side are the Oratorios, low chambers of black marbles for the royal family, and on these are the so-called **Enterramientos Reales*, kneeling bronze-gilt groups by *Pompeo Leoni*. On the l. are Carlos V, with his wife Isabel (mother of Philip II), his daughter María and his sisters Leonor and María. On the r. kneel Philip II, Ana, his fourth wife, Isabel, his third wife, and María, his first wife, with her son Don Carlos. Mary Tudor, Philip's second wife, is conspicuous by her absence.

In the S.E. corner a door admits to a vestibule, beyond which, and passing through the *Antesacristía*, with its arabesque ceiling, we enter the **Sacristía**, a handsome room, with arabesque ceiling-paintings by *N. Granelo* and *Fabricio Castello*. The presses contain vestments; above are mirrors, including one presented by Anne of Austria; and on the walls are paintings by *Ribera, Luca Giordano, Titian*, and others.

At the end of the room is the *Retablo de la Santa Forma*, behind which is preserved the host or wafer, which is said to have bled at Gorcum in Holland when trampled on by Zwinglian soldiers in 1525. Bas-reliefs on the altar represent the miracle and the presentation of the wafer to Philip II by Rudolph II of Germany. The painting on the retablo, by *Claudio Coello*, depicts the reception of the relic in this sacristy. The heads are portraits: Carlos II, who erected the altar, kneels in the centre; behind him are the dukes of Medinaceli and Pastrana; the prior is Santos, historian of the Escorial; of the Escorial; and low down on the l. is the painter. The host is enshrined in a bronze-gilt tabernacle presented by Isabel II, in the *Camarín*, a richly decorated chamber behind the altar.

The **Coro Alto**, situated above the Coro Bajo and overlooking the W. end of the church, is now closed to the public, but permission to visit may be obtained from the Augustin Fathers. It contains 124 stalls, carved in seven sorts of wood, after Herrera's design. Here Philip II, in his stall at the S.W. angle, would frequently join in the devotions of the monks. The *Old* church, however, was more likely where, according to the story, he received the news of the momentous victory of Lepanto without moving a muscle, and at the end of the service ordered a Te Deum to be chanted. The *Choir*, decorated with frescoes by *Cincinnato* and *Luqueto*, contains a wonderfully poised lectern, a rock crystal chandelier, and the four organs (1578), which until 1650 were the biggest in the world, and built by Gilles Brebos. They were badly 'modernized' in the 1920s, and have been restored recently, but are musically uninteresting. The Glory on the vault is by *Luca Cambiaso*. In the *Antecoros* are kept 216 huge parchment choir books, some with illuminations by *Andrés de León* and his pupil *Julián de la Fuente*.

From the Antesacristía we return to the vestibule, off which is the *Bajada a los Panteones*, a staircase to the royal tomb-chamber. As we descend we pass the entrance to the Panteón de los Infantes and further down the door of the *Pudridero*, or rotting-place, a vault in which the royal corpses remained for ten years before being commited to their final resting places. At the foot of the staircase we enter the **Panteón de los Reyes**, an octagonal vault c. 9 m. in diameter, situated directly beneath the Cap. Mayor. This chamber was left in bare and dignified simplicity by Philip II; the marble and gilt bronze decoration was added by Philip III and Philip IV. Begun in 1617, this enrichment was designed by *G. B. Crescenzi*. The body of Charles V was transferred here c. 1634 from the old church and here lie all later Spanish monarchs, except Philip V and Fernando VI with their queens, buried respectively at *La Granja*, and *Sta Bárbara* (Las Salesas Reales), Madrid. Opposite the entrance is an altar, with a crucifix by *Pietro Tacca*; and on six sides are horizontal recesses with 24 black marble sarcophagi in antique style, each bearing the name of the occupant. Kings (including Isabel II) lie to the l. of the altar, queens who have been mothers of kings lie to the r. Above the door are two more sarcophagi, one containing the remains of Francisco de Asis, consort of Isabel II. Alfonso XIII, buried in Rome, is to be transferred here.

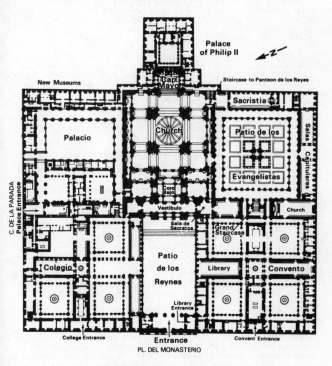

El Escorial

Philip IV would lie in the niche destined for his corpse while mass was celebrated over him, while his son, the moronic Carlos II, would gaze for hours at the mummified remains of his ancestors, which he had caused to be displayed.

The *Panteón de los Infantes* contains the tombs of princes and of queens ineligible for the royal vault. In the 5th chamber is the marble tomb, with recumbent effigy, of Don Juan of Austria (1547–78), half-brother of Philip II and victor at Lepanto, and in the last is interred Don Carlos, son of Philip II (1545–68).

We reascend to the Antesacristía and thence enter the *Lower Cloister* (*Claustro Principal Bajo*) surrounding the gardens of the *Patio de los Evangelistas*, which takes its name from the statues of the Evangelists (by *Monegro*) on the Doric temple in the centre.

The frescoes in the cloister are of little value. On the S. side are the **Chapter Rooms** (*Salas Capitulares*). The Pompeian ceiling is by *Granelo* and *Castello*. Among the paintings displayed here are: *After Velázquez*, Innocent X; *Ribera*, Holy Trinity; *Carducho*, Visitation; flower paintings by *Daniel Seghers*; *Navarrete*, Martyrdom of Santiago and four other works; an early El Greco (?) of St John the Baptist and St John the Evangelist.

In the end room are some embroidered vestments, and among other objects: a silver-gilt retablo; an ivory diptych and casket of the 10C; embroidered book cover; enamel casket of the 12C; an ivory diptych of the 14C; Church plate; a bishop's mitre in Mexican work (16C); and an alabaster figure of St John the Baptist by *Nic. Vergara*.

At the S.W. angle of the cloister is the *Old Church* (Iglesia Vieja), containing three paintings attr. to *Titian* (Adoration; Ecce Homo; Martyrdom of St Lawrence). On the walls are mortuary crowns of Spanish kings.—A grand *Staircase* (Escalera Principal), designed by *Juan Bautista Castello* (El Bergamasco), ascends from the W. side of the Lower Cloister to the Upper (closed to the public, but see above). The friezes, painted by *Luca Giordano*, depict the Battle, Siege, and Surrender of St Quentin, and Philip II and his architects planning the Escorial. Also by *Giordano* is the ceiling-painting. 'La Gloria' or 'St Lawrence ascending to Heaven'; among his companions may be recognized portraits of Charles V, Philip II and Carlos II.

On leaving the cloister we pass through the *Sala de Secretos*, so-called from its peculiar acoustic properties, back to the vestibule at the main entrance of the monastery, and thence ascend to the **Library*, a long vaulted room with a marble pavement. The frescoes (in colours 'too gaudy for the sober books', remarked Richard Ford) by *Tibaldi* (ceiling), and *Carducho*, refer to the liberal arts and sciences. In the bookcases, made by *José Flecha* from Doric designs by *Herrera*, the older books stand with their front edges bearing their titles turned outward, as arranged by Arias Montano (1527–98), the first librarian. Clarke relates that the illiterate Jeronimite monks into whose hands the library later fell were inordinately suspicious of anyone showing sufficient interest as to copy anything, saying 'if you copy our Manuscripts, the originals will then be worth nothing'!

Among the treasures displayed in glass-cases are: Missals of Charles V, Fernando and Isabel, and Philip II; the Codex Aureus, richly bound, with the Gospels in gold letters, made for the Emp. Conrad II and Henry III (early 11C); the Codex Albeldensis (976); a 15C Virgil, written in Spain; 15C Apocalypse, with elaborate illustrations; and the Cantigas de Sta María, by *Alfonso el Sabio*. The globe belonged to Philip II. The library, in spite of vicissitudes in the past, contains c. 40,000 printed volumes. The *Biblioteca de Manuscritos*, shown by special permission, contains c. 2000 valuable Arabic MSS., among others.

We leave the monastery by the main portal and, turning to the r., proceed to the middle of the N. façade, to enter the **Royal Palace** (*Pal. Real*). Visitors mount to the first floor and await the guide who 'escorts' them. The series of small rooms first shown are notable for their tapestries, mostly made at Madrid after *Teniers*, *Wouwerman*, *Goya*, *Bayeu*, and others.

At this N.E. angle of the building is a small suite of richly decorated private apartments known as the ***Habitaciones de Maderas Finas** (fine woods), for which a special entrance ticket should be requested. The quality of the cabinet work and marquetry of the doors, floors, panelling, and furniture, etc., is incomparable. Work on these rooms, which should not be missed by the connoisseur, dates from the reign of Carlos IV, and was completed in 1831.

We shortly reach the Sala de las Batallas, with a huge fresco by *Granelo* and *Fabricio Castello* (1587) of the Battle of Higueruela in 1431. The costumes in this fresco, copied from an earlier work found in the Alcázar at Segovia, are of historical interest. Between the windows and at the ends of the room are other military and naval scenes.—We descend to the next floor and the **Palace of Philip II**, first visiting the rooms of the Infanta Isabel, daughter of Philip II, which contain historical relics, including a portative organ (1575) by Gilles Brebos, used by Charles V at Yuste, and a 16C Flemish Virgin and Child. The room in which the king gave audience and received ambassadors has whitewashed walls, Talavera tiling, and contains two Brussels tapestries from the Spheres series (16C), some interesting views of Royal residences and battle-pieces, while in the adjoining room, with magnificent *Marquetry Doors (German), and a curious Sundial on the floor, are portraits by *Pantoja*.

Adjacent is the simple bedchamber, but the austere monarch is said to have expired (Sept. 1598) in a small recess commanding a view (through movable shutters) of the high altar in the church, upon which his dying gaze was fixed. A copy of the Haywain by *H. Bosch* (original in the Prado), Philip II as an old man, by *Pantoja*, and works of the Flemish and German Schools are also displayed here, together with the litter that carried the king on his last painful journey to the Escorial.

Returning to the rooms of the Infanta Isabel, we descend to the **New Museums**, a series of vaulted rooms, in which have been installed most of the finer paintings of the Escorial Collection. R I *Patinir*, Landscape with St Christopher; *H. Bosch*, Mocking of Christ, a copy of a panel from the Garden of Delights (original in the Prado), and two Temptations of St Anthony from the school of Bosch; *Gerard David*, triptych of the Deposition; and some studies of natural history by *Dürer*, restored. R II is devoted largely to the work of *M. Coxcie* (1499–1592), while R III displays *Titian*, Burial of Christ, St Jerome, and an Ecce Homo; and *P. Veronese* (?), Annunciation. R IV *Titian*, Last Supper (painted in 1564 for the refectory of the Escorial), mutilated and retouched; works by *Veronese, Bassano, G. Reni, Zuccaro*, and a St Jerome by *Palma Vecchio*. R V contains some outstanding paintings by *Ribera*, including St Jerome, Jacob guarding Laban's flock, Aesop, St. Francis, and the Burial of Christ; and R VI *Velázquez*, Joseph's Coat of many colours (painted in Italy c. 1630); *A. Cano*, Virgin and Child; *Valdés Leal*, Nativity; *Carreño* (?), Carlos II as a child, and Mariana de Austria.

We shortly reach a subsidiary range of rooms devoted to the *Architectural History of the Escorial*, with numerous designs, plans, engravings, models, etc., and a collection of tools and machines used in the construction of the monastery.—Hence we ascend to three larger rooms containing further important paintings; outstanding are *R. Van der Weyden*, Christ on the Cross between the Virgin and St John, and a copy by *Coxcie* of his Descent from the Cross, the original of which is in the Prado; *El Greco*, *St Maurice and the Theban Legion (1582), and the 'Gloria de Felipe II' (Philip II's dream of heaven and hell), among other works. Also preserved here are ten tapestries of the Conquest of Tunis by *G. Pannemaker* (completed 1554), and a 16C tapestry copy of *Bosch's* 'Garden of Delights'.

To visit the Casita del Principe, we turn r. on leaving the palace and walk through the Jardines del Principe. The **Casita del Principe**, or *Casita de Abajo*, a miniature country house in the style of the Casa del Labrador at Aranjuez, was built in 1772 by *Juan de Villanueva* for Carlos IV when prince. The elaborately decorated rooms contains numerous objects of art and paintings of the Spanish, Italian and French schools. Some of the ceilings are painted in the Pompeian style, and one room is decorated with over 200 plaques of Buen Retiro porcelain showing mythological scenes.—The smaller *Casita de Arriba*, also by *Villanueva*, restored and refurnished, lies a short distance to the W. of the monastery.

The 18C *Real Teatro de Coliseo* has recently been restored.

EXCURSIONS FROM THE ESCORIAL.

A road (off which we turn to reach the *Silla del Rey*, an eminence with steps and benches hewn in the rock, from which Philip II used to view the gradual rise of his great building) leads S.W. to join the new road to *Las Navas del Marqués* (3500 ft,) with the ducal residence built by Pedro de Ávila. Marqués de las Navas. Beyond, we enter the extensive pine forest planted by the Duque de Medinaceli, to *Navalperal* (3700 ft), and may continue W. to Ávila.—Another road bears S. from the Escorial and climbs through the foothills of the Gredos range viâ (15 km.) *Robledo de Chavela*, with a church containing a retablo of 17 panels, probably by *Antonio de Rincón* (late-15C) to (16 km.) *Navas del Rey*, see p.408.—The C 600 leads S. from the Escorial to (11 km.) *Valdemorillo*, where the 12C church was altered by Herrera, and past (15 km.) *Brunete* (p.408) to (15 km.) *Navalcarnero*, on the N. V. Tourists travelling from Segovia and La Granja to Toledo viâ the Escorial may find this road a convenient way—should they wish to do so—of by-passing Madrid.

Some 9 km. N. of the Escorial, to the l. of the C 600 as it approaches the village of Guadarrama, stands the entrance to the **Valle de los Caidos** (the Fallen). A grandiose expiatory monument to those slaughtered in the Civil War, lies 5 km. to the W., below a gigantic *Cross* of reinforced concrete encased in stone and rising to a height of 150 km, the base of which is approached by a rack-railway.

After a period of 20 years, this work of supererogation was completed in the Fascist taste, using political prisoners in its construction, by *Diego Méndez*, following the designs of *Pedro Muguruza*, and inaugurated in 1959. The massive subterranean *Basilica* (250 m. long) is entered through a short vaulted passage hewn through the rock. Appropriately, below the cupola, lies the Falangist martyr José Antonio Primo de Rivera (1903–36), while in the crypt repose the remains of unknown victims of the war, ostensibly of every political conviction. Francisco Franco (1892–1975), the late dictator of Spain, also chose to be interred here beneath a symbolically whited sepulchral slab near the altar. Beyond lies a courtyard, round which stand a *Centre of Social Studies*, and a *Monastery* (the Benedictines of which serve the Basilica).

We may regain the N VI by following a road E. opposite the entrance, or by turning l. to *Guadarrama*, see p.322.—Hence the C 600 climbs the lower slopes of the range which have been disfigured during recent years by the uncontrolled erection of chalets to (10 km.) *Navacerrada*, see p.322.

C   ARANJUEZ

For the road from Madrid to (48 km.) Aranjuez, see Rte 54A, p.457.

ARANJUEZ, a seedy oasis in the tawny Castilian plain and formerly a favourite pleasance of the Spanish court, is well-known for its gardens, luxuriant elms and plane-trees, water springs, nightingales, asparagus and strawberries.

The town (31,400 inhab.; *Hotel*), of no great interest, is laid out on the chess-board plan. Close to the palace, is the Pl. de S. Antonio, bounded on one side by the *Casa de Oficios* (1584–1762), the courtiers' quarters, on the other by the *Jardín de Isabel II* and the *Casa del Infante*. In the centre is the *Fuente de Diana* or *de las Cadenas* (the chains), at the S. end the chapel of *S. Antonio*, by *Bonavia*, and at the N. end the Parterre de Palacio. At the E. end of the avenue facing the palace is the church of *Alpajés*, (1680; completed by *Bonavia* in 1749); while to the S. is the *Pl. de Toros*, beyond which rises the *Mirador de Cristina*, commanding a wide view. Aranjuez was formerly an important horse-breeding centre, but the *Caballerizas Reales*, or royal stables, are now empty.

The **Palace**, in its present state, is a somewhat spiritless 18C building in the style of Louis XIV.

History. The summer residence built here in 1387 by Lorenzo Suárez de Figueroa, Grand Master of the Order of Santiago, became royal property under Fernando and Isabel. Charles V made it a shooting-box, and Philip II, whose architects were *Juan Bautista de Toledo* and *Juan de Herrera*, enlarged it to a palace, but this was practically destroyed by fires in 1660 and 1665. The present edifice is a reconstruction of 1715–52, designed for Philip V by *Pedro Caro*, with two wings added in 1775–78 by Carlos III. Philip II introduced elms from England, and subsequent monarchs contributed to the embellishment of the palace and grounds. Schiller places the scene of his '*Don Carlos*' at Aranjuez.

Late 18C travellers remarked that the local wild boar were so tame that they were fed in the streets, while another exotic sight was of camels carrying wood about the town, 21 of which remained of those imported earlier in the century. It was often visited for the excursion from Madrid, and here grandees 'appropriately mounted on asses, performed *borricadas* in the woods'—so wrote Ford—'for when a Madrileño on pleasure bent gets amongst real trees, he goes as mad as a March hare. . .'. Lady Holland had a private audience with María Luisa here, who enumerated the children she had had, and those she had lost—6 remained of a total of 22—her favourite, Don Francisco, bearing 'a most indecent likeness to the Prince of the Peace' (Godoy). It was at Aranjuez that Carlos IV, in March 1808, abdicated in favour of his son, Fernando VII.

From the W. entrance, visitors are escorted through a long series of apartments containing frescoed ceilings and miscellaneous paintings, besides some fine chandeliers, clocks, furniture, mirrors, and inlaid woodwork. The most interesting room is that covered by plaques of *Buen Retiro porcelain designed in the Japanese taste for Carlos III by *Giuseppe Gricci* of Naples c. 1763. The mirrors made in the factory at La Granja add to the sumptuous effect. A small *Museum of Costume* has been installed in the palace, which also includes a collection of fans, and curious nursery furniture.

To the E. lies the ornamental Parterre laid out in 1746 by *Étienne Boutelou*. At the palace end two small bridges span the overflow canal (La Ría) to the *Jardín de la Isla*, designed by *Seb. Herrera* in 1669. Its avenues and walks abound in ornamental fountains in the 18C taste. The main jet of the *Fuente del Reloj* serves as the gnomon of a sundial, and in a walk overlooked by the palace are surprise waterworks known as the *Burladores*. One of the finest avenues is the Salón de los Reyes Católicos, with its plane-trees, which skirts the Tagus. At the W. end of the garden is the *Jardín de la Isleta*, whence we return along the bank of the Ría.

The *Bridge*, which carries the Madrid road across the Tagus, was built in 1834. From the broad open space at its S. end the C. de la Reina, an avenue of plane-trees and elms, runs E. up the valley, skirting the Jardín del Príncipe and passing (c. 1.5 km.) the entrance (l.) to the **Casa del Labrador**, built in 1803–05 in emulation of the Petit Trianon at Versailles for Carlos IV, to the designs of *Isidro González Velázquez*. Visitors are escorted round the apartments, elaborately decorated and furnished, containing a number of curious works in the minor arts, including a series of paintings of La Granja by *F. Brambilla* (d. 1842). The ceilings are frescoed by *Vicente López*, *Maella*, and others. The

Sculpture Gallery, with a ceiling by *Zacarías Velázquez*, contains over twenty antique busts and hermae, Roman mosaics from Mérida, etc., and a musical clock in the shape of Trajan's Column. In the *Sala de María Luisa*, with a ceiling by *Bayeu* and *Maella*, are a table and chair of malachite presented by Prince Demidoff to Isabel II. The panelled walls of the *Gabinete de Platina* have bronze ornaments plated with gold and silver. Above the Service Staircase is a fresco by *Z. Velázquez* of the artist's wife and children on a balcony.

From the Casa del Labrador we may return to the town through the *Jardín del Príncipe*, between the C. de la Reina and the Tagus, a creation of Carlos IV before his accession. Shaded by large trees and embellished with fountains it includes various sections, among which, at its N.W. angle, is the *Florera* or English Garden, laid out by Richard Wall (1694–1778), an Irishman who served as Secretary of State in 1754–64. Here is the *Casa de Marinos*, originally built by Carlos III in connection with a scheme for improving the navigation of the river, but now a boat-house in which may be seen the decorated pleasure-boats of Carlos IV, Isabel II, Alfonso XII, and Alfonso XIII.

From a point 5 km. S. of Aranjuez the N 400 leads 40 km. S.W. to Toledo, see p.306; at 18 km. a road leads l. to (7 km.) *Villasequilla*, a picturesque walled village, to the E. of which are the vineyards that produce the white wine of Yepes.

D   ALCALÁ DE HENARES, AND GUADALAJARA.

Leaving Madrid by the N II, we pass (12 km. l.) the airport of *Barajas*, and (6 km., r.) *San Fernando de Henares*, 3 km. S., where a former palace (1740–49) of Fernando VII, used later as a cotton factory, stands deserted.—*Rivas de Jarama*, 6 km. S., and *Mejorada del Campo*, 4 km. E. of Rivas, have good 17C churches.—The N II now by-passes *Torrejón de Ardoz* (42,300 inhab.) scene of the victory of Narváez over Espartero in 1843, and temporarily a U.S. Airbase. The church contains a retablo by *Churriguera* and paintings by *Cl. Coello*. The early 17C, 'Casa Grande, 2 C Madrid,' once in Jesuit hands, has been restored and houses a restaurant, and a museum of Icons, etc.

13 km. S. lies *Loeches*, with the *Palace* and *Dominican Convent* (1636–64) to which the Conde-Duque de Olivares retired disgraced by Philip IV. In the church is the Pantheon whither his body was brought to be buried after his flight to Toro in 1643. The retablo mayor is of 1673.—9 km. E. of Loeches is *Pozuelo del Rey*, with a fine retablo of 1550 in its church, while 7 km. beyond, lies **Nuevo Baztán** (300 inhab.; *Hotel*), an interesting experiment, by Juan de Goyeneche, in 18C land-settlement and town-planning, with an enormous *Church* by *José Churriguera*, finished in 1722. The same architect also worked on the general design of the village, its plaza, and public buildings (1709–13).

13 km. **ALCALÁ DE HENARES** (100,600 inhab., which has almost doubled in size during the last decade; *Hostería Nac.; Hotel*), on the N. bank of the Río Henares, and birthplace of the author of 'Don Quixote', was once the seat of a famous university. Although seriously damaged during the Civil War, with the industrial expansion of Madrid it has regained some of its former prosperity, while there is talk of the return to Alcalá of some faculties from the University of Madrid.

History. Roman *Complutum*, further S. on the opposite bank of the Henares, seems to have disappeared with the decline of the Gothic kings, though St Fructuosus (not the martyr of that name) founded an important abbey here before 650. The Moors built a castle (*Al-Kalat*) on the present site, which was captured in 1118, by the bellicose Abp. Bernardo of Toledo, who also acquired the surrounding lands. Abp. Tenorio raised the walls (partially restored) and built a bridge over the Henares in 1389; and the great Card.-abp. Francisco Jiménez de Cisneros (1436–1517) founded the *University* (1508) which soon numbered 10,000 students, and printed the famous Complutensian Polyglot Bible (six vols; 1514–17), in Latin, Greek, Hebrew, and Chaldæan. With the transference of the university to Madrid in 1837 and the confiscation of the wealth of the monasteries, the importance of Alcalá declined, although even in the mid-18C the decline had set in. Baretti records that 'out of nineteen or twenty colleges . . . two-thirds are absolutely unhabitable', and that the walls of the Col. de Málaga, once with four or five courtyards, were falling into their cellars, and 'spiders form their webs in the clefts of the broken steps of the principal stair-case'.

Besides Miguel de Cervantes y Saavedra (1547–1616), it numbers among its natives Juan Ruiz (c. 1283– c. 1350), author of the 'Libro de buen amor'; Catherine of Aragón (1485–1536); the emperor Ferdinand I (1503–64); Francisco de Figueroa (1536–1617), the poet; Antonio de Solis (1610–86), the historian of Spanish America; Juan Martín Díaz (1775–1823). 'el Empecinado', the guerrilla general; Eugenio Lucas (1829–70), the painter, and Manuel Azaña y Díaz (1880–1940), the Republican president, 1936–38 (and translator of Borrow's '*The Bible in Spain*' into Spanish).

In the centre is the Pl. de Cervantes, the principal square, to the E. of which, in the *Pl. de S. Diego*, stands the **Col. Mayor de S. Ildefonso**, once the headquarters of the University, a magnificent Renaissance building begun for Card. Cisneros in 1498 by *Pedro Gumiel* and rebuilt in 1543–83 by *Rodrigo Gil de Hontañón*. It has been restored after severe damage in the Civil War.

The Plateresque *Façade (1537–53) bears the founder's arms supported by swans (*cisnes*, an emblem chosen by Cisneros), and the Franciscan cord, and is decorated with medallions of the Doctors of the Church. Of the three interior *Patios* the first (1662–76), with three stories and 96 columns, bears the statues and coats-of-arms of the founder and of St Thomas of Villanueva; the second has been destroyed; and the third, called '*El Trilingue*' (from the schools of Latin, Greek, and Hebrew which surrounded it), dates from 1557 and is by *Pedro de la Cotera*. Hence we enter the *Paraninfo*, or Great Hall, with an artesonado ceiling painted in red, blue, and gold, and Plateresque galleries (1518–19). The *Chapel*, Gothic in design and Plateresque in adornment, contains the tomb of Fr. Vallés, physician to Philip II.

To the S. of the plaza we may see the deteriorated façades of former colleges, which, together with conventual buildings, now house a variety of organizations, many being used as barracks.

Passing *Sta María la Mayor* (1449), destroyed in 1936, where Cervantes was baptized in 1547, the C. de Roma runs E. passing (r.) the *Col. de Málaga* (1610–43), the *Col. of the Augustinians* (17C), that of the *Dominicans* (16C), and the *Col. de Santiago* (1570); on the l. are the colleges of *Madre de Dios* (1566), with towers, of *Sta Balbina* (1513), of the *Trinitarios* (1525), and of *S. Bernardo* (1525), and the *Ermita de los Doctrinos* (1581; rebuilt c. 1700), containing a polychrome Christ attrib. to *Fr. Dom. Beltrán*. At the end of the street the *Conv. de Corpus Christi* begun in 1599, with a dilapidated Baroque church, faces the *Col. de los Basilios*, with a front of 1725. Behind the last is a *Carmelite Convent* founded in 1570 by Sta. Teresa.

From the Pl. de Cervantes the C. de la Trinidad runs S., passing the *Col. de la Trinidad Descalza* (1601) and the *Col. de los Carraciolos* (1604), with a Baroque church. In the C. de la Justa, the continuation of the C. de Roma, are (l.) the *Conv. de las Ursulas* (1564), with a Mudéjar timber roof to its church, while the *Col. de las Filipenas* preserves 14C fragments; and (r.) the *Conv. de las Magdalenas* (1589) has a mid-17C church. The C. de los Escritorios leads W. to the **Iglesia Magistral**, founded in 1136. The present building, erected in 1497–1509 for Cisneros by *Pedro Gumiel*, was gutted by fire in 1936–39, but has been restored.

Nearby, to the N., is the *Jesuit Church* of 1602–25. In this quarter, in the Callejón de los Colegios, are the *Col. de la Vizcaya* (1563), the *Col. de León* (1595; No. 29), and the façade of the *Col. del Rey* (1551; No. 31), by *J. Gómez de Mora*. To the S. are a number of 16-17C convents and other ecclesiastical buildings, notably (in the Pl. de la Victoria) the *Conv. de Minimos* (1553), in the style of Diego de Siloée.

The C. de Cisneros, or de los Coches, goes on to the classical *Pta. de Madrid.* We may turn to the r. (N.E.), skirting restored defensive walls to visit the former *Pal. of the Archibishops* (partially restored after a destructive fire in 1940). Of the first building, begun in 1209 by Abp. Rodrigo Jiménez, little remains apart from a pair of ajimez windows and a massive tower. Most of the existing edifice dates from the rebuilding begun by Abp. Tenorio (c. 1375) and continued by Abp. Contreras (1422–34), whilst the façade and patios were decorated by *Alonso de Covarrubias* in 1524–34 for Abps. Fonseca and Tavera. It now houses part of the National Archives.

Adjoining is the domed *Bernardine Church* (1613–26) and to the N. the *Pta. de S. Bernardo.* To the S. of the Pl. del Palacio is *S. Felipe Neri,* with a 17C front and church containing a statue of Sta Teresa by *Greg. Fernández,* while to the W. are the Mudéjar ruins of *S. Juan de la Penitencia.* In the long C. de Santiago, returning E. parallel to the C. Mayor, a tablet on the r. (near the *Capuchinos;* 1613) marks the site of the house in which Cervantes *could* have been born, but a similar claim is made for another in the C. Mayor itself, see below. The court-house at No. 1 in this street occupies the *Col. de la Madre de Dios* (1566), while *Santiago* has Churrigueresque retablos and interesting paintings. Further on (l.) is the *Col. de Aragón* (1611) with a good patio, then the *Conv. de la Juanas,* where the Baroque church contains a portrait and relics of Cisneros (in the sacristy) and paintings.

To the S. in the arcaded C. Mayor (running E. and W.) is the *Hosp. de Antezana* (1702) where the church has a carved Virgin (17C) and a portrait of S. Ignacio, who was infirmarer here. At No. 48 is a house built in 1955 on the site of one in which Cervantes *may* have been born, furnished in contemporary style, and containing a Cervantine museum and library.

On a hill near the S. bank of the Henares are the ruins of a Moorish castle called *Alcalá la° Vieja.*

At 8 km. we see, 5 km. N., the church of *Meco,* once a sanctuary for criminals, with star-vaults (1560), paintings by *Juan Correa,* three Churrigueresque retablos, and rejas of 1768, while some 14 km. to the S. stands the castle of *Santorcaz* where Cisneros and the Princess of Éboli were at one time prisoners.—4 km. *Azuqueca* (l.) is noted for apricots.

The N II bears r. to by-pass Guadalajara, while we fork l. and then r. over the Henares bridge (18C, on Roman foundations) to enter (13 km.) **GUADALAJARA** (45,050 inhab.; 14,000 in 1920; 21,000 in 1960; 31,000 in 1970; *Hotel*). It suffered severely during the Civil War, but retains a few buildings of interest. Minor industries have been developed in the area.

History. The Roman settlement of *Arriaca,* somewhere in the neighbourhood, has completely vanished, and Guadalajara first appears in history as a Moorish town—*Wad-el-Hajarah* (rivers of stones)—which was taken in 1085 by Alvar Fáñez de Minaya. In the 15-17Cs the house of Mendoza, Duques del Infantado, held their court here in almost royal state, and played the Maecenas to the authors and artists of Spain. Bernardino de Mendoza (c. 1540–1604), the historian, was appointed ambassador to England in 1578.

We approach the centre viâ the Pl. de los Caídos. On the r. is the attractive entrance to the *Hosp. Civil,* former *Conv. de Jerónimos,* founded in 1578. Further on are the *Academia de Ingenieros,* occupying an 18C building intended for a cloth factory, a disastrous experiment of Philip V. Even Thomas Bevan from Melksham, in Wiltshire, lured over from England with his fellow workmen, was unable to revive its expiring manufacture.

We shortly reach the **Pal. del Infantado,** the splendid Plateresque palace of the Mendozas. The *Façade,* studied with bosses, has a portal crowned by a huge armorial shield supported by satyrs, high above which is a row of graceful Mudéjar windows. The *Patio* is singularly effective, decorated with balustrades of twisted coulmns and the arms of the housès of Mendoza and Luna.

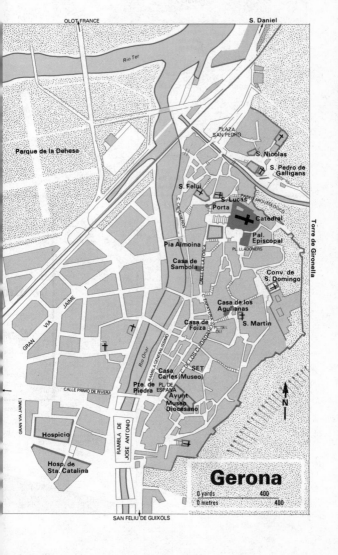

Gerona

0 yards	400
0 metres	400

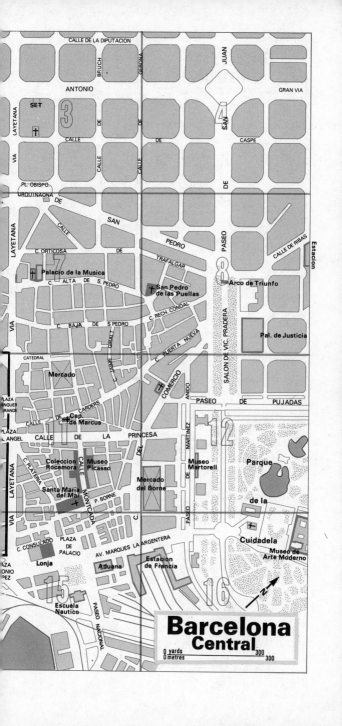

CALLE DE LA DIPUTACION

BRUCH
GERONA
JUAN

ANTONIO

GRAN VIA

SET

3

CALLE
DE
DE
SAN
CASPE

VIA LAYETANA

CALLE
CALLE
CALLE
DE

PL. OBISPO.
URQUINAONA
DE
CALLE
SAN

CALLE
C. ORTICOSA
DE
PEDRO
PASEO
CALLE DE RIBAS
Estacion

TRAFALGAR

Palacio de la Musica
7
8
Arco de Triunfo

VIA LAYETANA
C. ALTA DE S. PEDRO
San Pedro de las Puellas

C. BAJA DE S PEDRO
C. RECH. CONDAL

GIRALT
C. PUERTA NUEVA

SALON DE VIC. PRADERA

Pal. de Justicia

CATEDRAL
C. JAIME
COMERCIO

Mercado

PASEO
DE
PUJADAS

PLAZA
BINGUER
GRANDE
CALLE
DE
CARDERS
Cap. de Marcus

PLAZA
ANGEL
CALLE
DE
LA
PRINCESA

MARTINEZ

2

Museo Martorell
Parque

VIA LAYETANA
C. PLATERIA
Coleccion Rocamora
Museo Picasso

CALLE MONTCADA
Santa Maria del Mar
P. BORNE
Mercado del Borne
de la

C.

PASEO

PLAZA
DE
PALACIO
C. CONSULADO
Cuidadela

AV. MARQUES LA ARGENTERA
Museo de Arte Moderno

PLAZA
ANTONIO
LOPEZ
Lonja
Aduana
Estacion de Francia

15
16

N

Escuela Nautico
PASEO NACIONAL

Barcelona
Central

0 yards   300
0 metres   300

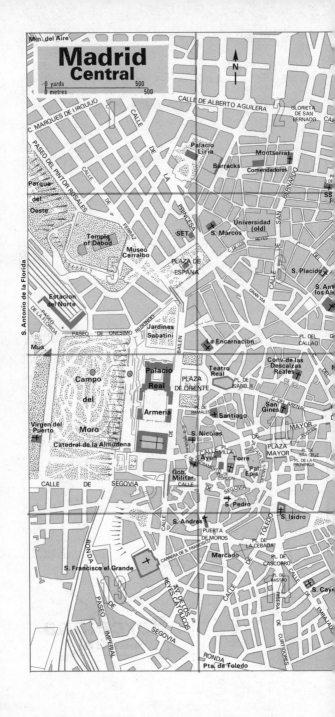

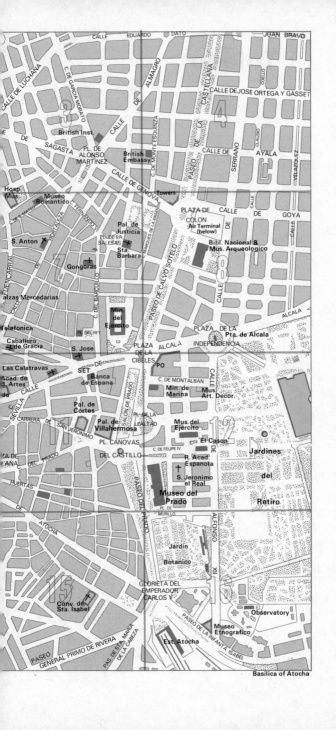

CALLE EDUARDO DATO — JUAN BRAVO

CALLE DE LUCHANA
C. DE GARCIA MORATO
CALLE

ALMAGRO
DE LA CASTELLANA
CALLE DE JOSE ORTEGA Y GASSET
COELLO

British Inst.
SAGASTA
PL. DE ALONSO MARTINEZ
CALLE DE MONTE ESQUINZA
CALLE DE
SERRANO
AYALA
VELAZQUEZ
CLAUDIO

British Embassy
CALLE DE GENOVA
Towers

Hosp. Mus.
Museo Romantico C. FERNANDO VI
PL. DE LA PRENSA
PLAZA DE COLON
Air Terminal (below)
CALLE DE GOYA

S. Anton
HORTALEZA
C. S. MATEO
Pal. de Justicia
PL. DE LAS SALESAS
Sta. Barbara
MARQUES DE LA ENSENADA
Bibl. Nacional & Mus. Arqueologico

FUENCARRAL
Gongoras
PASEO DE CALVO SOTELO
CALLE

alzas Mercedarias
C. DEL BARQUILLO

Telefonica
Min. del Ejercito
PL. DEL REY
PLAZA DE LA
Pta. de Alcala
ALCALA

Caballero de Gracia
S. Jose
PLAZA DE LA CIBELES
ALCALA INDEPENDENCIA

Las Calatravas
SET
Banca de Espana
PO
C. DE MONTALBAN

Acad. de B. Artes
CALLE
SEVILLA
Min. de Marina
Mus. Art. Decor.

Pal. de Cortes
SALON DE PRADO

CARRERA DE SAN VERONIMO
Pal. de Villahermosa
PL. DE LA LEALTAD
Mus. del Ejercito
El Cason
Jardines

PLAZA DE CANAL
DEL PRADO
PL. CANOVAS DEL CASTILLO
C. DE FELIPE IV
R. Acad. Espanola
S. Jeronimo el Real
del

HUERTAS
PASEO DEL PRADO
Museo del Prado
Retiro

DE
ATOCHA
MURILLO
PL. DE

Jardin Botanico
ALFONSO XII

PASEO
Conv. de Sta. Isabel
GLORIETA DEL EMPERADOR CARLOS V
PASEO DE LA INFANTA ISABEL
Observatory

GENERAL PRIMO DE RIVERA
PAS. DE STA. MARIA DE LA CABEZA
Est. Atocha
Museo Etnografico

Basilica of Atocha

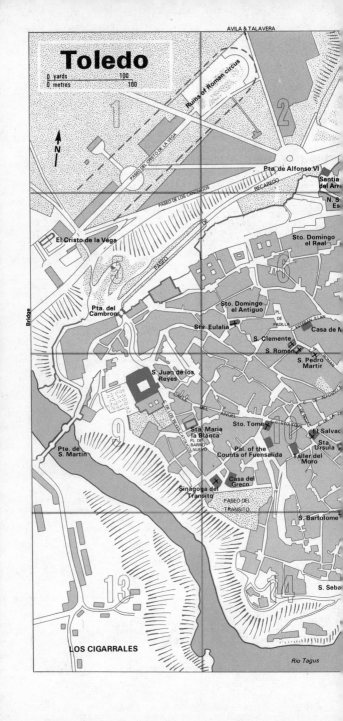

Toledo

0 yards 100
0 metres 100

N

AVILA & TALAVERA

Ruins of Roman circus

1

2

PASEO DEL CRISTO DE LA VEGA

Pta. de Alfonso VI

Santia
del Arra

RECAREDO

PASEO DE LOS CANONIGOS

N. S
Es

El Cristo de la Vega

Sto. Domingo
el Real

PASEO

6

Pta. del
Cambron

Sto. Domingo
el Antiguo

PL
DE
PADILLA

ESTEBAN ILLAN

Casa de M

Bridge

Sta. Eulalia

S. Clemente

S. Roman

S. Pedro
Martir

S. Juan de los
Reyes

CALLE   DEL   ANGEL

Sto. Tomé

CRISTO

El Salvac

9

Sta Maria
la Blanca

PL DE
BARRIO
NUEVO

Pal. of the
Counts of Fuensalida

10

Sta
Ursula

Taller del
Moro

Pte. de
S. Martin

Casa del
Greco

Sinagoga del
Transito

PASEO DEL
TRANSITO

S. Bartolome

13

14

S. Seba

LOS CIGARRALES

Rio Tagus

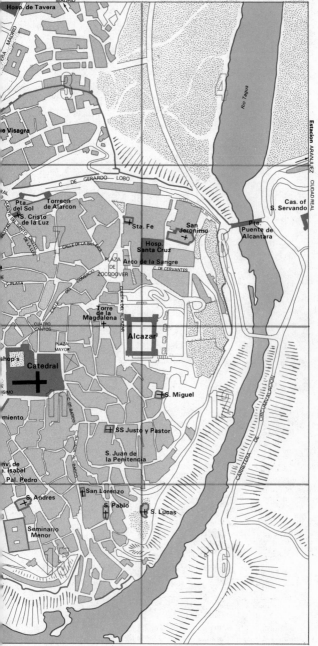

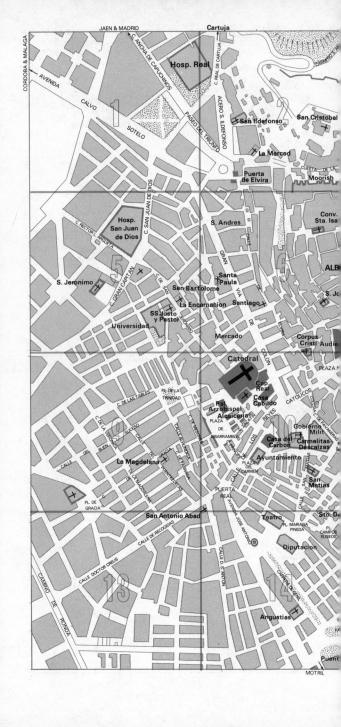

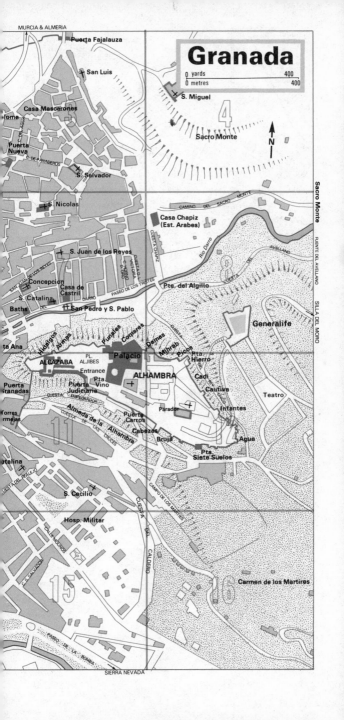

Granada

0 yards 400
0 metres 400

MURCIA & ALMERIA

Puerta Fajalauza

San Luis

Casa Mascarones

Puerta Nueva

S. Salvador

S. Nicolas

S. Juan de los Reyes

Concepcion

Casa de Castril

S. Catalina

Baths

San Pedro y S. Pablo

ta Ana

PASEO DE LOS TRISTES

Hidalgo

Arma

Puntales

Comares

ALCAZABA

PL ALJIBES

Entrance

Palacio

Demes

Mihrab

Picos

Pta. Hierro

Puerta Granadas

Pta Vino

ALHAMBRA

Cadi

Cautive

Puerta Judiciaria

Torres rmejas

Almeda de la Alhambra

Puerte Carros

Parador

Infantes

Teatro

atalina

Cabezas

Bruja

Agua

Pta Siete Suelos

S. Cecilio

Hosp. Militar

CALLE MOLINOS

15

16

Carmen de los Martires

PASEO DE LA BOMBA

SIERRA NEVADA

S. Miguel

4

Sacro Monte

N

CAMINO DEL SACRO MONTE

Casa Chapiz (Est. Arabes)

CUESTA CHAPIZ

Rio Darro

AVELLANO

8

Pte. del Algillo

Generalife

CUESTA DEL REALEJO

CAMPO DE LOS MARTIRES

CUESTA DEL CALDERO

Sacro Monte

FUENTE DEL AVELLANO

SILLA DEL MORO

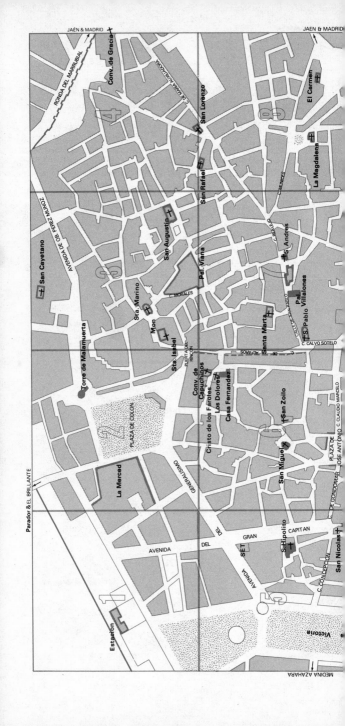

JAEN & MADRID

JAEN & MADRID

Conv. de Gracia

RONDA DEL MARRUBIAL

San Lorenzo

San Rafael

El Carmen

La Magdalena

San Cayetano

AVENIDA DE OB. PEREZ MUÑOZ

San Agustín

Pal. Viana

S. Andres

Sta. Marina

Pal. S. Pablo Villalones

Torre de Malamuerta

C. MORALES

Mon

Sta. Isabel

Santa Marta

C. CALVO SOTELO

Conv. de Capuchinos

Cristo de los Faroles

Casa Fernández

Los Dolores

San Zoilo

PLAZA DE COLON

La Merced

GENERALISIMO

San Miguel

PLAZA DE JOSE ANTONIO. C. CLAUDIO MARCELO

AVENIDA

DEL

GRAN

SET

CAPITAN

S. Hipolito

San Nicolas

C. CONCEPCION

Parador & EL BRILLANTE

AVENIDA

DEL

GRAN

Estación

Victoria

MEDINA AZAHARA

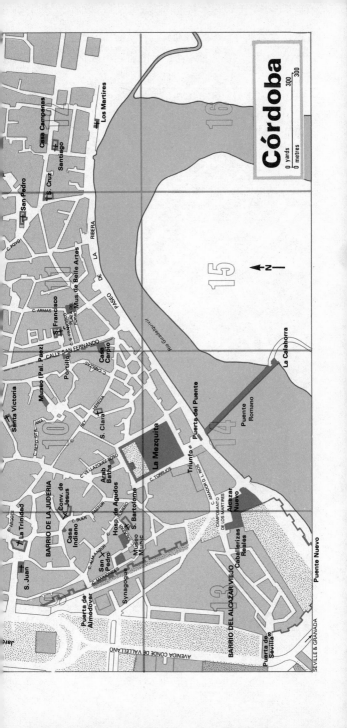

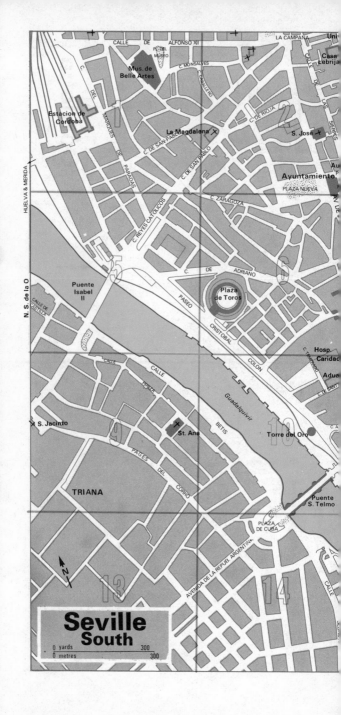

Seville
South

0 yards 300
0 metres 300

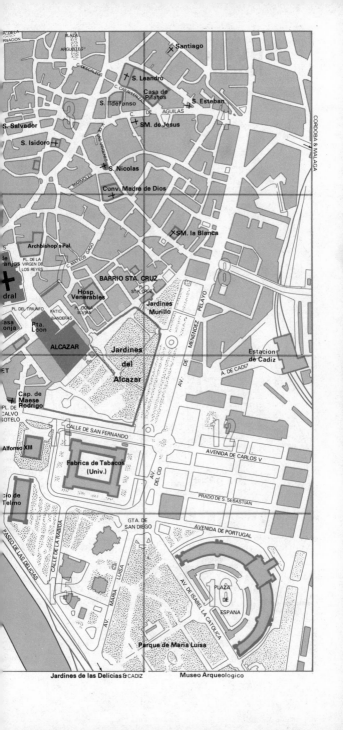

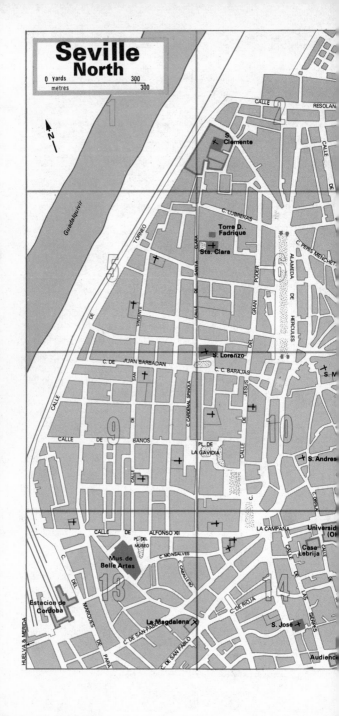

Seville
North

0 yards 300
metres 300

N

Guadalquivir

CALLE

RESOLAN

S. Clemente

CALLE

DE

C. LUBRERAS

Torre D. Fadrique

Sta. Clara

C. PERIS MENCHET

TORNEO

CALLE DE SANTA CLARA

PODER

ALAMEDA

GRAN

DE

HERCULES

DE VICENTE

DEL

S. Lorenzo

C. DE JUAN BARBADAN

C. C. BARAJAS

S. M

SAN

JESUS

CALLE DE CARDENAL SPINOLA

DE

S. Andres

CALLE

DE

BAÑOS

PL. DE LA GAVIDIA

C.

CALLE

CALLE

DE

ALFONSO XII

LA CAMPANA

Universid (O

PL. DEL MUSEO

Casa Lebrija

CALLE

DE

LAS

SIERPES

C. MONSALVES

Mus de Belle Artes

C. CABALLER

Estacion de Cordoba

C. DE RIOJA

S. Jose

C. DEL MARQUES DE

La Magdalena

HUELVA & MERIDA

C. DE SAN PABLO

C. DE SANTO PABLO

Audienc

PARIA

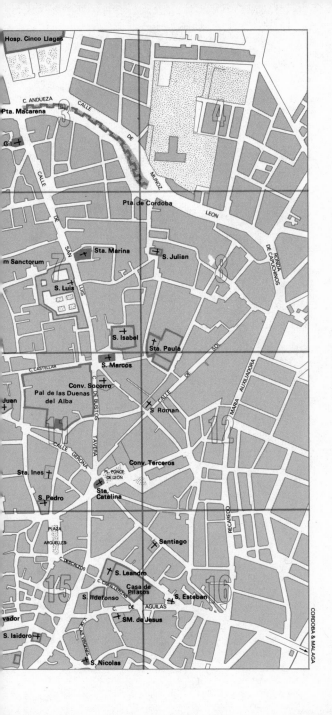

Hosp. Cinco Llagas

C. ANDUEZA

Pta. Macarena

CALLE

CALLE DE MUÑOZ

3

4

Gil

CALLE DE SAN LUIS

Pta. de Cordoba

LEON

RONDA DE CAPUCHINOS

m Sanctorum

7

Sta. Marina

S. Julian

8

S. Luis

S. Isabel

Sta. Paula

DE SOL

C. CASTELLAR

S. Marcos

Conv. Socorro

C. DE BUSTOS

Pal de las Duenas
del Alba

TAVERA

S Roman

CALLE DE

MARIA AUXILIADORA

Juan

11

12

CALLE GERONA

Sta. Ines

S. Pedro

PL. PONCE
DE LEON

Conv. Terceros

Sta.
Catalina

RECAREDO

PLAZA

ARGUELLES

C. DESCALZOS

Santiago

S. Leandro

15

C. CABALLERIZAS

16

S. Ildefonso

Casa de
Pilatos

S. Esteban

C. DE AGUILAS

vador

SM. de Jesus

S. Isidoro

PR. LAS VIRGENES

S. Nicolas

CORDOBA & MALAGA

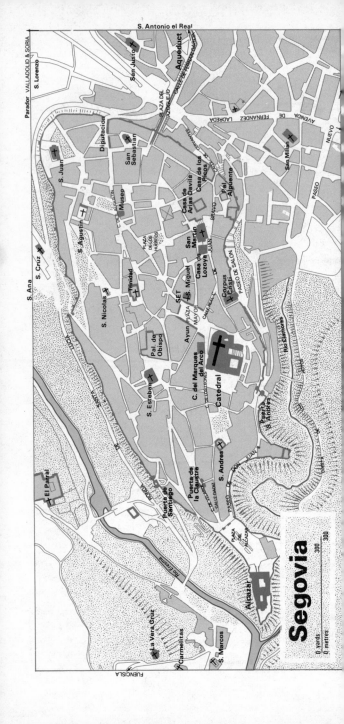

Segovia

S. Antonio el Real

Parador VALLADOLID & SORIA

S. Lorenzo

Aqueduct

San Justo

PLAZA DEL AZOGUEJO

CALLE DE

Diputación

San Sebastian

FERNÁNDEZ LADREDA

San Millan

AVENIDA DE

NUEVO

PASEO

S. Juan

Museo

Casa de Arias Davila

Casa de los Picos

Pal. Alpuente

S. Cruz

S. Ana

S. Agustin

C. DE S. AGUSTÍN

PLAZA DE LOS HUERTOS

San Martin

BRAVO

JUAN

Corpus Cristi

PASEO DE SALON

S. Nicolas

Trinidad

SET

S. Miguel

PLAZA MAYOR

Casa de Lozoya

CALLE REAL

DE

Ayun

Pal. de Obispo

C. del Marques del Arco

DE ISSTEVENS

Catedral

Río Clamores

S. Esteban

SANTA

MURALLA

Puerta de la Claustre

S. Andres

Puerta S. Andres

COLL. Y

El Paral

Puerta de Santiago

TOVAR

DON

JUAN

CALLEJADA

PASEO

PLAZA DE ALCAZAR

Río Eresma

FUENCISLA

La Vera Cruz

Carmelitas

S. Marcos

Alcazar

0 yards: 300

0 metres: 300

Sacked by the French in 1809, and burnt out in 1937, the palace, thoroughly restored when not actually rebuilt, now accommodates a singularly uninspired collection of paintings, mostly of religious subjects, perhaps the best of which is a S. Sebastián, by *Carreño*.

Begun in 1461 by *Juan* and *Enrique Guas* for Diego Hurtado de Mendoza, first Duque del Infantado, it was continued under his successors, and completed in 1492. Here the third duke entertained the captive Francis I, and in 1559 the marriage of Philip II with his third wife Isabel of Valois was celebrated in its chapel.

In the C. del Teniente Figueroa is *Santiago*, largely rebuilt, but preserving some 13–14C details and the late-15C vaults of the S. chancel chapel.—Opposite, the *Instituto*, once the nunnery of *La Piedad* (1524–30), preserves the ruined portal of its church, and a patio with an interesting staircase and balustrade. The main street leads to the Pl. Mayor, with the *Ayuntamiento*, behind which, in the Pl. de Dávalos, is a house with a Renaissance patio and fine artesonado ceilings.

To the N. of the Pl. Mayor is *S. Gil*, partly 15C, in whose portico the provincial council used to meet. Thence the C. Bardales leads to *S. Esteban*, the burial place of Álvar Fáñez (see above), built in a curious mixture of styles and noteworthy for its Toledan apse.

Following the C. Mayor, we pass *S. Nicolás* (1691) containing a 15C tomb brought from the monastery of *Lupiana*, see p.435. In the ugly Pl. de Gen. Mola is rebuilt *S. Ginés*, formerly in a Dominican monastery. The Renaissance tombs of Pedro Hurtado de Mendoza and his second wife, Juana de Valencia, and the Gothic tombs of the Conde de Tendilla, and his wife, have preserved their architectural form, but the statues are mutilated.—We may walk N., skirting the Parque de Calvo Sotelo to the *Maestranza*, within which is 15C. *S, Francisco*. In the crypt is the *Panteón*, or mausoleum of the Mendozas, whose 28 marble tombs 1696–1720) were rifled by the French in 1809.

The C. Ramón y Cajal leads W. to *Sta María de la Fuente* (15C) with a 13C Mudéjar tower, restored, containing the 15C tombs of Juan de Morales, treasurer to Fernando and Isabel, and Canon Yáñez de Mendoza; in front of the latter is the *Virgen de las Batallas*, said to have been carried by Alfonso VI on his expeditions against the Moors. Uphill to the W. is the *Cap. de los Urbinas*, a brickwork fragment of *S. Miguel* 1540). The C. Ramón y Cajal goes on past the *Conv. de Carmelitas de Arriba* (1591), with a Churrigueresque sacristy, whence the C. del Ingeniero Marino returns to the Pl. de los Caidos by way of the Carmelite *Conv. de S. José* (1615), containing an Ecstasy of Sta Teresa, by *Andrés de Vargas* (1644).

Crossing the N II a road leads 8 km. S. to *Chiloeches*, with a 16C church and 13C palace.—At 9 km. lies *Pozo*, with an ancient pillory, and 4 km. beyond, the 16C castle of *Pioz*.
For the continuation N.E. of the N II, see Rte. 19 in reverse.

26   FROM MADRID TO TOLEDO

Total distance, 71 km. (44 miles). N 401. 37 km. *Illescas*—34 km. **Toledo**
The first part of the road, of little interest in itself, is more often than not clogged with commercial traffic, and a motorway is still a long-term project; meanwhile travellers should give themselves plenty of time for the actual journey.

From the Glorieta del Emperador Carlos V, S. of the Prado, we bear
S.W., and follow the Paseo de Sta María de la Cabeza, crossing the
Manzanares, and shortly join the N 401, passing through a growing
industrial area.

To the W. lies *Carabanchel Alto,* where Teresa Caburrús (1773–1835; later Mme
Tallien) was born, when her father, the Conde de Caburrús (1752–1810) was a
minister of Carlos III.—The notorious prison is at *Carabanchel Bajo,* further to
the N.W.

At 13 km. we by-pass (l.) *Getafe,* with a Renaissance hall-church (1549–1645) by
Alonso de Covarrubias, containing paintings by *Coello* and a retablo by *Alonso
Cano,* and the *Hosp. de S. José* (1527).—14 km. *Torrejón de la Calzada,* has a 15C
church, while 3 km. E. at *Torrejón de Velasco,* are remains of a feudal castle and in
the 17C church, a 13C Virgin.

10 km. **Illescas.** *La Asunción* (12C, altered in the 16C) has a fine
Mudéjar tower (13C) and star vaults, while in the *Hosp. de la Caridad*
(1500, restored 1575–88) are five paintings of 1600–04 by *El Greco.*

In the C. Mayor is the house occupied by Francis I after his captivity in Madrid.
The town contains some 14C timbered houses, remains of a castle, and the
Mudéjar *Pta. de Ugena.*—At *Esquivias,* 8 km. E., Cervantes in 1584 married (in the
existing church) Catalina de Salazar y Palacios, by whom his pastoral of '*Galatea*'
is said to have been inspired.

We have a view (34 km.) *Toledo* as the Carretera de Madrid descends
towards its N. suburbs, passing (r.) the *Hosp. de Tavera* (p.309),
immediately beyond which we are joined (r.) by the N 403 from Ávila.
Ahead stands the *Pta. de Bisagra,* see p.307.

TOLEDO (51,400 inhab.; c. 25,000 in 1800; 31,000 in 1940, but which
was at one time as much as 200,000; *Parador Nac.* above the town to the
S.E.; *Hotels*), the ancient capital of Castile, finely situated on a rugged
bluff (1820 ft) washed on all sides but the north by a loop of the
impetuous Tagus in its deep gorge, is one of the most remarkable and
historic towns in Europe. In spite of a certain amount of modernization,
Toledo retains a Moorish stamp in its steep and tortuous lanes or wynds,
and in its outwardly plain houses with nail-studded doors guarding
hidden patios. A museum itself, the town is tourist-conscious, and the
main streets are disfigured by stalls overflowing with souvenirs of little
merit, including bogus antique Toledo ware.

Approaches. Although some of the main streets *may* be traversed by cars, it i
recommended that motorists park outside tte tld town, either near the Pta. de
Bisgara, or further W., near the Pta. del Cambrón. The main points of interest ar
at no great distance from either. Little has changed since the late 18C, whe
Swinburne observed that 'no stranger in his sober senses would venture up or dow
them in a carriage'.
The N 400 from Aranjuez, and the C 400 from Madridejos (on the N VI) whic
travellers from Andalucía will use, converge E. of the town near the railwa
station. On crossing the new bridge over the Tagus it is advisable to follow the roa
round to the Pts. de Bisgara.
Travellers from the Madrid train should cross the Pte. de Alcántara (p.308) an
ascend a flight of steps to the Paseo del Miradero, and there turn l. for the Pl. d
Zocodover.
A new road is under construction which will circle the S. side of the town abov
the N. bank of the Tagus.
Employment of Time. While it is preferable to spend at least two days in Toled
time often presses, and the following plan of visit is suggested. The visitor shoul
be able to guide himself by the principal buildings, most of which have their name
clearly displayed. The naming of the streets is erratic. An effort has been made t
show accurately on the plan (pp. 294-5) every twist and angle of the narrow lane
rather than to indicate their names.

Itinerary. Morning: starting from the Ll. de Zocodover, and passing the Cathedral, visit the *Taller del Moro* and *Pal. de Fuensalida;* (*Sto Tomé*); S. Juan de los Reyes; *Sta María la Blanca; El Transito; (the house of El Greco); S. Román.* Any spare time may be devoted to the *Alcázar,* open all day. In the afternoon: the *Cathedral; Hosp. de Santa Cruz* (museum; Cristo de la Luzt Santiago de Arrabal; and the Hosp. de Tavera (museum).

In the evening (after dark) the city takes on a different character, enhanced by a system of indirect lighting which has been installed, which displays many architectural details to advantage.

On Sat. and Sun. evenings, and on Fiestas, the major monuments are also floodlit.

Fiestas: Holy Week and Corpus Christi; 22 Jan. and 14-20th Aug.

History. Toletum, the chief town of the Carpetani, captured in 192 B.C. by the Romans, is described by Livy as 'urbs parva sed loco munita'. It was favoured by the Goths, and was established as their capital in the middle of the 6C. It was one of the few cities whose Roman walls were spared by Witiza, and Wamba, who built the first castle on the site of the Alcázar, is regarded as one of its first benefactors. Division among the Goths enabled the Moors to capture it in 712, and *Tolaitola* soon became a centre of trade, peopled largely by Jews and Mozarabic Christians, both of whom were allowed to exercise their worship undisturbed. An attempt to confiscate the wealth of the Jews led the latter to appeal to the growing Christian power for assistance, and Alfonso VI, aided by the Cid, entered Toledo in triumph in 1085, forthwith styling himself Emperor of Toledo. The Christian monarchs maintained the Moorish policy of religious tolerance despite the interference of bigoted prelates, and Toledo prospered as the capital of the kingdom and headquarters of renewed assaults against the Moors. At Toledo a famous school of translators worked, making known to Christendom the wisdom of antiquity and the Arab scientists.

In the 16C it was the main stronghold of the Comuneros against the absolutism of Charles V, and after their leader Juan de Padilla had been defeated at Villalar 1521) the town was defended by his widow, María de Pacheco, and by the archbishop, Antonio de Acuña. The Inquisition, which drove out the Jews, the transference of the court by Philip II to Madrid in 1560, and the expulsion of the Moriscos by Philip III put an end to its prosperity, although the immemorial secret of forging steel weapons still remains the peculiar property of the 'Ciudad Imperial y Coronada'. The Archduke Charles, unsuccessful rival of Philip V, thought of making Toledo once more the capital, but thenceforward it left little mark on history until the siege of the Alcázar in 1936. The Irish soldier of fortune George Dawson Flinter commanded the royalists here during the First Carlist War.

Among its natives are S. Ildefonso (607-67); Rabbi Ibn Ezra (?1093-1167); Alfonso X, ('El Sabio') the Learned, *not* Wise; 1221-84); Juana la Loca ('the Mad', 1479-1555); Juan de Padilla (1484-1521); Garcilaso de la Vela (1503-36), the poet; Francisco Cervantes de Salazar (?1514-75), historian of Mexico; Sebastián de Covarrubias (1539-1613), the lexographer; Francisco de Rojas (1607-48), the dramatist; and Anselmo Lorenzo (1841-1914), the anarcho-syndicalist. Doménico Theotocópulos (1541-1614), better known as *El Greco,* settled for life in Toledo c. 1575.

Perhaps because of the prohibition of Arabic in 1580, before which the city had been bilingual, a very pure Castilian is spoken in Toledo.

From the Madrid road we enter the town by passing round the **New Pta. de Bisagra,** (prev. *Visagra*), a double gateway dating from 1550. Above the inner gates beneath two towers roofed with coloured tiles, are the Imperial arms of Charles V, a design repeated above the outer gate, flanked by massive round towers. The *old* Bisagra Gate lies a little to the N., see p.309. To the r. is 13C **Santiago del Arrabal** (Pl. 2), with a Moorish tower (c. 1179) and recessed brickwork on the outside. The interior, entered from the W. doorway, displays unusual brick vaulting, and contains an elaborate arabesque pulpit (14C) and a restored artesonade ceiling.—Passing (r.) the 16C door of *N.S. de la Estrella,* we ascend the C. Real del Arrabal, which curves round to the l. to the battlemented **Pta. del Sol,** a Mudéjar gatehouse of the 12C, rebuilt by the Hospitallers in the 14C.

The central structure, flanked by a square and a semi-circlar tower, is adorned with interlaced arcades above. Within the tall outer Moorish arch, supported on two columns, is a lower arch, above which is a 13C relief of the presentation on the chasuble to S. Ildefonso.

The road now bears r. past the *Torreón de Alarcón*, and passing (l.) *Sta Fé*, with a 16C portal, soon enters the picturesque triangular **Pl. de Zocodover** (Pl. 7), with its arcades and cafés. The name of the square is derived from the Arabic *sûk ed-dawabb*, a horse market. Restored since the Civil War, it is still a centre of Toledan life and lounging as it was in the days of the Cervantes, and is a good point from which to explore the city. On the E. side opens the rebuilt Moorish *Arco de la Sangre del Cristo*, while to the S., on the highest point of the city stands the *Alcázar*, which may be reached easily from hence.

A   Environs: Bridges, Gates, and the Hospital de Tavera

It is recommended that visitors should drive round the **Carretera de Circumvalación (or** *Los Cigarrales*, from the Arabic 'Shagarât', meaning 'the place of trees') before entering Toledo, or at least, before leaving. The whole area is dotted with villas, usually in extensive grounds. The best comprehensive views of the town can be obtained from these heights to the S. and from the *Parador* (although El Greco's well-known panorama was taken from the N.W.) The views are particularly fine towards sunset.—From the Madrid road we drive round the Pta. de Bisagra, as if to ascend to the Pl. de Zocodover, and shortly fork l. down the C. de Gerardo Lobo towards the **Pte. de Alcántara** (pedestrians only), which bridges the rocky gorge of the Tagus in two unequal spans.

Dating from 1259 and restored in 1484, it replaces a Moorish bridge ('*e kantara*', i.e. the bridge) of 871, itself the successor of a Roman structure destroyed by Mohamed I in 854. At its W. end is a square tower of 1484, bearing a statue (by *Berruguete*) of S. Ildefonso, to whom Philip II dedicated the bridge (1575). Opposite (r.) is the blocked *Pta. de Alcántara*, with remains of Visigothic work. At the far end is a Rococo portal of 1721.

The river is commanded to the E. by the restored *Castle of S. Servando* (1380–84), with battlemented walls and cylindrical towers. We now cross the new bridge and then turn r.—To the l. are the remains of *Water Works* (Turbina Vargas) on the site of the *Arteficio* devised by the engineer *Juanelo Turriano* in 1568; to the r, are relics of a Roman *Aqueduct*.

The 'Mudéjar' *Railway Station* lies further to the l., overlooked by the new buildings of the *Military Academy*, while beyond the station (l.) is the restored '*Pal. de Galiana'*, once a Moorish villa. Begun in the 11C, it shows remains of a 13C rebuilding, and wall-paintings of c. 1362–75. It stood on the Huerta del Rey, site of the Cortes of 1085 held here before Alfonso VI, when the Cid complained of his sons-in-law, the Counts of Carrión.

The Carretera de Circumvalación now climbs above the Tagus and we shortly pass below the *Parador gnac.*, from which bird's eye *Views of the town are obtained. We next pass the *Ermita de la Virgen del Valle* on the side of the curiously shaped hill called La Peña del Moro, beyond which are two or three miradors offering spectacular panoramic *Views. We soon descend past the *Ermita de la Virgen de Cabeza* to the **Pte. de S. Martín,** (pedestrians only) a narrow bridge of five spans, with a defensive tower at each end. The inner tower bears carved armorials with inscriptions of 1690.

It was begun in 1203 and restored at the end of the 18C. A story is told that during its construction the architect confided to his wife that when the centres were removed the arches would fall. She forthwith set fire to the centring, and when the whole fell the calamity was attributed to the accident of the fire.

A new road bridge spans the Tagus a short distance further W.

From the N. end of the old bridge we follow the town wall to the Pta. de Cambrón, passing (l.) the scanty ruins of an ancient bridge-head known to romance as the *Baño de la Cava.*

Here, according to the story, Florinda or La Cava, called by the Moors Zoraide, daughter of Count Julian, was bathing when Roderic 'the last of the Goths', saw her from the terrace above and seduced her. Julian, who was governor of Ceuta, invited the Moors to assist him in avenging the outrage who, not stopping at the defeat of Roderic at the Guadalete (711), swept north to conquer the rest of the Peninsula.

The **Pta. del Cambrón** (r.) 'the gate of the thornbush' was the Moorish *Bâb-el-Makara*, rebuilt by Alfonso VI, but its present form, with four towers, dates from a reconstruction in 1576. Passing through the gate we may approach *S. Juan de los Reyes* (p.316), and the W. quarters of the town.

Not far N.W. of the Pta. del Cambrón is *El Cristo de la Vega,* the successor (frequently restored) of the *Basilica de S. Leocadia,* founded in the 4C above the tomb of that saint. Over the portal (1770) is a statue of S. Leocadia by *Berruguete,* brought from the Pta. del Cambrón. The present name of the church refers to an ancient wooden crucifix above the altar, replaced by a modern copy. S. Ildefonso and the feast Moorish king of Toledo are said to be buried here. The painted 13C roof has been restored.

From the Pta. de Cambrón we follow the tree-lined Paseo de Recaredo, passing (r.) the neo-classical *Asylum,* by *Ignacio Haan* (1790-93), commonly called *El Nuncio,* from an earlier one founded on the site by the Papal Nuncio in 1483. We next pass a long stretch of *Moorish Walls;* beyond stands the **Pta. de Alfonso VI** (the *Old Bisagra Gate*) the only 9C Moorish gate now left, through which Alfonso VI and the Cid entered Toledo in 1085. Although the gate is partly built up, and its arches and columns have been restored, its flanking towers stand almost in their original state. The name is derived from the Arabic '*bâb*' (gate) and '*sahra*' (wasteland). We now return to the new Pta. de Bisagra, completing our circuit of the city.

To the N. of the Pta. de Bisagra is the *Paseo de Merchan,* an Alameda' planted in 1628, beyond which stands the unfinished **Hosp. de Tavera,** also known as the *Hosp. de S. Juan Bautista,* or *Hosp. de Afuera* (outside the walls; Pl. 3), built in 1541-99 for Card. Juan de Tavera, by *Covarrubias* and *Bart. Bustamente.* A colonnade dividing the spacious classical patio leads through a handsome white marble portal by *A. de Berruguete* to the chapel of 1624 by *Gonzáles de Lara.* Beneath the dome is the marble tomb of Card. Tavera (d. 1545), the last work (1559-71) of *Berruguete,* who died here. The pharmacy has been fitted up in the 16C style, but it is difficult to obtain access. The building also houses the *Museum* founded by the Duchess of Lerma, a reconstruction of a noble mansion of the 16C, with its contents, including some Flemish tapestries.

This is entered from the l. of the entrance hall, and visitors are shown a number of rooms on two floors, displaying works by *Luca Giordano* and *Bassano;* a 15C Flemish shipwreck caused by Devils; *Ribera's* famous Bearded Woman *Tintoretto,* Holy Family; *Ant. Moro.* Marqués and Marquesa de las Navas *Titian's* copy of his Charles V at the Battle of Mühlberg; a fine secular *Portrait by Zurbarán* of the Duque de Medinaceli; portraits by *Carreño* of Card. Sandoval y Rojas, and the Duques de Ferias; and works by *El Greco,* including a small polichrome wooden statue of Christ, and paintings of Card. Tavera (restored) S.Pedro, and a Baptism of Christ, his last work. The *Library,* with some interesting bindings, retains the archives of the Hospital from 1541.

Immediately to the E., on the far side of the Carretera de Madrid, in the suburb of Covachuelas, are remains of a *Roman Amphitheatre,* while to the W. between the Av.de la Reconquista and the Camino a la Fábrica Nacional, is the site of a *Roman Circus.* The latter road leads to the *Weapon Factory (Fábrica de Armas Blancas),* built by Carlos III in 1777–83. It is open to the public on weekday mornings. There are a number of other smaller 'Fábricas' in the town to which visitors are also admitted.

The manufacture of 'Toledo blades' is of unknown antiquity; they are mentioned by Grattius Faliscus (1c B.C.), and the industry has survived every vicissitude of Spanish history. The custom of decorating arms and armour with gold incrustation, probably a Visigothic introduction, was encouraged by the Moors especially by Abderrahman II. Some peculiar virtue in the water and sand of the Tagus, used for tempering and polishing, is said to give the swords of Toledo their pre-eminent quality, but more obvious is the damascened ornamentation of the blades and handles. In the early 18C it was apparently worked with the assistance of English tools, confiscated from English workmen who had been commissioned to raise water from the Tagus, and whose success raised the envy and jealousy of local engineers.

B   CATHEDRAL AND S.E. QUARTER

The narrow C. del Comercio, which begins at the S.W. angle of the Zocodover, is continued past the cross-roads known as the Cuatro Cantos, by the C. Ancha and the C. del Arco, direct to the Cathedral, whose W. Façade fronts the Pl. de Generalísimo.—From the Cuatro Cantos the C. de la Chapinería (or 'de la Feria') descends to the *Pta. del Reloj,* see below.

*Toledo Cathedral (Pl. 11), a worthy seat for the Primate of Spain, is mainly in the pure vigorous style of the 13C with later additions. French in inspiration, it rivals the great cathedral of France in design, while it surpasses them in richness of furniture and wealth of adornment.

Admission. The cathedral is open all day, but the chapels, coro, sacristy, treasury, tower, etc., are closed between 1.00 and 15.30.; for these, tickets are issued inside the *Pta. del Mollete.* The entrance to the tower, which is worth ascending for the view, is to be found by turning r. on leaving the cathedral, and r. again. The door is marked 'a las Campanas'.

History. The church on this site, which the Moors converted into their chief mosque on capturing the city, is said to have been founded in 587 by St Eugenius, first bishop of Toledo under King Reccared. When Alfonso VI took Toledo in 1085 he guaranteed the Moors the continued possession of their mosque, but during his absence in the following year, his French consort, Constance, and Bernardo, the first archbishop, forcibly reclaimed it for Christian worship Alfonso's threat to avenge the insult to his royal pledge by burning the archbishop was averted only by the good 'Alfaqui', Abu Walid, who consented to surrender the mosque. Fernando III pulled down the building and in 1227 laid the first stone of the present cathedral, completed in 1493. The chapels, the sacristy, and some other dependencies are of later date. The first architect was Maestro *Martín* (1227–34); he was succeeded by '*Petrus Petri*' (d. 1290), probably a Frenchman. In 1521 the cathedral was plundered by the Comuneros, and in 1808 by the French under La Houssaye. Most of the treasures removed in 1936 have been recovered.

EXTERIOR. The best view of the cathedral, which is hemmed in by buildings, is obtained from the W. side of the Pl. del Generalísimo. In the *W. Façade* (begun in 1418) are three portals, that in the centre, the *Pta. del Perdón,* with a pediment

relief of the Virgin bestowing the chasuble on S. Ildefonso. Above, extending
between the buttresses, is a representation of the Last Supper. To the r. is the *Pta.
de los Escribanos* or *del Juicio;* to the l. the *Pta. de la Torre* or *del Infierno*. The
bronze plates covering the door date from 1377. The *N. Tower* (1380–1440), 295 ft
in height, rises in five square storeys adorned with colonettes and supporting an
octagonal storey embellished with pinnacles and windows; it terminates in a spire,
encircled with three bands of horizintal rays symbolizing the Crown of Thorns.

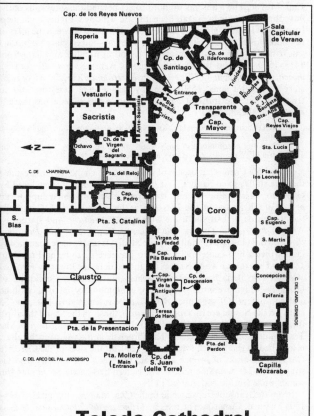

Toledo Cathedral

Begun by *Juan Alfonso,* it was continued by *Álvar Martínez,* and the lantern and
spire added by *Anequín de Egas* in 1448–52. The dome of the lower *S. Tower*
(1519, by *Enrique de Egas*), beneath which is the Cap. Mozárabe, was designed by
Jorge Manuel Theotocópulos, the son of El Greco, in 1631. On the *S. Façade* are
the *Pta. Llana* ('level', i.e. without steps), an incongrous design of 1800, and the
Pta. de los Leones, named from the shield-bearing lions on pillars in front it is
deeply recessed portal, elaborately ornamented with sculptures and carvings by
Anequín de Egas, Alfonso Fernández and *Juan Alemán* (1459–67). The bronze
doors were begun in 1545 by *Francisco de Villalpando,* but the upper part was
restored in the 18C. the *N. Façade* is concealed by cloisters, and the sacristies
added in the 17C. The transeptal *Pta. del Reloj,* known also as the *Pta. del Niño
Perdido* and *Pta. de la Feria,* is the oldest door in the cathedral (c. 1300).

INTERIOR. The usual entrance is the *Pta. de Mollete,* next to the N. Tower, which admits to the cloister (see p.315) from which we descend into the dark Cathedral through (r.) the Renaissance *Pta. de la Presentación* (1565–68), with a medallion relief by *Pedro Martínez de Castañeda* carved by *Pedro de Mena.* The NAVE of seven bays has double aisles, continued as a double ambulatory in the apse behind the Cap. Mayor. The transepts do not project beyond the side-walls of the nave, but terminate in portals beneath rose-windows. Eighty-eight piers formed of clustered shafts support the vaulting, and between the piers of the outer aisles are a series of chapels. The fine-stained glass *Windows* (most beautiful towards sunset) are c. 750 in number and date from 1418–1570. Among their chief designers were *Jacob Dolfin* (1418), *Joachim of Utrecht* (1429), *Alberto de Holanda* (1525), *Nicolás de Vergara* and his sons (1550). The nave has a large clerestory and no triforium, but the transept has a triforium on its E. side and there is another in the chancel.

Beneath the cathedral extends a vast crypt, with piers corresponding in number and arrangement to those above.
The building accommodates ten organs, including ones by Verdalanga and Echevarria (1755), and six portative and processional organs.

The whole **Coro** is a museum of sculpture, which makes it regrettable that the stalls are so badly lit. At the sides (*respaldos*) it is enclosed by elaborate 14C Gothic screens, the jasper pillars of which support an arcade of reliefs; and on the *Trascoro,* at the W. end, are a 14C statue of the Virgen de la Estrella, a medallion by *Berruguete,* and statues by *Nicolás de Vergara.* The reja which faces the Cap. Mayor is by *Domingo de Céspedes* (1547); originally silver-plated, it is said to have been hastily (and irrevocably) coated with iron to preserve it from the French in 1808.—The walnut-wood STALLS are in two tiers; the lower by *Rodrigo Alemán* (1495), is backed by 54 reliefs illustrating the conquest of Granada, which are interesting for the contemporary detail of costume and equipment. Of the upper tier, which was finished in 1543, the 35 stalls on the N. side are by *Philippe Vigarni;* those on the S. and the abp's throne, by *Berruguete.* Above the throne is a life-size group of the Transfiguration by *Berruguete.* The Virgen de la Blanca, over the altar, is ascribed to the French school of c. 1200. At the sides of the Coro are two reading-desks of bronze and iron, by *Nicolás de Vergara* and his sons (1572–74), with fine reliefs. The lectern by *Vicente Salinas* (1646), stands on a Gothic pedestal of 1425.

From the transept steps ascend to the CAP. MAYOR, enlarged in 1498–1504 by Card. Cisneros. The reja, by *Francisco de Villalpando* (1548), is flanked by two pulpits of gilt metal made from the bronze tomb prepared for himself by Álvaro de Luna but broken up in 1449 by the Infante, afterwards Enrique IV, in revenge for his defeat by Álvaro at Olmedo. The huge Gothic **Retablo** of larchwood, carved, painted, and gilded, was executed in 1502–4 by the combined efforts of numerous artists under the direction of *Enrique de Egas* and *Pedro Gumiel.* Beneath Gothic canopies on each side of the altar (1507) by *Diego Copin,* are the monuments of the Reyes Viejos; on the l. lie Alfonso VII, Sancho III (el Deseado), and the Infante Sancho, son of Jaime el Conquistador; on the r., Sancho II and the Infante Pedro, son of Alfonso VII. On the l. is also the Renaissance tomb, by *Andrea the Florentine,* of Card. Mendoza, the 'Tercer Rey' (1428–95), with his effigy, erected by Isabel the Catholic.—The outer walls of the chapel, begun in 1490 by *Juan Guas, Anequín de Egas*, and others, are embellished with statues and reliefs in canopied niches in a setting of gilded foliage and arabesques. Some of the statues are old works re-used, notably one of a king (?Sancho IV) dating from c. 1289. On the l. is the statue of Martín Alhaga, the mysterious shepherd of Las Navas de Tolosa, said to be designed by Alfonso VIII, for he alone saw the features of his guide. On the r. is a figure of Abu Walid (see history).

The theatrical Churrigueresque *Transparente* behind the Cap. Mayor, described by Richard Ford as a 'fricassée of marble', is the work of *Narciso Tomé* (1732). Although quite out of harmony with its surroundings, it displays considerable technical ability.

On the r. of the Cap. Mayor is the entrance (seldom open) to the underground *Cap. del Santo Sepulcro*, the altarpiece of which is an Entombment by *D. Copin*, painted by *Juan de Borgoña* (1514). To the l. of the Cap. Mayor, in the pavement of the outer ambulatory in front of the *Cap. de la Virgen del Sagrario*, a brass marks the tomb of Abp. Portocarrero (d. 1709), the prime mover of Philip V's succession.

From the 2nd bay of the outer N. ambulatory we may enter the **Sacristia,** a large chamber of 1593–1616 by *N. de Vergara*, with a ceiling fresco by *Luca Giordano*. The Altarpiece (Christ being stripped of his garments) is an early work (1579) of *El Greco*, who also painted the Apostles round the walls. Also here are *Goya,* Christ being taken by the soldiers; *Orrente,* the Nativity; and *Bassano,* the Deluge.—The adjoining *Vestuario* has a ceiling painted by *Coello* and *Donoso* (1671), and contains *Bassano,* Nativity, and Circumcision; *El Greco,* St. Francis; *Giov. Bellini,* Burial of Christ; and *Van Dyck,* Holy Family, and Clement VII.

In the *Ropería* are magnificent embroidered vestments, including a 13C silk cloak with the arms of Castile and León, the 14C English embroidered cope of Card. Albornoz, Moorish standards taken at Salado (1340), and the bed-hangings of Fernando the Catholic. Among illuminated MSS., note the Bible of the 13C in 3 vols. presented by St Louis of France to Alfonso X.

To the W. of the sacristy is the *Ochavo* (1630), a richly decorated 'Octagon' by the son of El Greco, containing relics, where it is planned to move the Cathedral 'Treasure', dormant riches—in the words of Edward Clarke—'which a mistaken piety has so absurdly set apart forever; which answers no rational purpose, and which neither serve to the glory of God, nor the good of man'. The ceiling-painting is by *Carreño.*—In the *Cap. de la Virgen del Sagrario*, built in 1592–1606 by the younger *Nic. de Vergara,* is an image of the Virgin, covered with jewellery and seated on a silver throne.

CHAPELS. A passage at the N.E. curve of the outer ambulatory leads to the Plateresque **Cap. de los Reyes Nuevos** (1531–34) by *Alonso de Covarrubias.* In the first bay is a Portuguese standard captured at Toro (1476). In the second, above the stalls, are niches containing the monuments of 'later kings', Enrique II and his descendants. On the r. Enrique II (d. 1379) and his wife Juana (d. 1381), on the l. Enrique III (d. 1407) and his wife Catherine of Lancaster (d. 1419) daughter of John of Gaunt. Juan II (d. 1454) whose kneeling statue by *Juan de Borgoña* is here, is buried at Miraflores near Burgos; he erected the original chapel for these kings on the spot now occupied by the *Cap. de la Descensión* in the N. Aisle. In the choir, beyond the reja by *Céspedes,* are statues of Juan I (d. 1390) and his wife, Leonor (d. 1382) by *Jorges de Contreras.* The altarpiece is by *Maella.*

The next two chapels described are usually locked, and application to visit them should be made to the sacristan, who will expect a tip, which should also cover the Cap. Mozarabe, see below. The **Cap. de Santiago** or *del Condestable* to the S. of the passage leading to the Cap. de los Reyes Nuevos, was erected in 1435–50, in the richest flamboyant Gothic, by Count Álvaro de Luna, master of the Order of Santiago, as his family burial place. The scallop shell of Santiago and the crescent moon (*luna*) of Álvaro's coat-of-arms abound.

The bronze effigies on the original tombs, destroyed by Enrique IV when infant, are said to have been so articulated as to rise from a recumbent to a kneeling position during mass. The Gothic marble Tombs, sculptured by *Pablo Ortiz* in 1488–89, were erected by Doña María, daughter of Álvaro. In the centre are th altar-tombs, with effigies of Count Álvaro (d. 1453) and his wife Juana de Pimente (d. 1488), possibly by *Sebastián de Almonacid*. In recesses on the l. wall are th tombs of Abp. Juan de Cerezuela (d. 1442) and Abp. Pedro de Luna (d. 1414) uncles of Álvaro; on the r. wall, that of Juan de Luna, his son. On either side of the central panel of the retablo of the high altar, by *Juan de Segovia, Pedro Gumie* and *Sancho de Zamora,* are portraits of Count Álvaro and Doña Juana.

Opposite the Transparente is the Gothic octagonal *Cap. de S. Ildefonso,* founded by Abp. Rodrigo, Alfonso VIII's fighting primate, and improved by Card. Gil de Albornoz (d. 1367), containing his mutilated monument, and sculptures relating to S. Ildefonso. Among several tombs are (r.) those of his grand-nephew, Bp. Alonso Carrillo de Albornoz of Ávila (d. 1514), by *Vasco del la Zarza,* and, beneath an arch, that of Iñigo López Carrillo de Mendoza (d. 1491), who died at the siege of Granada.

Sala Capitular de Invierno, or *Winter Chapter House.* A doorway (by *D. Copin*) at the S.E. curve of the ambulatory admits to an *Antesala,* with an artesonado ceiling, containing carved wardrobes, that on the l. dating from 1549–51, that on the r. from 1780. Thence, through a Mudéjar portal by *Benardino Bonifacio* (1510) with Renaissance doors, we enter the Sala Capitular proper. The artesonado ceiling is by *Diego López de Arenas* and *Francisco de Lara* (c. 1510) and the frescoes (1511) by *Juan de Borgoña.* Of the 'portraits' of the archbishops, only those from Card. Cisneros downwards have claims to authenticity. The stallwork, by *de Lara,* is of 1512. Above the Primate's stall, which is attr. to *D. Copín* (1514), is a Virgin and Child, attr. to *Gerard David.*

Several small chapels follow, including the *Cap. de los Reyes Viejos,* with a reja by *Domingo de Céspedes* (1529), and the retablos by *Comontes* (1539). Note the carving by *D. Copín* and others on the doors of the *Pta. de los Leones,* beyond which, on the wall, is the *Cristóbalon,* a fresco of St Christopher, repainted by *Gabriel de Rueda* in 1638, The *Cap. de S. Eugenio* contains a statue of St Eugenius by *D. Copín,* and an altarpiece of 1515, attr. to *Juan de Borgoña.* Here are the tomb and alabaster effigy of Bp. Fernando del Castillo (d. 1521) and the tomb of the alguazil Fernán Gudiel (d. 1278) with 'Moorish' decoration. The reja is from a design by *Enrique de Egas.*

Beneath the S.W. Tower is the **Cap. Mozárabe,** in which mass is celebrated according to the Mozarabic ritual (see below). The chapel, erected for Card. Cisneros (1436-1517) in 1504 by *Enrique de Egas,* has a reja by *Juan Francés* (1524), and an altarpiece in Roman mosaic (1794) of the Virgin and Child in a retablo of the Flemish school. The glass, with the cardinal's arms, is by *Juan de la Cuesta* (1513). The fresco on the W. wall, by *Juan de Borgoña* (1514), represents the battle of Oran (1509), a campaign planned, defrayed and headed by Cisneros in person.

Mozarabic liturgy. The Visigothic liturgy, later known as Mozarabic because preserved by the Mozarabic Christians in the churches allowed to them by the tolerant Moors, including six in Toledo, was the original national liturgy of the Spanish church. Card. Cisneros, who established the service in this chapel, did much to preserve the ritual from oblivion. The liturgy, not founded on the Roman use and differing from it in various points, is characterized by its simplicity and by a number and length of its hymns. According to the story, the rival claims of the Visigothic and the Roman ritual were subjected to trial by combat under Alfonso VI in 1086, the year after the conquest of Toledo. The Mozarabic knight was victorious, but a further ordeal by fire in the Pl. de Zocodover was demanded. The Mozarabic missal remained unconsumed in the flames, while the Roman missal leaped beyond their range. Since neither was injured, both were adjudged authoritative.

We cross the church to visit the *Cap. de S. Juan* or *de la Torre,* below the N.W. Tower. This Renaissance chapel with its elaborate roof, constructed by *Alonso de Covarrubias* in 1537, was reconstructed in 1890, and temporarily contains the *Treasury.* Displayed here are: a Sword said to have belonged to Alfonso VI; and another ascribed to Sancho IV ('el Valiente'); gold statuette of the Child, known as Juan de las Viñas; Mantle and Crown of the Virgen del Sagrario (1615); cross and ring of Card. Cisneros; Cruz de la Manga, silver gilt, by *Gregorio de Varona* of Toledo (16C); Cross planted by Card. Mendoza on the captured Alhambra in 1492; *Custodia of silver gilt (1515–24), the masterpiece of *Enrique de Arfe,* c. 3 m. high and adorned with 260 silver gilt statuettes besides precious stones. Here also are two silver allegorical figures on spheres, representing the quarters of the globe (1695), and silver reliefs by *Matías Melin.*

In the *Cap. de la Virgen de la Antigua,* in the 3rd bay of the N. Aisle, beyond the *Pta. de la Presentación,* is an ancient statue of the Virgin, in front of which the Christian banners were blessed before proceding against the Moors. Opposite, against a pier in the inner aisle of the nave, is the *Cap. de la Descensión de N.S.,* an altar beneath a Gothic canopy of open work by *Gregorio Vigarni,* brother of Felipe, erected in 1533 on the spot where the Virgin is said to have appeared to S. Ildefonso. On the r. encased in red marble, is the slab on which she alighted. The credulous kiss their fingers after touching the relic through the grating.

The legend is that the Virgin appeared to S. Ildefonso (d. 667), Abp. of Toledo, while he was celebrating mass at the high altar of the original church, and presented him with a new chasuble (*casulla*) in token of her approval of his treatise on the Immaculate Conception, and kissed the image of the Virgen del Sagrario (see above) as a faithful portrait of herself.

The *Cap. de la Pila Bautismal,* or *Baptistery,* has a reja by *Domingo da Céspedes* and retablos by *Francisco de Amberes* (Antwerp). From the N. Aisle, just beyond the *Pta. de Sta Catalina,* opens the Gothic *Cap. de S. Pedro,* built by Abp. Sancho de Rojas (d. 1422) and restored in the 18C. It contains a Statuette of St Francis by *Pedro de Mena,* 17C paintings on copper, 16C Flemish tapestries, and sketches by *Maella* and *Bayeu.* A few steps further on is the *Pta. del Reloj,* with 18C bronze doors.

The CLOISTERS have two storeys; the lower begun by Abp. Tenorio in 1389, the upper added by Card. Cisneros. Of the *Lower Cloister* only the S. walk is public. The frescoes on the walls are by *Bayeu* and *Maella.*

At the N.E. angle are the *Summer Chapter House* and the *Cap. de S. Blas,* with the tomb of Abp. Tenorio (d. 1399), by *Fernán González,* and ceiling paintings ascribed to *Arnaldo de Cremona,* a pupil of Giotto, although the only one signed is by *Juan Rodríguez de Toledo.*—The Cathedral *Library,* in the N. walk, is rich in early MSS., notably musical, shown by special permission only.

Opposite the cathedral is the 18C *Archbishop's Palace* in which the *Sala de los Concilios* has a rich artesonado ceiling. Hence the *Upper Cloister* of the Cathedral is reached by an archway crossing the street.

The *Ayuntamiento* (restored) on the S. side of the plaza, built under the Catholic Kings, was altered in 1599–1618 by *Jorge Manuel Theotocópulos*.

Behind the E. end of the cathedral is the *Posada de la Hermandad,* the late-15C doorway of which is a relic of the old prison of the Hermandad, a civic brotherhood established in the 13C to deal with robbers and murderers: it contains a small museum of contemporary art, but is of slight interest. Thence a short street leads N. to the undistinguished *Pl. Mayor.* At Nos. 27-31 *C. de la Tornerías,* N. of the plaza, are remains of a mosque on Visigothic foundations, under restoration. To the S. we may follow the *C.* del Barco, which is prolonged by the quaint *C.* Bajada al Barco. To the E. of the former is *SS. Justo y Pastor* with an apse covered with plaster decoration in the Mudéjar style (c. 1300); in the *Cap. del Cristo de la Columna,* founded by the architect Juan Guas, are portraits of Guas with his wife and children.—To the S. are the remains of *S. Juan de la Penitencia,* founded by Card. Cisneros in 1511 and burnt in 1936.—We may find our way to the S.E., by steep and narrow streets, to Mozarabic *S. Lucas* (late-13C), recently restored, and return thence N.W. passing *S. Pablo,* a Renaissance church with vaults in Gothic style to 12C *S. Lorenzo,* a few steps E. of the *C.* Bajada al Barco. More narrow and winding lanes lead us hence S.W. to *S. Andrés,* with a sanctuary of 1513 by *Juan de Borgoña,* a retablo by *Francisco de Amberes,* and Mozarabic ceilings. Immediately S. of S. Andrés is the *Seminario Menor,* a 14C Mudéjar mansion with Plateresque additions and, in its chapel, a retablo by *J. B. Vázquez* (1560). From S. Andrés we strike N. to the insignificant remains popularly believed to represent the *Pal. of Pedro the Cruel,.* These lie in the *C.* de Sta Isabel, which goes on N. to regain the Pl. del Generalísimo.

The *Conv. de Sta Isabel de los Reyes,* a short distance S. of the Ayuntamiento, founded in 1477 in two large houses of the Ayalas, has a fine artesonado ceiling, a stuccoed room of 1449, called the 'Dormitorio de la Reina' and 14C Mudéjar *S. Antolín* with a retablo mayor of 1572. To the S.W. of the convent is the brick apse of *S. Bartolomé* (14C); while in the extreme S. of the city are *S. Sebastián,* a Mozarabic parish church founded c. 602 and retaining its Visigothic columns, although rebuilt in the 13C; and picturesque *S. Cipriano,* rebuilt in 1613.

C   S.W. QUARTERS: STO TOMÉ, S. JUAN DE LOS REYES, STA MARÍA LA BLANCA, SINOGOGA DEL TRÁNSITO, AND CASA DEL GRECO

From the Zocodover to *S. Juan de los Reyes* on the W. side of the city, the direct route is viâ the *C.* del Comercio and *C.* de la Trinidad to *Sto Tomé.* On the l. at the end of the *C.* de la Trinidad is *El Salvador,* built on the site of a mosque, with a font of 15C porcelain and panelled retablo of the same period. The church of the Conv. de *Sta Úrsula,* to the E., is a Mudéjar work of 1360, altered in the 16C. In a side-street (l.) is **Sto Tomé** (Pl. 10), built in 1300–20, with a Mudéjar tower; the interior was restored in the 18C. Here is displayed *El Greco's* painting of the *Burial of Gonzalo Ruiz, Conde of Orgaz (d. 1323), which took place in this church. The work has been recently cleaned and replaced on a wall adjoining its previous site.

The figures bearing the corpse represent St Stephen and St Augustine who appeared at the burial to honour the count's piety in founding the church! The bystanders are portraits of distinguished citizens of Toledo of the time of the painting (1584–88), and include the artist himself, Alonso de Covarrubias (6th and 4th from the r.), and Diego de Covarrubias (above St Stephen). The acolyte is said to be the painter's son, Jorge Manuel.

The *C.* del Ángel prolongs the *C.* Sto Tomé to ***S. Juan de los Reyes** (Pl. 9), the church of a Franciscan convent founded by the Catholic

Kings in commemoration of the victory at Toro, and before the conquest of Granada, intended as their burial-place (comp. p. 488). The first architect was *Juan Guas,* and the main building was completed in 1480–92, but the N.W. Façade, begun by *Covarrubias* in 1553, was not finished until 1610. The exterior of the apse is richly decorated and is hung with fetters of Christian captives released during the final stages of the conquest of the Kingdom of Granada.—We first enter the two-storeyed *Cloisters* of 1494–1510, among the richest examples of Florid Gothic in Spain, whence we pass into the *Church,* the interior of which was damaged by the French in 1808 but has been restored. The aisleless nave is flanked by chapels, and around it runs a frieze of Gothic lettering referring to the foundation of the church. By the last pillars in the nave are openwork tribunes, bearing the interlaced initials of Fernando and Isabel. In the shallow transepts are statues of saints, between which are the escutcheons of Castile and Aragón, surmounted by eagles' heads and surrounded by the emblems of the Catholic Kings. The *Cap. Mayor* has a retablo of 1541–52 by *Felipe Vigarni* and *Fr. de Comontes.* The pulpit, entered by a passage in the wall, is supported by a petrified palm-stem.

To the S. E. of S. Juan the C. de los Reyes Catolicos leads through the old JUDERÍA, in which two synagogues remain of at least seven (in 1391). The first, in a small garden to the l., now *Sta María la Blanca,* was founded c. 1180 and rebuilt after a fire in 1250; it was seized by the Christians in 1405, at the instigation of S. Vicente Ferrer. In 1791–98 it was used as a barrack and storeroom, and later as a carpenter's workshop, but it has been well restored. The interior has double aisles, separated by octagonal pillars with elaborate capitals moulded in plaster and ornamented with fir-cones, etc. Above are Moorish arches. On the bases of some of the columns, the altar steps, and the pavement, are ancient azulejos. The door and ceiling are of larchwood. The sanctuary dates from c. 1550 and the retablo is by the Sevillans, *Bautista Vázquez* and *Nic. Vergara the elder* (1556).

A little further S.E., beyond the Pl. de Barrio Nuevo, we reach the Paseo del Tránsito (view). On the l. is the *Sinagoga del Tránsito (Pl. 10),* built in the Moorish style in 1366 for Samuel Levi, treasurer of Pedro the Cruel, who, despite the influence of his mistress María de Padilla, who was well-inclined towards Levi, terminated the connection by executing him and seizing his wealth. After the expulsion of the Jews in 1492, Isabel the Catholic presented the building to the Order of Calatrava, and it was dedicated first to St Benedict, and later to the Death of the Virgin (el Tránsito).—After the decades of neglect, work on its restoration was commenced at the instigation of Pérez Bayer in the mid-17C.—The galleried interior has no aisles; the frieze displays the arms of Castile and León. The Moorish arcade above, the arabesques, and the Hebrew inscriptions in praise of God, of Don Pedro, and of Levi, should be noted. Several Jewish tombstones are of the 14C. Part of the building now houses a small but interesting *Sephardic Museum* and *Library,* and displays a map indicating the situation of all Jewish communities in Spain prior to their expulsion.

The **Casa del Greco,** to the r. in the short C. de Tránsito, E. of the synagogue, owes its name to the fact that El Greco lived and died in part of the palace that once stood there. In the attractive garden-patio are fragments of archaeological interest, while the house, restored in 16C style by the Marqués de la Vega-Inclan, contains a somewhat miscellaneous collection of paintings, some in the so-called 'Studio of El Greco' upstairs, including: *Velázquez,* Four sketches; *Murillo,* Sta. Bárbara; *Carreño,* Mariana of Austria; *El Greco,* Bp. Covarrubias (son of Alonso), St Peter, *Pantoja,* Philip II, etc. Adjoining is the *Museo.*

Rooms on the ground floor to the r. contain *El Greco,* *View of Toledo (not to be confused with the more famous 'Storm over Toledo' in the Metropolitan Museum, New York), Christ, Twelve Apostles, Crucifixion, Portraits of Juan de Ávila and Alonso de Covarrubias, etc. In the rooms on the l. are *Herrera el Viejo,* St Andrew and other Saints; *Zurbarán,* Lament of St Peter; *El Greco,* St. Francis; *Tristán,* Crucifixion; *Del Mazo,* Mariana of Austria; *Carreño,* Carlos II. On the upper floor is a reference-collection of photographs of El Greco's works. Below the building are vaults of Roman masonry.

Continuing N. we return towards S. Tomé, to the S. of which, in the Pl. del Conde, is the **Pal. of the Counts of Fuensalida,** in which Isabel of Portugal, wife of Charles V, died in 1537. The fine two-storeyed patio of this 15C mansion preserves some Mudéjar decoration. Adjoining—and approached across a garden—is the ***Taller del Moro,** part of a late-14C building consisting of one large and two small rooms with the remains of attractive decoration. It was at one time the workshop (*taller*) of the cathedral masons, and now houses a small collection of carved woodwork and *azulejos,* and a 12C inscription on stone in both Latin and Arabic.

With the Taller del Moro is traditionally connected the massacre known as the 'Day of the Ditch'. The Moorish governor (a renegade Christian) invited, it is said, the leading Christian nobles and citizens to a banquet here, admitting them one by one. As each entered, his head was struck off and his body rolled into a ditch, until 400 in all were slain. Hence arose the proverbial expression '*Noche Toledana*'for a restless night (but comp. Huesca, p.189).

A short distance to the E. we regain *El Salvador,* see p.316.

D   N.W. QUARTERS: S. ROMÁN; SANTO CRISTO DE LA LUZ.

Opposite El Salvador is the C. de Rojas, which we may follow, and turning r. along the C. de Alfonso XII we reach the shaded Pl. Padre Mariana, and (l.) *S. Juan Bautista* (17C). To the W. the C. S. Román leads past the Dominican church of *S. Pedro Mártir,* mainly 16C, with tombs (including that of the poet Garcilaso de la Vega, d. 1536) and monuments from other buildings.

Nearby is ***S. Román** (Pl. 6; cons. 1221), with a Mudéjar tower (before 1166) and restored 13C murals. Probably built on the site of a Visigothic church, which was later converted into a mosque, it combines Christian and Moorish elements in a way that make it one of the most interesting and important Mudéjar churches in Toledo. It also houses a **Museum of Visigothic Art,** with a section covering the 6C Councils of Toledo, and a lapidary collection.—A short distance downhill to the l. is the imposing cloister of a convent, now a school. We pass (l.) the *Conv. de S. Clemente,* with a Renaissance doorway by *Alonso de Covarrubias,* before entering the Pl. de Padilla, a little to the N. of which is *St. Domingo el Antiguo* by *Herrera* and *Vergara* (1576), the burial-place of El Greco, with three paintings ascribed to his early period.—To the S. is *Sta. Eulalia,* a Mozarabic church founded in 589 and retaining Visigothic columns and horseshoe arches.—From the Pl. de Padilla the C. Esteban Illán leads E. At No. 9 is the **Casa de Mesa,** with remains of a Mudéjar mansion of the early 15C (if closed, apply next door). The interior, consisting of a saloon and a smaller room, is exquisitely decorated in the Moorish style, after the school of Granada, with delicate and complicated relief-work on the walls, fretted windows, friezes, artesonado ceilings, and a band of 16C azulejos around the base of the walls.—Further E. we pass (l.) the *Instituto,* the former University (1795–99), beyond which is the Pl. de S. Vicente, with a church of 1595. Behind *S. Vicente* the C. Sta Clara leads N. to the *Conv. de Sta Clara el Real,* with an altarpiece by *Luis Tristán* (1623).—To the l. is *Sto. Domingo el Real,* Baroque, with a Gothic cloister.

On the E. side of the Pl. de S. Vicente, the *Post Office* preserves a fine 16C doorway with the cord of St. Francis, while on the S. E. side are the 17C buildings of the *Conv. de las Gaitanas.*

To the N.E. the Cuesta de Carmelitas descends steeply to *Santo Cristo de la Luz (Pl. 7), formerly the mosque of Bâb-el-Mardom. This miniature mosque (987–999), built by Musa ibn Ali, probably on the site of a Visigothic chapel of which it incorporates some capitals, is one of the earliest examples of Moorish architecture in Spain. The interior is divided into nine square compartments, the remarkable vaults of which, formed by intersecting ribs, vary in design. In the middle are four low round columns, with sculptured capitals, from which spring heavy horseshoe arches. The transept and apse were added in the late 12C and contain remains of wall-paintings. The whole fabric deserves restoration and protection.

The name refers to the legend that, at the capture of Toledo (1085), Babieca, the famous charger of the Cid, knelt before his mosque and refused to move until the wall was opened and a recess revealed containing a crucifix and a still burning lamp. The first mass in the reconquered city was thereupon celebrated in the mosque, and Alfonso VI hung his shield above the altar.

The Cuesta del Santo Cristo de la Luz leads uphill S.E. towards the C. de la Silleria and back to the Pl. de Zocodover.

E.   N.E. QUARTER: HOSP. DE SANTA CRUZ; ALCÁZAR

Beyond the *Arco de la Sangre* on the E. side of the Zocodover, a flight of steps descends to the sloping C. de Cervantes, or Cuesta del Carmen Calzado.

Here is the site of the *Posada de la Sangre* (rebuilt) where Cervantes is supposed to have written the novel '*La Ilustre Fregona*'.
A lane behind the Gobierno Civil leads to the *Conv. de Santa Fé,* with a fine portal (16–17C) and a Churrigueresque retablo mayor, but retaining an 11C vaulted octagon from a Moorish palace, the *Cap. de Belén,* with 15C paintings, and the tomb of Juan Pôrez (d. 1280).

Further on, on the l., is the *Hosp. de Santa Cruz (Pl. 8), a remarkable Renaissance edifice, built in 1504–14, by Antón and Enrique de Egas for Card. Pedro Mendoza, and continued between 1524 and 1544 by Covarrubias. Above the rich Portal is carved the Adoration of the Cross, and the patio is enriched with the arms of the Mendozas. The Plateresque staircase, windows and balustrades are notable, as are the Mudéjar artesonado ceilings. There is also a small patio containing Visigothic capitals, part of an earlier palace on this site. The Lantern, destroyed in error by Republican bombs during the Civil war, has been replaced. The great wards of the building, forming a cross, and on two storeys, now house the Museo de Santa Cruz, and contain an extensive collection of Brussels' tapestries, furniture, and ecclesiastical art originally collected together for an exhibition devoted to Charles V and his time.

In the wing opposite the entrance are the blue silk standards of the Holy League, and a smaller pennant flown at Lepanto (1571). Among the more interesting works of art are an *anon*. Hispano-Flemish painting (16C) in the form of a triptych; *Morales*, Christ at the column; *Ribera*, Holy Family, and Descent from the Cross; *Orrente*, Self-portrait, and an Adoration; *Antonio Moro*, Calvary; an *anon*. Flemish diptych of the six children of Juana la Loca and Felipe el Hermoso; *Goya*, Crucifixion; *Pantoja*, Portrait of Charles V; and among examples of the very uneven work of *El Greco:* Christ stripped of his raiment, a version of the painting in the cathedral; St. Nicholas; *Santiago; La Veronica; and an Assumption, finished in the last few months of his life. Amongst the sculpture, note the bust of Juanelo Turriano, the engineer of Charles V, by *J. B. Monegro;* a marble bust of a Cardinal, by *Nic. de Busi;* and a polychromed wooden figure of St Martin (16C). There is also a notable series of Brussels tapestries of the Life of Alexander the Great (Early 17C).

An interesting *Archaeological Collection* is housed in rooms surrounding the patio, including Roman mosaics, one depicting fishing scenes (found near the Fábrica de Armas in Toledo); rope-worn marble Well-heads (Early 11C) and of baked clay (14C); Mudéjar *tinajas* or storage jars; *azulejos*, and carved beams; Visigothic capitals, etc. Collections of *Ceramics* and *Glass* may be visited in the galleries above.

A good view of the towering N. front of the Alcázar may be obtained on leaving the building.

Below the museum to the l., is the *Conv. de La Concepción Francisca,* with a brick tower (c. 1300). The gate at the l.-hand corner admits to the **Cap. de S. Jerónimo,** a fine example of Mudéjar building on a small scale, with elaborate decoration and a domed ceiling inlaid with tiles (1422). The main church dates from 1484, the raised coro from 1573.—
On returning to the Zocodover we turn l. and follow the Cuesta del Alcázar which ascends gently to the massive **Alcázar** (Pl. 11), which stands four-square on the highest point in Toledo.

History. The fort founded on this site by Alfonso VI after his capture of Toledo in 1085, developed under his successors into a castle and royal palace, receiving the title of Alcázar in the reign of Fernando III. Charles V practically rebuilt it in its present dimensions. It has been thrice burned: in 1710, during the War of Spanish Succession by Count Starhemberg, in 1810 by the French on evacuating Toledo, and in 1887 by accident. In the 1780s its apartments were fitted up with spinning-wheels and looms; from 1882 to 1936 it was occupied as a cadet school. In 1936, on adhering to the Nationalists, the small garrison—most of the cadets being on Summer leave—and a large civilian community were besieged under its commandant, Col. Moscardó, from 21 July to 28 Sept., when it was relieved by Gen. Varela. Gravely damaged by shell-fire and mining, the ruined fortress has again been virtually rebuilt.

Low towers stand at each corner of the building. The N. façade was the work of *Covarrubias* (1535–51); the E. façade, the main entrance, was ascribed to Fernando III (13C); the S. façade, with Doric pilasters, exhibits the classic work of *Herrera*; the W. façade, dating from the Catholic Kings, has a portal added by *Covarrubias*. The central *Patio* (1550–59), surrounded by a Corinthian arcade in two storeys, contains the bronze group of Charles V as conqueror of Tunis, a copy of the original by *Pompeo Leoni*. At the S. end is the wide state staircase designed for Charles V by *Villalpando* and *Herrera;* it was of this staircase that Charles exclaimed: 'When I climb it I feel myself truly Emperor'.

To the E. of the Alcázar are terraced gardens, while from the S. side the Cuesta de Capuchinos descends S.E. to the Corradillo de S. Miguel, overlooking the gorge of the Tagus, beside the late-Mudéjar tower of *S. Miguel*. Thence the Cuesta de S.

usto mounts S.W. to *S. Justo* and *S. Juan de la Penitencia*, see p.316.

To the S. W. of the Zocodover rises the Mudéjar tower of *La Magdalena* destroyed in 1936 and rebuilt in a different style), just beyond which is the *Corral de Don Diego*, with an interesting gateway, and remains of a 14C Moorish palace, with a well-preserved octagonal ceiling.

For Toledo to *Ciudad Real*, and Toledo to *Madridejos*, see Rte. 49B.

FROM TOLEDO TO GUADALUPE (174 km.), but see below. After crossing the Tagus djacent to the Pte. de. S. Martín, we turn r. and follow the C 401 S.W. At 13 km. we pass (r.) *Guadamur*, with a well-preserved *Castle* (1444–64) of the López de Ayala family, Counts of Fuensalida, with a solid square keep surmounted by six projecting turrets, containing a painted room with stucco decoration, and a lower wing with larger drum corner-towers, between which thrust triangular towers, each topped by turrets. At *Guarrazar*, near by, beside a fountain on the Toledo oad, was discovered in 1858 and 1861 the famous Visigothic royal treasure, now in the Archaeological Museum, Madrid.—3 km. *Polán* has a much-battered castle imilar to Guadamur.—14 km. *Gálvez*, with a 12C and 15C Mudéjar church.—At km. a road leads 5 km. N.W. to *Montalbán*, birthplace of Fernando de Rojas (c. 1465–1541), the author of 'La Celestina', where the large ruined castle with a huge entrance archway overlooks the ravine of the Torcón, a tributary of the Tagus. *S. Martín de Montalbán* has a church with a 13C Virgin and a retablo (1633) by *Diego Cerdán*.

At **Melque**, to the E. off the Torrijos road, is the ruinous but imposing Mozarabic church of *Sta María*, c. 862–930, displaying a number of horseshoe arches within sturdy Cyclopean walls. The tower, built over a dome, is probably a ater addition. Note the interior string courses, and the rounded corners of the exterior. The whole fabric is undergoing a careful restoration, but access is at present difficult, and application to visit should be made in advance to the Director of the Museo de Sta Cruz, Toledo.

AN ALTERNATIVE but minor road from Toledo meets our route just short of the crossroad leading to Montalbán. By turning l. and then r. after crossing the Tagus, we follow the Piedrabuena road, passing (8 km.) *Argés*, with an interesting church, and 3 km. beyond, *Láyos*, with a late-Gothic palace, to meet the C 402 after 19 km. Here we turn r. and enter *Cuerva*, where the church contains good paintings, while in the conv. de Carmelitas is a St Francis by *El Greco*.—6 km. S. lies *Las Ventas con Peña Aguilera*, with a 14C church. This road meets the C 403 and continues S. through wild and desolate country, crossing the Pto. de los Majales (2363 ft) to *Piedrabuena* (46 km. S. of Cuerva, and 26 km. W. of *Ciudad Real*).—At Cuerva we follow the C 402 W., and regain our route 8 km. beyond *Menasalvas*, with a fine church, 13 km. S.W. of which lies the ruined monastery of *S. Pablos de los Montes*.

19 km. *Navahermosa*, lying to the W. of the castle of *las Dos Hermanas*. Hontanar, to the S.W., retains the 14C *Torre de Malamoneda*, a ruined castle, and remains of a hermitage. At (21 km.) *Los Navalmorales*, we bear S.W. for (46 km.) *La Nava de Ricomalillo* to meet the C 503 from Talavera. Hence we continue to follow the N 401 as described in Rte. 44, to (58 km.) *Guadalupe*, see p.410.

FROM TOLEDO TO TALAVERA (81 km.) Driving N.W. on the N 403, at 27 km. we reach **Torrijos** (7100 inhab.; *Hotel*), with a richly ornamented Plateresque portal to its collegiate church of 1500. The semi-Moorish *Pal. de los Duques de Altamira*, by *Juan de Herrera*, has four fine saloons decorated with arabesques and artesonados. The great 16C architect, Alonso de Covarrubias (1488–1564) was born at Torrijos.—To the N.E. stands the imposing castle of *Barciense*, on the façade of which is carved a huge lion. At (12 km.) *Marqueda* (see p.409) we meet the N V and turn W. for (42 km.) *Talavera*, see Rte. 44. For the road from *Ávila* to *Marqueda*, see p.333.

27   FROM MADRID TO SEGOVIA

Total distance, 87 km. (54 miles) N VI. 40 km. *Villalba*—N 601. 22 km. *Navacerrada*—14 km. **La Granja**—11 km. **Segovia**.

Two main roads cross the Sierra de Guadarrama to Segovia. Although scenically the more attractive route, during winter months heavy snow-falls make the Navacerrada pass liable to intermittent closure, or accessible only with chains, which are obligatory. Notices to this effect are displayed at the exit from Madrid on the N VI. A new road has recently been completed, driving directly N. from the Pl. de Castilla by-passing *Colmenar Viejo* (see p.277) to join the Navacerrada road near the village of *Navacerrada.*

The granite SIERRA DE GUADARRAMA, the ancient *Montes Carpetani,* stretches with its continuations from S.W. to N.E. forming the border between New and Old Castile for a distance of c. 100 miles. It is prolonged to the N.E. by the Somosierra and the Sierra de Ayllón, and to the S.W. by the Sierra de Malagón, beyond which the lower mountains of Ávila form a connecting link with the Sierra de Gredos. Its mean height is over 5000 ft, and it culminates, near the centre, in the *Pico de Peñalara* (7894 ft).

THE ALTERNATIVE ROUTE VIÂ THE GUADARRAMA TUNNEL is much faster—94 km. (58 miles). We continue on the N VI past (40 km.) *Villalba,* the new autopista by-passing the village of *Guadarrama,* with a ruined church incorporating an early mosque.

Hence a road leads N. to the summer resorts of *Los Molinos* and (9 km.) *Cercedilla,* from which a rack-rail ascends to the Pto de Navacerrada (see below). The C 600 leads S.W. from Guadarrama past the *Valle de los Caídos* to (10 km.) *El Escorial,* see p.278.—The N VI now approaches and enters the *Guadarrama Tunnel* in fact two separate tunnels; pierced through the range in 1964 and 1972 respectively; toll.

The old road climbs steeply to the *Alto de los Leones* or **Pto. de Guadarrama** (4150 ft), where a stone lion commemorates the opening of the road in 1749. Napoleon himself led his army over the snowbound pass on Christmas Eve, 1808, in an attempt to trap the British army under Moore.—We by-pass (23 km. l.) *San Rafael,* and shortly fork r. onto the N 603, skirting the N. flank of the range.—A 18 km. a road (l.) leads 4 km. to the huge square château of *Riofrío,* begun in 1752 by *V. Rabaglio* for Isabel Farnese. Part of the building, similar in style to the palace in Madrid, houses a *Hunting Museum.* The estate, full of game, is an appropriate setting.—Segovia soon comes into view on the l., which we shortly enter.

Leaving Madrid near the *Pta. de Hierro,* we follow the N VI N.W. to (40 km.) *Villalba,* where we bear r. on to the N 601, and commence a gradual ascent. Fine views are obtained to the W., and S.W. towards the Escorial in the distance. At 13 km. we pass the village of *Navacerrada,* (*Hotel*), surrounded by chalet development. Entering pine forests, the road climbs up the flank of the range to (9 km.) the **Pto. de Navacerrada** (6053 ft) overlooked (r.) by the peak of *La Maliciosa* and (l.) by the *Sietepicos.*

The pass may also be reached by rack-rail from Cercedilla (see above) with intermediate halts, and after tunnelling through the range, the rail now continues to its terminus at the Pto. de los Cotos (see below).

At the pass, a popular centre for winter sports and starting point for excursions and ascents in the sierra, a good mountain road (C 604) leads r., and S. of the *Pico de Peñalara,* and crossing the Pto. del los Cotos, (with another winter-sports development), descends into the wooded valley of the Lozoya. At 25 km. we reach the Carthusian monastery of **El Paular,** at one time abandoned and used as a glass works, but recently reoccupied by Benedictines. It was founded by Enrique II in 1390 and built by *Rodrigo Alfonso,* architect of the cathedral of Toledo. The *church* (1433–40), by the Moorish architect *Abderrahman,* has a fine painted alabaster *Retablo* ascribed to Genoese sculptors of the 15C, a reja of 1500, by *Juan Francés,* and a main door and cloister (1475–1500), by *Juan Guas.* The *Cap. del Tabernáculo* (1719–24) is an extravagant Baroque work designed by *Francisco de Hurtado,* and with vaults painted by *Palomino.* Parts of the building have been converted to house a luxury *Hotel.* 2 km. beyond lies *Rascafría,* which may be reached also from *Miraflores de la Sierra* (p.277), or from *Lozoyuela* on the N I.

The N 601 now descends the N. flank of the range by a series of seven steep zigzags (*Las Siete Revueltas*) through the extensive pine forest of *Balsaín,* passing, at *La Pradera,* the remains of a palace built for Philip II in 1566, but burnt out early in the 18C.

14km. **San Ildefonso** (3900 ft), but now better known as **LA GRANJA** (see below), a small town and summer resort (4300 inhab.) at the foot of the Pico de Peñalara, has a flourishing glassworks. In the original *Fabrica de Cristales,* established here by Carlos III, were made the huge mirrors which adorn so many Spanish palaces, but the expense (and breakage) in their transport thence consumed any chance of profit. John Dowling, an Irishman who managed the works in the 1770s, also set up a cutlery manufactory there, with workmen brought over from Birmingham.

History. A hermitage dedicated to S. Ildefonso and a shooting-box built here by Enrique IV c. 1450 were presented by the Catholic Kings to the monks of El Parral in 1477; and around the grange (*granja*) or farmhouse arose a village. Philip V, the first Bourbon king of Spain and a lover of all things French, purchased the farm in 1720 and commissioned *Theodore Ardemans* to design a palace. His design was carried on by *Fr. de Ortega* and finished in 1723, but a recasing of the whole structure was begun in 1735 by *Juvara* and completed by *Sacchetti* in 1739—the result being, according to Richard Ford, 'a theatrical French château, the antithesis of the proud, gloomy Escorial, on which it turns its back'. The gardens, laid out by *Réne Carlier* and *Etienne Boutelou,* were not finished until the reign of Carlos III.
Here in Jan. 1724 Philip V abdicated the throne, only to resume it the following August; here in 1783 Carlos III received the Comte d'Artois (Charles X), when on his way to attack Gibraltar; Queen María Luisa is said to have preferred the apartments overlooking the courtyard in which her body-guard exercized; here in 1795 Godoy signed the treaty which virtually handed Spain over to France; here Fernando VII, during an illness in 1832, first revoked and then revived the Pragmatic Sanction of 1829, by which the Salic Law had been abolished, a vacillation precipitating the Carlist Wars in the reign of his infant daughter, Isabel; and here, in 1836, the Queen Regent Cristina was forced by mutinous sergeants to restore the democratic constitution of 1812. In 1918 a disastrous fire destroyed the N. wing of the palace and gutted most of the royal apartments, the chapel, and other dependencies, parts of which have since been restored.

By the Pta. de Segovia we enter the umbrageous Pl. del Palacio, opposite the rear façade, flanked by outbuildings for followers of the court. On the l. is the *Colegiata,* the palace chapel (1724) with frescoes by *Bayeu* and *Maella,* which suffered considerably in the fire. In a chapel beside the high altar are the tombs of Philip V (d. 1746) and his wife Isabel Farnese (d. 1766), while among the treasures is a processional cross of c. 1530. The organ is by José Otorel (c. 1850). The main *Façade* of the Palace, 150m. long, with a handsome portico surmounted by statues of the Seasons, fronts the gardens. The sparsely furnished royal apartments may be visited; of more interest is the important collection of Tapestries, some brought from Brussels by Charles V, including St Jerome at Prayer (16C), and some from cartoons by *Goya.*

The formal ***Gardens**, which including the plantations, cover 145 hectares, contain 26 elaborate fountains, designed mainly by *Frémin* and *Thierri,* with the same reliance on classical mythology as are the fountains of Versailles, but excelling these in magnificence.

In the middle of the 'Parterre' S.W. of the palace is the *Fuente de la Fama,* with a jet 30-36m. high, and at the end is the remarkable *Baño de Diana,* of which Philip V sardonically remarked 'it has cost me three millions and has amused me three minutes'. From the *Fuente de las Ranas* (Latona and the Frogs), c. 200m. S.E., the C. Larga, passing the *Pl. de las Ocho Calles* with its eight fountains, crosses the gardens to the fountains on the W. side. Some distance S.W. is the *Fuente de Andrómeda,* and further on in the same direction is *El Mar,* the artifical lake (170 ft above the Palace), whence the fountains are supplied with water. The *Casa de la Góndola* shelters a pleasure-boat of Carlos III.
The fountains play on certain days only, usually on May 30th, July 25th, Aug. 25th, and on the first Sunday in July, but it is as well to check beforehand.

We follow the N 601 N.W., shortly passing (r.) the royal domain of *Quita Pesares* (i.e. Sans-Souci), now an asylum, and near a 'Spanish' whisky factory, before descending gently to the Pl. de Azoguejo and Aqueduct of (11 km.) Segovia.

SEGOVIA (46,950 inhab; 16,000 in 1920; 32,000 in 1960; *Parador Nac;* 2 km. N.E. of the Valladolid road; *Hotels*), a characteristic Old Castilian town, crowns a rocky eminence (3297 ft) washed on the N. by the Eresma, and to the S. by the Clamores. The depression separating it from its suburbs on the E. is spanned by its famous Roman Aqueduct, which strides towards the medieval town picturesquely girdled by ancient walls, within which the Cathedral tower rises above a medley of narrow and irregular streets, while above its prominent W. apex towers the romantically perched Alcázar.

History. Segovia, the Roman *Segobriga,* a town of Iberian origin, rose to importance under the Romans by whom it was taken in 80 B.C. and under the Visigoths it became the seat of a bishop. It was occupied by the Moors, who are believed to have introduced the cloth-industry for which the town was long noted, but c. 1085, it reverted to the Christians, and became a royal residence during the 13C, although the palace caved in in 1258. In 1468 Enrique IV, repudiating his reputed daughter Juan la Beltraneja, publicly assumed his sister Isabel as his heir by leading her horse through the streets, and in 1474 Isabel the Catholic was here proclaimed queen. Next year her husband Fernando here took oath to respect the privileges of Castile. In the 14th and 15C the Cortes frequently met within its walls. In 1520 Segovia actively espoused the cause of the Comuneros, but its Alcázar remained loyal and untaken.

A duel took place here in 1758 on which Jovellanos based his play 'El Delicuente honrado'(1774). It was sacked by the French in 1808. An attempt was later made to restore its flagging woollen industry, but in 1829, when some improved machinery was introduced, it was forthwith destroyed by the boetian hand-loom weavers.

It was the birthplace of Andrés Laguna (1499-1560), the *converso* naturalist botanist and physician; Alonso de Ledesma (1562-1633), the 'Conceptista' poet Diego de Colmenares (1586-1651), the city's historian; and Arsenio Martínez Campos (1831-1900), the reactionary general whose *pronunciamento* at Sagunto in 1874 restored the Bourbon dynasty.

All roads entering Segovia converge on the enlarged *Pl. del Azoguejo,* crossed by the immense ***Aqueduct,** one of the largest antique structures in Spain. This massive aqueduct, known familiarly as 'El Puente', is built of huge blocks of Guadarrama granite, without mortar; of its total length of 813 m., 274 m. are in two stages, while the height of its 165 arches varies from 128 m. downwards according to the conformation of the ground. Note the slots in each stone, enabling it to be gripped by giant pincers, and raised by block and tackle or crane.

It has been assigned to the reign of Trajan (1–2C A.D.), and conducts the waters of the Riofrio to the city. Beginning near S. Gabriel, E. of Segovia, it spans the intervening depression and intersects the city towards the Alcázar, the latter part of its course being subterranean. In 1071–72 thirty-five of the arches were destroyed by the Moors, and they lay in ruins until 1483–89, when Isabel employed *Juan Escovedo,* a monk of El Parral, to rebuild them (letting him retain the scaffolding in lieu of payment); but apart from these and a few more modern restorations it is an untouched monument of ancient engineering genius. In 1520 images of the Virgin and S.Sebastián replaced those of Hercules in the niches above the loftiest pier. George Borrow waited under the 107th arch for the better part of an August day (1838) for his Spanish colporteur.

While the old town may be entered by car, it is more convenient to visit this area on foot, later driving round the walls, see p.327.

The C. de Cervantes, climbing N.W. from the Pl. del Azoguejo, is continued by the C. de Juan Bravo, or C. Real, the principal street, to the

Pl. Mayor and Cathedral. A short distance up the hill we bear r., passing the *Casa de los Picos,* under restoration, a fortified mansion of the 14C, which c. 1500 received the remarkable façade, studded with faceted stones, from which it takes its name. Beyond on the l., back from the street, is the *Pal. del Conde de Alpuente,* a 14C building with two *ajimez* windows, and decorated with the plaster pargetting, or *esgrafiado* work, which is still the favourite local style. Further on, steps lead down to the old *Alhóndiga,* or public granary, partly restored.

We shortly pass (l.) the so-called *House of Juan Bravo* (d. 1521), a leader of the Comuneros against Charles V. Opposite opens a plaza, the surrounding houses in which have been restored, and overlooked by the *Casa del Marqués de Lozoya* or *Mayorazgo de Cáceres,* with a 15C patio and tower. **S. Martín,** approached by a flight of steps, dating from the 12C, has a good W. Portal, an attractive exterior gallery of a local type, and a tower partly rebuilt after a fire in 1322. Within are interesting tombs, including one of alabaster, in the florid late-Gothic chapel of the Herreras (? by *Juan Guas*).

From the S. side of the plaza a lane descends to the tree-lined *Paseo de Isabel II,* above which stands a well-preserved section of the town wall strengthened by projecting *cubos.*

Continuing up the C. Real, we pass (r.) the former *Prison* (1737) housing a library and archives and (l.) *Corpus Cristi,* originally a synagogue, in plan resembling Sta María la Blanca at Toledo, but much plainer in detail, and consecrated as a Christian church in 1410. The street ends in the *Pl. Mayor,* an irregular old square, partly arcaded, with a dilapidated 17C *Ayuntamiento.* Opposite, *S. Miguel,* by *Rodr. Gil de Hontañón* (1588), has a Flemish triptych, and in the treasury a 16C processional cross by *Diego Muñoz.* The nearby Pl. de los Huertos is dominated by the patterned stucco tower of the 15C *Casa de Arias Dávila.*

The ***Cathedral,** the latest in Spain in the Gothic style, is built of a beautiful warm-coloured stone. Basilican in plan, with no projecting transepts, it terminates on the E. in a corona of seven polygonal chapels (1563–91) profusely adorned with pinnacles. At the S. angle of the plain W. Front rises a tall square tower (105 m.), terminating in a belfry chamber and cupola; and over the crossing is the *cimborio* (67 m.), the design of which, like the tower, heralds the Renaissance.

The previous 12C cathedral, which stood near the Alcázar, was wrecked during the insurrection of the Comuneros in 1520, and the present florid Gothic edifice was begun in 1525 and completed c. 65 years later. The architects were *Juan Gil de Hontañon* and his son *Rodrigo,* who followed the design of their cathedral at Salamanca.

The well-lit INTERIOR impresses by the wide span of its arches and the richness of the vaulting, but is disfigured by an ugly trascoro and respaldos (1784) by *Ventura Rodríguez,* and tastelessly decorated chapels in the ambulatory. The smaller of the two beautiful organs (1702, by Echevarria) is untouched; the larger one is by Pedro Liborna de Echevarria (c. 1760).

Some windows retain stained glass by the Fleming, *Pierre de Chiberry* (c. 1544). A pierced flamboyant balustrade takes the place of a triforium. The marble retablo mayor (1768–75) is by *Sabatini.* The nave is flanked by screened chapels, the first of which in the N. Aisle has a 16C mahogany reja. The *Cap. de la Piedad* (5th in the N. Aisle) contains a retablo designed by *Juan de Juni* (1571). The *Cap. de Santiago* (4th in the S. Aisle) has a retablo by *Pantoja de la Cruz,* with a portrait of Fr. Gutiérrez de Cuéllar by *Alonso de Herrera.* The next chapel (*del Cristo del Consuelo*), whence we enter the cloister, has two bishops' tombs and rejas from the old cathedral. In the Baroque *Cap. del Sagrario,* by *Manuel de Churriguera,* to the r. of the *Cap. Mayor, is* 'El Cristo de Lozoya', carved by *Alonso Cano,* while the *Cap. del Sepulcro* contains a recumbent Christ by *Greg. Fernández.*

The Gothic *Cloisters, built by *Juan Guas* in 1472–91 and transferred from the old cathedral, were re-erected after 1524 by *Juan Campero.* Both Rodrigo and Juan Gil de Hontañon are buried under plain slabs just near the entrance. At the S. W. angle is the tomb of María del Salto (d. 1237), a Jewess unjustly accused of adultery, who was hurled from the Peña Grajera and miraculously saved from death by the Virgin, whom she invoked as she fell.—The *Cap. de Sta Catalina,* at the base of the tower on the W. side contains the tomb of Don Pedro (d. 1366), the infant son of Enrique II, who was killed by falling from a balcony in the Alcázar. Here is also a silver custodia and gilt carriage of the 17C used at Corpus Christi.— The *Sala Capitular,* with a painted artesonado ceiling, contains Flemish tapestries from cartoons by Rubens; the series, with another, is continued on the stairs and in the *Library* above. Here, the badly-displayed *Museo Diocesano* contains illuminated MSS and incunables, vestments, ornaments, and among paintings, The Evangelists, by *Ribera.* The original Scale Drawings of the cathedral, on parchment, are of interest, but they are not generally on show. Here also is the case of a 17C Flemish harpsichord, possibly by Ruckers, which the guide insists is 'a *clavicornio* of the 13C' (sic)! It stood in the cloister until 1976, having long been used as a pigeon-cote!

Almost opposite the Cathedral entrance stands the *Casa del Marqués del Arco,* with a 16C patio, from which the C. de los Leones leads N.W. past *S. Andrés* (early 12C, modernized), with a Romanesque apse, to the Pl. del Alcázar.

The **Alcázar,** occupying the W. extremity of the ridge of the old town straddles, and looking sheer down into the valleys of the Eresma (N.) and the Clamores (W), is built possibly upon Moorish or even Roman foundations. Enlarged in 1352–58 by Enrique II, it was further extended by Catherine of Lancaster and her son, Juan II, in 1410–55, but in 1862, when occupied as an artillery school, it was so seriously injured by a fire that, apart from the towers, most of what we see dates from a restoration begun in 1882. The conspicuous features are the great *Torre de Juan II,* with its canopied windows, and bartizan turrets, and the *Torre de Homenaje,* with seven turrets, its roof providing panoramic *Views.*

Prince Charles (later Charles I of England) was entertained in the Alcázar in 1623 and supped, says the record, on 'certain trouts of extraordinary greatness'. The Torre de Homenaje was a state prison under Philip V, who in 1726 here confined his minister Ripperdá (1680–1737), who made his escape two years later.

The most interesting rooms are the *Salón de la Galera,* with a Mudéjar frieze (part of the works done for Queen Catherine in 1412), the *Salón del Trono,* the *Salón del Solio,* decorated in 1456 by *Xadel Alcalde,* and the *Pieza del Cordon.*

This last, decorated with the cord of St Francis, commemorates the story that Alfonso the Wise, having expressed the heretical opinion that the earth revolved around the sun, was so terrified by a thunderbolt that he immediately recanted and penitently assumed the cord of St Francis.—Also displayed are a 15C Flemish retablo, another by *P. Berruguete,* and some ancient armour and artillery.

A road descends S.E. to the *Pta. de Santiago,* by which we reach the Ronda de Sta Lucía, see p.327.—We may follow the Paseo de Don Juan II S.W. to the *Pta. del Socorro* or *Pta. S. Andrés,* a 12–13C city-gate bearing a tablet in commemoration of the picaresque heroes of Quevedo's novels, notably 'Don Pablo de Segovia'. Hence, bearing l. through the old *Judería,* we may regain the Pl. Mayor.—An alternative route from the Pl. del Alcázar follows the C. de Daóiz, passing the Romanesque *Pta de la Claustra,* the last of four which once separated the Alcázar quarter from the town, towards *S. Esteban,* see below.

From the N. end of the Pl. Mayor the C. Escuderos descends past the *Casa de Don Álvaro de Luna,* an ancient (?12C) mansion, restored, with an ornamental portal and interesting patio. It is said to have been occupied by Álvaro de Luna in 1445, and in the 16C was a local tribunal of the Inquisition.—At the far end of the C. Escuderos we turn r. to reach **S. Esteban,** with a noble 12C *Tower (rebuilt, and recently re-roofed) and a Romanesque exterior cloister. The church is 13C and contains a 13C Calvary from the destroyed church of Santiago. The *Bishop's Pal.,* opposite, has two curious reliefs on its granite façade. There is talk of it being converted to house a provincial museum of religious art.

Next to the *Cap. de S. Juan de Dios* to the W., in the C. de Desamparados, is a house in which from 1919 to 1931 lived the poet Antonio Machado (1875–1939). Following the C. de la Victoria, and passing (l.) a lane which descends to Romanesque *S. Quirce,* we come to a Dominican Convent in a fortified mansion built on Roman foundations, known as the *Casa de Hércules* from a figure which adorns its tower. Beyond is *La Trinidad* (12C), with its characteristic exterior arcade; the solemn interior contains an Isabelline chapel of 1513. To the E. *S. Nicolás* retains its apse and some mural paintings, but *S. Augustín,* late-Gothic, lies in ruins.

Following the C. de S. Augustín we pass (r.) the *Museo Provincial,* accommodated in a 16C house with Mudéjar decoration. The small collection includes a Holy Face by *Ambrosius Benson,* some interesting old views of the town, and polychrome sculptures from the destroyed church of Sta Columba, which once abutted the Aqueduct.—Just beyond, a lane (r.) leads past the over-restored *Casa de Apiroz* towards the 16C Herreran church of the *Seminario,* with a granite façade.

We shortly enter the small triangular Pl. de Conde de Cheste with the *Diputación,* and other typical mansions with sculptured doorways and patios, including the 14C *Casa de los Lozoya,* and *Casa de Segovia.*— Further E., in a lonely plaza, is the desecrated Romanesque church of *S. Juan de los Caballeros* (partially restored), with a good tower, triple apse, exterior arcade and Gothic W. Door. It is at present occupied by a ceramic factory (*Museo Daniel Zuloaga*).—Just S.W. of the Pl. del Conde de Cheste is *S. Sebastián,* a Franciscan church with a good apse and W. Doorway, while nearby is the N. end of the Aqueduct, from which we may descend by a flight of steps to the Pl. del Azoguejo.

A number of interesting buildings lie outside the walled town, and are perhaps best visited by car. Many picturesque views of Segovia may be obtained from the valleys of the Eresma and Clamores. From the Pl. de Azoguejo we drive N.E. vîâ the wooded *Ronda de Sta Lucía,* shortly passing the *Hospicio,* (under restoration), formerly the Dominican *Conv. de Sta Cruz,* founded by Fernando and Isabel beside a grotto said to have been a retreat of St. Dominic. The buildings, by *Juan Guas,* were erected in 1480–92.

Over the striking W. Portal of the church is a lunette showing the 'Catholic Kings' kneeling beside a Pietà, while their initials and emblems, the arrows and ox-yoke, occur in the exterior frieze of the apse.

A short walk E. Leads to Romanesque *S. Lorenzo,* with a Mudéjar tower, three apses, an arcade of coupled columns with interesting capitals, and a chapel of 1532 with a carved triptych by *Giralte.* The central plaza of this suburb has been restored. To the N. of S. Lorenzo, across the Eresma, lies the *Conv. de S. Vicente el Real.*

Continuing to follow the Ronda, we pass (r.) the *Casa de Moneda,* the old Mint, (now a Mill), in which all Spanish money was coined from c. 1586 until 1730. On the far side of the river is the Hieronymite monastery of *El Parral* (partly restored), founded in 1447 by Juan Pacheco, Marqués de Villena, on a spot where he had fought three successful duels, and afterwards famous for its vines and gardens ("las huertas del Parral, paraíso terrenal").

From the main cloister we enter the church built by *Juan Gallego* in 1494, with a tower finished in 1529 by *Juan Campero.* It contains the Plateresque Tombs of the founder and his wife and between them a retablo designed in 1528 by *Juan Rodríguez* and *Diego de Urbina.* The *Cap. Mayor* dates from 1472–85 (by *Juan Guas* and *Bonifacio);* the coro from 1494. In the side chapels (in which pigs were penned in 1848) are Gothic tombs of Segovían nobles, and beside the elaborate sacristy door is the tomb of Beatriz de Pacheco, illegitimate daughter of the founder. The stained-glass windows in the apse dated from 1494.

The Ronda crosses the Eresma a short distance further W.; we bear l. and r. onto the Zamarramala road to reach the remarkable Romanesque church of *La Vera Cruz,* built by the Templars c. 1204–08, with three apses and a richly moulded W. Doorway.In the centre of the twelve-sided nave is a walled chamber of two storeys built on the model of the Rotunda of the Holy Sepulchre in Jerusalem. It contains a retablo of 1516 and late-15C wall-paintings, and the tower should be ascended for the view.

At *Zamarramala* itself is a mute 18C organ, all its pewter pipes being removed in one hour in Oct. 1978, which has been the scandalous end of too many such instruments 'conserved' by the ecclesiastical authorities.
Further down the river, just beyond (l.) *S. Marcos* (12C), is (r.) the 17C *Carmelitas,* with the tomb of St John of the Cross (d. 1591), containing his head and trunk; his other limbs had already been dispersed as relics. Beyond lies the *Sanctuario de Fuencisla,* built in 1598-1613 by *Juan de Mora,* with a reja of 1764, while opposite rises the Pena Grajera (crag of the crows), the Tarpeian Rock of Segovia. Slightly further N. is the Baroque *Arco de Homenaje* (1704).

Crossing the nearby Pte. de S. Lázaro we may climb the l. bank of the Clamores by the Cuesta de los Hoyos, which commands an impressive *View of the 'prow' of the Alcázar, the city and its walls, later passing, on a spur, the old *matadero.* At the main crossroad W. of the town we turn l. Here Romanesque **S. Millán,** perhaps founded in the 10C, has a good doorway, the fine triple apse, and exterior arcades on each side, with carved capitals. Passing (r.) the façade of *S. Clemente,* in the Av. de Fernández Ladreda, we regain the Pl. de Azoguejo.

The most important building in the S. quarter is the **Conv. de S. Antonio el Reál.** It stands a short distance W. of the road to La Granja before reaching the Plaza de Toros, and may also be approached on foot by following the line of the Aqueduct to its termination, there bearing r. The convent was founded by Enrique IV in a country house, and rebuilt in 1455 by *Xadel Acalde.* The portal of the *church* (1488), the ceiling of the chancel, and the painted wooden Calvary with figures by a Flemish sculptor, are all remarkable. In the Convent (ring at the interior door), the magnificent artesonado *Ceilings* of the main *Cloister,* octagonal *Sala Capitular,* and *Sala de los Reyes* (Sacristia), are all in a perfect state of preservation.

Not far S.E. of the Pl. del Azoguejo stands *S. Justo,* with a good Romanesque tower and doorway, retaining some interesting murals (over-restored), while nearby *S. Salvador,* preserving Romanesque details, has a Baroque interior and a 16C Flemish Triptych.

The C.S. Francisco climbs S.W. from the Aqueduct past the *Artillery School* (established 1764), partly in the buildings of the Conv. de S. Francisco (founded in 1220), with a Plateresque patio. Continuing S. we pass *Sta Eulalia,* to the E. of which is the *Conv. de Sta Isabel,* florid Gothic, with a reja of 1537, while to the W. lies *Sto Tomás,* with Romanesque details, containing an Increduulity of St Thomas by *A. Herrera.*

28   FROM MADRID TO ÁVILA AND SALAMANCA

Total distance, 212 km. (131 miles). N VI. 83 km. *Villacastin*—N 501. 32 km. Ávila—N 403, 56 km. *Peñaranda*—41 km. **Salamanca.**

We follow the N VI as far as (83 km.) *Villacastín* (see Rtes 21 and 27), where we turn l. onto the N 501, which runs parallel to and N., of the Guadarrama range. At 32 km. we enter Ávila from the E., passing (r.) the *Parque de S. Antonio,* and bear l. viâ the Av. de Portugal to approach the fortified enceinte.

It is preferable to enter the *old* town on foot, as parking can be a problem.

ÁVILA (3500-3700 ft; 33,500 inhab.; 13,000 in 1920; 21,000 in 1950; *Parador Nac.* and *Hotels*), a 'provincial' capital famous principally for its impressive circuit of medieval walls and its fine Romanesque churches, stands on an abrupt spur above the river Adaja in the midst of a boulder-strewn plateau, overlooked by the Sierra de Ávila. Owing to its altitude, its winter climate is severe; but in summer the well-watered valleys of the neighbouring mountains offer a pleasant refuge from the drought of the Castilian plain.

History, The foundation of Ávila 'de los Caballeros' is lost in antiquity and is ascribed by legend to Hercules under the name of *Abula.* Known to the Romans as *Avela,* it was often a point of issue between Moors and Spaniards, but after the strengthening of the fortifications under Alfonso VI in 1090 it remained in Christian hands. It dates its decadence from the expulsion of the Moriscoes by Philip III (1607–10). Sta Teresa (1515–82) is the town's most famous native, while González de Ávila (1577–1658) a historiographer of some merit, and the great composer Tomás Luis de Victoria (1548–1611) were also born here; while although born in Madrid, Jorge Ruiz (George) Santayana (1863–1932), the philosopher, spent his youth here.

In the C. S. Segundo, skirting the E. side of the medieval town, we see the great castellated *Apse* of the Cathedral which forms a bastion in the city *Walls.* These were built in 1088–91 by Raymond of Burgundy, son-in-law of Alfonso VI, from the designs of *Cassandro,* a Roman, and *Florian de Ponthieu,* a Frenchman, and are in a remarkable state of preservation. They have 88 cubos, or cylindrical towers, and nine gates, the latter consisting simply of two towers close together connected by an arch and a battlement walk.

Just N. of the apse we may enter through the *Pta. del Peso de la Harina,* next to the *Casa de la Misericordia,* with its 16C doorway and statue of S. Martín. On our l. stands the granite **Cathedral,** the greater part of which was begun in 1157 and is in the earliest Gothic style. Its fortress-like appearance is due largely to Bp. Sancho (1188), who kept Alfonso IX in sanctuary there during his minority. The N. Doorway, with statues and a carved tympanum, dates from the 13C; the inferior W. Portal is of 1779 and is flanked by two early-Gothic towers, one unfinished; from the other is an extensive view. Guarding the entrance are two mace-bearers, *maceros,* like wild men of the woods.

The *INTERIOR*, containing curious red and white mottled masonry, has a narrow aisle *Nave* with a blind triforium and a large clerestory; the glazing (1535–36) is by *Nicolás de Holanda*. The *trascoro*, facing the entrance, bears coarse but vigorous reliefs by *Juan Rodríguez*. The *Coro* contains a remarkable *Silleria* by *Cornelis*, a Dutchman (1536–47), and the two gilt iron pulpits (15th and 16C) are also of fine quality. Near the older, by *Juan Francés* (on the S.), is the altar of *S. Segundo* with alabaster carvings; near the other, the marble altar of St Catherine.— The double-sided *Cap. Mayor* contains good glass (1495–97) by *Juan de Valdivielso;* the *Retablo Mayor* was painted by *Santos Cruz, Pedro Berruguete,* and *Juan de Borgoña* (1499–1508).

CHAPELS. In the N. Aisle is a 15C German font on a pedestal by *Vasco de la Zarza*. The chapel of *S. Nicolás* (N. choir aisle) contains the tomb of Bp. Bernardo (d. 1292). In the *Trassagrario* is the *Tomb* (1518), by *Vasco de la Zarza,* of Alfonso de Madrigal (1400–55), Bp. of Ávila c. 1450, nicknamed 'el Tostado' (the swarthy), showing the polymath prelate in the act of writing. In the S. Transept are several good Gothic tombs, and the sepulchre of Bp. Sancho Dávila, of Sigüenza (d. 1534). The stained glass of the transept (1532–38) is by *Alberto de Holanda* and *Diego de Ayala*.

The *Sacristy*, entered from the S. aisle, is roofed with a good octagonal vault, bedaubed with paint and gilding, and contains Renaissance marbles, with terracotta groups of the Passion above.—The *Relicario* contains a silver monstrance by *Juan de Arfe,* signed and dated 1571; an Italian enamelled chalice of the 14C, etc.—A Romanesque door on the S. side of the nave admits to the partially restored 13C *Cloister,* which, Townsend observed, was worthy of attention 'for its exquisite neatness, and elegant simplicity'. The *Cap. del Cardenal,* on the E. side, has good ironwork and painted glass (1498) by *Santillana* and *Valdivielso*.

Leaving the Plaza by the C. del Tostado, in which are some early houses, including a mansion with curious heraldic devices, we pass through the *Pta. de S. Vicente*. In this N.E. sector of the enceinte stood the *Juderia*. Not far to the E. is the *Museo Provincial,* housed in the *Casa de los Deanes* (Pl. Nalvillos 5), containing a collection of *bargueños,* and a triptych of the school of *Memling*.

Just outside the gate stands ***S. Vicente,** founded in 1307 on the site where the saint and his sisters (SS. Cristeta and Sabina) were martyred c. 303. On the S. side is a 13C portico with banded shafts protecting the 12C S. Door, which has curious capitals and an Annunciation on one of the jambs. The severe *W. Front* (C. 1170–90), with one tower partially completed in 1440, is remarkable for its double doorway surrounded by rich Romanesque sculpture. The central arched porch may be compared with that at Toro (p.355). The Romanesque interior is notable for the Tomb of the Patron Saints, a sarcophagus of c. 1180 on an Italian-Gothic base covered by a canopy of 1465. Beneath the triple apse (entrance in the N. Aisle) is a modernized crypt with the rock on which

the martyrs' bodies were exposed, and a 12C statue of the Virgin.

Below S. Vicente are Romanesque *S. Andrés,* with good S. and W.
Doorways and 12C apse; and *La Inclusa,* with a Renaissance portal and
sculptures ascribed to *A. Berruguete.*

Further N. are two convents *S. Francisco* with the restored star-vaulted *Cap. de
S. Antonio* (c. 1480), the 14C *Cap. de los Bracamontes,* and murals by *Sansón
Florentino* (c. 1500); and *La Encarnación* to the W., which was founded in 1478
and where Sta Teresa took the veil in 1533 and lived for 27 years.

Following the walls to the W. we pass the Romanesque tower of *S.
Martín* and chapel of *La Cabeza* (1210) before reaching, after a little
distance, **S. Segundo,** a Romanesque 'hermitage' overlooking the
Adaja, with a handsome roof, and apse with well carved capitals; the
interior was altered in 1579, but is worth visiting for the tomb-statue (by
Juan de Juni, 1572–73) of S. Segundo, the sturdy Bp. of Ávila who
hurled down a Moorish chief from the ramparts above.—Further S. are
the old and new bridges across the Adaja (fine views from the *Cuatro
Postes,* on the opposite hill, but the view *from* the walls is now spoilt by
the erection of an hotel on this previously desolate slope).—On the S.
side of the town are the restored Romanesque churches of *S. Nicolás* and
Santiago, the latter with a 14C tower and retablo of 1530; and the
abandoned hermitage of *S. Isidro.* Near Santiago is the *Conv. de la
Concepción,* much altered in the 16C, with stalls of 1400 and a Flemish
Pietà.

We may re-enter the town by the *Pta. del Rastro* and pass some of the
15–16C mansions for which Ávila is famous—on the r. the *Pal de
Abrantes,* on the l. the fortified *Torreón de Oñate* or *de Guzmanes.*
Keeping to the l. we reach the *Conv. de Sta Teresa* (Baroque) built on the
site of the birthplace of the saint. The church contains a Christ by *Greg.
Fernández,* and a museum.

Teresa de Cepeda y Ahumada (1515–82) of noble birth, and Jewish lineage,
destined herself to the Church from her earliest years. As a child of seven she
attempted to escape with her brother to seek martyrdom at the hands of the Moors,
and in 1533 she took the veil at the Carmelite convent of La Encarnación (see
above). Her inspired communication with her Heavenly Spouse has always been a
favourite subject with Spanish artists.

Just inside the *Pta. de Sta Teresa* is the handsome mansion of the
Duque de la Roca (Now the *Audiencia*), a 15C house with a front of
1541, and behind is a Romanesque *Sto Domingo* (closed).

To the N.W. is *S. Esteban,* an ancient hermitage with an interesting apse of the
early 12C; while nearer Sto Domingo are the 16C *Hosp. de Sta Escolástica* and
several old houses. Behind is the *Diputación.*

To the N. stands the mansion of the *Condes de Polentinos* (by *Vasco
de la Zarza,* 1520–35), with a good doorway and patio. The C. de
Vallespin leads r. to the *Pl. Mayor,* in which is *S. Juan* where Sta Teresa
was baptized, containing the tomb of Sancho Dávila (d. 1583), brilliant
commander of Philip II's armies, and a pietà of the school of Morales
(last N. chap.). The adjoining chapel of *N.S. de las Nieves* has 16C
glass.—Beyond the modern Ayuntamiento the C. de los Caños leads W.
to the *Parador Nac.,* while to the N. stands the ***Cap. de Mosén Rubí,**
a lofty cruciform chapel of 1516, with interesting tombs, and glass by *Nic.
de Holanda.* To the E., in the C. de López Nuñez, is the *Casa de los
Duques de Valencia* or *de los Águila,* while the Gothic doorway in the C.
del Lomo was perhaps that of the Synagogue.

In the S.E. quarter, near Jesuit *Sto Tomé,* is a group of medieval houses, known as the *Casas de los Dávilas;* to the N., in the C. de Alemania, is the *Casa de Gonzálo Dávila,* hero of the capture of Gibraltar in 1462.

We leave the city by the S.E. *Pta. del Alcázar* to visit **S. Pedro** in the Mercado Grande or Pl. de Sta Teresa (the scene of autos-de-fé), a 11–13C building resembling S. Vicente. The plain W. Doorway is surmounted by a beautiful *Rose-window and the apse is of the best Romanesque work. The retablo in the S. Transept is of the school of Berruguete (1536, and the sacristy contains an interesting treasury.

To the N.E. is the Carmelite *Conv. de las Madres* by *Fr. de Mora* (1607–15). Its church contains relics of Sta Teresa, and the tomb of her brother Lorenzo de Cepeda (1580). Opposite the latter are the monuments of Fr. Velázquez and of Bp. Álvaro de Mendoza (d. 1586) with a kneeling statue by *Est. Jordán.*—Beyond are the convents of *Sta Ana,* 16C, with remains of a church of 1350, and of *Las Gordillas* with the *Tower of María Dávila* (d. 1511) by *Vasco de la Zarza.*

The C. de Sto Tomás leads S.E. to the **Conv. de Sto Tomás,** founded by Fernando and Isabel and built by *Martín de Solórzano* in 1482–93. It was damaged by fire in 1949. After passing through the cloisters, we enter the church beneath a depressed arch bearing the *Coro* and see the high altar raised on a similar arch at the E. end. The *Retablo* of the high altar, the masterpiece of *Pedro Berruguete* (c. 1494–99), illustrating the life of St Thomas Aquinas, and the *Sillería,* especially the canopies of the royal seats, are delicately carved in flamboyant designs. Below and in front of the high altar is the exquisitely sculptured *Tomb of Prince Juan* (1478–97), only son of Fernando and Isabel, in white marble by *Dom. Fancelli* (1511–12). In the 3rd N. chapel are effigies of Juan Dávila and Juana Velázquez, attendants of the prince (1503), by an unknown master. In the sacristy is a plain slab marking the burial place of Tomás de Torquemada (1420–98), the inquisitor-general. The convent also houses some oriental antiquities.—We may return to the centre by way of the 15C *Cap. de las Vacas,* and the *Conv. de Gracia,* both with works by *Juan Rodríguez.*

On the edge of the town, is the *Conv. de S. Antonio,* founded in 1577. Its church includes the chapel of *N.S. de la Portería,* by *Pedro de Ribera* (c. 1725–31), a high altarpiece of 1719, and, in the sacristy a curious wax picture of 1670, by *Fray Eugenio,* and a portable organ in ebony and tortoiseshell.

Some 6 km. N. of Ávila is *Las Cogotas,* a famous type-settlement of the Iron Age, an acropolis within concentric walls (6–3C B.C.).

FROM ÁVILA TO MAQUEDA (FOR TOLEDO). We follow the N 403 S.E., shortly crossing the Pto. de Paramera before descending into the Alberche valley. At 41 km. a road leads 9 km. E. to *Cebreros,* with a large granite hall-church and the ruined *Conv. de S. Francisco.*—We cross the Alberche, passing the Embalse de Burguillo (r.), at 18 km. (l.) *San Martín de Valdeiglesias,* see p.408. 27 km. *Escalona,* with an imposing ruin of a castle built by Álvaro de Luna (1442) and colegiata church. Juan Manuel (1282–1348), the chronicler and poet, was born in an earlier castle on this site. At (10 km.) *Maqueda* (p.409) we meet the N. V. For the road from Maqueda to *Toledo,* 39 km. S.E., viâ *Torrijos,* see p. 321.

We leave Ávila by following either road skirting the walls, which meet beside the *Pta. del Puente* at the W. end of the town. Crossing the Adaja we turn r. (N 501), leaving the Palencia road to our l., see Rte 30. We have a fine retrospective view of the walled town as we climb out of the valley and before bearing N.W. through the rock-strewn hills of La Moraña.

At 33 km. a road leads 11 km. N. to *Fontiveros,* birthplace of St John of the Cross (1542–91), 'S. Juan de la Cruz', like Sta Teresa, of Jewish ancestry, where the church has a 12C nave and a 16C sanctuary by *Rodr. Gil de Hontañon.*—16 km beyond lies *Madrigal de las Altas Torres,* see p.353.

At 23 km. we reach the plain of Salamanca at **Peñaranda de Bracamonte,** a decayed town (6,100 inhab.) with two large plazas. The granite hall-church (undergoing restoration) has a curious altarpiece, and the *Carmelite convent* a pleasing patio.—The churches of *Zorita de la Frontera,* 13 km. due N., and *Macotera,* 10 km. S.W. on the C 610, have particularly fine ceilings, the latter artesonado. 4 km. beyond Macotera is another impressive church (15–16C) at *Santiago de la Puebla.*

From Peñaranda a deviation may be made by following a road S.W. to (28 km.) **Alba de Tormes** (4050 inhab.; *Hotel*), equally decayed, dominated by the *Torre de la Armería,* all that remains of the castle, which gave the ducal title to the Álvarez de Toledo family, of whom the most famous was Fernando, third Duke of Alba (1507–82), governor of the Netherlands. The *Tower* (restored in 1961) contains retouched frescoes (16C) of the battle of Mühlberg, in which the Duke saw action. In the *Carmelite Convent* here, which she had founded in 1570, Sta Teresa died twelve years later; the church contains a Mater Dolorosa by *Pedro de Mena* and a fine tomb by *Simón de Galarza. S. Juan* (12C) has a 14C Virgin, curious Romanesque sculptures of the Apostles, and a good retablo of 1771; *S. Miguel* and *Santiago* have 13–15C tombs, the latter an artesonado ceiling; and there are good sculptures in *S. Pedro* (rebuilt 1577 and 1686). The *Conv. de Sta Isabel* (1481) has a good artesonado and the tomb of Juan de las Vargas (d. 1525); while in *Las Benitas* are the 16C doorway and 15C tombs.—Not far S. are the ruins of Gothic *S. Leonardo* (1429–82) with a later cloister.—After crossing the Tormes and turning r. we approach (21 km. N.W.) *Salamanca,* passing as we near the city the two hills, *Los Arapiles,* which were the main bones of contention in the Battle of Salamanca, see p.346. This victory would have been complete, had not the Spanish force guarding the bridgehead at Alba de Tormes withdrawn contrary to orders, allowing the French to retreat across the river here.

Following the direct but less interesting road from Peñaranda, at 41 km. we enter **Salamanca,** see Rte. 32.

29 FROM SORIA TO MEDINACELI, SIGÜENZA AND GUADALAJARA

Total distance, 242 km. (150 miles) N III. 36 km. *Almazán*—40 km. *Medinaceli*—N II. 19 km. *Alcolea del Pinar*—C 114. 19 km. **Sigüenza**—C 204 for 27 km.—N II. 45 km. **Guadalajara**—56 km. **Madrid.**

SORIA (3460 ft; 27,600 inhab. 19,000 in 1960; *Parador Nac.* and *Hotels*), the capital of a province noted for the coldest climate in Spain, contains a number of fine medieval buildings, but modern development has impaired its once considerable charm, as celebrated in the poems of Antonio Machado (who lived here in 1907–13) and Gerardo Diego.

History. Of ancient foundation, Soria was restored after the Moorish invasions by Alfonso 'el Batallador' of Aragón, but later, ceded to Alfonso VII it became a capital of the march, ruled by twelve noble families (the 'Doce Linajes'). Untouched by the troubles of later centuries, until sacked by Ney in 1808, it long retained a strong provincial atmosphere. Its population in 1920 was merely 8000.

From the main Pl. de Ramón y Cajal the Paseo leads W. to the *Museo Numantino* with important material (badly displayed) from the excavations of Numancia, see p. 118, 8 km. N.E.

Opposite is the *Ermita de la Soledad* (16C), containing the Cristo del Humilladero. Behind this lies the Alameda de Cervantes, to the S. of which the church of the *Hospital* preserves a late-16C retablo (from ruined S. Nicolás) by *Fr. de Pinedo.*

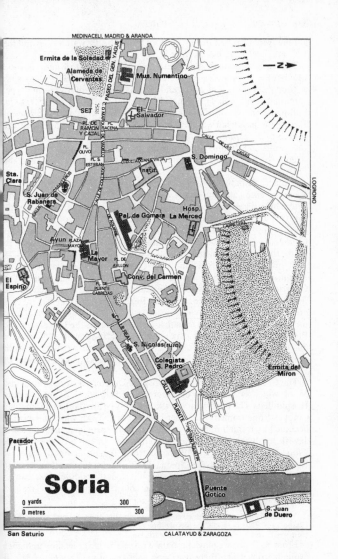

Soria

| 0 yards | 300 |
| 0 metres | 300 |

In the Pl. Aceña, N. of the Pl. Ramón y Cajal, is the house of the brothers Gustavo Adolfo and Valeriano Becquer, the 19C poet and painter. Behind it, a modern church retains the apse of Romanesque *El Salvador* (with a mid-16C retablo by *Fr. de Ágreda* and *Juan de Baltanas*).

Following the main street, the C. del Marqués de Vadillo. we pass (l.) the C. de la Aduana Vieja, where Romanesque *S. Clemente* has been torn down and replaced by the Telefónica. Among remaining mansions are the Renaissance *Casa de los Rios* (now a bottle warehouse) and the 16C *Pal. del Visconde de Eza.*

To the S. is a small plaza with the 16C *Pal. de Alcántara,* beyond which is the *Diputación.* Adjacent is **S. Juan de Rabanera** (c. 1200), with a good S. Front, and apse, and internal cupola of Byzantine type, containing (in the S. Transept) a Plateresque retablo by *Fr. de Ágreda.* Following the C. de Caballeros S.E. through what was the ancient *Judería,* we pass what was the *Conv. de Sta Clara* (16C), and beyond, the church of *El Espino,* in which lies Machado's wife, Leonor, retaining 16C vaults and a Churrigueresque retablo of 1686. Hence a road climbs steeply to the ruined Castle, commanding an extensive view, and the *Parador Nac.*

From El Espino we turn r. to reach the PL. MAYOR, with the 19C *Ayuntamiento,* and the old *Audiencia* (1796), bearing an inscription dated 1621 recording the privileges of the city. *N.S. de Mayor,* mainly 16C Gothic, retains fragments of Romanesque *S. Gil.* From the Pl. de S. Blas, to the W., the C. de Aguirre leads N.E. to the huge *Pal. de los Condes de Gómara* (1577–92), with a balustraded front, restored to house the new Audiencia.

Below, in the Pl. de Ayllón, is the *Conv. del Carmen,* (in the *Pal. de Beaumonte*) where Sta Teresa lived in 1580; the 17C church has Churrigueresque retablos.—By the C. del Carmen we may reach the Pl. de Fuente Cabrejas, hence the old C. Real descends, in which there are a number of derelict medieval mansions, passing the site of Romanesque *S. Nicolás,* little of which remains. To the N. stands the **Colegiata de S. Pedro,** a well-vaulted Gothic hall-church of 1520–73, with a 16C retablo mayor by *Francisco del Rio,* the Cap. del S. Saturio (with a triptych attrib. to *Correa de Vivar*), and three remaining wings of a Cloister of 1150-1205.

The C. del Puente descends to cross the Duero by a stone bridge, just N. of which is *S. Juan de Duero,* a ruined house of the Knights Hospitallers. The nave-altars of the 12C church are flanked by singular canopies (one domed, the other conical) of c. 1200, while the nave is occupied by a small museum of relics from the province, including 13C Jewish tombstones, etc. Note the well-preserved capitals. The curious *Cloister,* of which only the interlaced arcade remains, is one of the latest Romanesque buildings in Spain (13C). The columns change their character not at each corner (as is usual) but in the middle of each walk, with intersecting and horseshoe arches in which Mudéjar and Romanesque features are combined.

A little distance along the river in the other direction, beyond the Templar Chapel of *S. Polo* (13C), is the picturesque *Ermita de S. Saturio,* with 18C frescoes (restored), and a rock-cut crypt and staircase.

From S. Pedro we may climb the Travesia Exterior leading to higher ground, from which there is a good view (r.) of the *Ermita del Mirón* (1725) beside the Baroque *Obelisco de S. Saturio.* On our l. are late-Gothic *La Merced* with the *Hospicio,* retaining the front of the 16C convent in which lived Fr. Gabriel Téllez (Tirso de Molina, the dramatist; 1571–1648). Thence the C. de S. Tomé leads to *Sto **Domingo** (late-12C), with one of the finest Romanesque façades in Spain, including a magnificent doorway with sculptured capitals and tympanum and a deeply recessed wheel-window; note the musicians, the Massacre of the Innocents, etc. The interior, partly rebuilt in the 16C,

has Gothic vaults and Baroque retablos.—We descend to the centre by
the C. de la Aduana Vieja, passing the Instituto in the 18C *Casa de los
Castejones,* with a Baroque doorway.

From the Pl. de Ramón y Cajal we drive S. on the N 111, after 36 km.
reaching the fortified town of **Almazán** (5200 inhab.; *Hotel*),
on the left bank of the Duero. Important from its position on the
frontier of Aragón, Almazán a played a vital role in dynastic wars of the
14C, and was granted by Enrique de Trastamara to Bertrand Du
Guesclin, with many neighbouring fiefs.—Passing the octagonal *Ermita
de Jesús* (18C), we enter the town by the *Pta. de la Villa* which leads
directly into the *Pl. Mayor.* Here is late-12C *S. Miguel,* with a fine
*Mudéjar vault, and further W. is the medieval *Pal. de Altamira,* with a
Renaissance gallery overlooking the Duero. To the E. is late-Gothic *Sta
María,* not far from the twin-towered *Pta. de los Herreros.* In the centre
is *Santiago* (Renaissance), while other Romanesque churches of interest
are *S. Esteban* in the decayed S.E. quarter, dominated by a hill-top
Calvary; *N.S. del Campanario,* further W., with the *Pta. del Mercado*
beyond; and *S. Vicente* to the N.W.

The C 116 leads S.E. to meet (45 km.) the N II (Zaragoza-Madrid road) 7 km. N.
of *Sta María de Huerta* (p.212), passing (14 km.) *Morón de Almazán,* where the
church has a Platerésqué tower of 1540 dominating the plaza containing
Renaissance mansions, and (22 km.) *Monteagudo de las Vicarias,* encircled by
remains of ramparts, with a 15C castle, and a 16C church with a late-Gothic
doorway and a retablo of 1522.

FROM ALMAZÁN TO GUADALAJARA viâ ATIENZA (116 km.). A direct road (C 101)
follows the 'old' route S.W. across the Alto de Barahonda (3375 ft).—At 35 km. a
road leads 25 km. S.E. to *Sigüenza,* at 20 km. passing (1.) *Pozancos,* where the 13C
church has a 15C chapel with a fine reja, while to the r. lies *Palazuelos,* with a 15C
castle and old walls, and the Romanesque church of *Carabias,* 2 km. beyond.
Continuing S.W. on the C 101, we turn W. at 12 km. to enter (4 m.) **Atienza,**
successor of Celtiberian *Tutia,* a walled village (700 inhab.) with a ruined castle and
seven medieval churches, most of which were altered in the 16C, but nearly all
retain Romanesque portions, and sculpture, paintings, and plate.
From Atienza a poor road leads W. through mountainous country to (62 km.)
Ayllón (see p.341), passing (15 km.) *Albendiego,* where the Romanesque church
has remarkable windows of pierced stone, (14 km.) *Campisábalos* and (5 km.)
Villacadima, both with Romanesque churches.

18 km. **Jadraque** (1500 inhab.), with the 15C *castle* of the Duque de Osuna, and a
church containing alabaster tombs, and a Flagellation by *Zurbarán.*—20 km.
Hita, famous as the home of the medieval poet, the archpriest Juan Ruiz (d. 1353),
retains an old castle, a 12C gate and the ruined monastery of *Sopetrán.*—12 km.
N.W. lies *Espinosa de Henares.* Its 16C church has an artesonado roof, and there
are prehistoric and Roman remains near the chapel of *La Soledad.*—**Cogolludo,** 7
km. beyond, contains the noble *Pal. de Medinaceli* (1492–95) in the Florentine and
Renaissance style, a good 16C hall-church, and a ruined castle.—8 km. S. of
Cogolludo stands the church of *Mohernando,* with a 16C S. Francis, and the
remarkable tomb of the Eraso family, and 3 km. beyond, at *Cerezo,* a 16C church
with an artesonado ceiling.
At 23 km, we meet the N II and turn r. for (4 km.) **Guadalajara,** see p.288.

The N 111 climbs S. from Almazán to the Alto del Minguete. At 40
km. we may turn r. and after 1 km. enter the Moorish stronghold of
Medinaceli (3330 ft), now a mere village (1200 inhab; *Hotel,* and
Hosteria Nac.) perched above the Jalón valley, but containing a number
of attractive old mansions. Of the Roman city of *Ocilis* there remains a
Triumphal Arch of the 2nd or 3C, the only one with a triple archway to
survive in Spain.

Here in the 'city of Selim (?)', died the Moorish conqueror Almansor, in 1002 and here, after the Christian reconquest in 1124, was established the family of La Cerda, dukes of Medinaceli, who claimed the Spanish throne by right of descent from the Infantes de la Cerda, the sons of Alfonso el Sabio, who were dispossessed by their uncle, Sancho el Valiente.

Their imposing *Castle* still stands, and the *Church* (1520–40) contains many of their tombs. The *Beaterio de S. Román* was formerly a synagogue.

We now climb down into the valley to meet the N II, and turn r. for (1⁹ km.) *Alcolea del Pinar*. Here we bear r. again (C 114) for (19 km. *Sigüenza*, see below.

A direct but secondary road leads from just S. of Medinaceli to (24 km.) Sigüenza, passing N. of *Guijosa*, an old walled town with a 13C church. N. of this road, beyond the village of *Ambrona*, is a barn, or *Museo Paleontológico*, covering an excavated site in which are seen in situ the remains of elephants which roamed the area some 300,000 years ago. 4 km. E. of Alcolea, at *Aguilar de Anguita* is a Roman camp and a prehistoric cemetery.

15 km. S.W. of Alcolea, at *Torresaviñan*, is a 14C castle. At 18 km. the N II is joined by the C204 from Sigüenza. From this junction to (45 km. Guadalajara and (56 km.) *Madrid*, see pp.286–305 in reverse.

From the C 114 we turn r. to enter **SIGÜENZA** (3230 ft; *Parador Nac.)* an attractive old town of 6100 inhab., preserving the name of Celtiberian *Segontia*, said to have been founded by fugitives from Saguntum at *Villa Vieja*, a short distance N.E. The town is built on a steep slope, rising like an amphiteatre above the Henares, and is dominated by the Bishops' castle. It suffered from its position as an advanced post of the Nationalists during 1936–37.

Below the town, near the river, lies the *Alameda*, a pleasant park laid out in 1804 by Bp. Vejarano 'for the solace of the poor'.

To the W. stands the *Humilladero*, a Gothic chapel with a Renaissance doorway. To the N. lies N.S. *de los Huertos*, a fine late-Gothic church (1510–24) b Maestro *Juan*, whose self-portrait, kneeling in prayer, is in the cap. mayor.

By the E. end of the Alameda stands grandiose *S. Francisco* (c. 1594–1615), and S. of this is the Baroque chapel of *S. Roque*, in the street of that name, the main artery of a model suburb built for Bp. Díaz Guerra (1777–1800), on plans supplied by *Bernasconi*.

From S. Francisco, the C. de Medina leads uphill to the early-Gothic ***Cathedral.** Begun c. 1150 and consecrated in part in 1169, but considerably altered in the 13C, it is a plain building in a mixture of styles derived from France. The central lantern was added during reconstruction, since damaged by Nationalist gunfire in 1936. The *W. Front*, divided by massive buttresses and flanked by low square towers, has a fine round-arched door. On the l. is the *Chapter House* (by Fr. Baeza*, 1527). The S. Front is flanked by a slender tower of 1300 and has a 13C rose above *Bernasconi's* classical portal of 1797.

In the cathedral, the vault is supported by massive clustered piers. The *Sillería* (1490) is by *Rodrigo Duque, Fr. de Coca,* and others; the trascoro and altar are by *Juan Labera* (1665–88); against the coro is the Retablo de la Virgen de la Leche (1514). In the *Cap. Mayor,* with a reja of 1628–38, is the tomb of Abp. Bernardo of Toledo, first Bp. of Sigüenza (12C), and a retablo (1609–11) by *Giral. de Merlo.* The N pulpit is of 1495, the S. a masterpiece of *Martín de Valdoma* (1573). On the N. side is the *Portal* of the *Cap. de la Anunciación* (1510–16), an effective combination of Gothic, Renaissance, and Mudéjar ornament, while the adjoining *Chapel of S. Francisco Xavier* has a Plateresque portal. On the same side is the *Sacristy,* with a similar portal, a panelled ceiling by *Covarrubias* (1532–35) with 300 heads set in medallions, and some Nottingham alabasters of c. 1400. To the S. of the choir is the *Chapel of the Arce Family,* including the charming semi-recumbent *Figure (c. 1495) of Martín Vázquez de Arce, slain before Granada in 1486, and known as *El Doncel de Sigüenza.*—The Chapel of *S. Marcos* (c. 1511) contains a 15C triptych by *Fern. del Rincón;* in that of *Sta Librada* (patroness of Sigüenza) are the mausoleum of Don Fadrique de Portugal, (bishop here in 1512–32) drastically restored since 1936, and six 16C Italian panels. Off the late Gothic *Cloister,* on the N., by *Alonso de Vozmediano* (1503–07), a chapel contains 17C Flemish tapestries.

A *museum* stands opposite the cathedral, containing *El Greco's* Annunciation, *Zurbarán's* Inmaculada, and works attributed to *Salzillo, Morales,* and *Pompeo Leoni;* also some curious bronze crucifixes. The patio houses 15C figures of Adam and Eve.

The C. de Román Pascual, W. of the cathedral, passing the *Col. de S. Bartolomé,* or *Seminario Mayor* (1651; enlarged 1750–61), crosses the C. del Card. Mendoza to reach the Renaissance *Casa de la Inquisición,* C. de la Yedra 2. By this street we gain the C. del Peso (r.) with the late-16C *Casa del Pósito* and remains of the city wall. The wall continues along the C. del Hospital, where the *Hosp. de S. Mateo,* founded in 1445, preserves two good reliefs over the doorway.

The restored *Pl. Mayor,* S. of the cathedral, is surrounded by porticoes and balconies mostly designed by *Fr. Guillén* (1498 onwards). On the S. is the *Ayuntamiento* of 1511–12, by *Juan de Garay,* while to the E. the *Pta. del Toril* leads into open country across the 17C bridge and aqueduct called *Los Arcos* (view). The C. Mayor climbs steeply S., passing the picturesque Travesaña Baja (r.) and the ruined 12C church of *Santiago,* to reach the *Castle,* rebuilt in the 12th and 14-15C on the site of the Moorish Alcázar and restored to accommodate the *Parador Nac.* Below the castle the C. del Jesús leads to *S. Vicente* (12-13C); nearby is the *Casa del Doncel* (15C).

The C. Bajada de S. Jerónimo runs downhill to the *Seminario Menor* and the *Pal. Episcopal* built in 1624–25 to house a University, closed in 1837.

To regain the N II, 25 km. S.W., we follow the C 204, off which at 13 km., a road leands 5 km. N.W. to *Baides,* with the *Pal. of the Conde de Salvatierra.*—At *Pelegrina,* not far S. of Sigüenza, is a ruined castle and a Plateresque church.

For the continuation of this route to *Guadalajara* and Madrid, see pp. 286-305 in reverse, and p. 435.

30   FROM SORIA TO SEGOVIA, ÁVILA, AND PLASENCIA

Total distance, 408 km. (253 miles). N 122. 58 km. **El Burgo de Osma**—13 km. *San Esteban de Gormaz*—N 110. 47 km. *Riaza*—12 km. turn l. and follow N I for 5 km. then r.—58 km. **Segovia**—35 km. *Villacastin*—N 501. 32 km. **Ávila**—N 110. 78 km. *El Barco de Ávila*—70 km. **Plasencia.**

This long but interesting route follows the N. slope of the Sierra de Guadarrama and de Gredos, but should not be attempted in Winter, unless in good weather.

At 30 km. we pass (r.) **Calatanazor,** where according to tradition, Almanzor, the scourge of Christian Spain, was finally defeated by the Leonese in 1002. The picturesque village, surrounded by walls, has a ruined castle, while late Gothic *Sta Maria del Castillo* retains good Romanesque and earlier decoration, and a rare 16C organ in wood.

28 km. **EL BURGO DE OSMA,** a characteristic town of 5200 inhab., has crumbling medieval walls and arcaded streets. It was the birthplace of the poet Dionisio Ridruejo (1912–75). Facing each other in the Pl. Mayor are the *Casas Consistoriales* (1764–68) and the *Hosp. de S. Agustín,* with an interesting chapel and a front of 1700. The C. Mayor runs S. passing (r.) the 17C *Bishop's Palace.*

The *****Cathedral,** although small, is one of the finest in Spain for design and detail. Begun in 1232 by Maestro *Lope* and *Johan de Medina,* stonemason, to replace a church of 1101–10, it was finished by the end of the century. The *S. Portal,* enriched with statues (c. 1300), is modelled on the Pta. del Sarmental at Burgos, probably by the same craftsmen. The Baroque *****Tower* (1739–44) is by *Dom. Ondátegui.*—The *Coro* has a reja of c. 1500, bearing the Fonseca arms, stalls of 1589, and organ-cases of 1641 (S.) and 1787; the Renaissance *trascoro* dated from c. 1550, while the Gothic pulpit was given by Bp. Pedro González de Mendoza (1478–83). The *****Reja* of the *Cap. Mayor* is by *Juan Francés* (1505–15) and the retablo mayor by *Juan de Juni* and *Juan Picardo* (1550–54). An ambulatory and E. chapel were added in 1772–81 by *Juan de Villanueva.* In the N. Transept is the vaulted *Vestuario* (before 1281) beneath the *Cap. de S. Pedro de Osma* (1530–47). Two Romanesque windows opening onto the Cloister have been uncovered in the *Vestuario,* where lies the saint's *****Tomb* of 1258 of painted stone, unique in its period for naturalistic treatment and calculated lack of symmetry. To the E. is the transeptal chapel of the 12C *Cristo del Milagro,* while in the N. wall a door leads to the vaulted *Tesoro.*

Through the *Cloisters,* added in 1500–23 by *Juan de la Piedra,* we reach the Museo (escorted visit), containing a Panel of SS. Augustine and Dominic, attr. to *Nicolas Francés,* a collection of vestments (16–18C) and a piece of the Persian silk shroud of the patron (1199). From its important collection of codices, are displayed an illuminated Bible (13–14C) and a 12C Charter, thought to be the earliest example of Castilian, and a copy of the Apocalypse of Beatus of Liébana (1086). There are some good pictures in the *Sacristía Mayor* (1780), off the S. Ambulatory, and the *Sacristia de Santiago* (1551), at the W. end of the S. Aisle; the former contains a musical astronomical clock made in London for Bp. Calderón (1764–86). St Dominic (Domingo de Guzmán; 1170–1221), founder of the Dominican Order, took orders as a canon regular in the Cathedral chapter of Osma in 1194.

Beyond the W. end of the cathedral a gate leads to the old bridge, while the C. del Puente runs S. to the *Carmelite Convent* (1607). From the *Seminario* (1778), on the E. side of the town, the C. del Marqués del Vadillo leads back to the Soria road, on the other side of which stand the buildings of the former *University of Sta Catalina* (1541–55), with a good courtyard.—To the S. are twin hills, that on the E. bearing the ruins of a medieval castle (View). The other marks the site of Roman *Uxama Argelae,* which gave its name to the city of Osma, now a poor hamlet on the W. bank of the Ucero opposite El Burgo, originally a mere suburb.

Ucero, 26 km. N. of Osma, is commanded by a well-preserved castle, and 3 km. beyond, a track (l.) leads to the picturesquely sited 12C Templars' church of *S. Juan de Otero,* with remains of their house.

A road runs S. past the station of Osma to (25 km.) the remote village of *Caracena,* with a notable porticoed church (early 12C).

16 km. S.E. of El Burgo de Osma stands the huge Moorish *Castle of **Gormaz**,* with twin keeps and twenty-one other towers, dominating the landscape and well worth visiting for the extensive Views obtained from its windswept walls. A road now climbs to the summit. The castle, of 965, was altered in the 13th and 14Cs.—13 km. further E. lies **Berlanga de Duero,** commanded by an impressive 15C *Castle* with a 13C curtain wall. The *Colegiata* is a magnificent hall-church of 1526–30 by *Juan de Rasines.* The woodwork in the choir (1575–80) is by *Martín de Valdoma;* and there are good rejas and tombs, and an impressive Churrigueresque retablo.

7 km. beyond Berlanga is the curious 11C Mozarabic chapel of *S. Baudel,* where horseshoe arches radiate from a central column to which is fixed a tribune with a gabled oratory. It retains the faded remains of 12C murals, some of which are displayed in the Prado Museum, having been returned from the U.S.A., where they found their way in 1922, five years *after* its declaration as a National Monument!—Some 4 km. S.E. at *Caltójar,* is a Romanesque church with a retablo of 1570—*Andaluz,* 7 km. N.E. of Berlanga, and N. of the Duero, also contains a Romanesque church, *S. Miguel,* dated 1114, and signed by Subpirianus (i.e. Cipriano).

13 km. **San Esteban de Gormaz,** an old town (4200 inhab.) with an ancient bridge of 16 arches spanning the Duero, has two 12C churches, *San Miguel* and *del Rivero,* both with exterior galleries.

To the S.W. once stood an oakwood, the 'robredo de Corpes', where the Infantes de Carrión are said (in the 'Cantar de mio Cid') to have abandoned their wives.

22 km. N.W. lies *Alcubilla de Avellaneda,* with the ruined monastery of *La Espeja* nearby. Here the 16C church contains alabaster tombs of the Avellanedas. Immediately after crossing the bridge a road (l.) leads 35 km. S. to *Tiermes* or *Termancia,* the extensive site of a partially excavated Iberian town.

FROM SAN ESTEBAN TO ARANDA (45 km.) The N 122, runs due W. passing at 5 m. *Rejas de S. Esteban* (3 km. r.) with two Romanesque churches, (13 km.) *Langa de Duero,* with a medieval bridge, Gothic church, and castle-keep and (8 km.) *La Vid,* with an Augustinian church begun in 1542.—7 km, N. lies *Peñaranda de Duero,* see p.227—19 km. *Aranda de Duero;* see p.227.

At San Esteban we turn across the bridge onto the N 110 and gently climb S.W. out of the valley onto the plateau, from which magnificent views are obtained towards the Sierra de Ayllón and of the Guadarrama range further W.—27 km. **Ayllón,** a picturesque partly-walled village (1300 inhab.), with the *Pal. of the Contreras* (1497) and an irregular arcaded plaza, the church of *S. Miguel,* and the impressive ruins of *S. Juan;* those of the *Conv. of S. Francisco* lie to the N.W.—At 3 km. we pass (l.) *Santa María de Riaza,* with a church containing a good artesonado ceiling.

16 km. N.W. lies *Maderuelo,* on a rock ridge dominated by the interesting church of *Sta María; S. Miguel* is also basically Romanesque. A medieval bridge, sometimes covered by the reservoir, leads to *La Vera Cruz,* whence Romanesque murals have been removed to the Prado Museum.

17 km **Riaza,** a summer resort (1300 inhab.; *Hotel*) being spoilt by the erection of chalets, with a 16C church, 4 km. E. of which stands the chapel of *N.S. de Hontanares,* on the slope of the sierra with extensive views of the Castilian plateau.—To the S.W. lies the brash winter-sports development of *La Pinilla.*—At 3 km. a road forks r. direct to *Sepulveda* (see p.227) 24 km W., while at 19 km. we meet the N I (Burgos-Madrid,

see Rte 21A). Here we bear S. for 5 km. before turning r. onto the N 110, which continues to skirt the range.—From (18 km.) Arcones a road leads 9 km. N.W. to *Pedraza de la Sierra,* see p.228—24 km. r. *Sotosalbos* (p.228), 10 km. beyond which we look down on (10 km.) **Segovia,** see p.324.

Passing through the Aqueduct, we continue ahead at cross-roads and shortly turn l. onto the continuation of the N 110, passing (8 km. l.) *Madrona,* with a Romanesque church. At 27 km. we cross the N VI at *Villacastín* (see p.231) and follow the N 501. At (11 km.) *Aldeavieja* the road reaches the height of 3983 ft, with views (l.) of the sierras of Guadarrama and Malagon, before entering (21 km.) **Ávila,** see Rte 28. Crossing the Adaja W. of the town walls, we turn l. and gradually ascend the narrowing valley, with views S. of the Sierra de Gredos.

FROM ÁVILA TO ARENAS DE SAN PEDRO (85 km.). 6 km W. of Ávila the C 50 forks l., shortly climbing past the *Pto. de Menga* into the valley of the Alberche. A 6 km. we pass (8 km. S.) *Sotalbo,* with the 15C castle of *Aunquesospese,* and (6 km *Solosancho,* in the plaza of which stands a carved granite boar from the remarkable fortified site of *Ulaca,* 2 km. S.

At 33 km. the C 500 climbs W. to the *Parador Nac. de Gredos,* a favourite centr for excursions in the sierra, the wild goat *(Capra Pyrenaica)* of which were save from extinction through the initiative of Alfonso XIII, when only some two doze head had survived. *Hoyos del Espino,* 18 km, further down the valley of th Tormes, is the starting point for the easiest ascent of the *Circo de Gredos* (8504 ft) Beyond Hoyas, the road passes through a series of picturesque villages to (36 km. *El Barco de Ávila,* see below.

The C 502 climbs S. to the *Pto. del Pico* (4435 ft) with a Mirador, from which a magnificent *View S.W. is obtained, before we zigzag steeply down to the S. flan' of the range, passing (19 km. l.) the conspicuous *castle* of 1393 at *Mombetrán,* als with a 16C *hospital.*—At 3 km. a road forks r. for (6 km.) *Arenas de San Pedro* (se p.411, and for the road hence to *Plasencia).* The C502 continues S. to meet (34 km. the N V 7 km W. of *Talavera,* see p.409.

At 42 km. we cross the Pto. de Villatoro (4450 ft), with an attractive view S.W.—9 km. *Bonilla de la Sierra,* 5 km. to the N., contains an early 15C church covered by a pointed barrel vault of 16 m span.—6 km. **Piedrahita** (2250 inhab.; *Hotel*) has a good parish church with an 18C organ, and retains an 18C *Pal. of the Albas* (now a school).

21 km. **El Barco de Ávila,** an old town (2600 inhab.; *Hotel*), with ruined walls, a pleasant plaza, medieval bridge, and a late-15C castle (best seen from the bridge), has an early 14C church with good rejas and 15C paintings, a Virgin by *Vigarni,* and a relief by *Vasco de la Zarza.* In its 16C church is an unrestored 18C organ with five rows of trumpets in 'chamade'.

FROM EL. BARCO TO BÉJAR (28 km) The C 500 climbs W. through attractiv country, off which at 2 km. a road leads 8 km. N. to *El Tejado,* beyond which ar the extensive prehistoric ruins of *El Berrueco,* encircled by a wall. At 22 km. w turn l. on meeting the N 630 (from Salamanca to Plasencia, see Rte 46A), an enter (4 km.) *Béjar,* see p.421.

From El Barco the N 110 descends steeply S.W. by the *Pto. de Tornavacas* (4190 ft) into the long verdant valley of the Jerte, passing a 36 km. the attractive village of *Cabezuela del Valle.*—34 km *Plasencia,* see Rte 46A.

31   FROM VALLADOLID TO
SALAMANCA AND CIUDAD RODRIGO

Total distance, 232 km. (144 miles). N 620, 30 km. *Tordesillas*—85 km. **Salamanca**—88 km. **Ciudad Rodrigo**—29 km. *Fuentes de Oñoro.*

Crossing the Pisuerga, we follow the N 620 S.W. past (8 km) *Arroyo,* with a Romanesque church, to (3 km) **Simancas,** Roman *Septimanca* (1300 inhab.; *Hotel*) famous as the repository of the National Archives—some later used as kindling by Kellermann during the Peninsular War—transferred in 1545 to the moated slate-roofed castle. Here one may peruse the marriage contract of the future Philip II and Mary Tudor, that of Fernando and Isabel, and other important documents and autographs, etc. (permission to copy only with special authorization from the Archivero Mayor). In the plain below, Ramiro II defeated the Moors in 934. Hugh Roe O'Donnell (?1571–1602), Lord of Tyrconnel, died of poison at Simancas. The parish church has a Romanesque W. Tower and a retablo by *Inocencio Berruguete* and *Bautista Beltrán* (1563), painted by *Jerónimo Vázquez* (1571); the lierne vault (c. 1500) recalls English work.—A *Bridge* of 17 arches crosses the Pisuérga. Between Simancas and Tordesillas is the confluence of the Pisuerga and Duero, of which the proverb says: 'Duero tiens la fama y Pisuerga lleba el agua' (Duero gets the glory, Pisuerga brings the water: used with a much winder application).

19 km. **Tordesillas,** (6900 inhab.; *Parador Nac.* on the Salamanca road; *Hotel*), where the Duero is crossed by a picturesque bridge, was a centre of the Comunero rebellion. *S. Antolín,* above the bridge, contains a Crucifixion by *Juni* and the Alderete tomb (1550) by *Gaspar,* a local sculptor. *S. Pedro* (Gothic) and *Sta María* are other notable churches, the latter with a handsome Herreran tower.

The *Conv. de Sta Clara,** on a commanding site above the river, was once a palace of Pedro the Cruel. The building may be visited under escort. It was begun by Alfonso XI in 1340 (enlarged after 1360), and contains much fine Mudéjar work, including the *Patio of S. Pedro* and a beautiful artesonado ceiling over the *Cap. Mayor;* also a good retablo (Flemish, 15C), and, in the chapel, the founder's tomb (1435).

Note an early clavichord, and a square virginal (by Hans Bos of Antwerp) brought here c.1560 by Mary of Hungary. One of the 18C organs had its pipes removed in 1950 by the sacristan, who sold them to a local plumber!

The *little* portative organ was given to the church by Juana la Loca. This was restored in 1974 for a recording, but on condition that it was afterwards smashed, on the specific instructions of the Director of the Patrimonio Nacional!

Juana la Loca (the Mad; 1479-1555) mother of the Emperor Charles V, died at Tordesillas after 49 years of confinement. She is said to have occupied a small cell, without windows, but the story that she spent her time watching her husband's coffin is inaccurate.

In the town centre is a attractive arcaded *plaza.* Alonso de Castillo Solórzano (1584-1648), the author of picaresque stories and *entremeses,* and the braggart Nationalist general, Queipo de Llano (1875-1951), were born here.

14 km. to the N.W. of Tordesillas, 1 off the N VI, lies *Villalar,* where Juan de Padilla was defeated by the troops of Charles V (1521) in a battle which crushed the cause of the Comuneros; while 15 km. N., off the C 611, stands *Torrelobatón,* with a noble 15C *Castle** with a keep 45 m. high, and three drum towers, and a church with an altarpiece by *Adrian Álvarez.*

From Tordesillas to Toro and Zamora, see Rte 33. From Tordesillas N.W. to Benavente and S.E. to Medina del Campo, see Rte 36.

Beyond the bridge, we turn r. past the *Parador Nac.*, crossing the lonely undulating plain to (29 km.) **Alaejos,** with a ruined castle and two Renaissance churches, of which *Sta María* contains a retablo by *Est. Jordán* and *Fr. Martínez* (1604) and artesonados. Their towers dominate the region, which is noted for its sherry-like white wine ('Vino de Alaejos hace centar los viejos').

15 km. S.E. lies *Carpio,* home of the legendary hero, Bernardo del Carpio, nephew of Alfonso el Casto, while to the S. lies *Fresno el Viejo,* where *S. Juan,* the brick church of the Hospitallers (12-13C) contains a 15C Mudéjar tomb. Further S., (26 km. from Alaejos) at *Cantalapiedra,* the remarkable church is a former mosque, rebuilt in 1392–1405 and altered in the 18C.—11 km. E. of Alaejos is **Nava del Rey** (2700 inhab.). which may also be approached direct by a road (23 km.) forking l. off the N 620 some 4 km S.W. of Tordesillas. The great hall-church of *Los SS Juanes* (16-17C), is partly by *Rod. Gil de Hontañón,* with a splendid tower and good retablos, the retablo mayor being by *Greg. Fernández.* The church of the *Capuchinas* contains the Divine Shepherdess and other sculptures by *Carmona*

At 42 km. a turning (r.) leads 7 km. to *Palencia de Negrilla,* with a huge painted retablo (16C) in its church.

At 14 km. we enter **Salamanca,** see Rte 32.

On leaving the city, at 4 km. the C 517 forks r., off which (at 23 km.) a turning (r. leads 9 km. to **Ledesma,** an attractive old walled town (2000 inhab.) on the Tormes (to the N.W. forming the Embalse de Almendra), with a Bridge on Roman foundations; remains of Roman baths; *S. Miguel,* part-Romanesque, and *Sta María,* 13-16C, with fine tombs, overlooking an arcaded plaza, with an *Ayuntamiento* of 1606.—The C 517 continues past this junction to (41 km. *Vitigudino,* 7 km. to the S.W. of which is the Iberian site of *Yecla la Vieja,* while 4 km. W. at *Guadramiro* is a 15C palace.—At *Lumbrales,* 30 km. W. of Vitigudino are pre-Roman Walls, while there are various dolmens in the vicinity. The picturesque village of *S. Felices de los Gallegos,* 10 km. S., retains 16C fortifications; the church is partly Romanesque. **Ciudad Rodrigo** lies 39 km. S.E of S. Felices.

At 16 km. a road leads 3 km. N. to *Barbadillo,* near which is *S. Julián de Valmuza,* with important Roman ruins and mosaics.—3 km. *Calzada de Don Diego,* with a mansion of the Duque de Tamames.

64 km. **CIUDAD RODRIGO** (13,000 inhab.; *Parador Nac.* in the Castle), overlooking the Agueda, was founded in 1150 by Count Rodrigo González Girón and strongly fortified by Fernando II (c. 1190). Its walls are still standing, the circuit of which is recommended. The *Alcázar,* begun in 1372, dominates the bridge.

The town suffered two sieges in the Peninsular War, the first in 1810 when it was taken by Massena and Ney. In Jan. 1812 Wellington decided to secure the fortress as a base of operations. A lightning attack surprised the garrison, but the English were only masters of the fortress after a costly 11-days siege in which Gen Crauford (1764–1812), of the Light Division, lost his life in the breaches, while Wellington received an earldom and the Spanish title of Duque de Ciudad Rodrigo. Cristóbal de Castillejo (c.1491–1550), the poet, was born here.

The ***Cathedral,** a beautiful Gothic building of c. 1165–88, with 'Angevin' vaults begun in 1212, was damaged in 1812 by British fire from the Tesones, two knolls N. of the town, but has been restored,. It has three fine portals, particularly the richly sculptured *W. Doorway.* The jamb-statues of saints stand on little replicas of the Torre del Gallo at Salamanca, and beneath the Coronation in the tympanum are quaint carvings of the Last Supper, etc. It is proceded by a porch and steeple of 1760–65, Barosque work by *Sagarviñaga.* The solid-looking *INTERIOR contains elaborate capitals, and a wealth of sculpture. At the E. end, the central one of three apses was added in 1538–50. The choir stalls, with their grotesque carvings by *Rodrigo Alemán,* recalling those of

Plasencia and Zamora, should be observed. One organ, known as the Realejo' is 16C, and has a beautiful 'jeux de regal'; the other is 17C.

On the N. Side is a *Cloister* begun c. 1320; note the capitals and other carvings; a Crucifixion in the N.W. corner bears the name of the builder, *Benito Sánchez,* and on the Renaissance door leading into the garth are busts of a canon and of the architect, *Pedro Güemez,* who completed the N. and E. walks in 1525–38.

The *Ayuntamiento* (restored) facing the picturesque *Pl. Mayor,* is one of many 15-16C mansions, among which may be mentioned the **Pal. de los Castros,** with spiral pillars, where Wellington lodged after the siege near the E. gate). Also of interest are the *Cap. de Cerralbo* (1588–1685), with an altar-painting by *Ribera;* the church of the *Clarisas* by *Rodrigo Gil de Hontañón* (16C), *S. Pedro* and *S. Agustín.*

Some 4 km. downstream stands the *Monasterio de la Caridad,* with a fine façade (16C), and an 18C interior by *Sagarviñaga.*—Near *Zamarra,* 14 km S.E., are remains of a large pre-Roman town.

Crossing the Agueda, we drive W. throught pine woods. At 27 km., off the road to the l., lies **Fuentes de Oñoro,** the scene of Masséna's neffectual attempt in 1811 to dislodge Wellington from before the Portuguese fortress of Almeida, which led to the marshal's deposition from his command by Napoleon. The sanguinary battles (3–5 May) took place to the S. and E., and great losses were suffered by the French in crossing the rivulet of Dos Casas and in the narrow stone-walled alleys of the village.—The ruins of *Fort Concepción,* the pivot of Wellington's l. wing, lie not far N. of Fuentes de Oñoro, between the Dos Casas and the Portuguese border.—At 3 km. we reach modern *Fuentes de Oñoro,* with the Spanish Customs House.

Across the frontier at *Vilar Formosa* is the Portuguese Custom's station. From Vilar Formosa to *Guarda,* 53 km.; Guarda to *Porto,* 223 km.; Guarda to *Coimbra,* 166 km.; Coimbra to *Lisbon,* 199 km.; see *Blue Guide to Portugal,* forthcoming.

32   SALAMANCA

SALAMANCA (2635 ft; 131,400 inhab.; 32,000 in 1920; 87,000 in 1960; *Parador Nac,* and *Hotels*), standing above the river Tormes, is one of the most interesting cities in Spain, famous for its two cathedrals, and its university, the senior Spanish foundation of its kind. The area of the walled city in the Middle Ages was rather larger than Oxford and Cambridge combined. Although it has suffered much from fire and sword throughout the ages, and more recently from unrestricted building in the immediate suburbs, central Salamanca has preserved a multitude of fine old buildings, weathered to a beautiful golden brown. The climate is dry and sunny, but subject to violent extremes.

History. *Salmantica* was already an Iberian city of importance when captured by Hannibal in 217 B.C. The male defenders were disarmed, but the women, who had not been searched, supplied their men with weapons, enabling them to turn the tables on their captors and escape to the hills. Hannibal, impressed by their resource, allowed them to return unmolested. Under the Romans Salamanca was a station of the *Via Lata* (later known as the Via de la Plata) from Mérida to Astorga, and it rose once more to importance under the Goths. Taken by the Moors in 715 it was recaptured only in 1055, after 300 years of warfare which left the country between the Duero and the Tagus an uninhabited wilderness. Alfonso VI, the conqueror of Toledo, gave Salamanca to his son-in-law and daughter, Count Raymond of Burgundy and Doña Urraca, to repopulate (1085) and the city rose to high estate, aided especially by the foundation of the university c. 1220 by Alfonso IX of León. Despite this and other marks of royal favour, the Salmantines were continually in rebellion against the central authority, until the culminating insurrection of the Comuneros in 1521 was crushed by Charles V. The marriage of his son Philip II and Maria of Portugal was celebrated here in 1543, but the town and university, corrupted by the ultra-clericalism of the time, gradually decayed.

The final blow was struck by the French in 1811 when the entire S.W. quarter of the town, including numerous colleges and religious foundations, was demolished by Marmont to set up a fortification against Wellington, who was in turn obliged to besiege them. On the 22 July of the next year, however, Wellington, by his lightning victory of Salamanca (called *Arapiles* by the French and Spanish from the village and hills round which the battle centred, 7 km. S.) overturned in ¼ hr the fortunes of the entire French campaign in the Peninsula, but the following winter they returned to pillage the town again.

In 1832, Lt Col Badcock, a peninsula veteran, on enquiring why one section of the town appeared in a more derelict state than he remembered it, was told that the French had left a large deposit of gunpowder there, and that the Spanish garrison could find no better place to smoke than over the apertures of the store; the consequent explosion and devastation was as a matter of course blamed on the British!

Salamanca was the birthplace of Fernando Gallego (c. 1460–1550), the 'Spanish Van Eyck', Juan del Encina (1469–1529?), the playwright, poet, and musician; José Churriguera (1660–1725), the architect, and Diego de Torres Villarroel (1693–1770).

From the Valladolid (N 260) or Zamora (N 630) roads the central Pl. Mayor may be approached directly, while by turning l. at the Pl. de Ejército the centre may be by-passed by the Paseo de Canalejas, which then bears l. to cross the *Pte. Nuevo*, at the S. end of which is the junction for roads for Ciudad Rodrigo (N620), Plasencia (N 630), and Ávila and Madrid (N 501). From these roads the Pl. Mayor may be approached directly from the N. end of the bridge. A new bridge has been built W. of the Roman Bridge, which diverts traffic round the W. perimeter of the town. A new road is also to be constructed from this bridge towards the town centre.

The *Pl. Mayor, a handsome square, one of the largest in Spain, was built in 1720–33 by *And. García de Quiñones* and was the scene of bull-fights as lately as 1863, a tradition recently revived. The walks beneath its arcades are the fashionable promenade of the Salmantines. Two of the façades bear busts of kings and—with one exception—worthies of Spain, and on the N. side is the Churrigueresque front of the *Ayuntamiento*.

Just S.W. of the Pl. Mayor is 12C *S. Martín,* with a Romanesque N. Door surmounted by a group of S. Martín and the beggar, and a Renaissance S. Door (1586) with the same subject. Within are seven Gothic tombs (14-16C) and a retablo of 1731 by *Garcia de Quiñones.* Going on S. by the C. Meléndez and C. de la Compañia, or by the Rúa Mayor, we reach r., at a corner, the *Casa de las Conchas (under restoration) finished in 1483, one of the most complete of the 'solares' or mansions of the nobility which have survived. The exterior is studded with shells, and badge of its builder, a motive which is repeated in the remarkable grilles of the ground-floor windows and in some of the escutcheons in the patio, while over the principal doorway a shield with fleurs-de-lys is supported by a pair of lions.—At the opposite corner the **Seminario** or *La Clericía,* begun for the Jesuits in 1617 by *Gómez de Mora,* has a huge domed church (completed 1750) under restoration, a gateway of 1779 and a Baroque cloister. In the sacristy is a wooden figure of Christ at the column, by *Carmona.* Until recently a bus station occupied the Renaissance buildings of the adjacent *Conv. de S. Isidoro,* now being restored. The Pl. de Anaya, further S., has on its N. side *S. Sebastian* (1731; by *Alb. Churriguera*) and the *Facultad de Ciencias* (1760–65) by *José Hermosilla*, in the *Pal. de Anaya*, formerly the *Col. Viejo* or *S. Bartolomé*. The *Escuela Normal*, to the E., has a patio by *José Churriguera*.

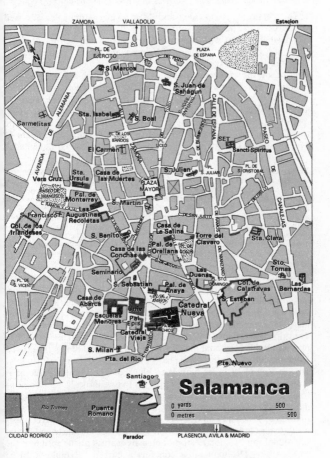

The S. side of the plaza is dominated by the ***Catedral Nueva,** an imposing Gothic pile begun in 1513 and opened for service in 1560, at the zenith of Salamanca's fame. In 1512 Bp. Francisco de Bobadilla summoned a conference of the chief architects in Spain, and the plans of *Juan Gil de Hontañón* were selected for the new church. At his death the work was carried on by his son. *Rodrigo,* and his assistant, *Juan de Álava.* A remarkable feature of the plan, is the square E. end.

EXTERIOR. The N. Door, facing the Pl. de Anaya, is known as the *Pta de Ramos,* or *de las Palmas,* from the relief of Christ's entry into Jerusalem. Further E. is the rather ineffective façade of the transept, plastered with pinnacles, etc. The *W. Front* (1513–31) is an extravagant example of late-Gothic decoration, especially the central *Pta. del Nacimiento.* with sculptured panels attr. to *Juan de Juni* and *Becerra.* The *S.W. Tower* (110 m.), modelled by *Rodrigo Gil de Hontañón* on the tower of Toledo Cathedral, was cased in masonry some years after the Lisbon earthquake of 1755, which weakened the structure. The central *Cupola,* begun in 1705 by *José* and *Joaquín de Churriguera,* was not finished until 1733.

The INTERIOR, 103 m. long and 49 in. wide, is imposing and well proportioned. The vault, supported by finely moulded piers and a pierced balustrade, with bust-medellions above and below, takes the place of a triforium. A gallery of Flamboyant Tracery runs round the aisle and transepts at the level of the capitals of the main arcade. The interior of the cupola is elaborately carved. The *Coro* (1725–33), contains stall decorated by *Alberto de Churriguera,* while in the *Trascoro,* by *Joaquín Churriguera,* are figures of St John the Evangelist, and St Anne with the Virgin, by *Juan de Juni.* The *Cap. Mayor* (c. 1588) retains Flemish glass and an Assumption by *Greg. Fernández.* Also note the organs, the smaller of 1588, and the huge Baroque instrument of 1745 (by Pedro Liborna del Echevarria), with its trumpets in 'chamade'.

The *Cap. Dorada* (2nd in the S. Aisle), founded by Francisco Sánchez de Palenzuela in 1524, contains rows of small saints, the effigy of the founder, fine azulejos, and a musicians' gallery. Adjacent to a door (at present blocked) leading to the CATEDRAL VIEJA is a Holy Family attrib. to *Morales.* From the Pta. del Patio Chico, we may step out into the *Patio Chico* to obtain an interesting view of the exterior conical cupola of the *old* cathedral, with its scaly tiles and crowned with a weathercock from which it took its name *Torre del Gallo.* In the 2nd chapel of the ambulatory is the entrance to the Sacristy (1715-55; closed). Passing the *Cap. de los Dolores* (4th), with a Pietà in wood by *Carmona,* we reach the *Cap. del Carmen,* containing the modern tomb of Bp. Jerónimo (d. 1120), and the wooden crucifix with which he used to exhort the Cid's troops. The N. Transept contains a crucifix by *Carmona..*

From a door in the S. Aisle steps decend into the *Catedral Vieja (cons. 1160), celebrated in the old Latin couplet—"Dives Toletana, pulchra Leonina, sancta Ovetensis, fortis Salmantina"—and in some ways one of the most interesting Romanesque churches in Spain. The mercenary practice of charging an entrance fee is enforced here. Traditionally founded by Bp. Jerónimo, its works were certainly in progress in 1152–89, and in general lines it is typical of the transitional Romanesque of Southern France. Some of the Romanesque windows on the N. and W. sides have been blocked. The beautiful *Dome is unusual in Western Europe, and appears to owe its design to Byzantine tradition, the ribbed vault being raised on two tiers of arcaded lights, quite unlike the dark cupolas of Aquitaine, but with similarities of style to those at Toro and Zamora. The main arcade is pointed, but the upper wall arcades are round-headed. The *Capitals* are curiously and boldly sculptured, and some are surmounted by statues at the spring of the corner-ribs.—The main apse contains a curved *Retablo, with 53 paintings by *Nicolás Florentino* (c. 1445–66); the lower frieze is attrib. to *Gallego.*

Above is a fresco, by *Nicolás,* of the Last Judgment, and above the altar is the gilt bronze Virgen de la Vega (13C). Among the tombs of the 13-16C preserved in the S. Transept, are those of Diego López, archdeacon of Ledesma (d. 1272), and Alonso Vidal, dean of Ávila. In the *Cap. de S. Martín,* or *'Del Aceite',* beneath the tower to the r. of the present entrance, are wall-paintings of c. 1300. The date (1262) of the inscription signed by *Antón Sánchez* of Segovia is hardly reconcilable with the surviving paintings.

The *Cloister,* entered from the S. Transept, was begun in 1177 but has been largely modernized, though some of the capitals have survived. It was the scene of numerous functions of the university in its great days. On the E. side are two chapels; the *Cap. de Talavera,* in which the Mozarabic ritual (comp. p.315) is still celebrated six times annually, with its founder's tomb (1517) and a curious dome with a star-shaped *Vault; the Cap. de Sta Bárbara* (1344–50) likewise has the tomb of its founder, Bp. Lucero, as well as other sepulchres and the chair from which degrees were conferred upon students of the university up to 1842. The *Chapter House* has a triptych of St. Catherine by *Gallego* among other paintings, and a curious carving of St Hubert. On the S. side is the *Cap. de S. Bartolomé,* erected in 1422 by Diego de Anaya, Abp. of Seville (d.1437) and founder of the Col. de S. Bartolomé. The vault is of English character, with tiercerons and ridge-ribs. In the centre is the archbishop's *Tomb surrounded by a magnificent 16C verja. Around the walls are other tombs of the Anaya family. The *Organ,* with its Mudéjar tribune, is possibly the oldest in Europe (1380). The soundboard is original. Note the painted doors (14C) and turrets. Among the musical instruments preserved in the cathedral are a set of shawms, but in the early 1970s their rarer cases were jettisoned by the ecclesiastical authorities as being of no consequence!

To the S.W. are the *Col. de S. Ambrosio,* with a façade of 1720 by *Manuel de Lara Churriguera,* and (further on) the *Col. de Carvajal* (1602).

From the W. Front of the Old Cathedral we may descend to the picturesque *Pta. del Rio,* on the l. of which is a section of the *Town Wall,* and thence passing Mozarabic *Santiago* (founded 1145), to the fine **Puente Romano,** a bridge of 26 arches crossing the Tormes. The nearest 15 arches are mainly of Roman work (rebuilt under Trajan and Hadrian), the rest date from 1499 and 1677. On the opposite slope stands the ungainly new *Parador Nac.*

Returning by the C. Tentenecio, we pass on the r. the restored front of the old cathedral and on the l. the *Bishop's Palace,* (used as a Nationalist H.Q. during much of the Civil War) before reaching the **University,** the entrance of which is in the *Patio de las Escuelas,* on the side farthest from the cathedral. Building was in progress between 1415 and 1529. In the centre of the square is a statue of Luis de León (1537–91), persecuted by the Inquisition for his advanced ideas.

Ford jocularly called the town 'Bull-ford', and numbered its students 'amongst the boldest and most impertinent of the human race, full of tags, and rags, fun, frolic, *Lice*nce, and guitars.'

History. Founded before 1230 by Alfonso IX of León in emulation of the Castilian university of Palencia, Salamanca absorbed the sister foundation in 1239 when the crowns of Castile and León were united in the person of Fernando III. In 1254 Alfonso el Sabio founded the law schools and the library, and from that date the university, acknowledged by Pope Alexander IV (1255) to be among the four greatest universities of the world, with Paris, Oxford, and Bologna, grew in importance. In the 15–16C is counted over 10,000 students and 25 colleges—four of them (S. Bartolomé, del Arzobispo, Cuenca, and del Rey) *Escuelas Mayores,* strictly reserved for aristocratic families, the rest *Escuelas Menores.* Columbus consulted the astronomical faculty which in the next century taught the Copernican theory, elsewhere regarded as heretical.

Among distinguished professors in the 15–16C were Luis de León. Francisco de Vitoria (d. 1546), defender of the American Indians, Beatriz de Galindo 'la Latina' (1475–1535), the first woman professor, who taught Queen Isabel Latin, Melchor Cano (d. 1560), and Juan Ribera (d. 1611), Abp. of Valencia; and among the less distinguished was Diego Torres Villarroel, author of a curious autobiography (1743). Aristocratic prejudice and religious bigotry brought about its decline. William Dalrymple, who passed this way in 1774, remarked that most of the colleges appeared 'as if they had been lately wasted and ruined by a ravaging army', and so depleted in numbers that in some he found only the head of the house, with one or two students, and in many, 'not above six or seven'. This decline was further precipitated by the demolition of colleges in 1811, but recent years have seen its revival, and it now numbers c.12,500 students.

The *Gateway of the University is one of the gems of Plateresque art, profusely adorned with escutcheons, medallions, and scrolls. The lowest medallions contain portraits of Fernando and Isabel, surrounded by a Greek dedicatory inscription. The interior is less remarkable, but among some old furniture is a rare portative organ (16C) probably used by Francisco de Salinas.

On the N. side of its patio is the *Lecture Room,* with the pulpit from which Luis de León lectured.

After five years of imprisonment by the Inquisition, his famous opening words to his audience were: 'Dicebamus hesterna die. . . '. (as we were saying yesterday)! Here also took place the historic confrontation (12 Oct. 1936) between Miguel de Unamuno, then Rector of the University, and the Nationalist General, Millán Astray, whose slogan: 'Viva la muerte', symbolized the military mind.

On the E. side is the *Chapel* (1767). The 16C *Staircase,* on the S. side, adorned with reliefs of bull-fights, etc., ascends to a gallery with an artesonado ceiling, whence we may enter the '*Old*' *Library* (containing c.130,000 vols., 462 incunables, and 2800 MSS) through an iron gate of the 16C.

Adjacent to the Gateway is the old *Rectoral,* where rooms on the first floor now contain the furniture and the library of Miguel de Unamuno (1864–1936), who had been Rector for the last 14 years of his life.

On the S. side of the Patio de las Escuelas are the two Plateresque doorways of the *Escuelas Menores;* the first door admits to the *Archives,* the second to a patio with curiously weak-looking arches. The building, of c. 1500–33, contains a museum displaying paintings done by *Fern. Gallego* in 1494 and transferred to canvas.

To the S. are the *Col. de S. Millán,* or *de los Ángeles* (1484), with a 16C Virgin in a niche, and the church of *S. Millán* (1480; Baroque doorway of 1635); while to the N.W. is the *Casa de Alvárez Abarca* (No.2, Pl. Luis de León), physician of Isabel the Catholic, and also entered from the Patio de las Escuelas. It now houses the **Museo de Bellas Artes.**

The building, restored in 1973, and preserving an artesonado from Duenas, contains a somewhat miscellaneous collection of paintings, the more interesting among which are: in **R2** an *anon.* Flemish Captain and harbequebusier, and a Knight of Malta. **R3** *School of Zurbarán,* Portrait of Fray Iñigo de Brizuela. **R4** Early copy of *Correggio,* Descent from the Cross, and *J.A. Beschey* (1710–86), Elevation of the Cross; and *anon.* Dutch landscapes. Steps ascend to **R7** *Rigaud,* Francisco L. de Borbon; View of the Jardin del Principe, Aranjuez; *Ranc,* María Ana Victoria de Borbon; 18C chairs from the Col. de S. Bartolomé. **R8** Hunting angels (Cuzco School); *M. Carbonero,* the Condesa de Pardo Bazan; *Zubiaurre,* Luncheon; *Bacarisas,* View of Segovia; *Zuloaga,* a Segovian. **R9** *Echevarria,* Portrait of Unamuno, and his sculpted head, by *Moises Huerta.* Some stelae may be seen in the garden.

Returning to the cathedral and passing between it and the Pal. de Anaya, we cross the C. S. Pablo to reach the Pl. de Sto Domingo. On the l. is the Plateresque portal (1553) of the Dominion nunnery of *Las Dueñas,* founded 1419, containing a Mudéjar doorway and an attractive 16C *Cloister,* an irregular pentagon of two storeys (restored) with grotesque capitals.

A footbridge leads r. towards *S. Esteban, assigned to the Dominicans when their previous building was destroyed by flood in 1256.

The Dominican monastery was famous for the asylum which it afforded Columbus in 1484–86 when he was seeking to interest the university in his projects for the exploration of a passage to the Indies. Diego de Deza (d. 1497), afterwards Abp. of Seville and Grand Inquisitor, recommended him to Isabel.

The present church, begun by *Juan de Álava* in 1524, has an imposing *W. Front,* which rivals that of the University. The relief of the Stoning of St Stephen is the work of *Juan Antonio Ceroni* (1610) of Milan. Note, among other delicate sculptures, the upper frieze of children and horses. We enter the monastery beneath the arcade on the r. Thence, passing through a cloister and ascending a staircase of 1533 in its N.E. corner, from the upper storey we may reach the raised coro with a feeble fresco by *Palomino* (1705). Redescending we enter the spacious church by a side door. At the E. end is the ornate retablo (1693) by *José Churriguera,* with statues by *Carmona,* a Martyrdom of St Stephen by *Coello,* and a 12C Limoges enamel Virgin. The tomb of Fernando Álvarez de Toledo, the great Duke of Alba (1507–82) has been moved to a chapel off the cloister. The *Sacristy,* by *Juan Moreno,* was begun in 1627.

To the E., in the C. Montejo, is the *Col. de Calatrava,* a dignified building, begun in 1717 by *Joaquín* and *Alberta Churriguera,* with a fine interior stair, and beyond, on the r., is *Sto Tomás,* a church with a Romanesque apse (1175–79), dedicated to St Thomas Becket four years after his martyrdom. To the E. lies the chapel of *Los Bernardas* (1552); while some distance to the S. stands the old *Conv. de La Vega,* now an asylum, with a garden containing ruins of a beautiful *cloister* of c. 1160.

Returning towards the centre by the C. S. Pablo, we enter (r.) the Pl. de Colón. No. 32 (l.), the *Pal. de Orellana,* is a fine 16C work, and No. 34, the *Casa de Abrantes,* has a 15C doorway, while at the N.E. corner is the *Torre del Clavero,* a castellated tower with eight bartizan turrets, built in 1480 by Francisco de Sotomayor, 'clavero', or key-warden of the knightly order of Alcántara. At the S.E. corner, *La Trinidad* or *S. Pablo,* of 1677, has good sculptures.—Continuing up the C. de S. Pablo is (l.) the *Casa de la Salina,* occupied by the Diputación. Built for the Fonseca family c. 1519–50, it has a majestic arched façade and an attractive patio whose projecting gallery is supported by consoles carved with remarkable wooden figures.

Retracing our steps past the Pal. de Orellana, we may make our way W. viâ the C. de Jesús and the C. de la Compañia to *S. Benito,* rebuilt in 1504, with an attractive doorway, and tombs of the Maldonado family. Further N. is *Las Agustinas Recoletas,* or *La Purísima,* built in 1626-36 by *Juan Fontana* for the convent founded by the Conde de Monterrey, viceroy of Naples. It is decorated with Italian marbles and contains good pictures of the Neapolitan school, notably a Conception, among other paintings by *Ribera.* Opposite the convent stands the imposing *Pal. de Monterrey* (begun 1540), crowned by a floreated balustrade (under restoration).

The C. de Ramón y Cajal, passing (l.) the Capuchin church of *S. Francisco* (1746-56), by *And. García de Quinones* with statues by *Carmona,* leads to the Paseo or Pl. de S. Francisco. On the l. is the ***Col. del Arzobispo** (or **de los Irlandeses**; now part of the Faculty of Medicine), founded in 1521 by Abp. Alonso de Fonseca and dedicated to Santiago. The Irish College itself, for the training of c. 30 priests, was founded in 1592, Joseph Townsend, who visited the college in 1786, reported that the course lasted eight years, and that the students, who had no vacations, rose every morning at 4.30! The building, by *Pedro Ibarra* and *Alonso de Covarrubias*, (mid-16C), is entered by an Ionic portal with the Fonseca arms and a relief of Santiago fighting the Moors. From the beautiful galleried courtyard, with medallions by *Berruguete*, a Plateresque doorway admits to the chapel by *Juan de Álava*, with a retablo (1531) probably also in part the work of *Berruguete*. The adjacent building, with a fine portal, is by *Juan de Sagarviñaga* (1760); while *S. Blas* (1772), opposite, retains a Romanesque apse.

In the quarter to the N. of the Monterrey palace is (r.) the *Casa de las Muertes* built by Abp. Fonseca (c. 1545) its façade decorated with busts of himself and his nephews, and with skulls. Unamuno died in the adjacent house. The apse of the conv, church of *Sta Úrsula*, opposite, is crowned by a fine balustraded mirador; within is the Tomb of Abp. Fonseca, by *Diego de Siloée;* the artesonados are noteworthy. Beyond the convent is the *Cap. de la Vera Cruz*, once a synagogue, but rebuilt in 1713, retaining a 16C doorway, and containing pasos by *G. Fernández* and *A. Carnicero* and sculpture by *J. de Juni* and *Fel. de Corral*. The *Adoratrices* convent opposite also has interesting sculptures (in the sacristy) and remains of a much altered 13C church.

Further N. (r.) off the Av. de Alemania, is the *Carmelitas,* a nunnery founded by Sta Teresa in 1570, with more works by *G. Fernández*. *S. Juan Bautista*, to the W., has 15C and later sculptures and remains of a Romanesque cloister; beside it is the 15C *Casa de Doña María la Brava*. The C. de Sta Teresa leads E., past the convent in which Sta Teresa lived in 1570-71, to the Pl. de los Bandos, with the church of *El Carmen* (1703) and two 16C mansions.—Thence the C. de Zamora leads N. to the *Conv. de Sta Isabel*, founded in 1433, with tombs of the Solis family, a painting of St Elizabeth of Hungary by *Nic. Florentino*, and a magnificent artesonado over the Coro. In the Pl. de S. Boal, on the other side of the street, is the *Casa del Marqués de Almaza*, where Wellington lodged in 1812, close to two 15C palaces and *S. Boal*, by *Alberto Churriguera* (1740).—The C. de Zamora ends near *S. Marcos* (1178-1202), one of the few round churches that have no connection with the Templars or Hospitallers.

In the E. quarter, beyond the C. de España, is *Sancti Spiritus* by *Rodr. G. de Hontañón*, with a fine roof over the coro and a richly chased portal by *Berruguete* (1541); the retablo mayor is of 1659 and there are notable sculptures of the 13-18Cs. In the same area, but further S., are the *Conv. de Sta Clara*, with a Gothic church containing Baroque retablos, the remaining arcades of its cloister now seen from the street; the *Col. de Josefinas,* with an early 16C patio; *S. Cristóbal,* Romanesque with Gothic and later sculpture; and (nearer the centre) *S. Julián*, rebuilt 1582 but retaining a 12C tower and doorway; within is a fine statue of S. Pedro de Alcántara by *Pedro de Mena*. In the *Casa de las Cadenas* (in the C. de Pozo) died Don Juan (1478-97), only son of the Catholic Kings, see p.333. Near by, in the C. de Bermejeros, stands the *Torre del Aire,* the only part remaining of the *Pal. de las Cuatro Torres,* with enriched window openings.

FROM SALAMANCA TO ZAMORA (62 km.). We drive N. on the N 630 across a monotonous plateau, passing (22 km. r.) *Villanueva de Cañedo,* with a late-15C fortified palace. Beyond (10 km.) *El Cubo* we pass (r.) the scanty ruins of the abbey of *Valparaiso,* where Fernando III was born in 1199, and descend gradually towards the Duero through the limestone hills of the Tierra del Vino.—At 23 km. a road leads 6 km. r. to *Arcenillas,* where the church contains 25 *Paintings of the Life of Christ (1490) by *Fernando Gallego,* restored in 1966-71. Originally there were 35. These were sold by the cathedral chapter of Zamora in 1715. Key at adjacent house.—Just before reaching the river we get a pleasant view of **Zamora,** see p.355.

From Salamanca to *Ciudad Rodrigo* and *Fuentes de Oñoro,* see Rte 31; to *La Alberca* and *Béjar,* p.421; to *Cáceres* and *Mérida,* Rtes 46A and B.

33   FROM MADRID TO TORDESILLAS, TORO, AND ZAMORA

Total distance, 248 km. (153 miles). N VI. 83 km. *Villascastín—*(44 km. *Arévalo)—* 32 km. *Medina del Campo—*23 km. *Tordesillas—*N122. 31 km. **Toro—**35 km. **Zamora.**

We follow the N VI N.W. through the Guadarrama tunnel, beyond which the extension of the autopista avoids the congested road junction at *San Rafael,* see Rte 27, p.322. We by-pass (r.) *El Espinar,* where the parish church contains a retablo (1565-73) by *Fr. Giralte,* and the chapel and convent of the *Cristo del Coloso.—*83 km. *Villacastín* (see p.231; also by-passed); at 27 km., *Adanero,* fork l. The N VI by-passes (16 km.) Arévalo, to enter which we bear l.

Arévalo (6100 inhab.; *Hotel*), situated on the bank of the Adaja, crossed by a Mudéjar bridge, is surrounded by fragments of former walls, and has remains of a royal residence in the 15-16C incorporated in the Conv. de *S. Bernardo el Real.* A castle (now a grain silo) dominates the town, which contains many ancient houses and churches, among which are Romanesque *Sta María,* with a high tower standing over a gate (*Arco de Sta María*) in the old walls; *S. Miguel,* with loopholed walls and blunt tower; *S. Martín,* with a Romanesque doorway and two brick towers; *El Salvador,* also of brick; and *Sto Domingo de Silos,* containing work of all periods from Romanesque to Renaissance, a 16C reja, a Baroque retablo, and, in the S. Aisle, a slate effigy with alabaster face and hands in the Burgos style. St Francis of Assisi is said to have founded the *Conv. de S. Francisco* in 1214, and in it lived S. Francisco Borja. An Egyptian Sarcophagus of green alabaster is preserved in the *Pal. de Villasanta,* and outside the *Casa de las Cardenas* is a carved stone bull of the Carthaginian period.—On the banks of the Arevalillo, not far S., is the site of the Cistercian nunnery of **N.S. de la Lugareta** with the remarkable fragment of its *Church, also known as that of *Gómez-Román.* Built early in the 13C, its dome, tower and apses form one of the most important monuments of the brick Romanesque of Castile.

28 km. to the W., reached by the C 605, lies **Madrigal de las Altas Torres** (2450 inhab.), birthplace of Isabel the Catholic (1451-1504), remarkable for the almost perfect circle of its ruinous *Walls (c. 1300), strengthened by towers that give the place its sobriquet, and pierced by four gates at the cardinal points, of which only that to the W., the *Pta. de Cantalpiedra,* is in good preservation. Others are in the process of over-restoration. In the Pl. del Generalísimo is *S. Nicolás de Bari,* Gothic with a brick tower; the artesonado roof of the nave is noteworthy, as are several tombs; a reja screens the *Cap. Dorada* (1543) and a 14C painted wood statue of St Anne with the Virgin in the chapel of the Virgen del Carmen.—*Sta María del Castillo,* on the site of the Moorish citadel, is Romanesque, internally rebuilt in the 17C, with a Baroque retablo, two Gothic paintings (15C) from an earlier retablo and a silver-gilt custodia of 1614. In the chapel of the *Hosp. Real,* founded in 1443, is the 13C Cristo de las Injurias. The *Conv. de las Agustinas* contains what remains of the small *Pal. Real,* where the alcove is shown in which

Isabel was born. The refectory, chapel, and other rooms are included in the visit.—Outside the walls is the abandoned Renaissance *Conv. de los Agustinos,* where Luis de León died in 1591.

The N VI may be regained at Medina del Campo, 26 km. N. of the C 610.

Returning to the N VI, N of Arévalo, we reach at 36 km., **MEDINA DEL CAMPO** (17,350 inhab.; *Hotels*), the 'city of the plain', a railway junction and centre of some of the finest corn-growing districts in Spain, but now a dull old town in spite of its great sheep market. Once it was *the* market town of Castile, and its fairs were long famous.

The Treaty of Medina del Campo (1489) between Ferdinand of Aragón and Henry VII of England, provided for true friendship and alliance between the signatory nations, the subjects of which might carry on commerce with, travel through, or remain in, either kingdom 'without general or special passport'. Among its natives were Bernal Díaz del Castillo (1492-1581) and José de Acosta (1539-1600), both historians of the conquest of Central America.

The 14C *Colegiata del S. Antolín*, S., of the Plaza, contains good carved retablos, that of the high altar being in part by *Berruguete* but mainly by *Juan Picardo, Juan Rodríguez* and *Cornelis de Holanda;* the *Cap. Mayor* is of 1503 and there is a Baroque chapel. The balconied *Casa Consistorial* of 1660 also stands on the *Plaza,* the scene during the ferias (Sept. 5-8th) of the eating of the traditional *tostón,* sucking-pig roasted on the spot. Adjacent to it, over an arch at the corner of the square, is the house in which Isabel the Catholic died in 1504. *S. Martín* contains a retablo painted by *Alonso Berruguete,* while in *Santiago* is a retablo by *Andrés Alvarez. S. Miguel* is a notable Mudéjar church with brick tower and apse, a portal of 1582 by *Martín de Répite* and retablo (1567) by *Leonardo de Carrión,* while *La Magdalena* was completed by *Rodrigo Gil de Hontañón* and has wall-paintings by *Luis Vélez* and a Crucifixion (c. 1570) painted by *Est. Jordán.* There is a brick *Hospital* (1591-1619) designed in the style of Herrera by the Jesuit *Juan de Tolosa,* with a chapel containing statues of the founder, Simón Ruiz, and his two wives, and a retablo by *Francisco de Rincón* and others.

Among ancient mansions the most notable is the brick *Casa de Las Dueñas,* attr. to *Andrés de Nájera,* with a Renaissance patio, staircases and artesonado ceilings. The medieval *Valladolid Gate* just W. of the station, and the basilican municipal *Slaughterhouse* of 1562 are also remarkable.—On the outskirts is the *Casa Blanca* of 1556-63, a curious Renaissance country house with rich carvings inside a tall central lantern-tower.—E. of the town rises the rose-coloured brick *Castillo de la Mota* (restored) with bartizan turrets, built by *Fernando de Carreño* for Juan II in 1440, and altered by *Alonso Nieto* in 1479, where in 1504-06 Caesar Borja was imprisoned at the instance of Pope Julius II and Gonzalo de Córdoba.

10 km. N.E. lies *Pozáldez*, with an octagonal belfry. At 23 km. we cross the Duero at *Tordesillas* (p.343) and turn W. onto the N 122.

At 17 km. a road leads 7 km. S.W. to *S. Román de la Hornija,* with an interesting 18C church, preserving part of the original structure founded by Chindasvinth (c. 750) and two sepulchres of Gothic kings. We may regain the main road at *Toro,* 10 km. N.W.

14 km, **TORO,** possibly Roman *Arbucala,* an interesting but decayed town (9500 inhab.; *Hotel*), on a long low hill, was once a place of importance.

History. In 1476 Fernando the Catholic and Afonso V of Portugal fought an indecisive battle nearby; the Portuguese withdrawal, however, put an end to the faction of La Beltraneja. Here in 1506 were held the Cortes by which the royal authority of Fernando was recognized after the death of Isabel. In 1645 the Conde-Duque de Olivares, the disgraced minister of Philip IV, died half-crazed at Toro.

The *Colegiata, or *Sta María la Mayor,* one of the finest Romanesque churches in Spain, built from 1160 to the 13C, is remarkable for its richly sculptured and painted *W. Doorway,* in perfect preservation. The N. Doorway, the capitals of the chancel arch and the sixteen-sided tower are also noteworthy. Compare the dome with those of the cathedral at Zamora, and the *old* cathedral at Salamanca. The tombs in the sanctuary include that of the warrior-Bp. Alonso de Fonseca, who fought beside Fernando at the battle of Toro. To the W. stood the ancient *Judería.*

Among the other interesting buildings are the *Col. de los Escolapios,* with a Plateresque courtyard, near the Pl. Mayor, with a *Casa Consistorial* of 1778 by *Ventura Rodríguez.* To the N. is *Sto Sepulcro,* with three Romanesque-mudéjar apses. Nearby is the *Torre del Reloj* of 1719. Among other churches of interest are *Sto Tomás Cantuariense* (much restored); *El Salvador* (13C Mudéjar); *S. Pedro del Olmo,* with a 14C brick nave, wall-paintings, and a tortoiseshell and ivory cross; of the mansion of the Marqués de Sta Cruz, where the Cortes of Toro were probably held, only a portico remains. *S. Lorenzo,* a late 12C brick church, has a retablo by *Fern. Gallego* and fine tombs in its 15C sanctuary; while in *Sancti Spiritus* (1316-15C) is the tomb of Beatriz of Portugal (d. c. 1410), queen of Juan I of Castile. The *Hospital* of c. 1500 has a good Gothic doorway, while the brick hermitage of *Sta María de la Vega* (cons. 1208), in the S. suburb, has 15C wall-paintings. Off the Paseo de S. Francisco is a privately-owned bull-ring of 1828 with covered wooden galleries.

At *Mixos,* N.W. of the town, is a church of c. 900, with Roman altars and good wall-paintings, while *Villalonso,* 10 km. N.E., has a well-preserved castle.

Leaving Toro, the road follows the N. bank of the Duero to enter (35 km.) historic **ZAMORA** (2065-2130 ft; 52,000 inhab.; 18,000 in 1920; 35,000 in 1950; *Parador Nac.; Hotels*), retaining fragments of its ancient ramparts which brought it the title of 'la bien cercada' ('the well-walled'), and a number of Romanesque churches, including an imposing cathedral.

History. Zamora owed its importance to its position on the Duero and was long a disputed frontier post. First taken from the Moors by Alfonso I in 748, it was violently assailed in 939 by Abderrahman III, who, it is said, left 40,000 of his warriors in the breaches of the seven walls which then guarded the city. From his failure arose the current proverb 'Zamora is not gained in an hour'. Almansor, more successful, captured and destroyed the place in 985, but Fernando I rebuilt it in 1065. Unhappily Fernando bequeathed Zamora as an appanage to his daughter Urraca, who resisted the demands to surrender to her brother Sancho II, Fernando's successor on the Castilian throne. The Cid, a foster-brother (some say a lover) of Urraca, refused to take up arms against her, and Sancho was lured to his death by Vellido Dolfos who pretending to lead the king to an unguarded postern in the W. wall, stabbed him in the back (1072).

Life at the convent of Sta María in the late 13C is amusingly described by Peter Linehan in his study of the Spanish Church in that epoch (see Bibliography). In the 15C Zamora was captured by the Portuguese supporters of Juana la Beltraneja, but was surrendered to Fernando the Catholic in 1476. In 1520 it was a stronghold of the Comuneros. It was the birthplace of the essayist Leopoldo Alas ('Clarín'; 1852-1901).

From the Tordesillas road we have a view of the walls before we enter the old town by the C. de Sta Clara. We soon reach the insignificant *Pl. Mayor*, with the *Old Ayuntamiento* of 1504 and the new Ayuntamiento. On the r. is *S. Juan*, with a florid Gothic S. window (bricked up), an early Renaissance door, and 16C retablos. To the N. in the Pl. de Zorilla, is the early 16C *Casa de los Momos*, now the Audiencia, with ajimez windows and a massive archway. From the Pl. Mayor, the C. Ramos Carrión leads to the Pl. de Cánovas. W. of the plaza is the huge *Hospital*, completed in 1662 and hiding *Sta. María la Nueva*, with some very curious Byzantine capitals (8C) on the apse, and wall-paintings, and containing a Christ by *Greg. Fernández*. Behind the church is a modern museum of *'Pasos'*.

On the r. of the plaza stands the *Parador Nac.* in what was part of the *Palace of the Condes de Alba Aliste* (15-16C) and later the *Hospicio* (1798), to the S.W. of which in an area once the *Judería*, is *La Concepción*, and Romanesque *S. Cipriano*, with early carving and an inscription of 1103. We shortly pass (r.) *La Magdalena*, a Romanesque building of c. 1165. The S. Doorway, with its recessed arches elaborately decorated, is surmounted by an attractive rose window, and within are two canopied tombs, that on the N. side (13C) having twisted columns and curious capitals.—*S. Ildefonso* (13-15C), S. of its plaza, has a front of 1798, and a raised coro.

Two bronze shrines hold the relics of S. Ildefonso (d. 666) and S. Attilano (d. 999), Bp. of Zamora; while in the sacristy is a Flemish triptych brought by Charles V in 1522.

At the extreme W. end of the town is the citadel, the stronghold of Doña Urraca, now modernized, enclosing the partly ruined *Castillo* and the Cathedral. The top of the keep commands a View of the Duero valley and surrounding plain; on the opposite side of the valley is the *Ermita de Santiago* (12C), said to mark the exact site of the murder of Don Sancho.

The *Cathedral, a comparatively small building, dates principally from the second half of the 12C (begun 1151; cons. 1174). The *Cap. Mayor*, however, is a Gothic addition of 1496-1506, and the N. Front, with the main entrance, was classicized by *Juan Gómez de Mora* in 1591-1621.

The characteristic features of the EXTERIOR are the bold *W. Tower*, foursquare for defence, with widening tiers of round-arched windows, and the *Dome, half-French, half-Byzantine, with corner-turrets like the Torre del Gallo at Salamanca, but with only one row of lights, (comp. also Toro). The French influence in the Romanesque work has been attr. to Bp. Jerónimo, afterwards translated to Salamanca, and his compatriot Bp. Guillermo (d. 1191). On the S. side is the delicate *Pta. del Obispo*, with scroll-like mouldings, the centrepiece of the 12C façade.

The INTERIOR is notable for the great mass of the columns, which are 2 m. across, while the nave itself is only 7 m. wide. On the *Trascoro* is a painting of Christ in Glory by *Fernando Gallego*. The *Cap. del Cardenal*, at the W. end, contains 15C tombs of the Romero family, and a damaged *Retablo by *Gallego* (1466). In the *Cap. de S. Juan*, at the S.W. corner, lies the elaborate tomb of Canon Juan de Grado (1507), while the *Cap. Mayor* contains an ugly 18C retablo, and the 15C tomb of Ponce de Cabrera, and a Virgin by *Bart. Ordóñez* (early 16C).—The interior of the Dome is a typical 'medio naranjo', the resemblance accentuated by the vault-ribs.—The *Coro* contains *Stalls (1490) attr. to *Rodrigo Alemán* or a pupil; the execution of the carvings, particularly of the misericords, is extremely delicate, and some—indelicate if not obscene satires on monastic life—were once nailed down by a sanctimonious bishop. His throne, the rejas, and the iron pulpits, are also of interest.

From the plain *Cloister* on the N. side, rebuilt in 1591-1621 by *Gómez de Mora,* a staircase ascends to a *Museum,* in which is a silver Custodia by *Juan de Arfe* and Maestro *Claudio* (c. 1515) and a magnificent series of 15-16C Flemish **Tapestries,* known as the 'Black Tapestries'; unfortunately they are badly displayed. The subjects of the tapestries are The Coronation of Tarquin; the Parable of the Vine; The Trojan War; and the Hannibal series, etc.

The remainder of the attraction of Zamora consists principally in its remarkable series of Romanesque churches. A walk descends across the ramparts behind the *Bishop's Palace* (S. of the cathedral), and the legendary *Casa del Cid* (11-12C), to *S. Claudio* (1100 and later), with a Romanesque door, and follows the river to the fine medieval *Bridge of* 17 arches. Thence (l.) past *S. Lucía* and a 16C palace, while further E. stands picturesque *Sta María de la Horta* (12C and 1495), with a square tower and two retablos. In the same quarter are *Sto Tomé* and the remains of *S. Leonardo,* both with Romanesque fragments. Hence we may make our way N. viâ wide-vaulted *S. Andrés* (16C) with good retablos, the **Monument to Antonio Sotelo* attrib. to Pompeo Leoni, and artesonado roof, *Santiago del Burgo* (c. 1200), and *S. Vicente* (13C) to the Pl. Mayor.

To the N.W. stands the *Pta. de la Feria,* whose archway bears an undecipherable inscription and bust said to represent Doña Urraca and her speech from the ramparts to the Cid, as quoted by the 'Romancero'. Following the Ronda de la

Feria to the r., we enter the old town again by the *Pta. de S. Torcuato,* and pass (r.)
17C *S. Torcuato* and the *Hospital,* with a doorway of 1526.

For *Arcenillas,* 7 km. S.E., see p.353.

The N 122 leads W. from Zamora, from which, at 12 km., a road forks
r. 9 km. to *Campillo* and *S. Pedro de la Nave,* whose Visigothic church
is of exceptional quality (c. 700, restored 907) and resembles those of the
Asturias. Owing to the construction of the Esla dam, the church has
been moved here from its original site.

36 km. due N. of Zamora, and 4 km. W. of *Granja de Moreruela,* on the N 630
for Benavente, 29 km. further N. lies the huge half-ruined Cistercian *Abbey* of
Moreruela, founded in 1131 (the first in Spain). The apse is particularly fine.

A longer excursion may be made to *Fermoselle* (64 km. S.W. on the C 527), near
the Portuguese border, here marked by the Duero, with an outstanding Gothic
church.

The N 122 continues W., crossing the Esla at 12 km. *Villacampo,*
5 km. S.W., has a Mudéjar church and the *Pta. de S. Andrés.* The nearby
ruins of the *Despoblado de Santiago* are of interest. Passing through
(37 km.) *Alcañices,* we reach the Portuguese frontier at (22 km.) *Rio
Manzanas* (Customs). *Bragança* lies 30 km. beyond. See the *Blue Guide
to Portugal,* forthcoming.

From Zamora to *Orense* and *Santiago,* see Rte 43. From Zamora to *Benavente*
see p.403.

34   FROM VALLADOLID TO LEÓN

Total distance, 134 km (83 miles). 38 km. *Medina de Ríoseco*—96 km. **León.**

We leave Valladolid by the N 601.

At 11 km. a road leads 8 km. W. to the village of **Wamba,** which commemorates,
by its name, the election there of Wamba to be king of the Visigoths in 672. He took
the oath on the tomb of his predecessor Recceswinth, who lies buried in the
Mozarabic church of c. 928, remains of which are incorporated in the 13C
structure.—7 km. to the E. of the N 601 lies *Fuensaldaña,* with a fine 15C castle
retaining a 13C gateway.

The road traverses the dreary Páramo de la Mudarra to (27 km.)
Medina de Ríoseco, an interesting but decayed old town (5000 inhab.;
Hotel), the Roman *Forum Egurrorum,* guarded by old walls, and
famous since the 14C for its cloth-fairs. Blake and Cuesta were defeated
near here by Bessières (14 July, 1808), who proceeded to sack the town;
nuns from the Conv. de Sta Clara were selected for a worse fate.

The picturesque winding arcaded *C. Mayor,* or de la Rúa, runs
through the town from N. to S. Near the centre is *Sta María del
Mediavilla,* a hall-church of 1490-1520 by *Gaspar de Solórzano,* with
good star-vaulting and a tower of 1738. The *Retablo Mayor,* by *Esteban
Jordán* (1590), was painted by *Pedro de Oña* (1603); the reja and
woodwork of the choir are from S. Francisco (see below); while the N.
chapel has a remarkable cupola in polychrome stucco by *Jerónimo del
Corral* (1548-54), Benavente tombs, an altarpiece by *Juni,* and a reja by
Fr. Martínez (1554). The treasury contains a Custodia by *Ant. de Arfe*
(1585) and a cross by *Leoni.*—The late 18C organ, by Francisco Ortega,
is under restoration. *Santiago,* to the N.E., is a fine example of
Plateresque, Renaissance, and Baroque styles, by *Rod. Gil de
Hontañón,* with a Churrigueresque retablo, a Mater Dolorosa by *Juni,*

and a series of *pasos*. At the S. end of the town *S. Francisco* (late-Gothic, restored 1531), has Plateresque retablos, a S. Sebastián and other terracotta statues by *Juni,* tombs with bronze weepers by *Andino* (1539), and a Renaissance organ-loft. *Sta Cruz* is being again restored, after its recently restored vaulting collapsed.

8 km. N.E. stands the early 16C castle of *Belmonte de Campos,* with a noble keep, while the castle of *Montealegre,* further E., but reached from the Palencia road (C 612), and *Meneses,* N. of the last, with a fortified church (15C), are of interest.

At 4 km. the C 611 forks r. to (13 km.) *Cuenca de Campos,* with the 13C brick church of *S. Justo,* with painted and gilded artesonado roofs, and an altarpiece by *Est. Jordán;* while there are good retablos in *Sta Maria del Castillo* (c. 1500) in the old fortress.—8 km. *Villalón de Campos,* noted for its cheese, for a stone pillory (*rollo*) of the early 16C, and its arcaded streets. We may follow the N 610 W. for 15 km. to regain the N 601.

At 16 km. we pass *Ceinos de Campos,* with a Templar's church, and at 17 km., *Mayorga,* on the Cea, with a brick Trans. church with a fine artesonado ceiling and a 15C retablo.—At 42 km. a road leads N.E. for *S. Miguel de Escalada,* see p. 226.

17 km. **LEÓN** (2740 ft; 113,300 inhab.; 22,000 in 1920; 59,000 in 1950; *Hotels*) capital of the ancient kingdom and of the modern province, is a sedate old city on the l. bank of the Bernesga. Its imposing cathedral ands other ancient buildings are eloquent of its former greatness.

History. León derives its name from the Roman *Legio Septima,* the legion quartered here by Augustus to defend the plains from the forays of the Asturian highlanders. It resisted the Gothic advance until 586 when it was taken by Leovigild, and although it fell before the first Moorish onrush in the 8C, it was recaptured by Ordoño I in 850. Ordoño II (913-23), fixed his court here. Almansor assulted and burned the city after a year's siege in 996, but after Calatañazor (1002) it was recovered; Alfonso V rebuilt the walls in *tapia* and assembled the Cortes here. Fernando I in 1037 was crowned king of León and Castile in the cathedral, and Alfonso XI in 1324 built the walls which now stand. After his death Pedro the Cruel removed the court to Seville, since when León lost much of its former political importance. Buenaventura Durruti (1896-1936), the Spanish anarchist, was born in León.

From the N 601 we enter the old town viâ the Av. de Madrid, off which (r.) leads the C. del Arco de Sta Ana, with its curious wooden 'rows'. The Av. de Madrid bears l. and its continuation, the C. de la Independencia, approaches the central *Pl. de Sto Domingo.* On the r. is *S. Marcelo,* founded in the 12C and rebuilt in 1588-1625 by *Baltazar Gutiérrez* and *Juan del Ribero,* with sculptures by *Greg. Fernández.* Behind it is the *Ayuntamiento,* by *Ribero* (1585). Nearly opposite S. Marcelo is the *Diputación* occupying the **Casa de los Guzmanes,** the solar of the family of Guzmán, built in 1559-66 by *Rodr. Gil de Hontañón* for Bp. Quinones y Guzmán on the site of the birthplace of Guzmán el Bueno (see p. 509). The patio and the grilles are noteworthy. At the back is the 16C *Pal. of the Marqués de Villasinta.* Nearby is the *Casa de Botines,* built by *Gaudí* (1892-94).

Hence the C. del Generalísimo leads E. to the *Cathedral (*Sta Maria la Regla*),* a magnificent example of the best type of Gothic construction.

Of the three cathedrals which preceded it, the second was built on part of the site of the palace which Ordoño II had constructed in the Roman thermae; the third, of which important remains have been discovered, was built in the 11C. The present building, begun in 1258, a Spanish translation of French 13C Gothic, was the work of the masters *Enrique* (d. 1277) and *Juan Pérez* (d. 1296), among others. It was probably completed c. 1303 under Bp. Gonzalo.

The building had been barbarously disfigured in the 15-17Cs, and Widdrington, who visited it in 1843, suggested that a 'Junta of conservation and purification could be established in Spain without much difficulty, which might banish by degrees all those altarpieces and other works unworthy of preservation.' During the restoration of 1868-1900 many of the accretions of previous centuries were removed. The roof was damaged by fire in 1966, but has since been repaired.

EXTERIOR. The *W. Front*, the finest of its kind in Spain, is of the late 13C. The three doorways, sepated by two narrow stilted arches, are supported on clustered shafts adorned with sculptures in the manner of the transeptal porches at Chartres. On the central shaft of the main doorway is the figure of N.S. la Blanca, and in the tympanum is Christ between the Virgin and St John, with the Last Judgment below. The side tympanums illustrate the life of Christ and the Virgin.—The *W. Towers*, 65m. and 68m. high, are of the 13-15C; the openwork spire on the *S. Tower* was built in 1458-72 by *Jusquín (Joosken van Utrecht)*, who completed the N. Transept in 1448. The three-storeyed *S. Portal* has three 15C doorways, above which is a statue of S. Froilán, Bp. of León in 990-1006. The *Apse*, with its flying buttresses, and the Plateresque wall of the sacristy, are best seen from the *Pta. del Obispo* (now a plaza) S.E. of the Cathedral.

The graceful INTERIOR is narrow in proportion to its length (90 m. long, 40 m. wide). The aisled nave is without flanking chapels, though a crown of them encircles the ambulatory. The main arcade, with its clustered piers, is surmounted by a graceful triforium, and clerestory, the latter lighted by beautiful *Stained Glass, of every period from the 13C onwards. Some of the finest fills the rose-windows of the W. and transeptal fronts, and the apse.—The *Coro* has two tiers of *Stalls* (1467-81), by *Juan de Malinas* and *Diego Copín de Holanda*. It is surrounded by a rich *Trascoro* of c. 1570-87 by *Juan de Badajoz, el Mozo*, of carved and gilded alabaster with painted figures by *Esteban Jordán*. The retablo in the *Cap. Mayor* is a modern composition containing paintings (after 1427) by *Nicolás Francés* of the life of S. Froilán and other subjects; to the N. is a Pietà by *Roger van der Weyden*.

The 16C silver custodias on the high altar contain the relics of S. Froilán. High up on either side of the 16C *Trassagrario* are the Renaissance tombs of Bp. San Pelayo (s.) and S. Alvito (N.). The chapels of the Ambulatory contain numerous tombs. On the r. beyond the S. Door, is the *Cap. del Carmen*, with the tomb of Bp. Rodrigo de Zamora (d. 1532), and beyond it the *Cap. del Calvario*, with a retablo of 1524 by *Juan de Valmaseda*. In the *Antesacristía* is another bishop's tomb, and opposite is the elaborate 15C *Pta. del Cardo*.—In the E. Chapel (*Cap. del Salvador*) is the 14C tomb of the Condesa Sancha de León, by Maestro *Marcos*, below which is represented in relief the punishment of her nephew and heir, who was torn in pieces by wild horses for the murder of his aunt, a benefactress to the Church.—Facing this chapel is the Tomb of Ordoño II (d. 932), with a 14C statue in a 15C frame. In the next chapel (*Concepción*) is the tomb of Bp. Manrique de Lara (d. 1232), long supposed to have been the founder of the cathedral, and in the following chapel (*Asunción*) is that of his successor, Bp. Arnaldo (d. 1235). In the E. corner of the N. Transept is the altar of *N.S. del Dado* (Our Lady of the Die), so called from the legend of an unlucky gambler who flung his dice at the Child, which miraculously bled.

The Plateresque *Pta. del Dado* admits to the vestibule of the cloister. On the l. is the *Cap. de Sta Teresa*, on the r. the *Cap. de S. Andrés*, with a late-13C sculptured portal, and beyond that the *Cap. de Santiago*, of 1492-1507, by *Juan de Badajoz, el Viejo*, with sculptured corbels and Flemish Glass in the E. windows.

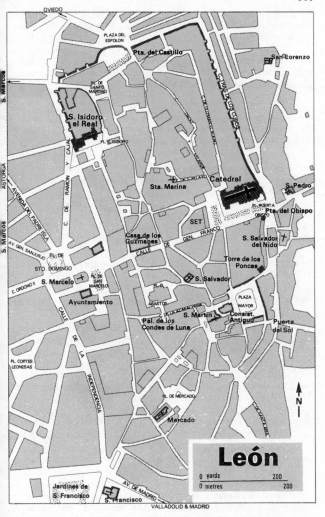

León

0 yards 200
0 metres 200

The *Cloisters,* originally of the 14C, but somewhat unskilfully altered c. 1540, are entered through finely-carved wooden doors. They contain tombs of cathedral dignitaries, and preserve remarkable *Mural Paintings* (probably by Florentine artists) of the Life of Christ (1459-70). In the N.E. corner is a Renaissance tomb, to the l. of which a Plateresque staircase (1525-34) ascends to the *Chapter House,* and further W. is the chapel of the Conde de Rebolledo (d. 1636). In the *Treasury* a small museum includes an 11C Antiphoner with Mozarabic musical notation, and a grant, in Romance, dated 959. On the S. side is the Virgen del Foro, an interesting piece of 11C sculpture, in an arched recess.

In the C. de Guzmán el Bueno, N. of the cathedral, is the *Conv. de Descalzas* (c. 1606-50), while in the C. Daóiz y Velarde an old doorway leads to the *Col. de Teresias* incorporating a two-storeyed 12C house, the *Casa de la Inquisición.* Following the C. de S. Pelayo (fine 13C doorway) we enter the picturesque quarter adjacent to *Sta Marina* (1571), which has for the centre of its retablo mayor a masterpiece of *Juan de Juni,* the Virgin with St John.

From the Pta. del Obispo we may visit, close by, *S. Salvador del Nido,* with a Pietà by *Bautista Vázquez,* and *S. Pedro* on the site of the old cathedral whose poverty awoke the generosity of Ordoño II. In this quarter are also a number of late-medieval timber-fronted houses, some with overhanging storeys.

Below the cathedral to the E., we may follow the C. tras de los Cubos to the N. in order to view the best-preserved portion of the *Walls,* remarkable for the close spacing of the solid semi-circular bastions (*cubos*), largely of the 11C, but restored in 1324. Some 31 of the original (perhaps) 80 towers remain. Near by (r.), stands *S. Lorenzo,* with paintings of 1537 by *B. Fernández.* Re-entering the old city at the *Pta. del Castillo,* crowned by a statue of 1579, we bear to the r. across the Pl. de Sto Martino beyond which is the collegiate church of *S. Isidoro el Real,* with a well-proportioned Romanesque tower (W. end).

Founded in the 11C by Fernando I and Doña Sancha as a shrine for the body of St Isodore of Seville (d. 636; S. Isidoro, the 'doctor egregius' of the Spanish church, not to be confused with S. Isidro Labrador, see p.257), the imposing W. narthex (1054-67) of the church remains, begun by their son Alfonso VI, (cons. in 1149 in the presence of Alfonso VII). The original architect was *Pedro de Deo,* but considerable alterations were made in the 16C.

We enter from the S. through a Romanesque doorway surmounted by a Renaissance coat of arms and a 16C equestrian statue of S. Isidoro; in the tympanum is a 12C sculpture of the sacrifice of Abraham. Further E. is the *Pta. del Perdón* with an 11-12C Descent from the Cross in the tympanum. The dark interior, although lighted by a large clerestory, is supported by massive pillars with richly sculptured capitals decorated with groups of animals. In the S.W. corner is a curious font (?11C), beside which is the plain sarcophagus of the architect, *Pedro de Deo.* From the N. Transept opens a 12C chapel with fragments of contemporary paintings. The *Cap. Mayor,* a late-Gothic work, was built in 1513 by *Juan de Badojoz,* but the apses on either side were left intact.

The high altar shares with Lugo the privilege of having the Host always visible (*manifestado*). In 1065 Fernando I, stricken with fever on the battlefield, breathed his last before this altar.

At the W. end, but approached by an adjacent entrance, is the *Panteón de los Reyes,* in the 11C *Cap. de Sta Catalina,* the burial place of the early kings of León and Castile. Here, until the chapel was desecrated by Soult's troops in 1808, rested the ashes of Alfonso V (d. 1028), Fernando I (d. 1065), his daughter Urraca de Zamora, and a score of other *infantes.* The *Vault-paintings,* representing the Lives of Christ and the Apostles, the Signs of the Zodiac, and the Months, are a remarkable example of early Spanish work (c. 1181-90).

The conventual buildings include the *Treasury,* in which are an enamel casket of the 12C, another of 1059 bearing ivory plaques, a 16C processional cross of silver, an 11C agate chalice, etc.; the modernized *Cloister;* and the Library, most of whose treasures were burned by Soult, but which still possess an illuminated Bible of 960. The vestibule, or *Cuarto de Doña Sancha,* preserves remains of 15C (?Florentine) frescoes.

On the E. side of the Pl. S. Isidore is a 14C palace. Turning to the r. after leaving S. Isidoro, we skirt another section of the ramparts.— Some minutes walk to the W. towards the Bernesga, takes us to the **Conv. de S. Marcos,** recently converted from its use as barracks to house a luxury hotel. Founded in 1168 for the Knights of Santiago, it was rebuilt in 1513-49 to the designs of *Pedro Larrea;* the sumptuous Plateresque *Façade (1533-41) has also been attributed to *Juan de Badajoz.* Over the elaborate main door is an equestrian figure of Santiago. Along the whole front runs a frieze of historical and mythological busts in high relief by *Juan de Juni.*—The nave of the *Church* (restored) is spacious and lofty. In the N. Transept is a doorway with plaster figures of the Virgin and saints. The *Choir Stalls,* in a gallery above the entrance, were carved by *Guillermo Doncel* in 1537-43, but clumsily repaired in 1723.

The *Museo Arqueológico Provincial* occupies the *Sacristy,* which has an elaborate vault, part of the modernized *Cloister* of *Juan de Badajoz,* which preserves one or two 13C shafts and capitals, and the *Chapter House* with its magnificent artesonado roof. Here is an important collection of sculpture; an ivory Christ (11C), a Crucifixion (12C), a 10C Mozarabic Cross, medieval textiles and vestments, ironwork, arms, and Roman and Renaissance statuary. Among the antiquities are memorials to the Seventh Legion, finds from *Corullón* in the Bierzo, and monuments of the 3C A.D. on which the horseshoe arch appears 500 years *before* the Moorish invasion. Off the upper storey of the cloister opens the cell in which Francisco de Quevedo was imprisoned from 1640-43 by Philip IV for his lampoons against Olivares. Broken in health, he died two years later.

Cutting diagonally S.E. through a modern quarter viâ the Pl. de Calvo Sotelo, or after following the river bank to the Glorieta de Guzmán and turning l. along the C. de Ordoño II, we return to the Pl. de Sta Domingo, from which we may visit old streets S. of the cathedral.

In the old *Pl. Mayor* is the dignified *Consistorio Antiguo* (1677) and behind it 13C *S. Martín,* restored in the 18C and containing sculptures by *Greg. Fernández* and a Pietà (1750) by *Luis Carmona.* Near the N.E. corner of the square is the massive *Torre de los Ponces,* recalling the great Leonese family of which Juan Ponce de León (?1460-1521), discoverer of Florida, was the most famous member. The C. de la Azabacheria leads W. to the Pl. del Conde de Luna with the *Pal. de los Condes,* with a 14C doorway, a Renaissance front with a tower, and unfinished patio. The tiny church of *S. Salvador de Palaz del Rey,* near by, has remains of c. 950 and 16C chapels.—Further S. in this area, the ancient *Judería,* is the Pl. del Mercado with its picturesque fountain and *N.S. del Mercado,* which preserves an 11C apse and 12-13C grilles in three S. windows. Beyond lies the *Jardín de S. Francisco* with the Neptune Fountain of 1784-87, and *S. Francisco,* in which is the Baroque retablo made for the cathedral in 1724.

FROM LEÓN TO ASTORGA (46 km.). This road forms part of the old pilgrimage route to Santiago (see p.224), which is described beyond Astorga in Rte 36A. Driving S.W. on the N 120, we traverse a monotonous plateau, after 6 km. passing the *Sanctuario de la Virgen del Camino,* with a modern façade and bronze sculptures by *José María Subirachs.*—At 23 km. we cross the Orbigo by a 13C *Bridge.*
This was the scene of the famous 'Paso de Honor', when during thirty days of the great jubilee of Santiago (July, 1434) Suero de Quiñones and his nine companions challenged every knight on the road who disputed the pre-eminent beauty of his lady. In all 727 courses were run, one knight was killed, and eleven were wounded, before Suero consented to remove the iron collar he wore in token of his vow.—At *Benavides,* 5 km. N., is a monastery containing important 13C tombs.—17 km. **Astorga,** see p.372.

35   FROM VALLADOLID TO SANTANDER

A Viâ Palencia and Reinosa.

Total distance, 247km. (153 miles). N 620. 37km. turn l. onto N 611—10km. **Palencia**—31km. *Fromista*—66km. *Aguilar de Campóo*—31km. *Reinosa*—46km. *Torrelavega*—24km. **Santander.**

Driving N.E. from Valladolid on the N 620, we follow a section (in reverse) of Rte 21B, as far as (37 km.) *Venta de Baños*, (see p. 229), where we bear l. onto the N 611.—At 2km. a road (l.) leads shortly to *Villamuriel de Cerrato,* with an early Templar's church.

8km. **PALENCIA** (62,200 inhab.; 20,000 in 1920; 41,000 in 1950; *Hotels*), the Roman *Pallantia,* now a somewhat characterless provincial capital on the river Carrión.

History. *Pallantia,* a town of the Iberian Vaccaei, put up a stout resistance before submitting to the Romans. In 457 it was taken by the Goths. The Moorish invasion extended to Palencia, but in 921 it was again in Christian hands, and in 1035 received its first bishop. In the 12th and 13C Palencia was a residence of the Castilian kings. The earliest university in Spain was founded here by Alfonso VIII in 1208 and numbered St Dominic among its students, but it was removed to Salamanca in 1239. Severely punished by Charles V for its share in the Comunero revolt (1520), th town gradually lost its importance.

Passing (r.) the Salón de Isabel II, we reach the C. Mayor. From this junction we may turn l. to follow the river bank by the Av. Gen. Goded, to the E. of which, beyond an area once the *Judería,* is the cathedral. By turning r. at this junction we skirt the town to reach the Santander road.

The arcaded *C. Mayor* intersects the town towards the Pl. de León, beyond which is *S. Pablo,* founded by St Dominic, begun c. 1230 and rebuilt in the 14-15C. Of the two fine tombs of the Rojas family, that on the r. of the altar, with kneeling figures of the Marqués de Poza (1577), and his wife, is by *Fr. Giralte.* On the S. is the *Cap. de Zapata,* with an altar of 1516; the retablo mayor dates from 1597.—To the W. of S. Pablo stands 16C *S. Marina* and the late-18C *Bishop's Pal.,* while to the S. is the *Cap. de las Dominicas* (17C) with a cupola of 1742. The C. Gen Mola leads S. to the Pl. de Cervantes and the cathedral.

The *Cathedral,* begun in 1321 and completed in the 16C on the site of an earlier church above the cave of St Antoninus (see below), is an interesting example of the Spanish late-Gothic and Transition style. It has no W. façade, but the transeptal portals are good, notably the *Pta. del Obispo* (S. Transept), richly sculptured by *Diego Hurtado de Mendoza* (late 15C). Between this and a small portal (the usual entrance) rises a massive square tower by *Gómez Día de Burgos* (mid-15C). In the N. Transept is the *Pta. de los Reyes.*

The *INTERIOR,* with its double transepts and rows of chapels on the N. side, contains interesting works of art, ill-lit, but light should be specifically requested for Vigarni's Retablo (see below). The main work of the nave (c. 1450-1516) is by *Bart. de Solórzano.* The triforium has curious tracery. The E. end, including the E. Transepts and the apse with its chevet of chapels, dates from the 14C; the remainder, with a new cap. mayor, was added in the 15th and 16C. The 2nd apsidal chapel on the S. has a reja of 1500. The *trascoro,* with sculptures and bas-reliefs (perhaps by *Simón de Colonia*), contains a fine *Retablo* by *Jan Joest* of Haarlem (1505) among others. A Plateresque staircase in front of the trascoro descends to the Visigothic *Crypt (c. 673, with a vestibule of c. 1075), in which Sancho the Great is said to have discovered the statue of St Antoninus (S. Antolín), martyred at Pamiers in the 2C.—The pulpit is Renaissance work by *Higinio de Valmaseda*. The *coro* has a reja of 1555-71 by *Gaspar Rodríguez*, and stalls of c. 1400-25 by *Luis Centellas*, completed in 1560 by *Pedro de Guadalupe*. High up in the S. Transept is a curious clock, with figures of a knight and a lion to strike the hours and the quarters. The 18C organ retains its beautiful Baroque case but the instrument has been ruined by 19C 'restoration'.

The *Cap. Mayor*, with a reja by *Cristóbal Andino*, has a beautiful five-tier *Retablo* by *Vigarni* (1505), with a Crucifixion of 1519 by *Juan de Valmaseda*. The 12 painted panels are by *Juan de Flandes* who undertook to complete them in three years from 1506. On the outside of the trassagrario are 15-16C tombs, including the sepulchre of Fr. Núñez, abbot of Husillos (1550). In the earlier cap. mayor, further E., are the tombs of Queen Urraca of Navarre (1189; high up on the l. wall) and Inés de Osorio (d. 1492). The vault dates from 1424.

Among the treasures—disgracefully neglected and displayed—in the *Sacristy* is a large custodia in chased silver, by *Juan de Benavente* (1581-85); paintings include a diptych by *Pedro Berruguete*. In the *Sala Capitular* are some Brussels tapestries of c. 1520-30.—The *Cloister* (c. 1500-20), by *Juan Gil de Hontañón*, lost its tracery in the 18C.

The Bajada de Puentecillas leads from the W. end of the cathedral to the river, crossed by an ancient *Bridge* with three arms.

Adjoining the cathedral is the *Hosp. de S. Antolín,* rebuilt in the 15C (doorway of 1580), and from the S. side of the plaza the C. Mayor Antigua leads to *S. Miguel* (13C; damaged by fire in 1966), with a crenellated Tower. In the unusual four-sided cap. mayor is an 11-14C crucifixion. The Cid and Doña Jimena were married in an earlier church on the site in 1074.

To the N.E., beyond the Seminario, is Jesuit *N.S. de la Calle* (1598) with Churrigueresque altars and a 15C Virgin enshrined in a natural wood retablo.
To the E. of the C. Mayor is the Pl. Mayor with the Ayuntamiento. At its E. corner is *S. Francisco* (13C, much altered in the 17C), preceded by a graceful Gothic arcade. Beyond the S.E. corner of the plaza stands the Diputación, housing a *Museo Arqueológico,* with a good Roman section, the Retablo of S. Millán c. 1400, and an early S. Sebastian (damaged) by *El Greco.* The C. de Colón leads S. to Plateresque *S. Bernardo,* passing (l.) the *Hosp. de S. Juan de Dios,* and the conventual church of *Sta Clara* (1378-1400), containing tombs of the admirals of Castile, 16C marble effigies of Beltrán de Guevara and Maria Fernández de Velasco, and a recumbent Christ.
FROM PALENCIA TO SAHAGÚN (64 km.). We follow the C 613 N.W., passing (14 km.) *Becerril de Campos,* birthplace of the historian and satirist Sebastián Miñano (1779-1845) with five (but two ruinous) churches, including *Sta María* with an attractive choir gallery, and (8 km.) **Paredes de Nava,** birthplace of the sculptor Alonso Berruguete (c. 1480-1561), and Jorge Manrique (1440-79), the soldier-poet. In Late-Gothic *Sta Eulalia,* with a spired tower, is a retablo by *Inocencio Berruguete* and *Esteban Jordán* (1557–60), with paintings by *Alonso Berruguete.* This, and the 'museum', largely devoted to the Berruguetes, was gutted of its paintings by thieves in Nov. 1979. Its *Organ* (1793) by Tadeo Ortega (who constructed that in *Sta María,* of 1791) is the most important parish organ in the Tierra de Campos (see below), a region containing more organs for its area than elsewhere in Spain. Both were restored in 1975-78. 5 km. **Cisneros,** which gave its name to the family of which Card. Cisneros, was the most famous member. The curious Mudéjar church (early 16C) of *S.S. Facundo y Primitivo* has fine ceilings, while in *S. Pedro* are a retablo mayor of 1545 by *Fr. Giralte,* a Mudéjar vault and

the tomb of Toribio Jiménez de Cisneros (1445), grandfather of the Cardinal. In the chapel of *Santo Cristo del Amparo*, is the 13C tomb of Gonzalo Jiménez de Cisneros, 'el buen caballero'.—*Mazuecos*, 6 km. S., has a good Renaissance church, and at *Villalcón*, 7 km. N., the church has fine artesonados.—10 km. *Villada*, with three Baroque churches, 3 km. to the S. of which lies *Villacidaler* where the brick church has a Plateresque retablo by *I. Berruguete*.—9 km. *Grajal*, with a 15C fort with corner towers (the earliest in Spain built to resist artillery), a palace of 1540, and an early 16C church containing a Christ by *Juan de Juni*.—8 km. *Sahagún*, see p.225.

There are a number of castles and churches of interest in the area S.W. of Palencia. The N 610 leads W. to (25 km. l.) *Baquerín*, with a finely carved retablo in its church, and (4 km.) *Castromocho*, with two 16C churches with notable roofs while 8 km. beyond and to the S., lies *Villarramiel*, with a Pietà of the school of Greg. Fernandez in its church (1176). At *Fuentes de Nava* to the S. are two organs by Tadeo Ortega, that in *S. Pedro* of c. 1788, and in *Sta María* of c. 1790, both restored in 1979; both churches are of interest.—At a point 15 km. W. of Palencia the C 612 forks l. from the N 610 to (15 km.) *Torremormojón*, with a 14-15C castle in ruins. That of **Ampudia** (1000 inhab.), 4 km. to the S., with its three square towers surrounded by a lower round-turreted curtain-wall, although besieged in turn by Comuneros and royalists in 1521, is better preserved and has fine state-rooms with artesonado ceilings. The Gothic church has a splendid *Tower*, called 'La Giralda de Campos', a Plateresque retablo and good tombs.—At *Villalba de Los Alcores* 13 km. S.W. of Ampudia, is a 12C castle altered in the 15C; while nearby lies the ruins of the once extensive Cistercian abbey of *Matallana*, with a church begun in 1228.

Driving N. from Palencia, the N 611 traverses the fertile but un-interesting TIERRA DE CAMPOS, the '*Campi Gotici*' of medieval writers, where the walls of most village houses are constructed with consolidated earth and chopped straw, or *tapia*, on a base of stone. At 7 km. we pass (r.) *Fuentes de Valdepero*, with 16C castle gallantly defended against the Comuneros in 1520 by Andrés de Rivera and the women of the village; and (3 km. l.) *Husillos*, on the W. bank of the Carrión, the seat of one of the oldest abbeys in Castile. The present building dates from the 12C.—2 km. *Monzón de Campos*, with the old *Pal. de Altamira*, is dominated by a *Castle*, now converted to house a *Hotel*.—At 2 km. a road leads 3 km. W. to *Rivas de Campos*, and the priory of *Santa Cruz*, with an early-Gothic *Church* and Romanesque chapter house.—5 km. *Amusco* has a large Romanesque church with a tall retablo of gilded wooden statues and a Mudéjar Pulpit in gesso. The poet and playwright Gómez Manrique (c. 1412-c. 1490) was born here.—*S. Cebrián de Campos*, 6 km. N.W., has a 16C tower and fine retablos.—Beyond (6 km.) *Piña de Campos*, near which are the remains of another castle, we cross the Ucieza and the Canal de Castilla, the latter bordered by a line of poplars, the most conspicuous feature of the landscape.

From Piña, with a fine Renaissance church (unfinished), a road runs 4 km. E. to the old walled village of **Támara**, where *S. Hipólito* (1334 and 15C) has an extraordinary 17C organ supported by a single wooden pillar; stalls, lectern, and font of 1577–82, and a tower designed by *Rodrigo Gil de Hontañon*. The *Iglesia del Castillo* of the 11C.—There is another good church (*S. Juan Bautista*) at *Santoyo*, 4 km. E., with a retablo of 1563–70 by *Manuel Álvarez*, and a beautiful 17C organ with human masks emitting the notes, beyond which (6 km. S.E.) lies *Astudillo*, surrounded by 13C walls, with the Mudéjar convent Church of *Sta Clara* (founded 1355), recently restored, and other late-medieval churches.—We may regain the N 611 at *Frómista*, 14 km. N.W.

6 km. *Frómista* (see p.225), on a cross-road of the Old Camino de Santiago, see Rte 20B.—6 km. *Marcilla de Campos* has a Baroque church possessing a seated Virgin of c. 1200 and a panelled sacristy.—6 km. r. *Las Cabañas de Castilla*, with a brick church and a medieval tower of the Counts of Osorno.—At 5 km. our road by-passes *Osorno*,

see p.225.—At 2km. a road leads 9km. N.W. to *Espinosa de Villagonzalo*, with a fine 15C doorway and 18C woodwork in its church.

Beyond (22km.) **Herrera de Pisuerga**, with its ruined walls and castle, the Cantabrian mountains appear on our l.

A road (C 627) connects Herrera with (40km.) *Cervera de Pisuerga* (p.394), passing many interesting churches; (5km.) *Villabermudo*, with a Romanesque church; (15km.) *S. Pedro de Moarbes*, where the Portal with its frieze of Apostles is notable; and (4km) *Olmos de Ojeda*. Here the monastic church of *Sta Eufemia* is a 12C barrel-vaulted building with a signed doorway of 1186–90, and there is a good church of 1270 at *Santibañez de Ecla*, 4km. S.E.—At 3km. a road (r.) leads shortly to the Romanesque churches of *Cozuelos de Ojeda* and *Vallespino de Aguilar*, finely carved.—At 4km. is *Perazancas de Ojeda*, with remains of wall-paintings in the roadside Chapel of *S. Pelayo.*.

8km. *Alar del Rey* stands at the head of the Canal de Norte, opened in 1759, while at *Nogales de Pisuerga*, on its outskirts, is a fine Romanesque church containing a 14C Calvary.—3km. S.E. lies the abbey of *S. Quirce* (1147) with a dome of Persian type.—At 4km. a poor road leads 8km. E. to *Rebolledo de la Torre* where the church porch has carvings by *Juan de Piasca* (1186).—3km. *Beccerril del Carpio* has two Romanesque churches and a 15C archpriest's house.—4km., r. *Mave*, where the monastery of *Sta María la Real* (1200–08) has apsidal wall-paintings, a Romanesque altar of walnut, and a 17C cloister. The scenery improves as we traverse the defile of Congosto, and enter the wine-growing valley of Cameta.

8km. **Aguilar de Campóo** (5200 inhab.; *Hotel*), perhaps Roman *Velliva*, has remains of walls and two ruined castles on two hills. It was made a Marquisate by the Catholic Kings in favour of Fernández Manrique, who here received Charles V in 1517 and 1522. *Sta Cecília* (1041 and c. 1200) and the *Colegiata of S. Miguel* contain interesting tombs and paintings. On the *Pta. de Reinosa* is an inscription in Castilian and Hebrew dated 1262; No. 17 C. del Puente is the *Casa Rectoral*, most notable of many medieval houses.

A visit may be paid to (3km. W.) the monastery of *Sta María la Real* (c. 1180–1213), under restoration, with a fine Romanesque cloister. A neighbouring grotto passes for the burial place of the legendary warrior Bernardo del Carpio and his squire Fernando Gallo.—*Villanueva de Pisuerga*, to the N.W., has a Roman Bridge and a remarkable Romanesque church Portal; while to the S.W. of the Embalse lies the Romanesque church of *Barrio de Sta María.*—*Barruelo*, 16km. N.W. of Aguilar, is the centre of a group of Romanesque churches, notably those of *Revilla de Santullán* with a carved portal; and *Villanueva de la Torre* (11C) to the S.W.

3km., r. *Cabria* has a doorway dated 1222. We pass the Pto. Pozazal before climbing down to reach (22km.) *Cervatos*, with a 12C church remarkable for its curious sculptures.—At (3km.) *Retortillo* and nearby *Bolmir*, are Romanesque churches, and beyond them, the great Embalse del Ebro.—3km. **Reinosa** (2790 ft) an old town (12,700 inhab.; *Hotels*) and summer resort among the Montañas de Santander.

From Reinosa a road leads N.W. past *Fontibre* and the headwaters of the Ebro and (r.) the ruined 15C castle of *Argüeso*, to (8km.) *Espinilla*, where it diverges l. (C 628), passing the tower of *Proaño*, and climbs towards the ski-slopes of Alto Campóo on the Peña Labra.—The r. fork (C 625) crosses the Pto. de Palombrera (4120 ft) and descends the Saja valley near picturesque *Bárcena Mayor*, to (40km.) *Cabuérniga*. 12km. beyond we meet the N 634 at *Cabézon de la Sal*, 18km. W. of *Torrelavega*, see p. 127.

Beyond Reinosa we cross the mountains, and follow a winding course down the valley of the Besaya. (16 km. l.) *Bárcena*, with old houses and a Romanesque church. We descend through a narrow gorge before entering the rich valley of the Buelna, a district noted for the huge Celtic disc-shaped stelae discovered there (and to be seen in the Museo de Prehistoria, Santander), often built into the walls of churches.—25 km. *Yermo*, with the late Romanesque church of *Sta María* (1203), beyond which lies (r.) the picturesque village of *Cartes*, with the 15C *Torre de los Manriques*.—5 km. *Torrelavega*, (p.127) through which runs the N 634 from Bilbao to Oviedo, see Rtes 5 and 39.—7 km. N.W. lies *Santillana* and the *Cueva de Altamira* (p.386), while our route bears N.E. parallel to the coast, to enter (25 km.) **Santander**, see Rte 38.

B   Viâ Burgos

Total distance, 276 km. (171 m.) N 620, 122 km. **Burgos**—N 623, 154 km **Santander**.

For the road from Valladolid to *Burgos*, see Rte 21, in reverse. From Burgos we drive N. on the N 623 shortly passing (r.) the former Monastery of *Fresdelval*, preserving an early 15C cloister and a Renaissance patio, and *Sotopalacios*, with a ruined castle, near *Vivar del Cid*, where Rodrigo Díaz de Vivar (c. 1040–99) may have passed his childhood. We enter the Montes de Oca, climbing to (35 km.) the Portillo del Fresno (3373 ft).—2 km. beyond, a poor road (r.) leads 10 km. to *Moradillo de Sedana*, with an attractive Trans. church (1188), from which we may regain the main road 9 km. N.W. viâ *Sedano.*— From (26 km.) *Escalada*, where we cross the Ebro, a side road (l.) ascends the valley for 14 km. to the Mozarabic and 12C church of *S. Martín de Elines*. At 25 km. we reach the E. end of the Embalse del Ebro, while at 5 km. the road is joined (r.) by the N 232 from Miranda del Ebro.

Beyond this junction the C 6318 leads 2 km. to *Corconte*, a small spa with fin views over the reservoir, and beyond skirting its N. bank, to (22 km.) *Reinosa*, se above.

The N 623 now crosses the main mountain ridge at the Pto. del Escudo (3240 ft), not infrequently closed by snow in Winter, and descends very steeply, in sweeping curves (views) into the Pas valley, at one time a district from which numerous wet-nurses or Pasiegas (see p.230) originated, to (37 km.) *Puente Viesgo*, from which the prehistoric caves of El Castillo and La Pasiega may be visited.—We shortly cross the N 634 and bear N.E., to enter (26 km.) **Santander**, see Rte 38.

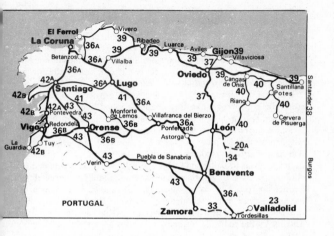

IV THE ASTURIAS AND GALICIA

The **Asturias** (the modern province of *Oviedo*), with a population of 1,102,000, has been much enriched in the last century by the exploitation of its mineral deposits. Its green valleys, with an Atlantic rainfall, are naturally fertile, while its apple orchards, fisheries, and the cattle of the upland pastures are likewise sources of prosperity, and game abounds among the more inaccessible Cantabrian mountains. With its rock-girt coast, and lofty ranges enclosing it on the south, the Asturias were in fact, until the coming of the railway, entered only with difficulty.

The neighbouring seaboard province of **Santander** (491,00 inhab.) resembles the Asturias in both its topography and its people, and although included politically in Old Castile, it is therefore described in this section. Both the Asturias and Santander (also known as *La Montaña*) are notable for their primitive churches which have survived almost intact from the early Romanesque period.

The Asturias takes its name from the Iberian tribe of the Astures, who put up a stout resistance against the Roman and Visigothic invaders of their mountain fastnesses. In 718, a small force of Moors, following the retreating Christians into these broken ranges, were ambushed in the glen of Covadonga and defeated (see p.393), since when the Asturias proudly claims to be the cradle of the Spanish kingdom. In 1388 Juan I, at the special request of John of Gaunt (who doubtless had in mind the newly-established title of Prince of Wales), conferred the title of Prince of Asturias on his eldest son before his marriage to John of Gaunt's daughter, which has been borne by the heir-apparent to the Spanish throne ever since.

Galicia, occupying the N.W. corner of the Iberian Peninsula, is divided into four provinces—*La Coruña, Lugo, Orense*, and *Pontevedra*. It is a wild and mountainous country with great expanses of heath separated by swift rivers (often flowing in deep gorges), of which the main ones are the Miño and its tributary the Sil. The coast is exposed to the Atlantic and has been broken up into innumerable sandy bays and estuaries (known as *rías*), shaded by fir and eucalyptus forests, which are its most attractive natural features. The climate of the coast is rainy and temperate and the lower valleys produce some of the best wine in Spain although in relatively small quantities, but the highlands on the borders of León and the Asturias are subject to extreme cold, and snow lies on the peaks almost throughout the year.

Everything that can be, is built of granite, down to the little farmyard storehouses (*hórreos*) like tiny chapels topped by a granite cross and festooned with golden maize, the vine props, and even the fences.

These hórreos (from the Latin *horreum*) are raised on stone o wooden pyramidal pillars or '*pegollas*', looking like large mushroom (called '*tornarratas*') to keep vermin from entering. They are also found in the Asturias in a different form. The latter are usually square in shape while those in Galicia are normally retangular like a large elongated kennel on stilts. We may still see and hear their notorious creaking oxcarts, whose heavy wooden axles emit a shrill whine as they are dragged slowly along the narrow lanes. Often single cows are seen grazing by the roadside, or being taken for a walk on a lead along the verge; and still we may notice women, wearing wooden clogs, balancing on their heads immense parcels of every description, milk-churns, etc Jardine, writing in the late 18C, remarked that perhaps the race was 'rendered short and thick by the custom of carrying burdens on their heads, particularly the women, who ... often carry the men across the rivers on their heads in a basket'!

This kingdom, founded by the Suevi in the N.W. of the Peninsula in 409, lost its independence to the Visigoths in 585 and to the Moors in 713. After the disastrous raid of Almansor at the end of the 10C which spread havoc over the whole of the kingdom of León, Alfonso VI was aided in the reconquest by Raymond and Henry of Burgundy. The latter was rewarded with the Duchy of Portugal (1095), which at that time extended from the N. coast to the Douro and included what is now Galicia. Owing to the intrigues of his wife with a Galician nobleman, his son Afonso Henriques in 1128 declared Portugal independent of Galicia and the countries thenceforward followed separate paths, the Spanish province becoming re-attached to León. Its ecclesiastical capital, Santiago de Compostela, was the object of one of the most frequented pilgrimages of the Middle Ages. In more recent years Galicia has been developed as a summer resort.

In language and customs, the people of Galicia closely resemble those of Northern Portugal; indeed, the Galician dialect is much near Portuguese than Castilian; moreover they share the Portuguese skill in improvization, and their lyric peotry, brought to a high pitch in the works of Rosalía de Castro, is very like the Portuguese in inspiration. An increasing number of books are published in Galician.

Although the total population of Galicia has increased comparatively little during the last fifty years, the Gallegos are a prolific race and the country is apt to be overpopulated, its fertile area being small, so that i is not surprising that Galicia supplies a large number of emigrants not only to America, and Northern Europe, but also to other parts of Spain The populations of the provinces of Orense and Lugo are lower than they were, but the ports of Vigo and La Coruña—233,000 and 206,000 inhab. respectively—have been growing rapidly.

Few of the villages of Galicia—unless well off the beaten track—are very attractive, and the houses built by the 'Americanos' (those who have returned home from abroad after accumulating a 'small' fortune) are usually characterless, and garishly coloured. And in recent years the sign-posts of many of them have been daubed over by some reactionary Galicians—in emulation of the Catalans—likewise wishing to perpetuate their dialect, but which can easily lead to the confusion of everyone else. The state of many of the roads in this province leaves much to be desired, but long overdue improvements are slowly being effected in certain areas, including the building of a motorway between El Ferrol and Túy.

36   FROM MADRID TO LA CORUÑA, SANTIAGO, AND VIGO

A   To La Coruña from Tordesillas.

Total distance, 604 km. (375 miles.) N VI. 182 km. *Tordesillas*—82 km. *Benavente*—62 km. **Astorga**—64 km. *Ponferrada*—80 km. *Becerreá*—39 km. *Lugo*—73 km., *Betanzos*—22 km. **La Coruña**.

From Madrid to Tordesillas, see Rte 33.

At 22 km. the N VI by-passes **Mota del Marqués**, with a ruined castle, the hall-church of *S. Martín* by *Juan Gil de Hontañón*, and a Renaissance patio in the *Pal. of the Marqués de Viesca.*

At 6 km. a side-road leads 5 km. E. to *S. Cebrián de Mazote*, with a Mozarabic church of c. 915, restored, with marble columns and capitals.—9 km. N. of S. Cebrián stands depopulated *Urueña*, on a height commanding a view to the N.W., with restored walls and castle. To the S.E. is a small Romanesque Basilica with an octagonal tower.—12 km. to the E. is the Cistercian monastery of *La Espina*, completed in the 14C, and restored after a fire in 1731, preserving a 17C cloister and a hostelry of 1789.—8 km. N. of Urueña is the castle of *Villagarcia de Campos,* which also has a fine alabaster retablo (1579-82) by *Juan Sanz de Torrecilla* in its 17C church. Padre José Francisco Isla (1703-81) author of 'Fray Gerundio', was a novice (from 1719) at the Jesuit monastery at Villagarcia.

27 km. **Villalpando**, with 12C walls, retains the impressive *Pta. de S. Andrés*, as well as Mudéjar *Sta María la Antigua*. A massive gateway also survives at *Villalobos*, some 10 km. N.W. At 21 km. we meet the N 630 from Zamora, and crossing the Esla by a Roman bridge, enter (5 km.) **Benavente** (11,600 inhab.; *Parador Nac.*). Only one tower (c. 515) survives of the stronghold of the Pimentel family, which was gutted by Moore's troops on their retreat to La Coruña. It had successfully resisted an Anglo-Portuguese attack in 1387 (in which Sir John Falconer, one of Lancaster's chief retainers, was killed. Before being dismantled in the 19C the 'vast shapeless pile, possessing the marks of great antiquity' completely dominated the town. The remaining tower, now roofed by an octagonal artesonado taken from a ruined church in the vicinity, has been incorporated into the Parador. Cruciform *Sta María del Azogue* (1170–1220) retains good doorways, five apses, and a lofty tower; the Baroque retablo and main porch are of 1735. *S. Juan del Mercado* (13C) preserves a good S. Door; while the *Hosp. de la Piedad* has a well-carved early-16C entrance and a pleasant cloister.

Valderas, 16km. S.E., sacked by Lancaster in 1387, retains vestiges of it. medieval walls.

FROM BENAVENTE TO LEÓN (70 km.). Following the N 630, we reach (17 km. N. *Villaquejida*, where the 16C chapel of *Sta Colomba* is paved with a 5C Roman mosaic, now in a poor state. The N 630 continues up the wide valley of the Esla, of which at 21 km. a road leads r. 6 km. to *Valencia de Don Juan* (3600 inhab.), with two interesting churches and a 15C castle of striking outline.—32 km. **León**, see p.359.

FROM BENAVENTE TO PUEBLA DE SANABRIA (84 km. W.) is a lonely drive along the undulating C 620, passing at 24 km. the 12C church of *Sta Marta de Tera*, before meeting the N 525 from Zamora at 28 km., see Rte 43.

We ascend the Orbigo valley to the N.W., through the country of the Maragatos (see below), with the Montañas de León looming ahead.— 41 km. *La Bañeza*, with two interesting churches, one with an unfinished tower. There are good paintings in the *Ermita de Jesús* and the *Cap. de las Angustias*, as well as on the ceiling of the church of *Soto de la Vega* (14C) to the S. There are a number of curious belfries in the vicinity.

21 km. **ASTORGA** (2850 ft; 12,200 inhab.), Roman *Asturica Augusta*, described as a 'Magnificent city' by Pliny, but no longer so. It was the birthplace of Francisco Villagrán (1507–63), the conquistador, and governor of Chile. It preserves *Roman Walls,* over 6 m. thick (battered, and stripped of their facing), behind which the Spaniards defied Junot for two months in 1810, the French in turn resisting Castaños for three (1812). The S.W. side, restored and laid out as a promenade, affords views of the Montañas de León. Until the early 19C, the carriage road from Madrid came to an abrupt end at Astorga.

The *Cathedral, at the N.E. corner of the town, begun in 1471 probably to the design of *Simón de Colonia* and continued (nave and transeptal chapels) by *Rodr. Gil de Hontañón* in 1530–59, is built of red and grey stone. Between its W. Towers, (of differing stone), is the Baroque portal (finished in 1693) bearing reliefs of the Life of Christ. The weathercock is a figure of Pedro Mato, a well-known Maragato. The well vaulted interior, lighted by a clerestory of 16C glass, contains a * *Retablo*, with its 'compartments of marble-sculpture in alto relievo, the figures as large as life', which had so impressed Edward Clarke in 1760. It is the masterpiece of *Gaspar Becerra* (1558–62), a pupil of Michelangelo. The reja is by *Lázaro Azcain* (1622), and the stalls of 1551 show good walnut carving. The Gothic *cloister* on the N. was restored in 1780. In the *Sacristy* (1772) the * *Treasury*, contains a 10C silvergilt casket, the 11C crystal chalice of Sto Toribio, a 12C reliquary, and a Crucifix by *Becerra*. The archives were destroyed by the French in 1810.

To the S.E. is the huge and incongruous *Bishop's Pal.*, by *Gaudí* and *Ricardo Guereta*, now housing a *Museum of the Pilgrimage Road*.

The basement contains a good collection of carved tombs, Roman capitals stelae, and coins; fragments of mosaic, glass, and terra sigillata, etc. The ground floor preserves pilgrims' medals, gourds, sticks, and shells, etc., while the upper floors contain a somewhat miscellaneous collection of polychromed statues processional crosses, ecclesiastical plate, ceramics, and glass.

In the arcaded Pl. Mayor is the * *Ayuntamiento* (1684) with a clock bearing two jaquemart figures in Maragato costume, before which on Corpus Christi and Ascension days, the Maragatos used to dance the curious *cañizo*. Behind and to the r. is Baroque *S. Julián*, with a late Romanesque doorway. To the N.E. of the Pl. Mayor is a vaulted Roman 'cryptoporticus' (now closed).

Some MARAGATOS, considered to be the descendants of the Berber highlanders ho came into Spain with Tarik and Musa, still inhabit the dreary moorland illages around Astorga, and others live in the town itself. Both men and women re handsome, and wore a characteristic costume, the former notable for the ouave-like breeches, the latter for their jewellery of peculiar design. The carrying ade of N.W. Spain was once mainly in their hands.

On leaving Astorga the new road climbs the E. slope of the Montañas e León to the Pto. de Manzanal (3750 ft), occasionally snowbound in an. and Feb., and descends into the Tremor valley.—44 km. *Bembibre* as a 15C church in a former synagogue, burnt down in 1934, and a astle of the Dukes of Frias. We descend above the gorge of the Boeza to 20 km.) **Ponferrada** (50,500 inhab.; 9800 in 1920; *Hotels*), also by-assed, the Roman *Interamnium Flavium*, rebuilt in the 11C as a refuge or travellers on the pilgrim road, and now a growing industrial and ining town. It is commanded by an imposing *Castle* (12C and c. 1340) f the Templars. In the Pl. Mayor is *N.S. de la Encina*, containing a *Magdalen* by *Greg. Fernández*, and 'Our Lady of the Oak', an ancient gure concealed behind the high altar, and said to have been iraculously discovered in an oak-tree. Nearby rise the towers of the *Ayuntamiento* of 1692.

On the outskirts is *Sto Tomás de las Ollas* (restored), with an oval apse and urious vault (c. 930), a dependency of the early monastery (c. 10 km. S.) of *S. Pedro de Montes*, which retains traces of 10C work, and valuable old chests in the eliquary chapel.—Beyond, on the S.E. slope of Monte Guiana (6070 ft), stands nspoilt Mozarabic *Santiago de Peñalba* of 931–37.

For the route from Ponferrada to *Vigo* viã *Orense*, see Rte 36B.

From Ponferrada the C 631 ascends the picturesque valley of the Sil to (64 km. N.E.) *Villablino* (14,300 inhab.), a coal-mining town in wild hill country, 20 km. .E. of which, at *Murias de Paredes*, is the 12C abbey of *Sta María de Sandoval*, estored in the 16-17C. For the road N.W. from Villablino to *Cangas de Narcea*, ee p.390.

The N VI now crosses the BIERZO, the saucer-shaped valley of an ncient lake now drained by the gorge of the Sil. The sportsman will find n abundance of fish in its streams and game in its forest.

Almost cut off by mountains and plentifully supplied with water, the Bierzo was favourite resort of medieval anchorites, who, led by S. Fructuoso in the 7C, built heir hermitages in its remote vales. Although harried by the Moors, the hermits eturned in the 9C, and ruins of their chapels, and of the convents which succeeded hem, abound.
A new road, driving due W. from Ponferrada, now by-passed Carcabelos, to ejoin the N VI. just before Villafranca.

14 km. *Carcabelos.*—A road leads 3 km. S. to one of the most nteresting of the Bierzo monasteries, at *Carracedo*, founded in 990 and ebuilt in 1138, with remains of a 13C royal palace, 16C domestic uildings, and a tower of 1602.—2 km. *Pieros*, ancient *Bergidum*, from vhich the Bierzo takes its name, has remains of Suevic fortifications still tanding to a height of 7.5 m. The N VI by-passes at 5 km. the icturesque town of **Villafranca del Bierzo** (6100 inhab.; *Parador Nac.*), t the confluence of the Valcarce and the Burbia, preserving a round-owered *Pal. of the Dukes of Alba* (16C), a collegiate church rebuilt in 726, a large *Franciscan Convent* founded by Pedro de Toledo, viceroy f Naples (1550), and a number of fine old house. It was the birthplace of Fray Martín Sarmiento (1695–1772), the scholar, and Feijóo's assistant.

The bee-hives here were once made of hollowed tree-trunks, about a metre high and covered with slate. Southey relates a tale told him by an English traveller, who going behind a *posada* one moonlight night and seeing one, 'congratulated himself that the people there were so far advanced as to have made such a convenience .. and was in a situation very unfit for making a speedy retreat when he took off the cover, and out came the bees upon him'!

At *Corullón*, 6 km. S.W. of Villafranca, are two 11-12C churches.— Beyond Villafranca the road, being improved by a new section, ascends the Valcarce valley, the line of Sir John Moore's retreat in Jan. 1809, when hundreds of his men perished of cold after their excesses in the wine-cellars of Ponferrada. The road continues to climb steeply up the E. side of the valley before reaching the summit of the Sierra de Picos at the *Pto. de Piedrafita* (3638 ft), where Moore's treasure chests containing 150,000 dollars were hurled into a ravine and Paget's rearguard beat off the pursuing cavalry. The descent into Galicia leads to (48 km.) *Nogales*, with an old castle and pre-Romanesque church, and (11 km.) *Becerreá*, on the Navia, with a ruined monastery (1162–66) and the Romanesque church of *Oselle*, and then across the Neira valley onto the rolling plain of Lugo.

FROM PEIDRAFITA TO SANTIAGO (185 km.). From the pass of Peidraíta, the old pilgrimage road diverges W. through *Cebrero*, where primitive *Pallazas* (see p.390 may be seen, to (40 km.) *Samos*. The famous Benedictine abbey of *S. Julián*, rebuilt in the 16C, was burnt out in 1951, but the church (after 1734) survives, with the Siren's Fountain in the cloister. This abbey was the home of the reformer Feijóo.— Beyond Samos, the road continues through (12 km.) *Sarría* (p.379) and (25 km. **Puertomarin** (*Parador Nac.*) a village reconstructed on an adjacent height above the Pantano de Belasar (1963), which would have covered its few monuments including the fortified Romanesque church of *S. Juan* and 12C *S. Pedro*.—13 km beyond Puertomarin we meet the N 540 between Orense and Lugo. At *Guntín* 8 km. N. of this junction, we turn l. and follow the C 547.—At 15 km. we reach *Palas del Rey* with the Romanesque monastic church of *Vilar das Donas*, with fine doorway, interesting tombs, and paintings of 1386.—15 km. **Mellid** (820 inhab.), market town of the area, in which *Sta María* has wall-paintings in its apse while *S. Pedro* (12-14C) contains good tombs. The *Ayuntamiento* occupies former Baroque chapel.—At 18 km. we reach *Arzúa*, beyond which the road continues W. across rolling country to (39 km.) **Santiago**, see Rte 41.

FROM MELLID TO BETANZOS (50 km.). We follow the C 540 N., off which a 16 km. a by-road runs 9 km. E. from *Corredoiras* to **Sobrado 'de los Monjes'**, with its *Monastery*, an imposing pile, long neglected, but which preserves a 13C kitchen and a sacristy of 1569-71 by *Juan de Herrera*. The Baroque *Church*, with front of 1676 by *Pedro de Monteagudo*, was consecrated in 1708, and preserves well-carved choir-stalls. The *Cap. del Rosario*, (1670-73) is by *Dom. de Andrade*. Adjacent is the late 12C *Cap. de la Magdalena*, with tombs of 1513. The *Hospederia* has a front of 1555 by *Dom. González* and a cloister of 1623-35. The *Great Cloister* was completed in 1744, off which opens the restored 12C *Capte house*, the *Claustro del Jardin* dates from 1753.

At 9 km. we pass *Villasantar*, where the 11-13C monastic church of *Sta María a Mesonzo* was founded by S. Pedro Mesonzo, Bp. of Compostela in 986, and author of the 'Salve Regina'. At 18 km. *Oza de los Rios* has an interesting Gothic church.—7 km. *Betanzos*, see p. 376.

42 km. **LUGO** (67,900 inhab.; 30,000 in 1920; *Hotels*), a provincial capital, stands on an eminence (1585 ft) overlooking the valley of the Miño. Of Celtic origin, it was known to the Romans as *Lucus Augusti* and was strongly fortified by them. The city was captured by Musa in 714, but retaken in 755. In 1809 it saw the retreat of Sir John Moore, and was later sacked by both Soult and Ney. Modern development has largely changed its character, and the walled enceinte is not noticable until nearly approached.

The ***Roman Walls**, built mainly of slate, and the most perfect of their ind, are 9-12 m. high and over 6 m. thick, with 85 semi-circular '*cubos*', nd girdle the old town in a rough square rounded off at the corners. The est preserved portion is near the Pta. del Carmen, on the W. A road lso circles the walls.

The N VI enters the town near the *Cathedral, which stands at the .W. corner. The three towers, which are a conspicuous feature of the andscape, and the W. Front, date from 1769–84, but the framework of ne building is late Romanesque, having been begun in 1129 by the ialican master, *Raimundo de Monforte*. The sanctuary and transept ere complete by 1177 but work on the nave continued for another entury. The whole fabric is undergoing an overdue restoration.

The N. Door, which has good wrought-iron hinges, is surmounted by a figure of 'hrist above a pendent capital with a curious representation of the Last Supper.

The INTERIOR, modelled on that of Santiago, has a long nave of nine ays with a pointed waggon-vault, and very low aisles. The deep riforium is lighted by round-headed windows, but towards the nave nows two pointed arches in each bay divided by coupled shafts. Off the . Transept is a vaulted Romanesque chapel, containing well carved ombs. Note also the retablos over the doors in the N. and S. transepts, nd the Rococo Lady Chapel. The ambulatory chapels and the chancel ere rebuilt in the 14C. The *silleria* in the *coro*, carved in walnut, is by *rancisco de Moure* (1624). The altar, like that of S. Isidoro at León, is nanifestado', i.e. has the privilege of keeping the Host always exposed. he *Cloister* on the S., is a spacious work of 1708–14 by *Fernando de :asas y Nóvoa*, who designed also the circular E. Chapel (*N.S. de Ojos irandes*) in 1726–35.

On the N. side of the cathedral is the *Bishops' Palace* (16-17C with a ront of 1743), while in the picturesque Pl. de Aureliano Pereira is an 8C fountain. Behind the Cathedral, in the Pl. de España, is the rococo rcaded *Ayuntamiento* (1736–38), by *L. A. Ferro Caàveiro*, and 18C *Sta Maria la Nova*. The C. de la Reina leads N. to *Sto Domingo* (14C) reserving good transepts and chancel. *S. Francisco*, to the W., is of c. 510, with a Romanesque cloister altered in 1452.

The *Diputación* in the C. de S. Marcos, N. of Sto Domingo, houses a *Museum*. esides tombs and inscriptions, some ship-models, and a collection of :ompostelan jet, it contains a 15C Mudéjar Doorway of plaster, a 12C seated 'hrist from S. Pedro Félix de Mujá, and an Effigy of a 15C abbot of Monforte.— A little distance to the N.W. is Baroque *S. Froilán*.

Outside the Santiago gate are some medicinal springs known to the Romans, nd below them, crossed by a fine old *Bridge*, flows the Miño (the Roman *Minius*, rom the vermilion found near it), the major river of Galicia, famous for its salmon, rout, and lampreys; indeed the latter were prized at the epicurean feasts of nperial Rome.

Some 15 km. S.W., reached by turning r. off the N 640 4 km. S. of .ugo, is the remarkable subterranean church (?) of *Sta Eulalia de 3óveda*, a building of three aisle with a porch (4-5C) entered through a orseshoe archway and preserving curious paintings and carvings of eligious dances.

From Lugo to *Ribadeo*, see p.391 24 km. S. lies *Puertomarin*, p.374.

Quitting Lugo by the N VI, we cross the Miño at 12 km. Hence the C 41 leads direct to (21 km.) *Villalba*, see p.391. We ascend the Ladra alley, joining at 12 km. the N 634 from Ribadeo and Mondoñedo, see

Rte 39.—At 7 km. a road leads l. to the Gothic church of *S. Alberto*, and (9 km.) the Castle of *Miraz*.—6 km. *Guitiriz*, a small spa, and (27 km. *Coirós*, with a 12C Gothic church, are passed before we descend to (6 km.) **Betanzos** (11,000 inhab.).

The *old* town stands on the site of Roman *Brigantium Flavium* on a low hill defended by medieval gates. *Sta María del Azogue* (1346–1447) has a fine doorway in the presistent local Transitional style; *S. Francisco* (after 1387) contains the *Tomb of the Conde de Andrade, resting on white marble boars. *Santiago*, rebuilt in the 15C, retains Romanesque work, while Romanesque *S. Martín*, above the town, commands a fine view of the ría and the richly-wooded countryside.

Excursions may be made from Betanzos to *Bergondo*, 4 km. N., with a 12C church, and (9 km.) the resort of *Sada*; hence a road leads W. to La Coruña; and (18 km. N.E., off the C 640), the derelict Cistercian monastery of *Monfero*, wit grandiose 17–18C buildings preserving a curious slate and granite façade.

FROM BETANZOS TO EL FERROL (38 km.). A motorway is under construction connecting La Coruña with El Ferrol, which passes near Betanzos, and will greatl improve communications in the area, at present badly served. We drive due N., a 8 km. meeting the direct road from La Coruña, which here crosses the estuary.— 23 km. **Puentedeume**, (8100 inhab.; *Hotel*, at *Cabañas*, N. of the river), preservin the ruins of a fine old bridge, once with 58 arches, and of the *Pal. of the Counts o Andrade* (1370–1400), as well as a 15C *Ayuntamiento*.—c. 15 km. E., and N. of th Eume, lies the collegiate church of *Caaveiro*, a ruined fortified building probabl of the 12C, including some Baroque work.—Crossing the Eume, we may at 32 km turn l. and cross the ría by the new bridge to (15 km.) *El Ferrol*, or alternativel circle the head of the ría, passing through the villages of *Neda* and *Jubia*, with th Cluniac Romanesque church of *S. Martín*.

El Ferrol (83,500 inhab.; 30,000 in 1920; *Parador Nac.; Hotels*) was original named from an ancient *'farol'* or light marking the entrance to its land-locke harbour. El Ferrol was chosen by Carlos III as a site for the royal naval Arsena and strongly fortified in 1769–74. The town, although of no special interest, has pleasant alameda alongside the arsenal wall, and retains a few 18C buildings. I 1800 a squadron under Gen. Pulteney attacked the port, but just as the garriso was on the point of surrender, the British troops were re-embarked and the relieve Spaniards left masters of the bloodless field. It is Spain's most important nava base, with extensive modern dockyards, and was the birthplace of Genaro Pére Villaamil (1807–54), the artist; Concepción Arenal (1820–93), the Spanis Elizabeth Fry; Pablo Iglesias (1850–1925), the socialist reformer; José Canaleja (1854–1912), the politician; and the ci-devant dictator of Spain, Gen. Francisc Franco y Bahamonde (1892–1975).

About 2 km. N.W. of El Ferrol is the curious church of *Chamorra*, surrounde by megalithic remains, and beyond, extensive sandy beaches. The area to the N.I is described in Rte 39.

We climb through eucalyptus woods before descending past (17 km. l.) *Cambre*, with *Sta María* of 1194, to enter the outer suburbs of (5 km. La Coruña. Crossing the tidal Mero, we may turn r. or climb the hill o Elviña and enter the town from the S.; both roads converge at the S. enc of the harbour before reaching the Cantón Grande.

LA CORUÑA—famous in English history as *Corunna*, and lon₂ known to British sailors as *The Groyne*—with a population of 206,80€ inhab. (64,000 in 1920; 128,000 in 1950; *Hotels*), is an active commercia port largely engaged in tinning, curing, and salting fish. It also has larg petrol refineries. It stands on the neck of a headland separating th sandy bay of Orzán (W.) from the Ría de la Coruña, but the old tow₁ occupies only a spur of this headland jutting out into the ría. Th characteristic *miradores*, or glazed balconies, give many streets th appearance of huge conservatories.

History. A port founded here by the Phoenicians (?) was captured by the Romans in 60 B.C. and named *Ardobicum Corunium*. It fell into Moorish hands in the 8C and again in the 10C until the defeat of Almansor in 1002. In 1370 the Portuguese occupied the town briefly. In 1386 John of Gaunt landed here to claim the crown of Castile in the right of his wife, daughter of Pedro the Cruel. Here Philip II embarked in 1554 on his way to marry Mary Tudor, and hence on July 26th, 1588, he despatched his 'invincible Armada' of 130 ships with 2630 cannon and 27,500 men, to crush her sister Elizabeth. Less than a year later Drake and Norreys landed in the harbour, burned the town, and drove back the relieving force.

Hugh Roe O'Donnell, Lord of Tyrconnel, landed here in 1602 after the disaster at Kinsale. Melchor de Macanaz, presecuted by his political enemies, was banished here for some years prior to his death in 1760.

It was long the port of disembarkation from the Falmouth packet, and here Edward Clarke (in 1760), and Robert Southey (in 1797), among other travellers, first landed in Spain. Alexander Jardine, author of 'Letters from Barbary', containing interesting observations on 18C Spain, was British Consul here from 1779–95. Alexander Humboldt sailed hence to Central America in May 1799.

On Jan. 16th 1809 Sir John Moore's army, retreating before Soult, having previously destroyed all supplies they were unable to load onto transports (including the blowing up of 4000 barrels of gunpowder), engaged in a gallant rearguard action on the heights of Elvina. Moore was mortally wounded, and the command devolved on Sir John Hope, who successfully embarked the army. In 1815–20 La Coruña was a centre of anti-monarchist agitation, in which Gen. Juan Porlier (1788–1815), one of the first Liberal martyrs 'pronouncing' against the king, was executed; but in 1823 it was occupied by the French troops supporting Fernando VII.

It was the birthplace of Emilia Pardo Bazán (1851–1921), the novelist, Eduardo Dato (1856–1921), the conservative politician; Ramón Menéndez Pidal (1869–1968), the polymath; and Salvador de Madariaga (1886–1978), the Liberal statesman, and exiled author.

While the life of the modern port centres on the lower town, the main interest and charm of La Coruña for the visitor lies in the picturesque **Ciudad Vieja** on the N. spur of the harbour. The latter has been fortified since the days of Enrique III, the principal strong point being the *Castillo de S. Antón*, built in 1589 on the site of a hermitage on the outermost reefs on the E. side, while to the S. stands the *Castillo de S. Diego*.

The old town is best approached from the N. end of the *Av. de la Marina*, an extension of the Cantón Grande, from which we may climb to the Pl. de Azcarraga, on the S. side of which is the 18C *Comandancia*. To the W. is *Santiago* (early 12C) with a wide nave, two interesting doorways, one with a relief of St James at Clavijo, and triple apse.

From the opposite corner of the plaza we reach *Sta María de Campo* of c. 1215–1302, but badly restored, with one pointed and two round-arched doorways and rudely-carved capitals. To the E. is the late-Gothic *Conv. de Sta Bárbara*, whose gateway is surmounted by a curious relief (?1613), including St Michael weighing souls. Just beyond is *Sto Domingo*, 18C Galician Baroque, with a Churrigueresque retablo. Hence the C. de S. Francisco leads S. to the *Jardín de S. Carlos*, in which is the granite **Tomb of Sir John Moore** (1761–1809). Some of the stanzas of Charles Wolfe's poem (first published in 1817) describing his burial are carved by the gate overlooking the harbour, as well as Galician verses by Rosalia de Castro. At the end of the peninsula the *Conv. de S. Francisco*, mainly rebuilt in 1651 but with the remains of its 14C chapel, stands above the well-preserved ramparts, with three sea-gates (16-17C). Below, in the *Castillo de S. Antón*, is a small *Archaeological Museum*.

At the end of the peninsula, N. of the town, rises the so-called **Torre de Hércules** (101 m.) a Roman pharos, probably rebuilt under Trajan by C. Servius Lupus, according to a damaged inscription on the rock (covered). It still serves as a lighthouse, but the exterior is a restoration of 1791. Edward Clarke remarked that the inscription referred to Mars, and was amazed that the Spaniards should be 'so perverse' as to give it to Hercules!

Returning to the Av. de la Marina we may turn r. into the large *Pl. de María Pita*, named after the city's heroine who displayed great bravery during the English attack of 1589. The plaza replaced a wall which formerly separated the Ciudad Vieja from the Pescadería, or fishermen's quarter, which once occupied the isthmus. To the N. of the plaza stands the triple-domed *Ayuntamiento*, to the W. of which, in the Pl. de Abastos, are the 18C churches of *S. Jorge* and *S. Nicolás*, the latter containing the Virgen de los Coruñeses. A little N., in the former *Real Consulado del Mar*, is the *Museo Provincial*, with paintings by *Goya* and *Ribera*, Galician ceramics from the Real Fábrica de Capuchinas, etc. In the nearby church of *Las Capuchinas* (18C Baroque) is a S. Francisco by *Zurbarán*. Parallel to the Av. de la Marina runs the C. Real, which leads back to the Cantón Grande, where, at No. 13, a tablet marks the house where Sir John Moore died.

FROM LA CORUÑA TO SANTIAGO (62 km.). The direct road (N 550) is of little interest, and the new motorway (A9) is a recommended alternative, even if slightly longer (74 km.). The first half of the former is somewhat winding, after which it traverses a typical stretch of Galician upland with views over open heaths, passing through (37 km.) *Ordenes*, before reaching (25 km.) **Santiago**, see Rte 41.

Those with plenty of time to spare should consider the route viâ CORCUBIÓN, described below, from which a number of small fishing villages may be approached. Climbing S.W. on the C 552, we pass (8 km.) *Oseira*, with a late-12C church, and (25 km.) *Carballo*, with mineral baths, to (26 km.) *Bayo*, connected with Santiago (54 km. S.E.) by the C 545.—From (9 km.) *Vimianzo*, once celebrated for its gold mines and with a restored castle and picturesque *paso*, a by-road (r.) leads 21 km. to *Camariñas*, on a beautiful ría, N. of which is Cabo Villánò, the wildest point on this savage coast. Opposite is *Mugía*, commanded by the pilgrimage church of *N.S. de la Barca*, reached by a by-road passing through *Cereijo*, with a 12C church, and *Ozón*, with an impressive *hórreo*, and *Moraime*, where Romanesque *S. Julián* has a porch copied from the Santiago 'Gloria'.— 26 km. *Corcubión*. (2000 inhab.; *Hotel*), a small village on a beautiful ría, has two dismantled forts. To the S.E rises Mte. Pindo, the best view-point for the coast.— 14 km. to the S.W. lies **Finisterre** (5200 inhab.) Here, in 1837, George Borrow was approached by the Justicia, assuming him to be the Carlist pretender. Just beyond is *Cape Finisterre*, the 'Land's End' of Spain, known to the Romans as *Promontorium Nerium*. Offshore, in 1747, Adm. Anson gained a victory over Adm. la Jonquière, and in 1805, Strachan overtook and captured French ships fleeing from Trafalgar.—From Corcubión we skirt the coast by the C 550, passing at *Carnota*. the longest *hórreo* in Galicia, before reaching the fishing-port of (43 km.) **Muros** (12,200 inhab.) an attractive place of narrow alleys and arcaded streets, and with the Gothic *Colegiata de S. Pedro*, and follow the N. shore of the Ría de Muros y de Noya.—At 28 km. we cross the 14C *Pte. Nafonso*, whose architect, Maestro *Alfonso*, is buried at the bridge-head.

5 km. **Noya** (12,800 inhab.) lies on the S. bank of its ría. The port, now silted up, was described by Froissart as 'the key of Galicia'. A medieval bridge crosses the Traba; *S. Martín* (before 1434) has a good rose-window and 16C towers; *S. María a Nova* is set in a picturesque churchyard with a curious chapel and several Calvaries; *S. Francisco*, begun in 1522, is Plateresque.

From Noya we may follow the C 543 climbing N.E. to (36 km.) **Santiago**. see Rte 41.

B   TO VIGO, FROM PONFERRADA

Total distance, from Madrid, 657 km. (408 miles.). N VI. 390 km. Ponferrada—N 120. 84 km. *Puebla de Trives*—77 km. **Orense**—29 km. *Ribadavia*—62 km. *Porriño*—15 km. **Vigo**. For the road from Madrid to Ponferrada, see Rte 33, and Rte 26A.

At **Ponferrada** (p.373) the N 120 bears S.W., passing (21 km. r.) at *Carucedo*, a small lake formed by a dike built by the Romans as part of extensive works to exploit the alluvial gold of the region, before following the valley of the Sil to (36 km.) *La Rua* (*Hotel*). This is however being replaced by a new road turning l. some 12 km. W. of *Ponferrada*, rejoining the old road at *La Rua*.

FROM LA RUA TO LALÍN (130 km.). We turn W. on to the C 533 and follow the r. bank of the Sil to (28 km.) **Quiroga**, with the Romanesque church of the Hospital containing fine tombs, while at nearby *S. Clodio*, on the opposite bank of the Sil, is another early Romanesque church.—*Torbeo*, to the S.W., has a good Romanesque and Gothic Church (restored).—We bear N.W. to (31 km) **Monforte de Lemos**, an ancient and picturesque town (20,100 inhab.) on the Cabé, also crossed by a medieval *Bridge*, beneath the castle-crowned hill (1255 ft) which gave it its name. Late-Gothic *S. Vicente del Pino* has a Renaissance doorway of 1539, and a cloister with a three-storeyed gallery, the top one glazed, and there are also two good Baroque churches. The *Chapel* of the immense *Col. del Cardenal* or *Instituto*, formerly a Jesuit convent (1592-1619), with two patios, contains an impressive 17C walnut retablo by *Fr. de Moure*, of Orense, to the l. of which is the kneeling figure of Card. Rodríguez (1500). Note also the good copy of a painting by Van der Goes. In another room are preserved two paintings ascribed to *Andrea del Sarto* (1524-25), two early paintings by *El Greco* (S. Francisco, and S. Lorenzo), and three of the School of Santiago.

In the Convent of *Sta Clara* (near the old bridge) a *Museum of Religious Art* has been recently installed, containing works by *Greg, Fernández, Pedro de Mena*, and a representative collection of reliquaries, vestments, plate, and a fine rock-crystal ark, etc.

From Monforte the C 546 leads N. to (67 km) *Lugo* through chestnut woods, with views on the r., as we approach (12 km) *Bóveda*, with an ancient palace.—22 km. **Sarriá** (12,000 inhab.), the Roman *Flavia Lambris*, has a fine Trans. church, the Gothic and Renaissance *Conv. de la Merced*, with important tombs, and remains of a castle. Hence the road continues N. to (33 km.) *Lugo*, see p.374.

The C 546 bears S.W. from MONFORTE TO ORENSE (48 km.), off which, at 11 km., a lane leads S. to the Romanesque church of *S. Fiz de Cangas*, passing the Romanesque *Abbey of Ferreira* (12-18C), with the tombs of two armed knights and a well-carved apse; N.W. lies *S. Miguel de Eiré*.—After crossing the Sil—here flowing through imposing gorges (Views)—at its junction with the Miño, a road (l.) leads to *S. Esteban de Ribas de Sil*, overlooked by an ivied convent begun in 1184, and the Romanesque abbey church at *Pombeiro*.—The C 546 follows the l. bank of the Miño to Orense, see p.404.

At 24 km. N.W. of Monforte, the C 533 meets the Miño, which is crossed by a Roman bridge. A little to the N. is the important Romanesque church of *S. Esteban de Ribas del Miño*, while to the S. are remains of the *Abbey of S. Pelagio Diomondi* (c.1170), approached by a rough road. After descending into the deep vine-terraced valley of the Miño, which we cross here, the road climbs steeply past (r.) *Asma*, with a Romanesque church, and at 9 km. we enter **Chantada** (10,100 inhab.).—To the N.E. lies *Pesqueiras*, with *Sta María* of 1121, while at *Taboada*, 14 km. N. on the N 540, the church has a carved tympanum of 1190, N.W. of which is *S. Pedro de Bembibre*, dated 1171. S.E. of Chantada, off the Orense road, at *S. Esteban de Chouzán*, the church is a relic of a double abbey of Benedictines founded c. 1155 and altered in 1314.—The C 533 leads W. from Chantada to (38 km) *Lalín* (p.406), on the N 525 from Orense to *Santiago*, see Rte 43.

At 2 km. we cross the Sil at *Petín*, on a bridge (la Cigarrosa) of Roman foundation, and bearing S.W., following the approx. line of a Roman road, we cross the Bibey on a three-arched bridge.

At 4 km. the C 533 bears S. towards (34 km.) **Viana del Bollo**, on the E. bank of the Embalse del Bao. an unspoilt old town (6300 inhab.) with arcaded streets and feudal keep. Beyond (19 km.) at *La Gudina*, it meets the N 525 from Puebla de Sanabria to *Orense*, see Rte 43.

21 km. **Puebla de Trives** (6250 inhab.; *Hotel*), a summer resort near the Navea, here passing through a gorge, which we cross and climb to the Alto de Cardeira (2730 ft), before descending to (25 km.) *Castro-*

Caldelas, with a 14C castle.—Hence an attractive road leads N.W., crossing the Embalse de S. Esteban (Views) direct to (24 km.) *Monforte de Lemos,* see p.379.

12 km. *Leboreira,* 6 km. S. of which at *Montederramo* are the ruins of a Cistercian monastery founded in 1124, including cloisters (one containing Gothic work) and a vast domed church finished in 1607.— We again climb, to the Alto de Rodicio (2835 ft; wide view).—Some 13 km. S. at *Los Milagros,* is a large Baroque church.—21 km. *Esgos,* close to the rock-hewn church of *S. Pedro de Rocas* (10-12C), entering, at 19 km., **Orense,** see p.404.

From Orense to *Pontevedra* viâ *Carballino,* see p.405.
From Orense to *Santiago,* see Rte 43.

Our route (N 120) follows the N. bank of the Miño to (29 km.) **Ribadavia,** a typical Galician town of 6600 inhab (*Hotel*), pleasantly placed at the confluence of the Avia and the Miño. It has a quaint plaza, an *Ayuntamiento* with elaborate ironwork, two churches, *Santiago* and *S. Juan,* preserving Romanesque remains, *Sta María* (Gothic, with interesting tombs), *S. Ginés de Francelos* (of Visigothic type; c. 800), and a Dominican monastery which was the residence of the Galician kings until c. 915. Remains survive of the town wall, castle, and palace of the courts. The sweet hams and the port-like wine of the district should be sampled.

The main road now bears away from the river valley, which shortly forms the frontier between Spain and Portugal.

A minor road skirts the r. bank of the Miño to *Túy,* at 9 km. S. of Ribadavia crossing the C 531 from Verín and Celanova (see p.404), which joins the N 120 at La Cañiza, 13 km. to the W.—At 23 km. we see the Portuguese town of *Melgaço* on the opposite bank, beneath the Outeiro Maior (4505 ft). The Miño here flows in a deep gorge.—22 km. Opposite the Spanish fortress of *Salvatierra de Miño* stands the Portuguese stronghold of *Monçao* and shortly we have a view of the abbey of *Ganfei* and the fortified town of *Valença* dominating the far bank, and further on of *Túy* (p.401), which we enter at 16 km. See also the *Blue Guide to Portugal,* forthcoming.

After passing through (10 km.) *Melón,* with ruins of a 12C Cistercian abbey, and (8 km.) *La Cañiza,* 4 km. beyond which the C 531 bears N.W. across country to (56 km.) *Pontevedra* (p.400), the N 120 climbs to the Pto. de Fuentefria (offering extensive views) and continues to wind through the hills to (24 km.) *Villasobroso,* with a castle.—At 7 km. a road leads 4 km. N. to *Mondariz,* a granite-built spa scattered among pine-woods above the banks of the Tea, from which we may regain our road 8 km. S.W. at **Puenteáreas** (15,800 inhab.) with a good parish church and beautiful old *Bridge.* We descend through broken wooded country to meet the N 550 at 13 km. Here we by-pass *Porriño* (*Hotel*), and climb across hills to (15 km.) *Vigo,* see p.400.

For the road S. from Porriño to *Túy,* and N. to *Pontevedra,* see Rte 42.

37   FROM LEÓN TO OVIEDO

Total distance, 118 km. (73 miles). N 630. 60 km. *Pto. de Pajares*—30 km. *Pola de Lena*—28 km. **Oviedo.**

A new **Motorway** is under construction, which will bear N.W. off the N630 just S. of León, and after skirting the Embalse de Barrios de Luna, will turn N., crossing the mountains to the W. of, and so avoid, the Pto. de Pajares. Communications between Oviedo, Avilés, and Gijón have recently been improved.

We drive N. on the N 630 through the valley of the Bernesga to (25 km.) *La Robla,* beyond which we follow the railway, and begin the ascent from the plateau into the heart of the CANTABRIAN MOUNTAINS which rise suddenly from the level land, and beyond (9 km.) *Pola de Gordón,* offer strange effects of tilted strata. We now enter a gorge in the foot-hills, emerging beneath the summits of the main ridge. The scenery is impressive. Both road and railway are protected by snowscreens.— 15 km. *Villamanín,* with a Templar chapel and remains of a Roman causeway *('Los Fierros').* Beyond (9 km.) *Busdongo* the road climbs to the *Pto. de Pajares* (4475 ft) affording magnificent views especially of the splintered crags and snowy ridges of the Peña Ubiña to the W. The area has been developed as a winter sports centre (*Parador Nac.*). Just above the pass rises the Pico de Arbás, beneath which is the monastery of *Sta María* at *Arbás,* enclosing a Romanesque church (c. 1216, reconstructed 1716), and recently restored.

We descend steeply into the valley of the Pajares and at 28 km. pass near (r.) the hill-top chapel of **Sta Cristina de Lena.* (Before climbing the stoney track uphill, ask for the key at the house immediately beyond the bridge.). This curious cruciform structure of 905–912 (or possibly as early as c.845), richly decorated in the Visigothic style, has a chamber opening off each side, and a remarkable iconostasis.—4 km. *Pola de Lena* marks the beginning of the industrial area of Oviedo. At 7 km. (1.) lies *Ujo,* with a partly Romanesque church.

To the r. a road ascends the valley of the Aller to (18 km.) *Cabañaquinta* and (7 km.) *Collanzo,* beyond which, by a mountain road crossing the Pto. de S. Isidro, we may reach *Lillo,* see p.394.—From Cabañaquinta the C 6310 Zigzags N.E. viâ *Tolivia,* with good views to the E. of the *Peña Mea* (5118 ft), descending into the Nalon valley at (16 km.) *Entralgo,* with a old house in which the novelist Palacio Valdés (1853–1938) was born. 1 km. beyond we meet the C 635, which ascends the Nalon (r.) to its head at the Pto. de Tarna (4975 ft) before climbing down towards *Riaño,* see p.392.—Turning l. at this junction we enter **Pola de Laviana** (15,350 inhab.) with argentiferous copper-mines, and follow the Nalon N.W. to (36 km.) *Oviedo,* see below.

The N 630 now by-passes (3 km.) **Mieres** (59,300 inhab.) an iron-smelting centre (beyond which the old road, further E., passes the Castle of *Olloniego*); bearing W. and then N. we enter (18 km.) *Oviedo.*

OVIEDO (159,700 inhab; 70,000 in 1920; 124,000 in 1960; *Hotels*) lying between the sea and the Cantabrian mountains, and situated near the centre of the Asturian coal and iron fields, is the ancient capital of the Asturias, and of the modern province. Part of the old town surrounding its Gothic cathedral, and the Asturian Romanesque churches on Mount Narranco, compensate for the ugliness of its industrial environs. The climate is moderate; the rainfall heavy. Note the curious way in which the otherwise flat cider is poured.

History. Founded in 757 by Fruela I as a fortress to guard the Pass of Pajares, Oviedo became the capital of the Asturian kings in 810, when Alfonso II, 'el Casto' (the Chaste), a native of the town, removed his court hither from Pravia, and two years later the episcopal see was established. Here were collected such relics of early saints as had been saved from the Moors, which earned for Oviedo the surname 'el Santo'; and here, when the Asturian kings were driven out of León, the capital of Christian Spain was again established. With the death of Almansor and the reoccupation of León (1002), the political importance of Oviedo vanished and its history was the uneventful record of the capital of a mountain province until the unresisting town was sacked by Marshal Ney and Gén. Bonnet in 1809. The city suffered severe damage and loss of life in the rigorously suppressed rising of the extreme socialists in 1934, and again in the siege of 1936–37, The Conde de Toreno

(1786–1843), a liberal, and historian of the Peninsular war; Ramón Pérez de Ayala (1881–1962), the novelist; and Idalecio Prieto (1883–1962), the socialist politician, were born in Oviedo.

On a slope in the town centre lies the umbrageous *Parque de S. Francisco,* a large alameda—containing a 12C portal from the old church of S. Isidoro—laid out on the site of the old hospital, W. of which stood the *Hospicio Provincial,* built by *Ventura Rodríguez* in 1752, and now a luxury hotel. From the E. corner of the park, the C. de Fruela leads past the ex-Jesuit church of *S. Isidoro* to the Pl. Mayor with the arcaded 18C *Ayuntamiento.* Hence we proceed due N. to the Pl. de la Catedral or de Alfonso II, passing (l.) the *Casa de la Rúa,* partly 14C.

To the S. of S. Isidoro lies the *Market,* beyond which stands the 18C *Pal. del Parque* or *de S. Feliz.* To the E., the conv.-church of *S. Domingo* has a late-16C nave and a porch designed by *Ventura Rodríguez* (late 18C).

The *Cathedral is a cruciform building in the 14C Gothic style, begun by Bp. Gutiérrez de Toledo in 1388. The original church was founded by Fruela I in 781 and enlarged by Alfonso el Casto in 802, but nothing of this remains but the *Camara Santa,* damaged in 1934. Nothing appears to have been done since that date to clean the building, which is black with grime.

EXTERIOR. The W. Front, though plentifully crocketed, and broken up by three deep porches (by *Pedro Bunyers;* 1508–12) has an unfinished air owing to the absence of statues from the niches and the incompleteness of the N. Tower which has not been carried above the nave. The *S. Tower, however, a feature of the landscape, is a masterpiece of late-Gothic detail and is crowned by an openwork pyramid spire with flanking spirelets (1556). Over the central doorway is a relief of the Transfiguration.

The INTERIOR, although small (67 m. by 22 m.) is beautifully proportioned and well lighted. The clustered piers spring straight from base to vault and their side colonnettes are broken only by simple foliage capitals. The triforium of the nave (1487–97) contains Flamboyant tracery, likewise the clerestory above it. The chapels in the aisles were 'modernized' in the 18C; the first on the l. contains the silver-gilt shrine of Sta Eulalia (? 11C) and the first on the r. a grille and stalls from the old coro. The *Cap. Mayor,* with brilliant *stained glass, contains the Coro, a short pillar on the r. of which bears an ancient figure of Christ (? 12C) and in its capital are pilgrims' cockle-shells. The *Retablo,* by *Giralte* and *Valmaseda,* dates from 1525, but has been clumsily repainted and regilt. To the l. is the effigy of Bp. Arias del Villar (d. 1490). The ambulatory is a 17C addition. The organ retains its 18C case.

Townsend, in 1786, was present when the Santissimo Sudario was exposed to some thousands of peasants who had come in from the surrounding villages, most of them with 'baskets full of cakes and bread, which they elevated as high as possible the instant the curtain was withdrawn, in the full persuasion that the cakes, thus exposed, would acquire virtues to cure or alleviate all disease'!
Opening off the N. Transept is the *Panteón del Rey Casto,* a tomb-chapel constructed by Alfonso II (d. 843) for the early kings of Asturias, but completely rebuilt in 1705–12 in the Baroque style. The inscription on the sarcophagi were ruthlessly obliterated, so that the attributions of burials recorded on a modern tablet are largely guesswork.

From the S. Transept steps lead to an ante-chapel, beyond which is the *Cámara Santa (much restored). The vault of the first chamber, remodelled by Alfonso VI (d. 1109), is supported by six pilasters, each bearing two statues of Apostles, with curious capitals above. The tessellated floor resembles Norman work of the 9C in Sicily. The inner chamber, the *Cap. S. Miguel,* probably the identical structure raised by Alfonso II in 802, retains its rough semicircular vault and barbaric capitals.

Until Aug. 1977, when some of the relics (saved from the French in 1809 at the cost of the more solid gold and silver plate) were stolen and smashed by a vandal, they were preserved here, including an 11C cedar chest or *Arca* covered with silver plates adorned with reliefs and a border of Cufic writing; the remarkable *Cruz de los Ángeles* (808), a Maltese cross adorned with gold filigree and precious stones; the *Cruz de la Victoria* (908), said to be that carried by Pelayo at Covadonga; a gold reliquary with agate inlay presented by Fruela in 910; and two curious ivory diptychs (?11C). Those items at present under restoration have been replaced by photographs.

The *Cloister* (c.1302–45 and 1487–97) containing 12-14C tombs, off which is the 13C *Chapter House,* is under restoration. The *Archives* contain the will of Alfonso II, and an illuminated 12C MS (El Libro Gótico).

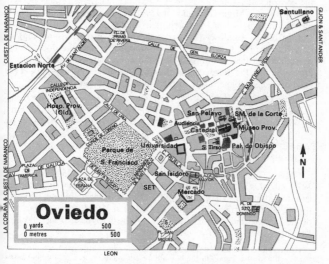

On making our exit and turning l. we pass modernized *S. Tirso,* the E. window of which (c.815) is visible from outside.—The lane opposite leads to the *Bishop's Palace,* built in the 16-18C on the site of a castle erected by Alfonso II. From this lane we can get a glimpse of the exterior of the *Cámara Santa,* showing a considerable portion of Alfonso VI's work and the Romanesque tower of c. 1070–80.

Hence the C. de S. Vicente leads behind the cathedral to the former *Conv. de S. Vicente,* rebuilt after 1493, with a cloister begun by *Juan de Badajoz* before 1550 but only completed in 1775. It houses the **Museo Provincial,* an impressive collection of local antiquities. The cell of the reformer Benito Jerónimo Feijóo (d. 1764) is also shown; his tomb is in adjacent 18C *Sta María de la Corte.* Beyond is the convent of *S. Pelayo,* while the C. del Paraíso, parallel to the E., follows the line of the old walls of Alfonso II.—The C. Martínez Vigil goes on downhill to approach **Santullano,** or *S. Julián de los Prados,* a curious building with three square apses, founded by Alfonso II, c. 830, containing important *Murals of a late Roman type.

W. of the Cathedral is the *University*, built in 1598–1604 by *González de Bracamonte* and *Juan del Rivero;* badly damaged in 1934, but since restored. The *Audiencia*, a few paces N., almost opposite the *Toreno Palace*, occupies the mid-18C *Pal. de Camposagrado.* Beyond is the 18C *Pal de Heredia.*

On the CUESTA DE NARANCO, c. 3 km N.W., reached either by road viâ the Av. de Galicia, off which we turn r., or (better for walkers) by the footbridge immediately W. of the Est. del Norte, is *Sta María de Naranco, built c. 842–50 as the hall of a palace and converted to a church after 905. It is a rectangular building with two external porches and the flat buttresses peculiar to Asturian Romanesque. At either end is a vestibule, and underneath is a crypt. A remarkable feature of the interior is the series of shield-like medallions arranged as though hanging from the consoles above them.

Nearby is *S. Miguel de Linio (or *Lillo*), a cruciform building founded in 848, one arm of which was rebuilt at a later date. The curious stone tracery of the windows (seen though rusting 'protective' netting) is noteworthy. The carvings on the column-bases and the door-jambs reproduce grotesque designs common on late-Roman consular diptychs, but the bordering arabesques are purely Visigothic.—The road above S. Miguel leads to the summit of the hill (view).

FROM OVIEDO TO GIJÓN (27 km.) There is also a motorway from Oviedo to (28 km. N.E.) *Gijón*, off which a branch leads N.W. to (29 km. N.W.) *Avilés*, each providing the faster route. We drive N.E. on the N 630, off which at 5 km., a road (l.) leads 10 km. to *Villardeveyo;* the Visigothic church (c.900) has a window with a rose above paired lights, an anticipation of Gothic tracery.

GIJON (236,700 inhab.; 57,000 in 1920; 111,000 in 1950; 185,000 in 1970; *Parador Nac.; Hotels).* What remains of the old town stands on an isthmus connecting the hill of Sta Catalina with the mainland, while to the W. lies the harbour extending to the *Puerto del Musel* on the far side of the bay, created in 1892, and since enlarged; to the E. is the Playa S. Lorenzo.

History. The Roman and Visigothic *Gigia,* of which little is known, was very briefly in Moorish hands in the 8C, but Pelayo's success at Covadonga caused them to abandon the coast. It was destroyed by fire in 1395. The harbour, founded in 1552 by Charles V, afforded a refuge to the shattered remnant of the Armada in 1588. It was later resorted to by the English 'for filberts and chestnuts', and also exported a little coal. A new quay was built in 1766, extended in 1859, and again since. In 1808 Toreno and the Asturian deputies sailed hence to seek British support against Napoleon. Borrow entered Gijón 'barefoot and bleeding' in 1837, having walked some 200 miles from El Ferrol under a continuous downpour of rain. The town was seriously damaged in 1934 and 1936, when the Nationalist-held barracks were under attack. Famous natives were Gaspar Melchor de Jovellanos (1744–1811), poet and statesman, Ceán Bermúdez (1749–1829), historian of Spanish art, and Evaristo San Miguel (1785–1862), the Liberal general.

Industrial Gijón contains few buildings of interest. At the E. end of the harbour is the Pl. del Marqués, with the *Colegiata* (16C) and *Pal. del Conde de Revillagigedo* (15C; altered in 1690–1702). From the former the C. del Instituto leads S. to the *Inst. Asturiano Jovellanos,* founded in 1797. Its collection of drawings by old masters, formed by Ceán Bermudez, was destroyed in 1936; while adjacent is a *museum* devoted to the *Gaita,* an instrument related to the bagpipes.—In the Campo Valdés, beneath the E. side of the hill of Sta Catalina, are the *Pal. de los

Condes de Valdés (1590), with two heavy towers, and *S. Pedro,* rebuilt in 1954, and nearby is the 16C *Casa de Jovellanos* (restored), containing works by Asturian artists, including *Nicanor Pinolé, Florentino Soria, A. Bartolomé; Sebastián Miranda's* carved Retablo de Mar, and an old wooden Model of Gijón—On the road E. towards *Villaviciosa* lie the vast buildings of the *Universidad Laboral,* while at *Deva,* to the N.E. is a restored Romanesque church of 1006.

38   SANTANDER AND ENVIRONS

SANTANDER (165,000 inhab.; 73,000 in 1920; 114,000 in 1960; numerous *Hotels*) is a cheerful modern town lying on the N. shore of its bay, looking S. towards the Cantabrian mountains. The proximity of the fashionable seaside suburb of *Sardinero* provides additional animation in summer, but it must be admitted, however, that Widdrington was not far wrong when he remarked in the 1830s that it was 'the only place in Spain of similar magnitude, where no artist, in any department, has left a memorial of his skill . . .'.

History. The name of Santander, Roman *Portus Victoriae,* is a corruption of *S. Emeterio,* a saint who was martyred along with S. Celedonio at Calahorra c. 300, and whose relics are preserved in the cathedral. Its first importance as a port dates back to 1248, when Fernando III set forth hence with a fleet to blockade Seville. In 1522 Charles V landed here on his second visit to Spain, and in 1623 Prince Charles, (later Charles I of England), embarked here after his visit to Madrid. The town was sacked by Soult in 1808; much damaged in 1893 by the explosion of a cargo of dynamite (300 people were killed); and a large area of the old city was destroyed by fire in 1941. In recent years there has been much rebuilding, and in 1945 the University of Menéndez Pelayo was founded. The historian Marcelino Menéndez Pelayo (1856–1912) was born in Santander, as were Joaquín Telesforo de Trueba (1799–1835), the novelist and playwright, who emigrated to England in 1823 and remained there until 1834; and the poet Gerardo Diego (1896-), while José María de Pereda (1834-1906), the novelist, was a native of *Polanco,* on the Torrelavega road.

From the central Pl. del Generalísimo the Av. de Calvo Sotelo leads E. past the Av. Alfonso XIII and Paseo de Pereda, skirting the bay and the 'Puerto Chico'. A flight of steps from beside the *Banco de España* (in the Av. Alfonso XIII) ascends to a vaulted passage beneath the Cathedral, in which is the entrance to the impressive early-Gothic *Crypt* (c. 1300), now used as a parish church. Going up the steps to the l. beneath another vault, we reach the entrance to the *Cathedral,* a 13C building altered in the 16 and 18Cs, and largely rebuilt in 1942–55. It contains the tomb of Menéndez Pelayo (see History). The 14C *cloister* (restored) survives on the S.—Emerging from the cathedral and leaving on the l. the remains of the old town, we follow the Av. de Calvo Sotelo.

By keeping straight on and bearing to the r. by the C. Cervantes we may visit (in the C. de Rubio, on the l.) the *Library* left by Menéndez Pelayo to his native town, and the adjoining *Municipal Museum,* containing a well-displayed collection of paintings, the ground floor of which is devoted to *Pancho Cossío, Francisco Iturrino,* and *María Blanchard.* The first floor contains the work of local artists; above are canvases by *Nicanor Piñole, Eduardo Chicharro, Solana's* 'Los Traperos', landscapes by *Agustín Riancho* (1841–1929), 19C portraits, a good *anon* portrait of Floridablanca, and of Carlos III, and a St Anthony of Padua (?) by *Carreño.*

Some distance to the E, near the end of the C. Hernán Cortes, is the *Museo de Prehistoria,* containing an extensive and important collections from Altamira and other sites in the province, including some huge stelae.

By the Av. de la Reina Victoria, a prolongation of the Paseo de Pereda, we reach **Sardinero,** with a huge *Casino* facing the fine sandy beach divided into two bays by a rocky promontory, the Punta del Rastro, whose flat top, laid out as a garden with tamarisk trees, commands the best view.

On the r. extends the peninsula of LA MAGDALENA, with the conspicuous *Pal. la Magdalena,* once a royal residence, and now a Summer School. On the S. side of the peninsula is a curious *Peña Horadada,* an island pierced by a natural arch.— The *International University buildings* lie not far W. of the Casino.—In the Paseo de Pérez Galdós, is the villa of *S. Quintin,* once owned by the novelist Benito Pérez Galdós (1845–1920).

The SHORT EXCURSION to *Santillana* and the *Caves of Altamira* (but see note below) may easily be made from Santander by following the N 611 S.W. parallel to the coast, towards *Torrelavega.*

At 22 km. *Barreda,* we turn r. Crossing the Besaya, we fork l. and pass (l.) *Vivenda* or *Queveda,* with the *Torre de la Beltraneja* (13-16C), once belonging to the poet Calderón de la Barca, accommodating a small private museum devoted to the art of José Gutiérrez Solana (1886–1935), before reaching (4 km.) **Santillana del Mar** (3800 inhab.; *Parador Nac.; Hotels*), still a picturesque old town, but in grave danger of excessive exploitation, preserving numerous stone mansions, mainly of the 15th and 16C, and a fine *Ayuntamiento.* Famous in fiction as being the birthplace of Gil Blas, of more interest is its Romanesque *Colegiata (late 12C) containing the tomb of Sta Juliana, a 4C martyr (of whose name Santillana is a corruption), a retablo of 1453, and a 17C silver altar frontal; in the sacristy some silver and embroidery are preserved. The *Cloister* (restored) with its coupled columns and elaborate capitals, was built slightly later than the church.

The 17C *Convent of Regina Coeli,* near the town entrance, now houses a *Museum.* From the cloister we may visit a number of rooms on two floors, displaying collections of religious art, including a retablo of enamelled plaques (16C), figures of S. Roque, carved and painted woodwork and furniture, polychrome sculpture, chalices, and crucifixes, etc.

Some 2 km. S. are the **Cuevas de Altamira,** a series of caves remarkable for their *Prehistoric Paintings* assigned to the Upper Magdalenian Age (c. 12,000 B.C.). The delineations of bisons, boars, deer, etc., painted in ochre and sometimes outlined by flint scratches, or shaped to the natural protuberances of the walls, are remarkably lifelike.

The caves were discovered in 1868, their entrance having fallen in at some remote date, but the paintings were not noticed until 1879. Some objects found here are housed in the adjacent museum.

Note. To avoid the further deterioration of the paintings, the number of visitors was strictly limited for some years, but it has been decided to close the caves entirely for a period of time, and a commission has been set up to study forms of preservation meanwhile, before the paintings are lost entirely to posterity.

39   FROM SANTANDER TO OVIEDO, LA CORUÑA, AND SANTIAGO

Total distance, 598 km. (471 miles). N611. 25 km. *Torrelavega*—N 634. 35 km. *San Vicente de la Barquera*—76 km. *Arriondas*—65 km. **Oviedo**—105 km. *Luarca*—66 km. *Ribadeo*—45 km. *Mondoñedo*—34 km. *Villalba*—at 17 km. meeting the N VI for 46 km. *Betanzos*—22 km. **La Coruña**—N 550. 62 km. **Santiago**. The route may be shortened by following the motorway direct from Betanzos to Santiago.

This long route should not be attempted in a day, *Oviedo* being a convenient stop en route.

For the road by-passing Santander, from *Laredo* to *Torrelavega* (N 634), see Rte 5. For the *Picos de Europa*, see Rte 40.

A short recommended detour, avoiding (25 km.) *Torrelavega*, may be made by turning r. for *Santillana* (see above), and there turning S.E. to regain the main road 3 km. W. of Torrelavega. The main road traverses the latter town (see p.127), where we turn r. onto the N 634.

The N 611 continues S. to *Reinosa, Palencia,* and *Valladolid;* see Rte 35A in reverse.
An attractive alternative route from Santillana, winding near the coast towards *San Vicente de la Barquera,* may be followed by continuing W. on the C 6316 to (17 km.) *Comillas* (*Hotels*), a small resort overlooked by the *Pal. of the Marqués de Comillas,* a number of ugly seminaries, and preserving a building known as 'El Capricho', by *Gaudí.* We regain the N 634 7 km. beyond.

At 18 km., *Cabezon de la Sal,* the C 625 (l.) leads past *Carrejo,* with ancient houses, and (7 km.) *Ruente,* with the 15C *Casa del Rey,* briefly the residence of Charles V. 5 km. beyond lies *Cabuérniga,* see p.367.— 5 km. *Treceño,* birthplace of Juan de Herrera, architect of the Escorial and of the didactic writer Fray Antonio de Guevara (c.1480–1525).— 11 km. *La Revilla,* where we meet the road from Comillas, see above, with *Views* towards the *Picos de Europa* across the tidal river, beyond which lies **San Vicente de la Barquera,** (4100 inhab.; *Hotels*) on a promontory approached by the long *Pte. de la Maza* (1433) with 28 arches. San Vicente, with the ruins of the 13C Franciscan convent where Charles V stayed in 1521, is a picturesque fishing port with arcaded streets overlooked by a battered castle. Some 16-17C mansions, 13C *N.S. de los Ángeles,* with a Romanesque doorway, an effigy of the inquisitor Ant. Corro (1524) by *Baut. Vázquez,* and a 15C tomb of the same family, are of interest.
The following 60 km of coast is particulary beautiful, with the Sierra de Cuera rising up to the S., and the Picos de Europa behind.—We cross the Nansa at (8 km.) *Pesués,* and 3 km. beyond enter **Unquera,** a good starting-point for the exploration of the *Picos de Europa* (see Rte 40), where the N 621 for *Potes* bears S.—We cross the Deva and enter the old kingdom of Asturias.—At 3 km. a track (r.) leads to the Cueva del Pindal containing paintings of the Altamira type. To the l., passing near *Colombres* (*Hotel*), as we approach Llanes, rises the bold Sierra de Cuero (c.4000 ft).

At 18 km. we follow the new road for the next 28 km, to *Llovio,* 3 km. S. of *Ribadesella,* see below. This avoids the picturesque but winding old road, which forks r. 2 km. to the industrial port of **Llanes** (15,000 inhab.; *Hotels*) with a 17C castle, medieval tower, and 15C church containing an early 16C retablo.—The main road passes (7 km. r.) *Celorio.* preserving ruins of the Romanesque monastery of *S. Salvador* (1017).—5 km. r. *S. Antolín de Bedón* (1251), near the Cueva de Lledias, with paintings of stags.—At 10 km. the old road turns r. to the small port of **Ribadesélla,** (7000 inhab.; *Hotels*), attractively situated at the mouth of the Sella, on the opposite bank of which is the stalactite cave of *Tito Bustillo,* containing prehistoric paintings.

FROM RIBADESELLA TO LUARCA (172 km.). From Ribadesella there is an alternative route to Oviedo viâ *Gijón* (only 27 km N.E. of Oviedo, see p.381) by the N 632, which runs roughly parallel to the coast, and continues past Gijón viâ Avilés to a point 11 km. E. of *Luarca,* where it joins the N 634 from Oviedo. From Ribadesella it passes through *Berbes* and (16 km.) *Caravia,* with old mansions and medieval towers, near the prehistoric site of Picos del Castro.—At 3 km. we pass (l.) the 9C church of *Gobiendas,* 6 km. beyond which is the Mirador de Fita, with extensive views.—4 km. *Colunga.* The fishing village of *Lastres,* with a 15C *Colegiata,* lies 4 km. to the N. At 10 km. we pass (1.2 km.) *Priesca,* with the church of *S. Salvador* (915–21), before following the estuary to (7 km.) **Villaviciosa** (16,400 inhab.), a good centre for the lover of romantic scenery or of Romanesque architecture. The streets of the old town preserve the atmosphere of the 16C, and at C. del Agua 31, Charles V stayed on his first visit to Spain in 1517, having landed at *Tazones,* 10 km. N.E. *Sta María* retains a 13C doorway with good statuary.

Many of the villages in the area possess curiously primitive Romanesque churches. Most notable of these is that of **Valdedios,* 9 km. S.W., consecrated in 893, adjacent to the ruinous Cistercian church of *Sta María* (1218), known as 'El Conventín'. Other curious examples are **S. Juan de Amandi* (1134; restored 1755), with a semicircular arcade at its entrance, and expressive capitals in its unusual apse; *Lugás;* and *Valdebarcena,* 2 km., 5 km., and 8 km. S., respectively. Also at *Fuentes,* 2 km. S.E.; and at *S. Andrés de Bedriñana* (9th and 13C) and *S. Lázaro de Lloraza* (11C). 3 km. N. and 8 km. N.W. respectively.

From Villaviciosa we may regain the N 634 some 21 km. E. of Oviedo, by following the C 638 to the S.W.—28 km. **Gijón,** see p.384, beyond which the N 632 crosses the neck of the Cabo de Peñas.

A faster road between *Gijón* and (23 km.) *Avilés* is now provided by a stretch of motorway, off which a branch leads S.W. to (28 km.) *Oviedo.*

At 6 km. a detour may be made by forking r. to the fishing village of *Candás* (*Hotel*), and (11 km.) *Luanco,* with a clock-tower of 1705, the *Pal. de los Pola,* and an early 18C church. Here, in 1786, Townsend spent ten days at the home of the Count of Peñalba, where 'the style of living resembled the old British hospitality and the long oak tables surrounded by strong oak benches, were every day well covered'.—The *Cabo de Peñas,* Roman *Arae Sextianae,* lies 10 km. N.W.— Passing near *Manzaneda,* with a Templars' church of the 12C, we may regain the N 632 at *Avilés,* see below.

After passing the great steelworks built as a metallurgical centre for the area, we enter (19 km.) **Avilés** (85,300 inhab.; *Hotel*), which, according to Townsend, possessed no manufacturers in his time 'except of copper and brass pans for the surrounding villages, and of some thread' for their own consumption. It was the birthplace of Juan Carreño (1614–85), the painter; Pedro Menéndez (1519–74), the mariner, and conquistador of Florida; and of the playwright and critic Francisco Antonio de Bances Candamo (1662–1704).

The conspicuous church of *La Merced,* originally of the 14C, is now mainly modern, with two tall towers. *S. Nicolás de Bari* (13–14C) contains the tomb of Menéndez, and the *Cap. de los Alas,* with a fine retablo and tombs; Romanesque *S. Francisco* has a 9C relief; while *Sto Tomás de Cantorbéry* (restored), is one of the first churches to be dedicated to Becket. Among old mansions the *Pal. de Valdecarzana* (or *Baragaña*), in the C. Herreria, is outstanding, with an unspoilt front of c. 1300; here Pedro the Cruel lodged in 1352. The *Pal. de Camposagrado* had a 17C Baroque façade of three orders; in the Pl. de España are the *Ayuntamiento,* a long arcaded building of 1670, and other 17-18C mansions.—N.W. of the town lies the resort of *Salinas;* to the S. stands the hill-top church at *Laspra,* retaining 9C work.

17 km. *Sota del Barco,* with the old *Castillo de Don Martin.*—8 km. upstream, in the beautiful Nalón valley, lies **Pravia** (12,200 inhab.), with a *Colegiata* of 1715 and *Casas Consistoriales* by *Manuel Requera* (late 18C). Nearby, at *Santianes,* the residence of the Asturian kings from c. 750 to the foundation of Oviedo, the 17C church preserves remains of a basilica of 774–83.—Crossing the Nalón, we pass through *Muros de Nalón,* with the *Valdecarzana palace* nearby. 4 km. beyond, at *El Pito* (r.), an altar of c.780 brought from Santianes is preserved in the crypt of its church, while in the *Pal. de Selgas* is a collection of paintings, which may be visited on previous application. To the r. is the attractive fishing village of *Cudillero,* huddled around its harbour; its Ayuntamiento in an old castle.—18 km. *Luiña,* whose church contains interesting inscriptions and a late-17C retablo. The coast road now becomes more hilly and winding before it joins the N 634 at (33 km.) *Canero.*—11 km. *Luarca,* see p.390.

From (6 km.) *Llovio,* the N 634 turns S.W. into the mountains, following the r. bank of the Sella to (15 km.) *Arriondas,* just before which the road to *Cangas de Onis* and *Covadonga* (p.393) bears S.E. We now follow the valley of the Piloña to (15 km.) *Villamayor,* with a ruined Romanesque church; old mansions survive here and at *Borines,* 6 km. N.—5 km. *Infiesto,* in a deep valley with marble quarries, has a curious sanctuary to the S., where three chapels are sheltered by a cave.—14 km. *Nava,* with the fortified *Pal. de la Cogolla.* The famous 12C church, destroyed during the Civil War, has been reconstructed. We traverse well-wooded and undulating country, passing collieries among the apple orchards, through (7 km.) *Lieres,* (8 km.) *Pola de Siero,* (37,100 inhab.) and (3 km. r.) *Noreña.* 13 km. **Oviedo,** see p.381.

From Oviedo we drive W., passing (7 km.) *Sograndio* and (r.) *San Claudio,* with Trans. churches, and (l.), near *Caldas,* the large Romanesque church of *S. Juan de Priorio* (late 11C).—At *Nora,* N. of (8 km.) *Trubia,* in the Nalón valley, is *S. Pedro* of c.900, restored.

From Trubia a road leads S. up the valley to (8 km.) *Tuñón,* with the abbey church of *S. Adriano* (891, restored 1108), and after traversing the defile of the *Peñas Juntas* we reach (11 km.) *Caranga,* where the valley divides. The l. branch follows the bank of the Embalse de Valdemurrio to the early churches of (7 km.) *Arrojo* (Trans.) and *S. Miguel del Bárzana* (pre-Romanesque), while the r. skirts the Embalse de Priañes to (3 km.) *La Plaza de Teverga,* with a *Colegiata* of c. 1070, and Romanesque churches at *Riello,* 2 km S.E., and *Villanueva,* 4 km. S.W.

12 km. **Grado** (12,800 inhab.), where another *Pal. de Valdecarzana* and the *Cap. de los Dolores* (18C) are of interest.—The C 632 leads 18 km. N. to *Pravia* (see above), passing *S. Román de Candamo,* with

cave-paintings in the cavern of *La Peña.*—At 10 km. the C 633 (l.) leads up the Pigueño valley to the picturesque town and ruined abbey of (21 km.) *Belmonte.*—1 km. *Cornellana,* with 11C *S. Salvador.*—9 km. **Salas** (9700 inhab.) with a 16C church containing a huge monument of 1568–82 by *Pompeo Leoni* to its founder, Card. Fernando de Valdés, a native of the place, and a cemetery with remains of the chapel of *S. Martín,* dating from a restoration of 951. At *La Campa* is the tower of the castle of Miranda. The road now climbs steeply for some 7 km. to (12 km.) *La Espina* before descending towards the coast, and (46 km.,) *Luarca,* see below.

FROM LA ESPINA TO LUGO (181 km.) The C 630 ascends S.E. towards (12 km.) **Tineo** (20,100 inhab.) with the 18C *Casa de Campomanes,* and a monastic church and cloister opposite.—At 10 km. and 18 km. to the W. of Tineo are the 12C abbeys of *Obona* and *Bárcena.*—The C 630 winds its way across country to (34 km.) *Pola de Allande,* near the Romanesque church of *Célon* with 14C murals, and 45 km. beyond, on the W. bank of the Embalse de Salime in the Navia valley, the village of *Grandas de Salimé,* whose church has important Romanesque features. The road continues through (33 km.) **Fonsagrada** (9800 inhab.), capital of this wild region, to (36 km.) *Castroverde,* with remains of one of the finest medieval castles in Galicia, and the church of *Villabad* (after 1452) with Baroque retablos.—21 km. **Lugo,** see p.374.

FROM LA ESPINA TO PONFERRADA (153 km.). Passing (r.) *Tineo,* see above, we follow the C 631 past (22 km.) the monastery of *S. Juan de Corias* (rebuilt 1773) containing two cloisters, and the tomb of its founder, Bermudo III (1027–37).— 4 km. **Cangas de Narcea** (20,100 inhab.) hemmed in by steeply scarped mountains, retains a crooked bridge, and a collegiate church of 1639–42. Leaving the valley we climb to the upland of Las Brañas, inhabited by a curious unassimilated pastoral race. Occasionally to be seen are the primitive thatched cabins or *Pallazas,* which were once the refuges of both man and beast, but mostly now derelict. At 37 km. we cross the *Pto. de Leitariegos* (4300 ft) in the Cantabrian chain, and begin a zigzag descent into the Sil valley, at (14 km.) *Villager,* meeting the C 623 from León. Here we turn S.W. and follow the river nearly all the way to (64 km.) **Ponferrada,** see p.373.

Luarca, a picturesque fishing port, (20,500 inhab.; *Hotel*) in a sheltered cove at the mouth of the Rio Negro, is overlooked by a chapel white-washed as a sea mark. We skirt the seaward ridges of the Sierra de Rañadoiro, passing (r.) *Puerto de Vega,* where Jovellanos died, in Nor. 1811, persecuted by his political enemies, and cross the Ría de Navia at (20 km.) **Navia,** the birthplace of the poet Ramón de Campoamor (1817--1901). Hence the C644 follows the Navia valley, much of it now filled with reservoirs, through quaint primitive slate-built villages, such as *San Estéban de los Buitres,* to (63 km.) *Grandas de Salimé* (see above). From approx. this point, the traveller will notice a difference in the shape of the *hórreos* (see p.370) from the square Asturian form to the oblong type of Galicia.—Some 5 km. S.W. at *Coaña* are remains of a Celtic village.—We shortly reach the estuary of the Eo, a magnificent natural harbour, and (31 km.) **Castropol,** (5500 inhab.) with Ribadeo facing it, to approach which, we circle the head of the ría at (8 km.) *Vegadeo.*

Hence the N 640 leads S.W. across the Sierra de Meira to (80 km.) *Lugo* viâ (45 km.) *Meira,* with a Cistercian monastery founded in 1144 and church cons. in 1258, but the ironwork of the W. Door is earlier. The Renaissance cloister now serves as the village plaza.

7 km. **Ribadeo** (8900 inhab.; *Parador Nac.*), has an 18C church and a two-towered castle, beyond which we skirt the coast to (20 km.) *Bareiros,* where the N 634 turns inland.

FROM RIBADEO TO BETANZOS, VIÁ VIVERO (169 km.). At Bareiros the C 642 crosses the Masma and continues W. past *Foz* (8400 inhab.) and (39 km. l.) *Sargadelos*, home town of Antonio Raimundo Ibáñez, first Marqués de Sargadelos, the 18C economist, to the sheltered port of (20 km.) *Vivero* (13,400 inhab; *Hotels*) famous for its sardine fisheries, and with a twelve-arched *Bridge* across the sandy mouth of the Androve. Four of its ten *Gates* have survived; one, the *Castillo del Puente* (1554), bearing the escutcheon of Charles V. *Sta María del Campo* is said to date from the 9C, while *S. Pedro* has Romanesque carvings. The *Franciscan Church* and church of *Valdeflores* are also of interest.—The road now bears N.W. and crosses the deep Ría del Sor, beyond which (r. 7 km.) is The Punta de la Estanca de Bares, the northernmost point of Spain. Skirting the shore of the rocky Ría de Sta Marta, we reach the resort of (31 km.) *Ortigueira* (18,800 inhab.). On the r. the coast runs out to Cape Ortegal, surrounded by dangerous reefs and surmounted by the *Ermita de S. Andrés de Teixido*, the scene of a pilgrimage with traditional songs and dances. Beyond (9 km.) *Mera* the road leaves the ría and runs inland.—At 6 km. the C 646 forks r. to follow the coast viá *Cedeira* (8100 inhab.) to (48 km.) *El Ferrol*, while the C 642 continues S.W., at 13 km. passing (5 km. l.) the castle of *Moeche* and (8 km.) *San Saturnino*, with former *Conv. de Sto Domingo*, and, 7 km. S., the 14C castle of *Narahío*. At 11 km. we meet the main road at *Jubia*, 8 km. S.W. of which is *El Ferrol*, see p.376. We bear l. for (32 km.) **Betanzos**.

From Bareiros we drive S.W. past (11 km.) *Lorenzana*, with a rebuilt Benedictine convent containing the 10C founder's tomb of Osorio Gutiérrez and a palaeo-christian tomb. The 17C church, by *Pedro de Monteagudo*, has a fine early-18C Baroque front by *F. Casas y Nóvoa*.

14 km. **Mondoñedo**, a sequestered town of 7200 inhab., in the lower part of which stands the *Cathedral, begun c.1220, with four 16C chapels at the E. end. The W. Front retains Gothic features based on Sigüenza, but was attractively cloaked in the local Baroque style in 1705. Note the sculpted St Jerome and the lion on its façade. In the S. Chapel is a wood carving of the Virgin and six seraphims, said to have been brought from St Paul's in London at the Reformation. The cathedral also contains a small museum. Note also the gilt and green Baroque organs (1759).

Near the *Bishop's Pal.* is a *Fountain* dated 1548. Adjoining the chapel of *N.S. de los Remedios* (12C; rebuilt 1738) is the *Hosp. de S. Pablo*, with a carved centrepiece of 1755. The *Conv. de·los Picos* and the *Seminario* are 17C—At *Alfoz*, 17 km. N.W., is the castle of *Castro de Oro*, and Romanesque *S. Martín* occupying the site of the early cathedral of the diocese (842–1112).

Our road crosses bleak uplands, with the Sierra del Gistral (4400 ft) on the r. to (34 km.) **Villalba** (17,100 inhab.), with a picturesque medieval tower accommodating the *Parador Nac.* Hence the C 641 leads 37 km. S. to *Lugo*, and 68 km. N.W. to *El Ferrol*. We continue S.W. to meet the N VI at 17 km., where we turn r.

At 19 km. the C 544 forks l. direct to *Santiago*, 69 km. to the S.W., see p.394. The N VI leads to (27 km.) *Betanzos* and (22 km.) *La Coruña*, see Rte 36A. From La Coruña to (62 km. S.) *Santiago*, the direct road (N 550) is described on p.378. An alternative route is that followed by the motorway from just W. of *Betanzos*, to *Santiago*.

40   THE PICOS DE EUROPA

From the N. this range is best approached from *Unquera* (p.387) or *Arriondas* (p.389), both on the N 634 from Santander to Oviedo, Rte 39. From *León*, to the S.W., a road led to Riaño, but extensive works are under way with the construction of a reservoir, and road communications in the area may be temporarily impaired. Riaño itself may be submerged.

At Unquera the N 621 turns inland and ascends the Deva valley, which soon narrows. We have a good view of the conical Peña Mellera as we approach (12 km.) *Panes*, with a Mozarabic chapel (c. 1000). To the r. is the gorge of the Cares, followed by the C 6312, see below.

FROM UNQUERA TO RIAÑO (94 km.). Our road now bears l. and we penetrate the impressive **Desfiladero de la Hermida*, to whose steep sides chestnut trees cling wherever they can find a hold.—20 km. *Urdón*, from which a rough track ascends S.W. through a gorge to the pastoral village of *Treviso*, whence we can reach *Sotres*.—A track also climbs W. from (2 km.) *La Hermida* to *Sotres*. At La *Hermida* the valley momentarily expands, and at 8 km. (l.) lies the Mozarabic church of **Sta María de Liébena* (before 924), with horseshoe arches and an exterior gallery.—9 km. **Potes** (1400 inhab; *Hotel*), in the mountain-girt valley of Liébana, is commanded by the square *Torre del Infantado.*— At 1 km. N. of Potes we meet the C 627 from Herrera de Pisuerga, see p.367.

3 km. S.W. of Potes a road (l.) ascends to *Sto Toribio de Liébana,* a monastic church of 1250 to which a Baroque chapel has been added, while just N. at *Puente Ojedo* is a Romanesque church with a Gothic retablo.—W. of Potes, a branch of the N 621 follows the Deva below the E. massif of the Picos to (20 km.) *Espinama,* overlooked to the S. by Coriscao, and 4 km. beyond to its source at *Fuente Dé* (*Parador Nac.*), a centre for the exploration of the high peaks of the central massif. At 3½ km. N. of Espinama is perched the *Refugio de Aliva* (3300 ft), accessible by a steep track (open to cars from May to Oct.), while a 'teleferico' ascends from Fuente Dé to a path W. of the Refugio.

From Potes the N 621 climbs S. up the Quivesa valley, and then S.W. (poor surface) towards the *Pto. de S. Gloria* (8301 ft), between the Peña Prieta massif to the S. and to the N. Coriscao, providing panoramic views on clear days. We descend to (36 km.) *Portilla de la Reina*, where another mountain road (r.) leades due N. across the Pto. de Pandetrave to *Santa Marina de Valdeón*, whence a track leads down to the *Posada de Valdeón* in the Cares valley, see below. The N 621 descends S.W. from Portilla to (18 km.) *Riaño*.

FROM UNQUERA TO CANGAS DE ONÍS (67 km.). From Panes, see above, we follow the C 6312 along the gorge of the Cares S. of the coastal Sierra de Cuera, to (22 km.) the village of *Alles*, in an attractive setting, with a picturesque spired church and remains of a Romanesque one.—14 km. *Las Arenas*, in the wild mountain region of *Cabrales*, noted for its goat's milk cheese, and its copper and zinc mines.

A road leads S. to *Camarmeña*, below the central massif of the Picos de Europa, where it diverges: l. towards *Sotres*, from which a track leads S. to the *Refugio de Aliva* and *Espinama;* and a rough path leads r., S.W., through a gorge to *Caín*, often isolated by snow, and the *Posada de Valdeón* (see above) lying between the central and Western massifs.

3km. *Carreña,* once a centre of pilgrimage and of the traditional dance called the 'corri-corri'; the town and neighbourhood are rich in ancient mansions.—11 km. 1. *Abamia,* with the small 12C church of *Sta Eulalia* (heavily restored) containing tombs traditionally those of Pelayo and his queen (but comp. *Covadonga).* At (13 km.) a road leads 6 km. S. to *Covadonga* (see below) before we enter (4 km.) **Cangas de Onís** (6400 inhab.; *Hotel*), once the residence of the Asturian kings, and notable for its chapel of *Santa Cruz,* founded in 735 by Favila on a Celtic tumulus, and for a 13C **Bridge* across the Sella. *Cangas de Onís* may also be reached from Arriondas, 7 km. N.W., by the N 634, see p.389. 3 km. N. of Cangas, at *Villanueva,* the ruined monastery of **S. Pedro* (under restoration), founded by Alfonso I in 746 and rebuilt in 1687, preserves a remarkable doorway whose capitals represent a bear-hunt. Much of the existing building is of the 12C, including the apse.

Covadonga *(Hotel)*, a commercialized hamlet occupying a beautiful site, is famous as the scene of the first reverse of the triumphant Moors in 718, and the beginning of almost 800 years of intermittent warfare ending in the conquest of Granada in 1492. Among the bands of fleeing Goths who had tanen refuge in the Cantabrian mountains the most powerful was that led by Pelayo, or Pelagius, who had been brought to bay with 300 men in the cul-de-sac of Covadonga. A small force of Moors sent to exterminate them was ambushed and defeated with heavy loss, and Pelayo was forthwith proclaimed king on the Campo del Rey below the village. The Moors, fearing for their communications, abandoned the N. Coast and diverted their attacks towards France, enabling the Asturian kingdom to consolidate its strength for a later sally into the plain of León.

The 16C *Colegiata* has a cloister containing two old tombs.—In the rock wall opposite, above a waterfall, is the shallow *Cueva* where, traditionally, Pelayo had his back to the wall, now approached by a flight of marble steps(!). Adjoining is the rebuilt chapel of the *Virgen de las Batallas* ('la Santina'), the successor of one built by Alfonso I that was destroyed by fire in 1777, and again in 1936. A recess in the cave wall contains the sarcophagus of Pelayo (d. 737) and his wife Gaudiosa, and at the back of the chapel is the tomb of his sister Ermesinda and her husband Alfonso I (d. 757). From the cave a tunnel leads to the terrace of the *Basilica of N.S. de las Batallas* (1877–1901), in 'Romanesque' style, with its twin spires, standing on a spur jutting out into the valley.

Beyond Covadonga, the road climbs steeply S.E. through wonderful scenery to (20 km.) the small **Lakes* of La Ercina and Enol, from which a track climbs S., over-looked by the massif of the *Peña Santa* (8485 ft), the N.W. buttress of the Picos de Europa. The district is reserved as a National Park for the preservation of the characteristic wild animals, such as bears, izards (the 'chamois' of the Picos de Europe), wild cats, ospreys, vultures, etc. The *Cruz de Priena,* on the mountain summit facing the cave at Covadonga, commands a fine view.

FROM CANGAS DE ONÍS TO RIAÑO (60 km.). The C 637 leads up the beautiful Sella valley, off which, at 25 km., a rough road (l.) leads to *Amleva,* from which tracks ascend into the Sierra de Beza. We now thread the **Defile of the Sella (de los Beyos),* at the S. end of which a road (l.) ascends to (4 km.) *Soto de Sajambre,* from which a track climbs to the head of the Dobra valley S. of the Peña Santa. Soon after leaving the main road there is a fine view S.W. towards the *Picos de Mampodre.*—The C 637 climbs steeply to (28 km.) the Pto. de Ponton (4520 ft).—Here a road leads 6 km. N.E. to the Pto. de Panderruedas, with views of the Picos de Europa to the N.E.; hence a track leads down the valley of the Cares to the Posada de Valdeón, see p.392—At 11 km. we meet the C 635 from Riaño to *Oviedo,* and 6 km. enter *Riaño,* at the confluence of the Yuso and Esla.

FROM LEÓN TO RIAÑO (93 km.) There are two routes from León to Riaño, and a third is projected. The most northerly (N 621) leads N.W. 25 km. to *Devesa,* at which point we turn l. and follow the Porma to (21 km.) *Boñar,* a small spa attractively situated in the Curueño valley.—5 km. S.E., at *Las Bodas,* is a church partly of the 11C.—Hence a rough road leads E. 20 km. to a point 3 km. N. of *Cistierna,* see below.—We continue N. and circle the E. bank of the Embalse de Porma, pass the mountain village of (25 km.) *Lillo,* with the ski-slopes of *S. Isidro* to the N.W., and climb to (15 km.) the *Pto. de Tarna* (4975 ft), where we meet the C 635 from Oviedo to Riaño. Here we turn r., and passing through *La Uña,* descend the upper valley of the Esla to (28 km.) *Riaño,* see below. A road is planned between the two halves of the N 621, from Devesa to Cistierna, 30 km. S. of Riaño, which will considerably shorten the route.

An alternative route from León may be followed by first driving S.E. on the N 601 for 13 km., then turning l., shortly passing *S. Miguel de Escalada* and *Gradefes.* Hence we bear N. parallel to the Esla to (47 km.) *Cistierna* and (33 km.) *Riaña.*—At *Pedrosa del Rey,* 4 km E. of Riaño, the C615, a mountain road leads S.E. to (30 km.) *Guardo* (see below), and *Saldaña,* 32 km. beyond, see p.225.

FROM CISTIERNA TO CERVERA DE PISUERGA (70 km.). We may drive E. through a coal, iron, and copper-mining area on the S. slopes of the Cantabrian mountains. After 8 km. we turn l. off the C 611 and wind along the flank of the *Peña Corada* (6007 ft).—At 9 km. a road leads N. 4 km. to the magnificent ruined *Pal. de Don Ant. Prado* (c. 1620) at *Renedo de Valdetejar*—16 km. *Guardo,* with a 16C church containing a Romanesque font, and several old mansions.—From *Velilla de Guardo,* 5 km. N. on the C 615, a mountain road skirts the N. bank of the Embalse de Camporredondo, below the Peña Prieta massif, and further E., that of the Embalse de Cervera.—22 km. *Pisón* has a church of 1100 with a 15C doorway; while 2 km. beyond. that of *Castrejón de la Peña* has a good retablo mayor and a 12C copper processional cross. There is an interesting church at nearby *Traspeña.*—13 km. **Cervera de Pisuerga**; the Renaissance church contains a retablo of 1513 by *Felipe Vigarni,* and a stone pulpit. A *Parador Nac.* has been recently built at *Fuentes Carriones,* not far to the N.

Cervera may be reached from *Herrera de Pisuerga,* 40 km. S.E. or from *Aguilar de Campo,* 28 km. E., both on the N 611, see Rte 35A.

From Cervera de Pisuerga we may approach the Picos de Europa by the C 627, leading N. and passing (16 km. l.) *San Salvador de Cantanuda,* with a 13C bridge, and a 12C church with an altar-slab with original columns. We climb to the Portillo de Piedrasluengas (4475 ft) before descending to (41 km.) *Potes* (p.392), passing (5 km. E.) *Piasca,* with a good 12C church.—From the Portillo a poor but picturesque mountain road (r.) descends the Nansa valley, past the hamlets of *Tudanca* and *Cosio* to (35 km.) *Puentenansa,* (11 km.) *Bielba,* with the *Torre de Obesa,* and (11 km.) *Pesués,* on the N 634 2 km. E. of *Unquera,* see p.387.

41   SANTIAGO DE COMPOSTELA

SANTIAGO DE COMPOSTELA (75,400 inhab.; 26,000 in 1920; 55,500 in 1950; *Hotels*), well described, in the words of George Borrow, as being 'a beautiful old town, in every respect calculated to excite awe and admiration', and one of the goals of medieval pilgrimage, stands on the summit of a low eminence in the midst of a green and hill-girt plain watered by the Sar and the Sarela. Not all visitors have been so charitable. Dalrymple, who passed that way in 1775, remarked that it swarmed with priests, 'who enjoy great incomes, live in luxury and every kind of dissipation'. It contains a University, and is noted for the rainiest climate in Spain. It is one of the few towns in Spain where mendicants or *Pordioseros* are noticeable.

Airport at *La Bacolla,* to the E.

Fiestas. 25 July; Ascension; Corpus Christi: and 31 Dec.

History. Legend relates that the body of St James the Great (*Santiago*), having landed in a stone (sic) coffin at *Padrón* (see p.400), was discovered in 813 by Theodomir, Bp. of Iria Flavia, directed by a miraculous star which appeared above a wood on the site where Santiago now stands (whence its surname *Compostela,* i.e. *Campus Stellae*). The chapel built here by Alfonso II was enlarged by Alfonso

III into a cathedral in 874–99, around which a town soon grew. This was destroyed by Almansor in 997, but the Moorish conqueror spared the saint's tomb, partly, no doubt, out of Moslem respect for a holy grave, partly in admiration of the courage of a friar who, along among the people of Santiago, remained beside the shrine.

Diego Gelmírez (1100–30), the first archbishop, in rebuilding the cathedral, incorporated the saint's bones in the foundations. The pilgrimage, already locally frequented as a result of Santiago's miraculous exploits against the Moors on the field of Clavijo, became universal and roads from the frontiers and seaports of Spain were made for the influx of pilgrims from foreign lands. The first recorded English pilgrimage to Santiago is that of Ansgot de la Haye of Burwell, Lincs., c. 1093. Chaucer's 'Wife of Bath' had been 'in Galica at Seynt Jame'.

The Church profited very considerably, and Santiago has been described by Peter Linehan as 'the anchorage of one of the great ecclesiastical pirates of thirteenth century Spain, Abp. Juan Arias' (1238–67). In 1386 John of Gaunt, claiming the throne of Castile in the right of his wife, daughter of Pedro the Cruel, invaded Galicia, and was crowned at Santiago. After the Reformation the popularity of the pilgrimage waned, although it is still visited, particularly in Compostelan years (when 25 July falls on a Sunday). In 1809 the treasury was plundered by Ney. but the spoil was disappointingly meagre, the offerings of pilgrims having been appropriated by the clergy to their own uses.

On entering Santiago from the N., a new approach road forks r. off the N 550 from La Coruña, and leads directly to the *Pl. de España,* a convenient central point from which to explore the town.

The **Pl. de España* is surrounded by imposing buildings. Facing the Cathedral is the *Pal. de Rajoy* (now the Ayuntamiento), built in 1766–72 as a seminary; to the N. is the huge ***Hospital Real,** built in 1501–11 by *Enrique de Egas* as a pilgrim-hostelry at the command of Fernando and Isabel.

In 1954 it was converted into a luxury hotel, the *Hostal de los Reyes Catolicos.* The main front of 1678, with a fine Plateresque portal, is crested by a series of well-designed mouldings. Within are two Renaissance patios, two later courts of the Doric order, and a *Chapel* with a reja of 1556 and a dome supported by pillars of the finest late-Gothic workmanship. The *Sala Real* was frescoed by *Arias Varela* (1783).

South of the square stands the *Col. de S. Jerónimo,* preserving a late 15C doorway (rebuilt 1662–65) in the Romanesque style. Behind is the *Escuela* or *Col. de Fonseca,* founded by Abp. Alonso III de Fonseca in 1525, with a good Plateresque doorway and a charming patio. The chapel and hall may also be visited.—On the N. side of the Cathedral is the *Pal. Arzobispal* (1759–1854) occupying the site of the ***Pal. of Abp. Gelmírez.** Some of the rooms are of interest, among them the vaulted *Salón de Fiestas* and the *Kitchen,* which date from this time (c. 1120) and from that of Abp. Arias (1235–66).

The fabric of the ***Cathedral** remains substantially as it was after the rebuilding begun by Bp. Diego Peláez c. 1075 and continued by Abp. Gelmírez and his successors in the 12C, but practically the whole of the exterior was recased in the 17-18C. It was consecrated c. 1128, but was not finished until 1211. The plan resembles that of St. Sernin at Toulouse, begun almost at the same time. It is curiously tufted with vegetation, as are many other buildings in this damp climate.

EXTERIOR. The ***W. Front,** or FACHADA DEL OBRADOIRO, by *Fernando Casas y Nóvoa* (1738–50), is a masterpiece of the Churrigueresque style, the overcharged detail being disguised by the great mass of the general plan. It is approached from the plaza by a quadruple flight of steps (1606) and flanked by two towers (70 m.).— Below the entrance is a Romanesque *Crypt* by *Mateo* (c. 1168–75).

The ***S. DOOR** (PTA. DE LAS PLATERIAS; 1104), facing the *Casa del Cabildo,* still displays some early work; the two outer doors have been concealed, one by the clock-tower (1676–80), the other by the E. wall of the cloister, which is surmounted by a delicate Renaissance balustrade. The huge corbel below the entrance on the l. is in the form of a cockle-shell. The marble outer shafts are carved with tiers of figures in niches and the jambs bear an inscription recording the erection.—At the E. end is the *Pta. Santa* (1611), opened only in jubilee years, approached through an outer doorway with figures from the original coro.—On the N. side is the *Pta. de la Azabachería* (jet-carvers), modernized by *Ventura Rodríguez* in 1765–70. We complete the circuit of the cathedral by a 12C vaulted passage beneath the *Archbishops' Palace,* see above.

The INTERIOR is 94 m. long, 60 m. across the transepts, 17.5 m. across the aisles, and 22 m. high. Immediately within the W. Front is the *Pórtico de la Gloria,* one of the most important works of sculpture surviving from the 12C and the masterpiece of *Mateo* (master of the works in 1168) whose kneeling figure is seen at the foot of the central shaft, which bears also the Tree of Jesse, and the figure of Santiago.

The credulous knock their heads against that of Mateo to obtain a share of his talents.—Over the main doorway is the Saviour in glory, encircled by elders with musical instruments. The side doors symbolize the Synagogue (l.) and the Heathen (r.) the arches are supported by the Apostles, etc. The columns rest on monsters. The carving is throughout admirable, and remarkable for the absence of the grotesque. The whole composition bears traces of polychrome painting of 1651.

Within the church the Romanesque work is striking in its plainness, with carving on the capitals only. The general lack of light is due to the absence of a clerestory, and the blocking-up of the S. windows. The triforium, with double-arched openings, is unusually deep and lofty. An octagonal cimborio (1384–1445), replaces the original lantern-tower. It is here that the *Botafumeiro,* the giant censer of 1602, is hung and swung. The *Cap. Mayor* has two bronze pulpits, the work of *J. B. Celma* (1578–84), and the **High Altar,** in the Churrigueresque style (1656–1703), bears a silver shrine (1715) with a seated *Statue of St James* (c. 1211), embellished with precious stones, and likened by Ford to 'a spider in the middle of its web, catching strange and foolish flies'.

Behind it is a stair ascended by the devout wishing to kiss the mantle of the figure, lit by a silver lamp, the gift of Gonzalo de Córdoba; while in a small crypt below are exposed the relics of Santiago and two of his disciples.—In the S. Transept, on the r. of the entrance to the cloister, is a 10C tympanum showing Santiago at the battle of Clavijo, the earliest representation of this subject.
The 18C organ has been gutted and contains an Italian electronic organ!

The SIDE CHAPELS were added mainly in the 16-17C and contain Baroque ornamentation. From the centre of the S. Aisle we enter an ante-room with entrances (l.) to the *Cap. de S. Fernando* (1521) and (r.) *de las Reliquias* (partially visible through a grille), in which are effigies of kings and queens, including Raymond of Burgundy (d. 1144; King of Galicia), Berenguela (d. 1149; wife of Alfonso VII), Fernando II (d. 1188), and Alfonso IX (d. 1230).

Among the treasures that adorn the modern retablo (replacing one destroyed by fire in 1921) are the Cross of Alfonso III (874), gold-plated and decorated with gems, a silver-gilt statue of Santiago (Parisian work of 1304); a silver head of 1322, said to contain the skull of St James the Less; the gold chalice of S. Rosendo (15C); and a remarkable Custodia by *Ant. de Arfe* (1539–46). On the wall)r.) are five English polychrome alabasters (1456).

Of the chapels opening off the ambulatory that of *S. Pedro* (r. of the Pta. Santa) has a reja of 1571–75, while that of *N.S. la Blanca,* on the l. of the E. Chapel, contains 13C tombs; in the *Cap. de S. Bartolomé* (on the N. side) is the Renaissance tomb of Canon Diego de Castilla (1521).

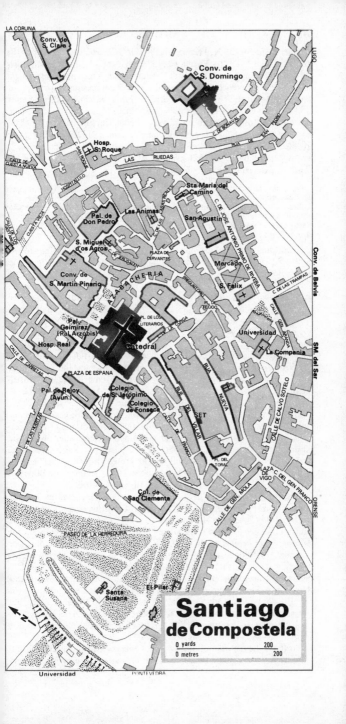

Santiago
de Compostela

| 0 yards | 200 |
| 0 metres | 200 |

On the E. side of the N. Transept is the *Cap. del Espíritu Santo,* with the tombs of Card. Pedro Varela (d. 1574; r.), Abp. Alonso de Moscoso (1383), and others of his family (l.). Adjacent steps mount to the *Cap. de la Corticela* entered by a finely sculptured Romanesque doorway and originally separate from the cathedral; within is the tomb of Card. Eanes (1342). The cruciform *Cap. del Cristo de Burgos* off the N. Aisle contains the tomb of its founder, Abp. Pedro Carrillo (d. 1667).—The *Sacristy,* off the S. Transept, by *Juan de Álava* (1527–38), has good furniture and plate. The late-Gothic **Cloister,** entered from the S. Transept, was begun in 1521 by *Juan de Álava* and finished in 1590 by *Rodr. Gil de Hontañón.*

On its W. side are the *Biblioteca,* and the *Sala Capitular,* containing a collection of Tapestries, mainly of the 17C, including Flemish pieces after Teniers and Rubens, and 19C Spanish tapestries from cartoons by Goya and Bayeu. Others are housed in a series of rooms on the upper floor. whence the *Torre de la Corona* (70 steps) may be ascended for the sake of the view. In the basement is a *Museo Arqueológico.*

From the Cathedral we may turn down any of the narrow flagstoned porticoed streets that surround it. To the N., opposite the Pta. de la Azabachería, the C. de Jerusalén leads N. to *S. Miguel d'os Agros Conv. de S. Martín Pinario,* the church of which, entered from the E., was designed before 1611 by *Gines Martínez,* but is badly damaged by damp. It contains a huge Churrigueresque retablo (1730–33) by *Casas y Nóvoa,* behind which is the coro, with stalls by *Mateo de Prado* (1639–47).—Further N. is the *Conv. de S. Francisco,* with remains of a 14C chapter-house. The church of 1742 has a monumental front of 1779–83.—Also in the northern quarter, once the *Judería* of Compostela, are the *Hospital de S. Roque* (1577; front of 1647) and, on the La Coruña road, the late-18C *Conv. de S. Clara,* with a remarkable 'Plattenstil' façade by *Simón Rodríguez,* and a Baroque altar-piece (1700) by *Dom. de Andrade* and carved stalls in the domed church.—In the N.W. quarter is the **Conv. de Sto Domingo** in which is an extraordinary staircase by *Andrade,* consisting of three separate spirals, each ascending to a different floor, but contained in the same tower. The Church has an apse of 1230, a 15C nave, a portal of 1667 by Andrade, and interesting tombs. The building at present houses collections of Galician ceramics, basket-work, and boats, etc.—In the C. de Boneval, just to the S., is a doorway of 1330, with a 13C Virgin.

Returning towards the centre by the C. de las Casas Reales, we pass (l.) *Sta María del Camino* (1770, with a 16C Gothic chapel) and reach the late 18C *Cap. de las Ánimas,* with a relief of Souls in Purgatory and (inside) life-size Passion scenes in coloured plaster by the local sculptor *Manuel de Prado y Mariño.*—From the Pl. de Cervantes, or Azabachería, the C. de Jerusalén leads N. to *S. Miguel d'os Agros* (1754), with a Gothic chapel, and curious carved angels in wood.— Nearby is the Gothic *Pal. de Don Pedro,* containing a small *Pilgrimage Museum.*—The Preguntoiro leads S. from the Pl. de Cervantes towards the Pl. de Feijóo and *S. Félix,* altered in the 17th and 18Cs, but preserving a 12C portal, tombs, and a silver-gilt Cross of c. 1400.—N. of the adjoining market place lies *S. Augustín,* by *González Araujo,* dating from 1633–48, with a cloister of 1618–23.

To the S. lie the old buildings of the *University,* founded in 1532, but rebuilt in 1769–1805 by *Melchor de Prado y Mariño.* The library contains 40 incunabula, an American collection, and the illuminated Book of Hours of Fernando I (1055). Just behind stands the church of *La Compañía* (1583–1673), with the tomb of its founder, Abp. Blanco (d. 1581) by *Mateo López*, and a retablo mayor by *S. Rodríguez*.

S.E. of the town just beyond the new by-pass, stands one of the most interesting buildings in Santiago after the Cathedral, the collegiate church of *Sta María de Sar. It is best approached (from the C. de Calvo Sotelo) by the C. de Sar. It is also advisable to check first at the Tourist Office for times of admission; the sacristan may be found in the house behind the church. This curious building of c.1133–70 is remarkable for the cant of its piers, probably caused by subsidence of the soil, although their inclination is so uniform that some have thought it intentional. The adjoining fragment of a beautifully sculptured *Cloister, the finest example of carving in Santiago after the Pórtico de la Gloria, contains tombs of priors (13-16C) and a granite font.

Also to the E. of the city is the *Conv. de Belvís*, originally built in 1305–13, but whose present church is a work of *Casas y Nóvoa* (1725–39).—S.W., in Baixo Sar, is *Sta María de Conjo*, preserving a Romanesque cloister; in its church (1609–71) are Churrigueresque retablos and a Christ by *Greg. Fernández*. *S. Lorenzo de Transouto*, further N., founded in 1217 and rebuilt c. 1700, contains interesting tombs.

To the E. of the Cathedral lies the *Pl. de los Literarios*, its side being taken up by the *Monasterio de S. Pelayo*, while to the S. stands the *Casa de los Canónigos*. Adjacent is the *Pl. de las Platerías*, with the *Casa del Cabildo* (by *Fernández Sarela*, 1747–58). Off this plaza leads the *Rúa del Villar*, one of the more picturesque streets, containing a number of old houses: No. 1, the *Casa del Dean* (1747–52) is also by *Sarela*. At its far end, in the Pl. del Toral, No. 2 is a late-18C mansion. We may return by the parallel *Rúa Nueva*, to the E., passing 12C *Sta María Salomé*, with a 15C front and a tower of 1701–43, or by the C. del Franco to the W.

Nearby is the animated Pta. Fajera and adjacent *Alameda*, from which we may follow the shady Paseo de Herradura ('horseshoe'), affording pleasant vistas. We pass, to the N., the classical front of the *Col. de S. Clemente*. From the Mirador, to the W., we have a good view below us of the new University quarter. On the summit of the hill stands 12C *Sta Susana*, from which we may regain the Alameda, passing (r.) *El Pilar*, of 1717–20.

Another panoramic view of Santiago may be enjoyed from the summit of *Monte Pedroso* (2155 ft, N.W.), on which is the *Ermita de S. Payo* (1260) with an early image of St Francis of Assisi.

42   THE RÍAS BAJAS

A. The N 550 runs S. FROM SANTIAGO TO TÚY (121 km.), passing through (20 km.) *Padrón*—(37 km.) **Pontevedra**—(20 km.) *Redondela*, where we diverge for (14 km.) **Vigo**, and regain the road 15 km. N. of Túy. By by-passing Vigo we may reduce the length of this route by 15 km. A motorway from just S. of Pontevedra now crosses the Ría de Vigo at its narrowest point, the only section at present (1979) completed between Santiago and Túy, which will eventually join up with the completed section between La Coruña and Santiago.

B. The C 543 leads S.W. from Santiago to *Noya*, where we meet the C 550, which closely follows the indented coastline. The length of this route is considerably greater than route A, but not every peninsula need be skirted. This coastal route may easily be shortened by driving direct from Santiago to (20 km.) *Padrón*—(34 km.) *Cambados*—(47 km.) **Pontevedra**—(20 km.) *Redondela*—(14 km.) **Vigo**—(21 km.) *Bayona*—(31 km.)*La Guardia*—(27 km.) **Túy** a total of 214 km. While various alternative routes may be taken, those described below are the direct road (A) and the coastal road (B).

A   FROM SANTIAGO TO PONTEVEDRA, VIGO AND TÚY

From Santiago we follow the N 550 S. past (14 km.) the Baroque pilgrimage church of *N.S. de la Esclavitud*, formerly a place of sanctuary for criminals; it contains a good retablo of 1688.—6 km. **Padrón,** (8300 inhab.) with an attractive alameda, was the Roman *Iria Flavia*, and the legendary landing-place of the body of Santiago (comp. p.394). The *Colegiata* has a nave of 1690–1714 and contains the tombs of 28 bishops. The *Casa del Obispo de Quito* (1666), by *Melchor de Velasco,* is notable among the old mansions. Padrón is the birthplace of the writer Camilo José Cela (1916-) and here also the poetess Rosalía de Castro (1837–85) lived and died.—We cross the Ulla to *Puentecesures* on a bridge built by Maestro *Mateo* of Compostela (d.1217) on foundations of the Roman *Pons Caesaris.*—18 km.   **Caldas de Reyes** (8900 inhab.) has a Romanesque church containing tombs of the Camoens family, and the old *Torre de Doña Urraca.*

21 km.   **PONTEVEDRA** (60,300 inhab.; 29,000 in 1920; *Parador Nac.; Hotels*) near the head of the lovely Ría de Pontevedra, is a granite town with arcaded streets and ancient houses bearing armorial shields. In the central Pl. de Orense is *S. Francisco,* begun c. 1274, with the tomb of its founder Gómez Charino (d. 1304), admiral and poet.—From the square the Pasantería descends to the Pl. de la Leña. Here, in a typical Gallego house of 1760 is the *Museum,* containing collections of ornaments from local churches and prints and documents illustrating Galician history.—To the N. are *S. Bartolomé* (Baroque; after 1686), with a Magdalen by *Greg. Fernández,* and, to the E., the *Conv. de Sta Clara* (Gothic).—Between the Pl. de Orense and the C. Michelena is the conspicuous round *Cap. de la Peregrina* (1778–92). In the Alameda, at the other end of the C. Michelena, are the *Ayuntamiento* and the ruins of the *Conv. de Sto Domingo* (c. 1331–83) consisting mainly of the E. end of the church with five polygonal apses containing old stone crosses, etc. To the r., beyond the Alameda, is 16C *Sta María la Mayor* with a front of c. 1545–59 by *Cornelis de Holanda,* and a carved interior W. Doorway.

From Pontevedra to *La Cañiza,* see p.380; to *Orense,* p.405.

At 6 km., a road (r.) leads 8 km. to a Mirador offering panoramic views.—At 5 km. we cross the Oitaven at *Puente Sampayo,* W. of the Roman Bridge. 1 km. beyond, a road leads 3 km. E. to the 15C castle of *Sotomayor.*—We skirt the head of the Ría de Vigo before entering (9 km.) **Redondela** (25,000 inhab.), with a Gothic parish church, while the *Conv. de S. Lorenzo Justiniano* dates from 1501. The N 550 continues S. to (28 km.) *Túy* (see below), but we diverge S.W.

14 km.   **VIGO** (233,300 inhab.; 53,000 in 1920; 199,000 in 1970; *Hotels*), one of the most important ports on the Spanish coast, is a lively modern town attractively situated on the S. shore of its deep land-locked ría. Protected from the full force of the Atlantic by the Cies islands, and

surrounded on the landward side by hills, it looks across the ría to the mountains above Cangas. Its quays are busy with factories engaged in curing and preserving fish. As a commercial and industrial centre it has grown rapidly in recent years, and has pretensions to replace Pontevedra as the provincial capital.

Regular FERRIES to Cangas, Moana, San Adrián and Domayo. The *Airport* lies 9 km. E.

History. Vigo has always been famous as a harbour of refuge and was known to the Romans as *Vicus Spacorum;* as a bathing resort it can boast probably the first record in Europe—in a song by the early Galician 'joglar', Martin Codax (early 13C). In 1585 and 1589 Sir Francis Drake raided the harbour, and in Oct, 1702 the Duke of Ormonde, Stanhope, and Rooke attacked the French and Spanish treasure-fleet, just returned from the River Plate. Eleven ships were captured and most of the rest sunk in the harbour, although the Comte de Château-Renaud escaped with some French vessels during the action. Various abortive attempts have been made to salve the sunken bullion. The port was again attacked by the English in 1719 under Lord Cobham, when the licentious sailors wantonly plundered and set fire to the town.

Vigo is visited less for its own interest than for the beauty of the surrounding country. From the landing-stage the C. del Carral ascends to the Pta. del Sol (or Pl. Capitán Carrero), where the two principal streets of the town meet, the C. del Principe being a favourite promenade of the Vigueses. The Parish Church of *Sta María*, a short distance N., is a neoclassical work by *Prado Marino* (1814–16). Lower down is the old town, a network of steep narrow lanes with 16–18C granite houses, some tarred on the windward side to resist the damp. Below, near the *Dársena del Berbés,* the fishing harbour, are a few old arcaded houses. Between it and the landing-stage is the *Mercado de la Lage,* where the fish are sold.—It is worth while for the sake of the *View to climb to the *Castillo del Castro* (453 ft), dominating the town.

The Parque de Quiñones de León (or Castrelos), to the S.W., contains the *Museo*, with a good local collection, installed in a *pazo* of 1670, a little to the E. of which is the *Pal. de Sto Tomé.*

From the Pl. de España, S. of the town, the Av. de Madrid joins the N 120, which climbs down to crossroads at (15 km.) *Porrino,* 14 km. S. of Redondela. Orense lies 90 km. to the E. At Porrino we turn r. for Túy, 15 km. S.

TÚY (*Parador Nac,* 1 km. S.) a frontier town (14,100 inhab.) guarding the passage of the Miño opposite *Valença* (Spanish Customs at the border), occupies a pleasant site above the mouth of the fertile valley of Louro.

Túy, once known as *Tude,* is of unknown antiquity. It was selected by the Gothic king Witiza as his capital c. 700, and was held by the Moors in 716-40, but the present town occupies a new site chosen by Fernando II in 1170. It suffered severely from earthquakes in the 16th and 18C, and in 1809 witnessed the repulse of Soult's attempt to cross the Miño by the Portuguese garrison of Valença. Bp Lucas (c. 1160–1249) the credulous historian, was perhaps the most famous incumbent of the See (from 1239).

The fortress-like *Cathedral,* undergoing restoration, was begun c. 1180, but the only 12C work remaining is the N. Tower and doorway and the lower part of the chancel and transepts. The capitals in the S. Transept are curiously carved. The *nave* (1218–39) is French in style; the W. Doorway is of 1225–87; but the upper part of the choir and the W. Front were not completed until the 15C, although in characteristic Galician fashion their style appears some 200 years older.

The INTERIOR, with Renaissance rejas, is heavily braced as a precaution against earthquakes. The sillería in the coro is boldly carved.

To the E. of the S. Transept is the chapel of *S. Telmo* (the Blessed Pedro González, d. 1240), the patron of the cathedral and of Spanish mariners, and the British sailors' 'St Elmo', whose fire-balls clinging to the yards have always been regarded as a favourable omen. The kneeling figure in the chapel is that of the founder, Bp. Diego de Torquemada (1579). Nearby is the grave of Bp. Lucas. The huge organ case is empty. The *Cloister*, to the S. (1264, altered 1408–65), has been marred by the addition of an upper storey..

At the E. end of the Alameda stands *Sto Domingo* (1330–1415), with a good 14C E. end, two interesting tombs in the N. Transept, and reliefs in the cloister. The platform behind commands a charming view across the Miño. *S. Bartolome* is Romanesque; neoclassical *S. Francisco* preserves remains of its Gothic predecessor; while the *Cap. de S. Pedro Telmo* is an interesting specimen of the 18C Portuguese style.

Valença, a picturesque fortified town on the Portugese bank of the Miño, may be approached by the two-storeyed *Pte. International* (1885; 333 m. long), built by the French engineer *Eiffel*, and should be visited for the fine views of Túy obtained from its commanding height. See the *Blue Guide to Portugal*, forthcoming.

Oporto lies 124 km. beyond. From Túy to *Orense*, see Rte 36B; *La Guardia* lies 27 km. S.W., see p.403.

B   THE COASTAL ROUTE.

From Santiago to (36 km.) *Noya*, see p.378; and from thence to *Muros, Corcubió*, and *Finisterre*, in reverse.

From Noya we follow the S. shore of the Ría de Muros y de Noya parallel to the Sierra de Barbanza, to (36 km.) *Santa Eugenia de Ribeira*, the most westerly town on the Ría de Arosa, the entrance to which is guarded by the *Isla de Sálvora*. We follow the road N.E., enjoying fine views (r.) across the ria towards Cambados and Villagarcia, and at 40 km. enter **Padrón**, see p.400. Crossing the Ulla, we turn seaward again through eucalyptus and pine woods to (22 km.) **Villagarcia** (29,300 inhab.). A good view of the ría may be obtained from the top of *Mte. Lobeira*, 4 km. S. We pass (r.) **Villanueva de Arosa** (14,200 inhab.), birthplace of Ramón María del Valle-Inclán (1866–1936), poet and playwright, and with a view of the *Isla de Arosa*, before entering (12 km.) **Cambados** (11,800 inhab.; *Parador Nac.*) with the galleried *Pal. de Fefiñanes* and picturesque ruined church of *Sta Marina*.—*Armenteira*, 10 km. S.E. has a restored Romanesque abbey (1164–81) with an 18C cloister.—The road now circles round the peninsula of EL GROVE, at the neck of which (17 km.) a road leads r. for 7 km. to **La Toja**, a fashionable resort (*Hotels*) with thermal springs known to the Romans. Driving S. from the peninsula, we see to the W. the *Isla de Ons*, and to the N.W., the *Isla de Sálvora* and numerous smaller islets and rocks scattered across the entrance of the Ría de Arosa. We shortly pass the resort of *Sangenjo*, and (19 km. r.) picturesque but unkempt **Cambarro**, a typical old Galician fishing village. At 2 km. l., lies *Poyo*, with a monastery and Neo-classical church.

9 km. **Pontevedra** (p.400), bearing S.W. from which we skirt the N. coast of the Morrazo peninsula through (8 km.) **Marin**, (20,900 inhab.) with a harbour and naval training college; (12 km.) *Bueu*, with a small nautical museum, and (11 km.) *Hío*, with a Romanesque church. From 3 km. *Cangas*, with a church of 1542, and a view across to Vigo, we

follow the N. bank of the ría, spanned by a new bridge, which we may cross to avoid circling the head of the ría viâ *Redondela.*

c. 22 km. **Vigo** (p.400), S.W. of which we have a near view of the *Islas Cies,* and at 14 km. pass (r.) *Mte. Ferro* jutting into the Atlantic to the N. of the extensive *Playa de América.*—7 km. **Bayona,** an attractive resort (9000 inhab.) with an interesting 12C church, and on a fortified wooded promontory, the *Castillo de Monte Real,* converted into the *Parador Nac..* The road now skirts the rock-bound coast to (19 km.) *Oya,* with a ruinous monastery and Trans. Church (c. 1246) with a font of 1740 and a 16C cloister.—12 km. **La Guardia** (9200 inhab.), at the foot of pine-clad *Mte. Tecla,* crowned with ruins of a pre-Roman town (and with an Archaeological Museum). From its summit we have a good *View along the coast and across the mouth of the Miño, on the opposite bank of which lies the Portuguese town of *Caminha.* Turning N.E., we drive through woods, and parallel to the river, to (27 km.) *Túy,* see p.401.

43   FROM ZAMORA TO ORENSE AND SANTIAGO

Total distance, 385 km. (239 miles). N 630 for 21 km., then N 525. 89 km. *Puebla de Sanabria*—91 km. *Verin*—71 km. **Orense**—30 km. *Lalin*—83 km. **Santiago.**

From Zamora we drive N. on the León road (N 630) across desolate country, at 21 km. bearing l. onto the N 525. The N 630 continues N. to *Benavente,* 43 km. beyond, see p.371, passing near the deserted medieval fortress (l.) of *Castrotorafe* (1175), with a 14-15C castle at its N.W. corner. On a parallel road to the W., 9 km. from Zamora, lies *La Hiniesta,* where the early 14C church has an immense vaulted porch.

We cross the Embalse del Rio Esla near the ruins of the 13C *Pte. de la Estrella* and enter (22 km.) *Tábara,* where the church of 1132–37 has a fine tower and a rebuilt sanctuary (1761), before bearing N.W. over a shoulder of the viper-infested Sierra de Culebra (3600–4200 ft) by the Portillo de Sazadón (2608 ft).—At 11 km. a road leads 16 km. N. to Romanesque *Sta Marta de Tera,* with notable sculpture (c. 1150), on the C 620 from Benavente, which joins our road after 15 km.—5 km. *Mombuey,* with a 13C church tower and spire. At 17 km. we meet the C 622 from León and La Bañeza before bypassing (10 km.) **Puebla de Sanabria** (1800 inhab; *Albergue Nac.),* with a castle, a good church, and galleried *Ayuntamiento,* on a hill above the modern village.

The Lago de Villachica, 13 km. N.W., is a small deep lake with sulphur springs, the largest of several tarns on the S. slopes of the roadless Sierra de Cabrera (6710 ft). At *S. Martin de Castañeda,* N. of the lake, is a large triple-apsed Romanesque Church of c. 1150 with a W. façade of 1571, a relic of a Benedictine monastery of 916.—18 km. from Puebla de Sanabria, and W. of the lake, lies *Ribadelago,* approached by a road skirting its S. shore.—The N 622 leads 22 km. S.W. from Pueblo de Sanabria to the Portuguese frontier (Customs post) and 20 km. beyond, to *Braugança;* see the *Blue Guide to Portugal,* forthcoming.

The N 525 now runs parallel to the border, climbs to the Portilla del Padornelo (4462 ft) and shortly enters Galicia. The road from this point to Verín, although very considerably improved, is still winding and undulating.—43 km. (l.) *Pereiro,* with an important Romanesque church, 9 km. beyond which, at *La Gudina,* we meet the cross-country

C 533 from Ponferrada, see Rte 36B. Hence we bear S.W. through the hills to (39 km.) **Verín** (9500 inhab.; *Parador Nac.; Hotels*) on the Támega. The town is overlooked from the N. by the fortified village and *Castle of Monterrey,* with its 13C church. The portal and other details are finely sculpted. A panoramic View may be had from the citadel and from the adjacent hill, on which stands the *Parador.*—At *Mijós,* c. 4 km. N. of Verín, is a 9C church containing mural paintings.

From Verin the C532 leads 15 km. S. to the frontier (Customs post), and 12 km. beyond, to *Chaves;* see *Blue Guide to Portugal,* forthcoming.

The N 525 now commences a long ascent before crossing the Pto. Estivadas and climbing down to (33 km.) *Ginzo de Limia* (10,200 inhab.) at the S. end of the Laguna de Antela.

From Ginzo de Limia to La Cañiza (67 km.). The C 531 winds 27 km. N.W. to **Celanova** (8450 inhab.), itself an interesting old town—see the C. de Abajo—the centre of a rich agricultural region and the birthplace of the Galician poet Manuel Curro Enríques (1851–1908). The huge Benedictine *Conv. de S. Salvador* (now a college) presents a Baroque front to the characteristic *Pl. Mayor.*
The *church* (1678-81) contains a splendid retablo, late-Gothic choir stalls, and 11C tombs, while of the two cloisters the larger was begun in 1550 and finished in the 18C; the other (1611–1722) has a balcony or *'paleiro';* behind, in the garden is the Mozarabic chapel of *S. Miguel* of c. 940–70.—There are Romanesque churches at *S. Munio de la Veiga,* to the S.E., and at *Paizás,* N.W., while *Villanueva de los Infantes,* on the Orense road, has an old tower and the Baroque sanctuary of the *Virgen del Cristal.* Some 4 km. from Celanova is the Celtic fort of *Castromau.*
From Celanova the poor cross-road (N 540) from Orense (26 km. N.) towards Portugal, passes through wild country to (16 km. S.) **Bande** and the little spa of *Baños de Bande,* ancient *Aquis Querpuenis,* on the W. bank of the Embalse de las Conchas. Some 10 km. beyond is **Sta Comba,* a remarkable Visigothic church on the Greek-cross plan, with a square sanctuary built c. 700 to house the strine of *S. Torquato,* and restored c. 872. The road follows the Limia valley to (13 km.) *Lovios,* some 10 km. beyond which is the Portuguese frontier.

The C 531 leads N.W. from Celanova through *Milmanda,* with an ancient bridge, ruined castle, and the church of *Sta María de Alázar,* beyond which we continue across country, bridging the Miño at *Cortegada,* to meet the N 120 at (40 km.) *La Cañiza,* see Rte 36B.

Beyond (6 km.) *Sandianes,* with a ruined castle, we bypass (12 km. l.) **Allariz** (8300 inhab.), with the 12C church of *Santiago* and 18C *Conv. de Sta Clara,* containing tombs of the children of Alfonso X. There are old churches at *San Martiño de Pazó* (10C, restored) to the W., and 7 km. E. at *Junquera de Ambia* (1164) with Renaissance stalls and a 16C cloister.—At 7 km. a road leads 3 km. E. to the Trans. church of *Sta Marina de Aguas Santas.*

13 km. **ORENSE** (80,200 inhab.; 18,000 in 1920; 55,000 in 1950; *Hotels*), an ancient town and modern provincial capital, with an early Gothic Cathedral and a medieval bridge, stands above the W. bank of the Miño in a basin surrounded by vine-clad hills.

History. Orense, taking its name from its hot springs, the Roman *Aquae Urentes,* was the capital of the Suevi in the 6-7C, and the scene of their first conversion to Christianity. In 716 it was destroyed by the Moors but was rebuilt by Alfonso III, c.900. John of Gaunt held his court here during the few months of his 'reign' as king of Castile in 1386–87. In May 1809 it was the starting-point of Soult's advance into Portugal after the embarkation of Moore's column, and a few months later it saw his army in retreat, shattered by Wellington at Oporto. Orense was the birthplace of the Benedictine reformer, Benito Jerónimo Feijóo (1676–1764).

A by-pass has been constructed, which crosses the Miño downstream from the old bridge, while the N 525 enters the town by the Av. del Generalísimo, from which the Av. de Pontevedra leads to the *Pl. Mayor* (see below) and continues downhill past (l.) the pilgrimage chapel of *N.S. de los Remedios* (1522, rebuilt 1584), containing a remarkable series of ex voto tablets. Beyond is the beautiful seven-arched *Bridge*, standing 40 m. above the normal level of the Miño, with a central span of 45 m. built by Bp. Lorenzo in 1230.

To the N.E. of the arcaded Pl. Mayor stands the *Cathedral*. Founded in 572, it was rebuilt in 1132–94, and again, in its present form, in 1218–48, by Bps. Seguino and Lorenzo. The façade, once covered with elaborate 13C decoration, was badly restored in the 16–17C; the *Portal* beneath the narthex, called *El Paraiso*, imitated from the Pórtico de la Gloria at Santiago, preserves some of its original painted ornament. On the l. is a crude fresco of *Cristóbalon,* or St. Christopher. The long nave and aisles are 13C work, and the transeptal doorways are boldly sculptured. The transepts, chancel, and ambulatory (1620) were rebuilt on a 12C foundation, and the cimborio, by *Rodrigo de Badajoz,* was built in 1499–1505. In the arched recesses round the walls are numerous tombs. There is good wood-carving in the chapels, and the *Coro* has a Plateresque reja and carved stalls (1587–90). In the *Cap. Mayor,* with another good reja, is a retablo by *Cornelis de Holanda* with a figure of S. Martín, and at the sides are reliefs of the martyrdom of Sta Euphemia (S.) and SS. Facundus and Primitivus (N.), marking the site of their graves. In the N. Aisle is the chapel of *S. Juan Bautista,* built in 1468 by the Conde de Benavente in recompense for damage wrought in the cathedral during the feud between his house and the Condes de Lemos. Its window tracery shows English influence, and it contains the tomb of Card. Quevedo y Quintana (d. 1586), with a statue by *Solá*. The *Cap. del Cristo Crucificado* (1567), E. of the N. Transept, contains a Crucifix, resembling the Cristo de Burgos, brought from a church at Finisterre in 1330; the silver Altarpiece is of Churrigueresque design. Opening off the S. Aisle is a fragment of a 13C *Cloister,* now used as a vestry.

The *Sacristy* contains a copy of the Monterrey missal (1494), the first book printed in Galicia, Limoges enamels, a processional cross attr. to *Enrique de Arfe,* spoilt by regilding and the addition of some coarse gems, and early 18C silver altar frontals by *Pedro Garrido*.

To the S., adjoining the old *Bishop's Palace,* containing the provincial *Archaeological Museum,* is ancient *Sta María la Madre,* restored in the 18C, with a 17C high altar by *Moure* and interesting sculptures. Further S. is *La Trinidad,* with a curious 16C towered front.

Above the cathedral to the E. stands the *Conv. de S. Francisco,* now barracks; permission should be asked to view the attractive *Cloister* (1311–32), whose 60 arches are supported by coupled columns with capitals sculptured with foliage and figures.

The church, with Gothic and Renaissance tombs in its triple apse, was rebuilt on a new site further N., in 1928.—*Loiro,* 10 km. S. along the N 540, has a Romanesque church.

For Orense to *Vigo* and *Túy,* see Rte 36B.

From Orense there are two routes N.W. to *Santiago.* An alternative road (N 541) to the N 525 viâ *Lalin* (see below) forks r. off the N 120 13 km. W. of Orense to (14 km.) *Carballino* (*Hotel*) At (3 km. l.) *Moldes,* and at *Boboras,* 2 km. beyond, are 12C Templars' churches. We cross the Sierra de Montes and at 17 km. fork r. the l. fork leads to *Pontevedra*, 43 km. to the S.W., passing after 8 km., *Cerdedo* with a Baroque church.—At 6 km. a road leads r. 7 km. to *Acebeiro*, with ruins of a Cistercian monastery founded in 1170.—Passing through (28 km.) **La Estrada** (29,600 inhab.), in the centre of a fertile countryside set with charming Baroque country houses or '*Pazos*', we cross the Ulla at *Puentevea*, and at 18 km. ente *Santiago*, see Rte 41.

The main road from Orense (N 525) climbs above the Miño valley to (11 km.) *Cambeo*, where the N 540 bears r. to *Chantada* (p.379) and *Lugo*, 95 km. to the N.— At 13 km. a road leads r. 9 km. up an umbrageous valley to the Cistercian monastery of *Osera. Founded in 1135 and finished in 1239, it was largely rebuilt after a fire in 1552, but the church retains Romanesque and Gothic features and the main cloister is 15C. After Baroque additions Osera became known as 'the Escorial of Galicia'-

The main façade of the monastery, with its four Salominic columns and statue of St Bernard kneeling before the Virgin, dates from 1708, at right-angles to which i that of the Church (1637), flanked by its two towers. There are three cloisters, tha 'de los medallones' reconstructed in 1553; the Gothic 'Patio de los pináculos'; and that 'de los Caballeros' (17C). Between the former two the imposing monumenta staircase (1644–47) ascends to the upper floor, off which are the kitchens and refectory; it also provides access to the *Library* (1776), retaining some of it original walnut cases. The *Church*, off which opens the low vaulted *Sacristy*, wa consecrated in 1239; the *Chapter-house*, with 'palm-vaulting' rising from twisted columns, is 14C; the *Choir* was added in 1675. The crossing and ambulatory approached through two Baroque retablos, received polychrome decoration in the early 17C. Off the N. transept is the 12C chapel of S. Andrés. Note also the painted altars in other chapels. The work of restoration continues.

On regaining the Santiago road, we cross the Alto de Sto Domingo (views) and descend to (33 km.) **Lalin** (20,500 inhab.; *Hotel*), the centre of the region of Deza.—14 km. *Silleda*, some 7 km. N. of which (sign-posted), in a bend of the Deza, stands the picturesque ruins of the monastery of *S. Lorenzo de Caboei:a, with a Romanesque church of 1171–92.—We may regain the main road at *Bandeira.*—At 18 km., 1 km. to the l. is the *Pazo de Oca*, with attractive formal gardens and moss-covered water-tanks.—Crossing the Ulla, we shortly pass (r.) the *Pico Sacro* (2250 ft;), the summit of which, with the 11C cave-chapel of *S. Sebastián*, commands a view of **Santiago**, which we enter at 24 km.; see Rte 41.

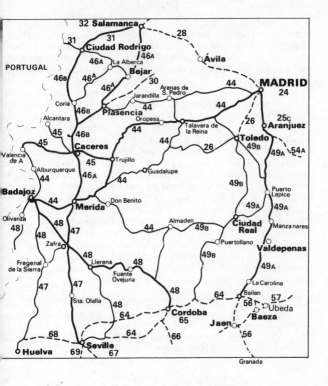

V   NEW CASTILE AND ESTREMADURA

New Castile (*Castilla la Nueva*) includes the modern provinces of *Madrid, Guadalajara, Toledo, Cuenca,* and *Ciudad Real.* Apart from its famous towns, it is, to the ordinary eye, perhaps the bleakest and least beautiful of Spanish provinces, although its desolate, sun-scorched and wind-swept plateaux, almost treeless and almost rainless, have an attraction of their own. Its most characteristic region is that of *La Mancha,* the home of Don Quixote and the scene of many of his adventures. On the N. and E. New Castile is separated from Old Castile and Aragón by the Sierras of Gredos, and Guadarrama, and the Montes Universales, and in its more scenically attractive uplands rise the Tagus and Guadiana, which flow through Estremadura to Portugal. The swamps which once bordered the sluggish Guadiana have recently given place to projects of reclamation associated with the 'Badajoz Plan' (see below). The soil is naturally fertile and responds to irrigation, but wide regions are deserted or used mainly for pasture. The Castiles owe their name to the many castles *(castillos)* erected against the Moors, and the name of *New* Castile recalls that it was the first of the Moorish territories to be annexed to the Castilian kingdom, after the reconquest of Toledo in 1085.

407

Estremadura, or *Extremadura*, extending from New Castile to the Portuguese frontier, embraces the provinces of *Cáceres* and, to the S., *Badajoz*, which represent respectively the old districts of ALTA EXTREMADURA, the basin of the Tagus, and BAJA EXTREMADURA, the basin of the Guadiana. For centuries it was a 'no man's land', between the Christians of León and the Andalucian Moors. The soil is not infertile, but the climate is subject to severe droughts. Agriculture, for long at a low ebb, has been stimulated to a limited extent in recent years, especially by widespread irrigation, the construction of reservoirs and hydro-electric stations, and schemes of afforestation. Based on the natural resources of the Guadiana valley, these works are known generally as the 'Badajoz Plan'. Characteristic features in the landscape are the extensive heaths of gum-cistus. Sheep-farming is still important although the annual migration of large flocks from their winter quarters in the lower districts to the more mountainous regions in this and the neighbouring provinces has largely died out. Almost as important are the herds of swine which find their food in the oak, chestnut, and beech forests. Hernán Cortés (d. 1547), conqueror of Mexico, and Francisco Pizarro (d. 1541), the conqueror of Peru, among many other *conquistadores*, were both 'Extremeños', and their fame encouraged the emigration of the more ambitious inhabitants from a province whose position was too remote to command any direct advantage from the wealth of the Americas.

With the exception of the province of Madrid—and not including the capital itself—the population of every province of New Castile and Estremadura has decreased during the last 25 years. Again (not including the province of Madrid), the total *depopulation* of this huge area during the last 25 years is now 625,000, and the population now amounts to mere 2,400,000, 40,000 *less* than it was in 1920.

44   FROM MADRID TO TRUJILLO, MÉRIDA AND BADAJOZ

Total distance, 400 km. (248 miles) 114 km. **Talavera**—32 km. *Oropesa* (for *Guadalupe*)—32 km. *Navalmoral* (for *Yuste*)—70 km. **Trujillo**—90 km. **Mérida**—62 km. **Badajoz.**

We drive S.W. on the N V.

FROM MADRID TO ARENAS DE SAN PEDRO (138 km.). At 15 km., the C 501, now much improved, forks r. off the NV towards the Sierra de Gredos.—9 km *Villaviciosa de Ordón*, with a castle of the Counts of Chinchón, where Fernando VI (d. 1759) passed the last melancholy years of his life.—9 km. r. *Brunete*, rebuilt since the battle of 1937, when the poet Julian Bell (driving an ambulance) was killed at the adjacent village of *Villanueva de la Cañada*.—18 km. *Chapinera*, with a church built with the surplus material of the Escorial, and a bishop's palace.—17 km. S.W. lies *Villa del Prado*, with a 15C church.—Beyond (3 km.) *Navas de Rey* the road climbs and then descends into the valley of Alberche and (r.) the Embalse de S. Juan.—9 km. *Pelayos*, with (r.) ruins of a Cistercian abbey, with remains of 12C work, 15C cloisters, and a 16C church.—13 km. S.W. lies *Cadalso de los Vidrios*, with the *Pal. de Villena* (16-18C).

At 5 km. we by-pass **San Martin de Valdeiglesias** (4600 inhab.) beneath the E spur of the SIERRA DE GREDOS (5250 ft), retaining a few old houses, an unfinished church by *Herrera*, and the restored castle of Alvaro de Luna. Regrettably this and other villages on this road, are being rapidly spoilt by the erection of weekend 'chalets'. Just beyond we meet the crossroad (N 403) from Ávila (59 km. N.W.) to Toledo.

We continue to follow the C 501, passing (r.) the 14C monastery of *Guisando*, where in 1468 the Castilian nobles proclaimed Isabel the Catholic queen. Close by stand some of the famous prehistoric stone-hewn animals known as the '*Toros de Guisando*'.—beyond (17 km.) *Sotillo de la Adrada* (*Hotel*), where the C 503 leads 44 km. S.W. to Talavera, we descend the Tiétar valley, passing the castle of *La Adrada*, to (10 km.) *Piedralves*, a summer resort (*Hotel*) amid pine woods, with good fishing. The road skirts the S. flank of the Gredos range to meet the C 502 from Ávila to Talavera at 38 km.—5 km. N.W. lies *Arenas de San Pedro* see p.411.

19 km. from Madrid the N V by-passes what now is the ugly dormitory town of *Móstoles*, the alcalde of which (Andrés Torrejón) was supposedly the first in Spain to proclaim war against Napoleon in 1808.—At 5 km. a road leads S. for 5 km. to *Arroyomolinos*, where the 15C ruined castle has a Mudéjar keep.—Beyond (7 km.) **Navalcarnero,** (7100 inhab; also by-passed), where Philip IV married Anne of Austria in 1649, in the interesting church containing a silver altar frontal, we pass through dull rolling country providing views of the Sierra de Gredos to the N.W.—15 km. S.E. of Navalcarnero lies the castle of *Batres.*—We meet the Ávila-Toledo road at (41 km.) **Maqueda** (*Hotel*) whose castle has a Mudéjar archway and battlements of Moorish tiles; *Sta Mariá* has a Mudéjar apse.

At 36 km. we cross the Alberche. To the N. lies the *battlefield of Talavera* (July 28th 1809), scene of the defeat of the French under Victor and Jourdan by Sir Arthur Wellesley (created Viscount Wellington in recognition of this success), aided intermittently by Cuesta's Spaniards, who pillaged the baggage of their allies before making a precipitate retreat. The town fell to Nationalist forces advancing from Mérida, on 3 Sept. 1936.

8 km. **TALAVERA DE LA REINA** (56,000 inhab.; 22,500 in 1950; *Hotels*), the ancient *Talabriga*, is a rapidly-growing dusty town long famous for its porcelain, but not as 'full of nice bits for the sketch book' as it was in Ford's time. Juan de Mariana (1536–1624), the historian, was born here. The 15C Bridge over the Tagus built by Card, Mendoza, is now in ruins. By the Madrid road is the high-domed *Ermita del Prado*, with attractive azulejo decoration in the entrance porch and inside. In the adjacent Plaza de Toros was killed the famous bullfighter Joselito (1920). In the arcaded Pl. Mayor is the *Arco de S. Pedro*, a Roman gateway, and among the houses rise the *Torres Albarranas*, relics of the 10C Moorish wall. Near the river is derelict *S. Mariá* (1400), with a rose window of 1470, and the *Conv. de S. Jerónimo* (1369, altered in the 16-17C). Also of interest are the conv.-churches of *S. Francisco*, with a Mudéjar tower, and *Sto Domingo*, with Renaissance tombs of the Loaisa family. *S. Salvador* is Romanesque, while late-Gothic *Santiago*, to the N., has a good W. Doorway (c. 1400). At the W. end of the town is a *Museo de Cerámica* in the *Fábrica del Carmen*.

FROM TALAVERA TO GUADALUPE (105 km.). The direct road (C 503) crosses the Tagus by the new bridge and climbs into a range of hills to the S.—At 47 km., *La Nava de Rico-Malillo*, we join the C 401 from Toledo.

The C 503 continues S. across the Pto. del Rey (2018 ft), skirts the W. bank and crosses the Embalse Garcia de Sola near *Castilblanco*, where on the last day of 1931 the detested Civil Guard were murdered by the villagers when attempting to prevent the holding of a Socialist meeting, which gained the place some notoriety, At 72 km. we enter *Herrera del Duque*, with a castle and fortified church.

We turn S.W. across the Sierra de Altamira, and at 22 km., just below the Pto. de S. Vicente (2648 ft), meet the road from Oropesa and El Puente de Arzobispo, see below. At the pass, with extensive views to the S. over thickly-wooded lower ranges, the winding road enters Estremadura and continues to zigzag through the foothills of the Sierra de Palomera.

36 km. **GUADALUPE** (3000 inhab.; *Parador Nac.*; *Hostal* in the monastery precincts), superbly sited, retains attractive arcaded cobbled streets but is spoilt by the traffic of the religious souvenir industry.

The town is dominated by the celebrated fortified Hieronymite *Monastery, founded in 1340 on Oct 29th, the date of the Battle of Salado, to house an ancient image of the Virgin. It was sacked by the French in 1809, and abandoned in 1835, but since 1908 has been occupied by Franciscans. Opposite the *Parador*, with a Mudéjar cloister, stands the *New Church* (1730), under restoration. To the W., facing the picturesque *Pl. Mayor*, is the richly decorated façade of the old *Church* (open all day) of 1389–1412, built by *Juan Alfonso*, whose monumental tablet (an azulejo) is on the l. pillar of the entrance. Steps ascend to the doors, plated with bronze, which were new in 1433. Entering the nave under a wide arch, we see (r.) a magnificent wrought-iron Reja of 1510–14 by *Fray Fr. de Salamanca*; the crestings over the screens of the aisles survive from the 15C. The *Cap. Mayor*, ornamented with 17C marbles by *J. B. Semeria*, a Genoese, and *Bartolomé Abril*, a Swiss (both brothers of the community), has a classical retablo by *Juan Gómez de Mora*, with statues by *Giraldo de Merlo* and paintings by *Vic. Carducho* and *Eugenio Cajés* (1615–18). Above the high altar the image of N.S. de Guadalupe may be seen enthroned (but see Camarín, below). The *Cap. de Sta Catalina* contains the tombs of Prince Denis of Portugal and his wife Joana (1461), and the *Cap. de Sta Ana*, beside the entrance-vestibule, contains the monument of Alonso de Velasco by *Anequín de Egas*. Behind a reja W. of the entrance is a bronze *Font* of 1402 by *Juan Francés*.

Adjacent to the church entrance is that to the *Monastery*. One is obliged to follow a perfunctory 'guided' tour; but *take your time*. we first visit the Mudéjar **Cloister** (1402–12) of two storeys entirely of brick with horseshoe arches, in the centre of which is a fountain surmounted by a pavilion known as the *Glorieta* or *Templete*, of 1405, capped with an octagonal spire, rising in three diminishing stages, each with gables, blind-arcaded, and with a ground-work of green and white tiles. Here also is the tomb of Bp. Illescas of Córdoba, by *Anequín de Egas* (1458) and in the S.W. corner, a 15C polychrome Calvary. Adjoining is the *Old Refectory*, containing a *Needlework Museum*. Among the sumptuous 14–17C vestments and altar-frontals, etc., that of Enrique II (No. 61) is outstanding. Hence we are conducted to the *Chapter House*, with a 16C arabesqued ceiling, accommodating a collection of 86 choir-books, some with fine miniatures, missals, and bindings, and a 15C alabaster Virgin. Among the paintings, many deteriorated, are the following attributions: a triptych by *Isambrandt*, a Baptism by *Juan de Flandés*, a Nativity by *Juan Correa*, and a small painting by *Goya*. We next enter the raised *Coro* of the church, with Churrigueresque Stalls (1742–44) by *Alejandro Carnicero*, a 14C wooden Candelabrum, and remarkable organ-cases.

Passing through the *Antesacristia*, r. of the high altar, we enter the lavishly decorated ***Sacristia** (begun 1638), which contains— unfortunately badly lit—eight paintings (1638–47) by *Zurbarán*, some illustrating the life of St Jerome; others being portraits of monks of the Order. In Widdrington's opinion, these paintings, 'untouched and uninjured' should have been moved to the Prado before they suffered the same fate as had the library, and where they might be *seen* to better advantage; never less, it is remarkable to see such masterpieces still in the position designed for them. That of Fray Gonzalo de Illescas seated at a table, is outstanding. The windows and pictures are identical in size and are identically framed, and both wardrobes and mirrors form part of the design. In the adjacent chapel are further paintings, including *Zurbarán's* Apotheosis of St Jerome, and a Temptation of the saint of the school of Zurbarán (and also attr. to Ribera). Note the similarity of the temptresses to the richly-clothed saints in the Seville Museum. A Turkish ship's lantern captured at Lepanto also hangs here. From the adjoining *Cap. de Sta Catalina* we enter the octagonal *Relicario* (1595; by·*Nic. de Vergara the Younger*) in which the engraved silver-gilt box by *Juan de Segovia* (mid-15C) with earlier enamels, is the most interesting object.

Red jasper stairs ascend to the *Joyero* of 1651, containing an ivory crucifix which belonged to Philip II, a Christ by *Morales*, paintings by *Luca Giordano*, and eight polychrome biblical figures by *Luisa Roldán*, including an enchanting Ruth. Adjoining is the *Camarín* (1688–96; by *Fr. Rodríguez*) where, seated on a hideous modern gyrating enamelled throne, is the gaudily-dressed smoke-blackened image of N.S. de Guadalupe.

Although not included in the tour, one should ask to be led to the *Gothic Cloister* (1502–24), now somewhat mutilated, round which the Hostal has been installed. From its entrance we may walk round the exterior of the Monastery, its solid bulk lightened by slender turrets, their pinnacles decorated with green and white tiles, to regain the Pl. Mayor.

The heaths around Guadalupe are overlooked by the *Cabeza del Moro* (4735 ft). From the early 15C chapel of *El Humilladero* (on the Oropesa road), we may approach to the *Arca del Agua*, a fountain of 1350 which supplies the monastery. A pleasant walk leads W. to the *Granja de Mirabel*, a palace rebuilt in 1486, while the *Granja de Valdefuentes*, S.E. built for Philip II in 1551–54, has an interesting chapel.

The N V may be regained by following the C 401 which winds across the Guadalupe range to the Pto. Llano (2106 ft) through *Cañamero*, producer of the local turbid wine, and (29 km.) **Logrosán** (3750 inhab.), in a narrow glen at the foot of the Sierra, and long famous for its rich deposit of lime phosphate found in the hard black schist whose sharp slaty rocks once protruded uncomfortably in the village streets. The church has a good apse and retablo and there is a 14C chapel of *N.S. del Consuelo*. On the neighbouring hill of S. Cristóbal are a ruined castle and remains of a pre-Roman town.

21 km. *Zorita*, 19 km. S. of which lies *Madrigalejo*, where Fernando the Catholic died in 1516. From Zorita we may turn N.W. and cross lonely and uncultivated country by the C 524 to (28 km.) *Trujillo* (Rte 45), or continue S.W. to meet the N V at (26 km.) *Miajadas*.

FROM TALAVERA TO PLASENCIA VIÃ ARENAS DE SAN PEDRO AND YUSTE (163 km.). 6 km. beyond Talavera the C 502 forks r. and gently climbs N. after crossing the Tiétar, entering (39 km.) *Ramcastañas*, where the C 501 from San Martín de Valdeiglesias joins our road from the E., see p.409. For the C 502 from *Ávila*, see p.342. Here we fork l. for (5 km.) **Arenas de San Pedro** (6400 inhab.), a summer resort and centre for excursions into the foothills of the Sierra de Gredos. It has a large *castle* (c. 1400), the granite church of *N.S. de la Asunción*, a Gothic bridge, and old houses. Nearby is the 18C Franciscan *Santuario de S. Pedro Alcántara* by

Ventura Rodríguez, and in the adjacent valleys to the N.W. are the picturesque villages of *Guisando* and *El Arenal*.—From Arenas the N 501 leads S.W., first climbing the N. side of the Tiétar valley (the district of LA VERA) through thickly wooded hills, to (20 km.) *Candeleda*, near the sanctuary of *N.S. de Chilla*, on the S. slope of *Almanzor* (8727 ft) the highest peak of the range. The road crosses a number of *gargantas* or huge boulder-strewn torrent beds, passing (or by-passing) (11 km.) *Madrigal de la Vera*, (10 km.) *Villanueva de la Vera* with an attractive plaza, (10 km.) *Valverde de la Vera*, with a restored plaza, and (10 km.) *Losar de la Vera*, with old houses, a 15C church and a chapel (El Cristo), containing a 16C crucifixion.

9 km. **Jarandilla** (2900 inhab.), with a large church, and a *castle* where Charles V lived while his quarter at Yuste were being prepared. This has been converted to house *Parador Nac.*—11 km. **Cuacos**, with ancient houses and a 14C church containing an organ and woodwork from Yuste, is the nearest village to the Hieronymite ***Monastery of Yuste** (2 km. W.) founded in 1404 and celebrated as the place of retirement of Charles V, from Feb. 1557 until death in Sept. 1558. Some parts of the original buildings, which were sacked in the Peninsular War have been restored, for it was virtually gutted in 1820, and fell into further decay, after the suppression of monasteries in the 1830s. No longer may one sleep 'the slumber of a weary insignificant stranger', as did Ford, in the room in which the emperor died, when he rode that way in 1832. William Stirling (later Stirling-Maxwell), who so well described the ex-emperor's life at Yuste, visited it in 1849.

A short avenue of eucalyptus trees leads to the *church* (1508). The two-storeyed cloister may be seen but not entered. In the crypt, under the altar, is Charles V's first coffin, in which his body remained for 16 years, before being transferred to the Escorial. A ramp, which the gouty monarch could mount on horseback, ascends to a terrace over-looking a fish pond. Hence his apartments, in the wing which he had specially built in 1554 by Fray *Ant. de Villacastín*, may be visited. The view across the valley of La Vera, which charmed the dying emperor, recalls his enthusiastic description, 'Ver ibi perpetuum'—'Here is eternal spring'.—N 501 winds on viâ (8 km.) *Jaraiz de la Vera*, with a 13C church, before climbing down to (35 km.) *Plasencia*, see Rte 46A.

At *Garganta la Olla*, 7 km. N.W. of Jaraiz, the church contained another early 16C Organ, taken from Yuste, which after years of wilful neglect was in 1973 deliberately destroyed by the village priest, and its smaller pipes distributed among children as 'penny whistles' for correctly repeating the Catechism!

32 km. l. **Oropesa** ((3200 inhab.), with a *Parador Nac.* in its restored *Castle* of 1366–1402), commanding a fine *View of the Tagus valley and the Gredos range rising abruptly to the N. It was the birthplace of Alonso de Orozco (1500-91) and Juan de los Angeles (1536-1609), both mystics.

From Oropesa a road leads S. to (86 km.) *Guadalupe* viâ (13 km.) **El Puente del Arzobispo**, with pottery works. The old *Bridge*, built in 1338 by Abp. Tenorio, and once fortified, was crossed by Wellington's army after the battle of Talavera. In *Sta Catalina*, burnt by the French and reconstructed in the 19C, are well-carved stalls.—We pass, near *Navalmolejo*, (8 km. l.) the ruins of *Vascos*, of. Roman origin, but abandoned in the 12C, before, at 26 km., joining the C 401 to (39 km.) *Guadalupe*, see p. 410.

3 km. l. *Lagartera* (2200 inhab.), famous for its striking embroidered costumes worn on Sundays.—At 29 km. the road by-passes **Navalmoral de la Mata**, (11,000 inhab.), with a stone pillory and two churches of interest; *S. Andrés* (15-16C) and *Las Angustias*.—From Navalmoral a road leads N.W. to (33 km.) *Jarandilla* and *Yuste*, see above, with a branch turning N.W. to *Plasencia* through a district devoted to the cultivation of tobacco, and dotted with drying sheds.

11 km. S.W. stands the 13-16C castle of *Belvis de Monroy* overlooking the Embalse de Valdecañas, while not far S.E. of Navalmoral, at *Bohonal de Ibor*, stand six columns of a portico moved from the submerged ruins of Roman *Talavera la Vieja*.—Beyond Navalmoral the N V bears S.W. to (12 km.) **Almaraz** (near which a nuclear power-station has been constructed), with an interesting church

and a fine *Bridge* over the deep gorge of the Tagus, the scene of Lord Hill's brilliant exploit in 1812 in severing French communications.

Unfortunately, over twenty years passed before it was restored, and in times of flood, travellers were occasionally obliged to wait for *days* at a neighbouring posada (much to the posadero's satisfaction) before the river had subsided sufficiently to make the crossing.

A well-engineered road now climbs steeply to the *Pto. de Miravete* (2180 ft), with magnificent retrospective views, and shortly passes (32 km.) *Jaraicejo*, with a handsome church, and providing extensive vistas towards the S.W., with *Trujillo* on a height in the distance. We shortly pass a medieval, and later a 17C bridge, and (l.) the *Pal. Real del Carrascal*, and at 27 km. enter **Trujillo**: see Rte 45, and for the road beyond to *Cáceres* and *Valencia de Alcántara.*

13 km. *Santa Cruz de la Sierra*, with prehistoric and Moorish ruins, and a domed church and (10 km.) *Villamesias*, with an imposing church, are passed before we meet the C.401 from Guadalupe at (18 km.) *Miajadas.*

FROM MIAJADAS TO CASTUERA (68 km.). At 19 km. the C 520 leads S. to (14 km.) **Medellín** (2600 inhab.), Roman *Metellinum*, named after Metellus Puis) see Bilbilis), once a flourishing town and birthplace of Hernán Cortés (1485–1547), conqueror of Mexico, but it has never recovered from its sack by Victor in 1809. The ruined castle commands a fine view of the Guadiana, here crossed by a bridge of 1636.

To the E. lies (8 km.) **Don Benito** (26,300 inhab.) an ancient town with the late-Gothic Hall-church of *Santiago* and interesting old streets, and 8 km. beyond, **Villanueva de la Serena**, (20,800 inhab.), birthplace of Pedro de Valdivia (1500–54) founder of Santiago de Chile, with a Gothic parish church, the *Conv. de S. Bartolomé*, and a neo-classic *Palace* of the Order of Alcántara.—From Villanueva the C 420 bears S.E., off which, at 12 km., a road (r.) leads 8 km. to *Magacela*, with a ruined castle.

26 km. **Castuera** (8500 inhab.), the chief town of LA SERENA, an arid and backward upland surrounded by mountains, was once guarded against the Moors by the '*Siete Castillos de la Serena*', seven forts at equal distance from each other in a semicircle 80 km. in extent. The reactionary religious writer Donoso Cortés (1809–53) was born here.—At *Zalamea de la Serena* (6300 inhab.), 16 km. S.W., the church tower incorporates part of a Roman temple. The place gave the title to the play 'El Alcalde de Zalamea', by Calderón (c. 1643).—Beyond Castuera the road deteriorates, but leads 32 km. E. to *Cabeza del Buey*, passing (9 km. l.) the chapel of the *Virgén de Belén*, formerly a Templar's church, and r., *Almorchón*, with a ruined Moorish castle.

49 km. **MÉRIDA**, (37,300 inhab.; 15,500 in 1920; *Parador Nac.*; *Hotels*) has grown considerably in recent years, after centuries of vegetation. Once the capital of the Roman province of Lusitania, it contains more important remains of Roman antiquity than any other town in Spain.

History. In 23 B.C. the legate Publius Carisius founded *Augusta Emerita* as a settlement for veterans of the Iberian wars. Under the Visigoths it remained capital of Lusitania, but in 711 or 713 it was taken by the Moors under Musa, and most of its monuments destroyed. Reconquered by Alfonso IX of León in 1228, it was presented to the Order of Santiago, but never recovered its importance. The poet, rabbi, general, Shemuel la-Levi ben Yosef Nagrella 993-1056) and Juan Pablo Forner (1756-97), the writer and polemicist, and José María Calatrava (1781-1847), the Liberal politician, were born here.

Mérida is by-passed to the S.E. by the N V, which crosses the Guadiana on a new bridge of eight spans (1960).—We fork r. and pass (l.) the *Circus Maximus* restored in 337–50, and which could hold 26,000 spectators; excavations have laid bare some rooms in which gladiators may have been housed. We soon reach the Av. Teniente Coronel Yagüe,

by which we circle the town to the sluggish river, here crossed by a
*Roman Bridge of 64 granite arches, dating from the time of Trajan,
repaired in 686 by the Visigothic king Erwic and Sala, duke of Toledo,
and again in 1610 by Philip III. Some of the arches, broken down in 1812
to retard Marmont's attempted relief of Badajoz, have been repaired.

On the sandbank upstream are the remains of a Roman work called *El Tajamar*,
built to protect the bridge-piers from floods. The bridge that crosses the
Albarregas (Alba Regis) a little downstream, is also built on Roman foundations.

Adjacent to the old bridge stands the *Alcazaba*, partly restored to
house a museum, successively a Roman, Visigothic and Moorish castle
(in 835), an episcopal palace, a house of the Templars, and the residence
of the 'provisor' of the Knights of Santiago. It was gutted by the French
in 1808; within may be seen a courtyard and steps descending to a huge
Visigothic cistern. Hence we approach the 16C arcaded *Pl. Mayor*, on
the l. of which is *Sta María* with Romanesque and Plateresque details
and an 18C retablo. On the W. side of the square is a Plateresque house,
known as the Casa de Vera.—Behind and to the N. of Sta María is a
Museum of antiquities housed in the former *Conv. de S. Clara*,
including Roman statues (mainly from the Theatre); note Marcus
Agrippa and a Mithraic mosaic; also remarkable Visigothic fragments,
among which are some pre-Moorish horseshoe windows.—The *Arco de
Santiago*, to the r., is a triumphal arch 'of Trajan' 13.5 m. high, but
stripped of its marble casing. We return thence to the Pl. Mayor and
follow the C. Sta Eulalia, to the N.E.—A turning on the r. leads to the
Casa del Conde de los Corbos, built inside a temple (said to be of Diana),
preserving the peristyle of granite Corinthian columns. The Plateresque
balcony is in interesting contrast to the Roman work. The C. de Sta
Eulalia and Rambla del Generalísimo continue N.E., passing a statue of
the saint on a column made up of four Roman altars superimposed, to
Sta Eulalia, which dates mainly from the 13C but preserves in the nave
some Visigothic capitals from an earlier church on the same site.
Opposite is the *Hornito*, a chapel decorated with Roman fragments,
claiming to be the oven in which the child martyr Eulalia (292–304) was
roasted alive. The porch incorporates material from a temple of Mars.

Some distance to the W., parallel to the Cáceres road, are ***Los
Milagros**, the imposing remains of a Roman aqueduct, 10 arches of
which still stand and now serve as the headquarters of the storks of the
Guadiana valley. It is possible that it red brick courses were laid to
cushion the effects of earth tremors.

The aqueduct once conveyed into the town the waters of the *Lago de Proserpina*,
of *Charca de la Albuera*, to the N.W., which preserves its granite retaining wall and
staircase towers.—A smaller reservoir, the *Albuera de Cornalbo*, near *Trujillanos*,
(reached by a road leading l. off the N V, 14 km. N.E. of the town), has steps
arranged in rows as though for a naumachia.

Following the C. José Ramón Melida from the N. end of the C. Sta
Eulalia, we reach the area of the great ROMAN MONUMENTS. The
Amphitheatre, which had room for 15,000 spectators, dates from A.D. 8.
The ***Theatre**, called *Las Siete Sillas* from the seven wedges into which
its seats are divided, and dating from 24 B.C., is one of the finest Roman
monuments extant in Spain.

The vomitoria, or entrance passages, are in perfect condition, and the stage, with
its elegant colonnade, in a remarkable state of preservation. Remains of a temple
of Serapis and of a Roman-Christianbasilica have likewise been discovered.

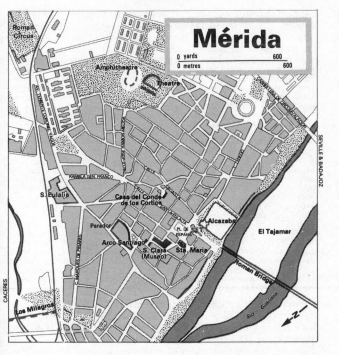

17 km. S.E. of Mérida, E. of the Embalse de Alange, lies *Alange*, with two domed chambers of a Roman bath.

From Mérida to *Seville,* see Rte 47; *Cáceres* lies 68 km. N.

At the junction S. of the Roman bridge and the by-pass, we turn W. along the S. bank of the Guadiana in its fertile vega, recently greatly increased in area by the irrigation scheme of the Vegas Bajas, fed from the Montijo dam below Mérida.—At 28 km. a road leads 6 km. N. to *Montijo* (12,400 inhab.) the ancestral home of the Condesa de Montijo (1826l920), later Empress Eugénie, wife of Napoleon III.—To the S.W., in the church of *Puebla de la Calzada*, are Passion scenes painted by *Morales.*—16 km. *Talavera la Real,* inappropriately named, where *Sta María de la Ribera* incorporates early Christian remains. A by-pass now circles S. of Badajoz towards the Portuguese frontier, crossing the Guadiana by a new bridge, while we fork r. and enter the town at 18 km. by the *Pta. de la Trinidad* (1680), just short of which we may turn r. below the walls to reach the *Pte. de Palmas* spanning the Guadiana. From the Pta. de la Trinidad the Av. de José Antonio (l.) follows the line of the dismantled fortifications S. and W. of the town.

BADAJOZ (102,800 inhab.; 41,000 in 1920; 76,000 in 1950; *Hotels*), the ancient capital of Estremadura, was once reckoned the key of Portugal, and is famous for its sieges, particularly that of 1812, one of the most sanguinary episodes of the Peninsular War. The town, which contains little of interest, has increased in size and importance since the 'Badajoz Plan' of harnessing the waters of the Guadiana has improved the economy of the area.

History. Badajoz, whose name has been derived from the Roman *Pax Augusta*, rose to prominence in 1009 when the Aftasside Moors formed an independent principality at *Bataljoz* after the break-up of the emirate of Córdoba. Subdued later by the Almoravides, the town was a focus of the struggle between Moors and Christians in the 12-13C, and was finally secured by Alfonso IX in 1229. Its position on the Portuguese frontier has exposed it to many sieges; by the Portuguese in 1660; by the Allies in the War of the Spanish Succession (1705); and by the French in 1808 and 1809. More important was Soult's siege of 1810–11, unsuccessful until the death of Rafael Menacho, the gallant commander. The perfidy of his successor, José Imaz, admitted the French and delayed for a year the relief of Andalucía. Beresford failed to recover the place in 1811, and in 1812 Wellington launched a surprise attack on 16 March. After dreadful carnage in the breaches the British forced their way into the town, which they then sacked. The defenders lost 1200 men out of 5000, the attackers 5000 out of 15,000. It was again the scene of tragedy when captured by Nationalist forces in Aug 1936, when its Republican defenders were herded into the old bullring and massacred.

Badajoz is the birthplace of many famous men, including the conquistadors Pedro de Alvarado (1485–1541), lieutenant of Cortés, and Seb. Garcilaso de la Vega (1500–59), protector of the Indians, who married an Inca princess; here also were born the painter Luis Morales (1506–86), and Manuel Godoy, Príncipe de la Paz (1767–1851), favourite of Carlos IV and lover of his queen. The town of Ladysmith, in South Africa, is named after a young girl of Badajoz, Juana María de los Dolores de León, rescued from the sack by Harry Smith, who married her, and who later became governor of the Cape. Here in Jan 1836, George Borrow spent his first ten days in Spain, mostly in the company of the local gypsies. Arturo Barea (1897–1957), the author, was also born here.

From the unimpressive Pl. de España in the centre of the old town, we may enter the **Cathedral**, erected by Alfonso el Sabio in 1232–84. It has a later façade (1619) with Ionic columns; the tower (1240–1419) was altered in the 16C. The interior is blocked by the Renaissance coro of 1558, by *Jerónimo de Valencia*, with good carvings on the organ galleries; the two 18C organs have been well restored; and there are some depressing paintings by *Morales*, *Mateo Cerezo*, and *Zurbarán*. The high altar of 1708 is Churrigueresque. The chapel of the *Duques de Figueroa* (2nd on the N.) contains good tombs and a 16C retablo, and in the next is a 15C Italian Madonna. In the transept is another Virgin painted on panel. On the S. side is the *cloister* of 1509–20, with interlacing arches, on the N. side of which is the bronze tomb-slab of Lorenzo Suárez de Figueroa (d. 1506), by *Alessandro Leopardi* of Venice. The *chapter house* contains paintings by *Zurbarán, Ribera*, and others.—On the E. side of the C. Moreno Nieto, S. of the cathedral, is the *Bishop's Palace*.

Other churches of interest are *S. Andrés* (17C), with a triptych by *Morales*, to the E.; *La Concepción*, to the N.E., with two retouched paintings by *Morales*; and *S. Agustín*, to the N., with the grotesque 18C monument of the Marqués de Blai, a general of Philip V. The *Castillo*, or *Alcázaba*, rising N.E. of the town, a mass of Moorish (c. 1170) and later ruins, commands a good view. At the foot is the arcaded Pl. Alta and, further S., the Moorish *Torre Espantaperros*, with an *Archaeological Museum*. On the W. side of the town is the *Conv. de Sto Domingo*.

From the Pl. de España we may follow the C. de Hernán Cortés and C. de Gabríel, passing the *Diputación*, with a *Museum* containing paintings by *Morales*, *Zurbarán*, and others, and the *Conv. de Decalzadas*, to reach the *Pta. de Palmas*, and *Pte. de Palmas*, designed by *Herrera* in 1596.

Beyond the river rises the fortified hill of S. Cristóbal. At the far end of the bridge the N V turns l. to join the by-pass before reaching the Portuguese frontier (and Customs post) only 4km. W. In Portugal, *Elvas* lies 13km. further W. on the direct road to *Lisbon*, 231km. beyond; see the *Blue Guide to Portugal*, forthcoming.

From Badajoz to *Zafra* and *Córdoba*, see Rte 48, p.426.

FROM BADAJOZ TO VALENCIA DE ALCÁNTARA (76km.). After crossing the Guadiana we turn r. and then fork l. off the Cáceres road (N 523) onto the C 530, ascending the valleys of the Gevora and Zapatón parallel to the Portuguese frontier.—44km. **Alburquerque**, a picturesque fortified town (7100 inhab.), is a centre of cork-production. It ruined *castle* (1314), famed in the wars between the Portuguese and the Moors, the Gothic church of *Sta María*, and *S. Mateo*, are of interest. To the W. is *El Risco de S. Blas*, with remarkable rock-paintings of human figures. In this region is the site of the battle of Zalaca, or Sacrialis, where Yusuf I defeated Alfonso VI in 1086. The castle of *Piedrabuena* lies c. 15km. N.E. on a poor road, while off the C 521, c 15km. E., is perched the castle of *Azagala*.—32km. *Valencia de Alcántara,* see p. 420; for the road beyond, see the *Blue Guide to Portugal*, forthcoming.

45   FROM TRUJILLO TO CÁCERES AND VALENCIA DE ALCÁNTARA

Total distance, 140km. (87 miles). N 521. 48km. **Cáceres**—92km. *Valencia de Alcántara.*

TRUJILLO (9400 inhab.; *Hotels*), an ancient and 'monumental' town, one of the most interesting for its size in Spain, and dominated by its castle, stands on a low hill N. of the N V. Its name is a corruption of *Turgalium,* and it claims to have been founded by Julius Caesar.

History. It was the birthplace of many conquistadores, including Francisco Pizarro (1476–1541), the brilliant and treacherous subjugator of the Incas; his half-brothers Hernando (?1478-1557) and Gonzalo (1511/13-48), who shared his adventures; Francisco de Orellana (1511–46), first explorer of the Amazon; and Diego García de Paredes (1466–1530), the right hand of Gonzalo de Córdoba.

Many seignorial mansions and towers (some restored, including those of the *Chaves-Mendoza*, and *de los Bejaranos*, towards the W.) built by the returned conquistadores, may be seen in the narrow streets of the old town. This is best visited on foot from the picturesque *Pl. Mayor*, overlooked to the N. by *S. Martín*, with fine vaults and good tombs. Near by are the magnificent solares of the *Duque de San Carlos*, and of the *Conde del Puerto*. To the W. of the plaza stands the 17C *Pal. de la Conquista*, and beyond, to the S.W., the *Pal. de Orellana-Pizarro*, with a Plateresque patio. On the S. side of the Pl. Mayor is the arcaded *Pal. Piedras Albas*, while a short distance further S. is *S. Francisco* (16C) and to the S.E. the *Pal. de Sofraga*.—To the W. of S. Martín we may ascend past (l.) the 16C *Casa de los Chaves* or *Torre del Alfiler*, to *Santiago*, with an early crucifix and a statue of the patron by *Greg. Fernández*. Higher up is *Sta María la Mayor* (15C), with a good doorway and an older tower (over-restored), containing the tomb of Diego de Paredes and a retablo attrib. to *Fernando Gallego*. From Santiago we may climb to the r. towards the huge *Castle* (restored in part, and spoilt by the addition of a Virgin over the entrance), preserving square Moorish towers and latter additions, from the parapets of which extensive views are obtained. The best stretch of *Walls* may be seen at the N.W. corner of the town, N.of which lies the *Conv. de S. Francisco el Real*.

A pleasant excursion may be made to *Montánchez*, 40 km. S.W.; see p.423.

From Trujillo we bear due W. on the N 521, traversing pastures and olive-groves, with a distant view of the Gredos range to the N., to (48 km.) Cáceres, its ancient towers dominating the growing modern town, as the road circles N. to the tree-lined Av. de España.

CÁCERES (1550 ft; 58,900 inhab.; 20,000 in 1920; 40,000 in 1950; *Hosteria Nac*; *Parador Nac.* projected; *Hotels*), is a pleasant provincial capital retaining a well-preserved medieval town of considerable charm, whose fertile environs produce corn, fruit, and wines; and its hams are excellent.

History. Its Roman name was *Colonia Norbensis Caesarina*. From the 9th to the 13C it was a bone of contention between Moors and Christians and was finally taken in 1229, becoming proverbially famous for the number of knights quartered there. It was the birthplace of many conquistadores, including Francisco Hernández Girón (?1505-53), afterwards a rebel leader in Peru, and of José de Carvajal y Lancáster (1698-1754), minister of Fernando VI.

From the Av. de España we ascend (l.) the C. S. Antón and C. S. Pedro, passing 15C *S. Juan*, which contains Baroque retablos. Below, the C. Generalísimo leads to the partially arcaded *Pl. Mayor* (Pl. Gen. Mola) dominated by the *Arco de la Estrella* (1726), by *Manuel de Lara Churriguera*, with the Roman *Torre de Bujaco* near by.

N.W. of the Pl. Mayor lies the *Conv. de Sto Domingo* (1524), the 16C *Casa de Galarza* and *Pal. de la Isla*, and, at the end of the C. de Cervantes, the *Seminario Viejo* or *Col. de S. Pedro* of 1589-1604.

From the Pl. Mayor we ascend into the ***Old Town.**

This remarkable quarter, almost deserted except by storks, is still surrounded by its Roman walls with their gates and towers. It is traversed by narrow stepped lanes lined with the grim-looking solares of the conquistadores and their descendants, and is best visited on foot. Almost any of its alleyways will repay the unhurried wanderer, but the itinerary which follows takes in the most remarkable buildings. If possible, a second visit to the old town should be made after dark, when its medieval atmosphere is more strongly felt. Many of the patios may be viewed. A small tip to the servant is appreciated.

On entering the ramparts, we pass (l.) the *Pal. Episcopal*, built for García de Galarza, Bp. of Coria, in 1587, and reach *Sta María la Mayor*, mainly of the 16C, with a good retablo of 1547-51 by *Guillén Ferrón* of Seville and the Fleming *Roque de Balduque*. The tower was designed in 1554 by *Pedro de Ibarra*. In the plaza round the church are imposing houses, including (W.) the 16C *Torre de Mayoralgo*; and (N.) the *Pal. de Ovando*, with a Plateresque portal and a fine patio. In the N.W. angle of the town walls stands the *Casa de Toledo-Moctezuma*, once the home of the descendants of Juan Cano, follower of Cortés and husband of the daughter of the last Aztec emperor.

Santiago, outside the walls to the N.E., by *Rodrigo Gil de Hontañón* (1550-56), has a splendid reja by *Fr. Núñez* (1563) and a retablo by *Berruguete* (1557-63). Opposite Santiago is the *Pal. de Godoy* (1594; by *Jerónimo Gómez*) with a fine front and corner balcony.

No. 1 in the Cuesta de la Compañía, ascending S. to the *Jesuit church* and *College* (1698-1750), is the remarkable *Casa de los Golfines de Abajo* (late 15C) with mosaic decoration. Opposite is the 16C granite front of the *Casa de los Becerras*.

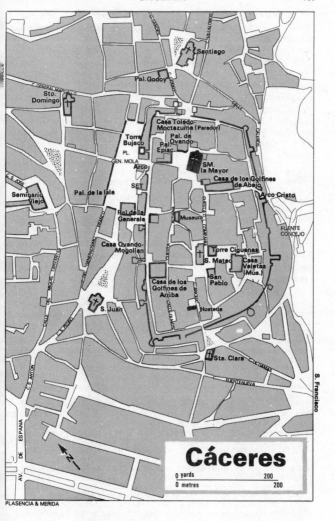

Hence it is worth while to descend E. to the *Arco del Cristo*, most complete of the Roman gates, beyond which is the picturesque *Fuente del Concejo*. The *Virgén de la Montaña*, a chapel on a hill (2113 ft) further E. commands good view. The sanctuary contains a retablo by *José Churriguera*.

The Cuesta Aldana, to the W., contains a Mudéjar house with ajimez windows, and the *Museo Provincial*, its contents of no great interest, but attractively displayed in an old palace. Approaching, at the top of the hill, *S. Mateo* (15C), with a striking tower, and containing the tomb of the Marqués de Valdepuentes (16C), we pass the *Casa del Mono*, *Casa de Aldana*, (l.) the *Casa del Sol*, with a 16C façade, and (r.) the *Pal. de Roda*. To the E. is the *Casa de las Veletas*, incorporating part of the 12C Moorish *Alcázar*, and retaining its *algibe*, or cistern. Here too are the battlemented *Torre de las Cigüeñas* of 1477, and the late-Gothic *Conv. de S. Pablo*. A little N.W. of S. Mateo lies the *Casa de los Golfines de Arriba* (15C; with a notable tower of 1515); to the E. stands the 17C front of the *Casa de Ovando-Mogollón*, and a little further N. is the 15C *Pal. de la Generala.*—The C. Ancha, descending S. from S. Mateo, flanked by the *Casa Ulloa*, *Casa Paredes-Saavedra*, and *Casa de Sánchez de Paredes*, leads to the *Conv. de Sta Clara* (just outside the walls) with a portal of 1614, from which the C. de Damas leads S. to the great *Conv. de S. Francisco*, founded in 1472, with a fine late-Gothic church and cloister.

At *Cáceres el Viejo* to the N. of the town, is the Roman camp of Q. Cecilius Metellus, dating from the war of 79 B.C. against Sertorius.

From Cáceres to *Plasencia, Salamanca,* and to *Mérida,* see Rte 46A; to *Ciudad Rodrigo*, Rte 46B, or viâ Alcántara, see below. A direct road (N 523) leads 89 km. S.W. to *Badajoz*, traversing a wild and depopulated region.

At the far end of the Av. de España we turn r. and then l. on to the N 521. The direct road to *Valencia de Alcántara*—92 km. to the W.— crosses a deserted landscape, but an interesting detour may be made to take in Alcántara, as described below:

FROM CÁCERES TO ALCÁNTARA (104 km.) 13 km. W. of Cáceres the C 523 forks r. off the N 521 to (7 km.) *Arroyo de la Luz*, or *Arroyo del Puerco*, whose church contains a *Retablo* adorned with works by *Morales*, and a St John by *Pedro de Mena*. There is also an old *Pal. of the Counts of Benavente* and, to the N., the pilgrimage chapel of *N.S. de la Luz.*—At 22 km. a road forks r. to (14 km.) *Garrovillas*, on tne S. bank of the Embalse de Alcántara with a curious white-washed arcaded plaza. The 15C church of *Sta María* and that of *S. Pedro* are of interest, and in the vicinity are prehistoric sites.—Beyond (6 km.) *Brozas*, birthplace of several conquistadores and Francisco Sánchez de las Brozas ('el Brocensé; 1523–1601), the humanist, where the fine Gothic church (16C) of *Sta María* has a notable tower and 18C retablos and rejas, the road descends into the Tagus valley.

15 km. **Alcántara** (2500 inhab.) takes its name from its **Bridge* (Arabic, *el kantara*) over the Tagus, which spans the gorge in six arches of uncemented granite, the two main arches 33.5 m. wide and 64 m. above the normal level of the river; the total length is 204 m. It was built for Trajan by Caius Julius Lacer A.D. 105. One of the arches, destroyed by the Moors in 1213, was rebuilt by Charles V in 1543; the second arch from the r. bank was blown up by Gen. Mayne in 1809, and temporarily repaired with woodwork. It was impassable from 1836, when the wooden arch was destroyed by the Carlists, until 1860, when the whole bridge was restored. A great dam holding back the waters of the Embalse de Alcántara has recently been constructed in the gorge a short distance E. of the Roman bridge. On the l. bank is a Roman temple with a memorial of the architect, and in the centre a triumphal arch.—The town, once the headquarters of the knightly order of Alcántara (transferred hither from Ciudad Rodrigo in 1218), whose function was to defend the frontier against the Moors, has ruins of the castle, and a 13C parish church containing tombs of Grand Masters of the order and paintings by *Morales*. The *church* and *Conv. de S. Benito* (1499–1577), begun by *Pedro de Ibarra*, with a dignified cloister and fine apse, is being restored.

For the road N.W. to *Castelo Branco,* see the *Blue Guide to Portugal,* forthcoming.

6 km. S. of Alcántara a road leads W. to (27 km.) *Membrio*, where we may regain the N 521, 25 km. N.E. of *Valencia de Alcántara*. *Moraleja*, on the C 526 for *Ciudad Rodrigo*, lies 50 km. N.

Valencia de Alcántara (8200 inhab.; Customs-post). The walled town preserves *N.S. de Roque Amador* (16C) within a 13C castle. 13C *La Encarnación* has a Mudéjar doorway; its 17C organ has been converted into a chicken-run! The *Ayuntamiento* dates from the late 16C. Not far off are the remains of the Roman city of *Julia Contrasta*.

14 km. beyond the town lies the actual frontier, from which the main road passes between *Marvao* (N.) and *Portalegre* (S.), and leads viâ *Abrantes* to *Lisbon*, 242 km. beyond; see the *Blue Guide to Portugal*, forthcoming.

46 FROM SALAMANCA TO CÁCERES AND MÉRIDA

A ViÂ PLASENCIA

Total distance, 278 km. (172 miles). N 630. 70 km. *Béjar*—59 km. **Plasencia**—81 km. **Cáceres**—68 km. **Mérida**.
La Alberca (see below) may be approached direct from Salamanca by the C 512.—At *Vecinos*, 22 km. S.W. of Salamanca, we fork r. for *Tamames* and then turn S. viâ *El Cabaco* for (45 km.) La Alberca.

Following approx. the line of the Vıa LATA (locally called *Camino de la Plata*), the Roman road which ran from Mérida to Salamanca and Astorga—fragments of its paving can be traced here and there—we drive due S. on the N 630.—7 km. *Arapiles*: for the *battlefield of Salamanca*, see p.334. At 11 km. a road leads 11 km. E. to *Alba de Tormes*, see p.334.—We skirt the W. bank of the Embalse de Sta Teresa, and climb to (48 km.) *Vallejera de Riofrio*, just beyond which we are joined by the C 500 from El Barco de Ávila.

10 km. **Béjar** (3077 ft; 17,300 inhab.; *Hotel*), with ancient Moorish fortifications restored in the 12C. The *Alcázar del Duque de Osuna* is a fine feudal palace with a 16C classical patio. *Sta María* (early 13C) has a Virgin by *Carmona*; while *S. Salvador* (1554) has a good retablo.—4 km. E. lies the picturesque village of **Candelario** (1400 inhab.), with its balconied houses overhanging steeply climbing streets; an unusual feature are the double lower doors to numerous houses; the ancient coiffure of the region may still be seen here.

From Bejar we may explore the *Sierra de Peña de Francia*, named, it is said, in honour of the French colonists brought to Salamanca by Raymond of Burgundy in 1085, and the wild region of *Las Hurdes*.

FROM BÉJAR TO CIUDAD RODRIGO (90 km.). We climb N.W. on the C 515, passing (9 km., l.) *La Calzada*, with a Roman fortress and remains of an ancient causeway. At 17 km. we are joined by the C 512 from Vecinos (see above) and bear W., above the gorge of the Alagón.—At 10 km. a left fork leads shortly to picturesque **Miranda del Castañar**, with a castle and Romanesque church, but we turn r. and climb steeply through the wooded hills, with views to the E., to (15 km.) *La Alberca*. An alternative approach may be made on the C 515 viâ *Sequeros*. Nearby, at *San Martín de Castañar*, are medieval walls and a castle.
La Alberca (3937 ft; 1400 inhab.; *Hotel*), a large, and until recently, unspoilt village of Moorish origin, contains many ancient houses flanking cobbled streets, an arcaded Pl. Mayor, and a 17C church. The Ofrenda a la Virgen and the Loa (a mystery play) are performed here on Aug 15-16, when local costumes and jewellery are displayed. A monument commemorates Maurice Legendre, whose pioneering study of the area was published in 1927.
5 km. N.W. of La Alberca we may turn l. and make the steep ascent to the monastery of *N.S. de la Peña de Francia*, at the summit of a conical peak (5653 ft), commanding a magnificent *View of the region.—Further N., at *El Cabaco*, we regain the C 515 which leads W., viâ *Tenebron*, to (34 km.) *Ciudad Rodrigo*, see p.344.

FROM LA ALBERCA TO CORIA (76 km.). Crossing the Portilla de la Alberca to the S.W. we descend into the rugged valley of *Las Batuacas*, which, with the three parallel valleys of *Las Hurdes*, was notorious in legend as late as the 16C as the home of savage and evil spirits, the latter exorcized by the foundation of a Carmelite monastery in 1599 in the valley. Some Hurdanos helped with the cutting of the Panama Canal. Bowles reported that the holy fathers of the convent were 'seldom in a hurry to open their doors' to a distressed traveller, unless provided with a letter from the provincial or general of their Order.

Near (13 km.) *Las Mestas* we meet the C 512 and turn r. To the S.E. the Alagón has been dammed to form the Embalse de Gabriel y Galán. We wind our way through the holm-oak woods below the Sierra de Gata to (17 km.) *Pinefranqueado* and (17 km.) *Villanueva de la Sierra*, 17 km. S.E. of which, at *Montehermosa*, local costumes may be seen at the Romería of S. Bartolomé (Aug 24).—Some 15 km. W. of Villanueva lies *Santibáñez*, and *Gata* (to the N.), see Rte 46B.—At 7 km. we turn r. (rough road) to (22 km.) **Coria**.

From Béjar, the N 630 ascends to the Pto. de Béjar (3215 ft), off which, at 11 km. a road leads 6 km. W. to *Montemayor del Rio*, with a Roman bridge and medieval castle.—4 km. an abrupt r. bend—*Baños de Montemayor*, a thermal resort since Roman times, with a leaning church tower. To the l. the *Sierra de Gredos* rises to 7875 ft, as we pass (2 km.) **Hervás** (3550 inhab.), an attractive village 3 km. S.E. amongst olive-groves and cherry orchards, with Baroque retablos in *S. Juan*, and with a well-preserved *Judería*.

At 7 km. the C 513 forks r. to (4 km.) *Abadía*, with a *Templars' Castle* converted into a Cistercian abbey, retaining a 13C cloister of horseshoe arches (restored), and to the S.W., remains of a palace built for the Duke of Alba in the 16C by Flemish and Italian craftsmen.—**Granadilla*, a fortified village, 14 km. beyond, on the E. bank of the Embalse de Gabriel y Galán, has a fine castle of 1400, but at present it can only be approached, with difficulty, by foot. The village itself is deserted, but has been the object of restoration.

At 15 km. a road (r.) leads shortly to *Cáparra,* with a four-square triumphal arch, and in the valley, a bridge, relics of Roman *Capera*.—Some 7 km. further W. lies *Guijo de Granadilla*, with a bridge on Roman foundations, and where the regional poet José María Gabriel y Galán (1870–1905) lived and died.

At 20 km., after passing the *Arcos de S. Antón,* a medieval aqueduct of 53 arches, we enter **PLASENCIA,** an attractively situated provincial town, (28,000 inhab.; *Hotel*) on the N. bank of the Jerte, which descends from the snow-capped Sierra de Gredos to join the Alagón. It was founded by Alfonso VIII in 1190 on the site of Roman (?) *Ambracia* or *Dulcis Placida,* destroyed by the Moors, and retains traces of ramparts, but most of the 68 semicircular towers (cubos) have been built against, and are hardly recognizable as fortifications. The pious founder gave the town the motto 'Ut deo placet', from which its modern name may be derived.

The river is spanned by the *Pte. de S. Lázaro* (1498) and the *Pte. Nuevo* (1500–12). Above the bridges rises the ornate but sombre Gothic **Cathedral** begun in 1498 by *Enrique de Egas* and continued in 1513–37 by *Juan de Álava,* but remained unfinished. The *Pta. del Enlosado,* on the N., in the style of Berruguete, dates from 1558. Inside, the size and unbroken shafts of the pillars and the delicacy of the vaulting is remarkable. The *Cap. Mayor,* finished by *Fr. de Colonia* and *Juan de Álava* (1513–22), contains a retablo by *Greg. Fernández* (1626) with paintings by *Fr. Rizi.* To the l. is the tomb of Bp. Ponce de León (d. 1573), by *Mateo Sánchez de Villaviciosa.* The *Reja* (1598–1604) is a masterpiece by *J.B. Celma,* but perhaps the most striking feature of the church is the **Sillería* by *Rodrigo Alemán* (1492–1520), an elaborate and beautiful piece of carving, with sacred and profane subjects incongruously jumbled together.

Abutting is a fragment of the old cathedral (c. 1320–1400), now called *Sta María;* the old *chapter house* has a 13C *dome,* of the type of the Torre del Gallo at Salamanca; the *Sacristy* contains an illuminated Bible (14C). From it a remarkable spiral *Staircase* ascends to a terrace. The *Cloisters* of the old cathedral date from 1416–38.

Facing the cathedral and in the C. de Obispo Casas are some old mansions, including the *Casa de Deán,* with a corner balcony. *S. Nicolás* (13-14C), to the N., contains to tomb of Bp. de Carvajal of Coria; opposite, is the *Pal. de Mirabel,* belonging to the Zuñiga family, with an attractive two-storeyed patio. *S. Ildefonso,* further N.E. has a fine effigy of Cristóbal de Villalba. *S. Martín* contains a 16C retablo by *Juan de Jaén,* with four paintings by *Morales* (1565). In the Pl. de S. Nicolás is the *Casa de las Bóvedos* (1550) with a saloon decorated with frescoes of the battles of Charles V. *S. Vicente* (1464–74), adjoining, contains the armed effigy of Martín Nieto (1597), but mutilated, a remarkable staircase of 1577, and good azulejos in the sacristy. In the arcaded *Pl. de España* stands the 16C *Ayuntamiento,* with a good artesonado in its main hall.

At the E. end of the C. del Marqués de la Constancia is *Sta Ana* (1556), while to the N. is *S. Salvador,* containing important monuments. To the S.E., by the Pta. del Sol, is *S. Pedro,* with the Teatro Romero occupying the site of the Council House in which Alfonso XI signed the Ordinances of Plasencia. Near the *Pta. de Coria is Sta María Magdalena* (Romanesque). The castle was destroyed during the Peninsular War.

From Plasencia to *Ávila,* see Rte 30; to *Yuste* and *Jarandilla,* Rte 44. *Montehermosa* lies 27 km. to the W.
Trujillo, 82 km. S.E., may be reached by climbing S. on the N 630 and then turning l. onto the C 524.—At 10 km. a road leads 6 km. 'N.E. to *Malpartida de Plasencia* (5100 inhab.) with a fine 16C church.—We cross the Embalse de Torrejon just below the junction of the Tietar and Tagus, the jagged gorge of which is overlooked by a ruined castle, and traverse a depopulated tract to *Trujillo,* seen from some distance away; see Rte 45.

From Plasencia the N 630 drives S.W.—At 16 km. a road leads 9 km. S.E. to *Mirabel,* with a 12C castle; while at 17 km. (r.) another leads shortly to *Palancar,* with a curious 16-17C monastery.'—7 km. *Cañaveral* (2100 inhab.; *Hotel*), with a Moorish tower, just beyond which we are joined by the C 526 from Ciudad Rodrigo (see below), before reaching the huge Embalse de Alcántara. Both road and rail meet to cross the reservoir by two-storeyed bridges. The ruins of the Roman bridge of *Alconétar,* destroyed by the Moors in 1232, are now partly submerged.—41 km. **Cáceres,** see p. 418.

From Cáceres we continue S. on the N 630, passing (10 km. l.) a fine medieval castle.—At 25 km. a road leads 15 km. N.E., climbing steeply to **Montánchez** (3100 inhab.), whose hams, famous in Estremadura, were much appreciated by Charles V during his retirement at Yuste, while the picturesque town preserves the extensive remains of a Moorish *Alcázar* (Views).—We descend into the Guadiana valley and at 33 km. enter **Mérida,** see p. 413.

B   VIÂ CIUDAD RODRIGO.

Total distance, 314 km. (195 miles) N 620. 89 km. **Ciudad Rodrigo**—C 256. 85 km. *Coria*—72 km. **Cáceres**—68 km. **Mérida.**

We follow the N 620 from Salamanca to (89 km.) *Ciudad Rodrigo*, see p. 344.

La Alberca (see p.421), may be visited by taking the C 515 towards *Béjar* viâ *Tenebron* and (39 km.) *El Cabaco.*

We drive S. from Ciudad Rodrigo on the undulating C 526 towards the Sierra de Gata, passing (13 km.) *El Bodón*, scene of skirmishing during the Peninsular War (25 Sept. 1811), and 11 km. S.W., *Fuenteguinaldo*, Wellington's H.Q. in the August of that year. Near by lie the extensive ruins and defensive walls of *Urueña*. We cross the Pto. de Perales. At 40 km. a road leads 11 km. l. to *Gata*, a fortified village with a good 16C church, while at 1 km. beyond this turning lies *Hoyos*, 4 km. W., also with a fine church.—25 km. beyond lies *Valverde del Fresno*. In the picturesque village of *San Martín de Trevejo*, 9 km. E., the church contains three paintings by *Morales.*

19 km. E. of this crossroad, on a height, stands the curious village of *Santibáñez el Alto* (providing panoramic *Views*).

The road continues to descend past (16 km.) *Moraleja*; hence a by-road leads S.W. viâ (30 km.) *Zarza la Mayor* to (20 km.) *Alcántara*, see Rte 45.

15 km. **Coria** (10,600 inhab.), a dilapidated old town on the Alagón. Its granite *Walls* incorporate materials from Roman *Cauria*, and the 12C *castle* has a noble 15C pentagonal tower. The rebuilding of the **Cathedral** as a church of a single span (17 m.) was begun in 1496 by *Martín* and *Bart. de Solórzano*, and completed in 1570 by *Pedro de Ibarra*. It contains stalls of 1489 and of 1515 (by *Martín de Ayala*), a reja (1503) by *Hugo de Santa Úrsula*, a Baroque retablo mayor by *Juan* and *Diego de Villanueva* (1745–49), an 18C organ by Verdalanga, and *Tombs* designed by *Diego Copín* and *Juan Métara*. The tower was rebuilt in 1756–60, and the cloister dates from c. 1450–73.—Below the cathedral a medieval bridge crosses the old course of the Alagón.

12 km. *Torrejoncillo*, a decayed town once noted for its cloth workers, beyond which, after passing at *Portezuelo* a Moorish castle, later reconstructed. We meet at 20 km. the N 630 S. of *Cañaveral* (*Hotel*) where we turn r.

For the road hence to *Cáceres* and *Mérida*, see Rte 46A.

47   FROM MÉRIDA TO SEVILLE

Total distance, 196 km. (122 miles.). N 630. 30 km. *Almendralejo*—26 km. *Zafra* (4 km. to the r.)—68 km. *Santa Olalla*—72 km. **Seville.**

Crossing the Guadiana we bear l. on to the N 630, to (30 km.) **Almendralejo** (22,300 inhab.), birthplace of José de Espronceda (1808–42), the Romantic poet. The church of *La Purificación*, by *Fr. Morate* and *Salvador Muñoz*, dates from 1539.—At *Los Santos*, nearby, was found the disc of Theodosius, now in the Real Academia de la Historiá, Madrid, see p.247. 14 km. *Villafranca de los Barros* preserves a number of old houses, and *Sta María* displays a fine Gothic façade. 9 km. E. is *Ribera del Fresno*, birthplace of the poet Juan Meléndez Valdés (1754–1817).—11 km. S.W. of Villafranca lies *Fuente del Maestre*, with the interesting church of *N.S. de la Candelaria*, containing a curious Retablo Mayor.—We ascend the Sierra de Jerez.

At 12 km. a road leads 4 km. W. to *Zafra* (p.427), passing (r.) *Los Santos de Maimona* (8100 inhab.) a Roman site with Gothic *Los Ángeles*, and a *Zurbarán* in the chapel of *N.S. de la Estrella.*—From Zafra the N 435 leads S.W. to *Huelva* (see below), off which after 10 km., the C 4311 turns W. to (28 km.) *Jerez de los Caballeros*, see p.426, through attractive hilly country viâ (19 km.) *Burguillos de Cerro*, overlooked by a castle, possibly of the Templars, restored.—At 7 km. we cross the N 432 from Badajoz to *Córdoba*, see Rte 48.

12 km. r. *Calzadilla de los Barros* has a good church, while at 6 km. *Fuente de Cantos*, the parish church contains a Baroque retablo. Zurbarán was born here in 1598. A Roman ruin lies some 4 km. S.W.; while *Montemolín*, 13 km. S.E., retains a Moorish castle, and old houses.—18 km. **Monestério**, 7 km. W. of which, at *Calera de León*, is a medieval monastery of the order of Santiago, with a Gothic church and a two-storeyed cloister, while to the S.W. in the Sierra de Tudia, is the monastery of *Sta María de Tentudia*, founded in the 13C, containing azulejos (1518) by *Niculaso Pisano*, and a Mudéjar cloister. We cross the Pto. de las Marismas, the easiest route through the convoluted SIERRA MORENA into Andalucía, passing (25 km.) *Santa Olalla* and (23 km.) *El Ronquillo*, to reach (r.) the Embalse de la Minilla.—At (14 km.) Venta del Alto, we meet the N 433 which leads N.W. viâ *Aracena* to *Rosal de la Frontera*, see p.561. We now descend into the Guadalquivir valley and soon discern Seville to the S.E.—At 24 km. r. we pass *Itálica* (see p.557) before entering (11 km.) **Seville,** see Rte 67.

FROM ZAFRA TO HUELVA (195 km.). We follow the N 435 S.W. to (42 km.) **Fregenal de la Sierra** (6700 inhab), birthplace of Arias Montano (1527–98) the humanist, and of the politician Juan Bravo Murillo (1803–73), attractively situated, and with an ancient castle, 23 km. N.W. of which lies *Jerez de los Caballeros*, see p.426. At *Segura de León*, 14 km. S.E., is a 13C castle, *La Asunción* (14C), and the 17C *Ermita del Santo Cristo de la Reja.*—At 15 km. a road (l.) leads 4 km. to *Cumbres Mayores*, with a late-14C castle.—26 km. We meet the cross-road (N 433) from Seville to Rosal de la Frontera, see p.561. Just S. of this junction, at *Jabugo*, with a reputation for its hams, is a good 17C church.—At 12 km. a road leads 6 km. W. to *Almonaster*, with a ruined castle and an interesting 16C church.

33 km. *Zalamea la Real*, 6 km. E. of which lies **Riotinto,** the centre of one of the oldest mining districts in the world. There are two townships, *Riotinto* itself and *Nerva* (5 km. E.) with a number of surrounding villages. The 'Rio Tinto' flows from the area S. through barren hilly country to the sea, its waters coloured by the copper and iron oxides washed into it. The mining area extends roughly from the Seville-Mérida highway to the Minas de São Domingos, beyond the Portuguese frontier.

The *Riotinto mines* were worked probably by the Phoenicians and certainly by the Romans from Nerva to Honorius (96–400 A.D.). The workings were broken up by the Visigoths and remained practically derelict until 1725, when they were leased by Philip V to Liebert Wolters, a Swede, from whose successors they reverted to the crown in 1783. After nearly a century of indifferent success they were again leased to a syndicate out of which arose the *Rio Tinto Company*, largely a British concern. In 1954 the property reverted to Spanish ownership, but the British Rio Tinto-Zinc Corporation retains a one-third interest. Between 3000 and 4000 tons of ore (iron pyrites containing some copper) are extracted daily (over a million tons annually). The mines and metallurgical works may be inspected only by previous written permission from the head office of the Company in Madrid. D. Avery's recent study, entitled 'Not on Queen Victoria's Birthday', gives the full history of the mines.

At 6 km. a road leads 17 km. E. to *Berrocal*, with a 15C church.— 15 km. *Valverde del Camino*, (10,550 inhab.) 18 km. N.W. of which, at *Calañas*, is the chapel of *N.S. de España*, in which Roderic, the last king of the Goths is said to be buried. At 24 km. we by-pass *Trigueros*, near the rock carvings of the Dolmen de Zancarrón de Soto, before descending to *San Juan del Puerto* and (22 km.) **Huelva,** see Rte 68.

48   FROM BADAJOZ TO ZAFRA AND CÓRDOBA

Total distance, 272 km. (169 miles). N 432. 24 km. *La Albuera*—53 km. **Zafra**— 41 km. *Llerena*—62 km. *Fuenteovejuna*—92 km. **Córdoba.**

We drive S.E. on the N 432 to (24 km.) **La Albuera** (1800 inhab.), the scene of the bloody battle of 16 May, 1811, immediately W. of the village, in which Beresford defeated Soult, although he failed to relieve Badajoz. Under Beresford were 35,000 allied troops, of whom 9000 were British; Soult's army numbered 24,000. The casualties on each side were 6000, and between 7000 and 8000 respectively.

27 km. W. lies the once strongly fortified town of **Olivenza** (9300 inhab.), which may also be approached direct from Badajoz (26 km. N.). It was taken from Portugal in 1801, and some of its architecture is distinctively Manueline. The *castle* dates from 1306, and in the 15C *Misericordia* the chapel has good azulejos dated 1723. The churches of *La Magdalena*, with spiral pillars, *Sta María*, the *Hosp. de la Caridad*, and the Doorway of the *Municipal Library*, are of interest.—20 km. S. of Olivenza stands the castle of *Alconchel*, and 18 km. beyond, *Villanueva del Fresno*, with a customs post, opposite the Portugese town of *Mourão*, 15 km. W.; see the *Blue Guide to Portugal*, forthcoming.

FROM LA ALBUERA TO JEREZ DE LOS CABALLEROS (49 km.). The N 435 forks r. to *Almendral*, with a fortified church, 7 km. E. of which is the well-preserved castle of *Nogales* (1438). At (24 km.) *Barcarrota*, birthplace of Hernándo de Soto (?1500– 1542), the conquistador, the old castle accommodates the Plaza de Toros. Good views to the S.E. are obtained as the road winds down to (25 km.) **Jerez de los Caballeros** (10,300 inhab.), an attractive and characteristic old frontier town, and birthplace of Vasco Núñez de Balboa (?1475–1519) discoverer of the Pacific. It is now a centre of the cork industry, and is renowned for its hams. Jerez preserves remains of 13C walls and six gates, and a 14C *Castle* of the Knights Templar (Caballeros Templarios), who took the place from the Moors in 1229. Beside the castle is *Sta María*, built in the 13C on a Visigothic site, but reconstructed in the 16C and later adorned in the Baroque style. Close to the Clock Tower is disused *La Vera Cruz*, now a wine-vault. Slightly below the castle, on the saddle between the twin hills on which the walled town was built, lies the *Pl. Mayor*, with the *Casas Consistoriales* of 1632, and *S. Miguel* partly of the 15C, but much altered, with a magnificent *Tower* of carved brick, completed in 1756, and a Baroque S. Doorway of 1719. The interior contains the choir of the Order of Santiago, which succeeded the Templars, and has a wrought-iron pulpit and a Baroque retablo mayor; the sanctuary is flanked on the N. by a *Camerín* of 1791, with interesting sculptures, and on the S. by a chapel of 1782.

Steep streets lead N, to *S. Bartolomé,* mainly 16C, but altered in 1739, with a W. Front of azulejos in the Portuguese style and a splendid *Tower* (1759) with vaulted ramps internally, similar to the Giralda of Seville; the exterior is of coloured stucco studded with azulejos and embossed blue glazed tablets. The baptistery is a late Gothic chapel (15C), and there are good effigies of Vasco de Jerez and his wife in the *Cap. de la Ánimas.*—To the S. W., outside the walled town, is *Sta Catalina,*with the third of the three 18C 'Torres Giraldinas' which crown the hill; mainly of the 16C, the church contains a retablo mayor and sculptures of the 17C, notably a Pietà and statues of S. Pedro Alcántara and S. Diego de Alcalá.—In the *C. del Hospital,* E. of the Pl. Mayor, is the Gothic doorway of the roofless chapel of the *Hosp de Transuentes,* while N.E., the C. de Vasco Núñez de Balbao leads to the *Pta. de Burgo* and is continued to the Pl. de Vasco Núñez, with the picturesque *Fuente de Caballos* beside the road.— *The Dolmen de Toniñuelo,* engraved with solar symbols, is c. 5 km. N.W.

23 km S.E. lies *Fregenal de la Sierra* (p.425), where we meet the N 435 from Zafra to Huelva.

53 km. Zafra, a decayed town (12,400 inhab.; *Parador Nac.*) full of reminders of its former importance, was the Iberian *Segada,* and the Roman *Julia Restituta.* It was called *Zafar* by the Moors. Manuel García (1805–1906), the famous singing-teacher, was born here. The granite *Pta. del Acebuche* leads to the towered *Alcázar,* E. of the town, the Gothic *Pal. of the Dukes of Feria,* built by Lorenzo Suárez de Figueroa in 1437–43 and gutted by the French in 1811. The impressive Patio was altered in the 16C. The palace has been well converted to house the Parador. The fig-leaf device of the Figueroas appears on this and many other buildings.

In the adjoining chapel of *Sta Marina* is the tomb (1601) of Lady Margaret Harrington, erected by her cousin Jane Dormer, Duchess of Feria and maid of honour to Mary Tudor. The tomb of the duchess and of her husband, the Spanish ambassador to England, is in the 15C *Conv. de Sta Clara,* S of the town.

The nearby C. Mayor leads to the arcaded *Pl. Grande* and adjacent *Pl. Chica* (both restored), an attractive and characteristic area.—The *Casa Grande* and the tower of the *Colegiata* are imposing although unfinished buildings in the Ionic style, the latter containing paintings by *Zurbarán.* The 14C church of *La Candelaria* has good 17C fittings, and the *Hosp. de Santiago* a fine portal.

For the route from Zafra to *Huelva,* see p.425.

38 km. S.W. of Zafra lies *Jerez de los Caballeros* (see above), approached by turning r. of the N 435 after 10 km. and after 9 km. traversing *Burguillos del Cerro,* see p.425.

At 7 km. we cross the N 630 and at 34 km. pass (r.) **Llerena** (5200 inhab.), preserving old walls, a pleasant Pl. Mayor, and interesting churches, particularly *N.S. de la Granada,* with a fine tower, 55 m. high, topped by a giralda, and a two-storeyed exterior gallery. The 15C *Pal. de Luís de Zapata* has been restored.

FROM LLERENA TO CARMONA (116 km.). We bear S.E. on the C 432 towards the Sierra Morena, passing (5 km. r.) a ruined Roman fortress called *Castillo de la Reina,* and enter a mining district (lead, coal, and iron) of which the main centres are (20 km.) *Guadalcanal* (6550 inhab.), birthplace of the statesman and dramatist Adelardo López de Ayala (1829-79). and (11 km.) *Alanís,* with a 14C church, old fortifications and houses.—17 km. S.W. of Alanís is *Cazalla de la Sierra* (6550 inhab.), where *La Consolación,* in Gothic-Mudéjar style, and the chapel of the *Virgén del Monte,* are of interest.—At (26 km.) *Constantina* (10,150 inhab.), delightfully sited, some Roman inscriptions survive, while in the parish church of *Las Navas de la Concepción,* 22 km. N.E., is a Baroque altarpiece and some interesting woodwork from the ruined *Conv. de S. Antonio del Valle.*—27 km.

Lora del Rio, on the C 431 from Córdoba to Seville, running parallel to the N. bank of the Guadalquivir, see Rte 64. We cross the river and bear S.W. to (27 km.) **Carmona,** 33 km. E. of *Seville.*

At Llerena the N 432 turns E. to (31 km) **Azuaga** (10,600 inhab.), an ancient town with ruined castles, in one of which, called *Miramontes,* the daughters of Trajan are said to be buried.—11 km. *La Granja de Torrehermosa,* whose parish church has a fine Mudéjar tower of c.1500. 20 km.—**Fuenteovejuna** (7300 inhab.; Carthaginian *Mellaria*), attractively situated on the brow of a hill, its famous for the rising in 1476 celebrated in Lope de Vega's play. There are remains of 13-15C fortifications, while the church contains interesting paintings and a fine custodia by *Enrique de Arfe.*

The road hence to *Cazalla* (73 km. S.W.; see above) is *not* recommended, although the surface is good, and it traverses wild and lonely ranges of the Sierra Morena.

We gently descend into the valley of the Guadiato to (15 km.) **Puebloneuvo** and adjacent **Peñarroya** (together 13,700 inhab.), still the centre of a mining district (lead, iron, and copper) although some buildings appear to be derelict.—We pass through (7 km.) *Belmez,* overlooked by a hill crowned by a Moorish castle, (20 km.) *Espiel,* with an interesting church, and (22 km.) the ruined Moorish castle at *El Vacar,* before crossing the Sierra de Córdoba. Passing (13 km.) *Cerro Muriano,* with copper mines, amid ancient Iberian settlements, we climb down steeply into the Giadalquivir valley near (15 km.) **Córdoba,** see Rte 65.

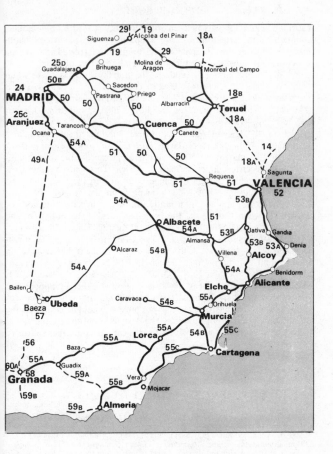

VI NEW CASTILE, VALENCIA, AND MURCIA

For **New Castile**, see description on p.407. The old kingdom of **Valencia**, consists of the modern provinces of *Valencia*, *Alicante*, and *Castellón*, and has perhaps the finest climate of any part of Spain; to the Moors it was Paradise a part, fallen down on earth, of the Heaven which they imagined to be suspended over it. It was finally taken from them by Jaime el Conquistador in 1238, but the indigenous population was allowed to cultivate the land in peace until 1609 when 2t0,000 of them were expelled by Philip III. Enough old men were left behind to hand down to the Valencians the shstem of irrigation which they had brought to a state of perfection.

The '*riego de las aguas*'—the complex irrigation system—is literally the life blood of the kingdom; the water, flowing down from the snows of the mountain barrier that wards off the rigours of the Aragonese or

Castilian winter, is divided up with the utmost skill among canals, channels, and irrigation drains, a special court of justice being maintained to ensure fair division. The huerta thus fertilized and vivified by continual sunshine produces an unending series of crops—fruit, wine, oil, hemp, almonds, and, in the marshy districts, rice, while Mulberry trees are grown for silkworm culture. The populations of both the provinces of Valencia and Alicante have doubled in size since 1920, their capitals having grown from 247,000 to 708,000 and from 63,000 to 215,000 respectively.

Murcia, the ancient *Reino de Murcia*, subdivided into the inland province of *Albacete* and, to the S., *Murcia*, is one of the driest parts of Spain, and its maritime portion, in climate, tropical productions, and general aspect, resembles a Spanish Africa. This seatoard region is subject to violent changes of temperature and to the scourge of the parching '*leveche*', a hot wind blowing from the Sahara. The soil, naturally fertile, is made luxuriantly productive by skiful methods of irrigation, while Cartagena, the principal port, is the outlet for the produce of an exceptionally rich mineral district. Under the Romans, Murcia was included in *Hispania Tarraconensis* and in the Moorish period it was at first part of the emirate of Córdoba but afterwards an independent kingdom. Under Fernando III it became a vassal state of Castile and was occupied in 1243.

The corn-growing plateau of Albacete grow bleaker a it approaches the boundary of New Castile. Extensive wind-blown tracts here, bare of trees, are used for pasture, and the province is as cold in Winter, as the coastal zone is baked in Summer. The population of the rural areas of Albacete is less than it was in 1920, but the capital has more than tripled in size.

49   FROM MADRID TO BAILEN

A   Viâ Aranjuez and Manzanares.

Total distance, 295 km. (183 miles), N IV. 48 km. *Aranjuez*—16 km. *Ocaña*—30 km. *Tembleque*—79 km. *Manzanares*—29 km. *Valdepeñas*—93 km. *Bailén*.
  For travellers wishing to drive S. direct from Toledo, there are two alternative routes, see below. Rte 49B.

We follow the N IV from Madrid viâ *Aranjuez* (Rte 25C) and *Ocaña,* see Rte 54. Here we bear due S.—13 km. S.W. lies *Yepes,* retaining old fortifications and a church of 1552 with a reredos containing paintings by *Luis Tristán* (1616).—We pass (20 km.) troglodyte *La Guardia,* 5 km. N.E. of which is the hermitage of the *Santo Niño,* claimed to have been crucified there in 1490 by Jews.—10 km. r. **Tembleque** (2500 inhab.) has an attractive wooden-galleried **Pl. Mayor.* We continue to traverse the monotonous steppes of LA MANCHA, exposed to wintry blasts and scorched by summer heat , by-passing (28 km.) *Madridejos*, with an imposingly buttressed bullring, 8 km. W. of which we see the castle of *Consuerga* on a ridge studded with white 'pepper-pot' windmills.—14 km. *Puerto Lápice* (*Hotels*), where we cross the N 420 from Mota del Cuervo (on the N 301) to *Ciudad Real,* 63 km. S.W.

FROM PUERTO LÁPICE TO ALMAGRO (54 km.). Forking r. here the N 420 crosses the Campo de Calatrava, the most fertile part of La Mancha, which belonged o the

Knights of Calatrava, to (32 km.) **Daimiel** (17,100 inhab.) with a good Gothic church, *Sta María*, and classical *S. Pedro*. To the N. are the lakes known as 'Los Ojos del Guadiana'. 22 km. to the S., on the C 417, on a cross-road (C 415) between Ciudad Real and Valdepeñas, lies the white town of **Almagro** (8700 inhab.; *Parador Nac.* projected in the Conv. de S. Francisco). It preserves an attractive *Pl. Mayor, a 16C * Theatre* (restored), and the *Conv. of the Knights of Calatrava*, with a good staircase and Plateresque cloister, in addition to a number of imposing doorways flanking its unspoilt cobbled streets, The 16C chapel of *S. Blas* was built at the expense of Jakob Fugger and his nephews, and there is a Last Supper of the same period in *S. Bartolomé*. Diego de Almagro (1478/9-1538), conquerer of Chile, is said to have been discovered at Almagro as a foundling.

From Almagro, the C 417 continues viâ *Granátula,* with a Roman bridge, the birthplace of Gen. Espartero (1792–1879), to (20 km. S.) *La Calzada de Calatrava* with two old castles, that of *Salvatierra* close to the town, and *Calatrava la Nueva,* c. 8 km. S.W. near the near the Pto. de Calatrava. The latter is a splendid ruin of the 13th and 15C, and includes a conventual church with a rose-window, and other monastic buildings.

From *La Calzada* we may follow the C 410 viâ *Viso del Marqués (see below) to regain the N IV at Almuradiel,* 36 km. S.E.

FROM VILARTA DE SAN JUAN TO RUIDERA. At (11 km.) *Villarta* a road leads 31 km. S.E. to **Argamasilla de Alba** (7100 inhab.), where Cervantes is said to have written or at least conceived the earlier chapters of 'Don Quixote' in a prison which is still shown (*Casa de Medrano*; rebuilt), is generally accepted as the authentic birthplace of the 'Knight of the Rueful Countenance', and Don Rodrigo de Pacheco, a local hidalgo, whose portrait is preserved in the church, is not improbably regarded as the original of that importal hero.

Tomelloso (26,300 inhab.) 8 km. to the E., is the centre of the local wine and cloth trade.—From Argamasilla an attractive road runs S.E., skirting the Embalse de Peñarroya, and passing the castle of *Peñarroja* to *Ruidera,* the scene of Don Quixote's adventure with the puppets, where the Guadiana rises in a series of small lakes known as the *Lagunas de Ruidera.* The main stream disappears W. of the Embalse, rising again to the surface at 'Los Ojos Del Guadiana' near Daimiel, see above, S.E. of Ruidera, at the head of the uppermost lake, is the *Cave of Montesinos,* apparently an ancient Roman copper-mine; to the S. extends the CAMPO DE MONTIEL, where Don Quixote sought adventure, and where Pedro the Cruel was defeated and killed by Henry of Trastamara in 1369.

At 26 km. we by-pass **Manzanares** (15,300 inhab.; *Albergue Nac.; Hotels*), on the site of a castle built after the battle of Las Navas de Tolosa. It was here that George Borrow met the famous blind improvisor known as 'La Ciega de Manzanares' or the 'Manchegan Prophetess', who used regularly to meet the Madrid diligence. The old town has a large late-Gothic church, and to the S.E. is the 13C castle of *Peñas Borras.*

At 29 km. we by-pass **Valdepeñas** (23,200 inhab.; *Hotels*), famous for its wines, which should be tasted in one of the numerous bodegas or wine-cellars. The resinous flavour, or *'borracha',* is due to the pitch with which the wineskins are coated inside.

At *Infantes,* 33 km. on the Albacete road (C 415), is the tomb of the poet Francisco de Quevedo y Villegas (1580–1645).—*Torrenueva,* 13 km. S.E., was the scene of Don Quixote's liberation of the galleyslaves.

Beyond (15 km.) *Santa Cruz de Mudela* (by-passed) with a 15C church, and an antimony mine once worked by the eminent 18C printer Antonio Sancha, we begin the gradual ascent of the SIERRA MORENA, at 15 km. passing *Almuradiel* (*Hotel*), a post founded by Carlos III in 1768 to suppress brigandage in the Sierra.—A road leads 6 km. W. to **Viso del Marqués**, with a large *Palace* built for Álvaro de Bazán, Marqués de Santa Cruz, begun in 1564 by *J. B. Castello* (*el Bergamasco*) and continued after 1585 by Genoese masters. The conventual church contains the tombs of María Figueroa and Alonso de Bazán.—12 km. the *Venta de Cárdenas* recalls Don Quixote's penance.

Now we enter the notorious ***Desfiladero de Despeñaperros**, a magnificent and extensive rocky defile, often the scene of highway robbery in the past, whose name signifies 'overthrow of the dogs', i.e. the infidels. Here, at the *Pto. del Rey*, according to John Talbot Dillon, writing in the late 18C, a toll was paid 'for monkies, parrots, negroes, and guittars unless played upon at the time: married women unless in company with their husbands or producing certificates . . . '. The well-engineered road traverses the pass in sweeping curves to *Santa Elena* (*Hotel*), before reaching (24 km. l.) the insignificant village of *Las Navas de Tolosa*, celebrated for the crushing victory, in 1212, of Alfonso VIII (miraculously guided through the sierra: comp. p.313) over the Andalusian Moors under Mohammed ibn-Abdallah en-Nasir.

At 3 km. we pass **La Carolina** (17,000 inhab.; *Hotel*), the most important of the settlements colonized in 1768 by Carlos III and his minister Pablo de Olavide (1725–1803) with Swiss and German immigrants in order to reduce the lawle sness of the Sierra Morena foothills. With the dismissal of Olavide it foundered, although Swinburne suggests that it was 'from eating unwholesome herbs, and drinking too much wine and brandy' that half the Germans died.

Hence the C 3217 bears S.E. to (53 km.) *Úbeda*, see Rte 57, while at 12 km., *Guarromán*, (*Hotel*) another leads 13 km. S.E. to *Linares*.—At 6 km. a road bears W. to (6 km.) *Baños de la Encina*, close to the Embalse del Rumblar, with a fine *castle* built in 967–68 by Hakam II.

6 km. **Bailén** (14,400 inhab.; *Parador Nac.; Hotels*), the scene of the fortuitous victory on 18 July, 1808, of the Spaniards under Castaños over Gén. Dupont with 22,000 French whose unexpected capitulation for days later, together with *S. Marcial* (comp. p.108), is celebrated in *Spanish* annals of the Peninsular War.

An anecdote is repeated that when Dupont delivered his sword to Castaños, he said: 'You may well, General, be proud of this day; it is remarkable that I have never lost a pitched battle till now,—I, who have been in more than twenty, and gained them all'. 'It is the more remarkable', replied dryly the sarcastic Spaniard, 'because I never was in one before in my life'.

From Bailén to *Jaén* and *Granada*, see Rte 56; to *Córdoba* and *Seville*, Rte 64. The N 322 leads E. from Bailén to 13 km. *Linares* (p.473), from which we bear S.E. to (33 km.) *Baeza*, and 9 km. beyond, *Úbeda*, see Rte 57, p.476.

B   Viâ Toledo and Ciudad Real

Total distance, 326 km. (202 miles). For the road from Madrid to (71 km.) **Toledo**, see Rte 26. Hence the N 401, 119 km. *Ciudad Real*—73 km. *Almuradiel*—63 km. *Bailén.*

An alternative route from Toledo meets the N IV at (70 km.) *Madridejos*. From Toledo we follow the N 401 to the E., and shortly climb S.E., after 4 km. turning l. onto the C 400.—At 5 km. *Nambroca*, the church contains a St Francis by *El Greco*, and (12 km.) *Almonacid de Toledo* is dominated by a ruined castle with an 11C keep within a double curtain wall; while at (5 km.) *Mascaraque* are slight remains of a 14C castle of the Padillas.—6 km. *Mora* (9600 inhab.), a thriving but ugly town, has a 15C church with a Plateresque retablo, and a castle built for Alfonso VII, commanding a wide view.—From (3 km. r.) *Manzanque*, with a 14-15C castle, we follow the road S.E. to (27 km.) *Consuegra*, with a conspicuous castle, before descending to (8 km.) *Madridejos,* see Rte 49A.

Following the N 401, at 9 km. S.E. of Toledo we pass *Burguillos*, where the 17C church contains Baroque retablos, while at (9 km.) *Ajofrín*, the Pl. Mayor has a fountain attrib. to *Alonso Cano*; the parish church has a Mudéjar tower, Churrigueresque retablos, and a reja of 1611; and the Dominican convent contains 16C sculpture.—4 km. S.W. at *Mazarambroz* is a tower of a 14C castle and a church with a Mudéjar roof.—4 km. The church of *Sonseca* has an altarpiece painted by *Luis Velasco* with carvings by *P. Martínez de Castañeda* (1574–88), 4 km. S. of which, at *Casalgordo*, are the slight remains of the Visigothic chapel of *S. Pedro de la Mata* (c. 675), with a horseshoe-arched entrance.—The road bears S.E. to (12 km.) **Orgaz**, a pleasant town (2900 inhab.) with an arcaded *Plaza*, a large granite *Church* of 1741–62, the uncompleted last work of *Alberto Churriguera*, the imposing 14C *Castle* of the Pérez de Guzmán, and a Roman bridge.—We climb olive-covered slopes and windmill-topped hills (Views) to (9 km.) **Los Yebenes** (6100 inhab.; *Hotel*), formerly a possession of the Knights of Malta. *S. Juan* has a 16C Mudéjar tower, while *Sta María* contains a retablo by *Martínez del Arce*.—At 18 km., just after passing (l.) the castle of *Guadilierzas*, a road leads 8 km. E. to *Urda*, with black marble and jasper quarries.—We cross the Sierra de la Serrona and descend towards the Guardiana.

At 42 km. *Fernancaballero*, we may fork l. to cross the river 7 km. beyond, passing on its banks the ruined castle of *Calatrava la Vieja*, at 7 km. meeting the N 420 at *Carrión de Calatrava*, the original headquarters of the Knights of Calatrava, a religious military order founded in 1158 to defend the southern frontier of Castile. The order was suppressed by the Catholic Kings and its possessions were vested in the crown in 1523, but the name survives as a titular order of merit. It was claimed by the Nationalists that in 1936 some hundreds of their supporters were rounded up from villages in the province and thrown down a mine shaft here.— *Alarcos*, to the W., was in 1195 the scene of the defeat of Alfonso VIII by the Moors, which was avenged 17 years later at Las Navas de Tolosa.—10 km. S.W. lies *Ciudad Real*.

At 8 km. we cross the Guadiana and climb again before entering (8 km.) the dull provincial capital of **CIUDAD REAL** (45,000 inhab.; 19,000 in 1920; *Hotels*), which scarcely merits the praise of Cervantes, who called it 'imperial, the seat of the god of smiles', and few would disagree with Gerald Brenan, who condemned it as a 'dull, one-horse little place'.

History. It was founded, as *Villa Real*, by Alfonso el Sabio in 1252 and received the title of city from Juan II in 1420. It was one of the earliest towns to possess a *Hermandad*, or brotherhood, to protect its roads against robbers. Similar associations arose in other parts of Spain (sometimes to protect citizens against the nobility), but by the Catholic Kings the *Santa Hermandad* was developed as a general police force, with para-inquisitorial powers—a precursor of the Guardia Civil. Hernán Perez del Pulgar (1451–1531), a hero of the siege of Granada, was born here.

Of the crumbling walls which once surrounded the city, not much else but the *Pta. de Toledo* remains, a gate in Mudéjar style built in 1328 to guard its N. entrance. From here the C. de Toledo runs S., with the *Audiencia* on the l., and the *Diputación* and *La Merced* (17C) on the r., to the arcaded Pl. del Generalísimo. At the N.E. corner is the old *Ayuntamiento* of 1619, while at the other end is the *Casa Consistorial* (1869). To the W. is the Paseo del Prado, with the former *Cathedral* (c. 1490–1580), or *Sta María del Prado*, containing good choir-stalls and retablo by *Giraldo de Merlo* (1616). The 17C tower was heightened in the 19C; of an earlier church there remains the blocked 12C W. Doorway.

To the N.E. lies *Santiago* (14C) but largely rebuilt, and a short distance E. of the central square is *S. Pedro*, a Gothic building (14C) with a Flamboyant rose-window, a Baroque retablo, and an alabaster wall-tomb in the S. chapel (c. 1500).—At *Miguelturra*, 4 km. S.E. on the Valdepeñas road, stands the curious 17C chapel of the *Cristo de la Misericordia*.

From Ciudad Real we may reach the N IV by driving 60 km. S.W. on the C 415 viâ *Almagro* (p.431) towards *Valdepeñas*, or 73 km. viâ *La Calzada de Calatrava* and *Viso del Marqués* to *Almuradiel*, and hence to (63 km.) *Bailén*, see Rte 49A.

FROM CIUDAD REAL TO CÓRDOBA VIÂ PUERTOLLANA (191 km.). We drive S.W. on the N 420, passing (19 km.) *Caracuel*, with a ruined castle, as has **Puertollano** (50,200 inhab.; *Hotel*), a coal-mining town with a huge but over-restored church, 17 km. beyond. We turn W. through (6 km.) *Almodóvar del Campo*, another colliery town, with a 13C church, before bearing S.W. for the Pto. de Niefla (3020 ft) and Pto. de Valderrepiso to (57 km.) *Fuencaliente*, a centre of prehistoric remains including the neolithic rock-paintings of *Peña Escrita* and *La Batanera* in the Sierra Madrona. Still following the N 420, we pass (16 km.) the *Venta de Cardeña*, and descend into the Guadalquivir valley, reaching the N IV at (36 km.) *Villa del Rio*, 8 km E. of *Montoro*. From Montoro to *Córdoba*, 41 km. W., see Rte 64.

From the Venta de Cardeña, the C 420 leads W. to (29 km.) **Villanueva de Córdoba** (11,200 inhab.), an interesting old town with Roman and Moorish remains.—*Conquista*, 16 km. N.E., a former estate of Pizarro, contains bismuth mines. There are forests of cork-oak, pine, and eucalyptus in the nearby valley of the Guadalmez to the N., here the boundary of Andalucía.—12 km. **Pozoblanco** (13,700 inhab.), birthplace of Juan Ginés de Sepulveda (c.1490–1573), the theologian, and adversary of Las Casas. It was also renowned for its woollens, 9 km. N.E. of which is the village of *Pedroche*, capital of the district of 'Los Pedroches', retaining ruined walls and a 15C church with a tower by *Hernán Ruiz*, while *Dos Torres* (8 km. N.W.) has fine old houses and a late-Gothic church.—21 km. **Alcaracejos**, a junction of minor roads and a lead-mining centre, has a Plateresque church and ruins of the *Cerro del Germo*, a Visigothic basilica of the 6C. *Almadén* (see below) lies 49 km. N. on the C 411. 28 km. S. is *Espiel*, see Rte 48; and 33 km. S.W. *Pueblonuevo*, while 21 km. N.W., on the C 420, lies **Hinojosa del Duque**, (9000 inhab.), where the Plateresque church contains a Churrigueresque retablo. 8 km. further N. is the impressive ruined *Castle of Belalcázar*, built in 1445 by *Gutiérrez Sotomayor*. It is probable that the conquistador Sebastián de Benalcázar (c. 1480-1551), also known as Belalcázar, was born here.

FROM CIUDAD REAL TO ALCARACEJOS VIÂ ALMADÉN (159 km.). We drive S.W. on the N 420, after 16 km. forking r. onto the C 424. The first section of road is in poor condition. It later improves, before twisting through a range of hills and entering the *Valdeazogues* (Vale of Quicksilver), in which we pass (r.) the derelict furnaces of *Almadenejas*.—86 km. **Almadén** (10,200 inhab.), Roman *Sisapo*, the centre of the richest mercury deposit in Europe. The mines lie to the W. of the town, in itself of little interest. Its name is a corruption of the Arabic words signifying 'the quicksilver mine', they were known to the Moors (whose castle of *Retamar* is preserved), but their present exploitation dates from the 16C, when they were pledged by Charles V to the Fuggers of Augsburg (known in Spain as Los Fúcares) as security for loans. The mercury is found both in the virgin state and in cinnabar ore, and the deepest shaft descends more than 1100 ft underground. Widdrington, in 1843, was one of the few English travellers who ever visited this remote area.

From Almadén, the road turns S. to (31 km.) *Santa Eufemia*, commanding extensive views, with ruined fortifications on a height to the W., and a 14C church, and passes near the castle of *Madroñiz*, before entering (26 km.) *Alcaracejos*, see above. There is a good road from Santa Eufemia to *Belalcázar*, 28 km. W.; see above.

50   FROM MADRID TO CUENCA

Total distance, 167 km. (104 miles). NIII. 82 km. *Tarancón*—N400. 85 km. **Cuenca.**
An alternative cross-country route is that from MADRID TO CUENCA VIÂ
GUADLAJARA AND SACEDON (236 km.). Some of the cross-country roads on this
longer route are in poor condition, and communications have been impaired,
temporarily, by the construction of the extensive Embalse de Buendia.
From Madrid to (58 km.) *Guadalajara*, see Rte 25D, p.286, where we turn r. on
to the N 320, which leads into the district known as LA ALCARRIA.—At 9 km. the road
leads 5 km. N.E. to the *Monastery of S. Bartolomé* at *Lupiana*, founded in 1370,
the mother-house of the Hieronymite order. The ruined church was completed in
1632, and there is an impressive three-storeyed Renaissance cloister. The buildings
are now private property, but may be visited on application—3 km. r. *Horche*, a
picturesque village with a 15C church containing good walnut stalls.—9 km. r.
Armuña, on the Tajuña, has a ruined castle and a fortified church.
In 1 km. we come to cross-roads.—7 km. to the S.W. lies *Aranzueque*, with a
Plateresque church.—20 km. S.E. lies **Pastrana** (2050 inhab.) once noted for its
silk-weaving. The Gothic *Çolegiata* contains a large retabio by *Juan de Borgoña*,
tombs of the Princess of Éboli (d. 1592) and her family, good choir-stalls, a rich
treasury, and magnificent **Tapestries* woven in the 15C to record the taking of
Tangier and Arzila by the Portuguese. The *Ducal Palace* (under restoration) was
begun in 1541.—12 km. beyond lies *Zorita de los Canes* (with a nuclear-power
station), retaining a restored castle within which is a small Romanesque church;
and at the nearby *Cerro de la Oliva*, remains of the Visigothic city of *Recopolis* (c.
580). 4 km. S.E. is *Almonacid de Zorita*, an ancient walled village, and adjacent
Albalate (*Hotel*) with a good 16C hall-church with reticulated vaults.—From
a cross-road 5 km. N.W. of Almonacid we may follow the C 204 N. for 23 km. to
regain the N 320 a short distance W. of *Sacedón*, see below.
From Armuña we turn E. through (5 km.) the arcaded main street of *Tendilla*
and (15 km) *Alhóndiga*, to reach (6 km.) *Auñón*, and further on, the Tagus, which
we cross to enter (13 km.) **Sacedón** (1800 inhab.), with a Renaissance hall-church
covered by fine Gothic vaults. To the N. lies the *Embalse de Entrepeñas* while a
road leading due S. skirts the W. bank of the huge *Embalse de Buendia*, also
known as *'El Mar de Castilla'*, and likely to be marred by chalet development. This
road is continued to *Huete*, 44 km. S. of Sacedón, and 13 km. N. of *Carrascosa del
Campo*, on the Tarancón-Cuenca road, see below.
The N 320 climbs E. from Sacedón over the Sierra de Altamira to reach (6 km.)
Córcoles, with a 15C church and the ruined Benedictine monastery of *Monsalud*,
of which the Chapter House (13C) and tombs in the 16C cloister are noteworthy.—
At 8 km. we fork l. for *Alcócer*, with remains of a castle and ramparts, and an
outstanding church with a Romanesque W. Doorway, nave of 1260, and a late-
Gothic crossing and sanctuary. The reservoir has now cut the direct road to
Cuenca and we must make a detour to the N. to (37 km.) *Priego*, where the rebuilt
church contains a painting of the Virgin given by Pius V after the battle of Lepanto
(1571). The remote *Conv. de S. Miguel de la Victoria*, 4 km. to the E., contains 18C
statues by *Carmona*.—We now turn S.E. to regain the N 320 at (20 km.)
Cañaveras, where we bear r., crossing the foothills of the Sierra de Bascuña to join
the N 400 6 km. W. of (46 km.) **Cuenca**, see below.

We follow the N III to (82 km.) Tarancón, see Rte 51, p.440, where we
turn E. onto the N 400 and strike off across the high bracken country of
the Serranía, passing (13 km. r.) *Huelves*, with an early castle.—15 km.
Carrascosa del Campo, sacked in 1808, is the centre of a depopulated
region sprinkled with ruined churches and castles. The church, however,
preserves an elaborate 16C portal and good retablos.—13 km. N., on the
C 202, lies **Huete**, ancient *Istonium*, pleasantly situtated in a hill-girt
plain, in which stands a ruined castle. *S. Esteban* has a handsome coro,
and *S. Lorenzo Justiniano* a good façade, while *Sto Domingo* contains a
15C tomb, and in the Conv. church of *La Merced* is a painting by *El
Greco*. The *Bishop's Palace* is of the 13C.

The road climbs through attractive wooded country to the Pto. de Cabrejas and descends into the valley of the Júcar where at 51 km. we meet the N 320 from Priego, see above. We cross the river by the *Pte. de S. Antón* to enter (6 km.) Cuenca. On the N. bank, opposite the bridge, stands the *Conv. de S. Antón* (14C), with a 16C Plateresque doorway, a church with good 18C decoration, and an elliptical dome.

CUENCA (3025 ft), a modern provincial capital (36,800 inhab,; 13,000 in 1920; *Hotels*), conserves a picturesque medieval town which is romantically situated on the rocky spur of S. Cristóbal; and isolated from the Serranía de Cuenca by the deep defiles of the Júcar and its tributary the Huécar. Old walls and towers overhang both streams, and from its seven gates narrow lanes wind up towards the cathedral.

History. Cuenca. Roman *Conca,* was given by Ibn Abet, king of Seville, to Alfonso VI as the dowry of his daughter, Zaida. The city rebelled, but was subdued by Alfonso VIII in 1177 after a nine-months siege. The influential *Fueros* date from 1189-90. In 1808 Cuenca was the victim of reprisals by the French; in 1873-74 it was sacked by the Carlists, and suffered further damage in 1937. It was the birthplace of Card. Gil de Albornoz (c. 1310–67), the papal general: Alonso de Hojeda (c. 1468–1515), companion of Columbus and explorer of Guiana; Andrés Hurtado de Mendoza (c. 1490–1561), viceroy of Peru, the *converso* brothers Juan (c. 1491–1541) and Alfonso de Valdés (c. 1490–1532), pioneers of church reform, and Hernán or Fernando Yáñez (fl. 1500–20), the painter.

The main artery of the uninteresting modern town runs S. from the Pte. de S. Antón, passing the *Beneficencia Municipal* of 1777 and, further on (r.), the *Hosp. de Santiago,* a 15C foundation, to the Pl. del Generalísimo. Here, 14C *S. Francisco* (or *S. Estebán)* contains some primitives and good 18C sculpture. Hence the C. Aguirre and its continuation runs N.E. to cross the Huécar at the *Pta. de Valencia*— whence we may walk up into the old town—and turns r. along the bottom of the gorge (views of the *Casas Colgadas)* before climbing to *S. Pablo,* see below.

While the *old* town may be visited by car—a road turning l. not far S. of the Pte de S. Antón climbs up to the Pl. Mayor and beyond to the Pl. del Castillo—much of this area can only be explored on foot.

From the Pl. de Caivo Sotelo, halfway along the main street, pedestrians should follow the C. de Fray Luis de León, which runs E. towards the old town. Crossing the Huécar, we climb the C. de la Correduria, lined with Casas Solariegas, the ancestral mansions of the Conquistadores, and adorned with their escutcheons; in the side streets are timbered houses with overhanging storeys. At the E. end of the bridge is the old *Almudí* (public granary), and some distance above it to the E. stands *S. Salvador,* with interesting retablos. Still farther W. is Baroque *S. Felipe* (gutted by fire in 1936) with embossed doors and a Pietà attr. to *Salzillo,* and *S. Andrés,* with Baroque retablos and an Ecce Homo by *J. Tores* (1648).

We continue to ascend, now by the C. Alfonso VIII, and see on the l. before passing through the arches leading to the Pl. Mayor, *La Merced,* with a reja by *Beltrán* and good polychrome sculptures, and beyond it the 17C portal of the *Seminary.* The hospital of the *Ancianos Desamparados,* opposite, has a Crucifixion by *Gerard David* and a Flemish triptych, while beyond is the *Torre de Mangana,* a relic of the Moorish fortress.

Passing through the arches supporting the *Ayuntamiento* of 1760, we see the unfinished white stone W. Front of the Cathedral on the r. At the N. end of the *Pl. Mayor* is the *Conv. de Petras*, with an elliptical church designed by *Ventura Rodríguez* and *A.G. Velázquez*, with a ceiling of 1759; thence a lane leads down to the *Conv. de Descalzas*, over-looking the Jucar gorge (plunging views); and beyond to the chapel of *N.S. de las Angustias.* Another path leads directly W. down to *S. Miguel* (restored).

The **Cathedral** (best seen in the morning) was founded by Alfonso VII. The nave (c. 1208–50), crossing, and W. part of the choir (c. 1197–1208) are a good example of simple Gothic work, containing features of Anglo-Norman character. The W. Front, clumsily rebuilt in 1664–69, has been tastelessly restored (after a plan made by *Vicente Lampérez*) since the partial collapse of the N. Tower in 1902. The old doors, with their bronze bosses, survive.

In the INTERIOR (which is in the process of being thoroughly cleaned, and the ugly gilt and whitewash removed), the capitals and the vault above the crossing are note-worthy. The apse is an elaborate late-Gothic construction with a strong suggestion of Moorish influence in the shape of the arches and the arrangement of the columns; it was built between 1448 and 1490, perhaps to the designs of *Anequín de Egas.* The clerestory of the nave has widely spaced interior tracery, and in the rose-window of the N. Transept is good stained glass; little of the other glass in the building merits attention. The 18C organ is by Julián de la Orden.

The modernized *Coro* has a *Reja* and eagle lectern by *Hernando de Arenas* (1557), and 18C stalls. The *high altar* of 1785, adorned with the variegated jasper of the neighbourhood, is a commonplace classical work by *Ventura Rodríguez;* the Virgin is by *Pedro de Mena;* behind it is the heavy *Transparente,* dedicated to S. Julián (1127–1208) first bishop of Cuenca, with four serpentine columns from Granada and an urn from Carrara, by *Fr. Vergara* (1758).

The SIDE CHAPELS are interesting for their Renaissance furniture; and particularly the iron Rejas of the *Cap. de los Apostoles* and *Cap. S. Juan* (3rd and 6th in the S. Aisle). In the S. Transept are tombs of the Montemayor family (15-16C), and in the *Cap. S. Martín,* beyond the transept, tombs of early bishops. On the S. side of the ambulatory are the *Sagrario,* with jasper columns and an image carried by Alfonso VII, and the *Sacristy,* with a remarkable vault, carvings of the Mater Dolorosa and a Virgin by *Pedro de Mena,* and two enamelled coffers. The *Sala Capitular,* entered from the sacristy, has a Plateresque portal, walnut doors and stalls carved in the manner of Berruguete, and a coarsely over-painted artesonado ceiling. The *Treasury* contains medieval plate, a fine byzantine diptych, and among the paintings, two by *El Greco*.

The E. Chapel, or *Cap. del Espíritu Santo,* possesses an outstanding *artesonado ceiling* and a painting of the Virgin in the primitive Flemish style, and in the *Cap. S.Juan Bautista* is a retablo by *Cristóbal Salmerón* (fl. 1630). The large *Cap. de los Caballeros* contains two retablos by *Hernan Yáñez* (c. 1526), tombs of the Albornoz family, including those of Card. Gil de Albornoz and his mother, Teresa de Luna, a reja by *Fernando de Arenas* (1526) and door by the Frenchman *Xamete* (1546). At the end of the N. Transept are a late-Gothic arch and Plateresque portal (by *Xamete,* 1546–50), decorated with Christian and pagan motives.

The *Cloister*, temporarily a workshop, was designed by *Juan Andrés Roc* (1577–83) in the simple classical style of Herrera. Off it opens the *Chapel of th Mendozas,* including the tomb of Diego Hurtado de Mendoza, viceroy of Siena (c 1566).

Opposite the 16C *Bishop's Pal.,* S.E. of the cathedral, is an old mansion now housing the *Museo Provincial,* containing an interesting archaeological collection, including finds from *Valeria* (see p.438) among them examples from its mint, and from *Segóbriga* (see p.440)

Hence a lane leads to the much-photographed **Casas Colgades** (or *Hanging Houses*), corbelled out above the gorge, and to ruined *St Cruz.* The Casas Colgadas contains a tastefully designed private *Museum of Abstract Art,* opened in 1966 and since extended, and a good restaurant.

Among the exhibits, frequently changed, are representative works by *Chillido Tapies, Zóbel, Torner, Manrique, Pons, Chirino, Romero, Sempere, Lorenzo Rueda,* and *Feito,* and others of the contemporary Spanish school.

Beyond, to the l., is the dizzy *Pte. de S. Pablo,* a footbridge 105 m long, thrown across the Huéscar at a height of 45 m. for the convenience of the Dominicans of *S. Pablo,* the 16C convent seen on the opposite bank.

From the Pl. Mayor, it is worth while to go on ascending, past the 17C *Carmelite Convent,* to the round church of *S. Pedro* (17C) and the battered *Pta. del Castillo,* and to descend steps to the r. towards a wilderness of oddly-shaped rocks, for the sake of the impressive *Views of the old town, with its perpendicular cliffs of houses, and the Huécar gorge

The wild hills W. and N.W. of Cuenca repay exploration by the walker an angler and excursions may be made to the geological curiosities of the **La Ciuda Encantada,** 36 km. N., and *Los Torcas.* The former are reached by crossing the Pte de S. Antón, turning r., and following the Jucar to *Villalba de la Sierra,* beyon which the river is bridged, then continue through pinewoods to *Vetano a Villalba* (View) to the keeper's lodge from which the Enchanted City' is visite with the help of guides. The cretaceous rock has been weathered by atmospheri exposure into fantastic forms; streets, buildings, monsters, and the like.—Henc one may circle E. to *Tragacete,* see p.439.

For *Las Torcas* we take the Teruel road (N 420), turning l. at *Mohorte,* 11 km S.E. of Cuenca. Climbing through pinewoods, the road reaches the first of th *'torcas'.* These, some 25 in all, are large sinkings in the ground due to the action o subterranean rivers; they vary from 45 m. to c. 700 m in width and from 10 m. t 75 m. in depth.

FROM CUENCA TO MOTILLA DE PALANCAR. Travellers wishing to regain th Valencia road (N III) may follow the N 420 S. past (30 km.) *Baños de Valdegang* crossing the Júcar at *Puente de Castellar* alongside the hump-backed Roma bridge.—We pass (14 km.) *San Lorenzo de la Parrilla,* whose church contains fine Gothic Virgin, and at 23 km. meet the N III at *La Almarcha.* Here we turn l. fc *Motilla del Palancar,* 48 km. to the E., see Rte 51.

An alternative road from Cuenca to Motilla (N 320) forks r. off the Teruel roa (N 420) 4 km. S. of Cuenca, climbing through pinewoods. At 8 km. we may bear through *Arcas,* with a Romanesque church, to approach (31 km.) *Valera a Arriba,* with the important ruins of Roman *Valera,* still in the process o excavation, with remains of a castle and church on a wind-blown height. It was bishop's see until the 8C. Another church contains the alabaster tomb of Hernand de Alarcón (d. 1582). We may regain the main road 14 km. to the E.

At 39 km. (from Cuenca) we pass near (l.) the castle of *Monteagudo de la Salinas.*—10 km. *Almodóvar del Pinar* has a church preserving good sculpture Here we may fork r. for (20 km.) *Motilla,* or keep l. viâ *Campillo de Altobuey an* (10 km.) *Puebla del Salvador,* with a 16C church, to meet the N III at (9 km *Minglanilla.*

FROM CUENCA TO TERUEL viâ ALBARRACÍN (160 km.). This attractive alternative route crossing the MONTES UNIVERSALES—not recommended in Winter—may be followed by driving N. up the picturesque Jucar valley past (r.) the *Ciudad Encantada*, see p.438. At 65 km., 5 km. S. of the mountain village of *Tragacete*, we climb E. Descending the far side of the range, we turn r. and shortly pass the source of the Tagus, and follow the road through *Frias de Albarracín* and *Calomarde*. At 50 km. we enter *Albarracín* (p.206), 45 km. S.E. of which lies *Teruel*.

FROM CUENCA TO TERUEL viâ CAÑETE (153 km.). We drive S. on the N 420, forking l. up a wide valley after 4 km. At 7 km. the road to *Las Torcas* (see p.438) bears l.—The road climbs up to open rolling country, at 7 km. passing *Fuentes*, where the church has Romanesque remains, to reach (26 km.) *Carboneras*, with remains of a former Dominican convent.

From Carboneras, a road, following the same general direction as the railway, leads S. to (22 km.) **Cardenete**, where the church has an enormous artesonado roof 43 m. long, and a good 15C triptych; the castle dates from 1522.—19 km. S.E. on the W. bank of the *Embalse de Contreras*, stands *Enguidanos* with a ruined castle and a 15C Virgin in its church.—The road continues S.E. from Cardenete to meet the N III at (68 km.) *Utiel*, see Rte 51.

From Carboneras the picturesque road now veers N.E., and beyond (7 km. l.) *Pajaroncillo*, with its marble quarries, follows the *Valley of the Cabriel, here an impressive pine-shaded gorge of tumbled rock. A track crosses the river to the *Rambla del Enear*, with perhistoric rock-paintings.—22 km. **Cañete**, a walled town (1000 inhab.), overlooked by a mid-15C castle of the Constable Álvaro de Luna.—11 km. *Salinas de Manzano*. To the N. rises the *Muela de S. Juan* (6135 ft), the massif in which the Tagus, the Guadalaviar, and the Júcar have their source, and at 31 km. we meet the Teruel-Utiel road (N 330).

6 km. S., reached by a twisting road, is **Ademuz** (1900 inhab.), an ancient hillside village of narrow medieval alleys, with a curious twin-domed church near its N. entrance. Hence the N 330 continues S. to meet the N III at (80 km.) *Utiel*, passing (after 30 km.) *Landete*, 5 km. N. of which lies *Santo Domingo de la Moya*, a fortified village with a 13C castle and 15C goldsmiths' work in the church treasury.

We follow the defile of the Guadalaviar N., shortly passing (r.) *Torre Alta*, a hamlet with a medieval tower, and (23 km.) *Villel*, with ruins of a castle set on an isolated peak, and the birthplace of Francisco Tadeo Calomarde (1773–1842), the reactionary minister of Fernando VII. The road provides a good view of the curious geological formation of the surrounding area as we approach (15 km.) *Teruel*: see p.206.

51   FROM MADRID TO VALENCIA

Total distance, 354 km. (220 miles). N III. 82 km. *Tarancón*—103 km. *Alarcón*—16 km. *Motilla de Palancar*—81 km. *Requena*—72 km. **Valencia**.

The main road to Valencia is by no means fast, and its improvement is long overdue.

We leave Madrid by the N III, a somewhat uninteresting road, at least for the first half, driving S.E., by-passing (l.) *Vicálvaro*, with stone quarries, and (r.) *Vallecas* with a 16C church with a brick tower, altered in the 18C. We cross the Jarama and climb past (28 km.) **Arganda** (17,350 inhab.) with a hospital in a transformed castle of 1400, and Churrigueresque altars in its church of 1525.

The C 300 bears S. passing the castle of *Casasola*, to (24 km.) **Chinchón**. (3900 inhab.; *Hosteria Nac.* in the restored 17C. Augustinian convent), an attractive village likely to be crowded at weekends, with a picturesque but over-restored Pl. Mayor, a 16C church containing a painting by *Goya*, and castle. Quinine derived its name from Chinchona, after a Marquesa de Chinchón had discovered its properties. 'Chinchón', the local *aguardiente* or eau de vie, is based on aniseed.—6 km. beyond (S.E.) lies *Colmenar de Oreja*, with an arcaded plaza and 16C church.

9 km. *Perales de Tajuña*.

Hence a road (l.) ascends the r. bank of the river past a series of rock grottoes painted and engraved in Neolithic times, to (12 km.) *Carabaña*, where the 15C church contains a Renaissance retablo, and good monuments.—14 km. beyond, a road leads 5 km. E. to **Mondéjar**, where the Parish Church (1516) by *Cristóbal de Adonza* and his son *Nicolás*, has a tower of 1560. Ruined Gothic *S. Antonio* (1487 -1509), with a beautiful doorway, is the earliest in Castile to show Renaissance decorative motives.

We climb in zigzags to the *Peñas Gordas* (2605 ft; views) and pass *Villarejo de Salvanés*, with a 13C church and an old castle keep.—At 26 km., by the bridge over the Tagus, stands the ruined 11C castle of *Fuentedueña del Tajo*. We climb S.E. out of the valley to by-pass (19 km.) **Tarancón** (8200 inhab.; *Hotels*), overlooking the Riansares. The church, otherwise spoiled by Philip II, has an elaborate late-Gothic façade. Here Queen Cristina built a château after her marriage with Muñoz, a guardsman whom she created Duque de Riansares.

It was the birthplace of the theologian Melchor Cano (1509–60).—*Horcajo de Santiago*, 19 km. due S., was that of the polymath Lorenzo Hervás y Panduro (1735–1809).

At 8 km. a road leads 6 km. N.E. to **Uclés**, near which Sancho, only son of Alfonso VI of León, was slain in battle by the Moors in 1100, at a spot known as 'Sicuendes' ('sete condes') from the seven counts who fell with the youthful *infante*. The large *Monastery* above Uclés was founded in 1174, and sacked by the French under Victor in 1811.

The buildings, begun in 1529 (E. Front and sacristy), were extended (N. and W. Fronts) by *Fr. de Mora*, whose work here gave the place its name 'el Escorial de la Mancha'. In the S. Front is a Baroque entrance of 1735, and in the church are monuments of the 15–16C notably those of the Infanta Doña Urraca and the poet Jorge Manrique (d. 1479), and 16C paintings. The refectory has a fine artesonada of 1548.—Two towers remain of the adjacent castle.

Near (11 km.) *Saelices*, (*Hotel*), at *Cabeza del Griego*, are the important Roman ruins of *Segóbriga*, including a theatre and amphitheatre (under restoration) and remains of a 6C Visigothic basilica. The museum is of interest.—Beyond (14 km.) *Montalbo*, with ruins of a castle of the dukes of Gandia, we climb through the picturesque Cañada del Estrecho to reach the watershed (3173 ft) between the Atlantic and Mediterranean.—At (38 km.) *Almarcha* we cross the N 420 from Cuenca to Alcázar de San Juan.—2 km. S. stands the castle of *Garcimuñoz*, with a church within its walls. Jorge Manrique (see above) died fighting here in 1479.—Passing *Honrubia*, we skirt the great Embalse de Alarcón in the Júcar valley.—At 32 km. (r.) lies the village of **Alarcón**, well sited on a rocky ridge with a small 14C castle converted to house the *Parador Nac.*, four derelict churches and *La Trinidad* (13-15C), restored.

16 km. **Motilla de Palancar**, (4400 inhab.; *Hotels*), with a late-16C hall-church, stands on the crossroad (N 320) from Cuenca to Albacete. There is a good 16C church and ruined fortifications at *Villanueva de la Jara*, 15 km. S.

Iniesta, some 10 km. S. of the main road, was the birthplace of Enrique de Villena (1384–1434), astrologer, the first translator of Dante's 'Divina Commedia' into Castilian, and a writer on cookery.

30 km. *Minglanilla*, with salt-mines to the S., soon after which the scenery increases in attraction as we descend into the Cabriel valley, and traversing several tunnels, enter the province of Valencia.—38 km. **Utiel** (11,900 inhab.), surrounded by vineyards, has a church (1521–48), by

Juan de Vidaña, with a doorway of 1517 by *Martín de Areche* and a Baroque retablo of before 1690. Old houses and parts of the town-wall survive.

At 13 km. the road by-passes **Requena**, an ancient town (17,800 inhab.) retaining some 15C houses and a ruined castle. Its churches were badly treated during the Civil War, including *El Salvador* (1480–1533) with a Baroque interior of 1710–12, noble tower, Isabelline doorway, and good ironwork on the doors; *Sta María* (c. 1470, restored c. 1730) also has a fine portal; and *S. Nicolás* (13C, altered 1787). The *Ayuntamiento* occupies the *Conv. del Carmen,* whose church, partly of c. 1480, contains the 13C Virgen de la Soterrana.

FROM REQUENA TO ALMANSA (83 km.). The N 330 drives S. across country to (33 km.) **Cofrentes**, at the confluence of the Cabriel and Júcar, dominated by a 14C castle, and climbs to (29 km.) *Ayora*, with ruins of a castle.—21 km. *Almansa*, on the N 430, see Rte 54A.

Slightly to the S. at 30 km., lies *Buñol,* with a ruined castle in which Francis I was briefly imprisoned, and a church with sculptures by *Ign. Vergara*, situated in the so-called 'Valencian Switzerland', a region abounding in springs and caves.—We next pass (10 km.) **Chiva**, commanded by the ruin of a Moorish castle whose chapel contains a vaery early carved Virgin and two 15C paintings. The church, built, in 1733–81 by *Ant. García*, has frescoes by *José Vergara*, and retains its Romanesque belfry.—The C 3322 runs S.E. towards *Carlet* (p.455), passing the ruined castles of (25 km.) *Montroy*, and *Aledua*.

We traverse the fertile huerta, with deep green citrus trees showing against the brilliant orange-red soil, and leave *Cheste*, with a fine domed 18C church, on the l., and (19 km, r.) *Aldaya*, where the Gothic church is restored in Churrigueresque style, before crossing the recently canalized river Turia, on entering the outskirts of (13 km.) **Valencia**, see below.

Until the A7 motorway circling to the W. of Valencia is completed, travellers wishing to by-pass Valencia must turn off immediately on crossing the canal to join, further S., the commencement of the N 332 or N 340 to *Alicante*, see Rte 53A and B, the former already providing an approach to the A7 S. of Valencia.

52   VALENCIA AND ENVIRONS

The N III (from Madrid) enters the town from the W. by the Av. del Cid to meet the Gran Via at its intersection with the C. S. Vicente. The latter leads N. towards the centre. The N 340 from Barcelona enters from the N.E. and by-passes the centre by the *Pte. Angel Custodia,* but by turning r. along the N. bank of the Turia and crossing the *Pte. de Aragón,* and then bearing r. again, we may reach the C. de la Paz.

VALENCIA (707,900 inhab.: 247,000 in 1920; 504,000 in 1950; numerous *Hotels*), the third largest city in Spain, and the ancient capital of the kingdom wrested by the Cid from the Moors, stands c. 3 km. from the Mediterranean in the midst of a fertile huerta watered by the Turia (or Guadalaviar) now canalized and carried round the S. of the city. For nine months of the year it enjoys a fine climate, but the summer is extremely sultry. The centre of Valencia has been largely modernized and rebuilt, but some narrow streets, low houses, and two town gates of the medieval city still survive. Many of its numerous churches, mostly disfigured in the 17-18C, were seriously damaged in 1936.

Air Services from *Manises* airport.
Steamers from El Grao to the Balearics.
Tourist Offices at the airport, Ayuntamiento, and C. de la Paz 46.
British Institute, C. Pascual y Genís 12.

History. Valencia founded on the site of a Greek settlement by the Roman Consul Decius Junius Brutus in 139 or 138 B.C. for the defeated soldiers of the Lusitanian general Viriathus. Sacked by Pompey after his victory over Sertorius in 75 B.C., it was rebuilt and became a Roman colony. *Valentia Edetanorum.* S. Vicente suffered martyrdom here in 304. It fell into the hands of the Goths in 413 and of the Moors in 714. In 1012 Valencia was declared an independent kingdom by Abd-ul-Aziz, grandson of Almansor. In 1092 it was conquered by the Almoravides, but Alfonso VI of León, smarting under his own recent defeat at Zalaca (1086), allied himself with the partisans of the deposed king of Valencia, and despatched a half-Christian, half-Moorish army under the Cid, who, after a siege of 20 months, entered Valencia in 1094 and ruled it until his death in 1099. In 1101 his widow, Jimena, was expelled by the Moors, who re-occupied the city until the advance of Jaime el Conquistador in 1238. For 400 years Valencia was among the most flourishing cities in Spain and in 1474 it saw the establishment of the first Spanish printing-press, while that of Benedict Monfort produced some imposing work in later centuries.

In the 17-18C, however, its prosperity suffered greatly, first from the expulsion of the Moriscos by Philip III and later from the displeasure visited by Philip V on those cities that resisted his succession. In 1762 it was still a maze of 428 'streets', mostly unpaved, and the night watchmen, or *Serenos*, established by Joaquin Fos in 1777, were the first of their kind, later universal in Spanish towns. Its population in 1800 was c. 80,000. In 1808 Valencia rose against the French and, under the government of Padre Rico, repulsed the attack of Moncey; in 1812, however, it was captured by Suchet. In 1871 the battlemented walls erected by Pedro IV in 1356 were pulled down to give employment to the poor. The city took an active part in the republican movements of 1868, 1869 and 1873; was the scene of extremist revolutionary activity in 1932–36; and was a seat of the Republican Government during the Civil War.

Among its natives were S. Vicente Ferrer (1350–1419); Juan Luis Vives (1492–1540), friend of Erasmus and tutor of Mary Tudor; Luis Beltrán (1525–81), Apostle of the Indies; Guillén de Castro (1569–1631), playwright; Juan Ribalta (1597–1628), the painter (son of Francisco); Francisco Pérez Bayer (1714–94), the Hebraist and educationalist; Ignacio Vergara (1715–76), sculptor; José Vergara (1726–99), the painter; Ant. de Cavanilles (1749–1804), the botanist; Tomás Lopéz Enguidanos (1773-1814), the engraver; Vicente Salvá (1786-1849), the bibliographer; Joaquín Sorolla (1863–1923), the painter; and the novelist Vicente Blasco Ibáñez (1867–1928).

Fiestas have long been a characteristic part of Valencian life among them those of March 17-19th, the *Fallas de S. José.* These are elaborate structures set up in the streets, with life-size figures and groups, which are burned at midnight on March 19th. The traditional custom originated with the Carpenters of Valencia, who thus wished to perpetuate the story of their patron making toys for Christ in his childhood. The *Fiestas de Mayo,* in honour of the Virgen de los Desamparados, include civil and religious processions, floral festivities, bull-fights, etc. At *Corpus Christi* take place religious processions, typical features of which are the 'giants' and ancient 'coaches' peculiar to Valencia. The *Feria* takes place from July 24th until the first week in Aug. Another feria, of ancient origin is held from Dec. 24th to Jan. 22nd.

A THE CATHEDRAL AND N.W. QUARTERS.

At a central point in the city lies the *Pl. de la Reina,* at the junction of the C. de la Paz and the C.S. Vicente, to the N. of which stands the *Cathedral* (Pl. 6), dominated by the **Miguelete.**

This octagonal bell-tower was built in 1381–1429 by *Andrés Juliá* and *Juan Franch,* and completed by *Pedro Balaguer* who in 1414 journeyed to Lérida, Narbonne and other distant towns to study the best models. The tower gets its name from the great bell baptized on Michaelmas Day, 1418; the present bell is of 1539. The energetic may climb the 207 steps to the summit for the view. The tower is entered by the small door between the *Cap. de la Trinidad* and the 1st chapel of the l. aisle of the cathedral; the passage has a ribless Gothic vault.

The *Cathedral is built on the site of a Roman temple of Diana, occupied by a church under the Goths and by a mosque under the Moors. The present building was begun by Bp. Andrés Albalat in 1262 to the designs of *Arnau Vidal,* continued by *Nicolás de Autun* (or Ancona?; fl. 1303), and extended to its present size in 1480. It was appointed a metropolitan church by Innocent VIII in 1492, and the first archbishop was Rodrigo Borja (Borgia), afterwards Pope Alexander VI. As it now exists it is a Gothic building with a partly Corinthianized interior by *Antonio Gilabert* dating from 1744–79.

EXTERIOR. The concave *Main Portal 'De los Hierros'* adjoining the Miguelete, is an unsuccessful Baroque experiment begun by the German *Konrad Rudolf* in 1703 and completed chiefly by *Francisco Vergara* in 1713. The *Pta. del Palau,* facing the Archbishop's Palace, is a dignified example of 13C Romanesque, with receding orders supported on slender colonnettes. The ironwork of the doors dates from 1481.

On the opposite side, beneath a rose-window and opening on the Pl. de la Virgen is the *Pta. de los Apóstoles* (1330–54; restored in the 15C), adorned with good but mutilated sculptures now undergoing restoration. In this ancient doorway, every Thursday about noon, meets the *Tribunal de los Acequieros,* or *de las Aguas,* a court that has been in existence since the 10C at least, and claims as its founder the caliph Hakam II. Here all disputes connected with the irrigation of the huerta are settled in the simplest and most patriarchal fashion. The disputants and witnesses are conducted within a portable railing and their case is heard by eight 'peasant' judges. No oaths are taken nor records kept, but the decisions of the court are final.

The INTERIOR was wantonly damaged in 1936, when many works of art perished. The sanctuary, decorated in Churrigueresque style by *J. B. Pérez* in 1682, now contains the walnut stalls (1604) carved by *Dom. Fernández Ayarza,* and organs of 1511–13. On the N. side is the late Gothic pulpit. The 18C casing of the six southernmost columns of the nave have been removed to display the original Gothic masonry and ogival arches, above which the old brick roof may be seen. Over the crossing is the cimborio (14C; finished in 1430 by *Martín Llobet),* with windows filled with sheets of alabaster. The *High Altar,* accidentally burned in 1469 during a ceremony in which a dove bearing lighted tow represented the Holy Ghost, was restored in 1498 and modernized in 1862. The door panels of 1506 were painted by *Hernán Yáñez* and *Fernando Llanos.* The 16C Virgin within the retablo niche is by *Ign. Vergara* and comes from the Cartuja de Portacoeli. The altar is sheltered by a baldacchino made from part of the destroyed Trascoro.

Above the font to the l. of the main door is a Baptism (1535) by *Vicente Macip the Elder;* on the other side is the chapel of the *Sagrado Corazón* with the tombs of Diego de Covarrubias (d. 1604) and his wife. A passage leads to the *Cap. del Santo Cáliz* and **Museum,** situated in the OLD CHAPTER HOUSE (1356–69) covered by an octagonal vault. It contains the chains carried off from the port of Marseilles by the Aragonese fleet in 1423 and the tomb of Abp. Pérez de Ayala (d. 1496). In the Gothic niches of the S. wall, flanking the altar, have been placed alabaster reliefs (1417–24) by the Florentine *Giuliano* (? *da Poggibonsi).* Above the altar is the *Santo Cáliz,* a remarkable agate cup with gold handles and jewelled bands. Brought to the cathedral in 1437 from S. Juan de la Peña (see p.192) where it was hidden during the Moorish invasion, it is said to be the Holy Grail itself; certainly of Roman origin, it bears traces of alterations in the 9th, 15th and 16Cs. The Museum also contains paintings by *Juan de Joanes* and others of the Valencian School, including the Incredulity of St Thomas (1400) by *Andrés Marzal de Sax.*

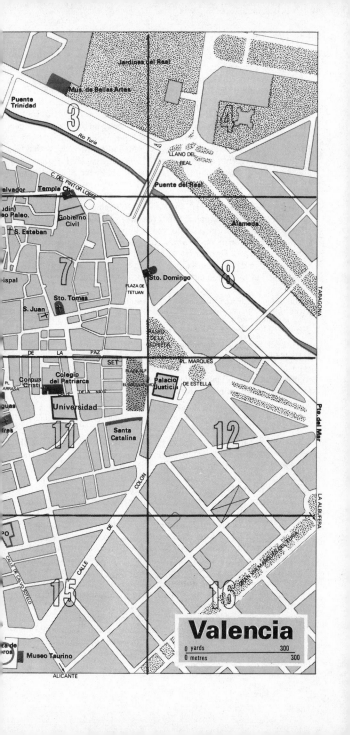

The 1st chapel in the r. aisle has a reja of 1647 by *Juan Pont Aloy,* and portions of the original alabaster high altar. In the next chapel the paintings over the altar, by *Maella,* and the two side paintings, by *Goya,* illustrate the life of S. Francisco Borja. The 4th, dedicated to S. Tomás de Villanueva (d. 1555), abp. of Valencia, contains a painting of the saint by *José Vergara,* who also executed the paintings in the r. transept, in which is the tomb of the great 15C poet, Ausias March. The fine panels from the organs, carved in 1511–13 by *Luis Muñoz* to designs by *F. Yáñez,* are now in the Ambulatory, off which is the *Sacristy,* with a fine vault, entered beneath a painting by *Ribalta* of Christ bearing the Cross. The chapel of *S. Dimas* contains the 'Cristo de la Buena Muerte' by *Juan Muñoz.* Adjacent stands the 15C alabaster *Virgin of Cadira.*

In the 3rd chapel of the l. aisle as we return is the tomb of St Louis of Anjou, Bp. of Toulouse (1274–97), and a S. Sebastián by *Orrente.*

Leading off this chapel is the **Treasury**, containing a magnificent *Portapaz, or ciborium, in gold and coloured enamels, by *Benvenuto Cellini;* a Pyx made by *Bartolomé Coscolla* in 1398; portions of a retablo of SS. Cosmas and Damian by *Yáñez* and *Llanos;* a Bible annotated by S. Vicente Ferrer; a crucifix that belonged to St Francis de Sales; a Virgin carried by Jaime el Conquistador, and Renaissance jewellery.

Connected with the cathedral by a vaulted footbridge is the modern *Archbishop's Palace,* facing the N. side of which is the *Pal. del Marqués del Campo,* with good iron gates. At No. 14 in the C. del Palau is the *Casa del Almirante* (15C), the only genuine Gothic mansion in the city.

Another bridge connects the cathedral with the chapel (1652–67) of **N.S. de los Desamparados** (Our Lady of the Helpless), of unpretentious exterior, designed by *Diego Martínez Ponce de Urrana,* but with an elliptical interior of lavish decoration by *Vicente Gasco* (1756), and weak vault frescoes (1701) by *Palomino.*

The original figure of La Virgen de los Desamparados, the patron saint of Valencia since the 17C, was carved in 1416 by *Vicente de S. Vicente* such for the chapel of the first lunatic asylum in Spain; the present image is a reconstruction.

The Pl. de Moncada behind (r.) leads to the old *Almudín,* or public granary of the 14C, altered in 1517, occupied by the *Museo Paleontológico,* with a collection of extinct S. American fauna. Further on, opposite the 16C *Casa de los Escribá,* is *S. Esteban* of 1472–1515, decorated in 1681–89 in the Churrigueresque style by *J. B. Pérez,* containing paintings of interest, including four panels of the school of *Jacomart* in the sacristy.

To the N. of the cathedral extends the Pl. de la Virgen, to the W. of which rises the old *Audiencia* or *Pal. de la Generalidad* (Pl. 6), a dignified building of 1481–1510 by *Pedro Compte* and now occupied by the Diputación. The tower of 1518–79, by *Gaspar Gregori,* is a notable example of the transitional styles of its century. Within are shown two rooms on the entresol with elaborate ceilings of 1534–35, and, on the first floor, the *Salón de las Cortes,* a beautiful room adorned with mural canvases (1591–93), mainly by *Juan Sariñena, Vicente Mestre,* and *Francisco Pozzo,* representing the assembly of the Provincial Estates. Below the paintings runs a dado of azulejos (1568–74), while above is a narrow gallery supported on elaborately carved shafts (1563–66). The artesonado ceiling (1536–66) was carved by *Ginés Linares, Pedro Martín,* and *Gregori.*

In this quarter lying N.E. of the Audiencia are many ancient houses, and 16C *El Salvador* which retains a 13C tower. Further on is Churrigueresque *S. Lorenzo*, designed by *José Mingues*, with a fine tower.

The C. de Caballeros, with many senorial houses and curious patios, leads W. from the Audiencia. *S. Nicolás,* in a side street (l.) built on the site of a mosque in the 14C and enlarged in 1455, was transformed (1693) by *J. B. Pérez*; the vault has a fresco (1697) by *Dionis Vidal*, aided by his master *Palomino*; the tower was added in 1755. The church contains a Crucifixion (1476) by *Rodrigo de Osona the elder,* a Last Supper and eight smaller paintings by *Macip,* and other pictures of his school. In the *Sacristy* are heads of Christ and the Virgin, by *Macip,* and a 15C silver chalice said to have been presented by Alexander VI in memory of his uncle Calixtus III, who was a priest at this church and later Bp. of Valencia.

The C. del Portal de Valldigna, named after a Moorish archway and running parallel to the N. of the C. de Caballeros, contains a house (No. 15) in which the first printing-press in Spain was set up (comp. history).

From behind the Audiencia we travers the Pl. de Manises, lined with 16-17C mansions, one housing the *Museo de Prehistoria,* and reach the Baroque tower of *S. Bartolomé,* rebuilt by *J. B. Pérez* in 1666-83.

At the end of the C. de Serranos, running N., rises the impressive **Torres de Serranos** (Pl. 2), a town gate built in 1391-98 by *Pedro Balaguer,* whose summit comands a good view. Beyond lies the Turia, usually all but dried up, yet subject to sudden floods, crossed by the *Pte. de Serranos,* the oldest bridge in Valencia, rebuilt in 1517-18. The river has now been canalized to the W. and S. of the city. Swinburne remarked that it contained 'scarce enough water . . . to wash a handkerchief'.

The C. de Roteros, which diverges on the l. before we reach the gate, leads to *Santa Cruz,* with a classical façade (17C) by *Gaspar de Santmarti,* and is prolonged by the C. del Museo, in which are the buildings of the *Conv. del Carmen* (suppressed 1835), now the *Escuela de Bellas Artes,* with remains of 13C work and a Renaissance cloister.

In the western quarter of the city, in the C. de Cuarte, an extension of the C. de Caballeros, is the second survivor of the town gates, the **Torres de Cuarte** (Pl, 5), built in 1441-60 by *Pedro Bonfill* in the style of the Castel Nuovo at Naples, which retain marks of the French sieges of 1808 and 1812.

Beyond are (r.) the *Jardín Botánico,* founded in 1633 and moved here in 1802; and (l.) *S. Sebastián,* a church of 1725-39 by *Jerónimo Cardona,* remarkable only for its azulejos.

B CENTRAL AND N.E. QUARTERS

In the *Pl. del Mercado* (or *del Guerrillero Romeu*), once the scene of bull-fights, tournaments, and executions, rises the *Mercado* with stalls heaped in brightly coloured profusion with the products of the huerta. On the N.E. side is the beautiful ***Lonja de la Seda** (*Silk Exchange;* Pl. 10), erected in 1483-98 by *Pedro Compte* and *Juan de Iborra*.

A low square tower divides the Gothic façade into two parts of which the r. half has an ogee-crowned doorway and windows with elaborate tracery (restored) and bears the escutcheon of Aragón, while the l. half has square-headed windows and an elaborate upper gallery (1498–1548), begun by *Compte*. The gargoyles and the crowned battlements are also noteworthy. Within is the *Salon de Contratación, whose fine roof is supported by 8 twisted columns and 16 pilasters without capitals. A door on the l. admits to a curious spiral staircase by which we may ascend the tower, while in an upper room is the magnificent artesonado ceiling of 1427 made by *Juan Llobet* and *Andrés Tanón* for the 'Sala Daurada' of the old Ayuntamiento.

Behind the Lonja is the *Iglesia de la Compañía,* with a Conception (1578) by *Juan de Joanes.*

Opposite the Lonja rises **Los Santos Juanes** of 1362–68, rebuilt in 1603–28 by *Vicente Garcia* with a Churrigueresque front (1693–1700). The interior, gutted in 1936, has been restored, but the vault-paintings by *Palomino* were destroyed.—Further W. rises the large azulejo dome of the *Escuelas Pias,* or *S. Joaquín* (1767–71) by *José Puchol.* The sculptures on the front are by *Esteve* and those within by *Ignacio Vergara.*

The C. de Trench, at the S. end of the Mercado, leads E. past (r.) the *Pl. Redonda* to 14C *Sta Catalina* with its graceful hexagonal Tower (1688–1705) by *J. B. Viñes.* Just beyond is the Pl. de Zaragoza, at the junction of two main streets of the old town—the C. S. VICENTE, which leads S.W., and the C. DE LA PAZ which leads E. A few steps along the former is *S. Martín,* a Gothic shell of 1372 covered with Baroque decoration. Over the doorway (1740 by *F. Vergara*) is a bronze equestrian statue of the saint dividing his cloak (1494), attr. to the Fleming *Piers de Becker.* The interior was seriously damaged in 1936. We may follow the alley along the S. side of the church to the Pl. de Villarrasa, on the r. of which is the 18C **Pal. del Marqués de Dos Aguas** (Pl. 11), a remarkable Baroque mansion with a grotesque *Portal* of 1740–44, supported by crouching figures, designed by *Hipólito Rovira* and carved in white translucent alabaster by *Ign. Vergara.* It now contains a *Ceramic Museum* complementary to that in the Ayuntamiento. Among other exhibits, the *Tiled Kitchen is particularly attractive.

In the area just to the N., and on either side of the C. de la Paz, was situated the ancient *Judería* of Valencia.

Not far S. lies **S. Andrés** (1602–84), with a Baroque doorway, attr. to *Juan Bautista Pérez.* To the E. of S. Andrés, on the S. and N. respectively of the C. de la Nave, are the old University and the Col. del Patriarca. The *Universidad* (founded in the 15C), occupies an early 19C building enclosing a Doric courtyard. One of the treasures of its *Library* is a copy of '*Les Trobes*', the first book printed in Spain (comp. History and p.447). In the chapel of 1737 is a retablo (1516) by *Nicolás Falcó.*

The **Col. del Patriarca** (Pl. 11), built in 1586–1610 by *Guillem del Rey,* with a two-storeyed Renaissance patio, was founded by Juan de Ribera (1533–1611), persecutor of the Moriscos, who is buried in the S. Transept of the adjoining church. On the r. of the entrance is the dark *Cap. de la Concepcion,* with Flemish tapestries (16C) and paintings by *Sariñena,* while the *Museo* on the first floor contain works by *Macip, Morales, El Greco, Dirk Bouts* (a small copy of his triptych at Granada), *Ribalta, Correggio,* and *Piombo.*

At the S.W. corner of the building is the richly decorated church of **Corpus Christi,** with some *Ribaltas'* including (1st N. chapel) the Vision of S. Vicente Ferrer, and above the high altar (of 1600–03 by *Fr. Pérez*) the Last Supper (1606).

The Miserere Service on Fri. is a curious ceremony; as the chanted Miserere begins, the painting of the Last Supper is lowered, and its place taken by dark purple veils; four veils are withdrawn in turn, and behind the last, against a gilded fretwork screen, appears the figure of Christ on the Cross, a 15C wooden Crucifix of unknown (?Florentine) origin.

At the end of the C. de la Nave is the Pl. de Alfonso el Magnánimo adjoining the Paseo de la Glorieta adorned with a fountain of 1700 by *Ponzanelli* of Genoa. In the angle between the two squares is the massive *Pal. de Justicia* (1768–1802), by *Felipe Rubio,* which served as a custom-house until 1828, then as a tobacco factory until 1910. At the N. end of the Glorieta, facing the *Pte. del Real,* is the Pl. de Tetuán, with several mansions, of which No. 3 is famous as the scene of the abrogation of the Constitution of 1812 by Fernando VII and of the abdication of the regency by María Cristina in 1840.

On the E. side stands **Sto Domingo,** founded in 1239. The Gothic *Cap. de los Reyes* (1437–62) by *Fr. Baldomar* and *Pedro Compte,* with a ribless vault, contains the tombs of Rodrigo Mendoza (d. 1554) and his wife. The church of 1772–81 contains frescoes by *José Vergara.* In the *Cap. del Capitulo* S. Vicente Ferrer assumed the Dominican habit. He was born in a house nearby (No.61, now converted into a small museum, at the corner of the C. del María and C. de María Carbonell). A double spiral staircase ascends the church tower, which commands a close view of the azulejo dome. The Gothic *cloister* (late 15C) and *chapter house* may be viewed with a permit from the adjacent *Capitania.*

The C. de Conde Montornés leads W. from the plaza to *Sto Tomás,* with a Baroque front of 1725–36 by *Ign. Vergara,* and to *S. Juan del Hospital* (restored) built in 1300–16 by the Knights of St John of Jerusalem. The interior has remains of decorations (1685) by *J. B. Pérez* and a 14C stone statue of the Virgin. Close by is the early Gothic chapel of the Knights, and in the priests' hospice (1356) on the other side of the street an 18C staircase with good azulejos. Further on is the Churrigueresque *Cap. del Milagro* of 1686, containing fine azulejos of c. 1700. A few paces N.W. are remains of the Moorish *Baños del Almirante* (11-12C).

At the end of the Pl. de Tetuán we leave on the l. the C. del Pintor López, which leads shortly to the *Gobierno Civil* and the *Temple Church,* both originally parts of the Templars' Convent. The present building (1761–70) is by *Miguel Fernández*; it contains a tomb of 1544 and frescoes by *José Vergara.*

We cross the river by the *Pte. del Real,* finished in 1598 and restored in 1682–83. Straight ahead are the Jardínes del Real, while to the r. is the *Alameda,* scene of the battle of flowers and other festivities of the July Feria. Further E. the river is crossed by the 16C *Pte. del Mar,* rebuilt in 1772–82, and other bridges.

Between the N. end of the *Pte. del Real* and the *Pte. de Trinidad* (further W.) are the buildings of a Baroque convent designed by *J. B. Pérez,* now housing the ***Museo de Bellas Artes** (Pl. 3), ranking among the most important galleries of Spain, and containing many paintings of the Valencian School, largely collected from suppressed convents. Passing through the vestibule we enter the cloister containing reliefs, sculptures, etc., of various periods, and turn r. In the floor of R VI is set a large mosaic of the Nine Muses from Moncada, and nearby crouches the 5-4C B.C. Iberian *Lioness of Bocairente.* Other rooms display medieval sculpture, and beyond lie galleries of more modern sculpture including works by *Mariano Benlliure* (1862–1947).

The First Floor is reached by the main staircase at the N.E. corner of the cloister, and R XXIV is the first of a range devoted to medieval paintings.—R XXV *Jaime Baçó, Jacomart,* Santiago and S. Gil;

Maestro del Grifo, Altarpiece of the life of S. Vicente Ferrer (c. 1500); *Felipe Pablo*, Panels from retablo mayor of Sto. Domingo (1523), with scenes from the life of St. Dominic; *J. J. de Espinosa*, Jerónimo Mos; R XXVIII *Rodrigo de Osona the younger*, Christ before Pilate; *Rodrigo de Osona the elder*, Piedad. Panels and predella of retablo of the Virgin from Portacoeli, attr. to *Juan Reixach*.—R XXI *Mastro de Bonastre*, Annunciation; Altarpiece of Fray Bonifacio Ferrer (c. 1400), formerly attr. to *Lorenzo Zaragoza*, but more likely the work of an Italian painting in Spain; *Maestro de los Marti de Torres* (? *Gonzalo Pérez*), Altar-piece of St Martín with St Ursula and St Anthony Abbot; *Maestro de Gil y de Pujades*, History of the Holy Cross, Formerly attr. to Pedro Nicolau.—R XXX *Hieronymus Bosch*, Triptych (Passion scenes); *Pupil of Fernando de Llanos,* Holy Family (c. 1520); *Pinturicchio*, Virgin and Child, with the donor, Bp. Juan Borja.—R XXXIII Altarpiece from the Ermita of Puebla Larga, attr. to the *school of Andrés Marzal* and *Pedro Nicolau* (c. 1430); *Maestro de Artés*, The Last Judgment (c. 1500).—R XXXII? *Nicolás Falcó*, with sculptures by *Damián Forment*, Retablo from the Conv. de La Puridad; *Maestro de Perea*, Adoration (c. 1491); *Maestro de Martínez Vallejo*, Virgin and Child.—R XXXVI A number of works by *Juan de Joanes*: El Salvador; Mystic betrothal of Sta Inés with the Ven. Agnesio (c. 1553); Ecce Homo; SS. Vicente Ferrer and Vincent Martyr; El Salvador.—R XXXV *Nic. Borrás*, Holy Family.—R XXXVI *Hernán Yañez de la Almedina*, Resurrection.—R XXXVII Mainly works by *Fr. Ribalta*: S. Isidro Labrador; St John The Evangelist; St Augustine; Last Supper; St Bruno; St Paul; St Peter;—R XXXIX *Van Dyck*, Francisco de Moncada.—R XL *El Greco,* St John the Baptist; *Ribera,* S. Sebastián; *Murillo* (?) Portrait of an unknown man.

RR XLI-XLVI, and LI-LV form the upper gallery of the cloister.—R XLII *Damián Forment*, carved alabaster altarpiece; R XLIV *Gaspar Requena* and *Pedro Rubiales*, altarpiece from the Conv. de La Puridad (1540); R XLVII *J. J. de Espinosa*, St Peter of Nola interceding for two friars; R XLVIII *Velázquez*, self-portrait; R XLIX *Goya*: Children's games; Francisco Bayeu, brother-in-law of the artist; Joaquina Candado, Goya's housekeeper; Rafael Esteve, the Valencian engraver; R LI *Orizonte*, Landscapes; R LII *José Avrial* (1807–91), Pl. de la Paja, Madrid; RR LIV and LV, portraits by *Vicente López*: Carlos IV; Josefa Ortiz; and Manuel Monfort.—The second and third floors contain a miscellaneous collection of more modern works.

C S. and S.E. QUARTERS.

E. of the C.S. Vicente lies the *Pl. del Caudillo*, with its flower-market. On the W. side stands the *Ayuntamiento* (Pl. 14), a building of 1758–63 with a modern façade. Within is the *Museo Histórico*, illustrating Valencia's history and customs.

The exhibits include: Plan of Valencia (1704) by *Padre Tosca*; Last Judgement, by a follower of Roger van der Weyden, bought for the city in 1493; 'Libre del Consolat de Mar', illuminated by *Domingo Crespi* (1407); the banner known as 'La Senyera' said to have been given by Jaime I after the reconquest of 1238; sword-blade regarded since the 15C as that of Jaime I; illuminated 'Libre dels Furs' (1329). A room is devoted to the 'Taula de Cambis', or first bank of exchange and deposit, established in 1407. The library contains some fine bindings.

Beneath are rooms housing the *Archaeological* and *Ceramic Collections*, the latter comprising a good representative collection of the wares of Paterna and Manises; of particular interest are the pieces recovered by excavation of the early kilns.

The Av. del Marqués de Sotelo leads S. to the *Estación del Norte* and *Plaza de Toros*, (with a *Museo Taurino*), passing (r.) the *Inst. Luis Vives* in a 17C Jesuit college, surmounted by a Baroque cupola of 1721. A little W. is restored *S. Agustín* (14C) containing paintings attr. to *Ribalta* and *V. Macip*, a 15C chasuble, and Gothic pyx. To the S. is Churrigueresque *S. Valero* (18C, restored).

D   ENVIRONS OF VALENCIA.

El Grao, the adjacent port, lies 3 km. E., and in the *Villanueva del Grao* are remains of the *Atarazanas* or medieval shipyards, five arcaded ranges begun in 1331, and rebuilt in 1410. The harbour lies immediately N. of the mouth of the Turia. Further N. lie the Playas de Levante and de Malvarrosa, the main beaches. S. of the port is the Playa de Nazaret, reached by the coast road to (9 km. S.E.) *Saler (Parador Nac.; Hotel)*.

To the S. lies the freshwater lagoon of **La Albufera** (Arab: *el-buhera*), fed by the Turia and the Acequia Real, bounded on its landward sides by rice-fields. It is separated from the sea by a narrow pine-clad bar called *La Dehesa*, although connected to it by two outlets. It abounds in waterfowl and fish, especially eels. During the shooting season (Nov-March) the stands ('puestos') for wildfowl shooting are sold by auction, but on Nov. 11th and 25th the shooting is free to the public ('tirada de S. Martín' and 'de Sta Catalina'). Unfortunately the area is in danger of being spoiled irremediably by the depredations of coastal developers. The title of Duc d'Albufera was bestowed by Napolean on Marshal Suchet in 1812.

At *Benetuser*, 5 km. S. of Valencia on the old Alicante road, is the 16C *Pal. de los Rabassa de Perelló*, while 2 km. beyond at *Catarroja*, the church has a fine steeple and contains 15C paintings.—9 km. W. lies *Torrente* (46,600 inhab.; *Hotel*), where the church contains Gothic paintings and a Baroque retablo, and the *Ayuntamiento* incorporates a castle-keep.—Just N. of Torrente lies *Alacuás*, with the magnificent *Pal. de la Casta* (1577–84), a huge hollow square with towers at the angles. The Baroque church (1694) has a retablo mayor (1597–1600) with paintings by *Crist. Lloréns*, and sculptures by *Esteve Bonet*.

Not far W. of Valencia lies *Manises* and *Paterna*, with a combined population of 51,400, S. and N. respectively of the Turia. The former was famous under the Moors for its metallic lustre ware, and is still a centre for the manufacture of majolica and glazed tiles (the factories are usually open to the public).—14 km. beyond Manises lies *Ribarroja*, with a medieval castle, and nearby, the extensive ruins of Roman *Pallantia*, known as *Valencia la Vella*.—*Paterna*, where green and blue pottery is manufactured, retains an old *Palacio*, while in the vicinity caved-dwellings and a medieval watch-tower.

FROM VALENCIA TO CHELVA (67 km.). N.W. of Paterna, the C 234 leads to (19 km.) *Puebla de Vallbona*, with a Baroque church containing a fine retablo and a Gothic chapel.—At 3 km. we pass the 15C stronghold of *Benisanó*, retaining its medieval walls. The church has a painting by *Juan de Joanes*.—2 km. **Liria** (12,400 inhab.), ancient capital of the Edetani (*Lauro* or *Edeta*), preserves the church of *La Sangre*, a 14C building with contemporary fittings. *El Buen Pastor* has a Gothic wall-painting in the presbytery, while the Baroque *Parish Church* of 1627–72 by *Martín Orinda*, has a grandiose front by *Tomás Lleonart Esteve*. There is also a municipal bakehouse, a medieval survival, and other early houses, two with 16C azulejos. The *Ayuntamiento* occupies the Renaissance *Pal.* of the Dukes of Berwick and Alba.—Beyond Liria the C 234 climbs the S. slope of the sierra, at 33 km. passing near *Domeño*, with remains of a Roman fortress.—10 km. **Chelva**, with a monumental Baroque church and the Roman aqueduct of *Peña Cortada*. The road goes on to meet the N 330 at (43 km.) *Sta Cruz de Moya*.

N.W. of Valencia lies *Godella*, whose Renaissance church has Trans. remains, and *Rocafort*, with 17C azulejos in the church. Beyond (19 km.) lies *Bétera*, with a Moorish castle, while 12 km. further is the *Cartuja de Portacoeli* (founded 1272), situated amid pine-wooded mountains, with an early 15C aqueduct, a church altered in the 18C, decorated with frescoes, and Gothic cloisters (14C; rebuilt 1479).

FROM VALENCIA TO SAGUNTO (25 km.) **Sagunto** itself (p.179), may be more easily reached by the new road skirting the Mediterranean, passing (19 km. l.) *Puzol*, (10,300 inhab.; *Hotel*), whose church contains a 14C retablo and later paintings.

The old road (N 340) drives due N. from Valencia, shortly passing (r.) the former monastery of *S. Miguel de los Reyes*, founded in 1371 and again in 1546 for monks of the Hieronymite Order. The building dates from c. 1590–1644 and is from plans by *Alonso de Covarrubias*; the portal of 1632–44 is Baroque. Since 1859 it has been a prison.—At 4 km. lies *Burjasot*, a centre of silk-culture, with subterranean granaries of 1573 in the Arab style, covered with a flagged walk. The *Castillo del Patriarca* is a 15C building with artesonado ceilings; the church contains early paintings. There is a good view from the chapel of *S. Roque*.

The church at *Alboraya*, to the E., contains important plate, while at adjacent *Almacera* is the 17C *Pal. de Parcent*, and in the church, a 14C coffer known as the 'Milacre dels Peixets'.—Further N., off the old Sagunto road, lies *Meliana*, with a Baroque church containing fine azulejos; *Foyos*, with an 18C church; *Albalat del Sorells*, with a 15C palace, and (8 km.) *Masamagrell*, whose church has a Gothic retablo mayor.—4 km. N.E. lies *El Puig*, scene of Jaime el Conquistador's victory (1238), which gave him the mastery of Valencia, with a huge monastery and a Gothic church containing the tombs of Bernardo Guillén de Entenza, uncle of Jaime. On the hill is the ruined castle of *Entenza*.—7 km. *Puzol*, see above.

53   FROM VALENCIA TO ALICANTE

A   VIÂ THE COAST

Total distance 185 km. (115 miles). N 332. 39 km. *Cullera*—38 km. *Gandia*—(25 km. *Ondara*, for *Denia*, 7 km. E.)—(8 km. *Gata*, for *Jávea*, 9 km. E.)—21 km. *Calpe*—12 km. *Altea*—9 km. *Benidorm*—43 km. **Alicante**.

Motorway. The autopista between Valencia and *Alicante*, now virtually completed, runs approx. parallel to the main road, but further inland, and is recommended if time is a consideration. It should certainly be taken from a point just prior to *Altea*, in order to avoid the stretch between *Benidorm* and *Alicante*.

As all the coastal towns have museums *Hotels*, their presence is not indicated in this route.

The N 332 drives S., parallel to and E. of the N 340, as far as (14 km.) *Silla* (see p.455), there bearing S.E. through rice-fields to (20 km.) **Sueca** (22,500 inhab.), where the church has a notable retablo.—At 5 km. we are joined by the coastal road skirting the E. shore of the lagoon of *La Albufera* (p.451), and pass through the suburbs of **Cullera**, a growing resort (18,700 inhab.), on the mouth of the Júcar and dominated by its ruined castle, which commands a wide view of the coast. The road veers inland before running S.E. again parallel to the coast near (14 km., r.) *Tabernes de Valldigna*, noted for its strawberries.

At 10 km. we pass (r.) the *Castillo de S. Juan*, and (l.) the resort of *Playa de Gandía*, and enter (4 km.) **Gandía** (41,600 inhab.), an ancient town near the mouth of the Serpis, retaining part of its walls, and which gave a ducal title to the Borja family. It was the birthplace of the Catalan poet, Ausias March (1395–?1459). The *Pal. de los Duques* (16 and 18C), the birthplace and residence of S. Francisco Borja (1510–72), fourth Duke of Gandía and superior of the Jesuit Order, and now a Jesuit College, contains some attractive azulejos, including a Manises tiled floor of the Elements, but little else of interest. Close by is the 14-16C *Colegiata*, S.E. of which stands the *Ayuntamiento* of 1781. The *Escuelas Pías*, at the S. end of the town, founded by Francisco Borja in 1546, was rebuilt in 1782–88. In *S. José* are Baroque altars, and the *Conv. de Sta Clara* contains paintings by *Pablo de S. Leocadio*.

8 km. **Oliva** (18,500 inhab.) with the church of *Sta María* and the *Conv. de S. Francisco*, with a 13C Virgin. Gregorio Mayans y Siscar (1699–1781), the author and savant, was born here.

9 km. to the S. lies *Pego*, with an early 17C church, a tower of 1700, and good retablos. Beyond Pego, a mountain road crosses the jagged sierra before descending to (43 km.) *Callosa*, see below.

The huerta to the S. of Oliva is particularly rich in orange-groves, and it is also the country of muscatel grapes, which are dried to make the famous Valencia raisins (*pasas*).—At 17 km. we reach *Ondara*, beyond which rises the conical peak of *Mongó*.

Here we may diverge l. onto the C 3311 for (7 km.) *Denía*, situated between the isolated mountain and the sea. Of Iberian foundation, **Denía** (20,350 inhab.) was probably colonized by Greeks who called it *Hemeroskopeion*, from its position commanding the coast, or *Artemision*, from the temple of Artemis which stood beneath the castle hill. Its name is derived from that of the Roman *Dianium*, whose fine harbour, now much silted up, was chosen by Sertorius as his navel base. The prosperity of the town increased under the Moors, and the Aragonese captured it only after having erected a castle on the hill of S. Nicolás (1244). A decline set in with the expulsion of the Moriscos. It was twice besieged in 1707–8 during the War of the Spanish Succession, and twice bombarded in the Penisular War; in 1813 the French garrison was blockaded here for eight months.

Little remains of ancient Denía save a few battered ramparts and ruins of the *Castle* (view). The *Ayuntamiento* (1612) was restored in 1877; *Sta Maria* dates from 1734.—*Mongó* (2497 ft) is easily climbed and commands a magnificent *View extending in clear weather to the Balearic island of *Ibiza*, 65 miles to the E.

A road climbs round its S.E. flank before descending steeply to (16 km.) **Jávea** (10,200 inhab.; *Parador Nac. de 'Costa Blanca'*), lying between the capes of S. Antonio and S. Martín. The town, once walled, retains some old houses. Its fortified church of 1513 was designed by the Basque *Dom. de Urteaga*; an architecturally interesting modern church—built like a ship's hull—lies near the port. In the neighbourhood are some curious stalactite caves, and much of the local stone is quarried from its tide-washed rocks. Continuing to drive S.E. we pass the Parador, and some surprisingly attractive villa developments, before ascending the wooded heights of the Cabo de la Nao, the nearest point of the mainland to the Balearics.—Fron Jávea we may regain the N 332 at *Gata de Gorgos*, some 9 km. to the W.

At 15 km., after threading a short defile, a road (l.) leads 7 km. to *Moraira*, a small resort, from which we may skirt the coast through woods interspersed with villas, to *Calpe* (see below).—5 km. **Benisa** (6600 inhab.) with a fortified church, whence we veer S. towards the *Peñon de Ifach* (1275 ft) rising dramatically fron the sea, at the base of which lies **Calpe**, approached by a road diverging l. at 9 km. The village (6100 inhab.), spoilt by speculative building, retains a Mudéjar church. We pass through the Sierra de Bernia, which here juts out into the sea, and traversing a series of short tunnels, climb down to (8 km.) *La Olla*.

Hence a road (r.) leads 10 km. to *Callosa de Ensarría*, 11 km. W. of which on the steeply climbing C 3313, is the *Castle of Guadalest*, perched picturesquely on a crag above its village, and entered only through a rock-hewn tunnel. 4 km. S. of Callosa lies *Polop*, in the Sierra de Aitana, whence we may descend to the coast at (10 km. E.) *Altea*, or (11 km. S.) *Benidorm*.

4 km. **Altea**, an attractively situated resort (9800 inhab.), dominated by its blue-domed church, is protected from the S. by the Sierra Helada, while to the N. and W. are more conspicuous ranges.

9 km. **Benidorm** (with a local population of 22,800; 12,000 in 1970; rising dramatically in the summer), was once a small fishing village and port for goods smuggled into Alicante, standing on a promontory defended by a castle and old fortifications. It has grown prodigously into one of the largest resorts on the Spanish coast, and is now a stamping ground for package tourists throughout the year. The old village nucleus commands a disenchanting view of an interminable succession of hotels and apartments skirting its pullulating playas.

11 km. *Villajoyosa* (20,300 inhab.), another resort, retains some walls, and a Gothic church.—At 16 km. we meet a crossroad, where we may turn l. for the *Playa de S. Juan*, following the shore for some 10 km. before bearing S.W. to *Alicante*, 7 km. beyond.—The r. turning leads inland to (9 km.) *Busot* (790 ft) a spa set amid pine woods on the slopes of the Cabezón de Oro.—At 8 km. we pass (r.) the *Conv. de Sta Clara*, or *La Santa Faz*, built to enshrine one of the three '*sudarios*' or handkerchiefs of Sta Veronica (see also *Jaén*).

We see ahead, on a commanding height, the *Castillo de Sta Bárbara*, and gently descend to the waterfront of (8 km.) **ALICANTE** (214,800 inhab.; 63,000 in 1920; 102,000 in 1950.), once the strongest fortress in the kingdom of Valencia. An active and growing commerical port, it contains few buildings of interest, but is visited for its delightful winter climate, while the summer, though torrid, is not scourged by the parching *leveche* of Murcia.

History. Alicante is said to occupy the site of Roman *Lucentum*, but it played only a small part in history until attacked from the sea by Sir John Leake and defended by Gen. Daniel O'Mahony in 1706. It was besieged in the following year, when the French troops of Philip V blew up the Castillo de Sta Bárbara and with it the English garrison commanded by Gen. John Richards. It was long the residence of an English merchant colony, importing 'all sorts of bale goods, corn, and Newfoundland cod', and exporting wine and barilla, and was garrisoned by English troops throughout the Peninsular War. In 1844 an insurrection under Pantaleón Bonet was brutally subdued and the ringleaders shot without trial. The last (6th) Earl Powerscourt dies here in 1875. During the Civil War Alicante was a centre of the Republicans, and here (in the Dominican Convent) José Antonio Primo de Rivera (1903–36), founder and later martyr of the Falange, was incarcerated, and, after a hurried trial, shot by local bosses in case the sentence might be commuted by the Government. The poet Miguel Hernández (1910–42) was allowed to die from neglect in gaol here during Franco's regime. It was the birthplace of Ruperto Chapí (1851–1909), the composer of *zarzuelas*, and of Gabriel Miró (1879–1930) the novelist.

Roads from Madrid (N 330), Valencia, and Murcia, converge on the *Explanada de España*, an attractive palm-lined promenade which skirts the harbour. Parallel to it a tessellated pavement has been laid between a double line of trees, while side-streets, running inland, intersect the C. de S. Fernando. Here is the Pl. Gabriel Miró, with a garden, while further E., the Rambla, or Av. de Méndez Núñez, the main thoroughfare, leads N. to the lively market hall. Its entrance is in the Av. de Alfonso el Sabio, prolonged to the W. by the Av. Gen. Mola, in which is the *Diputación*, housing the *Museo Arqueológico*.

From the sea-front we may enter the old town, or *Barrio de Santa Cruz*, by turning up the C. Jorge Juan. On the r. a short flight of steps leads to Gothic *Sta María*, with a Baroque W. Front and towers of 1720.—To the W. is the *Pl. 18 de Julio*, in which stands the *Ayuntamiento*, an attractive Churrigueresque building of 1696–1760, with two square towers. By the next turning r. (archway) we enter the tiled *C. Mayor* (closed to traffic), to reach **S. Nicolás de Bari**, a collegiate church of 1616–62 with a well-proportioned dome, and galleries surrounding the apse and sides. The interior is a good example of the plain solidity of Herrera's style, restored since gutted in 1936. The cloister, and the chapel l. of the entrance, contain Churrigueresque decoration.—In the C. Gen. Sanjurjo, running N., are some interesting old houses, and at C. de Toledo 21, there is a private *Ceramic Museum*.

The *Muelles* or breakwaters that protect the harbour command striking views of the town, dominated by the **Castillo de Sta Bárbara**.

Beyond the beginning of the E. Muelle we reach the Paseo de Gomis, above the Playa del Postiguet, not far along which is the entrance to the Ascensor or Lift to the castle. Fron these extensive fortifications, on the summit of a brown and isolated rock, we may obtain panoramic *Views of the coast and sierra to the N., and also a good bird's eye view of the town itself, and the lower *Castillo de S. Fernando*, rebuilt during the Peninsular War, but now a ruin. The descent may be made by a path climbing down its N. and W. slopes to *Sta María* (see above), or by the lift. Sta Bárbara may also be approached from the Valencia road by a road ascending the N. slope of the hill.

B Viâ Játiva and Alcoy.

Total distance, 167 km. (104 miles.), N 340. 64 km. **Játiva**—25 km. *Albaida*—25 km. **Alcoy**—28 km. *Jijona*—25 km. **Alicante**.

We follow the N 332 towards (14 km.) *Silla* (*Hotel*) with an 18C church and a former castle, now the Ayuntamiento, just short of which we fork r. onto the N 340.—At 10 km. we pass *Benifayó*, with two Moorish towers, and (3 km.) *Algínet*, with its *Ayuntamiento* in a 16C palace, and where the church contains a retablo by *Corseto Sardo* (1564) and a 14C statue of St Peter.—At 8 km. we reach a cross-road (C 3322); 3 km. to the r. lies *Carlet*, a wine-growing town with remains of walls, and a carved retablo by *Vergara* in the parish church.

8 km. to the E. is **Alcira** (35,300 inhab.), Roman *Sucro* and the Moorish *El Gezira*, owing the latter name to its position on an island in the river. It preserves the part-Gothic churches of *Sta María* and *Sta Catalina*, while *S. Agustín* contains old paintings. In the council chamber of the *Ayuntamiento* (by *Fr. Piquer*; 1558–61) are a good artesonado and a retablo of 1497. The town is a centre of the production of oranges and rice.—In a valley of the Sierra de la Murta, to the E., are the picturesque ruins of a Hieronymite convent.—4 km. N. of Alcira is *Algemesi* (23,600 inhab.) with a church containing paintings by *Ribalta*; 3 km. S. lies *Carcagente*, formerly noted for silk culture, and now surrounded by orange-groves.

The N 340 by-passes (10 km.) *Alberique* (8700 inhab.), where the church (1696–1701) contains a fine retablo, and soon crosses the Júcar.—*Villanueva de Castellón*, 3 km. l. has a good Gothic church.—At 14 km. we turn l. to (5 km.) *Játiva* (see below). The direct road S. from *Carcagente* to Játiva passes between two hills on which are seen the ruins of the chapel of *El Puig* and the *Castle of Sta Ana*, to the W.

From Játiva to Almansa (58 km.). We may rejoin the N 430 6 km. to the W. at *Alcudia de Crespins*, S.E. of which is the castle of *Canals*, birthplace of Alfonso Borja, see below.—The Cueva de la Araña, with early rock-paintings, lies some 35 km. N.W. near *Bicorp*. At 6 km. rises the imposing ruins of the castle of *Montesa*, once the headquarters of the Military Order of Montesa, founded in 1318 after the suppression of the Templars. At 15 km. we pass *Mogente*, with a Moorish castle, and the site of one of the first 'paradores', set up at the turn of the 19C by the Marqués de la Romana, and at *Les Alcuses* nearby, the ruins of an Iberian settlement of the 5C B.C. The Montesa valley which we ascend, is bounded to the S. by the Sierra Grosa.—At 14 km. a road (l.) leads 3 km. to *Fuente la Higuera*, birthplace of Juan de Joanes (Vicente Juan Macip, c. 1506–79), who painted the fine retablo of the parish church.—We cross the Pto. de Almansa and at 9 km. meet the Madrid-Alicante road (N 330), 8 km. beyond which lies *Almansa*, see Rte 54A.

JATIVA is an attractive and well-situated town (22,400 inhab.; *Hotel*); indeed Ford considered it 'one of the most picturesque towns in Spain, not excepting Granada'. It is famous for paper-making since

1150, and may have been the first place in Europe where paper was manufactured.

History. Roman *Saetabis*, but of Phoenician origin, was also known for its linen handkerchiefs, whose manufacture had been introduced from Tyre. Fortified by the Moors, who took it in 714 and called it *Xátiva*, it fell in 1244 to Jaime el Conquistador. In its castle were immured the Infantes Alfonso and Fernando de la Cerda, the heirs to the Castilian throne dispossessed by their uncle, Sancho el Valiente, in 1284; and the Duke of Calabria (1512–22) and Caesar Borja (1504–05), both by order of Gonzalo de Córdoba, who broke his word rather than disobey his master, Fernando the Catholic. The Borja family, so prominent in Italian history in the 15-16C as the Borgias, moved here from Borja (in Aragón) in the 14C. Alfonso Borja (1377–1458), afterwards Pope Calixtus III, was previously abp. of Valencia; his nephew Rodrigo (1431–1503), notorious as Alexander VI, was the father of Caesar and Lucretia and also of Juan, father of S Francisco Borja and ancestor of the dukes of Gandiá. Játiva resisted the accession of Philip V so stubbornly that, when the castle at last fell (1707), the city's name was changed to *San Felipe*, The old name was revived in 1834. José Ribera (c. 1589–1652), the painter, also known as 'El Españoleto', was born here, although he spent most of his life in Italy.

From the Alameda we may ascend to the parallel C. Moncada, the main street of the old town, with some typical Valencian houses, and the *Conv. de Sta Clara*. The C. de la Pta. de Sta Tecla goes on to the *Colegiata* of 1596, noted for its marble decoration, a 15C triptych attr. to *Jacomart*, and a Custodia given by Alexander VI. Opposite is the rich Plateresque façade of the *Hospital*, with Gothic flights of angels over the door. The *Museo Municipal* (C. José Carchano) contains interesting archaeological collections. Higher up the hill is the cypress-planted *Calvario*.

On the W. hill, above the walled-up *Pta. de la Aljama*, is the Mozarabic *Ermita de S. Félix* or *Feliú*, preserving a round-headed doorway and six antique columns, and a 15C retablo. Above rises the *Castillo*, mostly of the 15C although on a site fortified since Iberian days, commanding panoramic views.

Among the extensive ruins may be seen the prison and the *Salón del Duque* above it, where the Duke of Calabria was confined. Legend relates that Hannibal's wife Hamilce bore him a son in the castle whie he was besieging Saguntum.

The N 340 climbs through picturesque country, off which (12 km.) a road leads 5 km. E. to *Benigánim*, with a mosque converted into a church.—We ascend to (13 km.) **Albaida** (5200 inhab.) with a triple-towered *palace*.

From Albaida to Villena (46 km.). The C 320 leads to (8 km.) **Onteniente** (26,300 inhab.), in the upland valley of the Clariano, preserving a few fragments of its once formidable ramparts, and a good 16C church. Here we turn S. onto C 3316 to thread a defile before reaching (10 km.) r.) **Bocairente** (4700 inhab.), perched on a hill-top, with paintings by *Juan de Joanes* in its church, and in the neighbourhood, Iberian cave-tombs re-used as cells by early Christian anchorites. The road continues S.W., gently descending the wide valley of the Vinalopó, at 7 km. passing (3 km. l.) *Bañeres*, with a Gothic church, towards (21 km.) *Villena*, see Rte 54A.

We climb to the Pto. de Albaida (2060 ft), with fine views to the E. on our descent, before entering (18 km.) **Cocentaina** (1425 ft; 10,000 inhab.), preserving an imposing turreted *Palace of the Dukes of Medinaceli. Sta María* has paintings by *Nic. Borrás*. and there are good sculptures in the *Conv. de Clarisas*. To the W. stands *Moncabrer* (3568 ft), the highest point of the Sierra de Mariola.

7 km. **Alcoy** (910 ft), a picturesquely situated and flourishing town (60,400 inhab.) on a promontory between the rivers Molinar and Barchell at the foot of the Sierra de Mariola, contains a number of churches of the Valencian Baroque type. It has manufactures of paper and cotton and woollen goods and is noted for its *'peladillas'* or sugared almonds.

About St George's day (Apr. 22-24th) a sham fight between 'Moros' and 'Cristianos' commemorates the battle of 1227, when St George is said to have lent his aid to the Christian troops defending the town.

From Alcoy, an attractive drive may be made to the coast at *Benidorm* by following the C 3313, which climbs E., with fine retrospective views, to (14 km.) *Benasau.*—Here a side road leads S. 4 km. to the walled village of *Penáguila.*—The road ascends to the Pto. de Confrides before climbing down to (22 km.) *Guadalest* (p.453) and (12 km.) *Callosa,* 15 km. N. of *Benidorm,* see Rte 53A.

Another road to Villena leads off the N 340 8 km. S. of Alcoy viâ **Ibi** (17,750 inhab.), 8 km. beyond which is the cross-road for (1 km. S.) *Castalla,* with a castle and late Gothic churches; and 2 km. N., *Onil,* with a palace of 1539.—11 km. further W. lies *Biar* (p.460) and 24 km. beyond, *Villena.*

The N 340 now climbs to the *Pto. de Carrasqueta* (3418 ft), commanding fine panoramic *Views as we zigzag down to (20 km.) **Jijona** (1510 ft), an old hill-town (8400 inhab.) with an imposing castle, and Gothic church. It is renowned for its *turrón* (see p.84), and raisins. The road bears S.E. across barren country before descending gently to meet the N 332 some 8 km. N. of (25 km.) **Alicante**, see Rte 53A.

54   FROM MADRID TO ALICANTE, AND CARTAGENA

A   To Alicante viâ Albacete and Almansa.

Total distance, 426 km. (264 miles). N IV. 48 km. *Aranjuez*—16 km. *Ocaña*—N 301. 78 km. *Mota del Cuervo*—73 km. *La Roda*—36 km. **Albacete**—N 430. 11 km. *Chinchilla*—63 km. *Almansa*—18 km. turn r. on to N 330—30 km. *Villena*—63 km. **Alicante.**

We leave Madrid by the Paseo de las Delicias and the N IV, much improved as far as Ocaña, shortly passing (r.) *Villaverde*, with a 15C church containing a Gothic sanctuary, and Mudéjar roof and tower.— At 14 km. (l.) is the *Cerro de los Ángeles*, a low hill surmounted by a monument replacing another blown up in 1936, and regarded as the geographical centre of Spain.—At (6 km., r.) *Pinto*, is the 15C castle in which Philip II imprisoned the intriguing Princess of Éboli (see p.435), and a good Plateresque church door.—7 km. *Valdemoro* (*Hotel*) where the 16C church contains paintings by *Goya*, *Bayeu*, and *Cl. Coello.*—At 3 km. a road leads 5 km. E. to *Ciempozuelos*, also with works by *Coello* (1682) in its church. 4 km. beyond, at *Tituleia*, four retablos with paintings by *El Greco* and his son, Jorge, may be seen.—We descend into the valley of the Jarama and Tagus, to enter (18 km.) **Aranjuez**, see Rte 25C.

We climb steeply S.E. and shortly (16 km.) reach **Ocaña,** also by-passed, an antiquated town (5200 inhab.), sacked by the French under Soult in 1809, who had routed the Spaniards on the plain to the S., and also damaged during the Civil War.

To the S. of the arcaded *Pl. Mayor* (1782–91) are the remains of the Mudéjar *Pal. de Santiago* (15–16C). The *Pal. de Frías* is in the Isabelline style of 1500, and a

Theatre occupies the former Jesuit church. *S. Juan*, in the centre, is a Gothic-Mudéjar church (13-15C) with 16C retablos. Among other buildings of interest are ruinous *S. Martín* to the N.E., retaining a 16C tower; its portal may be moved elsewhere; *Sta María* (N.W.) with a Plateresque retablo, a good reja, and ten 'processional' suits of armour (16-17C). There is also a curious fountain (*Fuente Nueva*), and an aqueduct (restored) built by *Herrera* for Philip II (1574–78). Daniel O'Mahony, a general in the Spanish service during the War of the Succession, died here in 1714.

From Ocaña the N VI drives due S. to *Bailén*, see Rte 49; the N 400 leads E. to *Tarancón*, see Rte 50.

The N 301, which we follow, bears S.E. across the monotonous plain of LA MANCHA, at 60 km. by-passing **Quintanar de la Orden**, (8600 inhab.), noted for its cheese.

Sir Charles Wogan (1698?–1752?), a Jacobite soldier of fortune and a colonel in the Spanish service from 1723, was a governor of La Mancha during his last years. *El Toboso*, home of the peerless Dulcinea, with a museum and library of editions of 'Don Quixote', lies 7 km. S., 18 km. beyond which, near *Campo de Criptana*, on its hill, are seen some of the windmills that grind the corn of the district, and among these one may seek to identify the actual mills at which Don Quixote tilted.—8 km. W. of Campo de Criptana, on the road to Puerto Lápice, lies **Alcázar de San Juan** (27,100 inhab.; *Hotel*), a busy wine centre, which takes its name from a Moorish castle that afterwards became the headquarters of the Military Order of San Juan. The restored *Torre de Don Juan de Austria* and Romanesque *Sta María* are of interest.

18 km. *Mota del Cuervo* (*Hotel*) with a ruined castle of the Order of Santiago, lies at the cross-road of the N 420.

16 km. N.E. stands **Belmonte**, birthplace of Fr. Luis de León (1528–91), with a superbly situated and elegant *Castle*, built for the Marqués de Villena (1456), which in plan is based on the equilateral triangle and five-pointed star. The old church of *S. Bartolomé* (14C on Romanesque foundations) contains tombs of the Pacheco family.—The church of *Villaescusa de Haro*, 5 km. beyond, contains a fine Isabelline chapel, but admittance is not easy to obtain.

22 km. *Las Pedroñeras* (*Hotel*), the church of which contains a painting by *El Greco*. We soon enter a region of pinegroves, and at 17 km. reach crossroads.

San Clemente (6300 inhab.), 9 km. N.E., contains an attractive 16C *Ayuntamiento* and Pl. Mayor, while in well-vaulted *Santiago el Mayor* is a remarkable Gothic alabaster crucifix, unfortunately in a vile setting. The squat *Torre Vieja* in the nearby Pl. de Carmen Martínez is also if interest, while various old convents remain.—13 km. S.W. of the crossroads lies *Villarrobledo* (20,200 inhab.; robledo = oak grove), trading extensively in saffron, with an *Ayuntamiento* of 1599, and 16C *S. Blas*.

34 km. *La Roda*, with a hall-church of 1564, and ancient mansions; 14 km. *La Gineta* also has a 16C church.

At 22 km., in the centre of a flat, uninteresting plain, lies the dull provincial capital of·**ALBACETE** (2250 ft; 101,250 inhab.; 32,000 in 1920; 70,000 in 1950; *Parador Nac.* not far S. of the town; *Hotels*).

History. Of Moorish origin (Al-basit = the plain), it witnessed two bloody battles between Moors and Christians (1145–46), in the second of which Abu Jafar, emir of Córdoba, met his death. The town is famous for its '*puñales*' (daggers) and '*navajas*' (clasp-knives with spring-blades), whose handles were decorated with coarse inlay and with blades often engraved. Albacete is also the centre of the trade in saffron, of which Spain is the world's main producer. It attained its present importance only since the malarial swamps which surrounded it were drained by the Canal de María Cristina (1805). During the Civil War it was for some time H.Q. of the International Brigades.

Largely rebuilt, Albacete hardly retains a single old edifice, with the exception of the so-designated 'cathedral', or *S. Juan Bautista*, a 16C hall-church completed by Diego de Siloée, but entirely restored since 1936. A new *Provincial Museum* has recently been inauguarated.

For the road hence to *Murcia* and *Cartagena*, see Rte 54B.

FROM ALBACETE TO ALCARAZ AND UBEDA (208 km.). We strike S.W. across the plain on the N 322, passing (23 km. r.) *Balazote*, after which we ascend to Robledo and climb to the Pto. de los Pocicos.—At 56 km., just S. of the road, lies **Alcaraz** (2600 inhab.), dominated by the ruins of an extensive castle taken from the Moors in 1213 and rebuilt in 1507. Below the castle are the remains of Gothic *Sta María*, while in the town are *La Trinidad* (1544), with a good S. Door and ruined cloister, and the adjacent *Torre del Tardón* (1568); further along the main street is *S. Miguel* (16C); the *Ayuntamiento* of 1588 overlooks the *Plaza*; and old houses abound. Many of these buildings are from the designs of the native architect *Andrés de Vandaelvira* (1509–75).— At 1 km. the C 415 runs due W. towards *Villanueva de los Infantes* to meet the N IV just W. of (88 km.) *Valdepeñas*, see Rte 49A.

We descend into the valley of the Guadalimar through the wild hills linking the Sierra Morena with the Sierra de Alcaraz to (51 km.) *Puente de Génave*.

Just before, the C 321 bears l. After 11 km. a turning leads 5 km. E. to the hill village of **Orcera**, and beyond, to **Segura de la Sierra**, below its ancient, but restored, castle.—At 13 km. we turn r. to skirt the W. bank of the Embalse del Tranco de Beas, and crossing the Guadalquivir, follow the deep valley due S. between the well-wooded SIERRA DE CAZORLA and the SIERRA DE SEGURA massif to the E. 52 km. after turning off the N 322 we reach a junction; the l. fork leads 8 km. to a *Parador Nac.;* the r. fork, after crossing the Pto. de las Palomas and passing the castle of *Iruela*, enters (17 km.) *Cazorla*, see Rte 57. Hence the main road may be regained 9 km. E. of *Úbeda*, at (37 km.) *Torreperogil*, viâ (15 km.) Peal de Becerro.

A turning (r.) at 39 km. climbs shortly to the picturesque village of *Iznatoraf*, commanding panoramic views.—At 6 km. the N 322 by-passes **Villacarrillo** (12,050 inhab.), with an 18C *Ayuntamiento* and a church ascribed to *Vandaelvira*. The road now follows the S. slope of the *Lomo de Úbeda*, enjoying magnificent **Views* across the Guadalquivir valley and of the Sierra de Cazorla beyond, before traversing (23 km.) *Torreperogil* and entering (9 km.) **Ubeda**, see p.478.

From Albacete we follow the N 430, the Valencia road, commanded by a castle-crowned hill (2946 ft) and the ancient town of **Chinchilla de Monte Aragón** (5200 inhab.), which is by-passed by the main road, but may be entered at 11 km.

Chinchilla is somewhat dilapidated, but the old streets rising from the Pl. Mayor towards the *Castle* (15C; View) are lined with interesting houses in Gothic and Mudéjar styles. The 18C *Ayuntamiento*, on the E. of the plaza, preserves a front of 1590, while the *Prison* opposite bears inscriptions of 1605 and 1637. Unfinished *Sta María del Salvador*, largely built c. 1440, has an apse with remarkable Plateresque decoration (c. 1540), a reja of 1503, and 17C woodwork in the sacristy. To the E. is the ruinous *Conv. de Sto Domingo* (14C), with a disfigured Gothic cloister. In the other direction are the *Col. de N.S. de las Nieves* and the *Hosp. de S. Julián*, in the C. de los Benefactores below the castle.

The road now climbs, and at 27 km. crosses the Pto. los Altos, in a barren steppe-like landscape.—At 27 km. a road leads 10 km. N. to *Alpera*, near which, in the Cueva de la Vieja and Cueva del Queso are prehistoric rock-paintings, while on the *Puntal de Meca* (3996 ft) are remains of an Iberian town.—After passing (l.) *El Mugrón* (3993 ft) dominating the area, at 4 km. we see (r.) the *Embalse de Almansa*, a reservoir constructed by the Moors, nearly one mile square and confined by a great masonry dam.

5 km. **Almansa** (18,600 inhab.), by-passed by the main road, is commanded by a castle of Moorish origin but rebuilt in the 15C, standing on an isolated limestone hill. The *Parish Church* (late 15C) has

a good tower and a Renaissance portal, while the *Pal. of the Condes de Cirat*, adjoining, is a robust work of 1575 (façade and patio). Behind, the *Conv. of the Agustinas* is adorned with a Baroque door of 1704.

Almansa is noted for the victory of the French under the Duke of Berwick, fighting for Philip V, over the English partisans of the Archduke Charles, commanded by Ruvigny, Earl of Galway, and the Marqués de la Mina (25 April, 1707).
To the S.W., between Montealegre and Yecla, rises the *Cerro de los Santos*, the ancient *Ello*, famous for the Graeco-Phoenician (?) sculptures (4C B.C.), now in the Madrid Archaeological Museum, and in the museums of Albacete, Murcia, Valladolid, and Yecla.

At 8 km. we turn S. off the Valencia road (see p.455, in reverse) onto the N 330 and wind down the valley of the Vinalopó.—At 17 km. a road leads 6 km. S.W. to *Caudete*, with good retablos in the chapel of the *Pal. del Rosario* (1510) and in the parish church.

13 km. **Villena**, lying in a fertile valley, is an ancient town of 27,400 inhab., whose narrow streets retain a number of solares with armorial decorations. Dominating the town is the 15C *Castle*, with a large square tower. *Santiago* (1492–1511) preserves some unusual spirally-fluted columns, a polychrome wooden retablo of 1540, by *Jerónimo Quijano*, and interesting W. Door. *Sta María* is of the 16C; the *Ayuntamiento*. dating from 1707, houses an *Archaeological Museum* containing the important gold treasure discovered in 1963 by José María Soler, founder of the museum.

7 km. E. lies *Biar*, dominated by its 13C concentric castle with a large dungeon, and with a church with a sculptured portal of 1519 and an imposing tower (1698–1733) by *Blas Aparicio*.

FROM VILLENA TO CIEZA (81 km.). The C 3314 shortly passes near the Gothic sanctuary of *Las Virtudes* before entering (21 km.) **Yecla** (23,300 inhab.), an olive-growing town with a ruined castle. The church of the *Asunción* (1512) has a curious frieze of heads on its tower, while *S. Francisco*, damaged in 1936, contains a carving of 1764 by *Salzillo*. In the *Col. de los Escolapios* are some Iberian sculptures from the Cerro de los Santos.—26 km. **Jumilla**, a wine and oil producing centre (20,200 inhab.), has a good 15C church, *Santiago*, a castle, and Renaissance houses. The ancient prison, now the *Ayuntamiento*, has a gallery with spiral columns. To the S. are the ancient vaulted chapel of *El Casón* and beyond, the *Monastery of Sta Ana*, containing *Salzillo*'s Christ at the Column.—At 23 km. we meet the N 301, where, turning S., we soon reach (11 km.) **Cieza**, see Rte 54B.

At 11 km. we pass *Sax* (6500 inhab.), whose ruined castle is strikingly perched on a pinnacle of rock, and shortly by-pass **Elda** (48,700 inhab.; *Hotel*), an industrial town and birthplace of Juan Sempere y Guarinos (1754–1830), the literary critic. It retains a ruined *Alcázar* and a tall green-domed church. Nearer the by-pass is the ruined Moorish *Castle* of *Petrel* (20,400 inhab.).

8 km. S.W. lies *Monóvar* (10,850 inhab.), birthplace of Azorín (José Martínez Ruiz,1873–1967), the writer, with a museum incorporating his library, a Moorish castle, and a church of 1750.—In the valley between Monóvar and *Novelda*, and approached from the latter, stands the curious triangular tower of the *Castillo de la Mola*, or *de Luna*. Novelda itself (18,900 inhab.) birthplace of Adm. Jorge Juan y Santacilia (1713–73), is by-passed as we cross the foot of the Sierra del Cid.—At *Aspe*, 8 km. S. of Novelda, the road forks l. to (12 km.) *Elche* (see Rte 55A), and r. to (13 km.) *Crevillente*.

The main road bears l. through (29 km.) Montforte del Cid and traverses a bare hilly district before descending through flatter country towards the industrial outskirts of (23 km.) **Alicante**, see Rte 53A.

B   From Albacete to Murcia and Cartagena

Total distance, 449 km. (279 miles). N IV. 64 km. *Ocaña*—N 301. 187 km.
Albacete—61 km. *Hellín*—44 km. *Cieza*—45 km. **Murcia**—48 km. **Cartagena.**

For the road from Madrid to (251 km.) *Albacete*, see Rte 54A. Hence the Murcia road (N 301) runs S. across the dreary plateau with the rocky Peñas de S. Pedro in the distance to the W.—53 km. *Tobarra*, dominated by a Franciscan *Convent* and a ruined castle. Far to the W. rises the *Sierra de Alcaraz* (5875 ft).—8 km. **Hellín** (22,600 inhab.), with a 16-17C hall-church, is the ancient *Illunum*, known to the Romans for its sulphur mines rediscovered in 1564, which lie to the S. Melchor de Macanaz (1670–1760), the 18C political economist, was born here.

From Hellín the C 3212 climbs to *Elche de la Sierra* 36 km. to the W., whence mountain roads lead through a picturesque region passing near the huge Embalse de Cenajo; the C 415 runs N.W. to *Alcaraz* (94 km. beyond; see p.459), and S.E. to (69 km.) *Caravaca* (see p.468), while the C 3212 continues S.W. to (35 km.) **Yeste**, a remote town (6800 inhab.), near the Embalse de la Fuensanta, with a late-Gothic church (c. 1600) and 16C *Ayuntamiento* of interest.

10 km. r. *Minateda*, near which is a prehistoric rock-shelter with notable wall-paintings.—At 2 km. the C 3213 leads E. 28 km. to *Jumilla*, see above.—We now traverse the Sierra de las Cabras and enter the province of Murcia, at 21 km. meeting the cross-road (C 3314) from Jumilla to *Calasparra*, 24 km. to the r.

Calasparra, of Iberian origin, with a ruined castle, lies in the valley of the Segura, bounded by curiously shaped hills and which contains rice-fields.—22 km. beyond to the S.W., lies Caravaca, see p.468.

11 km. **Cieza**, (29,300 inhab.), rises above the fertile valley, while on the opposite hill are the slight ruins of a Moorish castle. The N 301 now rins parallel to the Segura, passing (21 km.) *Archena* (10,050 inhab.; *Hotel*), 4 km. W. on the far side of the river, which preserves remains of Roman and Moorish baths, was a Russian tank base during the Civil War.—*Ulea*, 5 km. N. of Archena, has a fine Mudéjar roof to its church.

The Segura valley above Archena, or *Valle de Ricote*, was the last part of Spain to be inhabited—until 1505—by unchristianized Moors, and remains of their fortress-towers survive. The conforming Moriscos, too, remained here for four years after the general expulsion of 1609.

Near (5 km. r.) *Lorquí*, Roman *Ilorci*, Publius and Gnaeus Scipio were defeated and slain by Carthaginian forces (211 B.C.). Oranges and lemons abound in the valley.—3 km., r. *Alguazas* has a 16C church with a Mudéjar ceiling. To the S., near the confluence of the Mula with the Segura, stands the medieval *Pal. of the Bishops of Murcia* (1337–51). We now traverse the dusty outskirts of Murcia, and at 16 km. enter the city centre, dominated by the Cathedral tower.

MURCIA (262,100 inhab.; 142,000 in 1920; 218,000 in 1950; *Hotels*), lies on the Segura, in the midst of a *huerta* rivalling that of Valencia. Extensive rebuilding is taking place in the suburbs surrounding the old town, which now has a less dilapidated air than a decade ago. On all sides rise barren hills, *Monte Agudo* (N.E.) and the *Monte de Fuensanta* (S.) being the salient features. The climate is erratic; the torrid summer is often affected by the parching dust of the *leveche*, while the winter nights are occasionally chilled with sudden frosts. Murcia subsists largely on the produce of its market gardens, and the canning of its considerable fruit crop. Less important now is the production of Silk Worm Gut, an industry fomented by the Estación Sericiola, a government establishment at *Alberca*, 5 km. S.E., to which interested visitors may obtain admission.

Fiestas: During Holy Week the 'pasos' of *Salzillo* (see p.464) and other figures are paraded on 'tronos' through the street, while in Spring a Battle of Flowers is celebrated, followed by the 'Burial of the Sardine'. Feria, Sept. 8–15th.

History. Little is known of Murcia before its rebuilding by the Moors at the beginning of the 8C, from the materials of an older town (? Roman or Iberian). It was named *Mursiyah*, and the river, the ancient *Tader*, was called *Sekhurah*. In 1224, at the disintegration of the Almohade empire, it became capital of a small Moorish kingdom soon overrun by Fernando III (1240); rebellion on the part of the inhabitants being finally crushed by the future Alfonso el Sabio in 1243, and the town was largely repopulated by Catalans. During the War of the Spanish Succession the city was saved from the Archduke Charles (1707) by its bishop, Luis de Belluga, who laid the environs under water and beat off the assailants with a handful of peasantry. The population was c. 40,000 in 1800. In 1810 it was sacked by Sebastiani; and in 1829 and 1879 it suffered severely from earthquake and flood. In 1936 the churches, with the exception of the Cathedral and S. Andrés, were looted and burnt. Among eminent Murcians were Ibn Al-'Arabi (1165–1240), the mystic, Francisco Salzillo or Zarcillo (1707–83), the sculptor, and the Conde de Floridablanca (1728–1808), minister of Carlos III, and prime mover in the expulsion of the Jesuits from Spain.

The *Pte. Viejo*, built in 1718–42, crosses the Segura opposite the Pl. de Martínez Tornell, an open space better known as *El Arenal*.

There is little interest S. of the river; the road first crosses the *Pl. de Calvo Sotelo*, previously the *Pl. del Marqués de Camachos*, built in 1756 and formerly a Plaza de Toros. Beyond is the *Jardín de Floridablanca*, at the far end of which is hhe restored church of *El Carmen* (1721–69) containing the Cristo de la Sangre (1693), the masterpiece of *Nic. de Busi*, a predecessor of Fr. Salzillo.

From the Arenal, the Gran Via leads N. through the old town, while riverside *paseos* diverge on either side. To the E. is the Glorieta de España; to the W. beyond the Plano S. Francisco, the MALECÓN (embankment), flanked by a botanical garden. In the Plano S. Francisco is the *Audiencia* of 1618–28, originally the corn-exchange, with parts of an earlier building of 1554–75, beyond which is the market. From the Glorieta, we pass between the *Ayuntamiento* (l.) and the *Bishop's Palace* (1748), completed by *Baltasar Canestro*, with a graceful patio.

The short passage between these buildings lead to the *Cathedral, on the E. side of the Pl. del Card. Belluga. Originally it was a plain Gothic building of 1394–1465, but additions in the 16C and the construction of new front after a destructive flood of the Segura in 1735, have completely changed its external appearance.

The valuable jewels of the Virgen de la Fuensanta, placed here for safe-keeping, were stolen in Jan. 1977.

EXTERIOR. The **W. Front**, a fine example of Baroque decoration, was built in 1736–54 from the designs of *Jaime Bort*. Pyramidal in design, it has Corinthian columns below, Composite above, and is adorned with figures of saints with flowing drapery. The *N. Portal*, the elegant Italianate *Pta. de las Cadenas* (1512–15), is ascribed to *Juan de León* and *Francisco Florentino*. On the N. side rises also the imposing **Tower** (90 m.), in five diminishing storeys. Begun in 1521–26 by *Francisco* and *Jacobo Florentino*, two Italian artists, it received a second stage (1526–46) from *Jerónimo Quijano*; but it was not completed until 1765–92, by *Juan de Gea*, *José López*, and *Ventura Rodríguez* (fine view from the summit, reached by an easy ramp and spiral staircase; apply at the Diocesan Museum). At the S.E. corner of the cathedral is the octagonal **Vélez Chapel** (c. 1495–1507), recalling the Manueline style, bearing large escutcheons and carved chains, the badge of the Vélez family. The *Pta. de los Apóstoles*, the S. Portal, is a restored doorway of c. 1440, by *Alonso Gil*. Beyond it is the Plateresque *Junterones Chapel* (1526–29), by *Quijano*.

The INTERIOR is Gothic in general effect, with rich ogee arches in the aisles, but incorporates some fine Plateresque and Renaissance decoration. The *Coro*, which blocks up the nave, contains stalls of 1567–71 (from the abbey of S. Martín de Valdeiglesias, W. of Madrid). The *Cap. Mayor* has a reja of 1497 by *Ant. de Viveros*. On the l. is a niche with an urn (? by *Jac. Florentino*) containing the entrails of Alfonso el Sabio. In the *Cap. de los Junterones* (4th in the S. Aisle) the altarpiece is a Nativity (early 16C Italian).

The remarkable *Cap. de los Vélez (5th in the ambulatory) with a beautiful screen and rich vaulting, is a good example of Plateresque decoration in its most lavish mood (1507). The *Sacristía Mayor*, entered by a Plateresque door at the base of the tower, in the N. ambulatory, is a fine domed room, by *Jac. Florentino*, with woodwork of 1527. The *Baptistery*, in the N. Aisle, is a Renaissance chapel of 1541.

From the W. side of the N. Transept we may enter the interesting **Diocesan Mueseum**, containing the sculptured Retablo de las Musas; a re-used sarcophagus-front (3-5C); a marble Virgin (17C); S. Jerónimo by *Salzillo*, and other sculptures; paintings, including the double Retablo of St Lucy and of the Virgin, by *Bárnaba da Módena* (fl. 1365–1400); a collection of charters, including that of Sancho IV authorizing the transfer of the see from Cartagena to Murcia (1291); a custodia of 1677 by *Ant. Pérez de Montalto*, and chalices (late 15C; 17C silver filigree), etc.

From the Pl. de las Cadenas, on the N. side of the Cathedral, leads the TRAPERÍA. This and the PLATERÍA, which diverges on the l. about mid-way, two of the principal streets, recall the C. de las Sierpes of Seville, and are likewise closed to traffic as are others in the area. At the N. end of the Trapería, passing (r.) the *Casino*, fin de siècle in style, and with a lavishly decorated ballroom, stands (l.) a Renaissance mansion known as the '*Casa de los Salvages*', and just beyond is the large unfinished church of *Sto Domingo* (1543–1742), restored. Thence the Gran Via Alfonso el Sabio passes between (r.) the *Conv. de Sta Ana* (with a church of 1728) and l. the Baroque front and dome of the *Conv. de Sta Clara*, where the church (c. 1755) contains works by *Salzillo*, to reach the *Museo Arqueológico*.

From Sta Clara the C. Acislo Díaz runs W. past Jesuit *S. Esteban*, completed in 1569, with a side-portal in the style of Quijano, and a figure of S. Francisco Xavier by *Busi* (1700). The building now houses a small museum of regional costume. The *Misericordia*, alongside, with a graceful patio, occupies the former *Casa de la Compañía*. Opposite is *S. Miguel* (c. 1676), with a retablo mayor (1731) by *Jacinto Perales* and *Fr. Salzillo*, and other sculptures by the latter and by his father *Nic. Salzillo*. Further on a narrow lane leads N. to the 13C *Ermita de Santiago* (restored), the oldest church in Murcia.

From the Trapería the Platería leads W., passing (l.) *S. Bartolomé*, containing *Salzillo's* Virgin de las Angustias (1741), and ends beyond the Gran Via near *Sta Catalina*, of 1594 and later, with figures by *Nic. Salzillo*. From the adjoining square to the S.W., where *S. Pedro* has a retablo by *Roque López*, we follow the C. S. Nicolás N.W. to sumptuous *S. Nicolás*, of 1736–43, which contains a Figure of St Anthony in Capunchin dress, by *Alonso Cano*.

Hence we may work our way W. towards *S. Andrés* (1630–1762), adjoining which is the round *Ermita de Jesús* of 1696, housing the

*Museo Salzillo, an impressive collection of *Pasos*, or figures carried in the Holy Week processions, by *Francisco Salzillo* (1707–83).

We first visit rooms containing works other than Pasos; small statues of Saints, a Child Jesus, the painted Holy Face, and the *Bethlehem*, comprising over 1500 minature figures.—The chapel has been arranged so as to display the Pasos in the encircling side-chapels. The realistically coloured life-size groups, together with his Bethlehem, betray Salzillo's Neapolitan origins by their resemblance to the popular 'Presepi' of the churches of Naples. The scenes represent the events of Holy Week; the figures of St John and St Veronica, and the Last Supper, are the most successful. Behind the altar stands the 16th or early-17C figure of Jesus the Nazarene, the only work not by Salzillo.

We return to the Arenal by the C. de Sagasta and C. de S. Francisco, passing the *Conv. de las Teresas*, and (l.) behind the market, that of *Las Verónicas*, with a Baroque front of 1727–55.

To the S. of the cathedral, between it and the river, is a block of buildings comprising the *Seminario de S. Fulgencio* (1592–1701); the *Instituto*, founded in 1724 as the *Col. de S. Isidoro*; and the *Hosp. of S. Juan de Dios* with an elliptical Rococo chapel of 1745–81. Beyond the last we reach the head of the *Pte. Nuevo*.

The C. Ceballos leads N. from the hospital, leaving to the r. *S. Juan Bautista* (18C) with statues by *Busi* (S. Isidro) and others of the school of Salzillo. Adjoining are the 18C mansions of the Floridalblanca and Saavedra Fajardo families.

Further N.E. is *Sta Eulalia* (c. 1765–79), beyond which is the *Museo de Bellas Artes* containing paintings of the Murcian school, a St Jerome by *Ribera*, and more recent canvases.

We pass N. of the P.O., the *Conv. de S. Antonio* (partly 16C) to reach *S. Lorenzo*, a cruciform church of six domed bays, completed by *V. Rodríguez* in 1810, behind which, to the N.E., is *La Merced*, an early Rococo work of 1713–27 notable for a series of paintings of the Order of Mercedarians by two local artists of the early 17C, *L. Suarez* and *C. Acebedo*. The conventual buildings, with a Renaissance patio, now house the *University*. Thence the C. de la Merced leads W. to the *Jardin de Sto Domingo*, at the top of the Trapería, see above.

EXCURSIONS may be made into the surrounding huerta. To the S. lies the pilgrimage chapel of *La Fuensanta* (1694), designed by *Toribio Martinez de la Vega*; close by are the monasteries of *Sta Catalina del Monte* (16C), and *La Luz* (18C), with a St Anthony by *Salzillo*. *Espinardo*, to the N., has a 16C palace, and a good retablo and custodia in the parish church.

N. of the Alcantarilla road lies the monastery of *La Nora*, now occupied by Jesuits. It was originally Hieronymite, and the Baroque church contains a St. Jerome (1755) by *Salzillo*. The name is derived from an ancient 'noria', an Arab irrigation-wheel for raising water to a higher level. At *Alcantarilla* also is the *Museo de la Huerta*, containing local furniture, ceramics, textiles, etc.

For the road to *Caravaca*, see p.468.

From Murcia the Cartagena road (N 301) after crossing the huerta, abounding with orange groves, ascends the Pto. de la Cadena (1125 ft) and then runs S.E. to enter (48 km. from Murcia, and 449 km. from Madrid), the arsenal and naval base of **CARTAGENA** (155,200 inhab.; 97,000 in 1920; *Hotels*).

In ancient times the strongest fortress in Spain, Cartagena now retains few relics of its past, but is still the main channel for the export of minerals from the surrounding hills, while its beautifully situated harbour is the safest on the Spanish Mediterranean coast, its narrow

entrance guarded by the forts of *Galeras* (W.) and *S. Julián* (E.)
Cartagena was seriously damaged during the Civil War, and the *old*
town has a somewhat decrepit appearance.

History. Founded, or more probably rebuilt, by Hasdrubal, son-in-law of
Hamilcar Barca, c. 243 B.C., *Carthago Nova* became the cente of Carthaginian
power in Spain, and its gold and silver mines worked by slave labour were an
important source of wealth. In the Second Punic War it was the principal objective
in Spain of the elder Scipio Africanus, and his siege and capture of it in 210-209 B.C.
are described by Livy and by Polybius. It retained its importance under the
Romans and was nicknamed *Spartaria*, from the abundance of esparto-grass, but
its official title was *Colonia Victrix Julia Carthago Nova.* The harbour was of little
use to the Goths, but at the time of the Moorish invasion a duchy of uncertain
extent under Theodomir seems to have maintained a partial independence under
the suzerainty of the Caliph.
    Moorish *Kartajanah* fell to Fernando III in 1242, but was recaptured and finally
secured only in 1265 by Jaime el Conquistador. In 1585 it was raided by Francis
Drake, who carried off its guns to Jamaica. Swinburne considered that the arsenal
had hardly sufficient equipment 'to fit out a frigate', when he visited the place,
which 'were it not for its celebrity. . .scarce deserves a minute's attention from a
curious traveller'; while Widdrington, some fifty years later, also found it much
decayed, containing only a corvette for sale, which no one would buy. In 1873
Communists held out for over six months against the Republic at Madrid, a
resistance which, although eventually subdued by bombardment, contributed to
the final discredit of the government. The Nationalist cruiser '*Baleares*' was sunk
off Cartagena in March 1938 by the torpedoes of Republican destroyers based
there.
    Isidoro de Sevilla (c. 560–636), the encyclopaedist, was born here, as was
Fernando Garrido (1821–83), the socialist revolutionary.

The N 301 passes through modern suburbs to the N. before reaching
the C. Real, skirting the Arsenal, hidden by a high wall, leading to the
Ayuntamiento and the *Muelle de Alfonso XII,* the principal quay. Here
stands *Isaac Peral*'s submarine of 1888. In front extends the *Harbour*,
whose entrance is protected by two breakwaters. On the quay, to the r.,
lie Harbour Offices and barracks. Adjoining is the entrance to the
extensive *Arsenal* (no admission), built in 1733–82, overlooked and
protected by the *Castillo de la Atalaya* (W.) and *Castillo de Galeras*
(S.W.).

To reach the *Castillo de la Concepción,* the highest point in the town
(which may also be approached by car from the *Muralla del Mar*), we
ascend the C. de Aire (roughly parallel to and E. of the *C. Mayor,* closed
to traffic), which climbs through a derelict area past 13C *Sta María la
Vieja*, the *Catedral Antigua,* in ruins since the Civil War. Roman
inscriptions have been discovered among the foundations of the ruined
fortress (rebuilt by Alfonso X) which occupies the probable site of the
Roman arx. It commands a panoramic *View of the town, harbour and
circumjacent heights, each crowned by a fort. The ruins of dismantled
forts—*de los Moros, de Despeñaperros*, and *de S. José*—on lower hills
to the N.E., may also be discerned.

    From the N. end of the C. Mayor we may reach, viâ the C. Tomás Maestre and
C. Sta Florentina, the *Archaeological Museum.*—The *Torre Ciega,* a Roman
monument N. of the station (l. beyond bridge over railway), preserves fragmentary
decoration. The 4-5C *Necropolis, of S. Anton* has recently been excavated, while
part of a Roman amphitheatre has been discovered on the site of the Pl. de Toros.

55   FROM ALICANTE TO GRANADA, AND ALMERÍA

A   To Granada viâ Murcia, Lorca, and Baza.

Total distance, 353 km. (219 miles) N 340. 199 km. **Elche**—(34 km. **Orihuela**)—22 km. **Murcia**—64 km. **Lorca**—16 km. *Pto. Lumbreras*—96 km. *Baza*—47 km. *Guadix*—55 km. **Granada**.

The N 340 traverses the rich huerta of Alicante, planted with vines, figs, pomegranates, almonds, etc., diverging from the coast road (N 332) after 4 km., see below (Rte 55B). Passing (6 km. l.) the airport, we soon enter the palm-forest of Elche.

9 km. **ELCHE**, a busy town of 148,500 inhab. (73,000 in 1960; 12,300 in 1920; *Hotels*), stands on the Vinalapó.

History. Elche, probably of Iberian origin, was an important settlement of the Graeco-Phoenicians under the name of *Helike*, and to the Roman it was known as *Colonia Julia Ilici Augusta.* The 'Dama de Elche' (now in the Archaeological Museum, Madrid), a remarkable stone bust discovered at *La Alcudia* in 1897, is attributed to an Iberian sculptor of the 5C b.c. A Mosaic floor, bearing Latin inscriptions, was found on the same estate in 1959.

Blue-domed *Sta María,* begun in 1673 by *Fr. Verde,* reconstructed since 1936, preserves a Baroque Portal by *Nic. de Busi,* and a tall tower commanding a view of the exotic landscape. A tower-house stands W. of the church; another, with an escutcheon, at C. Obispo Rocamora 6, to the S., while the 15C *Pal. de Altamira* lies to the N. The 17C *Ayuntamiento,* S. of Sta María, has a vaulted gateway incorporating part of the original building of 1443–44; *El Salvador,* further on, has a fine 18C Retablo.—In the Municipal Park, N. of the town, the small museum contains a life-size stone lioness of the 4C b.c.

The main interest of Elche is the **Palm Forest**, the only example of its kind in Europe, which extends around the town on three sides. The forest, really a series of separate plantations (*palmerales* or *huertas*), many unenclosed, consists of over 125,000 date-palms (18-24 m. high) planted alongside canals of brackish water which are fed by a reservoir further up the Vinalapó. In the **Huerta de Castaño** or **del Cura**, 15 min. walk from the Pl. Mayor, is the curious *Palmera del Cura* or *Palmera Imperial,* a male palm c. 150 years old with seven smaller stems clustered round the main trunk.—About 10 min. further on is the *Villa Carmen* with a belvedere commanding a remarkable view over the tops of the palms.

Only the female trees bear fruit (about November); they are fertilized, often artificially, by the pollen of the male trees, which flower in May. Besides the fertile date-palms the male trees and barren female trees are valuable for the 'palms' (*ramilletes*) which they provide for processions and decorations on Palm Sunday. The branches intended for this purpose are bound up and concealed from the light so that they become bleached; each tree can produce about ten 'palms' every fourth year.

10 km. *Crevillente* (20,050 inhab.; *Hotel*), has a reputation for its hemp-fibre mats.

At 12 km. we may diverge l. to pass through *Cox,* with a ruined castle, and *Callosa de Segura* (14,000 inhab.), with a Gothic hall-church of 1553. After 13 km. we regain the main road just prior to entering Orihuela.

By-passed by the N 340, **ORIHUELA** (48,100 inhab.; *Hotels*), standing on both banks of the Segura, was largely rebuilt after the earthquake of 1829. More recent building has caused most of its once unspoilt atmosphere to be dispersed. It claims to be the Gothic *Orcelis,* but the name is more probably derived from the Roman *Aurariola.* The town is the 'Oleza' of Gabriel Miró's novels, and the birthplace of the poet Miguel Hernández (1910–42): see Alicante. Its Huerta, irrigated by the Segura, is particularly fertile as attested by the proverb 'Llueva ó no llueva, trigo en Orihuela' ('Rain or no rain, corn in Orihuela').

Bearing l. off the N 340 at 12 km., we approach the town through a palm-grove which leads past a gate adjacent to the **Col. de Sto. Domingo,** with a fine façade. This former University was begun in 1552 by *Juan Anglés* for Bp. Loaces and continued by *Agustín Bernaldino* in the 17C. The stairs and refectory (with good azulejos) and the two cloisters are of this period. The adjoining Baroque *church* (1654–59) by *Pedro Quintana,* has a richly decorated ceiling. We follow the C. de S. Juan past the *Conv. de S. Juan* to the C. de Loaces, and crossing the Segura, soon reach the Glorieta de Gabriel Miró and park.

From here we see the ruined *Castle* on its height, and on the hill-side, the 18C *Seminario de S. Miguel,* from which a fine panoramic view is obtained. The hill may be ascended from a small plaza in the C. de Sargent, parallel to the C. Mayor.

Just N. of the Glorieta, the C. de S. Pascual leads l. and after crossing another bridge we turn l. to *Sta Justa* (1319–48) with a dome and tower of c. 1500 and unfinished Baroque front. Beyond is the *Salesas,* bearing headless statues by the Genoese *Santiago Baglietto* and containing paintings by *V. López* and others. *El Carmen,* set back in a small square, contains a Virgin by *Salzillo.* To the N., is *Santiago,* with a late-Gothic front and nave, and a transept of 1554–1609. The C. de Santiago is prolonged beyond *N.S. de Monserrate* (1748) and past (r.) the church of the *Capuchinos,* with a retablo by *J. Esteve Bonet* and a statue of S. Félix de Cantalicio by *Salzillo,* to reach the Murcia road.

From *Sta Justa* we may approach the C. Mayor, at the E. end of which is the *Pal. Episcopal* (18C), with an umbrageous courtyard. Opposite stands the ***Cathedral** built in 1305–55, with a remarkable transept of c. 1500, of which the vault has spirally twisted ribs. The N. Front (c. 1550) is attr. to *Jerónimo Quijano;* the W. Doorway, or *Pta. de las Cadenas,* and that on the S. (*Pta. de Loreto*) are Gothic. The ambulatory chapels were added after the church was raised to cathedral rank in 1564. It contains a fine sillería, an untouched organ of c.1720, and good rejas, but many paintings were lost in the 1829 earthquake.

To the E. of the cathedral is a small two-storey *cloister* transferred here from the damaged Conv. de la Merced after the Civil War, and open to the street. The *Diocesan museum* contains the Temptation of St Thomas by *Velázquez* and *Alonso Cano,* works by *Ribera* and *Morales,* and a silver processional Custodia. To the N. and in the C. Sta Lucía (further E.) are a number of old buildings. We may return to the C. Loaces via the C. Alfonso XIII, passing the Public Library and Archives housed in what was the *Pal. of the Conde de Luna,* containing also the curious Paso known as 'La Diablesa' by *Nic. de Busi* (1688). To the E. of this quarter, near the Segura, lies *La Trinidad,* with a relief of the Trinity (1580) over the W. Door.

At 17km. we pass *Monteagudo,* a rocky eminence crowned by a Moorish castle incorporating Roman remains (and surmounted by a poor modern monument), and at 5km. enter **Murcia,** see Rte 54B.

FROM MURCIA TO CARAVACA (73km.). At 9km., beyond Alcantarilla, we fork r. onto the C 415. We shortly enter the Mula valley, at 27km. reaching **Mula** itself (14,400 inhab.) with a fine castle of the Vélez (15-16C) on a hill. Its churches were ruined in 1936. It was the birthplace of Ginés Pérez de Hita (c.1544–c. 1619), historian of the wars of Granada.—20km. *Cehegín,* with many 16-18C mansions in the local red marble, preserves also a mid-16C hall-church and the *Ermita de la Concepción,* whose Mudéjar roof dates from 1556.
7km. **Caravaca** (2425 ft), a mountain-town (20,150 inhab.), is famed for an appariation of the Cross in 1232, twelve years *before* its occupation by the Christians; the cross was stolen in 1935. The town is commanded by a large *Castle* (restored), mainly 15C, and once a Templars' stronghold, surrounding the church of *Santa Cruz* (1617) in the 'Escorial' style, but its fantastic *Portal of 1722 is almost Mexican in manner. *S. Salvador,* near the main square, is a hall-church of 1534–1600.—*Moratalla,* 13km. N.W., has another fine church, begun in 1521 by *Fr. Florentino,* but never finished.

Leaving Murcia the N 340 follows the railway up the N. side of the Sangonera valley, by-passing *Alcantarilla* (see p.464).—24km. *Librilla,* a picturesque village divided by a ravine, was once the headquarters of the Murcian gipsies.—8km. *Alhama de Murcia,* a sulphur spa of very ancient origin (12,100 inhab.), lies below a Moorish fort.—11km. *Totana* (16,900 inhab.), where the valley narrows between the Sierra de Espuña (N.W.; 5200 ft) and the Sierra de Almenara, has a church (before 1587) with a 17C Baroque portal, a Mudéjar roof, and a 16C retablo. The *'tinajas'* (water-jars) made here have a local reputation.

The *Ermita de Sta Eulalia,* in the sierra, has a fine Mudéjar roof and mural paintings of 1624, while *Aledo,* a medieval village 9km. N.W., is noted for its wine and for its ruined castle held by the Knights of Calatrava in 1085-1160 in the heart of the Moorish dominion.

To the N. of the ugly modern suburbs of (21km.) **LORCA,** (59,300 inhab.; *Hotel*), is the more interesting but somewhat decayed centre, its older buildings undergoing restoration, the *Eliocroca* or *Ilucro* of the Romans and the *Lurkah* of the Moors. After its re-conquest by Alfonso el Sabio in 1244, it remained an outpost against the Moors of Granada. Its school of painting in the late 17th-early 18C, enjoyed some reputation. Lorca was also famed for its horses and its needlework, as well as for the processions of Holy Week, with elaborate 'pasos' rivalling in splendour those of Murcia. Most of its churches were looted in the Civil War. When Townsend passed through Lorca in 1787, he considered its public walks resembled those of Oxford, 'but upon a more extensive scale, and more beautiful'. It was the birthplace of the Carlist general, Rafael Maroto (1783–1847).

Before crossing the Guadalencín, we pass 18C *S. Cristóbal.*

In the C. López Gisbert, sands the *Casa de los Guevara,* with a portal with wreathed spiral columns of 1694; the *Casa de los Musso Valente,* opposite, has a fine portal and patio (1600). Not far W. stands domed *S. Mateo* (18C), and the *Pal. de S. Julián* (16C). Beyond (r.) is the *Hosp. de S. Francisco,* whose chapel contains Churrigueresque retablos with paintings by *Manuel Caro* (c. 1759).

Further W. is the *Carmen,* of 1712 with Rococo plasterwork; beyond it in the C. Pérez Cases is the *Ermita de Gracia* (16C) and higher up (r.) the *Calvario,* commanding an extensive view.

To the E. is the *Corredera*. with the 16C portal of the *Rosario* church, the *Bishop's Palace*, and more old houses. Uphill lies the Pl. de Santiago, with its 17C church, while the closely-built quarter on the slope contains Renaissance houses, and the remains of Gothic *S. Ginés* (13C), and *S. Jorge* (15C).

Lorca is commanded by a fine *Castle* (restored), partly of Moorish origin (12C), although the *Torre Alfonsina*, named in honour of Alfonso el Sabio, and in bad repair, is Spanish (15C). Below are (W. to E.) ruined *S. Pedro* (15th and 18C), *Sta María* (Gothic with a doorway of 1596), and *S. Juan Bautista* (Baroque). In the restored Pl. Mayor are the *Ayuntamiento* (17-18C) flanked to the N. by the large **Colegiata de S. Patricio,** with Baroque decoration, begun c. 1550 but not finished until 1776, and sculptures on the main front of 1627–1710. The S. Portal is an elegant work of c. 1600, while the Baroque tower, by *Fray Pedro de S. Agustín,* was completed in 1772. Within should be noted the ironwork of the sanctuary, especially the lectern (1716), and the unusual Christ, by the Guatemalan, *Manuel Santiago España* (1749).

Lorca is supplied with water by the *Pantano de Puentes,* 15 km. W., a reservoir built in 1785–91, which burst in 1802 and flooded the town.

16 km. *Puerto Lumbreras* (1320 ft; 8000 inhab.; *Albergue Nac., Hotels*), where the Granada and Almería roads separate. At the entrance of the gorge of the Nogalte stands a Moorish tower, *La Torrecilla,* the legendary scene of a bloody battle before the conquest of Granada. We follow the N 342 to the r. and ascend the Rambla Casarejos, scene of devastating floods in Oct. 1973.—29 km. *Vélez Rubio* (2750 ft; 8350 inhab.), has a notable church of 1753.

Hence a side-road (C. 321) climbs 6 km. N. past the Cueva de los Letreros, with pre-historic wall-paintings, to the impressive ***Castle of Vélez Blanco,** built by Italians in 1506–15 on an unusual polygonal plan. Regrettably, the Renaissance interiors were removed to New York in 1903, and have recently been re-erected in the Metropolitan Museum of Art.

We now ascend the Rambla de Chirivel, entering the province of Granada at (29 km.) *Las Vertientes* (3937 ft).

From (17 km.) *Cúllar de Baza* (2780 ft) an old town of 6300 inhab., the C 3329 bears N. through (20 km.) *Galera*, near the Iberian cemetery of *Tútugi* (60 B.C.) to (7 km.) **Huescar** (3125 ft; 10,100 inhab.) with a fine hall-church of the late 16C. Mountain roads radiate from here through the grand but lonely scenery of the Sierra de Segura.

38 km. **Baza** (2850 ft; 20,100 inhab.). Roman *Basti* and Moorish *Bastah,* was taken by Isabel the Catholic in 1489, and some of her cannon are preserved as posts on the Alameda. The Gothic *Colegiata* (1529–61), begun by *Pedro Urrutia,* has an 18C brick tower. Nothing remains of the Moorish *Alcazaba,* but the town retains some picturesque balconied streets. In 1971 an extraordinary statue (4C B.C.), somewhat similar to the Dama de Elche, was found here, and is exhibited at the Museo Arqueológico, Madrid. In the *Javalcón* (4720 ft), a hill to the N., are cave-dwellings.

The road onwards traverses a curious country of pointed sandy hillocks, on which only esparto grass will grow, and eventually we leave the valley of the Gallego and cross a bare and stony region. The distant summits of the *Sierra Nevada* come into view on the l.

47 km. **Guadix,** a town of 19,300 inhab., was the Moorish *Wadi-Ash,* which replaced the Iberian and Visigothic city of *Acci,* to the S.E. It was once of importance for its silver mines.

At Guadix was born the poet known as Shushtari (c. 1212–69) and (two years before the city was retaken from the Moors) Pedro de Mendoza (d. 1537), first founder of Buenos Aires in 1535; the dramatist Antonio Mira de Amescua (c. 1574 -1644); and Pedro de Alarcón (1833–91), author of 'The Three-cornered hat' and other works.

Besides the Moorish *Alcazaba,* which overlooks the town, the only building of any interest is the red-sandstone *Cathedral,* a hall-church, designed by *Diego de Siloée* in 1549, with a chevet added in 1574 by *Juan de Arredondo,* the building being completed in 1701–96 by *Vicente Acero* and *Gaspar Cayón.* The Renaissance *Pl. Mayor,* damaged in 1936–39, has been spoiled when reconstructed. The church of the *Conv. de Santiago* (c. 1540) has a Plateresque porch and artesonado ceiling.

Behind the town is the curious quarry-looking *Barrio de Santiago,* containing a large number of dwellings scooped out of the tufa, which cuts like cheese; and behind some of the entrances extend four-roomed caves, occasionally with two storeys. A few of them only are occupied by gipsies.—*Benalúa,* 6 km. to the N.W., has a similar cave district.

At 6 km. we pass through *Purullena,* also with numerous troglodyte homes, but the village is spoilt by an excessive display of pottery to tempt the passing tourist.—At 8 km. the N 324 diverges r. for *Jaén* (see p.473), 103 km. N.W.—We commence to climb up the valley of the Fardes to (6 km.) *Diezma,* with magnificent panoramic *Views towards the Sierra Nevada massif to the S. We soon pass the Pto. de la Mora (4688 ft) and continue to wind through attractive country, with extensive views to the l.—At 26 km. a road (r.) leads 2 km. to *Viznar,* with a palace (c. 1800) containing a frescoed gallery.—We shortly commence the steep descent to (9 km.) **Granada,** see Rte 58.

B   TO ALMERÍA VIÂ LORCA AND VERA.

Total distance, 294 km (182 miles) N 340. 139 km. **Lorca**—62 km. *Vera*—93 km **Almería.**

From Alicante to Lorca, see Rte 55A.

Leaving Lorca by the N 340, we fork l. at 16 km. (Puerto Lumbreras), where the Granada road diverges r., strike across the Sierra de Enmedio, and at 25 km. enter *Huércal-Overa* (12,450 inhab.), with a fine church.

At 6 km. the C 323 ascends (r.) the valley of the Almanzora, winding between brown heights on which brown villages are scarcely distinguishable from their background, at 18 km. passing *Albox,* with its old castle.—13 km. *Cantoria,* 3 km S., has an ancient church; thence a mountain road (C 3325) crosses the Sierra de lo Filabres to meet the N 340 11 km. before *Tabernas,* see p.471.—We pass marble cutting works, supplied from the quarries of (15 km.) *Purchena,* which lies on the opposite bank of the Almanzora, below a ruined castle, and enter the iron-mining district of Cuevas Negras, the central depot for ore being (17 km.) *Serón,* before reaching the head of the valley and descending to (30 km.) *Baza,* see Rte 55A.

The N 340 crosses the Almanzora and follows an undulating course through the hills of La Ballabona to (16 km.) **Vera** (ancient *Baria;* 5100 inhab.). The town was taken from the Moors of Granada in 1488, but in 1512 was destroyed by an earthquake. The parish church retains a good retablo, and the surrounding district is rich in antiquities.

10 km. S.E. lies *Garrucha*, a small port (*Hotel*) with a pleasant beach and a 16C coastal fort. 5 km. beyond, the road approaches **Mojácar** (1700 inhab.; *Parador Nac.; Hotels*), a hill-top town of flat-roofed white-washed houses recently developed as a tourist resort, and in danger of losing its original attraction.— Hence we may drive S.W. along the coast to (20 km.) *Carboneras* (*Hotel*), there turning inland to (37 km.) *Nijar* (see below), and (39 km.) *Almería*.

From Vera, the Almería road crosses the Sierra de los Yesares by steep zig-zags to (38 km.) *Sorbas* (4600 inhab.), picturesquely perched on a rock.

At 7 km. a mountain road turns S. to wind round the Sierra de Alhamilla to (25 km.) *Nijar* and then descends to the coast not far E. of *Almería*.

From (38 km.) *Tabernas* (4100 inhab.), where the ruined Moorish *alcazaba* is the most important in the province after that of Almería, we descend the Rambla de la Galera to the orange-groves of Rioja, just N. of *Pechina*, and close to the Iberian and Roman town of *Urci*, and at (26 km.) *Benahadux* join the N 324 for *Granada* from Almería (see p.497), 14 km. S.

C   From Alicante to Vera viâ Cartagena

Total distance, 231 km. (143 miles). N 332. 106 km. **Cartagena**—88 km. *Águilas*—37 km. *Vera*.

The coast S. of Alicante, although flat and uninteresting, is undergoing extensive development, and there are a number of growing resorts, particularly near the MAR MENOR. After 4 km. the N 332 forks l. off the N 340 to (14 km.) *Santa Polo* (*Hotel*), and the remains of the necropolis of *Ilici*, which has yielded a quantity of Roman and Iberian relics.

To the S. W. lies the small island of *Tabarca*, with restored 18C fortifications.

At (14 km.) *Guadamar*, we cross the Segura and pass between two large *salinas* or salt pans in the vicinity of (16 km.) **Torrevieja** (10,800 inhab.; *Hotels*), and at 20 km. enter the province of Murcia at *San Pedro de Pinatar*, in whose church is a St Peter by *Salzillo*. We shortly pass the N. end of the **Mar Menor**, a shallow salt lagoon c. 19 km. long and 11 km. broad, containing a number of small islands, and separated from the Mediterranean by narrow spits of land, to be joined by a road connecting San Pedro to *Cabo de Palos* at its S.E. corner, in turn serving '*La Manga*' and other tourist developments in the area (*Hotels*).

13 km. *Los Alcazares*, with remains of Roman and Moorish baths, just beyond which the road, skirting the W. rim of the lagoon, turns l. towards *Cabo de Palos*, while we enter a mining region, the centre of which is (13 km.) *La Unión* (12,900 inhab.; *Hotel*) whose zinc and argentiferous lead mines were worked by both Carthaginians and Romans.—12 km. **Cartagena**, see p.464

Continuing on the N 332, we turn inland before striking the coast again at (34 km.) *Puerto de Mazarrón* (*Hotels*). Mazarrón itself (9950 inhab.) 6 km. beyond, is an ancient centre of lead and iron mining, with a ruined castle of the Vélez and a Mudéjar church The coast here, between Cartagena and Águilas, is lined with 16-17C *atalayas*. Our road keeps some distance inland beneath the metalliferous Sierra de Almenara (2893 ft), and at 35 km. leaves on the r. the C 3211 for (23 km.) *Lorca*, and 4 km. beyond, a by-road for (22 km.) *Puerto Lumbreras*, see Rte 55A.

The coast is regained at (9 km.) **Águilas** (18,800 inhab.; *Hotels*) engaged in the export of esparto and the products of neighbouring mines. The town, with its ruined castle on a rocky headland, lies in a delightful situation between two bays. Practically deserted in the Middle Ages on account of the inroads of Barbary pirates, it was refounded on a regular plan by the Conde de Aranda in 1765. Ascending, we leave on the l. the Sierra de Almagrera, noted for its silver mines, and climb down to *Los Lobos* to reach the mining centre of (31 km.) **Cuevas de Almanzora**. The *Castle*, built in 1507 by Pedro Fajardo, first Marqués Vélez, as a protection against corsairs, was rebuilt under Philip II; here also is a curious quarter of cave-dwellings.

To the S.E., towards the mouth of the Almanzora, are the despoblado of *Almizaraque*, a hill which has yielded many late-Neolithic finds, and *Villaricos*, on the coast, where remains from the Carthaginian to the Moorish periods have been discovered. It was off the coast here, near the village of *Palomares*, that a thermonuclear bomb was jettisoned by the Americans, causing an international scandal.

6 km. *Vera*, see p.470.

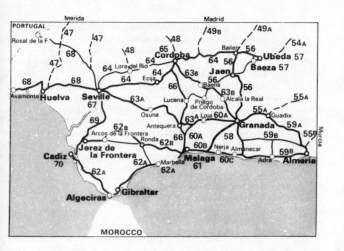

VII ANDALUCÍA

Andalucía (anglicized as *Andalusia*), the great southern province, stretching from Murcia on the E. to the Portuguese frontier on the W., is divided into the eight modern provinces of *Almería, Granada, Jaén, Córdoba, Málaga, Cádiz, Sevilla*, and *Huelva*. Physically it consists mainly of the wide basin of the Guadalquivir, the *Wadi el Kebir* ('great river') of the Moors and the *Baetis* of the Romans, which rises 4495 ft above the sea in the province of Jaén and enters the Atlantic at Sanlúcar after a course of 300 miles. On the N. the province extends up the S. slopes of the Sierra Morena, while on the S. the valley of the Guadalquivir is separated by the Penibetic mountain system from the sun-drenched Mediterranean. Within these limits, which include the eternal snows of the Sierra Nevada as well as the sugar plantations of the coast, the range of scenic beauty, as of climate, and of botanical interest, is extensive. Except in the desert maquis of the Sierra Morena and in the Alpine regions of the sierras the soil of Andalucía is extremely fertile, and the southern districts especially produce luxuriant crops of oranges and lemons, vines, olives, etc., as well as tropical plants such as palms and sugar cane. The mineral wealth of the provinces includes the lead, copper, and coal deposits of the Sierra Morena (Rio Tinto, Tharsis, Linares, etc.) and the lead of Almería. The sherry of Jerez de la Frontera needs no commendation.

Andalucía, whose name is derived from the brief Vandal occupation (409–429), has been identified with the *Tarshish* of the Bible (the *Tartessos* of the ancients); as the Roman province of *Baetica* it purveyed luxuries of every sort to the connoisseurs of imperial Rome. From 711 to 1492 it was the centre of one of the most highly developed civilizations of the Middle Ages—the Western Moorish empire. Andalucía, however, was rarely united under one ruler, and the internecine strife of the emirs of Córdoba, Jaén, and Granada led to the collapse of Moorish power before the increasing pressure of the Christian kingdoms of the north.

The expulsion of the Moriscos from Spain in 1609, little more than a century after the fall of Granada, was followed by a rapid decline in commercial and agricultural prosperity. Only six Morisco families were allowed to remain in every village of more than a hundred houses, to preserve Moorish agricultural methods.

The waves of colonization—Phoenician, Greek, Roman, and Moorish—sweeping successively over the country have left their traces upon the people as well as on the land. The effects of eight centuries of Islamic supremacy are detected in the Arabic forms in place names, in local expressions, and in the Andalusian pronunciation of Spanish as well as in the tendency to oriental exaggeration with which the province is sometimes reproached. A somewhat different background of tradition is still perceptible within the kingdom of Granada (provinces of Málaga, Granada, and Almería) from the rest of Andalucía, which had been extensively settled from the north before 1300. After the elections of April 1979 Andalucía was granted a certain measure of regional autonomy.

While the populations of the provinces of Granada, Córdoba and Jaén (particularly) have decreased during the last two decades, and while that of Almería has again reached its population of 1920, the other provinces of Andalucía have shown an increase. As far as the provincial capitals are concerned, the population of Córdoba has increased over 50 per cent since 1950, as have Almería and Huelva; Seville has grown from 374,000 to 590,000, and Málaga from 275,000 to 408,000 during the same period.

56   FROM BAILÉN TO JAÉN AND GRANADA

Total distance, 145 km. (90 miles.). N 323, 40 km. **Jaén**—105 km. **Granada**.
  For the road from Madrid to (295 km.) Bailén, see Rte 49.
  13 km. due E. of Bailén, on the N 322. lies **Linares** (52,860 inhab.), with rich lead and copper mines worked in part by English companies, who had imported their machinery from Britain. The ugly town retains a few old houses, and a good *Ayuntamiento*. *S. Juan de Dios* has a remarkable Baroque façade; in *Sta María* are Plateresque chapels. The *Museo Arqueológico* contains finds from nearby *Cazlona* or *Cástulo*, an Iberian settlement where Scipio Africanus won a victory over the Carthaginians in 208 B.C. Andrés Segovia, the exponent of the guitar, was born here in 1894, and it was in the Plaza de Toros of Linares that Manolete was killed in 1947.

Úbeda (see Rte 57) lies 29 km. S.E. of Linares.

We drive due S. on the N 323 from Bailén, crossing the Guadalquivir just short of (15 km.) *Mengibar*, after which the undulating road climbs towards (25 km.) **JAÉN** (1880 ft; 82,050 inhab.; 33,000 in 1920; 65,000 in 1960; *Parador Nac.; Hotels*). It is now largely a modern town of little intrinsic interest, above which the narrow straggling lanes of the older town climb the lower slopes of Mte. Jabalcuz. Its walls have practically disappeared, but it is still dominated by the castle, see below. Much of its prosperity is derived from the production of olive oil. The climate is hot in summer, but windy.

  History. Jaén, identified with Roman *Aurinx*, was the centre of the small Moorish principality of *Jayyan*, which fell to Fernando III in 1246. On Sept 7th, 1312, Fernando IV died here suddenly, 30 days after the unjust execution of the brothers Juan and Pedro Carvajal, who summoned him to meet them before God's

judgement-seat on that day; hence his surname '*El Emplazado*' ('the Summoned').
It suffered severely in an earthquake in 1712, and in 1808 it was sacked by the
French. It was the birthplace of the grammarian Ibn Malik (d. 1274).

We enter the modern town by the Av. de Madrid, passing (r.) the
Museo   Provincial,   with   an   interesting,   and   well-displayed
*Archaeological collection on the ground floor, including a Palaeo-
Christian sarcophagus from Martos, and a 'bull' capital from Bruñel-
Quesada. On the upper floors is a collection of paintings, including a
Christ at the column by *Pedro Berruguete*; the 19-20C works are of
slight merit.

At (l.) the C. del Rastro we reach the boundary of the old walked
town. From the Pl. Quiepo de Llano, to the W., the C. Millán de Priego
follows a line of ancient ramparts of which fragments remain, before
meeting the Córdoba road further N.W.—We shortly reach the central
Pl. de José Antonio.

The Pescadería (r.) passes the arcaded Renaissance front of the *Casa
de Vilches*, now a hotel. The C. Figueroa (l.) leads to *S. Ildefonso*, with a
façade designed by *Ventura Rodríguez;* internally the building is 14C
Gothic, containing Baroque retablos, that of the high altar being by
Pedro and *José Roldán*.

In the E. part of the town is the 17C *Conv. de Bernardas*, by *J. B. Monegro*, and
the Alameda, providing a good mountain *View.

Keeping straight on, we reach the Pl. de S. Francisco, where the
Ayuntamiento has an attractive 17C loggia. Opposite rises the
Renaissance **Cathedral,** built mainly from the plans of *Andrés de
Vandaelvira* (1534). The noble W. FRONT flanked by two towers 62 m.
high, added in 1667-88 by *Eufrasio López de Rojas,* is its best feature.

A Gothic sanctuary of 1512–19 was demolished except for its E. wall, and the
new work did not start until 1540. Vandaelvira's work included the sacristy (1555–
79), but much of the church, notably the S. Front, was built by *Juan de Aranda* in
1634–54; the lantern was added in 1654–60 by *Pedro del Portillo*, and the Sagrario
by *Ventura Rodríguez* as late as 1764–1801.

Within, the walnut *Coro* (c. 1500–30) was sculptured by *Gutierre
Gierero* (a German), *López de Velasco*, and *Jerónimo Quijano*; the
trascoro bears a Holy Family, by *Maella*. A coffer by the high altar
contains the Santo Rostro or Santa Faz (another of Sta Verónica's
napkins, comp. p.454), and on the altar is a tabernacle of serpentine and
crystal. The 18C organs incorporate remains of one probably played on
by Francisco Correa de Arauxo. In the Sacristy (S. Transept) are 16C
reliquaries and a custodia by *Juan Ruiz*. The *Museo* contains paintings
by *Ribera* and *Valdés Leal*, among other examples of religious art, while
in the *Sala Capitular* is a retablo by *Pedro Machuca*.

From the Pl. de Sta María, below the W. Front, the C. Maestra,
leaving the *Bishop's Palace* on the l., leads with its continuations to the
N. extremity of the old town, best visited on foot. We shortly pass (r.) the
Casino Primitivo, which incorporates the *Pal. del Condestable*
decorated in the 15C by Moorish artists from Granada. The C. de
Coches leads uphill to the curious *Arco de S. Lorenzo*, with a chapel of
the 15C in Moorish style and a vaulted sacristy.—A r.-hand fork leads
off the C. Maestra to *S. Bartolomé* (15–16C) with a good artesonado
roof, and ceramic font.

Further on, we pass (l.) *S. Juan*, with an early tower, to the E. of which
is the *Conv. de Sta Clara*, where the church has a fine artesonado roof,

while in the Pl. de los Caños, is a picturesque fountain-head of 1648.—
Beyond S. Juan a lane leads r. to Mudéjar *S. Andrés,* with a vaulted
cupola; the Sta Capilla of 1515 is closed by a beautiful *reja by Maestro
Bartolomé. We next reach the *Conv. de Sta Teresa (Hospicio de
Mujeres),* beneath which extensive remains of 11C *Moorish Baths* have
been discovered. To the r. alleys lead to the so-called *Casa de la Virgen,* a
mansion of c. 1500, and to the *Hosp. de S. Juan de Dios,* with a
Renaissance doorway, while the C. Sto Domingo bears l. past the *Conv.*
(now Hosp.) *de Sto Domingo* (doorway of¹ 1578 by *Vandaelvira*) to
Gothic *La Magdalena,* built on the site of a mosque, containing a
remarkable retablo by *Jacobo Florentino,* while the cloister walk
incorporates Roman tombstones in its walls. Beyond is the *Pta. de
Martos* and remains of ramparts on the Córdoba road. Nearby is the
early 16C *Casa del Cadiato,* and the *Casa de los Priores,* in the C. de
Hospitalico (uphill to the l.).

From the Pl. de Sta María, by the Cathedral, the C. Juan Montilla
leads S.W., passing (l.) the surviving *Conv. de Carmelitas Descalzas,* a
nunnery founded in 1615, which preserves the original MS. of the
'Cántico Espiritual' of St John of the Cross. Opposite is a stretch of the
town wall with two towers, beyond which (l.) is the former *Conv. de
Carmelitas Descalzos.* The C. de la Merced Alta (r.) leads to *La Merced,*
in which is the venerated figure of 'Jesús de los Descalzos'.

To the W., crowning a rocky crag, whence panoramic views may be
enjoyed, is the impressive **Castillo de Sta Catalina,** where the recently
enlarged but pretentiously decorated *Parador Nac.* is situated, easily
approached by a good road. It stands on Moorish foundations but was
almost completely rebuilt after the Reconquest. Beside the tall Torre del
Homenaje is the *Cap. de Sta Catalina* in one of the towers of the curtain
wall (early 14C).

For the route from Jaén to *Lucena,* see below.

From the Pl. de José Antonio we follow the Granada road (N 323),
which soon circles S., passing (r.) *La Guardia* with a ruined castle, and
threading a narrow valley, before climbing through rugged country to
the Pto. de Zegri (3565 ft).—At 68 km. a road leads 4 km. E. to *Iznalloz*
(2530 ft), with a hall-church of 1549. 10 km. beyond, at *Piñar,* are a
stalactite grotto and ruined castle.—We shortly pass the Embalse de
Cubillas and enter the fertile vega of Granada, with a fine view of the city
with the Sierra Nevada in the background as we approach it from the
N.W.—37 km. **Granada,** see Rte 58.

From Jaén to Lucena (114 km.). We follow the N 321 W. from the town to
(17 km.) *Torredonjimeno,* with an interesting church, where we turn S. for (6 km.)
Martos (21,550 inhab.) the *Colonia Augusta Gemella* or *Tucci* of the Romans. The
prison, of 1577, now the *Ayuntamiento,* has a fine classical gateway. To the E. is
the precipitous Peña de Martos, down which the Carvajal brothers were
condemned to be thrown by Fernando IV (comp. p.474). Restored *Sta María de la
Villa* is of little interest.

25 km. *Alcaudete,* see p.522. We turn r. onto the N 432, and at 8 km. fork l.,
winding through hilly country to (19 km.) **Priego de Córdoba,** a picturesque town
(21,200 inhab.; *Hotel*), noted for is extravagantly Baroque churches, best visited
on foot from the central plaza. Niceto Alcalá Zamora (1877–1948), President of
the Spanish Republic in 1931–36, was born here. A short distance N.E. of the Pl.
Calvo Sotelo stands the *Castle,* and further on, *La Asunción,* with its magnificent
stuccoed *Sagrario* of 1782 and a verja of 1575 at the W. Door. To the E. on the l. of
the Carrera de Álvarez are the *Cap. de S. Nicasio* (1771), known as 'La Aurora',
with remarkable plasterwork and a Baroque retablo; and *S. Francisco* with a

curious marble and plaster front decorated with geometrical patterns, and also containing fine retablos, and Christ at the Column by *Montañés*.

In the C. de los Héroes de Toledo, running S. from the main square, are the *Colegio*, with a noble front, and the *Cap. de las Angustias* (1775) on the r.; on the l. is *El Carmen* with a neo-classical tower. Beyond is the *Fuente del Rey* (1782), by *Alvarez Cubero*, with over 180 jets, and higher up, the *Fuente de la Salud* (1753). From above the fountains the C. de José Antonio leads back to the Pl. de Calvo Sotelo, passing (r.) twin-towered *N.S. de las Mercedes*, with another interior of Baroque stucco. On the E. side of the plaza stands the *Hosp. de S. Juan de Dios*, with a Doric patio of 1637 and Baroque church.

Below the Plaza to the N. and W. of the castle, is the *Lonja*, with a pleasant front and Doric patio, while near by is *S. Pedro*, with a polychrome stucco Camarín. From the neighbouring *Adarves*, or ramparts, panoramic views may be obtained.—In the upper town stands the half-ruinous church of the *Virgen de la Cabeza*.

To the S., beyond Priego, a mountain road crosses the Sierra de Priego to (52 km.) *Loja*, see Rte 60A.

From Priego we turn W. and climb through the hills to (8 km.) *Carcabuey* (3150 inhab.) dominated by its castle, and (21 km.) **Cabra** (20,450 inhab.), the ancient *Aegabrum*, a rambling old town whose marble quarries furnished many of the columns for the Mezquita at Córdoba. The ruined *Castle*, *S. Juan*, formerly a mosque, containing colonnades of stilted arches, and *Sto Domingo* (1550), are of interest. It was the birthplace of the blind minstrel Mukaddam Ibn-Muafa (9-10C) originator of the '*zajal*' stanza and a forerunner of the troubadors, and of Juan Valera (1824–1905), the writer.

10 km. *Lucena* (see Rte 66) on the main road from Córdoba to Málaga.

From Lucena the C 338 descends towards the Puente Genil, crossed at *Puente Genil* (25,400 inhab.; *Hotel*), of no interest, but famous for its *membrillo* (see p.84), near the Moorish castle of *Anzur*, 10 km. beyond which, at *Herrera*, we turn l. for (37 km.) *Estepa*, on the main road (N 334) from Granada to *Seville* viâ *Antequera* and *Osuna*, see Rte 63A.

57   ÚBEDA AND BAEZA

Úbeda may be approached from the N IV from Madrid by forking l. onto the C 3217 at *La Carolina* (see Rte 49A), or by taking the N 322 driving E. from *Bailén*, see Rte 56. It is also on the direct road from Albacete to Jaén, 57 km. S.W. Baeza lies only 9 km. W. of Úbeda.

ÚBEDA (*Parador Nac.*), a picturesque old town (30,200 inhab.) preserving a number of imposing old mansions, was first taken from the Moors by Alfonso VIII in 1212, and recaptured by Fernando III in 1234. St John of the Cross (S. Juan de la Cruz) died here in 1591. Amongst its natives was the artist José Elbo (1804–44). In the centre of the town is the Pl. del Gen. Saro, where the medieval *Torre del Reloj* has a 17C cupola. To the N.W. in the C. del Obispo Cobos is *S. Isidro*, with a Gothic doorway; while from Baroque *La Trinadad*, to the N.E., the Corredera de S. Fernando descends, passing (l.) the market-hall, from behind which we climb to **S. Nicolás de Bari** (15C) with a S. Doorway of 1509 and a W. Portal by *Vandaelvira* (1566). Within are the *Cap. del Deán Ortega*, with an entrance of 1537 and a Reja of 1596 by *Juan Álvarez de Molina*. Note the highly-patterned esparto carpets, or *ubediés*, for which the town is famous.—Further uphill (N.W.) is the curious 16C *Casa de los Salvages*.

From the central plaza the C. Queipo de Llano (or de la Cava) leads S. passing the square towers of the old *town wall* embedded in houses on the l. Through a breach in the wall we reach the *Pal. de la Rambla*, a balconied Renaissance mansion with a patio by *Vandaelvira*.

Further down, the C. del Condestable Dávalos leads to the *Casa de las Torres* (or *Pal. Dávalos)* with a two-storeyed patio (1530–40). Not far E. is disused *Sto Domingo* with a Gothic choir-vault and an artesonado roof to the nave. S. of the Casa de Cas Torres is ivy-clad *S. Lorenzo* (adjacent *Views*), whence we turn E., traversing a picturesque plaza, and passing through gates, bear half-r. to approach the striking *PL. VÁZQUEZ DE MOLINA*. To the N. stands the **Ayuntamiento,** the former *Casa de las Cadenas,* built by *Vandaelvira* for Philip II's secretary, with an imposing front and patio. **Sta María de los Reales Alcázares,** opposite, although cloaked with classical façades, is mainly of the late 15C, and has fine rejas by Maestro *Bartolomé* and part of a Gothic Cloister. Note also the arabesque ceilings painted blue. Close by are the *Cárcel del Obispo* (16C) and the *Pal. de Mancera,* with a square tower. To the S. is the site of the old Alcázar, with remains of its walls.

Beyond the Ayuntamiento stands the *Pal. de los Ortegas,* with a restrained 17C front (now housing the *Parador*). **El Salvador,** built in 1540–59 by *Vandaelvira* from designs by *Diego de Siloée* (1536), contains statues by *Berruguete,* saved from his retablo, which was destroyed during the Civil War, and a Reja of 1557, and a chalice saved from its looted treasure. In the circular crypt is the grave of the founder, Fr. de Cobos, secretary to Charles V. Behind are ruins of the *Hosp. de Ancianos.* Further E., the Redonda de Miradores commands panoramic *Views.

To the N. lies the Pl. del Generalísimo, with the porticoed *Escuela de Artes* (once the Ayuntamiento) and **S. Pablo.** This has a 13C W. Front and a polygonal apse of 1380, with a *mirador,* while the side façades date from 1490 (N.) and 1511 (S.), and the Plateresque tower from 1537. Stucco vaults were added within in 1763, but the *Cap. del Camarero Vago* has a fine doorway of 1536 and a retablo of 1538. In the C. Rosal and C. Montiel, N.E. of S. Pablo, are old mansions with attractive façades, one, the 'Casa Mudéjar', recently opened as a museum, and containing interesting Roman heads, and a model of a fortress. The C. Rosal leads down to a 14C Mudéjar *Town Gate.*

In the centre of the town are *S. Pedro* (partly Romanesque) and *Sta Clara* (Gothic doorway), and in the C. del Real Viejo stands the *Pal. de Vela de los Cobos,* with unusual balconies and an open loggia above.

In the Av. del Cristo Rey (the Baeza road), is the huge **Hosp. de Santiago** of 1562–75, by *Vandaelvira,* with a colonnaded patio, a grand staircase retaining original frescoes, and a reja of 1576 in the chapel, badly damaged in the Civil War.

Úbeda is a good centre from which to explore the beautiful and well-stocked *Sierra de Cazorla,* the most direct approach to which is by following the N 322 N.E. to (9 km.) *Torreperogil,* with a Renaissance church, 5 km. N. of which lies *Sabiote,* with a Moorish castle converted into a palace in 1543.—From Torreperogil we bear S.E. to (22 km.) *Peal de Becerro,* near the Iberian necropolis of *Tugia* (6-3 B.C.).

Beyond Peal, the C 323 climbs S.E. into the mountains, passing (12 km.) the walled town of **Quesada** (10,600 inhab.), containing a small museum devoted to the local artist *Rafael Zabaleta* (1907–60), before reaching the craggy Pto. de Tiscar (Views), beyond which a winding road slowly descends to (31 km.) *Pozo Alcón,* and after another 40 km. enters *Baza,* see Rte 55A.

At Peal we may turn E. to follow the C 328 to (15 km.) **Cazorla** (10,100 inhab.), a picturesque town with two medieval castles, and a ruined Plateresque church. It was the Treaty of Cazorla (1179) which prescribed the limit of Aragonese expansion into Andalucía.—The *Parador Nac.* is situated some 24 km. further to the S.E., approached by a sinuous mountain road, occasionally providing extensive views.

7km. N.W. of Úbeda on the N322 lies a Churrigueresque pilgrimage chapel at *La Yedra,* while 3km. beyond, dominated by a medieval castle of the Order of Calatrava ('modernized' in the 16C, and again recently) lies *Canena.* The road is continued to (20km.) *Linares* and (11km.) *Bailén,* see Rte 56.

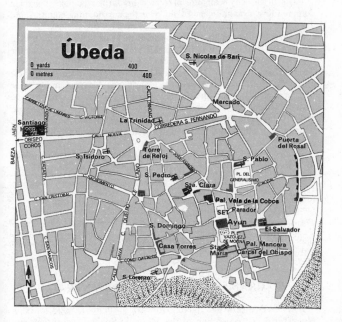

Leaving Úbeda on the N 321, with impressive panorámic views to the S., we soon enter the old cathedral town of *Baeza,* only 9km. to the W.

BAEZA (15,100 inhab.) Roman *Vivatia,* and sacked by Fernando III in 1239, was the birthplace of Gaspar Becerra (1520–70), the sculptor. Antonio Machado, the poet, lived here in 1913–19.

The main axis of the town is the C. de S. Pablo, part of the road from Úbeda to Jaén, in which there are several fine buildings, including the Plateresque *Casino* (No. 18). and Gothic *S. Pablo,* where Pablo de Olavide (1725–1803), promoter of the repopulation of the Sierra Morena, is buried. At its S.W. end is the PASEO, an attractive arcaded plaza, and (l.) the *Torre de Aliatares,* a relic of 13C fortifications. At the far end of the Paseo are the *Arco del Pópulo,* the Renaissance *Casa del Pópulo* (c. 1530), and the *Fuente de Leones,* by the beginning of the Jaén road.

In the S. quarter are the ruins of *La Compañia* (17C), and *Sta Cruz,* with a Romanesque doorway. In the street to the r. is the former *University* (16C). Adjacent is the **Seminario,** or *Pal. de Benavente,* or *de Jabalquinto,* with an imposing Isabelline *front, 16C cloister, and monumental stair; and the *Fuente de Sta María* (1564). Close to the last are the former *Ayuntamiento (Pal. de Cabrera),* and the **Cathedral,** rebuilt in 1567–93 to the designs of *Andrés de Vandaelvira.* Survivals of the earlier building on the site are the Isabelline *Pta. del Perdón* and the *Pta. de la Luna,* with a horseshoe arch. There are some good retablos, stallwork of 1635, and a reja attr. to Maestro *Bartolomé*. Remains of a mosque have been discovered in the cloister. In the sacristy is a Baroque custodia of 1714.

Parts of the city walls are preserved here, the track skirting them commanding a magnificent *View* over the surrounding country, and Jaén may be discerned to the S.W. on fine days.

From S. Pablo (see above) the C. del Rojo leads N.W. to *Sta Ana* and *S. Andrés* (1500–20), the latter with a Plateresque S. Portal bearing the arms of Bp. Suárez. The tower is of 1523–35, the N. Portal of 1555–60, and the Cap. Mayor (c. 1562) was designed by *Vandaelvira*. In the choir are stalls from the destroyed Sta María del Alcázar, and a large Triptych. Further on is the 17C church of the *Descalzos*. The C. de **S.** Francisco leads downhill past the ruins of *S. Francisco* (by *Vandaelvira;* 1546). Beyond are the Renaissance *Hosp.* and the *Ayuntamiento* (1559), with a notable Plateresque front and loggia, and containing a huge silver and gilt Custodia.

At *Ibros*, 5 km. N. on the direct road to Linares, are slight remains of a 'Cyclopean' fortress, in the Callejon de Peñones.

FROM BAEZA TO JAÉN (49 km.). The N 321 descends S.W. through olive groves and with extensive views ahead, passing (4 km. r.) *Begijar*, with a medieval castle converted into an episcopal palace, and shortly crosses the Guadalquivir by the ramped *Pte del Obispo* (16C).—41 km. Jaén, see Rte 56.

An ALTERNATIVE ROUTE, FROM ÚBEDA TO JAÉN (78 km.) runs S. to (23 km.) *Jódar* (11,700 inhab.), equivocally named, with a ruined Moorish castle, and an old church, 4 km. beyond which we turn r. through (6 km.) *Bedmar*, (7 km.) *Jimena*, and (19 km.) *Mancha Real* (8150 inhab.) with a large 16-17C church.—20 km. Jaén.

58   GRANADA AND THE SIERRA NEVADA

GRANADA (214,200 inhab.; 104,000 in 1920; 155,000 in 1960; *Hotels*), the last possession of the Moors in Spain, is an ancient city situated on the slopes and at the foot (2200 ft) of three low mountain spurs that descend from the S. and E. towards the broad and fertile vega bounding the city on the W. To the S.E., a beautiful background, stretches the snowy crest of the Sierra Nevada. On the central and highest spur, which presents a precipitous face towards the town, rise the walls and towers of the Alhambra. The depression occupied by the Alameda de la Alhambra separates this, on the S., from the Monte Mauror, crowned by the Torres Bermejas; while, on the N. it is divided from the low hill of the Alcazaba and Albaicín quarters by the gorge of the *Darro,* a scanty mountain steam flowing through the city (in a partly-covered channel) to join the *Genil* on the S., which irrigates the Vega.

During recent decades the city and region have found a new prosperity based on improved irrigation and intensive agriculture. The *Gitanos* (gipsies), who have been settled here since the 16C, are still a characteristic element in the population, who in general prey on the tourist.

Hotels: As package tours appear to take priority, individuals should book well in advance, although a pension can often provide reasonable alternative accommodation.

The *Airport* lies c.15 km. W. of the town.

Tourist Office, Casa de los Tiros, C. Pavaneras 19.

Tourist Office, Casa de los Tiros, C. Pavaneras 19.

Festivals. The main festivals are those of Corpus Christi; Holy Week, and 3 May; the anniversaries of the Surrender of Granada (2 Jan. 1492), and the naval battle of Lepanto (7 Oct 1571). A Festival of Music and Dancing, instituted in 1952, is held near the Generalife (June-July).

History. Already an Iberian settlement, named *Elibyrge,* in the 5C B.C., and known as *Illiberis* to the Romans and Visigoths, Granada emerges from obscurity only as a Moorish city and, growing in importance as the Moslem fortunes waned at Córdoba and Seville, finally fell to the Christian in 1492. For c. 60 years after the fall of the Ommeyads at Córdoba in 1031, Granada was the capital of an independent kingdom under the family of the Zirites, but later was subject successively to the Almoravides and the Almohades. When the power of the Almohades declined, Ibn Hud, a descendant of the Moorish kings of Zaragoza, established in 1235 an independent authority in southern Spain, extending from Algeciras to Almeria. On his death in 1238 he was succeeded by his rival Mohammed Ibn-Yusuf Ibn-Nasar, commonly known as Ibn el-Ahmar, who, when Jaén was captured by Fernando III in 1246, removed his capital to Granada, and, as Mohammed I (d. 1272), founded the Nasrite Dynasty that reigned there for 250 years. Ibn el-Ahmar found it politic to remain on friendly terms with Castile and even assisted Fernando III in the capture of Seville, while he devoted his attention to the development and improvement of his kingdom. Under this ruler and his successors Granada rose to an unexampled pitch of material prosperity and Moorish art in Spain here reached its apogee. Refugees from towns captured by the Christians flocked to this last stronghold, bringing with them their handicrafts and their industry; trade and commerce flourished; the fertile vega was developed by elaborate irrigation; and art, letters, and science were fostered. During this period the population rose to 200,000, over four times that of London. To Yusuf I (1334–54) and Mohammed V (1354–91) are ascribed the principal parts of the Alhambra. The decline of Granada, weakened by internal dissensions and threatened by the proselytizing enthusiasm of the Catholic Kings, may be dated from the reign of Muley Hassan (1462–85), who lost Alhama in 1482.

The romantic story has often been told. Muley Hassan, captivated by the charms of Isobel de Solis, a beautiful *Muladie* (see p.49) known by the Moorish name of Zoraya, aroused the jealous fears of his first wife Ayesha for the future of her young son Abu Abdallah (Boabdil); and the city was rent by the feuds of the Abencerrages, who supported Ayesha, and the Zegris, who favoured Zoraya. Ayesha fled with her son to Guadix; Boabdil ('el Rey Chico', the little king) was there proclaimed king, and succeeded after various vicissitudes, in dethroning both his father Muley Hassan and his uncle Ez-Zagal, who had ruled for a time in Málaga and at Granada. Boabdil meanwhile twice fell into the hands of the Spaniards—at Lucena in 1483 and at Loja in 1488—and regained his liberty only by accepting terms which held him passive while the Catholic Kings made further inroads into Andalucia.

When the evacuation of Granada was demanded in 1491 Boabdil could offer only a token resistance and on Jan 2nd, 1492 the Cross and the banner of Castile were planted on the Alcazaba. Boabdil and his followers retired to the Alpujarras, S.E. of Granada (see p.500), after Fernando and Isabel, in *Moorish* costume, had received the infidel's surrender. The capture of Granada was hailed as a triumph throughout Christendom and was celebrated at St Paul's in London by a special 'Te Deum'. But under the Christians the town fell on evil days; religious intolerance, culminating in Philip III's expulsion of the Moriscos in 1609, robbed it of its most industrious citizens, and the lost glory was never recaptured. By 1800 its population was as low as c. 40,000. The number of Republican sympathizers shot here during the Civil War was particularly high, and Granada has long had a reputation for being reactionary and its citizens irascible.

Although the name of Granada, derived from its Moorish name *Karnattah,* has no connection with the Spanish word for pomegranate ('*granada*'), a pomegranate, stalked and proper, has been adopted as the canting arms of the city.

Among eminent natives of Granada are Abu Haiyan (d. 1345), the philologist; the explorer Johannes Leo 'Africanus' (Hassan ibn Mohammed el-Wezaz, 1494–1552); Fr. Luis de Granada (1504–88), the prose writer; Diego Hurtado de Mendoza (1503–75), historian and humanist; Alonso Cano (1610–67), painter and sculptor; Francisco Martínez de la Rosa (1787–1862), the author; Ángel Ganivet (1865-98), philosophic novelist, and Manuel Goméz Moreno (1870-1970), the Arabist.

EMPLOYMENT OF TIME. The *Alhambra,* together with its dependencies, is open almost all day (10.00 to 18.00 in winter; 9.00 to 20.30 in summer) and the tourist, depending on the time of his arrival, may well wish to visit this area first, before the *Cap. Real* and *Cathedral.* Another day may be devoted to the rest of the city. If possible—although time often presses—a second visit to the Alhambra and Generalife should be made in the evening or towards sunset.

The roads from Madrid and Jaén (N 323), from Murcia and Guadix (N 343), and those from Córdoba (N 432) and Málaga (N342) converge at the N.W. corner of the town, which is entered by the Av. de Calvo Sotelo and its continuation, the Gran Via de Colón. At the Pl. de Isabel de Católica we turn r. along the C. de los Reyes Católicos to the Pta. Real. This is approached directly from the Motril road (N 323). A by-pass, the Camino de Ronda, skirts the W. suburbs connecting the Córdoba road with that to the coast.

The C. DE LOS REYES CATÓLICOS (Pl. 10), which runs N.E. from the *Pta. Real,* an irregular square retaining the name of a vanished gate, to the *Pl. Nueva,* forms the base-line for our description of the town.

Motorists are advised against taking their cars into the warren of narrow alleys of the *Albaicín* (see p.493) in the N.E. quarter of the town.

A   THE ALHAMBRA AND GENERALIFE.

Admission. While the hill of the Alhambra (Pl. de los Aljibes, etc.) is open free daily, the buildings may only be visited within stated hours, by tickets obtained near the entrance of the palace.. The Moorish Palace, the Pal. of Charles V. the Enciente Towers, and the Generalife are open daily; the Museums are closed in the afternoons. On Sunday afternoon, parts of the buildings are accessible free. Tickets for admission are normally available for two successive days, but higher charges apply for visiting the Alhambra at night, if the palace is illuminated. The price is further increased on Tues, Thurs, and Sat nights from April to Sept, when the whole Alhambra is illuminated.

The hill of the **Alhambra,** the 'Red Fort' (*Al Qal'a al-Hambra),* a steeply scarped ridge, rises abruptly from the valley of the Darro to the N. and W.; it rears above the trees of the Alameda to the S.W., and to the N.E. it is cut off by the Cuesta del Rey Chico—a ravine perhaps partly artificial—from the Cerro del Sol, on whose slopes rises the Generalife. The Moorish palace of the 'Alhambra' covers but a small part of its plateau, which, already fortified by nature, is encircled by a line of walls and towers closely following the configuration of the ground.

The direct approach road ascends from the Pl. Nueva by the steep Cuesta de Gomérez to the *Pta. de las Granadas* (Pl. 11), a kind of triumphal arch erected c. 1536 by Charles V from designs of *Pedro Machuca* on the site of the Moorish *Bâb el-Ajuar,* a gate in the wall that once united the Torres Bermejas (see below) with the Alcazaba. On the top are three open pomegranates (*granadas*). An inscription to the r. commemorates Ibn el-Ahmar (see History). This arch is an entrance to the **Alameda de la Alhambra,** a delightful wood in the Valle de la Asabica, umbrageous with the dense foliage of closely planted elms.

Beyond the Pta. de las Granadas the Paseo de la Alhambra ascends straight on through the wood, but cars are directed by a roundabout route to the *Pta. de los Carros.* Walkers take the Cuesta Empedrada, the footpath on the l. of the Pta. de los Granadas, and climb in c. 5 minutes to the Pta. Judiciaria, passing the Renaissance wall-fountain known as the *Pilar de Carlos V,* designed by *Machuca* and carved by the Italian *Nic. del Corte* in 1545.

To the r., off the central path, is the *Pta. de Bibarrambla,* which once stood by the plaza of that name, see p.490.
The Cuesta de las Cruces, the footpath on the r., ascends by the S. edge of the wood to the Campo de los Mártires, with lovely views towards the Sierra Nevada.

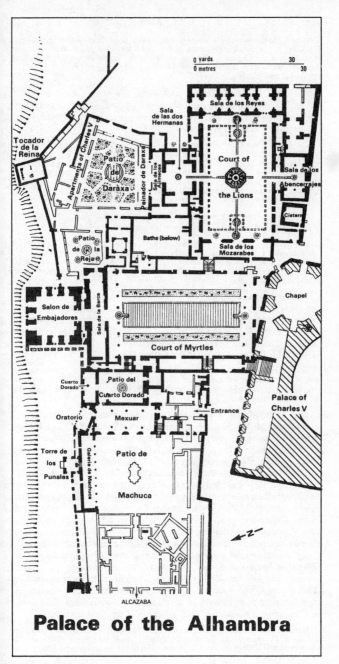

Palace of the Alhambra

Beyond is the *Carmen de los Mártires,* a park in the grounds of a former monastery (founded 1573), of which St John of the Cross was once prior. From near the beginning of the Cuesta a path mounts (r.) to the **Torres Bermejas** ('Vermilion Towers'), on Monte Mauror, a Moorish fortified outwork, perhaps earlier than the Alcazaba, but restored in the 16C.

The **Pta. Judiciaria** or **de la Justicia**, the main entrance to the Alhambra, is a strong gate-tower built in 1348 by Yusuf I. It has an outer and an inner archway, and the vaulted passage makes three bends so as to obstruct a hostile entrance.

The statue of the Virgin in a niche over the outer archway was made in 1500–01 by *Roberto Alemán.* Over the outer great horseshoe arch is engraved an open Hand and over the inner arch is carved a Key. The open hand is probably a talisman against the evil eye, and the key a symbol of power. At the upper end of the passage is now a Christian altar; a mural inscription records the capture of Granada and the appointment of Mendoza, Conde de Tendilla, as first alcalde, The inner archway retains its Moorish doors, iron-clad and nail-studded.

Ascending from the Pta. de la Justicia we see, on the r., the **Pta. del Vino**, so called because used as a wine store in the 16C.

This gateway, probably the oldest part of the Alhambra, built under Mohammed II (1272–1302), and embellished with later carving and inscriptions including the name of Mohammed V, perhaps stood in a wall shutting off the W. end of the hill, known as the Alhambra Alta, with the residences of court functionaries and others.

The open space on the top of the hill is the **Pl. de los Aljibes** ('square of the cisterns'; Pl. 11), so called from the immense reservoir constructed below part of it by the Catholic Kings. On the E. side of the square is the *Pal. of Charles V,* with the *Pal. of the Alhambra* behind it; on the W. side is the *Alcazaba*; and on the N. side a parapet, whence we have a plunging view of the Darro, with the Albaicín beyond.

In the *Patio de Machuca* (named after Charles V's architect), W. of the Moorish palace, excavations have revealed vestiges of buildings; and the *Galería de Machuca,* together with the 14C *Torre de los Puñales* or *de Machuca,* to which it led, have been restored.

The *****Pal. of the Alhambra** (Pl. p.484) is the most remarkable monument of Maghribian Moorish art in Spain. Built, partly on artificial foundations, close to the N. verge of the hill, its simple exterior gives no promise of the graceful and fairy-like beauty which—although much is modern restoration after centuries of neglect—still reigns in an interior designed as the luxurious abode of an Oriental monarch and his harem. But it is not as an architectural structure but as an achievement in ornamentation, and that mainly with such fragile materials as wood and plaster, that the Alhambra is famous. The richness and variety of the arches and ceilings, with stalactite pendentives and marvellous honey-comb cupolas, are a delight, and no less the lace-like diapers in plaster that cover many of the walls above the dados of richly coloured azulejos. In the courts slender white marble columns support elegant arcades of stilted or horseshoe arches, with spandrels of delicately perforated tracery. The inscriptions in Cufic characters or in the more decorative Naskhi script, which play a large part in the ornamentation, are mainly pious sentiments or eulogies of the builder and the buildings. 'God alone is Conqueror' (Walā ghaliba ill' Allah) is of frequent occurrence.

History. The Alhambra dates mainly from the 14C. Although Ibn el-Ahmar (1232–1272), founder of the Nasrite dynasty, took up his residence on the Alhambra hill, little of his work or of that of his immediate successors remains; the principal builders of the palace were Yusuf I (1334–54), who built the Court of the Myrtles, and Mohammed V (1354–91), to whom is due the Court of the Lions. Mohammed VII (1392–1408) decorated the Tower of the Infantas. The Catholic Kings, after the conquest of 1492, repaired and strengthened the palace, but Charles V pulled down part of it to make room for his still unfinished palace. A powder explosion outside the walls injured the Court of the Lions and the adjoining Sala de los Mozárabes in 1591, and though the damage was repaired the structure and decoration gradually deteriorated from gross neglect. Henry Swinburne, who visited the Alhambra in 1775, observed that the governor, who lived in a small corner of the palace, employed his many leisure hours, not in profound speculation of learned researches, but in emptying as many bottles of wine as his only arm (for he had but one) had steadiness to pour into his glass! It was visited by Châteaubriand in 1807. In 1812 an unsuccessful attempt to blow up the building was made by the French under Sebastiani on their retirement from Granada.

In 1829 Washington Irving spent three months in the palace, where he began his romantic tales and sketches of the Moors and Spaniards, in which he immortalized Francisca de Molina, 'Tia Antonia', who commenced tidying up the dilapidated Alhambra. In 1831 Richard Ford spent the first of two summers there, while on Aug 30th, 1836, it was visited by George Borrow. W. G. Clark, who visited the palace in 1849, complained of the guide of the time, who would keep up a running commentary, of the very smallest talk, recklessly confusing dates and facts, nations and personages; and for any special absurdity, audaciously appealing to the authority of *Vasindon Eerveen. . . .*' Intermittently, from 1828, haphazard attempts at repairing the damage were initiated, when it was not being pillaged by rapacious governors, but any serious modern work of restoration did not commence until 1862, and has since been brought more or less successfully to a conclusion.

Having obtained a ticket (see p.482), from the entrance we first visit (l.) the *Mexuar*, or council–chamber, converted into a chapel in 1537–44, but now restored. Adjoining is a small oratory. On the E. side is the *Patio del Cuarto Dorado*, originally built for Mohammed V, at the N. end of which is a 16C arch admitting to the *Cuarto Dorado*, decorated in the Mudéjar style by the Catholic Kings. From this Patio we enter the *Court of the Myrtles (de los Arrayanes)*, known also as the *Patio de la Alberca* ('of the pond'), an open court (110 by 78 m.), down the centre of which extends a narrow fish-pond between hedges of myrtle. At each end is a graceful arcade supported by six slender columns, and within these are alcoves with fine stalactite vaulting.

Above the S. arcade is another gallery, with pierced woodwork, which belonged to the part of the building removed to make room for the Pal. of Charles V. The E. side was destroyed by fire in 1890, but has been restored. On both sides are doorways and windows surmounted by rich ornamentation.

The **Sala de la Barca**, at the N. end of the court, is said to have been named from its ceiling, shaped like the inverted hull of a boat (*barca*), but the name is perhaps derived from Arabic *baraka,* a benediction. It was also damaged in 1890. By a decorated arch, beneath which in the thickness of the wall, are recesses for water-coolers or flower vases, we enter the **Hall of the Ambassadors** (Salón de Embajadores), the largest and one of the finest rooms in the Alhambra, occupying two storeys in the interior of the *Torre de Comares*, forming a square of 11 m. with a dome 23 m. above the floor.

This was the audience chamber, with the throne occupying the recess facing the entrance. Every inch is decorated. Above a dado of azulejos the walls are covered with an exquisite polychrome veil of interlaced patterns and inscriptions stamped upon the plaster. The inscriptions name Yusuf I as the builder. The ceiling is a curiously wrought and coloured dome of larch-wood. The windows deeply recessed in the enormous thickness of the walls, command enchanting prospects, which is said to have prompted Charles V's comment: 'Ill-fated was the man who lost all this'.

Towards the S. end of the Court of the Myrtles (from which we may also visit the octagonal crypt of Charles V's chapel) a door admits to the *Sala de los Mozárabes*, which suffered severely from an explosion in 1591, but its decorations and original ceiling are being restored. This hall is the ante-chamber to the *Court of the Lions (Patio de los Leones), a hypaethral court (28 m. by 16 m.), begun in 1377 under Mohammed V, and surrounded by an arcade of stilted arches, supported by 124 white marble columns, the elaborate capitals of which show traces of colour. At each end a graceful pavilion projects into the court, with cupolas in the media naranja style. The walls within the arcades are decorated with plaster fretwork patterns, but the ceilings are modern.—In the centre of the court stands a *Fountain*, resting on the backs of twelve diminutive lions conventionally carved in grey marble.

Around the edge of the twelve-sided basin, 4 m. in diameter, runs an inscription in thanksgiving for the beauties of the Alhambra and its plentiful supply of water. Gautier claimed to have camped in the courtyard for four days, keeping his bottles of sherry cool in the fountain.

Adjoining are several fine apartments; on the S. is the **Sala de los Abencerrajes**, with its marvellous stalactite roof, and inlaid larch-wood doors. The decoration of the walls is in part a 16C restoration.

The **Sala de los Reyes**, or *Sala de la Justicia*, to the E., has elaborate media naranja vaulting and rich stalactite arches. In three of the alcoves are remarkable *ceiling paintings* on leather, attributed to Christian artists of the late 14C. In the central alcove appear ten Moors seated at a council, while in the others are chivalric, romantic, and hunting scenes. They are at present (1979) under restoration.

To the N. is the *Sala de las Dos Hermanas ('of the two sisters'), named from twin slabs of white marble in the pavement. This room, perhaps part of the harem, is unequalled for the beauty and richness of its decoration. The window opposite the door retains its Moorish shutter, the only one of its kind remaining in the palace. Above the dado of azulejos the walls are covered with a lacework of patterns in stucco, and above is a *Honeycomb Dome*, the largest and most elaborate of its kind, said to include over 5000 cells.

Adjacent is the *Sala de los Ajimeces* with a fine ceiling and two ajimeces on its N. side, and beyond is the **Mirador** or **Peinador de Daraxa**, a prettily decorated belvedere overlooking its romantic patio, while to the E., a window overlooks the *Patio de la Sultana*, with its four cypresses.

A corridor on the W. side leads to the *Apartments of Charles V*, two rooms modernized c. 1527, where in 1829 Irving took up his quarters. At present under restoration, reached by a modern corridor, is the *Peinador** or **Tocador de la Reina** (Queen's Dressing Room), a mirador or belvedere at the top of the *Torre del Peinador*, where the sultanas of the harem were later succeeded by Elizabeth of Parma, wife of Philip V. Encircled by an outer gallery (superb *view) is a pavilion embellished with Italian paintings (1539–46), by *Julio de Aquilés* and *Alexander Mayner* (restored); on the outside are scenes from Charles V's expedition against Tunis. In one corner is a perforated marble slab through which perfumes may have been wafted from below.

From the Apartment of Charles V, we enter a gallery whence a staircase descends to the *Patio de la Reja* (or *de los Cipreses*), with its fountain and four tall cypresses. The name refers to the grille or *reja* (1655) of the upper windows.

On the E. side of this garden is the *Sala de los Secretos*, the centre of a number of low chambers forming a whispering gallery, from which a door admits to the **Baths**, dating from Yusuf I. The *Sala de las Camas* ('of the divans'), with its alcoves and gallery, was the reposing room. Its decoration dates from 1843–66. Beyond are four rooms of different sizes, with vaulted roofs pierced with star-shaped openings, once possibly filled with coloured glass. In the innermost, two marble baths remain.

Hence we enter the adjoining *Patio de Lindaraja*, a relic of the old Moorish inner garden, planted with cypresses, orange trees, and box edgings, crossing which we pass into the main gardens of the Alhambra.

On our l. is the *Torre de las Damas* (previously known as the *Casa Sánchez*), adjacent to which Richard Ford lived during the summer of 1833. Opposite is a large pool fed by two lions. Many of the towers in the enceinte surrounding the E. part of the Alhambra hill, one in ruins, have been restored, and several preserve interesting decorations. The second we pass is the *Torre del Mihrab*, beside which is a small mosque (c. 1350), with restored decoration. We next reach the *Torre de los Picos* of c. 1300, so-called from its battlements; below is the *Pta. de Hierro*. We pass the *Torre del Cadí* before entering the ***Torre de la Cautiva** ('of the captive'), a beautiful work dating from Yusuf I. Isabel de Solis (see History) is fabled to have been the prisoner to which the tower owes its modern name. The nearby *Torre de las Infantas* was once the residence of Moorish princesses; its decoration, of the reign of Mohammed VII (1392–1408) is sumptuous but shows signs of decadence. The *Cuesta del Rey Chico* is now spanned by a footbridge allowing direct access to the Generalife, see p.489.

Those wishing to make a complete circuit of the walls will continue past the *Torre del Agua*, at the S.E. angle of the ramparts, which marks the spot where the aqueduct from the Darro enters the Alhambra. On the S. stretch of wall are several towers blown up by the French in 1812, including the *Pta. de los Siete Suelos* ('of the seven floors'), the ancient *Báb al-Gódor*, which was believed to have seven subterranean floors or stages. Boabdil is said to have quitted the Alhambra for ever by this gate, which was afterwards walled up at his request. We eventually reach an iron gate, the *Pta. de Secano*, a short distance S.E. of the Pta. de los Carros.

The ***Pal. of Charles V** (Pl. 11), designed by *Pedro Machuca* (d. 1550), is an imposing edifice in Italian Renaissance style, but incongruous in its surroundings. Begun in 1526, with money extorted from the Moors as the price of certain privileges, the building operations progressed slowly for over a century before they were finally abandoned, leaving the roof unfinished. In the early 18C, part of the structure was used as a powder magazine, without lightening conductors. On three sides (each 63 m. in length) are elaborate façades, each with a basement in rustica masonry and an upper storey with Ionic pilasters between the windows. The portals on the S. and W. date from 1538–54 (S.) and 1550–63 (W.), the sculptures being by *Nic. del Corte*, on the S., and *Juan de Orea* and *Antoine de Leval*, on the W., with (higher up) additions of 1586–92 by *Juan de Minjares*. The circular *Patio*, completed in 1616, and 30 m. in diameter, is surrounded by an arcade of 32 Doric columns of conglomerate stone from a quarry near *Sta Fé*—although originally intended to be of marble—supporting an upper storey with Ionic columns separating recesses intended for sculptures. Here bull-fights once took place. At the N.W. angle is a staircase, and at the N.E. angle an octagonal *Chapel* (c. 1540–99), designed to be surmounted by a dome. The retablo, of Genoese marble, dates from 1546, while the painting of the Magi was executed in 1630.

Provisionally (1979) the palace accommodates two museums, but since the erection of extensive new museum premises to the E. of the Alhambra, there appears to be a considerable conflict or confusion of interests, and the present collections, among others in the city, may well be translated to this new site, but they may remain as they are. Until some agreement is reached they will be given comparatively brief descriptions.

On the ground floor is the *Museo Nac. de Art Hispano-Musulman*, an extensive collection of material from the area, much of it from the Alhambra itself, including the *Alhambra Vase*, the finest existing specimen of 15C Hispano-Moresque ware; while among other exhibits are a Cordoban marble ablution-bowl (10C), with curious carvings of eagles, and of lions devouring gazelles. Also on display are numerous examples of Moorish ceramics in all their variety, and likewise stucco-work, and glass; tombstones; carved wood; carved capitals; fountain-heads; bronzes; and fabrics, etc.

On the upper floor is the **Museo de Bellas Artes**. Among the more important works in RRI–VIII are (RI) the 'Triptico del Gran Capitán' (c. 1500), in Limoges enamel, by *Nardon Pénicaud*; a polychrome wooden Entombment (from S. Jerónimo), by *Jacobo Florentino*; Wooden relief from stall-work, by *Diego de Siloée*; and paintings by *Pedro de Raxis, el Viejo*. RII A Portal from vanished S. Gíl, by *Siloée* and his school; stalls from the Conv. de la Santa Cruz (1590) by *Juan de Orea* and *Fr. Sánchez*. RIII Works by *Juan Sánchez Cotán* from the Cartuja. RIV *Estéban de Rueda*, Denial of Peter; Still Lifes, including The Thistle (*el Cardo*), by *Mateo Cerezo, Antonio Arias Fernández* (d. 1684), and *Juan de Van der Hamen* (1596–1682). RV Polychrome busts by *Alonso Cano* and *Pedro de Mena*. RVI Paintings by *Juan de Sevilla*; *Diego de Mora*, Polychrome bust of Christ and the Mater Dolorosa. RVII Works by *Pedro Bocanegra* (1638–89). RVIII 18C miniature sculptures.

RRXIX–XI (the former with a Fireplace of Carrera marble depicting Leda and the Swan) contain a miscellaneous collection of 19–20C paintings, including works by *Carlos Haes, José Gutierrez de la Vega, José Roldan. Vicente López*, and *Vázquez Díaz*, etc.

At the S.W. angle of the Pl. de los Aljibes is the **Alcazaba**, the citadel of the Moors as early as the 11C, and, although little remains beyond the exterior walls and towers, parts of these may go back to the time of Ibn el-Ahmar (1238–72). It occupies the precipitous W. extremity of the Alhambra hill, which seems to have been divided from the rest by a depression now occupied by the cistern below the Pl. de los Aljibes. The E. wall of the citadel, facing the plaza, is strengthened by the *Torre Quebrada* and the *Torre del Homenaje*; on the N. side is the *Torre de las Armas*; and at the N.W. angle rises the *Torre de la Vela*. Turning to the l. on entering, we pass through the *Jardín de los Adarves*, a hanging garden on the S. rampart, to a platform sheer above the Pl. Nueva, nearly 500 ft below. An easy staircase ascends the **Torre de la Vela** (26 m.), on which, on Jan 2nd, 1492, the Christian flag was hoisted by Card. Mendoza, after 777 years of Moorish rule.

The Torre de la Vela enjoys panoramic *Views*. On the N. we have a bird's-eye view of the patios and winding streets of the Albaicín; to the N. and W. stretches the modern city, with the Vega beyond, studded with villages and guarded by a wall of mountains, while to the S.E. rises the Sierra Nevada.

In a turret on the upper platform hangs the Campana de la Vela, a huge bell cast in 1773, which is rung at intervals throughout the night to regulate the opening and shutting of the irrigation canals in the vega. In times of trouble the bell was rung to call the citizens to arms, but it is now heard by daylight only twice a year. On Jan 2nd it commemorates the taking of Granada, and from noon on the first Sat. in October until sunset on the following day it peals in honour of the victory of Lepanto (Oct 7th, 1571).

To the E. of the Pal. of Charles V stands *Sta María* (1581–1618), on the site of a mosque. This church, designed by *Herrera*, was built, on a smaller scale, by *Juan de Orea*. The heraldry of the portal was carved by *Martínez de Aranda* in 1616; the retablo of 1671 by *Juan López Almagro*, whose design was influenced by Cano. The column (1590) in front of the church commemorates two Franciscans martyred in 1347.—The C. Real leads to the former *Conv. of S. Francisco*, founded in 1495 but several times altered. In 1929 it was converted into a *Parador*, recently enlarged and meretriciously furnished. Within its *church* rested the bodies of Fernando and Isabel until their transference to the *Cap. Real*, see p.490.

Leaving the Alhambra we may follow (l.) the wall to reach the outer entrance of the Generalife, also conveniently approached by a footbridge from the N. side of the Alhambra gardens; see p.487. Thence an avenue leading through a striking vista between close-set clipped yews and cypresses, brings us to the inner gate, passing an *Open-Air Theatre* (1953).

The ***Generalife** (Pl. 8), once the summer palace of the sultans, lies on the slope of the Cerro del Sol, overlooking the Alhambra and the city. The restored buildings have suffered from alterations, and their decorations, older than those of the Alhambra, have been injured by past neglect, but the exquisite *Garden, with its trimmed hedges, its orange-trees and tall cypresses, and its characteristic fountain-jets and pools, recalls the reposeful refinement of its halcyon days.

The name (pronounced Heneralif *not* General Life, as has been overheard) is derived from the Arabic *Jennat al-Arif*, meaning 'garden of the architect' (or of Arif) but the builder of the palace, the original work of which dates from c. 1250, is unknown. An inscription records its decoration in 1319 by the Sultan Abul Walid.

Down the centre of the first court (*Patio de la Acequia*; 49 m. long), with its luxuriant flowers and shrubs, stretches a narrow aqueduct bordered by slender fountain-jets. We follow the arcade on the l. side, from the middle of which opens a mirador with good but damaged plaster ornamentation. At the end of the court rises a graceful arcade of five arches (restored), commanding good views. We next enter the so-called *Patio de los Cipreses*, a romantic enclosed garden, with a pool, and numerous fountain-jets, the legendary trysting place of Boabdil's sultana and her lover Hamet. To the N. is a gallery on two levels built in 1584–86.—On the slope behind this patio is the upper garden, from the successive terraces of which we may climb to a belvedere of 1836. One of the more delightful descents is by the *Camino de las Cascadas*; runnels of water, forming miniature cascades, flow down conduits formed by its balustrades.

Higher still, and outside the limits of the garden, is a knoll known as the *Silla del Moro,* which may be ascended for the view. Here are the remains of what was perhaps a mosque, and in the neighbourhood are traces of Moorish reservoirs.

B   S.W. GRANADA, THE CAP. REAL AND CATHEDRAL.

The C. de los Reyes Católicos, a main artery of traffic, is built over the covered channel of the Darro. Walking W. from the Pl. de Isabel la Católica, we first pass, facing the end of an alley, the restored *Casa del Carbón* (Pl. 10), originally a *khan* (erarly 14C), afterwards a granary (*alhóndiga*), then a theatre, and used in the 17C as a coal-weighing office. Unique in Europe it is a notable example of the type of hostelry still found throughout the Moslem world.—Adjacent stands the *Casa de los Duques de Abrantes* (early 16C).

The *Ayuntamiento,* facing the Pl. del Carmen, incorporates a patio of 1622 and remains of a Carmelite convent, and contains a small museum, with banners of 1493 and 1621, silver maces (1619), etc.

Opposite the Pl. del Carmen the C. del Príncipe leads N. to the once picturesque *Pl. de Bibarrambla,* the scene of jousts, bull-fights, and fiestas. The 17C fountain was brought from the demolished Conv. de S. Agustín.

The Moorish gate (*Bab ar-Ramla,* the sand gate), where the hands and ears (*orejas*) of malefactors were exposed, became known as the *Pta. de las Orejas* many years before a platform collapsed here at a festival in 1621, when it was later said that the mob tore earrings from the ears of ladies involved in the disaster, an episode giving rise to yet another fable. Removed in 1873, it was reconstructed in 1935 in the alamedas of the Alhambra. In the Zacatín, the street leading E. from the S.E. angle of the square, is the *Alcaicería,* a former Moorish silk-bazaar, burnt down in 1843 and rebuilt in a crude attempt to copy the original style.

The *Archbishop's Palace* in the N.E. angle of the square, dates mainly from the 17C. The *Curia,* further N., seat of the university until 1679, was built in 1527–44 to the design of *Diego de Siloée,* but its portal (1530) is by *Juan de Marquina,* and the Doric patio (1534) by *Seb. de Alcántara.*—A turning off the Alcaicería leads shortly to the entrance of the *Capilla Real,* adjoining the Cathedral (see below), which may also be approached direct from the Gran Vía.

On the S.E. side of the Capilla Real is the Plateresque *Lonja,* or *Exchange* (1518–22), built against the wall of the Sagrario and, like the façade of the chapel, designed by *Enrique de Egas* and built by *Pradas.* Opposite the Cap. Real is seen the remarkable painted *façade* (an addition of 1722–29) of the *Casa del Cabildo Antiguo,* or old Ayuntamiento. This was originally the *madresa* or university of the Moors, built in 1349, and containing an octagonal Moorish room with a dome, and the *Sala de Cabildos* (1512–13), with a good Mudéjar ceiling.

The late Gothic *Capilla Real* (Pl. 10), was built by *Enrique de Egas* in 1506–21 as a mausoleum for the Catholic Kings, superseding the royal burial chapel of S. Juan de los Reyes at Toledo, already partially completed, see p.316. The chapel was finished thirteen years after the death of Isabel and one year after that of Fernando, and in 1521 their remains were transferred here from the church of S. Francisco (p.489). Philip the Handsome and Juana 'the Mad', parents of Charles V, are also interred here.

The S. or S.E. Façade, adorned with elegant open-work balconies and pinnacles, but in a filthy condition, fronts the Pl. de la Lonja (see below). A central window is surmounted by the escutcheon of the Catholic Kings. Flanking the Plateresque portal (1527), by *Juan García de Pradas*, are statues by the French sculptor *Nicolás de León*.

We first enter the **Sacristy,** which contains the Treasury of the chapel and important paintings, mainly from the collection of Isabel: *Roger van der Weyden,* Nativity, and Pietà; *Master of the Legend of St Lucy,* Mass of St Gregory; *Memling,* Holy Women, The Virgin, Pietà, Descent from the Cross, Virgin and female saints; *Botticelli,* Christ in the Garden; *D. Bouts,* the Virgin, Head of Christ; Virgin and angels; *P. Berruguete,* St John on Patmos; and a number of anonymous 15C works of high quality.

In glass cases are the sceptre and crown of Isabel; her mirror converted into a custodia; an illuminated missal written for the queen by Francisco Flórez (1496); embroideries worked by Isabel; the sword of Fernando: banners used at the conquest of Granada; and a Tapestry by *Marcos de Covarrubias* of the Crucifixion between the sun and the moon; also a fine Altar Cross.—A staircase ascends to the raised choir at the W. end of the chapel, with Plateresque stalls by *Jacobo Florentino* completed by *Martín Bello* in 1521. Some of the choir-books have illuminations by *Lorenzo Florentino* (c. 1545).

Within the adjoining *Chapel* itself, a superb *Reja,* designed by *Juan de Zagala* and *Juan de Cubillana* and made by *Bartolomé de Jaén* (1520), separates the nave from the chancel, in which are the white marble **Royal Monuments,** executed in the style of the Italian Renaissance, with recumbent effigies and elaborate sculptured decoration. On the r. is that of Fernando (d. 1516) and Isabel (d. 1504), by *Domenico Fancelli* of Florence, made in Genoa and finished in 1517. On the l. is the slightly higher monument of Philip I (d. 1506) and Juana (d. 1555), designed by *Bartolomé Ordóñez* (1519–20).—Steps descend to the simple leaden coffins of the monarchs seen in a small vault beneath the chancel—'small room for so great glory', as Charles V remarked. The candle to be kept perpetually lit before Isabel's tomb, in accordance with her will, has been recently replaced by a dim electric light bulb.

The great **Retablo* is by *Felipe Vigarni* (1520–22); at the foot are kneeling statues of Fernando and Isabel, perhaps by *Siloée* and remarkable as portraits. Below these, in painted panels, is depicted the success of their ambitions—the conquest and conversion of the infidel. The *Relicarios* or side altars in the chancel are by *Alonso de Mena* (1630–32). In the N. Transept is a retablo of 1521 by *Jacobo Florentino el Indaco,* incorporating paintings by him and by *Pedro Machuca,* and also a fine triptych by *Dirk Bouts.*

From the Cap. Real we may visit the Cathedral, which is entered from the Gran Via de Colón, a short distance to the E., for the main W. entrance is usually closed.

The grandiose **Cathedral** (Pl. 10) adjoins the later Sagrario and earlier Cap. Real. Its construction, begun in 1521 in the Gothic style by *Enrique de Egas,* was taken over in 1528 by *Diego de Siloée* (d. 1563), who continued it in the early Renaissance style, and who was in turn succeeded by *Juan de Maeda.* It was consecrated in 1561 but the vaults were not completed until 1704 and work on the W. Front lasted until 1714. Twiss remarked (1773) that the interior had been recently 'entirely encrusted with the finest marbles . . . and enriched with bronze gilt', but all executed in a 'wretched and despicable manner'; and many will agree that this ungainly edifice is (in the words of John Harvey) 'one of the world's architectural tragedies, one of the saddest of wasted opportunities'.

EXTERIOR. The heavy W. Façade, facing the Pl. de las Pasiegas, with its massive pillars bearing figures of the Apostles, was designed in 1667 by *Alonso Cano* and built after his death by *José Granados*. Over the *Pta. Principal* is a relief by *José Risueño* (1717) and over the side doors are reliefs by *Michel* and *Louis Verdiguier* (1782–83). The Doric lowest stage of the N. Tower is due to *Juan de Maeda* (c. 1576), the Ionic and Corinthian stages above to *Ambrosio de Vico* (c. 1610).

The S. Tower was never built . On the N. side are the *Pta. de S. Jerónimo* (1532) and the *Pta. del Perdón* (finished 1537). *Diego de Siloée* designed the lower portions of both, but the former was completed by *Maeda*, the latter by *Ambrosio de Vico*. At the S.E. end of the ambulatory is the *Pta. del Colegio Eclesiástico*, built in 1530 by *Sánchez del Cerro* to the design of *Siloée*, who in 1531 carved the Ecce Homo above it.

INTERIOR. To the r. is the *Sacristy*, containing a Crucifixion by *Montañés*, a carved Conception (1656) by *Alonso Cano*, an Annunciation by *Cano*, and the Virgin appearing to St Julian, by *Pedro de Moya.*—The adjoining *Sala Capitular* leads to a Churrigueresque oratory with a carving of the Virgin and child by *Cano*, and altar-piece attr. to *Duque Cornejo*.

We enter the Cathedral proper through a doorway by *Siloée* (1534).

The *Nave* has double aisles off which open side chapels. The groined roof is supported by huge pillars with engaged Corinthian columns. At the E. end a bold arch opens upon the circular *Cap. Mayor*, behind which is an ambulatory with chapels. The huge organs (1745–46) were made by *Leonardo de Ávila*, but the acoustics of the building are bad, with a 5 second echo. The coro has been removed from the nave and the 16C stalls placed in the sanctuary. In the nave, close to the site of the old minaret, are buried Mariana Pineda (see p.495) and Alonso Cano (1601--67), who became a minor canon (*racionero*) of the cathedral.

The elaborately decorated **Cap. Mayor** has a dome supported by a double tier of Corinthian columns. The high altar has a modern silver tabernacle, but the lamps before it, designed by *Cano*, were made by *Diego Cervantes Pacheco* in 1653–54. Besides the pillars of the entrance arch are kneeling statues of the Catholic Kings, by *Pedro de Mena Medrano* (1675–77), and above the Baroque marble pulpits, by *F. Hurtado Izquierdo*, 1713–17, are carved Heads of Adam and Eve, by *Alonso Cano* (later coloured).

On the lower tier of columns in the chapel are figures of the Apostles (1612), by *Alonso de Mena* and *Martínez de Aranda*, and above are paintings by *Bocanegra* and *Juan de Sevilla*. The seven paintings (1652–54) between the columns of the upper tier are by *Alonso Cano*. Still higher are stained-glass windows, by *Theodor de Holanda*, and the cupola lighted by windows (1559–61) designed by *Siloée* and executed by *Juan del Campo* (Jan van Kampen).

Turning l. on entering the Cathedral we pass the *Cap. de Santiago*, with statues of saints. The Baroque Retablo, designed by *Hurtado Izquierdo* and made by *Juan de la Torre* in 1707, contains an equestrian statue of Santiago by *Alonso de Mena*, and, above it an ancient painting of the Virgen de los Perdones, presented by Innocent VIII to Isabel.—Continuing down the S. AISLE, we reach the *Altar de Jesús Nazareno*, whose retablo, designed by *Marcos Rodríguez Raya* (1722), contains: *Cano*, St Augustine, the Virgin, Via Dolorosa; and *Ribera*, Martyrdom of St Laurence, the infant Jesus appearing to St Anthony, and a

Magdalen. *Altar de la Trinidad:* Altar-piece and other works by *Cano;* Death of Joseph, by *C. Maratta. Cap. de S. Miguel,* with decorations of 1804–07 by *Fr. Romero de Aragón; Cano,* Virgen de la Soledad. In the last chapel are works by *Cano,* including a Head of St Paul.

Crossing to the N. AISLE, we enter, at the basement of the tower, the *Tesoro* which contains a Custodia presented by Isabel, vestments including a remarkable green set in Mudéjar style (1544), chalices, choir-books etc.; the doorway is by *Juan de Maeda* (c. 1560); the sculptured group of Charity is ascribed to *Diego de Pesquera.—Cap. de la Virgen del Pilar,* adjoining: *Juan Adán,* Virgin appearing to St James. *Cap. de N.S. del Carmen:* the Virgin of the retablo is by *Juan de Mora.* Further on is the *Pta. del Perdón.* AMBULATORY. The windows are by *Theodor de Holanda* (1556) and *Juan del Campo* (1554–59). The *Cap. de N.S. de la Antigua* contains a 15C wooden statue of the Virgin; and Baroque Retablo (1716–18) is by *Pedro Duque Cornejo.* The *Cap. de S. Cecilio* (E. end) contains carvings by *M. Verdiguier* (c. 1780). *Cap. de S. Sebastián: Juan de Sevilla,* Martyrdom of S. Sebastián. *Cap de Sta Ana:* Retablo of 1615, by *Gaspar Guerrero,* incorporating a painted 16C group of the Virgin and Child and St Anne, by *Diego de Pesquera;* and two paintings by *Bocanegra* (1674).

The **Sagrario,** a Renaissance structure abutting the Cathedral, was built as a parish church by *Hurtado Izquierdo* in 1750–59, on the site of the mosque which had been used as a Christian church until the middle of the 17C.

It contains a remarkable Renaissance *Font* (1520–22) by *Francisco* of Florence and *Martín* of Milan.—The *Cap del Pulgar* commemorates Hernán Pérez del Pulgar (1451–1531), a Spanish knight who secretly entered Granada by night in 1490 pinning to the mosque door a parchment bearing the words 'Ave María'. He was honoured by burial beside the royal vault, near the site of his exploit.

C   N.E. GRANADA.

The C. de los Reyes Católicos leads E. to the long *Pl. Nueva* (Pl. 10). The *Audiencia,* formerly the Chancillería, was built c. 1531, with a façade of 1584–87 by *Juan de la Vega,* perhaps with Herrera's assistance. The top balustrade was added in 1762. Within are an arcaded patio and a staircase with a fine stalactite ceiling of 1578.—At the end of the plaza appears **Sta Ana,** a Renaissance church of 1537–48, by *Siloée,* with a graceful minaret-like tower (1561–63) and a beautiful Plateresque portal (1542–47) by *Seb. de Alcántara* and his son Juan. Within are statues by *José de Mora* (1671).

In the Pl. de Sta Ana is the *Pilar del Toro,* a fountain carved by *Siloée* c. 1558. Opposite the church, N. of the Carrera del Darro, is the *Casa de los Pisas,* with a Gothic doorway, where S. Juan de Dios died in 1550 (see p.496).

On the hill which rises to the N. of the gorge of the Darro, lies the **Albaicín,** the oldest part of Granada, which derives its name from the Arabic *Rabad el-Bayyazin,* 'the quarter of the falconers', or from the fact that it was later settled with Moors from Baeza after the town had been sacked by Fernando III. Bounded on the W. by the C. de Elvira and retaining part of its Moorish wall on the N., the Albaicín is now a poor but characteristic region of narrow and crooked streets, with a few churches of minor interest and many Moorish houses whose unpretentious exteriors occasionally veil interiors and gardens (*carmenes*) of considerable charm.

From the Pl. de Sta Ana, the narrow and picturesque Carrera del Darro follows the r. bank of the stream, with the Alhambra looming high above on the r. Near the second bridge a fragment of masonry on the far bank survives as a relic of the Moorish *Bridge of the Cadi* (11C), across which passed the ancient approach to the Pta. de las Armas of the Alhambra. At No. 31 in the Carrera are remains of 11C *Moorish Baths* and the *Conv. de Sta Catalina de Zafra,* further on, built in 1520–40, incorporates a Moorish house. The **Casa de Castril** (No. 43), has an elaborate Plateresque façade showing the date 1539, probably by *Seb. de Alcántara* and patios with carved wooden columns.

The building now houses archaeological collections, including Punic alabaster vases from Almuñécar, stone bulls from Arjona (Jaén), a lamp from the mezquita of Medina Elvira (9C), and miscellaneous cinerary urns, lamps, metalwork, ceramics, etc.

SS. Pedro y Pablo, opposite, was built in 1560–67 by *Juan de Maeda,* although the tower and sacristry were not finished until 1593, while the main portal is by *Pedro de Orea* (1589). The fine artesonado ceilings are by *Jerónimo Vilchez* and the classical tabernacle (1790) by *Dom. Aguado.*

A short street climbs up to **S. Juan de los Reyes** built in the Gothic style by *Rodrigo Hernández* c. 1520 but retaining the 13C minaret (altered) of the mosque of Ataibín which became the first Christian church in Granada.

In the C. de S. Juan de los Reyes, W. of S. Juan, are the *Conv. de la Concepción* (1523), with a Gothic doorway and a church of 1644; and the late-16C *Casa de Ágreda.*—Uphill to the N.W. is **S. José,** on the site of an ancient mosque pulled down in 1517, but whose minaret is incorporated in the tower. Some 10C work has been exposed, including the oldest horseshoe arch in the city (S. wall). The church was built by *R. Hernández* in 1517–25, but the western coro, with an artesonado roof by *Dom. de Frechilla,* was added in 1540–44. Another artesonado covers the cap. mayor, whose red marble retablo (1788–89) was designed by *Ventura Rodríguez.* Also in the church are a Crucifix by *José de Mora;* Christ at the Column by *Siloée;* a retablo of c. 1540 by the *Maestro del Pulgar;* and another ascribed to the Fleming *Pedro de Cristo,* who worked in Granada in 1507–30.

To the N. of S. Juan de los Reyes is Gothic *S. Nicolás* (Pl. 7) by *R. Hernández* (rebuilt since a fire in 1932), the plaza of which commands a celebrated *View of the Alhambra.—To the N.E. is *S. Salvador* (16C) incorporating remains of the principal mosque of the Albaicín, on whose site it stands. The Ionic portal of 1543 was designed by *Siloée;* the brick tower was completed in 1592.—To the W. of S. Nicolás is the *Conv. de Sta Isabel la Reál,* founded by Isabel in 1501, with a domed church, the Florid Gothic portal of which is ascribed to *Enrique de Egas.* The artesonado ceiling is notable. The convent replaces the Pal. of Dâr al-Horra, residence of Moorish princesses, the considerable remains of which, in a parallel alley to the N., have been well restored.—To the S. is the *Casa del Gallo,* mentioned in Irving's 'Tales of the Alhambra'.

To the N.W. of Sta Isabel stands the 10C *Pta. Monaita,* whence the Cuesta de la Alcazaba leads N.W. to high-lying *S. Cristóbal* commanding a fine view, and W. to the *Paseos del Triunfo,* see p.495.

Some interesting buildings survive among the tangled lanes of the N. part of the Albaicín. A short distance N. of S. Nicolás we pass through the *Pta. Nueva* or *Arco de las Pesas* in a section of the town walls, beside the remains of the 8C gateway called *Hizna Román,* and enter the *Pl. Larga,* from which the C. Panaderos strikes E. to *S. Salvador* (see above). Going on N. by the C. del Agua we pass Moorish houses (notably No. 37) to reach at the end of the street the picturesque *Casa de los Mascarones,* home of the poet Pedro Soto de Rojas (d. 1655) and later of José de Mora, the sculptor (d. 1725). Another practically untouched Moorish house can be seen close by at No. 32, C. del Pardo. To the W. stands *S. Bartolomé* of 1542–70, by *Fr. Hernández de Móstolas,* with fine artesonados. Further N.E. are the remains of 16C *S. Luis,* burnt in 1933, and the *Pta. Fajalauza* (14C) in the outer city wall. No.

27 in the C. de S. Luis, and No. 2 in the nearby C. de Yanguas, are both Moorish houses.

The Carrera del Darro is continued E. by the Paseo de los Tristes (now Paseo de Padre Manjón) to the *Pte. del Algillo.*

Hence the Cuesta del Rey Chico climbs up the ravine between the Generalife and the Alhambra, while the Cuesta del Avellano ascends by the bank of the stream to the *Fuente del Avellano* ('of the hazel-tree'), commanding a fine view; and in the steep lanes climbing the hill (l.) are remains of Moorish houses, notably No. 14 C. del Horno de Oro and No. 9 Cuesta de la Victoria.

We turn N. at the bridge, to ascend the Cuesta del Chapiz, a road taking its name from the *Casa del Chapiz* (No. 14), a 16C mansion retaining remains of a patio and Mudéjar decoration restored to house the *Escuela de Estudios Arabes.*

From this point a footpath zigzags up to the high-lying *Ermita de S. Miguel el Alto,* with a magnificent *View of Granada and the Alhambra backed by the Sierra Nevada. Built in 1671–73 on the site of a Moorish tower, the chapel was rebuilt in 1815.

The Casa del Chapiz is situated at the corner of the CAMINO DEL SACRO MONTE, which leads to the E. along a hill-side covered by a luxuriant growth of prickly pear. Here, flanking the road, open the CUEVAS, inhabited mainly by gipsies, who will endeavour to extort what they can from the tourist, who they regard as their lawful prey. Their humble homes are not all so poverty-stricken as they look. Some distance beyond the Casa del Chapiz we reach a group of houses whence a sloping approach (l.) ascends in 10–12 min. more to the **Conv. of the Sacro Monte**, a magnificent view-point. The original buildings by *Pedro Sánchez,* were completed in 1610, but have been much enlarged. The choir-stalls (1615–17) are carved by *Fr. Díaz del Rivero.*

The human remains discovered in 1594 in caves on this site were credulously assumed to be the bones of S. Cecilio and his fellow martyrs, and early in the following century the convent was founded by Abp. Pedro de Castro, whose tomb is in the church.

A steep footpath descending from the Sacro Monte and finally following the line of the Moorish wall leads eventually to *S. Miguel el Alto,* see above.

D   N.W. GRANADA.

From the Pl. Nueva the narrow C. de Elvira runs N. parallel to the Gran Via, passing (r.) the church of the *Hosp. de Corpus Cristi,* with a doorway of 1654 by *Cano;* to the l. are *Santiago,* and *S. Andrés,* begun by *Rodrigo Hernández* (c. 1525 and 1528), beyond which we reach the mutilated *Pta. de Elvira* (11C), once the main gate of Granada.—The Gran Via itself was cut through a congested part of the old town at the beginning of this century, and passing near (l.) the *Conv. de Sta Paula,* finished in 1540, leads to the PASEOS DEL TRIUNFO, laid out as gardens, just N. of the Pta. de Elvira.

To the E., barracks occupy the restored *Conv. de la Merced* (1514–30); while *S. Ildefonso* (1553–55), beyond, designed by *Siloéc,* contains fine timber roofs. In the Paseos are a column with a statue of the Virgin, by *Fr. de Potes* and *Alonso de Mena* (1626–31), and an insignificant monument marking the spot where Mariana Pineda was unjustifiably executed in 1831 for the 'crime' of possessing an embroidered banner of the Liberals.

To the N. is the **Hosp. Real** (Pl. 1), an imposing Renaissance edifice with fine Plateresque windows, begun in 1511 by *Enrique de Egaz,* and completed in 1536 by *Juan García de Prades.*

The C. Real de Cartuja, passing the E. side of the Hospital, leads N. from the Pta. de Elvira to (c. 1 km.) the **Cartuja** (beyond Pl. 1), once a wealthy Carthusian convent, founded in 1506 on an estate granted by Gonzalo de Córdoba and moved to the present site in 1516. From the *Cloisters* we enter the Gothic *Refectory* (begun 1531), the *Chapter Room* (1517–19), and the later *Chapter House* (1565–67), preserving paintings of Martyrdoms, etc. by *Sánchez Cotán* and *Vicente Carducho*. The *Church* contains paintings by *Bocanegra*. The statues in the church were added in 1662; a screen of 1750 by *José Manuel Vázquez*, with paintings by *Cotán*, separates the monks' choir from that of the lay brothers.

The **Sagrario*, behind, richly adorned with marble, jasper, and porphyry by *Hurtado Izquierdo* (1704–20), has a cupola painted in fresco by *Palomino*. The **Sacristy** (1725–c. 1783), designed by *Izquierdo*, continued by *Luis de Arévalo*, and decorated by *Cabello*, is an extreme example of the Churrigueresque style, with its elaborate and extravagant decoration in brown and white marble and stucco; its door and cupboards inlaid with silver, tortoiseshell, and ivory, by *Vázquez*, who worked here in 1730–64. The statue of St Bruno on the high altar is by *José de Mora*, a pupil of Alonso Cano.

A short distance to the S.W. of the Paseos del Triunfo stands the **Hosp. de S. Juan de Dios**, founded in 1552, after the death of the saint commemorated in its name.

Juan de Dios or *de Robles* (1495–1550), 'St John of God', was a native of Montemor-o-Novo, in Portugal, and of Jewish lineage, who devoted his life to the succour of captives, foundlings, and the sick. He founded the Order of Charity for the Service of the Sick (approved by the Pope in 1570), and was canonized in 1691.

Over the portal, by *Jerónimo Vilchez* (1609), is a kneeling statue of S. Juan, by *Mora*, in the attitude in which he died. Between the two courts of the hospital, over a staircase, is a fine artesonado ceiling. The Baroque *church* of 1738–59, has a front by *José Bada*, while its Churrigueresque retablo is by *J. F. Guerrero*. In the camarín beyond the apse are a silver urn containing relics of S. Juan and a painted wooden head of the Baptist, attr. to *Alonso Cano*.

Not far beyond is **S. Jerónimo** (Pl. 5), founded by the Catholic Kings, and long neglected. The church was begun before 1519, continued from 1525 from the designs of *Jac. Florentino*, and completed in 1528–47 by *Diego de Siloée*. The portal in the main front was added in 1590 by *Martín Díaz de Navarrete* and *Pedro de Orea*. The tower has been recently restored.

At the sides of the high altar are Statues of Gonzalo de Córdoba, 'the Great Captain' (d. 1515), and María Manrique, his widow, whose remains are in the vault below. The carved and painted retablo, begun in 1570 by *Juan de Aragón* and *Lázaro de Velasco*, was finished by *Orea* and others in 1605. The stalls (1544), by *Siloée*, and the stained glass should be noted. The frescoes are by *Juan de Medina* (1723–35) and others. The great *Cloister*, a Gothic work with doorways by *Siloée*, was finished in 1519; the second patio, a curious mixture of Moorish, Gothic and Renaissance motives, in 1520.

From this church the C. de la Duquesa leads S. to the **University**, founded in 1526, which has occupied the present building, formerly a Jesuit college, since 1769. On the E. side is the Pl. de la Universidad, and *SS. Justo y Pastor*, with a nave of c. 1575–89 by *Martín de Baceta*, a Baroque doorway (1740) by *Alfonso Castillo*, and containing retablos (c. 1630) by *Díaz del Rivero* and frescoes of 1728 by *Martín de Pineda*. On the opposite side of the C. de S. Jerónimo is the *Conv. de la*

Encarnación (1524) and further N. are (l.) the university college of *S. Bartolomé*, in a 16C building, and (r.) the Renaissance *Pal. de Caicedo*.

The C. de la Duquesa ends at the Pl. de la Trinidad, whence we regain the Pta. Real by the C. Mesones or the C. Alhóndiga.

In the C. de las Tablas (W. of the Pl. de la Trinidad) are (l.) the *Pal. de las Infantas*, and the neoclassical *Pal. de Luque*. Off the C. Alhóndiga, leading S. from the Pl. de la Trinidad, is the C. de Gracia. At No. 3 C. de Parraga, to the l., Théophile Gautier briefly resided in 1843. Further along the C. de Gracia (l.) *La Magdalena* (1677–94), by *J. L. Ortega*, occupies the former Augustinian nunnery; and at the end, in the Pl. de Gracia, is the old *Trinitarian Conv.* of 1620–35.

E   S.E. GRANADA.

Diverging from the C. de los Reyes Católicos by the C. Colcha, we reach a little plaza. The C. del Marqués de Portago, the first turning on the r., leads to the *Conv. of the Carmelitas Descalzas*, founded in 1582 and incorporating the house in which the 'Great Captain' died. This street goes on (as the C. S. Matías) towards the Pl. Mariana Pineda, passing *S. Matías*, built in 1526–50. The rich portal of 1543 was made by *José de Luque* to designs of *Seb. de Alcántara*. Within is one of the finest retablos of Granada (1750), by *Blas Moreno*.—We retrace our steps to follow the C. de Pavaneras in which are the *Casa de Casablanca* (No. 11), with Plateresque stuccoes, and the **Casa de los Tiros** (Pl. 10), a Mudéjar house of c. 1505, with a curious façade.

The name is due to the muskets (*tiros*) projecting from the top windows. It formerly belonged to the Campotéjar family, late owners of the Generalife. The mansion now houses the *Tourist Office*, and an interesting *Museum of Local History*.

Further on the C. de Carnicería turns r. from the C. de Pavaneras for *Sto Domingo* (1512–32), with a raised choir and Gothic vaults. The marble tabernacle is by *Fr. Rodríguez Navajas;* the retablo in the N. Transept is by *Blas Moreno* (1726–56). The *Casa de los Girones*, at the corner of the C. de Sto Domingo, is a Moorish house of the 13C, with interior decoration in coloured stucco, and a staircase, gallery, and tower added in the 16C. Thence lanes lead S. to the Pl. de los Campos Eliseos in which is the entrance gate of the *Cuarto Real de Sto Domingo*, a late-13C Moorish palace in which Torquemada the Inquisitor is said to have lived, of which only one tower remains, and said to retain magnificently decorated rooms, untouched by the restorer, but admission is difficult to obtain.

Beyond the Casa de los Tiros, the Cuesta del Realejo, climbing towards the Alhambra hill, passes the *Conv. de Sta Catalina* (1530), beyond which we bear r. to reach *S. Cecilio*, built in 1528–34 by *Pedro Rios* with a Plateresque portal by *Juan de Marquina*.

The Av. de José Antonio, leading S. from the Pta. Real, is continued by the Carrera de Genil and other promenades on the bank of the river. The Campillo Alto, opening on the l., occupies the site of a Moorish gate; and the adjacent *Diputación* (1764), with its curious red and grey façade and quaint figures of soldiers, replaces the Castillo de Bibataubín, built by the Catholic Kings.

In the C. de S. Antón, parallel with the Avenida on the W., are the *Conv. del Ángel Custodia* (1626), with works by *Alonso Cano*, and *S. Antonio Abad* (1656, with a Baroque dome of 1747 by *Alf. Castillo*), with statues by *Pedro de Mena*.

The *Carrera del Genil* with its plane trees, is known also as the *Alameda* and as the '*Paseo de Inviernos*', or winter promenade. *N.S. de las Angustias* on its W. side, built in 1664–71 under *J. L. Ortega*, contains statues (1714–18) by *Pedro Duque Cornejo* and the 'Patrona de Granada', an image of the Virgin. The portal of the main front (1665–66) is by *Bernardo* and *José de Mora*.

On the r. is the Pl. del Humilladero where Fernando and Isabel with their retinue fell on their knees when they saw the silver cross and the banner of Castile displayed on the Torre de la Vela (p.489), the signal of the surrender of the Alhambra (Jan. 2nd. 1492).

The *Pte. de Genil*, replacing an older bridge, here crosses the river to the *Paseo del Violón* at the W. end of which is the *Ermita de S. Sebastián*, once a mosque, where Boabdil took leave of Fernando and Isabel on quitting his kingdom. *Roman walls* have been uncovered in this area. A short distance beyond, on the r, is the *Alcázar de Genil*, on the site of and including attractive remains of a palace built c. 1340–50 for the Moorish queens, and sold by Boabdil's mother Ayesha to the Catholic Kings. To the E. of the Pte. de Genil is the *Conv. de S. Basilio*, founded in 1614, with a church (1755-76) by *Luis de Arévalo*.

The *Paseo del Salón*, S.E. of the Pl. de Humilladero, shaded by elm-trees, is the summer promenade. It is continued by the *Paseo de la Bomba*, with its fountains and villas, ending at the *Pta. Verde*.

F   Excursions From Granada.

The rich VEGA, well irrigated since the days of the Moors, stretches W. and S.W. of Granada. At *La Zubia*, 5 km. S., Isabel narrowly escaped capture by the Moors on St. Lewis's Day (Aug. 25th, 1491), and in gratitude founded the *Conv. de S. Luis*, now represented by a 17C church. *Gabia la Grande*, 6 km. S.W., has remains of a 5C Byzantine baptistry and a curious 15C tower known as *El Fuerte*.—*Atarfe* lies 8 km. N.W., and near it are the ruins of *Elvira*, perhaps Roman *Illiberis*.

To THE SIERRA NEVADA. A good mountain road—in its upper reaches the highest in Europe—leads S.E. from the Paseo de la Bomba, ascending the narrowing valley of the Genil. We now start to climb in a series of zigzags to (35 km.) the *Parador Nac. de Sierra Nevada*, and the adjacent *Albergue Universitario*. The area of the *Peñones de San Francisco* (8530 ft) has been much developed as a winter sports centre. From the *Prado Llano* (6405 ft) with the *Solynieve* development, chair-lifts, cable-cars and ski-tows ascend towards the peaks. Beyond the Parador the road continues to climb to the *Collado de Veleta* (10,725 ft; S. of the *Veleta*). It is prolonged to the S. base of *Mulhacén*, and descends to join the road through the Alpujarras between *Trevélez* and *Órgiva* (see Rte 59A), but normally is only passable between Aug. and Oct. It is planned to deface the summit by the erection of a radio-telescope.

The snow-clad **Sierra Nevada**, the main link in the long Penibetic mountain system that separates inland Andalucía from the luxuriant Mediterranean coast, is c. 70 miles long, with peaks rising over 11,000 ft. Beginning near *Fiñana* (p.500), it runs E. to the *Contadero* (10,235 ft), then sweeps towards the S. in a magnificent cirque with the headwaters of the Genil descending from the culminating peaks of the *Mulhacén*, and the *Veleta* (see below), and finally bends S.W. towards the *Cerro del Caballo* and ends on the W. near *Padul* (p.501). Parallel with the Sierra Nevada, between it and the sea, is the much lower *Sierra Contraviesa*, the S. boundary of the Alpujarras.

The **Picacho de Veleta** (11,246 ft) may be ascended in 5-6 hrs from the Sierra Nevada chalet. **Mulhacén** (11,420 ft), the highest summit of the Sierra, is ascended in 12 hrs from the chalet by several routes, or from the S. in 5 hrs from Trevélez, which is connected by road with *Órgiva*, see Rte 59A. The *Alcazaba* (11,187 ft) is rather a continuation of Mulhacén than a separate mountain.

The *Cerro del Caballo* (10,590 ft), to the S.W., is best climbed from *Dúrcal*, see p.501. Its slopes are reserved as a National Park.—The barrancos or ravines of the *Circo de Genil*, overhung by the precipitous N. face of the sierra, down which fall innumerable cascades, repay exploration.—Visits to the *Corral de Veleta* and the *Laguna Larga* (one of several small lakes near the summit of the Veleta) are easy in summer, while there are many other picturesque valleys in the Sierra. In that of the *Monachil*, on the N.W. side, we may visit the striking cañon of *Los Cahorras*, at one point in which the flanking cliffs meet to form the natural tunnel known as

the *Pte. de las Palomas*, through which the river rushes. In the beautiful valley of
the Dilar we may ascend to the Dehesa de Dilar at the foot of the Veleta and to the
Salto de la Espartera, commanding a wonderful panoramic view.

59   FROM ALMERÍA TO GRANADA

A   Viâ Guadix.

Total distance, 166 km. (103 miles.). N 234. km. **Guadix**—55 km. **Granada.**

ALMERÍA (120,100 inhab.; 51,000 in 1920; 87,000 in 1960; *Hotels*)
has grown rapidly in recent years, but the old town, with its narrow
streets and peeling paint-work, still retains a characteristically Moorish
appearance, above which rises the castle backed by the slopes of the
Sierra de Enix, while seaward the bay is bounded by the Cabo de Gata to
the S.E. and Punta Elena or del Sabinal to the S.W. The winter climate is
warm and dry, although windy, but in summer the hot inland winds raise
the shade temperature to 97° Fahr. (36° cent.). Among its exports are
grapes, esparto grass, and ore from neighbouring mines.

The *Airport* lies some 9 km. E.

History. Almería was the Roman *Portus Magnus* and the *Al-Mariyat* of the
Moors, under whom it attained such prosperity (and with a population perhaps of
300,000) as to boast that 'Cuando Almería era Almería Granada era su alquería'
('Almería was Almería when Granada was but its farm'). For a time (c. 1035–91),
between the fall of the caliphate and its subjugation by the Almoravides, Almería
was the most important capital in Moorish Spain. Its pirates under Ibn Maimûn
were dreaded as much as those of Algiers. Momentarily captured by Alfonso VII in
1147, Almería was not finally taken until 1488, by Fernando the Catholic, since
when its importance declined until the opening of the railway in 1899. Long in
Republican hands, it was shelled by a German naval squadron in 1937.

The roads from Granada viâ Guadix (N 324) and from Murcia (N 340) meet N.
of the town, which is approached by an extension of the Rambla del Obispo
Orberá. The coast from Motril approaches Almería from the W. skirting the port
by the tree-lined Andén de Costa, which meets the Rambla near its junction with
the Paseo del Generalísimo, the main shopping street, pullulating with persistent
bootblacks.

At the N. end of this Paseo is the *Pta. de Purchena*, now a busy central
plaza, from which the C. de las Tiendas leads S.W. past (l.) *Santiago*,
with its tall 16C tower, and (r.) *Sta Clara* (18C), towards the PL. VIEJA
(r.) and further S., the *Episcopal Pal., Seminary*, and the fortress-like
Cathedral. Its construction was begun in 1524 on the site of the great
mosque (converted into a cathedral in 1490, but shattered by the
earthquake of 1522). Its four massive towers and a Corinthian façade
(1550–73) are by *Juan de Orea*. The interior contains walnut stalls
carved by the same artist (1558–80), elaborately but without much taste.
In the chapel behind the high altar is the 16C Tomb of Bp. Diego
Fernández Villalán, the founder.

Between the cathedral and the Paseo del Generalísimo, *Sto Domingo*
(18C; restored) is the sanctuary of the Virgen del Mar, patroness of the
town, whose image was found in 1502 on the beach of Torre García. *S.
Pedro*, to the N., and *S. Juan*, occupy the sites of ancient mosques.

From the Pl. Vieja, we may climb W. to reach the extensive Moorish
Alcazaba (under restoration), dominating the town, built in the 10C by
Abderrahman III, and enlarged later, but which was also ruined by the
earthquake of 1522. The principal remains were the *Torreón del*

Homenaje, erected by Fernando and Isabel, and a mosque converted into a chapel. The colourful gardens are a welcome relief from the dusty town.

A curtain-wall with towers links the castle with the neighbouring heights of S. Cristóbal, crowned by an ugly modern monument on the site of a chapel built by the Templars after the conquest of 1147. The C. Antonio Vico leads down to the Pta. de Purchena, near which is *S. Sebastián* (1684).

An excursion may be made to the *Cabo de Gata* (i.e. agate cape), 36 km. S.E., with its lighthouse, and caves noted for crystals. The wilderness further inland is the background for many foreign films made in Spain.

We drive N. on the N 324, at 14 km. forking l., still following the valley of the Andarax, to (4 km.) *Gádor*, with Moorish ruins and the great prehistoric cemetery of *Los Millares*, and traverse the gap between the Sierra de Alhamilla (r.) and the Sierra de Gádor, a district rich in lead and sulphur.—At 6 km. a road climbs W. viâ (24 km.) *Canjáyar* and (22 km.) *Laujar de Andarax* to (23 km.) *Ugíjar*, see Rte 59B.

After 24 km. a road leads r. 7 km. to *Gérgal*, with a castle commanding the pass between the Sierra Nevada and the Sierra de Baza, and prehistoric remains.

24 km. *Fiñana*, with a noble ruined castle.—24 km. **La Calahorra**, 3 km. S., has a magnificent 16C *Castle* with domed angle towers, built in 1500–13 for Rodrigo de Vivar y Mendoza, Marqués de Cenete (the legitimized son of Card. Mendoza) by *Lorenzo Vázquez*, and decorated within the Italian Renaissance style. Regrettably, it has since been gutted of much of its decoration.—After passing through the Llanos del Marquesado de Cenete, rich in minerals, we enter (14 km.) **Guadix** (see p.470), and thence follow Rte 55A to (55 km.) **Granada**, see Rte 58.

B   VIÂ MOTRIL

Total distance, 183 km. (113 miles). N 340. 53 km. *Adra*—59 km. *Motril*—N323. 71 km. **Granada**.

Leaving Almería behind us, we skirt the rock-bound coast to (11 km.) *Aguadulce* (*Hotels*), where a road leads S. towards *Roquetas de Mar* (15,100 inhab.; *Hotels*).—Climbing inland into the arid flat-topped Sierra de Gádor, we can reach the villages of *Enix* and *Félix*, both enjoying extensive views.—The N 340 strikes inland across the dreary Campo de Dalias to join the coast again before (42 km.) **Adra**, Phoenician *Abdera*, an ancient port (15,600 inhab.), with ruins of a Moorish castle.

From a point 3 km. short of Adra the C331 runs N. to (14 km.) *Berja*, with its lead mines and into LAS ALPUJARRAS, a hilly and previously a somewhat inaccessible district between the Sierra Nevada and the Sierra Contraviesa, whose beautiful and sometimes impressive valleys are rich in figs, oranges, lemons, and vines, and abound in mineral springs.

By the Treaty of Granada in 1492 the Alpujarras were assigned to Boabdil and his vanquished followers, but in 1499 the Moriscos were presented with the alternative of Christian baptism or exile. Eventually, after a desperate revolt, crushed by Don Juan of Austria in 1570, they were forcibly dispersed throughout Spain.

At 15 km. we turn l. onto the C 332, to approach (14 km.) the pleasant village of *Ugíjar*.—A difficult mountain road passing through magnificent scenery leads N. over the Sierra Nevada viâ the Pto. de la Ragua (E. of the Pto. del Lobo) from a point 6 km. E. of Ugíjar, to *La Calahorra*, see Rte 59A.

10 km. **Yegen** (2450 inhab.), the home of Gerald Brenan for some years before the Civil War and described well in 'South from Granada'. Among his visitors were Lytton Strachey, Carrington, Leonard and Virginia Woolf, Roger Fry, David Garnet, Bertrand Russell, and Augustus John.

The road continues to wind along the southern flank of the range through exotically named *Mecina Bombarón*; hence one may bear r. through *Berchules*, with extensive views to the S., or l., dropping down to *Cadiar*.

At 4 km. a mountain road (r.) leads 18 km. to **Trevélez**, (5600 ft; 1300 inhab.) renowned for its witches and snow-cured ham. and a starting-point for the ascent of Mulhacén from the S.E.

19 km. beyond, this is joined by a new road descending in zigzags round the sothern slopes of the massif, through the villages of *Capileira* and *Pampaneira*— supposedly repopulated by Gallegos—before climbing down to (30 km.) *Órgiva* (see below) 67 km. W. of Ugíjar.

Órgiva may also be approached by remaining on the N 332, which skirts the S. side of the valley of the Cardiar W. of Yegen.

From Adra the N 340 skirts the Mediterranean, its shores defended by ancient *atalayas* or watch-towers, viâ (16 km.) *La Rábita*, the resort of (21 km.) *Castell de Ferro*, and the fishing village of (10 km.) *Calahonda*, before entering (12 km.) **Motril** (35,400 inhab.; *Hotel*), some 2 km. from the sea, and a centre of the local wine and almond trade, and of the sugar industry. The collegiate church of *N.S. de la Encarnación* has a Gothic nave and Renaissance transeptal sanctuary. *N.S. de la Cabeza* is well sited.

From Motril to Málaga, see Rte 60B.

FROM LA RÁBITA TO LANJARÓN (62 km.). A beautiful mountain road (C 333) leads N.W. viâ (8 km.) *Albuñol* to (44 km.) *Órgiva*, after climbing in zigzags to the *Pto Camacho* (3690 ft). Crossing the Sierra Contraviesa, it commands a fine view of both the Sierra Nevada and the Mediterranean coast. In the *Cueva de los Murciélagos*, near Albuñol, important neolithic remains were discovered in 1857. **Órgiva** (5400 inhab.), picturesquely situated at 1370 ft overlooking the Guadalfeo and facing the Sierra Contraviesa, is a good starting-point for excursions into the Alpujarras. It has an interesting church and the fortified mansion of the Condes de Sástago.

10 km. to the W. lies **Lanjarón**, an attractive town (4100 inhab.) commanding fine views, with mineral springs and a ruined castle perched on a mountain shelf (2300 ft) below the Cerro del Caballo amid terraces of figs, oranges, peaches, and pomegranates. 7 km. beyond we meet the N 323 some 30 km. N. of Motril.

At Motril we climb inland on the N 323, through carnation plantations, and traversing the defiles of the Sierra de Lújar, we pass (12 km.) *Vélez de Benaudalla*, with a ruined castle. After crossing the Guadalfeo we ascend the lower slopes of the Sierra Nevada, where, at 18 km., the C 333 leads E. to *Lanjarón* (see above) and into the Alpujarras.

We now climb through the valley of Lecrin between *Dúrcal* and *Padul*, with its almonds, lemons, and oranges, called 'the happy valley' (*de la Alegria*) by the Moors, to reach the Puerto, 'El Ultimo Suspiro del Moro' (2840 ft), a hillock on the watershed between the Genil and the Mediterranean. Here, it is said, when Boabdil turned to take his last look at Granada, his mother reproached him with the words 'weep not like a woman for what you could not defend like a man'. We descend into the fertile vega, and approach the suburbs of (41 km.) **Granada**, see Rte 58.

60   FROM GRANADA TO MÁLAGA

A   Viâ Loja

Total distance, 126 km. (78 miles). 52 km. *Loja*—N 321. 74 km. **Málaga.**

The road (N 342), from which we get a fine view of Granada behind us outlined against the Sierra Nevada, soon by-passes (10 km.) the suburb of **Santa Fé** (10,750 inhab.), the original settlement built (it is said) within eighty days, by Fernando and Isabel while besieging Granada. Some town walls still stand, with three of their four gates surmounted by chapels.

Here the capitulation was signed in Nov 1491, and here in the following April, Isabel made the agreement with Columbus before his first voyage to America. The carving of a lance and a sheet of parchment with the words 'Ave Maria' over the door of the church (1773) is an allusion to the chivalrous story of Hérnan Perez del Pulgar, see p.493.

Not far to the N. lie two estates, each of c. 1,800 hectares, granted by the Cortes (from the confiscated property of Godoy) to the Duke of Wellington after the victory of Salamanca. One, *Soto de Roma,* had been owned previously by Ricardo Wall, the famous minister (of Irish origin) of Fernando VI and Carlos III, and included part of the village of *Fuente Vaqueros,* birthplace of the poet Federico García Lorca (1895–1936), who, it is supposed, was murdered at *Fuente Grande,* near *Viznar* (p.470), 7 km. N. of Granada. In 1933–43 almost all of this estate, having been let to smallholders, was sold to them at a very low figure; the other property, called *Molino del Rey,* is still in the possession of the family, and lies to the N.W. near *Illora,* beneath the bleak wall of the Sierra de Parapanda.

At 12 km. we pass *Láchar,* with the curious but neglected castle-palace of the Duque de San Pedro de Galantino, containing a number of horse-shoe arches.

At 11 km. the C 335 leads N. for 25 km. to picturesque **Montefrío** (10,300 inhab.) with an abandoned church of the type of the Cap. Real (Granada), designed by *Diego de Siloée* (1543-72).

19 km. **Loja** (22,200 inhab.), now of no great interest, was once of military importance as the key of Granada, guarding the entrance to the vega, but was taken in 1488 by Fernando and Isabel, aided by the English archers of Sir Edw. Woodville. Gen. Narváez (1800–68), the rival of Espartero, was a native of Loja. The town is dominated by the walls of the ruined Moorish *Alcazaba.* The *Iglesia Mayor (Sta Maria;* early 16C) is built on the site of the mosque, while *S. Gabriel* (1522–66), from designs by *Siloée,* has a fine artesonado roof.

To the E. is the gorge of Los Infiernos de Loja, which frets the Genil, while to the N.W. lies the Embalse de Iznajar.

The *old* road to Málaga forks l. shortly after Loja, towards the Pto. de los Alazores (3370 ft), but apart from offering plunging views of (77 km.) Málaga on its eventual descent, is not particularly recommended. The *new* road (N321) veers off to the l. at 15 km., to join the main road from Antequera to Málaga at (28 km.) the Pto de las Pedrizas. For the road thence to (31 km.) Málaga see p.537; and for **Málaga** itself, Rte 61.

B   Viâ Alhama

Total distance, 136 km. (84 miles). 54 km. *Alhama*—52 km. *Vélez Málaga*—30 km. **Málaga.**

We fork r. off the Motril road (N 323) 5 km. S. of Granada onto the C 340 and cross the vega towards the S.W., viâ *Gabia la Grande* (see p.498). Beyond (12 km.) *Mulá* we reach the mountains, passing (25 km.) the Pantano de Bermejales.—12 km. **Alhama de Granada** (7250 inhab.) picturesquely perched on a cliff high above the ravine of the foaming Marchan, was one of the keys of Granada, and its romantic capture in 1482 is the subject of a balled translated by Byron ('Ay! de mi Alhama'). The parish church (c. 1500–26) was built by *Pedro de Azpeitia* and *Enrique de Egas,* with a tower added by *Siloée.* The sacristy contains vestments said to have been embroidered by Isabel the Catholic.

Below the town are the *Baños de Alhama.* The *Baño de la Reina* may date from Roman times; the Moorish *Baño fuerte,* so called from the heat and strength of its water, has been incorporated into a hotel. At *Alhama Nuevo* is another spring that appeared after the earthquake of 1884, which devastated Alhama and the surrounding area. The posada at Alhama was condemned by Richard Ford as being 'truly iniquitous; diminutive indeed are the accommodations, colossal the inconveniences'.

At (18 km.) *Ventas de Zafarraya* we begin the descent through the Vélez valley to (34 km.) *Vélez Málaga,* see p. 504, and thence turn W. to (30 km.) **Málaga,** see Rte 61.

C   Viâ Motril.

Total distance, 177 km. (110 miles). N 323. 71 km. *Motril*—N 340. 23 km. *Almuñécar*—32 km. *Nerja*—21 km. *Vélez-Málaga* lies 4 km. N.)—30 km. **Málaga.**

Driving S. on the N 323 we follow the road to (71 km.) *Motril* described (in reverse) in Rte 59B. Here we turn W. onto the N 340, which traverses a region of rich southern vegetation, with sugar-cane, palms, and tropical plants. The coastal scenery, particularly between Almuñécar and Nerja, is impressive, the road climbing high above the shore commands some plunging views, but although many of the sharper turns are being modified, the road still demands careful driving, particularly in summer. As all the resorts on this stretch of coast contain numerous hotels of every category, their presence will be ignored in this route.

8 km. **Salobreña** (8200 inhab.) retains its Moorish *Castle* (restored), below which nestles the town, beyond which the road commences to climb.—15 km. *Almuñécar* (15,050 inhab.), the Phoenician *Sexi,* preserving Phoenician and Roman remains, known as the *Cueva de Siete Palacios,* and a ruined aqueduct, is a good example of a coastal resort ruined by unrestricted exploitation, and now offering little more than dirty beaches.

The road climbs steeply to its highest point in the Sierra Almijarra, with sheer cliffs towards the sea, before descending to (29 km.) *Maro.* Here a road leads shortly to the fine stalactite *Cueva de Nerja,* also containing palaeolithic paintings, while at 3 km. we enter the resort of **Nerja** (10,100 inhab.), its *Parador Nac.,* planned to overlook the bay from an isolated height, now being inexorably encroached upon by recent uncontrolled development.—6 km. inland, approached by a picturesque road, is *Frigiliana* (2200 inhab.), perched on its hillside, and with an orchid farm.—9 m. further W., and 4 km. inland, lies *Torrox* (9000 inhab.), of Roman origin, and probable birthplace of Almansor (940–1002) the scourge of the Christians.

At 21 km. a road leads 4 km. N. to **Vélez-Málaga** (38,000 inhab.), a centre for vine, and sugar-cane culture. It possesses the ruins of a Moorish castle; *Sta María* preserves considerable remains of a mosque, and *S. Juan Bautista* contains a jewelled chalice, and sculptures by *Pedro de Mena*. The sanctuary of *N.S. de los Remedios* (1640) is also of interest. The local gingerbread *(mostachón)* is worth trying. Here was born Joaquín Blake (1739–1827), a Spanish general of Irish descent, and a great loser of pitched battles during the Peninsular War.

The road hence to Málaga (30 km. to the W.) is now flanked by little less than a continuous chain of resorts each endeavouring to follow the examples set by Torremolinos, etc., and none offering any attraction other than a good climate. Eventually we gain glimpses of Málaga set against its mountain background, and enter its sprawling E. suburbs, including once-fashionable *La Caleta,* to reach the *Paseo del Parque* of **Málaga** itself: see below.

61   MÁLAGA

Most roads approaching Málaga eventually reach the umbrageous *Paseo del Parque,* skirting the inner harbour, which is conveniently near most sites of interest. There is an ambitious project to entirely by-pass the city from a point some 12 km. E., which circling to the N., will cross the Antequera road and form the first section of a motorway skirting the Costa del Sol.

MÁLAGA (408,450 inhab.; 150,000 in 1920; 275,000 in 1950; 361,000 in 1970; *Parador Nac.* and *Hotels*), with an important harbour, is well placed on its bay, surrounded by luxuriant sub-tropical vegetation and backed by a semi-circle of sunny hills. The chief products of its fertile vega are muscatel grapes, exported mainly as raisins or in the form of Malaga wine, oranges, lemons, prickly pears, sweet potatoes, custard-apples, and other fruit and vegetables; and sugar-cane, whose successful growth is assured by the entire absence of frost. The town is divided by the seasonal torrent of the Guadalmedina (i.e. 'river of the city'), which is now regulated by the Agujero dam to prevent inundations.

With a delightful climate, which is its main attraction, Málaga has long been the haunt of valetudinarians, and a Winter resort with a character of its own, while during recent years the mushroom growth of the town and the nearby resorts on the Costa del Sol have brought increased material prosperity to the area.

There have been strictures with regard to its inhabitants, who even two centuries ago were condemned, by Francis Carter who had lived there some years, for their 'love of dissipation', and 'as their traffic is lucrative, and their property extensive, each seems to vie with his neighbour in show and expence, and every one endeavours to move and maintain himself in a sphere above him: the mechanic appears a tradesman; the shop-keeper, a merchant; and the merchants, nobles'.

Townsend, when he visited Málaga in 1787, was told that the heat in summer was such that the inhabitants remained indoors until the evening, but after dark the young people would bathe for hours in the sea, but the sexes strictly segregated. To prevent intrusion, the girls were guarded by sentinels with loaded muskets, but nevertheless, the determined would go disguised as a female attendant, and in that character pass unobserved!

It was later a depot for delinquents or *'presidarios'*, who on their return after imprisonment on the African shore, were let loose on the town, which in the opinion of William Mark, the British Consul there in the early 19C, gave it a good claim to be entitled the sink of Spain in respect of vice and the almost total demoralization of the lower classes.

As early as the 1840s it claimed to have an ultra-civilized hotel, owned by a Mr Hodgson, where pale ale and Stilton cheese might be had for the asking. Here, wrote Ford, the bells which were hung would 'ring the knell of nationality'...while vague rumours were abroad that 'secret and solitary closets are contemplated, in which, by some magical mechanism, sudden waters are to gush forth...'. By 1850 there were c. 120 permanent English residents in Málaga, many engaged in the wine trade, and it was visited by some 300 English travellers annually, a number wintering there. Augustus Hare considered it the dearest place in Spain, being the most Anglicised.

AIR SERVICES from *El Rompedizo* airport; REGULAR STEAMERS to the Canaries, etc.

History. The Phoenician foundation of *Malaca* is attested by Strabo, but the city transferred its allegiance from Tyre to Carthage, and again, on the victorious advances of Scipio, it made terms with the rising power and became a Roman municipium. Although harassed by the barbarian invasions, it maintained a brisk trade with Byzantium and was the see of a bishop before the arrival of the Moors. After the battle of Guadalete (711) it fell to Tariq. under whose successors it flourished as the principal port of Granada, and Arab georaphers vied with each other in lauding it as an earthly paradise. It fell to Fernando the Catholic in 1487 after a dreadful siege followed by wholesale confiscation and autos-da-fé, and it lost much of its properity with the expulsion of the Moriscos after the insurrection of 1568.

In 1810 it was taken by Sebastiani, and in 1831 it was the scene of the unsuccessful rising of Gen. Torrijos, who, with his 52 companions was captured at Alhaurin, and executed by the absolutist governor, Gen. Moreno. The Liberal proclivities of the town showed themselves again in 1868 and 1873 in insurrection against the central government, while in 1931 Málaga was a Republican stronghold, and remained so until its capture by Nationalist forces in 1937. Both in 1931 and 1936 extremists pillaged and burnt its convents and churches.

Among Malagueños were the Jewish philosopher Ibn Gabirol (Avicebron; c. 1021–c.1057); while the Moorish poet Ar-Rusafi died here in 1177; Serafín Estébañez Calderon (1799–1867), author of many descriptions of Andalucian types and customs (a 'Costumbrista'); Andrés Borrego (1802–91), the historian and journalist; the statesman Antonio Cánovas del Castillo (1828–97); Pablo Ruiz Picasso (1881–1973), the artist, at Pl. de Merced 6; and the poets Emilio Prados (1899–1962); and Manuel Altolaguirre (1905–59).

Between the *Paseo del Parque,* with its palm-trees, laid out on land reclaimed from the sea, and the *Paseo de la Alameda,* further W., is busy Pl. del Gen. Queipo de Llano, aswirl with traffic. Just beyond, the main thoroughfare of the older town, the C. Marqués de Larios, leads N. to the Pl. José Antonio. On its N. side stands the *Consulado* of 1782 by *J.M. Aldehuela,* with a pleasant patio and still preserving the important library of the Soc. Económia de Amigos del País. Adjacent is domed *Sto Cristo* (17C), containing the tomb of the sculptor Pedro de Mena (1628–88). Further N. is *Santos Martires,* begun for the Catholic Kings, with a tower of 1548, and 18C carvings by *Fernando Ortiz* in the Baroque interior. To the S.W. is *S. Juan,* with a tall tower, completed in 1598 but altered in 1770. The C. de S. Juan leads S. through part of the old town, many narrow streets of which are now closed to vehicles, to regain the Alameda at the Pta del Mar, no longer a gate. A few paces to the W. just N. of this junction, in the C. Atarazanas, and now built into the S. wall of the *Mercado,* erected on the site of the Moorish arsenal, is preserved a white marble horseshoe *Gateway,* built for Yusuf I (1333–54).

To the W. beyond the bridge across the Guadalmedina, works are in progress to extend the Alameda through the newer W. quarters to the by-pass.
The quarter of EL PERCHAL on the W. bank of the Guadalmedina, contains four churches of slight interest; *El Carmen* with a brick front; *S. Pedro* with Baroque details; Renaissance *Sto Domingo;* and *S. Pablo,* incorporating remains of c. 1500.

A short distance N. of the W. end of the Paseo del Parque, overlooking the Pl. Obispo, flanked by the *Bishop's Pal.* (with a Baroque front of 1772 by *José Bada,* and three patios), is the **Cathedral.** A nondescript building, mainly Corinthian in character, it was begun in 1528 by *Diego de Siloée* and continued by *Diego de Vergara the Elder* (from 1549) and *the Younger* (after 1588). Having been partially destroyed by an earthquake in 1680, it was completed in 1719, except for the façade, by *José Bada,* added in 1719–88.

The W. Front, adorned with Corinthian columns and coloured marble, is flanked by two towers, only one of which (domed) has been carried above the second storey, leaving the other an ugly stump.

Twiss considered the cathedral 'one of the handsomest and neatest in Spain', not an opinion unanimously supported. His contemporary, Carter, found its N. and S. entrances 'immensely heavy, ill-shaped, and void of beauty', while the interior prespective was 'obstructed by a heavy, massy stone choir'; indeed, it displayed a 'want of symmetry, and frequent deviation from the rules of architecture'.
The dark INTERIOR with its overcharged vaulting, is singularly ineffective, and the pictures in the chapels are of little interest, apart from the Virgin of the Rosary in the 3rd S. chapel, by *Alonso Cano.* The *Cap. de los Reyes* (S. of the ambulatory) contains a figure of the Virgin carried, it is said, by Fernando V in battle, on either side of which are statuettes of Fernando and Isabel (1681) by *José de Mora.* The *Coro,* begun by *Vergara the Younger* in 1592, was not completed until 1662. But far the best thing in the church is the **Silleria del Coro* (1592–1658), by various hands, working under *Luis Ortiz* and, later, *José Micael,* including figures by *Pedro de Mena* and *Alonso Cano.* The custodia and other contents of the treasury disappeared in 1936. The huge organ (1781–85, by Julian de la Orden), partly restored, is still half mute.

Just to the N. of the present edifice is the separate *Sagrario* (containing a Plateresque retablo by *Balmaseda),* incorporated into the N. wall of which is the worn Isabelline Portal of the Gothic church which formerly stood here, erected on the site of a mosque.

From this point we may follow the C. S. Agustín N.E. to (r.) the *Pal. de Buenavista,* or *de Luna,* built c. 1525–50, housing the **Museo Prov. de Bellas Artes.**

In a patio adjacent to that near the entrance are Roman mosaics from Cártama. The paintings include works by *Luis de Morales,* and *Luca Giordano; Ribera,* Martyrdom of St Bartholomew, and a St Francis de Asis attrib. to him; *Zurbarán,* St Benedict, and St Jerome; *Murillo,* S. Francis de Paula; *Antonio del Castillo,* Adoration; and *Pedro de Mena,* Apparition of the Virgin to St Anthony. The upper floor is devoted to a miscellaneous collection of 19C paintings, including *Sorolla,* and *Muñoz Degrain,* Picasso's master, among them his Basque drunkard. A very few early works by *Picasso* (c. 1895) are also on display.

Leaving the museum we turn r. past *Santiago* (17-18C), preserving a Mudéjar tower of 1490–1545, to reach the Pl. de la Merced, the church of which has been domolished. Hence we may turn S. along the C. de la Victoria towards the Alcazaba (see below).

This street leads N.E., passing (r.) an 18C. *Cap. de la Expiación* and *S. Lázaro,* built on the site of a leper hospital, with some gruesome murals in its crypt. Some distance beyond is *La Victoria* (1518; rebuilt in 1694).

La Victoria is supposedly erected on the site where Fernando pitched his tent at the siege of Málaga; and the iron-work of its rejas is said to have been wrought from chains struck off liberated Christian slaves.

The retablo is sculptured with scenes from the life of St Francis of Paula, founder of the Minims, and behind the high altar is a profusely decorated *camarín* of 1693–95 with a Mater Dolorosa by *Pedro de Mena.* In a crypt are tombs of the counts of Buenavista. The adjoining military hospital occupies the former conventual buildings.

Near the S. end of the C. de la Victoria, partially *built over,* are the slight remains of a Roman *Theatre.* At the end of the street is the *Customs House* or *Aduana* of 1788–1829, abutting the Paseo del Parque. Between the two is the entrance to the **Alcazaba,** once the citadel *(al-Kasba),* a huddle of ruins which has been rather too thoroughly 'restored', but which incorporates a number of Moorish gates. A pleasant climb brings one to the main buildings arranged around patios and gardens, in which a *Museo Arqueológico* has been installed. Among the somewhat miscellaneous collection of statuary, mosaics, azulejos, plasterwork, ceramics, etc. is a maquette showing the possible distribution of the original buildings.

The Alcazaba was connected by a double wall with the **Gibralfaro,** the castle which crowns the summit of the hill (550 ft) to the E., rebuilt by Yusuf 1 on the site of the Phoenician fortress, below which stands the *Parador Nac.* The name, *Jebel Faro* (mountain of the lighthouse) recalls the beacon it once bore. Zigzag walks through gardens climb up the S. slopes to the summit, which may also be ascended by road, whence a panoramic *View may be enjoyed.

At the E. end of the Paseo del Parque is the *Fuente de Neptuno,* said to have been presented to Charles V by the Republic of Genoa (1560), just beyond which is the *Hosp. Noble,* a seaman's hospital founded by Dr. Noble (1799–1861). an English physician who died at Málaga. Immediately behind it is the *Plaza de Toros,* with a *Museo.* The high-rise blocks recently erected just S. of this point have effectively blocked off much of the sea view from the centre. The lighthouse on the old *mole* commenced as early as 1588 and extended in 1900, commands a good view of the harbour, however.

Further E., on the N. side of the main road a few minutes walk beyond the Plaza de Toros is the *English Cemetery,** in the umbrageous centre of which now stands the small Anglican *Church of St. George's.*

This, the first Protestant cemetery in Spain, was founded in 1830 by the British consul, William Mark (1782–1849), who had lived in Málaga since 1816 and had been consul since 1824. One of the first graves in it was that of Capt. Robert Boyd, a partisan of Torrijos (see History). Previously, according to Ford, bodies of such heretics were buried upright in the sand below low water-mark, but the orthodox fishermen feared that their soles might become infected. David Roberts, the artist, who visited the cemetery in 1833, was 'captivated by the views' hence: he would be less captivated now!

The original walled enclosure, later much extended, contains some of the earlier graves, many embellished with shells. Among those buried in the cemetery, including four victims of World War II washed ashore on this coast, are Mr. Hodgson (see p.505), and in a common grave, 62 survivors from the German training-ship 'Gneisenau', which in 1900 sank outside Málaga harbour.

It may be convenient to list here all the other British Cemeteries in mainland Spain, which have been laid out since in a number of unlikely places. With certain exceptions they have not been visited by the Editor, but some may contain sepulchral monuments of interest. They are listed in approx. date order, but do not include the battle sites of the War of the Spanish Succession, the Peninsular War (in which some 40,000 British dead were buried where they fell), and the First Carlist War (of which the plot on the N. slope of Mte Urgull at San Sebastián survives): *Cádiz* (1832); *Cartagena* (1846); *Valencia* (1849); *Tarragona* (1850); *Madrid* (1853); *Alicante* (1854; transferred to a new plot in 1962); *Seville* (1855); *Pasajes de San Juan* (mid 19C); *Puerto de Santa María* (1866); *La Coruña* (1870); *Huelva* (1874); *Águilas* (1883?); *Villagarcía* (1914–18?); *Bilbao* (1929; but containing remains transferred from another site, including a grave dated 1806); *Almería* (1973). There are others at *Jerez de la Frontera* and *Linares*.

62   FROM MÁLAGA TO CÁDIZ

A   Viâ Algeciras.

Total distance, 263 km. (163 miles). N 340. 13 km. *Torremolinos*—16 km. *Fuengirola*—28 km. **Marbella**—26 km. *Estepona*—43 km. *San Roque*—13 km. *Algeciras*—22 km. *Tarifa*—(48 km. *Véjer de la Frontera*)—40 km. *San Fernando*—14 km. **Cádiz**.

This route traverses the **Costa del Sol**, a narrow coastal strip flanking the Mediterranean and sheltered by the Sierra Bermeja and its extensions, where the climate well justifies the name given to this region by its exploiters. Accessible only with difficulty as recently as 1930, this coast has become a popular holiday area in recent decades. With popularity, it has lost most of its individual charm, as newer and more sophisticated pleasures have supplanted the delights of remoteness. New hotels, restaurants, clubs, villas, marinas, 'estates', shops and blocks of flats continue to spring up every day. Motorists are warned against dust clouds blown from building sites and unfinished works, etc. when passing through the coastal resorts.

A motorway between Málaga to a point beyond Estepona is projected, which will run roughly parallel to the present coast road, but slightly further inland.

As every resort has numerous *Hotels* (besides a *Parador Nac.* at Torremolinos) of every category, their presence, as far as Gibraltar, will not be noted.

The N 340 leads S.W. from Málaga, skirting industrial and maritime districts, and crossing the Guadalhorce, passes the airport.—At 8 km. the C 344 to Coín and Ronda turns off to the W., see Rte 62B, p.514.

Better by-passed, **Torremolinos**—described by William Jacob in 1810 as 'a delightful village'—is now an overgrown and cosmopolitan purlieu of Málaga, with a beach crowded throughout the year. We pass a succession of similarly congested resorts strung out along the coast, once the quietest part of the region.

From (17 km. r.) *Benalmádena* (9000 inhab.), with a museum of Pre-Columbian art, a road climbs into the the Sierra de Mijas, but 'urbanización' and speculative development has also extended to the once unspoilt village of **Mijas** (11,300 inhab.; the subject of Ronald Fraser's study, 'The Pueblo', 1973), whose Republican mayor remained concealed in his own house for 30 years after the Civil War, as described in the same author's 'In Hiding'.

4 km. **Fuengirola** (25,000 inhab.)—also by-passed—the Phoenician *Suel*, with remains of an old castle, was originally a small fishing port lying beneath the sierra, and the scene of Gen. Blayney's disastrous expedition of 1810, who made his dispositions 'with the utmost contempt of military rules'. Several *atalayas*, which served to guard the coast from Algerine pirates, may still be seen as we approach the most fashionable part of the Costa del Sol, passing (16 km.) *Calahonda*, centred on (12 km.) **Marbella** (50,400 inhab.; 12,000 in 1960).

Francis Carter, who passed that way in 1773, remarked that although the town lay in an 'exceedingly pleasant' position, its inhabitants 'bear the character of an uncivil inhospitable people, many of them descendants of the moors, who still resent the ill-treatment of their forefathers'. Those who have gained from recent changes are no doubt now reconciled.

Still, where not built over, surrounded by orange groves and sugar plantations, the older town preserves a 15C palace and fragments of its walls.

Hence the C 337 climbs steeply through beautiful scenery to (9 km.) *Ojén*. Beyond to the W., is the *Refugio Nac.*—At 10 km. lies *Monda*, and 11 km. beyond, *Coín*, on the main Málaga-Ronda road, see Rte 62B.

6 km. We pass (l.) the sophisticated marina of *Puerto Banús*.

From (3 km.) *San Pedro de Alcántara*, with ruins of a Moorish castle, the C 339, an attractive but winding road offering extensive views, turns inland and climbs into the Sierra Bermeja to *Ronda*, 54 km. N.W., see p.514.—Just beyond San Pedro (l.) are remains of a Roman Villa destroyed by an earthquake in 365, and of a Visigothic basilica.

After 1 km. a minor road climbs inland 8 km. through a gorge to the village of *Benahavis*.—The coast road continues to (16 km.) **Estepona** (22,450 inhab.), once a quiet fishing port in the same luxuriant vega. We may see Gibraltar ahead.—At 6 km. a road climbs inland 14 km. to the picturesquely-sited hill-town of **Casares** (3650 inhab.).

Beyond (2 km.) the *Castillo de la Duquesa*, we enter the province of Cádiz. We cross the Guadiaro and run parallel to the coast near the fashionable *Sotogrande* development, to by-pass (35 km.) **San Roque** (20,200 inhab.), founded in 1704, and with an early 18C church, containing a good 18C organ (restored). It was the birthplace of Luis de Lacy (1775–1817), the Spanish general and Liberal martyr of Irish descent.

Rochfort Scott, writing in the 1830s, repeats an anecdote concerning some garrison wives who walked out to San Roque from Gibraltar wearing trousers, much to the astonishment of the locals; and the famous bandit José Maria robbed one fair wearer of such inexpressibles merely to show his wife, and make her laugh!
Here the road divides: that towards Gibraltar bears l. viâ (6 km.) **La Linea** (*de la Concepción*; 53,900 inhab.), long a 'frontier-town' trafficking with Gibraltar, and a favourite resort of sailors. It was once fortified, but only the ruins of the castles of *S. Felipe* and *Sta Bárbara*, erected by Philip V in 1731, remain to guard either shore. They were dismantled by the British in 1810 at the request of the Spanish to make them untenable by the French. Beyond is the Spanish Customs Station, and the *Neutral Ground* on the isthmus, here c. 550 m. wide.

The physical appearance of the ***Rock of Gibraltar**, being such a conspicuous feature of the land and seascape, is described below, together with a brief historical summary, although the rock itself cannot yet (1979) be visited directly from the Spanish mainland, since the latest Spanish blockade commenced in June 1969.

History. *Calpe*, the Greek corruption of the Phoenicians' name for their trading-station on the rock of Gibraltar, was the northern bastion of the Pillars of Hercules in the Straits of Gibraltar, beyond which no other trader was allowed to venture until the decline of the Phoenician power. The rock bears the name of its Berber conqueror. Tariq ibn Zeyad, who landed here on April 30th, 711, and named the rock *Gebel Tarik*, the mountain of Tariq. Gibraltar was first taken from the Moors in 1309 by Guzmán el Bueno; they regained it in 1333; and it was finally captured for Spain by another Guzmán, Duke of Medina Sidonia, in 1462. In 1552 Charles V had the fortifications strengthened by the Milanese *Giambattista Calvi*, to protect it from from the raids of Barbarossa,the Moorish pirate.

On July 24th, 1704, during the War of the Spanish Succession, Sir George Rooke and Sir Clowdisley Shovell attacked the fortress suddenly and finding it with a garrison of only 150, took it in the name of the Archduke Charles of Austria, but hoisted the British flag. It was besieged by the French and Spanish in the following winter and again by the Spanish in 1727, but the Treaties of Utrecht (1715) and of Seville (1729) confirmed the British in its possession. The last and most famous siege of Gibraltar lasted from Aug. 1779 to Feb. 1783, when Gen. Eliott was governor. In a last great assault in Sept. 1782 the Spanish and French made use of floating batteries, which it was claimed, could neither be burnt, sunk, or taken, yet were totally annihilated by the British gunners who used red-hot shot. José Cadalso, the poet and satirist, was killed during the siege, a fortnight after being promoted colonel. Gibraltar palyed a passive part in both World Wars, but in 1939–45 the defences, especially underground, were enormously strengthened. 'The Rock of Contention', by George Hills, is a good historical study.

The **Rock**, rising to 1396 ft in the peak, known as *Highest Point*, is a mass of grey limestone with a few sandstone beds, heaved up by volcanic action at a comparatively recent epoch, a marine beach having been discovered 450 ft above sea-level. It is 4 km. long and slightly over 1 km. wide, and is separated from the mainland by a sandy isthmus, projecting off which is an airstrip. The N. and E. faces are precipitous, but elsewhere it descends in terraces to the sea. Gibraltar's supply of drinking-water depends largely on rainfall, and extensive catchment areas have been formed on the E. face, draining to reservoirs, with a capacity of 15 million gallons, hewn in solid rock. Its flora is surprisingly varied considering the barrenness of the rock, which is also inhabited by a small colony of Barbary apes, while rabbits and partridges abound. Apart from the garrison, the Jews, and Indians, etc., the indigenous population is a very mixed race, who have been engagingly stigmatized as 'Scorpions' by the Spanish and others who have had dealings with them. Indeed their selfish interest in fomenting the smuggling industry— with considerable connivance on both sides—has long been (and not without reason) a major cause of resentment on the part of the Spanish Government. To the latter, the Rock, symbolizing imperialist power and inviting uncomplimentary comparison, has always been a thorn in the flesh. No doubt the political and territorial issues at stake will be resolved eventually; but whatever the result, it must be admitted that apart from certain undeniably well-contrived features which will impress the military traveller, and the views obtained from its battle-scarred heights, the Rock of Gibraltar is singularly uninteresting.

The town itself faced Algeciras. The intervening bay which opens off the Strait of Gibraltar in a horseshoe between *Europa Point*, the S. extremity of the peninsula, and *Cabo Carnero*, in Spain, affords poor anchorage, being exposed to S.W. winds, but a commodious enclosed harbour was made at Gibraltar by the construction of huge moles. Few ships now proudly ride at anchor here, since fleets and flotillas have become superfluous.

The **Straits of Gibraltar**, the channel connecting the Mediterranean with the Atlantic, are only 9¼ miles (15 km.) wide at their narrowest, between the *Punta Marroqui*, S. of Tarifa, (see below), and the *Cuchillos de Siris*. The W. entrance between *Capes Trafalgar* and *Spartel*, is nearly 45 km. wide. The strong surface-current, setting in from the Atlantic at the average rate of 4 km. per hour, combined with the prevalence of N.W. winds, made navigation difficult in the day of sailing-vessels.

The PILLARS OF HERCULES—*Calpe* (*Gibraltar*) on the N., and *Abyle* (*Monte Hacho*, beside Ceuta) on the S.—fabled to have been raised by Hercules or Heracles on his expedition to seize the cattle of Geryon, were for ages the W. limit of the known world, beyond which lay the lost continent of Atlantis and the Islands of the Hesperides. Heracles, the tutelar of the Straits, was the Greek counterpart of the Phoenician deity Melkarth. The Romans do not appear to have ventured beyond the *Fretum Gaditanum* until the 2nd C. B.C. The Moorish name for the straits was *Bab ez-Zakak*—the narrow gate.

At 3 km. a road leads l. to **El Rocadillo**, a farm on the bank of the Guadar-ranque, marking the site of *Carteia*, originally an Iberian settlement, later colonized by the Greeks, and occupied by the Romans in 206 B.C. In 171 B.C. it was sacked by Scipio Africanus the Younger and re-peopled with the illegitimate descendants of Roman legionaries and Spanish women. Hither the younger Pompey fled after his defeat by Caesar at Munda (45 B.C.), but the ruins of the once important city, as described by Francis Carter in the 1770s, among others, long used a quarry for the building of San Roque, have almost disappeared.

At 5 km. the C 440 climbs N.W., crossing the Ptos. de la Cebada and del Judio to (50 km.) **Alcalá de los Gazules**, a picturesque town (6600 inhab.) of Moorish aspect, with a ruined fortress and 15C church tower studded with azulejos, and beyond to (24 km.) *Medina Sidonia*, see p. 512.

5 km. **Algeciras**, an ugly modern town (87,100 inhab.; 19,500 in 1920; *Hotels*) standing at the mouth of the Miel beneath the Sierra de los Gazules, although historically important, is without interest. The view of the Rock across the bay is impressive, however. There are some arches of a Moorish *aqueduct* a short distance inland along the railway. During the winter of 1927–28 W.B. Yeats convalesced briefly at the *Reina Cristina Hotel*, one of the few relics of a more expansive era.

History. Algeciras, the Roman *Portus Albus*, was the 'Green Island' (*el Gezira el-Khadra*) of the Moors, whose name is preserved in the offshore *Isla Verde*. Its successful assault by Alfonso XI in 1344 was reckoned among the greatest achievements of Christian chivalry. Presence at the siege was a title to knightly fame, and Chaucer records of his knight that 'in Gernade at the sege eek hadde he be of Algezir' (Prol. 54, 55). In 1760 the town was rebuilt by Carlos III on a rectangular plan. Pomponius Mela (1st C. A.D.), the geographer, was born at Tingentera, on the bay of Algeciras.

From Algeciras the winding hilly road climbs S.W. through cork-woods, crossing the Guadalmecí and affording magnificent retrospective *views of Gibraltar and the African coast.

22 km. **Tarifa** (14,150 inhab.; *Hotels*), occupies the site of Punic *Josa* and Roman *Julia Traducta*, and is named after Tarif ibn Malik, leader of the first band of Moors despatched by Tariq to Spain in 711.

History. Tarifa, captured by Sancho el Valiente in 1292, was defended against counter-attacks by Alonso Pérez de Guzmán. On the Moorish side was the traitor Infante Don Juan, brother of Sancho, to whom Guzmán's young son had been entrusted as a page. Juan brought the boy beneath the walls and threatened to kill him if Tarifa was not forthwith surrendered. Guzmán contemptuously tossed him a dagger and withdrew, preferring 'honour without a son, to a son with dishonour'. On hearing the cry of horror from the battlements when the boy was murdered, Guzmán stoically observed: 'I feared that the infidel had gained the city'. The king honoured him with the surname 'el Bueno', and he became the founder of the ducal house of Medina Sidonia.

In 1811 Gen. Campbell defended Tarifa against the superior forces of Victor, until relieved by Gough and the 87th, who beat back the French in a single night.

Tarifa retains portions of crumbling Moorish walls pierced by horseshoe gateways, surrounding its narrow winding lanes. Between the town and the sea is the Alameda; the Moorish *Alcázar* lies E., but the *Torre de Guzmán* is more modern than the tower from which the hero threw down his dagger. The *Castillo*, parts of which may be visited, affords good views from the wall-walks. A Cufic inscription records the building of the Moorish fortress in 950–60. The church of *S. Mateo*, built in the site of a mosque, has blocked 15C windows, quaint gargoyles, and a Baroque W. Front, and contains a Visigothic tablet dated 674 found some few kms away.

The peninsula S. of Tarifa ends at the *Punta Marroquí*, the southern extremity of Spain (36° N.), off which Adm. Saumarez defeated a French and Spanish squadron under Linois in 1801.

The road beyond Tarifa keeps near the sea, affording a good view of the Moroccan coast backed by the peaks of Atlas, before bearing inland through attractive country.—At 15 km. a road leads W. to the coast, sheltered by Cabo Camarinal, where lie the extensive ruins of the Roman town of *Belo* or *Bolonia* retaining temple and remains of a theatre.—We cross a marshy plain where Wallia the Visigoth defeated the Vandals in 417, driving them thence into Africa, and where Alfonso XI crushed the united armies of Yusuf I of Granada and Abul-Hassan of Fez in 1340. This battle saw the first cannon ever used in Europe, brought from Damascus by the Moors.—At 15 km. a road leads 11 km. W. to the fishing village of *Zahara de los Atunes* (2850 inhab.; *Hotel*). A little inland from the drained *Laguna de la Janda*, Tariq first encountered Roderic (711), and began the campaign which ended in the disaster of the Guadalete, see. p.563. At 18 km. we pass below (l.) the white Moorish-looking hill-town of **Véjer de la Frontera**, (13,500 inhab.), with a partially restored castle, Gothic church with a good rose-window, and an abandoned *Conv. de las Monjas*, which may have been built on the site of a Roman temple.

Just short of the ascent to Véjer, a road turns l. for (9 km. S.) *Barbate de Franco*, with ruins of a castle on the shore; while further W. along the coast, and 14 km. S.W. of Véjer, reached by a poor road, is **Cape Trafalgar** (*Tarif al-Ghar*, cape of the cave), the sandy bluff off which on Oct 21st, 1805, Nelson, with 27 ships of the line and 4 frigates, beat the allied French and Spanish fleet (33 ships of the line and 7 frigates) under Villeneuve and Gravina. Both the British and the Spanish commanders were mortally wounded.

20 km. N.E. of Véjer lies *Casas Viejas*, where an anarchist rising took place in 1933, some 8 km. S.E. of which is a gorge called *Tajo de las Figuras*, with caves containing prehistoric paintings of the Altamira type.—Some 5 km. beyond lie the romantic ruins of the Carmelite convent of *S. José de el Cuervo* (1713–70), abandoned in 1835.

At 16 km. a road leads to the tunny-fishing port of **Conil** (3 km. S.W., 11,900 inhab.; *Hotel*), with two medieval castles.—16 km. **Chiclana de la Frontera**, (31,900 inhab.; *Hotel*). On the r. is the knoll of *Barrosa* where Gen. Graham defeated the French under Victor in March, 1811.—The beach of *Sancti Petri*, 8 km. W. of Chiclana, is protected by the island of Farallón Grande, on which are remains of a castle built in the 13C on the ruins of a classical temple.

From Chiclana the C 346 leads E. 22 km. to **Medina Sidonia**, Roman *Asido*, a well-situated but decaying town (14,600 inhab.), once the chief seat of the Guzmán family, dukes of Medina Sidonia. The seventh duke (1550–1615) was commander-in-chief of the Invincible Armada. Leonor de Guzmán, mistress of Alfonso XI and mother of Enrique de Trastamara, fled here from the fury of Alfonso's son, Pedro the Cruel; and here in 1361 Pedro put to death his own wife, Blanche of Bourbon.

The town retains part of its rampart wall, and the Moorish *Arco de la Pastora*, a Ducal *Palace*, and Renaissance *Ayuntamiento*. 15C *Sta María*, with a good doorway and a tower completed by *Agustín de Arguello* in 1623, has a Retablo carved *J. B. Vázquez* (1575); *Santiago el Mayor* is of the 16C. Ford hardly considered it worth visiting, for it was like so many such hill-fort towns which, 'glittering in the bright sun. . .appear in the enchantment-lending distance to be a fairy residence', but which were in reality 'dens of dirt, ruin, and poverty': and in many cases the same stricture applies today..—37 km. N. lies *Arcos de la Frontera* (see Rte 62B); 36 km. N.W., *Jerez de la Frontera* (see Rte 69), and 24 km. to the E., *Alcalá de los Gazules*, see p.511.

We cross the Caño de Sancti Petri (see below) and meet the Seville road circling the Bay of Cádiz. Here we turn l., and cross onto the ISLA DE LEÓN. On both sides are seen pyramids of salt, obtained by evaporation from the winding creeks of the marsh. Juan van Halen (1788–1864), the Liberal general and adventurer, was born on the island.

The **Isla de León**, granted in 1459 to the Ponce de León family but resumed by the Crown in 1484, includes a larger S. portion, on which stands *San Fernando*, and the rocky peninsula of Cádiz to the N., together with the isthmus that unites them. The road from Algeciras to San Fernando crosses the Caño de Sancti Petri by the *Pte. Zuazo*, reputed to have been originally a bridge-aqueduct built by Cornelius Balbus the Younger of Cádiz, but destroyed by the Moors in 1262 and restored or rebuilt by Sánchez de Zuazo in the 15C. Near the bridge stands the modernized *Castillo de S. Romualdo*, built by Moorish engineers for Alfonso XI in 1325–28, and of interest for its regular rectangular plan and heavy square towers. The Isla de León was the legendary pasture of the red cattle of Geryon, which were stolen by Hercules; and at *Torregorda*, at the beginning of the isthmus, stood a celebrated temple of the Phoenician Hercules.

8 km. **San Fernando** (62,650 inhab.; *Hotel*), a headquarters of the Spanish Naval authorities, was founded in 1776, and contains an *Observatory* of 1793, while the *Ayuntamiento* is by *Torcuato Cayón*. In the *Teatro de las Cortes* the Cortes Constitucionales held their first meeting in 1810. It was the birthplace of Francisco Serrano (1810–85), general and politician.

The town shared the name of *Isla de León* until 1813, when in honour of the heroic resistance by the Spanish army in 1810–12, under the command of Diego Alvear y Ponce de León, to the French assaults on Cádiz, it was re-christened San Fernando.

To the N.E. lies the arsenal of *La Carraca*, founded in 1790. Passing (l.) the watch-tower of Torregorda (see above) the road follows the narrow sandy isthmus which is the land approach to Cádiz. To the l. stands the Fort of *Cortadura*; on the r., beyond the Fort of *Puntales*, appears the peninsula of Trocadero, from which the direct road from Seville crosses the Bay of Cádiz by the new bridge (1971). We enter the extensive outer suburbs of modern Cádiz, passing (r.) domed *S. José* (1783), and soon reach the old fortifications of 1639, improved in 1755 under *Torcuato Cayón*.—14 km. **Cádiz**, see Rte 70.

B   VIÂ RONDA.

Total distance, 248 km.—(154 miles). N 340 for 8 km.—C 344. 29 km. *Coín*—65 km. **Ronda**—C 339 for 40 km.—N 342. 44 km. *Arcos de la Frontera*—31 km. **Jerez de la Frontera**—N 1V. 31 km. **Cádiz**.

The direct road (C 344) turns r. off the N 340 8 km. S.W. of Málaga, passing *Churriana*, with the luxuriant *Hacienda de la Consula*, and (22 km.) *Alhaurín el Grande*, set amid orange and lemon groves, and noted for its marble quarries, to enter (7 km.) **Coín**(21,100 inhab.), with similar quarries. Hence the C 337 leads S. to *Ojén* before decending to *Marbella*, see Rte 62A—Beyond Coín the road continues to climb into the Serranía de Ronda viâ *El Burgo*, reaching at 65 km., *Ronda* itself, see below.

VIÂ THE GARGANTA DEL CHORRO (112 km.) This alternative and slightly longer route leads directly W. from Málaga, following the N. bank of the Guadalhorce. At 17 km. we pass, 3 km. S. on the far bank of the river, once navigable up to this point, *Cártama* (10,100 inhab.), Roman *Cartima*, with a ruined Moorish castle. Carter remarked that its ancient remains had been barbarously treated, and Roman statuary had been 'jammed into the walls of houses to keep off carts'.

At 13 km., *Pizarra*, a road forks l. and ascends past *Casarabonela* to join the C 344 at *El Burgo*, 20 km. N.W. of Coín.—At Pizarra, we continue N. to (7 km.) **Alora** (14,300 inhab.) perched above the river, famous for its manzanilla olives, oranges and lemons. It possesses a ruined castle converted into a cemetery, rising on a twin peak. The parish church of 1600 has a wooden roof supported by cylindrical columns.—We bear l. and follow the W. bank of the Guadalhorce through a luxuriant sub-tropical valley where the characteristic vegetation includes olives, oranges, and palm trees, with thick hedges of prickly pear and aloe, before entering (14 km.) the S. end of the *Garganta del Chorro.

This magnificent defile, through which the Guadalhorce forces its way to the sea, and through which the railway is carried in a series of 15 tunnels and 6 viaducts, affords some striking scenery.

Just beyond its N. end a l.-hand turning climbs up into the still remote *Mesa de Villaverde*, off which, by clambering down an unsignposted path to the l. we may approach the remains of the basilical Mozarabic *Church* of **Bobastro**, cut into the sandstone rock, with a curious sanctuary of horseshoe plan (c. 898–917). The road continues to climb past the high-lying reservoir supplying the hydro-electric works below the garganta, and c. 1 km. beyond comes to an abrupt halt. On the summit to the r. are the slight remains of the fortress founded in 884 by Omar Ibn Hafsun (Views).

Regaining the main road, we turn l. and shortly climb above the Embalse de Guadalhorce (Views) to reach *Ardales*, attractively sited, and bear N.W. to meet the C341 after 11 km., near *Teba* (see p.536).

We now ascend the valley of the Guadateba, with a distant view of *Cañete la Real* perched on the flank of a range of hills to the r., and shortly after meeting the C 344 from El Burgo (see above) enter (61 km.) *Ronda*.

RONDA (2450 ft; 30,050 inhab.; *Hotels*), one of the most romantic and picturesquely-sited towns of Spain, is famous for the mountains views it commands and for its extraordinary *Tajo*. It stands, surrounded by an amphitheatre of limestone hills, on a rocky bluff or shelf whose sheer walls fall on three sides to a depth of 400 ft,while in the midst of the town itself the vertiginous gorge of the *Guadalevin* (called *Guadiaro* lower down), a stupendous rent 250–300 ft wide, separates the old Moorish *Ciudad* from the new quarter of the *Mercadillo*, founded by the Christians after the reconquest. Below the Ciudad, on the S., is the *Barrio de S. Francisco*.

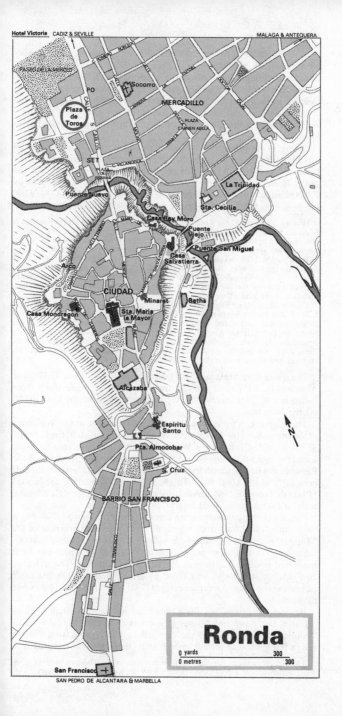

In the Serranía de Ronda the wild goat (*capra pyrenaica*) is preserved, while to the S.E. are the groves of a rare species of pine *(Abies pinsapo)*, unique examples in Europe of this prehistoric tree. Ronda is also famed for its fruit, especially cherries, peaches, and apples. The Rondeños of today are the descendants of the most redoubtable smugglers of the Andalucían hills, and though they have lost their unenviable notoriety as masters of knife-play they maintain their reputation as horse-breeders.

Owing to its proximity to Gibraltar, Ronda was often visited by officers of the garrison—it was a salubrious summer residence for their families—and by English tourists during the 19C and since, but the *Hotel Reina Victoria* (1906), once British-owned, no longer retains its Edwardian atmosphere. Momentos of Rainer Maria Rilke (1875–1926), the poet who was one of its more famous guests, are preserved.

History. Some probably Roman substructures, discovered in the foundations of Moorish buildings, may represent Roman *Munda,* on the site of Celtic *Arunda;* but the present town owes its importance to the Moors. Thanks to its almost impregnable position, Ronda remained the capital of an isolated Moorish kingdom until 1485, when it was surprised by a secret march on the part of Fernando the Catholic; the siege was the first occasion on which Spanish artillery used metal cannon-balls. The Maestranza, or Corporation of Knights, formed here in 1493 for the supervision of bull-fighting. became the model for later societies of the kind all over Spain.

Vicente Martínez de Espinel (1550–1624), musician and poet, and author of the Life of Marcos de Obregón, who is alleged to have invented the ten-syllable line called 'espinela', and added the fifth string to the guitar, was born in Ronda, as was Francisco Giner de los Ríos (1839–1915) the educationalist and founder of the *Institucion Libre de Enseñanza.* Pedro Romero's name is inseparable from the Plaza de Toros, and this great 18C matador is credited with the invention of the classical bull-fighting style of the School of Ronda.

The roads from Málaga (C 344), San Pedro de Alcántara (C 339) and Algeciras (C 341) enter the old town from the S.; while those from Antequera (C 341) and Seville (C 339) approach the centre from the N. viâ the Mercadillo.

The *Alameda,* a pleasant garden completed in 1806 at the N.W. edge of the town above the Guadalevin, commands a fine view of the *Cerro de S. Cristóbal* (5420 ft) to the W., where vultures may be seen hovering over the vega on the look-out for carrion. Some 500 prisoners of the Republicans (led by a mob from Málaga) were thrown alive over the cliff here early in the Civil War. To the S. of the Alameda is the elegant *Plaza de Toros, of 1784, second oldest in Spain after that of Seville, and with an exceptionally wide ring of 66 m. diameter.

Passing the *Ayuntamiento* we come to the **Pte. Nuevo** (1740–88), a single span of 33.5 m. from which we have the finest prospect of the *Tajo or Gorge of the Guadalevin, with the river foaming along its rocky refuse-choked bed 90 m below, the main stream of which has been harnessed to drive the turbines of a small power-station. The architect, *José Martín Aldehuela,* was killed by falling from the parapet while inspecting the work. An earlier bridge (1735) had collapsed, killing some fifty people.

Beyond the bridge lies the **Ciudad,** an intricate Moorish town of tortuous lanes and tiny houses with doors of walnut. We take the C. Tenorio (r.) which leads to the *Campillo,* a plaza (view) from which a rough track, forking almost immediately, descends into the gorge.

The branch on the r., passing the *Arco de Cristo,* a Moorish gateway of c. 1300, leads down to the *Upper Mill,* from which we have an extraordinary *View upwards of the Tajo and the Pte. Nuevo.—The path on the l. at the fork leads to the *Lower mills,* whence, crossing the river by stepping-stones, we may find our way downstream to a flight of steps ascending near the *Hot. Reina Victoria.* Or from the lower mills we may retrace our steps and take a path to the r., which ascends gently to the gateway between the Alcazaba and the Barrio de S. Francisco.

From the Campillo, the Ronda de Gameros leads to the *Casa de Mondragón,* whose two patios are decorated with moulded brick arches and glazed tiles. A gallery with a Moorish roof commands a plunging view of the valley. Further on, in the attractive Pl. de la Duquesa de Parcent, is the 16C hall-church of **Sta María la Mayor,** originally a mosque, of which the mihrab (13C) has been discovered. The church, with a high E. Transept, has an elegant tower (the ancient minaret), and contains a large retablo and Renaissance stalls. Further S. beyond the *Alcazaba,* blown up by the French in 1809, and *Espíritu Santo* (15C) is the suburb of S. Francisco, with the curious Moorish *Pta. de Almocobar.*

Returning to the Alcazaba, we follow the C. Méndez Núñez. Near the corner of the C. del Marqués de Salvatierra (r.) stands the minaret of the destroyed church of *S. Sebastián.* Nearby, at No. 6 C. del Gigante, are remains of a 14C Moorish house. Bearing r. we descend the hill towards the *Casa del Marqués de Salvatierra,* with a Renaissance façade. The curious figures supporting the pediment over the portal seem to show colonial influence.—Further down the hill we pass through a Renaissance archway to reach the *Pte. Viejo* (1616), built on Roman foundations, and the *Pte. S. Miguel.* Both bridges afford good views of the Tajo. By the river to the r. are remains of *Moorish Baths.* Keeping to the r. as we reascend the hill, we pass the so-called *Casa del Rey Moro,* built in 1709 on earlier foundations. From the terraced garden, which commands a fine view of the Tajo, the *Mina de Ronda,* a subterranean stair of 365 steps cut in the solid rock, climbs down to the river bed.

Two favourite excursions from Ronda may be made from a point 14 km. N.W., on the C 339. To the r. a bridle-path leads 7 km. to **Ronda la Vieja,** on the site of Roman *Acinipo,* with ruins including a theatre with a 'frons scenae' like that at Mérida, but the main attraction of the expedition is the fine mountain scenery.— From the same crossroad we may drive S. to visit the **Cueva de Gato,** a long stalactite cavern, which should be entered with caution, and at 15 km. beyond *Benaoján,* the *Cueva de la Pileta,* with palaeolithic rock-paintings of the Altamira type.

FROM RONDA TO ALGECIRAS (99 km.). We climb down from Ronda through olive groves and fruit trees by the C 341 to (38 km.) **Gaucin** (2500 inhab.), romantically situated on a cleft ridge; here Guzmán el Bueno was killed in 1309. Its Moorish castle commands a good View of Gibraltar, with Africa looming behind. Crossing the Guadiaro we enter (20 km.) **Jimena de la Frontera** (8600 inhab.), a white town standing on a hill above the Hozgarganta, at the foot of which is the sanctuary of *N.S. de los Ángeles,* with an ancient image. Its Moorish *castle,* captured in 1431, which dominates the town, is entered through a triple horseshoe-arched gateway in which Roman tombstones have been incorporated.—21 km. *Almoraima* has a 17C convent, 8 km. N.W. of which stands the extensive Moorish castle of **Castellar de la Frontera** with its village of white-washed houses.—We now descend through a region of cork-woods and soon traverse the Campo de Gibraltar, lying between the Sierra de Bermeja (l.) and the Sierra de los Gazules, at 10 km. meeting the N 340, Here we turn r., and 10 km. beyond, reach **Algeciras,** see Rte 62A.

Driving N.W. through the hills from Ronda by the C 339, we descend towards the valley of the Guadalete.

At 5 km. a mountain road ascends 10 km. W. to **Grazalema,** the ancient *Lacidula,* a small town of 2500 inhab., with a good Gothic church, and described by Ford as a 'cut-throat den. . .fastened like a martlet's nest on the face of a mountain'. It was the subject of Julian Pitt-Rivers' sociological study 'The People of the Sierra' (1954).—19 km. to the S.W. is *Benaocaz,* with a church tower possibly that of an earlier mosque, a Baroque Ayuntamiento, and ruined fortifications.—3 km. beyond lies **Ubrique** (14,750 inhab.) with the 'Virgen de la O' by *Jerón. Hernández* (1575) in its church. Its leatherwork is noted.—From above Grazalema, we descend to *El Bosque* (*Hotel*), also with a Gothic church, where the C 344 is regained, which leads 32 km. due W. to *Arcos de la Frontera,* see below.

We meet the N 324 37 km. N.W. of Ronda, near *Algonales,* after passing (15 km. l.) picturesque *Zahara de los Membrillos* ('of the Quinces'), perched below its ancient castle, once a Moorish stronghold, offering superb views.

23 km. N.E. of this junction, and reached by turning r. and following the N 324 through the Sierra de Algonales, lies **Olvera,** (11,800 inhab.), whose remote valley was once famous as a refuge for bandits and *'male gente'* generally, so that the proverb was coined *'mata al hombre y vete a Olvera',* i.e. 'kill your man and fly to Olvera'. In the darkest recesses of a posada here, George Cayley, in 1851, encountered a Cambridge friend on honeymoon, with his wife romantically disguised as a younger brother, and they had thus ridden all the way from Cartagena! Here an imposing church, and remains of a Moorish castle dominate the town from a rocky crag. The nearby village of *Torre-Alhaquime* is perched equally precipitously.—**Setenil,** on a rough road between Ronda and Olvera (and 12 km. S.E. of the latter), is one of the more curious villages in the area, many of its troglodyte dwellings huddled beneath impending rocks. The diminutive 'old' *Ayuntamiento* has an artesonado ceiling; ask for the key at the new Ayuntamiento. Isabel the Catholic gave birth to a child at Setenil during the siege of Ronda.

We turn W. towards (33 km.) **Villamartín** (12,500 inhab.) noted for a wine called *'pajarete',* and cross the Embalse de Bornos. A road leads 26 km. N.W. to meet the N IV 45 km. S. of Seville. We pass *Bornos* (7600 inhab.), on the N. bank of the reservoir, a summer-resort, clustering round a Moorish castle and two monasteries.

21 km. **Arcos de la Frontera** (*Parador Nac.*), an attractive steep-streeted town (25,100 inhab.), of Iberian foundation on a sharp ridge above a loop of the Guadalete, was known to the Romans as *Arcobriga,* and as *Medina Arkosh* to the Moors, who were dislodged from this almost impregnable stronghold by Alfonso el Sabio in 1264. A colony of English officers of the 99th Regiment of Foot were confined here on parole for three months in 1780, after the capture of a naval convoy, as described by Richard Croker.

From the Ronda road the C. del Generalísimo climbs past the former *Conv. de S. Francisco* (17C) and the *Hosp. de S. Juan de Dios* (c. 1600). We continue past the *Pal. de Águila,* with an Isabelline Mudejar front to the fortified *Pal. of the Dukes of Osuna* in a small plaza to the r. Here stands *Sta María de la Asunción,* with a good W. Front of the time of the Catholic Kings and an unfinished tower (1758) by *Vic. Bengoechea.* A hall-church with star vaulting, it displays 15C wall-paintings, a retablo mayor by *Jerónimo Hernández* (1586), and stalls of 1734–44. Opposite the S. Door is the *Ayuntamiento* with a Mudéjar artesonado, once part of the adjoining *Castle.* A mirador to the E. commands a glorious *View over the *'tajo'* above the Guadalete, where we may see numerous lesser kestrels (*Falco naumanni*) wheeling above the vertiginous cliff. Adjoining is the *Parador.* The former *Hosp. de la Encarnación* (1529), N. of Sta María, has a late-Gothic portal.

Continuing up the main street we pass the Isabelline front of the *Misericordia* chapel, founded in 1490, to reach **S. Pedro,** built at the edge of the cliff on the site of the Moorish fortress. This church has an important retablo (1539–42) by *Fernando Sturm* and others, and paintings by *Zurbarán* and *Pacheco*.

Retracing our steps, we turn sharply downhill by the picturesque Cuesta del Socorro, passing *S. Agustín* (closed), having on our l. a second cliff (Peña Vieja) plunging down to the N. loop of the river. Continuing our descent, we pass through the old *East Gate*, beyond which, in the Pl. de la Caridad, is the *Asilo de la Caridad*, a delightful Baroque work of 1740–64, with good brick detail and a pretty patio.

From Arcos we follow the N 342 across the Llanos de Caulina, through vineyards and olive groves, passing (20 km., r.) the Moorish *Torre de Melgarejo,* reconstructed in the 14C, and at 11 km. enter *Jerez de la Frontera,* see Rte 69. Hence we may drive S.W. to (31 km.) **Cádiz,** see Rte 70.

63   FROM GRANADA TO SEVILLE

A   Viâ Osuna

Total distance, 258 km. (160 miles.). N 342. 52 km. *Loja*—47 km. **Antequera**—N334. 72 km. **Osuna**—87 km. **Seville**.

From Granada to *Loja,* see Rte 60A, p.502, beyond which we leave the Málaga road on our l. and follow the N 342 to (14 km.) **Archidona** (by-passed), a town of 10,200 inhab. on the slope of a curiously shaped mountain. Buildings of interest include the *Col. de Escolapios* and *Sto Domingo*, while its small octagonal *Plaza*, often overlooked, deserves a visit.—We soon cross the Guadalhorce in a pleasant valley studded with white farmhouses, and approach the conspicuous *Peña de los Enamorados*.

From this abrupt rock a Moorish maiden and a Christian knight hurled themselves, it is said, to escape from the pursuing vassals of her father, as told in Southey's balled of 'Leila and Manuel'.

23 km. **Antequera,** see Rte 66. We now turn N.W. onto the N 334.— After 7 km. a continuation of the N 342 bears W. to (25 km.) *Campillos*, beyond which the road will eventually lead to *Olvera* (see p. 518), *Arcos,* and *Jerez,* but see Rte 62B.—We pass (25 km.) *La Roda de Andalucía*, and (3 km. r.) *Casariche*, with Roman mosaics, before entering (16 km.) **Estepa** (9400 inhab.), Iberian *Astapa* or *Ostippo*, whose natives rivalled the Numantians in their stubborn resistance to the Romans in 207 B.C. It contains the interesting churches of *Sta María* (Gothic), *La Asunción* (early 17C), *El Carmen*, and the Baroque *Pal. de los Cerverales*; while its *Castle* commands a wide view. It is also known for its confections called *polverones* or *mantecados*.

We pass through (12 km.) *Aguadulce,* named from its 'sweet waters', which create an oasis in a saline wilderness, before entering (12 km.) *Osuna*.

OSUNA (19,000 inhab.), famous for its carnations, which once covered the slope of its hill, retains a number of attractive streets and imposing old mansions. It was the *Urso* of the Romans, honoured with the title of *Colonia Gemina Urbanorum* when it was garrisoned by two legions from Rome itself. The Moorsn who called it *Ushuna*, lost it to Fernando III in 1240. Swinburne somewhat unfairly condemned it as 'a large stinking town'. In fact it is now one of the most *un*-spoilt towns of its size in Andalucía, and well deserves exploration.

In the town centre is the PL. DE ESPAÑA, with the Ayuntamiento, partially but soberly modernized, to the N. of which is the *Market,* with its patios. Continuing N., we pass (r.) *Sto Domingo* (1531), with Renaissance and Baroque retablos, beyond which is the *Audiencia*, with a Doric patio, and opposite, *N.S. de la Victoria* (1584), with a tall steeple. A few steps beyond is the *Arco de la Pastora* (late 18C). Opposite Sto Domingo is the *C. S. PEDRO, retaining a number of imposing Baroque mansions, including the *Pal. de Gomera*, and the *Cabildo Colegial* (1775). In the C. José Antonio, two streets to the S., is the *Pal. de Puerto Hermoso* or *Juzgado*, with its Salomonic columns, the convent of *Sta Caltalina* (16C, containing 18C dados), and the steeple of *S. Carlos el Real* (1664).

Returning to the Pl. de España (just S. of which in the C. Calvo Sotelo, is the *Pal. de los Cepedas*) we may continue E., ascending past (r.) the *Torre Cartigines*, containing a small but interesting *Archaeological museum*, largely a collection of Roman and Visigothic carvings and sculpture; also three Iberian heads; coins from the local mint; and glass and ceramic collections, etc.

Continuing the ascent, we reach the hill-top, dominated by the old *University*, founded in 1549 and suppressed in 1820, with its blue-tiled turrets, and cloister. To the E. are remnants of a Roman fortress; to the W., overlooking the town, the *Colegiata, of 1534–39, the entrance to which is now through the Plateresque patio (to be restored) on the N. side. One is led to the private chapel and lugubrious pantheon of the Dukes of Osuna (the first of whom received his title from Philip II in 1562) before entering the Sacristy, with a carved wooden ceiling, and containing four paintings by *Ribera* (of Saints Bartholomew, Jerome, Peter, and Sebastian); also pointed out is a Christ by *Juan de Mesa*, and a St Jerome attrib. to *Pietro Torregiano*. Other rooms preserve an extensive collection of chalices, custodias, processional crosses, etc.; some Flemish paintings, and a Christ by *Morales*. The *Church*, an impressive edifice, the cleaning and restoration of which has been recently completed, contains two marble pulpits, a very rare portative organ (late 16C), a retablo by *Sebastián Fernández*, and a Crucifixion (restored) by *Ribera*.

To the N., downhill opposite to the entrance to the Colegiata, stands the Convent of *La Encarnación* (1549), with a Baroque church and steeple (1775), also containing a small collection of religious art (note the pelican in the *Sagrario;* a polychromed alabaster Christ; and a S. Francis de Paula by *Juan de Mena*), but of more interest is the tiled *Dado* or *zocalo* surrounding both the 18C cloister and the gallery above. Note the section depicting the Alameda de Hércules in Seville.

At 17km. *La Puebla de Cazalla,* is a wine-growing centre (10,300 inhab.), with a Baroque altar-piece in its church.

At 15km. we reach a road junction; 7km. to the r. lies Marchena on the direct road from Écija to *Utrera* (see Rte 69) and *Jerez*. **Marchena** is an ancient town (18,600 inhab.) granted by Fernando V to the house of Ponce de León, Dukes of Arcos. The more interesting part is to the N. within the Moorish walls, where stood the *Pal. of the Dukes* and Gothic *S. Juan* (partly restored), with a carved cedar coro and a 16C retablo. *Sta María* has a tall tower covered with azulejos in the Portuguese manner, while in the newer town to the S. are *S. Augustín* and *S. Sebastián,* with Baroque details.

17 km. to the S. at this junction lies **Morón de la Frontera** (26,200 inhab.), on the Guadaira, commanded by the extensive ruins of a once impregnable Moorish *Castle*, built on the foundations of a Roman fort. Its *tortas* (fruit-cakes) are excellent. The steep and often stepped streets radiate from the *Ayuntamiento* in the centre. Eastwards the C. Joaquín Janer leads to *S. Ignacio*, or *La Campaña*, with a good carved frontal, and to the late-Gothic *S. Miguel*, with a tower recalling the Giralda. The noble keep and ramparts of the castle rise to the S., while on a low hill to the N. a curious monument of plucked cock commemorates the downfall of a tax-collector. In a parallel street on this side are some old mansions. Streets lead S. from the centre to the *Hospital*, in a former convent, passing the *Posada Lecilla*, with a relief of the Giralda on its portal (1744). To the W. of the town is *N.S. de la Victoria*, with an artesonado roof and a round tower with a hexagonal belfry.

At 4 km. a road leads 2 km. N. to *Paradas*, where the Renaissance church has a tower studded with azulejos.—5 km. *El Arahal* (15,900 inhab.) preserves the 15C *Hosp. de la Caridad* and two interesting churches. Beyond the town we fork r. for Seville; the l. fork leading 22 km. S.W. to *Utrera*, see Rte 69. We follow the N. bank of the Guadaira, passing *Gandul*, with a Moorish castle and prehistoric remains, and then by-pass (30 km.) *Alcalá de Guadaira* (38,700 inhab.), the Phoenician *Hienippe*. The Moorish Castle, which surrendered to Fernando III in 1246, retains its subterranean corn-magazines, several cisterns, its inner keep, and a huge donjon added by the Spaniards, who carried out extensive works in 1424 and 1470–77. In 1332 Alfonso XI presented it to Doña Leonor de Guzmán, and it was later used as a state prison. Another relic of Moorish times is a small ruined mosque, afterwards the church of *S. Miguel*, on whose day the town was taken. In the conv. church of *Sta Clara* is a retablo with six small reliefs by *Montañés*.

Passing near the *Caños de Carmona*, fragments of a Roman or Moorish aqueduct, we enter the E. surburbs of (16 km.) **Seville**, see Rte 67.

B   Viâ Córdoba.

Total distance 94 km. (182 miles.). N 432. 51 km. *Alcalá la Real*—27 km. *Alcaudete*—27 km. *Baena*—61 km. **Córdoba**—N IV. 128 km. **Seville**.

We leave Granada by the N 432, shortly (8 km. r.) passing the ruins of *Elvira* (perhaps the *Illiberis* of the Romans), where traces of an acropolis, a subterranean aqueduct, etc., have been found.

In this neighbourhood the Infantes Pedro and Juan (uncles of the youthful Alfonso XI) were defeated and slain by the Moors in 1319. Among the fallen was a 'Lord of Ilkerinterrah', of England. Don Pedro's skin is said to have been stuffed and put over the gate of Elvira. This defeat was amply avenged in the same neighbourhood by Álvaro de Luna in 1431, at the battle of La Higueruela, so-called from the little fig-tree (*higueruela*) under which Juan II bivouacked.

6 km. *Pinos Puente*, with a quaint chapel on an ancient *Bridge* over the Cubillas. It was here that Columbus was recalled by Isabel's messenger just as he was setting out in desperation to offer his services to Henry VII of England.

At 12 km. a road leads 8 km. S.W to *Illora*, with a church containing Roman columns (possibly from Elvira) and a ruined castle, called by the Moors the 'Eye (ojo) of Granada'.—At 4 km. a road leads 4 km. E. to *Moclin*, an interesting and well-preserved Moorish fortress.—We now climb to the Pto. Lope before descending to (21 km.) **Alcalá la Real** (20,700 inhab.), a picturesque place commanded by the Moorish castle of *La Mota* and by the extensive ruins of *Sta María*; it also contains one or two other churches of slight interest, and a 16C abbot's palace. Martínez Montañés (1568–1649), the sculptor, was born here.—Hence the road climbs through the hills to (27 km.) **Alcaudete** (12,500 inhab.), with a ruined Moorish castle, and the churches of *Sta María* and *S. Pedro*, the latter with a good retablo and 18C stalls. From Alcaudete we follow the N 432 W., passing the castle of *Venceaire*.—27 km. **Baena**, a curious old town (20,400 inhab.), the birthplace of José Amador de los Rios (1818–78), historian of Spanish literature, is dominated by the ruined Moorish castle which once belonged to Gonzalo de Córdoba, with an unusual dome. In the upper walled town, known as the Almedina, are Renaissance mansions, Gothic *Sta María*, burnt in the Civil War and being restored, and the *Conv. de la Madre de Dios*, in Mudéjar style with artesonados, and, in the late-Gothic porch, a carving of the Annunciation. In the lower town are *S. Bartolomé* and (further E.) *N.S. de Guadalupe* (c. 1540), the latter with an octagonal artesonado ceiling in its Cap. Mayor.

19 km. **Castro del Rio** (10,100 inhab.), with a ruined castle and walls. The church of *La Asunción* has a Plateresque doorway, while the *Ayuntamiento* preserves the prison of Cervantes, whose son was born here.—8 km. *Espejo*, Roman *Ucubi*, dominated by the Mudéjar castle of the Dukes of Osuna, and with a retablo by *Pedro Romano* in its 14C church.

We now descend into the valley of the Guadalquivir, with the Sierra Morena beyond, and at 34 km. enter **Córdoba**, see Rte 65.

From Córdoba to (128 km.) Seville, see Rte 64, below.

64   FROM BAILÉN TO CÓRDOBA AND SEVILLE

Total distance, 241 km. (150 miles). N IV. 28 km. *Adújar*—75 km. Córdoba—50 km. *Ecija*—55 km. **Carmona**—33 km. **Seville**.
For Bailén, see p.432. Hence we drive W. on the N IV.

At 22 km. a road leads 31 km. N.W. high up into the Sierra Morena to the *Santuario de la Virgen de la Cabeza* (founded 1277) whose besieged buildings (restored) were destroyed in 1936–37.

5 km. **Andújar** (35,600 inhab.; *Hotel*), perhaps the Iberian *Iliturgis*, has a *Roman Bridge* of fifteen arches at the S.W. angle of the walled town. Part of its industry is the manufacture of pottery, especially the large porous '*alcarrazas*' or '*jarras*' for drinking-water common throughout Spain. On the W. side of the town is *S. Bartolomé* (c. 1500) with good doorways, star vaults, and an 18C tower. We skirt the S. walls; at the E. end, by the Madrid road, stands the *Conv. de Capuchinos*. In the central Pl. de España are the *Ayuntamiento*, some Renaissance mansions, a Baroque fountain, and late-Gothic *S. Miguel* with an 18C tower. The C. Maestra leads back to the Madrid road, passing the fine front of the *Casa de Don Gomé*; while the C. de la Feria leads W. to the old *Clock Tower* and the Gothic hall-church of *Sta María*, with a Plateresque façade of 1559, on the site of a mosque. The town retains fragments of the Moorish Castle, and several old houses.

At 26 km. the C 327 leads 18 km. S.E. to *Porcuna* (8500 inhab.), Roman *Obulco*, once the centre of Mithraic rites, while Boabdil was held prisoner in the castle of the Knights of Calatrava.

We pass (3 km.) *Villa del Río,* where a Moorish palace has been converted into a church. There is a *Roman Bridge* E. of the town and one of the 18C across the Arroyo de Diablo.—8 km. **Montoro** (11,250 inhab.), famous for its olives, has a 16C bridge across the Guadaliquivir, some curious Romanesque capitals—unique in Andalucía—in *Sta María,* and a fine tower and rich stallwork in Gothic *S. Bartolomé*.

Bujalance (9350 inhab.) which lies 13 km. S., has a seven-towered castle built for Abderrahman III in 935, and was notorious for its legendary bagpiper, who charged a peseta to start playing and ten to stop. *Cañete de las Torres,* 8 km. E. of Bujalance, has a Moorish castle and an interesting church.

19 km. l. *El Carpio* has a Moorish tower and a palace of the Dukes of Berwick and Alba, while the church of *La Asunción* preserves a fine reliquary. We soon cross the Guadalquivir. leaving on the r. the *Bridge of Alcolea* where Dupont beat the Spaniards in 1808, and scene of the victory of Marshal Serrano over the troops of Isabel II in 1868, which compelled her abdication, and shortly enter the E. suburbs of (23 km.) **Córdoba,** see Rte 65, p.526.

From Córdoba to Seville viâ Lora del Rio (140 km.). This alternative but minor road (C 341) from Córdoba follows the N. bank of the Guadalquivir. The chain of the Sierra Morena approaches nearer the N. side of the valley, and the *Conv. de S. Jerónimo* is seen on its slopes. Also on the r., in the region known as *Córdoba la Vieja* (the site of Medina Azahara, see.p.534), are the breeding grounds of bulls intended for the ring, the smaller enclosures being used for testing young heffers. The picturesque Moorish *Castle of Almodóvar del Rio* (Roman *Carbula*) 22 km. from Córdoba, standing high above the river (View), and fortified by Pedro the Cruel as a Treasury for his spoils, has been restored, and may be visited by arrangement with the office of the S.E.T. in Córdoba.

We cross the Guadiato and pass (10 km.) *Posadas,* with its bell-towers.—At 11 km. a road leads 10 km. N.W. to *Hornachuelos,* with another ruined castle, while at 10 km. (3 km. to the S.) lies **Palma del Río** (17,500 inhab.) on the S. bank of the Guadalquivir at the confluence of the Genil, famed for its oranges, and which has some interesting churches.—6 km. *Penaflor,* Roman *Ilissa,* retains an old tower, while a little further on is seen the ruined castle of *Setefillas.*—17 km. **Lora del Río** (16,100 inhab.), preserves a chapel with a good W. Doorway, a Churrigueresque *Ayuntamiento,* and ruined Moorish castle. The road (C 432) from *Constantína* (see p.427) enters the town from the N. and leads S.W. 27 km. to *Carmona,* see p.524.—13 km. *Alcolea del Rio,* S. of which, at *La Peña de la Sal,* are the ruins of Roman *Arva,* with baths and a cemetery.—18 km. *Cantillana,* colonized by Mudéjars from Seville in 1345, retains the ruins of its ancient walls, while the *Ermita de S. Bartolomé* and the *Castillo de Mulva* are of interest.—At 19 km., *Alcalá del Río,* the road crosses the Guadalquivir and runs due S. to (14 km.) **Seville.**

Leaving Córdoba, we cross the Guadalquivir and turn r. The N IV bears S.W. away from the river, ascending the Cuesta del Espina.— 32 km. **La Carlota** (7900 inhab.) was one of the *'nuevos poblaciones'* colonized by Carlos III with Swiss and Germans, comp. p.432.

At 22 km. we turn r. off the by-pass to enter **ÉCIJA, a** very ancient town (33,400 inhab.), the Roman *Astigi,* displaying a fine series of tall steeples studded with azulejos.

Under the Visigoths Écija became the see of a bishop, but it owes its walls to the Moors, from whom it was retaken in the mid 13C. Notorious for its grilling heat and known as 'la Sarten (frying-pan) de Andalucía', the town was once the headquarters of a famous band of outlaws, 'los Siete Niños de Écija; and birthplace of Luis Vélez de Guevara (1579–1644), poet, playwright, and satirist.

Crossing the bridge over the Genil, we turn l. near the *Conv. de Terceras,* whose church *(Sta Ana),* built c. 1740–63, has a picturesque corbelled tower decorated with azulejos, and circle round to the S. side of the town, turning r. along the C. de Cervantes towards the Pl. Mayor. A short distance to the r. after turning towards the centre, lies *La Merced,* with a retablo of 1608–15 designed by *Juan Ortuño* and with carvings by *Felipe Vázquez,* a camerín of 1739, and Baroque paintings. At the S.E. corner of the plaza is *Sta Bárbara* (1790) by *Ignacio Tomás,* with a battlemented belfry, Roman columns, and good stalls.

Just to the S. the C. de los Caballeros runs E., flanked by mansions and palaces, of which the most notable are the *Pal. de Peñaflor,* with a Doric portal of 1721 and a galleried front with frescoed paintings; No. 41, the Renaissance *Pal. de Torres Cabrera* (c. 1530), and (No. 47) the *Pal. de la Marquesa de Alcántara,* with a balconied Baroque portal. S. of the Peñaflor palace is *S. Gil,* founded in 1479 but altered in 1765–70, with a fine tower (1777–79), and containing the Cristo de la Salud (c. 1550). N. of the Pal. de Peñaflor the great tower of *S. Juan* (c. 1730–45) rises above its church, largely in ruins.

Further N. stands *S. Pablo* (1728–76) with the Baroque chapel of the Virgen del Rosario. *Sta Cruz* (1776–1836), a short distance W. of S. Pablo, with a brick tower, contains a paleo-Christian sarcophagus, and arabic inscriptions recording the setting up in 929 and 977 of public fountains, the second the gift of Princess Subh, a Basque by birth, and mother of Hisham II.

Beyond the walls to the N. lies *La Concepción* (1641–84), with a twin-towered front of 1745. In the N.E. quarter of the town *Sta Florentina* has a good Baroque S. Doorway (1759), to the S. of which is the Churrigueresque *Conv. de Descalzos* (1718–70). From the N.W. corner of the Pl. Mayor the C. de José Antonio leads past (r.) the Isabelline front of the *Conv. de las Teresas,* which occupies a 14C Moorish palace, and the Isabelline *Hosp. de la Concepción* (1592–98), while some distance further W. beyond the Pta. Cerrada lies *El Carmen,* with a tall tower of 1637, a 15C recumbant Christ, and a Pietà of c. 1500. Just S.W. of the Pl. Mayor, beyond a smaller plaza, stands *Sta María* (1755–78), with a splendid tower of 1717. Within are good retablos and tombs, and in front is a Baroque triunfo of 1766. Nearby is the *Conv. de S. Francisco.*

Returning to the S. perimeter of the town, and turning r., we pass (l.) the *Conv. de la Victoria,* with a brick steeple (1757), and (r.), Gothic *Santiago* (c. 1500), restored, with an Isabelline Retablo Mayor, a Crucifixon by *Pedro Roldán,* good paintings in the N.E. chapel, and a Renaissance patio. To the r. as we drive W. out of Écija, is the Plaza de Toros, built on the site of a Roman amphitheatre, and near a Roman necropolis.

Just W. of the town the C 333 bears S.W. to (39 km.) *Marchena* (see Rte 63A) on the direct road to Utrera and Jerez.—16 km. *La Luisiana* is another of Carlos III's colonies (see *La Carlota,* above). After passing, slightly to the S., the Infantado *Pal. de Moncloa,* the road crosses a deserted region before entering (39 km.) *Carmona,* standing on a height overlooking the plain.

CARMONA (21,950 inhab.; *Parador Nac.*), the Roman *Carmo* and Moorish *Karmuna,* was captured by Fernando III in 1247. Immediately outside the Roman *Pta. de Sevilla* (2C; altered under the Moors), is *S. Pedro,* begun c. 1466, with a rich interior, whose tower (1704) is an imitation of the Giralda at Seville. Above it towers the imposing ruin of the *Alcázar de Abajo,* a Moorish fortress on Roman foundations, and here we may enter the old town, passing *S. Bartolomé,* which retains a Gothic sanctuary and a S. Doorway with dog-tooth ornament. Bearing l. uphill we reach the *Pl. Mayor* with the *Juzgado* of 1588, and the *Ayuntamiento,* which contains a number of Roman mosaics. Further on (r.) stands Churrigueresque *El Salvador* (1700–20) by *Diego Romero* and his sons, while to the l. is **Sta María,** a late-Gothic church, built between 1424 and 1518 on the site of the Great Mosque, of which a patio survives. The *Sanctuary* (1525–51) contains the high altar with a retablo and a terracotta frontal; while in the baptistery is a 15C triptych by *Alejo Fernández;* in the coro is good 17C woodwork.

Beyond the *Pta. del Sol,* S.E. of Sta María, is the *Pal. del Marqués de los Torres* of 1755, while on the N. are the *Ayuntamiento Viejo* (C. Martín López 39), with a front of 1697, the *Conv. de Descalzas,* founded in 1620, and *La Trinidad* (1721-48). Further E. are **Sta Clara* (1460), with artesonado roofs and a blocked Gothic W. Doorway, and the polychrome brick chapel of *La Caridad* (1510). Above them is *Santiago,* with a steeple adorned with azulejos, and a fine sanctuary (c. 1350). The street descends to the *Pta. de Córdoba* (c. A.D. 175), altered by the Moors and provided with Renaissance fronts in 1668.

The old Córdoba road, now a track, falls steeply into the valley to a ruined Roman bridge of five arches.

The top of the hill is dominated by the extensive ruins of the *Alcázar de Arriba,* an early fortress with an imposing entrance gate, converted by Pedro the Cruel into a luxurious palace, but abandoned after the earthquake of 1504. Part of it is the site of the newly constructed *Parador,* whence magnificent *Views are gained over the valley of the Corbones. From the Alcázar we may return to the Pta. de Sevilla past the ruins of Renaissance *S. José,* and Gothic and Mudéjar *S. Felipe* (1456–73; by *Martín García*) through a picturesque quarter of of narrow cobbled streets.

Also of interest is *Sto Domingo* (or *Sta Ana;* c. 1522) now serving as a cemetery chapel, with a Renaissance nave and a vaulted Gothic sanctuary, and higher, in the N. suburb, *S. Blas* (14C), rebuilt in 1726-27.

Immediately W. of Carmona (at the fork of the Seville and Alcalá roads, turn sharp r., then l.), and between two Roman roads, lies an important ***Roman Necropolis** (2C B.C.-4C A.D.) with a small museum of glass, ceramics, cinerary urns, and bronzes etc., and including a very 'modern' marble *Head (female).

The subterranean rock-hewn family tombs, approached by narrow stairways or perpendicular shafts, are generally arranged in groups. Before each is its crematorium, and a few have vestibules; the most interesting are those called 'del Olivo', 'del Columbario', 'de Prepusa', and 'de Póstumo', with the Triclinio del Elefante, a stone figure of an elephant, and a circular domed mausoleum. The remains of a temple-tomb c. 30 paces long with columns surrounding a galleried patio have also been excavated and known as the Tumba de Servilia. Close by are some prehistoric tumuli.

From Carmona we may drive S.W. on the C 432 viâ (11 km.) *Viso del Alcor,* with an old *Ayuntamiento,* and (4 km.) *Mairena del Alcor,* with a 15C castle containing a small archaeological museum, to meet the N 334 at *Alcalá de Guadaira,* see Rte 53A.

The NIV soon passes (23 km. l.) the airport of San Pablo and enters the E. suburbs of (6 km.) **Seville,** see Rte 67.

65   CÓRDOBA AND ENVIRONS

CÓRDOBA (250,900 inhab.; 73,000 in 1920; 190,000 in 1960; *Hotels*) is situated on the r. bank of the broad but shallow Guadalquivir, in a plain overlooked on the N. by the Sierra de Córdoba, a spur of the Sierra Morena. The climate is extremely hot in summer, with abundant rain in winter, which is sometimes frosty. Once the magnificent capital of Moorish Spain, it still retains its wonderful mosque or Mezquita; but apart from this and its Moorish bridge, it contains few other memorials of its departed greatness. The older streets are narrow and labyrinthine, passing along which flower-decked patios may often be discerned. Under the Moors it was noted for its silver-smiths' work and for Córdoban leather, whence comes the English word 'cordwainer' for shoemaker, and excellent leather goods are still produced here including stamped, printed, or gilded leatherwork known as '*guadamecil*' ware. The last 50 years have seen a new wave of prosperity and a great expansion of the city.

History. Córdoba, the Roman *Corduba,* an Iberian town of importance, was made a Roman colony by the consul Marcus Marcellus in 152 B.C., and enjoyed the title of *Colonia Patricia* and the dignity of capital of Hispania Ulterior. After the battle of Munda (45 B.C.) it was punished by Julius Caesar for its adherence to Pompey; but under Augustus it became the prosperous capital of the province of Baetica, and the largest city in Spain. Its bishop, Hosius (Osio; 257–337) presided in 325 over the Council of Nicea which gave Christendom the Nicene Creed. During the Visigothic period (5–8C) it was the seat of a bishop subordinate to Toledo; together with most of Baetica it was re-annexed to the Byzantine Empire under Justinian c. 534, but it was again taken by Leovigild in 572.

The Moors, on invading Spain, soon made themselves masters of Córdoba, aided by its disaffected Jewish inhabitants. In 756 Abderrahman I (d. 788), surviving scion of the Ommayyads of Damascus, here established an independent emirate, which as the Caliphate of Córdoba, governed most of the Peninsula. Under his successors, especially under Abderrahman III (912–961) and Hakam II (961–976), the city attained a pitch of wealth, luxury, and culture, the description of which taxed even the hyperbolic pen of Oriental writers, while Almansor (d. 1002), the powerful minister of the titular caliph Hisham II (976–1012), added military glory. At this period 'Córdoba with its half-million inhabitants, its three thousand mosques, its three hundred public baths, and its twenty-eight suburbs, yielded in size and magnificence only to Baghdad, a city indeed to which its inhabitants loved compare it.' At the beginning of the 11C internal dissensions and revolt prepared its decadence.

The Ommayyad dynasty came to an end in 1031 with the abdication of Hisham III; the caliphate split up into numerous petty kingdoms or *taifas,* and the city passed successively to the Almoravides in 1094 and to the Almohades in 1149. When Córdoba was captured by Fernando III in 1236, many of its inhabitants fled, and its decline was hastened by Christian indifference to industry, trading and agriculture.

It remained a dull provincial capital for some centuries, and its provincial nobility spent most of their time in each others houses, enjoying 'genteel refreshments, merry good-natured conversation, and some low card-playing' according to Swinburne (1775), who added that as a class, he wondered 'how they ever learned to read or write, or having once attained so much, how they contrived not to forget it'. According to Twiss, a high proportion of their carriages and furniture came from England. In the municipal elections of April 1979 it was the only town in Spain to return a Communist mayor.

Córdoba boasts a long roll of eminent natives: Seneca the Elder (d. 39 A.D.), his son Seneca the Younger (d. 65) and grandson Lucan (39-63), author of the 'Pharsalia'; Ibn 'Abd Rabbih' (860-940) the poet; Ibn Faradi (962-1012) and Ibn Hayyân (988-1076) historians; Ibn Hazm (994-1064), statesman and philosopher; Ibn Guzman (c. 1078-1160), poet; Averroes (1126-98), the famous Arab philosopher; Moses Maimonides (1135–1204), the rationalistic Jewish rabbi; Pero Tafur (c. 1410–c. 1484), author and traveller; the historian, Ambrosio de Morales (1513–91); the poets Juan de Mena (1411–56), Luis de Góngora (1561–1627), and the Duque de Rivas (1791–1865); and among painters, Pablo de Céspedes (1538–1608) and Juan Valdés Leal (1631–91). The fame of Manuel Rodríguez ('Manolete'; 1917–1947), the torero, is in no way eclipsed by the recent fashion for 'El Cordobés' (born in Palma del Río in 1936). Garcilaso de la Vega (El Inca; 1539–1616) also died in Córdoba.

Ziryab (789–857), the greatest musician and arbiter of taste of his age, came to Córdoba in 822 and died there, having introduced into Europe from the Abbasid court of Baghdad the proper ordering of meals, from soup to dessert, through regular courses of meat, poultry, and sweets.

From the Madrid road we pass (r.) the Mudéjar church of *El Carmen* (1580) containing a recently discovered retablo with 12 paintings by *Valdés Leal*, before reaching the N. bank of the Guadalquivir near the *Ermita de los Mártires*, to the E. of which lies *N.S. de la Fuensanta*, a pilgrimage church of 1641. Skirting the river, we pass (r.) the Pl. del Potro (see p.532) and then the Pte. Romano, adjacent to the Mezquita (see p.528), to which visitors will first direct their steps. A short distance beyond the bridge are (r.) the walls of the Alcázar (see p.531), and the New Bridge, at the far end of which the road diverges r. for *Seville* and *Málaga*, and l. for *Granada*, see Rtes. 64, 66, and 63B (in reverse).

The new Av. de Carlos III also turns off the Madrid road to circle N. of the town, passing (l.) the RONDA DEL MARRUBIAL, preserving a long stretch of the old city *Walls* and towers. On the r. stands the *Conv. de S. Cayetano* of 1580–1614, founded by St John of the Cross. Beyond, we pass through the Torre de la Malmuerta (see p.534) to enter the Pl. de Colón, from the N.W. corner of which the Carret. del Brillante climbs towards the attractive N. suburbs, the *Parador Nac.*, and *Las Ermitas* (see p.535). The W. side of this plaza is flanked by the highly-coloured Baroque buildings (1745) of the *Conv. de la Merced*. Hence the Av. del Generalísimo leads S.W., crossing the Av. del Gran Capitán, and shortly enters the spacious tree-lined Jardínes de la Victoria, the S. extension of which joins the riverside road at the New Bridge. Further S.W. lies the *Parque José Cruz Conde*. From the N. end of the Jardínes de la Victoria the C 431 leads W. towards *Medina Azahara*, see p. 534.

A THE JUDERÍA, MEZQUITA, ALCÁZAR, AND MUSEO ARQUEOLÓGICO

Visitors should not attempt to enter by car the maze of narrow streets of the old town. Convenient parking sites may be found in the vicinity of the *Jardínes de la Victoria*, from which the **Barrio de la Judería** may be entered on foot by the *Pta. de Almodóvar*, a good specimen of a Moorish town-gate. The *Walls* running S. have been well-restored, and the gardens skirting them are attractively laid out.

The whole area well repays a second visit after dark, when the strongly shadowed streets and lantern-lit patios are displayed to great effect. See also the *Cristo de los Faroles*, p.534.

Not far E. of the *Pta. de Almodóvar* is the Moorish façade of the 15C *Casa de los Ceas* or *del Indiano*, while further E. lies the *Conv. de Jesús Crucificado* (1496–1588) with outstanding artesonado ceilings, and patio containing Roman, Visigothic, and Moorish capitals. After turning l. up the C. de Valladares, we may diverge to the r. by the C.

Argote, passing *La Trinidad* (17C), and remains of a small minaret (c. 840) which survives from the mosque which became the church of *S. Juan,* now a convent, largely of 1576. Continuing N. along the C. de S. Felipe, we pass (l.) the 16C *Gobierno Militar,* attr. to *Alonso Berruguete,* to reach the S. end of the Av. de Gran Capitán, and r., the animated PL DE JOSÉ ANTONIO.

Passing through the Pta. de Almodóvar, we may also turn r. down the C. Maimonides, passing (No. 18) the remains of a *Synagogue* of 1315 in the Mudéjar style, but which cannot compare with those of Toledo. Beyond (l.) is the *Museo Municipal,* attractively housed in a 16C building, which includes a small display of leather and silver-work, but is devoted primarily to Bull-fighting. The C. Salazar leads E., passing the *Hosp. de Agudos* (undergoing restoration), whence we may enter the *Cap. de S. Bartolomé* of c. 1275, with Gothic vaults, friezes of Moorish alicatados, and a fine 15C pavement. To the N. is *S. Pedro de Alcántara,* built in 1690–96 by *Luis de Rojas.* The C. Romero leads S.E. to the *Cathedral,* (Pl. 14) which may also be approached from the main road skirting the river.

The Cathedral, better known as *La Mezquita* ('The Mosque'), and originally the great mosque of the Ommayyad caliphs of Córdoba, ranked among the largest and most sumptuous of Moslem shrines. Its ground-plan, orientated N.W. and S.E., is rectangular (174 by 137 m.) and it is entirely surrounded by a massive battlemented wall, 9–18 m. in height, strengthened by solid square buttresses.

Twenty-one doorways in this wall admitted to the mosque and its forecourt, but several have been filled up or destroyed, and those that remains have been restored and redecorated almost too completely.

Above the N. wall rises the *Belfry* (93 m. high), a tapering square tower of five storeys crowned by a figure of St Raphael. This, replacing the Moorish minaret, was begun by *Hernán Ruiz the Younger* in 1593, completed by *Gaspar de la Peña* in 1664 and repaired after the earthquake of 1755.

The Mezquita is closed to the public during services, which are usually held in the S.E. corner of the building, entered from the adjacent street.

History. The building of the Mezquita extended over two centuries, and four distinct stages are represented in it (comp. Plan). When the Moors entered Córdoba in 711 they contented themselves with half of the Visigothic church of S. Vicente as a place of worship, but some 70 years later Abderrahman I purchased the other half from the Christians and, clearing the site, he began in 785 the erection of a mosque which was to rival all others in splendour and was to save his people the arduous pilgrimage to the tomb of the Prophet at Mecca. This original mosque, divided by rows of columns into 11 vertical aisles running N. and S. and 10 or 11 narrower cross aisles running E. and W., and completed in 796 by Hisham I, forms only the N.W. quarter of the present building. The increasing population soon demanded a larger shrine, and Abderrahman II (833–848) extended the mosque to the S. by adding 7 more cross aisles.

A second and much greater extension was made by Hakam II, whose addition (961–966) of no less than 14 cross aisles, nearly doubling the area of the mosque, prolonged it to the present S. wall and established the *Mihráb* (prayer recess) in its present position. Up to this point the mosque had retained a symmetrical ground-plan, with the entrance and the mihráb at opposite ends of the main axis of the building and connected by the central vertical aisle, wider than the others. The third and last extension, which was completed in 990 by Almansor, deprived the mihráb of its central postion. For, as the nature of the site forbade further extension on the S. Almansor added 8 new vertical aisles on the E. side, without any counterbalancing extension on the W.

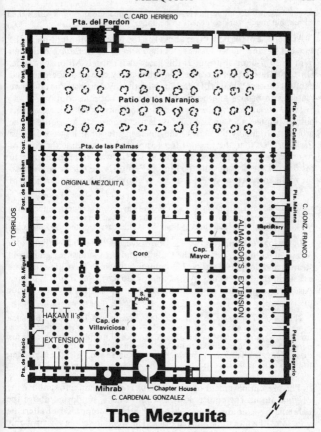

The Mezquita

After the capture of Córdoba (1236) the mosque became the Christian church of the *Virgin of the Assumption,* chapels were built against the interior walls, and the N. Front, hitherto open to the forecourt, was filled up, leaving as the main entrance the Pta. de las Palmas. Some years later a number of columns in the S.W. part of the mosque were removed to make way for a chapel, with a coro and a high altar situated approximately on the site of the second mihráb, where the Cap. de Villaviciosa now is.

In 1523 the cathedral chapter, unhappily fortified by the authority of Charles V against the enlightened opposition of the city council, began the erection of the incongruous cruciform church that now occupies the centre of the mosque. This structure, designed by *Hernán Ruiz the Elder* and completed nearly a century later, is a Renaissance building 55 m. long, with a coro and cap. mayor, a transept (crucero) 15 m. across, and a lofty and richly decorated roof; but its situation is inappropriate and its construction involved the removal of about 60 ancient columns. When Charles V in 1526 saw the mischief he had unwittingly been induced to permit, he reproved the chapter: 'You have built here what you or anyone might have built anywhere else, but you have destroyed what was unique in the world'. But the emperor himself had destroyed part of the Alhambra to provide an enplacement for his own palace.—The present vaulting in the mosque dates from 1713, but in the principal aisle a portion of the original flat wooden ceiling, carved and painted, has been restored to view. Restorations have rescued and revealed many other interesting features of the original mosque, both without and within, but much work still needs to be done.

At the base of the belfry (see above) on the N. side of the mosque, is the **Pta. del Perdón,** by which we enter the *Patio de los Naranjos.* Although built in 1377 under Enrique II this gateway is entirely Moorish in style. On the exterior it is decorated with delicately carved arabesques and exhibits the escutcheons of Córdoba with the royal crown. The doors are plated with bronze and bear both Cufic and Latin inscriptions.

The *Patio de los Naranjos,* the Moorish Court of Ablutions, with its palms, orange trees and fountains, is a characteristic vestibule to the mosque. Originally the ends of the nineteen interior aisles were open to the court, so that the lines of trees appeared to continue the rows of columns within, an arrangement which it was once proposed to restore.—Directly opposite the Pta. del Perdón is the *Pta. de las Palmas,* the main entrance, a Moorish doorway above which is a square attic of 1531.

An Arabic inscription on the r. of the doorway records the restoration of this front by Abderrahman III in 958 and gives the names of the superintendent of the works, Abdallah ibn-Badr, and of Said ibn-Ayub, carver of the inscription.h

INTERIOR. On entering we find ourselves in the subdued light of a forest of columns, with arched alleys and cross-alleys extending in strange and delightful vistas. The columns, of which there are said to be c. 850, in the 19 N. and S. Aisles, and the 36 narrower E. and W. Cross Aisles, average c. 4 m. in height, but are uniform neither in material nor in style.

The majority originate in Spain (Córdoba, Seville and Tarragona), but some come from as far afield as Narbonne and Nismes, Carthage and other Roman towns of N. Africa, and Istanbul. Many varieties of marble, jasper, breccia and porphyry occur; most of the shafts are smooth, through a few are spiral; the capitals are mainly Byzantine or Moorish, but Roman and Visigothic capitals are to be seen in the older parts.

The present pavement of marble slabs is more than a foot above the original floor. The roof is low (c. 12 m.) and is supported above the columns by a double row of Moorish arches, composed of alternate voussoirs of white stone and red brick. The wooden ceiling was probably originally all of *alerce* (larch), transported hence from Morocco. To the r. of the entrance is a font support from the Visigothic church of S. Vicente (see History).

The mihrábs of the successive mosques lay in the axis of the aisle leading S. from the Pta. de las Palmas. The First Mihráb, of Abderrahman I, has vanished. The *Second Mihráb,* due to Abderrahman II, and beyond the present coro, is distinguished by its fine arches and dome. This was apparently also the position of the high altar of the earliest Christian church. Adjoining on the E. is the elevated ***Cap. de Villaviciosa** (regrettably inaccessible), a Mudéjar chapel of 1371 (restored 1892). The unprotected inscriptions on tombstones on the W. wall of the chapel have been defaced by graffiti, while many of the columns have been similarly mutilated. This may have originally been the second *maqsura,* or elevated platform, on which the caliphs would pray on Fridays. To the E. of this chapel is the *Cap. de S. Pablo,* enclosed by 16C rejas, in front of which is the tomb of Pablo de Céspedes (d. 1608), artist of the retablo.

At the end of the aisle is the **Third Mihráb,** one of the most remarkable achievements of Moorish art, dated 965. Its vestibule is surrounded by interlaced arches upon marble columns; the walls are covered with coloured mosaics, and it is roofed by a fine octagonal cupola. Here the faithful prayed with faces turned to the *mihráb,* which in fact lies W. of the true direction of Mecca. The ** Mihráb,* an octagonal recess c. 3.3 m. in diameter, with arches supported by coloured columns, beneath a shell-shaped dome hollowed from a single block of marble, is still more gorgeously decorated.

Beneath the dome runs a Cufic inscription giving the date of its construction by Hakam II, with the names of the works committee, headed by Jafar ibn-Abderrahman, major-domo of the palace. The walls, encrusted with carved marble, and the pavement are worn by pilgrims circling the holy place seven times on their knees, in imitation of the practice at Mecca.

The side chamber on the E., formerly the *Cap. de la Cena,* has been restored to its original state, as have the chaples to the W.; these constituted the third *Maqsura,* or royal gallery of the caliph.

Off the *Chapterhouse,* to the E. of the Mihráb, is the *Treasury,* containing a fine Gothic Custodia in silver gilt by *Enrique de Arfe* (1510–18), a crucifix attr. to *Alonso Cano,* a 14C Mudêjar reliquary, and other examples of ecclesiastical art, while in the *Crypt* below the chapterhouse are two embroidered Frontals, illuminated choirbooks, etc.

In the *Sala Capitular,* opening off the sacristy, are the tomb of its founder, Card, Pedro de Salazar (d. 1706), and a Virgin attr. to *Alonso Cano.* The Annunciation, on a pillar outside the *Cap. de la Encarnación* (E. of the Sacristy) by *Pedro de Córdoba* (1475) is in a sad state of repair.

The **Coro** of the degenerate church erected in the middle of the mosque was built by *Hernán Ruiz* in 1523–39. The elaborately carved Churrigueresque *Stalls* (1747–58) are the work of *Pedro Duque Corrnejo* (1677–1757), while the *Pulpits* supported by symbols of the Evangelists, are by *Michel Verdiguier* (1760). In the *Cap. Mayor* of 1547-99 the Retablo is by *Alonso Matías* (1618-28), with paintings by *Palomino.* The massive silver chandelier is said to weigh over 400 lbs (180 kg). The 17C organ is unplayable.

Bp. Leopold of Córdoba (d. 1557), son of the Emperor Maximilian and brother of Philip the Handsome, is buried in the middle of the transept. On the wall of the Trasaltar are some 16C Italian reliefs of the Passion.

In the C. de Torrijos, which skirts the W. side of the Cathedral, is the beautiful Portal (1512) of *S. Jacinto,* forming part of the *Casa de Expósitos* or Foundling Hosp. (*'La Cuna'*). To the l., beyond the house in which the chronicler Morales died, is the *Episcopal Palace,* the oldest part of which is of the 15C, but which occupies the site of the palace of Roman and Visigothic governors, and alcázar of the caliphs. The latter is undergoing excavation and restoration. The *Sala de los Obispos* contains a collection of 16C tapestries.

The street ends on the S. at the Churrigueresque *Triunfo,* a monument to the tutelar S. Rafael, by *Michel Verdiguier* (1765–81); some of his other works had been destroyed the night after their erection by the barbarous populous, to the great mortification of the *Corregidor,* who had commissioned them, according to Jardine.

Hence the C. Amador de los Ríos leads W. to the **Alcázar Nuevo,** on the site of a palace begun for Alfonso X in the late 13C, enlarged for Alfonso XI in 1328, and occupied by the Inquisition in 1482–1821. The interior is of architectural interest and contains remains of the Roman and Moorish period (mosaics and baths; the latter dating from 1328), and a Sarcophagus of C. A.D. 200.

Attractive gardens lie to the S.W., while the open space to the N., called *Camposanto de los Mártires*, is the legendary scene of Christian martyrdoms under the Moors. Further W., beyond the *Caballerizas Reales*, lies the Barrio del Alcázar Viejo, a district of narrow lanes leading to the 10C *Pta. de Sevilla*.

To the S. of the Triunfo stands the *Pta. del Puente*, a Doric archway erected in 1571 for Philip II, to design by *Hernán Ruiz*, on the site of the Moorish *Bâb el-Kantara*. Beyond it the **Bridge**, 238 m. long and 6 m. broad, crosses the river to the southern suburbs.

Its sixteen arches on Roman foundations of the Augustan age were ruined by the Visigoths, but were rebuilt by the Moors in the 8C and have been many times restored. The central statue of S. Rafael is by *Bernabé Gómez del Río* (1651).

As a tête de pont at its S. end and in the direct axis of the bridge stands the crenellated *Torre de la Calahorra* (1369) housing a small museum with interesting plans and documents, and commanding a view from its battlements. Downstream we can see the remains of Moorish *Mills;* the northernmost (*Molino de la Albolafia*) incorporates fragments of an Almohade palace built over the river, and until 1492 housed the great wheel that raised water for the Alcázar gardens.

Returning to the Triunfo, we may skirt the S. and E. walls of the Mezquita and continue N. along the C. Velázquez Bosco, where, between Nos. 4 and 6, survive *Moorish Baths* (11C); others have been excavated to the N. of the Alcázar. The C. Saavedra leads N. past (r.) the *Pal. del Marqués de Fuensanta*, with a front of 1551, to the Pl. de José Antonio (p.534), but we turn r. along the narrow C. Alto de Sta Ana, and climb down to a small plaza overlooked by the elaborate Renaisance portal (1540–45) of the *Pal. de Jerónimo Paéz* (Pl. 10), designed by *Hernán Ruiz the Elder*. This attractive building houses the well-displayed ***Museo Arqueológico**, with important collections of prehistoric, Roman, Visigothic, Moorish and Gothic antiquities. Outstanding among the exhibits is an inlaid bronze Stag from Medina Azahara, originally added by Abderrahman III to a fountain given him by the Byzantine emperor Constantine VII (945–959).—Not far to the S.W., in the C. de Rey Heredia, the *Conv. de Sta Clara* preserves a minaret of c. 1000.

B   EASTERN CÓRDOBA.

From the Archaeological museum we may continue S.E. towards the C. de S. Fernando (or de la Feria) which we enter by passing through the *Portillo*, an archway opened in the wall which once divided the two parts of the city; the ALMEDINA (W.) and the AJARQUÍA. To the r., just before reaching the Portillo, in the C. Cabezas, is the 15C *Casa de los Marqueses del Carpio*. Opposite, an archway admits to a small plaza in front of the *Convm de S. Francisco*, founded by Fernando III, but now a Churrigueresque building containing a St Andrew by *Valdés Leal* among other works. To the S. the C. de S. Francisco leads to the Pl. DEL POTRO, with another monument to S. Rafael by *Verdiguier* (1772), and a celebrated fountain adorned with a colt (*potro*), of which mention is made in 'Don Quixote'. Cervantes is supposed to have lodged at an inn (restored) on the l. The nearby *Posada de la Herradura* is another similar survival.

On the E. side of the plaza stands the **Museo del Bellas Artes** (Pl. 11), established in an old hospital, with a Plateresque portal.

On the ground floor are miscellaneous paintings and sculptures by late 19th and early 20C Spanish artists. In the corridor are two heads in fresco (c. 1280) from the Mezquita, while on the first floor are works by *Alejo Fernández*, *Pablo de Céspedes*, *Ribera*, *Murillo*, *Morales*, *Zurbarán*, and *Alonso Cano*, and two protraits by *Goya* (Carlos IV and María Luisa). There are also several paintings by members of the Córdoban family of Castillo Saavedra, among them *Antonio del Castillo* (1616–68), a pupil of Zurbarán.—On the other side of the courtyard is a small museum devoted to the Córdoban artist *Julio Romero de Torres* (1885–1930).

A detour may be made towards the E. along the riverside Paseo de la Ribera, where, opposite the *Molinos de Martos,* we turn l. to *Santiago,* retaining the 10C minaret of a former mosque, an artesonado ceiling of 1635, and also containing a Santiago by *Lorenzo Cano*, an Assumption of the school of Marcellus Coffermans, and a 15C stone Virgin. Nearby is the Mudéjar *Casa de las Campanas* (14C) and the 15C *Casa de los Caballeros de Santiago* (once a bodega and now a school) with two Mudéjar patios. Returning to the centre we pass (l.) the *Conv. de la Santa Cruz* (founded 1435) and (r.) **S. Pedro** (13C) on the site of the earlier mozarabic cathedral, but extensively altered in 1542–75. The Churrigueresque *Cap. de los Mártires* contains a silver reliquary of 1790 by *Cristóbal Sánchez y Soto* and a hanging lamp (1602) by *Lucas de Valdés*. Hence the C. de Poyo leads N.W. to the *Pl. Mayor*, see below.

From the Pl. de Potro. the C. Armas leads N. to the brick-built PL. DE LA CORREDERA (or *Pl. Mayor*) of 1683, restored after the removal of an unsightly market-house. From its N.W. corner we may reach, viâ the C. Calvo Sotelo—where, behind the *Ayuntamiento*, a late *Roman Temple* is in the course of excavation—the Romanesque conv.-church of **S. Pedro** (Pl. 7), founded in 1241, with a Baroque frontal (1706), and within, Mudéjar capitals and ceiling (1537), and the Gothic chapel of the Rosary (1409) with a Baroque camarín. The central plaza lies a short distance to the W.

C NORTHERN CÓRDOBA

Sta Marta, to the N.E. of S. Pablo, completed in 1471, has a good Gothic portal and contains a St Jerome carved by *Fray Miguel Bellver*. The C. de S Pablo leads E. past the impressive front of the *Pal. de los Villalones* (1560) and the Plateresque *Casa de Hernán Pérez de Oliva* (1542), to *S. Andrés* (13C, but largely rebuilt in 1733) with a good retablo of the Córdoban school of c. 1500 in a side chapel. The C. Muñices leads S.E. to Gothic *La Magdalena*, with a Baroque interior and 18C tower. To the N.E. stands **S. Lorenzo** (14C), with a fine Rose-window, and a tower added in 1555. The interior dates from 1678, but an artesonado ceiling survives above the vaults and 15C wall-paintings adorn the apse. Further N.E. lies the *Conv. de los Padres de Gracia* (1607).

From S. Lorenzo we may work our way W. past *S. Rafael* (1796) and *S. Agustín*, a 14C building much altered in the 16C and later, to the 17C *Pal. del Marqués de Viana*, with 13 patios (and containing a private Museum). Hence the C. Morales leads N. to **Sta Marino**, Gothic with a Renaissance tower, containing paintings by the Castillo family, and the 15C Mudéjar *Cap. de los Orozcos*, altered in 1751–56. Opposite the W. Front stands a *Monument to Manolete*. The C. Conde Priego leads

S.W. past the *Conv. de Sta Isabel*, founded in 1491, with a simple front of 1576, to the Pta. de Ricón, from which steps ascend to *Los Dolores*, containing a revered wooden Virgin. We pass the Plateresque front of the *Casa de los Fernández de Córdoba*, while opposite stands the 17C *Conv. de Capuchinos*, with doors of Mudéjar inlay. The plaza contains the picturesque **Cristo de los Faroles** (Pl. 6), which should be visited a second time after dark. From the W. end of the plaza we may turn r. into the Pl. de Colón, at the N.E. corner of which stands the **Torre de Malamuerta** (1406–08) which owes its name to a garbled tradition that it was built as the price of a pardon from Enrique III by a knight who had murdered his wife.

The tower is, in fact, linked by an underground passage to the *Casa del Conde de Priego*, in which took place c. 1455 the murder by Fernando Alfonso de Córdoba of his wife and household, immortalized by Lope de Vega in 'Los Comendadores de Córdoba'. The tower became in the 18C the observatory of the astronomer Serrano, and later a powder magazine.

From the Cristo de los Faroles we may turn S. along the C. Conde Torres Cabrera towards the Pl. de José Antonio, passing (l.) the Baroque church of *Las Capuchinas* (1655), (r.) *S. Miguel*, 13C but altered in 1749, and to the E., the Baroque chapel of *S. Zoilo* 1740). From the S.E. corner of the **Pl. de José Antonio** (Pl. 6), the main square of the older town, thronged with cafés, we may approach the church of *La Compañía*, built in 1564–69 by the Jesuit *Alonso Matías*, with a Baroque retablo by *Pedro Duque Cornejo*.

At No. 5 Pl. de la Compañía, a short distance S.E.n below the remains of the church of S. Domingo de Silos, are shown four fragmentary Roman (3C) mosaics of the Seasons (apply at the Bodega de la Compañía). Further S. is *Sta Victoria*, a neo-classical church begun in 1701 by *Baltasar Graveton* and completed in 1772–88 by *Ventura Rodríguez*.

The C. Gondomar leads W. fron the plaza towards the attractive octagonal tower, completed in 1496, of *S. Nicolás*, Within are artesonados of 1580, Baroque retablos, a baptistery of 1554 by *Hernán Ruiz. el Mozo*, and a Renaissance door to the Sacristy.

The C. Concepción leads W. from S. Nicolás to enter the Jardínes de la Victoria at a point not far N. of the Pta. de Almodóvar.
Av. de Gran Capitán leads N. from S. Nicolás, on the l. of which stands *S. Hipólito* dating from 1348. It contains an Ecce Homo by *Valdés Leal* and, in the choir, the sarcophagi of Alfonso XI (d. 1350), the chivalrous hero of Tarifa and Algeciras, and his brother Fernando IV (d. 1312). The nave was added in 1726–36 and the tower begun in 1773. The cloister contains the grave of Ambrosio de Morales (1531–91), the chronicler.

EXCURSIONS FROM CÓRDOBA.

About 6 km. N.W. of Córdoba, turning r. off the C 431, on a site known as Córdoba la Vieja, are the remains of *Medina Azahara, an extensive palace complex begun c. 936 by Abderrahman III for his favourite wife Zahra or Zahara ('Flower'). Excavations have traced the line of the rectangular bounding wall and the sites of many of the principal buildings. Near the entrance is a small display of fragments of columns, mosaics, and other relics, but the more important are now in the Archaeological Museum in Córdoba.

The description of the size, luxury, and splendour of Medina Azahara by the Arab historian El-Makkari recalls the 'Arabian Nights'. Its construction employed 10,000 men with 2,600 mules and 400 camels for 25 years; it included not only a magnificent palace with gardens and fish-ponds, but also a great mosque, baths, and schools of learning; marble, jasper, and other costly materials were lavishly used, and of its 4300 splendid columns some were brought from Carthage and other ancient cities. It had a garrison of 12,000 men, while 4000 servants waited in the palace and 2000 horses stood ready in its stable. In 1010 all this magnificence was destroyed by rebel Berber mercenaries and for centuries the site was marked only by scattered debris.

The sensational discovery in 1944 of the *Royal Apartments*, containing the fallen materials of their arches and roofs, has been followed by a meticulous reconstruction which enables us to appreciate the architectural magnificence of a Moorish throne-room of c. 947–57. More recent excavations have laid bare the outline of its mosque.

The neighbouring *Conv. de S. Jerónimo* (c. 1408; now a private residence) where Morales was a monk, was built from the remains of the palace, and contains a Moorish fountain. There is a Gothic cloister, but the church was rebuilt c. 1794.— At *Alamiría*, W. of Medina Azahara, stood the remains of a country house of Almansor (c. 990) until destroyed in 1926.

Another favourite excursion from Córdoba, mainly on account of the fine views en route, is that to **Val Paraíso**, a convent situated on a foot-hill of the Sierra c. 10 km. N. of the city. Its hermitages or cells, 13 in number, date from c. 1709 and are grouped beside a church within a walled enclosure. The finest viewpoint is known as the *Silla del Obispo*.

Other excursions may be made to the N.W. (by the road crossing the railway W. of the station) to *Sta María de Trassierra*, an Almohade mosque of c. 1200 converted to a chapel, within a ruined castle. Further on is a Moorish bridge of nine arches crossing the Guadiato near its confluence with the Guadalmuno.

By the Carretera del Brillante we may reach the *Huerta de los Arcos*, a beautiful garden containing Moorish remains, while a side-road leads to *Sto Domingo de Scala Dei*, a convent (15-18C) which had Fray Luis de Granada (1504–88) as prior.

66   FROM CÓRDOBA TO MÁLAGA

Total distance, 175 km. (108 miles). N IV for 19 km.—N 331. 28 km. *Montilla*— 28 km. *Lucena*—52 km. **Antequera**—N331 and then N321. 48 km. **Málaga.**

Crossing the Guadalquivir we follow the Seville road (N IV) for 19 km. before forking l. on to the N 331.—12 km. l. *Fernán Nuñez* (by-passed) has a ducal palace with an old tower, and in the church is a crucifix carried by the earliest missionaries to Japan.—At 10 km. a road leads 4 km. S.W. to *La Rambla*, with Renaissance churches and a ruined castle.—6 km. l. **Montilla** (21,900 inhab.; *Hotel*) perched on two hills, is perhaps Roman *Munda Baetica*, where Caesar defeated the sons of Pompey in 46 B.C. The palace near the town belongs to the Duke of Medinaceli; *Santiago* and the *Conv. de Sta Clara*, in Mudéjar style, are of interest.

The surrounding district, including the Sierra de Montilla, is celebrated for a delicate white wine, quite unlike the type of sherry to which is given the name 'amontillado'. The latter is a blended wine of Jerez, whereas Montilla is the classical Córdoban table-wine.

Montilla was the birthplace of Gonzalo Fernández y Aguilar (1453–1515) known as Gonzalo de Córdoba, after serving with distinction against the Moors, and who also earned the title of 'El Gran Capitán' by his brilliant campaign (1495-

98) in Italy against the French. In 1502–04 he expelled them from Neapolitan territory, and was the first of the long line of Spanish viceroys to Naples.

8 km. *Aguilar de la Frontera* (14,300 inhab.; *Hotel*) is prettily situated among olive-groves and vineyards, with a picturesque hill-top plaza; its parish church, Moorish castle, and the Baroque chapel of the *Conv. de las Descalzas* are of interest. The Málaga road bears S.E. to (20 km.) **Lucena,** a busy town of 29,400 inhab., scene of the capture of Boabdil in 1483 by the Conde de Cabra, and famous for its apricots, olives and pottery. It was populated almost entirely by Jews in the Moslem era until driven out by the Almohades and settled in Christian territory. Amongst its churches are *S. Mateo* (15C) in the Pl. Nueva with good artesonados, a Renaissance high altar and exuberant Baroque Sagrario; *Santiago*, a Gothic doorway and curious Baroque turret; the *Agustinas Recoletas,* a Baroque portal; and *S. Francisco,* further N., an octagonal lantern, Baroque retablo, and charming patio with fountain. Another patio, with curious wall-paintings, is at the *Hosp. de S. Juan de Dios*, whose church contains a fine retablo, as does the chapel of the *Cristo de la Sangre*. On a height to the S. stands the shrine of *N. S. de Araceli*. Hurtado Izquierdo, the architect, was born here in 1669, and died at nearby by Priego in 1728; another native was the poet Luis Barahona de Soto (1548–95), author of a treatise on hunting.—20 km. S.E. lies *Rute* (9300 inhab.) near remains of a Visigothic city, on the direct road via *Iznájar*, with a castle dominating the new reservoir, to (60 km.) *Loja*, see p.502.

From Lucena we descend into the valley of the Genil and climb again before reaching an improved section of road and (51 km.) **Antequera** (1680 ft; 40,200 inhab.; *Albergue Nac.; Hotel* 7 km. N.), preserving a number of churches and mansions of carved brick.

Originally a Roman station (*Anticaria*), Antequera was taken from the Moors in 1410 by the Infante Fernando, afterwards Fernando I of Aragón, who was thenceforth known as 'el de Antequera'. Gunpowder is said to have been used for the first time in Spain on this occasion.

The *Torre Mocha* (13C) of the ruined Moorish *Castle* commands a fine view, while the old *Pta. de Málaga* forms the *Ermita de la Virgen de Espera*. Adjacent is *Sta María la Mayor*, a hall-church of 1503–50, with an interesting W. Front, artesonado roof, and 14C retablo. *S. Sebastián* (mid-16C) has a brick steeple of 1709, while other churches are *S. Juan Bautista* (1489–1584), containing a remarkable Crucifix; *S. Pedro* (1522–74); *S. Francisco*, finished in 1507; and *S. Agustín*, with well-carved stalls. The *Pal. de Nájera* houses a small collection of antiquities and inscriptions The *Arco de S. María de los Gigantes* (1585), erected in the Pl. Alta, incorporates some Roman inscribed stones.

More interesting is the *Cueva de Menga*, a double dolmen some few minutes N.E. of the town. Close by is the *Cueva de Viera*, another dolmen; while a third, the *Cueva del Romeral*, stands on the Cerrillo Blanco in the vega.

A 'natural' curiosity, approached from Antequera by the C3310 climbing S., off which a track leads r. after c. 12 km., is *El Torcal*, a labyrinth of red limestone, resembling in their form the buildings and streets of a ruined city.

FROM ANTEQUERA TO (89km.) RONDA AND ARCOS. At first bearing N.W., we shortly turn l. onto the N342 for (32 km.) *Campillos* (7100 inhab.), with a Baroque façade to its parish church, where we fork r. for Ronda.—Hence the N342 is being extended to the W. to *Olvera* (see. p.518).—The C341 descends towards the

Embalse del Guadalhorse, at 11 km. leaving on a height to the r. the picturesque walled town of *Teba* (4850 inhab.).

Here in 1330 Sir James Douglas, on his way to Jerusalem with the heart of Robert Bruce, fell in battle with the Moors. The casket, containing the heart, which Douglas had flung before him as though to lead the way into the thickest of the fight, was recovered and Bruce's heart now rests in Melrose Abbey in Scotland.

After (4 km.) we meet the road from *Alora* and the *Garganta del Chorro*; see p.514. This road is longer, but a far pleasanter and more interesting road from Antequera to Alora than the more direct C331.—*Ronda* lies 42 km. to the S.W., for which, and the road thence to *Arcos*, see pp.514 and 518.

Some 4 km. N.E. of Antequera we turn r. onto the N331, climbing steeply to the Pto. de las Pedrizas, where we are joined by the new N321 from Granada. This has virtually superseded the older road. (C340), which continued S.E. through *Colmenar* and the Pto. de León, before its complicated descent, but providing panoramic views, to Málaga. The new road, immediately commencing its descent down the valley of the Guadalmedina, is certainly a considerable improvement, but is less interesting. In the lower valley it passes the estates of *S. José* and *La Concepción*, remarkable for their tropical vegetation, which may be visited; Roman remains from Málaga and Cártama have been incorporated into the 'Grecian' temple at the latter.

For *Málaga* itself, see Rte 61.

67   SEVILLE AND ENVIRONS

SEVILLE (in Spanish—*Sevilla;* 589,700 inhab.; c. 96,000 in 1800; 206,000 in 1920; 302,000 in 1940; 442,000 in 1960; 546,000 in 1970; numerous *Hotels*), the fourth city of Spain, and the capital of Andulucía, is situated on the l. bank of the Guadalquivir in the flat and fertile Tierra de María Santísima. Its Cathedral, the Giralda, and the Alcázar are among the famous buildings of Spain, and it is rich in churches and works of art, while one of the more attractive features of the city are the number of plazas and streets shaded by orange trees. Not without justification is the boast 'quien no ha visto Sevilla no ha visto maravilla'. George Borrow considered it 'the most interesting town in all Spain', standing beneath 'the most glorious heaven. . .'.

Although it is 70 miles from the sea, the Guadalquivir admits sea-going vessels to its quays, although its main stream has been taken in a widened arc to the W. behind the suburb of *Triana.*

Many of the older houses have an entrance porch (*zaguán*) with open-work iron gates (*cancela*). The windows are protected by iron gratings, whence the phrase 'to live on iron' (*comer hierro*), once used of the cloaked gallants who in the evening sought to woo the señoritas caged within. The square inner patio, with a fountain in the centre and *corredores* supported by pillars at the sides, is covered in summer by an awning (*toldo*) and used as a living-room; the family migrating upstairs in winter.

The arms of Seville present S. Fernando (Fernando III) between S. Leandro and S. Isidoro, with the badge known as 'El Nodo' (the knot) above and the motto 'muy noble, my leal, muy heróica, y invencible.' *El Nodo*, which is seen carved and painted everywhere, is a rebus, consisting of a double knot (*madeja*) between the syllables NO and DO, to be read 'no m'ha dejado', i.e. 'it has not deserted me', and commemorates the fidelity of Seville to Alfonso X.

RAILWAY STATIONS. *Est. de Córdoba*, on the W. side of the city, for Mérida, Huelva, etc.; *Est. de Cádiz* for the Talgo to Córdoba, Madrid, Cádiz, Granada, Málaga, etc.

Air services from *S. Pablo airport,* to the E.

P.O., Av. Queipo de Llano 40.

British Institute, C. Federico Rubio 7.

History. Seville, Roman *Hispalis* and the *Ishbiliya* of the Moors, was originally an Iberian settlement. Julius Cæsar, who entered it in 45 B.C., made it an assize town, and gave it the title of *Colonia Julia Romula*; and in the early imperial epoch it was one of the leading towns in the flourishing province of Bætica. Under the Visigoths (5–8C) it belonged to the kingdom of which Toledo became the capital. Hermengild, viceroy at Seville, abjured the Arian heresy and was put to death as a rebel by his father Leovigild (586), but when the orthodox creed triumphed he was canonized together with S. Leandro and S. Isidoro, brothers and successive archbishops of Seville, now tutelars of the city. After the defeat of Count Roderic on the Guadalete in 712, Seville was captured by the Moors under Musa, the lieutenant of Tariq, and was included later in the Caliphate of Córdoba, rivalling that capital both in material prosperity and as a seat of learning. When the western caliphate broke up in the 11C, Seville proclaimed its independence (1023) under the family of the Abbadites, who were dispossessed in 1091 by the Almoravides, who were in turn succeeded in 1147 by the Almohades, under whom the city enjoyed a new period of prosperity and saw many fine buildings erected, including the Giralda.

In 1248 Seville was reconquered by Fernando III, the Saint, who died and was buried there, after dividing among his followers (many of them from Burgos, Palencia, and Valladolid) the possessions of, it is said, some 300,000 citizens who had depopulated the city by seeking voluntary exile. Seville, alone among Spanish towns, remained faithful to Alfonso X during the revolt of his son, Sancho, and it became the favoured residence of later kings, especially of Pedro the Cruel (1350–69). The discovery of the New World by Columbus in 1492 raised Seville to the pinnacle of its fortunes, but during the reign of Philip IV (1621–65) its prosperity began to decline. The city suffered from the rivalry of Cádiz under the first Bourbon kings, from the loss of the Spanish colonies, and from the troubled state of Spain in the 19C. From 1808 until 1812 Seville was occupied by the French under Soult; and in 1843 it was bombarded by Gen. Espartero. At the commencement of the Civil War the Nationalist Gen. Queipo de Llano seized Seville by a fortuitous *coup de main* and hence he made his notorious braggart broadcasts.

It has again grown in importance with the partial autonomy of Andalucía.

Seville was the birthplace of the writers and historians Bartolomé de las Casas (1474–1566), historian of the Spanish conquest and 'Apostle of the Indies'; Lope de Rueda (1500–65); Pedro de Cieza de León (1518–54), historian of Peru; Fernando de Herrera (1534–97); Mateo Aleman (1547–1615), author of 'Guzmán de Alfarache'; the humanist Argote de Molina (1548-98); Rodrigo Fernández de Ribera (1579–1631); Francisco de Rioja (c. 1583–1659); Diego Jiménez de Enciso (1585–1634?); Nicolás Antonio (1617–84), the bibliographer; Alberto Lista (1775–1848); Joseph Blanco White (1775–1841), the theological writer, who lived from 1810 in England; Pascual Gayangos (1809–97), the Arabic scholar; Gustavo Adolfo Bécquer (1836–70); Antonio Machado (1875–1939), Vicente Aleixandre (1898-); and Luis Cernuda (1902–1963).

Among painters Franciso Pacheco (1571–1654); Francisco de Herrera the Elder (el Viejo; 1576–1656) and the Younger (el Mozo; 1612–85); Diego de Velázquez (1599–1660); Bartolomé Esteban Murillo (1618–82), Antonio Esquivel (1806–57); José, Joaquín, and Valeriano Domínguez Bécquer (1805–41, 1817–79, and 1834–70 respectively); and Manuel Cabral Bejarano (1827–91).

Among composers Cristóbal de Morales (c. 1500–53); Francisco Guerrero (1528–99); and Joaquín Turina (1882–1949); and Manuel García (1775–1832), the singer and composer of *tonadillas*, and father of Malibran and Pauline Viardot. In 1828 Washington Irving was painted in Seville by David Wilkie; here, two years later, Richard Ford spent his first winter in Andalucía, while George Borrow spent his last months in Spain (1839–40) at No. 7 Plazuela de la Pila Seca, which lay near the old Pta. de Jerez. Julian Williams, a great collector of paintings, was British Vice-Consul here for many years of the second quarter of the 19C. Seville (viâ Beaumarchais, admittedly) supplied the background to Mozart's '*Mariage de Figaro*' (1786) and '*Don Giovanni*' (1787), Rossini's '*Barbiere di Siviglia*' (1816), Bizet's '*Carmen*' (1875); while Byron's '*Don Juan*' (1818) was a hidalgo of Seville.

Church Festivals. Some of the ecclesiastical functions of Seville, although verging on the Mariolatrous, are curious and spectacular, particularly during the celebrations of Semana Santa (Holy Week), when the city is overcrowded, and accommodation is difficult to find unless booked well in advance.

Holy Week. The following ceremonies take place in the cathedral, but it is as well to check beforehand the times at which they are performed. *Palm Sunday*: c. 9.00. Blessing of palms and olive-branches. *Wednesday*: c. 10.00, Mass followed by the rending of the Veil of the Temple (*Velo Blanco*) to the sound of thunder; in the afternoon gradual extinction of the lights on the Tenebrario; at 21.00. Eslava's 'Miserere'. *Maundy Thursday*: c. 7.00. Blessing of the Sacred Oils; procession bearing the Host to the Monumento; in the afternoon, Washing of Feet, at 22.00 Eslava's 'Misere'. *Good Friday*: at 6.00. Passion sermon at the Monumento; mass, followed by black-robed procession; vespers in darkness. *Saturday*: 7.00. Blessing of the Paschal Candle; at 10.00 Revelation of the Altar by the rending of the veil (*Velo Negro*), with the singing of the Gloria in Excelsis, the sound of thunder, and the ringing of bells, the 'Tocado de la Gloria', when (at 12.00) all the bells of the city are rung; illumination of the Tenebrario. During the following night the Giralda bells ring between 2.00–4.00. *Easter Sunday*: Mass and processions.

The **Dance of the Seises** before the High Altar in the Cathedral may be seen daily during the octaves of the festivals of Corpus Christi and the Immaculate Conception and on the last three days of the Carnival. This dance, a slow minuet, is performed by 10 choristers (originally 6, i.e. *seis*), wearing 17C costumes, with plumed hats and carrying castanets. It is said to be a survival from the Mozarabic ritual or to have originated in the rejoicing of Christian youths on the reconquest of Seville, but appears to date in fact from 1508.

Pasos. On four days in Holy Week (Palm Sunday, Wednesday, Maunday Thursday, and Good Friday) members of various brotherhoods (*Cofradías*) clad in the forbidding hooded dress of penitents (*nazarenos*), and carrying candles, pass through the streets, accompanying large and elaborately adorned carved groups representing saints, or scenes from the Passion, or one of Seville's numerous Virgins, etc., which are borne on the shoulders of as many as thirty men. These ponderous floats or '*pasos*', each starting from the church of its brotherhood, approach the Pl. de la Falange viâ the C. de las Sierpes, slowly defile before a stand erected for civic dignitaries in front of the Ayuntamiento, and follow the Av. de José Antonio and Av. Queipo de Llano to the cathedral, through which they pass to return to their starting-points. *Halts are frequent, and monotony can soon set in*. Seats, which may be booked at various sites for the series of four days, and other positions of vantage, should be taken up in good time, having checked in advance the approximate hour at which the pasos pass. The '*saetas*', ostensibly spontaneous exhibitions of religious fervour, are often sung by professionals as part of the pageant.

Feria. Seville is crowded and prices are raised during its great fair, which is held between April 18th–23rd on the Prado de S. Sebastián. If these dates clash with Easter, the Feria is postponed for a week. Although originally a cattle-market (founded 1848), the *Feria* is more interesting as a characteristic scene of Sevillian merrymaking—a natural reaction to the inhibiting solemnity of Easter. Bull-fights take place in the late afternoons and fireworks at night, while in the '*casetas*'—wooden or canvas huts erected for the occasion—revelry continues well into the early hours.

A   SOUTHERN SEVILLE

Flanking the central PL. DE LA FALANGE (or *de S. Francisco*), and separating it from the larger PL. NUEVO (or *S. Fernando*) is the **Ayuntamiento** (Pl. 2), designed by *Diego de Riaño*, begun under his direction in 1527–34 and completed c. 1564 (restored in 1891). The elaborate ornamentation of the exterior, notably the E. Façade, was a masterpiece of the Plateresque style, but its filthy and unkempt condition reflects the occupants' lack of interest in too many monuments in Seville, which deserve better care.

The chapel was built in 1571 under *Benv. Tortelli*.

The interior contains handsome rooms, and houses some Roman, Visigothic, and Moorish antiquities. The *Sala Capitular* has a vaulted coffered ceiling, while in the *Library* are preserved civic archives and a municipal banner (15C), etc.

From the Pl. de la Falange, flanked on the E. by the *Audiencia* (1606), the parallel C. Hernando Colón and Av. de José Antonio, both lead S. to the C. Alemanes, whence the *Pta. del Perdón* admits us to the *Patio de los Naranjos* within the architectural group formed by the *Cathedral* and its dependencies (Pl. 7).

The **Pta. del Perdón** dates from Moorish times and retains its Mudéjar bronze doors, but it was altered in 1522 by *Bartolomé López*. The terracotta statues and the relief over the horseshoe arch are by *Miguel Perrin*, a French sculptor trained in Italy (1519–20). The top storey is comparatively modern. The arcades opposite the gate were once the haunt of Seville's *escribanos* or scrivenors.

The **Patio de los Naranjos**, the picturesque but neglected court of the old mosque (p.541), shaded by orange-trees, retaining the fountain at which the Moslems performed their ritual ablutions, is a frequented thoroughfare, the exit being the *Pts. de Oriente*, at the base of the *Giralda*. This N.E.angle of the patio deserves restoration. As we enter the patio, we see (r.) the *Sagrario*, and (l.), the *Biblioteca Colombina*, while two doors admit to the *Cathedral*, see below. The *Pta. del Lagarto* (Lizard), to the S.E., is partly concealed by an archway of Mudéjar stucco-work, belonging to the *Cap. de N.S. de Granada*, which contains six Visigothic capitals.

The portal takes its name from a stuffed crocodile (replaced by a replica) which hung in the vestibule, an unconventional offering which accompanied a request from the Sultan of Egypt for the hand of the daughter of Alfonso X in 1260. The elephant's tusk, also hanging there, is said to have been unearthed in the amphitheatre at *Itálica*.

The *Sagrario*, entered also from the cathedral, and now used as a parish church, was designed by *Miguel de Zumárraga* in 1616 and continued by *Lor. Fernández de Iglesias*. The retablo, brought from the destroyed Conv. de S. Francisco, was made in 1664–69 by *Fr. Dionisio de Ribas* and contains sculptures by *Pedro Roldán*.

The **Biblioteca Colombina** was founded in 1552 from the bequest of Fernando Colón (d. 1539) of the manuscripts of his father, the great Columbus, and over 3000 vols. collected by himself. With these are kept the chapter library of c. 60,000 vols. including Illuminated Missals. other rare manuscripts and autographs.
The *Columbus MSS., exhibited in the second room, include the treatise drawn up by the navigator to prove that his plans of discovery were not antagonistic to Scripture, and his annotated copy of the 'Tractatus de Imagine Mundi' by Card. Pierre d'Ailly. Other cases contain Books of Hours (13th and 15C); the Bible of Alfonso the Wise, by Pedro de Pamplona; Pontifical of Bp. Juan de Calahorra (1390); Missale Hispalense (15C); Missals of Card. Hurtado de Mendoza (14C), and of Card. González de Mendoza (16C), etc.

Above the N.E. angle of the cathedral towers the incomparable ***Giralda** (309 ft), originally the minaret of the mosque. The lower part, 54 ft square with walls 8 ft thick, was begun in 1184 by *Ahmed ibn Baso* to the order of the Almohade sultan Yusuf II, at whose death the works were stopped at the level where the stone courses cease. It was continued in brick for Yakub I by *Ali de Gómara*, who completed the tower in 1198. The four sides are relieved by elegant balconied ajimeces, flanked by panels of diapered brickwork (*ajaracas*). On the N. side are some faded paintings by *Luis de Vargas*. The Renaissance open bell-chamber and the diminishing stages above were added in 1560–68 by *Hernán Ruiz*, while on the pinnacle is an oscillating bronze figure of La Fé (Faith). Cast by *Bartolomé Morel* in 1568 from a model by *Diego de Pesquera*, this is the 'Giraldillo' (i.e. vane), from which the tower takes its name.

The Ascent, made by a succession of easy inclined planes, is rewarded by an extensive view (best towards evening). Each stage or 'cuerpo' has its distinctive name. In the Cuerpo de Campanas are the 24 bells, each of which is formally christened; 'Sta María', the largest, dates from 1588; the oldest, of 1400, is all that survives of the first public clock set up in Spain. The bell on which the hours are struck today dates from 1764.—The first Christian knight to ascend the minaret after the conquest of Seville was Lawrence Poore, a Scotsman. In 1839 George Dennis outclimbed most travellers, for not content with the prospect from the belfry, he shinned up an iron post, squeezed through a grating, and 'standing only on a small projecting stone, and clinging to the walls for support', found himself immediately below the figure of Faith herself. It was from here that 'Dr Disillusion' in Fernández de Ribera's 'Los anteojos de major vista' saw the world.

To the E. is the Pl. de la Virgen de los Reyes, flanked to the N. by the *Pal. Arzobispal* (1664–1717), with a Baroque central feature of 1704. Off the S.E. side of the plaza a small cul-de-sac and patio may be entered; while at No. 6 in the nearby C. de los Abades, l. off the C. de Mateos Gagos, is the *Casa de Abades* (16C), with a patio in the Mudéjar style. This narrow street had a reputation for also accommodating the concubines or *barraganas* of the celibate clergy.

To the S.E. of the Cathedral opens the irregular *Pl. del Triunfo*, at one end of which a *Monument* (1767) marks the spot where mass, interrupted in the cathedral by the earthquake of 1755, was concluded.

The *Cathedral is the largest *Gothic* church in the world, of which grandeur is the distinctive quality as elegance is of León, strength of Santiago, and wealth of Toledo. Crowned by numerous pinnacles and with graceful flying buttresses, the massive structure preserves the oblong quadrilateral plan of the mosque on whose site it arose. Its architectural interest is enhanced by the works of art that it contains, but its exterior has a reprehensibly neglected appearance. It also shelters the tomb of Christopher Columbus.

Admission. The cathedral itself is usually open free, but entry to the Chapter House and Giralda, etc. is by ticket during specific hours. The lighting of the side-chapels has been improved, byt they are not always illuminated. To obtain a close look at their contents, it is advisable to seek out the sacristan.

History. After the reconquest of Seville in 1248, the mosque begun by Yusuf II in 1171 was dedicated to Sta María de la Sede and continued to be used, but as the Christian cathedral. In 1401 the chapter resolved to erect on its site an entirely new building, 'such and so good that it never should have its equal', and this ambitious project, begun in 1402, was accomplished in 1506. The name of the first architect is not recorded, but he was probably a Frenchman acquainted with the details of St-Ouen at Rouen and thus perhaps identical with the Charles Galter of Rouen (in Spain generally known as Carli), who worked at Barcelona and Lérida and was in charge of the works here at any rate from the 1430's, until his death in 1454. The design is remarkable for its eclecticism and for the knowledge shown of French Gothic and of developments in Aragonese and Castilian architecture. The lantern collapsed in 1511 and was rebuilt (by *Juan Gil de Hontañón*; 1519). Later earthquakes weakened the fabric, and in 1888 part of the central roof fell in, but since then the cathedral has been thoroughly restored. The Sala Capitular, the principal sacristies, and the Cap. Real, were added in the 16C.

Exterior. In the W. or principal Façade is the modern *Pta. Mayor*. The *Pta. del Bautismo* or *de S. Juan* (l.) and the *Pto. del Nacimiento* or *de S. Miguel* (r.) are adorned with figures by *Lorenzo Mercadante* (1464–67) and *Pedro Millán* (c. 1500).—The *Pta. de la Lonja* or *de S. Cristóbal*, on the S., dates from 1877–95. To the E. are the *Pta. de las Campanillas* and the *Pta. de los Palos*, both with 16C sculptures by *Miguel Perrin* (1522–23). Opening from the Patio de los Naranjos, on the N., are the *Pta. del Lagarto* and the 19C *Pta. de los Naranjos*.

INTERIOR. Notwithstanding the immense area and the towering clustered columns of the cathedral, rising to a balustraded gallery, the first general impression as we enter is one of sombre grandeur rather than of great size. The enormous proportions are only realized later as the eye becomes accustomed to the gloom. The ground plan shows a nave with double aisle, off which open side-chapels; the transepts do not project beyond the side wall; in the middle are the Cap. Mayor and Coro. The original brick floor was replaced in 1789–93 by the present marble paving. Most of the 93 windows contain stained glass (16–19C), the earliest by *Cristóbal Alemán* (1504); the most brilliant are the Ascension, Christ and Magdalen, Lazarus, and the Entry into Jerusalem, by *Arnao de Flandes* and his brother (1525), and the Resurrection, by *Carlos de Bruges* (1558), in the *Cap. de la Visitación*.

The richly adorned **Cap. Real**, at the E. end, was designed in 1550 by *Martín Gaínza* and completed by *Juan de Maeda* in 1575, on the site of an earlier royal burial chapel. Above the Reja by *Seb. Van der Bovart* (1771) Fernando III el Santo, on horseback, receives the keys of Seville. Within, the chapel is embellished with statues designed in 1553–54 by the Dutch painter, *Pedro Campana*. On the l. is the tomb of Alfonso the Wise (d. 1284), on the r. that of his mother, Beatrice of Swabia, wife of Fernando III; both tombs are modern. The high altarpiece behind contains the richly dressed *Virgen de los Reyes*, a wooden image of archæological interest, but much restored, said to have been presented by Louis IX of France to Fernando. Fernando (d. 1252) lies in the shrine of silver and bronze made in 1717 by *J. L. de Pina*, which stands in front of the altar.

A flight of steps descends to a vault, with an altar on which stands the *Virgen de las Batallas*, an ivory statuette of French workmanship, which Fernando III is said to have carried on his saddle-bow. Below this altar is his original coffin, and in glass cases around are those of Pedro the Cruel, his mistress María de Padilla, the Infante Fadrique (see p.546), and other royalty. The pennon and sword of Fernando are also preserved here. In the Sacristy is a Mater Dolorosa by *Murillo*.

The **Sala Capitular**, immediately S. of the *Pta. de las Campanillas*, the S.E. door of the cathedral, is entered through the *Cap. de la Purificación*. In the *Anteroom* are exhibited choir books (15–17C). The fine illuminations of the earlier volumes show Flemish and Giottesque influence. The reliefs here (1587–90) are by *Diego de Pesquera* and *Marcus Cabrera*. The chapter house proper, an eliptical saloon by *Riaño* and *Gainza* (1530–92), has a fine ceiling, and is adorned with marble reliefs (1587) by *J. B. Vázquez, Diego Velasco* and *Cabrera*. The frescoes by *Pable de Céspedes* (1538–1608), may have been retouched by Murillo. Above the Bishop's Throne is a Fernando el Santo (on copper) by *Pacheco*, and higher up is a Conception by *Murillo*, who painted also the eight ovals between the windows. Adjacent is a room displaying a collection of vestments.

The **Sacristía Mayor**, to the W. of the chapter house, is in the Plateresque style, begun in 1535 from designs by *Riaño* and *Gainza*. On the doors are carvings by Maestro *Guillén* (1548). It contains the *Treasury* and two paintings of the Virgin by *Zurbarán*; *Pedro Compana*, Descent from the Cross; *Pacheco*, Conception, etc. In a recess to the l. of the entrance is preserved a fine silver Custodia by *Juan de Arfe* (1580–87) on a pedestal by *Juan de Segura* (1668), while opposite is the TENEBRARIO, a bronze candelabrum, made (1559–62) by *Pedro Delgado*

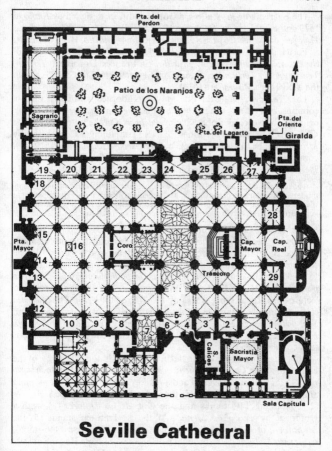

Seville Cathedral

and *Bart. Morel* to designs by *Hernán Ruiz*, which during Holy Week is placed between the coro and the high altar.

Small cupboard rooms contain smaller treasures and relics. Among these, besides monstrances, censers, and ornaments, are the *Alphonsine Tables, an elaborate reliquary in the form of a triptych, bequeathed by Alfonso the Wise c. 1280; a cross said to be made from the first gold brought from America by Columbus; a Gothic cross of 1580, by *Francisco Merino*; a head of St John the Baptist, by *Martínez Montañés*; an agate chalice of S. Clement; a rock-crystal cup belonging to Fernando el Santo, and the keys presented to him when Seville surrendered.

The silver gilt key given by the Moors is inscribed 'May Allah render eternal the dominion of Islam in this city'; on the iron gilt key surrendered by the Jews are the words 'The King of Kings will open, the King of all the earth will enter'.

The **Sacristía de los Cálices**, a Gothic addition, designed by *Riaño* in 1529 and completed by *Gainza* in 1537, and entered from the *Cap. de los Dolores*, contains: *Goya*, SS Justa and Rufina; *Murillo*, Head of Christ, S. Fernando, Holy Family; *Morales*, Pietà; *Valdés Leal*, Deliverance of St Peter; *J. Núñez*, Pietà; *Murillo*, St Frances Dorothea; *Tristán*, Trinity; *Alejo Fernández*, Adoration, St Peter; etc. The Crucifixion on the altar is by *Montañés* (1614).

The *Trascoro*, facing the Pta. Mayor, is adorned with Doric marble columns, and reliefs. The altarpiece is the *Virgen de los Remedios* (15C); below is the Surrender of Seville by *Pacheco*. On the outer sides of the *Coro* are four alabaster shrines, one (S.) containing a Conception by *Montañés*. The **Coro**, with a Reja by *Francisco de Salamanca* (1519–23), contains Gothic Stalls by *Nufro Sánchez* and the Flemish sculptor *Pieter Dancart* (1475–78) and a lectern by *B. Morel* (1570).

Above is the organ, with attractive cases, parts of which date from 1478. It was modernized at the turn of the century and later electrified, but only the upper organ is used during services, and produces a 5 second echo. The building also houses a very rare 'English' claviorgan of 1787, deserving restoration.

The raised **Cap. Mayor** has a Reja (1518–33) by *Francisco de Salamanca* and *Sancho Muñoz*. The Gothic * *Retablo* (recently cleaned) unequalled in Spain for size and elaborate detail, was begun in 1482 by *Dancart* and finished by other hands in 1525; the wings were added in 1550–64. In the centre is the *Virgen de la Sede* (late 13C).—The iron pulpits of 1531 are by *Fr. de Salamanca*, while the tabernacle and lecterns are Renaissance works by *Fr. Alfaro* (1593–96). The *Sacristía Alta*, behind the altar, has an artesonado ceiling by *Pedro López* and *Seb. Rodríguez* and contains three early paintings by *Alejo Fernández*.—On the exterior walls of the Cap. Mayor are numerous terracotta statues.

SIDE CHAPELS: **S. Aisle**. We begin our round in the S.E. angle of the cathedral at the *Cap. de la Purificación* or *del Mariscal* (**1**), which has a reja (1555) by *Pedro Delgado* and a retablo of 1555 by *Pedro Campana* and *Ant. de Alfián*.—Following the S. Aisle we pass the *Cap. S. Andrés* (**2**) containing 14C tombs and the *Cap. de los Dolores* (**3**), with a Dolorosa by *Pedro de Mena*.—At the S. Transept stands (**5**) the *Monument of Christopher Columbus* (Cristóbal Colón; c. 1446–1506), by *Arturo Mélida* (1891), brought with his remains from Havana in 1899 after the independence of Cuba was declared.—On the E. side of the transept is the Altar de la Piedad (**4**), with a Descent from the Cross, by *P. Fernández de Guadalupe* and *Alejo Fernández*, and on the W. is the Altar de la Gamba (**6**), with an altarpiece (1561) by *Luis de Vargas*. The reja, designed by *Juan Méndez*, was finished in 1562 by *P. Delgado*. Beside the *Pta. de S. Cristóbal* is a huge fresco of St Christopher by *Mateo Pérez de Alisio*.—*Cap. de la Antigua* (**7**), Fresco of the Virgin, Byzantine in style but ascribed to the 14C; Plateresque Tomb of Abp. Hurtado de Mendoza, by *Dom. Fancelli* (1509).—*Cap. de S. Hermenegildo* (**8**); Gothic Tomb of Abp. Juan de Cervantes (d. 1453), by *Lorenzo Mercadente 'de Bretaña'* (with a reja of 1537); the statue of St Hermengild is by *Bart, García de Santiago* (c. 1700); the late 15C glass by *Cristóbal Alemán*.—*Cap. de S. José* (**9**); Marriage of the Virgin, by *Valdés Leal*; fine Stained Glass by *Crist. Alemán* above the door.—*Cap. de S. Ana* (**10**); Gothic retablo of 1504; Virgin and child with St Anne, 17C Neapolitan.

W. Side. At the Altar del Nacimiento (**12**) are an Adoration by *Luis de Vargas*.—Before reaching the door of the *Cap. de S. Isidoro* (**13**) we pass the Altar de la Virgen de la Cinta, with a terracotta of c. 1500, and go on to the Altar de la Virgen del Madroño, with sculptures of 1454 by *Mercadante*.—Adjoining the *Pta. Mayor* are (l.) the Altar del Ángel (**14**), with the Guardian Angel, by *Murillo*, and (r.) the Altar del Consuelo (**15**), with a Virgin and saints by *Alonso Miguel de Tobar*, a pupil of Murillo.—At the Altar de la Virgen de la Alcobilla is a 15C terracotta group.—Altar de la Visitación (**18**), Retablo by *Pedro Villegas de Marmolejo* (16C).—From the *Cap. de los Jácomes* (**19**) we may enter the Sagrario.

In the pavement of the nave, between the *Pta. Mayor* and the *Trascoro*, is the Tombstone (**16**) of Fernando Colón (1488–1539) son of Columbus, 'who', remarked Richard Ford (repeating Bourgoing) 'would have been considered a great man had he been the son of a less great father'. It is inscribed A CASTILLA Y A LEON MUNDO NUEBO DIO COLON.

N. Aisle. In the *Cap. de S. Antonio* or *del Bautisterio* (**20**) is *Murillo*'s St. Anthony of Padua's Vision (1656)—skilfully repaired since the kneeling figure of the saint was cut of the canvas in 1874, to be recovered some three months later in New York—while above is a Baptism by *Murillo*. Among other paintings are: *Jordaens*, Circumcision, Nativity; *Valdés Leal*, Scenes from the life of St Peter; *Pacheco*, Conception; *Zurbarán*, SS. Justa and Rufina. The glass dates from c. 1670 and is by *Juan Bautista de León*.—*Cap. de Escalas* (**21**); with a reja of 1564; Cenotaph of Bp. Baltasar del Río (d. 1540) with a Genoese marble altarpiece of 1539; terracotta relief of the Virgen de Granada, by *Andrea Della Robbia*.—*Cap. de Santiago* (**22**); Juan de Las Roelas, Santiago riding over Moors (1609); *Valdés Leal*, St Lawrence. Tomb of Abp. Gonzalo de Mena (d. 1401). The stained glass (1550–60) is by *Vicente Menardo*.—*Cap. de S. Francisco* (**23**); *Herrera el Mozo*, Apotheosis of S. Francisco; *Valdés Leal*, the Virgin presenting the chasuble to S. Ildefonso. On the W. wall are numerous Flemish works. The glass in this, and the next two chapels, is by *Arnao de Flandes* (1534).—At the Altar de la Virgen de Belén (**24**) is a Virgin and Child by *Alonso Cano*.—The *Cap. de las Doncellas* (**25**) has a reja of 1579 and Baroque retablo.—The *Cap. de los Evangelistas* (**26**) has a retablo by *Ferdinand Sturm* (1555), with a view of the old Giralda in the lowest panel on the l.—At the Altar de N.S. del Pilar (**27**) is a painted wooden statue of the Virgin by *Pedro Millán* (c. 1500).

E. Side. *Cap. de S. Pedro* (**28**); Retablo (1625) by *Zurbarán;* the glass dates from 1778.—*Cap. de la Concepción Grande* or *de S. Pablo* (**29**); (beyond the Cap. Real), has a Baroque retablo of 1658 designed by *Fr. de Ribas* with sculptures by *Alfonso Martínez*; the glass is by *Menardo* (1526); the reja is of 1560.

The **Casa Lonja* or *Exchange* (Pl. 7), in a severe classical style, was designed by *Herrera* and erected by *Juan de Minjares* in 1584–98 in order to accommodate the vociferous merchants who previously conducted their business in the Patio de los Naranjos. The main entrance is on the W. façade.

Within is an arcaded patio, while a handsome red marble staircase (1787) ascends to the *Archivo de Indias*, founded in 1785, an immense and not yet fully explored collection of some 36,000 files of documents relating to the discovery of America and to the history and administration of Spain's American colonies. A changing exhibition of maps and other material is usually on view in at least one of its imposing, vaulted galleries.

To the S., in the '*old*' *Chapter House* (1770; attrib. to *Pedro de Silva*) a *Museum of Contemporary Art* has been installed, containing a representative collection of the works of Spanish (and particularly Sevillian) artists, among them *Millares, Zobel, Lucio Muñoz, César Manrique, Quixart, Manuel Rivera, Rafael Armengol, Joaquín Saenz, Canogar, Subirach*, and *Francisco Farreras*.

On the S.E. side of the Pl. del Triunfo lies the *Alcázar* (Pl. 7), the Mudéjar palace of Spanish Kings for nearly seven centuries. The successor of a more extensive citadel and palace, founded perhaps under the Abbadites in the 11C and enlarged by the Almohades in 1171–76, much of the present structure dates from Pedro the Cruel (1364–66), who employed Moorish architects for his restoration or rebuilding and incorporated fragments from earlier Moorish buildings. Subsequent additions, alterations, and restorations (rarely happy) mingling Christian with Moorish motifs, have impaired its claim to be regarded as a true monument of Moorish art, but, although inferior to the Alhambra, it is still a captivating building.

Some parts exist of the Almohade citadel into which Fernando III forced his way in 1248, but few traces remain of the Moorish palace within it, which is supposed to have been built on the site of a Roman prætorium c. 1171 by an architect named *Jalubi*. In the alcázar rebuilt by Pedro I, Isabel the Catholic constructed the chapel on the upper floor. Charles V, who was married to Isabel of Portugal in 1526 in the Hall of Ambassadors, added several rooms and laid out the garden. A thorough restoration of the building was made by Philip IV c. 1624; and Philip V, who resided here in morbid seclusion for two years, built the pillared *Apeadero* and dug the fish pond c. 1733. The offices over the Bath of Padilla date from Fernando VI. Damaged by earthquake in 1755 and by fire in 1762, the palace was neglected until the 19C, when it was crudely restored.

The monarch especially connected with the Alcázar is Pedro the Cruel, who lived here with María de Padilla. Here he caused the assassination of his half-brother Fadrique, Master of the Order of Santiago, in 1358, and murdered his guest, Abu Said of Granada, for the sake of his jewels. One of these, an uncut ruby, presented by Pedro to the Black Prince in 1367, was worn by Henry V at Agincourt and adorns the Imperial Crown of Great Britain.

From the S.W. angle of the Pl. del Triunfo we enter the *Pta. del León*, a narrow archway above which is a lion in glazed tilework. The adjacent curtain walls are Almohade work of 1171–76. The first courtyard (the *Mexaur* of the Moorish palace) is called the *Patio de la Montería*, the court of the 'Monteros de Espinosa' (see p.126), the royal lifeguard.

To the l. is the old *Sala de Justicia*, built c. 1345 for Alfonso XI, through which is reached the *Patio de Yeso*, a relic of the Almohade palace, not normally on view.

A wall pierced by three arches divides us from the inner court, or *Patio del León*, on the far side of which is the main façade of the Alcázar proper, see below.

To the r. is the *Cuarto del Almirante, Casa de Contratación*, or *Casa del Océano*, founded by Isabel in 1503 as the official centre for organizing expeditions and regulating the relations between Spain and the new territories overseas. The qualification *de las Américas* was only later added. Passing through the arcade which supports the upper floor, we enter a hall hung with 17–18C tapestries and communicating with the *Sala de Audiencia* and the *Chapel*, with an artesonado ceiling.

On the end wall hangs the Virgen de los Mareantes or Navegantes (Seafarers), executed by *Alejo Fernández* for this position in 1531–36. Beneath the Virgin's cloak are figures of (r.) Columbus and the brothers Pinzón and (l.) Charles V (or the Admiral of Castile) and officials of the Casa de Contratación. A frieze beneath the ceiling displays the arms of Admirals from the institution of the office in 1248.

From the Patio we may ascend to the least interesting part of the palace, the *State Rooms* and the *Royal Apartments* used since the time of Charles V, whose motto 'Plus Ultra' appears on the tiles lining the staircase walls. The outermost antechamber, or *Saleta*, with a ceiling displaying the yoke-and-arrows badge of the Catholic Kings, has tapestries from cartoons by Teniers and Wouwerman.—Beyond a square chamber with an octagonal Mudéjar ceiling we reach the *Oratory of Isabel the Catholic*, where the retablo of painted azulejos is by *Fr. Niculoso of Pisa* (1504).—Returning towards the Saleta we enter (r.) an anteroom admitting to the *State Dining Room*, and passing through a further series of rooms, often with fine ceilings, with balconies overlooking the gardens, and containing royal portraits, we reach the *Bedroom of Pedro the Cruel*. The skulls painted over the door are said to record the fate of five unjust judges executed by the King. The artesonado ceiling is notable. Through the upper gallery of the Patio de las Doncellas, we reach the *Music Room of Isabel II*, with several portraits by *Mengs* and *V. López*. More portraits hang in the *Bedroom of Isabel II*, which leads to the Mudéjar *Hall of Audience*, another survival from the 14C palace. The *Antechamber*, hung with Brussels Tapestries by *Juan de Raes* and containing 18C French furniture, leads back to the Saleta, whence we descend to the Patio del León.

On our r. is the main *Façade* of the Alcázar, the central part of which, decorated with arabesques, is surmounted by a boldly projecting cornice above a row of windows with cusped arches, flanked on either side by open galleries with slender marble columns amid Moorish arches.

Above the window over the square-headed main portal (*Pta. Principal*) an inscription records that 'these castle and façades' were built by Pedro I in 1364. The rectangular cartouche surrounded by this inscription bears, eight times repeated in formalized Cufic, the Arabic 'God alone is Conqueror' (see p.484), the motto of the tributary Nasrite king of Granada, Mohammed V, who sent his best craftsmen to carry out the work.

From the *Vestíbulo*, with its marble columns, a passage on the extreme l. admits to the **Patio de las Doncellas** ('maids of honour'), a charmingly decorated court surrounded by an arcade of cusped arches on coupled marble columns, with open arabesque work above. The columns, in the Renaissance style, and the upper storey date from a mid-16C restoration. Charles V's motto frequently recurs. The brilliant azulejos (14C) on the walls, the stucco-work, and friezes should be noted. On the l. we enter the *Salón de Carlos V*, which has a fine coffered ceiling and tasteful azulejo decoration, both dating from the 16C. Adjoining are the three *Apartments of María de Padilla*.

The ***Salon de Embajadores**, ('of the Ambassadors'), 10 m. square, with a 'media naranja' dome, is the most splendid room in the Alcázar; walls, arches, and doorways being covered with elaborate and intricate Moorish decoration in delicate polychrome colouring. Special features are the triple doorways and the ornamented blind arcade forming the frieze. The incongruous balconies are due to Charles V; and the frieze of royal portraits at the same level, to Philip II. Adjoining, l., are a *Comedor* (dining-room), and in front, the *Apartment of Philip II*.

Beyond the latter is the **Patio de las Muñecas** ('dolls'), taking its name from two minute medallion faces at the spring of one of the smaller Moorish arches of the arcade. The upper part of the court dates from 1856. Adjoining this patio are the *Bedroom of Isabel*, the *Salón del Principe* (Don Juan, her only son, born in the Alcázar in 1478), and the *Dormitorio de los Reyes Moros*.

From the Patio de las Muñecas a narrow passage brings us back to the Vestíbulo. Leaving the main entrance we bear r. to enter a gallery leading to the *Patio de María de Padilla*, altered for Philip V (c. 1727–32). This area was the site of the Gothic palace built after 1248, of which little remains beyond the so-called *Pal. de Carlos V*, altered in the 18C.

In the basement is a vaulted gallery with the alleged *Baños*, in which the beautiful María is said to have bathed. The gallants of Don Pedro's court used to drink her bathwater in exaggerated homage, but one excused himself, lest 'having tasted the sauce, he might covet the partridge'.

The first of the apartments here contains a magnificent series of *Tapestries* recording Charles V's Tunis expedition of 1535. The cartoons were drawn by *Jan Vermayen*, who accompanied Charles throughout the campaign, and the tapestries were woven by *Willem Pannemaker* of Brussels. Completed in 1554, they were exhibited in London in connection with the marriage of Philip II and Mary Tudor. Of the twelve panels, two are copies made in Madrid in 1740 shortly before the originals disappeared; on the map of the Mediterranean, the figure leaning against the column on the r. represents Vermayen.— Beyond is the vaulted *Salón del Emperador*, retaining its Gothic form, with walls enriched by a dado of azulejos (1577-79) painted by *Cristóbal de Augusta*.

The **Alcázar Gardens**, with their perfumed orange-groves and palm-trees, roses, brick walks with 'surprise waterworks', alleys shaded by box and myrtle hedges, are a delightful spot to while away an hour. Next to the palace is the *Estanque*, a square pool beside which is a wall of Baroque masonry with grotesque frescoes. Steps descend to the *Jardín de la Danza*, beyond which are the gardens of Charles V. In the lower garden is the semi-Moorish *Pabellón* built by *Juan Hernández* in 1543, beside an ancient orange-tree said to have been planted in the days of Pedro the Cruel; beyond is a labyrinth of myrtles and cypresses enclosing the open-air 'Baths of the Sultanas'. Further on, in a wilder part of the gardens, is another pavilion, while the *Pta. de Marchena* is a fine doorway of c. 1500, brought here when the palace of the dukes of Arcos at Marchena was demolished in 1913. The gate now serves as an entrance to the Huerta del Retiro, with flagged walks and rosebeds. We leave the gardens by the 18C *Apeadero*, a hall of marble columns, and the *Patio de Banderas*, planted with orange-trees, adjoining the S.E. angle of the Pl. del Triunfo.

To the E. of the Alcázar, reached from the S.E. angle of the Patio de Banderas by an archway and passage, are the *Jardines de Murillo*.

To the N. are the narrow lanes of the **Barrio de Santa Cruz**, the old *Judería*. Murillo was buried in 1682 in the old church of Santa Cruz, destroyed by Soult. The whole area evokes the 'Romantic' view of Seville, the scene *par excellence* of so many operas and dramas, for which it is indeed a perfect setting. It is also, with its maze of alleys, its cool patios and plazuelas, a delight to wander through at any time of day or night, although an area further N. is less sophisticated.

In the C. Mezquita, leading E. from the Pl. de Santa Cruz, is the house occupied by Washington Irving in 1828. *Sta María la Blanca*, to the N.E., a synagogue until 1391, and rebuilt as a Baroque church in 1659, contains a Pietà (1564) by *Luis de Vargas*, a Last Supper by *Murillo*, and an Ecce Homo by *Morales*. The **Hospicio de Venerables Sacerdotes**, in the Pl. de los Venerables, a little N.W. of the Pl. de Alfaro, has an attractive patio decorated with azulejos, and a chapel of 1675–98 containing works by *Valdés Leal*, and wall-paintings by *Lucas Valdés*.

A little to the W. is the attractive *Pl. de Doña Elvira*, from the N.W. corner of which we may return, viâ the Pl. de la Alianza, to the Pl. del Triunfo.

S.W. of the Lonja, from the far side of the Av. de Queipo de Llano, the C. Jurado and C. de Santander lead to (r.) the C. Temprano and (Pl. 6) the **Hosp. de la Caridad* (for the sick and aged poor), with a colourful façade, and of interest for the paintings by Murillo and Valdés Leal in its chapel. The chapter-house (*cabildo*) and crypt are also shown on request. The arches in the grounds are remains of the medieval *atarazanas* built by Alfonso X, occupying the site of earlier Moorish shipyards.

Don Miguel de Mañara (1626–79), a profligate noble of Seville, turning from the frivolities of life, joined the fraternity of the Caridad, whose function was to provide Christian burial for executed criminals, and devoted his life and fortune to the establishment of this hospital, completed in 1674 from plans by *Bernardo Simón de Pineda*. Murillo, a friend of Mañara, is said to have designed the five large azulejos on the façade of the church. Mañara is buried at the foot of the high altar.

Six of the series of paintings executed by *Murillo* in 1660–74) for the Chapel remain; five others were carried off by Soult (one is now in the Nat. Gallery, London). S. Wall: Miracle of the Loaves and Fishes; below it, Medallion of the Infant Saviour; on the opposite wall: Moses striking the rock; below it, John the Baptist as a child; Annunciation; and S. Juan de Dios bearing a sick man to the hospital. At the high altar (1670) is a Deposition by *Pedro Roldán*. Two cadaverous paintings by *Valdés Leal* flank the W. Door: Corpses of a bishop and of a knight of Calatrava, and Death quenching the light of Life. They have been much improved by recent cleaning.

In the *Chapter House* are portraits of Elder Brethren of the fraternity, including that of Mañara by *Valdés Leal*; also the sword and death-mask of Mañara.

Beyond the Jardines de la Caridad, the Paseo de Cristóbal Colón skirts the river northwards, passing the colourful **Pl. de Toros* built in 1760–63 by *Vic. Sanmartin*, and a market, perhaps on the site of the prison in which the sculptor Torrigiano died (1522) under the ban of the Inquisition. An old house, which deserved restoration, in the adjacent C. de Antonia Diéz, was recently demolished by the authorities, who heed not the condemnation of architects of taste for their continuing destruction of 'old' Seville. A few paces further on the *Pte. de Isabel II* (1852) spans the river to *Triana*, see p.556.

On the bank of the Guadalquivir, S. of the C. de Santander, stands the **Torre del Oro**, a twelve-sided battlemented tower, built in 1220 on the wall of the Alcázar citadel and known to the Moors as the 'golden tower' from the colour of its azulejos. The round uppermost stage and the lower windows with balconies date from 1760. Used by Pedro the Cruel as a prison, it now contains a small *Maritime Museum*.

Following the river bank southwards, we pass the *Pte. de S. Telmo* to the *Pal. de S. Telmo*. Now a seminary, with a Churrigueresque portal

(1734), it dates from 1682–1796, and was originally a naval college. The present appearance is due to *Leonardo de Figueroa* and his son *Matías*.

Here, according to William Jacob (1809) 'pretentions' were made 'to teach geography, algebra, geometry, and trigonometry; but having neither books, nor instruments, nor professors possessing any knowledge, their progress is very trifling'.

Immediately to the N. is the grandiose *Hotel Alfonso XIII* at the corner of the C.S. Fernando and close to the Pl. de Calvo Sotelo or Pta. de Jerez, where there is now no gateway. It was here, abutting the S.W. wall of the Alcázar, that Borrow lived in 1839–40, at No. 7 Plazuela de la Pila seca, but the area is now built over.—On the N. side of this square is the **Cap. de Maese Rodrigo** (c. 1505–14), built under *Antón Ruiz* and *Martín Sánchez* for the Antiguo Seminario founded by Rodrigo de Santaella, and containing a Retablo by *Alejo Fernández* (1520), fine azulejos, and a good artesonado ceiling.

Just E. of the hotel, rises the huge square bulk of the **Fábrica de Tabacos** (Pl. 11), built in 1750–66 to the designs of the Flemish engineer *Sebastian van der Borcht*. At one time 10,000 '*cigarreras*' were employed here, but 'Carmen' has left only a romantic memory, for the building now houses the **University**—the 'weed' making way for 'grass'. These cigarreras were reputed by Ford to be 'more impertinent than chaste', and were obliged to undergo 'an ingeniously-minute search on leaving their work, for they sometimes carry off the filthy weed in a manner her most Catholic majesty never dreamt of'.

Beyond is the open PRADO DE S.SEBASTIÁN, still the scene of the annual Feria, and previously the *Quemadero*, site of the Inquisition's autos-de-fe. To the N.E. beyond the Estación de Cádiz, is neo-classical *S. Bernardo* (1780–95), by *José Álvarez*, containing Baroque retablos by *Fernando de Barahonda* (c. 1690) and a Last Judgment by *Herrera the Elder* (1628–29).

From the Pal. de S. Telmo the wide Paseo de las Delicias runs S., shortly skirting the **Parque de María Luisa** (l.), until 1893 part of the grounds of *S. Telmo,* and the smaller *Jardínes de las Delicias* (r.), attractively laid out with palms, orange-trees, roses, etc. In 1929 a Spanish-American exhibition was held in and beside these gardens and some buildings then erected remain. To the E. opens the *Pl. de España*, within an immense hemicycle of buildings now accommodating the *Capitanía General* and the *Gobierno Civil*.

To the S. is the **Museo Arqueológico**.

BASEMENT. Collections of the Paleolithic period, including **R 2** Campaniform vases from *Écija*; idol-plates or pendents (c. 2000 B.C.) from the *Cueva de la Mora* (Jabugo), and owl-like idols from *Morón*. **R 3** Arrow-heads, some of rock-crystal. **R 4** Funerary steles (8C B.C.), from *Carmona*: Bronze fibulas, etc. **R 5** Artefacts from *Carambola*, including (in **R 6**) reproductions of the gold Tartessian treasure (8C B.C.), and a seated statuette of Astarte. **R 8** Bronze plaques and pectorals from *Punta de Vaca* (c. 7C B.C.), of Punic or Phoenician origin; Phoenician ceramics from *Rio Tinto*. **R 9** Punic amphoras, and metal and bone objects. **R 10**, Bronze ex-votos.

Ascending to the GROUND FLOOR, we turn r. into **R 11**, with an impressive collection of stone Lions from *Bornos, Estepa*, and *Utrera* (2–3C B.C.), and Bulls; also a relief of two soldiers (*Estepa;* 1C A.D.). **R 12** Mosaics; a puteal from *Trigueros*, and Heads of Paris and Minerva, among others, and bronze objects and figures. **R 13**. Statues from *Italica*, and the Mosaic of Cacchus (*Écija*; 3C A.D.). **R 14** Statues of Diana and of Mercury, both Roman copies of hellenistic originals. **R 15** Glass an sculpted fragments from *Italica*, including a beautiful hand. **R 17**. a Roman copy of a statue of Venus, from *Italica*. Note the unusual ex-votos of feet displayed on the wall, possibly those of pilgrims. **R 18** Terracotta lamps, etc. **R 19**

Funerary inscriptions, steles, etc., and a Roman copy of a statue of Diana. **R 20** (central oval), displaying large statues and busts from *Italica*. **R 21** Ritual ara, including funerary steles (note No. 43) and (No 52), a Pedestal of Isis; cinerary urns, and amphoras. **R 23** Artefacts and capitals, etc. from *Carteia*. **R 24**, Glass and jewellery (1–11C); a head of a woman from *Mulva* (2C), and material from *Munigua* (near Villanueva del Rio y Minas). RR 22 and 25 are closed. **R 26** Palaeochristian sculpture, sarcophagi, and capitals, etc.; also material from *Medina Azahara,* and bronze thimbles. **R 27** Moorish tiles, jars, well-heads (from *Seville*), and woodwork, from which we make our exit onto a veranda, displaying tombs.

On the opposite side of the gardens is the **Museo des Artes y Costumbres Populares**, with its interesting collections.

Near the entrance is a Map of Seville dated 1771. **R 1** (r.), displaying a range of Costumes and smaller objects, including purses, waistcoats, rosaries, jewellery, hat-pins, rattles, and 'grilleras' (cricket-cages). **R 2** Costumes used at Carnival and Corpus, including that worn for the Dance of the Seises (see p. 539) in the Cathedral; and frilled and flounced 'flamenco' dresses, and examples of the *Manta* and *Saya* of Tarifa. **R 3** Musical instruments, including *zambombas*. **R 4** Agricultural implements, including a *trillo* with its seat; saddles and stirrups, etc; branding irons; basketwork, including esparto *redendels*, for drying grapes; shepherds' carvings; firearms; ceramics, and bull sculptures by *Mariano Benlluire*. **R 5** a collection of ecclesiastical plate (anteolas); **R 6** Embroidery and lace, and an extensive *Collection of camisas* or chemises. **R 7** Individual rooms of differing types of furniture, including a 'Casita de Feria'; note the Mudéjar box. **R 8** Ceramics, mostly late 19C.—In the BASEMENT are a series of alcoves and rooms displaying weights and measures; tin-work (*hojalatería*) candle-holders; wine and oil-presses; implements for the cleaning and softening of leather; copper and brasswork; ceramics, including *tinajas* or large earthenware storage-jars, *búcaros* or water-jugs and *botijos* or pitchers, Pharmacy jars, and ware from Triana, showing Japanese influence, and an extensive *Collection of tiles, some with a metallic lustre.—On the GROUND FLOOR are Exhibition Rooms.

B   WESTERN SEVILLE

The narrow **C. de las Sierpes**, a famous pedestrian thoroughfare which leads N. from the Pl. de la Falange, is said to take its name ('of the serpents') from the sign of an ancient tavern. Here, and in the vicinity, the life of the Sevillanos may still be seen at its most characteristic, although progressively less so. At No. 52 stood a prison in which Cervantes was once incarcerated, while in the C. Jovellanos (l.) is the Baroque **Cap. de S. José** of c. 1690, with a portal of 1766. The original work, a fine example of the richest Sevillian style of the period, is attr. to *Pedro Romero*.

At the N. end of the Sierpes (*La Campana*) we turn l. and follow the C. de Alfonso XII to the Pl. del Museo (formerly del Conde de Casa Galindo). The ***Museo de Bellas Artes** (Pl. 13) occupies the buildings of the *Conv. de N.S. de Gracia*, or *de la Merced*, built around three patios and completed in 1612 by *Juan de Oviedo*.

The museum is in the protracted process of being entirely reformed, and only a proportion of its paintings are at present on view. The previous description has therefore been retained meanwhile, as giving some indication of its normal contents. It contains a number of important works, particularly of the Sevillian school, besides more modern canvases. The nucleu of the collection consists of paintings rescued by the exertions of Dean Manuel López Cepero from the convents suppressed in 1836.

At the entrance is a gallery (r.) displaying examples of 16–17C azulejos. We pass the enclosed *Patio del Aljibe* and turn l. to enter RRI–II, containing a number of fine works and retablos of the medieval period, including: *Franz Frutet*, Triptych of the Crucifixion; *Marten de Vos the Elder*, Last Judgment; *School of Alejo Fernández*, Virgin with SS Michael and Bartholomew; and eight Saints from the Retablo of the Military Orders of the church of S. Benito de Calatrava.—R III contains an anonymous Baptism and two good Calvaries, two sculptures by *Pedro Torrigiano*, and works by *Crist. de Morales*, among others, while R IV contains *El Greco's* portrait of his son, and religious paintings by *Fr. Pacheco* (1571–1634).—R V displays a Romería by *Jan Brueghel*; *Alonso Cano*, S. Francisco Borja; *Tristán*, Conception; and *Ribera*, *Santiago Peregrino, and Sta Teresa. We enter the great cloister (*Patio de los Bojes*) adjoining which is the convent *Church* (RR VI-VIII) containing works by *Herrera the Elder*, *Montañés*, *Zurbarán*, including his *St Hugh and Carthusian monks at table, and the Apotheosis of St Thomas Aquinas (on the l. is Abp. Deza; on the r. Charles V, and behind him, Zurbarán), and conspicuously, *Bartolomé Murillo* (1616–82), mostly painted for the Old Capuchin convent, notably *St Thomas of Villanueva, while in an adjacent side chapel is displayed his 'Madonna de la Servilleta' said to have been painted on a napkin (*servilleta*) for the convent cook. The dome over the crossing was painted in tempera by *Dom. Martínez* (18C).

We pass a charming *Series of luxuriously dressed female saints of the school of Zurbarán on the cloister wall as we approach the main staircase, at the head of which we turn l. into the upper cloister, in which, together with R IX, are examples of the art of *Juan de Valdés Leal* (1622–90). In R X, adjoining, is the Virgin presenting the chasuble to S. Ildefonso, by *Velázquez*, and his portrait of Cristóbal Suárez de Ribera. We may follow the upper cloister to R XII, accommodating eight large paintings showing the celebrations at the accession of Fernando VI and Barbara de Braganza in 1747, which are of historical interest.—R XI, adjacent, contains a small display of ceramics, while from the far end of R XII steps ascend to R XIII in which is *Goya's* *Portrait of José Duarzo, and a still-life by *Meléndez*.—R XIV contains a fine collection of *Portraits by *Antonio María Esquivel* (1806–1857).

We now pass through a series of rooms (XV–XVIII) devoted to 19C works; R XIX displays paintings by *Gonzalo Bilbao* (1860–1938), while in R XX are a number of 20C works, including a *Sorolla*. In the adjoining upper cloister (RR XXI and XIV) and R XXII are foreign paintings, including *Cornelio Schut*, Portrait of the Dominican Fray Domingo Bruselas, and two fine 17C battle scenes. Among recent acquisitions is a Calvary by *Lucas Cranach*.

At the end of the C Alfonso XII, N.W. of the museum, is the site of the Pta. Real, by which Fernando III entered Seville.—Due N. of the museum is *S. Vicente* (14C; largely rebuilt in the 18-19C), preserving a retablo mayor (1690-1706) by *Cristóbal de Gaudix*, a Descent from the Cross carved by *And. de Ocampo* (1603-04), and the Virgen de los Remedios, by *Villegas Marmoléjo*.

From the S.E. angle of the Pl. del Museo runs the C. Monsalves, where stood a house in which Richard Ford resided during the winter of 1831–32. To the r. is the C. Férnan Caballero, where at No. 14 lived the novelist 'Fernán Caballero' (Cecilla Bohl von Faber; 1796–1877). At the corner of the C. S. Pablo stands **La Magdalena**, the church of the former Conv. de S. Pablo, built in 1692–1704 by *Leonardo de Figueroa*, and with a fine mudéjar cupola. The church is rich in frescoes by *Lucas Valdés* and has a Baroque retablo mayor, with a figure of the Magdalen by *Felipe Malo de Molina*, 1704; and two paintings by *Zurbarán* in the Cap. Sacramental.

Hence we may return N.E. to LA CAMPANA. At No. 18 in the C. de Cuna, parallel to and E. of the C. de las Sierpes, is the **Pal. de la Condesa de Lebrija**, with three patios containing Roman mosaics pillaged from Itálica, and an artesonado ceiling (over the staircase) brought from the destroyed palace of the dukes of Osuna at Marchena.

Among the mosaic pavements is an attractive octagonal one round an interior fountain; other bits of mosaic have been 'framed'. The rooms contain a jumble of artefacts likewise collected from Italica, but the building is otherwise of slight interest, although certain walls have pleasant early tiles.

A short distance further E. (until its removal to the Fábrica de Tabacos, see p.550), stood the old University, which since 1771 had occupied a Jesuit convent built in 1565–79 by Fray *Juan de Carvajal*, probably to designs by Fray *Bartolomé de Bustamante*. It was demolished in the 1970s and replaced by the modern buildings of the School of Bellas Artes.

Originally a school established in 1256 by Alfonso the Wise, it was raised to the rank of a university in 1502 by the Catholic Kings. The **University Church** has been recently restored. In the centre of the retablo mayor, made by Fray *Alonso Matias* soon after 1600, is a Holy Family by *Roelas*, flanked by his Nativity, and an Adoration by his pupil, *Fr. Varela*; above, an Annunciation, by *Ant. Mohedano*, and the two SS. John, by *Alonso Cano*. The statues of S. Francisco Borja and S. Ignacio, in front, by *Montañés* (1610), were painted by *Pacheco*. To the l. of the high altar are the brasses of Francesco Duarte de Mendioca (d. 1554) and his wife. In the l. transept, the Tomb of Lorenzo Suárez de Figueroa (d. 1409). In the r. transept are the effigy (1606) of the humanist Arias Montano, and a monument to Gustavo Adolfo Bécquer, who, with his brother Valeriano, is interred in the crypt. In the nave are the Italian Renaissance tombs (1520) of Pedro Enríquez and his wife, Catalina de Rivera, by the Genoese *Antonio Aprile* and *Pace Gagini* respectively. In the pavement between these, a brass of Pedro Afán de Rivera (d. 1571). The Altar del Cristo de la Buena Muerte has a Crucifixion (1610) by *Juan de Mesa*.

A short distance N., approached by the C. Orfila, is **S. Andrés** (14–15C) with Mudéjar chapels, a Conception by *Cano*, a nave altarpiece by *Andrés de Castillejo* (1587), and SS. Michael and Lucy (1520) by *Cristóbal* (?) *Mayorga*. Further N. is *S. Martín*, built in the early 15C, with a high altar of 1606–08 by *López Bueno* and *Ocampo*; the paintings of the tutelar, once ascribed to Herrera the Elder, are the work of the Italian *Girólamo Lucente*, of Corregio (1643).

C NORTHERN SEVILLE

From LA CAMPANA, we may work our way N.W. to the Pl. Gavidia, and turn N. along the C. Card. Spinola to **S. Lorenzo**, rebuilt in the early 17C, but retaining traces of Gothic and Mudéjar work. In an adjoining chapel is the image of Jesús del Gran Poder by *Juan de Mesa* (1620). The church contains a retablo by *Montañés* (1638–39) with figures by *Felipe* and *Fr. Dionisio de Ribas*, paintings by *Pedro Villegas de Marmolejo* (1520–97), who was buried here, and a mural (c. 1345) of N.S. de Rocamador. The chapels flanking the high altar have Baroque retablos of 1682–89 by *Fernando de Barahona*, while lateral chapels contain works by *Pacheco* (1624).

The church of the **Conv. de Sta Clara** further N. founded 1260, is entered from No. 40 in the street, admitting to a charming orange-shaded patio. It contains an artesonado ceiling, and a retable by *Montañés* and his school (1621–23). The doorway of 1622 is by *Diego de Quesada*, while the interior is adorned with azulejo dadoes, those in the sanctuary by *Alonso García* (1575), the rest added by *Hernando de Valladares* in 1622.—A Gothic gateway on the l. of the church admits to a yard or 'corral' in which rises the battlemented **Torre de Don Fadrique** (1252), a relic of the Pal. of Don Fadrique, brother of Alfonso X, and unique in Andalucía as a specimen of transitional Gothic style.

At the N. end of the C. de Sta Clara is the ***Conv. de S. Clemente el Real** (Pl. 13), founded by S. Fernando on the site of a Moorish palace, but rebuilt in the 18C. The earlier church has a huge and impressive artesonado ceiling and azulejos of 1588, while the walls higher up bear frescoes (c. 1700) by *Lucas Valdés*, The Plateresque high altar of 1639 is the masterpiece of *Felipe de Ribas*. On the r. of the entrance is a statue of St John the Baptist, by *Gaspar Núñez Delgado*, and on the N. side of the high altar is the monument of María of Portugal, wife of Alfonso XI.

To the E. of S. Lorenzo lies the *Alameda de Hércules*, a promenade designed by *Asensio de Maeda* in 1574. At its S. end are two antique columns (comp. p.556) bearing statues of Julius Caesar and Hercules, by *Diego de Pesquera* (1574).

The N.E. QUARTER of Seville contains many characteristic churches with their combination of Moorish and Renaissance architecture. From the N. end of the Alameda de Hércules, we pass *Omnium Sanctorum* in the C. Peris Mencheta, with Gothic portals, a pentagonal apse with battlemented eaves, and a partially Moorish tower with arabesques. Thence the C. de la Feria (the scene of a rag-fair on Thurs.) leads l. towards the Paseo de Resolano and (r.) the *Pta. de la Macarena*. The latter, named after a Moorish princess, was rebuilt in 1795. Within the gate is S. Gil, with remains of 13–14C work and a rich dado of geometrical alicatados (c. 1300) in the presbytery; in the adjoining *Basilica de la Macarena* is the *Virgen de la Esperanza*, the cherished cult-image of Seville, ascribed to *Pedro Roldán* or his daughter *Luisa* ('la Roldana').

Outside the gate appears the classical façade of the **Hosp. de Cinco Llagas** ('of the Five Wounds'), or *de la Sangre* ((of the Blood'), much extended since its foundation at the expense of Enríquez and Catalina de Rivera. Although founded in 1500, its buildings were not begun until 1546, to a design by *Martín Gainza*, after whose death they were continued by *Hernán Ruiz*. The church he designed in 1560 was completed by *Asensio de Maeda* in 1613. The medallions on the church are perhaps by *Torrigiano*; within are a retablo with paintings by *Alonso Vázquez*, and other paintings by *Jerónimo Ramirez* and *Est. Márquez*.

Between the *Pta. de Macarena* and the *Pta. de Córdoba* we skirt a well-preserved fragment of the **City Walls** built of tapia with square towers and battlements, belonging to the Almoravide refortification of c. 1100. These, together with the walls of the Alcázar gardens, are all that remain of the ramparts, which once included 166 towers and 12 gates, mostly demolished in the mid-19C. Re-entering the city at the latter gate we pass *S. Julián*. *Sta Marina*, to the W., has a Mudéjar tower, but to all appearances, is gutted, while opposite is Baroque *S. Luis* (1709–32) by the *Figueroas*, with frescoes by *Lucas Valdés*. To the S. is the façade of **S. Marcos** (14C Gothic) with an attractive Mudéjar portal, built on the site of a mosque, on the base of whose minaret rises a Mudéjar tower of c. 1350. Adjacent is the *Conv. de S. Isabel* of 1602–09, by *Alonso de Vandaelvira*, with retablos (1610–24) by *Montañés*, *López Bueno*, and *Juan de Mesa*.

A few paces E. is the **Conv. de Sta Paula**, founded in 1475, the Gothic portal of which exhibits the arms and motto of the Catholic Kings, and glazed terracotta embellishments by *Niculoso de Pisa* surrounding medallions by *Pedro Millán*. The church has a good artesonado ceiling and some of the finest azulejos in Seville, and several late-Gothic tombs. The statues of the two SS.John (1635–38) are by *Alonso Cano* and *Montañes*. From an adjacent door we may visit a small museum of religious art, including a S. Jerónimo by *Ribera*, and a Christ attrib. to *Guido Reni;* and in a pleasant room with an artesonado ceiling, overlooking a patio, some good furniture, and statues are by *Alonso Cano.*

To the S. of S. Marcos stands the *Conv. del Socorro* whose church contains a retablo by *Montañes* (1610-20).

To the W. stands the huge **Casa del Duque de Alba** (Pl. 11), also called *Casa de las Dueñas,* a Mudéjar palace begun by the *Pineda* family in the 15C and embellished later by the *Riveras,* with a Gothic chapel containing fine azulejos, and a beautiful patio. A short distance N.W. is *S. Juan de la Palma,* an ancient mosque, with a Gothic doorway, and minaret of 1085.

A short distance E. of the Old University (see p.553) and not far S. of the Casa del Duque de Alba (see above) rises the campanile of Gothic **S. Pedro** (Pl. 11), rebuilt in the early 17C, in which Velázquez was baptized on June 6th, 1599. The retablo mayor (1641–66) is by *Felipe de Ribas;* in the first chapel on the r. is a painting by *Roelas,* and at the end of the l. aisle is a retablo with paintings by *P. Campana.*—Abutting S. Pedro is the *Conv. de Sta Ines,* with a Gothic chapel, and 17C organs.

E. of S. Pedro is *Sta Catalina* with a Mudéjar tower (c. 1350) and a chapel with a fine artesonado ceiling (c. 1400). The retablo mayor (1624–29), designed by *Diego López Bueno,* has paintings by the brothers *Sarabia,* while in a chapel to the l. is a Scourging of Christ by *P. Campana.* On the other side of the Pl. Ponce de León is the *Conv. de Terceros,* with unusual Baroque features ascribed to the Portuguese Fray *Manuel Ramos,* and a retablo by *Fr. de Ribas.* At the end of the N. Aisle is the *Cap. Sacramental,* a magnificent early 18C work by the *Figueroas.*

To the S. of S. Pedro, off the PL. DE ARGÜELLES, the conventual church of *El Buen Suceso* contains a Virgin and St Anne, by *Montañés* (1632–33) and figures of Sta Teresa and S. Alberto by (?) *Alonso Cano.*

From this plaza we follow the C. Descalzos and C. Caballerizas to *S. Ildefonso,* rebuilt in 1794–1841. It contains a fresco of c. 1375 from the church of the Virgen del Coral, a relief in the baptistery, by *Montañés* (1609), and figures by *Felipe de Ribas,* from the retablo of 1637, on the arch of the coro. The *Conv. de S. Leandro,* opposite, rebuilt c. 1600 by *Juan de Oviedo,* has retablos by *Montañés* in the nave chapels (c. 1621).

At the end of the C. Caballerizas is the ***Casa de Pilatos** (Pl. S.4 or N.15) the property of the Duque de Medinaceli, a dignified mansion in the Mudéjar style showing in its architecture and ornamentation a pronounced intermingling of Moorish, Gothic and Renaissance motifs, while the interior is profusely adorned with azulejos.

Begun c. 1480 for Pedro Enríques de Rivera, it was continued by his son Fadrique, first Marqués de Tarifa, and finished by Pedro Afán de Rivera (1504–71), Duque de Alcalá and viceroy of Naples. Under the third Duque de Alcalá, a patron and collector of art, the house was the intellectual centre of Seville. It is called 'House of Pilate' from the popular belief that Don Fadrique, who visited the Holy Land in 1519, planned it as a copy of Pilate's house in Jerusalem.

Beyond the Plateresque portal (by *Ant. María de Aprile;* 1529–33) we cross a court to enter the beautiful **Patio,* with marble columns and graceful arcades embellished with azulejos. In the angles of the court are Roman statues from Itálica, and on the walls in the arcade are 24 busts, some antique. To the r. is the so-called *Praetorium,* notable for its azulejos, inlaid ceiling, and window. Facing the entrance of the patio is the *Judgment Hall* (with fine azulejos and stucco ornamentation), a vestibule to the *Chapel,* with a Gothic roof and Gothic-Moorish ornamentation. To the l. of the vestibule and opening directly l. from the patio is a *Gabinete Particular*, giving on the garden, with an artesonado ceiling and a table of marbles. The magnificent *Staircase*, which ascends from the N.W. corner of the patio, has a remarkable dome and a finely-carved ceiling by *Cristóbal Sánchez* (early 16C). On the first landing is a copy of Murillo's 'Virgen de la Servilleta' by *Alonso Cano*. A small 'museum' has recently been installed.

Adjacent is *S. Estaban* with 14–15C Gothic and Mudéjar remains and interesting paintings, including several works by *Zurbarán*, dispersed parts of the former retablo mayor of 1629, *Santiago* (1789), further N., preserves Baroque retablos.

The C. de Águilas leads W. from the Casa de Pilatos, passing (l.) the conv. church of *Sta María de Jesús* (1690), containing a Virgin by *Torrigiano* and azulejos of 1589. The C. de las Virgenes leads S. to *S. Nicolás* (1781) and the **Conv. de la Madre de Dios**. The church, probably designed by *Hernán Ruiz the Younger*, and finished in 1572 by *Pedro Díaz de Palacios*, is roofed with magnificent artesonados begun in 1564.

At the main entrance is a relief medallion of 1590 by *Juan de Oviedo*, while the Baroque high altar (1684–90) is by *Fr. Barahona*. *Jerónimo Hernández* carved the Virgin of the Rosary and the Calvary (1573), also the retablo in the N. Aisle. In this church are buried the widow and daughter of Hernán Cortés, commemorated by effigies (1590) by *Miguel Adán* and *Juan de Oviedo*. The reja of the *Cap. del Correo* (1571–73) is by *Pedro Valera*.

To the W., at the end of the C. Mármoles, are three granite columns known as *Las Monolitos*, remnants of a Roman temple, which supplied also the columns in the Alameda de Hércules (see p.554).

To the N.W. is **S. Isidoro**, perhaps the oldest church in Seville (c. 1360), built on the spot where the saint is believed to have died (636). The high altarpiece was painted by *Roelas* (1613), while the *Cap. de los Maestres* (N.) contains the 14C Cristo de la Sangre.—During the winter of 1830–31 Richard Ford lived in a house which stood in the Pl. S. Isidoro.

In a plaza further W. stands **S. Salvador**, built in 1671–1712 on the site of the first grand mosque of Seville and incorporates part of the minaret in its tower. It contains statues of Christ (1618–19) and St Christopher (1597) by *Montañés*. The Baroque retablo mayor of 1770–79 is by *Cayetano Acosta*. In a chapel on the l. is the 'Cristo de los Desamparados' ('the forsaken'); a cufic inscription records the re-building of the minaret in 1079 after an earthquake. At No. 3 in the C. de Cuna, which leads N., is the mansion of the Marqués de Montilla, a descendant of Lawrence Poore (see p.541), while a few paces S.W. is the Pl. de la Falange.

D   TRIANA.

Triana, Roman *Trajana*, on the r. bank of the old Guadalquivir, now a backwater, was known since early antiquity for its potteries, and more recently for its Gipsy population, but it is now little more than a residential suburb.

The Virgin martyrs SS. Justa and Rufina were potters here in the 3C, and here, later, the beautiful azulejos of Seville were made. Triana now lies on the l. bank of the 'new' Guadalquivir, united to Seville by a broad artificial causeway and the Av. del Cristo de la Expiración and, lower down, by bridges.

From the *Pte. de Isabel II*, the usual approach, the C. de la Pureza leads S. to **Sta Ana**, a church in a Mudéjar-Gothic style, built in 1276–80. Apply at No. 90 in this street for admission. The architect was probably a master from Burgos cathedral, whose vault-plan, with the unusual (English) feature of a longitudinal ridge-rib, has been followed. At the high altar is a Plateresque retablo, by *Nic. Jurate* and *Nufro Ortego* (1542), with paintings (1548–57) by *Pedro Campana* and others, and sculptures by *Delgado*. On the wall of the l. aisle; *Fernando Sturm* (?) SS. Justa and Rufina, Adoration; at the other end of the aisle, *Campana* (?) St Francis of Assisi. On the trascoro, *Alejo Fernández*, Virgen de la Rosa. Near the end of the r. aisle, a terracotta tomb by *Niculaso of Pisa* (1503).

From the bridge the C. de Castilla leads N. past **N.S. de la O** to the *Cap. del Patrocinio* in which is the 'Cristo de la Expiración', a polychrome statue carved by *Francisco Antonio Gijón* in 1682, popularly known as 'El Cacharro', and carried in procession on Good Friday.

Returning to Pte. Isabel II we turn W. to reach *S. Jacinto*, built by the Dominicans and completed in 1775, containing paintings by *Arteaga*. It is the centre of several Cofradias, whose pasos include the 'Virgen de la Esperanza de Triana'. We may return to the centre by skirting the river by the C. de Betis and crossing the *Pte. de S. Telmo*.—Just beyond the bridge is the *Conv. de los Remedios* (1632–1700). In 1519 Magellan sailed from this point to Sanlúcar de Barrameda at the start of the first circumnavigation of the globe.

Also of interest is the *Cartuja*, to reach which it is now necessary to cross to the W. bank of the new course of the Guadalquivir and follow a rough track (r.) immediately beyond the bridge.

The **Cartuja**, founded in 1401 as a Charterhouse, has been a busy pottery since 1841, and was long controlled by the English firm of Pickman and Son, when its owner built two 'willow-pattern' summer-houses in its adjacent orange-groves (now vanished). Extensive remains of the conventual buildings were altered for use as warehouses and workshops. *N.S. de las Cuevas* remains intact, where the body of Columbus (d. 1506), brought from Valladolid, rested from 1507 to 1542. It was then removed to Haiti, and in 1796 to Havana, whence it was returned to Seville (see p.544). A good artesonado ceiling may be seen adjacent to another church, near brick kilns in use until c. 1950. The pottery is to be removed in 1980 to a new site off the Badajoz road, and there is an ambitious project to restore some of the older buildings, which may then be very close to a site being laid out to accommodate the *Feria*.

Also W. of the Guadalquivir, but approached from the W. of Triana, lies *San Juan de Aznalfarache* (21,100 inhab.), with remains of Roman walls and a ruined castle. The church has a good retablo, paintings by *Juan del Castillo*, and a Mudéjar font.

E   SANTIPONCE AND ITÁLICA.

We follow the N 630 N.W. to (8 km.) **Santiponce**. The church belonged to the *Conv. de S. Isidoro del Campo*, founded in 1298 by Alfonso Guzmán 'el Bueno', as a Cistercian house but transferred in 1431. to the Hieronymites. It possesses a retablo of 1613 with figures of SS. Isidore and Jerome by *Montañés*, who carved also the effigies (1609) on the tomb of Guzmán and his wife. In a second Mudéjar church, added c. 1350 by the founder's son, is the latter's tomb, with those of Doña Urraca Osorio, burned by Pedro the Cruel for rejecting his addresses. This was the first resting-place of the body of Cortés, before its removal to Mexico (see below). In the two-storeyed *Patio de los Muertos* are wall-paintings of the 15–16C, while the *Patio de los Evangelistas* has a remarkable frescoed dado (1431–36).

About 1 km. N.W. in the old Campos de Talca, are the ruins of **Itálica**, founded in 206 B.C. by Scipio Africanus as a home for his veterans and later a colonia under Hadrian, and which enjoyed considerable prosperity in the 2nd and 3C. It claims to be the birthplace of three Roman emperors, Trajan (52–117), Hadrian (76–138), and Theodosius (c. 346–75), but the latter may have been born at Coca (Segovia). *Itálica* was abandoned by the Visigoths in favour of Seville, and its remains were used as a quarry, but the *Amphitheatre (built for 40,000 spectators), over which crops of wheat long waved their golden ears, still retains a few rows of seats, underground passages, and dens; and there are traces of a *Forum*. Continuing excavation has brought to light remains of two *Thermae,* a theatre, and laid out on a grid of streets, numerous villas.

Among the mosaics to be seen (surrounded by rusting barbed wire, and entirely unprotected from the elements) are a colourful one of Birds; another of Neptune (discovered in 1970); that in the so-called Casa de Planetario; and a number with geometric patterns. Others were grubbed up by pigs or removed by dilettante during the course of centuries (see the *Pal. de la Condesa de Labrija,* p.553, or the *Archaeological Museum,* Seville, p.550, to which most of the smaller antiquities have been transferred, although there is an apology for a museum at the site entrance).

68   FROM SEVILLE TO HUELVA AND AYAMONTE

Total distance 156 km. (97 miles). 18 km. *Sanlúcar la Mayor*—44 km. *Niebla*—32 km. **Huelva**—62 km. *Ayamonte*.

Motorway. An autopista (A 29) is under construction between Seville and *Huelva,* running parallel to and S. of the N 431.

We follow the N 431 W. across the Guadalquivir to (6 km.) *Castilleja de la Cuesta* where in the *Conv. de las Irlandesas,* Hernán Cortés (1485–1547) died. A small Moresque castle, built in the 18C on the site of his house in the C. Real, contains a few souvenirs of the conquest of Mexico. Castilleja occupies the site of the Iberian *Osset* and Roman *Julia Constantia,* whose ruins served as a quarry for the building of *S. Juan de Aznalfarache,* see above.

At 8 km. a road leads 4 km. N. to *Valencina,* with the Cueva de Matarrubilla, a large chambered tomb, while at *Castilleja de Guzmán,* to the E., is the smaller Cueva de la Pastora.

9 km. *Espartinas,* an old town, beyond which we pass (r.) the *Conv. de N.S. de Loreto,* while at *Olivares,* 5 km. N., the church contains a Crucifixion by *Montañés* and damaged paintings by *Roelas,* who died in 1625, a canon of the Iglesia Mayor.—At *Umbrete,* 1 km. S., the church has a fine azulejo dome, while 4 km. beyond, at *Bolullos de la Mitación,* there is an 11C mosque converted into a chapel.—3 km. **Sanlúcar la Mayor** (7100 inhab.) was the Roman *Solis Lucus,* while the fertile country below was known as the 'Garden of Hercules'. The town preserves an azulejo tower, a ruined Alcázar, the Mudéjar churches of *Sta María* (13C) on the site of a mosque, *S. Pedro* (12C), built like a fortress, and with a monumental staircase to its altar mayor, and *S. Eustaquio.*

Aznalcázar, 11 km. S.W. of Sanlúcar, has a church with ornamental battlements and spire, and the shell of a castle. Thence a road, crossing the Guadiamar by a Roman bridge, goes on to (4 km.) *Pilas,* with a house where Murillo lived, and (6 km.) *Villamanrique de la Condesa,* with a palace, on the edge of the Marismas, see below.

13 km. *Carrión de los Céspedes* 2 km. S. was a fief of the Knights of Calatrava, while at 13 km. *Villalba del Alcor,* Gothic *S. Bartolomé* is built at right-angles to the earlier mosque.—At 6 km. the road by-passes *La Palma del Condado* (8800 inhab.), with a Plateresque church and interesting *Ayuntamiento.*

Almonte (*Hotel*) 15 km. S., also reached by a road direct from Seville, is noted for the Whitsun pilgrimage to the chapel of *N.S. del Rocío* (Our Lady of the Dew), 15 km. further S. on the edge of the Marisma.

The road has been continued to (30 km.) *Torre de la Higuera* on the Atlantic, whence the coast road turns N.W. to *Mazagón* (see below). LAS MARISMAS, the area S. of El Rocío, bounded by the ocean on the W., and the Isla Mayor to the S.E. beyond which flows the wide stream of the Guadalquivir, is now designated the **Nature Reserve of the Coto Doñana** or *Parque Nac. de Doñana*. While much of the wild-life inhabiting the Coto Doñana can be seen without actually entering the protected area, permission to visit the reserve itself should be obtained by writing well in advance either to the Director of the Estación Biologica de Doñana, Paraguay 1, Sevilla, or to the Secretary of the World Wild Life Fund, 2 Caxton St., London S.W.1. An introduction, at short notice, *may* be obtained from the S.E.T. office at Seville. The *Pal. de Doñana*, inside the Reserve, is best reached by turning l. 10 km. S.W. of El Rocío.

12 km. Niebla, Roman *Ilipla*, on the r. bank of the Rio Tinto, is an interesting but decayed town (4050 inhab.) with a castle and ruinous but complete **Walls*. The bridge is a well-preserved Roman structure, and within the walls are some Moorish houses. *Sta María de la Granada* has some Mozarabic details (10C) and a good tower; close to it is the *Hosp. de N.S. de los Ángeles*, with a pretty cloister.

Niebla was the birthplace of the Arab poet Ahtal ibn-Numara (d. c. 1080); it was captured in 1262, and the district was made a 'condado' in favour of Juan Alfonso de Guzmán on his marriage with Doña Beatriz, daughter of Enrique II (1396).

We now follow the eucalyptus-shaded river.

At 15 km. a road leads S.W. past (6 km.) *Moguer* to (9 km.) *Palos* and 4 km. beyond, *La Rábida*, see p.560, which may be approached also from Huelva direct, see below.—**Moguer** (8900 inhab.), a decayed port, was the birthplace of the poet Juan Ramón Jiménez (1881–1958) and his donkey Platero (small museum in his house). On the Pl. Mayor are the neo-classical *Ayuntamiento*, and *N.S. de la Granada*, with a Giralda-type tower and some good retablos. In the *Conv. de la Esperanza* (rebuilt 1482) are fine azulejos and a Baroque altarpiece with a Holy Family by *P. de Céspedes*. On the N. outskirts is the remarkably preserved **Conv. de Sta Clara**, a foundation of 1348. The brick buildings are in a Mudéjar-Gothic style, and the church contains a unique series of Choir-Stalls in Granadine style on a base of azulejos, tombs of the Portocarrero family, 15C painted doors, a Sienese diptych, and many other works of the highest quality. In the refectory is a Last Supper, by *Pedro de Córdoba*, and in the cloister, a well.

1 km. *S. Juan del Puerto*, where the N 435 from Zalamea and Zafra join us from the r., see pp.425-6.

16 km. HUELVA, a flourishing port (112,100 inhab.; 34,000 in 1920; 75,000 in 1960; *Hotels*), with a pleasant winter climate, stands on the navigable Odiel above its confluence with the Rio Tinto. It is of commercial importance as the main channel of export of the rich pyrites-mines inland, and its fisheries are considerable, while extensive oil-refineries have been constructed further S. near La Rábida. The original railway and pier were constructed in 1873–76 by George Barclay Bruce.

Huelva preserves few traces of antiquity although it occupies the site of Roman *Onuba* and probably an earlier Phoenician settlement, and was recaptured from the Moors in 1257. The most interesting buildings surviving the earthquake of 1755 are 16C *S. Pedro*, which incorporates fragments of a mosque, and has a good tower, and reja of 1585; and a disused *Aqueduct*, N. of the town, probably of Moorish construction. A new *Provincial Museum* has been installed at Alameda Sundheim 13, largely devoted to archaeology, especially to Tharsis (see below), but also containing a section on the fine arts.

In *La Concepción*, near the centre, are two paintings by *Zurbarán* and good stalls; further E. beyond the Pl. de José Antonio (or de las Monjas), stands the conventual church of *Sta María de Gracia* (1500); while a block to the S.E. is 16C *S. Francisco*, with paintings by *Pacheco* and *Montañés*. The *Conv. de la Merced*, with an unusual façade of 1605, near the N. end of the town and used for years as barracks, has been restored. The Av. de Manuel Siurot leads N.E. to the *Santuario de N.S. de la Cinta*, visited by Columbus, with good artesonado roofs and commanding a wide view.

Motor launches ply to **Punta Umbría** (7050 inhab.; *Hotels*), a popular resort on the W. side of the Odiel estuary.

FROM HUELVA TO LA RÁBIDA. Driving S. along the E. bank of the Odiel we cross the Rio Tinto to the Franciscan **Conv. de la Rábida** (*Hotel*), whose name is derived from an Arabic word meaning 'watch-tower'. It is famous as the refuge of Columbus in 1491, when his ideas had been rejected, after long negotiation, by Isabel and her advisers. On his way to Huelva to take ship for France he arived at La Rábida in a somewhat desperate plight. The prior, Juan Pérez de Marchena, who had been the queen's confessor, recognized the probability of Columbus's scheme, and by his influence Isabel was induced to reverse her decision. The Conv. Buildings (restored 1892) date in part from the 14C (apse of the church). The artesonado roof of the nave, the 15C Mudéjar cloister, and the room in which Columbus lodged, are of interest, while the sacristy has mural decoration by *Vázquez Díaz* (1930). A late-Gothic Processional Cross is also preserved.

Palos de la Frontera, 4 km. N.E., now a decayed village (5100 inhab.), was the port from which Columbus set sail on 3 Aug, 1492, in the 'Santa María' and hither he returned in the following March. His second voyage likewise started from Palos in Sept. 1493, and here Cortés landed in May, 1528, after the conquest of Mexico. It was thanks to two well-to-do citizens of Palos, Vicente and Martín Pinzón, that Columbus was able to obtain crews for his ships; the Pinzóns commanded his other vessels, the 'Niña' and the 'Pinta'. The church of *S. Jorge* (1473) has remains of wall-paintings, an iron pulpit, a fine 15C Crucifix, and 14–15C alabasters.

Moguer (see above) lies 7 km. N.E.—Driving S. from Palos we reach (12 km.) *Mazagón* (*Parador Nac.*), 24 km. beyond which lies *Torre de la Higuera* and the N limit of the Coto Doñana Reserve, see p.559.

A new road bridges the Odiel just W. of Huelva, and the detour to the N. along the l. bank of the river through orange-groves and ricefields to (14 km.) *Gibraleón*, may now be avoided.

From Gibraleón, dominated by its ruined castle, the C 443 leads N.W. to (15 km.) *Bartolomé de la Torre*, with an ancient castle, and (18 km.) **Tharsis**, whose name recalls that of *Tartessos* or *Tarshish*, probably the Phœnician name for Andalucía. The copper-mines here, worked by Phœnicians and Romans, were leased to Liebert Wolters by Philip V, but reverted to the crown in 1783. In private hands from 1829 to 1873, when it was bought by a British concern, since 1952 it has again reverted to Spanish control. Hardly any trace of copper has been found in the ancient slag-heaps, showing how perfect was the Roman system of smelting. See 'The Mines of Tharsis', by S.G. Checkland (1967).

At 20 km. we by-pass *Cartaya* (8900 inhab.), once a Phœnician settlement, with a ruined castle, and (7 km.) *Lepe* (12,600 inhab.), Roman *Leptis*, with a Gothic church.—At 10 km. a road leads 6 km. S. to *Isla Cristina* (*Hotels*), a centre of sardine and tunny-fishing.

11 km. **Ayamonte** (13,900 inhab.; *Parador Nac.; Hotel*), on the E. bank and near the mouth of the Guadiana, which here forms the frontier with Portugal. Apart from the Moorish castle, its churches are of interest; *N.S. de las Angustias*, with an attractive façade, a 16C retablo, and Mudéjar roof; the convent church of *S. Francisco* (1527), with a fine tower and ceilings, rich in Mudéjar detail; *El Salvador*, with another good tower; and the 16C *Conv. de S. Clara*.

Here is the Spanish Customs Station. Car and passenger ferries link Ayamonte with *Vila Real de Santo Antonio*, the Portuguese town which faces it across the estuary.—*Faro* lies 53 km. to the W. while *Lisbon* is 310 km. N.W. of Faro; see the *Blue Guide to Portugal,* forthcoming.

FROM SEVILLE TO ROSAL DE LA FRONTERA (159 km.), FOR LISBON. We follow the Mérida road (N 630) N.W. through rolling country to (35 km.) *Venta del Alto,* where we fork l. onto the N 433.—At 18 km. a road leads 30 km. W. to *Riotinto,* see p.425. We ascend into the Sierra Morena.—At (22 km.) *Higuera de la Sierra* the church contains paintings by *Alonso Miguel de Tobar.*

14 km. **Aracena,** (2400 ft) a picturesque town of 6500 inhab., is dominated by a ruined Moorish castle (12C; later partly reconstructed by the Templars) from whose mosque the minaret survives as the tower of *N.S. de los Dolores* (late-13C), with a noble doorway and a polygonal apse. Below, in the Herreran parish church of *La Asunción,* is a carving by *Montañés.* But the main attraction of the place, apart from its pleasant climate and surroundings, is the nearby *Gruta de las Maravillas,* a large stalactite cavern.

At 9 km. a road leads 5 km. S. to *Alájar,* close to the Peña de los Ángeles, where Philip II visited Arias Montano; a cave called the *Sillita del Rey* is supposed to mark the site of their interview.—At 9 km. we cross the N 435 from Zafra to Huelva (see p.425) and at 9 km. pass **Cortegana** (7900 inhab.), Roman *Corticata,* with an old castle and an interesting church in beautiful surroundings.—14 km. l. *Aroche,* (5000 inhab.) in a district rich in prehistoric remains, is the *Aruci* of classical times, preserving its walls, a Moorish castle and 18C church. We now descend the Chanza valley to (29 km.) **Rosal de la Frontera,** the Spanish frontier town (Customs-post), 3 km. from the border. *Beja,* 63 km. to the W., lies on the route to *Lisbon,* 192 km. beyond; see the *Blue Guide to Portugal,* forthcoming.

69 FROM SEVILLE TO JEREZ AND CÁDIZ

Total distance, 131 km. (81 miles). N IV. (29 km. *Utrera* lies 13 km. E.)—69 km. **Jerez de la Frontera**—33 km. **Cádiz.**

Motorway. The latter commences some 17 km. S. of Seville, and is well signposted. Roads lead off after 11 km. for *Utrera;* at 22 km. for *Lebrija,* 15 km. S.W.; at 34 km. for *Jerez,* 6 km. S.W.; and *Arcos de la Frontera,* 25 km. E.; and at 26 km. for *El Puerto de Santa María,* 9 km. N.W.—13 km. **Cádiz.**

We leave Seville by the Paseo de las Delicias, and follow the N IV S., to (29 km.) *Los Palacios y Villafranca.*

13 km. to the E. of this junction lies **Utrera** (39,700 inhab.), Roman *Utricula,* the centre of an agricultural and cattle-rearing district, famous for its bulls. From the town centre, close to the remains of the Moorish *Alcázar,* the C. Gen. Queipo de Llano leads to the Pl. Mayor and 15C *Santiago,* with a Flamboyant W. Doorway. *Sta María de la Asunción,* to the S.E., dates from 1369 and has a Gothic nave, a Plateresque coro, a tall 18C tower, and contains the tomb of Diego Ponce de León. On the N.E. outskirts is the *Conv. de los Minimos,* or *Santuario de N.S. de la Consolación.* The plain W. Front has a 16C portal and a slender tower, while within are notable stalls, a fine Mudéjar artesonado ceiling, and a carved retablo. Rodrigo Caro (1573–1647), the antiquary and poet, and the dramatists Serafin (1871–1938) and Joaquín (1873–1944) Álvarez Quintero were natives of Utrera.

The *Castillo de las Aguzaderas,* beyond *El Coronil,* 18 km. to the S.E., was built in 1381.

13 km. *Las Alcantarillas,* with ruins of a fortified Roman bridge. At 7 km. we are joined by the direct road (N 333) from Écija, and soon bear S.W., with a view of the Sierra de Gibalbin, and beyond, the Serranía de Ronda.—At 9 km. a road leads 6 km. W. to *Las Cabezas de San Juan,*

where Col. Rafael Riego began the 'pronunciamento' that developed into the Liberal revolution of 1820 (see p.565)—At 18 km. another road leads 8 km. N.W. to **Lebrija**, the *Nebrissa Veneria* of Pliny and Moorish *Nebrishah*, a well-situated town (22,350 inhab.), surrounded by walls and crowned by a castle, and overlooking the Marismas. The humanist and lexographer Antonio de Nebrija (1444–1522) was born here.*Sta María* (or *N.S. de la Oliva*), or originally an Almohade mosque, and with an early 19C tower modelled on the Giralda, contains a cedar and mahogany retablo carved by *Alonso Cano* (1630-36). The church of *Vera Cruz* may house a Crucifixion by *Montañés*. The *Castle Chapel*, a mixture of Mudéjar and Renaissance motives, has a good timber roof.

22 km. **JEREZ DE LA FRONTERA** (167,000 inhab.; 65,000 in 1920; 131,000 in 1960; *Hotels*), formerly *Xeres*, probably the Roman *Asido Caesaris*, whose surname was corrupted by the Moors into *Sherish*, from whom it was recaptured in 1264 by Alfonso X. The town is famous throughout the world for its white wines, known in English as *sherry*, which was first exported to England in the reign of Henry VII, and many of the bodegas are owned by descendants of English families who have since intermarried with their own and with Jerez society. At the turn of the century W. J. Buck, co-author of *Wild Spain* and *Unexplored Spain*, was the British Vice-consul here. The town retains some attractive old mansions, while through a number of doorways one may still see delightful vistas of flower-filled patios shaded by orange trees and palms.

Sherry. The *Bodegas*, lofty one-storey buildings filled with impressive rows of wine-butts, are a characteristic feature of Jerez, and at most of the important establishments visitors are courteously shown round and afforded an opportunity of tasting the various types of sherry. Among the principal shipping firms are *Messrs. Williams and Humbert, González Byass, Pedro Domecq, Sandeman, Garvey*, and *Marqués del Merito*.

At the vintage in Sept. the small white grapes are crushed at the vineyards in the '*lagares*' or presses, large wooden trays 50 cm. deep, being first trodden and afterwards subjected to hydraulic pressure. The must thus produced is left in casks to ferment right out, thus converting the sugar in the grape-juice into alcohol. About two months later, when fermentation has ceased and the lees have fallen to the bottom of the cask, the clear new wine is racked off into clean casks, and is then either stored in a bodega to mature alone or is used to refresh one of the '*soleras*'. These 'soleras' are the mother wines that are never moved. When some of the wine is taken out for making up blends or for shipping, younger wine of the same year is used to refresh the solera and to be 'educated' by the older wine and its impregnated cask.

Several kinds of sherry are used in making up shipping blends (*Amontillado, Fino, Palo Cortado, Oleroso*, etc.), and several kinds are used for blending in the bodegas, such as '*color*', made by boiling down three butts of must to make one butt of 'vino de color'; 'P.X.', made by sun-drying the small sweet grape of that name until it is almost a raisin and then pressing it and adding a little wine-alcohol to arrest the fermentation; and '*Moscatel*', made in the same way from Muscat grapes. Sherry is generally shipped to England in butts (108 gallons), hogsheads (54 gal.), or quarter casks (27 gal.), approx 490, 245, and 122 litres, respectively, and bottled there.

There is a by-pass W. of the town, but from the Seville road we enter by the C. Julio Ruiz de Alda, which passing (l.) *Sto Domingo*, a large conventual church burned in 1936, but restored, leads us along the C. de José Antonio to the *Pl. de los Reyes Católicos*, the main square, planted with palms, beyond which is the Alcázar, a medieval fortress-palace once belonging to the Duque de S. Lorenzo, partially restored.

Below it, to the N.W., stands the **Colegiata**, or *S. Salvador*, begun in 1696–1705, and completed (1706–65) on the plans of *Torcuato Cayón de la Vega*, with an elaborate sculptured portal; the isolated belfry is in a Moorish-Gothic style. The church possesses a good library and coin-collection, and, in the sacristy, 'The Sleeping Girl' by *Zurbarán*.— A flight of steps leads down to a small plaza with the fine Baroque doorway of the *Bertemati palace*.

S. Miguel, a short distance S.E. of the main plaza, is a Gothic building of c. 1430–1569, whose W. Front is masked by an ornate classical façade of 1672–1701 adorned with azulejos. The elaborately decorated transepts and bold pillars of the main arcade are worthy of note. The retablo mayor (1613–47) is by *Montañés* and *José de Arce*; that of the sagrario is a Rococo work of c. 1750.

Returning to the plaza we may follow the C. de Calvo Sotelo to the N. to the *Casa del Cabildo Vieja*, formerly the **Ayuntamiento**, built in 1575 by *Andrés de Ribera*, with a façade adorned by a graceful frieze with bold sculptures, but marred by a later balustrade. The building houses a valuable library and a small *Archaeological Museum* containing a Greek helmet (7C B.C.) found on the banks of the Guadalete. In the Plaza is *S. Dionisio*, a Moorish-Gothic church founded by Alfonso X but transformed internally in 1728–31, with Rococo retablo mayor, while adjacent is the Mudéjar *Torre de la Atalaya* (1449), each side with individual decoration.

From the Pl. de Villavicencio behind, the C. González Quijano and its continuations lead W. to the heavily restored Gothic church of *Santiago* (c. 1500; tower of 1663). The C. de la Merced leads S.W. to the *Hosp. de la Merced* (16C), whose church has a retablo mayor (1654) by *Fr. Ribas* enclosing the Gothic Virgen de la Merced; the silver altar-frontal (1730) was worked in relief in Guatemala. Amid the winding lanes of the old town are: *S. Mateo*, late Gothic, with remarkable vaults over the chapels; *S. Lucas*, Mudéjar, altered in 1715–30 by *Diego Díaz*; and *S. Juan* (c. 1423) with Mudéjar vaulting and other details. Near S. Juan is the *Casa de Ponce de León*, with a Renaissance patio and oriel (1537). Returning in a N.E. direction, we reach *S. Marcos* (c. 1480), with a front of 1613, fine *alicatados* forming an altar-frontal, and a dado in the sanctuary.

Some 5 km. S.E. on the C 440 to (36 km.) *Medina Sidonia* (see p.512), is the **Cartuja de Jerez**, a celebrated monastery, for many years derelict, and now undergoing heavy restoration, founded in 1477 by Álvaro Overtós de Valeto (d. 1482). The monastery, with an impressive patio, is still in clausura, and male visitors may view the richly decorated Baroque *Façade (1667) of the Gothic church.

Below the Cartuja rolls the Guadalete, on whose banks was fought the battle (711) in which Tariq beat Roderic, 'the last of the Goths', after which the Moors soon subjugated the Peninsula.

A pleasant detour may be made to *Sanlúcar de Barrameda*, 24 km. N.W. on the C 440, at the mouth of the Guadalquivir. **Sanlúcar** (44,000 inhab.; *Hotel*), the ancient *Luciferi Fanum*, surrounded by orange-groves, is the principal depot for the export of *manzanilla* wine which is produced in the neighbouring sandhills.

Reconquered in 1264, it was granted to the family of Guzmán el Bueno, but was reassumed as royal property by Philip IV in view of the growing importance of the transatlantic trade. Columbus sailed hence in 1498 on his third voyage to America, and in 1519 the Portuguese mariner Magellan weighed anchor here to circumnavigate the globe. Wyndham Beawes, author of a ponderous 'Civil, Commercial, Political, and Literary History of Spain', was long the British Consul here in the late 18C.

To the W. of the town is *Sta María de la 'O'* (14C), with a Mudéjar portal and *alfiz*, and other admirable details including artesonado ceilings and a screened private pew. Further along the long main street, where 'Fernán Caballero' (see p.553) had a house, and with numerous bars serving Manzanilla, is domed *Sto Domingo* (16C), well-vaulted, and with a stone retablo; and beyond, *S. Francisco*, founded by Henry VIII in 1517 as the *Hosp. of St George* for English sailors, opposite which is *S. Nicolás*. On the Cuesta de Belén is the former *Pal. of the Duc de Montpensier*, with fantastic decorations in its Gothic arcades, and the *Pal. of the Duque de Medina Sidonia* (restored, and containing archives) are of interest. The *Castle* commands a good view, while two gates of the town walls are preserved.

4 km. N. lies the little port of *Bonanza*, while 9 km. S.W. is *Chipiona* (11,000 inhab.) ancient *Turris Cœpionis*, with a lighthouse marking the river mouth. Hence we may follow the coast road to *El Puerte de Sta María*, passing *Rota* (19,300 inhab.; *Hotels*), temporarily a U.S. base, having the aspect of a concentration camp. It is still noted for the red sacrament wine (*tintillo*) known in England as 'tent wine'. There are good stalls and azulejos in the church.

The main road (N IV) from Jerez goes on to (12 km.) **Puerto de Sta María**, or *El Puerto*, the Roman *Portus Menesthei*, a wine-exporting town (47,350 inhab.), at the mouth of the Guadalete, with a Moorish castle and several sherry bodegas which may be visited, including those of Messrs. Caballeros, Duff Gordon, Terry, and Osborne. Twiss mentioned that he met the Marqués de la Cañada here, a gentleman of Irish extraction, whose name was Tyrry, who had a fine library of English books, and a collection of paintings. Washington Irving stayed at No. 57 C. de los Reyes Católicos in 1828, writing 'The Alhambra'. The poet Rafael Alberti was born here in 1902. N.E. of the town is the *Conv. de la Victoria* (16C), now a prison. Keeping to the r. bank of the Guadalete, we reach the *Hosp. de S. Juan de Dios*, behind which the C. José Navarrete runs inland, passing the *Castillo de S. Marcos* (restored), with an attractive mansion opposite.

Beyond stands the *Iglesia Mayor Prioral,* or *N.S. de los Milagros* of 1265, rebuilt in the 17C, with a Renaissance S. Portal. Further W. is the *Casa del Marqués de Purallena,* now gutted of its ballroom, but previously the best of the mansions with which the town abounds, and *S. Francisco*, with a Baroque retablo and sculptures by *Juan de Mesa*. From the Pl. de España the C. Vicario and C. Gen. Mola lead to *S. Joaquín*. In the C. de José Antonio, leading back towards the river, is the 18C church of the *Concepcionistas*, while the domed church of the *Conv. de Capuchinas*, in the C. Larga, has a Baroque retablo and remarkable Crucifix. There is a fortified church just E. of the port.

Leaving El Puerto we turn S. and cross the Guadalete and the Rio de S. Pedro, enjoying a view of Cádiz across the bay to the r. The new approach to Cádiz from the N.E. turns r. along the peninsula, passing *Trocadero* on the creek of the same name, surrounding a fort famous for the stubborn resistance it made to the Duc d'Angoulême's troops in 1823. Adjoining is the construction yard of *Matagorda*, and wharves.

We now cross the bay by the new bridge (1971), before bearing r. to enter (21 km.) *Cádiz*, itself, see below.

While the autopista enters from this direction, the NIV continues to circle the bay, at 21 km. from Jerez passing through **Puerto Real** (21,500 inhab.), Roman *Gaditanus*, rebuilt by Isabel the Catholic in 1483, and surrounded by salt marshes. The 16C classical church of *S. Sebastián* is its most interesting building. 11 km. beyond we meet the N 340 from Algeciras, and at 2 km. reach *San Fernando*, see p.513. Hence we follow the road N.W. along the peninsula to enter (15 km.) **Cádiz**.

70   CÁDIZ

CÁDIZ (140,900 inhab.; 76,000 in 1920; 115,000 in 1960; *Hotels*), one of the principal ports of Spain, is also one of the oldest towns in Europe, but it retains little air of antiquity. With tall white houses characterized by their miradors and roof-terraces (*azoteas*), and narrow intercrossing streets, *old* Cádiz, standing on its isolated rock and surrounded by sea-walls except towards the harbour and its S. entrance, was likened by Ford to a 'sea-prison', but it retains a certain faded charm of its own, which is preferable to its modern suburbs strung out along the isthmus.

History. The Phœnician settlement of *Gaddir* (i.e. an enclosure), known to the Greeks as *Gadeira*, is said to have been founded as early as 1100 B.C., and in the 7C it was a market for the tin of the Cassiterides and the amber of the Baltic. About 501 B.C. it was occupied by the Carthaginians, and here Hamilcar Barca landed in 237 before his conquest of the Mediterranean coast of Spain. With the rise of the power of Rome the city deserted its ancient masters. Julius Cæsar, whose first magistracy was a Spanish quaestorship, recognized the importance of *Gades* as the key of the Mediterranean and as dictator he endowed its inhabitants with Roman citizenship and the city with the title of *Julia Augusta Gaditana*. It also had the monopoly of the salt-fish trade with Rome. With the fall of Rome came the fall of Gades; both under the Visigoths and under the Moors it remained insignificant, and in 1013 it was harried by Norman pirates; so that when Alfonso el Sabio reconquered *Jeziret Kádis* (1262) he found it almost depopulated, and recolonized it from the province of Santander.

With the discovery of America, Cádiz rose once more, and on several occasions in the 16C it repelled the attacks of Barbary corsairs. Drake was more successful in 'singeing the King of Spain's beard' in 1587, and in 1596 Lord Essex captured 13 men-of-war and 40 galleons in the inner bay, and sacked the town, although later English retaliatory expeditions, in 1625 and 1702, were failures. Between 1720 and 1765 it enjoyed a monopoly of the Spanish American trade. Alexander O'Reilly (?1722–94), a Spanish general of Irish descent, was governor of Cádiz in 1775–88 and did much to improve the town, which had been described previously as being 'insufferably stinking'. It was blockaded by a British fleet from Feb. 1797 to April 1798, and was bombarded by another squadron in 1800. At that time the population was as high as c. 70,000

In 1805 it saw the return of a shattered fleet after the battle of Trafalgar, see p.512. Throughout the Peninsular War Cádiz was the seat of the Cortes, and in 1810-12, under the Duque de Albuquerque, maintained a heroic resistance against the French until relieved by Gen. Spencer. It was during the siege that the Liberal Constitution of March, 1812, was issued. In 1820 Rafael Riego here defended the standard of liberalism, and the liberal movement was arrested only in 1823 when Trocadero fell to another French army under the reactionary Duc d'Angoulême.

The Editor has not personally experienced the *Solano*, an unpleasantly dry East wind, which, in the words of C.A. Fischer (1802) disarmed the *gaditanas* and caused all the senses to be 'involuntarily inebriated'; when 'an irresistable instinct becomes authorised by example and is excited by solicitation'. To moderate this ferment of the blood, the sexes would go sea-bathing, the women strictly guarded by cavalry!

Cádiz was the birthplace of Lucius Cornelius Balbus (or 'Balbus Maior; fl. 40 B.C.), the first provincial to be a Roman consul; his nephew Balbus Minor constructed a dockyard at Cádiz (fl. 40 A.D.). Other natives were Columella (fl. 40 A.D.), the agricultural writer; Ibn Tufail (c. 1105–85), the philosopher; José Celestino Mutis (1732–1808) the celebrated botanist; José Cadalso (1741–1782) the author;

Antonio Alcalá Galiano (1789–1865) author and politician; Juan Alvarez Mendizábal (1790–1853), the Jewish financier responsible for the expropriation of Spanish monasteries in 1836; Francisco Javier Isturiz (1790–1870), the Liberal politician; the republican leader Emilio Castelar (1832–99); Segismundo Moret (1838–1913) the liberal statesman; and Manuel de Falla (1876–1946), the composer.

A modern town has grown S. along the narrow isthmus on which, in the suburb of *San José*, is the *English Cemetery* (undergoing restoration), founded by John Brackenbury, British Vice-Consul in 1822–40. The road enters the old town by the *Pta. de Tierra*, constructed by *Torcuato Cayón* (1751–55). In 1947 an explosion of submarine mines destroyed a large section of the defensive wall in this area.

Bearing r. past the station and quays we reach (l.) the palm-bordered Pl. de S. Juan de Dios, flanked by the neo-classical *Ayuntamiento*.—Ahead, the Av. Ramón de Carranza leads to the *Diputación*, built as a custom house in 1764–73 to designs by *Juan Caballero*.

Behind the buildings facing the harbour runs the C. de S. Francisco, towards the S. end of which is *S. Agustín*, with a façade of 1647, a Christ attr. to *Montañés*, and a retablo of 1666 by *Alfonso Martínez*. *S. Francisco*, on the E. side of the street, with some good details and Mudéjar stuccoes, was restored in the early 17C; while at No. 11 in the C. de S. Francisco is the entry to the *Santa Cueva*, a late 18C elliptical chapel by *Benjumeda*, containing frescoes (1793–95) by *Goya*. The main front is in the parallel C. del Rosario.

Beyond the Diputación extends the Pl. de España, from which the C. Antonio López leads N.E. to the Pl. del Generalísimo, once the garden of a Capuchin convent. The *Academia de Bellas Artes*, on the S.E. side of the plaza, accommodates the **Museo de Pinturas** (undergoing reformation), containing works by *Alejo Fernández, Rubens, Van Orley, Frans Francken, Alonso Cano, Luca Giordano, Murillo, Ribera,* and *Zurbarán*, royal portraits by *Carnicero*, and *Lawrence*, Adm. Ignacio María de Álava (?). But far more important are the series of *Saints by *Zurbarán* from the Cartuja at Jerez.

These are: St John the Evangelist; St Luke; St John the Baptist; three of St Bruno, one 'in ecstasy'; St Lawrence; St Mark; St Matthew; St Anthelm, Bp. of Belley; St Hugh of Grenoble, a Carthusian saint; Bl. John Houghton, prior of the London Charterhouse, martyred in 1538; St Hugh of Lincoln; and Card. Nic. Albergati.

The **Museo Arqueológico**, on the ground floor, contains the few extant relics of the Phœnician *Gaddir*, including a Sarcophagus, Greco-Phœnician in style and other finds from the necropolis at *Punta de la Vaca*, and the *Mariquita del Marmolejo*, a headless Roman statue from Lebrija, once worshipped as a Virgin.

From the opposite side of the Pl. del Generalísimo the C. S. José leads to the C. Duque de Tetuán. To the r. is the Pl. José Antonio with 18C *S. Antonio* (restored). This plaza, Rochfort Scott (writing in the 1820s) considered 'a kind of treadmill, that fashion has condemned her votaries to take an hours exercise in after the fatigues of the day'. Ahead is the **Oratorio de S. Felipe Neri**, a chapel of 1679–1719, where the Cortes sat in 1811–12. Within are a Conception by *Murillo*, and a terracotta head of St John attr. to *Pedro Roldán*. Next door is the *Museo Histórico Municipal*, with pictures and souvenirs of 1810–12, and containing a magnificent wooden *Model of Cádiz (1779).

To the l. in the nearby C. del Sacramento, is the *Torre Vigía de Tavira*, an old semaphore tower or observatory, still in use, which according to Twiss, contained instruments 'chiefly made in London by Mr Dolland

and Mr Bird'. The *Hosp. de Mujeres* or *de N.S. del Carmen*, in the C. Obispo Calvo y Valero (to the r., just short of the tower), with a fine patio of 1740, contains in its chapel an Ecstasy of St Francis, by *El Greco*.

Beyond the Torre Vigía the C. del Sacramento goes on to the Pl. de Castelar from which the C. de Santiago leads past *Santiago*, with 17C Baroque altar-pieces, and the adjacent *Bishop's Palace* (18C) to the Pl. de la Catedral. Hence the C. Alfonso el Sabio turns E. past the *Arco del Pópulo*, an old city gate surmounted by a chapel rebuilt in 1621, back to the Pl. de S. Juan de Dios.

The **Catedral Nueva**, with a conspicuous dome of glazed yellow tiles, is a Baroque building begun in 1722 by *Vic. Acero* and continued intermittently after 1753 by *T. Cayón*. Townsend (1787) considered it 'a disgrace to taste', while Ford compared it to 'a stranded wreck on a quicksand'! The upper part of the front (by *Manuel Machuca*) and the W. Towers (by *Juan Daurá*) are neo-classic works of 1789–1853. It was for this cathedral that Haydn wrote the *Seven last Words from the Cross*. De Falla was buried in the crypt.

The INTERIOR, containing Stalls (1702) by *Agustín* and *Miguel Perea* and *Juan de Valencia*, brought from the Cartuja at Seville, is at present closed for extensive restoration necessitated by the friable nature of its masonry. But even in 1776 Swinburne had ominously remarked that in one chapel the work was so coarsely done and 'the squares. . . so loosely jointed and ill fitted, that in a few years the facing will be quite spoilt'.

The adjacent *Museum*, likely to be transferred to a nearby site, contains a Custodia by *Ant. Suárez* (1648–74) with a car of 1740 by *Juan Pastor*; another known as 'El Cogollo' attr. to *Enrique de Arfe*, and two later processional custodias; a Processional Cross by *Juan de Arfe*, saved from the sack of 1596; a 15C chalice; an ivory Crucifix by *Alonso Cano*; and the jewel encrusted 'Custodia del Millón (1721) by *Pedro Vic. Gómez de Ceballos*. Apart from a collection of Vestments, there are a number of paintings including works by *Ribera, Morales, Valdés Leal, Alejo Fernández, Zurbarán,* and *Murillo,* and a copy of the latter's Conception attr. to *Clemente de Torres*.

To the S.E. lies the *Catedral Vieja*, or *Parroquia de Sta Cruz*, with a massive tower. Built after 1265, it was almost entirely destroyed by Essex in 1596, and rebuilt in 1602. The retablo mayor (c. 1650) is by *Alfonso Martínez* and *Alejandro de Saavedra*; a coffin of solid silver used in the pasos of Good Friday may also be seen.

In the quarter to the S.E. are *Sta María*, with azulejos painted in Delft in 1679 by Armenian artists; *Sto Domingo*, a conv. church with a doorway of 1675 and a marble retablo of 1694; and *La Merced* (1629) with paintings by *Pacheco* and *Clemente de Torres*.
To the W. a large hospital incorporates the chapel of *Los Capuchinos*, or *Sta Catalina*, which contain the Marriage of St Catherine, the last work of *Murillo*, who fell from the scaffolding when the painting was almost finished, and died at Seville shortly afterwards from his injuries; and a Calvary carved by *Salzillo*.

At the S.W. corner of the ramparts is the *Pta. de la Caleta*, while projecting out to sea is the *Castillo de S. Sebastián*, with a square tower built in 1613 on Phœnician or Carthaginian foundations, and now a military prison. We turn N., passing the huge *Hospicio*, built in 1740–72 by *Torquato Cayón*. Beyond the *Hosp. Mora* we leave the *Castillo de Sta Catalina* on the l., and reach the *Parque Genovés*, with its palm-avenues and open-air *theatre*.

Passing the Artillery Barracks, we round the Punta de Candelaria, with the military governor's residence on the r., and reach the Alameda

Marqués de Comillas in which is the Churrigueresque *N.S. del Carmen* (1737–64), containing the grave of Adm. Gravina (1756–1806), commander of the Spanish fleet at Trafalgar, who died from wounds received in the Battle. The Alameda was once 'as much resorted to by ladies of easy virtue as our St James's Park', noted Twiss, and the only place in Spain where he had seen 'bare-faced licentiousness and libertinism'. At the end of the Alameda we reach the *Pl. de Argüelles*, which in turn leads us back to the Pl. de España.

INDEX

Topographical names are printed in Roman or **bold** type; the names of eminent persons, and of the principal Spanish artists, sculptors, and architects (together with their dates, and including foreign artists working in Spain), are printed in *Italics*. The founding proclivities of kings, nobles, prelates, and saints, are usually ignored. Subject entries are printed in CAPITALS. Persons mentioned in the preliminary essays are only indexed if also referred to in the text. For ease of reference, in certain cases persons are indexed under their second name, i.e. *Lorca, Federico García* rather than the first—*García Lorca, Federico*—although the latter is the correct Spanish form.

NOTES

NOTES

NOTES

NOTES

key page to Map numbers

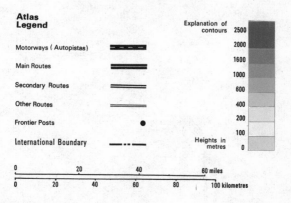

Atlas Legend

Motorways (Autopistas)	━ ━ ━
Main Routes	━━━
Secondary Routes	═══
Other Routes	───
Frontier Posts	●
International Boundary	━ ┅ ━

Explanation of contours

2500	
2000	
1600	
1000	
600	
400	
200	
100	
0	

Heights in metres

0 20 40 60 miles
0 20 40 60 80 100 kilometres

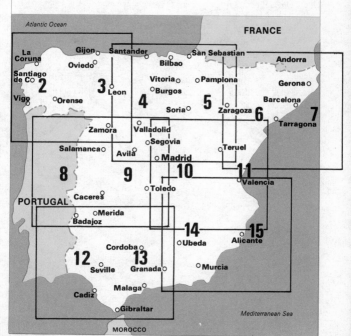

Atlantic Ocean

FRANCE

La Coruña
Gijon
Santander
San Sebastian
Andorra

Santiago de Co
Oviedo
Bilbao
Gerona

2
Leon
Vitoria
Pamplona
Barcelona

Vigo
Orense
Burgos
3
5
Zaragoza
6
7
Tarragona

4
Soria

Zamora
Valladolid
Segovia
Teruel

Salamanca
Avila
Madrid
11

8
9
10
Valencia

Caceres
Toledo

PORTUGAL
Merida
Badajoz
14
15

Cordoba
Ubeda
Alicante

12
13
Seville
Granada
Murcia

Cadiz
Malaga

Gibraltar
Mediterranean Sea

MOROCCO

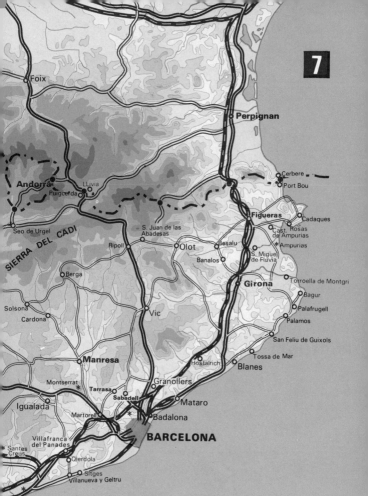

7

Foix

Perpignan

Cerbere
Port Bou

Andorra
LLivia
Puigcerda

Figueras
Cadaques
Seo de Urgel
S. Juan de las
Abadesas
Cast. Rosas
de Ampurias
SIERRA DEL CADI
Ripoll
Olot
Besalu
Ampurias
Banalos
S. Miguel
de Fluvia
Berga
Girona
Torroella de Montgri
Solsona
Vic
Bagur
Cardona
Palafrugell
Palamos
San Feliu de Guixols
Manresa
Hostalrich
Tossa de Mar
Montserrat
Granollers
Blanes
Tarrasa
Sabadell
Igualada
Mataro
Martorell
Badalona
Villafranca
del Panades
BARCELONA
Santes
Creus
Olerdola
Sitges
Villanueva y Geltru

Mediterranean Sea